Contemporary Authors®

Explore your options!

Gale databases are offered in a variety of formats

The information in this Gale publication is also available in some or all of the formats described here. Your Gale Representative will be happy to fill you in. Call toll-free 1-800-877-GALE.

GaleNet

A number of Gale databases are now available on GaleNet, our new online information resource accessible through the Internet. GaleNet features an easy-to-use end-user interface, the powerful search capabilities of BRS/SEARCH retrieval software and ease of access through the World Wide Web.

Diskette/Magnetic Tape

Many Gale databases are available on diskette or magnetic tape, allowing systemwide access to your most-used information sources through existing computer systems. Data can be delivered on a variety of mediums (DOS-formatted diskettes, 9-track tape, 8mm data tape) and in industry-standard formats (comma-delimited, tagged, fixed-field).

CD-ROM

A variety of Gale titles are available on CD-ROM, offering maximum flexibility and powerful search software.

Online

For your convenience, many Gale databases are available through popular online services, including DIALOG, NEXIS, DataStar, ORBIT, OCLC, Thomson Financial Network's I/Plus Direct, HRIN, Prodigy, Sandpoint's HOOVER, the Library Corporation's NLightN and Telebase Systems.

ISSN 0010-7468

Contemporary Authors®

A Bio-Bibliographical Guide to
Current Writers in Fiction, General Nonfiction,
Poetry, Journalism, Drama, Motion Pictures,
Television, and Other Fields

SCOT PEACOCK,
Editor

volume 159

GALE

DETROIT · NEW YORK · TORONTO · LONDON

Contents

Indexing note: All *Contemporary Authors* entries are indexed in the *Contemporary Authors* cumulative index, which is published separately and distributed with even-numbered *Contemporary Authors* original volumes and odd-numbered *Contemporary Authors New Revision Series* volumes.

As always, the most recent *Contemporary Authors* cumulative index continues to be the user's guide to the location of an individual author's listing.

Preface

Contemporary Authors (*CA*) provides information on approximately 100,000 writers in a wide range of media, including:

- Current writers of fiction, nonfiction, poetry, and drama whose works have been issued by commercial publishers, risk publishers, or university presses (authors whose books have been published only by known vanity or author-subsidized firms are ordinarily not included)

- Prominent print and broadcast journalists, editors, photojournalists, syndicated cartoonists, graphic novelists, screenwriters, television scriptwriters, and other media people

- Authors who write in languages other than English, provided their works have been published in the United States or translated into English

- Literary greats of the early twentieth century whose works are popular in today's high school and college curriculums and continue to elicit critical attention

A *CA* listing entails no charge or obligation. Authors are included on the basis of the above criteria and their interest to *CA* users. Sources of potential listees include trade periodicals, publishers' catalogs, librarians, and other users.

How to Get the Most out of *CA:* Use the Index

The key to locating an author's most recent entry is the *CA* cumulative index, which is published separately and distributed with even-numbered original volumes and odd-numbered revision volumes. It provides access to *all* entries in *CA* and *Contemporary Authors New Revision Series* (*CANR*). Always consult the latest index to find an author's most recent entry.

For the convenience of users, the *CA* cumulative index also includes references to all entries in these Gale literary series: *Authors and Artists for Young Adults, Authors in the News, Bestsellers, Black Literature Criticism, Black Writers, Children's Literature Review, Concise Dictionary of American Literary Biography, Concise Dictionary of British Literary Biography, Contemporary Authors Autobiography Series, Contemporary Authors Bibliographical Series, Contemporary Literary Criticism, Dictionary of Literary Biography, Dictionary of Literary Biography Documentary Series, Dictionary of Literary Biography Yearbook, DISCovering Authors, DISCovering Authors: British, DISCovering Authors: Canadian, DISCovering Authors: Modules* (including modules for Dramatists, Most-Studied Authors, Multicultural Authors, Novelists, Poets, and Popular/Genre Authors), *Drama Criticism, Hispanic Literature Criticism, Hispanic Writers, Junior DISCovering Authors, Major Authors and Illustrators for Children and Young Adults, Major 20th-Century Writers, Native North American Literature, Poetry Criticism, Short Story Criticism, Something about the Author, Something about the Author Autobiography Series, Twentieth-Century Literary Criticism, World Literature Criticism,* and *Yesterday's Authors of Books for Children.*

A Sample Index Entry:

Name (parentheses denote parts of name not used for publication)	Birth date (and death date, if applicable)	Volume containing most recent sketch (*CA/CANR* entries come first if they exist; no acronym means *CA* volume)

Kinnell, Galway 1927- CANR-34
Earlier sketches in CA 9-12R, CANR-10
Interview in CANR-34
See also CLC 1, 2, 3, 4, 13, 29
See also DLB 5
See also DLBY 87
See also MTCW

- Volumes containing previous *CA* and *CANR* sketches

- Volumes of *Dictionary of Literary Biography* and *DLB Yearbook* containing entries on author

- Volumes of *CA/CANR* containing unique interviews with the author

- Volumes of *Contemporary Literary Criticism* containing entries on author

- *Major Twentieth Century Writers* contains entry on author

How Are Entries Compiled?

The editors make every effort to secure new information directly from the authors; listees' responses to our questionnaires and query letters provide most of the information featured in *CA*. For deceased writers, or those who fail to reply to requests for data, we consult other reliable biographical sources, such as those indexed in Gale's *Biography and Genealogy Master Index,* and bibliographical sources, including *National Union Catalog, LC MARC,* and *British National Bibliography*. Further details come from published interviews, feature stories, and book reviews, as well as information supplied by the authors' publishers and agents.

An asterisk (*) at the end of a sketch indicates that the listing has been compiled from secondary sources believed to be reliable but has not been personally verified for this edition by the author sketched.

What Kinds of Information Does an Entry Provide?

Sketches in *CA* contain the following biographical and bibliographical information:

- **Entry heading:** the most complete form of author's name, plus any pseudonyms or name variations used for writing

- **Personal information:** author's date and place of birth, family data, ethnicity, educational background, political and religious affiliations, and hobbies and leisure interests

- **Addresses:** author's home, office, or agent's addresses, plus e-mail and fax numbers, as available

- **Career summary:** name of employer, position, and dates held for each career post; resume of other vocational achievements; military service

- **Membership information:** professional, civic, and other association memberships and any official posts held

- **Awards and honors:** military and civic citations, major prizes and nominations, fellowships, grants, and honorary degrees

- **Writings:** a comprehensive, chronological list of titles, publishers, dates of original publication and revised editions, and production information for plays, television scripts, and screenplays

- **Adaptations:** a list of films, plays, and other media which have been adapted from the author's work

- **Work in progress:** current or planned projects, with dates of completion and/or publication, and expected publisher, when known

- **Sidelights:** a biographical portrait of the author's development; information about the critical reception of the author's works; revealing comments, often by the author, on personal interests, aspirations, motivations, and thoughts on writing

- **Biographical and critical sources:** a list of books and periodicals in which additional information on an author's life and/or writings appears

Obituary Notices in *CA* provide date and place of birth as well as death information about authors whose full-length sketches appeared in the series before their deaths. These entries also summarize the authors' careers and writings and list other sources of biographical and death information.

Related Titles in the *CA* Series

Contemporary Authors Autobiography Series complements *CA* original and revised volumes with specially commissioned autobiographical essays by important current authors, illustrated with personal photographs they provide. Common topics include their motivations for writing, the people and experiences that shaped their careers, the rewards they derive from their work, and their impressions of the current literary scene.

Contemporary Authors Bibliographical Series surveys writings by and about important American authors since World War II. Each volume concentrates on a specific genre and features approximately ten writers; entries list works written by and about the author and contain a bibliographical essay discussing the merits and deficiencies of major critical and scholarly studies in detail.

Available in Electronic Formats

CD-ROM. Full-text bio-bibliographic entries from the entire *CA* series, covering approximately 100,000 writers, are available on CD-ROM through lease and purchase plans. The disc combines entries from the *CA, CANR,* and *Contemporary Authors Permanent Series* (*CAP*) print series to provide the most recent author listing. The *CA CD-ROM* is searchable by name, title, subject/genre, nationality/ethnicity, and personal data, as well as by using Boolean logic. The disc is updated every six months. For more information, call 1-800-877-GALE.

Contemporary Authors is also available on CD-ROM from SilverPlatter Information, Inc.

Online. The *Contemporary Authors* database is made available online to libraries and their patrons through online public access catalog (OPAC) vendors. Currently, *CA* is offered through Ameritech Library Services' Vista Online (formerly Dynix).

GaleNet. *CA* is available on a subscription basis through GaleNet, an online information resource that features an easy-to-use end-user interface, the powerful search capabilities of the BRS/Search retrieval software, and ease of access through the World-Wide Web. For more information, call 1-800-877-GALE.

Magnetic Tape. *CA* is available for licensing on magnetic tape in a fielded format. The database is available for internal data processing and nonpublishing purposes only. For more information, call 1-800-877-GALE.

Suggestions Are Welcome

The editors welcome comments and suggestions from users on any aspects of the *CA* series. If readers would like to recommend authors for inclusion in future volumes of the series, they are cordially invited to write: The Editors, *Contemporary Authors,* 835 Penobscot Bldg., 645 Griswold St., Detroit, MI 48226-4094; call toll-free at 1-800-347-GALE; or fax at 1-313-961-6599.

CA Numbering System and Volume Update Chart

Occasionally questions arise about the *CA* numbering system and which volumes, if any, can be discarded. Despite numbers like "29-32R," "97-100" and "158," the entire *CA* print series consists of only 146 physical volumes with the publication of *CA* Volume 159. The following charts note changes in the numbering system and cover design, and indicate which volumes are essential for the most complete, up-to-date coverage.

***CA* First Revision**

- 1-4R through 41-44R (11 books)
  Cover: Brown with black and gold trim.
  There will be no further First Revision volumes because revised entries are now being handled exclusively through the more efficient *New Revision Series* mentioned below.

***CA* Original Volumes**

- 45-48 through 97-100 (14 books)
  Cover: Brown with black and gold trim.
- 101 through 159 (59 books)
  Cover: Blue and black with orange bands.
  The same as previous *CA* original volumes but with a new, simplified numbering system and new cover design.

***CA* Permanent Series**

- *CAP*-1 and *CAP*-2 (2 books)
  Cover: Brown with red and gold trim.
  There will be no further *Permanent Series* volumes because revised entries are now being handled exclusively through the more efficient *New Revision Series* mentioned below.

***CA* New Revision Series**

- *CANR*-1 through *CANR*-60 (60 books)
  Cover: Blue and black with green bands.
  Includes only sketches requiring significant changes; **sketches are taken from any previously published *CA*, *CAP*, or *CANR* volume**.

If You Have: You May Discard:

If You Have:	You May Discard:
CA First Revision Volumes 1-4R through 41-44R **and** *CA Permanent Series* Volumes 1 and 2	*CA* Original Volumes 1, 2, 3, 4 Volumes 5-6 through 41-44
CA Original Volumes 45-48 through 97-100 **and** 101 through 159	**NONE:** These volumes will not be superseded by corresponding revised volumes. Individual entries from these and all other volumes appearing in the left column of this chart may be revised and included in the various volumes of the *New Revision Series*.
CA New Revision Series Volumes *CANR*-1 through *CANR*-60	**NONE:** The *New Revision Series* does not replace any single volume of *CA*. Instead, volumes of *CANR* include entries from many previous *CA* series volumes. All *New Revision Series* volumes must be retained for full coverage.

A Sampling of Authors and Media People
Featured in This Volume

Alfred Adler

A former protege of Freud's, Adler broke ranks with the Vienna Psychoanalytic Society after developing the humanistic approach to psychology described in *The Practice and Theory of Individual Psychology*.

Melba Pattillo Beals

Overcoming violence and isolation, Beals helped fulfill a 1957 Supreme Court desegregation order by attending an all-white high school. She reflects on this turbulent experience in *Warriors Don't Cry: A Searing Memoir of the Battle to Integrate Little Rock's Central High*.

Ruth Behar

Behar, an acclaimed anthropologist and author, merges the discipline of social science with personal experience in the ethnography *Translated Woman: Crossing the Border with Esperanza's Story*.

Alan Berlow

An award-winning journalist for National Public Radio, Berlow reports on a case of human rights abuse in *Dead Season: A Story of Murder and Revenge on the Philippine Island of Negros*. The book exposed a cover-up and forced a new government investigation.

Carol Botwin

With such titles as *The Love Crisis: Hit and Run Lovers, Jugglers, Sexual Stingies, Unreliables, Kinkies, and Other Typical Men Today,* Botwin has issued a series of controversial books that discuss sex and relationships.

Alain de Botton

Considered one of the rising young British novelists of the 1990s, de Botton is the author of *The Romantic Movement: Sex, Shopping, and the Novel* and *How Proust Can Change Your Life: Not a Novel*.

John Denver

A singer, songwriter, and environmental activist, Denver earned praise and popularity during the 1970s for a string of recordings. Two years before his death, Denver saw publication of his 1995 autobiography *Take Me Home*.

Gayatri Devi

Devi, the Maharani of Jaipur, describes her life among the royalty of India in the memoir *A Princess Remembers*. In the years following India's independence from Great Britain, Devi served as a parliament member of the new government.

Dagoberto Gilb

Gilb, whose tales reflect the struggles of working-class Mexican-Americans, wrote for ten years in obscurity before the publication of his first book. Gilb's short story collection *The Magic of Blood* has since met with considerable critical success.

Michael Henry Heim

A prolific translator, Heim has rendered into English the work of such prominent Central and Eastern European writers as Milan Kundera, Anton Chekhov, and Danilo Kis.

Jonnie Jacobs

A mystery novelist, Jacobs is the author of such titles as *Murder among Us* and *Evidence of Guilt*. In both the "Kate Austen" and "Kali O'Brien" series of novels, Jacobs's lead characters are female sleuths.

Haing S. Ngor

Ngor, who won an Academy Award for his role in *The Killing Fields*, a film concerning the Cambodian genocide, authored *A Cambodian Odyssey,* a memoir of his own suffering under the brutal Pol Pot regime.

John Scarne

An expert on gaming as well as illusions, Scarne has written numerous guides on dice, poker, casino gambling, and magic tricks. *The Odds against Me*, published in 1966, is Scarne's autobiography.

Jon Michael Spencer

Spencer's work explores various aspects of African-American culture, particularly in its relationship between music and religion. His books include *Black Hymnody: A Hymnological History of the African-American Church*.

Simone Weil

A controversial religious thinker, Weil inspired the philosopher Jean-Paul Sartre as well as the poet T. S. Eliot. Among her more influential writings are *Waiting for God, Letters to a Priest,* and the omnibus *Simone Weil Reader*.

Frederick Wiseman

In celebrated film documentaries like *Titicut Follies, High School, Hospital, Juvenile Court,* and *Welfare*, Wiseman avoids traditional narrative by employing the techniques of cinema verite to reveal the inner workings of his chosen topics.

A

Indicates that a listing has been compiled from secondary sources believed to be reliable, but has not been personally verified for this edition by the author sketched.

ADLER, Alfred (F.) 1870-1937

PERSONAL: Born February 7, 1870, in Penzig, Austria; immigrated to United States, 1935; died of a heart attack, May 28, 1937, in Aberdeen, Scotland; son of Leopold Adler (a merchant); married Raissa Epstein; children: four. *Education:* University of Vienna, earned medical degree, 1895. *Avocational interests:* Music.

CAREER: Psychiatrist and author. Worked in hospital, c. 1895-98; worked as physician specializing in eye problem, then became physician in private practice, c. 1900. Founded children's clinic in Vienna, Austria, 1919; visiting professor at Columbia University, New York City, 1926; held chair in medical psychology at Long Island College of Medicine, New York City, 1932. *Military service:* Worked in military hospital during World War I.

MEMBER: Society for Individual Psychology (founding member), Vienna Psychoanalytic Society (founding member; president, 1910-11).

WRITINGS:

BOOKS IN ENGLISH TRANSLATION

Studie ueber die Minderwertigkeit von Organen, 1907, translation by Smith Ely Jelliffe published as *Study of Organ Inferiority and Its Psychical Compensation,* Nervous and Mental Disease Publishing, 1917.

Ueber den nervoesen Charakter: Grundzuge einer vergleichenden Individual-Psychologie un

Psychotherapie, J. F. Bergmann, 1912, translation by Bernard Glueck and John E. Lind published as *The Neurotic Constitution: Outline of a Comparative Individualistic Psychology and Psychotherapy,* Moffat, Yard, 1926.

Praxis und Theorie der Individualpsychologie: Vortraaege zur Einfuehrung in die Psychotherapie fuer Aerzte, Psychologen, und Lehrer (essays), J. F. Bergmann, 1920, translation by P. Radin published as *The Practice and Theory of Individual Psychology,* Harcourt, 1924.

Menschenkenntnis, 1927, translation by Walter Beran Wolfe published as *Understanding Human Nature: A Key to Knowledge,* Breenberg, 1927.

Die Technik der Individualpsychologie: J. F. Bergmann, Volume 1, *Die Kunst eine Krankengeschichte zu lesen,* 1928, Volume 2, *Die Seele schwereziehbren Schulkinder,* 1929, translation of Volume 2 by Guy Daniels published as *The Problem Child: The Life Style of the Difficult Child Analyzed in Specific Cases,* introduction by Kurt A. Adler, Capricorn, 1963.

The Case of Miss R., translated by Eleanore Jensen and Friedrich Jensen, Greenberg, 1929.

Individualpsychologie in der Schule: Vorlesungen fur Lehrer und Erzieher, S. Hirzel, 1929, translation published as *Individual Psychology in the School: Lectures for Teachers and Educators.*

Problems of Neurosis: A Book of Case Histories, edited by Philippe Mairet, preface by F. G. Crookshank, Cosmopolitan, 1929.

The Science of Living, edited by Heinz L. Ansbacher, Greenberg, 1929.

The Education of Children, translated by Eleanor Jensen and Friedrich Jensen, Greenberg, 1930.

The Pattern of Life, edited by W. Beran Wolfe, Kegan Paul, Trench, Trubner, 1930.

1

(Editor) *Guiding the Child on the Principles of Individual Psychology,* translated by Benjamin Ginzburg, Greenberg, 1930.

Das Problem des Homosexualitat, 1930, translation published as *The Problem of Homosexuality.*

The Case of Mrs. A.: Diagnosis of a Lifestyle, C. W. Daniel, 1931.

What Life Should Mean to You, edited by Alan Porter, Little, Brown, 1931.

(With Ernst Jahn) *Religion und Individualpsychologie: Eine prinzipelle Auseinandersetzung ueber Menschenfuehrung,* Wien & Leipzig, 1933, translation published as *Religion and Individual Psychology.*

Der Sinn des Lebens, R. Passer, 1933, translation by John Linton and Richard Vaughan published as *Social Interest: A Challenge to Mankind,* Faber & Faber, 1938.

The Individual Psychology of Alfred Adler: A Systematic Presentation in Selections from His Writings, edited by Heinz L. Ansbacher and Rowena R. Ansbacher, Allen & Unwin, 1956.

The Education of the Individual, foreword by Carleton Washburne, Philosophical Library, 1958.

Superiority and Social Interest: A Collection of Later Writings, edited by Heinz L. Ansbacher and Rowena R. Ansbacher, biographical essay by Carl Furtmuller, Routledge & Kegan Paul, 1965, Northwestern University Press, 1970.

Sex, Personality, and the Establishment—Guidelines for Social Re-Education (essays), edited by George H. La Porte, prologue by Albert Reissner, 1970.

Cooperation Between the Sexes, 1978.

OTHER

Die andere Seite: Eine massenpsychologische Studie ueber die Schuld des Volkes, L. Heidrich, 1919.

Contributor to periodicals. Founding editor of *International zeitschrift fuer individual psychologie.*

SIDELIGHTS: Alfred Adler is a key figure in the development of psychoanalytic theory. He was born in Penzig, a suburb of Vienna, Austria, in 1870. Childhood illnesses, together with the traumatic death of a younger sibling, compelled Adler to pursue a medical career, and in the 1890s he studied medicine at the University of Vienna. After graduating, Adler worked in a hospital for three years. He then worked as an eye specialist before commencing a more general private practice. During this period

Adler distinguished himself as a physician with decidedly socialist concerns, and he published various articles advocating social reform.

A turning point in Adler's career came when he attended a series of lectures by the influential psychiatrist Richard von Krafft-Ebing. As a result of Krafft-Ebing's presentations, Adler was inspired to research and treat various psychological disorders. In the early 1900s Adler came to the attention of pioneering psychoanalyst Sigmund Freud, who invited him to became a part of the group that eventually became the Vienna Psychoanalytic Society. Although Adler was an active member of the society, and even became its president in 1910, he remained aloof from Freud's pervasive influence. Whereas Freud perceived human behavior as driven by sexuality and the pursuit of basic biological needs, Adler believed human conduct was a consequence of ideas and values.

Adler's essentially humanistic perspective is evident in his first publication, *Studie ueber die Minderwertigkeit von Organen* (translated as *Study of Organ Inferiority and Its Psychical Compensation*), where he explicates the influence of physical ailments on neurotic behavior. In this volume Adler argues that humans biologically compensate for physical weaknesses. A *Times Literary Supplement* reviewer, writing in 1958, noted, "This hypothesis of compensation has found broad acceptance in modern medicine."

In 1912 Adler published *Ueber den nervoesen Charakter: Grundzuge einer vergleichenden Individual-Psychologie un Psychotherapie* (translated as *The Neurotic Constitution: Outline of a Comparative Individualistic Psychology and Psychotherapy*), where he appropriates the notion of compensation and articulated neurosis as a consequence of psychological compensation. Furthermore, Adler characterizes neuroses as extremes of normal traits. According to Adler, in the neurotic—as Wayland F. Vaughan noted in a *Journal of Abnormal and Social Psychology* essay—"there are certain traits that appear in exaggerated prominence, such as egotism and anxiety, which express themselves in intense modes of self-assertion that are peculiarly characteristic of this type of person." In effect, with *The Neurotic Constitution* Adler merely extended the earlier premise of compensation from *Study of Organ Inferiority and Its Psychical Compensation.*

Adler further delineated his concept of humanistic—or what he described as "individual"—psychology in

Praxis und Theorie der Individualpsychologie (translated as *The Practice and Theory of Individual Psychology*), a volume that prompted *Dial* reviewer H. M. Kallen to draw parallels to the philosophy of Friedrich Nietzsche, who developed the notion of the "will to power." According to Kallen, Adler believed that "the psyche . . . is always to be considered an organic and indissoluble unity." The psyche's essence is delineated by Adler as the pursuit of unity, or what Kallen, acknowledging Hegelian thought, calls the "whole." Kallen observes that the psyche's essence "is to be a goal, generating the means of its attainment by its reactions upon its environment."

In developing such radical notions, Adler had found himself increasingly outside the Freudian mainstream of psychoanalytic thought, for if Freud characterized neurosis as unavoidable, Adler saw it as correctable. Ultimately, as Clarence J. Karier observed in his *Scientists of the Mind: Intellectual Founders of Modern Psychology,* "Adler's deviations were bitterly resented by Freud, who repeatedly referred to his once highly respected student as a 'malicious paranoiac.'" According to Karier, "Freud described Adler as a shallow thinker who constantly reduced psychanalysis to the 'commonsense' simplicity of the man in the street." Karier added, however, that "Adler would not have been insulted by such a remark."

By 1920, when *The Practice and Theory of Individual Psychology* appeared, Adler had broken from the Vienna Psychoanalytic Society and Freud's circle and had founded, instead, the Society for Individual Psychology. After World War I, when Adler worked in a military hospital, he founded several children's clinics in Vienna. He became increasingly involved in children's mental health and even practiced what has since become known as family counseling. For Adler, mental health is directly related to social interest, which must be fostered in childhood for greatest benefit. If neurosis derives from social dysfunction, "wholeness" comes from social harmony.

To facilitate wellbeing, Adler encouraged therapists to diagnose dysfunctional individuals through considerations of dreams, memories, and birth order. Since neurosis is a manifestation of dysfunction, Adler believed, dysfunction is a consequence of the individual's distorted self-image in relation to the outside world. The therapist's task, therefore, is the guiding of the dysfunctional individual towards personal—and, thus, social—harmony. Adler expressed

as much in such works as *Menschenkenntnis* (translated as *Understanding Human Nature*) and the two-volume *Die Technik der Individualpsychologie* (of which the second volume, *Die Seele schwereziehbren Schulkinder,* was translated as *The Problem Child: The Life Style of the Difficult Child Analyzed in Specific Cases*).

In some of his ensuing writings Adler aimed at the "commonsense" reader denigrated by Freud. Notable among such works is *The Pattern of Life,* an examination of twelve schoolchildren with various emotional problems. In addition, Adler produced various writings targeted for the educational community. In works such as *Guiding the Child* and *The Education of Children,* he provided specialized accounts of theories and methods pertaining to children's therapy.

Critics have been disinclined to rank Adler's later books among his most significant efforts. A *Times Literary Supplement* reviewer observed, "In his later works Adler tended increasingly to address himself to the educator and the layman rather than to the medical world." For this reviewer, works such as *The Pattern of Life* "were books aimed at the new post-war public avid for psychological enlightenment. They presented their author as an effective populizer of his own brand of psychological self-help. No doubt they had influence in their time. Today they are virtually forgotten." Similarly, Edward Hoffman wrote in *The Drive for Self: Alfred Adler and the Founding of Individual Psychology,* that *The Education of Children* "offered little that was really new to Americans familiar with individual psychology."

While Adler continued to publish prolifically, Europe was undergoing an extreme upheaval. Nazism had begun spreading in Germany and its neighboring countries. By the early 1930s, Austria had become disturbingly unstable, so Adler, who had grown accustomed to life abroad as a result of various stints as a lecturer and teacher, immigrated to the United States and began teaching at the Long Island School of Medicine. But he also continued to lecture elsewhere. And though his rate of publishing new works now diminished, he continued to train others in Adlerian methods. In 1937, while on a speaking tour in Scotland, Adler suffered a fatal heart attack. He was sixty-seven years old.

In the years since Adler's death, he has continued to be recognized as a leading figure in psychoanalysis and the field of psychotherapy, and his methods remain in practice. As Edward Hoffman wrote in *The Drive for Self,* "Today, Adlerian institutes and therapeutic training centers are growing modestly throughout the United States, Central Europe, and elsewhere. Although he surely would be dissatisfied with Freud's unquestionably greater impact upon Western civilization, it seems likely that Adler would be content to see how much of his impassioned life's work has proven beneficial to the world."

BIOGRAPHICAL/CRITICAL SOURCES:

BOOKS

Bottome, Phyllis, *Alfred Adler,* Putnam, 1939.
Hoffman, Edward, *The Drive for Self: Alfred Adler and the Founding of Individual Psychology,* Addison-Wesley, 1994.
Karier, Clarence J., *Scientists of the Mind: Intellectual Founders of Modern Psychology,* University of Illinois Press, 1986, pp. 226-254.
Mosak, Harold H., editor, *Alfred Adler: His Influence on Psychology Today,* Noyes Press 1973.
Orgler,Hertha, *Alfred Adler: The Man and His Work,* Sidgwick & Jackson, 1973.
Twentieth-Century Literary Criticism, Volume 61, Gale, 1996.

PERIODICALS

American Journal of Sociology, September, 1928, pp. 391-93.
Criterion, July, 1932, pp. 733-735.
Dial, March, 1925, pp. 236-239.
Journal of Abnormal Psychology, January-March, 1927, pp. 358-371.
Times Literary Supplement, November 21, 1958, pp. 665-666.*

*   *   *

ADRIAN, Edgar Douglas   1889-1977

PERSONAL: Born November 30, 1889, in London, England; died August 4, 1977, in Cambridge, England; son of Alfred Douglas Adrian (legal counsel to the London Local Government Board) and Flora Lavinia Barton. *Education:* Cambridge University, graduated (with first class honors), 1911; St.

Bartholomew's, bachelor of medicine, 1915; received M.D., 1919.

CAREER: Neurophysiologist and writer. Cambridge University, Trinity College, Cambridge, England, fellow, 1913-19, appointed head of the laboratory, 1919-29, elected Foulerton Professor of the Royal Society, 1929-37, became professor of physiology, 1937-39, appointed to Medical Research Council, 1939-51, became master of Trinity College, 1951-65, vice chancellor of the University, 1957-59; Rockefeller University, New York, elected trustee, 1962; served on committees of the World Health Organization. *Military service:* British Army, served during World War I, assigned to the treatment of nerve injuries and disorders of servicemen at the Hospital for Nervous Diseases.

MEMBER: Royal Society (president), British Association for the Advancement of Science (president), Royal Society of Medicine (president).

AWARDS, HONORS: Nobel Prize in physiology or medicine (with Sir Charles Scott Sherrington), 1932, in recognition of their work on the role of neurons in the stimulation of muscles and sense organs, which made possible the development of electroencephalography; Royal Medal, 1934; British Order of Merit, 1942; Copley Medal from the Royal Society, 1946; Albert Gold Medal from the Royal Society of the Arts, 1953; knighted First Baron Adrian of Cambridge, 1955; Harben Medal, 1955; French Legion of Honor, 1956; Medal for Distinguished Merit from the British Medical Association, 1958; Jephcott Medal from the Royal Society of Medicine, 1963.

WRITINGS:

The Basis of Sensation: The Action of the Sense Organs, Christophers, 1928.
The Mechanism of Nervous Action, University of Pennsylvania Press, 1932.
The Physical Basis of Perception, Clarendon Press, 1947.

Contributor to journals and periodicals, including *Journal of Physiology.*

SIDELIGHTS: Lord Edgar Douglas Adrian, noted Cambridge University physiologist, won renown for his research on the functions of the brain and the nervous system. With Sir Charles Scott Sherrington, he received the Nobel Prize in physiology or medicine in 1932 in recognition of his work on the role of neurons in the stimulation of muscles and sense organs. Adrian's research also made possible the development of electroencephalography, or the measurement of electrical activity in the brain.

Born in London on November 30, 1889, Adrian was the son of Flora Lavinia Barton and Alfred Douglas Adrian. His father was legal counsel to the Local Government Board in London and saw to it that his son had a good education. Adrian attended London's Westminster School and in 1908 won a science scholarship which opened the doors of Cambridge University's Trinity College to him. Besides taking courses in other natural sciences, he studied physiology under the direction of the physiologist Keith Lucas. Lucas was researching the reactions of muscles and nerves to electrical stimulation. When Adrian joined in this pursuit, he set his course for a lifelong career investigating the nervous system. He graduated from Trinity College in 1911 with first-class honors in five subjects.

His work in neurophysiology with Lucas led Adrian into the analysis of the functioning of neurons (nerve cells) in the stimulation of muscles and sense organs. The physiologist Sherrington had already made discoveries in this field, which Adrian was to advance further. His early research with Lucas resulted in his election as a fellow of Trinity College in 1913. Adrian earned his bachelor of medicine degree in 1915 at St. Bartholomew's in London and was able to pursue his interest in the nervous system when he served in the British Army during World War I. He was assigned to the treatment of nerve injuries and disorders of servicemen at the Hospital for Nervous Diseases. The effect of shell shock was a particular area of study. The young doctor's efforts to get assigned to a post in France were unsuccessful, however.

Adrian's career took an unexpected turn when Lucas died in an airplane crash during the war and Adrian was appointed to take charge of his laboratory in 1919, the same year he received his doctor of medicine degree. In the laboratory, he resumed his work on nerve impulses and began using advanced electrical techniques. He was able to amplify by five-thousand times the impulses in a single nerve fiber and single end organ in a frog's muscle. Adrian published his first observations on these nerve stimuli experiments in 1926 and came forth with definitive conclusions in 1928. Impulses that led to the sensation of pain were of particular interest to Adrian, and he directed his attention to a study of the brain.

He found that the regions of the brain leading to a particular sense organ varied between species of animals. In pigs, which use their snouts to explore their environment, for instance, almost the entire region of the cortex dedicated to touch is taken up with nerve endings of the fibers that lead to the snout. In humans, a large area is taken up with the endings of fibers leading to the hands. Adrian's work cast new light on the nature of the nervous impulse, the action of the neuron and the physical nature of sensation. Today's understanding of the human nervous system is to an important extent informed by Adrian's findings.

In 1929, Adrian was elected Foulerton Professor of the Royal Society. He made a trip to New York, where he worked with Detlev Wulf Bronk on converting electrical impulses to sound. Returning to Cambridge, he continued his investigations of how sensory impulses reach the brain. One of his aims was to develop a practical method of reading the brain's electrical wave patterns. His work laid the foundation for the development of clinical electroencephalography, which could accomplish such brain analysis. The electroencephalogram (EEG) made it possible to study such conditions as epilepsy and brain tumors.

It was announced on October 27, 1932, that Adrian and Sherrington were to share the Nobel Prize in physiology or medicine. The news was greeted enthusiastically throughout the scientific world and hailed particularly by the British press. Adrian was named professor of physiology at Cambridge in 1937 and was appointed to the Medical Research Council in 1939. From 1951 to 1965, he held the post of master of Trinity College and from 1957 to 1959 was also vice chancellor of Cambridge University. During these later years, he also served terms as president of the Royal Society, president of the British Association for the Advancement of Science, and president of the Royal Society of Medicine. He served on committees of the World Health Organization and, in 1962, was elected a trustee of Rockefeller University in New York.

Among the many awards received for his research achievements were the Royal Medal (1934), the British Order of Merit (1942), the Copley Medal from the Royal Society (1946), the Albert Gold Medal of the Royal Society of the Arts (1953), the Harben Medal (1955), the French Legion of Honor (1956), the Medal for Distinguished Merit of the British Medical Association (1958) and the Jephcott Medal of the Royal Society of Medicine (1963). In 1955, he was knighted First Baron Adrian of Cambridge. Adrian did not confine his activities to the laboratory or lecture hall. He and his wife enjoyed mountain climbing. He also enjoyed fencing, sailing and fast bicycle riding. He took a strong interest in the arts, particularly painting. The exhibit of eighty of his works in Cambridge marked the high point of his hobby. When he retired from Trinity in 1965, he continued to live in the college's Neville's Court almost until his death on August 4, 1977.

BIOGRAPHICAL/CRITICAL SOURCES:

BOOKS

Fox, Daniel M., Marcia Meldrum, and Ira Rezak, editors, *Nobel Laureates in Medicine or Physiology,* Garland, 1990.
Magill, Frank N., editor, *Nobel Prize Winners, Physiology or Medicine,* Volume 1: *1901-1944,* Salem Press, 1991.*

*   *   *

AFZAL, Omar   1939-
     (Athar, a pseudonym)

PERSONAL: Born March 13, 1939, in Dudhara, Basti, India; naturalized U.S. citizen; son of Husain (an educator) and Najma (a homemaker) Afzal; married June 15, 1966; wife's name, Salma; children: Bushra, Iqbal, Samina, Sadia, Marya. *Ethnicity:* "Asian/Caucasian." *Education:* Aligarh Muslim University, M.A. (English language and literature), 1965; Delhi University, M.A. (linguistics), 1971; Cornell University, Ph.D. (linguistics), 1978. *Politics:* "Republican/Humanist." *Religion:* Islam. *Avocational interests:* Public speaking, research.

ADDRESSES: Home—1069 Ellis Hollow Rd., Ithaca, NY 14850. *Office*—180 Kroch Library, Cornell University, Ithaca, NY 14853; fax 607-255-8438. *E-mail*—oaiz@cornell.edu.

CAREER: Gauhati University, Dibrugarh, India, teacher of English literature, 1965-68; American Institute of Indian Studies, teacher of Urdu and Hindi, 1970-72; Delhi University, Delhi, India, teacher of English language and literature, 1972-73; Cornell University, Ithaca, NY, Southeast Asia assistant, 1973—, chairperson of Center for Research

and Communication, and adviser to MECA. Crescent Observation International, committee chairperson; Forum, national coordinator, 1981-96.

MEMBER: Association for Asian Studies.

AWARDS, HONORS: Order of Merit, Aligarh Muslim University, 1965; University Gold Medal, Delhi University, 1971.

WRITINGS:

The Life of Muhammad (biography), Al-Hasanat Rampur (Delhi, India), 1971.
Aap ki uljhane, Maktaba Islami (New Delhi, India), 1972.
Issues in the Lunar Calendar, Afkar-i Islami (Karachi, Pakistan), 1988.
Calculating Prayer Times, MCC (Chicago, IL), 1993.
(Editor, with Nimat Hafez Barazangi and M. Raquibuz Zaman) *Islamic Identity and the Struggle for Justice,* University Press of Florida (Gainesville, FL), 1996.

Author of poetry under pseudonym Athar. Special correspondent, *Radiance,* 1992—. Contributor of stories to magazines, including *Kanti.* Editor, *Message,* 1982—.

WORK IN PROGRESS: Research on issues in Islamic banking, Islamic legal reform, and the Islamic calendar.

SIDELIGHTS: Omar Afzal told *CA:* "I write because of the need for re-assessing three major issues in Islamic jurisprudence: gender, astronomical calculations, and monetary contracts."

*   *   *

ALEKSANDROV, Pavel S(ergeevich)   1896-1982

PERSONAL: Born May 7, 1896, in Bogorodsk, Russia; died November 16, 1982, in Moscow, U.S.S.R. (now Russia); son of Sergei Aleksandrovich (a doctor) and Tsezariia Akimovna Zdanovskaia Aleksandrov; married Ekaterina Romanovna Eiges, 1921 (divorced). *Education:* University of Moscow, undergraduate degree, 1917, Ph.D., 1934.

CAREER: Mathematician and writer. Leader of the mathematical society in Moscow for thirty years.

WRITINGS:

(With Heinz Hopf) *Topologie I,* Springer-Verlag, 1935.
Combinatorial Topology, three volumes, Graylock Press, 1956-60.
An Introduction to the Theory of Groups, Hafner, 1959.

Aleksandrov's autobiography was published in the journal *Russian Mathematical Surveys,* volume 34, number 6, 1979, pp. 267-302; and volume 35, number 3, 1980, pp. 315-358.

SIDELIGHTS: Pavel S. Aleksandrov laid the foundation for the field of mathematics known as topology. In addition to writing the first comprehensive textbook on the subject, Aleksandrov introduced several basic concepts of topology and its offshoots, homology and cohomology, which blend topology and algebra. His important work in defining and exploring bicompact (compact or locally compact) spaces laid the groundwork for research done by other mathematicians in these fields.

The youngest of the six children of Sergei Aleksandrovich Aleksandrov and the former Tsezariia Akimovna Zdanovskaia, Pavel Sergeevich Aleksandrov was born in Bogorodsk, Russia, on May 7, 1896. A year later the family moved to Smolensk, where Aleksandrov's father became head doctor in the state hospital. Although educated mainly in public schools, Aleksandrov learned German and French from his mother, who was skilled in languages.

In grammar school Aleksandrov developed an interest in mathematics under the guidance of Aleksandr Eiges, his arithmetic teacher. Aleksandrov entered the University of Moscow in 1913 as a mathematics student, and achieved early success when he proved the importance of Borel sets after hearing a lecture by Nikolai Nikolaevich Luzin in 1914. Aleksandrov graduated in 1917 and planned to continue his studies. However, after failing to reach similar results on his next project—Georg Cantor's continuum hypothesis (since acknowledged unsolvable; that is, it can be neither proved nor disproved)—Aleksandrov dropped out of the mathematical community and formed a theater group in Chernigov, a city situated seventy-seven miles north of Kiev, in the Ukraine. Besides participating in the theater group, he lec-

tured publicly on various topics in literature and mathematics. He also was involved in political support of the new Soviet government, for which he was jailed briefly in 1919 by counterrevolutionaries.

Later that same year, Aleksandrov suffered a lengthy illness, during which he decided to return to Moscow and mathematics. To help himself catch up, he enlisted the help of another young graduate student, Pavel Samuilovich Uryson. The two immediately became close friends and colleagues. After a brief, unsuccessful marriage in 1921 to his former teacher's sister, Ekaterina Romanovna Eiges, Aleksandrov joined some fellow graduate students in renting a summer cottage. There, he and Uryson began their study of the new field of topology, the branch of mathematics that deals with properties of figures related directly to their shape and invariant under continuous transformation (that is, without cutting or tearing). In topology, often called rubber-sheet geometry, a cylinder and a sphere are equivalent, because one can be shaped (or transformed) into the other. A doughnut, however, is not equivalent to a sphere, because it cannot be shaped or stretched into a sphere. No textbooks were available on the subject, only articles by Maurice Frechet, Felix Hausdorff, and a few others. Nonetheless, from these articles, Uryson and Aleksandrov came up with their first major topological discovery: the theorem of metrization. Metrization is the process of deriving a specific measurement for the abstract concept of a topological space. In order to do this, Aleksandrov and Uryson first had to develop definitions of topological spaces. They initially defined a *bicompact* space (now known as compact and locally compact spaces), whose property is that for any collection of open sets (or groups of elements) that contains it (the interior of a sphere is an example of an open set). There is a subset of the collection with a finite number of elements that also contains it. Prior to their work, the concept of space was too abstract to be applicable to other mathematical fields; Aleksandrov and Uryson's research led to the acceptance of topology as a valid field of mathematical study.

With this result, the pair rose to fame within the mathematical community, gaining the approval of such notable scholars as Emmy Noether, Richard Courant, and David Hilbert. In 1924 Uryson and Aleksandrov went to Holland and visited with Luitzen Egbertus Jan Brouwer, who suggested that they publish their studies on topology. Aleksandrov and Uryson went on to the seaside in France for a spell of work and relaxation that ended tragically when Uryson drowned while swimming. In the aftermath of his friend's death, Aleksandrov lost himself in his work, conducting a seminar on topology that he and Uryson had begun organizing in 1924, and spending 1925 to 1926 working with Brouwer in an attempt to get his research into a form suitable for publication. During this time he further developed his theories of topology and compact space, with an eye to applying topology to the investigation of complex problems.

In 1927 Aleksandrov left Europe for a year to continue his work with a new friend and colleague, Heinz Hopf, at Princeton. Aleksandrov had met Hopf during the summer of 1926 in Gottingen, which along with Paris was considered to be the mathematical hub of Europe. It was in Gottingen in 1923 that Aleksandrov and Uryson first presented their results outside the U.S.S.R., and it was Aleksandrov's preferred summer residence until 1932. There he worked with others, including Noether, who gave the topological work of Aleksandrov and Hopf its algebraic bent. This may have led to Aleksandrov's growing interest in homology, the offshoot of topology incorporating algebra. Homology had first been developed by the French mathematician Jules Henri Poincare, but only for certain types of topological spaces. In 1928 Aleksandrov made a major step in expanding the field when he was able to generalize homology to other topological spaces.

In 1934 Aleksandrov at last received his doctorate from the University of Moscow. The next year, he would issue his most famous work. After much difficult research, the first volume of Aleksandrov and Hopf's still-classic work *Topologie* was published (the remaining two volumes would not be published until after World War II, though they were completed sooner). In the tome they outlined, often for the first time, many basic concepts of this branch of mathematics. They also introduced the definition of cohomology, which is the "dual" theory, or mirror image, of homology. Cohomologists consider the same topics as homologists, but from a different vantage point, providing different results. The publication achieved, Aleksandrov settled in a small town outside of Moscow with his friend and colleague Andrey Nikolayevich Kolmogorov. They stayed together here, teaching at the University of Moscow, for the rest of their lives.

Always concerned with the younger generation of mathematicians, Aleksandrov in later years crafted ground-breaking textbooks in the fields of topology, homology, and group theory, which studies the properties of certain kinds of sets. He guided his students—noted mathematicians such as A. Kuros, L. Pontriagin, and A. Tikhonov—to great heights. He also led the mathematical community in Moscow, presiding over that city's mathematical society for more than thirty years. In 1979 Aleksandrov wrote his autobiography. He died three years later in Moscow on November 16, 1982.

BIOGRAPHICAL/CRITICAL SOURCES:

BOOKS

Boyer, C., and Volume Merzbach, *A History of Mathematics,* second edition, Wiley, 1989.
Brown, Ronald, *Elements of Modern Topology,* McGraw-Hill, 1968.
Dictionary of Scientific Biography, volume 17, Scribner's, 1990, pp. 11-15.
Fang, J., *Mathematicians from Antiquity to Today,* volume 1, Paideia Press, 1972, p. 156.
Temple, George, *100 Years of Mathematics,* Springer-Verlag, 1981.

PERIODICALS

Russian Mathematical Surveys, vol. 31, no. 5, 1976, pp. 1-13.*

*   *   *

ANDERSON, Philip Warren   1923-

PERSONAL: Born December 13, 1923, in Indianapolis, IN; son of Harry Warren (a professor of plant pathology) and Elsie (Osborne) Anderson; married Joyce Gothwaite, 1947; children: one daughter. *Education:* Harvard University, B.S. (summa cum laude), 1943; M.S., 1947, Ph.D., 1949.

ADDRESSES: Office—Princeton University, Princeton, NJ 08544.

CAREER: Physicist and writer. Bell Telephone Research Laboratories, Murray Hill, NJ, physicist, c. 1949-75, consulting director, 1975-84; University of Tokyo, visiting professor, 1953-54; Cambridge University, conducted research with Nevill Mott in his laboratory, 1967-75; Princeton University, Joseph Henry Professor of Physics, 1975—. *Wartime service:*

Worked on the design of radio and radar antennae at the Naval research Laboratory, Washington, DC, during World War II.

AWARDS, HONORS: Oliver E. Buckley Prize from the American Physical Society, 1964; Dannie Heineman Prize from the Gottingen Academy of Sciences, 1975; Nobel Prize for physics (with Nevill Francis Mott and John Van Vleck), 1977, for contributions to the study of magnetism and disordered states; Guthrie Medal from the London Institute of Physics, 1978; National Medal of Science, 1982.

WRITINGS:

Concepts in Solids, W. A. Benjamin, 1963.
Basic Notions of Condensed Matter Physics, Benjamin/Cummings, 1984.

Contributor to journals and periodicals, including *Physical Review.*

SIDELIGHTS: The 1977 Nobel Prize in physics that Philip Warren Anderson shared with Nevill Francis Mott and John Van Vleck was given not so much for one specific discovery but for his contributions over a number of years to the study of magnetism and disordered states. In fact, Anderson's interests have extended well beyond those areas and have included work on the broadening of line spectra, electron tunneling, and superconductivity.

Anderson was born in Indianapolis, Indiana, on December 13, 1923, but he grew up in Urbana, Illinois. Anderson came into a family that boasted a number of teachers, including his own father, Harry Warren Anderson, who was a professor of plant pathology at the University of Illinois. Anderson's mother, the former Elsie Osborne, was herself the daughter of another teacher, a professor of mathematics. Anderson graduated from University High School in Urbana in 1940 and was then awarded a scholarship to Harvard University. He graduated from Harvard with a B.S., summa cum laude, in 1943.

World War II prevented Anderson from beginning his graduate studies immediately. Instead he accepted a job at the Naval Research Laboratory in Washington, D.C., where he worked on the design of radio and radar antennae. At the war's conclusion, Anderson returned to Harvard to begin his graduate studies in physics. His doctoral advisor there was the

physicist John Hasbrouck Van Vleck, later to share a Nobel Prize with Anderson.

Anderson's graduate studies focused on the problem of line spectrum broadening. The term *line spectrum* suggests a spectrum in which electron transitions within an atom result in the formation of clear, distinct lines. In fact, that type of event is often not the case. Interactions among atoms and among molecules often cause slight variations in the emission of energy from an atom, variations that result in a "smearing" of lines. Anderson found that modern quantum theory, which posits that energy exists in discrete units, provided a means for developing a quantitative explanation of the broadening effect. For this line of research, Anderson was awarded his M.S. degree in 1947 and then his Ph.D. in 1949 from Harvard.

Anderson's first job after graduation was with the Bell Telephone Research Laboratories in Murray Hill, New Jersey. Perhaps the most exciting work then taking place at the Bell Labs focused on solid-state physics, especially the research on superconductivity (the tendency of a material to lose all resistance to the flow of an electrical current, usually at temperatures close to absolute zero). Anderson, however, was at first involved in studies on magnetism. Once again, he used the techniques of quantum mechanics to show how the properties of individual atoms and electrons could be used to explain magnetic properties on a macroscopic scale. This work was one of the fields singled out by the Nobel Prize committee in its award of the 1977 physics prize to Anderson.

The atmosphere at Bell was such, however, that Anderson could hardly have avoided some contact with studies on superconductivity, particularly with reference to its occurrence in semiconductors (materials that are neither good insulators nor good conductors). In 1964, for example, he designed and carried out an experiment that demonstrated the existence of electron tunneling in semiconductors with AC currents. He also examined the effects of impurities in semiconductors, as predicted by quantum theory.

During the academic year 1953-54, Anderson was a visiting professor at the University of Tokyo. At a conference on theoretical physics held in Kyoto during the year, Anderson made the acquaintance of Nevill Mott (later, Sir Nevill Mott), an English physicist with interests similar to Anderson's. Mott suggested that Anderson visit him at his own laboratories at Cambridge University. The two eventually worked out a plan whereby Anderson could spend half of each year at Cambridge and half at the Bell Laboratories.

The topic to which Anderson and Mott devoted much of their attention was the behavior of electrons in amorphous solids. Traditionally, physicists had done most of their research on ordered solids, that is, crystals in which ions and electrons occupy relatively clearly defined positions. The mathematics of such systems, while not always simple, was at least easier than for systems in which ions and electrons are more randomly distributed through a material.

In 1958 Anderson published a paper, "Absence of Diffusion in Certain Random Lattices," in which he announced a new theory of disordered solids. The behavior of electrons in such solids as well as the properties of the solid itself can best be understand, he said, by acknowledging that electrons are often "tied" to specific locations within the solid and are not free to move throughout it. This phenomenon has become known as Anderson localization and has made it possible to design materials with very specific and desirable properties. The use of relatively inexpensive amorphous silicon in place of the more expensive pure silicon in semiconductors is one example of the practical applications of Anderson's discovery. The analysis of disordered solids was the second basis for the Nobel Prize committee's decision to award the 1977 physics prize to Anderson.

Anderson commuted to Mott's laboratory from 1967 to 1975 and then abandoned that practice in order to become consulting director at Bell Labs and Joseph Henry Professor of Physics at Princeton University. He held his Bell post until his retirement in 1984, although he continued to teach at Princeton. Retirement did not mean an end to Anderson's research work, however. Indeed, one of his most important accomplishments was the development of a new theory of superconductivity, announced in 1987, in which he was able to explain the recent discovery of high-temperature superconducting materials.

Anderson was married in 1947 to Joyce Gothwaite. The couple has one daughter. In addition to the Nobel Prize, Anderson has been awarded the Oliver E. Buckley Prize of the American Physical Society (1964), the Dannie Heineman Prize of the Gottingen Academy of Sciences (1975), the Guthrie Medal of

the London Institute of Physics (1978), and the National Medal of Science (1982).

BIOGRAPHICAL/CRITICAL SOURCES:

BOOKS

Magill, Frank N., editor, *The Nobel Prize Winners: Physics,* Volume 3, 1968-1988, Salem Press, 1989, pp. 1133-1142.
McGraw-Hill Modern Men of Science, Volume 1, McGraw, 1984, pp. 11-12.
Wasson, Tyler, editor, *Nobel Prize Winners,* H. W. Wilson, 1987, pp. 20-22.

PERIODICALS

Physics Today, December 1977, pp. 77-78.
Science, November 18, 1977, pp. XX.*

*   *   *

ANFINSEN, Christian Boehmer   1916-

PERSONAL: Born March 26, 1916, in Monessen, PA; son of Christian (an engineer) and Sophie (Rasmussen) Anfinsen; married Florence Bernice Kenenger, 1941 (divorced, 1978); married Libby Esther Schulman Ely, 1979; children: (with Kenenger) three. *Education:* Swarthmore College, B.A., 1937; University of Pennsylvania, M.S. (organic chemistry), 1939; Harvard University, Ph.D. (biochemistry), 1943. *Avocational interests:* Sailing, music.

CAREER: Biochemist and writer. Harvard Medical School, instructor in biological chemistry, 1943-44, associate professor, 1948-50, 1962-63; United States Office of Scientific Research and Development, chemist, 1944-46; Medical Nobel Institute, Sweden, American Cancer Society senior fellow, 1947-48; National Institutes of Health National Heart Institute Laboratory of Cellular Physiology, head of laboratory, 1950-62, Laboratory of Chemical Biology at the National Institute of Arthritis, Metabolism and Digestive Diseases, director, 1963-81; Weizmann Institute of science, member of staff, 1981-82; Johns Hopkins University, professor of biology, beginning in 1982.

MEMBER: National Academy of Sciences, American Society of Biological Chemists, Royal Danish Academy.

AWARDS, HONORS: Rockefeller Public Service Award, 1954; Nobel Prize for Chemistry (with Stanford Moore and William Howard Stein), 1972, for establishing the relationship between the structure of an enzyme and its function; awarded honorary degrees from seven universities, including Georgetown University and New York Medical College.

WRITINGS:

The Molecular Basis of Evolution, Wiley, 1959.

SIDELIGHTS: Biochemist Christian Boehmer Anfinsen is best known for establishing that the structure of an enzyme is intimately related to its function. This discovery was a major contribution to the scientific understanding of the nature of enzymes. For this achievement, Anfinsen shared the 1972 Nobel Prize for Chemistry with the research team of Stanford Moore and William Howard Stein.

Anfinsen was born on March 26, 1916, in Monessen, Pennsylvania, a town located just outside of Pittsburgh. He was the child of Christian Anfinsen, an engineer and emigrant from Norway, and the former Sophie Rasmussen, who was also of Norwegian heritage. Anfinsen earned his B.A. from Swarthmore College in 1937. Subsequently, he attended the University of Pennsylvania, earning an M.S. in organic chemistry in 1939. After earning his master's degree, Anfinsen received a fellowship from the American Scandinavian Foundation to spend a year at the Carlsberg Laboratory in Copenhagen, Denmark. Upon his return in 1940, he entered Harvard University's Ph.D. program in biochemistry. His doctoral dissertation involved work with enzymes; he described various methodologies for discerning the enzymes present in the retina of the eye, and he earned his Ph.D in 1943.

After earning his Ph.D., Anfinsen began teaching at Harvard Medical School in their department of biological chemistry. From 1944 to 1946 he worked in the United States Office of Scientific Research and Development. He then worked in the biochemical division of the Medical Nobel Institute in Sweden under Hugo Theorell as an American Cancer Society senior fellow from 1947 to 1948. Harvard University promoted him to associate professor upon his return, but in 1950 he accepted a position as head of the National Institutes of Health's (NIH) National Heart Institute Laboratory of Cellular Physiology. He

served in this position until 1962. Anfinsen returned to teaching at Harvard Medical School in 1962, but he returned to NIH a year later. This time he was named director of the Laboratory of Chemical Biology at the National Institute of Arthritis, Metabolism, and Digestive Diseases. He held this position until 1981; he spent a year at the Weizmann Institute of science and then in 1982 accepted an appointment as professor of biology at Johns Hopkins University.

Anfinsen began his research concerning the structure and function of enzymes in the mid-1940s. Enzymes are a type of protein; specifically, they are what drive the many chemical reactions in the human body. All proteins are made up of smaller components called peptide chains, which are amino acids linked together. Amino acids are, in turn, a certain class of organic compounds. The enzymes take on a globular, three-dimensional form as the amino acid chain folds over. The unfolded chain form of an enzyme is called the primary structure. Once the chain folds over, it is said to be in the tertiary structure. From one set of amino acids for one particular enzyme there are one-hundred different possible ways in which these amino acids can link together. (Only certain amino acids can "fit" next to other amino acids.) However, only one configuration will result in an active enzyme. In general, Anfinsen's research concerned finding out how a particular set of amino acids knows to configure in a way that results in the active form of the enzyme.

Anfinsen chose to study the enzyme ribonuclease (RNase), which contains 124 amino acids and is responsible for breaking down the ribonucleic acid (RNA) found in food. This reaction enables the body to recycle the resultant smaller pieces. He felt that by determining how a particular enzyme assumes its particular active configuration, the structure and function of enzymes could be better understood. He reasoned that he could determine how an enzyme protein is built and when the enzyme becomes functional by observing it adding one amino acid at a time. He utilized techniques developed by Cambridge University's Frederick Sanger to conduct this research. Another research team headed by Stanford Moore and William Howard Stein was working simultaneously on the same enzyme as Anfinsen, ribonuclease; in 1960, using ribonuclease, Moore and Stein were the first to determine the exact amino acid sequence of an enzyme. However, Anfinsen remained more concerned with how the enzyme forms into its active configuration.

Anfinsen eventually changed his methodology of research during an opportunity to study abroad. While at the NIH, Anfinsen took yet another leave of absence when a Rockefeller Public Service Award allowed him to spend 1954 to 1955 at the Carlsberg Laboratory studying under the physical chemist Kai Linderstrom-Lang. Anfinsen had been studying ribonuclease by building it up; Linderstrom-Lang convinced him to start with the whole molecule and study it by stripping it down piece by piece. Anfinsen began with the whole ribonuclease molecule and then successively broke the various bonds of the molecule. The process is called denaturing the protein or, in other words, causing it to lose its functional capacity. By breaking certain key bonds, other bonds formed between the amino acids resulting in a random, inactive form of ribonuclease. By 1962 Anfinsen had confirmed that when this inactive form is placed into an environment that mimics the environment in which ribonuclease normally appears in the body, that inactive form would slowly revert to the active configuration on its own and thus regain its enzymatic activity. This discovery revealed the important fact that all the information for the assembly of the three-dimensional, active enzyme form was within the protein's own sequence of amino acids.

For uncovering the connection between the primary and tertiary structure of enzymes, Anfinsen received half of the 1972 Nobel Prize for Chemistry. Moore and Stein and were awarded the other half. In addition to his numerous journal articles on protein structure, enzyme function, and related matters, in 1959 Anfinsen issued a book entitled *The Molecular Basis of Evolution*. After receiving the Nobel Prize, Anfinsen began focusing his research on the protein interferon, known for its key role as part of the body's immunity against both viruses and cancer. He has succeeded in isolating and characterizing this important human protein.

Anfinsen's other honors received after winning the Nobel Prize include being the recipient of seven honorary degrees from universities including Georgetown University and New York Medical College. Anfinsen is a member of the National Academy of Sciences, the American Society of Biological Chemists, and the Royal Danish Academy. He married Florence Bernice Kenenger in 1941, and together they had three children before divorcing in 1978. In 1979, Anfinsen married Libby Esther Schulman Ely. Outside the professional world, his interests include sailing and music.

BIOGRAPHICAL/CRITICAL SOURCES:

BOOKS

Wasson, Tyler, editor, *Nobel Prize Winners,* H. W. Wilson, 1987, pp. 24-26.

PERIODICALS

New York Times, October 21, 1972, p. 14.
Science, November 3, 1972, pp. 492-493.*

*   *   *

ASHEIM, Lester E(ugene)   1914-1997

OBITUARY NOTICE—See index for *CA* sketch: Born January 22, 1914, in Spokane, WA; died after suffering from Alzheimer's disease, July 1, 1997, in Chapel Hill, NC. Librarian, educator, and author. Asheim devoted his career to the study of library science. In his early career, he held reference posts at the University of Washington in Seattle, at the U.S. Federal Penitentiary at McNeil Island, and with the U.S. Federal Public Housing Authority. In 1948 he joined the faculty at the University of Chicago as an assistant professor. By 1952 he had risen to the rank of associate professor and dean. In 1961 he began work at the American Library Association (ALA) as director of its international relations office; he became the ALA's director of the Office for Library Education in 1966. In 1971 he returned to the University of Chicago as a professor, then he left for the University of North Carolina three years later. At the latter post, he served as William Raud Kenan, Jr., Professor of Library Science, becoming professor emeritus in 1984. He wrote, edited, and contributed to numerous books during his career. Among them are *Library's Public* (with Bernard Berelson), *Forum on the Public Library Inquiry, The Future of the Book, The Humanities and the Library* (with others), *Differentiating the Media* (with Sara Fenwick), *Reading and Successful Living* (with D. Philip Baker and Virginia Mathews), and *The Reader-Viewer-Listener*. He was the recipient of several honors, including the Joseph W. Lippincott Award in 1976.

OBITUARIES AND OTHER SOURCES:

BOOKS

Who's Who in America, Marquis, 1990.

PERIODICALS

Chicago Tribune, July 8, 1997, sec. 1, p. 9.
Library Journal, August, 1997, p. 32.

*   *   *

ATHAR
  See AFZAL, Omar

*   *   *

ATTEMA, Martha 1949-

PERSONAL: Born December 22, 1949, in Menaldum, the Netherlands; immigrated to Canada, 1981; daughter of Wilke (a farmer) and Romkje (a homemaker; maiden name, Noordenbos) Hoogterp; married Albert Attema; children: Romkje, Sjoerd, Rikst. *Education:* Attended a teacher's college in the Netherlands, 1966-70; Laurentian University, B.A., 1986, B.Ed., 1989. *Avocational interests:* Sewing clothes, crafts.

ADDRESSES: Home—376 Voyer Rd., Corbeil, Ontario, Canada P0H 1K0. *E-mail*—martatte@Via Net. on.ca.

CAREER: Kindergarten teacher in Giekerk, the Netherlands, 1969-73; teacher of kindergarten and grade one in North Bay, Ontario, Canada, 1987—.

MEMBER: Canadian Society of Children's Authors, Illustrators, and Publishers, Writers' Union of Canada—North Bay Children's Writers Group, North Bay Writers Club.

AWARDS, HONORS: Blue Heron Award for Young Adults, 1996, and shortlist, Geoffrey Bilson Award for Historical Fiction, Canadian Children's Book Centre, 1996, both for *A Time to Choose.*

WRITINGS:

The Unhappy Pinetree (picture book), privately printed, 1992.
A Time to Choose (young adult historical novel), Orca Book Publishers (Victoria, British Columbia), 1995.

A Light in the Dunes (young adult novel), Orca, 1997.

Contributor to periodicals.

WORK IN PROGRESS: Research on the Germanic people in Northern Europe during prehistoric times.

SIDELIGHTS: Martha Attema commented: "Writing has always been part of my life. In my teenage years I wrote poetry to sort out the world and my personal problems and to find an outlet. During those years I began to envy my grandfather, who was a published playwright and poet. When I became a teacher and later a mother, I wrote stories, poems, and puppet plays for my students and for my own children. My writing was all in the Frisian language. Friesland is one of the northern provinces in the Netherlands. The Frisians are a proud and stubborn people who have their own language (not a dialect).

"After I moved to Canada with my family in 1981, I continued to write in my mother tongue. Several years later I felt myself between languages. I didn't get enough exposure to the Frisian language, and I wasn't proficient enough in English to feel comfortable writing stories and poems in this language. A creative writing course at the local college inspired me. The instructor and my other classmates gave me hope and encouraged me to market my stories.

"I knew what I wanted to write about. After I came to Canada, I decided to share some of my Frisian background and culture with young people here. My first book, *Is That You, Sinterklaas?,* is a novel for middle graders about the legend and traditions surrounding Saint Nicholas. To this day, I haven't been able to publish this story.

"*A Time to Choose* is a young adult historical novel, based on facts and stories from survivors of World War II. I am pleased that I was able to preserve some of the stories from a generation of people who will not be here much longer to tell their own stories. It gives me great satisfaction that *A Time to Choose* is a contribution to the evidence that this war was real. I am glad to be able to tell young people not to forget this war or any other war, that in every war the conflicts are not just between the good and bad guys, that war is much more complex and conflicts occur within families and among friends.

"The Frisian language is a rich language, full of sagas, legends, and folktales. In my young adult novel *A Light in the Dunes* I have used an old legend from one of the islands off the coast of Friesland and have woven this legend through a contemporary story of a young girl who is unhappy about the fact that she was named after the witch in the legend. I owed our youngest daughter this story, for she was also named after the witch in the legend.

"In my future writing I hope to preserve more history, folktales, and legends by giving these tales and facts new life in young adult novels and picture books. Besides writing, I enjoy research and reading. I collect folktales and legends from Friesland and I love to read about the history of the area where I grew up. As a teacher of grade one, I'm exposed to many excellent picture books. By sharing these picture books as well as my own stories and poems, I hope to foster a love for reading and writing in my students.

"I never dreamed that I would actually become a published author. I always thought the language would be a major handicap and a drawback. Now that I have become an author, I encourage young people never to give up their dreams, but to be determined and try hard to fulfill them."

BIOGRAPHICAL/CRITICAL SOURCES:

PERIODICALS

Quill and Quire, January, 1996, p. 369.

*   *   *

AvZ
  See Von ZELEWSKY, Alexander

B

BABBITT, Susan E. 1953-

PERSONAL: Born February 13, 1953, in Washington, DC; Canadian citizen; daughter of Jack D. (a physicist) and Dorothy (Rooney) Babbitt. *Education:* University of Ottawa, B.A. (English), 1982, B.A. (philosophy; with honors), 1983, M.A. (philosophy), 1985; Cornell University, M.A., 1988, Ph.D., 1991. *Politics:* "Socialist/feminist." *Religion:* None. *Avocational interests:* Skiing.

ADDRESSES: Home—13 St. Catherine St., Kingston, Ontario, Canada K7K 3R9. *Office*—Department of Philosophy, Watson Hall, Queen's University, Kingston, Ontario, Canada K7L 3N6; fax 613-545-6545. *E-mail*—babbitts@qucdn.queensu.ca.

CAREER: Queen's University, Kingston, Ontario, Canada, assistant professor of philosophy, 1990—.

MEMBER: Canadian Society for Women in Philosophy, Canadian Philosophical Association, American Philosophical Association.

AWARDS, HONORS: Beatrice Brown Award for Women's Studies, Cornell University, 1989; Grants for research in Cuba, Queen's University, 1993-96; grants from Canadian International Development Agency, 1996, and Social Sciences and Humanities Research Council of Canada, 1996-99.

WRITINGS:

(Contributor) *Feminist Epistemologies,* edited by Elizabeth Potter and Linda Alcoff, Routledge & Kegan Paul (New York City), 1992.

Impossible Dreams: Rationality, Integrity, and Moral Imagination, Westview Press (Boulder, CO), 1996.

(Contributor) *A Question of Values: New Canadian Perspectives on Ethics and Political Philosophy,* edited by Tracy Isaacs, Michael Milde, and Samantha Brennan, Rodopi (Atlanta, GA), 1997.

Contributor of articles and reviews to scholarly journals, including *Hypatia, The Philosophical Review, Journal of Aesthetics, Philosophical Studies,* and *Queen's Quarterly.*

WORK IN PROGRESS: Artless Integrity: Reflections on Moral Imagination; research on women and development in Cuba.

*　　*　　*

BACON, Melvin (L.) 1950-

PERSONAL: Born December 9, 1950, in Denver, CO; son of Joe M. (an optician) and F. Miriam (Baughman) Bacon; married Deborah A. Booz (a teacher), October 12, 1974; children: Sarah E., Joseph M. *Education:* Metropolitan State College-Denver, B.A., 1973; University of Northern Colorado, M.A., 1983. *Politics:* Republican. *Religion:* American Baptist. *Avocational interests:* Antique/classic automobiles, western U.S. history (ghost towns), stamps, coins, photography.

ADDRESSES: Home—771 South 11th Ave., Brighton, CO 80601.

CAREER: Educator and writer. Education Department of Western Australia, Perth, Australia, high school social studies teacher, 1975-76; Brighton School District, Brighton, CO, teacher (of history, literature, geology, and creative writing) and social studies curriculum coordinator, 1977—.

MEMBER: National Council for the Social Studies, Colorado Council for the Social Studies, Ye Olde Car Club (chapter of Antique Automobile Club of America), Kaiser-Frazer Owners Club International, Colorado Ghost Town Club.

AWARDS, HONORS: Outstanding Social Studies Educator, Colorado Council on Social Studies, 1990; Outstanding American History Teacher, Colorado State Society of the Daughters of the American Revolution, 1992; Outstanding American History Teacher, Colorado Daughters of Colonial Wars, 1993.

WRITINGS:

(With Daniel Blegen) *Bent's Fort: Crossroads of Culture on the Santa Fe Trail,* Millbrook, 1995.

Also author of published fiction and poetry.

WORK IN PROGRESS: Frontier Ghost Towns. Researching everyday life in frontier communities.

SIDELIGHTS: As a costumed interpreter at historic Bent's Fort along the old Sante Fe Trail in Colorado, history teacher Melvin Bacon gained valuable insights into the lives of nineteenth-century traders and travelers, even enjoying the experience of sleeping under the stars in a Buffalo robe. Bacon's research and fascination with the old west resulted in his first book, *Bent's Fort: Crossroads of Cultures on the Sante Fe Trail,* co-written with Daniel Blegen. *School Library Journal* contributor Julie Halverstadt offered a favorable assessment of the book, noting that its "personal accounts make the history of this bustling stop come alive." Halverstadt also commended the book's detailed description of the fort itself, adding: "There's an amazing amount of information in this attractive volume."

BIOGRAPHICAL/CRITICAL SOURCES:

PERIODICALS

Booklist, January 1, 1996, p. 820.
Horn Book Guide, spring, 1996, p. 152.
School Library Journal, November, 1995, p. 109.

BAKIS, Kirsten 1968(?)-

PERSONAL: Born in c. 1968.

ADDRESSES: Agent—c/o Farrar, Straus, 19 Union Square W., New York, NY 10003.

CAREER: Writer.

WRITINGS:

Lives of the Monster Dogs (novel), Farrar, Straus & Giroux (New York City), 1997.

SIDELIGHTS: Kirsten Bakis's first novel, *Lives of the Monster Dogs,* was published in 1997 and was well-received by critics. An animal fantasy in the tradition of Mikhail Bulgakov's *Heart of a Dog* or, even more closely, H. G. Wells's *The Island of Dr. Moreau,* the novel describes the arrival on Manhattan Island, in the year 2008, of a group of 150 canines who have been surgically transformed into cultured, intelligent beings. Their creator, like Mary Shelley's Dr. Frankenstein, whose influence several critics noted, is a German surgeon named Augustus Rank. After being emotionally scarred by a lonely childhood, Rank has attempted to create a race of superdogs who will give him the unconditional love he has always craved and never received. However, when his dogs realize that they are slaves, they rebel and escape to New York City. There they are welcomed as the latest fashion by high society and touted by the media. Their prosthetic hands and voices enable them to mingle among humans, even to the point of composing and staging an opera. Eventually New York society loses interest in the dogs, and their canine traits emerge. The dogs are befriended by a young journalist, Cleo Pira, who narrates their story. They are her companions at a time of personal difficulty, and she is witness to their ultimate decline.

Many critics were enthusiastic about *Lives of the Monster Dogs,* including M. G. Lord, who reviewed Bakis's novel for the *New York Times Book Review.* Lord offered high praise for the novel, asserting, at the end of the review: "This is not one of those flashy novels that ultimately prove hollow. . . . Never violating its internal logic, the book unfolds like a rich, resonant dream that you can't stop thinking about the following day. . . . Ms. Bakis has produced a dazzling, unforgettable meditation on what it means to be human." The novel was also, Lord averred, "laugh-aloud funny" at some points.

Other reviewers were not as laudatory as Lord, but nonetheless gave Bakis praise. In a review in *Time,* for instance, John Skow claimed that the mechanics of the dogs' surgical transformations defied common sense; nevertheless, he maintained that the novel's sad, mysterious ending worked well and that the book left "a melancholy stillness as it is put back on the shelf." *People* contributor Melissa Stanton asserted that the conclusion of *Lives of the Monster Dogs* "drags a bit," but on the whole the novel was a "fantastic, skillfully told story" and a "poignant, mostly magnificent" book. *Wall Street Journal* reviewer Brooke Allen characterized *Lives of the Monster Dogs* as "an effective fantasy in the tradition of Robert Louis Stevenson and Mary Shelley," and lauded Bakis's handling of German Romantic themes. Though Allen asserted that Bakis was not entirely successful in making the dogs "human," she found the novel "consistently attractive."

BIOGRAPHICAL/CRITICAL SOURCES:

PERIODICALS

New York Times Book Review, March 9, 1997, p. 4.
People, April 21, 1997, p. 31.
Time, March 3, 1997.
Wall Street Journal, March 3, 1997.

OTHER

amazon.com, March 31, 1997.
salonmagazine.com, February, 1997.*

*   *   *

BARBEAU, Edward J(oseph) 1938-

PERSONAL: Born June 25, 1938, in Toronto, Ontario, Canada; son of Edward Joseph (a firefighter) and Vera Grace (Arthur) Barbeau; married Eileen Mary Jones, June 17, 1961; children: Judith Barbeau Gargaro, Paul. *Education:* University of Toronto, B.A., 1960, M.A., 1961; University of Newcastle-upon-Tyne, Ph.D., 1964. *Religion:* Anglican. *Avocational interests:* Music (organ, piano).

ADDRESSES: Home—130 Mona Dr., Toronto, Ontario, Canada M5N 2R6. *Office*—Department of Mathematics, University of Toronto, Toronto, Ontario, Canada M5S 3G3; fax 416-978-4107. *E-mail*—barbeau@math.utoronto.ca.

CAREER: University of Western Ontario, London, Ontario, Canada, assistant professor of mathematics, 1964-66; Yale University, New Haven, CT, postdoctoral research fellow, 1966-67; University of Toronto, Toronto, Ontario, assistant professor, 1967-69, associate professor, 1969-88, professor of mathematics, 1988—.

MEMBER: Canadian Mathematical Society, Canadian Society for History and Philosophy of Mathematics, National Council of Teachers of Mathematics, American Mathematical Society, Mathematical Association of America, American Mathematical Society.

AWARDS, HONORS: David Hilbert Award, World Federation of National Mathematics Contests; Adrien Pouliot Award, Canadian Mathematical Society; fellow, Ontario Institute for Studies in Education.

WRITINGS:

Polynomials, Springer-Verlag (New York City), 1989.
(With Murray Klamkin and William Moser) *Challenging Mathematical Problems: High School and College,* Mathematical Association of America (Washington, DC), 1993.
After Math: Puzzles and Brainteasers, Wall & Emerson (Toronto, Ontario), 1995.
(With Klamkin and Moser) *Five Hundred Mathematical Challenges,* Mathematical Association of America, 1995.
Power Play, Mathematical Association of America, 1997.

SIDELIGHTS: Edward J. Barbeau told *CA:* "I write for two reasons: first, to bring mathematics to a wider audience; and second, to help interested students reach beyond the regular school curriculum to see mathematics in a broader context, appreciate its structure, and be challenged by interesting problems. I like to create situations in which the reader is forced to reflect upon mathematics and gain a feeling of accomplishment that comes with understanding. My books are the putting together of material that I have used in particular situations, such as presentations to students, teachers, or the general public. My future plans are to prepare resource material that might be useful to teachers. Mathematics should be like music, in that more than ninety-five percent of the population should be able to engage in it at some level. In both cases, the highest levels of creativity are accessible to very few, but there is a wide spectrum to cater to amateurs of all levels of background, ability, and perseverance."

* * *

BARNETT, Robert W(arren) 1911-1997

OBITUARY NOTICE—See index for *CA* sketch: Born November 6, 1911, in Shanghai, China, to American parents; died of cancer and pneumonia, July 25, 1997, in Washington, DC. Educator, diplomat, and author. Barnett devoted much of his career to work with the U.S. State Department in China and Europe. He also served as deputy assistant secretary of state for East Asian and Pacific affairs. He began his career as an educator, first at the University of North Carolina at Chapel Hill, then at the Institute of Pacific Relations. In 1941 he became program executive officer for United China Relief in New York City. In 1945 he began four years with the Far Eastern Commission for Occupation of Japan as a U.S. member of its economics and reparations committees. He joined the State Department in 1949, first serving as officer in charge of China economic affairs. Other stints followed, including posts in Europe, the Netherlands, and Belgium.

In addition he served in other capacities, such as officer in charge of European economic organizations, deputy director of foreign economic advisory staff in the office of the under-secretary of state, and ultimately as the deputy assistant secretary of state for East Asian and Pacific affairs. In 1970 he became vice president and director of the Asia Society's Washington Center. Nine years later found him as a resident associate with the Carnegie Endowment for International Peace. During his career, he was investigated by Senator Joseph McCarthy during the Red Scare; he was accused of being a security risk and Communist sympathizer. Barnett spoke firmly about the "preposterous" charges and was cleared. He also found time to write a dozen books, including *Wandering Knights: China Legacies Lived and Recalled, The Industrial Revolution: China and Great Britain, British Foreign Policy with Respect to the Russo-Japanese War, Quemoy: The Use and Consequences of Nuclear Deterrence, Economic Shanghai: Hostage to Politics, Beyond War: Japan's Concept of Comprehensive National Security,* and *The United States and China.*

OBITUARIES AND OTHER SOURCES:

BOOKS

Who's Who in America, Marquis, 1996.

PERIODICALS

Chicago Tribune, July 28, 1997, sec. 1, p. 10.
New York Times, July 27, 1997, sec. 1, p. 30.

* * *

BAYLISS, William Maddock 1860-1924

PERSONAL: Born May 2, 1860, in Wednesbury, Staffordshire, England; died August 27, 1924, following a long illness; son of Moses (an iron manufacturer) and Jan (Maddock) Bayliss; married Gertrude Starling, 1893; children: one daughter, three sons (one named Leonard). *Education:* Attended University College, 1880-85; Wadham College, first-class degree in physiology, 1888.

CAREER: Physiologist and writer. University College, London, England, teaching and research assistant, 1888-1903, assistant professor, 1903-12, professor of general physiology, 1912-24.

MEMBER: Royal Society (member of council), Royal Academy of Belgium, Royal Danish Academy of Science.

AWARDS, HONORS: Elected fellow of the Royal Society, 1903; Copley Medal from the Royal Society; Baly Medal from the Royal College of Physicians; knighted, 1922; awarded honorary degrees from Aberdeen University, Oxford University, St. Andrews University, and others.

WRITINGS:

The Nature of Enzyme Action, Longmans, Green, 1908.
Principles of General Physiology, Longmans, Green, 1914.
Intravenous Injection in Wound Shock, Longmans, Green, 1918.

Contributor to journals and periodicals, including *Journal of Physiology, Archives des sciences biologiques,* and *Proceedings of the Royal Society.*

SIDELIGHTS: The name William Maddock Bayliss is inevitably linked with that of Ernest Starling for the duo's collaborative scientific research on the digestive, nervous, and vascular systems. Their 1902 investigations into the trigger mechanism for the release of pancreatic digestive juices led to the discovery of an entirely new class of chemical messengers which they called hormones. Additionally, Bayliss's pioneering work with enzymes and the innervation of the heart and intestines made important contributions to the understanding of physiology. In 1914, Bayliss authored *Principles of General Physiology,* a basic physiology textbook that is still considered a landmark in biological literature. His long and distinguished career won for him the Copley Medal of the Royal Society, the Baly Medal of the Royal College of Physicians, and, in 1922, a knighthood.

Bayliss was born on May 2, 1860, in the town of Wednesbury, Staffordshire, England. His father, Moses Bayliss, who was a wealthy iron manufacturer, and his mother, the former Jan Maddock, lived in the affluent industrial midlands between Birmingham and Wolverhampton. Bayliss attended a local private school and entered his father's firm for a short time after graduation. However, finding that he was more interested in science than manufacturing, Bayliss decided to study medicine, and was apprenticed to a local physician for training.

In 1880 the family moved to a prosperous home on four acres of parkland in Hampstead, London, where Bayliss entered University College to study physiology and anatomy. However, after pursuing a degree in medicine, Bayliss decided instead to devote his life to a study of the then-emerging science of physiology—a branch of biology that analyzes bodily functions. At University College, he was influenced by both John Burdon-Sanderson in physiology and Ray Lankester in zoology. In 1885 Bayliss's studies took him to Wadham College in Oxford where, in 1888, he took a first-class degree in physiology, then returned to University College as a teaching and research assistant. He remained at University College for the rest of his life, becoming assistant professor in 1903, and, from 1912 to his death, professor of general physiology, a chair created specifically for him.

In 1890 Bayliss met E. H. Starling, a fellow physiologist, and the pair began a long professional collaboration and personal friendship; within three years Bayliss married Starling's sister, Gertrude.

Following the death of Bayliss's father in 1895, the couple moved into the Hampstead home and raised one daughter and three sons, the youngest of whom, Leonard, also went on to become a physiologist. Bayliss was left financially secure by his father, and the family entertained a good deal at the Hampstead home where Bayliss, a lover of music, often played the violin. In addition, Bayliss was an experienced photographer, and his pictures were published as illustrations for his professional books and papers.

Bayliss and Starling collaborated first on a project in electrophysiology, charting the electrical changes of the mammalian heart. Using a new instrument called a capillary electrometer, the researchers studied the hearts of mammals to observe cardiac cycles. Next they turned to the vascular system, recording nerve-controlled dilation and contraction of blood vessels. This work resulted in the development of an improved device for measuring blood pressure called a hemopiezometer. Yet another area of interest for Bayliss and Starling was intestinal movements. This study led to a description of the peristaltic wave—a function of the intestines which contracts and relaxes to propel the contents of the intestines forward during the process of digestion. At about this same time, 1892, Bayliss followed an independent line of study into the physiology of the depressor nerve, leading to a general examination of vasomotor reactions (nerves which dilate or constrict blood vessels) and their coordination.

By far the best known achievement of Bayliss and Starling was the discovery, in 1902, of hormones. Following up on the work of the famous Russian physiologist Ivan Petrovich Pavlov, who had shown that pancreatic secretions were created by a stimulation of the vagus nerve, Bayliss and Starling experimented with dogs whose nerves to the upper intestine had been severed. At the time, the only known means to excite glands to secretion was the action of secretory nerves. However, when the researchers introduced dilute hydrochloric acid (HCL) into the dog's duodenum—the first part of the small intestine which connects to the stomach—they discovered that pancreatic digestive juices were still secreted, and concluded that communication with the pancreas could only be through the bloodstream. In a further experiment in which dilute HCL was injected into the jugular vein of an anesthetized dog, they found a chemical substance activated in the epithelial cells, or the tissue covering the surface or lining of the duodenum. They called this chemical substance "secretin," because, when it was released into the bloodstream, it came into contact with the pancreas and stimulated it to secrete a digestive juice into the intestine. Starling went on to coin the term "hormone"—from the Greek *horman,* "to set in motion." This discovery proved that a hormone secreted by one internal organ could have a direct effect on another internal organ.

After 1903, Bayliss and Starling collaborated for one more paper, this one on enzyme action, studying the activation of the enzyme trypsin in pancreatic digestive juice. Bayliss then worked on his own to demonstrate how trypsin was formed in the small intestine. He measured the time required for a trypsin solution to digest specific amounts of proteins and established, in the course of the studies, that enzymes acted as catalysts. He proved, further, that much of the enzymes' effect came from being in a colloidal or emulsion state (substances that do not dissolve when dispersed). This latter conclusion prompted Bayliss to continue with a general study of colloids in the properties of membranes and in surface action.

Bayliss applied physical chemistry to physiological problems. One of Bayliss's findings during World War I was that the intravenous use of a gum saline solution to replace lost blood was effective in treating soldiers in danger of wound shock. The use of these saline injections prevented the onset of surgical shock by maintaining an equal colloidal osmotic pressure in the blood circulation. It was a practice that saved many lives.

Bayliss's book *Principles of General Physiology,* which appeared in 1914, secured his lasting reputation. It was a landmark publication in a fledgling science. Bayliss was honored for his work from many quarters. In 1903 he was elected a fellow of the prestigious Royal Society and served on its council for three years. He was awarded honorary degrees from such universities as Aberdeen, Oxford, and St. Andrews, and was a member of the Royal Academy of Belgium and the Royal Danish Academy of Science. Bayliss died on August 27, 1924, following an illness of some months.

BIOGRAPHICAL/CRITICAL SOURCES:

BOOKS

Perspectives in Biology and Medicine, Volume 4, University of Chicago Press, 1961, pp. 460-479.*

BEADLE, George Wells 1903-1989

PERSONAL: Born October 22, 1903, in Wahoo, NE; died June 9, 1989, in Pomona, CA, from complications of Alzheimer's disease; son of Chauncey Elmer and Hattie Albro Beadle; married Marion Cecile Hill, c. 1927 (divorced); married Muriel Barnett, 1953; children: (with Hill) David. *Education:* University of Nebraska, B.S. (biology), 1926; Cornell University, Ph.D. (genetics), c. 1931.

CAREER: Geneticist and writer. California Institute of Technology, Pasadena, CA, member of Thomas Hunt Morgan's genetics laboratory staff, 1931-35, professor and chair of the division of biology, 1946-61; Institut de Biologie Physico-Chimique, member of Boris Ephrussi's genetics laboratory staff, 1935-36; Harvard University, instructor of genetics, 1936-37; Stanford University, Stanford, CA, professor of biology, 1937-46; University of Chicago, Chicago, IL, chancellor, 1961-68; American Medical Association, Institute for Biomedical Research, director, beginning c. 1968.

AWARDS, HONORS: Lasker Award, 1950, from the American Public Health Association; Nobel Prize for Physiology or Medicine (with Edward Lawrie Tatum and Joshua Lederberg), 1958, for work on the "one gene-one enzyme" concept; Albert Einstein Commemorative Award in Science, 1958; National Award, 1959, from the American Cancer Society; Edison Award (with wife, Muriel Beadle), 1967; awarded memberships in several academic societies; awarded over thirty honorary degrees from various American universities.

WRITINGS:

(With A. H. Sturtevant) *An Introduction to Genetics,* W. B. Saunders, 1939.
(With others) *The Place of Genetics in Modern Biology,* Massachusetts Institute of Technology, 1959.
(With wife, Muriel Beadle) *The Language of Life: An Introduction to the Science of Genetics,* Doubleday, 1966.

Contributor to journals and periodicals, including *Cornell University Agricultural Experimental Station Memo, Proceedings of the National Academy of Sciences,* and *Physiological Review.*

SIDELIGHTS: Early in his professional life, George Wells Beadle worked in the laboratory of Thomas

Hunt Morgan, the geneticist who helped to revolutionize what we know about genetics—the inheritance of characteristics by the deoxyribonucleic acid (DNA) found in the chromosomes of cells. Beadle's innovative research on such diverse living things as corn, fruit flies, and bread mold helped to demystify the activities of genes, making it possible to reduce the inheritance of a particular characteristic to a series of steps needed for the manufacture of biochemicals, notably enzymes. For his work on the "one gene-one enzyme" concept, he shared the Nobel Prize for Physiology or Medicine with Edward Lawrie Tatum and Joshua Lederberg in 1958.

Beadle was born in Wahoo, Nebraska, on October 22, 1903, to Chauncey Elmer and Hattie Albro Beadle. He probably would have worked on the family farm if not for a high school science teacher who advised him to go on to college. At the College of Agriculture at the University of Nebraska, Beadle gained an interest in genetics, especially that of corn. He received his undergraduate degree in biology in 1926, then left for Cornell University in New York where he earned his doctorate in genetics. During this time Beadle married Marion Cecile Hill. They would have one son, David.

In 1931 Beadle went to work in the genetics laboratory of Thomas Hunt Morgan at the California Institute of Technology (Caltech) in Pasadena, California. Morgan had pioneered genetics work on the fruit fly, *Drosophila melanogaster*. As Beadle studied inherited characteristics such as eye color, he began to think that genes might influence heredity by chemical means. When he left California for Paris in 1935, he continued this line of work with Boris Ephrussi at the Institut de Biologie Physico-Chimique. Carefully transplanting eye buds from the larvae of one type of mutant fruit fly to larvae of another, Beadle showed that eye color in the insects is not a quirk of nature but the result of a long chain of chemical reactions. For all the relative ease of working with fruit flies, however, Beadle sought a simpler organism and a simpler set of chemical reactions to study.

Several years later, Beadle found what he was looking for. When he returned from Paris in 1936 he briefly taught genetics at Harvard and then went on to Stanford University in California, where he remained from 1937 to 1946. As a professor of biology there, he began working with a red bread mold, *Neurospora crassa*. He would work with neurospora for seventeen years. In 1941 he began collaborating with Edward Tatum, and their work eventually won them—with Joshua Lederberg, who later worked with Tatum at Yale—the Nobel Prize.

Neurospora crassa, once the bane of bakers, became a boon for geneticists Beadle and Tatum. Not only does the mold have a short life cycle and grow on a basic sugar medium, but it reproduces both sexually and asexually. Also, the final cell division that produces its reproductive cells, known as ascospores, leaves them in a linear arrangement along the pod-like ascus (spore case), making the trail of inherited characteristics very clear to follow.

Taking a hint from fellow geneticist Hermann Joseph Muller, who in the mid-1920s had shown that the rate of mutation increases with exposure to X rays, Beadle and Tatum grew thousand of cultures of molds in which they had induced mutations. The wild strain of the mold can grow on a medium containing very few nutrients. With just some sugar sprinkled with a little biotin (a growth vitamin) and inorganic salts, a wild-type mold can synthesize all the proteins it needs to live. A mold with a mutation, however, loses the ability to make a particular compound it needs to grow, such as a specific amino acid (amino acids are the building blocks of proteins such as those used to construct DNA). Beadle expected that a missing amino acid would have to be supplied to the mold, but found to his surprise the mold was sometimes able to convert a similar compound to the necessary amino acid. Through a process of trial and error, Beadle was able to deduce the sequence of chemical steps involved in the work of conversion.

Once Beadle had pieced together the pathways of chemical production, his ideas could be applied to other molds. One immediate application was to use his techniques to mass-produce the antibiotic penicillin. Penicillin and other antibiotics are derived from compounds produced naturally by certain molds, which use them as a defense against invading bacterial cells.

Beadle also crossed two different mutant strains of mold and found that the resulting hybrid could produce a particular amino acid that neither parent strain could produce alone. This was because one mutant lacked genetic coding for a certain enzyme (a protein that can encourage or inhibit chemical reactions), causing a breakdown in the chemical synthesis along one spot in the sequence, while the other mutant lacked different coding for an enzyme from another spot along the sequence. When crossed, the resulting mold could produce the missing amino acid because it had inherited both genetic patterns, one from each parent. Beadle concluded that specific genes (sequences of protein groups in DNA serving as functional units of inheritance) controlled each step in the sequence. Each gene held the information for the manufacture of a single enzyme, a concept that became known as "one gene, one enzyme."

Extended to other plants and animals, Beadle's theory could be used to explain all of genetic inheritance in terms of chemical reactions. Different genes control the different stages of chemical reactions. For example, cells must be able to produce the pigment that gives an animal's eyes their color. The production of pigment might occur in several steps, with enzymes used to hasten each chemical reaction. If the gene for any one of the enzymes is missing, the cells cannot produce the pigment.

The one gene-one enzyme concept caused a breakthrough in genetic research during the 1940s by shifting the study of genetics away from physical characteristics of organisms to the production of biochemicals. On the heels of this line of research, the compound deoxyribonucleic acid (DNA) was analyzed, and the mechanism of the genetic code was pieced together in the early 1950s. Beadle and Tatum parted ways when Tatum left for Yale University in 1945. Using the same mutation induction techniques on bacteria, Tatum worked along with Joshua Lederberg to show how genetic information can be transferred from one bacterium to another.

Beadle became professor and chairman of the division of biology at Caltech in 1946 and stayed on until 1961. For his work in genetics he won the Lasker Award of the American Public Health Association in 1950. He and his first wife divorced, and he then married Muriel Barnett in 1953. With his second wife he wrote several books on genetics for a general audience. Recognition for years of work came in 1958 when Beadle, Tatum and Lederberg won the Nobel Prize. In that same year Beadle won the Albert Einstein Commemorative Award in Science, and in the following year he received the National Award from the American Cancer Society.

In the 1960s Beadle renewed his interest in the genetics of corn. He became a player in the "corn wars," a debate among geneticists and archaeologists over the domestication of corn or maize in the Americas. Beadle contended that modern corn comes from a Mexican wild grass rather than a now-extinct species of maize. Beadle drew his conclusion from the corn remains that show that domestication occurred at the time of the Mayans and Aztecs.

In 1961 Beadle left California for Chicago, Illinois, where he became the sixth chancellor of the University of Chicago. He remained there until he retired in 1968. By then he had accumulated over thirty honorary degrees from many universities around the country and been awarded memberships into several prestigious academic societies. For their work in popularizing genetics, he and his wife Muriel won the Edison Award in 1967. In the late 1960s Beadle became director of the American Medical Association's Institute for Biomedical Research. He died on June 9, 1989, in Pomona, California, at age eighty-five from complications of Alzheimer's disease.

BIOGRAPHICAL/CRITICAL SOURCES:

BOOKS

The Annual Obituary, 1989, St. James Press, 1990, pp. 336-339.*

*   *   *

BEALS, Melba Patillo
  See BEALS, Melba Pattillo

*   *   *

BEALS, Melba Pattillo   1941-
  (Melba Patillo Beals)

PERSONAL: Born in 1941, in Little Rock, AR; daughter of Lois Pattillo (a teacher); surrogate child of George (a professor and founder of Sonoma State University) and Carol McCabe; married a soldier, c. 1961 (divorced, c. 1968); children: Kelley (daughter). *Education:* Attended Horace Mann High School, Little Rock, then Central High School, Little Rock, AR; graduated from Montgomery High School, Montgomery, CA; studied journalism at San Francisco State University; Columbia University, graduate degree (broadcast journalism and film).

ADDRESSES: Agent—c/o Pocket Books/Simon & Schuster, 1230 Avenue of the Americas, New York, NY 10020.

CAREER: Writer. Former television news reporter for National Broadcasting Corporation (NBC), KQED-affiliate, San Francisco, CA; Media Exposure (a public relations and marketing firm), owner, Sausalito, CA.

AWARDS, HONORS: Martin Buskin Lecturer, Educational Writers Association, 1995; honored by President Clinton, 1997, for attending Central High School, Little Rock, AR, to execute the Supreme Court's decision in Brown v. Board of Education.

WRITINGS:

Expose Yourself: Using the Power of Public Relations to Promote Your Business and Yourself, Chronicle Books (San Francisco, CA), 1990.

Warriors Don't Cry: A Searing Memoir of the Battle to Integrate Little Rock's Central High, Pocket Books (New York City), 1994.

SIDELIGHTS: Melba Pattillo Beals was thrust into the spotlight at the early age of fifteen as one of the "Little Rock Nine." She, along with eight other African-American students, was selected to attend Little Rock, Arkansas's all-white Central High School. Originally eighteen black students agreed to attend, but by the actual day, only nine were left. Realizing the ground-breaking Supreme Court decision of Brown vs. Board of Education, these nine teenagers endured violence and isolation as they became among the first black Americans to challenge openly the practice of segregation in the American South. According to Clarence Petersen's Chicago Tribune Books review of her 1994 work, *Warriors Don't Cry: A Searing Memoir of the Battle to Integrate Little Rock's Central High,* Beals "emerged from the struggle strengthened by faith, courage, and hope." Beals was encouraged and went on to become a television news reporter for the National Broadcasting Network (NBC) in San Francisco, a public relations expert, and eventually a writer.

In her first book, 1990's *Expose Yourself: Using the Power of Public Relations to Promote Your Business and Yourself,* Beals utilized her personal experience with national attention and her public relations experience, as well as her academic credentials and training, to construct an informative book aimed at helping the reader learn the art of public relations. According to Leighton Klein in the *Bloomsbury Review,* Beals's book depicts "quite simply—how to manipulate the media." Her knowledgeable perspectives, both on screen and off, made her a qualified guide to the secrets of attracting media attention. Although David Rouse of *Booklist* found fault with the title, he did praise the helpful information in *Expose Yourself.* Using a straightforward approach in *Expose Yourself,* Beals created "a work [that] will be useful to anyone seeking a self-help guide to publicity," commented Robert Logsdon in *Library Journal.*

Warriors Don't Cry is a coming-of-age story, both for the young Beals and for the nation. To assist Beals in understanding the powerful events, she began the book shortly after the events occurred. From the time of her experience to the book's release in 1994, Beals manuscript went through at least twelve rewrites. Millicent Ellison Brown in *Women's Review of Books* lauded Beals for "shar[ing] her own transformation from confident, happy-in-my-own-world teen, to someone who dared to believe that you can be neither happy nor in your own world if that space is prescribed by others solely based on race." *Warriors Don't Cry,* a memoir of Beals's experience as one of the "Little Rock Nine," addresses the personal and cultural battles that took place surrounding the historical event. Beals details the events through excerpts from her own diary entries as a sixteen-year-old girl and through newspaper clippings. According to Keith Dixon in the *New York Times Book Review,* this vivid and moving memoir serves as a reminder of the pain and suffering caused by racial segregation. Although many critics assessed *Warriors Don't Cry* as a fine read, some reviewers argued that the memoir would have benefitted from more information about Beals's personal life. Jervey Tervalon of the *Los Angeles Times Book Review* maintained, in his review of *Warriors Don't Cry,* that he "wanted more self-reflection from Beals: more than the four- or five-page summation of the rest of her life, less of the daily account of the cruelty inflicted upon her."

Other reviewers expressed opinions similar to Brown, who asserted that the memoir resembled a "fictionalized account" more than an in-depth look into the effects of the events of Central High on Beals herself, both then and now. Reviewer David Holmstrom of *Christian Science Monitor* found the work to be "a powerful, chilling account of what it was like to endure howling, redneck mobs, to be attacked physically and verbally, to be shot at, and to be continually hated and threatened."

Through the depiction of numerous family conversations, including one that inspired the title of *Warriors Don't Cry,* Beals illustrated the strength and resolve of her family during that traumatic time. Both her mother and grandmother played a prominent role in guiding the young Beals forward and supporting her attendance at Central High. Tervalon wrote: "Beals's grandmother, India, is a follower of Ghandi's teachings and impressed upon her granddaughter the importance and need for personal sacrifice to accomplish even modest social change; this willingness to sacrifice is a major theme of the book. Beals is in every sense a nonviolent warrior of integration." *Warriors Don't Cry* also addresses the sacrifices endured by Beals, the eight other black students at Central High, and the students' families. In a review in *Washington Post Book World,* Judith Paterson declared that in *Warriors Don't Cry* "the political story that threatened the unity of the nation parallel[s] the personal one threatening the adolescent identity of the narrator." Eventually, to remove Beals from an environment of death threats from the Ku Klux Klan in Little Rock, she was taken in by the white George and Carol McCabe family in Occidental, CA, whom she refers to as her ma and pa. She graduated from Montgomery High School in California, attended college at San Francisco State University, and earned a graduate degree from Columbia University in New York. Beals makes her home in California.

Beals's life took an abrupt turn when she signed the petition against segregation in the small southern town of Little Rock, Arkansas. Calling upon the same strength, grace, and determination that allowed her to walk through the angry mobs at Central High on the first day of class in September, 1957, she has documented her experiences and has created what Brown called an "effective tool for better understanding one of America's bleakest eras." A commentator from *Kirkus Review* praised Beals' "immediacy" pointing out that "the well-crafted account makes the events seem like they happened yesterday." Petersen in Chicago *Tribune Books* summarized the deeply personal memoir as "riveting."

BIOGRAPHICAL/CRITICAL SOURCES:

PERIODICALS

Belles Lettres, spring, 1995, pp. 68-69.
Bloomsbury Review, May/June, 1990, p. 14.
Booklist, March 15, 1990, pp. 1401-1402.
Christian Science Monitor, June 7, 1994, p. 13.

Kirkus Reviews, March 14, 1994.
Library Journal, March 15, 1990.
Los Angeles Times Book Review, July 3, 1994, pp. 2, 7.
New York Review of Books, April 20, 1995, pp. 34-35, 44-49.
New York Times Book Review, June 19, 1994, p. 33.
Press Democrat (Santa Rosa, CA), September 24, 1997.
Tribune Books (Chicago), February 12, 1995, p. 8.
Washington Post Book World, May 29, 1994, pp. 3, 12.
Women's Review of Books, December, 1994, pp. 13-15.

OTHER

www.booknotes.org
www.boston.com/dailyglobe*

*　　*　　*

BEASLEY, Bruce　1958-

PERSONAL: Born January 20, 1958, in Thomaston, GA; son of Harold and Dorothy (Leming) Beasley; married Suzanne Paola, September 7, 1992; children: Jin. *Education:* Oberlin College, B.A., 1980; Columbia University, M.F.A., 1982; University of Virginia, Ph.D., 1993. *Religion:* Roman Catholic.

ADDRESSES: Office—Department of English, Western Washington University, Bellingham, WA 98225. *Agent*—c/o University Press of Colorado, P.O. Box 849, Niwot, CO 80544.

CAREER: Poet, c. 1988—. Western Washington University, Bellingham, WA, associate professor of English, 1992—.

AWARDS, HONORS: Ohio State University Press/ *The Journal* Award, 1993, for *The Creation;* Colorado Prize, 1997, for *Summer Mystagogia;* National Endowment for the Arts fellowship, 1992.

WRITINGS:

POETRY

Spirituals, Wesleyan University Press (Middletown, CT), 1988.

The Creation, Ohio State University Press (Columbus, OH), 1994.

Summer Mystagogia, University Press of Colorado (Niwot, CO), 1996.

Also contributor of poems to periodicals, including *Poetry, Yale Review, Kenyon Review,* and *Gettysburg Review.*

SIDELIGHTS: Poet Bruce Beasley, who grew up in Georgia, has penned three collections of poetry, two of which have won awards. His first book, *Spirituals,* saw print in 1988 and established his frequently used theme of Christianity. Beasley is also known for his poems concerning grief and loss—some of which describe his childhood with alcoholic parents—as well as his use of tales from classical mythology. In addition to his book-length collections, his poetry has appeared in such periodicals as *America, Poetry,* and the *Yale Review.*

Spirituals was well-received by critics. Staige Blackford in the *Virginia Quarterly Review* hailed it as "a beautiful first book," and observed that though many of Beasley's pieces tell a story, "their strength is in their lyricality." Mark Jarman in the *Hudson Review* praised the poet's "original imagination and style in the way he retells Biblical stories," and cited "Death of Lazarus" as a "particularly effective" example. Blackford concluded his critique by asserting that "*Spirituals* is a book of apprenticeship in which one can see the potential for genius." Besides the aforementioned "Death of Lazarus," the volume includes selections such as "Novice," "From Grace"—a retelling of the Genesis story of the fall of man—and "Elegy," an account of Christ's Last Supper that Jarman lauded for its "fresh portrait" of a well-known Biblical scene.

Beasley's second volume, 1994's *The Creation,* garnered him the Ohio State University Press/*The Journal* Award. In addition to religious poems such as "Tracing the Angel," *The Creation* includes "Going Home to Georgia," a personal tribute to Beasley's childhood home. The collection also features the classically-themed "Eurydice in Hades" and "Zeta Hercules." B. Wallenstein, reviewing *The Creation* in *Choice,* singled out "The Instrument and Proper Corps of the Soule" for particular attention, applauding it as "a free-wheeling, five-part meditation on the brain." Though Wallenstein asserted that Beasley did not quite measure up to the standards of such great poets, Wallenstein compared his works to metaphysical and religious poets T. S. Eliot and W.

H. Auden. Molly McQuade in *Publishers Weekly* also complimented *The Creation,* proclaiming it "a gracefully lush reverie on matters of earth and spirit." She further noted that Beasley "shares what he knows as our fellow traveler, and not as a guide." Blackford, in a *Virginia Quarterly Review* assessment, described Beasley's "approach" as "always measured, yet sure," and finished with the declaration that *The Creation* "is filled with thoughtful and serious poems."

For *Summer Mystagogia,* his 1996 collection of poems, Beasley was awarded the Colorado Prize. The poet defines the last word in his title as "the period immediately following the initiation into a mystery." Citing the title poem and another labeled "The Monologue of the Signified" as worthy examples from the volume's pages, Daniel Tobin, a contributor to the *Boston Review,* assessed Beasley's work in *Summer Mystagogia* as "a wonderfully resilient and hard-won poetry of witness."

BIOGRAPHICAL/CRITICAL SOURCES:

BOOKS

Beasley, Bruce, *Summer Mystagogia,* University Press of Colorado, 1997.

PERIODICALS

Boston Review, February/March, 1997.
Choice, October, 1994, p. 278.
Hudson Review, winter, 1989, pp. 734-735.
Publishers Weekly, April 25, 1994, p. 65.
Virginia Quarterly Review, summer, 1988, pp. 99-100; autumn, 1994, p. 136.

*   *   *

BEDARD, Michael   1949-

PERSONAL: Born June 26, 1949, in Toronto, Ontario, Canada; married; wife's name, Martha; children: four. *Education:* University of Toronto, B.A. (English and philosophy), 1971. *Avocational interests:* Collecting books (particularly stories of the supernatural), cooking vegetarian meals, baseball.

ADDRESSES: Home—Toronto, Ontario, Canada. *Agent*—Linda McKnight, Westwood Creative Artists, 94 Harbord St., Toronto, ON M5S 1G6, Canada.

CAREER: St. Michael's College Library, Toronto, Ontario, Canada, library assistant, 1971-78; pressman at a small press, 1978-81; full-time writer, 1982—.

AWARDS, HONORS: Book of the Year, Canadian Library Association, Governor General's Literary Award for Text, 1990, National Chapter of Canada IODE Violet Downey Book Award, and Young Adult Canadian Book Award runner-up, both 1991, International Board on Books for Young People (IBBY) Honor List, 1992, all for *Redwork;* National Chapter of Canada IODE Violet Downey Book Award, 1991, for *The Nightingale.*

WRITINGS:

JUVENILE

Woodsedge and Other Tales (fairy tales), Gardenshore Press, 1979.
Pipe and Pearls: A Gathering of Tales (fairy tales), Gardenshore Press, 1980.
A Darker Magic (novel), Atheneum, 1987.
The Lightning Bolt, illustrated by Regolo Ricci, Oxford University Press, 1989.
Redwork (novel), Lester, 1990, Atheneum, 1990.
The Tinderbox (retelling), illustrated by Regolo Ricci, Oxford University Press, 1990.
The Nightingale (retelling), illustrated by Regolo Ricci, Oxford University Press, 1991.
Painted Devil (novel), Lester, 1994.

BIOGRAPHY

Emily, illustrated by Barbara Cooney, Lester, 1992, Doubleday, 1992.
The Divide, illustrated by Emily Arnold McCully, Doubleday, 1997.
Glass Town, illustrated by Laura Fernandez and Rick Jacobson, Atheneum, 1997.

SIDELIGHTS: "We sat there spellbound as it flowed and eddied about the room, transforming all it touched." In his stories for children and young adults, Michael Bedard uses vivid, sometimes disturbing prose, as in this description of a magician's spell in *A Darker Magic.* Bedard's work is filled with mystery and magic as he investigates themes of freedom, self-determination, and imagination. His novels often investigate the supernatural, but they don't fit neatly into one category. They have been variously described as "realistic," "fantasy," "dark-fantasy," "mystery," "psychological thriller" and

"mystical prose-poetry." Joanne Findon explained in *Canadian Children's Literature* that Bedard masters a number of difficult ideas in a sophisticated manner. "One of the most intriguing aspects of Bedard's work is his richly textured representation of evil," Findon says. "In fact, Bedard prefers to speak of 'darkness'—a term which expands his symbolic range considerably and allows him to deploy a series of double-edged images throughout his novels."

Bedard's major works include *A Darker Magic, Redwork,* and *Painted Devil.* In *Redwork,* his main characters are an alchemist and two teenagers who form an unlikely friendship. In *A Darker Magic* and *Painted Devil* the protagonists face demonic characters. Bedard has also written several picture books reworking the traditional folk and fairy tales of Hans Christian Andersen and the Brothers Grimm with endings that evoke much more optimism than the originals.

Bedard's work has been heavily influenced by Emily Dickinson's poetry and exhibits a keen focus on extremes and what lies beneath the surface of things. Bedard's fiction, picture books, and retellings of fairy tales and folk stories have earned him a reputation as an important writer of fiction for children, but because his writing is detailed it is sometimes viewed as challenging for young readers.

Bedard is best known for writing suspense novels for young adults, a natural audience for someone who has been around children all his life. He was born the oldest of five children and was raised in Toronto, Canada, where he still lives. Stories became a fascination for him when he was four, and he pored over Currier and Ives prints and later through comic books that he lugged with him wherever he went. Books were a scarce commodity in Bedard's household, so when he was a young boy he was thrilled to inherit six books from an uncle. These classics sent him on adventures with Tom Sawyer, Huck Finn, Long John Silver and Tarzan. They were the seeds from which his writings would grow. "It was not until I was seventeen or so and fell under the spell of poetry that I first began to write," Bedard explains in *Seventh Book of Junior Authors and Illustrators.* "We had a teacher that year with a passion for poetry that proved infectious. . . . By the end of the year I had begun to write. I knew right then what I wanted to do with the rest of my life."

He went on to attend the University of Toronto and earned a Bachelor of Arts degree in English and philosophy, graduating in 1971. The next several years he worked at a university library and began a family. Bedard later took a job as a pressman at a small printing shop and while working there published two collections of original fairy tales for children, *Woodsedge and Other Tales* and *Pipe and Pearls: A Gathering of Tales.* All the while he seemed to be building a foundation for his lifetime passion of becoming a full-time writer, which he realized in 1982.

In his first novel, *A Darker Magic,* Bedard tells a story about a magician who takes away children's souls. It centers around an elderly teacher, Miss Potts, who fifty years earlier, as a young girl, persuaded her parents to take her to a magic show in the waiting room of a railway depot. A magician, Professor Mephisto, materializes on the makeshift stage; his performance has deadly results. Five decades later, a handbill appears in one of the schoolroom desks where Miss Potts teaches, announcing there will be a show by Professor Mephisto in the old railway depot. As the date of the show draws closer, Miss Potts begins to remember what happened that fateful night when she was a young girl. Miss Potts and one of her students, Emily Endicott, must work together to thwart Mephisto's evil plans.

Bedard's debut novel was well-received by critics. According to a reviewer in *Children's Book News,* "*A Darker Magic* is rich in imagery and unexplained incident all woven together to make a totally captivating story which will engross—and probably frighten—its readers. It's not a book to be missed." David Gale, writing in *School Library Journal,* similarly stated that the author's "well-paced narrative is rich in language and riveting in tone; it brims with a sense of foreboding that is sustained throughout." Other reviewers questioned the appropriateness of the work for children. In *Books in Canada,* Welwyn Wilton Katz commented that "all of the children of this book are either victims or potential victims," adding, "There is no light in *A Darker Magic.*"

Bedard drew from his own upbringing when creating the characters for *A Darker Magic.* In an interview with Marie C. Davis in *Canadian Children's Literature,* Bedard says the relationship between Emily and her younger brother Albert paralleled his family life. "I was often called upon to watch the younger kids because there is a seventeen-year gap between me and the youngest. . . . The younger sibling offers a reminder of where you came from and is helpful in developing where you are going to go."

Two years after *A Darker Magic* was published, Bedard's *The Lightning Bolt* was released. In this reversal on Grimms' tale of *The Fisherman and His Wife,* Bedard features an old, poor woman who frees a little man from a tree in the woods. He gives her a stick that grants wishes and a cap that reveals others' secret thoughts. Quietly keeping the cap, she gives her bullying husband the stick and he greedily obtains more and more gifts. Her husband continues to mistreat her and decides to kill her, but because she has the cap she knows his secret thoughts and saves herself by returning the gifts to the little man. Finally, the wicked husband is returned to the roots of the tree where the woman found the little man.

A year later Bedard retold another story, *The Tinder Box* by Hans Christian Andersen. In this tale, a soldier finds a witch's magical tinder box and with it reaps fortune and the hand of a beautiful princess. The soldier understands that his wealth attracts false friends, but instead of being bitter, he remembers his poor beginnings and makes donations to the poor. "Bedard's satisfyingly zestful narrative allows us to enjoy the soldier's successes without letting us forget the unsavoury greed that motivates him, for the soldier is not a perfect hero," according to Ulrike Walker in *Canadian Children's Literature.*

There is a similarity between writing fairy tales and writing novels, Bedard explains to Davis: "I began my work by writing poetry and fairy tales. I think perhaps that is still what I'm doing. The form has changed, but the intent is the same. . . . That is what moves us in a piece of poetry, a fine sculpture, a beautiful dance; we see the harmony of inward and outward, the finite and the infinite, eternity and time." Critics believe Bedard achieved this harmony in his second novel, *Redwork,* which was published in 1990 and is generally considered his most accomplished work. "There is simply too much that is good here to cover in a review," according to Laurence Steven in *Canadian Children's Literature.* The story unfolds as fifteen-year-old Cass and his single mother, Alison, move into an unkept old house. Their landlord is Mr. Magnus, a reclusive World War I veteran, who lives on the floor below. Meanwhile, Cass feels a strange bond between the house and Mr. Magnus. Cass and his new friend Maddy discover that Mr. Magnus is an alchemist and take part in his quest to make a philosopher's stone.

Patrick Jones declares in *Voice of Youth Advocates* that in *Redwork,* "Everything is described with detail, every point is made with dialogue, and each scene is fleshed out considerably." The theme of the novel, like many of his other works, delves into the dark roads people must take during life's travels, which reflects William Blake's writings. This influence is most obvious in *Redwork,* but the idea of descending into death is also present in Bedard's *A Darker Magic* and *Painted Devil.* Despite the dark images in his stories, Bedard says he believes that childhood is a time of innocence. "The child's vision is one of wonder and awe," he tells Davis. "The child is fully imaginative. As the child becomes more accommodated to the world and more self-conscious—around ten, eleven, twelve—some of their initial lights begin to go out. Suddenly it is not enough to just be themselves; it is very important how they are perceived. So these original openings that the child had are curbed or curtailed."

Bedard's next work, *The Nightingale,* is adapted from the original classic written by Hans Christian Andersen. Bedard "uses descriptive and colorful language to relate the ancient tale of a Chinese emperor who ruled over a huge empire and lives in the most magnificent palace in the world," according to Gwen Maguire in a review for *CM: A Reviewing Journal of Canadian Materials for Young People.* Visitors come from around the world to see the palace and city where the emperor ruled. They are impressed with what they see, but they are enraptured by the song of a nightingale. When the emperor learns this, he has the bird captured and kept in a cage. A mechanical, bejeweled bird patterned after the real nightingale is sent as a gift from a Japanese emperor and is equipped to sing one of the songs sung by the real nightingale. The emperor soon cherishes this replica more than the real one. By the story's end, however, it is the real nightingale that gives the dying emperor life.

In his next work, *Emily,* Bedard incorporates two passions, one for reclusive poet Emily Dickinson, and the other for his unquenchable thirst to explore new areas of knowledge. After researching Dickinson's life, "the idea for the picture book *Emily* came to me, as I imagined what it might be like for a young child to move in across the street from this remarkable woman," Bedard explains in the *Seventh Book of Junior Authors and Illustrators.* In *Emily,* a young girl's mother is invited to play the piano at Dickinson's house. A brief encounter between Emily and the child involves an exchange of gifts—lily bulbs for a bit of paper with a handwritten poem.

"The story is very quiet but beautifully crafted, with a clarity of observation and a delicately tart edge, that creditably emulate Emily herself," according to a contributor in *Kirkus Reviews.* Bedard explains in the Davis interview that Dickinson was elusive: "The embodiment of mystery. But, she teaches you very deep lessons. On the surface she lived a very limited life in a very limited world. But she opened that out in incredible ways. She saw into the small things of life with a passion and a depth that someone in a larger world might not have seen comparably."

It is precisely the same eye for detail that Stephanie Zvirin referred to in a *Booklist* review. She explains that Bedard "knows how to create chilling atmosphere" in his novel *Painted Devil.* "Recurring imagery and precise descriptions are part of his technique, and he's a master at manipulating tension," Zvirin says. *Painted Devil* centers around Alice, who accepts a summer job helping produce a Punch and Judy puppet show at the library. Alice's parents are preoccupied with her mother's troubled pregnancy and leave a lot of the care of little Lela to her. Frightening events occur as the puppet show is about to begin and only Alice's Aunt Emily (Emily Endicott from *A Darker Magic*), who is odd and secretive, knows that these happenings are part of an ancient satanic spirit's unrelenting plot, and that the only way to avoid doom is to destroy the devil puppet. A reviewer in *Publishers Weekly* commented: "Bedard's intensely dark, moody yet handsomely wrought prose lends itself well to this sophisticated thriller." Zvirin noted that the author "invokes a sense of mystery and foreboding so vividly that the story is hard to put down."

Bedard tapped on his experience working in a library, as he sets the plot around the home and local public library. He states in the Davis interview that he must be able to see a scene to describe it to the reader. "When I stop being able to see the scene, I must stop writing," he says. "I'm not a writer who can somehow prompt the scene by the act of writing the words." According to the critics, the format works. "*Painted Devil* is a well-written novel that depicts good and evil forces at play, and the positive results that ensue when fears (real or imagined) are met and conquered," according to Irene E. Aubrey in a *Quill and Quire* review. "Bedard successfully creates a mood of unease and foreboding, and his complex characters capture the reader's imagination." Steven summed up Bedard's writing: "The subtlety of Bedard's handling of relationships represents maturity missing in a great deal of adult fiction, not to speak of the plethora of superficiality aimed at teens. Michael Bedard is worth reading."

Bedard explains in his interview with Davis that there is an important relationship between him and the reader. "The reader is really a co-creator," Bedard says. "It is not up to me to detail everything to such an extent that I put the reader's imagination out. It's rather up to me to sketch things and to touch on detail to the extent that I bring the piece alive, but beyond that the reader comes in and fleshes it out."

BIOGRAPHICAL/CRITICAL SOURCES:

BOOKS

Bedard, Michael, *A Darker Magic,* Atheneum, 1987.
Bedard, Michael, autobiographical essay in *Seventh Book of Junior Authors and Illustrators,* edited by Sally Holmes Holtze, H.W. Wilson, 1996.
Twentieth-Century Children's Writers, St. James Press, 1995, p. 78.

PERIODICALS

Booklist, March 1, 1994, p. 1249.
Books in Canada, April, 1988, p. 36; December, 1992, pp. 30-32.
Canadian Children's Literature, no. 63, 1991, pp. 72-73, 83-87; no. 70, 1993, pp. 92-94; no. 82, 1996, pp. 69-79.
Children's Book News, winter, 1987, p. 11.
CM: A Reviewing Journal of Canadian Materials for Young People, May, 1988, p. 85; October, 1991, p. 306; January, 1993, p. 20.
Horn Book, May-June, 1990, p. 367; January-February, 1993, pp. 72-73.
In Review: Canadian Books for Children, October, 1979, pp. 30-31; February, 1980, p. 34; August, 1981, p. 28.
Junior Bookshelf, August, 1990, pp. 164-165; August, 1991, p. 141.
Kirkus Reviews, November 1, 1990, p. 1528; March 1, 1992, p. 320; December, 1992, p. 26.
Publishers Weekly, March 14, 1994, p. 74.
Quill and Quire, November, 1989, p. 15; August, 1990, p. 14; September, 1990, p. 20; December, 1992, p. 26; April, 1994, pp. 38-39.
School Librarian, August, 1991, p. 99.
School Library Journal, October, 1990, p. 139; November, 1992, p. 88.

Voice of Youth Advocates, December, 1990, p. 293; April, 1993, p. 34.*

*   *   *

BEHAR, Ruth   1956-

PERSONAL: Born November 12, 1956, in Havana, Cuba; immigrated to the United States, 1962; naturalized citizen, 1986; daughter of Alberto Behar and Rebecca (Glinsky) Behar; married David Frye, June 6, 1982; children: Gabriel Frye-Behar. *Ethnicity:* "Latino." *Education:* Wesleyan University, B.A., 1977; Princeton University, M.A., 1981, Ph.D., 1983. *Religion:* Jewish.

ADDRESSES: Home—Ann Arbor, MI. *Office*—c/o Department of Anthropology, University of Michigan, 1020 LSA Building, Ann Arbor, MI 48109.

CAREER: University of Michigan, Ann Arbor, assistant professor, 1986-89, associate professor, 1989-94, professor of anthropology, 1994—.

AWARDS, HONORS: MacArthur fellowship, 1988-93; Guggenheim fellowship, 1995-96.

WRITINGS:

Santa Maria del Monte: The Presence of the Past in a Spanish Village (nonfiction), Princeton University Press (Princeton, NJ), c. 1986, reprinted as *The Presence of the Past in a Spanish Village: Santa Maria del Monte,* Princeton University Press, 1991.
Translated Woman: Crossing the Border With Esperanza's Story (nonfiction), Beacon Press (Boston, MA), 1993.
(Editor) *Bridges to Cuba/Puentes a Cuba* (literary anthology), University of Michigan Press (Ann Arbor, MI), 1995.
Las Visiones de una Bruja Guachichil en 1599: Hacia una Perspectiva Indaigena Sobre la Conquista de San Luis Potosai, Centro de Investigaciones Histaoricas (San Luis Potosai), 1995.
(Editor with Deborah A. Gordon) *Women Writing Culture* (nonfiction), University of California Press (Berkeley, CA), 1995.
The Vulnerable Observer: Anthropology That Breaks Your Heart (nonfiction), Beacon Press, 1996.

Contributor of poetry to *Tikkun, Michigan Quarterly Review, Prairie Schooner, American VOICE, Bridges,* and *Witness;* contributor of articles to journals, including *Kenyon Review, Chronicle of Higher Education,* and *Natural History;* contributor to anthologies including *Little Havana Blues: A Cuban-American Literature Anthology* and *Sephardic American Voices: Two Hundred Years of Literary Legacy.*

SIDELIGHTS: Educator and author Ruth Behar was born in Havana, Cuba, and raised by Eastern European and Sephardic Jewish grandparents who had immigrated there after the passage in 1924 of the Immigration and Nationality Act (through which the United States sought to limit Jewish immigration). This background led to her interest in anthropology; her academic home for the past several years has been the University of Michigan's anthropology department. Though she has also written poetry and edited a literary anthology of Cuban writers, Behar has become known for her anthropological works which blur the line between social science and personal involvement with the people she studies, including the well-received 1993 book *Translated Woman: Crossing the Border With Esperanza's Story.* Behar explained her philosophy of the "involved participant" in anthropology in her 1996 collection of personal essays *The Vulnerable Observer: Anthropology That Breaks Your Heart.*

Behar's first full-length anthropological work, however, is *Santa Maria del Monte: The Presence of the Past in a Spanish Village,* published in 1986, and subsequently reprinted with the title and subtitle reversed. In this generously illustrated volume, Behar examines a Spanish village which had remained in isolation from modern Spain longer than most other settlements. By the time she wrote her book, however, it was finally becoming encroached upon by a nearby development of holiday 'chalets.' The people of the village of Santa Maria in the province of Leon, Spain, felt "the presence of the past" and had a long tradition of literacy, thus Behar was aided in her study by well-kept village records dating back to the eighteenth century. Her chronicle portrays what Sandra Ott in *Times Literary Supplement* describes as "long term cultural continuity" rather than the more fashionable anthropological depiction of modern social and economic change, and includes the conventions of inheriting private property as well as some methods of control by the "concejo" (village council) over communal property. D. D. Caulkins, reviewing *Santa Maria del Monte* in *Choice,* noted that "this admirable work sets a high standard for

historical ethnography." Ott greeted it as "a welcome step forward in Iberian anthropology." Similarly, James S. Amelang in the *New York Times Book Review* complimented it as "an impressive foray into historical ethnography."

Translated Woman began when Behar was working on a very different project—archival records of women affected by the Mexican Inquisition. She went to a cemetery near the town of Mexquitic and attempted to photograph a Mexican-Native American woman placing flowers on the graves of her children. The woman, to whom Behar assigned the name Esperanza in the book, questioned her about what she was doing. The two struck up an acquaintance, and Esperanza bargained with Behar. If Behar and her husband would serve as godparents to one of her living children, Esperanza would tell her story to Behar and provide the anthropologist with intimate details of the life of women in Mexquitic.

Esperanza's story does appear in *Translated Woman,* and it is a tale of suffering and abuse. Her first memory is of her father beating her mother; later, she herself is battered by her own first husband. Esperanza credits the rage this produced within her with spoiling her breast milk, and thus causing several of her infant children to die of malnutrition. When her husband—who is not only abusive but an adulterer as well—is suddenly and mysteriously stricken with blindness, Esperanza is labeled a witch by the rest of her community. She is already somewhat on the outside of society because of her poverty and her Native American heritage, but the suspicion of witchcraft places her further outside the circle of community.

At the end of *Translated Woman,* Behar provides an autobiographical chapter, comparing her own life to Esperanza's and claiming outsider status as well—as a granddaughter of Jewish emigrants in Cuba, as a Cuban refugee in the United States, and as a woman difficult to classify in academia. This has proven the most controversial section of the work. Victor Perera in the *Nation* cautioned that "it is disingenuous to compare the suffering Mexican village society inflicts on Esperanza for rebelling against its strictures with the ordeal of having to accept tenure at a prominent university," while Nancy Scheper-Hughes in the *New York Times Book Review* determined that "the metaphor is contrived and the lesson is clear: the lives of anthropologists are rarely as rich and fascinating as those of their subjects." Conversely, Louise Lamphere in the *Women's Review of Books* observed that "the difficulties of articulating the connections between the American woman academic and Mexican female street peddler, the sense of contradictions in tension, and the lack of an easy resolution are perhaps, paradoxically, the most satisfying aspects of Behar's book." Emma Perez in the *Journal of American History* observed: "Behar has offered a gift. . . . Rarely do academicians engage their contradictions so honestly."

On the value of *Translated Woman* as a whole, critics were clear. Perez predicted that "the book will become a model for ethnographers, historians, and other scholars crossing disciplines to reconstruct life histories." Lamphere held the volume up as "postmodernist writing at its best," while Scheper-Hughes offered appreciation for the fact that "Behar has broken many taboos and inhibitions in writing an experimental ethnographic text that has for its subject a poor native Mexican woman who refuses to be a pitiful victim, or a saint, or a Madonna, or a whore, or a Joan of Arc." Perera praised *Translated Woman* as "a ground-breaking Latina feminist ethnography" and a "powerful and brilliant study."

Reviewing *The Vulnerable Observer* in the electronic magazine *Salon,* Sally Eckhoff explained Behar's new method of anthropological study: "Combine traditional fieldwork with a researcher's personal experience . . . and you come up with a mode of study that informs the intellect as it grips the emotions—without smashing the delicate subject(s) flat, the way conventional research often does." Eckhoff went on to report that Behar structures *The Vulnerable Observer* in such a way as to first explain and defend her position, then illustrate its benefits with specific essays that have resulted from her method. Included in this section is a piece about studying elderly villagers in Spain while simultaneously worrying about her own elderly grandfather's decline in Miami, Florida. Diane Cole, discussing *The Vulnerable Observer* in the *New York Times Book Review,* congratulated Behar on the "insight, candor and compassion" of "her vision."

The volumes Behar has edited or co-edited have attracted critical notice as well. *Bridges to Cuba/ Puentes a Cuba* contains literary contributions both from writers living in Cuba and from writers living in exile from that nation. R. Ocasio, reviewing the anthology in *Choice,* observed that "Behar introduces readers to the diaspora of the rich literature of Cuba" and concluded by recommending the book for most libraries. *Women Writing Culture,* which Behar

edited with Deborah A. Gordon, contains essays by women anthropologists and discusses important contributions to that field by women which have been often overlooked. Kate Gilbert, holding forth on the essay collection in the *Women's Review of Books,* protested "the way some contributors, largely successful in academic anthropology, rush to claim outsider status," but found most of the individual essays to be useful contributions to the field. C. Hendrickson in *Choice,* however, concluded that "this lively and important book . . . challenges readers to rethink ethnographic traditions in the face of experimental feminist writing."

BIOGRAPHICAL/CRITICAL SOURCES:

PERIODICALS

Belles Lettres, summer, 1993.
Bookworld, March 21, 1993.
Choice, October, 1986, p. 346; June, 1996, pp. 1649, 1690-1691.
Journal of American History, September, 1994, pp. 836-837.
Nation, September 20, 1993, pp. 290-292.
New York Times Book Review, September 28, 1986, p. 27; September 5, 1993, p. 22.
Times Literary Supplement, January 16, 1987, p. 64.
Women's Review of Books, May, 1993, p. 14; June, 1996, pp. 21-22.

OTHER

nytimes.com, March 23, 1997.
salonmagazine.com, April 15, 1997.

—Sketch by Elizabeth Wenning

*   *   *

BEN-YEHUDA, Nachman 1948-

PERSONAL: Born March 8, 1948, in Jerusalem, Israel; son of Itzhak (an accountant) and Dina (a practical nurse) Ben-Yehuda; married August 29, 1973; wife's name, Etti (an administrator); children: Tzach, Guy. *Ethnicity:* "Jewish." *Education:* Hebrew University of Jerusalem, B.A. (cum laude), 1972; University of Chicago, M.A., 1976, Ph.D., 1977. *Religion:* Jewish. *Avocational interests:* Science fiction, astronomy, movies, naval warfare.

ADDRESSES: Home—3 Heler St., Apt. 15, Givat Mordechai, Jerusalem 93725, Israel. *Office*—Department of Sociology and Anthropology, Hebrew University of Jerusalem, Jerusalem 91905, Israel; fax 02-532-4339. *E-mail*—msnahman@pluto.mscc.huji.ac.il.

CAREER: Hebrew University of Jerusalem, Jerusalem, Israel, member of faculty of sociology, 1978—. Visiting professor at State University of New York at Stony Brook, 1983-84, University of Toronto, 1990-91, and London School of Economics and Political Science, London, summers, 1996, 1997. U.S. National Council of Drug Abuse, international member of board of advisers, 1976-80; Israeli Interministerial and Interinstitutional Committee on Drug Abuse, director of Drug Abuse Unit, 1979-82; Israeli Ministry of Education, member of Interministerial Committee on Cults in Israel, 1982-85; National Committee on Police Violence, member, 1993-94; National Committee on Reforms in the Government Civil Service, member, 1996; consultant to U.S.-Israel Binational Science Foundation and Israeli Academy of Science. *Military service:* Israel Defense Forces, active duty in Military Police Investigation Department, 1966-69, 1973-74, reserve duty, 1969-96; became major.

MEMBER: Israeli Sociological Association, American Sociological Association, American Society of Criminology, U.S. Naval Institute.

WRITINGS:

Deviance and Moral Boundaries: Witchcraft, the Occult, Deviant Sciences and Scientists, University of Chicago Press (Chicago, IL), 1985.
The Politics and Morality of Deviance: Moral Panics, Drug Abuse, Deviant Science, and Reversed Stigmatization, State University of New York Press (Albany, NY), 1989.
Political Assassinations by Jews: A Rhetorical Device for Justice, State University of New York Press, 1993.
(With Erich Goode) *Moral Panics: The Social Construction of Deviance,* Blackwell, 1994.
The Masada Myth: Collective Memory and Mythmaking in Israel, University of Wisconsin Press (Madison, WI), 1995.

WORK IN PROGRESS: A book on deception and why people lie, using politics and archaeology as the central illustration; a book on treason; research on deviance among ultra-orthodox Jews.

SIDELIGHTS: Nachman Ben-Yehuda told *CA:* "I like to do research and write. Writing a book forces me to crystallize and focus my ideas, an activity that I have learned to cherish. My interest in deviance dates back to my days as an undergraduate. I have always been interested in conceptualizing how societies and cultures work. One interesting way of doing that is to look at some of the myriad contrasts that are characteristic of the way cultures are made. These contrasts set boundaries which, in turn, define the variety of the symbolic-moral universes of which complex cultures are made. Examining deviance and non-deviance allows me to look at some of the most fascinating and powerful of these contrasts.

"I have written about drug abuse, witchcraft, deviant sciences and scientists, politics, assassinations, positive deviance, moral panics, radio astronomy, UFOlogy, mythmaking, deception, and treason. My choices of subject matter were dictated by my desire to select phenomena of deviance that can be used to understand central cultural processes of change and stability. I typically begin writing only after the data collection process is complete. I outline what I want to say, create the structure of the book, and begin writing."

*   *   *

BERLOW, Alan 1950-

PERSONAL: Born January 25, 1950, in East Orange, NJ; son of Melville J. (an attorney) and Rose (Berkowitz) Berlow; married Susan Blaustein (a composer and journalist), December 27, 1988. *Education:* Attended New College (Sarasota, FL), c. 1972.

ADDRESSES: Home—9 East Melrose St., Chevy Chase, MD.

CAREER: Reporter, National Public Radio, 1979-89; freelance writer, 1989—.

AWARDS, HONORS: Overseas Press Club Award, 1985, for reporting from Honduras; Edward Weintol Award for Diplomatic Reporting from the School of Foreign Service, Georgetown University, 1986, for reporting from the Philippines; Major Armstrong Award, Columbia University, 1987, for reporting from the Philippines; World Hunger Award, World Hunger Foundation, 1987, for reporting from the

Philippines; Major Armstrong Award, Columbia University, 1989, for reporting from Cambodia.

WRITINGS:

NONFICTION

Dead Season: A Story of Murder and Revenge on the Philippine Island of Negros, Pantheon (New York), 1996.

SOUND RECORDINGS FOR NATIONAL PUBLIC RADIO (NPR)

Genetic Screening/Genetic Engineering, July 27, 1981.
Watergate, Ten Years After, June 22, 1982.
Vietnam Veterans in the Wake of War, November, 1982.
Vietnam Veterans' Memorial Dedication, November 13, 1982.
Reagan Administration Nuclear Weapons Policies, Parts I-V, March, 1983.
The Hotel Intrigue: The United States and Human Rights in Honduras, April 22, 1984.
Mexico City Earthquake, October 8, 1985.
The Philippines, 1986.
Davao City, Philippines: Laboratory for a Revolution, February 4, 1986.
New Hope for Philippine Democracy, September 18, 1986.
The New People's Army on Negros, February, 1987.
Land Reform in the Philippines, April 14-15, 1987.
Cambodia Ten Years after "Liberation", December 17, 1988.
The War against Rangoon, 1989.

Author or numerous other sound documentaries for NPR.

WORK IN PROGRESS: Detestable Villainy, a screenplay about a slave rebellion in the eighteenth century.

SIDELIGHTS: The subject of *Dead Season* by Alan Berlow, a former journalist for National Public Radio (NPR), is a series of inter-related murders which occurred on the Philippine island of Negros, in a barrio named Mambagaton (literally, "the place of the ghosts").

The book explores the surprising links between the massacre of Moret De los Santos, his wife Cerila, and their three small children, and three other deaths in the same town: that of a soldier who participated

in the massacre and was allegedly murdered two weeks later as part of a military cover-up; the assassination of the town's wealthiest landlord, Serafin "Batman" Gatuslao; and the kidnapping and murder of an alleged military informant whose name Cerila De los Santos inscribed in her own blood, only moments before she died, on a little wooden box in which her husband kept his "magic" snake. The narrative also dissects a cover-up of the massacre by the Armed Forces of the Philippines.

Based on the findings in *Dead Season,* Philippine President Fidel V. Ramos ordered the investigation into the De los Santos massacre reopened in December, 1996, more than six years after it had been shelved.

Seth Mydans, writing in the *New York Times Book Review,* remarked that *Dead Season* is "a book filled with sometimes shocking detail and personal intimacy, the kind of book about life in the Philippines that so many reporters wish they could leave their daily routines to write." The result of five years of research and writing based on more than two hundred interviews with witnesses, survivors, and the murderers themselves, the book illuminates the ways in which a single human rights abuse eventually corrupts every segment of society. Elected officials at the barrio and provincial level as well as the president of the republic, Corazon C. Aquino, are all swept into a whirlwind of deceit, and all are ultimately complicitous both in ensuring that there would be no justice for the victims and in contributing to an environment in which murder and disappearances are committed with impunity.

Berlow lived for five years in the Philippines while setting up and reporting for the Manila bureau of NPR and various newspapers and magazines. His intimate and telling expose of the murders of the De los Santos family propelled him to investigate Philippine politics—both local and national—as well as the economic and cultural problems of Philippine society, such as failed attempts at land reform, the ambiguous role of the Catholic Church, and the communist insurgency. "Ultimately, *Dead Season* is a case study of the corrosive effects of human rights violations on the very underpinnings of democracy," Berlow told *CA.* By deconstructing the De los Santos massacre, the book illustrates just how difficult it is to cultivate a democracy at the end of the twentieth century in the poisoned soil of feudalism, colonialism, and dictatorship.

Dead Season is "rich in telling detail and revealing a thorough understanding of the local culture," stated James A. Rhodes in *Publishers Weekly.* Jose Magadia, a contributor to *Commonweal,* commented that the book "reads like a mystery thriller. . . . A truly impressive piece of investigative journalism."

Berlow told *CA:* "Like many ordinary newspaper readers, I find it almost impossible to ignore the almost daily human rights horror stories, whether they be from Bosnia, Rwanda, East Timor, Tibet, of wherever. What I find most striking about much of the reporting on these incidents is how easily the victims are relegated to 'body counts.' In the end, it seems that the bigger the body count, the more 'significant' the human rights violation and, paradoxically, the more difficult it is to actually understand anything about either the victims or perpetrators.

"In 1988, when I was reporting for National Public Radio, I stumbled on one of these human rights stories on the Philippine island of Negros, and decided that I would attempt to learn everything there was to know about the characters involved. This meant tracking down not only survivors and their friends and family members, but government officials, businessmen, church leaders, and the men who were actually responsible for the murders. My hope was that in 'deconstructing' a single human rights case, the massacre of the De los Santos family, I might be able to understand a society and culture that seemed to routinely tolerate the most horrendous crimes without raising a finger of protest.

"The title of my book is taken from what residents of Negros call the *tiempo muerto,* or 'dead season,' the post-harvest period when sugar workers have no income, their children have little to eat, and, as a result, there is a high incidence of infant and child mortality. The dead season is an annual phenomenon that literally defines life on Negros. Because the book deals with a series of murders that take place within this environment, *Dead Season* seemed a fitting title."

BIOGRAPHICAL/CRITICAL SOURCES:

PERIODICALS

Asiaweek, December 13, 1996, p. 49.
Commonweal, February 14, 1997, p. 19.
Defense and Foreign Affairs, October 31, 1996.
Far Eastern Economic Review, February 20, 1997, p. 49.

IRE Journal, March/April, 1997.
Islands, March/April, 1997.
Library Journal, July, 1996, p. 138.
New York Times Book Review, October 20, 1996, p. 32.
Publishers Weekly, June 3, 1996, p. 68.
Washington Post Book World, October 6, 1996, p. 6.
Worldview, fall, 1996, p. 32.

*   *   *

BERRY, Leonidas Harris   1902-1995

PERSONAL: Born July 20, 1902, in Woodsdale, NC; died in 1995; son of Lewellyn and Beulah Anne Harris Berry; married Opheila Flannagan Harrison, 1937 (marriage ended); married Emma Ford Willis, 1959; children: (with Harrison) Judith Berry Griffin. *Education:* Wilberforce University, B.S., 1924; University of Chicago, B.S., 1925, M.D., 1930; University of Illinois, M.S. (pathology), 1933.

CAREER: Physician and writer. Freedmen's Hospital, Washington, DC, intern, c. 1930; Cook County Hospital, Chicago, IL, resident physician in internal medicine and gastroenterology, c. 1933-35; Provident Hospital, staff physician, 1935, founder of division of gastroenterology, c. 1936; chair of division of gastroenterology, c. 1936-70, chief of gastrointestinal endoscopy service, 1966-74; University of Illinois Medical School, instructor, 1950-57; Cook County Graduate School of Medicine, instructor, c. 1957-67; U.S. Department of State, traveled as a foreign cultural exchange lecturer to East Africa, West Africa, Japan, Korea, the Philippines, and France, 1965, 1966, and 1970; United States Department of Health, Education, and Welfare national advisory council on regional medical programs in heart disease, cancer, and stroke, member of council, 1966-68. Organizer and coordinator of clinics for medical counseling on narcotics for the Illinois Department of Health; founder of the Council on Medical Careers; chair of health committee for Chicago Commission on Human Relations; organizer of Flying Black Medics in Chicago and Cairo, IL.

AWARDS, HONORS: Rudolph Schindler Award, 1977; Leonidas Berry Society for Digestive Diseases organized in Berry's honor, 1983; Rush Medical College graduates and staff members established a scholarship fund in Berry's name in 1993; Clinical Achievement Award from the American College of

Gastroenterology; professional achievement and distinguished service awards from the Cook County Physicians Association; Marshall Bynum Service Award from the Chicago brand of the National Association for the Advancement of Colored People (NAACP); received two honorary doctorate degrees.

WRITINGS:

(Senior author and editor) *Gastrointestinal Panendoscopy* (textbook), Thomas, 1974.

I Wouldn't Take Nothin' for My Journey: Two Centuries of an Afro-American Minister, Johnson, 1981.

Contributor to journals and periodicals, including *Journal of the National Medical Association* and *Gastrointestinal Endoscopy.*

SIDELIGHTS: As a leading physician and educator, Leonidas Harris Berry was an active force in the Chicago-area medical community for more than forty years. The first African American internist at Cook County Hospital and the first black doctor at Michael Reese Hospital and Medical Center, Berry was an inspiration to minority medical students throughout his long career. In 1955 Berry invented the gastrobiopsyscope, a first-of-its-kind instrument for exploring the digestive tract, now part of the medical collection at the Smithsonian Institution. In 1993 a scholarship fund was established at Rush Medical College in Berry's name.

Berry was born on July 20, 1902, in Woodsdale, North Carolina, to Lewellyn and Beulah Anne Harris Berry. He received a B.S. degree from Wilberforce University in Ohio in 1924. At the University of Chicago, he earned a second B.S. in 1925 and an M.D. in 1930. The University of Illinois awarded him an M.S. in pathology in 1933. After an internship at Freedmen's Hospital in Washington, he served a residency in internal medicine and gastroenterology, then joined the medical staff at Cook County Hospital in Chicago. Following his residency, he joined the medical staff of Provident Hospital in 1935, founded the division of gastroenterology, and served thirty-four years as its chairperson. For eight of those years, 1966 to 1974, Berry also was chief of Cook County Hospital's gastrointestinal endoscopy service. He taught at the University of Illinois Medical School from 1950 to 1957, then at the Cook County Graduate School of Medicine until 1967. In 1955 he invented the direct-vision gastrobiopsyscope, the first instrument for viewing the inside of the digestive tract.

Long active in medical and civic affairs from the local to the international level, Berry organized and coordinated clinics for medical counseling on narcotics for the Illinois Department of Health, helped found the Council on Medical Careers, served as chairperson of the health committee for the Chicago Commission on Human Relations, and organized Flying Black Medics in Chicago and Cairo, Illinois. At the national level he served from 1966 to 1968 on the U.S. Department of Health, Education, and Welfare's first national advisory council on regional medical programs in heart disease, cancer, and stroke. Sponsored by the U.S. Department of State, he traveled to East Africa, West Africa, Japan, Korea, the Philippines, and France as a foreign cultural exchange lecturer in 1965, 1966, and 1970.

Berry also served as senior author and editor of the textbook *Gastrointestinal Panendoscopy,* published in 1974, and contributed various articles to medical publications and books. He conducted research on racial, sociological, and pathological aspects of tuberculosis, on gastroscopy techniques, gastrobiopsy instrumentation, therapy for chronic gastritis and peptic ulcer, gastric cancer, and narcotic rehabilitation. In 1977 he was the recipient of the Rudolph Schindler Award. Berry wrote a personal chronicle entitled *I Wouldn't Take Nothin' for My Journey: Two Centuries of an Afro-American Minister,* published in 1981.

In 1937 Berry married Opheila Flannagan Harrison, with whom he had a daughter, Judith Berry Griffin. After the marriage ended, he wed Emma Ford Willis in 1959. For his energy, dedication, and achievement in the medical profession, Berry received two honorary doctorate degrees and many other awards and honors. Chief among these are the first Clinical Achievement Award from the American College of Gastroenterology; professional achievement and distinguished service awards from the Cook County Physicians Association; and the Marshall Bynum Service Award from the Chicago branch of the NAACP. The Leonidas Berry Society for Digestive Diseases was organized in his honor in 1983. In 1993 graduates and members of the staff of Rush Medical College established a fund in Berry's name to provide scholarships to promising minority students, and kicked off a fund-raising campaign on the occasion of his ninety-first birthday. Berry died in 1995.

BIOGRAPHICAL/CRITICAL SOURCES:

PERIODICALS

Exposition, 1977, p. 30.
Jet, December 13, 1993.*

* * *

BERRY, Ron(ald Anthony) 1920-1997

OBITUARY NOTICE—See index for *CA* sketch: Born February 23, 1920, in Rhondda, Glamorganshire, Wales; died July 16, 1997. Novelist, short story writer, and author of television shows. Berry is remembered as one of Wales' important postwar novelists who wrote in English. His writings often concerned the seamy side of society in post-industrial South Wales. Berry, who served in the British Merchant Navy and Army during World War II, also worked as a miner, fitter, football player, boxer, and carpenter. Writing was his main pursuit as he crafted poems, essays, short stories, and novels. His first novel was *Hunters and Hunted,* which was set in the fictional mining village of Blaenddu in Wales.

Other works followed, including *Travelling Loaded, The Full-Time Amateur, Flame and Slag, So-Long, Hector Bebb,* and *Peregrine Watching.* He also wrote for radio and television. These productions included the radio program *Everybody Loves Saturday Night* and television plays such as *But Now They Have Fled, Death of a Dog, Uncle Rollo,* and *Where Darts the Car, Where Floats the Wrack.* Several of his books were also optioned for film, including *The Full-time Amateur.* During his career, Berry also covered soccer for *The Observer* in London. His stories were featured in periodicals including *New Welsh Review* and *Planet.* His last book, *This Bygone,* was published in 1996.

OBITUARIES AND OTHER SOURCES:

BOOKS

Writers Directory, St. James Press, 1995.

PERIODICALS

Times (London; electronic), July 24, 1997.

BERS, Lipman 1914-1993

PERSONAL: Born May 22, 1914, in Riga, Latvia; emigrated to the United States, 1940; died in 1993; son of Isaac A. (an engineer) and Bertha Weinberg Bers; married Mary Kagan, 1938; children: one son, one daughter. *Education:* Attended University of Zurich, 1932; attended the University of Latvia, 1932-34; University of Prague, Ph.D., c. 1934.

CAREER: Mathematician and writer. Brown University, Providence, RI, researcher, 1940-42, research director, 1942-45; Syracuse University, Syracuse, NY, assistant professor, 1945-51; Institute for Advanced Study, Princeton University, Princeton, NJ, researcher, 1949-51; New York University, New York City, assistant professor, 1951-53, professor, beginning in 1953; City University of New York, New York City, visiting professor, 1984-88.

MEMBER: American Mathematical Society (president, 1975-77).

AWARDS, HONORS: Steele Prize, 1974, from the American Mathematical Society.

WRITINGS:

Theory of Pseudoanalytic Functions, New York University Press, 1952.
Introduction to Several Complex Variables, Courant Institute of Mathematical Sciences, 1964.
Calculus, Holt, Rinehart and Winston, 1969.
(Editor with Irwin Kra, and contributor) *A Crash Course on Kleinian Groups,* Springer-Verlag, 1974.

SIDELIGHTS: Lipman Bers has had a long and prolific career as a mathematician which has covered nearly all aspects of the field of analysis, or theoretical calculus. His work in the mathematical aspects of gas dynamics, partial differential equations, and complex function theory has redefined several applied mathematical fields. The American Mathematical Society recognized his achievements in 1974 when they awarded him the Steele Prize. A leader in the mathematical community, Bers has also used his position to speak out for human rights and equality.

Born in Riga, Latvia, on May 22, 1914, his youth was less than ideal. His parents, Isaac A. Bers and Bertha Weinberg Bers, separated when Bers was still very young, and he spent much time being shuttled back and forth between his father, who was an engineer, and his mother, who was studying to be a psychoanalyst in Berlin. While in Berlin, the eleven-year-old Bers was told by a teacher that he was destined to be a mathematician. Bers did not believe him, and it was only in high school, after discovering that he had unknowingly duplicated the results of the mathematician Kamke, that he withdrew his application to engineering school.

Bers entered the University of Zurich in 1932 to study mathematics, but for economic reasons he was only able to stay in Switzerland for one term. He returned home and entered the University of Latvia. The mathematics department there was poor, however, and Bers devoted much of his time to underground political activities. He became involved in the socialist youth and anti-fascist movements, which made it dangerous for him to stay in Latvia after the coup by the fascists in 1934. Bers escaped to Czechoslovakia, where he completed his schooling at the University of Prague. His dissertation adviser, Karl Lowner (later known as Charles Loewner) was an important mentor, and Bers would have an opportunity to help him in the future.

By 1938, the shadow of Hitler and the Nazis had fallen across Czechoslovakia. It was clear that the country would not be a haven for Bers, who was Jewish, for long; his mother had already left Latvia for America. Bers married Mary Kagan in 1938, and they tried to emigrate to the United States. However, conditions all over Europe had worsened, and the pair could only get as far as France, where they spent a tense time waiting and wondering, as war broke out and France seemed about to fall. Their first child, a daughter, was born during this period; their son, however, would be born in America. After the fall of Paris, Eleanor Roosevelt convinced her husband to issue special visas for European intellectuals who wished to escape the Nazi regime. In an interview with the *College Mathematics Journal,* Bers has said, "I literally owe my life to Mrs. Roosevelt." He and his wife reached the United States in December of 1940.

But the country was still in an economic depression at that time and jobs were scarce. Bers could only manage to find a poorly paid summer research appointment at Brown University. The couple had to live with Bers's mother, who was in New York City practicing psychoanalysis. But the need for applied mathematicians increased when America entered World War II, and in 1942 Bers was appointed research director at Brown.

The war work Bers did at Brown was largely concerned with gas laws and fluid dynamics, as well as applications of partial differential equations to these fields. His research during this time not only furthered the American war effort, it laid the foundation for his later insistence on the importance of applied as well as theoretical mathematics. Bers also had the pleasure of welcoming his former mentor, Charles Loewner, to Brown. R. G. D. Richardson, Brown's graduate dean, had rescued Loewner from a position at the University of Louisville where he had a heavy teaching load, including remedial classes. Bers and Loewner would continue to work together for many years at various institutions.

After the war, Bers accepted an assistant professorship at Syracuse University, where he remained from 1945 to 1951. Many excellent mathematicians were there, including Loewner and Paul Erdos, and Bers found the atmosphere stimulating. He also did research at the prestigious Institute for Advanced Study at Princeton University between 1949 and 1951. During this time, Bers began to publish his first major research papers, which dealt with partial differential equations, analytic functions, and the mapping of "minimal" surfaces (so called because a minimal surface generally defines the smallest area spanned by a curve).

In 1951 Bers moved to New York University, where he gained a full professorship in 1953. During 1953 he also published the first of a series of important papers on his theory of pseudoanalytic functions and their applications, which he termed quasi-conformal mappings. This theory involved a series of exceptions to classical analytic functions, whose applications are called conformal mappings. Conformal mappings display a smooth curvature when graphed, but the pseudoanalytic functions described by Bers had irregularities—breaks or changes of direction—that necessitated new rules and a new terminology.

Before Bers did his research on pseudoanalytic functions, engineers and other applied mathematicians had been forced to utilize the classical framework when confronted by these exceptions in practical situations, and often their results were imperfect. Bers's quasi-conformal mappings were more readily suited to practical problems. But his theories were not simply practical; they also dealt with the more abstract topological concept of Riemann surfaces, providing connections between the fields of topology and differential equations.

In the late 1960s, Bers published a textbook, *Calculus,* which was a standard for many years. His continuing interest in topology, however, led his research in new directions, and he began the study of Kleinian groups. Kleinian groups are an algebraic method for describing rotations and motions of objects. Bers lectured on this subject at a 1974 meeting of the American Mathematical Society, where he was presented with the Steele Prize.

Also during 1974, *Contributions to Analysis* was published in honor of Bers's sixtieth birthday, written by his colleagues and former students. In the dedication, the editors commented not only on Bers's mathematical achievements, but also on his activism in support of human rights and his love of literature and the theatre. The members of the American Mathematical Society showed their appreciation by electing him president from 1975 to 1977. One of Bers's most important contributions to the field of mathematics was his encouragement of women students. The Association of Women in Mathematics has honored him by holding a symposium on his teaching.

In 1988, Bers retired from teaching at the City University of New York, where he had been visiting professor since 1984. He continued to give lectures and seminars on various subjects, from Kleinian groups to his experience with the Nazi regime, until his death in 1993.

BIOGRAPHICAL/CRITICAL SOURCES:

BOOKS

Ahlfors, L., I. Kra, B. Maskit, and L. Nirenberg, editors, *Contributions to Analysis: A Collection of Papers Dedicated to Lipman Bers,* Academic Press, 1974.
Furtmuller, L., and M. Pinl, *Mathematicians under Hitler,* Secker and Warberg, 1973.

PERIODICALS

College Mathematics Journal, September, 1987, pp. 266-290.*

*   *   *

BERTHELOT, Helen Washburn   1904-1996

PERSONAL: Born November 29, 1904, in Lakeville, MA; died of a pulmonary embolism, May 6, 1996, in Livonia, MI; daughter of (William) Clarence (a farmer) and Helen (Whitmore) Washburn; widowed; children: Margarette H. Berthelot Beagle, Douglas R. *Education:* Attended Bridgewater State College, one year. *Politics:* Democrat. *Religion:* Baptist.

CAREER: Union activist, political manager, and lobbyist. Michigan Bell Telephone Company, telephone operator, beginning 1923 and again c. 1930s; Communications Workers of America, organizer, c. 1930s, lobbyist in Washington, DC, 1953-69. Managed numerous democratic election candidates, including G. Mennen Williams, campaign for Michigan state governor, 1950, 1954, and 1958, and campaign for U.S. Senate, 1966; Neil Staebler's campaign for Congress, 1962, and campaign for state governor, 1964; Hubert Humphrey, presidential campaign; and did post-victory organizing for President Jimmy Carter, 1976. Served as a delegate to Democratic presidential nominating conventions in 1952, 1956, and 1960; served as vice president of the Michigan State Fair Commission in 1958.

WRITINGS:

Win Some, Lose Some: G. Mennen Williams and the New Democrats, Wayne State University Press (Detroit, MI), 1995.

WORK IN PROGRESS: Communications Workers of America union activities. A second book, concerning the development of the labor movement in Michigan, was completed before the author's death.

SIDELIGHTS: Helen Washburn Berthelot is remembered as a woman whose hard work and dedication in improving the lives of workers brought her to the forefront of the Michigan political scene for many years. Born and raised in rural Massachusetts, Berthelot came to Detroit, Michigan, in 1923, and worked for a while as a telephone operator at the Michigan Bell Telephone Company. She then married, had two children, was widowed, and returned to work for Michigan Bell in the 1930s. Quickly fed up with working conditions at Michigan Bell, Berthelot began organizing for the Communications Workers of America (CWA). Upon her death in 1996 at age ninety-one, *CWA News* remarked that Berthelot "is credited with helping to build a national union in the communications industry."

Berthelot's activism in the CWA led first to elected positions in local government, then to a stint as a lobbyist in Washington, D.C., from 1950 to 1969, which made her the first woman labor lobbyist in United States history. During that time, Berthelot also ran successful campaigns for G. Mennen Williams to the office of governor of Michigan, making her the first woman campaign manager of a statewide campaign in either national political party. Berthelot's 1995 memoirs, *Win Some, Lose Some: G. Mennen Williams and the New Democrats,* is "an intimate account of the activism that brought the Democrats out of the 'smoke-filled room' and Williams into power in Lansing," according to *Detroit Free Press* staff writer Matt Helms.

OBITUARIES:

CWA News, May/June, 1996.
Detroit Free Press, May, 1996.*

* * *

BICKHAM, Jack M(iles)   1930-1997
(Jeff Clinton, John Miles, George Shaw)

OBITUARY NOTICE—See index for *CA* sketch: Born September 2, 1930, in Columbus, OH; died of lymphoma, July 25, 1997, in Norman, OK. Journalist, educator, and author. Bickham was a prolific writer of western, mystery, and adventure novels, including *The Apple Dumpling Gang, Gunman's Gamble, Hangman's Territory,* and *Katie, Kelly and Heck.* In all, his books totaled around seventy-five. In addition to writing as Jack M. Bickham, he used pseudonyms such as Jeff Clinton, John Miles, and George Shaw. In his early career, he worked for the *Norman Transcript* as a reporter from 1956 to 1960. For the next six years, he was the assistant Sunday editor on the *Daily Oklahoman.* After working as managing editor of the *Oklahoma Courier* from 1966 to 1969, he joined the faculty at the University of Oklahoma. He also taught journalism at Oklahoma City University in the 1960s. Among his other books are *The Padre Must Die, The Night Hunters* (as Miles), *A Question of Ethics, I Still Dream about Columbus, Wanted: Wildcat O'Shea* (as Clinton), *Wildcat on the Loose* (as Clinton), *Miracleworker, Ariel, Day Seven,* and *Tiebreaker.* Several of his novels were turned into films. These include *The Apple Dumpling Gang, Dinah, Blow Your Horn, Baker's Hawk,* and *Katie, Kelly and Heck.* Sigma Delta Chi named him editor of the year in 1969, the Oklahoma Writers Federation awarded him the trophy for best novel several times, and the Florence

Roberts Head Memorial Award was bestowed on him for *I Still Dream about Columbus.*

OBITUARIES AND OTHER SOURCES:

BOOKS

Writers Directory, St. James Press, 1995.

PERIODICALS

Washington Post, July 28, 1997, p. B4.

* * *

BIEL, Steven   1960-

PERSONAL: Born October 30, 1960, in Cleveland, OH; son of Morton (a teacher and administrator) and Claire (a speech and language pathologist; maiden name, Diamond) Biel; married Jean Kolling (an attorney), June 23, 1990; children: Jacob, Olivia. *Education:* Brown University, B.A., 1983; Harvard University, M.A., 1985, Ph.D., 1990.

ADDRESSES: Home—4 Hillside Avenue, Wakefield, MA 01880. *Agent*—c/o W.W. Norton and Company, 500 Fifth Ave., New York, NY 10110. *E-mail*—sbiel1030@aol.com.

CAREER: Writer, historian, and teacher. Harvard University, Cambridge, MA, lecturer of history and literature, 1990-93, preceptor, expository writing, 1994-96; Brandeis University, Waltham, MA, lecturer, 1997-98;

WRITINGS:

Independent Intellectuals in the United States, 1910-1945, New York University Press (New York City), 1992.
Down with the Old Canoe: A Cultural History of the Titanic Disaster, Norton (New York City), 1996.

Contributor to periodicals, including *TV Guide.*

SIDELIGHTS: Steven Biel is the author of well-received nonfiction volumes. His 1992 work, *Independent Intellectuals in the United States, 1910-1945,* is a survey of leading American thinkers in the first half of the twentieth century. For Biel, intellectuals such as Van Wyck Brooks, John Reed, Max

Eastman, and Margaret Sanger distinguished themselves in shaping an autonomous intelligentsia. Leonard Wilcox, writing in the *Journal of American History,* noted that "Biel's study brings new interest to [these intellectuals] by focusing on their pioneering work in defining an independent and socially engaged intellectual life." Wilcox, who described Biel's prose as "dense yet elegantly written," called *Independent Intellectuals in the United States, 1910-1945* an "important book" and added that it "contributes something new to our understanding of the significance of the intellectual of the 1910s."

Another reviewer, Elaine Orr, declared in *American Literature* that Biel's book constitutes "a textured history, one in which . . . intellectuals emerge as serious, passionate, and very human workers grappling with the twin dragons of American materialism and self identity." *American Historical Review*'s Bruce Clayton observed that "Biel's book has the merit of bringing to life, in a brisk and accessible format, a brilliant group of men and women who preferred to do good rather than well and left a rich legacy of creative thought."

In *Down with the Old Canoe: A Cultural History of the Titanic Disaster,* published in 1996, Biel appraises various interpretations of the purportedly unsinkable luxury liner that met with disaster on its maiden voyage in 1912. Biel notes that the Titanic disaster has been mythologized along racial, economic, political, and even sexual lines. Milton Garrison wrote in the *New York Times Book Review* that "Biel combines scholarly research with an ear for the telling phrase to show how those myths have been exploited." Likewise, *New York Times* reviewer Michiko Kakutani affirmed that Biel "does a nimble job of assessing historical attitudes towards the Titanic, showing how its meanings 'are contingent and contextual rather than inherent or timeless.'"

Biel told *CA:* "In both my books, though in very different ways, I have tried to raise questions about the lines we tend to draw between highbrow, middlebrow, and lowbrow, between intellectuals and popular culture. *Independent Intellectuals* is concerned with critics who often disparaged popular culture while working within it. *Down With the Old Canoe* suggests that the resonance of the Titanic disaster defies the categories of high and low culture. I also tried to write *Canoe* in a way that scholars, 'general' readers, and buffs would find equally engaging."

BIOGRAPHICAL/CRITICAL SOURCES:

PERIODICALS

American Historical Review, December, 1993, pp. 1694-1695.
American Literature, September, 1993, pp. 584-585.
Book World, November 24, 1996, p. 7.
Boston Globe, October 2, 1996, p. D2.
Evening Standard, April 14, 1997, p. 30.
Financial Times, April 19/20, 1997.
Houston Chronicle, March 30, 1997, p. 22, 26.
Independent on Sunday, April 13, 1997, p. 34 *Journal of American History,* December, 1993, pp. 1125-1126; June 1997.
London Review of Books, June 5, 1997, p. 12.
New Statesman, April 18, 1997, p. 47-48.
New Yorker, October 14, 1996, pp. 94-98.
New York Times, October 29, 1996, p. C16; April 13, 1997.
New York Times Book Review, January 26, 1997, p. 19.
Philadelphia Inquirer, October 13, 1996, p. Q2.
Sunday Times (London), April 29, 1997.

*   *   *

BILLETDOUX, Raphaele   1951-

PERSONAL: Born February 28, 1951, in Paris, France; daughter of Francois (a dramaturge) and Evelyne (a homemaker; maiden name, Colin) Billetdoux; children: Augustin Guilbert. *Ethnicity:* French.   *Religion:* Roman Catholic.

ADDRESSES: Office—Editions Grasset, 61 Rue des St. Peres, 75006, Paris, France.

CAREER: Novelist and screenwriter. Director of the film *La Femme-enfant,* with Klaus Kinski, 1979.

AWARDS, HONORS: Bourse del Duca, 1971, for *Jeune fille en silence;* Prix Louise de Vilmorin, 1973, for *L'ouverture des bras de l'homme;* Prix Interallie, 1976, for *Prends garde a la douceur des choses;* Cannes Film Festival Prize, 1980, for *La Femme-enfant;* Bourse de la Fondation Valentine de Wolmar de l'Academie Francaise, 1981, for *Lettre d'excuse;* Prix Renaudot, 1985, for *Mes nuits sont plus belles que vos jours.*

WRITINGS:

Jeune fille en silence (novel; title means "Silent Girl"), Editions du Seuil (Paris), 1971.

L'ouverture des bras de l'homme (novel; title means "The Man's Embrace"), Editions du Seuil, 1973.

Prends garde a la douceur des choses (novel; title means "Beware the Sweetness of Things"), Editions du Seuil, 1976.

La Femme-enfant (screenplay; title means "The Woman-Child"), 1979.

Lettre d'excuse (novel; title means "Letter of Apology") Editions du Seuil, 1981.

Mes nuits sont plus belles que vos jours (novel), Editions Grasset (Paris), 1985, translation by Derek Mahon published as *Night without Day,* Viking (New York City), 1987.

Entrez et fermez la porte (novel; title means "Come in and Close the Door"), Editions Grasset, 1991.

Melanie dans un vent terrible (novel; title means "Melanie in a Terrible Wind"), Editions Grasset, 1994.

WORK IN PROGRESS: "Chere Madame ma fille cadette," a narrative, for Editions Grasset, expected in 1997.

SIDELIGHTS: Although French author and screenwriter Raphaele Billetdoux has written a handful of award-winning novels, only the French best-seller *Mes nuits sont plus belles que vos jours* has appeared in English, as *Night without Day.* In this love story and psychological thriller, which the novel's translator Derek Mahon in *New Statesman* called "vigorous and lyrical," Billetdoux tells the story of a chance encounter and an obsessive three-day liaison between Lucas, a university student of languages, and Blanche, a concert violinist and singer. The two meet while they are both vacationing at a beach resort in Normandy, France. Lucas would have Blanche give up everything for his sake, but Blanche has other plans, and the troubled romance ends in savage tragedy.

The work's subject and prose style earned mixed reviews from critics. "*Night without Day* isn't a romantic souffle, but a dark story of pathological sexual obsession, played out in the feverish perceptions of Lucas. . . . Told in the superheated language of a man who delves for the meaning beyond the meaning in everyday conversation, *Night without Day* is incantatory, surrealistic, full of overextended metaphors and psychedelic images," wrote Elaine Kendall in the *Los Angeles Times.* While a *Publishers Weekly* reviewer praised the author for her depiction of erotic obsession, several commentators bemoaned the prose style of the work. Deborah Mason, in the *New York Times Book Review,* compared the language of the novel as translated to the extremism of its characters, finding the prose "clotted and hyperbolic, lurching from apocalypse to ennui and back again." "Billetdoux seems to write standard-issue pulp-purple, with ineffable feelings and mental states indicated by ellipses every other line or so," stated William Grimes, writing in the *Village Voice.*

While *Night without Day* was marked by more florid language and imagery, Billetdoux has also experimented with other literary approaches with varying degrees of success. She utilized the format of an epistolary novel in 1981 to chronicle the failure of a marriage in *Lettre d'excuse.* Her 1994 work, *Melanie dans un vent terrible,* is presented with a more reserved style of language than *Night without Day.* In the novel, a psychoanalyst's insanity is discovered by one of his patients, Melanie Vechart. "For this novel, Raphaele Billetdoux chose a cold and impersonal style that perfectly matches the clinical rapport of Dr. Fourrey," asserted Dominique S. Thevenin in *French Review.*

The entree of a young woman into the adult world has been a recurrent theme in Billetdoux's works. Her first novel, *Jeune fille en silence,* published in 1971, and the 1976 work *Prends garde a la douceur des choses* are coming-of-age stories, the first being semi-autobiographical. This topic is also explored in the 1979 film *La Femme-enfant,* which Billetdoux wrote and directed. The movie won a prize at the celebrated Cannes Film Festival in 1980 and was distributed in Europe and the United States.

BIOGRAPHICAL/CRITICAL SOURCES:

PERIODICALS

Booklist, October 1, 1987, p. 216.
French Review, April 1996, pp. 844-845.
Kirkus Reviews, September 15, 1987, p. 1336.
Library Journal, September 1, 1987, p. 197.
Los Angeles Times, January 5, 1988.
New Statesman, December 20, 1985, p. 60.
New York Times Book Review, December 27, 1987, p. 18.
Publishers Weekly, October 2, 1987, p. 82.
Village Voice, December 15, 1987, p. 124.

BLACK, MaryAnn
  See EASLEY, MaryAnn

* * *

BLAKEY, Nancy 1955-

PERSONAL: Born October 12, 1955, in Moscow, ID; daughter of Charles D. (a potato broker) and Betty (a homemaker; maiden name, Burns) Holt; married Gregory B. Blakey (an owner of a fish processing company), August 12, 1976; children: Jenna, Ben, Daniel, Nick. *Education:* Attended Washington State University, 1974-75; attended the University of Washington, Seattle, 1984-86. *Politics:* "Independent (left leaning)." *Religion:* Episcopalian. *Avocational interests:* Hiking, skiing, golf, kayaking, "anything that keeps you moving, outdoors."

ADDRESSES: Home and office—15890 Euclid Ave., Bainbridge Island, WA 98110.

CAREER: Author, journalist, and columnist. Worked as able-bodied seaman on ferry boats in and around Seattle, WA, 1974-84. Professional model in Australia and in Seattle, 1978-80.

MEMBER: Bainbridge Astronomical Association.

WRITINGS:

The Mudpies Activity Book: Recipes for Invention, illustrated by Melissah Watts, Northwestern Parent Publishing, 1989; reprinted by Tricycle Press (Berkeley, CA), 1994.
More Mudpies: 101 Alternatives to Television, illustrated by Watts, Ten Speed Press/Tricycle Press (Berkeley, CA), 1994.
Lotions, Potions, and Slime: Mudpies and More!, illustrated by Watts, Tricycle Press, 1996.

Author of "Mudpies," a column in *Seattle's Child,* also syndicated nationally, 1987—. Contributor to *Reader's Digest.*

WORK IN PROGRESS: Monstercide, about a boy who has trouble with monsters and how he solves his problem; *A Graduate's Guide to Life,* a life skills book for graduating seniors.

SIDELIGHTS: Nancy Blakey commented: "I was not born a natural writer; that is, I never bowled the teachers over with talent. My essays and papers were stiff with prose, too full of enchanting words I had discovered. No, any seeds of future talent lay in the river of ideas that ran through my head. The ideas would keep me awake at night. They ran headlong and unchecked for as long as I can remember. It was the momentum of these ideas that led me to write science, art, and craft projects. There is nothing else in my background to explain it. I never took an art class in high school or college. I did not consider myself particularly imaginative or creative. Science bored me. I kept the writer inside alive with small writing jobs, but I did not have a clear idea of what was before me.

"In the years that our four children were born, the idea possessed me that I could help our daughter defy the cultural odds stacked against girls. I would raise her to love science. I began to adapt science experiments and projects to tickle the interests of toddlers. With nothing more than the unmeasured energy of four small children and a few ideas, we collected rocks and blew bubbles in winter air. We popped. We fizzed. We soaked chicken bones in vinegar. We measured and planted and took small machines apart. We asked 'What if?' What if we lit twelve candles under the jar instead of one? What if we froze a balloon? What if we took a newly lost tooth and soaked it in vinegar? I was not a scientist. I was often unable to answer the children's questions. I decided to follow their curiosity willingly to the answer. At times it led to nothing more than a mess—a puddle, Jello between fingers, solutions that stank, and broken eggs. Most times we learned something, a germ of something, that we took with us into our lives. We grew to love science.

"This newly born love was instrumental when I applied for a job as a columnist writing science and art activities for children in a regional magazine. The column was called 'Mudpies.' The river of ideas forever chasing me had found a home.

"Trying out projects with four small children restricted my range (so many little pairs of hands and restless energy!) but, in the end, worked in my favor. Most of the activities I wrote about were great fun, but very simple. They were so simple, in fact, that the projects required very little adult supervision. Through this, I discovered that the most successful art and science projects, the ones that children love, that live beyond the time they take to create, were those that surrendered all stages of the activity to the child. The more I interfered or 'helped,' no matter how wonderful the end product, the less interested my children were in doing them. They scattered, refused to participate, sighed and snorted, and declared the project *boring!* The column absorbed these tenets cast by my children. Process was everything. The column evolved. Books were born. Mudpies sprang from a mother, not a professional, and that is where the heart and soul of my writing lies.

"In my books and columns, I want to find the words to convince parents that creativity is vital for children, for all human beings. A well stretched and limber imagination leads to positive risk-taking and fresh discoveries for solving old problems. It leads to larger thoughts and ideas for a better life. There is no room for hopelessness and resignation in imagination. Imagination is a place where possibilities are entertained, possibilities that can change the course of a life, the same possibilities that fostered dreams in a young girl from Idaho that she could become a writer. If it can be imagined, it can be."

BIOGRAPHICAL/CRITICAL SOURCES:

PERIODICALS

Parents Magazine, April, 1994, p. 184.
Publishers Weekly, March 11, 1996, p. 66.
Small Press, spring, 1994, p. 351.

*   *   *

BLATCHFORD, Claire H. 1944-

PERSONAL: Born January 3, 1944; daughter of John I. (a banker) and Nelda A. (an artist) Howell; married Edward W. Blatchford (a headmaster), April 6, 1968; children: Laurel, Christa. *Education:* Bennington College, B.A., 1966; Adelphi University, M.A., 1968; Columbia University, M.A., 1970. *Avocational interests:* Pottery, weaving, tennis, gardening, hiking, canoeing, "taking groups of young people on backpacking trips, studying contemporary young adult literature."

ADDRESSES: Home—113 Sam Hill Rd., Guilford, CT 06437.

CAREER: Caritas Day Classes for Deaf Children, Rockville Center, NY, teacher of kindergarten and art, 1970-72; writer, 1972—. Arts and crafts teacher at elementary schools and public libraries, 1980-94; has also worked as a substitute teacher.

WRITINGS:

Listening: Notes from a Kindergarten Journal, Alexander Graham Bell Association for the Deaf (Washington, DC), 1972.
Yes, I Wear a Hearing Aid, illustrated by Barbara Rothenberg, Lexington School for the Deaf (New York), 1976.
All Alone (Except for My Dog Friday), David C. Cook (Elgin, IL), 1983.
Down the Path, illustrated by Mike Eagle, Dushkin (Guilford, CT), 1992.
A Surprise for Reggie, illustrated by Eagle, Dushkin, 1992.
Shawna's Bit of Blue Sky, illustrated by Eagle, Dushkin, 1992.
Nick's Mission, Lerner (Minneapolis, MN), 1994.
Full Face, Butte (Oregon), 1997.
Many Ways of Hearing, J. Weston Walch (Portland, ME), 1997.
Going With the Flow, Carolrhoda (Minneapolis, MN), 1997.

Work represented in anthologies, including *No Walls of Stone: An Anthology of Literature by Deaf and Hard of Hearing Writers,* edited by Jill Jepson, Gallaudet University Press (Washington, DC), 1992, and *Of Cabbages and Kings 2: The Year's Best Magazine Writing for Kids,* edited by Kimberly Olson Fakih, Bowker (New Providence, NJ), 1992. Contributor of stories and articles to magazines, including *Spider, Hip, Catholic Digest, Flyfisher, Cricket,* and *Better Health.*

WORK IN PROGRESS: A sequel to *Nick's Mission.*

SIDELIGHTS: Claire H. Blatchford commented: "I lost my hearing overnight at the age of six when I had the mumps. My parents put me back in public school, and I stayed there, even though I didn't get a hearing aid until I was twelve (because there was nothing powerful enough). There were no oral or signing interpreters in those days. No one took notes for me, and there was no closed captioning on television or TTYs (telephone typewriters for the deaf), so I read a lot to keep up with my classmates. I was also a pretty good bluffer!

"At age eleven I knew I wanted to write, in fact *had* to write. When I read, and when I wrote, all the hassles of being deaf were instantly removed. I could understand what everyone said without having to ask people to look at me or repeat what they were saying. I could hear animals, plants, angels, elves, gnomes, and other mysterious creatures speak. Words took me all over the world, out into space, deep down in the chambers of the heart, high up in the towers of the mind, forward and backward in time. They still do. I feel privileged to work with words and hope the ones I use ring true and call forth the best in others."

BIOGRAPHICAL/CRITICAL SOURCES:

PERIODICALS

Booklist, November 15, 1995, p. 559.
School Library Journal, October, 1996, p. 120.

*   *   *

BLOOM, Steven   1942-

PERSONAL: Born May 29, 1942, in Brooklyn, NY; son of Ruby (a candy store owner) and Anne (a homemaker; maiden name, Kabakow) Bloom; married Dolores Nobles, 1962 (marriage ended); married Sara Gothelf (a singer), 1968; children: Zoe Bornhoeft-Bloom, David. *Education:* Brooklyn College of the City University of New York, B.A., 1964; New York University, M.A., 1966, Ph.D., 1973.

ADDRESSES: Home—Bogenstrasse 5, 69124 Heidelberg, Germany. *Agent*—Ronald Goldfarb, 918 16th St., N.W., Washington, DC 20006.

CAREER: University of Heidelberg, Heidelberg, Germany, part-time teacher, 1992—. Also worked as part-time teacher at New York University, Fordham University, and University of Maryland's European Division; lecturer on American topics in Germany, 1977—.

AWARDS, HONORS: Award from Associated Writing Programs, 1995, for *No New Jokes.*

WRITINGS:

No New Jokes (novel), Norton (New York City), 1997.

Also author of short stories.

WORK IN PROGRESS: Two novels, *Give Me a Question* and *Human Frailty.*

SIDELIGHTS: Steven Bloom told *CA:* "*No New Jokes,* a much rejected novel, is structured around approximately a hundred jokes. There is also a good deal of banter. It is primarily a novel about the feeling of powerlessness. Writing fiction, like telling jokes, is one way of dealing with this feeling.

"Walter Goodman, in the *New York Times Book Review,* wrote that 'Mr. Bloom has a perfect ear for competitive quipping. In these back and forths, he manages to deliver both laughs and character.' This, of course, was my intention. Roger Miller, in the *Virginia Pilot,* commented that the jokes 'nearly all are funny (even the groaners) and nearly all express pain: pain revealed—and relieved—through humor and self-mockery.' A reviewer in *Publishers Weekly* remarked that 'the novel speaks volumes about Jewish humor—or any humor.'

"Although *No New Jokes* is my first published novel, I have been writing fiction for twenty-five years. I am not conscious of having any particular style, although everyone must have one. As a reader of Joyce, Faulkner, and Nabokov, I suppose I have learned from them, rather than from films, but probably no one growing up watching movies can entirely escape their influence. A producer thinks he can turn *No New Jokes* into a film. I wish him the best of luck."

BIOGRAPHICAL/CRITICAL SOURCES:

PERIODICALS

Jerusalem Post, July 4, 1997, p. 25.
Kirkus Reviews, February 1, 1997.
Library Journal, March 1, 1997.
New York Times Book Review, May 18, 1997, p. 19.
Publishers Weekly, February 17, 1997, p. 211.
Virginian-Pilot, June 29, 1997.

*   *   *

BOLOTIN, Norman (Phillip)   1951-

PERSONAL: Born September 14, 1951, in Seattle, WA; son of Sam (a machinist) and Anita (Levey) Bolotin; married Christine Anne Laing (an author and editor), August 8, 1982; children: Jacob Laing

Bolotin, Zachary Laing Bolotin, and Hannah Laing Bolotin. *Education:* University of Washington, B.A., 1972.

ADDRESSES: Home—17122 N.E. 160th Ct., Woodinville, WA, 98072. *Office*—16250 N.E. 80th St., Redmond, WA 98052.

CAREER: Publishers Professional Services, Seattle, WA, editorial director, 1973-77; Alaska NW Publishing, Edmonds, WA, editor, 1978-84; KC Aly & Co. Communications, Bellevue, WA, partner and vice president, 1984; Laing Communications, Redmond, WA, president, 1985—. University of Chicago, Business of Publishing Course, director, 1995—; Western States Arts Federation, trustee; Pacific Northwest Writers Conference, trustee.

MEMBER: Western Writers of America, Society of American Baseball Research.

AWARDS, HONORS: Governor's Award for Literature (Washington).

WRITINGS:

Klondike Lost, Alaska Northwest Books, 1980.
A Klondike Scrapbook: Ordinary People, Extraordinary Times, Chronicle Books, 1987.
The World's Columbian Exposition: The Chicago World's Fair of 1893, Preservation Press, 1992.
For Home and Country: A Civil War Scrapbook, Dutton/Lodestar, 1995.

WORK IN PROGRESS: Two baseball books; preliminary research on several other history books.

SIDELIGHTS: Norman Bolotin asserted that he has "an abiding interest in Americana and American history." The focus of Bolotin's writings reflect that interest. In a preface to *The World's Columbian Exposition,* Bolotin and his coauthor and wife Christine Laing wrote: "Our hope is simply to take readers on a fun and fascinating journey back to an event that their grandparents might have considered the experience of a lifetime. *The World's Columbian Exposition* shares their thrilling experience—if only through imagination. . . . As authors, we have a passion for first-person histories. When we develop, write, and design history books—on the Civil War, the Klondike gold rush, or the World's Columbian Exposition—we want to breathe it, understand it, feel it. We want our readers to do the same."

In reviews of his work, Bolotin's passion for his subjects and his thoughtful presentation of their stories have been acknowledged. Ray Olsen, in a review in *Booklist,* called *A Klondike Scrapbook* "a very appealing and browsable look at daily life during the last great North American gold rush." Elizabeth Bush of the *Bulletin of the Center for Children's Books* remarked of *For Home and Country: A Civil War Scrapbook:* "This browsers' delight takes a broad, topical view of military life from muster to demob, and examines civilian efforts to cope with wartime privation." Margaret A. Bush, reviewing the same title for *Horn Book,* commented: "From the outset, the reader becomes absorbed in the portrayal of actual people as they lived through the realities of war." Bush continued, "the well-chosen topics are skillfully researched and described with intelligent consistency."

BIOGRAPHICAL/CRITICAL SOURCES:

BOOKS

Bolotin, Norman and Christine Laing, preface to *The World's Columbian Exposition,* Preservation Press, 1993.

PERIODICALS

Booklist, October, 1987, p. 359.
Bulletin of the Center for Children's Books, October, 1995, p. 47.
Horn Book, November/December, 1995, p. 753.

*   *   *

BONONNO, Robert   1949-

PERSONAL: Born May 16, 1949, in Flushing, NY; son of Mario and Sarah (Bertolini) Bononno. *Education:* New York University, B.A.; Graduate Center of the City University of New York, M.A. *Politics:* Independent. *Religion:* "Undecided."

ADDRESSES: Home—109 East Second St., New York, NY 10009; fax 212-982-3249. *E-mail*—rb28@ 154.nyu.edu.

CAREER: Freelance photographer in New York City, 1972-85; freelance translator, New York City, 1983—. New York University, adjunct professor of translation studies; Graduate Center of the City University of New York, lecturer.

MEMBER: American Translators Association, American Literary Translators Association, PEN, ASTM.

AWARDS, HONORS: Photography grant, Creative Artists Public Service (CAPS), 1975.

WRITINGS:

TRANSLATOR

Braque: Complete Graphic Work, Alpine Fine Arts (New York City), 1983.

Anna Lorme, *A Traitor's Daughter,* Holmes & Meier (New York City), 1993.

Michel Brun, *Incident at Sakhalin: The True Mission of KAL 007,* Four Walls Eight Windows, 1996.

Herve Guibert, *Ghost Image,* Sun and Moon (College Park, MD), 1996.

Pierre Levy, *Collective Intelligence: Mankind's Emerging World in Cyberspace,* Plenum (New York City), 1997.

Contributor of translations to periodicals, including *Grand Street, Translation,* and *Paintbrush.*

OTHER

Contributor of articles to magazines, including *Photography* and *Language International.*

WORK IN PROGRESS: Translating Levy's *The Virtual World,* publication by Plenum expected in 1998; translating *Isabelle Eberhardt: Seven Years in the Life of a Woman,* edited by Eglal Errera; translating *Le cygne de Proust,* by Henri Raczymow, for Editions Gallimard (Paris, France); research on concept styles and classification in terminology and on computer-based methods of terminology management.

SIDELIGHTS: Robert Bononno told *CA:* "My career as a translator began—like that of most translators, it would seem—rather haphazardly. I became involved with a Frenchwoman, living in New York City, who had a house in the French countryside, an ancient, crumbling cottage in a corner of paradise. My intent was to spend my vacation there doing photography. The location, an island off the coast of Brittany, was wonderful, and I am still proud of the work I did there, but I was more or less helpless with the language.

"I returned to France every year for several years, each year spending a little more time there. My French kept getting better, and I was reading more. In 1983 or 1984 a friend, who was working as an editor for a publisher in New York City, told me that they were going to publish a book on Braque, and they needed a translator. Would I be interested in submitting a sample? I said 'Sure!' This was my first professional assignment. I knew nothing about translation as a profession, nothing about contracts, nothing about 'work for hire' or PEN, and next to nothing about publishers. Fortunately I avoided making a complete fool of myself.

"Photography accounts for a substantial portion of my life—some fifteen years or so—and was the source of considerable satisfaction and modest artistic success. I grew bored, however, and started to grow disillusioned about the photography market. In 1989 I learned about a graduate program in translation at the Graduate Center of the City University of New York. I talked it over with some friends, who encouraged me to give it a try.

"While in graduate school I began working for translation agencies on a part-time basis. I hadn't yet chosen a specialization, but I quickly learned that there were certain areas of translation that I wanted no part of, including law and finance. It made sense finally to capitalize on what I had learned as an undergraduate studying chemistry and to build on that core of knowledge. Although I would never be a chemist, I had been trained as a scientist and was familiar with scientific literature and language.

"As a technical translator I have more or less focused on a core set of technologies, along with terminology, which I feel is critical to good translation. I am primarily concerned with terminology management tools and visualization, perhaps because of my interest in computers, and with integrating such tools into a translator workstation. Since I have begun teaching terminology, however, I have developed a much deeper interest in the theory of terminology, especially the theory of the concept (on which terminology is built) and classification.

"Concomitant with the hard core and eminently practical side of my work, is my interest in translation history and theory and translation pedagogy. As a full-time technical translator, I'm often frustrated by what I feel is the abstractness and lack of relevance of much contemporary theory. I feel its use of linguistics has not always been beneficial for translation, nor has it appreciably helped our understanding of the translation process. As a literary translator with an interest in theory, however, I am happy to investigate anything that adds to the body of knowledge about translation. (It has been my impression, purely subjective, that most literary translators don't give a hoot about translation theory, either, again fragmenting the field into theory versus practice.)

"Since leaving graduate school I have continued to work on literary and business projects, with the bulk of my time devoted to commercial endeavors. I try to promote my literary projects when I have a moment, but it is a slow procedure, and my time is limited. Recently I have been doing 'quasi-literary' translations for magazines and periodicals, mostly about contemporary politics. It's hard to classify this material as literature, strictly speaking, but I tend to lump most publishable material into the literary category. I haven't had the opportunity to translate any published scientific texts, but would like to.

"It is strange to be back teaching at the City University of New York, after all the years since graduate school. Nothing much has changed about the place. It is still the same, except the carpets are threadbare now, and I am more aware of how depressing some of the classrooms are. I keep wondering, is this a step forward or a step back?"

*   *   *

BORDO, Susan (Rebecca) 1947-
   (Susan R. Bordo)

PERSONAL: Born January 24, 1947, in Newark, NJ; daughter of Julius and Regina (Siegal) Klein; married, 1968; divorced, 1971. *Education:* Carleton University, B.A., 1972; State University of New York at Stony Brook, Ph.D., 1982. *Avocational interests:* "Movies, culture-watching, my dogs (two collies, a border collie, and a Jack Russell terrier)."

ADDRESSES: Office—Department of Philosophy, University of Kentucky, Paterson Office Tower, Lexington, KY 40506. *Agent*—Beth Vesel, Sanford Greenberger Associates, 55 Fifth Ave., New York, NY 10003.

CAREER: Duke University, visiting associate professor, graduate faculty, women's studies, 1989; Le Moyne College, Syracuse, NY, associate professor of philosophy, 1987-93, Joseph C. Georg professor, 1991-94; University of Kentucky, Otis A. Singletary Chair in the humanities, professor of philosophy, 1994—.

MEMBER: American Philosophical Association, Society for Phenomenology and Existential Philosophy, Society for Women in Philosophy, American Studies Association.

AWARDS, HONORS: Visiting scholar in women's studies, Douglass College, Rutgers University, 1985; American Council of Learned Studies/Ford Foundation fellowship, 1988; Rockefeller Humanist in Residence, Duke University/University of North Carolina Center for Research on Women, 1987-88; Scholar of the Year Award, Le Moyne College, 1990; *Unbearable Weight* named as a Notable Book of the Year by the *New York Times,* and as the University of California Press nominee for the Pulitzer Prize, 1993; Distinguished Publication Award, Association for Women in Psychology, for *Unbearable Weight,* 1994.

WRITINGS:

The Flight to Objectivity: Essays on Cartesianism and Culture, State University of New York (Albany, NY), 1987.
(Editor, under name Susan R. Bordo, with Alison M. Jaggar) *Gender/Body/Knowledge: Feminist Reconstructions of Being and Knowing,* Rutgers University Press (New Brunswick, NJ), 1989.
Unbearable Weight: Feminism, Western Culture, and the Body, University of California Press (Berkeley, CA), 1993.
Twilight Zones: The Hidden Life of Cultural Images from Plato to O. J., University of California Press, 1997.
(Editor) *Feminist Interpretation of Descartes,* for Pennsylvania State Press, in press.

WORK IN PROGRESS: My Father's Body and Other Unexplored Regions of Sex, Masculinity, and the Male Body, probable publication in 1998 by Farrar, Straus.

SIDELIGHTS: Susan Bordo is a feminist philosopher whose works examine the philosophical roots of Western culture's attitudes toward gender and the body. In the words of Susan Squier, professor of literature at Penn State University, Bordo's writings "can be said to have catalyzed the birth of the new interdisciplinary field of work known as 'body studies.'" Bordo relates gender inequality in the West to the mind/body split postulated by many philosophers and theologians. According to Bordo, Western culture positively associated the mind and reasoning with the male, while the body became negatively associated with the female. Bordo's works examine manifestations of this split in historical and contemporary Western culture. Though her conclusions are sometimes questioned, Bordo's scholarship and provocative insights have been praised by many commentators.

Bordo's first book, *The Flight to Objectivity: Essays on Cartesianism and Culture,* examines seventeenth-century philosopher Rene Descartes' version of the mind/body split and places it in historical context. *Choice* contributor M. Andic, while questioning some aspects of Bordo's reading of Descartes, nevertheless praised the author's "illuminating" ideas. Andic recommended *The Flight to Objectivity* for library collections on epistemology and feminism. Jane Duran, in her book *Toward a Feminist Epistemology,* has described Bordo's analysis of Descartes as "enormously influential because the very Cartesian tradition . . . is painted by her in careful, textured strokes."

In *Unbearable Weight: Feminism, Western Culture, and the Body,* a series of essays on contemporary Western culture and its attitudes toward the female body, Bordo looks at the social causes of eating disorders and other contemporary issues. She calls attention to a variety of American cultural influences, from the media to the courts to medical and psychological research. According to Carole M. Counihan's summary in the *Women's Review of Books,* these influences "continually reproduce a mind-body dualism that defines women and their bodies as evil and dangerous." Counihan further commented, "Women's obsession with thinness results from their internalizing the negative meanings of fat, hunger and desire."

Unbearable Weight was widely praised. Sue Fisher wrote in *American Journal of Sociology*: "*Unbearable Weight* is a wonderful read. In it Western culture, the body, and different theoretical perspectives are woven together to display how the ongoing production, reproduction, and transformation of culture shift through historical changes in relations of power, modes of subjectivity and the organization of life." Carol Gilligan in the *London Review of Books* observed, "Bordo's calm and steady analysis of this

history [of Western culture's treatment of women] and its implications opens the way to a radical formulation, which she stops just short of stating: to bring the body and women from the margin into the central arenas of Western culture would transform its stabilizing mind/body dualism, and this is the task of feminism." Janet Sayers in *Radical Philosophy* noted, "Bordo is precise, rigorous and eloquent in exposing the gendered character of Cartesian dualism," while a *Publishers Weekly* contributor found *Unbearable Weight* to be a collection of "brilliant, scholarly yet accessible essays." Maud Ellmann in the *New York Times Book Review* remarked, "What makes this book different from the standard rants against prescriptive images of women is its historical and philosophical depth," but also found that "the picture [Bordo] paints is too depressing to be complete." Other critics similarly noted the book's failure to recognize women's ability to resist cultural messages, or to give sufficient weight to the cultural, class, and racial differences among women.

Despite some reservations, Mimi Nichter in *Contemporary Sociology* called the book, "an engaging and insightful study of ideological domination at the site of the body," and concluded that *Unbearable Weight* "is extremely well written and thought-provoking." Many critics found *Unbearable Weight* to be not just thought-provoking, but a watershed book. Susan Hekman in *Hypatia* wrote that Bordo's "analyses of cultural phenomena from the perspective of gender are persuasive and compelling. The analyses of anorexia nervosa and bulimia in particular are on the cutting edge of feminist theory. Bordo's thesis is that these phenomena require detailed analysis, that they cannot be explained simply by reference to the cult of slenderness prevalent in the contemporary West. Unlike many commentators on these phenomena, however, Bordo then goes on to supply just such a detailed analysis. . . . It is impossible to read this book without being gripped by the power of Bordo's arguments and outraged at the plight of the victims of our cultural constructions of self." Ellen Annandale, reviewing the book in *Social History,* commented: "This is a superb collection of essays which combines theoretical sophistication with an engaging interpretation of media images and women's experience. . . . This book without doubt demonstrates that Bordo is one of the best, if not the best, contemporary writer on the body and the politics of gender."

Bordo told *CA:* "All of my writing, in one way or another, has been about the suppression of the body in Western culture. I think that I have been drawn to this area because of my deep belief in the edification, relief, and communication that become possible when we talk openly (and intelligently) about those aspects of life that hold the most shame for us, that are most taboo. The first time I said the word 'thigh' in a philosophical lecture, there was an audible gasp! And although twentieth-century American popular culture may seem more body-loving than Plato or Augustine, in fact we clearly have deep problems with accepting the vulnerability and imperfection of the body. My work on women's body-issues has helped me to understand myself, and now—working on a book about the male body—to enter men's experiences empathically as well as analytically.

"For me, women's studies is a part of gender studies, and gender studies is a part of cultural studies. Looking at men and masculinity, at race, at cultural developments that seem to have nothing to do with gender, is vital to the way that I approach the study of gender. But neither gender studies nor cultural studies can be of much significance unless they reach outside the academic world. To do this, academics need to unlearn a good deal of what we were taught in graduate school, not only in our language but also in our sense of disciplinary territoriality and arrogance. This slow unlearning has been my second and ongoing education since I finished my first one."

BIOGRAPHICAL/CRITICAL SOURCES:

BOOKS

Duran, Jane, *Toward a Feminist Epistemology,* Rowman and Littlefield, 1991, pp. 88-89.

PERIODICALS

American Journal of Sociology, July, 1994, pp. 109-11.
Choice, June, 1993, p. 1588; December, 1987, p. 634.
Contemporary Sociology, January, 1995, pp. 42-43.
Hypatia, fall, 1995.
London Review of Books, March 10, 1994, pp. 6-7.
New York Times Book Review, September 26, 1993, p. 14.
Publishers Weekly, July 12, 1993.
Radical Philosophy, May/June, 1995.
Social History vol 8 no 1, 1995.
Women's Review of Books, December, 1993, p. 19.

BORDO, Susan R.
  See BORDO, Susan

*   *   *

BOTWIN, Carol   1929-1997

PERSONAL: Born Carol Dariff, 1929, in New York, NY; died of cancer, April 15, 1997, in New York, NY; married Edward Botwin (a real estate broker; divorced, 1983); children: William, Alexandra. *Education:* New York University, B.A.; Columbia University, pursued graduate studies.

CAREER: Author and social critic. Columnist.

WRITINGS:

Sex and the Teenage Girl, Lancer (Flushing, NY), 1972.
The Love Crisis: Hit and Run Lovers, Jugglers, Sexual Stingies, Unreliables, Kinkies and Other Typical Men Today, Doubleday (Garden City, NY), 1979.
Love Lives: Why Women Behave the Way They Do in Relationships, Bantam (New York City), 1983.
Is There Sex After Marriage?, Little, Brown (Boston, MA), 1985.
Men Who Can't Be Faithful: How to Pick Up the Pieces When He's Breaking Your Heart, Warner (New York City), 1988.
Tempted Women: The Passions, Perils and Agonies of Female Infidelity, William Morrow (New York City), 1994.

Contributor to periodicals, including *This Week, Girl Talk, Woman, Redbook, Cosmopolitan,* and *New Woman.*

SIDELIGHTS: Carol Botwin, a leading sexologist and social critic of the Depression-era generation, has written books on sex and marriage as well as several advice columns on the subject. Her most popular books, dealing with male and female infidelity, have been translated into more than a dozen languages. In the 1960s, Botwin served as a columnist for *This Week* and *Girl Talk* magazines prior to publishing her first book, *Sex and the Teenage Girl,* which was considered a prototype for future guides dealing with questions about sex. Though this guide was well-received, the adult-oriented text titled *The Love Crisis: Hit and Run Lovers, Jugglers, Sexual*

Stingies, Unreliables, Kinkies and Other Typical Men Today was criticized by a commentator for *Kirkus Reviews* as "ugliness blown up to the point where . . . reality [is] distorted." *The Love Crisis,* Botwin's primer for how to deal with the modern male, is based on the pain she weathered after her first marriage ended in divorce, according to her agent Barbara Lowenstein. However, Lena Williams in the *New York Times* described the book as "the precursor to such 1990s best sellers as *Men Are From Mars, Women Are From Venus.*"

During the 1980s, Botwin wrote an advice column for *New Woman* and *Woman* magazines and continued conducting research on relationships and sex. Published in 1985, the book *Love Lives: Why Women Behave the Way They Do in Relationships* divides women into categories such as the Princess, the Chameleon, and the Technicolor Lady. A review in *Publishers Weekly* questioned what the reviewer saw as Botwin's double standard. Although purporting to advocate liberation for women, the reviewer stated, Botwin "reinforces stereotypes and encourages dependence on man" with her tacit endorsement of the traditional women's role—wife and mother. *Los Angeles Times Book Review*'s Don Strachan lamented Botwin's labels: "If Botwin were a man, we'd call her a male chauvinist pig."

Also published in 1985, *Is There Sex After Marriage?* presents views from leading sex therapists and psychotherapists, in addition to interviews with men and women who discussed their sexual behavior with Botwin. A reviewer for *Publishers Weekly* called the work a "solid, intelligent book about marital dynamics." Ray Olson in *Booklist* hailed the guide as a "no-nonsense discussion of how married couples can maintain good sex together throughout their lives." Sharon G. Nathan in *Library Journal* called the book "a well-written, sophisticated, but still very accessible volume."

In 1988, Botwin again identified men through the use of labels in her book *Men Who Can't Be Faithful: How to Pick Up the Pieces When He's Breaking Your Heart,* which was serialized in the magazines *Redbook, Cosmopolitan,* and *New Woman.* A *Publishers Weekly* critic assessed, "Of special value is Botwin's advice on dealing with the anger, pain, self-blame and jealousy." The book sparked heated debates on the talk show circuit due to Botwin's report that sixty to seventy-five percent of American men cheated at least once in their married lives.

The controversial *Tempted Women: The Passions, Perils and Agonies of Female Infidelity* is the last book by Botwin published in her lifetime. Several reviewers expressed disappointment that Botwin's research had not delved deeper into the intriguing topic of female infidelity, especially after claiming that fifty percent of married women have cheated. The book also hypothesizes that women are more likely than men to end a marriage over an affair and less likely to end the affair, and that affairs usually start as friendships.

Botwin, diagnosed with cancer in 1994, died in 1997. She had been preparing to write a book about her battle with the disease.

BIOGRAPHICAL/CRITICAL SOURCES:

PERIODICALS

Booklist, March 1, 1985, p. 912.
Book World, July 2, 1972, p. 13.
Glamour, March 1985, pp. 226-227.
Kirkus Reviews, August 15, 1979; September 15, 1988, p. 1372; November 15, 1993, p.1429.
Library Journal, December 1993, p. 150.
Los Angeles Times Book Review, March 27, 1983, p. 12.
Publishers Weekly, May 15, 1972, p. 55; January 14, 1983, p. 74; January 25, 1985, p. 81; January 3, 1986, p. 51; August 12, 1988, p. 435; November 29, 1993, p. 48.

OBITUARIES:

New York Times, April 16, 1997, p. D22.
Time, April 28, 1997, p. 27.*

*   *   *

BOURINOT, Arthur Stanley   1893-1969

PERSONAL: Born October 3, 1893, in Ottawa, Ontario, Canada; died January 17, 1969; son of Sir John George Bourinot (a reporter and clerk for the House of Commons). *Education:* University of Toronto, B.A., 1915; Osgoode Hall (Toronto), called to the bar in 1920.

CAREER: Poet and author. Practiced law, 1920-59; *Canadian Poetry,* editor, 1948-54 and 1966-68; *Canadian Author and Bookman,* editor, 1953-54, associate editor, 1957-60. *Military service:* Served in World War I, 1915-19.

MEMBER: Royal Society of Literature (fellow).

AWARDS, HONORS: National Poetry Competition Prize, 1919, for *Canada's Fallen;* Governor General's Literary Award, Canada Council, 1939, for *Under the Sun.*

WRITINGS:

Laurentian Lyrics and Other Poems, [Ottawa, Ontario, Canada], 1915.
Poems, [Ottawa], 1921.
Lyrics from the Hills, [Ottawa], 1923.
Pattering Feet: A Book of Childhood Verses, Graphic Publishers (Ottawa), 1925.
Selected Poems, [Ottawa], 1935.
La Salle: Written on the Occasion of the 250th Anniversary of the Death of the Great Explorer, [Ottawa], 1937.
Eleven Poems, [Ottawa], 1937.
Under the Sun, Macmillan (Toronto, Ontario), 1939.
Canada at Dieppe, [Ottawa], 1942.
Collected Poems, [Ottawa], 1947.
More Lines from Deepwood, [Ottawa], 1949.
Treasures of the Snow, [Ottawa], 1950.
The Green Earth, [Ottawa], 1953.
Tom Thomson and Other Poems, [Ottawa], 1954.
Ten Narrative Poems, [Ottawa], 1955.
Everything Must Die, [Ottawa], 1955.
A Gathering of Poems, [Ottawa], 1959.
Harvest from Deepwood, [Ottawa], 1962.
To and Fro in the Earth: Poems, [Ottawa], 1963.
Watcher of Men: Selected Poems (1947-66), [Ottawa], 1966.

EDITOR

Some Letters of Duncan Campbell Scott . . . Archibald Lampman & Others, Quality Press (Montreal, Quebec), 1959.
More Letters of Duncan Campbell Scott with Some Personal Recollections by the Author, [Ottawa], 1960.

Compiler and editor of books, including *Five Canadian Poets,* 1954; *Edward William Thomson, 1849-1924: A Bibliography with Notes and Some Letters,* 1955; *Letters of Archibald Lampman to Edward William Thomson (1891-1897),* 1956; *Letters of Edward William Thomson to Archibald Lampman, 1890-1898,* 1957; *At the Mermaid Inn,* 1958.

Producer, with Marius Barbeau and Arthur Lismer, *Come a Singing!* (a collection of folk songs), 1947.

SIDELIGHTS: Award-winning poet Arthur Stanley Bourinot wrote reflectively for more than fifty years, publishing his first chapbook of poetry, *Laurentian Lyrics and Other Poems,* in 1915 at the age of twenty-two. In 1919, after serving in the first World War, his *Canada's Fallen* won the National Poetry Competition Prize. Twenty years later, in 1939, the Canada Council granted him the Governor General's Literary Award for *Under the Sun,* a book that the *Oxford Companion to Candian Literature* found to be more experimentive in nature and that "reveals a new versatility in its terse rhythms and free verse, and in its frank poems about the Depression and [World War II]." Besides writing, Bourinot practiced law in Ottawa, Canada.

In addition to publishing numerous books and chapbooks of poetry, Bourinot also compiled and edited the works of others in books such as *Five Canadian Poets,* which includes the works of Duncan Campbell Scott, Archibald Lampman, Charles Sangster, George Frederick Cameron, and William Marshall. Bourinot presented the writings of Scott, with *More Letters of Duncan Campbell Scott with Some Personal Recollections by the Author,* Lampman, with *Letters of Archibald Lampman to Edward William Thomson (1891-1897,* and others.

Bourinot was active in the Canadian literature community throughout his life. He was editor of the magazine, *Canadian Poetry,* and of *Canadian Author and Bookman.* In 1950, Bourinot became a fellow of the Royal Society of Literature. His last book of poems, *Watcher of Men: Selected Poems (1947-66),* was published in 1966, just three years before he died in 1969.

BIOGRAPHICAL/CRITICAL SOURCES:

BOOKS

Story, Norah, *Oxford Companion to Canadian Literature,* Oxford University Press (Toronto, Ontario), 1967.
Toye, William, editor, *Oxford Companion to Canadian Literature,* Oxford University Press, 1983.*

BOURLIERE, Francois   1913-1993

PERSONAL: Born December 21, 1913, in Roanne, Loire, France; died November 9, 1993; son of Gabriel (in business) and Marie (Deroche) Bourliere; married Jacqueline Butez, October 2, 1942; children: Jacques, Catherine, Marc. *Education:* Studied at Institution Saint-Joseph a Roanne; University of Paris, M.D.; New University of Ulster, D.Sc; Agrege de medecine experimentale et biologie medicale. *Avocational interests:* Wildlife photography.

CAREER: Biologist, educator, and author. Paris hospitals, Paris, France, intern, 1937-44; Institut National de la Sante et de la Recherche Medicale (INSERM; also known as National Institute for Health and Medical Research), University of Paris, Paris, research assistant in medicine, 1942, professor, 1949-58, professor of gerontology, 1959-83, chairperson of physiology, 1969-83; School of Medicine, Roanne, Paris, professor of physiology, 1946-49. Director, Centre de Gerontologie Claude-Bernard, 1956-84; convener, International Biological Programme (Terrestrial Ecology), 1964-69; director, National Foundation of Gerontology, 1968-80; president, Special Committee for the International Biological Programme (ICSU), 1969-74; chairperson, International Coordination Committee, Man and the Biosphere Program, United Nations Educational, Scientific, and Cultural Organization (UNESCO), 1971-75; chairperson, Interdisciplinary Research Programme on Environmental Problems, Conseil National de Recherche Scientifique (CNRS; also known as International Council of Scientific Unions), 1981-83; chairperson, United Nations Educational, Scientific, and Cultural Organization; chairperson, International Council of Scientific Unions.

MEMBER: International Association of Ecology (INTECOL; president, 1982-86), International Union for the Conservation of Nature and Natural Resources (president, 1963-66), Societe National de Protection de la Nature (president, 1972-82), Maison de la Chasse et de la Nature.

AWARDS, HONORS: Chevalier of the French Legion of Honor, 1970; Commander of the Order of the Golden Ark (Netherlands), 1974; Officier Ordre National du Merite, 1978; Officier Legion D'Honneur, 1989; Commandeur de L'Arche d'Or (Pays-Bas).

WRITINGS:

Elements d'un guide bibliographique du naturaliste, two volumes, Protat (Macon, Paris), 1940-41.

Formulaire technique de zoologiste, P. Lechevalier (Paris), 1941.

Vie et moeurs des mammiferes, Payot (Paris), 1951, published in U.S. as *The Natural History of Mammals,* translated by H. M. Parshley, Knopf (New York City), 1954, third edition, 1964.

Le monde des mammiferes, Horizons de France (Paris), 1954, published in the U.S. as *Mammals of the World: Their Life and Habits,* Knopf, 1955.

Titres et travaux scientifiques, [Paris], 1955.

(With Leon Renee Binet, M. Aubry, and others) *Precis de gerontologie,* Masson (Paris), 1956.

Senescence et senilite: principes d'hygiene et de therapeutique, Doin (Paris), 1958.

(With Jacques Verschuren) *Introduction a l'ecologie des ongules du Parc National Albert,* Foundations pour Favoriser les Recherches en Afrique (Brussels, Belgium), 1960.

(Editor) *Ecology and Management of Wild Grazing Animals in Temperate Zones,* International Union for the Conservation of Nature and Natural Resources (Warsaw, Poland), 1960.

(Editor with Francis Clark Howell) *African Ecology and Human Evolution,* Aldine Publishing (Chicago, IL), 1963.

The Land and Wildlife of Eurasia, edited by members of *Life,* Time Inc. (New York City), 1965, second edition, 1978.

(Editor with Maxime Lamotte) *Problemes de production biologique,* Masson, 1967.

(With C. Balier, J. D. Barbey, H. Beck, P. Berthaux, and others) *Progres en gerontologie,* Editions Medicales Flammarion (Paris), 1969.

(Editor with Maxime Lamotte) *Problemes d'ecologie: l'echantillonnage des peuplements animaux des milieux terrestres,* Masson, 1969.

The Assessment of Biological Age in Man, World Health Organization (Geneva, Switzerland), 1970.

(Editor with Maxime Lamotte) *Problemes d'ecologie: l'echantillonnage des peuplements animaux des milieux aquatiques* (also known as *Problemes d'enchantillonnage des peuplements animaux aquatiques*), Masson, 1971.

(With Jacques Verschuren) *Institut national pour la conservation de la nature de la Republique du Zaire: exploration du Parc national des Virunga,* Foundation pour favoriser les recherches scientifiques en Afrique, 1972-83.

Mecanismes du vieillissement moleculaire et cellulaire (title means "Molecular and Cellular Mechanisms of Aging"), Editions INSERM (Paris), 1973.

Zoologie, Volume 4, Pleiade, 1974.

(Editor with Maxime Lamotte) *La Demagraphie des populations de vertebres* (also known as *La Demagraphie des populations sauvages de vertebres*), Masson, 1975.

Gerontologie: biologie et clinique, 1982.

(Editor with Maxime Lamotte) *Problemes d'ecologie: structure et fonctionnement des ecosystems terrestres,* Masson, 1983.

(Editor) *Tropical Savannas,* Elsevier Scientific (New York City), 1983.

(With Annie Gautier-Hion) *A Primate Radiation: Evolutionary Biology of the African Guenons,* edited by Jean-Pierre Gautier, Cambridge University Press, 1988.

(Editor with M. L. Harmelin-Vivien) *Vertebrates in Complex Tropical Systems,* Springer-Verlag (New York City), 1989.

Editor of the periodicals *Gerontologia: International Journal of Gerontological Research* (Basel, Switzerland), and *La Terre et la vie: revue d'ecologie appliquee* (Paris).

BIOGRAPHICAL/CRITICAL SOURCES:

PERIODICALS

Choice, September, 1983, p. 122; February, 1986, p. 835.*

* * *

BRANCH, Muriel Miller   1943-

PERSONAL: Born April 10, 1943, in Montclair, NJ; daughter of Frank Adolph and Missouri Walthall Miller; married Willis L. Branch, Sr., 1974; children: Willis, Jr., Kenneth, Chery A., Margaret Lewis, Sonja Evette. *Education:* Virginia State University, B.S., 1964, M.Ed., 1978; additional studies at Appalachian State University, Virginia Commonwealth University, James Madison University, and the University of Virginia. *Religion:* Baptist.

ADDRESSES: Home—9315 Radborne Rd., Richmond, VA 23236.

CAREER: Richmond Public Schools, Richmond, VA, library media specialist, 1967—. Maggie L. Walker Historical Foundation, secretary, vice president, and president.

MEMBER: National Storytelling Association, Society of Children's Book Writers and Illustrators, Virginia Breast Cancer Foundation, Virginia Historical Society, Virginia Area Chapter Pi Lambda Theta International Honor Society, Virginia Educational Media Association, Richmond Story League.

AWARDS, HONORS: Rudolph and Esther Bonsal Award for Teaching Excellence, Greater Richmond Community Foundation, 1991; Virginia Hero, Virginia Heroes Incorporated, 1996; "Children's Book of the Year" citation, Bank Street Child Study Children's Book Committee, 1996, for *The Water Brought Us: The Story of the Gullah-Speaking People;* 1997 Cable Educator of the Year.

WRITINGS:

(With Dorothy Rice) *Miss Maggie: The Story of Maggie Lena Walker,* Marlborough House, 1984.

(Compiler, with Earlene G. Evans) *Hidden Skeletons and Other Funny Stories,* illustrated by Dennis R. Winston, Brunswick, 1995.

(With Earlene G. Evans) *A Step Beyond: Multimedia Activities for Learning American History,* Neal-Schuman, 1995.

The Water Brought Us: The Story of the Gullah-Speaking People, photographed by Gabriel Kuperminc, Cobblehill, 1995.

Freedom Day: The Story of Juneteenth, Cobblehill, 1997.

(With Dorothy Rice) *Pennies to Dollars: The Story of Maggie Lena Walker,* Linnet Books, 1997.

Articles published in professional journals.

SIDELIGHTS: Muriel Miller Branch grew up in rural Cumberland County where she didn't have access to a library or bookstore. The stories she grew up with were told by her father, brothers, and cousins. The family would gather in the living rooms about once a week and swap stories. Many of the stories were about her great-great-grandmother who had been a slave.

When Branch finally did set foot inside of a library, she made up for lost time by staying up late at nights to read as many books as she could. Her deep appreciation for the library influenced her to become a librarian, while her love for the historical stories she heard as a child convinced her to try her hand at writing. After publishing *Miss Maggie: The Story of Maggie Lena Walker,* she collaborated on two other books before writing *The Water Brought Us: The Story of the Gullah-Speaking People,* her first solo work.

In 1991, Branch won an award for teaching excellence from the Greater Richmond Community Foundation that allowed her to travel. Among the places she visited was the Sea Islands. There she conducted research on the Gullah-speaking people, descendants of slaves whose isolated island communities have developed a unique culture based in large part on traditions of handcrafting and storytelling handed down from their West African forebears. Branch's book *The Water Brought Us* draws on formal resources as well as the author's experiences among the people of the Sea Islands "to explore the history, heritage, and culture of these descendants of slaves," a *Kirkus Reviews* critic observed.

The book's "very ambitious aim," Kay McPherson said in *School Library Journal,* is to relay the distinctive history, culture, and language of the Gullah. Despite admitting "the writing often substitutes adulation for detail," Roger Sutton remarked in the *Bulletin of the Center for Children's Books* that "the historical chapters are strong." McPherson likewise praised the historical section, but noted that Branch fails to successfully incorporate her anecdotal material with her objective tone in the sections on contemporary life on the islands. A reviewer in *Booklist,* whose response to *The Water Brought Us* was also mixed, nonetheless concluded that the merits of Branch's subject matter outweighed the flaws in her presentation, saying "many readers will find the place and people of compelling interest."

BIOGRAPHICAL/CRITICAL SOURCES:

PERIODICALS

Booklist, September 15, 1995, p. 149.
Bulletin of the Center for Children's Books, November, 1995, p. 85.
Companion, May, 1996, p. 36.
Kirkus Reviews, August 1, 1995, p. 1107.
School Library Journal, October, 1995, p. 143.
Voice of Youth Advocates, February, 1996, p. 405.

BREDERO, Adriaan H(endrik) 1921-

PERSONAL: Born September 22, 1921, in Utrecht, the Netherlands; son of Adriaan H. (a director of a building company) and Johanna A. (Jaspers) Bredero; married Gerda Johanna Hoogstraten, October 26, 1950; children: Gerlien, Johanna, Bernard, Adriaan, Louise. *Education:* Attended University of Utrecht and University of Ghent; Catholic University of Nijmegen, doctorate, 1960; also studied in Rome. *Religion:* Roman Catholic.

ADDRESSES: Home—Hoge Ham 55 zwart, 5104 JB Dongen, the Netherlands.

CAREER: Bonifatiuscollege, Utrecht, the Netherlands, professor of history, 1948-66; Theological Faculty, Tilburg, the Netherlands, professor of church history, 1967-75; Free University, Amsterdam, the Netherlands, professor of medieval history, 1976-86.

MEMBER: Medieval Academy of America.

WRITINGS:

(Editor) *Christendom and Christianity in the Middle Ages,* Eerdmans (Grand Rapids, MI), 1994 (originally published in Dutch, 1986).
Bernard of Clairvaux, Eerdmans, 1996 (originally published in Dutch, 1993).

Author of more than a hundred other publications.

*   *   *

BROOKS, Ron(ald George) 1948-

PERSONAL: Born April 12, 1948, in Pambula, New South Wales, Australia. *Education:* Attended Bairnsdale Technical School, Swinburne Technical School, Swinburne Institute of Technology, and Royal Melbourne Institute of Technology, Australia.

CAREER: Author and illustrator of books for children, 1972—. Has also worked as a freelance designer and illustrator for advertisers and publishers.

AWARDS, HONORS: Best Picture Book of the Year, Children's Book Council of Australia, 1974, for *The Bunyip of Berkeley's Creek,* and 1978, for *John Brown, Rose, and the Midnight Cat;* Picture Book of the Year, Highly Commended, Children's Book Council of Australia, 1975, and Best Children's Visual Arts Book of the Year Award, 1976, for *Annie's Rainbow*.

WRITINGS:

SELF-ILLUSTRATED

Annie's Rainbow, Collins, 1975.
Timothy and Gramps, Collins, 1978.

ILLUSTRATOR

Joan Phipson, *Bass & Billy Martin,* McMillan, 1972.
David Martin, *Hughie,* Blackie, 1972.
Jenny Wagner, *The Bunyip of Berkeley's Creek,* Kestrel, 1973.
Wagner, *Aranea: A Story about a Spider,* Kestrel, 1975.
Wagner, *John Brown, Rose, and the Midnight Cat,* Kestrel, 1977.
(Contributor of illustrations) Mitsumasa Anno, *All in a Day,* Philomel, 1986.
Maurice Burns, *Go Ducks Go!,* Scholastic, 1987.
Rosalind Price and Walter McVitty, *The Viking Bedtime Treasury,* Viking, 1987.
Price and McVitty, *The Bedtime Story Book,* Orchard Books, 1992 (published in Australia as *The Macquarie Bedtime Story Book,* 1987).
Julia McClelland, *This Baby,* Oxford University Press, 1993, Houghton Mifflin, 1994.
Wagner, *Motor Bill and the Lovely Caroline,* Viking, 1994, Ticknor and Fields, 1995.
Margaret Wild, *Old Pig,* Allen and Unwin, 1995, Dial Books, 1996.

SIDELIGHTS: In 1974, author-illustrator Ron Brooks received the top honor from the Australian Children's Book Council for his illustrations in *The Bunyip of Berkeley's Creek* written by Jenny Wagner. This initial success convinced him to concentrate his efforts on children's literature full time. Since then, he has illustrated many books by other well-known authors and written two of his own, *Annie's Rainbow* and *Timothy and Gramps.*

Brooks was born in Pambula, New South Wales, Australia, in 1948. He lived in several remote locations in Australia during his childhood years, including the Gippsland Lakes region on the continent's south coast. In comments provided to Grace Allen Hogarth for *Illustrators of Children's Books, 1967-76,* Brooks noted that the freedom he experienced as

a boy strongly influenced his decision to write and illustrate books for children: "When I wasn't in school, I was out on the sand dunes, creeks, lakes, islands, exploring the miles of beautiful coastline." He recalled building numerous forts and tree houses, and floating on nearby rivers and lakes using homemade rafts and canoes.

At the age of fifteen, Brooks moved to Melbourne to study art. He attended several art schools and colleges in Australia over the next six years. After working as a freelance designer in the advertising and publishing industries, he began writing and illustrating picture books in 1972. The most satisfying aspect of writing for children, as he explained to Hogarth, was that his young readers had the ability to enter and become a part of his stories. "I like to view my art as like that of a maker of windows," he noted, "which each reader, once having entered, is then able to explore, use and reapply his experiences in his own individual way."

Brooks's first self-illustrated book, *Annie's Rainbow,* was published in 1975. In this fantasy story, Annie is a prim little girl in a white dress who longs to capture a rainbow. She spends most of her time in the garden, waiting for a rainbow to appear and then trying in vain to catch it. One day, she sees a particularly beautiful rainbow and ventures into the woods to find its source, a shining fountain. There she meets a sympathetic artist who helps her to achieve her dream by giving her a picture of the rainbow. A *Publishers Weekly* reviewer praised Brooks's "simple story" and "lovely paintings," noting that "misty colors accentuate the dreaminess" of the tale. Similarly, a *Booklist* commentator called *Annie's Rainbow* "a visual treat plus a curiously satisfying tale."

Brooks's next self-illustrated work, 1978's *Timothy and Gramps,* tells the story of a young boy who feels like an outsider at his school in Dorset, England. Timothy finds relief from the loneliness and isolation by taking long walks with his lively grandfather and exchanging imaginative stories with him. Finally, Timothy persuades his grandfather to accompany him to school and speak to his class for "show and tell." After his grandfather entertains the class with colorful tales, Timothy begins to feel more comfortable relating to the other children, and they begin to accept him. Although *Timothy and Gramps* did not prove as popular as Brooks's previous works, it did earn some positive reviews. Janet French of *School Library Journal* claimed that the book "lacks action or deeply felt emotion," but nonetheless praised Brooks's pen-and-ink drawings, noting that they were "warmed with the soft colors of the English countryside." Writing in *Growing Point,* Margery Fisher also commended the illustrations in *Timothy and Gramps* for their "elegant precision" and their success in communicating the "zest and richness" of the relationship between the two main characters.

Brooks has also illustrated a number of well-received books by other authors, including *This Baby* by Julia McClelland, published in 1994. The story concerns a family of bear-like wombats who are preparing for the arrival of a new baby. Andrew—a toddler and the only child up to this point—is alternately angry, frightened, and jealous as his parents' attention is diverted to the upcoming event. He reacts by throwing tantrums, sulking, and having bad dreams, while his loving parents try to reassure him. Finally, when they make Andrew realize how small and helpless the infant will be, he begins to look forward to becoming a big brother. In a review for *School Library Journal,* Susan Hepler praised Brooks's decision to show the family from a position above their den in his watercolor illustrations, which gave "the fat ursines an even more compressed and cozy look. It's as if readers are looking in on this family drama." Jo Goodman of *Magpies* called *This Baby* a "sheer delight," adding that the "text and illustrations complement each other perfectly."

Brooks also received high praise for his pastel watercolor illustrations in 1996's *Old Pig,* by Margaret Wild. The poignant story, which a *Publishers Weekly* reviewer called "a winning addition to the many books that help children cope with the loss of a loved one," follows a grandmother pig as she prepares to face the end of her life. After living happily with her granddaughter for many years, one day Old Pig has trouble getting up in the morning to begin the day's routine. When she realizes that her death is near, she prepares herself by returning books to the library, closing her bank account, and paying her bills. Then she takes a walk with her granddaughter in order to enjoy the wonders of nature—such as the play of light on the trees and the taste of rain—one last time. The book's final picture shows the granddaughter alone. In a review for *Booklist,* Ilene Cooper noted that "the soft watercolors are entirely childlike and unpretentious, but Brooks manages to mix the everyday with a beauty that transcends chores and meals." Likewise, Betsy Hearne of the *Bulletin of the Center for Children's Books* noted that Brooks's illustrations "cast a golden glow over this gentle farewell to life and love," while Christina Dorr of *School Library Journal* added that the drawings "successfully extend the unspoken portions of the story."

BIOGRAPHICAL/CRITICAL SOURCES:

BOOKS

Kingman, Lee, Grace Allen Hogarth, and Harriet Quimby, compilers, *Illustrators of Children's Books, 1967-1976,* Horn Book, 1978.

PERIODICALS

Booklist, January 1, 1977, p. 663; March 15, 1994, p. 1374; January 15, 1995, p. 940; May 15, 1996, p. 1587.
Bulletin of the Center for Children's Books, May, 1994, p. 293; March, 1996, p. 247.
Growing Point, March, 1976, p. 2857; January, 1979, p. 3448.
Junior Bookshelf, April, 1979, p. 92; April, 1995, p. 68.
Kirkus Reviews, May 1, 1996, p. 695.
Magpies, July, 1993.
Publishers Weekly, December 13, 1976, p. 62; January 9, 1995, p. 62; June 3, 1996, p. 82.
School Library Journal, September, 1979, p. 104; August, 1994, p. 140; April, 1995, p. 119; April, 1996, p. 121.*

*   *   *

BROWNRIDGE, William R(oy)   1932-

PERSONAL: Born October 14, 1932, in Rosetown, Saskatchewan, Canada; son of Roy Harper (a railroad station agent) and Theresa Vivian (a teacher; maiden name, Cochlan) Brownridge; married Barbra Irene Orsted (an artist), September 6, 1960 (divorced, 1984); children: David, Leanne, Nancy, Beth, Boyd. *Education:* Southern Alberta Institute of Technology and Art (now Alberta College of Art), Graphic Arts Diploma. *Politics:* New Democrat. *Religion:* Unitarian. *Avocational interests:* Painting, hockey, nature, books, music.

ADDRESSES: Home—705 145 Point Dr. N.W., Calgary, Alberta T3B 4W1, Canada.

CAREER: KB Graphic Design, Calgary, Alberta, Canada, partner for fourteen years; Francis, Williams & Johnson (advertising and public relations firm), Calgary, associate creative director for twenty years. Artist. Artwork has been represented in a national touring exhibition, 1978-79, at Burnaby Print Show, Young Contemporaries of Canada, Red River Exhibition, National Museum of Science and Technology, and at Canada House Banff, 1996; artwork included in Calgary's print and film presentation for the 1988 Olympic Winter Games; designer of uniforms for the Calgary Flames hockey club, 1993.

MEMBER: Art 17 Society (chair of arts committee, 1992-95).

AWARDS, HONORS: Canada Council grant, 1975-76.

WRITINGS:

The Moccasin Goalie (self-illustrated children's book), Orca (Victoria, British Columbia, Canada), 1995.

WORK IN PROGRESS: The Final Game, a sequel to *The Moccasin Goalie; Trucking the Iron Horse.*

BIOGRAPHICAL/CRITICAL SOURCES:

PERIODICALS

Quill & Quire, September, 1995, p. 72.
School Library Journal, January, 1996, p. 76.

*   *   *

BRYANT, Jennifer F(isher) 1960-

PERSONAL: Born May 13, 1960, in Easton, PA; daughter of Charles Holcombe (a mortician) and Elizabeth (a homemaker; maiden name, Starczyk) Fisher; married Neil Bryant, June 12, 1982; children: Leigh. *Education:* Attended Rutgers University, in Tours, France, 1980; Gettysburg College, B.A., 1982; attended Beaver College, 1996; attended West Chester University, and University of Iowa. *Politics:* Democrat. *Religion:* Presbyterian. *Avocational interests:* Swimming, cycling, cross-country skiing, bird-watching, travel.

ADDRESSES: Home—Glenmoore, PA. *Office*—P.O. Box 816, Uwchland, PA 19480.

CAREER: Writer, 1989—. Substitute high school teacher of English and foreign languages; writing instructor for public school gifted education programs; Pennsylvania Council on the Arts, artist in residence.

MEMBER: Society of Children's Book Writers and Illustrators, National League of American Pen Women, Philadelphia Children's Reading Round Table, Phi Beta Kappa.

AWARDS, HONORS: Books for the Teen Age, New York Public Library, 1995, for *Louis Braille: Inventor;* Young Alumni Achievement Award, Gettysburg College, 1997.

WRITINGS:

"WORKING MOMS" SERIES; PHOTOGRAPHS BY PAMELA BROWN; PUBLISHED BY TWENTY-FIRST CENTURY BOOKS (FREDERICK, MD)

Anne Abrams, Engineering Drafter, 1991.
Ubel Velez, Lawyer, 1991.
Sharon Oehler, Pediatrician, 1991.
Zoe McCully, Park Ranger, 1991.
Jane Sayler, Veterinarian, 1991.
Carol Thomas-Weaver, Music Teacher, 1991.

"EARTH KEEPERS" SERIES; PUBLISHED BY HENRY HOLT

Marjory Stoneman Douglas: Voice of the Everglades, illustrated by Larry Raymond, 1992.
Margaret Murie: A Wilderness Life, illustrated by Antonio Castro, 1993.

"PHYSICALLY CHALLENGED" SERIES; PUBLISHED BY CHELSEA HOUSE

Louis Braille: Inventor, 1994.
Henri de Toulouse-Lautrec: The Artist Who Was Crippled, 1995.

"GREAT ACHIEVERS" SERIES; PUBLISHED BY EERDMANS (GRAND RAPIDS, MI)

Lucretia Mott: A Guiding Light, 1996.
Thomas Merton: Poet, Prophet, Priest, 1997.

OTHER

Birds of a Feather (adult nature anthology), Peter Pauper Press (White Plains, NY), 1993.

Contributor to periodicals, including *Earth's Daughters, Kinesis, The Schuykill Valley Journal, The Pegasus Review, The Forum, Disabilities Digest,* and *Highlights for Children.*

WORK IN PROGRESS: A book of poems; several articles on historical women.

SIDELIGHTS: A nonfiction writer for middle grade and high school-age students, Jennifer F. Bryant has written an array of biographies on people of achievement from various walks of life. Included in this league are women's rights activist Lucretia Mott, environmental advocate Marjory Stoneman Douglas, inventor Louis Braille, and nineteenth-century artist Henri de Toulouse-Lautrec. Bryant's well-received *Louis Braille: Inventor* was commended by *School Library Journal* contributor Margaret C. Howell as a "solid reference resource on the history of handicapping conditions as well as a biography of a man who overcame a challenge." *Booklist* reviewer Karen Simonetti maintained that "Bryant . . . meticulously chronicles Braille's profound optimism, tenacity, and commitment to making the world more accessible for the blind."

Bryant's 1996 biography *Lucretia Mott: A Guiding Light* has also drawn a favorable response from critics. *Voice of Youth Advocates* contributor Joyce Hamilton praised the author's study of the abolitionist and women's rights advocate, calling the book "informative and highly readable." Bryant's "Men of Spirit" series entry *Thomas Merton: Poet, Prophet, Priest* was similarly cited as a "remarkable biography" by a *Kirkus Reviews* commentator, who added that young people "may come away from this book not only with a real sense of the man and his writings, but courage enough for their present and future struggles as well."

In addition to these more famous figures, Bryant has also written about everyday heroes, specifically working moms. Within the "Working Moms" series, Bryant presents women pursuing their career—from an engineering drafter to a veterinarian—while also raising children. Each volume allows readers to ride along with the featured mom for a day, so they can understand the rewards and demands of balancing work and family. When needed, Bryant provides additional material, such as information about the woman's field, its ups and downs, and training requirements. In a review of *Sharon Oehler: Pediatrician,* a critic in *Kirkus Reviews* commented: "There's a substantial amount of information here, well-organized and appealingly presented." "As career guidance," noted Denise Wilms in *Booklist,* "the books give positive examples of how young women might look forward to pursuing careers and motherhood."

Bryant commented: "Human behavior has always fascinated me. The choices people make, their fears, fantasies, struggles, and achievements provide an endless pool of stories for nonfiction writers and biographers. Researching and writing biographies gives me a chance to explore the lives of unique individuals and to share their stories with young readers. When they read biographies, children inevitably absorb important lessons and concepts from history, science, philosophy, and even religion.

"Most well-written biographies also present positive role models for service and achievement, thereby counteracting some of the negative images presented through the media. Readers also learn that no one leads a charmed life or begins with perfect circumstances, and that all great achievers encounter failure, frustration, and setbacks. Every biography I've written has taught me something new. Each one has given me a deeper appreciation for what it means to be human."

BIOGRAPHICAL/CRITICAL SOURCES:

PERIODICALS

Appraisal, autumn, 1992, pp. 48-49.
Booklist, June 15, 1991, p. 1958; July, 1994, p. 1938; May 1, 1996, p. 1496.
Children's Book Watch, May, 1991, p. 12; February, 1992, p. 7; April, 1992, p. 5.
Kirkus Reviews, May 1, 1991, p. 602; June 1, 1992, p. 726; December 1, 1995, p. 1700; May 1, 1997, p. 717.
Main Line Today, January, 1997, pp. 16-17.
MultiCultural Review, March, 1993, p. 28.
School Library Journal, June, 1991, p. 114; July, 1991, p. 77; June, 1992, p. 128; July, 1993, p. 89; August, 1994, p. 160; June, 1996, p. 154.
Science Books and Films, May, 1992, p. 116; August/September, 1992, p. 181.
Skipping Stones, summer, 1995, p. 30.
Voice of Youth Advocates, October, 1996, p. 226.

BUTLER, Geoff 1945-

PERSONAL: Born January 13, 1945, in Fogo, Newfoundland, Canada; son of Isaac (a member of the clergy) and Julia (a homemaker; maiden name, Earle) Butler; married Judith McClare (a teacher), August 17, 1976; children: Tegan, Kirsten, Leah, Sean. *Education:* Memorial University of Newfoundland, B.A., 1966; Syracuse University, M.A., 1969; attended Art Students League, New York City, 1972-73.

ADDRESSES: Home—P.O. Box 29, Granville Ferry, Nova Scotia B0S 1K0, Canada. *E-mail*—gbutler@auracom.com.

CAREER: Artist and writer, Granville Ferry, Nova Scotia, 1980—. Soccer coach, Annapolis Royal, Nova Scotia, 1994—.

MEMBER: Writers Federation of Nova Scotia, Visual Arts Nova Scotia (member of board of directors, 1995-96).

AWARDS, HONORS: Ruth Schwartz Children's Book Award, picture book category, Canadian Booksellers Association and Ontario Arts Council, 1996, for *The Killick; The Killick* was also shortlisted for the Governor General's Award and the Amelia Francis Howard-Gibbon Award in 1995 and 1996, respectively.

WRITINGS:

Art of War: Painting It out of the Picture, privately printed, 1990.
(Self-illustrated) *The Killick: A Newfoundland Story* (children's book), Tundra Books of Northern New York (Plattsburgh, NY), 1995.

ILLUSTRATOR

Peter Wyman, *Dear Don,* privately printed, 1985.

Creator of book cover illustrations.

WORK IN PROGRESS: The Hangashore, "a children's story set in Newfoundland, relating how a magistrate and an intellectually challenged boy regard their respective front pews in church"; *Mouth Music,* a children's story about a fiddler set in Newfoundland; *Wise Acres,* a story set in Nova Scotia contrasting outdoor pond hockey with organized indoor rink hockey; a portfolio of songs, poems, and stories to accompany the author's angel paintings, titled *Angels: Behind the Picture.*

SIDELIGHTS: Geoff Butler commented: "Someone with natural talents in a particular field is said to be born, not made, that way. It was not until I was in my mid-twenties that I attended an art class for the first time, so, in terms of technique at least, I am a 'made' artist; or, perhaps I just took a long time being born. For some reason, I did feel some kind of kinship with painting, and so I pursued it as a career. For more than twenty years now I have been a visual artist in the fine arts. Only recently have I turned to writing and illustrating children's books.

"For me, the process involved in creating a painting or forming a story is very similar. It involves striving toward that indefinable quality that makes something work. In *The Killick,* my training in visual arts helped to determine the course of the narrative. As the story was about dehumanization and calling names, I used the children's verse about sticks and stones. A killick, being a homemade anchor, is also sticks and stones, and this became the focal point of the story. The killick at the beginning of the story is not what it is at the end, however. It is given a new life. What was a simple anchor becomes, as the story unfolds, a memorial to the innocent victims of war.

"I sometimes used to bemoan the time I thought I had lost in being a late bloomer. I realize now that there is more to becoming an artist than just learning the techniques of art. One must have something to paint and write about. That is largely determined by the experiences one has had in all facets of life, and by the type of person one has become and continues to be. So, time growing isn't really lost.

"I relish the privilege I have in being an artist, but I am mindful also of the responsibility that goes with it: to be creative and open-minded, to follow one's voice without being egotistical about it, and to strive to do one's best. In my case, I use art as a means of self-expression. Particularly I think, when one reaches middle age and gets a sense of one's own mortality, one is driven to do only what is meaningful and not to waste what time one has left on things that don't really matter.

"For most of the 1980s, I worked on a series of paintings on the subject of war and militarism. It was summarized by a tombstone I made to celebrate the death of war. This mostly satirical project culminated in my self-published book *Art of War.* I am reminded of someone's comment that Picasso's feelings about war that he expressed in his large painting, *Guernica,* were probably not much different from those that General Sherman expressed in his short, simple phrase, 'War is hell.' Each of their expressions, however, carries its own impact. Since there is always a need to voice our opinions on such issues, I also decided to offer mine in the form I thought could best express it.

"I do not hold the view that profundity can only be expressed by dealing with negative issues. My second series of paintings dealt with the subject of angels. For me, they are but one of the symbols we use to represent our search for enlightenment. Perhaps even a worldly matter like warfare can be brought to heel by an enhanced spiritual dimension to our lives, by what is otherwise known as art."

BIOGRAPHICAL/CRITICAL SOURCES:

PERIODICALS

Atlantic Books Today, fall, 1995.
Canadian Materials, March, 1991, p. 110.
Globe and Mail (Toronto), December 23, 1995.
Maclean's, December 11, 1995.
Quill and Quire, November, 1995, p. 46.
Times Educational Supplement, December 8, 1995, p. 12.

C

CALDWELL, Grant 1947-

PERSONAL: Born March 6, 1947, in Melbourne, Australia.

ADDRESSES: Agent—c/o Hale & Iremonger, 19 Eve St., Erskineville, New South Wales 2043, Australia.

CAREER: Secondary school teacher, 1971-73; worked in London, Morocco, and Spain, 1974-77; imprisoned for drug smuggling in Morocco, 1975-76; *SCOPP* (literary magazine), Sydney, Austrailia, editorial reader, 1977-79; freelance writer, c. 1979—; *MEUSE* (art and literature magazine), editor and publisher, 1980-82; Angus and Robertson Publishers, editorial reader, 1982-84; Darlinghurst Non-School of Writing, teacher and director, 1984-87; *Going Down Swinging* (literary magazine), guest editorial reader, 1992; Literature Board fellowship, category B, 1992, category A, 1994; Victoria College of the Arts, writer and teacher, 1995-97. Performed and read work in numerous venues, including schools, theatres, universities, pubs, clubs, and festivals.

AWARDS, HONORS: Shortlisted for *The Age* Book of the Year, 1996, for *You Know What I Mean.*

WRITINGS:

POETRY

The Screaming Frog That Ralph Ate (poetry), Saturday Centre Books (Cammeray, Australia), 1979.
The Bells of Mr. Whippy (poetry), East End Art, 1982.
The Nun Wore Sunglasses (poetry), Glandulon Press, 1984.

The Life of a Pet Dog (poetry), Five Island Press, 1993.
You Know What I Mean (poetry), Hale & Iremonger (Erskineville, New South Wales, Australia), 1996.

OTHER

The Revolt of the Coats (short stories), Angus and Robertson, 1988.
Malabata (autobiography), A & R, 1991.

Also contributor of stories to periodicals, including *Going Down Swinging* and *Far Out.* Poetry, prose, and stories published in magazines, anthologies, and newspapers, and broadcast on television and radio in numerous countries, including the United States, Australia, Canada, Ireland, Germany, Colombia, and Brazil.

WORK IN PROGRESS: The Long Road Turning (autobiographical novels series); *The Heads of Arnold Grey* (novel), for Hit & Miss Press, 1998.

SIDELIGHTS: During a foreign sojourn undertaken for the purpose of self-discovery, Australian author Grant Caldwell was arrested for attempting to smuggle hashish out of the Moroccan city of Tangier late in 1975. He was subsequently sentenced to six months in one of that country's prisons, and was also fined the equivalent of four thousand dollars in Australian currency. While enduring his incarceration, Caldwell suffered abuse and torture, including what is known as "bastinada"—beatings applied to the soles of a person's feet. Although Caldwell is known primarily as a poet—his first published book after his release from prison was the 1979 volume of poetry

The Screaming Frog That Ralph Ate, and his poetry has won him great acclaim in his native Australia—he chronicled his experiences in a foreign prison in his 1991 nonfiction tome, *Malabata.*

In *Malabata,* named for the prison that held him, Caldwell's readers are provided with details such as the way in which special compartments had been welded into his car in which to smuggle the hashish, how some of the welding was done in a hotel parking lot and noticed by a prostitute, who informed on Caldwell, and how he used yoga to cope with the cold night-time temperatures within the prison. The author also discusses his relationship with his fellow prisoners, some of whom were European and some of whom were Moroccan. He describes one incident in which he had to prove his courage to the other inmates by sticking his arm down a toilet clogged with human waste; in another incident he details how the guard who has taken the largest part in his torture offers him a hamburger.

Caldwell confesses he had been somewhat lost in his life before his arrest; Andrew Peek, critiquing *Malabata* in the *Australian Book Review,* cited the "list of books [Caldwell] published since imprisonment" and inferred that the author's time in prison "seems to have played a major role in his becoming a writer." Peek went on to praise *Malabata,* maintaining that its "narrative is carefully shaped and contains some fine writing."

Caldwell's poetry collections have included titles such as *The Bells of Mr. Whippy* and *The Nun Wore Sunglasses.* One of his later volumes, published in 1996, is titled *You Know What I Mean. You Know What I Mean* made the 1996 shortlist for *The Age* magazine's Book of the Year, and is composed primarily of poems meant to be read aloud. Subject matter ranges from ants to the homeless, from bus drivers to betting on horse races. A critic for *The Age* hailed the collection as "poetry of clarity" and "keen observations," while Beate Josephi, discussing *You Know What I Mean* in the *Australian Book Review,* compared it to performance art as practiced in the Australian city of Melbourne and observed: "Calling Caldwell's poems accessible does not mean that they are simplistic. Far from it."

In addition to his achievements in poetry and autobiography, Caldwell has also penned short stories. His short fiction, categorized in the genre groups of science fiction, fantasy, and horror, has appeared in publications such as *Going Down Swinging* and *Far Out.*

BIOGRAPHICAL/CRITICAL SOURCES:

BOOKS

Caldwell, Grant, *Malabata,* A & R, 1991.

PERIODICALS

Australian Book Review, April, 1991, pp. 18-19; May, 1996, p. 51.

OTHER

The Age, http://www.theage.com.au/special/book/intindex.htm, April 8, 1997.

* * *

CAMERON, Meribeth E(lliott) 1905-1997

OBITUARY NOTICE—See index for *CA* sketch: Born May 22, 1905, in Ingersoll, Ontario, Canada; died July 12, 1997, in South Hadley, MA. Educator, historian, and author. Cameron gained acclaim in the field of Chinese history and for her work in Asian studies. Much of her life was spent teaching history. She began her lengthy educational career in 1928 at Reed College in Oregon. Over the next forty-two years, she taught at such schools as the Flora Stone Mather College of Western Reserve University in Cleveland, Milwaukee-Downer College, Stanford University, and Mount Holyoke College in Massachusetts. Between 1958 and 1961 she served as a member of Massachusetts State Advisory Committee to the U.S. Commission on Civil Rights. She also served as the founding editor of *Far Eastern Quarterly* (now called *Journal for Asian Studies*).

In 1970 Cameron became professor emeritus and dean emeritus at Mount Holyoke College. In addition to contributing numerous articles to trade journals, she wrote *The Reform Movement in China, 1898-1912* and was the coauthor of *China, Japan and the Powers.*

OBITUARIES AND OTHER SOURCES:

BOOKS

Directory of American Scholars, R. R. Bowker, 1982.

PERIODICALS

Chicago Tribune, July 18, 1997, sec. 1, p. 10.
New York Times, July 17, 1997, p. B10.

*   *   *

CANFIELD, Jack   1944-

PERSONAL: Born August 19, 1944, in Fort Worth, TX; son of Fred C. (stepfather; in sales) and Ellen T. (a homemaker) Angelis; married Judith Ohlbaum (divorced); married Georgia Lee Noble; children: (first marriage) Oran David, Kyle Dania, Christopher Noble. *Ethnicity:* "Anglo American." *Education:* Harvard University, B.A., 1966; University of Massachusetts at Amherst, M.Ed., 1973. *Politics:* Democrat. *Religion:* Christian. *Avocational interests:* Tennis, skiing, running, billiards, reading.

ADDRESSES: Home—929 Via Fruteria, Santa Barbara, CA 93110. *Office*—P.O. Box 30880, Santa Barbara, CA 93130; fax 805-563-2945. *E-mail*—soup4soul@aol.com. *Agent*—Jeff Herman, Jeff Herman Agency, Inc., 500 Greenwich St., Suite 501-C, New York, NY 10013.

CAREER: High school social studies teacher in Chicago, IL, 1967-68; Clinton Job Corps Center, Clinton, IA, director of teacher program, 1968-69; W. Clement and Jessie V. Stone Foundation, Chicago, IL, associate director of education, 1969-70; New England Center, Amherst, MA, founder and director, 1971-77; Institute for Wholistic Education, Amherst, MA, founder and director, 1975-80; Insight Training Seminars, Santa Monica, CA, director of educational services, 1981-83; Self-Esteem Seminars, Santa Barbara, CA, president, 1983—. Foundation for Self-Esteem, chairperson of board of directors, 1986—. Maui Writers School, faculty member.

AWARDS, HONORS: Honorary Ph.D., University of Santa Monica, 1981; American Booksellers Book of the Year (ABBY) Award, *Body, Mind, and Soul* Book of the Year Award, *Storytelling World* Honor Award (tellable adult stories category), 1995, American Family Institute Nonfiction Literary Award, 1996, all for *Chicken Soup for the Soul: 101 Stories to Open the Heart and Rekindle the Spirit;* named Southern California Book Publicist of the Year, 1995; *Storytelling World* Book Award (tellable adult stories category), 1996, for *A Second Helping of Chicken Soup for the Soul: 101 More Stories to Open the Heart and Rekindle the Spirit;* Distinguished Author Award, Radio and Television Interview Report, 1996; Motivator of the Year Award, *Business Digest,* 1997.*

WRITINGS:

(With Harold C. Wells) *About Me: A Curriculum for a Developing Self,* Encyclopedia Britannica (Chicago, IL), 1971.

(With Wells) *100 Ways to Enhance Self-Concept in the Classroom: A Handbook for Teachers and Parents,* Prentice-Hall (Englewood Cliffs, NJ), 1976, revised edition, Allyn & Bacon (Boston, MA), 1993.

Personalized Learning: Confluent Processes in the Classroom, privately printed (Newington, CT), 1976, published as *Loving to Learn,* Self-Esteem Seminars (Culver City, CA), 1997.

(With Marie Reese, Ron Rowland, Sandie Limina, and others) *Self-Esteem in the Classroom: A Curriculum Guide,* Self-Esteem Seminars, 1986.

Self-Esteem and Peak Performance: A Transcript, CareerTrack (Boulder, CO), 1991.

(With Frank Siccone) *101 Ways to Develop Student Self-Esteem and Responsibility in the Classroom,* Allyn & Bacon, Volume I: *The Teacher as Coach,* 1992, Volume II: *The Power to Succeed in School and Beyond,* 1992, published in one volume, 1994.

Los Angeles Dodgers Team Esteem Program: A Self-Esteem Curriculum Guide, Los Angeles Times (Los Angeles, CA), 1992.

(Compiler, with Mark Victor Hansen) *Chicken Soup for the Soul: 101 Stories to Open the Heart and Rekindle the Spirit,* Health Communications (Deerfield Beach, FL), 1993.

(With Hansen) *Dare to Win,* Berkley Books (New York City), 1994.

(With Karen Goldberg) *Follow Your Dreams: A Goals Setting Workbook,* Dream Time Project (Wayne, PA), 1994.

(Compiler, with Hansen) *A Second Helping of Chicken Soup for the Soul: 101 More Stories to Open the Heart and Rekindle the Spirit,* Health Communications, 1995.

(With Hansen) *The Aladdin Factor: How to Ask for and Get Everything You Want in Life,* Berkley Books, 1995.

(Compiler, with Hansen and Diana Von Welanetz Wentworth) *Chicken Soup for the Soul Cookbook: Stories and Recipes from the Heart,* Health Communications, 1995.

(Compiler, with Hansen) *A Third Serving of Chicken Soup for the Soul: 101 More Stories to Open the Heart and Rekindle the Spirit,* Health Communications, 1996.

(With Jacqueline Miller) *Heart at Work: Stories and Strategies for Building Self-Esteem and Reawakening the Soul at Work,* McGraw (New York City), 1996.

(Compiler, with Hansen, Patty Aubery, and Nancy Mitchell) *Chicken Soup for the Surviving Soul: 101 Stories of Courage and Inspiration from Those Who Have Survived Cancer,* Health Communications, 1996.

(With Hansen and Barry Spilchuk) *A Cup of Chicken Soup for the Soul,* Health Communications, 1996.

(Compiler, with Hansen and Patty Hansen) *Condensed Chicken Soup for the Soul,* Health Communications, 1996.

(Compiler, with Hansen, Marci Shimoff, and Jennifer Hawthorne) *Chicken Soup for the Woman's Soul: 101 Stories to Open and Hearts and Rekindle the Spirits of Women,* Health Communications, 1996.

(Compiler, with Hansen, Martin Rutte, and others) *Chicken Soup for the Soul at Work: 101 Stories of Courage, Compassion, and Creativity in the Workplace,* Health Communications, 1996.

(Compiler, with Hansen, Hanoch McCarty, and Meladee McCarty) *A Fourth Serving of Chicken Soup for the Soul: 101 Stories to Open the Heart and Rekindle the Spirit,* Health Communications, 1997.

(Compiler, with Hansen and Kimberly Kirberger) *Chicken Soup for the Teenage Soul: 101 Stories about Life, Love, and Learning,* Health Communications, 1997.

(Compiler, with Hansen, Aubery, and Mitchell) *Chicken Soup for the Christian Soul,* Health Communications, 1997.

(Compiler, with Hansen, Shimoff, and Hawthorne) *Chicken Soup for the Mother's Soul: 101 Stories to Open the Hearts and Rekindle the Spirits of Women,* Health Communications, 1997.

Author of "Chicken Soup for the Soul," a weekly column, *Woman's World,* 1995—. Canfield's books have been published in Chinese, Czech, Bulgarian, Japanese, Croat, Dutch, Finnish, German, Greek, Hebrew, Hungarian, Icelandic, Indonesian, Italian, Polish, Portuguese, Slovakian, Slovenian, Spanish, Swedish, Thai, and French.

WORK IN PROGRESS: Compiling *Chicken Soup for the Laughing Soul,* with M. Hansen and Joel Goodman;

Chicken Soup for the Grieving Soul: 101 Stories to Heal the Aching Heart, with M. Hansen; *Chicken Soup for the Country Soul: 101 Stories to Open the Heart and Rekindle the Spirit,* with M. Hansen and Ron Comacho; *Chicken Soup for the Ocean Lover's Soul: 101 Stories to Open the Heart and Rekindle the Spirit,* with M. Hansen and Wyland; *Chicken Soup for the Jewish Soul: 101 Stories to Open the Heart and Rekindle the Spirit,* with M. Hansen and Rabbi Dov Elkins; *Chicken Soup for the Pet Lover's Soul: 101 Stories to Open the Heart and Rekindle the Spirit of Pet Lovers,* with M. Hansen and Martin Becker; *Chicken Soup for the Recovering Soul: 101 Stories to Open the Heart and Rekindle the Spirit,* with M. Hansen, Pam Finger, and Robin Kotock; and *Chicken Soup for the Loving Couples Soul: 101 Stories to Open the Heart and Rekindle the Spirit,* with M. Hansen and Barbara DeAngeles, publication of all titles by Health Communications expected in 1998 or 1999.

SIDELIGHTS: Jack Canfield told *CA:* "I started my writing career as a high school teacher who collected and published classroom activities to build self-esteem in my students. Three books later, I started to give motivational talks to schools and to corporations. One day, an audience member said, 'You have the best stories I have ever heard anywhere. Have you ever thought of putting them in a book?' With that prompting, I began to write down the stories that, three years later, with the help of Mark Victor Hansen, became *Chicken Soup for the Soul.*

"When our agent tried to sell the book in New York, we were rejected by thirty-three publishers. Later, at the American Booksellers Convention, we were turned down by another hundred and fourteen publishers! Finally Health Communications agreed to publish the book. It took fourteen months for the word of mouth to take hold, and then the book made the *New York Times* Bestseller List, where it stayed for a hundred and twenty-five weeks. In that two-year period the book had gone on to sell over six-million copies in twenty-three languages. The book also won the American Booksellers ABBY Award.

"As a result of placing a request for more stories in our first book, we now receive in the mail more than fifty stories a day from readers all over the world. This has led to twelve additional 'chicken soup for the soul' books, with combined sales of more than fifteen-million copies.

"What motivates us to continue to work so hard compiling, editing, and writing these books are the thousands of letters I receive that describe the powerful impact the books have had on so many lives, including prisoners, students, teachers, managers, parents, cancer survivors, and numerous others.

"Mark Hansen and I have a policy that a portion of all the proceeds from our books goes to such charities as the American Red Cross, Literacy Volunteers of America, Habitats for Humanity, the National Arbor Day Foundation, and others. Our most cherished project is Soup Kitchens for the Soul, which places tens of thousands of uplifting and inspiring books in jails and prisons."

*   *   *

CANNING, Peter 1937-

PERSONAL: Born January 25, 1937, in New York, NY; son of Elisha (a telephone company executive) and Florence (a nurse; maiden name, Crooke) Canning; married Mary Cook, July 24, 1965 (divorced, May, 1980); married Gaelen Brooke, November 20, 1982; children: Elizabeth, Joshua. *Education:* Harvard University, B.A. (magna cum laude), 1959. *Politics:* Democrat. *Religion:* Protestant. *Avocational interests:* Biking, kayaking, fishing.

ADDRESSES: Home—2032 Main Road, Westport Point, MA 02391-0041. *Agent*—Sterling Lord Literistic, 65 Bleecker St., New York, NY 10012.

CAREER: Reader's Digest, Pleasantville, NY, 1965-88, managing editor, 1980-88. *Military service:* U.S. Army, 1959-63, served in counterintelligence.

MEMBER: Authors Guild.

WRITINGS:

American Dreamers: The Wallaces and Reader's Digest: An Insider's Story, Simon & Schuster (New York City), 1996.

WORK IN PROGRESS: Why So High?: What Every Family Should Know About Drugs, Dependence, and Addiction, expected in 1999.

SIDELIGHTS: Peter Canning told *CA:* "After twenty-five years as a magazine editor, patiently advising aspiring writers about their chosen craft, I decided a few years back to see if I had the slightest idea what

I had been talking about. It was also true that I had a natural story to tell (about the sad last years of DeWitt and Lila Wallace, and how their vast publishing empire was overrun by greedy profiteers) and the motivation of a long-time Wallace admirer to see that the truth was told. The result—*American Dreamers: The Wallaces and Reader's Digest: An Insider's Story*—was published by Simon & Schuster in 1996, to considerable critical acclaim."

Unfolding the saga of the founders of the *Reader's Digest* empire, from the magazine's exciting start-up in the Greenwich Village of the Roaring Twenties to the dismal final days of the Wallaces' lives, *American Dreamers* was singled out as one of the year's "most interesting books" by David Walton in the *Dallas Morning News.* Walton, who noted that Canning was a former employee of *Reader's Digest,* stated that the author "covers this history briskly, without much ax-grinding." Describing the book's impact on readers as "haunting," Kathy Balog in *USA Today* termed the work "as much a cautionary tale as it is a business success story"—one that "documents all the brilliance and decadence, generosity and pettiness of [the] founding couple."

The *Reader's Digest* was born from DeWitt Wallace's idea to publish summaries of Agriculture Department pamphlets and, later, shortened versions of already published articles. Tracing the path of the magazine's huge growth in circulation, *American Dreamers* also discloses the Wallaces' accumulation of great wealth and its trappings as well as their generosity to *Digest* staff, DeWitt's resistance to change, how the *Digest's* content was influenced by governmental organizations, the couple's failing health and final isolation in their great mansion, the changes made to the original business and its guiding philosophy, and the redirection of the Wallace fortune by opportunists with their own agendas.

"The fall of the house of Wallace was brought on by greed and corporate modernization," James Ledbetter pointed out in the *Washington Post Book World.* "Canning's skill is in documenting how those indomitable forces combined to make a very American tragedy." The book "distinguishes itself by giving a view from deep inside the RD world . . . that thankfully avoids the superficiality associated with the average memoir," the critic observed. A contributor to *Publishers Weekly* found *American Dreams* "a sad and bitter story, magnificently told, with a full sense of its implications for contemporary 'bottom line' America."

The recognition accorded *American Dreamers* was "a pleasant surprise," acknowledged Canning. "But the real surprise had nothing to do with critics or reviews.

"As a first-time author, I was astonished by how much writing added to my life. There was me (there had always been me), but there was now also the book. And while I worked on the book everything else I encountered—every novel, newspaper, movie, play, conversation—took on new significance. Things that were meaningful in their own right became doubly meaningful for the potential they had to contribute to the book. There was an edge to things. Life was more intense, more organized.

"I have recently started work on a new project—about the national madness known as the War on Drugs—and already that subliminal edge is coming back. I can't wait to get deeper into my research, to discover whatever it is I'm going to discover. My only regret is that I spent so many years talking about this process instead of doing it."

BIOGRAPHICAL/CRITICAL SOURCES:

PERIODICALS

Dallas Morning News, November 17, 1996, pp. 8J-9J.
Publishers Weekly, October 7, 1996, p. 51; November 1, 1996, p. 42.
USA Today, March 25, 1997, p. 4B.
Washington Post Book World, February 23, 1997.

* * *

CARLIN, Martha

PERSONAL: Female. *Education:* Bryn Mawr College, A.B., 1975; University of Toronto, M.A., 1976, Ph.D., 1984.

ADDRESSES: Office—Department of History, University of Wisconsin at Milwaukee, P.O. Box 413, Milwaukee, WI 53201.

CAREER: Historian and writer. University of Wisconsin at Milwaukee, assistant professor, 1990-95, associate professor of history, 1995—, director of graduate studies, 1996—.

MEMBER: Royal Historical Society (fellow).

WRITINGS:

Medieval Southwark (monograph), Hambledon Press (Rio Grande, OH), 1996.
(Editor, with Joel T. Rosenthal) *Food and Eating in Medieval Europe,* Hambledon Press, 1997.

WORK IN PROGRESS: Research on medieval England, urban history, the history of London, food history, and the history of domestic technologies.

* * *

CARR, Emily   1871-1945

PERSONAL: Born December 13, 1871, in Victoria, British Columbia, Canada; died March 2, 1945; daughter of Richard (a merchant) and Emily Carr. *Education:* Educated at home until age seven; attended local primary and secondary schools, and private art lessons; attended California School of Design (San Francisco, CA), 1891-95; attended Westminster School of Art (London, England), 1899-1904; attended Academie Colarossi (Paris, France), 1910-11.

CAREER: Painter, illustrator, author of memoirs, letter writer, and craftsperson. Oil paintings and other works housed in museums, galleries, and collections, including Vancouver Art Gallery. Illustrated (with others) a book on Indians by Marius Barbeau, 1928. Taught art in Victoria; dismissed because of Fauvist style. Beginning in 1913, ran a boarding-house, made pottery and carpets, and bred sheepdogs.

AWARDS, HONORS: Governor-General's Award, best Canadian nonfiction book, 1942, for *Klee Wyck.*

WRITINGS:

Klee Wyck, Oxford University Press (Toronto and New York City), 1941.
The Book of Small, Oxford University Press (Toronto), 1942, (London and New York City), 1943.
The House of All Sorts, Oxford University Press (Toronto and London), 1944.
Growing Pains: The Autobiography of Emily Carr, Oxford University Press (Toronto), 1946.
Pause: A Sketch Book, edited by Ira Dilworth, with illustrations by Carr, Clarke, Irwin (Toronto), 1953, Stoddart Publishing (Toronto), 1995.
The Heart of a Peacock, edited by Ira Dilworth, Clarke and Irwin, 1953, reprinted 1986.

Hundreds and Thousands: The Journals of Emily Carr, edited by Phyllis Inglis, Clarke, Irwin, 1966.

Fresh Seeing: Two Addresses by Emily Carr, preface by Doris Shadbolt, introduction to the 1930 speech by Ira Dilworth, Clarke, Irwin, 1972.

Dear Nan: Letters of Emily Carr, Nan Cheney, and Humphrey Toms, edited by Doreen Walker, University of British Columbia Press (Vancouver), 1990.

The Emily Carr Omnibus, with introduction by Doris Shadbolt (includes *Klee Wyck, The Book of Small, The House of All Sorts, Growing Pains: The Autobiography of Emily Carr, The Heart of a Peacock, Pause: A Sketch Book,* and *Hundreds and Thousands: The Journals of Emily Carr*), Douglas & McIntyre (Vancouver), 1993, University of Washington Press, 1993.

Carr's papers are stored in the Public Archives of British Columbia.

SIDELIGHTS: "Three things are true of anything Emily Carr makes, be it book or picture: she has something to tell, it is something of her own, and it is a Canadian something." These were the words of a *Canadian Forum* reviewer heralding the appearance of Emily Carr's second autobiographical book, *The Book of Small,* in 1942. At that time, in her eighth decade, three years from the end of her life, Carr had only recently achieved celebrity in her native land with the 1941 publication of her first book, *Klee Wyck.* Belated fame had somewhat overwhelmed her after years of obscurity as a painter of the Canadian Northwest. Her progress toward maturity as a visual artist had been a long, difficult one, and her writings told about it in prose of strikingly visual quality, where things described and things concealed were sometimes equally fascinating.

Carr was born in 1871 in Victoria, British Columbia, a small, growing city which physically faced the Pacific but spiritually looked east to England for its cultural roots. Carr's father, Richard, a prosperous merchant of conservative views, had emigrated from England after a sojourn in the gold fields of California; British Columbia's own gold rush had occurred in the 1850s and 1860s. Both of Carr's parents died during her adolescence; from that point she was raised primarily by her strict older sister. Frustrated by her sister's opposition to her artistic aspirations, Carr won permission from her legal guardian to travel to San Francisco to study art at the age of twenty. (Eleanor Munro, in the *Los Angeles Times Book*

Review, related the tale—one of the distortions found in Carr's writings—that Carr ran away to San Francisco at age sixteen.) Almost four years at the San Francisco School of Design had little effect on Carr's art, according to George Woodcock in the *Dictionary of Literary Biography.* Repeated journeys to the shores of northern Vancouver Island, for sketching purposes, brought her into contact with Indian villagers and exposed her to the totemic art which she painted so powerfully in later years.

Studies in England and France in the second decade of the twentieth century brought Carr into contact with modernist as well as academic painting. She suffered at least one emotional breakdown in England, and returned to Victoria in 1911, at the age of forty. She painted and gave art lessons in her home, but was unable to support herself through art and was compelled to take in boarders for the next twenty-five years. She also supplemented her income by making crafts for tourists and by breeding sheepdogs for sale. As Woodcock observed in a *Quill & Quire* column, Carr, who was socially and sexually shy and fearful, constructed a persona that was viewed as eccentric by her fellow citizens: "She wandered through the streets of Victoria pushing a pram filled with dogs and a monkey, and perhaps a parrot on her shoulder." As Hal Quinn put it in a 1992 *Maclean's* article, "She confronted, and affronted, Victorian sensibilities," by habits that included smoking and riding a horse men's-style rather than sidesaddle. She was also beginning to attract some local attention as a regionalist painter. Until 1927, Carr's other duties prevented her from painting except during summer trips to Indian villages. It was only then, at age fifty-six, that she received her first significant one-person show, in the National Gallery in Ottawa. The exhibition, in turn, brought her into contact with a group of Canadian painters called The Seven, who accepted her warmly.

The next decade is considered to be Carr's greatest creative period. She painted large canvases of the coastal rain forests and of totem poles; in Woodcock's words in the *Dictionary of Literary Biography,* "developing her own striking color spectrum and mastering the strange alterations of shadow and light that characterize the coastal world." Major paintings included *Stumps and Sky; Big Raven; Cedar; In a Circle;* and *Scorned as Timber, Beloved of the Sky.* In Quinn's view, "Carr is now widely acknowledged as one of Canada's finest painters ever," and her work, as of 1992, had sold for almost 300,000 dollars (Canadian) per canvas.

In 1937, however, Carr suffered the first of a series of heart attacks. This and other health problems made it substantially more difficult for her to travel and paint. She had heretofore kept journals and written letters, but at that point she began writing for publication. Her first book, *Klee Wyck,* describes her 1898 trip to the Indian villages of Vancouver Island and subsequent interactions with Indians in the forests, along the rivers, and in the cities of British Columbia. The title conveys the name the Indians gave Carr; it means "Laughing One," and rather than meaning that Carr laughed a lot, it "connotes sharing, understanding, and knowledge, the promise of a closer kind of contact achieved outside of verbalization," in the opinion of scholar Roxanne Rimstead, as expressed in *Canadian Literature.*

Klee Wyck was a smash success in Canada, and helped reinforce Carr's growing reputation as a painter. "There is vividness and poignancy as well as spontaneity in the enlightening collection which makes this book," wrote a reviewer in the *New York Times Book Review,* calling Carr "a natural-born writer." The reviewer concluded that Carr "saw, and catches in a few words, the characteristics and atmosphere of lonely islands and wilderness settlements. And she writes with a brisk and sensitive originality, as if she were smiling, or sighing, to herself." Peter Sanger, casting a backward look at Klee Wyck and Carr's four subsequent autobiographical volumes in a 1987 essay for the *Antigonish Review,* found them to be "written with wit, concision, respect and love. They also offer some of the finest passages of natural description in Canadian prose." This, despite Sanger's view that Carr had crucially distorted her inner life, and some facts of her outer life as well, in those books. Carr underestimated her age at important times in her life, for example, and understated her hostility toward her boarders and other characters. Rimstead, more sympathetic toward Carr, admitted the lack of reliability in Carr's memoirs, but added, "*Klee Wyck* as text, however, is valuable history—not simply because it explains the journey behind some of Canada's most esteemed artworks—but because Carr's subjective expression challenges our colonizing history by telling stories about marginal realities which we have never liked to hear." In particular, Rimstead pointed out, *Klee Wyck* reveals the considerable extent of female power in Northwest Coast Indian society.

One year after *Klee Wyck* was published there appeared *The Book of Small,* Carr's memoir about her childhood. A *Canadian Forum* critic called it possibly "Canada's book of the year." The 1944 *The House of All Sorts,* episodic in form like the two previous books, dealt with her experiences as a landlady to boarders. Its view of the boarders is often satirical and critical, for as Kathleen Coburn phrased it in *Canadian Forum,* "Her landladyhood burned into her like caustic, and left scars." Calling Carr's candor "at times almost brutal," Coburn wrote, "She smiles at herself often. But the general effect of the book is of suffering, more because of what is concealed or only hinted at than what is expounded." In the posthumously published volume *Growing Pains* (1946), Carr created a more traditional autobiography; Woodcock, in *Dictionary of Literary Biography,* called it "the most substantial of Carr's memoirs," and stated, "It is written with vigor and a good deal of humor." Coburn, complaining of a paucity of facts and dates and of Carr's failure to describe the causes of her breakdown, found the book's strength to be in an "admirable" reticence that implied much. "Readers will find the unconscious self-exposure almost too poignant to be borne," averred Coburn. Terming the book "quite devoid of self-dramatization," she claimed that, while more uneven than Carr's earlier books, it still left its author "the best of our [Canada's] essayists." Coburn singled out two chapters, "English Spring" and "The Clearing," for praise.

In 1953 came two posthumous volumes, both edited by Carr's friend Ira Dilworth. *Pause: A Sketch Book,* with illustrations by Carr, describes the author's interlude in a British tuberculosis sanitorium after her emotional breakdown in 1903. Upon the book's republication in 1995, Barbara Robertson, in *Canadian Book Review Annual,* praised its "freshness of observation," and opined, "Carr enthusiasts will simply delight in the fact that *Pause* is once again available, for you cannot have too much of a national treasure." The other book from that year, *The Heart of a Peacock,* consists largely of stories and sketches about animals, and conveys, in the process, what a *Times Literary Supplement* reviewer called "a picture of the writer as a girl who had a passion for wild life, great hardihood in bearing its vicissitudes, a peculiar power of taming animals and birds, and an understanding of Indians." Praising the book's lack of sentimentality, the reviewer wrote, "The delicate flavour of individuality and wild life will be enjoyed by all who have any taste for either."

The next Carr book to reach the public did not appear until 1966; it was *Hundreds and Thousands: The Journals of Emily Carr.* Here, readers found Carr expressing her private thoughts about her art, in passage after passage that opened a window into the creative spirit. This aspect of the book made *Dictionary of Literary Biography* contributor Woodcock call the edited journal, "though the least consciously planned of Carr's writings, perhaps the best." Some critics have been ambivalent about the journals, and David P. Silcox, reviewing them in *Saturday Night,* found them poorly written and "humourless," although he added, "I suppose we ought to be thankful to have anything by great people." David Watmough, in *Canadian Literature,* was equally aware of the limitations of Carr's literary style, but much more charitably so. Carr's prose, he found, spanned the range from realism to gushiness, and "there remains a down-to-earthness, a so-eminent humanity and an intimate tearing away of the veils that conceal any artist's true anguish." The journals, he found, evoked "a marvellous sense of period" in the hands of a writer with "an exceptional imagination." Summing up Carr's journal-making achievement, he enthused, "Emily Carr, this record reveals, knew herself better than most of us know ourselves. . . . The finished article is a compelling journal that manages to push sophistication to the wings and wrings genuine if containable emotions in steady succession from the read."

The 1990s saw two new volumes by Carr: the publication of her letters in 1990, under the title *Dear Nan: Letters of Emily Carr, Nan Cheney, and Humphry Toms,* and the 1993 compilation titled *The Emily Carr Omnibus* by a Vancouver publisher. The *Omnibus,* 1,200 pages long and containing an introduction by Carr biographer Doris Shadbolt, contained all the previously published memoirs plus the edited journals, and was greeted positively by reviewers on its issuance. The *Dear Nan* letters, meanwhile, earned an enthusiastic review from Woodcock in *Canadian Literature.* With regard to the self-portrait of Carr in the letters, Woodcock remarked, "What a marvellous projection of character it is, better than any of the great letter novels of the eighteenth century!"

BIOGRAPHICAL/CRITICAL SOURCES:

BOOKS

New, W. H., editor, *Dictionary of Literary Biography,* Volume 68: *Canadian Writers, 1920-1959,* Gale (Detroit), 1988, pp. 54-59.

Samuels, Peggy, and Samuels, Harold, *The Illustrated Biographical Encyclopedia of Artists of the American West,* Doubleday (Garden City, NY), 1976, pp. 82-83.

Twentieth-Century Literary Criticism, Volume 32, Gale (Detroit), 1989, pp. 115-131.

Wilson, Joyce M., editor, *Canadian Book Review Annual 1995,* CBRA (Toronto), 1996 p. 46.

PERIODICALS

Antigonish Review, 1987, pp. 211-239.
Canadian Forum, December, 1942, pp. 284, 186; April, 1945, p. 24; January, 1947, pp. 234-235.
Canadian Literature, summer, 1967, pp. 72-75; summer, 1991, pp. 236-237; Autumn, 1991, pp. 29-59.
Essays on Canadian Writing, summer, 1984, pp. 152-174.
Maclean's, July 6, 1992, p. 70.
New York Times Book Review, June 7, 1942, p. 24.
Quill & Quire, December 25, 1993, p. 25.
Saturday Night, November, 1966, pp. 54-56.
Times Literary Supplement, July 9, 1954, p. 436.*

*   *   *

CASANOVA, Mary 1957-

PERSONAL: Born February 2, 1957, in Duluth, MN; daughter of Eugene (a business manager) and Joyce (a homemaker; maiden name, Anderson) Gazelka; married Charles Casanova (an insurance agent), July 1, 1978; children: Katie, Eric. *Education:* University of Minnesota, B.A., 1981. *Religion:* Judeo-Christian/Lutheran. *Avocational interests:* Reading, writing, cross-country and downhill skiing, camping, canoeing, hiking, running, horseback riding, and playing the piano.

ADDRESSES: Agent—Kendra Marcus, Bookstop Literary Agency, 67 Meadow View Rd., Orinda, CA 94563.

CAREER: Author, lecturer, and writing instructor. Eslinger Sleddog Races, International Falls, MN, volunteer; Voyageurs National Park, Artist in Residency Program, selection judge, 1996; junior high youth group leader. Has taught writing workshops at colleges, universities, and for the Institute of Children's Literature, West Redding, CT. Also worked variously as an immigrations clerk, horticultural worker, piano player, real estate agent, nursing home aid, maid, and English department assistant.

MEMBER: Society of Children's Book Writers and Illustrators, The Loft (a national writing organization), Toastmasters.

AWARDS, HONORS: Emily Johnson Award, Children's Literature Conference, 1990, for the short story "Father's Boots"; Career Development Grant, Minnesota State Arts Board, 1992; Career Opportunity Grants, Arrowhead Regional Arts Council, 1992-94; Fellowship in Literature, Arrowhead Regional Arts Council/Mcknight Foundation, 1995; *Moose Tracks* was selected as a Children's Book of the Month, 1995, and nominated for the Northeastern Book Award, 1995, the North Dakota Library Association Flicker Tale Children's Book Award, 1997, the Iowa Readers' Choice Book Award, 1998, and the Indian Paintbrush Book Award, 1998; *Riot* was nominated for the Minnesota Book Award for Young Adults, 1996, and the Northeastern Book Award, 1997, and was named a Junior Library Guild selection, 1996.

WRITINGS:

The Golden Retriever (nonfiction), Crestwood House/ Macmillan, 1990.
Moose Tracks (middle-grade novel), Hyperion, 1995.
Riot (middle-grade novel), Hyperion, 1996.
Wolf Shadows (middle-grade novel, sequel to *Moose Tracks*), Hyperion, 1997.
Stealing Thunder (middle-grade novel), Hyperion, 1998.
One Dog Canoe (picture book), illustrated by Carter Goodrich, Dorling Kindersley, in press.

Contributor of short stories and articles to *Cricket, Highlights,* and *Once upon a Time.*

SIDELIGHTS: Mary Casanova commented: "When I set out to write for children, I had two main goals: to write books that kids couldn't put down and to write books that matter. Coming from a family of ten children—seven boys and three girls—I was always active: riding horses, playing tag off the pontoon boat in the summer and ice-hockey with our own 'team' in the winter. I was also a reluctant reader. I loved being outside, and if a book was going to hold my attention it had to be a fast-paced story. *Moose Tracks,* my first novel, hooks the kind of reader I was.

"I love to throw my character in the midst of issues, issues I can't quite get my arms around. *Riot* is that kind of story. After living through a two-year labor dispute that erupted into violence in my small northern town in 1989, I knew I'd have to write about it and somehow make sense of it. The result is the fictionalized account of a riot through 12-year-old Bryan Grant's eyes; his father is increasingly involved in the fervor, protesting the work he doesn't get at the paper mill. Bryan's mother, on the other hand, is a union member and teacher who desires a peaceable solution to the dispute." "Casanova has created an exciting, realistic novel," Cheryl Cufari commented in a *School Library Journal* review of *Riot*. Although Elizabeth Bush complained in a review in *Bulletin of the Center for Children's Books* that "good guy/bad guy treatment of the labor action grossly oversimplifies the issues," Lauren Peterson concluded in a review in *Booklist* that "this fast-paced story poses challenging questions that have no easy answers."

Casanova fulfills her intention to write fast-paced stories centered on issues that make her young-adult readers think hard about important questions. In Casanova's sequel to *Moose Tracks, Wolf Shadows,* Matt, the protagonist, illegally shoots a wolf, causing a nearly insurmountable rift in his longtime friendship with Seth who vehemently opposes poaching. In *Kirkus Reviews* a critic wrote that "the attention-grabbing action and emotional struggles of the hero [in *Moose Tracks*] will hook reluctant readers." Centered on twelve-year-old Seth, who kills a rabbit in a protected wilderness area without his warden stepfather's permission, the novel stages a coming-of-age story in which Seth comes to question ideas he had formerly held about himself and his family. *School Library Journal* reviewer Todd Morning said that "Casanova's precise and evocative descriptions" add depth to the adventure story that culminates when Seth orchestrates the capture of poachers and confesses to his own misdeed.

BIOGRAPHICAL/CRITICAL SOURCES:

PERIODICALS

Booklist, November 1, 1996, p. 497.
Bulletin of the Center for Children's Books, January, 1997, p. 165.
Kirkus Reviews, May 15, 1995, p. 708.
Los Angeles Times, November 24, 1996, p. 1328.
Pioneer (Bemidji, Minnesota), May 14, 1997, p. 6.
Publishers Weekly, June 19, 1995, p. 60.
School Library Journal, June, 1995, p. 108; October, 1996, p. 120.
Star Tribune, October 22, 1995, p. F13.

CHAMBERLIN, Ann 1954-

PERSONAL: Born March 28, 1954, in Salt Lake City, UT; daughter of R. Eliot (a math professor) and F. Elizabeth Maud (a kindergarten teacher) Chamberlin; married Curt F. Setzer, September 14, 1978; children: Eliot, Harris. *Education:* Attended Brigham Young University, and the Universities of Virginia and Tel Aviv, graduated (Middle Eastern anthropology and archaeology), 1978. *Avocational interests:* Gardening, folk dancing, raising chickens.

ADDRESSES: Office—P.O. Box 71114, Salt Lake City, UT, 84171-1114. *Agent*—Virginia Kidd Agency, 538 East Hartford St., P.O. Box 278, Milford, PA 18337.

CAREER: Novelist and playwright.

MEMBER: Novelists Inc., Romance Writers of America, Utah Romance Writers, League of Utah Writers, Idaho Writers' League, Dramatists' Guild, Wasatch Mountain Fiction Writers (president, 1997).

AWARDS, HONORS: Winner, Utah Playwriting Competition, 1976, for *To Life,* 1977, for *A Faerie Tale,* and 1979, for *Ex Cathedra;* semi-finalist, Jane Chambers Playwriting Award, and Beverly Hills Theatre Guild—Julie Harris Playwright Award Competition, both 1991, both for *Shadow Play;* first choice in finalist category, ALBALT Play Search, 1992, for *Acting Heads of State;* semi-finalist, Shiras Institute/Mildred and Albert Panowski Award, 1993, for *The Piper Must Be Paid;* Festival of New Plays finalist, Cleveland Public Theatre, 1993, for *Someone Like No Other;* finalist, Dayton's Futurefest, and Shenandoah Playwright's Retreat, both 1995, both for *Every Woman Blues;* award for one of six best new scripts of the season, *Off-Off Broadway Review,* 1996, for *Jihad;* Best Foreign Historical and Best Cover, *Affaire de Coeur* Readers Poll, 1996, for *Sofia.*

WRITINGS:

NOVELS

The Virgin and the Tower, Pocket Books (New York City), 1979.
Tamar, Forge (New York City), 1994.
Sofia, Forge, 1996.
The Sultan's Daughter, Forge, 1997.
The Reign of the Favored Women, Forge, 1998.

PLAYS

To Life, produced in Salt Lake City, UT, Greenbriar Theatre, 1976.
A Faerie Tale, produced in Salt Lake City, UT, Salt Lake Acting Company, 1978.
Ex Cathedra, produced in Salt Lake City, UT, Theatre 138, and in Seattle, WA, La Pensee DISCOVERY! Theatre, 1980.
The Desert and the Sown, staged reading produced in Seattle, WA, La Pensee DISCOVERY! Theater, 1980.
The Lorlei, produced in Seattle, WA, La Pensee DISCOVERY! Theater, 1981, and in Lancaster, PA, The Independent Eye, 1988.
Someone Like No Other, staged reading produced in Woodstock, NY, Common Stage Theater, 1991.
Simoom, reading produced in San Rafael, CA, Theater Artists of Marin, 1991.
The Giantkiller, produced in Denver, CO, 1992.
The Sow's Bladder, reading produced in Rose Valley, PA, Hedgerow Theatre, 1993.
Pas De Deux, produced in Long Island, NY, Hofstra University, 1993.
A Christmas Wish, staged reading produced in Rose Valley, PA, Hedgerow Theatre, 1994.
Fire Exit, produced in Eureka, CA, Plays-In-Progress World Premiere Theatre, 1996.

Also author of unproduced plays, including *Shadow Play; Acting Heads of State; The Piper Must Be Paid; Every Woman Blues;* and *Jihad.*

WORK IN PROGRESS: Leaving Eden, expected in 1999; research on medieval France.

SIDELIGHTS: Ann Chamberlin told *CA:* "I believe that the purpose of storytelling—as of all true art as well as all true religion—is to support positions in exact opposition to the views prevailing in a culture's powerhouses, whatever those views happen to be. Nowhere is this more crucial than in the retelling of history. As Milan Kundera tells us, people in the powerhouses are not so interested in who will control the future as in who controls the airbrushes in the labs where the past's photos are retouched.

"Am I on a crusade? You bet. Only please, let's not call it crusade, jihad or even mission. In my books, I hope to wield my own airbrush, retell history from the points of view of people who did not get to tell their side because their side lost, usually for an excess of virtue, if anything. And the history of religions with crusades, jihads and/or missions are of particular fascination to me. I believe the notion of progress is the Great Lie. Sooner or later, I hope to offend everyone—everyone who fancies his position in a powerhouse way, anyway.

"I began writing before I could write, making my long-suffering mother write down my stories for me. I produced my first play at age four, inducing brother and sisters to act. I got my first rejection notice from a New York house at the age of seven. The theatre seemed a more promising avenue in my youth. There was always some amateur company hoping for some piece with parts for many women they didn't need to pay royalties on. To this day, I have found no greater high than the collaboration found in the rehearsals for a show I've written.

"My true calling, however, I date to my college days, a summer spent on an archeological excavation in Israel and the place—Sinai, of course, where all good epiphanies come. I went convinced of the superiority of western culture just like any other American girl—certainly convinced of the superiority of the opportunities it offered me and my sex. But in the desert I was hosted by a Bedouin family and the woman of the family. I never saw her face (she was heavily veiled), I never spoke a word to her (my Arabic at the time was worse than her English), nor did I ever learn her name (she was, of course, called only Umm Khalid, after her eldest son). But never in my life have I met a more confident, respected, powerful, *divine*, woman. The meeting sent my conviction of superiority into freefall. Her spirit enveloped me, continues to consume me. Moses, in the same vicinity, never had better.

"Mary Renault is my favorite all-time author and influence on my work. I also like Shakespeare (*Measure for Measure* most of all), Christopher Fry, Rudyard Kipling and the "J" part of the Bible. Of more recent authors I admire Cecelia Holland, Kathryn Harrison, Wilbur Smith, Morgan Llwelyn and—yes—Anne Rice.

"My first novel, *The Virgin and the Tower*, was just for practice. It is as close as I've been able to come to confronting my Mormon upbringing and combines the ancient Mesopotamian story of Gilgamesh with *Book of Mormon* stories. *Tamar* takes on the Biblical story of King David from the point of view of his Goddess-worshipping stepdaughter.

"*Sofia* begins a trilogy exploring the time in their history the Turks have named "The Reign of the Favored Women." *The Sultan's Daughter* and *The Reign of the Favored Women* will complete the series by 1998.

"As a writer with a passionate interest in gender roles, I find I always need a character who straddles those roles. The form of my story never appears clearly until I have found him/her. I am attracted to study societies that have very strongly enforced gender roles and find, without exception, that such societies always allow—often fiercely demand, in fact—the in-between role as well. An in-between role helps the society appreciate both sexes more. People in the modern U.S. certainly don't even appreciate femininity. Not unless it is the femininity that caters to the alpha male. I feel a need to counteract that."

* * *

CHAPMAN, Lynne F(erguson) 1963-

PERSONAL: Born March 14, 1963, in Los Angeles, CA; daughter of James (a professor of English) and Lorice (a library assistant and teacher; maiden name, Mittry) Ferguson; married Paul Chapman (a neuroscientist), June 21, 1986; children: Thomas, Samuel. *Education:* DePauw University, B.A., 1985. *Avocational interests:* Reading, watching films, cooking, playing games, drawing and graphic design, travel.

ADDRESSES: Home and office—7 Westbourne Rd., Cardiff CF4 2BP, Wales.

CAREER: Mayfield Publishing, Mountain View, CA, editorial assistant, 1985-87; Windsor Publications, Northridge, CA, photography editor, 1987-88; Dushkin Publishing, Guilford, CT, annual editions editor, 1988-89; freelance editor and writer, 1989—.

MEMBER: National Childbirth Trust, Eglwys Newydd Primary School and Parents Association (secretary, 1996—).

WRITINGS:

Sylvia Plath, photographs by Benno Friedman, Creative Company (Mankato, MN), 1994.
Leo Tolstoy, Creative Company, 1997.

WORK IN PROGRESS: Jane Austen and *The Bronte Sisters,* both for Creative Company.

SIDELIGHTS: Lynne F. Chapman commented: "Because both of my parents taught English, it was probably inevitable that I, after a proper period of teenage rebelliousness, would want to have a lot to do with books. Publishing seemed an obvious career choice, so I spent several years after college moving from one small publishing company to another as my husband pursued his academic career at various universities. Then I decided to take up freelance editing, not coincidentally before the birth of my first child, and I have worked at home ever since. While living in Minnesota, I was asked to try writing for a small, upmarket publisher of beautiful educational books. I wrote my first book with equal parts nervousness and delight, and three more followed. Now we have settled overseas, in Cardiff, Wales, and as my children get older, I hope to have more time for writing—although those nerves just won't go away!"

*   *   *

CHEN, Edwin 1948-

PERSONAL: Born in 1948.

ADDRESSES: Agent—c/o Carol Publishing, 600 Madison Ave., New York, NY 10022.

CAREER: Journalist. *Los Angeles Times,* science and policy reporter, correspondent in Washington bureau.

WRITINGS:

Cheating Death (nonfiction), Onyx (New York City), 1992.
Deadly Scholarship: The True Story of Lu Gang and Mass Murder in America's Heartland (nonfiction), Carol (New York City), 1995.

SIDELIGHTS: A science and policy reporter for the *Los Angeles Times,* Edwin Chen is also the author of nonfiction works recounting sensational murders. *Cheating Death,* published in 1992, details events leading to the 1988 murder of an unsuspecting California man who unluckily resembled the perpetrator of an insurance fraud scheme. Melvin Eugene Hanson, the owner of a sports clothing retail chain, enlisted his business partner and a physician to help him fake his own death and collect nearly 1.5 million dollars in insurance awards. Bill Kent in the *New York Times*

Book Review faulted Chen's account of the conspiracy for providing only "shallow portraits" of the story's central characters. Kent concluded that "Chen's just-the-facts style of reporting is long on information but short on analysis."

Chen followed *Cheating Death* in 1995 with *Deadly Scholarship: The True Story of Lu Gang and Mass Murder in America's Heartland,* another nonfiction work centering on a sensational murder. On November 1, 1991, Lu Gang, a brilliant but socially unsuccessful Chinese graduate student shot and killed several faculty members and his chief academic rival in the physics department at the University of Iowa before turning the gun on himself. Chen's exploration of the tragedy, which a *Publishers Weekly* reviewer called a "searching study," considers the various pressures on foreign graduate students and recounts the academic and social disappointments that culminated in Gang's shooting spree. A commentator for *Kirkus Reviews* called the work a "pedestrian retelling of a true crime case." According to the reviewer, "Chen's attempt to probe potentially interesting subjects yields little insight." John Greenya, however, offered a more favorable assessment of the work in the *Washington Post Book World,* stating, "Chen does a good job of tying it all together, of showing how a concatenation of events resulted in a horrible outcome."

BIOGRAPHICAL/CRITICAL SOURCES:

PERIODICALS

Kirkus Reviews, December 1, 1994, p. 1582.
New York Times Book Review, July 19, 1992, p. 20.
Publishers Weekly, December 5, 1994, p. 61.
Washington Post Book World, March 5, 1995, p. 6.*

*   *   *

CHONG, Denise

PERSONAL: Raised in Prince George, British Columbia, Canada; daughter of John and Hing Chong; married Roger Smith (a Canadian Television Network (CTV) journalist).

ADDRESSES: Home—Ottawa, Ontario, Canada.

CAREER: Writer and economist. Finance Department, Ottawa, economist; senior economic advisor to

Prime Minister Pierre Trudeau, 1980-84. Freelance writer in Beijing, Toronto, and London, England.

AWARDS, HONORS: Edna Staebler Award for Creative Non-fiction, 1995; City of Vancouver Book Award; VanCity Book Prize, 1995; nominated for Hubert Evans Non-Fiction Prize, 1995; shortlisted for Governor General Award, 1994; all for *The Concubine's Children: Portrait of a Family Divided.*

WRITINGS:

The Concubine's Children: Portrait of a Family Divided, Viking (New York City), 1994.

SIDELIGHTS: Denise Chong's biographical book, *The Concubine's Children: Portrait of a Family Divided,* outlines the lives of her Chinese ancestors. The research for the book is comprehensive. Hing, Chong's mother, provides the needed information which mostly revolves around Chong's grandmother, May-ying, a concubine. May-ying was sold to a Chinese immigrant named Chan Sam, who then brought her to Vancouver, Canada, where she worked in a tea house. May-ying was an alcoholic and for Hing the memories are hard ones. May-ying gave birth to three children, and two went to China to be raised while Hing remained in Canada with her mother. Not only was the family in a white society, but they also had to pay the living costs of the children in China. The racism and the hardships of life were difficult. May-ying's hard life and alcoholism led to a strained relationship for May-ying and Hing, which resulted in a strained relationship between Hing and Chong.

"As a work of history and memoir, *The Concubine's Children* has the narrative flow of fiction; as a work of invention, it has the persuasive force of the truth," remarked Jonathan Yardley in *Washington Post Book World.* David Guterson of *New York Times Book Review* described Chong's work as "beautiful, haunting and wise, it lingers in the mind like a portrait one returns to often in a family album, and elicits the same mysterious response of love, melancholy and pride."

BIOGRAPHICAL/CRITICAL SOURCES:

PERIODICALS

Los Angeles Times Book Review, April 9, 1995, p. 6.
New York Times Book Review, January 15, 1995, p. 24.

Washington Post Book World, January 8, 1995, p. 3.*

*   *   *

CHRISTOPHER, Renny (Teresa)   1957-

PERSONAL: Born March 4, 1957, in Newport, CA; daughter of Richard (a carpenter and boat builder) and Bebi (a hairdresser and bookkeeper) Christopher. *Ethnicity:* "Irish/German-American." *Education:* Mills College, B.A., 1982; San Jose State University, M.A., 1986; University of California, Santa Cruz, Ph.D., 1992. *Politics:* "Peace and freedom." *Religion:* None. *Avocational interests:* Horses, hiking.

ADDRESSES: Home—P.O. Box 3395, Turlock, CA 95381. *Office*—Department of English, California State University, Stanislaus, 801 West Monte Vista, Turlock, CA 95382; fax 209-667-3720. *E-mail*—rchristo@toto.csustan.edu.

CAREER: Horse Lovers' National, Burlingame, CA, features editor, 1976-79; *Literature of Liberty,* Menlo Park, CA, production editor, 1982; *Gilroy Dispatch,* graphic arts editor, 1983-84; San Jose State University, San Jose, CA, lecturer in English, 1986-87; Cabrillo Community College, Aptos, CA, instructor in English, 1988-95; California State University, Stanislaus, Turlock, assistant professor of English, 1995—. San Jose State University, lecturer, 1993-94; University of California, Santa Cruz, lecturer, 1992-95; University of Virginia, associate fellow of Institute for Advanced Technology and the Humanities. Sixties Project Collective (electronic bulletin board), member. *Viet Nam Generation: A Journal of Recent History and Contemporary Issues,* vice-president. Gives readings from her works.

MEMBER: PEN International, Modern Language Association of America (and its Radical Caucus), American Studies Association, Popular Culture Association, Asian American Studies Association, Association for Asian Studies, National Council of Teachers of English, Conference on College Composition and Communication, National Writers Union, Philosophical Association of the Pacific Coast, California American Studies Association.

AWARDS, HONORS: Winner, McHenry Library Book Collection Contest, 1988; outstanding service award, Alpha Gamma Sigma, 1993; book award, outstanding book on human rights, Gustavus Myers Center for the Study of Human Rights in North America, 1995, for *The Viet Nam War/The American War.*

WRITINGS:

(Contributor) *Understanding Others: Cultural and Cross Cultural Studies and the Teaching of Literature,* edited by Joseph Trimmer and Tilly Warnock, National Council of Teachers of English (Urbana, IL), 1992.

(Contributor) *Reading the Literatures of Asian America,* edited by Shirley Lim and Amy Ling, Temple University Press (Philadelphia, PA), 1992.

The Viet Nam War/The American War: Images and Representations in Euro-American and Vietnamese Exile Narratives, University of Massachusetts Press (Boston, MA), 1995.

(Contributor) *The Canon in the Classroom,* edited by John Alberti, Garland Publishing (New York City), 1995.

(Contributor) *This Fine Place So Far from Home,* edited by C. L. Barney Dews and Carolyn Law, Temple University Press, 1995.

My Name Is Medea (poems), New Spirit Press (Kew Gardens, NY), 1996.

Viet Nam and California (poems), Viet Nam Generation, 1997.

Poetry represented in anthologies, including *A Measured Response,* edited by Palmer Hall, Pecan Grove Press, 1993. Staff film critic, *Matrix Women's Newsmagazine,* 1990-92; film critic, *La Gazette,* 1992—. Contributor of articles, stories, poems, and reviews to periodicals, including *Journal of American Culture, Santa Clara Review, Viet Nam Generation, American Letters and Commentary, Journal of Women and Religion,* and *LIT: Literature, Interpretation, Theory.* Co-editor, *Women's Studies Quarterly,* spring, 1998; *Quarry West,* member of editorial board, 1987-90, fiction editor, 1990-92.

WORK IN PROGRESS: American Nightmares: U.S. Working Class Literature; A Carpenter's Daughter: A Working Class Woman in Higher Education.

SIDELIGHTS: Renny Christopher told *CA:* "I became interested in the war in Viet Nam out of personal acquaintance with Viet Nam veterans and with Vietnamese students. I wrote *The Viet Nam War/The American War* out of a deep frustration with the omnipresent racism that informs most U.S. discussions of the war. I have received several letters from

people—mostly veterans—who have told me that my book explained to them things about Viet Nam (the country, not the war) they hadn't understood, which helped them put their own experiences in perspective. This is exactly what I hoped to accomplish with the book.

"I am now undertaking a study of U.S. working class literature. My own experience is that of upward mobility, being the first person in my family to have a college degree. I am also writing a memoir, *A Carpenter's Daughter: A Working Class Woman in Higher Education,* which addresses my own experiences.

"However, although literary criticism is what I have best succeeded in publishing, I do not primarily think of myself as a scholar, but rather as a poet and fiction writer. I have had some modest success with poetry, but the piece I would most like to have published, a novel called *A Spy in the Land of the Living,* remains unpublished eight years after its completion, despite the efforts of two agents, my own attempts to place it with a small press, and a large number of 'encouraging' rejections. This remains the largest disappointment of my life."

*   *   *

CLAYTON, Elaine 1961-

PERSONAL: Born September 17, 1961, in TX; daughter of Robert (a doctor) and Bonnie (a home maker) Clayton; married Simon Boughton (a publisher), September 14, 1996. *Education:* Atlanta College of Art, B.F.A., 1984; attended Georgia State University, 1986; School of Visual Arts, New York City, M.F.A., 1996. *Avocational interests:* "Riding horses, western and English style, in-line skating, playing with my dog Ah Wing, traveling, learning to speak Italian."

ADDRESSES: Home and office—65 Sussex St., Jersey City, NJ 07302. *Agent*—William Reiss, John Hawkins and Associates, Inc., 71 West 23rd St., Suite 1600, New York, NY 10010.

CAREER: Illustrator and author. Cesar Chavez Migrant Camp, Mobile, AL, head start teacher, 1980; High Museum of Art, Atlanta, GA, gallery instructor, 1980-85; St. Anthony's Summer Camp, Atlanta, art instructor, 1983; Woodruff Memorial Arts Center

Gallery, Atlanta, gallery manager, 1984; Paideia School, Atlanta, assistant teacher and artist-in-residence, 1985-89; Mary Lin Elementary School, Atlanta, artist-in-residence, 1985; Atrium School, Water-town, MA, elementary teacher, 1990-94. Volunteer with Glen Mary Missionary. Has presented artwork at exhibitions, including Woodruff Memorial Arts Center, Atlanta, GA, 1984; The Visual Club, New York City, 1995; Art Directors Club, New York City, 1996; and The New York Women's Foundation, New York City, 1996.

WRITINGS:

(Self-illustrated) *Pup in School,* Crown, 1993.
(Self-illustrated) *Ella's Trip to the Museum,* Crown, 1996.
(Illustrator) *Six Haunted Hairdos* by Gregory Maguire, Clarion, 1997

Editor, "Puzzle Gallery Books," Crown, 1997. Contributor of reviews and illustrations to magazines and newspapers, including *Drawing, Raygun, Curio, Drawing Instructor, Southline,* and *New York Times.*

WORK IN PROGRESS: Picture books.

SIDELIGHTS: Elaine Clayton commented: "I grew up in a big family and learned the importance of lively conversation and storytelling. As I grew up, my private world was one involving characters I drew, whole families of people with stories I made up.

"Before and while studying art in college, I worked with children—never doing art without being at times surrounded by children to even out the intensity of painting and drawing, and never working with children without bringing my creative process (and theirs) to the forefront.

"Eventually, children asked that I put my stories on paper, not disposable marker boards or chalk boards where they disappear when story time is over. I had to do as they asked since, as a teacher, I expected stories from them on paper! This is when I began pursuing publication of my work, and I have loved the entire process. I make stories involving the same types of characters I made up as a child, always meeting new ones in real life along the way. I want more than anything to encourage children to delight in their view of the world and, through art and stories, change the world by showing us what they see."

BIOGRAPHICAL/CRITICAL SOURCES:

PERIODICALS

New York Times Book Review, May 19, 1996, p. 28.
Publishers Weekly, June 28, 1993, p. 75; June 3, 1996, p. 82.
School Library Journal, October, 1993, p. 97; June, 1996, p. 99.*

*   *   *

CLEARY, Brian P.   1959-

PERSONAL: Born October 1, 1959, in Lakewood, OH; son of Michael J. (in international business) and Suzanne Cleary; married Colleen (a teacher), August 21, 1982; children: Grace, Ellen, Emma. *Education:* John Carroll University, B.A., 1982.   *Religion:* Catholic.

ADDRESSES: Home—2084 Brown Rd., Lakewood, OH 44107. *E-mail*—baberuth60@aol.com.

CAREER: Humor writer, freelance copywriter.

AWARDS, HONORS: Children's Choice selection, International Reading Association/Children's Book Council, 1996, for *Give Me Bach My Schubert.*

WRITINGS:

Jamaica Sandwich?, illustrated by Rick Dupre, Lerner, 1996.
It Looks a Lot Like Reindeer, illustrated by Dupre, Lerner, 1996.
Give Me Bach My Schubert, illustrated by Dupre, Lerner, 1996.
You Never Sausage Love, illustrated by Dupre, Lerner, 1996.

Has also published humor articles, essays, features, and cartoons in local and national magazines.

SIDELIGHTS: Humorist Brian P. Cleary commented: "I believe that baseball is the perfect game.

"I believe that cats are smarter than dogs.

"I believe that *The Andy Griffith Show* will still have appeal one hundred years from now.

"I believe in Nestle Quik for milk and Hershey's syrup for ice cream.

"I believe some people were born to play tuba in the marching band.

"I believe you should have a game plan, and that you should write it in pencil.

"I believe that when someone says, 'Smell my hand,' that it's never good.

"I believe the world was just a little better place when men wore hats.

"I believe good teachers save more lives than good doctors, firefighters, and police officers combined.

"I believe humor increases vocabulary, ignites curiosity and, therefore, teaches."

BIOGRAPHICAL/CRITICAL SOURCES:

PERIODICALS

Publishers Weekly, February 26, 1996, p. 105.
School Library Journal, June, 1996, p. 120.

* * *

CLINTON, Jeff
  See BICKHAM, Jack M(iles)

* * *

CODER, S(amuel) Maxwell 1902-1997

*OBITUARY NOTICE—*See index for *CA* sketch: Born March 25, 1902, in Straight, PA; died July 23, 1997, in Chicago, IL. Theologian, editor, educator, and author. Coder devoted his career to the study of religion, eventually becoming editor-in-chief of Moody Press. Ordained in the Presbyterian ministry in 1938, he served as pastor at churches in Camden, New Jersey, Atlantic City, New Jersey, and Philadelphia, Pennsylvania, from 1935 until 1945. He joined the faculty of the Moody Bible Institute in Chicago in 1945 and remained on staff until 1969. While at Moody he became editor-in-chief in 1945, vice president and dean of education in 1947, and dean emeritus in 1969. He spoke at Bible and mission conferences worldwide.

Coder wrote and edited a number of books, including *Dobbie Defender of Malta, Our Lord Prays for His Own, God's Will for Your Life, The World to Come, Jude: The Acts of the Apostates, The Bible Science and Creation, Great Doctrines of the Bible* (with William Evans), *Nave's Topical Bible, Israel's Destiny, Christian Workers New Testament,* and *The Final Chapter.* He also put together the *Youth Triumphant* correspondence course. In addition, Coder worked with Wilbur M. Smith to edit the lengthy "Wycliffe Series of Christian Classics" for Moody.

OBITUARIES AND OTHER SOURCES:

BOOKS

Writers Directory, St. James Press, 1994.

PERIODICALS

Washington Post, August 3, 1997, p. B6.

* * *

COHEN, Sholom 1951-

PERSONAL: Born May 23, 1951, in Kansas City, MO; son of Eugene Joseph (a typographer) and Clara (Stillman) Cohen; married Bryna Chorner (a school administrator), August 21, 1978; children: Avraham, Chaim, Menachem Mendel, Yisroel, Nechama Dina, Sara Leah, Mushkie. *Education:* Massachusetts Institute of Technology, B.S., 1973; University of Michigan, M.L.S., 1974; attended University of Western Ontario, 1976-78; Columbia University, M.S., 1981. *Religion:* Jewish.

*ADDRESSES: Home—*6383 Douglas St., Pittsburgh, PA 15217. *Office—*Software Engineering Institute, Carnegie-Mellon University, Pittsburgh, PA 15213. *E-mail—*sgc@sei.cmu.edu.

CAREER: University of Western Ontario, London, Canada, music librarian, 1974-78; Columbia University, New York City, systems librarian, 1979-81; McDonnell Douglas Corp., St. Louis, MO, software engineer, 1982-88; Carnegie-Mellon University, Pittsburgh, PA, software consultant, 1988—.

WRITINGS:

"YITZ BERG FROM PITTSBURGH" SERIES

Yitzy and the G.O.L.E.M., HaChai Publications (Brooklyn, NY), 1992.
The Lopsided Yarmulke, HaChai Publications, 1995.

WORK IN PROGRESS: Additional books in the "Yitz Berg from Pittsburgh" series.

SIDELIGHTS: Sholom Cohen commented: "It had never occurred to me to write fiction, let alone a children's novel, until about six years ago. At that time, I hadn't written anything of a fictional nature in over twenty years, since high school. (That's apart from the technical reports I do for government sponsors, which might be considered fiction in some quarters.)

"My actual inspiration was the lack of appropriate fiction for my children. There is a void of meaningful fiction for and about Jewish kids in the preteen years. As a Chassidic Jew, I wanted something that was, in a sense, for and about religiously observant Jewish children growing up in contemporary America. At the same time, I wanted to avoid the stereotypical religious themes of some Jewish children's literature and provide something that would appeal to a non-Jewish audience as well. I have tried to develop characters and tell stories that are clearly about the Jewish experience, but that also explore the universal themes of friendship, trust, and honesty.

"I also wanted to use Pittsburgh as a setting. The urban locale offers so many opportunities for plot development, and I've tried to make the city a character in some ways. The exploration of Pittsburgh has given me the chance to share some of the city's unique features with readers.

"Over the past six years of writing for children, I've had the greatest pleasure in hearing from readers of my books. I never tire of the best question of all: 'When's the next book coming out?'"

*   *   *

COLTART, Nina   1927-1997

OBITUARY NOTICE—See index for *CA* sketch: Born November 21, 1927, in Shortlands, Kent, England;

died June 24, 1997. Psychoanalyst, psychiatrist, and author. Coltart devoted her career to the study of psychology, establishing herself as a psychoanalyst in private practice in 1961. She began her work after studies at Somerville College and St. Bartholomew's Hospital, as well as studies with the British Psychoanalytic Society. At St. Bartholomew's, she was the first woman to serve as editor of its *Barts Journal.* Later, she worked at various hospitals under the National Health Service. After qualifying for the British Psycho-Analytical Society as an associate member in 1964, she took on the responsibilities of training analyst and supervisor seven years later. She also directed the London Clinic of Psycho-Analysis for ten years. A Theravada Buddhism practitioner, she helped establish a Buddhist monastery near Petersfield, England. She wrote several books, including *Slouching Towards Bethlehem, The Baby and the Bath Water,* and *How to Survive as a Psychotherapist.*

OBITUARIES AND OTHER SOURCES:

BOOKS

Writers Directory, St. James Press, 1996.

PERIODICALS

Times (London; electronic), July 24, 1997.

*   *   *

CONSTABLE, Giles   1929-

PERSONAL: Born June 1, 1929, in London, England; became a naturalized citizen of the United States; son of William George and Olivia (Carson-Roberts) Constable; married Esther Van Horne Young, 1959; children: Olivia Renie, John Van Horne. *Education:* Harvard University, B.A., 1950, Ph.D., 1957.

ADDRESSES: Office—P.O. Box 3, Van Hornesville, NY 13475.

CAREER: Harvard University, Cambridge, MA, assistant professor, became associate professor, 1958-66; Lea Professor of medieval history, 1966-77; professor of history, 1977—. Dumbarton Oaks Research Library and Collection, Washington, DC, member of board of scholars, 1973-80; director, 1977—; senior fellow, 1980—. Center for Advanced Studies in

Medieval Civilization, Poitiers, France, lecturer, 1961; Catholic University of America, visiting professor, 1978—. *Speculum,* assistant editor, 1958-78. Writer and editor.

MEMBER: Medieval Academy of America (fellow, vice-president, 1978-79, president, 1979-80), Royal Historical Society (fellow), American Historical Association, New England Historical Association (vice-president, 1975-76, president, 1977-78), New England Medieval Conference (president, 1976-77).

AWARDS, HONORS: Guggenheim fellow, 1967-68. Honorary doctorate from University of Paris.

WRITINGS:

Monastic Tithes from Their Origins to the Twelfth Century, Cambridge University Press, 1964.
(Editor) *The Letters of Peter the Venerable,* two volumes, Harvard University Press (Cambridge, MA), 1967.
(Editor, with B. Smith) *Libellus De Diversis Ordinibus et Professionibus Qui Sunt in Aecclesia: Orders and Callings of the Church,* Oxford University Press (Oxford, England), 1972.
Medieval Monasticism: A Select Bibliography, University of Toronto Press, (Toronto, Canada) 1976.
Cluniac Studies, Variorum (London, England), 1980.
Attitudes Toward Self-Inflicted Suffering in the Middle Ages, Hellenic College Press (Brookline, MA), 1982.
(With A. P. Kazhdan) *People and Power in Byzantium: An Introduction to Modern Byzantine Studies,* Dumbarton Oaks (Washington, DC), 1982.
(Editor, with Robert L. Benson and Carol D. Lanham) *Renaissance and Renewal in the Twelfth Century,* Harvard University Press, 1982.
Monks, Hermits, and Crusaders in Medieval Europe, Variorum, 1988.
(Editor, with Theodore Evergates) *The Cartulary and Charters of Notre-Dame of Homblieres,* Medieval Academy of America (Cambridge, MA), 1990.
(Editor, with Elizabeth H. Beatson and Luca Dainelli) *The Letters between Bernard Berenson and Charles Henry Coster,* L. S. Olschki (Florence), 1993.
Three Studies in Medieval Religious and Social Thought, Cambridge University Press, 1995.

Author of introduction, *Apolgiae Duae,* edited by R.B.C. Haygens, Brepols (Turnholti), 1985. Editor of scholarly journals.

SIDELIGHTS: Giles Constable is a world-renowned scholar of medieval history who has written and edited several books in this field, including bibliographies, letter collections, and commentary. A *Times Literary Supplement* critic praised the his meticulous editing of the 1967 collection *The Letters of Peter the Venerable:* "The scholarship is of a very high order. There is no heaping up of irrelevant detail, but equally nothing is spared, nothing abbreviated." A reviewer in *Choice* found Constable's 1976 work *Medieval Monasticism: A Select Bibliography* to be a "thorough and discriminating guide" to its subject matter.

BIOGRAPHICAL/CRITICAL SOURCES:

PERIODICALS

Choice, October, 1976.
Library Journal, June 15, 1976.
Times Literary Supplement, March 7, 1968.*

*   *   *

COOK, Jean Thor   1930-

PERSONAL: Born March 10, 1930, in Little Falls, MN; daughter of Melvin H. (a construction company executive) and Florence (a teacher and homemaker; maiden name, Bohman) Thor; married Alan F. Cook (an automotive executive), August 5, 1950; children: Siri Cook Everett, Jodi Cook Nelson, Terry, Jill Cook Jensen, Jon. *Education:* Macalester College, B.S., 1951; University of Missouri, M.A., 1979. *Politics:* "Independent voter." *Religion:* Lutheran. *Avocational interests:* Travel, literature, sailing, relationships.

ADDRESSES: Home—325 Jack Boot Rd., Monument, CO 80132.

CAREER: Writer. St. Mary College, Kansas City, KS, publicity director for an inner-city adult baccalaureate program, 1978-80.

WRITINGS:

Hugs for Our New Baby, illustrated by Michelle Dorenkamp, Concordia (St. Louis, MO), 1987.
Butterflies for Grandpa, R.A.D.A.R., 1990.
Audrey and the Nighttime Skies, Concordia, 1994.
Jesus Calms the Storm, Concordia, 1994.

Sam, the Terror of Westbrook Elementary, Concordia, 1994.

Room for a Stepdaddy, illustrated by Martine Gourbault, Albert Whitman (Morton Grove, IL), 1995.

WORK IN PROGRESS: Who's under My Bed?; Calhoun becomes a Service Dog; Libby and Her Stepmommy; The Lopez Family Posada; Mrs. Pip's Wacky Tea Party; Where's Mama?; Molly's Wedding.

SIDELIGHTS: Jean Thor Cook commented: "My great love in writing is the picture book. I compare it to my son-in-law's creation of a fine French sauce. He begins with a variety of ingredients in a big kettle, simmered and stirred over several days until only a small amount of the original is left, then strained. Spices are added and *voila!* The broth becomes a superb, exquisite sauce to be savored with an entree.

"So it is with picture books as I write pages and pages, adding experiences, information, power words, the problems children experience, the things they like, the things they don't, relationship needs, a bit of the spiritual side of life, a pinch of how one can give something back to the world, and a big shake of humor. Then I put on my editing hat and start the torturous process of deciding what to keep. When my story is stripped down to bare bones, I add more words, better ones this time around, I hope, all the time reading the story aloud. Next I divide it into pages, making sure I have fruitful grist for an illustrator's imagination. Throughout this process I do my best not to be didactic, to keep the story entertaining, to find a dynamite beginning and a satisfying ending—all of this in less than a thousand words! Next I put the story aside for a few weeks, so I can have a fresh eye for the finishing touches before sending it on to the publishing companies. It's a challenge, but a process that I enjoy, just as my son-in-law does his French cuisine.

"My writing began when I took care of my elderly parents, folks in a health crisis. I had just finished a master's degree in adult education with an emphasis in counseling and was polishing my resume when I learned my life was going on a different highway. I wrote a manuscript about my experience, hoping that it would help others in the 'sandwich generation.' Then the road branched again as my husband took an early retirement. At this point we hoisted backpacks to travel extensively here and abroad, purchased a boat to sail in the Puget Sound and ultimately to Alaska, and pursued our hobbies, families, and friends.

"Then I discovered the picture book, and writing became a perfect accompaniment to this lifestyle, especially when grandchildren became the authentic spice for my stories. I wrote *Jesus Calms the Storm* off the shores of Canada when the wind blew up knee-knocking 'lumpy' seas, as the sailors call them. *Room for a Stepdaddy* came as a suggestion from a Minnesota bookstore employee whose life was in trauma. A Seattle grandchild was featured in *Audrey and the Nighttime Skies. Butterflies for Grandpa* was about my father's death. For one who has always done extensive community work, these stories have become my avenue to helping others. It's a wonderful way to mix pleasure and work. Have briefcase, will travel."

BIOGRAPHICAL/CRITICAL SOURCES:

PERIODICALS

School Library Journal, January, 1996, p. 77.

* * *

CORDELL, Alexander
See GRABER, (George) Alexander

* * *

COUSTEAU, Jacques-Yves 1910-1997

OBITUARY NOTICE—See index for *CA* sketch: Born June 11, 1910, in St. Andre-de-Cubzac, France; died after a long illness of respiratory infection and heart problems, June 25, 1997, in Paris, France. Underwater explorer, inventor, photographer, film and television producer, environmentalist, and writer. Cousteau fascinated the world with tales of explorations under the sea. He was a leader in marine research and is credited with turning oceanography into a popular science. Although he had no formal training in the field, Cousteau spent sixty years documenting life underwater, thrilling audiences with his films and adventure stories, technologically advancing the science of marine studies, and advocating the conservation of the Earth's resources. As a young man, Cousteau attended Ecole Navale, the French naval academy in Brest, beginning in 1930. In 1935 he began training as a flier with the French Navy, but a car accident prevented him from finishing. In 1936 he served in the artillery. It was at this time that Cousteau began conducting a series of diving experiments and developed a mask and fins used by French spear-fishermen. By 1942 World War II was well underway. Following the fall of France to the Germans, Cousteau joined the French Resistance where he put his camera skills to use by photographing enemy activities along the coast of France. For his efforts during the war, he received the Croix de Guerre and the Legion d'Honneur.

Also in 1942, Cousteau, along with Philippe Taillez and Federic Dumas, began experimenting with underwater photography and produced their first documentary film *Par dix-huit metres de Fond* (*Through Eighteen Meters of Water*). The making of the film was later chronicled when *Par dix-huit metres de fond: Histoire d'un film* (*Through Eighteen Meters of Water: History of a Film*) was published in 1946. The year 1943 proved instrumental not only for Cousteau, but for oceanography and marine studies. Cousteau and engineer Emile Gagnan developed and patented the "aqualung"—the first self-contained underwater breathing apparatus (SCUBA)—by inserting a modified gas valve, hooked to an oxygen tank, into a diving mask. It revolutionized underwater diving. In the mid-1940s Cousteau and Taillez formed the Groupe d'Etudes et Recherches Sous-Marines for the French Navy to develop diving equipment.

During the 1950s, Cousteau and his crew converted a minesweeper into a research vessel called the Calypso. For the next forty-plus years, Cousteau and the Calypso sailed in search of the mysteries of the deep, funded by such groups as the National Oceanographic Society, Monaco's Oceanographic Institute, and the French government. (Calypso was sunk off the coast of Singapore in 1996 when it was struck by a barge while in dock.) In the early 1960s, Cousteau developed and documented the Conshelf II experiment in which five men lived beneath the sea in a man-made structure for one month. Cousteau's documentary film about Conshelf II, *World Without Sun,* won an Academy Award. Throughout his life, Cousteau produced numerous films and television shows, in addition to his written works. *The Silent World,* published in 1953, was transformed into a documentary film, which received honors at the Cannes Film Festival as well as an Academy Award. From 1968 to 1976 the American Broadcasting Cor-

poration (ABC) aired *The Undersea World of Jacques Cousteau,* and later Cousteau produced shows for Public Broadcasting Service (PBS) and Turner Broadcasting System (TBS). His written works include *The Living Sea* (with James Dugan), *Jacques Cousteau's Amazon Journey* (with Mose Richards), *Jacques Cousteau—Whales* (with Yves Paccalet), and a twenty-volume encyclopedia titled *The Ocean World of Jacques Cousteau.* In the 1970s Cousteau founded the Cousteau Society in an effort to preserve marine life. His memoir, *Man, Octopus, and Orchids,* published in 1997, reflects his passion for protecting the Earth's water resources.

OBITUARIES AND OTHER SOURCES:

BOOKS

Who's Who in America, Marquis, 1997.

PERIODICALS

Chicago Tribune (electronic), June 26, 1997.
CNN Interactive (electronic), June 25, 1997.
Detroit Free Press, June 26, 1997, p. A12.
Los Angeles Times (electronic), June 26, 1997.
New York Times, June 26, 1997, pp. A1 and B7; July 1, 1997, p. D22.
Times (London; electronic), June 26, 1997; June 27, 1997; June 30, 1997.
USA Today (electronic), June 26, 1997.

*   *   *

CRAIG, Lee A(llen)

PERSONAL: Education: Ball State University, B.S., 1982, M.A., 1984; Indiana University—Bloomington, M.A., 1986, Ph.D., 1989.

ADDRESSES: Office—Department of Economics, North Carolina State University, 310D Hillsborough Bldg., Box 7506, Raleigh, NC 27695-7506. *E-mail*—craig@econbus2.econ.ncsu.edu.

CAREER: Center for Econometric Model Research, School of Business, Indiana University, Bloomington, research associate, 1985-89; North Carolina State University, Raleigh, assistant professor, 1989-94, associate professor of economics, 1994—. Duke University, postdoctoral fellow at Center for Demographic Studies, 1991-94.

MEMBER: American Economic Association, Economic History Association, Social Science History Association, Cliometrics Society, Business History Conference.

AWARDS, HONORS: Allan Nevins Prize, Economic History Association, 1988-89; fellow, National Bureau of Economic Research, 1991—; grant, National Science Foundation, 1994.

WRITINGS:

To Sow One Acre More: Childbearing and Farm Productivity in the Antebellum North, Johns Hopkins University Press (Baltimore, MD), 1993.
(With Douglas Fisher) *The Integration of the European Economy, 1850-1913,* St. Martin's (New York City), 1997.

Contributor of articles and reviews to economics, statistics, and history journals, including *Journal of Macroeconomics, Journal of the American Statistical Association, Journal of Economic History, Explorations in Economic History, Maryland Historical Review, American Studies, Business History Review, Economic History, Agriculture and Human Values,* and *Agricultural History.*

*   *   *

CREECH, Sharon   1945-
(Sharon Rigg)

PERSONAL: Born July 29, 1945, in Cleveland, OH; divorced once; married Lyle D. Rigg (headmaster at TASIS England American School, Thorpe, Surrey), 1981; children: Rob, Karin. *Education:* Hiram College, B.A.; George Mason University, M.A.

ADDRESSES: Home—c/o TASIS England, Coldharbour Lane, Thorpe, Surrey, England; and Chautauqua, NY. *Agent*—The Jonathan Dolger Agency, 49 East 96th St., Apt. 9B, New York, NY 10128; and Carol Smith.

CAREER: Affiliated with Federal Theater Project Archives, Fairfax, VA; *Congressional Quarterly,* Washington, DC, editorial assistant; TASIS England American School, Surrey, England, teacher of American and British literature, 1979-82, and 1984—; TASIS (The American School in Switzerland), Lugano,

Switzerland, teacher of American and British literature, 1983-85.

AWARDS, HONORS: Billee Murray Denny Poetry Award, Lincoln College, IL, 1988, for "Cleansing"; Best Books, *School Library Journal,* 1994, Notable Children's Books, American Library Association, 1995, Newbery Medal, American Library Association, 1995, and Young Readers Award, Virginia State Reading Association, 1997, all for *Walk Two Moons.*

WRITINGS:

FOR YOUNG PEOPLE

Absolutely Normal Chaos, Macmillan (England), 1990, HarperCollins, 1995.
Walk Two Moons, HarperCollins, 1994.
Pleasing the Ghost, illustrated by Stacey Schuett, HarperCollins, 1996, published in England as *The Ghost of Uncle Arvie,* illustrated by Simon Cooper, Macmillan, 1996.
Chasing Redbird, HarperCollins, 1997.

OTHER

The Center of the Universe: Waiting for the Girl (play), produced in New York City, 1992.

Also author, under pseudonym Sharon Rigg, of *The Recital,* published in England, 1990, and *Nickel Malley.*

SIDELIGHTS: "On February 6th, [1995]" recalled author Sharon Creech in comments reprinted in *Horn Book,* "I was home alone in England and had been wrestling all morning with a manuscript. Feeling ornery and frustrated, I fled to our backyard to vent one of my muffled screams (muffled because I am a headmaster's wife and it isn't seemly for me to scream too loudly). In the midst of that scream, the phone rang.

"A ringing telephone in a headmaster's house often signals a crisis," she continues, "and when it rings, I'm well-trained; I grab pencil and paper. . . . That afternoon, I scribbled: American Library Association and Newbery Med. . .

"The writing trails off there."

Walk Two Moons, the 1995 Newbery Medal winner, brought Creech instant celebrity in the United States, where her first novel for young adults, *Absolutely*

Normal Chaos, had not yet been published. "I still don't know how I feel about it," she confessed to Judy Hendershot and Jackie Peck in *Reading Teacher.* "It's like someone has given me this beautiful suit of Armani clothes. They look nice and everyone admires them, but I'm a little uncomfortable in them. I like to wear them for brief periods of time and then change back to my blue jeans."

Despite her years living and working in England, Sharon Creech is an American citizen. She was born and raised in Cleveland, Ohio, part of "a big, noisy family . . . with hordes of relatives telling stories around the kitchen table," she explained in the *Seventh Book of Junior Authors & Illustrators.* "Here I learned to exaggerate and embellish, because if you didn't, your story was drowned out by someone else's more exciting one." She was an enthusiastic writer throughout grade school and high school, and she was often captivated by the "instruments of writing: paper, pens, pencils, books. I hoarded them." She was an equally enthusiastic reader. "I don't remember the titles of books I read as a child, but I do remember the *experience* of reading—of drifting into the pages and living in someone else's world." "I loved myths—American Indian myths, Greek myths, and the King Arthur legends," she concluded, "—and I remember the lightning jolt of exhilaration when I read *Ivanhoe* as a teenager."

After receiving her bachelor's degree from Hiram College, Creech went on to George Mason University in Washington, D.C., for her master's. "During graduate school," she stated in the *Seventh Book of Junior Authors & Illustrators,* "I worked at the Federal Theater Project Archives and longed to write plays. Next I worked at *Congressional Quarterly,* as an editorial assistant, but this was not pleasant work for me, for it was all politics and facts." Nevertheless, Creech remained in Washington, D.C., for several years. She married, had two children, and was divorced. In 1979, she persuaded the headmaster of TASIS (The American School in Switzerland) England School, a grade school for the children of expatriate Americans in Thorpe, England, to hire her as a teacher of literature. "Before receiving an offer of employment, however," noted Creech's husband, Lyle D. Rigg, in *Horn Book,* "Sharon had to convince the headmaster that she, a single parent with two young children, could handle the considerable demands of teaching in an international day/boarding school in the suburbs of London. Although I have never read Sharon's letter to that headmaster, I have heard that it was a

masterpiece of persuasion and was instrumental in getting her hired."

Sharon Creech and Lyle D. Rigg were married about three years after they met. "I think it was a combination of our Buckeye roots and ice cubes that drew us together," Rigg recalled. "We met on our first day in England, when Sharon borrowed some ice—that rare commodity in Europe—from me." Rigg had been hired as assistant headmaster—the British equivalent of a school principal—and soon after he and Creech were married, they were transferred to the TASIS branch in Switzerland. In 1984, Rigg returned to Thorpe as headmaster of the English branch, and he and Creech have been there ever since (although they spend their summers in a cabin in Chautauqua, New York). "As a teacher of American and British literature to American and international teenagers," Rigg added, "Sharon has shared her love both of literature and of writing. She'd open up Chaucer's world in *The Canterbury Tales* and then head off to Canterbury with her students so that they could make the pilgrimage themselves. She'd offer *Hamlet,* and then off they would all go to Stratford-upon-Avon."

For many years Creech devoted her time almost exclusively to her teaching and her family. "In 1980, when my children and I had been in England for nine months," she recalled in *Horn Book,* "my father had a stroke. Although he lived for six more years, the stroke left him paralyzed and unable to speak. . . . Think of all those words locked up for six years. . . ." Creech started her first novel a month after her father's death in 1986, "and when I finished it," she continued, "I wrote another, and another, and another. The words rushed out."

Absolutely Normal Chaos, Creech's first book for young readers, was published in England in 1990. "When I wrote *Absolutely Normal Chaos,*" Creech told Hendershot and Peck, "I didn't know it was a children's book." *Absolutely Normal Chaos* deals with a variety of themes, some specific to adolescence (first love, growing up, schoolwork), and others that can apply to any period in life (dealing with relatives and friends, learning compassion and understanding). The book is the journal of one summer in the life of thirteen-year-old Mary Lou Finney of Easton, Ohio. At the beginning of the book Mary Lou begs her English teacher not to read the remainder of the story. Her summer, it becomes apparent, has been more bizarre than usual. "Her life is disrupted in more ways than one by the arrival of a gangling, uncommunicative cousin, Carl Ray, from

West Virginia, by his curious relationship with Charlie Furtz, the genial neighbour from across the road, who subsequently dies of a heart attack, and by her own budding romance with Alex Cheevey," explained Joan Zahnleiter in *Magpies*. These circumstances force Mary Lou to confront issues in her own life and to come to terms with her own family and its functionings. Throughout her summer, Mary Lou learns to confront such diverse issues as classic literature, death, questionable legitimacy, and family life. "Mary Lou is a typical teen whose acquaintance with the sadder parts of life is cushioned by a warm and energetic family," stated Cindy Darling Codell in her *School Library Journal* review. "Her entertaining musings on Homer, Shakespeare, and Robert Frost are drawn in nifty parallels to what is happening in her own life." Nancy Vasilakis of *Horn Book* added: "Her own hilarious brush with culture shock occurs when she accompanies Carl Ray on a trip to his home. This visit also provides Mary Lou with some insights into what her cousin has had to endure at her house. Mary Lou grows in a number of important ways throughout the summer, and the metaphors she now recognizes in the *Odyssey* could, she realizes, very well apply to her own life."

The same themes of growth and self-recognition appear in Creech's second novel (the first published in the United States), *Walk Two Moons*. In this story, Salamanca Tree Hiddle, another thirteen-year-old girl like Mary Lou, relates the plight of her friend Phoebe, whose mother has left home. What makes Phoebe's story particularly relevant to Sal is the fact that Sal's mother Sugar also left home and never returned. Sal is on a trip to Idaho with her grandparents to visit her mother. "Sal finds that recounting Phoebe's story helps her understand the desertion of her own mother," explained Deborah Stevenson in the *Bulletin of the Center for Children's Books*. "Creech skillfully keeps these layers separate but makes their interrelationship clear, and the plot moves along amid all this contemplation with the aid of a mysterious noteleaver, a local 'lunatic,' an eccentric English teacher, and Sal's budding romance."

Some of the elements of *Walk Two Moons* came from Creech's own experiences. "In every book I've done," she told Hendershot and Peck, "the characters are combinations of people. I do draw very much from my family, and so I've speculated that Salamanca and her mother are very much me and my own daughter combined." Creech explained that the idea that originally inspired the writing of *Walk Two Moons* came from a message she found in a fortune cookie: "Don't judge a man until you've walked two moons in his moccasins." The framework of the story was based on Creech's trip to Lewiston, Idaho with her family at the age of twelve. Sal's Native American ancestry was also inspired by the author's childhood experiences. "I inhaled Indian myths, and among my favorites were those which involved stories of reincarnation," she commented in her Newbery acceptance speech. "How magnificent and mysterious to be Estsanatlehi, 'the woman who never dies. She grows from baby to mother to old woman and then turns into a baby again, and on and on she goes, living a thousand, thousand lives.' I wanted to be that Navajo woman."

Sal's full name, Salamanca Tree, also evokes Creech's fondness for the outdoors. "I think I spent half my childhood up a tree," she recalled in *Horn Book*. "You could climb and climb, and you could reach a place where there was only you and the tree and the birds and the sky. And maybe the appeal of trees also lay in the sense that they live 'a thousand, thousand lives,' appearing to die each autumn." "The Indianness is one of the best things about this book," asserted *New York Times Book Review* contributor Hazel Rochman, "casual, contemporary and mythic, not an exotic thing apart. Sal is only a small part Indian, and she knows her parents gave her what they thought was the tribe's name but got it wrong. Still, the heritage is a part of her identity. She loves the Indian stories her mother told her, and they get mixed in with Genesis and Pandora's box and Longfellow and with family stories and, above all, with a celebration of the sweeping natural world and our connectedness with it." "For once in a children's book," Rochman concluded, "Indians are people, not reverential figures in a museum diorama. Sal's Indian heritage is a natural part of her finding herself in America."

One of the most dramatic themes common to both *Absolutely Normal Chaos* and *Walk Two Moons* is that of death, examined in relation to subsequent feelings of grief and loss. Mary Lou and Carl Ray have to come to terms with the loss of Charlie Furtz. Sal has to deal with death and her own sense of desertion and loss. These themes are also linked to Creech's life. "When I read Salamanca's story now, with some distance," the author revealed in *Horn Book*, "I hear such longing in her voice—for her mother, for her father, for the land—and I know that her longing is also my longing . . . for my children, my larger family, and for my own country."

Creech's next story, *Pleasing the Ghost,* directed to a somewhat younger audience, also deals with death and loss, but with a lighter touch. Nine-year-old Dennis is visited in his bedroom by a parade of ghosts—"but never the one I want." Hoping to encounter his late father, Dennis instead meets up with his Uncle Arvie, who wants the boy to help Arvie's widow, Dennis's Aunt Julia, find gifts and money he has left hidden for her. Mystery blends with comedy in Creech's tale as Dennis must first decipher his uncle's messages, jumbled due to a speech impairment caused by a stroke Arvie suffered before his death. "The book has several mythical elements: three wishes, magic, ghosts, a lonely young boy whose father has died, a quest and a satisfactory conclusion," asserted *School Librarian* contributor Ann Jenkin. A *Publishers Weekly* reviewer observed: "Arvie's earnest affection for Julia and Dennis make him a role model as well as a clown, and Creech's attention to nuances of feeling grounds this light tale in emotional truth." *Booklist* reviewer Michael Cart called *Pleasing the Ghost* an "engaging story that manages to deal lightheartedly with emotional loss by offering [Creech's] readers the enduring promise of hope."

Creech returns to the hills of Kentucky, the setting for the opening of *Walk Two Moons,* for *Chasing Redbird,* another well-received story of grief, loss, and discovery. Thirteen-year-old Zinnia Taylor, the third of seven siblings, enjoys escaping to the "Quiet Zone" of her neighboring aunt and uncle's home. The death of Zinny's aunt, however, causes her despondent uncle to engage in increasingly eccentric behavior as he succumbs to unrelenting grief, leaving Zinny to find solace elsewhere. The teenager soon becomes obsessed with her discovery of a long, winding trail near her home—a trail once used by trappers and Indians. As Zinny works to clear the trail, occasionally interrupted by the attentions of an older boy, she unearths markers and other indications of her ancestors' presence in the region. "Creech has written a striking novel, notable for its emotional honesty," declared Ethel L. Heins in a *Horn Book* review of *Chasing Redbird.* "In her Newbery Medal acceptance speech," Heins added, "the author spoke of her predilection for mystery and for metaphorical journeys; she has worked both into the novel and, in addition, once again bridges the gap between the generations and binds them together." A *Kirkus Reviews* commentator also had high praise for the book, maintaining: "Creech crams her novel full of wonderful characters, proficient dialogue, bracing descriptions, and a merry use of language." A *Publishers Weekly* reviewer called *Chasing Redbird* "Creech's

best yet," while Deborah Stevenson of the *Bulletin of the Center for Children's Books* concluded: "Creech again demonstrates her expertise at evoking physical and emotional landscapes and the connections between the two as Zinny blazes her way down literal and spiritual paths."

BIOGRAPHICAL/CRITICAL SOURCES:

BOOKS

Children's Literature Review, Volume 42, Gale, 1997.
Seventh Book of Junior Authors and Illustrators, edited by Sally Holmes Holtze, H. W. Wilson, 1996, pp. 67-69.

PERIODICALS

Booklist, November 15, 1994, p. 590; September 1, 1996, p. 125.
Bulletin of the Center for Children's Books, November 15, 1994, p. 590; January, 1995, p. 162; November, 1995, p. 87; March, 1997, p. 243.
Carousel, summer, 1997, p. 25.
Detroit Free Press, February 7, 1995, pp. 1C, 3C.
Fiction, May/June, 1996, pp. 34-35.
Horn Book, July/August, 1995, pp. 418-425, 426-429; March/April, 1996, pp. 204-205; May-June, 1997, pp. 316-317.
Kirkus Reviews, June 15, 1994, p. 832; February 1, 1997, p. 220.
Magpies, September, 1991, p. 32.
New York Times Book Review, May 21, 1995, pp. 24, 34.
Publishers Weekly, February 13, 1995, p. 16; March 20, 1995, pp. 24-25; July 22, 1996, p. 242; January 20, 1997, p. 403.
Reading Teacher, February, 1996, pp. 380-382.
School Librarian, February, 1997, p. 23.
School Library Journal, November, 1995, p. 119.
Teaching PreK-8, May, 1996, pp. 48-49.
Top of the News, spring, 1995, pp. 313-314.
Voice of Youth Advocates, February, 1995, pp. 337-338; June, 1996, p. 94.*

*   *   *

CROWELL, Jenn(ifer) 1978-

PERSONAL: Born April 19, 1978, in Hershey, PA; daughter of Robert K. Crowell, Jr. (a caseworker with the Pennsylvania Department of Welfare) and S. Jane Beck-Dettinger (a secretary). *Education:* Pursued a dual degree in English/Creative Writing and Women's Studies at Goucher College. *Politics:* "Left of center/Feminist." *Avocational interests:* Literature, art, music, travel, feminist theory and activism.

ADDRESSES: Agent—Jane Gelfman, Gelfman Schneider Literary Agents, 250 West 57th St., New York, NY 10107.

CAREER: Writer.

AWARDS, HONORS: Princeton Poetry Prize, Princeton University, 1995; Isabelle Kellogg Thomas English Prize, Goucher College, 1996.

WRITINGS:

Necessary Madness (novel), G. P. Putnam's Sons (New York City), 1997.

WORK IN PROGRESS: Novel, *Reykjavik Dreaming* (tentative title), G. P. Putnam's Sons, publication expected in December, 1998. Research into Icelandic culture and Anastasia Romanov.

SIDELIGHTS: Novelist Jenn Crowell attracted international attention with the 1997 publication of her first novel, *Necessary Madness*. Only seventeen when the manuscript was completed and accepted for publication by Putnam, Crowell pursued a dual degree in English and Women's Studies at Goucher College in Baltimore while working on her next fiction manuscript. In a March 1997 interview with Jennifer Weiner in the *Philadelphia Inquirer,* Crowell revealed that she began working with the central character of the novel when she was fourteen and later developed the plot with an interest in "the whole concept of grief and how it impacts children."

In the novel, a thirty-year-old American widow living in London comes to terms with the loss of her husband and her doubts about single parenthood through a reconciliation with her estranged mother and a newfound friendship with a widower who had known her late husband. While *Time* reviewer Paul Gray appraised the novel as "a generic weeper with a happy ending," he also noted that "certain passages . . . suggest that Crowell is ready to break free of conventions and find her own way." Donna Seaman, writing in *Booklist,* called *Necessary Madness* "an impressive and promising debut," noting that any weakness in the text could be "forgotten in

light of Crowell's fresh wit and keen psychology and her irresistible story's steady march toward catharsis." Adam Mazmanian, critiquing the novel for *Library Journal,* noted that despite the excessive amount of tragedy contained in the book, "Crowell never loses control of her material or tinctures it with sentiment." In the *Philadelphia Inquirer,* Weiner commented that "the plot is a sturdy workhorse, the characters are well drawn, the structure is meticulous, and some of the writing is fresh and inventive."

BIOGRAPHICAL/CRITICAL SOURCES:

PERIODICALS

Booklist, January 1-15, 1997, p. 778.
Library Journal, January 1997, pp. 144-145.
Time, March 3, 1997, p. 78.

OTHER

Philadelphia Inquirer (online), March 30, 1997.

*   *   *

CUDAHY, Sheila   1920-

PERSONAL: Born October 5, 1920, in Chicago, IL; daughter of Edward A. and Margaret (Carry) Cudahy. *Education:* Barnard College, B.A., 1943; Columbia University, M.A., 1944.

ADDRESSES: Home—101 Fifth Ave., New York, NY 10003-1008.

CAREER: Farrar, Straus-Cudahy, New York City, vice president, secretary, and editor; freelance writer, c. 1961—.

WRITINGS:

POETRY

Poems, Collins & Harvill (London), 1961.
Clod's Calvary, and Other Poems, Collins & Harvill, 1971.
The Bristle Cone Pine and Other Poems (includes title poem and "The Pack,"), Harcourt Brace Jovanovich (New York City), 1976.
(And translator) *Presence,* Paseo Press (Santa Fe, NM), 1994.

FICTION

The Trojan Gold (novel), Harper & Row (New York City), 1979.

Nectar at Noon: Stories, Harcourt Brace Jovanovich (San Diego, CA), 1989.

Crow Time (short stories; includes "The River's Story," and "The Pack"), Sun & Moon Press (Los Angeles, CA), 1995.

SIDELIGHTS: During the course of her career, Chicago-born Sheila Cudahy has held a number jobs in publishing in addition to publishing many of her own writings. Her first collection of poems, titled simply *Poems,* saw print under the auspices of a British firm in 1961. She produced another British collection, *Clod's Calvary, and Other Poems,* ten years later, then went on to see her first volume printed in the United States with 1976's *The Bristle Cone Pine and Other Poems.* Since that time, her focus has been predominantly on prose. A novel, *The Trojan Gold,* became available to readers in 1979. Cudahy has also authored two collections of short fiction, 1989's *Nectar at Noon* and 1995's *Crow Time.*

In *Nectar at Noon,* the reader finds a tale about a woman who awakes one morning enlightened about the meaning of the universe, but cannot find the words to share her epiphany with either her stressed and hurried husband or her fourth-grade students. Another protagonist keeps track of distant friends through weather reports from their various locations. In another story, a man obsessed with skywriting drives his wife away. When he tries to win her back by writing her name, Elaine, repeatedly in the sky, weather conditions distort the letters so they spell out "Pain," instead. Yet another story features a young girl having difficulties with her parents' adoption of another girl. Nina Sonenberg, critiquing *Nectar at Noon* in the *New York Times Book Review,* declared that "Cudahy has refined her gift for language into art," and called the volume "a sophisticated collection, rich in range and charm." A *Publishers Weekly* contributor noted the "careful, playful attention to the possibilities of imagination" contained in the stories and added that Cudahy's talents "bear real promise."

Crow Time contains stories of varied length. The shorter pieces include the paragraph-long "The River's Story," and reminded a *Publishers Weekly* reviewer of "prose poems." Among the longer tales, "Christmas People" concerns a young girl who feels she must summon Christmas snow for her strange, reli-gious new neighbors; "Best of Friends" describes two couples who are best friends until one of the women becomes pregnant; and "The Pack," apparently a prose re-working of the poem by the same name found in *The Bristle Cone Pine and Other Poems.* The fictive version depicts the torment of a girl at the hands of her female classmates, and her long-delayed revenge. Though *Publishers Weekly* expressed concerns about the believability of several sections of *Crow Time,* it conceded that "Cudahy's language flows smoothly and there are some satisfying entries."

Cudahy also produced a volume of poetry during the 1990s. Titled *Presence,* it combines the author's own creations with her translations of Italian poems.

BIOGRAPHICAL/CRITICAL SOURCES:

PERIODICALS

Choice, October, 1976, p. 978.
Library Journal, April 15, 1976, p. 1023.
New York Times Book Review, October 8, 1989, p. 12.
Publishers Weekly, July 21, 1989, p. 52; May 29, 1995, p. 81.
Times Literary Supplement, October 29, 1976, p. 1348.*

*   *   *

CURTIS, Christopher Paul   1954(?)-

PERSONAL: Born c. 1954, in Flint, MI; son of Herman (an auto worker) and Leslie Curtis; married Kaysandra (a nurse); children: Steven, Cydney. *Education:* University of Michigan-Flint, B.A., 1996.

ADDRESSES: Home—Windsor, Ontario, Canada.

CAREER: Writer. Fisher Body Plant, Flint, MI, assembly line, 1972-85; assistant to Senator Don Riegle, Lansing, MI; Automatic Data Processing, Allen Park, MI.

AWARDS, HONORS: Best Books, *Publishers Weekly* and *New York Times Books Review,* both 1995, Coretta Scott King Text Honor, Best Books for Young Adults, and Newbery honor, American Library Association, all 1996, all for *The Watsons Go to Birmingham—1963.*

WRITINGS:

The Watsons Go to Birmingham—1963, Delacorte (New York City), 1995.

ADAPTATIONS: The Watsons Go to Birmingham—1963 has been recorded on audiocassette, Ingram, 1996.

WORK IN PROGRESS: A novel about a sit-down strike in a Flint, Michigan, assembly plant, for Delacorte.

SIDELIGHTS: Christopher Paul Curtis wrote his first book, *The Watsons Go to Birmingham—1963,* at a table in the children's section of his local public library. The award-winning story of a closely knit African-American family that travels to the racially divided South during the civil rights era, Curtis's novel has literally changed its author's life. Praised by readers and reviewers and awarded a Newbery honor in 1996, *The Watsons Go to Birmingham* has allowed Curtis to fulfill his dream of becoming a full-time writer.

Raised in Flint, Michigan, like the characters in his first novel, Curtis worked in a local automotive assembly plant for more than a decade after graduating from high school. After putting his dreams of a college education on hold for several long years, he began attending classes at the University of Michigan part-time, while holding down another job, and finally graduated in 1996. During that time, encouraged by winning the University's Hopwood prize for a rough draft of his story, Curtis agreed with his wife Kaysandra's suggestion that he take a year off and see what he could do as a writer. With the strong support of his family—his wife assumed many of their financial responsibilities while son Steven typed his father's handwritten manuscript into the family's computer every night—the story was completed by the end of 1993, and Curtis entered his manuscript in a national writing contest, where it came to the attention of Delacorte editors. Although his story did not meet the content guidelines specified for contest eligibility, Delacorte editor Wendy Lamb responded favorably to the novel and began making arrangements to publish it.

The Watsons Go to Birmingham recounts everyday events in the life of Kenny Watson, a ten-year-old African American boy. Blessed with a quick wit and a crossed eye, Kenny lives in the blue-collar, industrialized city of Flint, Michigan, along with his parents, his little sister, and his bossy older brother, Byron. The novel's narrator, Kenny believes that everyone in his neighborhood must think his family is nuts—the "Weird Watsons." Byron, who has just turned thirteen, has made the transformation from bossy older brother to teenage juvenile delinquent almost overnight: he starts to behave very badly, flushing flaming tissue parachutes down the toilet, dying his hair bright red and then getting it "conked" (straightened), and generally bullying his younger siblings around—including little sister Joetta, a kindergartner trying to keep up with her older brothers.

During the summer of 1963, Kenny's parents decide to take a vacation to Birmingham, Alabama, the home of Grandma Sands, to see if she can discipline the obstinate and unruly Byron. After packing everything they'll need for the trip—roadside restaurants that served African Americans were very uncommon in the segregated South of the 1960s—everyone piles into the family car, the "Brown Bomber," to begin the long journey. In Birmingham, the mood of the novel shifts, as the lighthearted hijinks of the Watson brood suddenly become overshadowed by the racial tensions of the era. Kenny and his family experience racial violence first hand when four teens are killed after a bomb explodes in the Sunday school classroom where little Joetta has been. Although the young girl is physically unharmed, she and the rest of her family return to Michigan transformed by their experiences.

Remarking on the shift between the lighthearted first part of Curtis's novel and its tragic ending, Betsy Hearne wrote in the *Bulletin of the Center for Children's Books:* "The contrast is startling, innovative, and effective . . . showing how—and why—the Civil Rights movement affected individual African Americans." *Horn Book* reviewer Martha V. Parravano similarly asserted that "Curtis's control of his material is superb as he unconventionally shifts tone and mood, as he depicts the changing relationship between the two brothers, and as he incorporates a factual event into his fictional story." Kermit Frazier of the *New York Times Book Review* concluded *The Watsons Go to Birmingham—1963* "a marvelous debut, a fine novel about a solid and appealing family."

In addition to his talent for spinning an imaginative and entertaining tale, Curtis based parts of his book on memories of his own childhood, as well as on an historic event—the actual bombing of Birmingham's

Sixteenth Avenue Baptist Church in September, 1963. Although Curtis was not a witness to that event, he did a great deal of research in writing his novel. And he did not consciously prepare his tale for a certain intended audience. "Perhaps because Curtis didn't think the novel would be for children when he started it, there's nothing heavy-handed or preachy about the Watsons' brush with the civil rights movement," noted Linnea Lannon in an article on Curtis for the *Detroit Free Press.*

Curtis's debut novel has been praised for its warmly drawn characters and its vivid settings. "When the 'Weird Watsons' drive to Birmingham . . . to visit Grandma," related Ann Valentine Martino in the *Ann Arbor News,* "you feel like you're riding along in the back seat—with Kenny's little sister drooling in your lap." "I've read a lot of Chris' writing over the years," the author's sister, Cydney, told Lannon in the *Detroit Free Press,* recalling the "fibs" that her brother told as a child. "This is good," she exclaimed of *The Watsons,* "but I don't think it's his best. His best is yet to come."

BIOGRAPHICAL/CRITICAL SOURCES:

PERIODICALS

Ann Arbor News, April 8, 1996, p. D1.
Booklist, August, 1995, p. 1946.
Bulletin of the Center for Children's Books, January, 1996, pp. 157-158.
Detroit Free Press, December 27, 1995, pp. C1, C5.
Horn Book, March-April, 1996, pp. 195-196.
Kirkus Reviews, October 1, 1995, p. 1426.
New York Times Book Review, November 12, 1995, p. 23.
Publishers Weekly, October 16, 1995, p. 62; December 18, 1995, pp. 28-30.
School Library Journal, October, 1995, p. 152.*

CURTIS, Nancy 1947-

PERSONAL: Born June 6, 1947, in Duncan, OK; daughter of William H. (a rancher) and Edwina (a rancher) Johnson; married Douglas J. Curtis, July 23, 1966; children: Wendy. *Education:* Casper College, A.A., 1967; University of Wyoming, B.A., 1969; University of Denver Publishing Institute, graduated, 1984.

*ADDRESSES: Home—*P.O. Box 123, Glendo, WY 82213; fax (307)-735-4590.

CAREER: Platte County School District no. 1, Glendo, WY, English teacher, 1969-84; ranch, Glendo, WY, owner and operator, 1969—; High Plains Press, Glendo, WY, publisher and editor, 1984—. Platte County Library Board, 1993—, clerk, 1994—; Wyoming Council on the Arts, 1993—, chair, 1996—.

MEMBER: Wyoming Writers (served as president), Western Writers of America, Women Writing the West, Rocky Mountain Book Publishers Association.

AWARDS, HONORS: Wrangler National Cowboy Hall of Fame, 1991, 1993, for publishing an outstanding book of poetry.

WRITINGS:

(Editor, with Linda Hasselstrom and Gaydell Collier) *Leaning into the Wind: Women Write from the Heart of the West* (anthology), Houghton Mifflin (Boston, MA), 1997.

SIDELIGHTS: Nancy Curtis told *CA:* "Besides my literary life where I am a publisher, editor and author, I run a working cattle ranch. This influences my writing and focuses my interest in the land, women who work with the land and animals, and the history of the Old West."

D

DAIGON, Ruth 1923-

PERSONAL: Born March 3, 1923, in Winnipeg, Manitoba, Canada; immigrated to the United States, 1947; daughter of Nathan (a carpenter) and Rose (a homemaker; maiden name, Levin) Popeski; married Arthur Daigon (an English professor), April 11, 1952; children: Tom, Glenn. *Education:* University of Manitoba, B.A., 1943; Royal Conservatory of Toronto, diploma, 1946.

ADDRESSES: Home—29 Loring Ave., Mill Valley, CA 94941.

CAREER: Vancouver Symphony, British Columbia, Canada, soprano soloist, 1946-48; Temple Emanuel, New York City, soloist, 1949-54; New York Pro Musica, New York City, soprano soloist, 1950-54; Columbia Records, recording artist, 1950-56; Community Church, Great Neck, NY, soloist, 1952-63; *Camera Three,* CBS-TV, regular appearances, 1954-56; University of Connecticut at Storrs, recital and television artist, 1963-70. Editor, *Poets On:* (a poetry journal), 1976-96; organizer, poetry activities, Hartford [CT] Festival of Arts, 1980; organizer of poetry programs for Public Broadcasting Service, 1984-86; regular participant in Bay Area poetry readings, and in the Marin Summer Poetry Festivals, 1990—; participant in international poetry festival, BBC, 1991; guest artist on KPFA Radio Poetry Hour, Berkeley, CA.

MEMBER: PEN, Poetry Society of America, Poets and Writers, Academy of American Poets.

AWARDS, HONORS: Fellowship, Virginia Center for the Arts, 1987; Eve of St. Agnes National Award, Negative Capability Press (Mobile, Alabama) 1993; Ann Stamford National Poetry Award, University of Southern California, 1997.

WRITINGS:

Learning Not To Kill You (poems), Selkirk Press (Chaplin, CT), 1976.
(Editor, with husband Arthur Daigon and Marion Levine) *Put It in Writing* (anthology), Harcourt (Orlando, FL), 1978.
On My Side of the Bed, Omnation Press (Chicago, IL), 1980.
A Portable Past, Realities Library (San Jose, CA), 1986.
Between One Future and the Next, Papier-Mache Press (Watsonville, CA), 1994.
About a Year, Small Poetry Press (Pleasant Hill, CA), 1996.

Contributor of verse to poetry journals, including *Kansas Quarterly, Poet & Critic, Poet Lore, Shenandoah,* and *Southern Poetry Review,* and to periodicals in Australia, England, Israel, Chile, Canada, and Japan. Work represented in numerous anthologies, including *Poetry Society of America's 75th Anniversary Issue, The BBC's International Competition Winners, Life on the Line, Negative Capability,* and *If I Had It To Do All Over Again . . . ,* Papier-Mache Press. Has published extensively on the internet and is poet of the month on *Pares cum Paribus* (University of Chile), that published a chapbook of her poems with Spanish translations on the internet, 1997.

WORK IN PROGRESS: "Next large collection, *As if Time Were Nothing at All,* and three chapbooks, *The Moon Inside, Old Scores,* and *Somewhere in Another Country.*"

SIDELIGHTS: Ruth Daigon, former editor of the journal *Poets On:,* and the creator of accessible lyric poetry on themes of family, has published verse in the collections *Learning Not To Kill You, On My Side of the Bed, A Portable Past, Between One Future and the Next,* and *About a Year,* as well as in many anthologies and journals.

Daigon grew up during the 1930s in Winnipeg's North End immigrant community. The long winter months were filled with books, dancing, piano lessons, debating, glee club, and skating. On Sundays the family gathered in the kitchen and told stories, some from the Old Country, others of recent activities. Summers were spent north of the city—in the first Icelandic settlement in the new world, Gimili, on the shore of Lake Winnipeg—with the large extended family at a primitive cabin, where siblings and cousins swam, fished, hiked, told stories, and played cards.

Longing for more than domestic life, Daigon finished high school and attended the University of Manitoba. For her musical talent—which only she of all the Popeski children inherited from her mandolin-playing father—Daigon earned a full scholarship to the Royal Conservatory of Music in Toronto, where, as a soprano, she studied the classical repertoire, folk songs, and operatic arias with Emil Gartner. After graduation she moved to New York City. There she made a living singing and playing guitar at clubs, meetings, and banquets. During one of these singing engagements, the then Ruth Popeski met her future husband Arthur Daigon, a college student.

At the invitation of Noah Greenberg, Popeksi joined the newly formed New York Pro Musica, a choral group that specialized in Renaissance music. The group was very successful, making concert and television appearances and recordings for Columbia Records. Daigon continued to perform after her marriage, until her first child was born. When Arthur earned his doctorate in English and was offered a position at the University of Connecticut, Ruth found herself too far away to participate in the New York City music scene. For a few years she appeared on occasion with the Hartford Symphony or with a baroque trio of local talent, but she became bored with the domestic routine.

Daigon spent hours reading, keeping a diary, and writing letters. In the early 1970s, her husband suggested that she write poetry. Intrigued by the idea, Daigon read widely books of verse and books about verse. When she started to pen her own, it was with the same discipline that she had studied music for so many years. "There were no shortcuts to becoming a poet," she recalled in *Contemporary Authors Autobiography Series* (*CAAS*). "I went back to the way I studied and learned to become a singer, and I used everything I knew about music to discover poetry. In the performance of a Schubert *lied* the emotion is always carefully controlled and the tone as well. You give less but convey the feeling of great depth and an even greater reserve of energy. You never overpower your audience with sound for the sake of sound. It must always reflect the sense and poetry of the music and must always be a little understated." Daigon continued: "All of these musical imperatives seemed useful in the making of poetry. I developed what appeared to be my innate double vision that permitted me to see metaphorical possibilities. I am now quick to acknowledge that I have no allegiance to any words and if eliminating whole passages improves the poem, I have few regrets."

In her verse Daigon revisited her past, recreating personages and experiences; she made domestic life the subject of her poetry as well. She joined a local critique group and, although the men were skeptical and disparaging of what they called "Ruth's kitchen poems," she continued because she felt compelled. "I never dreamed that poetry would take over my life," she admitted in *CAAS.* When Daigon sent several poems to a friend for criticism, he passed them on to two young professors who were starting a new magazine, *The Far Point.* "Ma" and "Pa" were accepted, and Daigon launched her career as a published poet. She didn't wait long to bring her poetry to other audiences. Within a short period of time she began giving poetry readings, doing library programs, and speaking in classrooms. Her vocal training gave her the skills to interpret her poems with emotion and honesty.

For several years, writing and reading her poetry and singing satisfied Daigon, but the isolation of a small Connecticut town took its toll. Daigon needed a new challenge. In 1976 she and her husband inaugurated a poetry journal, *Poets On:,* to be published semiannually. Each volume deals with a particular theme. Daigon was flooded with manuscripts. Justifying acceptances and rejections made her determine standards for "good" poetry and apply those same standards to her own work. Daigon related that she looked for "poems that produce a sense of discovery, of new understanding." "I reject poetry that is declamatory, sloganeering, bathetic, or opaque. Nor am I interested in poetry as mere word games or technical exercises," she explained in *CAAS.* "The words must point to something more important than themselves and must move a reader in ways that discursive text cannot." From its debut, *Poets On:* was a success. "This journal . . . [is] cause for rejoicing . . . with clear and relevant poems on these themes," enthused a *Library Journal* critic. "Daigon is an important contributor to the small press scene," declared Richard Soos in *Small Press Review*. Daigon commented in *CAAS* about the twenty-year history of the journal: "After perusing thousands of poems, publishing some 1,600, working with and corresponding with 2,000 or more poets, I know the magazine, *Poets On:,* has been useful to many, and I also know their work has added new dimensions to mine."

In a review of the 1976 chapbook *Learning Not To Kill You,* a *Choice* critic called Daigon "a fresh voice which speaks authentically of the people of her roots," adding, "the poet . . . turns the knife of language with real precision." Writing in *Small Press Review,* D. Steven Conkle considered the 1986 volume *A Portable Past.* He called Daigon a "remarkably connected poet" and praised her "straightforward and unpretentious" diction and images that "flow naturally as they are demanded by the poem." He noted that many of the poems "succeed, some quite admirably." Daigon's *Between One Future and the Next* also garnered critical praise. "This is a well-balanced and unique collection" asserted *Belles Lettres* critic Linda Keegan, calling Daigon's work "accessible," her language "straightforward," and her subjects "solid in universal truth." "Without sentimentality or . . . bitterness, Daigon presents the family and its machinations without missing a note," lauded Elizabeth Gunderson in *Booklist.* Keegan concluded: "Her poetry speaks a truth that does not reduce to factual tidbits of the poet's own life; and this is, indeed refreshing." June Owens in *Iowa Woman* stated, "Daigon's poems vibrate with sound. They touch, thank God, whatever music remains in me."

Daigon told *CA:* "I never intended to be a writer. I was trained as a musician, a concert soprano at the Royal Conservatory of Toronto, and I sang with all the Canadian symphonies, toured Alaska, the Yukon, and Canada with an opera quartet. When I came to the United States, I was soloist with the New York Pro Musica specializing in Renaissance music, I was also guest artist on CBS's *Camera Three,* recorded for Columbia Recordings and was very active in music in and around New York. But when we moved to Connecticut and I had two small children, I was away from the red hot center, and although I still sang—the Hartford Symphony, University of Con-

necticut recitals, television, etc.—I needed more stimulation and it was natural to begin writing poetry. My reason for writing books is for the same reason that I performed. When I prepared a concert program, it was with performance in mind, and publishing poetry is also a performance otherwise one remains an amateur forever.

"I spend at least four to five hours a day writing. I get up, have my coffee and leave the dishes in the sink, and then go down to my desk exactly the way I used to go to the piano when I was singing full-time. For me, mornings are best. We have a basement office that looks out at the back garden and is my special place for writing. I start with a pen and notebook, because I feel that I'm totally involved and in control with the pen between my fingers, and my elbow moving from one side of the page to the other. When there's something or the beginning of something, I type it into the computer and see what must be done . . . PLENTY. I don't really look for distractions because I have such fun writing. Coming to poetry after a full-time career in singing is like having a chance at a second life. You don't want to run away from that. I do like other activities. I swim everyday when the weather is decent. We go for hikes . . . drive into San Francisco or Berkeley for plays, concerts, friends, etc. . . . but when it's time for writing, I write!

"I don't intend to die, but if and when that time approaches, I will keep on doing exactly what I'm doing. I can't think of a better way to live. After making it through the freezing climate of Winnipeg, the wet of Vancouver, the snow and frost of Toronto, New York and Connecticut, it's a pleasure to live in the Bay Area with all of its advantages . . . weather . . . action . . . interests . . . people . . . and certainly living with the same man, Artie, that I met so long ago in New York's Borscht Circuit on the dance floor of the Harmony Country Club. Add to that our sons Tom and Glenn and the life is complete."

BIOGRAPHICAL/CRITICAL SOURCES:

BOOKS

Contemporary Authors Autobiography Series, Volume 25, Gale (Detroit, MI), 1997.

PERIODICALS

Belles Lettres, January, 1996, p. 38.
Booklist, February 1, 1995, p. 987.

Choice, July-August, 1976, p. 660.
Iowa Woman, winter, 1995, p. 42.
Library Journal, February 1, 1995, p. 77.
Publishers Weekly, February 27, 1995, pp. 98-99.
Small Press Review, July-August, 1988, p. 11; May, 1995, p. 9.

*   *   *

DANAKAS, John 1963-

PERSONAL: Born September 26, 1963, in Winnipeg, Manitoba, Canada; son of Constadinos (a restaurateur) and Maria (a restaurateur; maiden name, Stamatakos) Danakas; married Sophia Aggelopoulos (a sales clerk), June 16, 1990; children: Costa. *Education:* University of Manitoba, B.A., 1986, M.A., 1994.

ADDRESSES: Home—7 Stanford Bay, Winnipeg, Manitoba R3P 0T5, Canada. *Office*—Public Affairs Office, University of Manitoba, 423 University Cres., Winnipeg, Manitoba R3T 2N2, Canada.

CAREER: Winnipeg Sun, Winnipeg, Manitoba, journalist, 1986-91; University of Manitoba, Winnipeg, media relations officer, 1996—. Dal's Restaurant, restaurateur.

WRITINGS:

Curve Ball, James Lorimer (Toronto, Ontario), 1993.
Lizzie's Soccer Showdown, James Lorimer, 1994.
Hockey Night in Transcona, James Lorimer, 1995.

WORK IN PROGRESS: The Case of the Missing Spirit Pipe; sequel to *Hockey Night in Transcona.*

SIDELIGHTS: John Danakas commented: "I love people, meeting them, getting to know them, finding out their personal stories. My writing is an attempt to communicate to others what I have learned about the people I have known, about what is important to them and why, about how they deal with the ordinary and extraordinary occurrences in their lives. Writing for young people is particularly rewarding because they are such appreciative readers. One of the best things about having published books for young readers is being able to visit schools and meet with many of my readers. They never fail to remind me just how intelligent, clever, and perceptive they are and that, if I want to ensure that my writing meets their standards, I should be prepared to work extra hard.

"I came to writing through reading. After reading a good book, I'd want to take a crack myself at telling a story through words on paper. Some of the writers whose books generated such a desire in me include William Saroyan, Harlan Ellison, Harry Mark Petrakis, Raymond Souster, Walter Dean Myers, Jack Schaefer, John O'Hara, and Daphne Du Maurier, to name only a few.

"I believe in young people and their dreams. I also believe that the best thing adults can do for young people—beyond ensuring their health and safety—is to let them be young—in body, mind, and soul—as long as possible."

BIOGRAPHICAL/CRITICAL SOURCES:

PERIODICALS

Books in Canada, April, 1995, p. 58.
Canadian Materials, September, 1994, p. 124.
Quill & Quire, January, 1994, p. 38; January, 1995, pp. 40-41; January, 1996, p. 44.*

*   *   *

DAVIS, Stephen R(andy) 1956-

PERSONAL: Born in 1956; married Jenny Davis; children: Kinsey.

ADDRESSES: Office—E-Systems, 10001 Jack Finney Blvd., Greenville, TX 75401-6056. *E mail*—srdavis@ACM.org.

CAREER: E-Systems, Greenville, TX, programmer, 1978—; freelance writer, c. 1985—.

WRITINGS:

NONFICTION

Turbo C: The Art of Advanced Program Design, Optimization, and Debugging, M&T Books (Redwood City, CA), 1987.
DESQview: A Guide to Programming the DESQview Multitasking Environment, M&T Books, 1989.
Hands-On Turbo C++, Addison-Wesley (Reading, MA), 1990.
C++ Programmer's Companion: Designing, Testing, and Debugging, Addison-Wesley (Reading, MA), 1993.

C++ for Dummies, IDG Books (San Mateo, CA), 1994.

More C++ for Dummies, IDG Books Worldwide (Foster City, CA), 1996.

Learn Java Now, Microsoft Press (Redmond, WA), 1996.

Also contributor of articles to periodicals, including *PC Magazine.*

SIDELIGHTS: Computer programmer and author Stephen R. Davis is responsible for several popular reference books on computer programming languages. He is especially knowledgeable about C and C++. His titles include *Turbo C: The Art of Advanced Program Design, Optimization, and Debugging; Hands-On Turbo C++; C++ Programmer's Companion: Designing Testing, and Debugging; C++ for Dummies; More C++ for Dummies;* and *Learn Java Now.* In addition, he has contributed articles to *PC Magazine,* and has served as a programmer for E-Systems in Greenville, Texas, for nearly two decades.

With his 1993 volume *C++ for Dummies,* Davis provides readers with a simplified guide to the language of the title, with as little use of technical jargon as possible. The book also reviews the C language, upon which C++ builds. Non-object-oriented features, classes, and object-oriented programming are discussed, as well as inheritance—an aspect of C++ which helps users streamline their efforts. In addition, Davis provides twenty-five minute review sessions in order for learners to test themselves upon their newly-gained proficiency. Another feature of *C++ for Dummies* are Top Ten Lists of various C++-related items, such as ways to avoid bugs and the most important compiler switches. Davis even lets his readers in on all of the optional features of C++.

BIOGRAPHICAL/CRITICAL SOURCES:

BOOKS

Davis, Stephen R., *C++ for Dummies,* IDG Books, 1994.*

*   *   *

DAVIS, Tim(othy N.)   1957-

PERSONAL: Born October 17, 1957, in Medina, NY; son of Everett (a pastor) and Linda (a homemaker; maiden name, Childs) Davis; married Rebecca Henry (a writer and editor), December 15, 1984; children: Katie, Stephen, Christiana, Joshua. *Education:* Attended Cedarville College, 1976-78; Bob Jones University, B.A. (cum laude), 1982. *Politics:* Conservative Republican. *Religion:* "Bible-believing Christian." *Avocational interests:* Writing, inventing games.

ADDRESSES: Home—60 Main St., Germantown, NY 12526.

CAREER: Bob Jones University Press, Greenville, SC, staff illustrator, 1982-91, elementary art director, 1986-91, advertising art director, 1989-91; freelance children's illustrator and writer, 1990—. Elementary school speaker, 1994—; pastoral intern, 1996-97.

AWARDS, HONORS: Mice of the Seven Seas was named a C. S. Lewis Noteworthy Book by the Christian School Children/Youth Book Awards in 1995.

WRITINGS:

SELF-ILLUSTRATED CHILDREN'S BOOKS; PUBLISHED BY BOB JONES UNIVERSITY PRESS (GREENVILLE, SC)

Mice of the Herring Bone, 1992.

Mice of the Nine Lives, 1994.

Mice of the Seven Seas, 1995.

Tales from Dust River Gulch, 1996.

Contributor of stories to elementary reading textbooks.

ILLUSTRATOR

The Cranky Blue Crab: A Tale in Verse by Dawn L. Watkins, Bob Jones University Press, 1990.

The Land of Tuppitry by Abigail Nunn, second edition, Victory Press (Monterey, CA), 1991.

Jellyfish Can't Swim, and Other Secrets from the Animal World by Marjorie Hodgson Parker, Chariot Books (Elgin, IL), 1991.

Grandpa's Gizmos by John Menken, Bob Jones University Press, 1992.

Pocket Change: Five Small Fables by Dawn L. Watkins, Bob Jones University Press, 1992.

Right-Hand Man by Connie Williams, Bob Jones University Press, 1992.

El Pato Paco: A First Look at Spanish by Anna Turner and Beth Kitching, Bob Jones University Press, 1993.

Once in Blueberry Dell by Dawn L. Watkins, Bob Jones University Press, 1995.

Illustrator of the "Darcy Doyle" book series, Zonder-van (Grand Rapids, MI) and *Tony Salerno's Good News Express*. Contributor of illustrations to magazines, including *Children's Playmate* and *Highlights for Children*.

SIDELIGHTS: Tim Davis commented: "I've always been an illustrator. For as long as I can remember, I've been drawing imaginary characters and scenes. Writing came much later, after graduating from Bob Jones University. My wife-to-be was a professional writer when we met. She challenged me to write a children's story. I did—and it was published! Since then I've tried to write when I can. My children are a constant source of inspiration, as well as a ready test audience for my stories.

"Growing up in a pastor's home, and now doing pastoral work myself, I've always had a strong sense of right and wrong. I believe this foundation underlies everything I write—though my stories are far from pedantic. I love fun and adventure too much! I write fanciful fiction of faraway places, but I try to make my heroes exhibit real character in what they do and say."

* * *

DAWSON, Robert MacGregor 1895-1958

PERSONAL: Born March 1, 1895, in Bridgewater, Nova Scotia, Canada; died July 16, 1958, in Bridgewater, Nova Scotia, Canada. *Education:* Dalhousie University, B.A., 1915, M.A., 1916; Harvard University, A.M., 1917; London School of Economics, M.Sc. Econ., 1921, D.Sc. Econ., 1922.

CAREER: Canadian political scientist. Dalhousie University, lecturer, 1921-1923; Carnegie Institute of Technology, 1923-1926; Rutgers University, 1926-1929; University of Saskatchewan, professor of political science, 1929-1937; University of Toronto, associate professor, then professor, of political science, 1937-1958.

MEMBER: Royal Society of Canada (elected fellow, 1935).

AWARDS, HONORS: Governor General's Award for best Canadian nonfiction book, 1949, for *Democratic Government in Canada.*

WRITINGS:

The Principle of Official Independence, [London], 1922.
The Civil Service of Canada, [London], 1929.
Constitutional Issues in Canada, 1900-1931, [London], 1933.
The Development of Dominion Status, [Toronto], 1937.
Canada in World Affairs: Two Years of War, 1939-1941, [Toronto], 1942.
The Government of Canada, [Toronto], 1947; three revised editions through 1963; fourth through sixth editions revised by Norman Ward; fifth edition, University of Toronto Press (Toronto), 1970; sixth edition published as *Dawson's The Government of Canada,* sixth edition, University of Toronto Press, 1987.
Democratic Government in Canada, University of Toronto Press and Copp Clark Publishing (Toronto), 1949; fourth edition, co-written by W. F. Dawson and revised by Norman Ward, University of Toronto Press, 1971; fifth edition, 1989.
William Lyon MacKenzie King, Volume 1: *A Political Biography, 1874-1923,* University of Toronto Press, 1958; republished with Volume 2: *The Lonely Heights, 1924-1932,* by H. Blair Neatby, and Volume 3: *The Prism of Unity, 1932-1939,* by Neatby, 1976.
The Consumption Crisis of 1944, [Toronto], 1961.

EDITOR

Problems of Modern Government, [Toronto], 1961.

SIDELIGHTS: Canadian political scientist Robert MacGregor Dawson is the author of *Democratic Government in Canada* and *Government of Canada,* two surveys of the Canadian government that have become standard texts. Dawson has also written the official biography of William Lyon MacKenzie King, one of Canada's most memorable prime ministers, and several other, more specialized works. A native Nova Scotian, Dawson was educated at some of the world's finest institutions of political science— Dalhousie, Harvard, and the London School of Economics—and spent the first years of his teaching career in U.S. universities before returning to Canada in his mid-thirties to take up a post at the University of Saskatchewan.

After several years at the University of Saskatchewan, Dawson found lifelong employment in 1937 at the University of Toronto, whose press oversaw the publication of most of his books. His 1947 survey, *The Government of Canada,* presents an account of that nation's political system in the form of chapters that stand as separate long essays. The book was extremely successful and was updated periodically in accord with new developments in Canadian history. Appraising the fifth edition, which was published in 1970, *Choice* referred to the work as "a classic in its field," and added that no other work on the subject covered the material as well as *The Government in Canada,* and that any library should consider it the primary source on the topics the book covers. On the publication of the sixth edition in 1987, Howard Hurt, a reviewer for *CM,* rejoiced that "it retains the essential goals and spirit . . . while bringing material up to date." Calling the volume "beautifully comprehensive," Hurt described it as "academic without being pedantic, polished without being difficult." It was a book, Hurt concluded, that every Canadian voter should own.

Two years after the publication of *The Government of Canada,* Dawson refashioned similar material into a 150-page introductory survey for college students and adults, *Democratic Government in Canada.* The book forms a continuous narrative made of short chapters. In response to the appearance of the fifth edition, in 1989, Louise Dick of *CM* attested that this "clear and well-organized" book "works well as a companion" to Dawson's larger opus.

Dawson's other major literary project was the official biography of Prime Minister William Lyon MacKenzie King. Unfortunately, Dawson lived to complete only the first volume, which dealt with King's formative period. King, a capable leader and an eccentric, served Canada as prime minister for twenty-one years and was leader of the opposition for many years as well. A "superb arbitrator and conciliator," in the view of Joseph A. Boudreau in *The Journal of American History,* King helped steer Canada through a period of Depression and world war, when England's influence on the Dominion was being supplanted by that of the United States. King did make some notable miscues, however, such as praising Mussolini and Hitler during the 1930s and saying that Canada ought not go to the aid of Europe. In his personal life, he was a bachelor who, after his domineering mother's death, continued to communicate with her through spirits. Other eccentricities included building artificial ruins at his country home and owning a series of

Irish terriers named Pat. Dawson's and Neatby's three-volume effort was praised by reviewers, including a critic for *Choice,* who called it "a fine, scholarly study."

BIOGRAPHICAL/CRITICAL SOURCES:

BOOKS

Wallace, W. Stewart, editor, *Macmillan Dictionary of Canadian Biography,* fourth edition, revised, enlarged, and updated by W. A. McKay, Macmillan of Canada (Toronto), 1978.
World of Winners, second edition, Gale Research (Detroit, MI), 1992.

PERIODICALS

Choice, January, 1971, p. 1576; April, 1977, p. 259.
CM: A Reviewing Journal of Canadian Materials for Young People, May, 1988, p. 104; December, 1989, p. 282.
Journal of American History, June, 1978, pp. 111-113.*

*   *   *

DAY, Shirley 1962-

PERSONAL: Born June 15, 1962, in Manila, Philippines; daughter of Salvador Dipasupil (a civil engineer) and Eden Miraflores (an accountant). *Education:* Attended University of Houston, 1980-84; University of South Florida, B.S., 1987.

ADDRESSES: Home—Tampa, FL.

CAREER: St. Petersburg Times, St. Petersburg, FL, marketing coordinator, 1990-93, senior copywriter, 1993-96; Staff Leasing, Bradenton, FL, marketing communications manager, 1996; Danka (office equipment distributor), manager of employee relations and community affairs, 1996-97.

AWARDS, HONORS: First place award, Southern Circulation Managers Association, 1991, for a newspaper carrier recognition campaign; first place awards, International Circulation Managers Association, 1992, for a quality control advertisement and for the advertisement "Real People, Real Stories," and 1993, for a t-shirt design; Gold ADDY Award, 1992, for a radio spot; Gold Award, Southern Classified Advertising Managers Association, 1993, for a "Yellow Pages" campaign; first place award, promotion/market development awards competition, Newspaper Association of America, 1994, for a "Santa Tracking" sales campaign.

WRITINGS:

Luna and the Big Blur: A Story for Children Who Wear Glasses, illustrated by Don Morris, Magination Press (New York City), 1995.

WORK IN PROGRESS: A children's story about a little girl from the Philippines.

SIDELIGHTS: Shirley Day commented: "My children's book *Luna and the Big Blur* sits on a local bookshelf because of one reason: swim season. A few years ago, swim season, which runs from August through November, kept my former husband away from home nearly every day. After working full-time as a high school teacher, he would head directly to the pool to coach the school's swim team. It was during one of his extended absences that I decided to write a book.

"At the time, I worked for a newspaper, where I was able to seek advice from published authors and from Don Morris, an artist who had illustrated children's books. I attended local writing conferences, researched the process, from writing an effective query letter to selecting publishers, and made frequent visits to the children's section in bookstores.

"I sent queries only to receive rejection letters. 'It could take decades,' I thought. It didn't matter, as long as I was trying. The drive to continue stemmed from my business marketing background. I found it challenging.

"The call from Magination Press, a psychotherapy publishing house, caught me by surprise. Apparently my timing was perfect. They were in search of a more mainstream story for four- to eight-year-old children. I was elated that *Luna* fit that slot. Magination also reviewed Don Morris's artwork and quickly agreed to let him illustrate the book. It was truly an exciting time."

BIOGRAPHICAL/CRITICAL SOURCES:

PERIODICALS

School Library Journal, January, 1996.

de BOTTON, Alain 1969-

PERSONAL: Born December 20, 1969, in Zurich, Switzerland; son of Gilbert and Jacqueline (Burgauer) De Botton. *Education:* Attended Gonville College and Caius College, Cambridge University.

ADDRESSES: Home and office—18 Caroline Terrace, London SW1W 8JT, England. *Agent*—Caroline Dawnay, Peters, Fraser and Dunlop, Chelsea Harbour, Lots Rd., London SW10 OXF; fax 0171-352-7356. *E-mail*—adb@netcomuk.co.uk.

CAREER: British novelist and journalist. Worked as a television reviewer for *New Statesman; Sunday Telegraph,* journalist.

WRITINGS:

Essays in Love, Macmillan (London), 1993, published in the United States as *On Love,* Atlantic Monthly Press (New York City), 1993.
The Romantic Movement: Sex, Shopping, and the Novel, Macmillan, 1994, Picador (New York City), 1995.
Kiss & Tell, Macmillan, 1995, Picador, 1996.
How Proust Can Change Your Life: Not a Novel, Pantheon (New York City), 1997.

Contributor of articles and book and television reviews to *The Daily and Sunday Telegraph, New Republic,* and other periodicals.

WORK IN PROGRESS: "A study of certain helpful, relevant ideas from key philosophers, entitled *The Consolation of Philosophy;* to be published in spring, 1999."

SIDELIGHTS: In his early twenties Alain de Botton became one of the most talked-about young British novelists of the 1990s with his debut, *Essays in Love,* which was published in the United States as *On Love.* The novel is plotted with deliberate simplicity and surrounded by an apparatus of witty, erudite commentary.

The plot involves a nameless male narrator who meets a women named Chloe on a plane flight and enters into a love affair with her, an affair which is ultimately terminated. The apparatus includes quotations from and allusions to an array of thinkers including Stendhal, Plato, Goethe, Kant, Mill, Freud, and a self-help writer named Dr. Peggy Nearly. There are also diagrams: a seating chart of the airplane, a graph of an orgasm, and more; and the novel's paragraphs are numbered in the style of a philosophical treatise. Indeed, as Gabriele Annan asserted in *The Spectator,* "The book is a psycho-philosophical treatise on love." Annan added, "Ingeniously pinpointed mundane details stop the novel from getting too abstract. It is witty, funny, sophisticated, neatly tied up, and full of wise and illuminating insights." The book was also, Annan added, "quite unusually optimistic." Many critics echoed that praise. A *Kirkus Reviews* critic called *On Love* "a tour-de-force pleasure of a first novel. . . . both intellectually stimulating and emotionally touching." Others, while generally admitting the author's talent and skill, assessed the novel's devices as tiresome. In the *New York Review of Books,* P. N. Furbank discerned "all sorts of bright jokes and nice silly-clever ploys" in the novel, and predicted: "This is not the last we shall hear of [de Botton]."

The following year, 1994, de Botton's *The Romantic Movement: Sex, Shopping, and the Novel* was published. More than one reviewer commented on the similarities between de Botton's first two books: poet and novelist Lisa Zeidner, reviewing *The Romantic Movement* for the *New York Times Book Review,* commented that the 1994 work followed the pattern of *On Love* "almost exactly." Again there is a straightforward plot involving a love affair between a bright, attractive young man and woman accompanied by philosophical commentary. "What's fresh here is the willingness to stretch the gag to this absurd length not once, but twice—since *On Love* was almost the very same book (with slightly more plot but fewer pictures)," said Zeidner. A more positive review came from travel writer Pico Iyer in *Time:* "Light as a souffle, and no less addictive, *The Romantic Movement* is that happiest of artifacts, a novel that smiles," he declared. *Times Literary Supplement*'s Helen Szamuely maintained that "the simplicity of the story serves as a framework for reflections on love which are both modern and original." John Updike, writing in the *New Yorker,* observed that "de Botton's method has much cultural vogue behind it" and that "potentially useful direct information about our love lives and historically determined romantic dispositions is contained in the talky pages of *The Romantic Movement.*"

As was the case with de Botton's first novel, more than one reviewer faulted *The Romantic Movement*'s techniques and style of humor. Tom Hiney of the *Spectator* coined the term "Novelisation X" to describe de Botton's genre. "When Alain de Botton hits the target, *The Romantic Movement* is a delight to read," he asserted, but noted that when de Botton's aim was off-target, he found it hard to take.

De Botton's third novel, *Kiss & Tell,* was published in 1995, and departed from the author's previous pattern in ways that critics maintained demonstrated continuity and an effort at growth. The novel is presented as the biography of an ordinary woman named Isabel. The narrator, having been told by his ex-girlfriend that he is narcissistic, has vowed to write the biography of the next person he meets, who turns out to be Isabel. The result resembles Vladimir Nabokov's *Pale Fire* or Steven Millhauser's *Edwin Mullhouse* in form; and in the words of *The Spectator's* Philip Glazebrook, it is an "engaging and delightful book. . . . so cultivated and witty and self-aware" that de Botton "could write the biography of a broomstick, as Dr. Johnson suggested, and it would come alive under his pen." The *Boston Review*'s Sara Kramer, calling *Kiss & Tell* "playful and adroit," found it a humorous exploration of the biographical form and human self-awareness. A *New Yorker* reviewer, describing the book as both "ingenious" and "wise," declared that *Kiss & Tell* "elicits an almost continual smile." Jason Cowley of the *Observer* found Isabel to be de Botton's "most appealing creation to date," and declared that the author "has a real flair for dialogue. Though expressing disappointment that de Botton had to that point written only in the tone of "playful cheerfulness," Cowley enthused that "De Botton clearly has talent to burn," and praised "the superb readability of his prose" and "his formal adventurousness and stylistic daring."

De Botton's fourth novel, 1997's *How Proust Can Change Your Life: Not a Novel,* comments on the mammoth French masterpiece *A La Recherche du Temps Perdu,* known in English as *A Remembrance of Things Past,* and on its author's personality, suggesting that the Proust's novel can be used as a self-help book. According to De Botton, *A La Recherche du Temps Perdu* works in such a capacity because it is "a practical, universally applicable story about how to stop wasting time and start to appreciate life." "It's a real pleasure to read someone who treats this sacrosanct subject as something that is still vital and vigorous," said a *Publishers Weekly* reviewer. Several reviewers used the term "engaging" to describe the book that David Futrelle called "not quite self-help, not quite literary criticism." Author Lev Raphael, writing for the *Detroit Free Press,* added that the book might serve as "a gentle incitement to scale the Proustian mountain."

BIOGRAPHICAL/CRITICAL SOURCES:

PERIODICALS

Kirkus Reviews, September 1, 1993, p. 1090.
Library Journal, September 1, 1993, p. 220.
Los Angeles Times, August 17, 1997.
Los Angeles Times Book Review, January 9, 1994, p. 6.
New Yorker, August 21 and 28, 1995, pp. 105-114; September 23, 1996, p. 95; July 2, 1997.
New York Review of Books, January 13, 1994, p. 35.
New York Times Book Review, June 11, 1995, p. 35; August 4, 1996, p. 18; May 22, 1997.
Observer, September 10, 1995.
Publishers Weekly, September 13, 1993, p. 84; March 3, 1997, p. 53; August 4, 1997.
San Francisco Chronicle, August 6, 1997.
Spectator, October 30, 1993, p. 41; August 27, 1994, p. 34; September 9, 1995, p. 41.
Time, June 12, 1995.
Times Literary Supplement, September 23, 1994, p. 24; September 15, 1995, p. 20.

OTHER

Boston Review, http://www-polisci.mit.edu:80/Boston Review/BR21.6/prosemicro/html.
Detroit Free Press, http://www.freep.com/browsing/books/qbrowse23.html, October 6, 1997.
Salon, http://www.salonmagazine.com/may97/sneaks/sneak970505.html, October 6, 1997.

* * *

DECHAUSAY, Sonia E.

PERSONAL: Born in Curacao, Netherland Antilles; daughter of Joseph Gabriel (a merchant) and Seraphine Marie (a merchant) Dechausay; children: Colette Sarah. *Education:* Concordia University, Montreal, Quebec, B.A., 1992.

ADDRESSES: Home—Winnipeg, Manitoba, Canada.

CAREER: Goodwill Junior High School, Commonwealth of Dominica, West Indies, kindergarten and primary schoolteacher, 1969-73; Dominica Banana Growers' Association, West Indies, assistant secretary, 1973-77; Protestant School Board of Greater Montreal, Montreal, Quebec, director's assistant and school coordinator, 1982-84, kindergarten extension educator, 1984-95, director of kindergarten extension and day care services, 1993-95. Quebec Board of Black Educators, Inc., member, 1982—, executive member, 1992-96, adult literacy program coordinator, 1995-1996; City of Montreal, member of the Division of Intercultural Affaires Round Table planning committee, 1996.

MEMBER: Federation of English Language Writers of Quebec, Montreal Association of Early Childhood Educators (member of board of directors, 1993), Concordia University Alumni Association (member of board of directors, 1996), Black Educators Association of Manitoba (vice president, 1996).

WRITINGS:

What's a Memory? (juvenile), illustrated by Daryl Anderson, Winston-Derek (Nashville, TN), 1995.

Member of editorial staff, *Kola.*

WORK IN PROGRESS: Jason's Red Box; Steven Is Not Hurryuping; The Best Storyteller in the World.

SIDELIGHTS: Sonia E. Dechausay commented: "I've always loved books. Both of my parents were avid readers who encouraged us, their children, to read. My mother and maternal grandmother were great storytellers. My brothers and sisters would listen for hours as my mom told us the stories her mother had told her, as well as stories she made up herself. Sometimes our friends would join us in the dining room of our house to listen to our mom. I enjoyed writing short stories. One day, my mom showed a customer copies of my stories. This customer was a writer and was also the owner and editor of a local newspaper. Her name was Mrs. Phyllis Sand-Allfrey. One of her books, *The Black Orchid,* I believe, was developed into a movie. She published a few of my short stories in the *Star,* her newspaper, and encouraged me to continue writing. I was thrilled when my first book *What's a Memory?* was published by Winston-Derek, making me the first Canadian author to sign with their publishing company. This was a dream come true."

* * *

DENVER, John   1943-1997

PERSONAL: Born Henry John Deutschendorf, Jr., December 31, 1943, in Roswell, NM; died October 12, 1997, in a plane crash, in Monterey, CA; son of

Henry John (an Air Force officer) and Erma Deutschendorf (a homemaker); married Ann Marie Martell (a psychotherapist), June 9, 1967 (divorced, 1983); married Cassandra Delaney, 1988 (divorced, 1991); children: (first marriage) Zachary, Anna Kate; (second marriage) Jesse Belle. *Education:* Attended Texas Technical University, 1961-64. *Avocational interests:* Aviation, golf, photography.

CAREER: Musician and writer. Member of Mitchell Trio, 1965-68. Performer on various television shows, including *The John Denver Special,* ABC, 1974; *John Denver's Rocky Mountain Christmas,* ABC, 1975; *John Denver in Australia,* ABC, 1978; *John Denver and the Muppets: A Christmas Together,* ABC, 1980; *John Denver: Music and the Mountains,* ABC, 1981; *John Denver's Christmas in Aspen,* CBS, 1988; and *In Performance at the White House,* PBS, 1989. Actor in films, including *Oh, God!,* Warner Bros., 1977. Narrator of *Fire and Ice,* Concorde, 1987. Founder of Windstar Foundation, 1976, and World Hunger Project, 1977. National UNICEF Day, chair, 1984. Appointed by President Jimmy Carter to Commission on World and Domestic Hunger, 1977.

MEMBER: National Space Institute, Cousteau Society, Friends of the Earth, Human/Dolphin Foundation, Save the Children Foundation, European Space Agency.

AWARDS, HONORS: Top Male Recording Artist Award from *Record World,* 1974-75; Entertainer of the Year Award from Country Music Association, People's Choice Award for favorite musical performer, Singing Star of the Year Award from American Guild of Variety Artists, and Male Vocalist of the Year Award from Academy of Country Music, all 1975; Emmy Award for Best Musical Variety Special from Academy of Television Arts and Sciences, 1976, for *An Evening with John Denver;* Golden Apple Prize from Hollywood Women's Press Club, 1977; and other awards. In the United States, Denver had four platinum and twelve gold records.

WRITINGS:

Alfie, the Christmas Tree (juvenile), illustrations by Jean Pidgeon, National Wildlife Federation, 1990.
(With Arthur Tobier) *Take Me Home* (autobiography), Harmony Books, 1994.

SONGBOOKS; ALL PUBLISHED BY CHERRY LANE

Anthology, edited by Milton Okun, 1982.
Dreamland Express, edited by Okun, 1985.

Classic John Denver, edited by Okun, 1988.
The Love Songs of John Denver, edited by Okun, 1988.
Best of John Denver: Easy Guitar, edited by Okun, 1995.
John Denver's Greatest Hits, edited by Okun, 1995.

RECORDINGS; AND PERFORMER

Rhymes and Reasons, RCA, 1969.
Take Me to Tomorrow, RCA, 1970.
Whose Garden Was This?, RCA, 1970.
Poems, Prayers, and Promises, RCA, 1971.
Aerie, RCA, 1972.
Rocky Mountain High, RCA, 1972.
Farewell Andromeda, RCA, 1973.
Back Home Again, RCA, 1974.
John Denver's Greatest Hits, RCA, 1974.
Rocky Mountain Christmas, RCA, 1975.
An Evening with John Denver, RCA, 1975.
Windsong, RCA, 1975.
Live in London, RCA, 1976.
Spirit, RCA, 1976.
I Want to Live, RCA, 1977.
John Denver's Greatest Hits, Volume 2, RCA, 1977.
John Denver, RCA, 1979.
A Christmas Together with the Muppets, RCA, 1979.
Autograph, RCA, 1980.
Some Days Are Diamonds, RCA, 1981.
Perhaps Love, RCA, 1981.
Seasons of the Heart, RCA, 1982.
It's About Time, RCA, 1983.
Collection, Telstar, 1984.
Dreamland Express, RCA, 1985.
One World, RCA, 1986.
Rocky Mountain Christmas, 1989.
Stonehaven Sunrise, RCA, 1989.
Take Me Home, Country Roads, and Other Hits, RCA, 1990.
The Flower That Shattered the Stone, 1990.
Earth Songs, 1990.
Different Directions, 1991.
Higher Ground, 1991.
The Best of John Denver Live, 1997.

OTHER RECORDINGS

(With Mitchell Trio) *That's the Way It's Gonna Be,* Mercury, 1965.

Also composer of scores for motion pictures, including (with others) *Fire and Ice,* Concorde, 1987.

SIDELIGHTS: John Denver, a prominent singer-songwriter, enjoyed immense popularity in the 1970s.

He began his music career in the early 1960s after attending Texas Technical University. He then headed for Los Angeles, where he found work as a performer preceding headliners at a nightclub. Although Capitol Records executives were sufficiently impressed to record Denver, they refrained from releasing the records. Denver then traveled to New York City and successfully auditioned for the Mitchell Trio. He appeared on the band's ninth recording, *That's the Way It's Gonna Be,* as a singer, guitarist, and banjo player. While with the trio Denver wrote "Leaving on a Jet Plane," which became a major hit when recorded by the folk trio Peter, Paul, & Mary.

After the Mitchell Trio ceased performing in 1968, Denver mined the success of "Leaving on a Jet Plane" and managed to tour the United States performing his songs. The next year RCA Records signed Denver and released his first single recording, "Rhymes and Reasons," which was featured later that year on an album of the same title.

In 1971 Denver scored a substantial success with his fourth album, *Poems, Prayers, and Promises,* which featured one of his most popular songs, "Take Me Home, Country Roads." The next year he achieved another success with *Rocky Mountain High,* which includes the popular song of the same title. The strength of such songs—coupled with his wholesome image and endearing personality—enabled Denver to soon realize considerable prominence in pop music. He began performing on various television shows and playing concerts in larger auditoriums. Within only a few years, he was able to produce an album entitled *John Denver's Greatest Hits.*

Denver's career peaked through the remainder of the 1970s, when he enjoyed continued success with both concerts and recordings such as *Back Home Again,* which featured the popular "Annie's Song" in addition to the prominent title tune. In 1975 he proved particularly popular, receiving the Entertainer of the Year Award from the Country Music Association, the People's Choice Award for favorite musical performer, the Singing Star of the Year Award from American Guild of Variety Artists, and the Male Vocalist of the Year Award from Academy of Country Music. In 1976 he also won an Emmy Award for his television special, *An Evening with John Denver.* And within a few years, Denver—who had begun working as an actor in various television shows—made his motion-picture debut opposite George Burns in the comedy *Oh, God!* By 1977, he had also released *John Denver's Greatest Hits, Volume 2.*

In the ensuing years Denver maintained a prominent position as a musician. He released a Christmas recording on which he performed with the Muppets, and he appeared with celebrated opera tenor Placido Domingo on the popular song "Perhaps, Love." In addition to performing and recording, Denver devoted himself to various environmental and social causes and participated in activities organized by such groups as the Friends of the Earth and the Save the Children Foundation.

In 1995 Denver published an autobiography, *Take Me Home,* in which he reflected on his social and environmental concerns; mentioned more personal considerations, including his first marriage, which ended in divorce; and discussed life as a touring and performing musician. Portions of the book also disclose the origins and inspirations behind some of Denver's most widely known songs. *Entertainment Weekly* reviewer David Browne remarked that *Take Me Home* made for less-than compelling reading.

On October 12, 1997, Denver was killed when the experimental aircraft he was piloting crashed into California's Monterey Bay. At the time of the accident, according to a *USA Today* contributor, he had been writing new songs in anticipation of an album release in 1998.

"He was the Jimmy Stewart of folk music," Mary Traverse of Peter, Paul & Mary told *People* magazine. *People* also spoke with Denver's former agent Jerry Weintraub who said: "If you give Elvis the '50s and the Beatles the '60s, I think you've got to give John Denver the '70s."

BIOGRAPHICAL/CRITICAL SOURCES:

BOOKS

Dachs, David, *John Denver,* Pyramid, 1976.
Fleischer, Leonore, *John Denver,* Flash, 1976.

PERIODICALS

Entertainment Weekly, November 11, 1994, p. 65.
People, October 27, 1997, pp. 82-86, 88.

OBITUARIES:

OTHER

Atlanta Journal & Constitution (website), access atlanta.com, October 14, 1997.

Chicago Tribune (website), chicago.tribune.com, October 14, 1997.

CNN (website), cnn.com, October 14, 1997.

Detroit Free Press (website), freep.com, October 14, 1997.

Los Angeles Times (website), latimes.com, October 14, 1997.

New York Times (website), nytimes.com, October 14, 1997.

Times (London; website), the-times.co.uk, October 14, 1997.

USA Today (website), usatoday.com, October 14, 1997.

Washington Post (website), washington.post.com, October 14, 1997.*

* * *

DEVI, Gayatri 1919-
(Maharani of Jaipur)

PERSONAL: Born May 23, 1919, in London, England; raised near West Bengal, India; daughter of Jitendra Narayan (the Maharajah of Cooch Behar) and Indiraraje Gaekwar (Princess of Baroda); married Sawai Man Singh Bahadur (the Maharajah of Jaipur), May 9, 1940 (deceased); children: Kumar Jagat Singh. *Education:* Educated at home by tutors; attended Shantiniketan University, 1933-34, Brilliamount School, Switzerland, and London College of Secretaries. *Politics:* Swatantra (Freedom) Party. *Religion:* Hindu. *Avocational interests:* "I am interested in education and in conservation and preservation. I love horses. My husband was a nine-handicap polo player. I like sports, particularly tennis and polo."

ADDRESSES: Home and office—The Lily Pool, Sawai Ram, Singh Rd., Jaipur 302004 (Raj.), India.

CAREER: Elected member of Indian Parliament, 1962-77; Maharajah of Jaipur Museum Trust, Jaipur, Rajasthan, India, trustee, 1959—. Has served as vice president of National Swatantra Party, vice president of Rajasthan state Swatantra Party, founder and chair of board of governors of Maharani Gayatri Devi Girl's Public School, Jaipur, Rajasthan, and chair of Rajasthan Tourist Development Corporation. Associated with Red Cross.

MEMBER: Badminton Association of India (president), All India Lawn Tennis Association (vice president), India Polo Association (vice president, 1984).

WRITINGS:

A Gourmet's Getaway (Indian cuisine), Orient Longman (Jaipur, India), 1969.

(With Santha Rama Rau) *A Princess Remembers: The Memoirs of the Maharani of Jaipur* (autobiography), Lippincott (New York City), 1976, Rupa and Co. (New Delhi, India), 1995.

SIDELIGHTS: In her autobiography *A Princess Remembers: The Memoirs of the Maharani of Jaipur,* written with Santha Rama Rau, Gayatri Devi depicts her royal life in India. Born in London, England, in 1919, to the Maharajah of Cooch Behar and the Princess of Baroda, the author, according to her account, led a charmed life with all of the extravagances befitting royalty. Helen W. Coonley in *Kliatt* commented that the memoir was "more fascinating than fiction" due to the enormous wealth of the family and the privileged life it provided. She recalls in her book, for example, that at age three she shopped alone at Harrod's department store in London, with the manager unquestioningly bagging her every selection. She details her lavishly appointed palace home, her fine clothes and other treasures, among them exotic birds that could perform amazing tricks, and numerous elephants, including one with diamond-studded tusks. Unlike many women in her country at the time—with thanks to her liberal parents—Gayatri Devi was blessed with an education. She was educated early by tutors in her home before attending a school in India, a finishing school in Switzerland, and the London College of Secretaries.

The princess's way of life grew even more opulent with her 1940 marriage to the Maharajah of Jaipur. His third wife and Maharani, Gayatri Devi shares in *The Princess Remembers* that she was also his social wife; his other wives observed the tradition of purdah, the seclusion of women from public observation. Liberated from purdah by her education, her own will, and her husband's permission, Gayatri Devi accompanied the Maharajah on safaris, entertained his guests, and hosted their resplendent parties. And to enable and encourage other Indian women to refrain from purdah, the Maharani founded a school for girls, as well as schools that taught sewing and handicraft skills.

After India gained independence from Great Britain in 1947, the status of Jaipur's royal family was altered, as the Maharajah was no longer sovereign. Eventually, the city of Jaipur joined other autocracies to become one state, Rajasthan, with the Maharajah serving as a ceremonial ruler of the state until 1956. With their loss of sovereignty, the Maharajah and Maharani lost much of their wealth, and they subsequently turned their palace into a hotel and made other investments that enabled them to live in the manner to which they were accustomed.

The changes enacted by India's new government also caused a political stirring in Gayatri Devi; she joined the Swatantra Party at its inception in 1959 to counter then-Prime Minister Indira Gandhi's Congress Party. In 1962, the Maharani was elected to the House of the People, the lower chamber of India's parliament, where as a voice for the Swatantra Party she sought to promote free enterprise within her country and lobbied for closer ties to the West. She served in the Parliament until 1977.

A Princess Remembers recreates Gayatri Devi's life from childhood to her election to Parliament. Reviewers found the book an interesting peek inside the life of an Indian royal, although most of the critics suspected that the world Gayatri Devi depicts is a fairy-tale rendition, with all its skeletons locked in their closets. She does not include, for instance, any mention of her 1975 imprisonment and subsequent trial for nondisclosure of income.

Peter S. Prescott observed in *Newsweek* that "the princess has a lot to tell us, but the glimpses she allows us of her life are formal and carefully posed, arranged like family photos in a presentation album. She means to be discreet, to promote for history views of her family with its make-up all in place. . . . On balance, her book seems to me a worthy enterprise, the kind of story that will perhaps not excite interest in its subject but which adequately repays any interest brought to it."

BIOGRAPHICAL/CRITICAL SOURCES:

BOOKS

Devi, Gayatri, and Santha Rama Rau, *A Princess Remembers: The Memoirs of the Maharani of Jaipur,* Lippincott (New York City), 1976.

PERIODICALS

Kliatt, winter, 1986, p. 36.
Newsweek, March 28, 1977, pp. 79-81.
New York Times Book Review, March 13, 1977, p. 5.

DIAMOND, Edwin   1925-1997

OBITUARY NOTICE—See index for *CA* sketch: Born June 18, 1925, in Chicago, IL; died of a pulmonary disorder, July 10, 1997, in New York. Journalist, educator, and author. Diamond devoted his career to the media, whether it was working as a reporter, providing on-air television news commentary, or offering criticism of the news media. Early in his career, he worked as a reporter for the City News Bureau and the *Chicago Herald American,* beginning in 1953. Shortly thereafter he joined the International News Service as a science writer until 1957. He then spent eleven years with *Newsweek* magazine, first as a science editor and later as a senior editor.

While at *Newsweek,* Diamond covered the U.S. space program and was an acknowledged authority on the subject. In 1970 he began eight years with *New York Magazine* as contributing editor, followed by two years at *Esquire* magazine in the same capacity. He joined the staff of the *New York Daily News* from 1980 to 1981, then hooked up with *Adweek.* Diamond also was a senior lecturer in political science at the Massachusetts Institute of Technology beginning in 1970 and founded the school's News Study Group in 1972. He served as a commentator with the *Washington Post-Newsweek* Stations, Inc. from 1970 to 1979, and also participated in the "Spectrum" series for CBS from 1974 to 1975. During his career, he was also a founding senior editor of the *Washington Journalism Review.* He joined the faculty at New York University in 1984, where he remained until 1997. As the Internet grew in popularity, Diamond also worked as a contributing editor of *PoliticsNow.com,* a political web site sponsored by the Washington Post Co., ABC News, and the Times Mirror Corporation. His column, "Medium Cool," was featured on the site weekly.

In addition to his journalism, Diamond wrote various books, including *The Media Show, The Science of Dreams, Good News, Bad News, Sign Off: The Last Days of Television, The Tin Kazoo: Television Politics and the News, Behind the Times: Inside the New York Times, Jimmy Carter: An Interpretive Biography, White House to Your House: Media and Politics in Virtual America, The Rise and Fall of the Space Age, The Spot: The Rise of Political Advertising on Television,* and *Telecommunications in Crisis: The First Amendment, Technology and Deregulation.* Among his honors were a Page One Award.

OBITUARIES AND OTHER SOURCES:

PERIODICALS
Chicago Tribune, July 12, 1997, section 1, p. 20.
Los Angeles Times, July 11, 1997, p. A18.
New York Times, July 12, 1997, p. A10.
Washington Post, July 12, 1997, p. B6.

* * *

DISNEY, Walt(er Elias) 1901-1966

PERSONAL: Born December 5, 1901, in Chicago, IL; died of lung cancer, December 15, 1966, in Burbank, CA; son of Elias (a building contractor and later a farmer) and Flora (a school teacher; maiden name, Call) Disney; married Lillian Bounds (one of his first employees), 1925; children: Diane Marie, Sharon Mae. Education: Attended Chicago Academy of Fine Arts, 1917, and Kansas City Art Institute, 1919. Politics: Republican. Religion: Protestant.

CAREER: Animation pioneer. Worked as a mail sorter, factory worker, newspaper deliverer, cartoonist, and commercial artist. Worked for the Kansas City Film Ad Company, c. 1920; founded (with Ub Iwerks) Laugh-O-Gram Films, 1922; founded Disney Brothers Studios, c. 1924. Creator of animated films, including the early cartoon series "Newman Laugh-O-Grams," 1920-22; "Alice in Cartoonland," 1923-26; and "Oswald the Rabbit," 1926-28. Walt Disney Productions (parent company of Walt Disney Music Co., Wonderland Music Co., Buena Vista Distributors, Buena Vista International, MAPO Inc., Walt Disney Travel Co., Walt Disney Educational Media Co., and Walt Disney World), Burbank, CA, president and chairman of the board, 1929-60, director, 1929-1945, and executive producer, 1960-66; Walter Elias Disney (WED) Enterprises (family entertainment and recreational company), founder and owner, 1952-65, creator (through his company) of the amusement park Disneyland, which opened in Anaheim, CA, 1955, and Disney World, which opened in Orlando, FL, 1971. Founder of the California Institute of the Arts (through the amalgamation of the Los Angeles Conservatory of Music and Chouinard Art Institute), 1961. Wartime service: Served in the Red Cross Ambulance Corps as an ambulance driver in France during World War I. Helped in the wartime effort in World War II by involving more than ninety percent of the facilities of Walt Disney Studios in the production of government-related films, such as Armed Forces training films, propaganda films (including der Fuhrer's Face), the 1943 feature film Victory Through Air Power, and a number of educational films that were distributed by the U.S. State Department.

MEMBER: American Society of the French Legion of Honor, Order de Molay, Variety Clubs International, Riviera Club of Santa Monica, Writers and Athletic Clubs of Hollywood, American Forestry Association (honorary lifetime member), American Guild of Variety Artists, American Institute of Cinematography, Art Workers Guild of London, Association of Cinematographers of Argentina, California State Park Rangers Association, Izaak Walton League of America, National Association of Children of American Colonists, National Congress of Parents and Teachers, Screen Directors Guild, Society of Motion Picture and Television Engineers, Southern California Academy of Sciences, Sierra Club.

AWARDS, HONORS: Recipient of over 950 awards and citations over his lifetime. Recipient of forty-eight Academy Awards (the first for Flowers and Trees, the first Technicolor animated film, which he produced in 1932) and seven Emmy Awards. Recipient of the Presidential Medal of Freedom, the Irving G. Thalberg Memorial Award, Legion of Honor from France, Most Noble Order of the Crown of Thailand, National Order of the Southern Cross for Brazil, Order of the Aztec Eagle from the Mexican Ministry of Foreign Affairs, Cross of Merit from the Federal Republic of Germany, Cecil B. DeMille Award, Outstanding Achievement Award from the Freedoms Foundation, and Ambassador of Freedom Award from the Freedoms Foundation, among others. Recipient of honorary degrees from Harvard University, Yale University, Chouinard Art Institute, University of Southern California, and University of California at Los Angeles. A commemorative stamp was issued by the U.S. Post Office in his honor.

WRITINGS:

FILMS AS DIRECTOR, ANIMATOR, AND PRODUCER

"Newman Laugh-O-Grams" series, 1920.
Cinderella, 1922.
The Four Musicians of Bremen, 1922.
Goldie Locks and the Three Bears, 1922.
Jack and the Beanstalk, 1922.
Little Red Riding Hood, 1922.
Puss in Boots, 1922.
Alice's Wonderland, 1923.

Tommy Tucker's Tooth, 1923.
Martha, 1923.

FILMS AS DIRECTOR, ANIMATOR, AND PRODUCER; *"ALICE IN CARTOONLAND"* SERIES

Alice and the Dog Catcher, 1924.
Alice and the Three Bears, 1924.
Alice Cans the Cannibals, 1924.
Alice Gets in Dutch, 1924.
Alice Hunting in Africa, 1924.
Alice's Day at Sea, 1924.
Alice's Fishy Story, 1924.
Alice's Spooky Adventure, 1924.
Alice's Wild West Show, 1924.
Alice the Peacemaker, 1924.
Alice the Piper, 1924.
Alice the Toreador, 1924.
Alice Chops the Suey, 1925.
Alice Gets Stung, 1925.
Alice in the Jungle, 1925.
Alice Loses Out, 1925.
Alice on the Farm, 1925.
Alice Picks the Champ, 1925.
Alice Plays Cupid, 1925.
Alice Rattled by Rats, 1925.
Alice's Balloon Race, 1925.
Alice's Egg Plant, 1925.
Alice's Little Parade, 1925.
Alice's Mysterious Mystery, 1925.
Alice Solves the Puzzle, 1925.
Alice's Ornery Orphan, 1925.
Alice Stage Struck, 1925.
Alice's Tin Pony, 1925.
Alice the Jail Bird, 1925.
Alice Wins the Derby, 1925.
Alice Charms the Fish, 1926.
Alice's Monkey Business, 1926.
Alice in the Wooly West, 1926.
Alice the Fire Fighter, 1926.
Alice Cuts the Ice, 1926.
Alice Helps the Romance, 1926.
Alice's Spanish Guitar, 1926.
Alice's Brown Derby, 1926.
Clara Cleans Her Teeth, 1926.
Alice the Golf Bag, 1927.
Alice Foils the Pirates, 1927.
Alice at the Carnival, 1927.
Alice's Rodeo (also known as *Alice at the Rodeo*), 1927.
Alice the Collegiate, 1927.
Alice in the Alps, 1927.
Alice's Auto Race, 1927.
Alice's Circus Daze, 1927.
Alice's Knaughty Knight, 1927.

Alice's Three Bad Eggs, 1927.
Alice's Picnic, 1927.
Alice's Channel Swim, 1927.
Alice in the Klondike, 1927.
Alice's Medicine Show, 1927.
Alice the Whaler, 1927.
Alice the Beach Nut, 1927.
Alice in the Big League, 1927.

FILMS AS DIRECTOR, ANIMATOR, AND PRODUCER; *"OSWALD THE LUCKY RABBIT"* SERIES

Trolley Troubles, 1927.
Oh, Teacher, 1927.
The Ocean Hop, 1927.
All Wet, 1927.
The Mechanical Cow, 1927.
The Banker's Daughter, 1927.
Great Guns, 1927.
Rickety Gin, 1927.
Empty Socks, 1927.
Harem Scarem, 1927.
Neck 'n Neck, 1927.
The Ol' Swimmin' 'ole, 1928.
Africa before Dark, 1928.
Rival Romeos, 1928.
Bright Lights, 1928.
Sagebrush Sadie, 1928.
Ozzie of the Mounted, 1928.
Ride 'em Plow Boy!, 1928.
Hungry Hoboes, 1928.
Oh, What a Knight, 1928.
Sky Scrappers, 1928.
Poor Papa, 1928.
The Fox Chase, 1928.
Tall Timber, 1928.
Sleigh Bells, 1928.
Hot Dog, 1928.

FILMS AS HEAD OF WALT DISNEY PRODUCTIONS, CO-DIRECTED WITH UB IWERKS; *"MICKEY MOUSE"* SERIES

Steamboat Willie (first synchronized sound cartoon; voice of Mickey Mouse provided by Disney), 1928.
Plane Crazy, released with synchronized sound, 1929.
The Gallopin' Gaucho, released with synchronized sound, 1929.
The Barn Dance, 1929.
The Opry House, 1929.
When the Cat's Away, 1929.
The Barnyard Battle, 1929.
The Plow Boy, 1929.
The Karnival Kid, 1929.
Mickey's Choo Choo, 1929.

The Jazz Fool, 1929.
Jungle Rhythm, 1929.
The Haunted House, 1929.
The Barnyard Concert (sole director), 1930.
Just Mickey (Fiddling Around) (sole director), 1930.
The Cactus Kid (sole director), 1930.

*ANIMATED FILMS AS HEAD OF WALT DISNEY PRODUC-
    TIONS, CO-DIRECTED WITH UB IWERKS; "SILLY SYM-
    PHONIES" SERIES*

The Skeleton Dance, 1929.
El Terrible Toreador, 1929.
The Merry Dwarfs (sole director), 1929.
Night (sole director), 1930.
The Golden Touch (sole director), 1935.

*ANIMATED FEATURE FILMS AS HEAD OF WALT DISNEY
    PRODUCTIONS*

Snow White and the Seven Dwarfs, 1937.
Pinocchio, 1940.
Fantasia (with live action sequences featuring the
    Philadelphia Orchestra), 1940.
The Reluctant Dragon (with live action sequences
    featuring Robert Benchley), 1941.
Dumbo, 1941.
Bambi, 1942.
Saludos Amigos (with live action sequences featuring
    Walt Disney), 1943.
Victory Through Air Power (with live action), 1943.
The Three Caballeros, 1945.
Make Mine Music, 1946.
Song of the South (with live action sequences featur-
    ing James Baskett and Bobby Driscoll), 1946.
Fun and Fancy Free (with live action), 1947.
Melody Time, 1948.
So Dear to My Heart (with live action sequences
    featuring Burl Ives and Beulah Bondi), 1948.
Ichabod and Mr. Toad, 1949.
Cinderella, 1950.
Alice in Wonderland, 1951.
Peter Pan, 1953.
Lady and the Tramp, 1955.
Sleeping Beauty, 1959.
101 Dalmatians, 1961.
The Sword and the Stone, 1963.
The Jungle Book, 1967.

*LIVE ACTION FILMS AS HEAD OF WALT DISNEY PRODUC-
    TIONS*

Treasure Island, 1950.
The Story of Robin Hood, 1952.

The Sword and the Stone, 1953.
Rob Roy, the Highland Rogue, 1954.
20,000 Leagues Under the Sea, 1954.
The Living Desert, 1954.
The Vanishing Prairie, 1954.
Davy Crockett, King of the Wild Frontier, 1955.
The Littlest Outlaw, 1955.
The African Lion, 1955.
The Great Locomotive Chase, 1956.
Davy Crockett and the River Pirates, 1956.
Westward Ho the Wagons, 1956.
Secrets of Life, 1956.
Johnny Tremain, 1957.
Perri, 1957.
Old Yeller, 1957.
The Light in the Forest, 1958.
Tonka, 1958.
White Wilderness, 1958.
Darby O'Gill and the Little People, 1959.
The Shaggy Dog, 1959.
Third Man on the Mountain, 1959.
Toby Tyler, or, Ten Weeks with a Circus, 1960.
Kidnapped, 1960.
Pollyanna, 1960.
Ten Who Dared, 1960.
The Swiss Family Robinson, 1960.
The Sign of Zorro, 1960.
Jungle Cat, 1960.
Babes in Toyland, 1961.
The Absent-Minded Professor, 1961.
The Parent Trap, 1961.
Nikki, Wild Dog of the North, 1961.
Greyfriars Bobby, 1961.
Big Red, 1962.
Moon Pilot, 1962.
Bon Voyage, 1962.
Almost Angels, 1962.
The Legend of Lobo, 1962.
In Search of the Castaways, 1962.
Son of Flubber, 1963.
The Miracle of the White Stallions, 1963.
Savage Sam, 1963.
Summer Magic, 1963.
The Incredible Journey, 1963.
The Misadventures of Merlin Jones, 1964.
A Tiger Walks, 1964.
The Three Lives of Thomasina, 1964.
The Moon Spinners, 1964.
Mary Poppins, 1964.
Emil and the Detectives, 1964.
Those Calloways, 1965.
The Monkey's Uncle, 1965.
That Darn Cat, 1965.
The Fighting Prince of Donegal, 1966.

Follow Me, Boys, 1966.
The Ugly Dachsund, 1966.
Lt. Robin Crusoe, U.S.N., 1966.
Monkeys, Go Home, 1967.
The Gnome-Mobile, 1967.
The Adventures of Bullwhip Griffin, 1967.

Many hundreds of artists, animators, story men, and technicians contributed to the achievement of Walt Disney Studios. Some of the major animators included Ub Iwerks, Disney's earliest collaborator, the designer of Mickey Mouse, and the man responsible for many of the studio's technical innovations (including the multiplane camera technique), Ward Kimball, Les Clark, Frank Thomas, Milt Kahl, John Lounsbery, Ollie Johnston, Marc Davis, Woolie Reitherman, Eric Larson, Norm Ferguson, Art Babbitt, Grim Natwick, Ham Luske, Freddy Moore, Bill Tytla, Fred Spencer, and Preston Blair.

The Disney Studios produced short subjects on a regular basis through the mid-1950s, reaching a total of some six hundred films, in addition to many more 16mm films and filmstrips for educational use, advertising purposes, and for television presentation.

TELEVISION

Walt Disney produced a weekly one-hour series, including drama, cartoons, mystery, action-adventure, educational programs, comedy, and nature and science. On ABC-TV: *Disneyland,* October, 1954, to September, 1958; *Walt Disney Presents* (three rotating series: "The Nine Lives of Elfago Baca," starring Robert Loggia and Robert Simon; "The Swamp Fox," starring Leslie Nielsen and Barbara Eiler; and "Texas John Slaughter," starring Tom Tryon and Harry Carey, Jr.), September, 1958, to June, 1959; *Walt Disney's Adventure Time,* September, 1958, to September, 1959; *Walt Disney's World,* October, 1959, to September, 1961; on NBC-TV: *Walt Disney's Wonderful World of Color,* September, 1961, to September, 1981.

Mickey Mouse Club, October, 1955, to September, 1959, ABC TV, daily one-hour series of varied entertainment for children, live and filmed, with Disney cartoons and episodic series (like "Spin and Marty" and "The Hardy Boys") produced in both thirty- and sixty-minute versions, hosted by Jimmy Dodd and featuring a cast of forty-four "Mouseketeers," including Annette Funicello, Kevin Corcoran, Tommy Kirk, Johnny Crawford, and Tim Considine. *Zorro,*

September, 1957, to September, 1959, ABC-TV, weekly thirty-minute dramatic series, starring Guy Williams, Richard Anderson, and Annette Funicello.

ADAPTATIONS: Hundreds of books have been adapted from Disney films, including *Pinocchio,* Random House, 1939; *Bambi,* Simon and Schuster, 1941; *Donald Duck in the High Andes* (from the film *Saludos Amigos*), Grosset, 1943; *Uncle Remus Stories* (retold by H. Marion Palmer [also known as Helen Geisel]; illustrations adapted by Al Dempster and Bill Justice), Simon & Schuster, 1947; *Mickey and the Beanstalk* (from the film *Fun and Fancy Free;* illustrations adapted by Campbell Grant), Grosset, 1947; and *Lady and the Tramp* (illustrations adapted by Claude Coats), Simon & Schuster, 1955.

SIDELIGHTS: He is a man known for lifting America's spirits through the Great Depression, a World War, and the post-war baby-boom, and he is still present in spirit today as his company, Walt Disney Productions, continues to lead in defining family entertainment in the United States. The legacy of Walt Disney strongly impacts the movie industry, toys, children's clothing and accessories like backpacks and toothbrushes, books and music, and vacation plans. In *Children's Books and Their Creators,* Terri Payne Butler wrote that "nearly three decades after his death, 'Disney' is no longer a name, but a conjuring word, summoning collective memories of poisoned apples, pumpkined carriages, and raucous blue genies."

Although his accomplishments are many, Disney is best known as the creator of the character Mickey Mouse, as the producer of a myriad of films for children and adults, and as the creator of the theme parks Disneyland and Disney World. In his lifetime, he also created and endowed a new university, the California Institute of the Arts, a professional school for the creative and performing arts.

Disney was born in Chicago, Illinois, in 1901, the fourth son in a family of five from a lower middle class family. His father, Elias, who was Canadian, was an unsuccessful farmer, carpenter, and businessman, and his mother, Flora Call, was a patient women who supported her husband through his numerous pursuits. Although it appears that his early life was not marked by harmony and stability, a happy family life is a recurrent theme in all of Disney's work.

In 1906 the Disneys moved from Chicago to a farm near Marceline, Missouri. Later, Disney would remember the friendliness of rural life, but also the hard work that he and his family were forced to perform in order to get the farm established. When his two older brothers left the farm and returned to Chicago, the farm began to fail. It was on the farm that Disney's interest in art began to show itself; he and his sister Ruth would take sticks dipped in tar and paint on the side of the family's white house. In *The Disney Version: The Life, Times, Art and Commerce of Walt Disney,* Richard Schickel quoted Disney as saying, "I recall when I was about seven. The doctor had a very fine stallion which he asked me to sketch. He held the animal while I worked with my homemade easel and materials. The result was pretty terrible, but both the doctor and his wife praised the drawing highly, to my great delight." Disney also used some of the farm animals as the basis for the animated animals that later appeared in his films. His mother taught him to read at home, but Disney's interest in classwork was minimal.

When the farm failed, the family moved to Kansas City, Missouri. It was 1910, and Elias Disney began to manage a paper route with the help of Walt, who was nine years old at the time. Again, the work was grueling, and Disney remembered delivering newspapers in the morning and evening in summer heat and winter snowstorms. He was not a good student, but his teachers at the Benton Grammar School in Kansas City encouraged Disney's interest in drawing. When his sister Ruth became ill, Disney designed a flip book in which figures appeared to move; this was his first effort in the world of animation. He also began to read the classics and enrolled in children's art classes at the Kansas City Art Institute.

The family moved again in 1917 when Elias Disney invested in a jelly factory in Chicago. Disney graduated from Benton Grammar School in June of that year, spent the summer working for the railroad selling refreshments to passengers, and met his family in Chicago in September, where he enrolled at McKinley High School and began to take art classes at the Chicago Institute of Art. But after a year of high school, Disney was restless and anxious to see more of the world. He was too young to join the military but decided, with his mother's permission, to join the Red Cross Ambulance Corps and become an ambulance driver. He spent most of his tour of duty delivering relief supplies and working in the motor pool; by the time he went overseas, World War I had virtually ended.

After the war, Disney headed to Kansas City. He decided to use his artistic talent to get a job, and he soon found work in advertising as an apprentice at a commercial art studio. It was there that he met a Dutch cartoonist named Ub Iwerks. Together, they left to form their own art studio, but it soon failed.

Next, the pair went to work for the Kansas City Film Ad Company, where they learned the basics of animation as they created one-minute animated cartoon commercials. They also created the concept of Laugh-O-Grams, which were short cartoons that combined a gag and a commercial announcement. Disney and Iwerks left to form Laugh-O-Gram Films in 1922, and the popularity of these Laugh-O-Grams caused them to be prosperous for a while. While at Laugh-O-Gram Films, they also produced several seven-minute animated cartoons based on fairy tales.

Because they had no experience in distribution, this company failed; however, Disney was determined to succeed, and he persuaded his brother Roy to invest in his third company, which would produce a series known as "Alice in Cartoonland." In this series, a live young girl appeared in adventures along with animated creatures and backgrounds. This company failed, too, and Disney and Iwerks declared bankruptcy.

By 1923, Disney was still determined to produce animated films. He moved to Hollywood and revived Laugh-O-Grams and the "Alice" series. Then, he convinced his brother Roy and Iwerks to join him in Hollywood and he formed Disney Brothers Studios. It was here that Disney began to demonstrate a remarkable ability to delegate responsibility to his staff. He became the main idea man behind stories, characterization, and film development. Iwerks took over the art department, and Roy Disney became the business manager. Iwerks was later replaced by a large staff of artists, but Roy and Walt Disney stayed in these respective positions throughout their careers. After this time, Disney never performed the actual tasks involved in cartooning and animation again; he found that he had a gift for creating visionary master plans and for directing others into seeing them through.

As his professional life became more settled, Disney's personal life did as well. In 1925, his company hired an inker and painter named Lillian Bounds. They fell in love, married that summer, and later had two daughters—Diane Marie, who was born in 1933, and Sharon Mae, who was born in 1936. Their marriage appeared to be happy and lasted until Disney's death.

The early years of Disney Brothers Studio were busy ones, as the company produced fifty-six "Alice in Cartoonland" shorts. By 1927, Disney began collaborating with Universal Studios to produce cartoons featuring the character "Oswald the Lucky Rabbit." Using new techniques for producing these films, the company created ten Oswald shorts in 1927 and sixteen in 1928. The humor was slapstick and the plots were simplistic, but the Oswald series was a popular one. When Disney attempted to negotiate a new contract with Universal Studios, he discovered that they actually owned the Oswald character. At this point, Disney vowed never to work on a property that he did not own again.

Next, Disney created his own star, which would become the most famous of all his characters. There are many myths about how the character of Mickey Mouse was created: some say that Disney dreamed up the character when he was working on the drawing board in Kansas City, and others say that the character was created by Disney on the train ride home after the Oswald dispute with Universal. The truth is that the development of the character was a collaboration between Disney, who developed the idea, and Iwerks, who drew the character and created his form. Disney wanted to call him Mortimer Mouse, but his wife thought that the name Mickey would be better. In *The Story of Walt Disney,* his daughter Diane Disney Miller remembered the conversation this way:

"'I think I've got something,' Father told Mother. 'It's a mouse. I'll call him Mortimer. Mortimer Mouse. I like that, Don't you?' "Mother thought it over and shook her head. 'I like the mouse idea,' she said, 'but Mortimer sounds wrong. Too sissy.' "'What's wrong with it?' Father asked. 'Mortimer Mouse, Mortimer Mouse. It swings, Lilly.' "But Mother didn't buy it. She couldn't explain why 'Mortimer' grated on her. It just did.

"'All right,' Father said. 'How about Mickey? Mickey Mouse?'"

In this way, the world's most famous cartoon character was born. In 1928, the studio produced three animated shorts using their new character Mickey. He was soon joined by a number of supporting characters, including Minnie Mouse, Pluto, Horace Horsecollar, and Donald Duck.

Although Donald Duck is also a popular character, Mickey, whose voice was done by Disney himself, is considered the most memorable of Disney's cre-

ations. According to M. Thomas Inge, writing in *Dictionary of Literary Biography,* Disney once said, "Mickey's a nice fellow who never does anybody any harm, who gets in scrapes through no fault of his own but always manages to come up grinning."

Mickey Mouse and friends became popular around the world, but Disney Brothers Studios was still experiencing financial problems. In his book *The Disney Version: The Life, Times, Art and Commerce of Walt Disney,* Richard Schickel quoted Disney as describing the problems in this way: "Each film we finished just about paid for getting out the next one. I kept adding new people to our staff, but in spite of that, I had to work over-time night after night myself."

Because Disney owned this group of characters that he had created, he licensed them for use in hundreds of products, including books, games, toys, and watches. Numerous comic strips were created, including an adventure strip based on Mickey that was developed by cartoonist Floyd Gottfredson and was published in daily newspapers from 1930 to 1950. Carl Barks, a former Disney animator, developed a popular comic book series about Donald Duck, Uncle Scrooge (who Barks created), and Donald's nephews that was published in Dell Comic Books from 1943 through the 1960s.

After his first six Mickey Mouse shorts were produced, Disney began working on his next project, a film known as *The Skeleton Dance,* which was produced in 1929. In this film, which is the first in the "Silly Symphony" series, the bony residents of a graveyard dance to "The Dance of the Dwarfs." In the next of the "Silly Symphonies," *Flowers & Trees,* Disney added color to the film. In November of 1932, he received an award for this animated cartoon from the Academy of Motion Picture Arts and Sciences.

By 1933, Disney had released his thirty-sixth film in the "Silly Symphony" series. This film was a popular one, primarily because of its upbeat message during the Depression and the memorable theme song "Who's Afraid of the Big Bad Wolf?" In addition to making the nation happy, *The Three Little Pigs* also made Disney wealthy when it grossed 125,000 dollars in its first year.

At this point, Disney decided to produce a feature-length animated film. This project was an ambitious one that would involve creating seven reels of action in Technicolor. To create this film, Disney introduced the multiplane camera, a machine that was able to photograph characters and settings through several planes, giving the animated cartoon a multidimensional effect. The film that Disney chose to produce was *Snow White and the Seven Dwarfs,* one of the best loved fairy tales from the Brothers Grimm.

Disney realized the gamble he was taking when he set out to work on *Snow White.* In *The Disney Version,* Richard Schickel quoted Disney as saying: "We've got to be sure of it before we start, because if it isn't good we will destroy it: If it is good, we shall make at least a million." The story was trimmed down, and much of the horror was eliminated from the original tale. The Disney film, which had an optimistic tone, was released a few days before Christmas in 1937. The film premiered at the Carthay Circle Theater in Hollywood, and later appeared at Radio City Music Hall in New York City. Thousands of moviegoers flocked to theaters to see the film, and *Snow White* earned eight million dollars, putting Disney Studios on solid financial ground for the first time. Although *Snow White* might have looked as though it was easy to produce, it took four years of hard work involving hundreds of talented people. The film won a special Academy Award in 1939, in the form of one large Oscar statue and seven little Oscar statuettes—one for each of the film's dwarfs.

Encouraged by the financial and critical success of his first feature-length animated film, Disney and his staff began working on *Pinocchio,* another full-length animated film. Taking a classic children's story written by Carlo Collodi in the late nineteenth century, Disney reworked the tale of a puppet who came to life and turned it into a Disney masterpiece that combines comedy, terror, artistry, and memorable music.

Pinocchio was still in production when Disney Studios began working on *Fantasia,* a revolutionary integration of imaginative visuals and some of the great works of classical music. In an August 1941 interview with *Who* magazine, Disney described his interest in *Fantasia* this way: "It seems I'm just finding out about music. . . . I never liked this highbrow stuff. It bored me. Honest, I just couldn't listen to it. But I can now. It seems to mean a little more to me. Maybe *Fantasia* can do the same for other people." The film was released in 1940, nine months after *Pinocchio,* but *Fantasia* was not as popular as Disney had hoped and only came into its own as it was re-released over the years.

The years that directly followed the release of these two films were not as magical for Walt Disney. Production costs on both films had been high, and *Fantasia* was basically a commercial failure. When World War II began, foreign film markets were closed. Additionally, Disney felt betrayed when many of his employees went out on a labor strike in 1941. The films *Dumbo* and *Bambi* were released in 1941 and 1942, respectively, but most of the work on these projects had been completed before problems set in at the studio. Both *Dumbo,* the story of a flying elephant that contains the surrealistic "Pink Elephants on Parade" segment, and *Bambi,* the rendering of the Felix Salten novel about the life of a fawn and life in the forest, were popular with moviegoers.

Disney took on many government contracts during the war years. He produced animated training films for all branches of the armed forces. At first, the treasury department did not like the idea of using Donald Duck to represent the average taxpayer in these films. In Diane Disney Miller's *The Story of Walt Disney,* Disney is quoted as saying: "You wanted me to get this message over, so I've given you Donald. At our studio, that's like MGM giving you Clark Gable. The Duck is well known to the American public and they'll go to theaters to see him. I can promise that they won't walk out on him and I wouldn't promise that they won't take a walk on your Mr. Taxpayer." Later, in a film designed to support a good neighbor policy with South America (*The Three Caballeros,* 1945), Disney combined live action and animation; this technique was so effective that it was later used in *Song of the South* (1946), a film collection of selected stories by Joel Chandler Harris. This film included some Old South stereotypes, but it did use some innovative film techniques to tell the stories of Brer Rabbit, Brer Bear, and Brer Fox.

In the years directly following the war, Disney continued to produce anthologies (*Make Mine Music,* 1946, and *Melody Time,* 1948), films that combined animation with music (*Fun and Fancy Free,* 1947) and films that retold old stories (*Ichabod and Mr. Toad,* 1949, *The Wind in the Willows,* 1949, and *So Dear to My Heart,* 1948). Disney Studios also continued to produce a number of short films, including cartoons featuring the popular characters Mickey Mouse, Donald Duck, Pluto, and Goofy. About 180 short films were produced in the 1930s, 150 in the 1940s, ninety in the 1950s, and twelve in the 1960s as theater managers lost interest in this medium. In addition to being shown in theaters, these films were also used when Disney introduced his first television special in 1951 and initiated his weekly show *Disneyland* in 1954. *The Mickey Mouse Club,* which was one of the most widely watched children's program of the 1950s, was introduced in 1955. Disney himself became a television personality when he served as host for *Disneyland* (which became the *Wonderful World of Color* in 1961).

In 1950, Disney Studios began to produce adaptations of classic fairy tales and children's stories, including *Cinderella* (1950), *Alice in Wonderland* (1951, based on the book by Lewis Carroll), *Peter Pan* (1953, based on the play by James M. Barrie), *Lady and the Tramp* (1955, based on the story by Ward Greene), *Sleeping Beauty* (1959), *101 Dalmations* (1961, based on the book by Dodie Smith), *The Sword and the Stone* (1963, inspired by T. H. White's retelling of the Arthurian legends), and *The Jungle Book* (1967, inspired by Rudyard Kipling's *Mowgli* stories). *The Jungle Book* was the last film that Disney actually supervised.

At the same time, Disney Studios was also hard at work producing a number of live action films, including *Treasure Island, 20,000 Leagues Under the Sea, Kidnapped,* and *Mary Poppins.* In a sixteen-year period, Disney oversaw the production of sixty-three live-action films. These films are considered great family entertainment and were generally box-office hits, but few of them are recognized as classics. Some exceptions include *Treasure Island* and *20,000 Leagues Under the Sea,* which are considered by many critics the best of these films, and *Mary Poppins,* which, in 1964, was nominated for thirteen Academy Awards and received five of them.

Disney is not without detractors. In 1965, Dr. Max Rafferty, California's superintendent of public instruction, wrote an article in which he described Disney as "the greatest educator of this century." This claim created a backlash, as educators and critics around the country described the way that Walt Disney had mishandled fairy tales and children's classics. Frances Clarke Sayers, who was director of children's services for the New York Public Library, wrote a letter to the *Los Angeles Times* in response to Dr. Rafferty's article. In it she said that Disney had "scant respect for the integrity of the original creations . . . manipulating and vulgarizing everything for his own ends. His treatment of folklore is without regard for its anthropological, spiritual, or psychological truths." "I call him to account for his debasement of the traditional literature of childhood, in

films and in the books he publishes," she wrote. She also commented that "the acerbity of *Mary Poppins,* unpredictable, full of wonder and mystery, becomes . . . one great marshmallow-covered cream-puff," and added that Disney "transformed *Pinocchio* into a slapstick sadistic revel." However, author and illustrator Maurice Sendak, writing in his 1988 collection of essays *Caldecott & Co.,* praised Disney's *Pinocchio.* "Collodi's book is of interest today," Sendak wrote, "chiefly as evidence of the superiority of Disney's screenplay." Writing in *People* in 1992, Ralph Novak also gave *Pinocchio* high marks. "While modern kids may find the ending too low-key or the whole production too low-tech, the film is to children what *Casablanca* is to adults," he observed.

As might be expected, Disney did not try to recreate fairy tales or children's classics faithfully. In the *Horn Book,* Betsy Hearne stated that Disney once said to one of his story men assigned to work on *The Jungle Book,* "The first thing I want you to do is not to read it," adding later, "You can get all bogged down with these stories."

One of Disney's proudest achievements was Disneyland, the amusement park that he built in Anaheim, California, in 1955. At the dedication, Disney said, "Disneyland will never be completed as long as there is imagination left in the world." In Diane Disney Miller's *The Story of Walt Disney,* she quoted her father as saying: "The germ of Disneyland was planted in my mind when you and your sister Sharon were little and I took you to amusement parks and to zoos on Saturdays and Sundays. Those days were among the happiest of my life." Although he planned it, he did not live to see Disneyworld, which was completed in Orlando, Florida, in 1971. (Disney died of lung cancer in 1966.) Nearly sixteen years after his death, Epcot Center, Disney's vast vision of a combination world's fair, theme park, and dream factory, opened in Orlando, Florida, at a cost of 900 million dollars.

In a 1993 interview with *Entertainment Weekly,* Adriana Caelotti, who was the original voice in *Snow White,* described Disney this way: "To me, he was just about the greatest man artistically. He seemed to understand what was correct with anything that had to do with art, with music. And I feel that he will never die."

Among his many accomplishments, Disney is best remembered for bringing about the innovative family amusement parks and for bringing animation to a new level of accomplishment. Today, his financial and cultural empire is secure, and young animators continue to bring forth new feature films every year. Disney characters are known throughout the world and Disney's influence is felt throughout society. Few have influenced popular culture more than Walt Disney.

BIOGRAPHICAL/CRITICAL SOURCES:

BOOKS

Bailey, Adrian, *Walt Disney's Wonderful World of Fantasy,* Dodd, Mead, 1985.

Beard, Richard R., *Walt Disney's EPCOT Center: Creating the New World of Tomorrow,* Abrams, 1985.

Butler, Terri Payne, *Children's Books and Their Creators,* edited by Anita Silvey, Houghton Mifflin, 1995.

Cole, Michael D., *Walt Disney: Creator of Mickey Mouse,* Enslow, 1996.

DiFranco, Joann, *Walt Disney: When Dreams Come True,* Dillon, 1985.

Disney, Walt, *Sketch Book/Walt Disney,* Applewood, 1993.

Eliot, Marc, *Walt Disney: Hollywood's Dark Prince,* Harper, 1994.

Fanning, Jim, *Walt Disney,* Chelsea House, 1994.

Finch, Christopher, *The Art of Walt Disney: From Mickey Mouse to the Magic Kingdoms,* Abrams, 1995.

Fisher, Maxine P., *Walt Disney,* F. Watts, 1988.

Ford, Barbara, *Walt Disney: A Biography,* Walker, 1989.

Greene, Katherine, *The Man Behind the Magic: The Story of Walt Disney,* Viking, 1991.

Inge, M. Thomas, "Walt Disney," *Dictionary of Literary Biography,* Volume 22: *American Writers for Children, 1900-1960,* Gale, 1983, pp. 124-135.

Italia, Bob, *Mickey Mouse,* Abdo & Daughters, 1991.

Jachnin, Boris, *Walt Disney,* ASF, 1990.

Jackson, Kathy Merlock, *Walt Disney: A Bio-Bibliography,* Greenwood Press, 1993.

Korman, Justine, *Walt Disney's Sleeping Beauty and the Prince: A Book about Determination,* Golden Book, 1988.

Miller, Diane Disney, *The Story of Walt Disney,* Curtis, 1956.

Mosley, Leonard, *Disney's World: A Biography,* Stein & Day, 1985.

Schickel, Richard, *The Disney Version: The Life, Times, Art and Commerce of Walt Disney,* Avon Books, 1968.

Schomp, Virginia, *Walt Disney: Making Dreams Come True,* Dillon Press, 1992.

Selden, Bernice, *The Story of Walt Disney: Maker of Magical Worlds,* G. Stevens, 1996.

Sendak, Maurice, *Caldecott & Co.: Notes on Books & Pictures,* Michael Di Capua Books/Farrar, Straus, 1988.

Sinyard, Neil, *The Best of Disney,* Twin Books, 1988.

Thomas, Bob, *Walt Disney: An American Original,* Hyperion, 1994.

Tietyen, David, *The Musical World of Walt Disney,* H. Leonard Publishers, 1990.

Uelmen, Amelia J., *Seeing the U.S.A.: The Landscapes of Walt Disney,* Georgetown University Press, 1991.

West, John, *The Disney Live-Action Productions,* Hawthorne & Peabody, 1994.

PERIODICALS

American Legion, September, 1996, p. 72.
Boy's Life, October, 1994, p. 15.
Entertainment Weekly, April 2, 1993, p. 57; July 9, 1993, p. 59.
Gentlemen's Quarterly, January, 1996, p. 105.
Horn Book, December, 1965, pp. 602-611; March/April, 1997, pp. 137-146.
Journal of American History, June, 1995, p. 84.
Life, fall, 1990, p. 26.
New York, October 22, 1990, p. 116.
New Yorker, January 6, 1992, p. 14.
People, July 6, 1992, pp. 14-15; November 21, 1994, p. 142.
Variety, April 19, 1993, p. 63; November 7, 1994, p. 142; September 9, 1996, p. 124.
Who, August, 1941.

OBITUARIES:

PERIODICALS

National Review, January 10, 1967.
Newsweek, December 26, 1966.
New York Times, December 18, 1966.
Time, December 23, 1966.*

* * *

DOSS, Erika

PERSONAL: Female. *Education:* Ripon College, B.A., 1978; University of Minnesota—Twin Cities, M.A., 1980, Ph.D., 1983.

ADDRESSES: Office—Department of Fine Arts, Campus Box 318, University of Colorado, Boulder, CO 80309-0318; fax 303-492-4886. *E-mail*—erika.doss @colorado.edu.

CAREER: Minneapolis College of Art and Design, Minneapolis, MN, instructor in art history, 1981-83; Carleton College, Northfield, MN, visiting assistant professor of art history, 1983-84; Cleveland State University, Cleveland, OH, assistant professor of art history, 1984-86; University of Colorado, Boulder, assistant professor, 1986-91, director of London Study Abroad Program, 1988, associate professor of art history and director of American Studies Program, 1991—. University of Minnesota—Twin Cities, instructor, 1983; University of Oregon, visiting assistant professor, 1984; University of Sydney, senior Fulbright lecturer, 1996; lecturer at Marquette University, Indiana University—Bloomington, Ripon College, Naropa Institute, University of Wyoming, Washington State University, North Carolina State University, Wayne State University, and Art Institute of Chicago. Boulder Arts Commission, member, 1992—.

MEMBER: American Studies Association, Association of Historians of American Art, College Art Association of America, Organization of American Historians.

AWARDS, HONORS: Arts and Criticism Award, Jerome Foundation, 1983; grant, National Endowment for the Humanities, 1985; Marshall Fishwick Award, Popular Culture Association, 1993, for the article "Raising Community Consciousness with Public Art: Contrasting Projects by Judy Baca and Andrew Leicester;" Charles C. Eldredge Prize, National Museum of American Art, 1993, for *Benton, Pollock, and the Politics of Modernism;* grant, Colorado Endowment for the Humanities, 1993; senior fellow, Wolfsonian Research Center (Miami Beach, FL), 1995; senior Fulbright scholar in Australia, 1995.

WRITINGS:

Benton, Pollock, and the Politics of Modernism: From Regionalism to Abstract Expressionism, University of Chicago Press (Chicago, IL), 1991.
Spirit Poles and Flying Pigs: Public Art and Cultural Democracy in American Communities, Smithsonian Institution Press (Washington, DC), 1995.
(Editor and contributor) *Looking at LIFE: Cultural Essays on America's Favorite Magazine,* Smithsonian Institution Press, in press.

Contributor to books, including *Independent Spirits: Women Artists of the West, 1890-1945,* edited by Patricia Trenton, University of California Press (Berkeley, CA), 1995; *The Icons of American Protestantism: The Art of Warner Sallman, 1892-1968,* edited by David Morgan, Yale University Press (New Haven, CT), 1996; and *The Architecture of Reassurance: Designing the Disney Theme Parks,* edited by Karal Ann Marling and Nicholas Olsberg, Centre Canadien d'Architecture (Montreal, Quebec), in press. Contributor of articles and reviews to academic journals, including *American Art, Woman's Art Journal, Landscape Architecture, International Sculpture, Artpaper,* and *Journal of American Culture.*

WORK IN PROGRESS: Twentieth-Century American Art, publication by Oxford University Press (London, England) expected in 1999; *Saint Elvis: Audiences and Cultural Production in Contemporary America.*

*   *   *

DUANE, Daniel   1967-
  (Daniel King Duane)

PERSONAL: Born in 1967, in Berkeley, CA. *Education:* Cornell University, B.A.; pursued graduate study in American literature at University of California at Santa Cruz.

ADDRESSES: Agent—c/o Farrar, Straus, & Giroux, 19 Union Sq. W., New York, NY 10003.

CAREER: Writer about outdoor subjects. Worked as teaching assistant, University of California, Santa Cruz. Worked in a mountaineering-equipment store, Berkeley, CA, after college.

WRITINGS:

(As Daniel King Duane) *Lighting Out: A Vision of California and the Mountains,* Graywolf Press (St. Paul, MN), 1994.
Caught Inside: A Surfer's Year on the California Coast, North Point Press/Farrar, Straus (New York City), 1996.

WORK IN PROGRESS: A novel about surfing and adventuring in the South Pacific.

SIDELIGHTS: With his first two books, Daniel Duane carved a niche for himself writing first-hand accounts of the thrills of dangerous outdoor sports, especially those popular with the demographic group referred to as Generation X. Born in Berkeley, California during the turbulent 1960s, and a child of civil rights activists, Duane was perhaps destined not to succumb, as many of his Cornell classmates did, to the temptations of a suit-and-tie job in the business world. He finished his undergraduate degree having spent his junior year in the Pyrenees instead of in Paris where he was supposed to be; and after graduating he returned to his home town to work in an outdoor outfitting shop.

As a child, under the influence of his father's personal library of mountaineering books, Duane became interested in mountain climbing. As a young man, he trained with his experienced father and uncle to conquer El Capitan, one of the most famous and perilous peaks in the Sierra Nevada range. The ascent succeeded, and Duane wrote a book about it, *Lighting Out: A Vision of California and the Mountains,* which was published in 1994. The book also contains observations of cafe life among the twenty-something crowd, and of Duane's love affair with a feminist organic gardener. A contributor to *Kirkus Reviews* applauded the descriptions of mountaineering and called the book "a sort of nouveau *Dharma Bums.*" Tim Markus, in *Library Journal,* described the book as "a captivating debut" and lauded Duane's "wonderfully deadpan writing style." Gregory McNamee, in the *Washington Post Book World,* felt that Duane's examination of his gen-eration's culture fell short, but he caught the author's "obvious, infectious joy at scrambling about in the high country" and commended his "talent for conveying the feel of a climb."

In the course of a year, during which he was a part-time teaching assistant at the University of California at Santa Cruz, Duane thoroughly learned the sport of surfing and became acquainted with several of its colorful adherents. The result was his 1996 book, *Caught Inside: A Surfer's Year on the California Coast,* which a *Kirkus Reviews* contributor described as a "testament to an obsession." Duane described the physical sensations of surfing (including that of nearly drowning), the technique and precision demanded by the sport (which the *Kirkus Reviews* critic averred he handled "with aplomb"), and the introspections of surfers on their way of life (which the *Kirkus Reviews* critic termed "utterly intriguing"). In summary, the reviewer for *Kirkus Reviews* declared, Duane had fashioned "poetry from the surf's chaos— wild and vital, supple and elegant." Even higher

praise came from John Murray in *Bloomsbury Review,* who announced the book's arrival as nothing less than that of the "natural spokesman and . . . nascent laureate" of a generation: "A book significant not only for its deft grasp of subject and style but also for the promise it holds for greater things to come from a writer so young and gifted."

Continuing in a similar vein, Murray, who appreciated the difficulties of both writing and surfing, commented, "This is a book to buy and read and share . . . he is, as they say, the real thing, and one has the continual sense that Duane is at the beginning of a fine career." Equally appreciative, although more moderate in tone, was praise from surfer-writer David Sheff, who assessed *Caught Inside* for the *Los Angeles Times Book Review.* Sheff found the "surferese" in the book excessive, but added, "the overall impact is nonetheless enthralling. Duane has an honest take on surf culture, seeing both the romance and the irony. . . . Duane has succeeded in creating a seductive journal that describes not only the complexities of this sport but offers a compelling glimpse into a profoundly different raison d'etre." Above all, Sheff admired Duane's "evocative, compelling observations about nature," which included "fresh and thrilling" descriptions of sharks, hawks, clouds, otters, pelicans, and more.

Further praises came from the nature magazine *Outside,* which discovered Duane's writing on surfing to be more than satisfactory: "thanks to Duane's keen eye, powerful prose and deft sense of humor, [surfing] feels great for the rest of us too." Though Bruce Barcott of *Salon* felt the book was less than substantial, he was in the minority as yet another reviewer, Louisa Kamps for *Boston Phoenix Review,* admired Duane's "lucid, lyrical prose" and "his smart, funny, eclectic impressions." Stephen Fowler for *HotWired,* who was expecting an uninteresting read, found out instead that "this book is an ideal piece of nonfiction . . . I found myself intrigued by it, then fascinated, then genuinely engrossed."

BIOGRAPHICAL/CRITICAL SOURCES:

PERIODICALS

Bloomsbury Review, May, 1996, pp. 18-19.
Kirkus Reviews, February 1, 1994, p. 110; April 15, 1996, p. 573.
Library Journal, March 1, 1994, p. 93.
Los Angeles Times Book Review, July 14, 1996, p. 4.
Washington Post Book World, May 8, 1994, p. 6.

OTHER

Boston Phoenix Review (website), www.bostonphoenix.com.
HotWired (website), wwww.hotwired.com/books.
Outside (website), outside.starwave.com.
Salon (website), www.salonmagazine.com*

* * *

DUANE, Daniel King
  See DUANE, Daniel

* * *

DUGGLEBY, John 1952-

PERSONAL: Born January 1, 1952, in Muscatine, IA; children: Katie. *Education:* University of Iowa, B.A., 1973.

ADDRESSES: Home and office—Duggleby Communications, 5322 Norma Rd., McFarland, WI 53558-9479. *E-mail*—duggleby@mailbag.com.

CAREER: Allstate Insurance, Northbrook, IL, magazine editor, 1976-78; American Telephone & Telegraph, Chicago, IL, member of corporate communications staff, 1978-81; Burson-Marsteller Public Relations, Chicago, member of creative staff, 1981-84; Duggleby Communications, McFarland, WI, owner, 1984—.

MEMBER: Society of Children's Book Writers and Illustrators, Wisconsin Public Relations Forum, Wisconsin Communicators Council.

AWARDS, HONORS: Awards from Illinois Press Association and International Association of Business Communicators; Children's Crown nomination from the National Association of Christian Schools.

WRITINGS:

The Sabertooth Cat, Crestwood House/Macmillan, 1989.
Pesticides, Crestwood House/Macmillan, 1990.
Doomed Expeditions, illustrated by Robert Andrew Parker, Crestwood House/Macmillan, 1990.
Impossible Quests, illustrated by Allan Eitzen, Crestwood House/Macmillan, 1990.

Artist in Overalls: The Life of Grant Wood, Chronicle Books (San Francisco, CA), 1996.

Contributor of numerous articles and poems to periodicals, including *Business Week Careers, Country Living, Home, Mature Outlook, Redbook,* and *Walden Books Kid's Club.*

SIDELIGHTS: John Duggleby commented: "I was the first baby born in Muscatine, Iowa, on New Year's Day in 1952. I was raised in the eastern Iowa Mississippi River town of Clinton, in the same general area of rolling hills and fields that Grant Wood painted. Interestingly, *American Gothic* began to re-emerge as a cultural icon while I was growing up, so Wood became sort of an Iowa hero. Though I grew up in town, several people in my family were, or had been, farmers. My grandfather, Red Harter, gave me accounts of farming in the 'old days' that were remarkably similar to those of Wood, which I uncovered in researching *Artist in Overalls: The Life of Grant Wood.*

"I went to the University of Iowa, where Wood first sneaked into art classes, and I graduated with a degree in journalism. I went through a series of jobs in my younger days, ranging from selling sporting goods to spending a summer lobster fishing in Long Island Sound, but I have made my living as a writer for the past twenty years. I began in newspaper work, was on the staff of a travel magazine, and did creative and public relations work before creating my own company, Duggleby Communications, in 1984.

"I now live just outside Madison, Wisconsin, in a little town called McFarland. It looks much like the Wood landscapes where I grew up, except there are more lakes and Holsteins. I am a single parent with a very cool daughter, Katie.

"Although I grew up among the Wood landscapes, I was no more than mildly interested in the artist until the mid-1980s. That's when a major retrospective of his work toured the country and stopped at Chicago, where I was living. His work absolutely bowled me over, and I wanted to know more about this relative unknown who painted what is arguably the most-recognized American artwork.

"As I learned more about this unique artist and the way his childhood so profoundly shaped his work, I thought he would make an excellent subject for a children's book. Wood's approach is very populist, and his work is very approachable. Wood himself was very childlike his whole life, and was interested in turning kids and other 'typical' people on to art. He believed art is for everyone, not just for a cultural elite and that art should be fun.

"I've witnessed the truth of these assertions firsthand, because, since the book was published, I've been a frequent guest of schools and libraries doing presentations on Wood's life and work. At the end of each program we all draw a live chicken—my co-star, Henrietta—and we definitely have lots of fun!"

BIOGRAPHICAL/CRITICAL SOURCES:

PERIODICALS

Booklist, April 15, 1996, p. 1435.
Kirkus Reviews, March 1, 1996, p. 372.
Publishers Weekly, April 1, 1996, p. 77.
School Library Journal, February, 1991, p. 87; May, 1996, p. 121.

*   *   *

DUNN, John M. (III) 1949-

PERSONAL: Born September 23, 1949, in Coral Gables, FL; son of John M., Jr. (a science teacher) and Carol J. (a preschool teacher) Dunn; married, wife's name Susan L. (a media specialist), July 10, 1973; children: Colleen Amy, Bridget Eileen. *Education:* University of South Florida, B.S., 1971; attended West Georgia College, 1976; attended Central Florida Community College, 1982; studied in Sindelfingen, West Germany. *Avocational interests:* Studying German, traveling (toured nineteen countries, from Turkey to Russia to the Arctic Circle), playing the acoustic guitar, hiking, reading, gardening, "talking to interesting people."

ADDRESSES: Home and office—222 S.E. 29th Terrace, Ocala, FL 34471.

CAREER: Writer and educator. Paulding Country Junior High School, Dallas, Georgia, English teacher, 1972-76; U.S. Department of Defense American Junior High School, Stuttgart, West Germany, English teacher, 1976-80; Asheville-Buncombe County Technical College, Asheville, NC, instructor in adult education and writing, 1980-81; Osceola Middle School, Ocala, FL, English teacher, 1981-82; Forest High School, Ocala, teacher of history, sociology, law,

and ethics, 1982—. Central Florida Community College, part-time instructor for Elder Hostel and Senior Institute programs, 1990-96. *Military service:* U.S. Naval Reserve, active duty, 1971-72, honorable discharge, 1976.

WRITINGS:

First Hero (play), first produced in Gainesville, FL, by the Fable Factory (theater company), 1991.
The Russian Revolution, Lucent Books, 1994.
The Relocation of the North American Indian, Lucent Books, 1995.
The Spread of Islam, Lucent Books, 1996.
Issues in Advertising, Lucent Books, 1997.

Contributor of articles to newspapers and periodicals, including *Europe Magazine, New Shelter, Off Duty, Overseas Life, R & R Entertainment Digest, Ladycom, Military Lifestyle, Sierra, Rotarian, Executive Review, St. Petersburg Times, Florida Trend, Florida Living, View, Ocala Today, Gainesville Business, Ocala Star Banner,* and *Dekalb Literary Arts Journal.*

WORK IN PROGRESS: A history of the civil rights movement, for Lucent Books.

SIDELIGHTS: John M. Dunn commented: "Like many other authors, I have a *compulsion* to write. If a day goes by and I don't get something down on paper, I experience a pang of regret. Why so many of us writers have this nagging urge to put things down in words, I don't know, but I do know that this need to write is common to most writers.

"Since childhood, I've enjoyed writing. Unlike most of the kids in my fourth-grade class, I thought it sounded like fun when the teacher instructed us to use all our spelling words in a story. I've been that way ever since, but it was while I was in college that I discovered I had the ability to write professionally. A great writing instructor gave me the corrective criticism and encouragement to try my hand at getting published.

"Though I write mostly nonfiction today, I have done some fiction work, too. I find that the creative process needed for both forms is pretty much the same. Writers take in raw facts and impressions from real life and then recreate the material with words expressed in their own unique ways.

"Another thing I share with most writers is that I must support myself and my family with another job.

In my case, I teach high school; it's something I enjoy very much. All my adult life, in fact, I've had one foot in the world of writing, the other in education. Often my two worlds intersect. What I learn from doing research for my writing projects often finds its way into my history, law, and sociology classes. Similarly, some of the attention-getting techniques that I use as a teacher find their way into articles and books that I write.

"My humble advice to any young person wanting to become a writer is this: be in love with words, write every day, and never quit trying. Perseverance brings success."

BIOGRAPHICAL/CRITICAL SOURCES:

PERIODICALS

School Library Journal, March, 1994, p. 242; March, 1995, p. 229.

* * *

DWYER, Jim 1949-
(Junkyard Moondog)

PERSONAL: Born July 21, 1949, in Seattle, WA; son of William C. (a machinist) and Ellen D. (a homemaker) Dwyer. *Ethnicity:* "Caucasian." *Education:* University of Washington, Seattle, B.A., 1971, M.L.S., 1973. *Politics:* "Democrat/Green." *Religion:* "Pantheist." *Avocational interests:* Environmental activism, poetry, music, dance, whitewater rafting.

ADDRESSES: Home—464 East Third Ave., Chico, CA 95426. *Office*—Meriam Library, California State University, Chico, CA 95929-0295; fax 916-848-4443. *E-mail*—JDWYER@OAVAX.CSUCHICO. EDU.

CAREER: State University of New York at Albany, librarian, 1973-76; University of Oregon, Eugene, librarian, 1976-82; Northern Arizona University, Flagstaff, librarian, 1982-86; Meriam Library, California State University, Chico, head of bibliographic services, 1986—. Sacramento River Preservation Trust, member of board of directors and secretary, 1959—; Chico Natural Foods Board, vice-president, 1992-93, president, 1993-94.

MEMBER: American Library Association, Association for the Study of Literature and the Environment, Western Literature Association.

AWARDS, HONORS: Ludlow Bushmutt Creative Writing Award, University of Washington, Seattle, 1971; named poet laureate, Adedexter Theatre, Dexter, OR, 1981.

WRITINGS:

Earth Works: Recommended Fiction and Nonfiction about Nature and the Environment for Adults and Young Adults, Neal-Schuman (New York City), 1996.

Poet, under the pseudonym Junkyard Moondog. Contributor of articles and poems to periodicals. Fiction reviewer, *Library Journal;* book review editor, *Topics;* contributing editor, *Technicalities.*

WORK IN PROGRESS: Research for a collection of essays on "ecofiction."

SIDELIGHTS: Jim Dwyer told *CA:* "In 1992 I wanted to edit a collection of essays on 'ecofiction,' exploring how the environmental movement has been influenced by contemporary fiction and vice-versa. I discovered that the field of 'ecocriticism' was just being established, but that there were no standard reference books or bibliographies for this field.

"*Earth Works* began as an annotated bibliography of ecofiction and personal nature essays. At my publisher's advice it was broadened to include nonfiction. The book is intended for the use of individual activists and scholars, schools, and libraries."

E

EASLEY, MaryAnn
(MaryAnn Black)

PERSONAL: Born November 8, in Los Angeles, CA; daughter of Wendell C. (an educator) and Sarah M. (a homemaker) Black; married Robert A. Knox (marriage ended); married Richard L. Easley (a teacher); children: (first marriage) Robert, Sherry Erickson, John, Tracy. *Education:* University of Redlands, Redlands, CA, B.A.; Chapman University, Orange, CA, M.A. *Politics:* Democrat. *Religion:* Christian.

ADDRESSES: Home—Oceanside, CA. *Office*—300 Carlsbad Village Dr., Suite 108A-355, Carlsbad, CA 92008.

CAREER: Fallbrook Union Elementary School District, Camp Pendleton Marine Base, CA, elementary school teacher. Also worked as a teacher in Alaska. Worked as an editor, typesetter, and circulation manager for a regional magazine. Fished commercially for salmon along the Pacific Northwest, 1976-82.

MEMBER: Society of Children's Book Writers and Illustrators, PEN, National Writers Association, National Education Association, Publishers Marketing Association, California Teachers Association.

AWARDS, HONORS: I Am the Ice Worm was an American Library Association Best Book and a Junior Library Guild selection, both 1997.

WRITINGS:

I Am the Ice Worm, Boyds Mill Press, 1996.

Also author of audio cassette learning programs for Achievement Dynamics, including *Miss Mary's SuperPhonics, SuperPhonics Plus, The New Verbal Advantage, Verbal Advantage Plus,* and *Verbal Advantage: Student Edition.* Contributor to national and regional magazines and newspapers, sometimes under the name MaryAnn Black.

WORK IN PROGRESS: Several young adult novels.

SIDELIGHTS: MaryAnn Easley commented: "I am concentrating most of my writing efforts at present for the ten-to-fourteen age group. The stories I write feature a fourteen-year-old heroine actively involved in her own survival. My stories deal with truths. As my heroine encounters one ordeal after another, she learns about the world and about herself. It is this journey that takes her one step closer to maturity. In *I Am the Ice Worm,* when the tiny bush plane carrying my heroine to her mother in the Arctic crashes and the pilot is killed, Allison's real journey begins. She encounters a strange new world and learns the true meaning of love and home.

"I have written for as long as I can remember, before I owned a typewriter and before computers existed. I have written everything from poetry to magazine articles to learning programs, but what I like best is writing novels for the young adult."

BIOGRAPHICAL/CRITICAL SOURCES:

PERIODICALS

Booklist, October 15, 1996, p. 420.
Kirkus Reviews, August 1, 1996, p. 1152.

EDWARDS, Vince   1928-1996

PERSONAL: Born Vincente Eduardo Zoino III, July 7, 1928 (some sources say July 9), in Brooklyn, NY; died March 11, 1996, in Los Angeles, CA, of pancreatic cancer; son of Vincente (a bricklayer) and Julia Zoino; married Kathy Kersh, June 13, 1965 (divorced, October, 1965); married Linda Ann Foster, 1967 (marriage ended); married Cassandra (an actress), 1980 (marriage ended); married Janet, 1994. Children (from second and third marriages): Angela, Nicole, Devera. *Education:* East New York High School, studied aviation mechanics; attended Ohio State University, 1946-48; attended University of Hawaii, 1948; studied theater at American Academy of Dramatic Arts, New York City. *Avocational interests:* Swimming.

CAREER: Actor, director, and writer. Appeared with the Honolulu Community Theater and the University of Hawaii Players, 1948. Made Broadway debut in the chorus of *High Button Shoes,* Century Theatre, New York City, 1947. Appeared as an actor on the New York stage, 1940s, and on live television, 1950s. Signed as contract player, Paramount Pictures, 1951. Appeared in films, including *Mr. Universe,* Eagle-Lion, 1951; *Sailor Beware,* Paramount, 1951; *Hiawatha* (title role), Monogram, 1952; *Rogue Cop,* Metro-Goldwyn-Mayer (MGM), 1954; *Cell 2455, Death Row,* Columbia, 1955; *The Night Holds Terror,* Columbia, 1955; *I Am a Camera,* Directors Corporation of America, 1955; *The Killing,* United Artists (UA), 1956; *Serenade,* Warner Bros., 1956; *The Hired Gun,* MGM, 1957; *Hit and Run,* UA, 1957; *Ride Out for Revenge,* UA, 1957; *Three Faces of Eve,* Twentieth Century-Fox, 1957; *Island Women* (also known as *Island Woman*), UA, 1958.

Murder by Contract, Columbia, 1958; *City of Fear,* Columbia, 1959; *The Scavengers* (also known as *City of Sin*), Valiant/Roach, 1959; *The Outsider,* Universal, 1962; *Too Late Blues,* Paramount, 1962; *The Victors,* Columbia, 1963; *The Devil's Brigade,* UA, 1968; *The Desperadoes,* Columbia, 1968; *Hammerhead,* Columbia, 1969; *The Mad Bomber* (also known as *Police Connection* and *Detective Geronimo*), Cinemation, 1973; *The Seduction,* AVCO-Embassy, 1982; *Deal of the Century,* Warner Bros., 1983; *Space Raiders* (also known as *Star Child*), New World, 1983; *The Fix* (also known as *The Agitators*), Reverie, 1985; *Sno-Line* (also known as *Texas Sno-Line*), Vandom, 1986; *Return to Horror High,* Balcor, 1987; *Cellar Dweller,* Empire, 1988; *The Gumshoe Kid,* 1990; *Son of Darkness: To Die For II,* 1991; and *The Fear,* 1995.

Appeared in roles on television, including title role, *Ben Casey* (series), ABC, 1961-66; title role, *Matt Lincoln* (series), ABC, 1970-71; voice characterization, *Punky Brewster* (animation), NBC, 1985; voice characterization, *The Centurions—PowerXtreme!* (animation), syndicated, 1986; and title role, *The Return of Ben Casey* (television movie), syndicated, 1988. Appeared in the television miniseries *The Rhinemann Exchange,* NBC, 1977.

Appeared in television pilots, including *Dial Hot Line,* ABC, 1970; *Firehouse,* ABC, 1973; *Cover Girls,* NBC, 1977; *The Return of Mickey Spillane's Mike Hammer,* CBS, 1986; and *Knight Rider,* NBC. Appeared in episodes of the television series *Undercurrent; Fireside Theatre,* NBC; *The Untouchables,* ABC; *General Electric Theater,* CBS; *Philco Television Playhouse,* NBC; *Adventures in Paradise* (also known as *James Michener's Adventures in Paradise*), ABC; *The Deputy,* NBC; *Studio One,* CBS; and *Alfred Hitchcock Presents,* CBS/NBC.

Appeared in television movies, including *Sole Survivor,* CBS, 1970; *Do Not Fold, Spindle, or Mutilate,* ABC, 1971; *Death Stalk,* NBC, 1975; and *Evening in Byzantium,* syndicated, 1978. Appeared in television specials, including *Saga of Sonora,* NBC, 1973; *ABC's Silver Anniversary Celebration,* ABC, 1978; *Circus of the Stars,* CBS, 1979; *National Off-the-Wall People's Poll,* NBC, 1984; *You Are the Jury,* NBC, 1986; and *Lifetime Informathon* ("Surviving a Heart Attack"), Lifetime, 1988.

Director of television productions, including *The Courage and the Passion* (pilot; also creator and co-executive producer, with David Gerber), 197; episodes of *The Hardy Boys Mysteries,* ABC, 1977-79, *David Cassidy—Man Undercover,* NBC, 1978-79, *B. J. and the Bear,* NBC, 1979-80, *Battlestar Galactica,* ABC, 1978-79, *Galactica 1980,* ABC, 1980, *In the Heat of the Night,* NBC, *Fantasy Island,* ABC, *Police Story,* NBC/ABC, and *Ben Casey,* ABC. Worked as singer; made six record albums, including *Vince Edwards Sings,* and appeared in clubs in Las Vegas, NV, Los Angeles, CA, and New York City.

AWARDS, HONORS: Sour Apple Award for least cooperative interviewee, Hollywood Women's Press Club, 1965.

WRITINGS:

SCREENPLAYS

(With Christian I. Nyby II) *Mission Galactica: The Cylon Attack,* Universal, 1979.

(With Marcu Demian; and director) *Maneater* (teleplay), ABC, 1973.

SIDELIGHTS: Vince Edwards, who died of pancreatic cancer in March, 1996, will be remembered by vintage television fans for his portrayal of the title role in *Ben Casey,* a popular medical drama series which aired on ABC from 1961 to 1966. Playing the neurosurgical resident Dr. Casey, Edwards became noted for his gruff, all-business demeanor and macho swagger, which was matched by an underlying compassion for humanity and an impatience with formalities. Outwardly, the sign of these character traits was the unbuttoned white tunic which displayed actor Edwards's chest hair, and which became widely imitated. The Ben Casey character was publicly seen as contrasting with the smooth Dr. Kildare (played by Richard Chamberlain), the title character of another medical drama that achieved equal popularity during the same era. Ratings wars between the two series, and wars of popularity between the two actors on the covers of fan magazines, were frequent at the time. Edwards himself, looking back on the phenomenon in a 1988 Associated Press interview, called his sudden rise from obscurity to fame "a cultural shock." Even though he was not well-known before 1961 Edwards had been a frequent presence on both the large and small screens.

Edwards was born in Brooklyn, New York, where he was christened Vincente Eduardo Zoino, the seventh child of an Italian-American bricklayer in a tough neighborhood. Although a skillful street-fighter as a youth, he wisely heeded his mother's advice to stay out of trouble, and turned his physical prowess toward swimming. At a New York Metropolitan championship meet where Edwards won the 100-yard backstroke, a swimming coach from Ohio State University spotted him and offered a scholarship. Entranced by swimming, Edwards transferred to the University of Hawaii after two years, but an attack of appendicitis ended his collegiate swimming career. By that time, he had already begun appearing in student and community theatrical productions, where his rugged good looks and athletic build helped make him a leading man.

Edwards returned to New York City to study acting at the American Academy of Dramatic Arts and began a long apprenticeship. As a working actor, he appeared in musicals, live television dramas, and many B-movies, the latter for Paramount, where he signed a contract in 1951. He also appeared in a handful of classic movies, such as director Stanley Kubrick's film noir *The Killing* (1956) and the award-winning drama *Three Faces of Eve* (1957). Ironically, Edwards's big break came at a time when he had "gone to ground," in the words of a *London Times* obituary, and was spending his time racing motorcycles. The producer of *Ben Casey,* James Moser, was looking for a rugged, sexy actor to play the title role, and was given Edwards's name by his agent; only with some searching was the obscure actor found at Malibu Beach.

After the finale of *Ben Casey* in 1966, Edwards's career declined, but he remained busy. His singing appearances in clubs were successful, and he recorded six albums. A second try at a series title role, *Matt Lincoln,* lasted one year, with Edwards playing a psychiatrist who runs a hotline for inner-city teens. He appeared in numerous television shows, including pilots, series episodes, and specials; the 1978 *Evening in Byzantium* was a notable television movie in which Edwards appeared. As director, Edwards guided episodes of various series, including *B. J. and the Bear, Fantasy Island, In the Heat of the Night,* and *Police Story.* He created and co-produced a prospective series, the *The Courage and the Passion,* the pilot of which he also directed. He coauthored a theatrical screenplay, the *Mission Galactica: The Cylon Attack,* and a TV script, the *Maneater.*

Edwards's life in later years was made difficult by a series of broken marriages and a gambling habit. However, his fourth marriage, in 1994, brought him fulfillment. He was able to reduce his gambling to a weekly poker game, where his tablemates included Sid Caesar and Milton Berle. He faced his brief final illness with courage, wishing to be seen as a role model; according to his wife Janet, quoted in *People* magazine, "he kept saying 'I love you' and blowing kisses" at the point of death. His manager, T. J. Castronovo, called Edwards "a sweetheart" and "really an easygoing guy"—a contrast to Edwards's gruff screen persona.

BIOGRAPHICAL/CRITICAL SOURCES:

Contemporary Theatre, Film, and Television, Volume 7, Gale (Detroit), 1989, pp. 113-114.

OBITUARIES:

PERIODICALS

Chicago Tribune, March 13, 1996, sec. 3, p. 14.
New York Times, March 13, 1996, p. B9.
People, March 25, 1996, p. 59.
Times (London), March 14, 1996, p. 23.
Washington Post, March 13, 1996, p. B4.*

*   *   *

EHRENBERG, John   1944-

PERSONAL: Born October 2, 1944, in New York, NY; son of Robert (a general contractor in the construction business) and Janice (a homemaker; maiden name, Dryfoos) Ehrenberg; married Kathleen Golding, November 16, 1968; children: Cassie, David. *Ethnicity:* "White." *Education:* Dartmouth College, B.A., 1965; Stanford University, M.A., Ph.D., 1975. *Politics:* "Left-socialist." *Avocational interests:* Baseball.

ADDRESSES: Home—474 13th St., Brooklyn, NY 11215. *Office*—Department of Political Science, Long Island University, Brooklyn, NY 11201; fax 718-488-1086. *E-mail*—jehrenbe@hornet.liunet.edu.

CAREER: University of New Mexico, Albuquerque, assistant professor of political science, 1972-77; St. John's University, New York City, assistant professor of political science, 1977-80; Long Island University, Brooklyn, NY, associate professor, 1980-85, professor of political science, 1985—.

MEMBER: International Political Science Association, American Political Science Association, Caucus for a New Political Science (president, 1994-96).

WRITINGS:

The Dictatorship of the Proletariat, Routledge & Kegan Paul, 1992.
Proudhon and His Age, Humanities (Atlantic Highlands, NJ), 1996.

Contributor of more than a dozen articles to scholarly journals.

WORK IN PROGRESS: A Critique of Civil Society, publication by Routledge & Kegan Paul expected in 1998.

*   *   *

ELIE, Lolis Eric   1963-

PERSONAL: Born April 10, 1963, in New Orleans, LA; son of Lolis Edward and Geri (Moore) Elie. *Education:* University of Pennsylvania, B.S., 1985; Columbia University, M.A., 1986; University of Virginia, M.F.A., 1991.

ADDRESSES: Home—P.O. Box 50160, New Orleans, LA 70150-0160. *Office*—3800 Howard Ave., New Orleans, LA, 70140. *E-mail*—TPElie@aol.com.

CAREER: Atlanta Journal, Atlanta, GA, staff writer, 1986-89; *Callaloo,* Charlottesville, VA, assistant managing editor, 1989-90; University of Virginia, Charlottesville, instructor of English, 1989-90; freelance journalist, 1986—; Wynton Marsalis Enterprises, Inc., New York City, road manager, 1991-93; *The Times-Picayune,* New Orleans, LA, metro columnist, 1995—.

WRITINGS:

Smokestack Lightning: Adventures in the Heart of Barbecue Country, photographs by Frank Stewart, Farrar, Straus (New York City), 1995.

Contributor to the anthology *That's What I Like about the South,* 1993. Contributor to periodicals, including *African American Review, Black Enterprise, Businessweek Careers,* and *Advertising Age.*

SIDELIGHTS: "Whenever pork and people come together," Lolis Eric Elie notes in his 1995 travel book *Smokestack Lightning: Adventures in the Heart of Barbecue Country,* "the rich people will end up with the hams and chops and the poor people will end up with the ribs, lips, foots, and chitterlings." Comparisons such as these are not new in literature; many writers have explored the relationship between food and society. Still, Elie finds a relatively unexplored niche for his musings: the uniquely American tradition of barbecue.

The inspiration for *Smokestack Lightning* came about during Elie's long sojourn through the American

Midwest and South while he served as musician Wynton Marsalis's road manager. He and his partner for *Smokestack Lightning,* photographer Frank Stewart, who was also a member of the Marsalis entourage, profess to have eaten so much barbecue over the course of that tour that a book on the subject seemed obligatory. While conducting research for the book, the coauthors returned to the heart of the barbecue belt, crossing from the Carolinas to Texas in Elie's beat-up Volvo, interviewing restaurateurs, touring famous and infamous barbecue havens, and constantly dining on countless barbecue dishes.

Like many other genuine remnants of Americana, barbecue inspires an almost religious fervor among its devotees. Elie and Stewart discuss a variety of barbecue-related subjects in *Smokestack Lightning,* from the preparation of the food itself to the various and distinct regional cultures of which barbecue is a part. According to critics, this breadth is the book's greatest strength and weakness, for while the authors "present . . . passionate and vivid profiles of individual restaurants and barbecue joints," according to *Library Journal*'s John Charles, they sometimes overwhelm the reader with detail.

For example, the authors delineate the often grisly process of preparing beef—specifically, cows' faces—and pork—including hogs' heads and intestines—for cooking, providing enough detail to make casual eaters consider avoiding barbecue altogether. As one critic noted in a *Publishers Weekly* review, "a little barbecue research, like barbecue itself, goes a long way."

Still, Elie succeeded in exploring the legend, lore, and tradition of barbecue. Dwight Garner declared in a review for *Salon* that Elie and Stewart "deliver some fine writing about what barbecue and its history have to say about race and class in America."

BIOGRAPHICAL/CRITICAL SOURCES:

PERIODICALS

Library Journal, June 15, 1996, p. 85.
Publishers Weekly, April 1, 1996, p. 66.

OTHER

Salon, http://www.salonmagazine.com, June 20, 1996.

*   *   *

EMERT, Phyllis R(aybin)   1947-

PERSONAL: Born May 2, 1947, in Philadelphia, PA; married Larry Emert (an administrative law judge), August 15, 1971; children: Melissa, Matt. *Education:* State University of New York at Stony Brook, B.A., 1969; Pennsylvania State University, M.A., 1971.

ADDRESSES: Home—Alta Loma, CA.

CAREER: Writer, 1975—. Suffolk County Department of Social Services, Bay Shore, NY, social caseworker for unmarried parents in Children's Division, 1969-70; National Association of Social Workers, Suffolk County Chapter, Huntington, NY, administrative assistant, 1971; University of California, Davis, administrative and project assistant in psychiatry, 1972; Yolo County Department of Public Welfare, Woodland, CA, eligibility worker in income maintenance, 1972; Yolo County Youth Services Bureau, Woodland, director, 1972-74.

WRITINGS:

FOR YOUNG PEOPLE

Jane Frederick, Pentathlon Champion, Harvey House (New York City), 1981.
The Illustrated Track and Field Dictionary for Young People, Harvey House, 1981.
Guide Dog, Crestwood House (Mankato, MN), 1985.
Hearing-Ear Dog, Crestwood House, 1985.
Search and Rescue Dog, Crestwood House, 1985.
Sled Dog, Crestwood House, 1985.
Military Dog, Crestwood House, 1985.
Law Enforcement Dog, Crestwood House, 1985.
Great Sports Heroes: Quarterbacks, Tor Books (New York City), 1989.
Great Sports Heroes: Running Backs, Tor Books, 1989.
Great Sports Heroes: Hitters, Tor Books, 1990.
Great Sports Heroes: Pitchers, Tor Books, 1990.
Mysteries of Ships and Planes, Tor Books, 1990.
Monsters, Strange Dreams, and UFOs, Tor Books, 1990.
Fighter Planes, Messner (New York City), 1990.
Transports and Bombers, Messner, 1990.
Helicopters, Messner, 1990.
Special Task Aircraft, Messner, 1990.
Sports Cars, Think Street (Indianapolis, IN), 1990.
Classic Cars, Think Street, 1990.
Fighters, Think Street, 1990.

Bombers, Think Street, 1990.
Mysteries of People and Places, Tor Books, 1992.
Ghosts, Hauntings, and Mysterious Happenings, Tor Books, 1992.
Mysteries of Bizarre Animals and Freaks of Nature, Tor Books, 1994.
Mysteries of Space and the Universe, Tor Books, 1994.
Mysteries of Strange Appearances From Beyond, Tor Books, 1995.
Mysteries of the Mind and Senses, Tor Books, 1995.
Women in the Civil War: Warriors, Patriots, Nurses, and Spies, Discovery Enterprises (Lowell, MA), 1995.
All That Glitters: The Men and Women of the Gold and Silver Rushes, Discovery Enterprises, 1995.
Colonial Triangular Trade: An Economy Based on Human Misery, Discovery Enterprises, 1995.
The Twenty-Five Scariest Places in the World, Lowell House (Los Angeles, CA), 1995.
Top Lawyers and Their Famous Cases, Oliver Press (Minneapolis, MN), 1996.
True Valor: World War II, Lowell House, 1996.
On the Homefront: World War II, Discovery Enterprises, 1996.
World War II: The European Theatre, Discovery Enterprises, 1996.
The Book of Nightmares, Roxbury Park Publishers, 1997.
Mysteries of Lost and Hidden Treasure, Tor Books, 1997.
Frightening Phantoms and Haunted Habitats, Tor Books, 1997.

OTHER

The Pretzel Book (for adults), Woodsong Graphics (New Hope, PA), 1984.

Contributor of stories to magazines, including *Hopscotch.*

SIDELIGHTS: Phyllis R. Emert commented: "From the time I was in the second grade, I knew I wanted to become a writer. That's why I take kids seriously when they tell me their plans for the future. I've written about animals, automobiles, airplanes, sports heroes, ghosts, mysteries, monsters, and historical figures and events. I try to listen to what kids have to say about what they like to read. It's especially worthwhile when I receive fan letters from young readers all over the country. These letters help me keep on top of what our young people consider to be

important. I've always tried to entertain my readers and hope they learn something along the way.

"One of my biggest thrills as a writer came when I saw my recent book *Top Lawyers and Their Famous Cases* in the gift shop of the United States Supreme Court."

BIOGRAPHICAL/CRITICAL SOURCES:

PERIODICALS

Booklist, September 1, 1996, p. 71.
School Library Journal, December, 1981, p. 85; August, 1986, p. 91; March, 1996, p. 203.
Wilson Library Bulletin, March, 1995, p. 111.

*　*　*

ERSKINE, John   1879-1951

PERSONAL: Born October 5, 1879, in New York, NY; died of a heart attack, June 2, 1951, in New York, NY; son of James Morrison (a textile merchant) and Eliza Jane Hollingsworth Erskine; married Pauline Ives (divorced, 1945); married Helen Worden (a journalist), c. 1946; two children from first marriage. *Education:* Columbia University, B.A., 1900, M.A., 1901, Ph.D., 1903, LL.D., 1929.

CAREER: Music educator and critic, and novelist. Amherst College, Amherst, MA, instructor in English, 1903-09; Columbia University, New York City, professor of English, 1909-37. Played as a soloist on piano with the New York Symphony Orchestra and Baltimore Civic Orchestra; Juilliard School of Music, New York City, president, 1928-37; Juilliard Music Foundation, president, 1948-51; Metropolitan Opera Foundation, director, 1935.

MEMBER: French Legion of Honor (officer).

AWARDS, HONORS: Received honorary degrees from Amherst College, 1923, University of Bordeaux, France, 1929, Rollins College, 1931, and Cornell College, 1935.

WRITINGS:

The Elizabethan Lyric, Macmillan (New York), 1903, Folcroft Library Editions (Folcroft, PA), 1974.

Actaeon, and Other Poems, Lane (New York), 1907.

Leading American Novelists, Holt (New York), 1910, Books for Libraries Press (Freeport, NY), 1966.

(With Helen Erskine) *Written English: A Guide to the Rules of Composition,* Century, (New York), 1910.

(With W. P. Trent) *Great American Writers,* Holt (New York), 1912.

The Moral Obligation to Be Intelligent, and Other Essays, Duffield (New York), 1915, revised edition published by Davies (London), 1921, reprinted by Books for Libraries Press (Freeport, NY), 1969.

The Shadowed Hour, Lyric (New York), 1917.

Democracy and Ideals, Doran (New York), 1920.

Hearts Enduring: A Play in One Scene, Duffield (New York), 1920.

The Kinds of Poetry, and Other Essays, Duffield (New York), 1920.

Collected Poems, 1907-1922, Duffield (New York), 1922.

The Literary Discipline, Duffield (New York), 1923, Books for Libraries Press (Freeport, NY), 1969.

The Private Life of Helen of Troy, Bobbs-Merrill (Indianapolis), 1925.

Sonata, and Other Poems, Duffield (New York), 1925.

Galahad: Enough of His Life to Explain His Reputation, Bobbs-Merrill (Indianapolis), 1926.

Adam and Eve: Though He Knew Better, Bobbs-Merrill (Indianapolis), 1927.

American Character, and Other Essays, Chautauqua Press, (Chautauqua, NY), 1927.

Prohibition and Christianity, and Other Paradoxes of the American Spirit, Bobbs-Merrill (Indianapolis), 1927.

The Delight of Great Books, Bobbs-Merrill (Indianapolis), 1928, Scholarly Press (St. Clair Shores, MI), 1974.

Penelope's Man: The Homing Instinct, Bobbs-Merrill (Indianapolis), 1928.

Sincerity, a Story of Our Time, Bobbs-Merrill (Indianapolis), 1929.

Cinderella's Daughter, and Other Sequels and Consequences, Bobbs-Merrill (Indianapolis), 1930.

Uncle Sam in the Eyes of His Family, Bobbs-Merrill (Indianapolis), 1930.

Unfinished Business, Bobbs-Merrill (Indianapolis), 1930.

Tristan and Isolde: Restoring Palamede, Bobbs-Merrill (Indianapolis), 1932.

Bachelor—Of Arts, Bobbs-Merrill (Indianapolis), 1934.

(Author of libretto) *Helen Retires: An Opera in Three Acts,* music by George Antheil, Bobbs-Merrill (Indianapolis), 1934.

Forget If You Can, Bobbs-Merrill (Indianapolis and New York), 1935.

Solomon, My Son!, Bobbs-Merrill (Indianapolis and New York), 1935.

The Influence of Women and Its Cure, Bobbs-Merrill (Indianapolis and New York), 1936.

Young Love: Variations on a Theme, Bobbs-Merrill (New York), 1936.

The Brief Hour of Francois Villon, Bobbs-Merrill (Indianapolis and New York), 1937.

The Start of the Road, Stokes (New York), 1938.

Give Me Liberty: The Story of an Innocent Bystander, Stokes (New York), 1940.

Casanova's Women: Eleven Moments of a Year, Stokes (New York), 1941.

Mrs. Dorratt, Stokes (New York and Toronto), 1941.

Song Without Words: The Story of Felix Mendelssohn, Messner (New York), 1941.

The Complete Life, Messner (New York), 1943, Books for Libraries Press (Freeport, NY), 1971.

The Philharmonic-Symphony Society of New York: Its First Hundred Years, Macmillan (New York), 1943.

The Voyage of Captain Bart, Lippincott (Philadelphia and New York), 1943.

What Is Music?, Lippincott (Philadelphia and New York), 1944.

The Human Life of Jesus, Morrow (New York), 1945.

The Memory of Certain Persons, Lippincott (Philadelphia and New York), 1947.

My Life as a Teacher, Lippincott (Philadelphia), 1948.

Venus, the Lonely Goddess, Morrow (New York), 1949.

My Life in Music, Morrow (New York), 1950, Greenwood Press (Westport, CT), 1973.

Also author of the short story "Cannibal King" published in *Second Mercury Story Book,* Longmans, Green (London), 1931; and author of "Remember the Sabbath Day, to Keep It Holy" published in *The Ten Commandments: Ten Short Novels of Hitler's War Against the Moral Code,* edited by Amin L. Robinson, Simon & Schuster (New York), 1943.

EDITOR

(Also author of notes and introduction) *Selections from Spenser's The Faerie Queen,* Longmans, Green (New York), 1905.

Selections from Tennyson's Idylls of the King, Holt (New York), 1912.

(Also author of introduction) Lafcadio Hearn, *Interpretations of Literature,* Dodd, Mead (New York), 1915.

(Also author of introduction) Lafcadio Hearn, *Appreciations of Poetry,* Dodd, Mead (New York), 1916.

(Also author of introduction) Lafcadio Hearn, *Life and Literature,* Dodd, Mead (New York), 1917, Books for Libraries Press (Freeport, NY), 1969.

(With William Peterfield Trent, Stuart P. Sherman, and Carl Van Doren) *The Cambridge History of American Literature,* four volumes, Putnam's (New York), 1917-21.

(Also author of introduction) Lafcadio Hearn, *Talks to Writers,* Dodd, Mead (New York), 1920, reprint, Books for Libraries Press (Freeport, NY), 1967.

(Also author of introduction) Lafcadio Hearn, *Books and Habits,* Dodd, Mead (New York), 1921.

(Also author of introduction) Lafcadio Hearn, *Pre-Raphaelite and Other Poets,* Dodd, Mead (New York), 1922, Books for Libraries Press (Freeport, NY), 1968.

(Also author of introduction) *A Musical Companion: A Guide to the Understanding and Enjoyment of Music,* Knopf (New York), 1935.

SIDELIGHTS: John Erskine excelled in a number of scholarly fields before his death in 1951. A popular professor of English at Columbia University for many years, Erskine was also an accomplished pianist who played as a soloist with several prominent orchestras; he later served as president of the prestigious Juilliard School. The titles listed under Erskine's name give evidence to a similarly wide range of interests. Early in his career as a writer, he penned essays and criticism of literary topics, later expanding into explorations of general social issues. He also translated plays and the works of others. Mid-career, Erskine resumed his study of the piano and became a well-regarded soloist; this point roughly coincided with his turn to fiction as a literary medium. He penned several "re-creations" of traditional tales or myths from history, giving them an innovative revamping that won their author both critical and commercial success.

Erskine was spent nearly all of his life in New York City. Born in 1879, the son of a textile merchant, he studied piano from his youth but pursuing this talent as a career was discouraged by his father. Erskine earned three degrees from Columbia University in quick succession, concluding with a Ph.D. in 1903. (He would later earn a law degree from his alma mater at the age of fifty.) Securing a teaching position at Massachusetts's Amherst College, he spent six years there but returned to New York City when Columbia hired him for its faculty in 1909. His classes were favorites among undergraduates because of his broad approach to the study of literature, combining it with matters of philosophy and history. By this point Erskine had begun to write poetry and scholarly essays, efforts published in the form of 1907's *Actaeon, and Other Poems* and *Leading American Novelists,* issued in 1910; he also edited works such as 1912's *Selections from Tennyson's Idylls of the King* and other literary volumes.

Erskine's examination of literary topics evolved into a wider exploration of social issues, reflecting the approach he took in his teaching career. He wrote numerous works on social and moral topics. These appeared as 1915's *The Moral Obligation to Be Intelligent, and Other Essays* and *Democracy and Ideals,* published in 1920. The World War I era also marked the beginning of a new project for Erskine, who was gaining acclaim in his field. He compiled and edited several volumes of writings and lectures by the American scholar Lafcadio Hearn, a writer of the macabre who left the U.S. in 1890 for Tokyo. Hearn had died in 1904, but his radical ideas—which stressed an emotional response to literature, as opposed to a purely academic one—and Erskine's editorship and introductory essays to *Interpretations of Literature* (1915), *Appreciations of Poetry* (1916), and *Life and Literature* (1917) introduced Hearn's views to the American literary public. They were followed by three other volumes, for which Erskine also served as editor and penned an introductory essay—*Talks to Writers* (1920), *Books and Habits* (1921), and *Pre-Raphaelite and Other Poets* (1922).

Erskine continued to expand his horizons, even as he entered middle age in the 1920s. After returning to the study of the piano with private teachers, he attained such a mastery that he was soon invited to solo with prominent musical bodies such as the New York Symphony Orchestra. Still a professor at Columbia, he also turned to the novel form and won great fame with his first attempt. *The Private Life of Helen of Troy,* published in 1925, posited the story of the infamous Greek mythic figure whose beauty was said to have launched the Trojan War. The novel takes place after Helen has returned home and primarily through dialogue between the frivolous Helen and her sober daughter. The work, wrote Lois Bragg in an essay on Erskine for *Dictionary of Literary Biography,* Volume 9, "is praiseworthy for its pervasive humor, a quality which had often been noted in Erskine's essays." Bragg also said that the protofeminist, generational conflict between Helen and her daughter was presented "in a way that readers in 1925 found decidedly modern."

Erskine repeated this formula of reprising historical tales and providing a more commonplace fictional "sequel," presenting what might have really happened, with several other titles. In 1926, *Galahad: Enough of His Life to Explain His Reputation* presented the exemplary Knight of King Arthur's Round Table as small-minded; *Adam and Eve: Though He Knew Better,* published in 1927, and the following year's *Penelope's Man: The Homing Instinct* were received less enthusiastically by critics.

Erskine continued in his teaching career at Columbia, played the piano, and took on the presidency of the Juilliard School of Music for a decade. He also earned a law degree in 1929. By this point he had ventured into more traditional fiction with works such as *Bachelor—Of Arts,* the 1934 tale of a Columbia undergraduate, and *The Brief Hour of Francois Villon,* a 1937 work based on a true story. Villon was both a crook and a poet who disappeared in 1463; Erskine's tale posits that he reinvented himself as a small-town notary. In 1938's *The Start of the Road,* Erskine sketches a young Walt Whitman in love in New Orleans in 1848.

After retiring from Columbia in 1937, Erskine continued to write prolifically. These include novels such as *Mrs. Dorratt* and biographies including *Song Without Words: The Story of Felix Mendelssohn,* both published in 1941; he also contributed a chapter to the 1943 cautionary tale, *The Ten Commandments: Ten Short Novels of Hitler's War Against the Moral Code.* Other contributors included Rebecca West and Thomas Mann; Erskine's inclusion "testifies to his reputation as a writer at the time," wrote Leonard Mustazza in an essay for *Dictionary of Literary Biography,* Volume 102. Before his death in 1951, Erskine completed four volumes of autobiography.

BIOGRAPHICAL/CRITICAL SOURCES:

BOOKS

Dictionary of Literary Biography, Volume 9: *American Novelists, 1910-1945,* edited by James J. Martine, Gale (Detroit, MI), 1981, and Volume 102: *American Short Story Writers, 1910-1945 (Second Series),* edited by Bobby Ellen Kimbel, Gale, 1991.*

* * *

ESPADA, Martin 1957-

PERSONAL: Born in 1957; son of Frank Espada.

ADDRESSES: Home—10 Lilac Ct., Cambridge, MA 02141. *Office*—Dept. of English, Bartlett Hall, University of Massachusetts, Amherst, MA 01003.

CAREER: Has worked as an attorney; University of Massachusetts, Amherst, English instructor.

AWARDS, HONORS: PEN/Revson Award, 1989, for *Rebellion Is the Circle of a Lover's Hands.*

WRITINGS:

POETRY

The Immigrant Iceboy's Bolero, with photographs by father, Frank Espada, Ghost Pony Press (Madison, WI), 1982.
Trumpets From the Islands of Their Eviction (includes "Trumpets From the Islands of Their Eviction," "Tiburon," "The Policeman's Ball," and "From an Island You Cannot Name"), Bilingual Press (Tempe, AZ), 1987; expanded edition, 1994.
Rebellion Is the Circle of a Lover's Hands (includes "Portrait of a Real Hijo de Puta," "The Savior is Abducted in Puerto Rico," "Jorge the Janitor Finally Quits," and "Cusin and Tata"), Curbstone Press (Willimantic, CT), 1990.
City of Coughing and Dead Radiators: Poems (includes "Coca-Cola and Coco Frio," "The Skull Beneath the Skin," and "When Songs Become Water"), Norton (New York, NY), 1993.
(Editor) *Poetry Like Bread: Poets of the Political Imagination From Curbstone Press,* Curbstone Press, 1994.
Imagine the Angels of Bread: Poems, Norton, 1996.

Also contributor to periodicals, including *Harper's, Progressive, Nation,* and *Ploughshares.*

SIDELIGHTS: Attorney, educator, and poet Martin Espada has dedicated much of his varied career to

Hispanic and other socially liberal causes. His critically acclaimed collections of poetry celebrate—or, in some cases, lament—the Hispanic experience. Whether it be Puerto Ricans and Chicanos adjusting to life in the United States, or Central and South American Latinos struggling against their own repressive governments to achieve social justice, Espada has put their "otherness," their powerlessness, poverty and enmity into verse. Espada's *Rebellion Is the Circle of a Lover's Hands,* earned him the 1990 PEN/Revson Award and the Paterson Poetry Prize.

Espada's first published book of poetry was 1982's *The Immigrant Iceboy's Bolero,* which was enhanced by photographs taken by his father, Puerto Rican-born Frank Espada. More widely reviewed, however, was his second collection, 1987's *Trumpets From the Island of Their Eviction.* Published with facing pages of Spanish translation by Arizona's Bilingual Press, *Trumpets* featured poems such as "Tiburon," which compares the United States' assimilation of Puerto Rico to a shark eating a fisherman; "The Policeman's Ball," which chants the tale of police brutality to a cadence; and "From an Island You Cannot Name," about an aged Puerto Rican veteran furious at his categorization as a negro by hospital authorities. There is also, the title poem, which includes a segment in which a Hispanic woman is evicted by her landlord after she sends him the ten mice she caught in her apartment, sealed in individual sandwich bags.

Linda Frost, critiquing *Trumpets From the Islands of Their Eviction* in the *Minnesota Review,* explained her view of Espada's poetic intent: "Espada uses his characters as excavated archetypes, cultural heroes who give names and faces to the members of this ignored community who have been 'evicted' from their original home of Puerto Rico . . . and their not-so-friendly new home in the United States." Frost went on to observe that "through both his swift kicks in our reading behinds and his detailed narratives, Espada takes us by the hand and leads us straight into the core of boredom, poverty, hostility and violence. He indeed gives a voice to the silenced, gathering together the tales of the ignored and forcing us to see the faces in the crowd." Noting that the poet aims his work at both English and Spanish speakers, she ended by declaring that "Espada writes to stir up the blood of those in despair and those in ignorance, and in these goals, he is indeed quite successful." Mireya Perez-Erdelyi, reviewing *Trumpets From the Islands of Their Eviction* in *Americas,* asserted that

the collection "demonstrates how a people survive in spite of the harshness and squalor of their reality." She concluded that *"Trumpets* moves us to take notice, to care, as the song of the victims of political and social oppression is played. It is a powerful song we cannot ignore."

The poet's next effort proved to be award-winning. The book's title, *Rebellion Is the Circle of a Lover's Hands* is taken from a poem in which a woman continues moving her hands with circular motions to complete the sewing of her wedding dress, though she has just learned her fiance has been killed. Other poems in *Rebellion* include "Portrait of a Real Hijo de Puta." The Spanish words of the title translate as "son of a whore," a common Spanish epithet, but Espada takes it literally, and discusses the life of a boy whose mother is a drug-addicted prostitute. "The Savior is Abducted in Puerto Rico" illustrates the metaphorical effects of the theft of a statue of a crucified Jesus from a Puerto Rican church, while in "Jorge the Church Janitor Finally Quits," a Honduran immigrant ponders the possibility that his white employers identify him completely with his mop. "Cusin and Tata" is a poem about Espada's own aunt and grandmother, who remained in Puerto Rico and survived abusive husbands and abandonment.

Roger Gilbert, taking notice of *Rebellion Is the Circle of a Lover's Hands* in the *Partisan Review,* reported that it is "continually informed by anger at social and economic injustices. This anger gives the book considerable moral urgency." Alan Gilbert, writing in the *Boston Review,* proclaimed that "the individuality of Espada's voice is one to which any attentive reader can respond. These poems deserve an audience." John Bradley in the *Bloomsbury Review* praised "the expansive humanity of Espada's vision" and his use of "the blade of humor." Leslie Ullman in the *Kenyon Review* concluded of *Rebellion* that "the poems in this collection tell their stories and flesh out their characters deftly, without shrillness or rhetoric, and vividly enough to invite the reader into a shared sense of loss."

In 1993's *City of Coughing and Dead Radiators: Poems,* Espada uses a more bitingly humorous approach to get his points across. "Coca-Cola and Coco Frio" is an autobiographical poem in which the young Espada on his first visit to relatives in Puerto Rico discovers he prefers cold coconut milk to cola, while the islanders have forsaken their more healthy native beverage for the exotic foreignness of soft drinks. "Skull Beneath the Skin" compares mangoes to the piled skulls of the victims of El Salvadoran death squads, and another poem, from the volume's last section "When Songs Become Water," features an ex-mental patient trying to make contact with an alien spaceship. According to Perez-Erdelyi, this time offering her opinions in the *Voice Literary Supplement,* the poet of *City of Coughing and Dead Radiators* "cuts like a sword through the submerged layers of conquest, colonialism, diaspora, violence, and madness to create supremely gutsy poems." Bessy Reyna, critiquing the same collection in the *MultiCultural Review,* judged that "Espada continues to give us poems that speak directly to the heart of the Latina/o community in the U.S., while reaching the hearts of everyone else, creating a bridge of understanding between all cultures."

Espada edited the 1994 anthology *Poetry Like Bread: Poets of the Political Imagination* for Curbstone Press. The poets included in this anthology hail from all areas of North and South America; many of them are Hispanic. They range from El Salvador's Roque Dalton, to Guatemala's Otto Rene Castillo, to Haiti's Paul Laraque, to Los Angeles' Luis Rodriguez. While noting the "diversity" of the poetic voices in the anthology, Chris Faatz in the *American Book Review* testified that "they all share one thing, an intense passion for justice." Faatz went on to applaud *Poetry Like Bread* as "art at its most meaningful and powerful; *this* is the embodiment of the 'artistry of dissent.'"

Imagine the Angels of Bread, another volume of Espada's own poetry, became available to readers in 1996. The book includes an elegy to Clemente Soto Velez, a Puerto Rican nationalist, and other poems between its covers tell of poor education in anachronous schools, and the violence encountered by Puerto Rican-Americans in prison. Barbara Hoffert in the *Library Journal* lauded Espada's "brutal and luminescent" language and pronounced the poet "able to take raw experience, and without losing the rawness distill it to a few lines."

BIOGRAPHICAL/CRITICAL SOURCES:

PERIODICALS

American Book Review, March/May, 1995, p. 9.
Americas, summer, 1990, pp. 119-121.
Bloomsbury Review, March, 1991, p. 5.
Boston Review, October, 1991, p. 29.
Kenyon Review, summer, 1992, p. 174-187.
Library Journal, June 1, 1996, p. 112.

Minnesota Review, fall, 1991, pp. 129-135.
MultiCultural Review, March, 1994, p. 74.
Partisan Review, winter, 1994, pp. 180-186.
Publishers Weekly, October 12, 1990, p .57.
Voice Literary Supplement, November, 1994, p. 16.*

—Sketch by Elizabeth Wenning

* * *

ESTEP, Maggie 1962(?)-

PERSONAL: Born c. 1962.

ADDRESSES: Agent—c/o Harmony Books, 201 East 50th St., New York, NY 10022.

CAREER: Writer; performance and recording artist. Has recorded the albums *No More Mr. Nice Girl,* c. 1994, and *Love Is a Dog from Hell,* Mouth Almighty Records, c. 1997. Has been variously employed, including as a maid for Holiday Inn. Appeared on Music Television (MTV) series *Spoken Word.*

WRITINGS:

Diary of an Emotional Idiot (novel), Harmony (New York), 1997.

SIDELIGHTS: Performance artist Maggie Estep has extended her opportunities for self-expression into the genres of sound recording and fiction. She has appeared on the Music Television (MTV) series *Spoken Word,* and released the albums *No More Mr. Nice Girl* and *Love Is a Dog From Hell.* In 1997 her first novel, the semi-autobiographical *Diary of an Emotional Idiot,* was published.

In *Diary of an Emotional Idiot,* readers meet protagonist Zoe as she lies in wait for her ex-boyfriend—whom she calls "Satan"—in his closet. She intends to tie him up with a bicycle chain and force him to perform degrading acts, but while Zoe waits for the right moment, she tells the story of her life. Details include her two main present means of earning a living—writing pornographic novels and serving as a receptionist for an agency offering dominatrix services—and incidents from her past. The latter range from her well-traveled childhood with her promiscuous father, to cleaning out her dealer's cat's litter box for free drugs, to whiling away her time in a rehabilitation facility by having sex on the bathroom floor. Zoe also describes her history with "Satan," who apparently broke up with her the day after her father was buried.

Diary of an Emotional Idiot has brought Estep accolades from critics. Though Meg Cohen Ragas in the internet magazine *Salon* labeled the book "yet another tale of love gone wrong too many times," she noted that it "is saved by its fierce irreverence, razor-sharp humor and the simple fact that it doesn't take itself too seriously." Sybil Steinberg of *Publishers Weekly* praised *Diary* as "a clever and cynical take on a young woman's life on the edge of urban society." Kevin Grandfield, writing in *Booklist,* responded favorably to the novel as well, concluding that "Zoe's story reminds the reader just how magical and random every person's journey is."

To a great extent, Estep's second album, 1997's *Love Is a Dog from Hell,* ties in with *Diary of an Emotional Idiot.* One track on *Love Is a Dog from Hell* is labeled "I'm an Emotional Idiot," and in a commentary offered on an internet web page for Mouth Almighty Records, Estep explained her feelings about various parts of the album. She stated that the first track, "Master of Lunacy" is "also sort of a plot synopsis of my novel." Of the next, "I'm an Emotional Idiot," Estep revealed that a friend told her "it ought to be the theme song for borderline personality disorder. He's right." Another piece, "Scab Maids on Speed," is excerpted from *Diary of an Emotional Idiot,* and stems from Estep's experiences working as a maid at a Holiday Inn. Noting its relation to her novel, she urged her audience to "rush out and buy" the book, "so that my future as an old cantankerous novelist is assured." Yet another track on the album is called "Stalk Me"; of this effort Estep commented: "My friend Jenny is really worried that people are going to follow me around and send me dead animal parts and doll heads as a result of this song but please, if you feel inclined to send me dead animal parts, think it through."

BIOGRAPHICAL/CRITICAL SOURCES:

PERIODICALS

Booklist, March 1, 1997, pp. 1109-1110.
Publishers Weekly, February 10, 1997, p. 68.

OTHER

Mouth Almighty Records, http://www.mouthalmighty
    .com/maggie1.htm, August, 1997.

Salon, http://www.salonmagazine.com/march97/sne
    aks/sneak970317.html, March, 1997.*

*   *   *

ESTEVEZ, Emilio 1962-

PERSONAL: Born May 12, 1962, in New York, NY; son of Martin (an actor; original surname, Estevez) and Janet Sheen; married Paula Abdul (divorced); children: Taylor, Paloma. *Education:* Graduated from Santa Monica High School, Santa Monica, CA.

ADDRESSES: Agent—Andrea Jaffe, Inc., 9229 Sunset Blvd., Suite 401, Los Angeles, CA 90069.

CAREER: Actor, screenwriter, and director. Film appearances include *Apocalypse Now,* 1979, *Repo Man,* 1984, *The Breakfast Club,* 1985, *St. Elmo's Fire,* 1985, *That Was Then . . . This Is Now,* 1985, *Maximum Overdrive,* 1986, *Young Guns,* 1988, *Young Guns II,* 1990, *Freejack,* 1992, *The Mighty Ducks,* 1993, and *Judgement Night,* 1995; television appearances include *In the Custody of Strangers,* 1982, *To Climb a Mountain,* and *Making the Grade;* stage appearances include *Echoes of an Era* and *Mister Roberts.* Director of motion pictures, including *Wisdom,* 1986, *Men at Work,* 1990, and *The War at Home,* 1996; executive producer, *National Lampoon's Family Dies.*

WRITINGS:

SCREENPLAYS

That Was Then . . . This Is Now (based on the novel
    by S. E. Hinton), Paramount, 1985.
Wisdom, Twentieth Century-Fox, 1986.
Men at Work, Triumph, 1990.

OTHER

Author of the play *Echoes of an Era,* produced at Santa Monica High School, Santa Monica, CA.

SIDELIGHTS: Emilio Estevez, best known for his performances in several popular motion pictures, is the son of noted actor Martin Sheen, whose surname was Estevez before he changed it for the stage name Sheen. (He is also the brother of actor Charlie Sheen, with whom he has co-starred in several films, including *Men at Work.*) Estevez began his career in films as an extra in Francis Ford Coppola's *Apocalypse Now,* which featured his father in the leading role. As one of Hollywood's busiest actors during the 1980s—when he was classed with a group of popular twenty-something actors known collectively as the "Brat Pack"—Estevez chose films that ran the gamut from high adventure to intimate discourses on teenage angst. His most notable roles include a high energy performance as Otto Maddox in *Repo Man,* the overachieving Andrew Clark in *The Breakfast Club,* Kirbo in *St. Elmo's Fire,* and as Billy the Kid in *Young Guns* and *Young Guns II.*

In the mid-1980s Estevez became one of the youngest writer/directors for a major Hollywood studio. Acting from his first screenplay, *That Was Then . . . This Is Now,* which he adapted from a novel by S. E. Hinton, Estevez played the lead role in the story of the unravelling friendship between a self-destructive delinquent and his buddy, a young man who has changed his ways and is ready for responsibility. Writing in the London *Times,* David Robinson described the backdrop of *That Was Then . . . This Is Now* "a surreal world peopled mainly by kids, with grown-ups making only fleeting and rarely welcome intrusions. Life is lived on the city streets, and mean they are in look and spirit. Violence and sudden death are facts of life. Delinquency is inescapable. Gang enemies are rife. Friendships though are as passionate as rage: love is a powerful and declared bond between the boys."

Estevez's second screenplay, *Wisdom,* portrays a modern-age Robin Hood working in defense of the common man. Playing the title role, John Wisdom, Estevez offers the story of an intelligent teenager who had a bright future until, on a whim, he stole a car. Now, with a police record, he can't find a job. Writing in the *Washington Post,* Paul Attanasio noted that *Wisdom* reflects a distinct genre with deep roots in the frustrations of the American underclass. Attanasio observed: "He [Wisdom] decides to become a sort of Robin Hood, bombing file cabinets full of loans that the evil banks intend to foreclose. He and his girlfriend become a sort of Bonnie and Clyde, riding cross country in a Subaru wagon, eating junk food, singing songs, making love."

Two happy-go-lucky sanitation workers are the protagonists in Estevez's comedic environmental spoof, *Men at Work.* The garbage men turn sleuths when they discover the dead body of a city councilman stuffed in an oil drum. From the moment of their discovery, the chase is on to reveal the greedy, polluting chemical company with its sights on the small beach-front community.

In addition to his work acting in and crafting screenplays, Estevez has directed several motion pictures.

BIOGRAPHICAL/CRITICAL SOURCES:

BOOKS

Contemporary Newsmakers 1985 Cumulation, Gale (Detroit), 1986.

PERIODICALS

American Film, March 1985, p. 42.
Nuestro, October 1985, p. 12.
People Weekly, February 28, 1983, p. 63.
Seventeen, July 1985, p. 49.
Teen, July 1985, p. 41.
Times (London), October 31, 1986.
Washington Post, January 1, 1987.*

*   *   *

EVANS, Douglas 1953-

PERSONAL: Born April 3, 1953, in Euclid, OH; son of Gerald David and Elizabeth Louise (Votypka) Evans. *Education:* Oregon State University, B.S., 1975; University of Oregon, M.Ed., 1977. *Religion:* None. *Avocational interests:* Travel (more than a hundred countries), music composition.

ADDRESSES: Home and office—2819 Piedmont Ave., Berkeley, CA 94705. *E-mail*—douglas@ emf.net.

CAREER: Writer, educator. Teacher of second grade at an elementary school in Veneta, OR, 1976-83; International School of Helsinki, Helsinki, Finland, teacher of second grade, 1983-84; American School of London, London, England, teacher of second grade, 1984-85; Orinda School District, Orinda, CA, teacher of second grade, 1987-97.

MEMBER: Society of Children's Book Writers and Illustrators.

WRITINGS:

Classroom at the End of the Hall, illustrated by Larry Di Fiori, Front Street (Arden, NC), 1996.

So What Do You Do?, Front Street, 1997.
The Truth About Teachers, Front Street, in press.

Contributor of stories to *Cricket*.

WORK IN PROGRESS: Cozy Up to the Blackboard, poems about the classroom, for Front Street.

SIDELIGHTS: Douglas Evans commented: "Having taught in a wide variety of schools—one in a small logging town, two international schools in Europe, a private school in Berkeley, and one in an upper-class American suburb, I've been able to collect many ideas and experiences about children and fellow teachers. For the past twenty summers, I've lived in Europe and traveled to over a hundred-twenty countries, where I've also gathered material for stories."

Evans's experience with a wide variety of children and educational settings forms the basis for the tongue-in-cheek humor of his first published book, *The Classroom at the End of the Hall*. "Though I finished the book in about a year's time," Evans explained to Sally Lodge in a *Publishers Weekly* interview, "often writing through the night, I collected bits and pieces of the stories over time. But they are based on types that every teacher knows: the class pain-in-the-neck, the daydreamer, the kid with the desk that is always messy. I'd see these kids year after year and began to think of magical ways that they could solve their problems."

Pleased with the positive response of students and fellow teachers to his work, Evans commented: "I consider teaching schoolchildren the noblest profession a person can have. I've had great fun writing about the classroom and spoofing teachers."

BIOGRAPHICAL/CRITICAL SOURCES:

PERIODICALS

Booklist, August, 1996, p. 1900.
Kirkus Reviews, July 1, 1996, p. 978.
Publishers Weekly, June 17, 1996, p. 65; July 1, 1996, pp. 35-36.

F

FEIN, Ellen

PERSONAL: Born in New York, NY; married; children: two. *Education:* New York University, B.A.; studied for M.A. in social work. *Religion:* Jewish. *Avocational interests:* "Dating."

ADDRESSES: Home—Long Island, NY. *Office*—The Rules, FDR Station, P.O. Box 6047, New York, NY 10152. *Agent*—Connie Clausen, Connie Clausen & Associates Literary Agency, 250 East 87th St., New York, NY 10128.

CAREER: Freelance writer, c. 1995—; dating consultant with Sherrie Schneider, 1995—. Has given lectures and seminars on relationship strategies throughout the United States; appeared on television programs, including *20/20,* ABC, and *The Oprah Winfrey Show,* syndicated.

AWARDS, HONORS: Named one of the Fascinating Women of 1996 by *Ladies Home Journal.*

WRITINGS:

NONFICTION

(With Sherrie Schneider) *The Rules: Time-Tested Secrets for Capturing the Heart of Mr. Right,* Warner Books (New York City), 1995.
(With Schneider) *The Rules II: More Rules to Live and Love By,* Warner Books, 1997.

Contributor of articles to periodicals, including *Cosmopolitan, Ladies Home Journal,* and *TV Guide.*

SIDELIGHTS: Ellen Fein and her friend, Sherrie Schneider, often discussed their theories about dating and relationships, even though each is married. They agreed that there were specific rules a woman should follow if she wanted to get married, and then decided they should write them all down in the form of a book. The result was not only the controversial 1995 best-seller, *The Rules: Time-Tested Secrets for Capturing the Heart of Mr. Right,* but what became a profitable consulting and speaking business for Fein and Schneider. Women pay two hundred and fifty dollars per hour to ask Fein or her coauthor about personal relationship issues, and the pair have made appearances and lectures all over the United States.

Reviewing *The Rules* in *America,* Catherine Walsh observed that "rule one tells a woman to be a 'creature unlike any other,' to rejoice in her individuality and build a full life regardless of whether or not she has found the right man." Meanwhile, other "rules" include never speaking to a man first, and only rarely returning his calls. Also, according to Fein and Schneider, a woman should never allow anything more intimate than a casual kiss on the first date. Nor should a woman accept a weekend date made later than a Wednesday. The authors also recommend that women hoping to gain marriage partners should grow their hair long and always wear sheer black pantyhose, put sex off as long as possible, and, in general, cultivate an air of mystery in the minds of the men they are dating.

Critical response to *The Rules* has been mixed. Elizabeth Gleick in *Time* declared that "a first reading of this book provokes a mix of outrage and hilarity." John Leo in *U.S. News and World Report* explained the volume's popularity, as "conservatives seem to be gratified that the book is essentially a collection of grandmother's traditional advice on courtship," yet "there is almost enough overlay of breezy '90s empowerment to soothe anti-traditionalists." Karina Rollins in the *National Review* lamented that *The Rules*'s advice to women not to date married men was based less on morality than on "utilitarian" reasons (the dating woman would get hurt and the man would lose respect for her): "As if *successfully* [her emphasis] stealing another woman's husband would be just fine." As Gleick reported, however, many of Fein and Schneider's readers swear by *The Rules*. The *Time* contributor quoted a Hollywood film producer named Kathy, who has put the volume's rules to the test, as saying: "The results of the Rules are wonderful.... I am weeding out the losers real quick."

Fein and Schneider also wrote a sequel to their bestseller, fittingly titled *The Rules II: More Rules to Live and Love By*. In this 1997 tome, the pair dole out more specialized advice, including tips for married women, women in long-distance relationships, women using dating services, and plans for winning back an ex-boyfriend or husband.

Fein told *CA* that she and Schneider had "met for years talking about the Rules in Chinese restaurants and decided it was time to write them down." She added that their primary influences are the hundreds of letters they receive from women, and that helping these women with relationships is the primary motivation for their writing.

BIOGRAPHICAL/CRITICAL SOURCES:

PERIODICALS

America, November 23, 1996, p. 9.
National Review, December 23, 1996, p. 58.
Time, September 30, 1996, p. 58.
U.S. News and World Report, October 21, 1996, p. 38.

OTHER

http://www.pathfinder.com/@WyJgRw UASxON 1bHO/twep/warner_books/authors/ellen_fein/ (web page), October 7, 1997.

FEINBERG, Leslie 1949-

PERSONAL: Born in 1949.

ADDRESSES: Agent—c/o Beacon Press, 25 Beacon St., Boston, MA 02108.

CAREER: Writer.

AWARDS, HONORS: Award for Gay and Lesbian Literature, American Library Association and Lambda Literary Award, both 1993, both for *Stone Butch Blues*.

WRITINGS:

Stone Butch Blues (novel), Firebrand Books (Ithaca, NY), 1993.
Transgender Warriors: Making History from Joan of Arc to RuPaul (nonfiction), Beacon Press (Boston), 1996.

SIDELIGHTS: Leslie Feinberg is a writer who underwent surgical and hormonal treatments to change from a female to a male. In 1993 she published *Stone Butch Blues,* an autobiographical novel about a masculine female and her unhappy experiences in a heterosexual culture. The novel's protagonist is Jess Goldberg, whom E. J. Graff described in *Women's Review of Books* as "an involuntary gender outlaw." After years of enduring the bewilderment of others regarding her own sexuality, Goldberg becomes open about herself and her preference. But her candor hardly leads to emotional fulfillment. Instead, Goldberg finds that lesbians are regularly targeted for abuse by heterosexuals. After having endured a rape while in high school, Goldberg now endures physical assaults from brutish law officers. Her devastation is such that she eventually determines to pose as a man. But this guise only leads to further problems, especially in her more intimate romantic interactions. Finally, Goldberg decides to live her life openly. Graff called this "the third stage of [Goldberg's] journey: a return to being visible, not clearly woman or man."

Stone Butch Blues, which appeared in 1993, has been hailed as a significant, revelatory novel. Graff called it "an astonishing accomplishment," and Gail Shepherd in *Belles Lettres* praised it as "a moving and important novel." Likewise, Maria Kuda, in her appraisal for the *San Francisco Review of Books,* deemed Feinberg's work "important and compelling." Victoria A. Brownworth, meanwhile, wrote in the *Village Voice* that "*Stone Butch Blues* takes the reader into previously unchartered territory" and added that "through the intimate and compelling drama of Jess's narrative, it forces an examination of gender definitions in a way no treatise on sexual politics could."

Feinberg is also the author of *Transgender Warriors: Making History from Joan of Arc to RuPaul,* a history of transgender. In this work she argues that much of the social denigration of non-heterosexuals is rooted in a male-centered culture. Feinberg provides personal anecdotes as well as comments from individuals spanning the range of transgender.

BIOGRAPHICAL/CRITICAL SOURCES:

PERIODICALS

Belles Lettres, winter, 1993-94, pp. 58-61.
San Francisco Review of Books, August-October, 1993, pp. 27-28.
Village Voice, May 25, 1993, p. 83.
Women's Review of Books, July, 1993, p. 25.*

*   *   *

FELSTINER, Mary Lowenthal 1941-

PERSONAL: Born February 19, 1941, in Pittsburgh, PA; daughter of Alexander and Anne (Fineman) Lowenthal; married John Felstiner, February 19, 1966; children: Sarah Alexandra. *Education:* Harvard University, B.A., 1963; Columbia University, M.A., 1966; Stanford University, Ph.D., 1971.

ADDRESSES: Office—Department of History, San Francisco State University, 1600 Holloway Ave., San Francisco, CA 94132.

CAREER: Stanford University, lecturer in history, 1970-71, 1972; Sonoma State College, lecturer, 1971-72; San Francisco State University, San Francisco, CA, assistant professor, 1973-76, associate professor of history, 1976—.

MEMBER: Pacific Coast Council on Latin American Studies, Coordinating Commission of Women in History Professions.

AWARDS, HONORS: Foreign Area fellow, 1964-66, Doherty fellow, 1967-68.

WRITINGS:

(Co-editor and contributor) *Chanzeaux: A Village in Anjou,* Harvard University Press (Cambridge, MA), 1966.
To Paint Her Life: Charlotte Salomon in the Nazi Era, HarperCollins (New York, NY), 1994.

Contributor to periodicals, including *Journal of Inter-American Studies* and *Hispanic American History Review.*

SIDELIGHTS: Mary Lowenthal Felstiner's book *To Paint Her Life: Charlotte Salomon in the Nazi Era* is the biography of German Jewish artist Charlotte Salomon, who was murdered at Auschwitz during World War II. Before her death at age twenty-six, Salomon drew on her own tragic family history and artistic talents to create a unique work of art. According the Jonathan Kirsch in the *Los Angeles Times,* Salomon "created more than seven hundred paintings and hundreds of other drawings, captions, playlets and operettas that amount to an autobiography in word and image." Salomon titled her work *Leben oder Theater?,* or *Life? or Theater?* It was published after her death and is acknowledged by many as an artistic masterpiece.

Peter Gay in the *New York Times Book Review* notes that Felstiner's biography of Salomon includes thorough and detailed interviews with the artist's friends and relatives. This research, according to Gay, "gives her account some independent value and will spread the word about a talented and tragic hostage to her family and her times." A *Kirkus Reviews* critic remarked that Felstiner "moves fluidly between biography, history (with a feminist angle), and art criticism as she fleshes out the brief life of Charlotte Salomon." Donna Seaman in *Booklist* wrote that the author "sheds light on little-known aspects of the Jewish massacre, particularly the treatment of women." Kirsch in the *Los Angeles Times* stated that "*To Paint Her Life* is something truly remarkable, a work of art in its own right and a masterpiece in the field of Holocaust studies."

About the biography's examination of the sociopolitical climate of Salomon's time, Gay in the *New York Times Book Review* further observed: "Ms. Felstiner tells this harrowing tale clearly and emotionally. Indeed, this in an angry book. Not content with recovering the life of this accomplished, attractive and driven victim, she devotes a great deal of space to the crimes of the Nazi regime and to the men responsible for Charlotte Salomon's death." Joan Weimer, writing in *Belles Lettres,* perceived resounding success in Felstiner's handling of the difficult material: "Even as she unearths and relates such horrifying events, she writes a beautiful book, as artful, lyrical, ironic, penetrating, and dramatic as its subject's own work."

BIOGRAPHICAL/CRITICAL SOURCES:

PERIODICALS

Belles Lettres, spring, 1995, pp. 98-99.
Booklist, July, 1994, p. 1912.
Kirkus Reviews, May 15, 1994, p. 681.
Library Journal, June 15, 1994, pp. 74-75.
Los Angeles Times, August 3, 1994, p. 4E.
New York Times Book Review, August 14, 1994, pp. 11-12.*

*   *   *

FIDO, Martin (Austin) 1939-

PERSONAL: Born October 18, 1939, in Penzance, Cornwall, England; son of Austin Harry (a statistician) and Enid Mary (a school teacher; maiden name, Hobrough) Fido; married Judith Mary Spicer (a college lecturer), June 21, 1961 (divorced, 1972); married Norma Elaine Wilson, December 16, 1972 (divorced, 1984); married Karen Lynn Sandel (a retired executive chef), December 17, 1994; children: Rebecca Mary, Abigail Joanna, Austin Charles. *Ethnicity:* "Anglo-Indian." *Education:* Lincoln College, Oxford, B.A., 1961, B.Litt., 1966. *Politics:* "Unattached Left." *Religion:* Quaker. *Avocational interests:* Walking tours, chamber music, religion, theology.

ADDRESSES: Agent—Richard Jeffs, Roger Hancock Ltd., 4 Water Lane, London NW1 8NZ, England.

CAREER: University of Leeds, Oxford, England, lecturer in English, 1966-72; University of West Indies, Barbados, reader in English and head of the Department of English and Linguistics, 1973-83; Hoevec Investors Ltd., Barbados, actor, 1981-83; writer, broadcaster, courier, guide-lecturer, 1983—.

AWARDS, HONORS: Scott Mancrieff Prize nomination, 1972.

WRITINGS:

NONFICTION

Charles Dickens, Routledge (London), 1968, Humanities Press (New York), 1968.
Charles Dickens: An Authentic Account of His Life and Times, Hamlyn (London), 1970, Feltham (New York), 1973.
Oscar Wilde, Viking (New York City), 1973.
Rudyard Kipling, Viking, 1974.
Shakespeare, Viking, 1978.
Oscar Wilde: An Illustrated Biography, Harper and Row (New York City), 1985.
Shakespeare, Hammond (London), 1985.
Murder Guide to London, Weidenfeld and Nicolson (London), 1986, Academy Chicago (Chicago, IL), 1990.
The Crimes, Detection, and Death of Jack the Ripper, Weidenfeld and Nicolson, 1987, Barnes and Noble (New York City), 1993.
Bodysnatchers: A History of the Resurrectionists, 1742-1832, Weidenfeld and Nicolson, 1989.
Murders after Midnight, Orion (London), 1990.
(With Keith Skinner) *The Peasenhall Murder,* Alan Sutton Publishing (London), 1990, A. Sutton (Wolfeboro Falls, NH), 1991.
(With Paul Begg and Keith Skinner) *The Jack the Ripper A to Z,* Headline (London), 1991.
The Chronicle of Crime: The Infamous Felons of Modern History and Their Hideous Crimes, Carroll and Graf (New York City), 1993.
Deadly Jealousy, Headline, 1993.
(With Paul Begg) *Great Crimes and Trials of the Twentieth Century,* Carlton (London), 1994.
Twentieth Century Murder, Carlton, 1995.
(With wife Karen Fido) *The World's Worst Medical Mistakes,* Carlton, 1996.
(With wife Karen Fido) *Our Family,* Carlton, 1997, Laurials (New York), 1997.
The World of Charles Dickens, Carlton, 1997, Barnes and Noble, 1997.

PLAYS

Let's Go Bajan!, produced in Barbados, 1983.

AUDIOTAPES, WRITER AND READER

Silence of the Lambs: The True Stories, Tring Long Island (Tring, England), 1992.

Guilty or Insane?, Tring Long Island, 1992.

The Kennedys, Tring Long Island, 1992.

On the Trail of Jack the Ripper, Tring Long Island, 1992.

Son of Sam, Tring Long Island, 1992.

Hell Hath No Fury, Tring Long Island, 1992.

10 Rillington Place, Connoisseur Collection (London), 1993.

Shady Ladies and Wicked Women, Connoisseur Collection, 1993.

The Yorkshire Ripper, Connoisseur Collection, 1993.

The Krays, Connoisseur Collection, 1993.

Classic Murders, Connoisseur Collection, 1994.

The Manson Family, Connoisseur Collection, 1994, reissued as *A Passion for Killing,* MCI (Watford, England), 1995.

The Truth about Jack the Ripper, Connoisseur Collection, 1994.

Serial Killers, MCI, 1995.

The Mob, MCI, 1996.

Who Killed JFK?, MCI, 1996.

Cults that Kill, MCI, 1996.

Contributor of reviews to periodicals, including the *Times Educational Supplement, Times Literary Supplement, Oxford Review,* and *Oxford Magazine.*

SIDELIGHTS: Professor and historian Martin Fido has made a career of writing about literature and crime. In the literary arena, he has written popular biographies of such figures as William Shakespeare, Rudyard Kipling, Oscar Wilde, and Charles Dickens. His writings have also investigated the realm of crime in books such as *Murder Guide to London; Crimes, Detection, and Death of Jack the Ripper; Bodysnatchers: A History of the Resurrectionists, 1742-1832; The Peasenhall Murder;* and *The Chronicle of Crime: The Infamous Felons of Modern History and Their Hideous Crimes.*

Fido's early biographies drew respectful notice from critics. Among these works was the 1985 volume *Oscar Wilde: An Illustrated Biography,* which a critic for the *Los Angeles Times Book Review* called "an authoritative study." Writing in the *Chicago Tribune Book World,* Richard Christiansen described Fido's 1978 work *Shakespeare* as a "prosaically written" book that successfully brings together facts about the life and writings of the English playwright. *Charles Dickens: An Authentic Account of His Life and Times* prompted a *Times Literary Supplement* critic to remark on Fido's "lively and accurate" writing as well as his selection of illustrations, which the reviewer praised as "well-chosen."

For tourists in London who want to visit sites where infamous murders occurred, Fido wrote *Murder Guide to London* in 1990. Thomas Swick, of the *New York Times Book Review,* found the murder guide to be "fascinating," and Dan Crawford, writing for *Armchair Detective,* called it "entertaining" and a "treasure trove." "Perhaps the most intriguing aspect of Fido's guide is the pattern he discerns between types of murder and social class, mores and architecture of the district in which it took place, a pattern which is perhaps predictable but still intriguing," commented P. D. James in the *Times Literary Supplement.* Citing the easy-to-read text, maps, as well as the high quality of the book's indexes and bibliography, Crawford found the volume to be a useful one, stating, "Anyone in need of a reasonably priced reference guide to murder in London would be well advised to pick this up."

The serial murders in 1888 of five women in the Whitechapel area of London by an assailant known as Jack the Ripper have been the subject of numerous books of both nonfiction and fiction. For the centennial of these murders, Fido added his own book on the topic, *The Crimes, Detection and Death of Jack the Ripper.* In this nonfiction work, Fido presents an argument that points to David Cohen, a Jewish tailor, as the murderer. Christopher Wordsworth, in the *Observer,* described Fido's tome as "interesting and knowledgeable on the police angle," and Patricia Highsmith in a review for the *Times Literary Supplement* praised the work as "well-documented and highly readable."

Bodysnatchers: A History of the Resurrectionists, 1742-1832 is a more scholarly work on the sensational subject of "burking"—murder by suffocation or strangling in order to obtain a body to be sold for dissection. In this work, Fido describes the activities of the firm of Messieurs Burke and Hare of Edinburgh, Scotland, who during the early nineteenth-century, pillaged burial grounds and burked victims to supply their clients. "Mr. Fido's excellent book abounds in strange characters, savage beyond belief, grotesques who seem to have stepped straight out of the frame of a Hogarth print," remarked Richard Whittington-Egan in *Contemporary Review.*

Fido told *CA:* "Between 1976 and 1983 I used my home leaves from the West Indies to study the transition from the concept of natural philosophy to the concept of exact science, and the ways in which this was reflected, encouraged and shaped by literature. Since it proved impossible for the university to grant me the sabbatical leave to which I was entitled, I resigned and returned to England to live on savings and complete the book. Unfortunately, all my notes and manuscript were destroyed in a warehouse fire while awaiting shipment. Given the impossibility of replacing the material in a year, and on the advice that I should be quite unable to earn a living by academic writing, I turned to writing crime history which has largely occupied me ever since."

BIOGRAPHICAL/CRITICAL SOURCES:

PERIODICALS

Armchair Detective, fall, 1990, p. 469.
Chicago Tribune Book World, December 10, 1978, sec. 7, p. 4.
Contemporary Review, February, 1989, p. 109-110.
Los Angeles Times Book Review, November 17, 1985, p. 1D.
New Statesman, November 13, 1987, p. 28.
New York Times Book Review, June 10, 1990, p. 49.
Observer (London), January 3, 1988, p. 22.
Times Literary Supplement, June 4, 1970; May 9, 1986, p. 508; December 25-31, 1987, p. 1427.

*   *   *

FINLEY, Joseph E(dwin)   1919-1997
(William L. Scott)

OBITUARY NOTICE—See index for *CA* sketch: Born August 7, 1919, in Portageville, MO; died of compilations after a severe fall, July 8, 1997, in Baltimore, MD. Lawyer, historian, writer. Finley established himself as an attorney and served as general counsel of the Office and Professional Employees International Union for more than forty years. He also became historian for the union. Before being admitted to the District of Columbia Bar in 1951 and the Ohio Bar in 1957, he served in the U.S. Army during World War II, eventually obtaining the rank of captain. He worked at Woll, Glenn and Thatcher in Washington, D.C., beginning in 1951, before turning to private practice in 1954. In 1961 he became part of the firm of Metzenbaum, Gaines, Finley and Stern in Ohio, where he remained until 1971 when he returned to private practice, this time in Philadelphia, Pennsylvania. In addition to his work for the Office and Professional Employees International Union, he also worked as general counsel for the International Brotherhood of Pottery and Allied Workers. He wrote several books, including the nonfiction books *The Corrupt Kingdom* and *White Collar Union* as well as the novel *Missouri Blue.* He also wrote books on racing as William L. Scott. These books included *Total Victory at the Track: The Promise and the Performance* and *How Will Your Horse Run Today?*

OBITUARIES AND OTHER SOURCES:

BOOKS

Who's Who in American Law, Marquis (New Providence, NJ), 1989.

PERIODICALS

New York Times, July 13, 1997, sec. 1, p. 26.
Washington Post, July 14, 1997, p. B4.

*   *   *

FLEMING, Candace   1962-
(Candace Groth-Fleming)

PERSONAL: Born May 24, 1962; daughter of Charles (a superintendent) and Carol (a homemaker; maiden name, Price) Groth; married Scott Fleming (in commercial real estate), November 9, 1985; children: Scott, Michael. *Education:* Eastern Illinois University, B.A., 1985. *Religion:* Lutheran. *Avocational interests:* Reading, collecting antiquarian books, camping, hiking, travel.

ADDRESSES: Office—415 East Golf Rd., Arlington Heights, IL 60005.

CAREER: Writer, 1990—. Junior Great Books coordinator, 1995-97; Harper College, Palatine, IL, adjunct professor, Liberal Arts Department, 1997—.

MEMBER: Society of Children's Book Writers and Illustrators.

AWARDS, HONORS: Highlights for Children History Feature of the Year, 1995; *Highlights for Children* Patriotic Feature of the Year, 1996; award from Chicago Women in Publishing, 1996, for *Women of the Lights.*

WRITINGS:

(As Candace Groth-Fleming) *Professor Fergus Fahrenheit and His Wonderful Weather Machine,* illustrated by Don Weller, Simon & Schuster (New York City), 1994.

Women of the Lights, illustrated by James Watling, Albert Whitman (Morton Grove, IL), 1996.

Madame LaGrande and Her So High, to the Sky, Uproarious Pompadour, illustrated by S. D. Schindler, Knopf (New York City), 1996.

Gabriella's Song, illustrated by Giselle Potter, Atheneum (New York City), 1997.

Westward Ho, Carlotta!, illustrated by David Catrow, Atheneum, 1998.

The Hatmaker's Sign, illustrated by Robert Andrew Parker, Orchard Books (New York City), 1998.

Contributor to magazines, including *Boys' Life* and *American Baby.*

WORK IN PROGRESS: When Agnes Caws, for Atheneum, scheduled for 1999; *A Big Cheese for the White: A True Tale of a Tremendous Cheddar;* research on eighteenth-century New England life.

SIDELIGHTS: Candace Fleming commented: "I remember the day I discovered the music and magic of words. It was the day my second-grade teacher, Miss Johnson, held up a horn-shaped basket filled with papier-mache pumpkins and asked the class to repeat the word 'cornucopia.' It sounded good. I said it again, and again, and I decided I loved that word. I loved its rhythm and cadence. I loved the way it felt on my tongue and fell on my ears. I skipped all the way home from school that day chanting 'Cornucopia! Cornucopia!' From then on, I really began listening to words—to the sounds they made, and the way they were used, and how they made me feel. I longed to put them together in ways that were beautiful, and yet told a story.

"Now, my family and close friends will tell you that I have always made up stories. My mother loves to tell of the time I regaled our next-door neighbor with tales of our family trip to Paris, France. So vivid were my descriptions of that romantic city that my neighbor believed every word I said. I can only imagine his chagrin when he learned I had never been beyond my home state of Indiana.

"I told many stories like this. My classmates heard the saga of my three-legged dog Tiger. My Sunday school teacher listened, wide-eyed, as I told the tale of the ghost in our attic. Lots of people heard my tall tales. Lots of people believed them.

"Technically, I suppose you could call this lying. Fortunately, I had parents who understood the difference between imagination and lies. They encouraged me to make up stories, but they strongly suggested that I not claim these stories as truth. Eventually, I took their advice.

"The result? My love of language and my need to tell a good story merged, and I became a writer. I filled notebook after notebook with my stories, poems, and plays. I couldn't stop the flow of words and ideas that rushed from my pencil, and I didn't try. Often, I arrived home from school, closed my bedroom door, and wrote for hours on end. When I wasn't writing, I was reading, and if something I read sparked my imagination, I would start writing all over again.

"I still have many of those notebooks today. I cherish them. They are a record of my writing life, from second grade to the present. In them I can see my struggle to tell a good and believable story. I can see my struggle to use musical language. I can't help but recognize that these are the same struggles I have as a writer today. They are also my goals. I want to tell you a good story. I want to tell it in a believable way. And I want to tell it with language that opens your ears to the music and magic of words."

BIOGRAPHICAL/CRITICAL SOURCES:

PERIODICALS

Booklist, October 15, 1994, p. 434; March 15, 1996, p. 1258; July, 1996, p. 1829.

Kirkus Reviews, May 1, 1996, p. 687.

Publishers Weekly, October 3, 1994, p. 68; June 24, 1996, p. 59.

School Library Journal, January, 1995, p. 86; April, 1996, p. 144; July, 1996, p. 59.

Smartkid, May, 1996, pp. 20, 45.

*   *   *

FORBES, Edith 1954-

PERSONAL: Born October 28, 1954; U.S. citizen. *Education:* Stanford University, B.A., M.A., 1978. *Avocational interests:* Sustainable agriculture, cross-country skiing and other outdoor sports, cooking, gardening.

ADDRESSES: Office—c/o Seal Press, 3131 Western Ave., No. 410, Seattle, WA 98121.

CAREER: TSC, Inc., worked as computer programmer; self-employed carpenter, farmer, and writer.

WRITINGS:

NOVELS

Alma Rose, Seal Press (Seattle, WA), 1993.
Nowle's Passing, Seal Press, 1996.
Exit to Reality, Seal Press, 1997.

WORK IN PROGRESS: Another novel.

BIOGRAPHICAL/CRITICAL SOURCES:

PERIODICALS

American Bookseller, July, 1997, p. 10.

*   *   *

FOX, Frank   1923-

PERSONAL: Born December 26, 1923, in Poland; became U.S. citizen; son of Samuel and Anna Fox; married Anne (a writer), January 8, 1946; children: Julian Fox, Nina Schapiro. *Education:* Temple University, B.S., 1950; University of Pennsylvania, M.A., 1952; University of Delaware, Ph.D., 1966. *Avocational interests:* Collector of posters.

ADDRESSES: Home and office—51 Merbrook Lane, Merion, PA, 19066.

CAREER: Professor of history, nonfiction writer, editor, and translator. Temple University, Philadelphia, PA, teacher, 1963-67; West Chester University, West Chester, PA, professor, 1967-89; occasional classes taught at University of Delaware, Newark, DE, and St. Joseph's University, Philadelphia, PA. *Military service:* U.S. Army, 1943-46, achieved rank of corporal. World Cultures Workshop lecturer, 1964; Iran Public Works (Peace Corps), lecturer on the Soviet Union, 1966; Higher Education Opportunity Program teacher, 1970; History Syllabus Committee, West Chester University, chair,

1980. Curator of Polish poster exhibits, including, Port of History Museum, Philadelphia, PA, 1984; Haverford School, Haverford, PA, 1990; Kosciuszko Foundation, Philadelphia, PA, 1994; Katonah Museum, Katonah, NY, 1996. Curator of Polish film poster exhibits, including Lincoln Center, New York City, 1985; West Chester University, West Chester, PA, curator, 1987. Posters of Wiktor Sadowski, curator, West Chester University, 1988. Interviewed on radio and television, including ABC Television, September 3, 1974; BBC, October 16, 1974; National Radio Network, October 24, 1974; and WTOP-TV, April 24, 1975. Pennsylvania Humanities Council Speakers Program, participant, 1986; Conference of the American Association for the Advancement of Slavic Studies, University of Delaware, speaker, March 20, 1993; "Ghetto Policemen: A Recent Memoir," Y.M.H.A., speaker.

AWARDS, HONORS: Grant-in-aid, Eleutherian Mills Library, DuPont, PA, for research, 1967, 1969; grant for research, American Philosophical Society, 1970; Faculty Development Fund Award, West Chester University, 1986.

WRITINGS:

(Editor and translator) *Am I a Murderer? Testament of a Jewish Ghetto Policeman* (memoir), by Calel Perechodnik, Westview (Boulder, CO), 1996.
Polish Posters: Combat on Paper, 1960-1990 (exhibit catalogue), Katonah Museum (Katonah, NY), 1996.

Also author, with Stephen Parker, of a series of articles on Watergate published in *New York* magazine, 1974-75; author of a series of articles on Polish art and culture in *World & I, Print,* and *Affiche;* author of history articles published in periodicals, including *French Historical Studies, Liberty, Welcomat, Inside, Midstream, St. Croix Review, Pennsylvania Magazine of History and Biography, East European Jewish Affairs,* and *Film Heritage.*

WORK IN PROGRESS: History Exhumed: Aerial Photography and the Katyn Massacre, The Polish Poster, and *Jan Sawka and His World,* all tentative titles. Research on the history of the Polish poster.

SIDELIGHTS: Frank Fox told *CA:* "Being born in Eastern Europe (Poland, to be precise) almost automatically guarantees an interest in history. Fortunately for myself (and I hope for my readers) I have cast my net over a fairly wide area of research. I have investigated such topics as Utopian history, the Watergate scandal, Polish poster art, Polish-Jewish relations, and the now extinct area of Soviet studies.

"I have been greatly influenced by two outstanding teachers, Professors Walther Kirchua and Ellis Rivkin. They inspired me not only to seek the facts of history, but even more important, the motivations of those who make events. I have added to that a healthy dose of ingredients that I consider most interesting—the effects of accidents, coincidences, and just plain human stupidity."

* * *

FRAENKEL, Abraham Adolf 1891-1965

PERSONAL: Born February 17, 1891, in Munich, Germany; died October 15, 1965, in Jerusalem, Israel; son of Sigmund and Charlotte (Neuburger) Fraenkel; married Malkah Wilhemina Prins, March 28, 1920; children: four. *Education:* Attended University of Munich; attended University of Marburg; attended University of Berlin; University of Breslau, Ph.D., 1914. *Religion:* Jewish.

CAREER: Mathematician and writer. University of Marburg, privatdocent (unsalaried lecturer), 1916-22, assistant professor, 1922-28; University of Kiel, professor, 1928-33; Hebrew University, visiting professor, 1929-31, professor, 1933-59. *Wartime service:* Served as a sergeant in the German medical corps, and also worked with the meteorological service during World War I.

WRITINGS:

Abstract Set Theory, North-Holland, 1953.
Integers and the Theory of Numbers, Scripta Mathematica, 1955.
Foundations of Set Theory, North-Holland, 1958.
Extension of the Number Concept, Scripta Mathematica, 1964.

Contributor to journals and periodicals, including *Scripta Mathematica* and the *Bulletin of the Research Council of Israel.*

SIDELIGHTS: Abraham Adolf Fraenkel was a set theorist who participated in the development of modern logic. He is best known for his work on

Ernst Zermelo's set theory and the introduction of "Ur-elements," which Wolfgang Pauli used to formulate the exclusion principle in quantum physics. Fraenkel's prose was clear and easy to read, and the accessibility of his writings only added to his influence. He began teaching in Jerusalem on sabbatical in 1929 and left Germany permanently in 1933, after Adolph Hitler was elected chancellor. He spent the rest of his life in Israel.

Born in Munich on February 17, 1891, Fraenkel's orthodox Jewish heritage had a strong influence on him from his youngest days. His great-grandfather, B. H. Auerbach-Halberstadt, had been widely known for his rabbinical teachings, and Fraenkel's parents, Sigmund and Charlotte (Neuburger) Fraenkel, made certain that the young boy was reading Hebrew by the age of five. Brought up in a literate family that placed such a strong emphasis on education, Fraenkel advanced quickly in his studies; he attended the universities of Munich, Marburg, and Berlin, and he earned his doctorate from the University of Breslau in 1914 at the age of twenty-three. During World War I, Fraenkel served as a sergeant in the German medical corps, also working with the meteorological service. Beginning in 1916, he accepted a position as privatdocent, an unsalaried lecturer at the University of Marburg, where he began his most important research. He married Malkah Wilhemina Prins on March 28, 1920; they would have four children.

Fraenkel had long been interested in the work of Ernst Zermelo, who in the early years of the century had published his innovative and controversial work on set theory. Specifically, Zermelo had conjectured that, given any set of numbers, a single element could be selected and that definite properties of that element could be determined; this was known as the axiom of choice, but the problem was that Zermelo offered little proof for much of his theory, insisting that mathematics could only progress if certain axioms were simply accepted. This radical notion was unacceptable to many of those working in mathematics. Though some, like Jacques Hadamard, agreed to accept Zermelo's theory until a better way could be found, Jules Henri Poincare and other mathematicians fought adamantly against it.

Instead of accepting or rejecting the theory outright, Fraenkel searched for ways to put Zermelo's work on a firmer foundation. Zermelo's theory already worked well in the case of finite sets. But for infinite sets, his assumptions were more questionable. What

Fraenkel did was substitute a notion of function for Zermelo's idea of determining a definite property of an item in a set. By doing so, he not only clarified much of Zermelo's set theory but rid the theory of its dependence on the axiom of choice, which had been one of the most controversial elements of the work.

Fraenkel's findings on set theory appeared initially in two separate works: a popular 1919 introductory textbook and a 1922 research article determining the independence of the axiom of choice. This latter work included as part of the proof a newly-defined term, Ur-elements—infinite and distinct pairs of objects which do not in themselves define a set. Although some mathematicians at the time questioned the validity of these Ur-elements, the physicist Wolfgang Pauli used them in his proof of the exclusion principle just three years later.

With these investigations, Fraenkel was propelled to the forefront of set-theory research. Over the course of the next several years, he published numerous articles on the subject while continuing to teach. He had been promoted to assistant professor at the University of Marburg in 1922, and in 1928 he accepted a full professorship at the University of Kiel. Although grateful for his position at Kiel, Fraenkel took a leave of absence in 1929 to become a visiting professor at the Hebrew University in Jerusalem. He taught at the Hebrew University for two years, but after a disagreement with the administration there he returned to Kiel.

When Fraenkel returned to Germany in 1931, the country was troubled. Racked by a brutal economic depression and the punishing conditions inflicted by the Treaty of Versailles, political factions had become increasingly intolerant. Although Fraenkel's position at Kiel seemed assured, he could not ignore the growing power of the Nazi party. In January of 1933, Adolf Hitler became chancellor, and a month later Fraenkel and his family left Germany. They went to Amsterdam, and after watching events unfold from there for two months, Fraenkel decided that the situation in his native country would not soon improve. He sent in his resignation to the University of Kiel in April of 1933, and the Hebrew University welcomed him back as a full professor despite their earlier disagreement. Fraenkel would never again live in Germany.

The experience of having to leave his homeland because of his religion marked Fraenkel for the rest of his life. Although he continued to publish texts on set theory over the course of his career, the focus of his research shifted. He became increasingly interested in the study of modern logic and the specific contributions Jewish scientists and mathematicians had made to their fields. Fraenkel had begun his work as a historian of Jewish mathematicians in 1930 and 1932, when he had written two long articles on the career of Georg Cantor, the founder of set theory, who was half Jewish. Cantor was then of interest to Fraenkel more due to the nature of his research than his ethnic background, however, and it was not until after he settled permanently into his position at the Hebrew University that he began a wider investigation of Jewish mathematicians and scientists. In the field of logic, Fraenkel investigated the natural numbers, describing them in terms of modern ideas of logic and reasoning. While he underscored the need for continuity in consideration of the number line, he was also interested in opposing arguments. After a discussion with Albert Einstein, who suggested the possibility that the atomistic conception of the number line might one day take precedence over continuity in mathematics, Fraenkel wrote an article explaining these views of the intuitionists, as they were known. He remained ultimately unconvinced, however, primarily because he considered mathematical continuity necessary to the foundation of modern calculus.

In 1958, Fraenkel published his last major work, *Foundations of Set Theory,* a textbook which served to summarize his work in this field. A year later, he retired from his teaching position at the Hebrew University. In celebration of his seventieth birthday in 1961, several members of the mathematical community assembled a collection of essays and research articles related to Fraenkel's work. Mathematicians from many countries contributed to the collection, *Essays on the Foundation of Mathematics,* but Fraenkel never saw it in its final form. He died in Jerusalem on October 15, 1965, just months before the book's publication.

BIOGRAPHICAL/CRITICAL SOURCES:

BOOKS

Biographical Encyclopedia of the World, Institute for Research in Biography, 1940, p. 201.

Gillespie, Charles Coulson, editor, *Dictionary of Scientific Biography,* Volume 5, Scribner (Old Tappan, NJ), 1972, pp. 107-109.

Hayden, Seymour and John F. Kennison, *Zermelo-Fraenkel Set Theory,* C. E. Merrill, 1968.

Pinl, Max, and Lux Furtmuller, *Mathematicians under Hitler,* Secker and Warberg, 1973, pp. 161-162.

Temple, George, *100 Years of Mathematics,* Springer-Verlag, 1981, pp. 263-264.*

*   *   *

FRANK, Lucy 1947-

PERSONAL: Born March 22, 1947, in New York, NY; daughter of Sidney (a dentist) and Viola (a teacher and photographer; maiden name, Sobol) Kantrowitz; married Peter C. Frank (a film editor), September 30, 1978; children: Michael. *Education:* Barnard College, A.B., 1968. *Avocational interests:* Reading, gardening, nature study.

*ADDRESSES: Home—*New York, NY. *E-mail—*Lucy_Frank@msn.com.

CAREER: Author of books for young adults. Assistant portfolio manager and marketing manager for a major mutual fund company, New York City, 1986-96; placement counselor for a temporary employment service, New York City, 1996—.

MEMBER: Society of Children's Book Writers and Illustrators, Authors Guild.

WRITINGS:

I Am an Artichoke, Holiday House (New York City), 1995.
Will You Be My Brussels Sprout?, Holiday House, 1996.

WORK IN PROGRESS: Additional young adult novels.

SIDELIGHTS: Lucy Frank is considered by many critics to be a promising new author whose tales of adolescent angst written for a young adult audience center on intelligent and funny characters going through realistic problems. Frank, whose own son was in early adolescence while she was writing her first published book, 1995's *I Am an Artichoke,* relied not only on her son's input ("I figured if he laughed we were OK," Frank told Bella Stander in a *Publishers Weekly* interview), but on her observa-tions of people she saw on the street and on buses in her hometown of Manhattan. "Part of getting the voice right is listening to kids," Frank told Stander, "and part of it is just letting my imagination rip." The draw of writing for young adults is that "the teenage point is where a lot is changing fast and emotions are running high," Frank continued. "Kids have a highly developed sense of the ridiculous or weird, which appeals to me."

In *I Am an Artichoke,* fifteen-year-old Sarah is bored with her dull suburban existence and decides that working in Manhattan as a mother's helper over the summer will be just what she needs. Thus begins her association with the dysfunctional Friedman family. Florence Friedman, a flamboyant magazine writer—"presented with a vividness that has a fingernail-across-the-chalk board effect on the reader," according to Dolores J. Sarafinski in *Voice of Youth Advocates*—hires Sarah in the hope that she will be able to cure twelve-year-old Emily's anorexia, an agenda that becomes painfully obvious only after Sarah accepts the job. "As the story evolves," noted Elizabeth S. Watson in *Horn Book,* "it becomes clear that, while Sarah can make a difference, she will not cure Emily or the myriad problems in the family."

"This accomplished first novel sparkles with deliciously wry humor," enthused a reviewer in *Publishers Weekly* about *I Am an Artichoke.* The novel was warmly received by other critics as well, who praised the author for consistent characterization, solid pacing, and thoughtful treatment of issues such as self-esteem, family, and friendship—all without losing track of her sense of humor. Susan Dove Lempke concluded her review in *Bulletin of the Center for Children's Books* with the following summation: "Tart, witty narration, strong characterization, and well-paced, realistic plot development make this writer's initial entry into fiction bode well for her future work."

The first example of Frank's "future work" was *Will You Be My Brussels Sprout?,* the sequel to *I Am an Artichoke* in which Sarah meets and falls in love with Emily's older brother David on one of her weekly trips to Manhattan to take cello lessons at the New York Conservatory of Music. Frank's account of first love is "punctuated with humor and witty dialogue and filled with all the angst any teen could ever want," remarked Lauren Peterson in *Booklist.* Some other reviewers were less enthusiastic, however, complaining, like Alice Casey Smith in *School Library Journal,* that the conclusion is "disappointingly open-ended." And, although reviewers generally commended the author's treatment of sex as responsible and age-appropriate, a critic for *Kirkus Reviews* concluded that Sarah's inability to break up with David, who pressures her for sex and undermines her musical ambitions, may leave some readers with the feeling that "all the sexual stereotypes they've been taught to recognize and resist have just been reinforced—in spades." Nevertheless, like *I Am an Artichoke*, *Will You Be My Brussels Sprout* garnered praise as a "well-paced [novel] with fresh characters and an appealing plot," from *Voice of Youth Advocates* reviewer Judy Sasges.

BIOGRAPHICAL/CRITICAL SOURCES:

PERIODICALS

Booklist, February 1, 1995, p. 999; April 15, 1996, p. 1433.
Bulletin of the Center for Children's Books, June, 1995, pp. 342-343.
Horn Book, September, 1995, p. 609.
Kirkus Reviews, January 15, 1996, p. 133.
Publishers Weekly, March 27, 1995, p. 86; July 3, 1995, pp. 31-32; April 15, 1996, p. 70.
School Library Journal, March, 1995, p. 222; April, 1996, p. 154.
Voice of Youth Advocates, August, 1995, p. 158; October, 1996, pp. 208-209.*

*   *   *

FRANKLIN, Michael J(ohn)   1949-

PERSONAL: Born August 15, 1949, in Cardiff, Wales; son of Leonard Charles and Irene (Daniels) Franklin; married, wife's name Caroline (a university lecturer), June 28, 1972; children: Geraint Leonard, Ieuan Maredudd. *Education:* University of Wales, University College, Cardiff, B.A. (with honors), 1972, Ph.D., 1997; University of York, M.Phil., 1977. *Politics:* Socialist. *Religion:* Anglican. *Avocational interests:* Medieval lyric, the romantics, preromanticism, India.

ADDRESSES: Home—6 Hen Parc Ave., Upper Killay, Swansea SA2 7HA, Wales. *Office*—Department of English, St. John's Comprehensive School, Glan Rd., Aberdare, Mid Glamorgan, Wales.

CAREER: Worcester Girls' Grammar School, Worcester, England, English teacher, 1974-83; University of Birmingham, Birmingham, England, extra-mural lecturer, 1982-83; University of Wales, University College, Cardiff, Wales, extra-mural lecturer in continuing education, 1989—, part-time lecturer in English, 1992-95. Trinity College, Carmarthen, Wales, part-time lecturer, 1994-95; St. John's Comprehensive School, Mid Glamorgan, Wales, head of English department.

MEMBER: British Association for Romantic Studies.

WRITINGS:

Sir William Jones: A Critical Biography, University of Wales Press (Cardiff, Wales), 1995.
(Editor) *Sir William Jones: Selected Poetical and Prose Works* (critical edition), University of Wales Press, 1995.

Contributor to books, including *Romanticism and Colonialism,* edited by T. Fulford and P. Kitson, Cambridge University Press (Cambridge, England), 1997; contributor to periodicals, including *Medium Aevum.*

WORK IN PROGRESS: Research on "The Johnson Circle" and orientalism.

SIDELIGHTS: Michael J. Franklin told *CA:* "I have always been fascinated by fourteenth-century literature, art, music, domestic and ecclesiastical architecture, and I was inspired to write on medieval lyric by my supervisors at York, the late Professor Elizabeth Salter and Professor Derek Pearsall.

"My love of the romantics and of Hindu culture inspired my researches into the orientalist Sir William Jones and his legal, judicial, and literary career. My two books on Jones have been enthusiastically reviewed, and this has encouraged me to develop plans to edit other orientalist works and to write a biography of Hester Lynch Thrale (also known as Mrs. Piozzi), the friend of Samuel Johnson.

"My chief inspiration is derived from my wife, whose books on Byron have been so well received, and my children, Geraint and Ieuan, whose music-making accompanies my writing."

G

GABRIEL, Adriana
 See ROJANY, Lisa

* * *

GALBRAITH, Stuart IV 1965-

PERSONAL: Born December 29, 1965, in Detroit, MI; son of Stuart E. and Mary A. Galbraith; married Anne Sharp, 1990 (divorced, 1994). *Education:* Eastern Michigan University, B.A. (magna cum laude); University of Southern California, M.A., 1997.

ADDRESSES: Home—7400 Hollywood Blvd., No. 516, Hollywood, CA 90046.

CAREER: Writer.

WRITINGS:

Motor City Marquees, McFarland (Jefferson, NC), 1994.
Japanese Science Fiction, Fantasy, and Horror Films, McFarland, 1994.
The Japanese Filmography, 1900-1994, McFarland, 1996.
Monsters Are Attacking Tokyo: The Incredible World of Japanese Fantasy Films, Feral House, 1997.

Author of "Video View," a weekly home video column in the *Ann Arbor News,* 1989-93. Contributor to magazines and newspapers, including *Filmfax, Cult Movies, Agenda,* and *Current.*

WORK IN PROGRESS: A book on the science fiction genre, 1977-1997.

SIDELIGHTS: Stuart Galbraith IV told *CA:* "Movies are my great passion, and my books and magazine articles are a means to learn more about those film areas of which I am especially fond. Also, I am attracted to subjects of which little has been written. In the case of my Japanese cinema books, I was frustrated that there was so little on this subject, other than film theory-type books or books that focus almost exclusively on so-called 'art house' films. I am amazed, for instance, there is yet to appear an English-language biography or filmography of Japan's greatest star, Toshiro Mifune.

"My interests and areas of expertise include classical Hollywood cinema, especially science fiction, horror, fantasy, comedies, musicals, and westerns; wide-screen and sound technologies and film exhibition or historic film theaters; postwar American film; and Japanese and British cinema. My influences include writers Bill Warren, Leonard Maltin, Kevin Brownlow, Donald Richie, the late Ron Haver, and Thomas Schatz; in any event, they have written some of the film books I like most. Several other associates of mine, notably writers Steve Ryfle, Ted Okuda, and R. M. Hayes have also been major influences, as have my film history professors Rick Jewell, David Shepard, and Drew Casper. The best film book I've read in a long time was Shawn Levy's *The King of Comedy;* I would like to write something as good as that some day.

"I write in a very straight-forward, matter-of-fact style. I abhor pretentiousness, particularly writing about film that ignores or dismisses the realities of how and why motion pictures are produced, released, and received by contemporary audiences and critics. I believe in exhaustive research, and for me the biggest kick about writing lies is finding those little nuggets of heretofore unknown information. I also try to inject my passion for film into my writing, while providing the reader with an entertaining and useful tool that he or she will want to keep near the video cassette recorder, one that will inspire people to seek out films they might otherwise overlook.

"Ultimately, I would like to be able to live reasonably from my writing, while working in the environment of a film archive or library."

*   *   *

GALVIN, Matthew R(eppert) 1950-

PERSONAL: Born July 24, 1950, in Seattle, WA; son of Ralph B. (an engineer) and Virginia R. (Reppert) Galvin; married Deborah Chernin (a modern dancer and choreographer), 1979; children: Joseph Chernin, Sarah Reppert. *Education:* Attended Westminster College (Fulton, MO), 1968-69; Indiana University-Bloomington, A.B. (with honors), 1975, M.D., 1979, postdoctoral study, 1979-83. *Politics:* Independent. *Religion:* Roman Catholic.

ADDRESSES: Home—8225 Meadowbrook Dr., Indianapolis, IN 46240. *Office*—Riley Child Psychiatric Services, 702 Barnhill Dr., Indianapolis, IN 46202-5200.

CAREER: Indiana University Medical Center, Indianapolis, fellow in child psychiatry, 1982-84, assistant professor, 1984-89, clinical assistant professor, 1990-92, 1993-95, clinical associate professor of psychiatry, 1995—. Larue Carter Hospital, staff psychiatrist, 1984-88, acting director of Youth Service, 1988-90; Indiana University Hospitals, staff psychiatrist, 1984—, assistant director of Psychiatric Services for Children and Adolescents, 1991—; Riley Child Psychiatric Services, staff child adolescent psychiatrist, 1990—, medical director of Child Adolescent Psychiatric Inpatient Program, 1991—; St. Vincent's Hospital, staff psychiatrist, 1993—; Methodist Hospital, staff psychiatrist, 1995—. Public speaker; guest on television and radio programs. *Military service:* U.S. Army, Medical Corps, 1970-76; served in Vietnam.

MEMBER: International Society for the Prevention of Child Abuse and Neglect, American Psychiatric Association (fellow), AACAP, American Society for Adolescent Psychiatry, National Alliance for the Mentally Ill (affiliate member), Indiana Council on Child and Adolescent Psychiatry (founding member; president, 1990-91), Phi Beta Kappa.

AWARDS, HONORS: Mosby Scholarship Book Award for the presentation "Neurochemical Investigations of Spinal Spasticity and Neurotransmitter Replacement Therapy"; award for teaching excellence, Indiana University psychiatry residents, 1995.

WRITINGS:

Ignatius Finds Help: A Story About Psychotherapy for Children, illustrated by Sandra Ferraro, Magination Press (New York City), 1988.
Otto Learns About His Medicine: A Story About Stimulant Medication for Children, illustrated by Ferraro, Magination Press, 1988, revised edition, 1995.
How Robby Really Transformed: A Story About Grownups Helping Children, illustrated by Ferraro, Magination Press, 1988.
Clouds and Clocks: A Story for Children Who Soil, illustrated by Ferraro, Magination Press, 1989.
(With Rosemary Collins) *Sometimes Y: A Story for Families With Gender Identity Issues,* illustrated by Ferraro, privately printed, 1993.

Contributor to medical books. Contributor to *Skipping Stones* and to medical journals.

WORK IN PROGRESS: The Conscience Celebration: A Story About Moral Flourishing, with Barbara Stilwell; *Grandma's Grade-A Gray Day* (tentative title); research on the development of conscience in children, adolescents, and young adults; research on the biopsychosocial consequences of maltreatment in children and adolescents; research on the high-risk offspring of bipolar parents.

SIDELIGHTS: Matthew R. Galvin commented: "Psychoeducation regarding various disorders has long been recognized as an important part of effective treatment. At Indiana University, Riley Child and Adolescent Psychiatric Services has an excellent tradition of developing and providing psycho-educational materials to children and their families. We routinely engage our child and adolescent patients and their parents in a biopsychosocial explanation of the specific disorder that affects them and, subsequently, of the treatment interventions.

"Over the seventeen years I have been associated with child and adolescent psychiatry, I've found my interest in traditional psychoeducation converging with my own experiences engaging children via narrative and teaching residents how to use children's favorite fairy tales and books, mutual storytelling, and therapeutic metaphor in psychotherapy. Stories mutually told and narrative organized around healing metaphors created in the context of psychotherapy do not necessarily lose their power when the case is closed, however. Sometimes they are recognized for being more universally relevant. Hence, there is a pathway with traces first discerned in sharing therapeutic metaphor and mutual storytelling with children on their way to healing and flourishing. It merges with another pathway discovered in the growth and development of people like my wife, myself and my own children, Joseph and Sarah and the family saga which we also mutually tell. It converges with still another pathway: the acquisition and transmission of sound, clinical knowledge. The final common pathway, I discovered, leads eventually to a psychoeducational special needs library. I and my colleagues and our families have been privileged to contribute to the collection therein.

"Our first effort along these lines was *Ignatius Finds Help,* which has found its place in the special needs collections assembled by clinicians who serve children and their families, and in school libraries. The publication of this and two additional books launched a new imprint of Brunner/Mazel Publishing called Magination Press, devoted exclusively to special needs/mental health literature for children and their parents.

"The success of *Ignatius Finds Help* has been modest, however, in comparison to our second book, *Otto Learns About His Medicine.* Like its predecessor, *Otto* came into print only after careful review by other child psychiatrists. It has sold over twenty-thousand copies and was even rendered into the format of a children's therapeutic drama. *Otto* was followed by *How Robby Really Transformed.* This book turned out to have very limited appeal, selling chiefly, we surmise, to clinicians serving the seriously and persistently mentally ill children who need out-of-home placement, case management, and play therapy. Drawing an analogy to medications that may benefit people with uncommon conditions, but which cannot be marketed successfully because of

limited demand, I think of *Robby* as our first 'orphan book.'

"Some of our other books deal with sensitive subjects, such as *Sometimes Y,* for children with gender identity and role issues. It became our second orphan, published in a limited printing, financed with royalties from our previous titles, and available to clinicians upon request. I am pleased to note that no one involved in the authorship, illustration, critical review, or contribution of introductory commentary has received compensation for this effort. The royalties have been used to pay for education (such as summer internships or travel expenses for visiting professors) and research at the Indiana University School of Medicine.

"Our Children's Psychoeducational Initiative took a new turn when Barbara Stilwell, who had been the principal investigator on the university's Conscience Project, retired from academia to devote herself full-time to rendering the results of our scholarly studies into the form of a suitable book for adults. We decided that we should also author a book for the children themselves. It would inform children about what they and their peers are experiencing as their consciences develop. It would be designed for use in the classroom and the school library. The result is *The Conscience Celebration.*

"Now, with access to the Internet through a departmental home page, we have an unprecedented opportunity to make a substantial contribution to public awareness of childhood mental illness and its treatments, to distribute psychoeducational materials to colleagues in the mental health field, and to develop our own electronic special needs library. This library will solve the dilemma posed by our orphan books. We propose to start with a book about depression in families, tentatively titled *Grandma's Grade-A Gray Day.* In future years we could expand the library to include books on such subjects as post-traumatic stress disorder, the consequences of maltreatment, and obsessive compulsive disorder. In addition, we can begin collecting the therapeutic metaphors that are so often used in psychotherapy in the clinic, the hospitals, and on the consultation service, making them available through our home page. We also envision additional activities in the future; for example, psychoeducational materials for teachers.

"The Children's Psychoeducational Initiative has an excellent tradition, which spans our component institutions and has flourished over the years in various forms. I have been privileged to collaborate with others in making contributions to psychoeducation. More can be accomplished in the age of the Internet, particularly if there is corporate sponsorship and support.

"More recently I have collaborated with my daughter on a story that we illustrated. 'Sheilah and Shimmer,' which has been published in *Skipping Stones,* is concerned with the recognition of religious intolerance in various forms, and with the moral valuation of religious differences. It addresses the experience from the point of view that respect for differences which cannot be reconciled has moral value for both parent and child. We hope the story will be of special value to children in religiously mixed families, because it positively frames the experience of being different in a very important respect from a very important attachment figure, and it models an approach to issues that children (and parents) from such families usually encounter, but may find difficult to discuss."

* * *

GANTSCHEV, Ivan 1925-

PERSONAL: Born January 4, 1925, in Tirnovo, Bulgaria; son of Stanco (a lawyer) and Jordana (a teacher; maiden name, Gadjanova) Gantschev; married May 12, 1965; wife's name, Rosemarie (a commercial clerk); children: Loreta, Igna-Marie. *Education:* Attended the Academy of Art in Sophia, Bulgaria.

ADDRESSES: Home—Bettinastrasse 33, 6000 Frankfurt 1, Germany.

CAREER: Writer. Freelance artist, Bulgaria, until 1966; J. Walter Thompson (advertising agency), Frankfurt, West Germany, illustrator, beginning 1968; freelance artist, 1989—.

AWARDS, HONORS: Oesterreichischer Kinderbuch-Illustrationspreis (prize for best illustrated picture book in Austria), 1982; Ehrenliste Oesterreichischer Kinder-und Jugendbuchpreis, 1983-84; Die schoensten Buecher Oesterreichs, 1982-84, Goldene Plakette Biennale Bratislava, 1985.

WRITINGS:

SELF-ILLUSTRATED; JUVENILE

The Volcano, Picture Book Studio (Saxonville, MA), 1981.
The Christmas Train, translated from the original German manuscript by Karen M. Klockner, Little (New York City), 1984.
Rumprump, Picture Book Studio, 1984.
Journey of the Storks, Picture Book Studio, 1986.
Otto the Bear, translated from German by Karen M. Klockner, Little, 1986.
Walk under the Rainbow, Burdett, 1986.
The Train to Grandma's, Picture Book Studio, 1987.
Where Is Mr. Mole?, adapted by Andrew Clements, Picture Book Studio, 1989.
Good Morning, Good Night, adapted by Andrew Clements, Picture Book Studio, 1991.
The Christmas Story by Father Christmas, c. 1992.
The Christmas Teddy Bear, text adapted by Andrew Clements, North-South Books (New York City), 1994.
Libby's Journey, c. 1995.

Also author of *The River, The Little Bird's Favorite Tree, The Cherrytree, When I Grow Up, The Story of the Rock, The Elephant, Old Woman and the Bear, Timmi and the Old Locomotive, Colors, Raindrop, The Tigers' Present, The Pear Tree, Hanibal,* and *The Adventure of the Mouse,* all published by Gakken (Tokyo, Japan).

ILLUSTRATOR

Hisako Aoki, *Santa's Favorite Story,* Picture Book Studio, 1982.
Oliver Gadsby, *The Moon Lake,* Picture Book Studio, 1985.
Robert Saunders, editor, *Two Islands,* Picture Book Studio, 1985.
Laurie Lattig-Ehlers, *Canoeing,* Picture Book Studio, 1986.
Kurt Baumann, *Three Kings: A Christmas Tale,* translated from German by Naomi Lewis, North-South Books, 1990.
Andrew Clements, *Noah and the Ark and the Animals,* Picture Book Studio, 1991.

OTHER

The Art of Ivan Gantschev, Itabashi Art Museum (Tokyo, Japan).

WORK IN PROGRESS: Der kleine kreis, to be published by Patmos (Dusseldorf, Germany); *Wo der Mond wohnt,* to be published by Neugebauer (Zurich, Switzerland); *The Dragonfly,* to be published by Gakken (Tokyo, Japan).

SIDELIGHTS: Ivan Gantschev told *CA:* "Why do I make picture books? Perhaps I believe that with beautiful books I can influence the future of the young inhabitants of this world, so that they may live their lives free of tyranny, stress, and war. Illusions? Perhaps I make picture books only for myself because I enjoy doing them so much!"

Whether for children or himself, Gantschev has created a wealth of picture books, many of which were originally written in German and translated into English, Spanish, and several other languages. Typically Gantschev's books explore the closeness of family, the importance of faith and timeless virtues, and the magic of love. His 1994 book, *The Christmas Teddy Bear,* for example, tells of a grandfather's love for his family as he braves a snowstorm on Christmas Eve to bring sugar for his wife's baking and a teddy bear for his grand-daughter's Christmas gift. Disoriented by the blinding snow, the grandfather, clinging to the teddy bear he chose for his beloved granddaughter, collapses and disappears into a drift. Fortunately, the teddy bear's bright red cap protrudes from the snow drift so his family can locate and rescue the grandfather. A *Publishers Weekly* reviewer deemed *The Christmas Teddy Bear* "fetching," and "clearly a labor of love."

Gantschev also recreates old-fashioned times and the gift of family in his 1984 book, *The Christmas Train,* which is based on a true story about the author's aunt, who as a child thwarted a Christmas Eve train wreck by setting her Christmas tree afire to signal the train conductor of looming danger. Writing in *Newsweek,* reviewer Laura Shapiro called Gantschev's story and illustrations "dream-laden and dazzling."

The magic of Christmas also inspired Gantschev to illustrate several other books on the holiday, among them Hisako Aoki's *Santa's Favorite Story,* in which Santa Claus brings peace to anxious forest animals by explaining the true meaning of Christmas, and Kurt Baumann's *Three Kings: A Christmas Tale,* the tale of a young musician, a blind storyteller, and a king who witness the birth of the Christ child.

BIOGRAPHICAL/CRITICAL SOURCES:

BOOKS

Gantschev, Ivan, *The Art of Ivan Gantschev,* Itabashi Art Museum (Tokyo, Japan).

PERIODICALS

Jugend Bulletin, 1996.
Newsweek, December 3, 1988, p. 88.
Publishers Weekly, September 19, 1994, p. 31.

*   *   *

GERRITSEN, Terry
  See GERRITSEN, Tess

*   *   *

GERRITSEN, Tess   1953-
  (Terry Gerritsen)

PERSONAL: Born June 12, 1953, in San Diego, CA; daughter of Ernest and Ruby (Tao) Tom; married Jacob Gerritsen, 1977. *Ethnicity:* "Chinese-American." *Education:* Stanford University, B.A., 1975; University of California, San Francisco, M.D., 1979. *Avocational interests:* Amateur violinist, gardener, "perpetual tourist."

ADDRESSES: Agent—Meg Ruley, Jane Rotrosen Agency, 318 East 51st St., New York, NY 10022.

CAREER: Physician in Honolulu, HI, 1979-89; freelance writer, 1989—.

MEMBER: Author's Guild, Mystery Writers of America, Romance Writers of America.

AWARDS, HONORS: Reviewers' Choice award, best Harlequin intrigue novel, *Romantic Times,* 1991-92, for *Never Say Die.*

WRITINGS:

NOVELS

Adventure's Mistress, SOS Publications (Los Angeles, CA), 1985.

Call after Midnight, Harlequin (New York City), 1991.
Never Say Die, Harlequin, c. 1990s.
Presumed Guilty, Harlequin, 1993.
(As Terry Gerritsen) *Peggy Sue Got Murdered,* HarperCollins (New York City), 1994.
Thief of Hearts, Harlequin, 1995.
Harvest (medical thriller), Pocket Books (New York City), 1996.
Keeper of the Bride, Harlequin, 1996.
Life Support (medical thriller), Pocket Books, 1997.

Also the author of other "romantic suspense" novels. Gerritsen's books have been published in nineteen foreign languages.

TELEPLAYS

"Adrift," *CBS Movie of the Week,* CBS, 1993.

WORK IN PROGRESS: Another medical thriller.

SIDELIGHTS: Tess Gerritsen told *CA:* "I began writing while working as a physician, as escape, as release, as a means of entertaining myself. After my children were born, writing was a means for me to remain home as a mother while pursuing a career more conducive to family life.

"I write to entertain and to move my readers' emotions. Books have always been my good friends, and I want readers to consider my books friends—something to turn to for excitement, to enliven an otherwise dreary day. My advice to aspiring writers? Read. Dream. Write what you *want* to write, not what you think you *should* write. The excitement will shine through!"

*   *   *

GIBSON, Richard G. 1953-

PERSONAL: Born October 12, 1953, in Atlanta, GA; son of Richard G., Sr., and Miriam (Healy) Gibson; married Karen Hillman, April 22, 1994; children: Sarah Elizabeth. *Education:* University of North Carolina at Charlotte, B.S.E., 1976, M.B.A., 1980; University of Maryland at College Park, M.S., 1990, Ph.D., 1992.

ADDRESSES: Home—2987 Lost Creek Blvd., Laurel, MD 20724. *Office*—Department of Computer Science and Information Systems, American University, 4400 Massachusetts Ave., Washington, DC 20016; fax 202-885-1479. *E-mail*—rgibson @american.edu.

CAREER: Queen City Plastics, Charlotte, NC, sales engineer, 1976-77, plant engineer, 1977-79, plant manager, 1979-81, general manager, 1981; Guilford Technical Community College, Greensboro, NC, instructor in industrial management, computer science, and office automation technology and coordinator of cooperative education, 1981-85; University of Maryland, European and Asian Divisions, instructor in business management, computer science, information systems, and mathematics, 1985-89, computer studies coordinator, 1988-89; University of Maryland at College Park, part-time instructor in computer science and information systems, 1991; American University, Washington, DC, instructor, 1992, assistant professor of computer science and information systems, 1993—. Consultant to Xerox Corp.

MEMBER: Information Resources Management Association, Decision Sciences Institute, Institute of Electrical and Electronics Engineers, Association of Computing Machinery, DC SPIN, Beta Gamma Sigma, Omega Rho, Upsilon Pi Epsilon (charter member).

AWARDS, HONORS: Macmillan Best Paper Award, 1993; grants from Center for International Business Education and Research and Mellon Fund.

WRITINGS:

(Editor with T. Bergin) *The History of Programming Languages II,* ACM (New York City), 1996.
(Contributor) Palvia, Roche, and Palvia, editors, *Global Information Technology and Systems Management,* Ivy League Publishing, 1996.

Contributor of articles and reviews to management and computer sciences journals. Member of editorial review board, *Journal of Global Information Management,* 1991—, and *Journal of End User Computing,* 1994—; member of editorial advisory board, *Journal of Database Management,* 1994-96, and *Information Management,* 1994—.

BIOGRAPHICAL/CRITICAL SOURCES:

PERIODICALS

Journal of Global Information Management, fall, 1996, p. 35.

GILB, Dagoberto 1950-

PERSONAL: Born in 1950, in Los Angeles, CA; married, wife's name Rebeca; children: Antonio, Ricardo. *Education:* University of California, B.A., M.A., 1976.

ADDRESSES: Home—Box 31001, El Paso, TX 79931.

CAREER: Los Angeles County, certified journeyman carpenter, 1976-91. University of Texas, Austin, Department of English, visiting fiction writer, 1988; University of Arizona, Tucson, Department of English, visiting writer in creative writing program, 1992; University of Wyoming, Laramie, Department of English, visiting writer, 1994.

MEMBER: Texas Institute of Letters, PEN/West, PEN American Center.

AWARDS, HONORS: James D. Phelan Award in literature, San Francisco Foundation, 1984; Dobie-Paisano fellow, Texas Institute of Letters/University of Texas, 1987-88; creative writing fellow, National Endowment for the Arts, 1992; Whiting Writers' Award, Mrs. Giles Whiting Foundation, 1993; Brazos Bookstore/Texas Institute of Letters Award for best short story, 1993; Jesse Jones/Texas Institute of Letters Award for best book of fiction, Texas Institute of Letters, 1993; PEN/Hemingway Foundation Award for First Fiction, Ernest Hemingway Foundation, 1994; PEN/Faulkner Award for fiction finalist, PEN American Center, 1994; Guggenheim fellowship, John Simon Guggenheim Memorial Foundation, 1995.

WRITINGS:

Winners on the Pass Line, Cinco Puntos Press (El Paso, TX), 1985.
The Magic of Blood, University of New Mexico Press (Albuquerque, NM), 1993.
The Last Known Residence of Mickey Acuna, Grove Press (New York City), 1994.

Contributor of numerous short stories and articles to magazines and anthologies.

WORK IN PROGRESS: 20 lbs, a novel.

SIDELIGHTS: In a 1995 *Los Angeles Times Magazine* interview with Lisa Broadwater, Dagoberto Gilb, author of *The Magic of Blood,* described himself as "the least likely writer." His life has been neither easy nor subdued, and these influences are reflected in his writing style and choice of subject matter.

The author's mother immigrated illegally from Mexico City, settling in Los Angeles, where she met his father, an ex-Marine of German ancestry. Their relationship was brief and stormy. The author's childhood was spent "in a part of Los Angeles that's pretty bad—near Washington High School, right next to Watts." He admits to running wild in his youth, but being lucky enough to avoid getting caught.

At the age of eighteen, Gilb decided to attend college, obtaining degrees in philosophy and religious studies. It was during this period that he began to keep personal notebooks. Following completion of a master's degree, he became a journeyman carpenter, which provided the flexibility to devote large blocks of time to writing. The author told Broadwater, "For me, a guy that likes to write, it was great. I could work six months and then take off for three and write some stories."

Broadwater noted that most literary magazines "weren't remotely interested in publishing Gilb's stories, which focus primarily on the professional and personal struggles of working-class Mexican Americans. They considered his work 'too colloquial.'" For ten years, attempts at publication met with frustration. The author's tenacity finally paid off in 1993 when his short story collection, *The Magic of Blood,* was accepted by a university press.

The following year, recognition abounded in the form of prestigious literary awards and a flood of critical attention for *The Magic of Blood.* Commenting that the book contained "wonderful, unsentimental stories" and prose that is "direct and strikingly honest," Robin Beeman of *Washington Post Book World* praised, "He is able to illuminate life's transforming moments with a delicate appreciation of their power and evanescence." In a reading list of new Chicano writing for *The Nation,* Ray Gonzales described Gilb's work as "disturbing" and declared that the stories, "written in fresh, startling language that says, 'I don't care. This is how it is,'" are the most powerful form of literature that a Chicano can write.

In 1994, Grove Press purchased rights to Gilb's *The Last Known Residence of Mickey Acuna,* a novel of inquiry into the lives of residents of a Texas YMCA, which closes with an unsettling conclusion. "I'm trying to give the experience of the Y, of living that life," explained Gilb in the *Los Angeles Times* interview with Broadwater. "And when you're done, with all your questions, you're just bitching about living there just like all the other people living there. So when you come away, you might have a view of what happened; but the fact is, you can't be sure what happened."

The Last Known Residence earned attention from reviewers. *New York Times* book critic Robert Cohen praised the novel and the author's "deft, ironic style that is all his own. He has conceived a bleak fable of a low-rent outlaw on the lam from someone who may only be himself—a man struggling, as we all do, to make transition yield transformation." In the *Bloomsbury Review,* Ray Gonzales noted, "We are lucky this prolific writer saved one of his most memorable and haunting characters for a longer work. . . . [He has] a drive for telling stories that inhabits the soul of a man like Mickey Acuna."

Though pleased with the positive recognition, Gilb is apparently content to keep the writing establishment at arm's length. As he said in the *Los Angeles Times Magazine* interview, "Art is about being a little wild, taking risks, not necessarily getting approval from somebody; it's the disapproval."

BIOGRAPHICAL/CRITICAL SOURCES:

PERIODICALS

Bloomsbury Review, March/April, 1995, p. 18.
Kirkus Reviews, August 1, 1993, p. 954.
Los Angeles Times Book Review, December 11, 1994, p. 2.
Los Angeles Times Magazine, November 12, 1995.
Los Angeles Times Mirror, c. 1994.
Nation, June 7, 1993, p. 772; December 27, 1993, p. 809; December 26, 1994, p. 816.
New York Times Book Review, October 31, 1993, p. 40; October 2, 1994, p. 15; December 4, 1994, p. 71; October 22, 1995, p. 44.
Publishers Weekly, July 25, 1994, p. 47.
Washington Post Book World, September 18, 1994.
World Literature Today, autumn, 1995, p. 794.*

*   *   *

GOLDBERG, Jacob 1943-
(Jake Goldberg)

PERSONAL: Born November 7, 1943, in Brooklyn, NY; son of Norman (a commercial artist) and Florence (maiden name, Frankenstein) Goldberg. *Education:* Harpur College, B.A., 1966. *Avocational interests:* Flying, fencing, chess, wilderness travel, progressive politics.

ADDRESSES: Home—423 11th St., Brooklyn, NY 11215.

CAREER: Crown Publishers, Inc., New York City, senior editor, 1970-90; Chelsea House Publishers, New York City, senior editor, 1990-96.

WRITINGS:

Rachel Carson: Biologist and Author (juvenile), Chelsea House (New York City), 1993.
Miguel Cervantes (young adult), Chelsea House, 1994.
Economics and the Environment (young adult), Chelsea House, 1994.
The Disappearing American Farm (young adult), Franklin Watts (New York City), 1995.
Albert Einstein: The Rebel behind Relativity (young adult), Franklin Watts, 1995.
Food (young adult), Franklin Watts, 1997.
Hawaii (juvenile), Marshall Cavendish, 1997.

Has also written under the name Jake Goldberg.

SIDELIGHTS: Jacob Goldberg commented: "I have wide-ranging interests, and I view the writing experience as an opportunity to research subjects I'd like to learn more about. I like to write for younger readers because I am forced to clearly explain all the components of my argument and carefully test my understanding of ideas I might otherwise have taken for granted."

Goldberg is the author of several nonfiction books for older elementary-school students and young adults. Critics praise Goldberg for presenting even the most controversial topics with clarity and objectivity. In his first book, a biography of Rachel Carson, *Bulletin of the Center for Children's Books* reviewer Zena Sutherland wrote that "Goldberg's tone is impartial" as he conveys Carson's apocalyptic theories about the damage being done to the environment by the pesticides commonly in use on America's farms. Goldberg also describes the strong resistance with which those theories were met by some.

Kathleen Beck, who reviewed Goldberg's *Economics and the Environment* in *Voice of Youth Advocates (VOYA),* praised the author for his "clear and provocative" narrative. In this book, the author "raises important questions, ones which are seldom addressed on a young adult level," Beck commented. However, the *VOYA* contributor questioned the author's objectivity on such issues as the effect of international banking on economic development in the Third World.

Goldberg offered a concise history of farming, with particular emphasis on federal subsidies of American farms, in his book *The Disappearing American Farm,* which received mixed reviews. A *Kirkus Reviews* critic felt that Goldberg's approach to his complicated topic lacked focus, and thus "does little to clarify the issues" raised. However, Eldon Younce wrote in *School Library Journal* that Goldberg does "an exceptional job" of recounting the history of his subject and objectively presents arguments both for and against federal subsidies.

BIOGRAPHICAL/CRITICAL SOURCES:

PERIODICALS

Bulletin of the Center for Children's Books, July, 1991, p. 262.
Kirkus Reviews, April 15, 1996, p. 601.
School Library Journal, June, 1996, p. 156.
Voice of Youth Advocates, June, 1993, p. 111.

*   *   *

GOLDBERG, Jake
  See GOLDBERG, Jacob

*   *   *

GRABER, (George) Alexander   1914-1997
  (Alexander Cordell)

OBITUARY NOTICE—See index for *CA* sketch: Born September 9, 1914, in Colombo, Ceylon (now Sri Lanka), to British parents; body found in a stream, July 9, 1997, near Llangollen, Denbighshire, Wales. Soldier, surveyor, author. Graber was a popular novelist who penned historical yarns under the pseudonym Alexander Cordell. The son of a British soldier, he also pursued military service first as a British Army sapper from 1932 to 1936, then with the Royal Engineers during World War II, becoming a major. From 1936 to 1939 and after 1945, Graber worked as a civil surveyor in Wales and eventually settled there. He was a member of the Welsh Nationalist Party and advocated self-government in his adopted country. He began his writing career in earnest in 1950 and at one time served as vice president of the Cardiff Writers' Circle. Credited with writing nearly thirty books, Graber is best remembered for his novel *Rape of the Fair Country,* which focused on the struggles of workers to obtain various labor rights. The book was part of the "Welsh Trilogy," which also included *Robe of Honour* and *Song of the Earth.* Among his other books are *A Thought of Honour, If You Believe the Soldiers, Sea Urchin, Siesta without Sleep, Rogue's March, Land of My Fathers, To Slay the Dreamer, Peerless Jim, Tales from Tiger Bay, This Proud and Savage Land, Tunnel Tigers, Requiem for a Patriot, Moll, The Dreams of Fair Women, Beloved Exile, Land of Heart's Desire,* and *Send Her Victorious.* He wrote a number of books for children, including *The White Cockade, Witches Sabbath,* and *The Healing Blade.* At the time of his death, his novel about Owain Glyndwr, a medieval Welsh prince, was incomplete.

OBITUARIES AND OTHER SOURCES:

BOOKS

Writers Directory, St. James Press, 1996.

PERIODICALS

Chicago Tribune, August 11, 1997, sec. 4, p. 8.
New York Times, August 10, 1997, sec. 1, p. 37.
Times (London; electronic), July 12, 1997.

*   *   *

GRANT DUFF, Shiela   1913-

PERSONAL: First name is sometimes spelled Sheila; born May 11, 1913, in London, England; daughter of Adrian (a soldier) and Ursula (an editor; maiden name Lubbock) Grant Duff; married Noel Francis Newsome, 1942 (marriage ended); married Michael Sokolov (a company director), 1952; children: Penelope Newsome, Jasper Newsome, Fiona Sokolov Rativ, Ivan Sokolov, Alexander Sokolov. *Education:*

Lady Margaret Hall, Oxford University, B.A., 1934. *Politics:* Liberal.

ADDRESSES: *Home*—Castlehaven, Castletownshend, Skibbereen, County Cork, Ireland. *Office*—c/o University Women's Club, 2 Audley Sq., South Audley St., London W1, England. *Agent*—Gill Coleridge, Anthony Sheil Associates Ltd., 43 Doughty St., London WC1N 2LF, England.

CAREER: *Chicago Daily News,* Paris, France, foreign correspondent, 1934-35; *Observer,* London, England, London correspondent, 1935, Prague correspondent, 1936-38, Czechoslovak expert in Foreign Research and Press Section of Foreign Office, 1939-61; editor of Czechoslovak section of European Service of the British Broadcasting Company, 1941-44.

MEMBER: University Women's Club.

WRITINGS:

German and Czech: A Threat to European Peace, New Fabian Research Bureau, 1937.
Europe and the Czechs, Penguin, 1938.
(Contributor) *Germany: What Next?,* Penguin, 1939.
A German Protectorate, the Czechs under Nazi Rule, Macmillan (London), 1942.
Fuenf Jahre bis zum Krieg, Beck (Munich), 1978.
The Parting of Ways: A Personal Account of the Thirties (historical autobiography), Peter Owen (London), 1982.
A Noble Combat: The Letters of Shiela Grant Duff and Adam von Trott zu Solz, 1931-1939, edited by Klemens von Klemperer, Oxford University Press (New York City), 1988.

SIDELIGHTS: Shiela Grant Duff told *CA:* "I have never really considered myself an author since it is not writing for itself that I am interested in but for a purpose. My first books were written as a foreign correspondent in Europe, where, like most of my colleagues, I desperately wanted to alert my fellow countrymen to the threat of war." One of the books she issued is *The Parting of Ways: A Personal Account of the Thirties,* which chronicles her years as a foreign correspondent, captures the turmoil of the war years, and portrays the colorful personalities who affected her life during that time.

Described by the author as "autobiography cum history," *The Parting of Ways* provides glimpses of Grant Duff's youth as the daughter of influential parents. Although her father was killed early in

World War I while the author was a still child, her memories of childhood are pleasant. She describes her rambling family estates in England and Scotland, her trips to visit friends at their equally magnificent homes, and her acquaintances with interesting classmates at preferred schools.

After her education at Oxford University, Grant Duff joined the London *Observer* as a foreign correspondent, serving first as an apprentice to several veteran correspondents, who informed her of Adolf Hitler's activities in Germany and the threat of Nazism's spread across Europe. Grant Duff then had a mission: to warn as many people as possible of the murderous Hitler and his comrades.

As she describes in *The Parting of Ways,* Grant Duff began a long association with Czechoslovakia in 1936 as a foreign correspondent. She quickly grew to love the country, and her fear of Hitler's threat to England soon expanded to include Czechoslovakia. A cousin to Winston Churchill's wife, Grant Duff used her family ties to gain information from Churchill about Nazism's threat to Czechoslovakia. That information, coupled with her first-hand observations, formed her book, *Europe and the Czechs,* which was published in 1938, after Czechoslovakia was ravaged by the Nazis.

Reviewing *The Parting of Ways* for *Times Literary Supplement,* Bernard Bergonzi declared that Grant Duff "records the intense anguish of a first-hand participant in the crisis and a passionate supporter of the Czech cause. . . . Shiela Grant Duff conveys her feeling about Czechoslovakia, certainly; but there are other interesting things about which she says very little, such as her dealings with her family and friends over her individualistic course of life. She says just enough about her relationship with Adam von Trott to make one wish for more."

Fulfilling that reviewer's wish, Grant Duff delivers more about Adam von Trott in her 1988 publication, *A Noble Combat: The Letters of Shiela Grant Duff and Adam von Trott zu Solz, 1932-1939,* which was edited by Klemens von Klemperer. Grant Duff met the young von Trott at Oxford, where he was a German Rhodes scholar studying law. Both politically-minded, Grant Duff and von Trott based their friendship on their love for their respective countries, which they hoped would remain friendly.

Upon leaving Oxford, von Trott returned to Germany, while Grant Duff embarked on her career as a journalist with the *Observer*. Some of her earliest assignments were covering the Saar plebiscite, when the citizens of the League of Nations's-held Saarland voted to reunite with Germany, and the German takeover of Sudetenland from Czechoslovakia. These events exposed the young reporter to the evils of Hitler's Nazi party, and her disgust with events in Germany eventually affected her relationship with von Trott, who she believed sympathized with Hitler's cause. Just before the outbreak of World War II, she ceased corresponding with her college friend. But von Trott, while loyal to his motherland, was actually involved in a plot to assassinate Hitler. Von Trott's letters, however, could not reveal his animosity towards the dictator, lest they be intercepted. Unfortunately, von Trott's involvement in the assassination plot was eventually uncovered and he was executed in 1944.

Grant Duff's *A Noble Combat* was made possible when von Trott's widow returned to Grant Duff the letters she had mailed to her friend. The collection is considered a colorful portrait of the pre-World War II era, and the book has been applauded by numerous critics, among them an *Economist* reviewer who deemed Klemens von Klemperer "an exemplary editor," and found that the book "illuminates not just the writers, but the 1930s in European history." Further praise was issued by Anne Chisholm in her *Spectator* review. Chisholm described *A Noble Combat* as "a remarkable exchange of letters" and observed that the letters shed light on the "complexity of Anglo-German relationships" on the eve of World War II.

BIOGRAPHICAL/CRITICAL SOURCES:

BOOKS

Grant Duff, Shiela, *A Noble Combat: The Letters of Shiela Grant Duff and Adam von Trott Zu Solz, 1932-1939*, edited by Klemens von Klemperer, Oxford University Press (Oxford, England), 1988.
Grant Duff, Shiela, *The Parting of Ways: A Personal Account of the Thirties*, Peter Owen, 1982.

PERIODICALS

Economist, July 9, 1988, p. 84.
English Historical Review, October, 1991, pp. 1058-1059.
Journal of Modern History, December, 1991, pp. 817-818.

Library Journal, April 15, 1988, p. 76.
Publishers Weekly, February 26, 1988, p. 188.
Spectator, December 3, 1988, p. 31.
Times Literary Supplement, March 12, 1982, p. 274.

* * *

GREEN, Anna Katharine   1846-1935
(Anna Katharine Green Rohlfs)

PERSONAL: Born November 11, 1846, in Brooklyn, NY; died April 11, 1935, in Buffalo, NY; buried in Forest Lawn Cemetery, Buffalo; daughter of James Wilson (a defense lawyer) and Catharine Ann (Whitney) Green; married Charles Rohlfs (an actor and furniture designer), November 25, 1884; children: Rosamond, Sterling, Roland. *Education:* Ripley Female College (Poultney, VT), B.A., 1867. *Religion:* Presbyterian.

CAREER: Author of nearly thirty mystery novels; poet, dramatist.

WRITINGS:

MYSTERY NOVELS, EXCEPT AS NOTED

The Leavenworth Case: A Lawyer's Story, Putnam (New York City), 1878, reprinted with a new introduction by Michele Slung, Dover (New York City), 1981.
A Strange Disappearance, Putnam, 1880.
The Sword of Damocles: A Story of New York Life, Putnam, 1881.
The Defense of the Bride, and Other Poems (poems), Putnam, 1882.
X.Y.Z.: A Detective Story, Putnam, 1883.
The Mill Mystery, Putnam, 1886.
Risifi's Daughter: A Drama, Putnam, 1887.
7 to 12: A Detective Story, Putnam, 1887.
Behind Closed Doors, Putnam, 1888.
The Forsaken Inn, R. Bonner (New York City), 1890, reprinted by Books for Libraries Press (Freeport, NY), 1971.
The Old Stone House and Other Stories, Putnam, 1891, reprinted by Books for Libraries Press, 1970.
A Matter of Millions, illustrated by Victor Perard, R. Bonner, 1891.
Cynthia Wakeham's Money, Putnam, 1892.
Marked "Personal", Putnam, 1893.
Miss Hurd: An Enigma, Putnam, 1894.

The Doctor, His Wife, and the Clock, Putnam, 1895.

Dr. Izard, Putnam, 1895.

That Affair Next Door, Putnam, 1897.

Lost Man's Lane: A Second Episode in the Life of Amelia Butterworth, Putnam, 1898.

Agatha Webb, Putnam, 1899.

A Difficult Problem, The Staircase at the Heart's Delight, and Other Stories, F. M. Lupton (New York City), 1900, reprinted by Garrett Press (New York City), 1968.

The Circular Study, McClure Phillips (New York City), 1900, reprinted by Garland (New York City), 1976.

Hand and Ring, Putnam, 1901.

One of My Sons, Putnam, 1901.

The Filigree Ball: Being a Full and True Account of the Solution of the Mystery Concerning the Jeffrey-Moore Affair, illustrated by C. M. Relyes, Bobbs-Merrill (Indianapolis, IN), 1903, reprinted by Arno Press (New York City), 1976.

The Amethyst Box, Bobbs-Merrill, 1905.

The Millionaire Baby, Bobbs-Merrill, 1905.

The House in the Mist, Bobbs-Merrill, 1905.

The Chief Legatee, illustrations by Frank T. Merrill, Authors and Newspapers Association (New York City,) 1906, also published as *A Woman of Mystery,* 1909.

The Woman in the Alcove, illustrated by Arthur I. Keller, Bobbs-Merrill, 1906.

The Mayor's Wife, illustrated by Alice Barber Stephens, Bobbs-Merrill, 1907.

Three Thousand Dollars, R. G. Badger (Boston, MA), 1910.

The House of the Whispering Pines, Putnam, 1910.

Initials Only, Dodd, Mead (New York City), 1911.

Masterpieces of Mystery (short stories, contains "Midnight in Beauchamp Row," "Room No. 3," "The Ruby and the Cauldron," "The Little Steel Coils," "The Staircase at Heart's Delight," "The Amethyst Box," "The Grey Lady," "The Thief," and "The House in the Mist"), Dodd, Mead, 1913, also published as *Room Number 3 and Other Detective Stories,* Dodd, Mead, 1919.

Dark Hollow, illustrated by Thomas Fogarty, Dodd, Mead, 1914.

The Golden Slipper, and Other Problems for Violet Strange (short stories), frontispiece by A. I. Keller, Putnam, 1915.

To the Minute, Scarlet and Black: Two Tales of Life's Perplexities, Putnam, 1916.

The Mystery of the Hasty Arrow, illustrated by H. R. Ballinger, Dodd, Mead, 1917.

The Step on the Stair; or, You Are the Man, Dodd, Mead, 1923.

Le Crime de La 5 Avenue, translated from English by Rene Lecuyer, J. Tallandier (Paris, France), 1931.

ADAPTATIONS: The Leavenworth Case: A Lawyer's Story was adapted for the stage and filmed as both silent and sound motion pictures.

SIDELIGHTS: Anna Katherine Green is often referred to as "mother of the detective novel," according to a contributor for *Twentieth Century Literary Criticism,* because her writing established many detective novel literary devices and brought "unprecedented" popularity to the genre. A decade before Sir Arthur Conan Doyle issued his renowned Sherlock Holmes tales, Green created her protagonist, Inspector Ebenezer Gryce, who made his debut in Green's *The Leavenworth Case: A Lawyer's Case* and continued his investigations as long as the author continued spinning her mysteries.

Educated in New York City and Buffalo, New York, public schools, Green attended Ripley Female College in Poultney, Vermont, where she actively participated in the literary society, making the acquaintance of such notables as Ralph Waldo Emerson, with whom she would later correspond. At this time, Green, the daughter of a prominent defense attorney, was pursuing her interest in poetry. But her love of Edgar Allan Poe's mysteries, coupled with her fascination with her father's defense cases, inspired her to begin writing her own mystery. Published in 1878, *The Leavenworth Case* was immediately relished by its readers, who bought more than half a million copies of the book that many credit with creating the popular mystery genre.

Many years after *The Leavenworth Case* was issued, critics were still discussing its merits. Although many wrote that Green's Victorian style seemed stilted and archaic, most applauded her variety of plots, use of scientific and medical evidence, and knowledge of police and legal procedures. Author Grant Overton, for example, wrote in an essay on Green in the book *The Women Who Make Our Novels:* "Without ever creating a character comparable with Sherlock Holmes, Anna Katherine Green constructed mysteries more baffling than those solved by Conan Doyle's detective. . . . When pained by the lack of literary quality in her writing, it is possible to recall that she filled all the drawers of a massive bureau with discarded manuscript in the effort to write well a single book, *The Leavenworth Case.* And in the end she wrote it very badly, and it mattered little, so ingenious and satisfying was the story she had to tell."

Reviewer Howard Haycraft echoed Overton's sentiments in the essay "America: 1890-1914 (The Romantic Age)," in *Murder for Pleasure: The Life and Times of the Detective Story*. "There are sufficient aspects of uniqueness about *The Leavenworth Case* to make it, despite some incredibly bad writing, one of the true historical milestones of the genre," Haycraft stated. "It sprang full-fledged from its author's head, without traceable antecedents; it contained a sound police detective Ebenezer Gryce, and a remarkably cogent plot; it was one of the all-time best-sellers in the literature; and above all it was written by a woman. . . . Her plots are models of careful construction that can still hold their own against to-day's competition. For this quality, and by virtue of precedence and sustained popularity, she occupies an undisputed and honorable place in the development of the American detective story."

Because of the immediate success of *The Leavenworth Case,* Green thereafter concentrated her literary efforts on the mystery genre, although she did publish at least one volume of poetry. As she created more mysterious cases to solve, she introduced other protagonists in addition to the ever-present Gryce, including Violet Strange and Amelia Butterworth, female detectives who have been cited, respectively, as inspirations for the girl-sleuth Nancy Drew and Agatha Christie's Miss Jane Marple.

Amelia Butterworth has been the subject of numerous modern essays on feminism in literature. Providing an in-depth reading of the detective as seen in Green's *That Affair Next Door,* essayist Cheri L. Ross wrote in the *Journal of Popular Culture* that Green's creation of Amelia Butterworth added "a new dimension to the detective novel while challenging the assumptions of society. Miss Butterworth, in her fifties, upper-middle class, and most respectable, is the first woman detective in American literature to challenge the accepted role of women."

Throughout *That Affair Next Door,* Ross explained, Green portrays Butterworth as a strong and wise woman who even convinces the traditional Inspector Gryce of her mental and detective skills. But representing the men of her day, Green allows Gryce to admire Butterworth's abilities with caution; although admitting she possesses a certain talent for unraveling mysteries, Gryce still counters many of Butterworth's hunches concerning the case they are

working on. Through the interactions of the two detectives, Gryce and Butterworth, Green illustrates the complexities of sex roles and perceptions, but, Ross asserted in her essay, "by the end of the novel, Miss Butterworth has not only proved to be Gryce's equal; she has also shown him up. She revels in her success, 'I admired him and I was sorry for him, but I never enjoyed myself so much in my whole life.' Gryce finally admits that she 'is a woman of genius,' and according to Miss Butterworth's sources, 'he has never been the same since the clearing up of this mystery.'"

Green's detective Violet Strange has also been viewed as an early feminist. In "A Case for Violet Strange," in *Images of Women in Fiction: Feminist Perspectives,* essayist John Cornillon looks at the stories in Green's collection *The Golden Slipper and Other Problems for Violet Strange,* observing: "Although Violet upholds the myth in public by conforming to the role expected of a young woman in her station in life, it is a hollow act, and in secret she lives a life in defiance of those role expectations. . . . Abstracting the plot from a feminist perspective we see Violet Strange breaking away from absolute dependence upon the patriarch and gaining economic independence by getting a job." Cornillon also found feminism evident in that Violet "earns money" and that by "using her mind," rebels against patriarchal order, and helps her sister look to her own talents, and not to a man, for economic survival. "Anna Katherine Green has used these stories to expose many of the ways women are oppressed by society's laws, conventions, attitudes and institutions," Cornillon stated, praising Green for not according her heroine "happiness that resulted from the salvation effected by some heroic Prince Charming."

Although Green produced some thirty detective novels and was widely read, her popularity waned at the turn of the century, as her Victorian mores and language became viewed as archaic. Still, her influence, critics noted, lives on in the works of today's masters of mystery. Writer Audrey Peterson detailed Green's achievements in the essay "Some Minor Voices," published in *Victorian Masters of Mystery: From Wilkie Collins to Conan Doyle,* noting: "Her work was widely read on both sides of the Atlantic and may well have had its effect upon the 'genteel' school of detective fiction which developed rapidly in Great Britain in the early years of the twentieth century. . . . Green's originality, the tightness of her plots, the attractiveness of her characters, and her astonishing consistency over a forty-five year span make her an author well worth a second look, while the old-fashioned qualities which banished her to obscurity have now, in an age of Victorian revival, taken on a patina of charm."

BIOGRAPHICAL/CRITICAL SOURCES:

BOOKS

Cornillon, John, "A Case for Violet Strange," in *Images of Women in Fiction: Feminist Perspectives,* edited by Susan Koppelman Cornillon, Bowling Green University Popular Press, 1973, pp. 206-215.

Harkins, E.F., and C.H.L. Johnston, "Ann Katherine Green (Mrs. Rohlfs)," in *Little Pilgrimages among the Women Who Have Written Famous Books,* L.C. Page & Co., 1902.

Haycraft, Howard, "America: 1890-1914 (The Romantic Age)," in *Murder for Pleasure: The Life and Times of the Detective Story,* D. Appleton-Century, 1941, pp. 83-102.

Overton, Grant, "Ann Katherine Green," in *The Women Who Make Our Novels,* Dodd, Mead, 1928, pp 167-173.

Peterson, Audrey, "Some Minor Voices," in *Victorian Masters of Mystery: From Wilkie Collins to Conan Doyle,* Frederick Ungar, 1984.

Twentieth-Century Literary Criticism, Volume 63, Gale Research (Detroit), 1996, pp. 133-160.

PERIODICALS

Journal of Popular Culture, fall, 1991, pp. 77-86.*

* * *

GREEN, Richard 1936-

PERSONAL: Born June 6, 1936, in Brooklyn, NY; son of Leo Harry and Rose (Ingber) Green; life partner of Melissa Hines; children: Adam Hines-Green. *Education:* Syracuse University, A.B., 1957; Johns Hopkins University, M.D., 1961; Yale University, J.D., 1987.

ADDRESSES: Office—Gender Identity Clinic, Charing Cross Hospital, London W6 8RF, England.

CAREER: Kings County Hospital, Brooklyn, NY, intern, 1962-64; National Institute of Mental Health,

Bethesda, MD, resident in psychiatry, 1965-66; University of California, Los Angeles, began as assistant professor, became professor of psychiatry, 1968-74 and 1986—, professor of law, 1988-90, part-time faculty member of law school, 1991-92; State University of New York, Stony Brook, professor of psychiatry and professor of law, 1974-85; Charing Cross Hospital, London, England, consulting psychiatrist in Gender Identity Clinic. University of Cambridge, Cambridge England, visiting scholar, 1980-81; fellow of Center for Advanced Study in Behavioral Sciences, Stanford, CA, 1982-83; visiting fellow of Institute of Criminology, Cambridge University, 1994; volunteer attorney for the American Civil Liberties Union, Los Angeles. Diplomate of American Board of Psychiatry and Neurology; admitted to the Bar of California, 1987, and Washington, DC, 1989.

MEMBER: International Academy of Sex Research (founding president, 1973), Society of the Science of the Study of Sex (fellow; served as president).

AWARDS, HONORS: Fulbright Scholar, King's College, London, and University of Cambridge, 1992.

WRITINGS:

(Editor, with John Money) *Transsexualism and Sex Reassignment,* Johns Hopkins Press (Baltimore, MD), 1969.

Sexual Identity Conflict in Children and Adults, Basic Books (New York City), 1974.

(Editor) *Human Sexuality: A Health Practitioner's Text,* Williams & Wilkins (Baltimore, MD), 1974.

(Editor, with Eli A. Rubinstein and Edward Brecher) *New Directions in Sex Research,* Plenum Press (New York City), 1976.

The "Sissy Boy Syndrome" and the Development of Homosexuality, Yale University Press (New Haven, CT), 1987.

Sexual Science and the Law, Harvard University Press (Cambridge, MA), 1992.

SIDELIGHTS: Psychiatrist and attorney Richard Green is the author of several books on sexual identity, including his 1987 publication, *The "Sissy Boy Syndrome" and the Development of Homosexuality,* which studies the connection between feminine behavior in males and the propensity towards homosexuality. Green issued his study based on interviews he conducted over fifteen years. One study group consisted of sixty-six boys who exhibited typically feminine traits, including dressing as girls, whom they also preferred as playmates, favoring girls' toys, such as dolls, and avoiding rough contact sports. The second group Green observed was traditionally masculine; the members enjoyed such activities as playing rough, and chose to play with cars and trucks.

Green conducted interviews with these boys and their parents during his fifteen-year study, and he includes excerpts from many of his interviews in *"Sissy Boy."* He also seeks to answer the most often asked questions regarding the emergence of homosexuality in boys, looking, for example, at the influence of a passive father on his son's sexuality. Does a weak or absent father cause a boy to develop homosexual tendencies, or does a father appear passive because he rejects his effeminate son? Green offers explanations to such questions, examining possible physiological, parental, and societal causes of homosexuality.

Green's *"Sissy Boy"* met with mixed reviews; some critics determined that the book offers too few concrete answers to explain why some boys become homosexuals. However, a *Spectator* reviewer, Anthony Storr, praised *"Sissy Boy,"* opining: "If more studies of this kind were available, we should know a great deal more about the huge number of variable, complex factors which go to form adult personality." Storr concluded that "many will find the case-histories and interviews of considerable interest," and predicted "professionals in the business of mental health will learn much, although unequivocal answers are still a long way off."

BIOGRAPHICAL/CRITICAL SOURCES:

PERIODICALS

Observer, February 8, 1987, p. 3.
Spectator, February 7, 1987, pp. 31-32.
Times Literary Supplement, March 27, 1987.
Village Voice Literary Supplement, February, 1987.*

* * *

GREENSIDE, Mark 1944-

PERSONAL: Born July 27, 1944, in Brooklyn, NY; son of Ernest (an attorney) and Dorothy (a teacher; maiden name, Kletter) Greenside; married Donna

Umeki. *Education:*University of Wisconsin—Madison, B.S. (history), M.A. (political science), 1968; attended University of California, Berkeley, 1971, and San Francisco State University, 1984-87. *Politics:* "Left(over)."

ADDRESSES: Home—6621 Ascot Dr., Oakland, CA 94611.

CAREER: Peralta Community College District, Oakland and Berkeley, CA, teacher of history, political science, English, creative writing, and humanities, 1971—, staff development officer, 1992-94, 1996-98. Vista College, director of "older adult program," 1978-84.

MEMBER: National Writers Union, American Federation of Teachers (chief grievance officer, 1985—; local president, 1987-89), PEN/Oakland, Faculty Association of California Community Colleges.

WRITINGS:

I Saw a Man Hit His Wife (short stories), White Pine Press (Fredonia, NY), 1997.

Work represented in anthologies, including *Gifts of Our Fathers,* edited by Thomas Verny. Contributor of stories to periodicals, including *Albany Review, Nebraska Review, Outerbridge, Soundings East, West End Review, Bellingham Review, McGuffin, New Laurel Review, Sun, Transfer, West Wind Review, Crosscurrents,* and *Beloit Fiction Journal.*

WORK IN PROGRESS: And the Good News Is . . . (tentative title), a collection of short stories, completion expected in 1999; research on the people, land, and culture of Brittany.

SIDELIGHTS: Mark Greenside told *CA:* "Questions of motivation and inspiration for my writing are interesting, because they have little to do with me. They seem to imply choice: choosing a subject, locating a modus operandi, neither of which I do. As much as I would like to say that I have chosen my subject, I cannot. It has chosen me. It speaks to me. If I wanted to invest thousands of dollars and hours into therapy, I might know why, but I'm not interested in doing that. The more I know why, the less I write, the worse I write. Not knowing why is what moves me. That is what's interesting, what I try to explore.

"To be sure, there are patterns in my writing. I write about time, about missed connections, about the search for place (in family, friendships, community, between lovers, parents and children, husbands and wives, siblings) in a world that is increasingly placeless, but that is not what starts me. What starts me is a voice or a picture. In my stories 'Jersey' and 'What Is It with Women, Anyhow?' I heard the voice of the narrator. In 'Father's Day' it was an image: the sight of a young boy holding his father's hand. In 'Inside and Out,' 'Beginnings,' and 'Fantasy,' it was a technical problem or an exploration of form that moved me. In 'Dreamers of Dreams' it was a story that an older woman told me, and in 'Mementos' it was something that happened to someone I knew, and I tried to imagine what that would be like.

"Who influences my work? Carver, of course, for his spareness; Flannery O'Connor for her sense of humor and meaning; Tobias Wolff and Ralph Lombreglia for their storytelling and characterizations; John Sayles for his generosity of spirit; Joyce Carol Oates for her bravery and her willingness to fail; Grace Paley, Bernard Malamud, Ethan Canin, Andre Dubus, Alice Munro, Gabriel Garcia Marquez, Bharati Mukherjee, Eudora Welty. Those are the biggies as far as short stories go, but there is the whole French world from Dada to absurdism to existentialism: Breton and Beckett and Sartre and Camus, without whom it is impossible to imagine thinking about anything. There is the world of the sixties: Ginsberg, Kerouac, Burroughs, Heller, Baldwin, Ferlinghetti, and so on.

"As for my writing process: I avoid. There is nothing more difficult than writing, except maybe not writing. I avoid and avoid and avoid until I am ready to burst—and then in frenzy and fear and exhilaration I begin to write, and sometimes I even like what I see. Those are the stories that make it to print. The others are waiting to be told."

*   *   *

GROTH-FLEMING, Candace
  See FLEMING, Candace

*   *   *

GRULIOW, Leo   1913-1997

OBITUARY NOTICE—See index for *CA* sketch: Born May 27, 1913, in Bayonne, NJ; died July 13, 1997,

in Columbus, OH. Journalist, educator, translator, author. Teaching himself the Russian language, Gruliow used his new skills to establish himself as a Soviet scholar and translator. Early in his career, he worked at the *Elizabeth Evening Times* as a reporter and the *New York Democrat* as a reporter and managing editor, before he found himself jobless during the Great Depression. He accepted a position with the *Moscow Daily News* as a technical consultant in 1933. The *News* was an English-language newspaper based in Moscow that was intended for tourists. In 1939 he became a Washington correspondent to the Transradio Press Service, then worked with New York's Russian War Relief during World War II. He then joined the Americans Friends Service Committee as a lecturer.

Stints as a guest lecturer followed at Grinnell College and the New School for Social Research. Gruliow also began work as a translator for the American Council of Learned Societies. In 1948 Gruliow began the *Current Digest of the Soviet Press* (now the *Current Digest of the Post-Soviet Press*) at Columbia University and served as its editor. More assignments as an educator followed at schools such as the Institut Universitaire de Hautes Etudes Internationales. Gruliow also served as a television commentator for the ABC and CBC television networks. Gruliow later founded Diorama Publications in New York City. Other career achievements included a stint with *The Christian Science Monitor* as its bureau chief in Moscow. He was the editor of several volumes of *Current Soviet Policies* and authored *Moscow.* Among his translations were Bulat Okudzhava's *A Taste of Liberty* and Aleksander Solzhenitsyn's *The Cancer Ward.* For his work providing relief to Russians after World War II, Gruliow was decorated by the Kremlin.

OBITUARIES AND OTHER SOURCES:

PERIODICALS

Chicago Tribune, July 21, 1997, sec. 2, p. 10.
New York Times, July 20, 1997, sec. 1, p. 26.

*   *   *

GUINNESS, Jonathan (Bryan)   1930-

PERSONAL: Born March 16, 1930, in London, England; son of Bryan Walter and Diana (Mitford) Guinness; married Ingrid Olivia Georgia Wyndham (divorced, 1962); married Suzanne Phillips, 1964; children: Catherine, Jasper, Valentine, Sebastian, Daphne. *Education:* Trinity College, Oxford, M.A., 1953. *Politics:* Conservative. *Religion:* Church of England.

ADDRESSES: Home—14 Porchester Terrace, London W23TS, England. *Agent*—Gillon Aitken, 29 Fernshaw Road, SW10-OTG England.

CAREER: Reuters, journalist, 1953-56; Erlangers Ltd., merchant banker trainee, 1956-59; Philip Hill, merchant banker trainee, 1959-62; Arthur Guinness Son & Co. Ltd., director, 1961-88; Leopold Joseph, executive director, 1962-64, non-executive director, 1964-91.

WRITINGS:

(With Catherine Guinness) *The House of Mitford* (biography), Hutchinson (London), 1984; Viking (New York), 1985.

Shoe: The Odyssey of a Sixties Survivor (biography), Hutchinson (London), 1989.

Requiem for a Family Business, Macmillan, in press.

SIDELIGHTS: Jonathan Guinness, along with his daughter, Catherine, put their own spin on the famous and infamous activities of their own Mitford family in the biography titled *The House of Mitford.* The work focuses on the seven well-born and connected Mitford children who came of age in England in the 1920s and 1930s. They include Nancy, the novelist and historian; Jessica, a writer and former Communist; Unity, a close friend of Adolf Hitler who shot herself when England went to war against Germany; and Deborah, who married the Duke of Devonshire. Jonathan Guinness is a businessman and the son of Diana Mitford, who spent time in prison for her support of fascism and whose second husband was the British fascist leader Sir Oswald Mosley.

The House of Mitford opens with a description of Bertie Mitford and Thomas Bowles, Jonathan Guinness's great-grandfathers, who were both Victorian eccentrics. Bertie was a scholar and diplomat who enjoyed travels in Japan, while Bowles was the owner of the magazines *Vanity Fair* and *The Lady.* Both were Conservative members of Parliament and members of the landed gentry. Next Guinness touches briefly on David and Sydney Mitford, his grandparents, and moves on to the next generation. Using previously unreleased letters from Unity to her parents and sister Diana and a memoir written

about Unity by her mother, Guinness sympathetically describes Unity's convictions about National Socialism and Hitler. On the other hand, he declares Jessica's convictions about communism dangerous.

In the *Washington Post Book World,* critic Victoria Glendinning called *The House of Mitford* a "hefty addition" to the Mitford mythology, while an *Atlantic* reviewer described it as a "fine group portrait." Anne Chisholm commented in the *New York Times Book Review* that *The House of Mitford* suffers from "rather laborious, overlapping and repetitive sequences," but admitted that the work is "ultimately highly revealing." "This is an enormously long book, but far from dull, despite the obvious constraints under which it was written," maintained E. S. Turner in the *Times Literary Supplement.* Betty Abel remarked in *Contemporary Review,* "Jonathan Guinness ably and amusingly traces the family history back to the 1890s." But Abel tempered her praise with the caveat, "Nothing in this excellently researched and entertaining book can, however, eradicate the spine-chilling impact of the tragically misguided Unity's passion for Hitler."

Several other commentators broached the subject of the authors' extreme right-wing biases in writing the work. The Guinnesses often try to excuse the activities of their ancestors on the grounds that their actions were understandable given the situation at the time. "Although Guinness writes well and is enormously entertaining, various sorts of bias inevitably intrude," commented Anne Smith in *New Statesman.* "Democracy is snubbed here, even in the telling of the story, and one puts this book down with a sinking feeling," declared Richard F. Shephard in the *New York Times.* "This family sparkles on the surface," commented Melvin Maddocks in *Time,* "but *The House of Mitford* refuses to probe the darkness, and by treating its subjects with too much charity, reduces their lives and careers to a series of gossipy, entertaining, but ultimately trivial pursuits."

BIOGRAPHICAL/CRITICAL SOURCES:

PERIODICALS

Atlantic, September 1985, pp. 114-115.
Contemporary Review, January 1985, pp. 52-53.
London Review of Books, December 6-19, 1984, pp. 11-12; May 18, 1989, p. 10.
Los Angeles Times Book Review, September 22, 1985, pp. 1, 6.
New Statesman, December 14, 1984, pp. 30, 32.

New York Times, July 29, 1985.

New York Times Book Review, August 18, 1985, p. 10.

Observer, November 18, 1984, p. 29; March 12, 1989, p. 45.

Spectator, December 8, 1984, pp. 37, 39.

Time, September 2, 1985, p. 71.

Times Literary Supplement, December 14, 1984, p. 1440.

Washington Post Book World, July 21, 1985, pp. 5-6.

*   *   *

GUNESEKERA, Romesh   1954-

PERSONAL: Born in 1954, in Colombo, Sri Lanka; raised in Sri Lanka, the Philippines, and England; children: two daughters.

ADDRESSES: Home—London, England.

CAREER: Novelist and short-story writer.

AWARDS, HONORS: Notable Book of the Year, *New York Times,* 1993, for *Monkfish Moon;* short-listed for Booker Prize, 1994, for *Reef;* Best First Work award, *Yorkshire Post,* 1994, for *Reef;* Premio Mondello, 1997, for *Reef;* nominated for New Voice Award.

WRITINGS:

Monkfish Moon (short stories), Granta Books (London), 1992, New Press (New York City), 1992.

Reef (novel), New Press (New York City), 1995.

The Sandglass (novel), Granta Books (London), 1998.

SIDELIGHTS: On the strength of his first volume of short stories, the 1992 *Monkfish Moon,* and his first novel, the 1994 *Reef,* Romesh Gunesekera was placed by critics in the select company of the most promising young British fiction writers; D. C. R. A. Goonetilleke declared him "arguably one of the top twenty young British novelists" in *Contemporary Novelists,* and poet-diplomat Guy Amirthanayagam, writing for *Washington Post Book World,* informed readers, "He bids fair to join the likes of V. S. Naipaul, Salman Rushdie, Timothy Mo and Kazuo Ishiguro." *Monkfish Moon* was less than one hundred and forty pages long—Suzanne Berne, in the *New York Times Book Review,* called it a "slender, evoca-tive book"—but as Goonetilleke pointed out, "each story is distinct in spite of a common motif of refurbishing dilapidated interiors and . . . an ironic theme of severance, parting, fracture, and failure."

Though several of the stories in *Monkfish Moon* are set in London, Sri Lankan life, and especially the civil war between Tamil and Sinhala forces, make themselves felt from across the sea. D. J. Taylor, reviewing the book for *New Statesman and Society,* felt that the stories were strongest when politics emerged quietly from the background as in "Batik" and "A House in the Country," rather than being placed in the foreground of the narration as in "Storm Petrel." Opined Taylor, "Gunesekera's forte is atmosphere: tiny intimations of disquiet, sudden adjustments to the psychological thermostat against a background of political turmoil. . . . [he] achieves his best effects in stories where character resists the thraldom imposed on it by environment." Taylor named the title story and "Carapace" as examples of this strength.

The novel *Reef* solidified Gunesekera's growing reputation. A coming-of-age story about a young domestic servant named Triton, it is set mainly in the 1960s but is narrated in flashback from the vantage point of thirty years later. As a boy, Triton is brought into the house of Salgado, a marine biologist obsessed with saving a local reef. Triton acquires the skills of cookery, and, within the limits of the experiences available to him, grows in sophistication. A worldly Sri Lankan woman, Nili, enters the household as Salgado's lover. The lovers part on bitter terms, after which Salgado and Triton move to London. In that city, Triton achieves a degree of independence as owner of a prosperous snack bar and eventually a restaurant. In the end, Salgado returns to the ravaged land of Sri Lanka to rejoin Nili, who has been psychologically maimed and rendered homeless by the communal violence.

Critics received *Reef* enthusiastically, praising in particular its language and characters. "The strength of the novel lies in its treatment of individual lives and personal relations and in its characteristic use of language," wrote Goonetilleke. "Gunesekera's style is sensuous and impassioned, almost incandescent," proclaimed Amirthanayagam. Travel writer Pico Iyer, in the *New York Review of Books,* was also impressed by the subtle beauties of Gunesekera's apparently simple prose, calling the book an "unusual prose-poem." Referring to the novel's "exquisitely sensuous surface," Iyer elaborated that the book was "lush" with descriptions of flora and fauna, of scents and sights: "The strength of *Reef,* in fact, lies in its unforced and convincing depiction of a self-contained universe." Iyer added praise for the novelist's supple technique: "The remarkable thing about this novel, indeed, is that it achieves nearly all of its effects silently, as it were, through almost imperceptible shadings of language and texture. . . . *Reef* proceeds so gently and lyrically—whispering around use like a murmurous sea—that it is easy to overlook just how subversive the book is." The subversiveness and "singular courage" of the book, Iyer commented, lay in its presentation of social corruption as deeper than ideology or fashion. All in all, *Reef* was, for that reviewer, "the best novel from the subcontinent since Rohinton Mistry's *Such A Long Journey.* . . . Calmly, it gives us a new and unexpected world, and gradually it makes it feel like home."

Neil Gordon, in the *Boston Review,* compared the central Christmas-dinner scene in *Reef* to James Joyce's novella *The Dead,* and called the young author "one of the two or three best writers I've encountered among my contemporaries." Like other critics, Gordon loved what he termed Gunesekera's "wholly original, very ambitious language," and applied the epithet "exquisite." Gordon doubted whether the novel succeeded in weaving topical political concerns organically into Triton's first-person narrative; however, he clarified, "emotional realities are what this book, in its perceptive, quiet voice, is most convincingly about."

Two reviewers alluded to the short-storylike nature of the novel. Julian Evans, who called *Reef* "a delightful novel," believed that it was "a long story more than a novel, a long episode of childhood that ends with the characters fading out into real life on the last page, a comedy with a vein of sadness." Aamer Hussein, a *Times Literary Supplement* reviewer, surmised that "the author, a natural short-story writer, has cunningly contrived to compose his novel of fragments structured like complete stories; but each story is deliberately deprived of an essential element, which is later revealed at the right moment."

Another aspect of Gunesekera's achievement that came in for praise was his creation of character, particularly the character of Salgado. Evans asserted, "Salgado himself, mysterious, kind, dreaming, depressive, is a complex creature on a par with [R. K.] Narayan's Margayya in *The Financial Expert* and

Yusef in [Graham] Greene's *The Heart of the Matter."* Richard Eder, in the *Los Angeles Times Book Review,* called Salgado "a wonderful mix of abstraction and urgency." Eder praised Gunesekera for saying so much within the deliberately confined scope of a first-person tale about a servant: "[He] has taken the risk of telling a large story in the tiny, almost cloying constriction of meals, recipes, furniture polishing and a boy's besotted reverence for the figure for whom he performed these tasks." The risk paid off, Eder implied, thus meriting its author respect both for courage and for achievement.

Gordon, a novelist himself, wrote of Gunesekera's work in the *Boston Review* concluding: "The perceptive, thrilling dram of his narration seems to burst the limits of his framing device, a tribute to the power of his story. I look forward to reading every word he writes, not only for the pleasure of following one of the two or three best writers I've encountered among my contemporaries, but also in the hopes of seeing his stories escape his rather tendentious narrative bias toward literary relevance and speak more simply and dramatically for themselves."

BIOGRAPHICAL/CRITICAL SOURCES:

BOOKS

Brown, Susan Windisch, editor, *Contemporary Novelists,* sixth edition, St. James Press (Detroit, MI), 1996, pp. 423-424.
Contemporary Literary Criticism, Volume 91: *Yearbook 1995,* Gale (Detroit, MI), 1996, pp. 33-44.

PERIODICALS

Boston Review, April, 1995, pp. 31-32.
Los Angeles Times Book Review, February 19, 1995, pp. 3, 11.
Manchester Guardian Weekly, July 17, 1994, p. 29.
New Statesman and Society, February 28, 1992, p. 47; September 2, 1994, p. 38.
New York Review of Books, June 22, 1995, pp. 30-31.
New York Times Book Review, August 1, 1993, p. 10; March 26, 1995, p. 29.
Spectator, March 7, 1992, p. 30.
Times Literary Supplement, June 24, 1994, p. 23.
Washington Post Book World, June 25, 1995, p. 5.

OTHER

Boston Review, http://www/polisci.mit.edu/Boston Review/BR20.2/Gordon.html, October 8, 1997.*

GUNETTI, Daniele   1963-

PERSONAL: Born January 16, 1963, in Turin, Italy; son of Luigi and Ugolina (Cirio) Gunetti. *Education:* Ph.D., 1995.

ADDRESSES: Office—Department of Computer Science, University of Turin, S.C.O. Svizzera 185, 10149 Turin, Italy; fax +39-11-751603. *E-mail*—gunetti@di.unito.it.

CAREER: Ministry of Communication, Turin, Italy, technician, 1983-87; University of Turin, Turin, technician, 1987-95, assistant professor of computer science, 1995—.

WRITINGS:

(With Francesco Bergadano) *Inductive Logic Programming: From Machine Learning to Software Engineering,* MIT Press (Cambridge, MA), 1995.

WORK IN PROGRESS: Research on computer security and machine learning.

H-I

HACKBARTH, Steven (L.) 1945-

PERSONAL: Born July 7, 1945, in St. Cloud, MN; son of Randall C. and Viola M. (Geisinger) Hackbarth; married Joyce Brown, September 11, 1965 (divorced, 1982); married Teresa F. Palacios (a UNICEF staff member), November 15, 1996; children: (first marriage) Valerie L. *Education:* California State University, Sacramento, B.A. (psychology), 1967, M.A. (psychology), 1968; University of California, Los Angeles, Ph.D. (philosophy of education), 1976; University of Southern California, M.S.Ed. (instructional technology), 1984; New York University, M.A. (special and elementary education), 1995. *Politics:* "Hillary Rodham Clinton, Nelson Mandela." *Religion:* "Christian." *Avocational interests:* History, anthropology, astronomy, philosophy, physics, theology, music, art, travel.

ADDRESSES: Home—Long Island City, NY. *Office*—Primary School 6, 45 East 81st St., New York, NY 10028. *E-mail*—hackbarths@aol.com. *Homepage*—http://members.aol.com/hackbarths.

CAREER: New York City Board of Education, Primary Schools 6 and 116, Manhattan, computer specialist teacher, 1994—; University of Southern California, director of office of student services, adjunct faculty member in department of policy, planning, and administration, 1977-91. Consultant to UNICEF, 1992—. Has served as youth softball coach, tennis coach, scout leader, and political campaign worker.

MEMBER: American Educational Research Association, Association for Educational Communications and Technology (National Membership Committee, 1994-97), Far Western Philosophy of Education Society (served as president, vice president, board member, and Program Committee chair), Phi Delta Kappa.

AWARDS, HONORS: Most Outstanding Doctoral Graduate of the UCLA School of Education, UCLA Doctoral Alumni Association, 1976; Certificate of Merit for Outstanding Contributions to the USC School of Education, 1989; Most Outstanding New Member award, Phi Delta Kappa, 1991; graduate education scholarship, New York University, 1995, for two years of study; finalist for Book of the Year Award, Association for Educational Communications and Technology, 1997, for *The Educational Technology Handbook: A Comprehensive Guide: Process and Products for Learning.*

WRITINGS:

The Educational Technology Handbook: A Comprehensive Guide: Process and Products for Learning, Educational Technology Publications (Englewood Cliffs, NJ), 1996.

Contributor to *Philosophy of Education in Cultural Perspective, The Educational Forum, Programmed Learning & Educational Technology, Phi Delta Kappan, Confluence in Education: Integrating Consciousness for Human Change, Educational Technology, Wired Together: Computer-Mediated Communication in K-12,* Volume 1: *Perspectives and Instructional Design, Web-Based Instruction, The Educational Media and Technology Yearbook 1997,* and *Tech Trends;* writer of reports and critiques for UNICEF (critiques are included on the UNICEF "Evaluation Database on CD-ROM"); special-issue guest editor, *Educational Technology.*

WORK IN PROGRESS: Second edition of *The Educational Technology Handbook,* for January, 2000. Research on the "role of disciplinary inquiry in Web-based learning" and on "using the problem-solving process of educational technology and electronic media to serve hard-to-reach populations."

SIDELIGHTS: In describing his career, Steven Hackbarth told *CA* that he has derived great satisfaction over the years from assisting in the writing of dissertations and reviewing reports for UNICEF on topics including sexual abuse and street children, gender equity in access to health and education, wife abuse, terminal cancer pain, female genital mutilation, child slavery, and AIDS orphans.

"While there is much satisfaction in writing to address such extreme and urgent issues, I have not moved to the front line of resolving them," he noted. "Rather, after thirteen years of working in a college office, I elected to seek certification to teach children having learning and emotional disabilities. My premise was that these children might benefit from using the sorts of electronic media I had been using and writing about the past two decades.

"My larger motivation is based on the fact that print and electronic media, along with parents and teachers, do much to influence the characters and aspirations of all people. Media messages today are shaped far more by commercial and political self-interest than by goodwill and noble ideals. Through sharing my expertise in the processes of learning and teaching as these relate to instructional design and media use, I have aspired to make positive contributions to the quality of education and thereby to the health and welfare of people everywhere and to our capacity to love joyfully many things and each other."

Written by a teacher for K-12 teachers, Hackbarth's *The Educational Technology Handbook: A Comprehensive Guide: Process and Products for Learning* is a guide to using technology to improve teaching and learning in the classroom. The book includes lists of resources and information on the development and use of instructional programs, the selection and use of products and media, advances in computers, and an educational technology start-up checklist.

The book helps teachers "make sense of the sea of advanced technology available to them," observed Karen Nelis in *New York Teacher.* Calling the book an excellent, comprehensive guide, George Marcoulides in *Educational Technology Review* lauded the author for doing "a fine job of synthesizing the prospects for educational technology in school systems" and providing "ample encouragement for educators to consider these new technologies."

The Educational Technology Handbook elicited praise from Rodney S. Earle in *Educational Technology Research and Development* for being user-friendly and bringing closer together the fields of instructional design and teacher planning, through the author's use of "models, language, and illustrations with which teachers can resonate." Hackbarth presents highly theoretical concepts "simply, in a manner that invites practical reflection," wrote C. A. Cunningham in *Choice. The Educational Technology Handbook* "is a well-balanced, extensively documented, encyclopedic work," declared James Rogers in *Computing Reviews,* hailing its informed yet tempered enthusiasm for the educational benefits of technology.

BIOGRAPHICAL/CRITICAL SOURCES:

PERIODICALS

Choice, December, 1996, p. 661.
Computing Reviews, December, 1996, p. 635-636.
Educational Technology Research and Development, vol. 44, no. 2, 1996, pp. 71-76.
Educational Technology Review, autumn, 1996, p. 28.
New York Teacher, April 29, 1996, p. 23A.

*   *   *

HADDAD, Bill
  See HADDAD, William F(rederick)

*   *   *

HADDAD, William
  See HADDAD, William F(rederick)

*   *   *

HADDAD, William F(rederick) 1928-

PERSONAL: Born July 25, 1928, in Charlotte, NC; son of Charles Frederick and Esther (Nowack) Haddad;

married Kate Roosevelt (divorced, 1973); married Noreen Breuer Walsh; children: (first marriage) Laura, Andrea, Camilla; (second marriage) Amanda Lee. *Education:* St. Petersburg Junior College (St. Petersburg, FL), A.A., 1952; Columbia University, B.A., 1954; conducted postgraduate studies, Columbia University, 1954, and Georgetown University, 1955-56. *Politics:* Democrat. *Religion:* Jewish. *Avocational interests:* Skiing, writing, vegetable gardening.

ADDRESSES: Home—Sedgewood Club, RD 12, Carmel, NY 10512. *Office*—Danbury Pharmacal, Inc., 131 West St., Danbury, CT 06810.

CAREER: Special assistant to Senator Estes Kefauver, Washington, DC, 1954-56, including assistant on world tour, 1955, political advisor on presidential primaries, 1955-56; administrative aide in vice presidential campaign, 1956; U.S. Senate Judiciary Committee, Washington, DC, public relations worker and staff director of the subcommittee to investigate juvenile delinquency, 1955; *New York Post,* New York City, investigative reporter, 1956-60; RCA, New York City, systems engineer of military applications, 1957; Council of New York Democrats, New York City, organizer, 1957; New York Committee for Democratic Voters, New York City, member of executive committee, 1959-60; 1960 presidential campaign, special assistant to Robert Kennedy, 1960; Peace Corps, Washington, DC, director of planning, coordination, and evaluation, 1961, associate director, inspector general, 1961-63; International Conference on Middle Level Manpower, 1962; *New York Herald Tribune,* New York City, investigative reporter, 1963-64; Office of Economic Opportunity, Washington, DC, associate director, inspector general, 1964-66; U.S. Research and Development Corporation, president, 1966, president and chief executive officer, starting in 1968; *Manhattan Tribune,* New York City, co-publisher, 1967-72; New York Board of Trade, NY, board of directors, vice chair, 1967-72; Robert Kennedy for President, campaign advisor, 1968; New York State Board of Continuing Education, NY, chair, 1968-70; New York City Diamond Jubilee, New York City, 1971; Sarah Lawrence College, Bronxville, NY, visiting lecturer, 1972-74; New York State Assembly, Albany, NY, director of Office of Legislative Oversight and Analysis, 1974-78; DeLorean Motor Company, New York City, consultant, vice president for planning and evaluation, 1979-81; Generic Pharmaceutical Industry Association, New York City, president, chief executive officer, then chair, 1981—; Generic Pharmaceutical

Industry Association Orphan Drug Foundation, chair, 1982—; Mario Cuomo for governor of New York, campaign advisor, 1982; *Generics* magazine, editor-in-chief and publisher, 1983—; Danbury Pharmacal, Danbury, CT, vice chair, chief executive officer, 1985—; Martin Luther King Memorial, State of New York, director, 1986—.

Cofounder, International Peace Corps; Ferre for governor of Puerto Rico, PR, campaign advisor; Waller for governor of Mississippi, MS, campaign advisor; Robert King High for governor of Florida, FL, campaign manager; Robert Kennedy for senator of New York, campaign research director; member of board of directors of Boys Brotherhood Republic, Crossroads Africa, Encampment for Citizenship, and New York Urban Coalition; American Jewish Congress, member of governing board. *Military service:* Merchant Marines, radio officer, 1945-54.

MEMBER: National Organization of Rare Disorders.

AWARDS, HONORS: Littauer fellow, 1957, 1964; George Polk Memorial award (with Joe Kahn), 1958, 1959, for outstanding metropolitan reporting; Heywood Broun award, American Newspaper Guild, 1959, 1966; Page One award, Newspaper Guild of New York, 1959, 1960; Byline award, Newspaper Reporters Association, 1961.

WRITINGS:

NONFICTION

(With Francis W. Goodwin and Richard N. Goodwin) *The Hidden Force: A Report of the International Conference on Middle Level Manpower, San Juan, Puerto Rico, October 10-12, 1962,* Harper & Row (New York City), 1963.
(Editor with G. Douglas Pugh) *Black Economic Development,* Prentice-Hall (Englewood Cliffs, NJ), 1969.
(As William Haddad; with Mel Roman) *The Disposable Parent: The Case for Joint Custody,* Holt, Rinehart, and Winston (New York City), 1978.
(As William Haddad) *Hard Driving: My Years with John DeLorean,* Random House (New York City), 1985.

GOVERNMENT REPORTS

(As Bill Haddad) *Political Dossiers: Memo for Stanley Steingut,* The Assembly, State of New York (Albany, NY), 1975.

(As William Haddad) *Preliminary Report on the New York State Lottery: To Stanley Steingut,* Office of Legislative Oversight Analysis, The Assembly, 1975.

(With Terry Lenzner, Carmine Bellino and Susan T. Mackenzie) *The Banks and the Municipal Crisis: Public Responsibility and Private Profit: Special Report to Honorable Stanley Steingut, Speaker, New York State Assembly,* Office of Legislative Oversight and Analysis, The Assembly, 1976.

(With Mel Roman) *No-Fault Custody: Special Report to Honorable Speaker Stanley Steingut,* The Assembly, 1978.

Contributor to periodicals.

SIDELIGHTS: William F. Haddad is a businessperson who has also worked as an investigative reporter, political aide, public relations consultant, and director of the Peace Corps. For fifteen years, he worked with John Z. DeLorean, the maverick automotive engineer who designed the highly successful, sporty Pontiac GTO, the first of the "muscle cars," and later tried to launch his own sports car venture, the DeLorean Motor Company. Haddad left DeLorean Motor Company shortly before it failed; DeLorean was later arrested, tried, and acquitted of drug dealing in a highly publicized case. In *Hard Driving: My Years with John DeLorean,* Haddad, presenting himself as a reluctant whistle-blower, ignores the drug matter and instead tells the behind-the-scenes story of the failed company. Wondering how he could have been fooled for so long by DeLorean's visions of an "ethical sports car," Haddad describes DeLorean as a charismatic con artist who only used his automobile company as a means of bilking money from a variety of sources, including the British government.

Commentators had much to say about the work, which was published at the same time as DeLorean's own apologetic memoir, *DeLorean.* Bill Hogan, a contributor to the *Washington Post Book World,* described *Hard Driving* as "a rather malevolent memoir," in which Haddad "concentrates his considerable investigative energies on documenting DeLorean's darker side." Writing in the *New York Times Book Review,* Ron Rosenbaum praised the work: "Mr. Haddad's account of the attempt by Mr. DeLorean's creditors to track down seventeen million dollars he supposedly shifted to a Swiss subsidiary makes a complicated international corporate detective story." In *Newsweek,* David Lehman maintained that Haddad "builds an impressive case against his former boss," adding that the author "writes more in sorrow than in anger, despite having plenty to be angry about."

BIOGRAPHICAL/CRITICAL SOURCES:

PERIODICALS

Los Angeles Times Book Review, December 22, 1985, p. 2.
New York Times Book Review, January 18, 1970, p. 9; October 20, 1985, p. 56.
Newsweek, October 28, 1985, p. 88.
Washington Post Book World, December 29, 1985, pp. 3, 13.*

* * *

HADDIX, Margaret Peterson 1964-

PERSONAL: Born April 9, 1964, in Washington Court House, OH; daughter of John Albert (a farmer) and Marilee Grace (a nurse; maiden name, Greshel) Peterson; married Doug Haddix (a newspaper editor), October 3, 1987; children: Meredith, Connor. *Education:* Miami University, B.A. (summa cum laude with university honors and honors in English), 1986. *Religion:* Presbyterian. *Avocational interests:* Travel.

ADDRESSES: Home—615 Timber Ln., Clarks Summit, PA 18411. *Agent*—Renee Cho, McIntosh & Otis, 310 Madison Ave., New York, NY 10020.

CAREER: Fort Wayne Journal-Gazette, Fort Wayne, IN, copy editor, 1986-87; *Indianapolis News,* Indianapolis, IN, reporter, 1987-91; Danville Area Community College, Danville, IL, adjunct faculty, 1991-93; freelance writer, 1991-94.

MEMBER: Phi Beta Kappa, Society of Children's Book Writers and Illustrators.

AWARDS, HONORS: Honorable mention, *Seventeen* magazine fiction contest, 1983; fiction contest award, National Society of Arts and Letters, 1988; Junior Library Guild selection, *American Bestseller* Pick of the Lists selection, nominee for Mystery Writers of America's Edgar Allen Poe award, listed as a Notable Children's Trade Books in the Field of Social Studies for 1996 by the National Council for Social Studies and the Children's Book Council, and listed as a Quick Pick for Reluctant Young Adult Readers and as a 1997 Best Book for Young Adults by the Young

Adult Library Services Association, all for *Running Out of Time;* Children's Book Award (older reader category), International Reading Association, 1997, and listed as a Quick Pick for Reluctant Young Adult Readers and as a 1997 Best Book for Young Adults by the Young Adult Library Services Association, all for *Don't You Dare Read This, Mrs. Dunphrey.*

WRITINGS:

Running Out of Time, Simon & Schuster (New York), 1995.
Don't You Dare Read This, Mrs. Dunphrey, Simon & Schuster, 1996.
Leaving Fishers, Simon & Schuster, 1997.
Among the Hidden, Simon & Schuster, 1998.

Short stories published in *Indiannual* and *The Luxury of Tears,* National Society of Arts and Letters, 1989.

WORK IN PROGRESS: A young adult novel.

SIDELIGHTS: Margaret Peterson Haddix commented: "I grew up on lots of stories, both from books and in my family. My father in particular was always telling tales to my brothers and sister and me—about one of our ancestors who was kidnapped, about some friends who survived lying on a railroad bridge while a train went over the top of them, about the kid who brought possum meat to the school cafeteria when my father was a boy. So I always thought that becoming a storyteller would be the grandest thing in the world. But I didn't want to just tell stories. I wanted to write them down.

"For a long time, I tried to write two different kinds of stories: real and imaginary. In college I majored in both journalism and creative writing (and history, just because I liked it). After college, I got jobs at newspapers, first as a copy editor in Fort Wayne, then as a reporter in Indianapolis. It was a lot of fun, especially getting to meet and talk to people from all walks of life, from homeless women to congressmen. And in the evenings and on weekends, I tried to write down the made-up stories that were accumulating in my head. But this was frustrating, because there was never enough time. So, in 1991, when my husband got a new job in Danville, Illinois, I took a radical step: I quit newspapers. I took a series of temporary and part-time jobs, such as teaching at a community college, and used the extra time to write.

"The first book I wrote was *Running Out of Time.* I'd gotten the idea when I was doing a newspaper story about a restored historical village. I kept wondering what it would be like if there was a historical village where all the tourists were hidden and the kids, at least, didn't know what year it really was.

"I wrote my second book, *Don't You Dare Read This, Mrs. Dunphrey,* when I was eight months pregnant with my first child, and feeling a little bored. The story should have been very difficult to write, because I had a happy childhood and wonderful parents, and should have had nothing in common with the main character—tough-talking, big-haired Tish, whose parents abandoned her. But I'd once worked on a newspaper series where I talked to more than a dozen abused and neglected kids, and their stories haunted me for years. So writing *Don't You Dare* was almost like an exorcism—I did feel possessed by Tish's spirit. Actually, in a way, everything I've written has felt like that, like being possessed. When I'm writing, I feel like I *must* write.

"I have two kids now, Meredith and Connor, and I'm amused that I felt like I didn't have enough time to write before they were born. It's much harder now. But I think I've found a balance. I write intensely when my kids are at play groups and preschool or taking naps. And a lot of times when I'm doing the ordinary things that go along with having two kids, a husband, and a house—cooking, playing chauffeur, running to Wal-Mart for diapers—I'm listening to a voice in my head insisting, 'Write about me!' or suggesting things like, 'What if Dorry's dad confronts her before she goes to the mall?' Now, I'll be the first to admit that it sounds a little weird to have voices talking in my head, but I wouldn't have it any other way."

Haddix's novels for young adults are built upon stories and scenarios she learned about while working as a newspaper reporter. While her books share little in terms of plot, setting, or theme, critics have commended the author's ability to involve even reluctant readers in the lives of her characters. In *Running Out of Time,* thirteen-year-old Jessie Keyser lives with her family in a frontier village in 1840, but when the town's children are stricken with diphtheria, Jessie's mother reveals that it is actually the 1990s, and the village is a tourist exhibit and scientific experiment gone awry. "The action moves swiftly, with plenty of suspense" as Jessie attempts to make her way through the modern world, looking for help for her family and friends, Lisa Dennis noted in *School Library Journal. Voice of Youth Advocates* critic Ann Welton, however, complained that Jessie's adjustment to the drastic shift in time "is far too smooth, resulting in a lack of narrative tension." In his review of *Running Out of Time, Bulletin of the Center for Children's Books* critic Roger Sutton concluded that "many kids . . . will be gripped by the concept, and the book, readable throughout, [is] exciting in spots."

Critics noted that Haddix relies on a much more familiar set-up when she places Tish Bonner, the main character in her second novel, *Don't You Dare Read This, Mrs. Dunphrey,* in an English class where she is required to keep a journal, giving the reader an insiders' view of her troubles. Since Tish has no one but her journal to confide in as she deals with an absent father, a depressed mother unable to care for her or her younger brother, and a part-time job where the manager subjects her to sexual harassment, "the tone here shifts only in terms of varying shades of anger," a reviewer observed in *Publishers Weekly.* "Tish's journal entries have an authentic ring in phrasing and tone and will keep readers involved," Carol Schene claimed in *School Library Journal.* The result, according to Jean Franklin in *Booklist,* is "a brief, gritty documentary novel, . . . a natural for reluctant readers."

BIOGRAPHICAL/CRITICAL SOURCES:

PERIODICALS

Booklist, October 15, 1996, p. 413.
Bulletin of the Center for Children's Books, November, 1995, p. 91.
Publishers Weekly, August 12, 1996, p. 85.
School Library Journal, October, 1995, p. 133; October, 1996, p. 147.
Voice of Youth Advocates, December, 1995, p. 302.

*   *   *

HALEY, Ken(neth) H(arold) D(obson)   1920-1997

OBITUARY NOTICE—See index for *CA* sketch: Born April 19, 1920, in Southport, England; died July 2, 1997. Educator and author. Haley was well versed in the field of Dutch and British politics of the seventeenth Century. After serving with the Royal Engineers of the British Army during World War II, Haley began a thirty-five-year career teaching history at the University of Sheffield in England. His first book, *William III and the English Opposition, 1672-74,* was published in 1953. His other works included *The Dutch in the Seventeenth Century, The British and the Dutch, Politics in the Reign of Charles II,* and *An English Diplomat in the Low Countries: Sir William Temple and John de Witt 1665-72.* He also wrote articles for historical journals and served as the editor of *The Historical Association Book of the Stuarts.*

OBITUARIES AND OTHER SOURCES:

BOOKS

Who's Who, St. Martins, 1997.

PERIODICALS

Times (London, electronic), July 21, 1997.

*   *   *

HALL, Lee   1934-

PERSONAL: Born December 15, 1934, in Lexington, NC; daughter of Robert and Florence (Fitzgerald) Lee. *Education:* University of North Carolina, B.F.A., 1955; New York University, M.A., 1959, Ph.D., 1965; Warburg Institute, University of London, postgraduate studies, 1965; University of North Carolina at Greensboro, D.F.A. (with honors), 1976.

ADDRESSES: Home—14 Silverwood Terrace, South Hadley, MA 01075.

CAREER: Artist, educator, and writer. New York State University College at Potsdam, NY, assistant professor of art, 1958-60; Keuka College, Keuka Park, NY, associate professor of art and chair of art department, 1960-62; Winthrop University, Rock Hill, SC, associate professor of art, 1962-65; Drew University, Madison, NJ, assistant professor, 1965-67, associate professor, 1967-70, professor of art, 1970-74, chair of art department, 1965-74; National Endowment for Humanities, consultant, 1969-75, panelist 1972-80; State University of New York College at Purchase, NY, dean of visual arts, 1974-75; Rhode Island School of Design, Providence, president, 1975-83; Academy for Educational Development, New York City, senior vice president and director of arts and communications, 1984-92. Oil and watercolor works have been exhibited in group shows in London, New York City, Winston-Salem, NC, and Eugene, OR.

MEMBER: Cosmopolitan Club, National Arts Club, PEN.

AWARDS, HONORS: Research grant, American Philosophical Society, 1965, 1968; Childe Hassam Purchase award, American Academy Arts and Letters, 1977; Athena medal, Rhode Island School of Design, 1983.

WRITINGS:

Wallace Herndon Smith: Paintings, University of Washington Press (Seattle, WA), 1987.
Abe Ajay, University of Washington Press, 1990.
Betty Parsons: Artist, Dealer, Collector, H.N. Abrams (New York City), 1991.
Common Threads: A Parade of American Clothing, Bulfinch Press (Boston, MA), 1992.
Elaine and Bill, Portrait of a Marriage: The Lives of Willem and Elaine de Kooning, Harper (New York City), 1993.
Olmsted's America: An "Unpractical Man" and His Vision of Civilization, Bulfinch Press, 1995.
Athena, Addison-Wesley (Reading, MA), c. 1997.

Contributor to professional journals, including *Art and Sexual Politics* and *Craft Horizons.*

SIDELIGHTS: Lee Hall is perhaps best known for her continuing efforts "to introduce readers to undervalued American artists," according to a reviewer in *Choice.* As a biographer, she has often explored how the beliefs and social values of the artist contribute to his or her work.

Hall's 1995 biography of Frederick Law Olmsted, *Olmsted's America: An "Unpractical Man" and His Vision of Civilization,* received much favor for its attention to the architect's beliefs and reasonings. According to Susan Salter Reynolds of the *Los Angeles Times Book Review,* "*Olmsted's America* neatly traces the evolution of Olmsted's thinking." Another critic, writing for *Publishers Weekly,* praised *Olmsted's America* for its thoroughness, noting how Hall "deftly provides the full social context in which Olmsted worked." William Huchting, a contributor to *Booklist,* remarked that the book possessed "narrative flair, fluid interpretation, and a superb set of illustrations."

As with *Olmsted's America,* Hall highlighted the interplay of art and politics in many of her other biographies, including *Abe Ajay* and *Betty Parsons: Artist, Dealer, Collector. Choice* reviewer G. A. Anderson deemed *Abe Ajay* a "discerning study" and "af-

fectionate examination." The *Publishers Weekly* reviewer remarked that the "richly illustrated" *Betty Parsons* "captures Parsons's many-faceted, whirlwind life."

In *Elaine and Bill: Portrait of a Marriage,* a biography of the artists Elaine and Willem de Kooning, Hall changed tone and direction from that of many of her previous biographies. This work focused more on the day-to-day trials and adventures of the artistic couple. Hall's evocative and emotive approach received mixed reviews. In a *Los Angeles Times Book Review,* Eleanor Munro remarked, "Hall's real obsession is with power wielded by a woman over men, ordinarily a cliche of anti-feminist tracts." David Anfam of the *Spectator* voiced a similar opinion, stating that *Elaine and Bill* possesses "two principal characters who ultimately emerge against the grain of the author's imagination." However, Jane Mendelsohn of the *Village Voice* had only praise for *Elaine and Bill.* She wrote, "Lee Hall tells the story of this turbulent couple and paints a picture as grisly and beautiful as any de Kooning."

Besides her more well-known biographies, Hall explored the art and politics of the American fashion industry in *Common Threads: A Parade of American Clothing.* One of Hall's earlier works, it "links dress inextricably to historic, social, political, economic, religious, and industrial forces," wrote M. F. Morris in *Choice.* Here she couples art (clothing and style) to the ideas and social values of the artist (the American public who set the style of the times). Writing in the *Library Journal,* Vicki Gadberry had similar praise for *Common Threads,* calling it an "informative and well-illustrated history" which details the "factors behind the changes and the roles of clothing." Even when not writing about people, Hall illustrates the importance of looking at art through the lens of the social and political leanings of the artist.

Athena, Hall's most recent book, published in 1997, recounts the mythical lore of a "complex" goddess whose wisdom was achieved, not inherited. According to a reviewer for *Kirkus Reviews,* Athena is transformed, in this legend, from a wily and venomous young goddess to the lovely, wise, and just luminary of our indulgent imaginings. "Hall contributes her own novelistic flair in the vivid retellings," The *Kirkus Reviews* contributor stated. And the various anecdotes, the reviewer contended, surrounding the goddess's emergence are equally "fresh and revealing," such as "how Hera's breast spewed out the

Milky Way." Hall, the *Kirkus Reviews* critic, concluded, "leaves one wanting to reread the ancients and think again about the gods."

BIOGRAPHICAL/CRITICAL SOURCES:

PERIODICALS

Booklist, June 1 and 15, 1995, pp. 1714-1715.
Choice, September, 1990, p. 92; April 1993, pp. 1377-1378.
Kirkus Reviews, April 15, 1993; March 01, 1997.
Library Journal, January, 1993, p. 110.
Los Angeles Times Book Review, July 18, 1993, pp. 2, 11; June 25, 1995, p. 6.
New York Times Book Review, August 1, 1993, p. 24.
Newsweek, July 5, 1993, p. 55.
Publishers Weekly, March 29, 1991, p. 83; May 8, 1995, p. 281.
Spectator, March 25, 1995, p. 33.
Times Literary Supplement, March 10, 1995, p. 20.
Village Voice, August 10, 1993, p. 38.*

*   *   *

HALLIBURTON, David (Garland) 1933-

PERSONAL: Born September 24, 1933, in San Bernadino, CA; married, 1960; children: three. *Education:* University of California—Riverside, B.A., 1955, M.A., 1963, Ph.D. (English), 1966.

ADDRESSES: Office Department of English, Stanford University, Stanford, CA 94305.

CAREER: University of California—Riverside, Riverside, CA, assistant professor of English, 1966-72, associate professor of English, comparative literature, and modern thought and literature, 1972-80; Stanford University, Stanford, CA, professor of English, 1980—.

MEMBER: Modern Language Association.

AWARDS, HONORS: Grant, American Philosophical Society, 1970; fellow, American Council of Learned Societies, 1971-72.

WRITINGS:

Edgar Allan Poe: A Phenomenological View, Princeton University Press (Princeton, NJ), 1973.

Poetic Thinking: An Approach to Heidegger, University of Chicago Press (Chicago, IL), 1982.
The Color of the Sky: A Study of Stephen Crane, Cambridge University Press, (Cambridge, England), 1989.
The Fateful Discourse of Worldly Things, Stanford University Press (Stanford, CA), 1997.

Contributor to periodicals, including *Modern Fiction Studies, Papers in Language and Literatures,* and *Studies in Romanticism.*

SIDELIGHTS: David Halliburton, a professor of comparative literature at Stanford University, has written studies on nineteenth-century American writers Edgar Allan Poe, Nathaniel Hawthorne, Herman Melville, and Stephen Crane, as well as twentieth-century German philosopher Martin Heidegger and other philosophical matters.

Halliburton's 1982 study of Heidegger's thoughts on poetry, *Poetic Thinking: An Approach to Heidegger,* garnered mixed reviews. "Halliburton's account is a generally faithful yet selective paraphrase of all Heidegger's important work" regarding the relationship in poetry between a word and the item the word signifies, "along with a number of helpful side-lights from other authors," asserted Gregory Desjardins in the *Times Literary Supplement.* "He has read the works on which he is commenting in the original, and frequently expresses what Heidegger writes in felicitous English. His interpretation stays close to the text, attempting to recover the direction and movement of Heidegger's own thought; nevertheless, in his restatement this direction is not always made clear enough and strategic distinctions are sometimes obscured."

Other reviewers gave *Poetic Thinking* varied criticism. A contributor to the *Virginia Quarterly Review* praised Halliburton for "presenting a clear exposition of Heidegger's philosophical meditations on art." Burleigh T. Wilkins, in a review for the *South Atlantic Quarterly,* found Halliburton to be "intelligent," and concluded that "the book is on the whole informative." Daniel O'Hara saw one drawback in the work. "The one reservation I have about Halliburton's fine introduction to an often difficult thinker concerns the price Heidegger clearly pays for his self-revision, his shift from systematic overcoming to playful evasion, a price Halliburton fails to estimate, even though he the account books right in his hands, so to speak," he wrote in *Comparative Literature.* "In any event," he concluded, "the clarity and precision of its presentation of a complex philosopher's most vexing and influential conceptions make *Poetic Thinking* likely to become the leading introduction to its subject."

In his 1989 work, *The Color of the Sky: A Study of Stephen Crane,* Halliburton discusses a wide variety of topics related to the works of Stephen Crane. Among them are titles, the architecture of the American West, and trains. The work received mixed reviews. "To some, David Halliburton's *The Color of the Sky: A Study of Stephen Crane* will be both intriguing and stimulating. To others, who are traditionally and historically inclined, it may be disappointing," predicted Thomas A. Gullason in *Modern Fiction Studies.* Writing in *American Literature,* Paul Sorrentino wrote that the book's "interdisciplinary method is often clear and enlightening, but Halliburton might have more thoroughly explained an occasional term and concept."

In *The Journal of American History,* Chester L. Wolford remarked that *The Color of the Sky* "raises no new questions or new explanations," and "old or new, Halliburton's enormous knowledge is everywhere apparent, sometimes too apparent." Sorrentino concluded that "despite these problems, Halliburton's insightful analysis reaffirms the importance of Crane in the canon of American literature." Likewise, Wolford stated that "Halliburton's book is a wonderful rough draft awaiting editing," and Gullason predicted that *"The Color of the Sky* will help students of Stephen Crane arrive at a fairer assessment of his writing talent."

BIOGRAPHICAL/CRITICAL SOURCES:

PERIODICALS

American Literature, June, 1990, pp. 337-338.
Choice, October, 1973, p. 1192; March, 1990, p. 1144.
Comparative Literature, winter, 1984, pp. 78-81.
Journal of American History, December, 1990, p. 1036-1037.
Library Journal, April 15, 1973, p. 1286; February 15, 1982, p. 461.
Modern Fiction Studies, winter, 1990, pp. 552-553.
South Atlantic Quarterly, autumn, 1983, pp. 459-460.
Sewanee Review, July, 1985, pp. 465-480.
Times Literary Supplement, January 14, 1983, p. 40.
Virginia Quarterly Review, summer, 1982, p. 81.*

HAMILTON, Carol (Jean Barber) 1935-

PERSONAL: Born August 23, 1935, in Enid, OK; daughter of Clarence DeWitt (an electrical engineer) and Ruby (a teacher of English and writing; maiden name, Settles) Barber; married J. Jefferson Hamilton (a legislator), August 25, 1956 (marriage ended, June 29, 1994); children: Debra Susan Hamilton Havenar, Christopher David, Stephen Anthony. *Education:* Phillips University, B.S., 1956; University of Central Oklahoma, M.A., 1978; also attended University of Oklahoma, Hiram College, University of Colorado, Rose State College, and Academia Hispano Americano. *Politics:* Democrat. *Religion:* "Christian Church (Disciples of Christ)."

ADDRESSES: Home—9608 Sonata Ct., Midwest City, OK 73130. *Office*—Creative Studies, Box 184, University of Central Oklahoma, 73034-0184.

CAREER: Elementary schoolteacher in North Haven, CT, 1957-60, Indianapolis, IN, 1970-71, and Tinker Air Force Base, OK, 1971-82; Academic Center for Enrichment, Pleasant Hill, OK, teacher of elementary gifted education, 1982-93; Rose State College, Midwest City, OK, adjunct professor of English, 1988-96; University of Central Oklahoma, adjunct professor, 1996—. Freelance writer and storyteller at camps, churches, libraries, and schools. Olympics of the Mind, local, regional, and state judge, 1985—. Artist in residence at Contemporary Arts Foundation and Warehouse Theater. Interpreter and teacher at medical missions in Mexico, Bolivia, Dominican Republic, and Oklahoma City, OK.

MEMBER: Association of Classroom Teachers (member of executive board, 1980-85), League of American Pen Women (state chair, 1988—; literary chair of Oklahoma City branch), Oklahoma Writers Federation (member of board of directors), Poetry Society of Oklahoma (president, 1984), Individual Artists of Oklahoma, Mid-Oklahoma Writers (past president).

AWARDS, HONORS: Southwest Book Award and Pegasus Award, both 1988, both for *The Dawn Seekers;* Oklahoma Book Award and Pegasus Award, both 1992, both for *Once the Dust;* grand prize, Poetry Society of Oklahoma contest, 1994; Cherubim Award, 1995, for *The Mystery of Black Mesa;* named poet laureate, State of Oklahoma, 1995.

WRITINGS:

Deserts, Dry Places, and Other Aridities (poems),

University of Central Oklahoma (Edmond, OK), 1978.

Daring the Wind, Broncho Press (Edmond, OK), 1985.

The Dawn Seekers (juvenile novel), illustrated by Jeremy Guitar, Albert Whitman (Morton Grove, IL), 1987.

Once the Dust, Broncho Press, 1992.

Legends of Poland, illustrated by Toni Britt, Central European Refugee Committee and Kirkpatrick Foundation, 1992.

Mystery of Black Mesa (juvenile novel), illustrated by John Roberts, Bob Jones University Press (Greenville, SC), 1995.

Contributor of more than three thousand articles, poems, and stories to periodicals, including *Christian Science Monitor, New York Quarterly, South Dakota Review, Astronomy, Revista Interamericana, Oklahoma Today, Voices International, Chiron Review, Arizona Quarterly,* and *Humpty Dumpty.*

WORK IN PROGRESS: When the Wolf Comes, a historical novel for young people; a poetry manuscript.

SIDELIGHTS: Carol Hamilton commented: "Writing began for me when I was a child and wrote scary stories to frighten my friends. My stories, unfortunately, scared me so much that I lay awake at night expecting them to come true. That habit has helped me over the years, for I've always written early in the mornings while the rest of the world is still sleeping.

"I began my writing and publishing career with articles and short stories. My first published piece in a national magazine, in 1965, was called 'Winnie the Pooh as Existentialist.' I never dreamed of writing poetry or children's literature, but these two fields have given me the most success and satisfaction over the years. Today, I still rise at five o'clock in the morning to write in various fields. I feel constantly challenged to shape words and experience into poetry and to create worlds of adventure and enchantment that children, and I count myself as one of them, will want to enter again and again."

BIOGRAPHICAL/CRITICAL SOURCES:

PERIODICALS

Booklist, May 15, 1987, p. 1446.
Kirkus Reviews, January 1, 1987, p. 56.
School Library Journal, March, 1987, p. 160.

HAMILTON, Richard 1922-

PERSONAL: Born February 24, 1922, in London, England; son of Peter and Constance Hamilton; married Terry O'Reilly, 1947 (died, 1962); married Rita Donagh, 1991; children: (first marriage) one son, one daughter. *Education:* Attended St. Martin's School of Art, Royal Academy Schools, and Slade School of Art.

ADDRESSES: Home—Northend Farm, Northend, Oxfordshire, RG9 6LQ, England. *Agent*—c/o Tate Gallery, Millbank, SW1P 4RG, London, England.

CAREER: Design Unit, jig and tool draftsman, 1941-42; Electrical and Musical Industries (EMI), 1942-45; Central School of Arts and Crafts, teacher of design, 1952-53; Institute of Contemporary Arts, member, Independent Group, 1952-55; Fine Art Department, Kings College, University of Durham (later University of Newcastle-upon-Tyne), lecturer, 1953-66; Royal College of Art, teacher of interior design, 1957-61. Numerous group, solo, and retrospective exhibitions in Europe and the United States.

AWARDS, HONORS: William and Noma Copley Foundation award for painting, 1960; Joint First Prize, John Moores Liverpool Exhibition, 1969; Talens Prize International, Amsterdam, 1970; World Print Award, 1983; Golden Lion, Venice Biennale, 1993.

WRITINGS:

Richard Hamilton: The Tate Gallery, 12 March-19 April 1970, Tate Gallery (London), 1970.

Richard Hamilton: Stedelijk Van Abbemuseum Eindhoven, 15 Mei-28 Juni 1970, Tate Gallery, 1970.

Polaroid Portraits, Volumes 1-3, Edition H. Mayer (Stuttgart, Germany), 1972, 1977, 1983.

Prints, Multiples, and Drawings (exhibition catalog), Whitworth Art Gallery (Manchester, England), 1972.

The Prints of Richard Hamilton (exhibition catalog), Petersburg Press (New York City), 1973.

Richard Hamilton (exhibition catalog), Guggenheim Museum (New York City), 1973.

(With Dieter Roth) *Collaborations of Ch. Rotham,* Edition H. Mayer, 1977.

Interfaces (exhibition catalog), Kunsthalle Bielefeld (Bielefeld, Germany), 1979.

Interiors, Waddington Galleries (London), 1979.

Drawings, Prints, and Paintings, 1941-55 (exhibition catalog), Anthony d'Offay (London), 1980.

Collected Words, 1953-1982, Thames and Hudson (London), 1982.

Richard Hamilton, Image and Process: Studies, Stage, and Final Proofs from the Graphic Works, 1952-82, Edition H. Mayer, 1983.

Teknologi, ide, konstverk: Richard Hamilton, Moderna Museet (Stockholm, Sweden), 1989.

Richard Hamilton: Exteriors, Interiors, Objects, People, (exhibition catalog), Kestner-Gesellschaft (Hannover, Germany), 1990.

Richard Hamilton (exhibition catalog), Tate Gallery, 1992.

Prints: A Complete Catalogue of Graphic Works, H. Mayer, 1984.

SIDELIGHTS: British painter and printmaker Richard Hamilton is widely known as one of the pioneers of Pop Art, a movement in art that finds its material in advertising, industrial design, photography, and the cinema, and which first developed in England during the mid-1950s. Although Hamilton has produced work in many different styles during his lengthy career, the common denominator is the art's complexity and intellectual content. His work has been shown in many exhibitions throughout Europe and in the United States.

Hamilton is also an expert on the work of French Dadaist and Futurist Marcel Duchamp. In 1965 and 1966, Hamilton spent a year making a full-scale version of Duchamp's *Large Glass.* He also wrote a lengthy and authoritative essay on Duchamp, which appeared in his 1982 volume, *Collected Words, 1953-1982.*

In a review of *Collected Words,* a *Choice* critic commented, "Hamilton writes well and is sometimes quite witty," adding that the book is of "interest limited to historians of art, critics, and advanced art students." A *Los Angeles Times Book Review Critic* remarked that *Collected Works* reveals Hamilton as "an important partisan critic on the interaction of art and mass culture," remarked a *Los Angeles Times Book Review* critic. Patricia Scott, reviewing *Collected Words* for *Library Journal,* commented that the was text too lean but added that she found the book to be "a well-designed, informative, and absorbing work."

BIOGRAPHICAL/CRITICAL SOURCES:

BOOKS

Dictionary of the Arts, Facts on File (New York City), 1994.

Leach, Dawn, *Richard Hamilton: The Beginnings of His Art,* Peter Lang (Frankfurt am Main, Germany), 1993.

Naylor, Colin, editor, *Contemporary Artists,* third edition, St. James Press (Chicago), 1989.

PERIODICALS

British Book News, March, 1983, p. 183; August, 1983, p. 473.

Choice, July, 1983, p. 1583.

Encounter, May, 1983, p. 62.

Library Journal, February 15, 1983, p. 386.

Los Angeles Times Book Review, October 9, 1983, p. 8.

Observer (London), November 28, 1982, p. 30.

Publishers Weekly, December 17, 1982, p. 67.

Times Literary Supplement, November 26, 1982, p. 1294.*

* * *

HAREVEN, Shulamith 1931-

PERSONAL: Born February 14, 1931, in Warsaw, Poland; immigrated to Israel, 1940; daughter of Abraham and Natalie (Wiener) Ryftin; married Alouph Eliahu Hareven, 1953; children: Ithai, Gail. *Education:* Attended Hebrew University. *Religion:* Jewish.

ADDRESSES: Home—Jerusalem, Israel. *Agent*—c/o Mercury House, 785 Market St., Suite 1500, San Francisco, CA 94103.

CAREER: Writer. *Military service:* I.D.F., 1950-52, served as combat medic, became lieutenant.

MEMBER: Academy of Hebrew Language.

AWARDS, HONORS: Wallenrod Prize, 1968; Schwimmer Prize; Israeli Prime Minister's Creativity Award, 1975, for *City of Many Days.*

WRITINGS:

Yeroshalaim Dorsanit, 1962.
Mekomot Nifradim, 1967.
Reshut Netuna, 1969.
'Ir yamim rabim (novel), 1972, translated by Hillel Halkin, published as *City of Many Days,* Doubleday (New York City), 1973, revised translation, Mercury House (San Francisco, CA), 1993.

Ani Ohev Lehariah (children's verse), 1976.

Sone ha-nisim (novel), translated by Hillel Halkin, published as *The Miracle Hater,* North Point Press (San Francisco, CA), 1988.

Ha-Navi (novel), translated by Hillel Halkin, published as *Prophet,* North Point Press, 1990.

Twilight and Other Stories, translated by Miriam Arad, Hillel Halkin, J. M. Lask, and David Weber, Mercury House, 1992.

The Vocabulary of Peace: Life, Culture, and Politics in the Middle East (essays), Mercury House, 1995.

Thirst: The Desert Trilogy (includes *The Miracle Hater, Prophet,* and *After Childhood*), translated by Hillel Halkin, Mercury House, 1996.

Translator of *Konrad Wallenrod* by Adam Mickiewicz. Also translator of works for theaters; contributor of articles to newspapers.

SIDELIGHTS: Known for her ironic humor, Shulamith Hareven is a prolific Israeli writer whose many works in Hebrew include novels, stories, poetry, plays, and essays. Her works have been translated into more than a dozen languages. Works that have appeared in English include *City of Many Days;* the *Thirst* trilogy, which is comprised of the three novellas *The Miracle Hater, Prophet,* and *After Childhood; The Vocabulary of Peace,* a collection of twenty-three essays on Middle Eastern life, language and culture; and *Twilight,* a collection of seven short stories.

City of Many Days, which won the Israeli Prime Minister's Creativity Award in 1975, is a historical novel that takes place in Jerusalem. It focuses on Sara Amarillo, a Sephardic Jew and nurse, who comes of age during the creation of the modern state of Israel at the close of World War II. *City of Many Days* is "volatile and aromatic" according to Martin Levin in the *New York Times Book Review.* Levin added that the prose is full of "sensuous images, pungent smells, street noises and tensions of Jerusalem." Less impressed by Hareven's work was Kenneth Turan of the *Washington Post Book World,* who considered the book, for all its violence and death, to be rather soft and emotional, marked by "atmospheric writing of a precious and delicate sort."

Hareven is perhaps best known in the United States for her *Thirst* trilogy. The first volume, *The Miracle Hater,* which first appeared in English in 1988, is a retelling of the biblical Exodus story, in which Moses leads the Hebrews out of slavery in Egypt. Hareven presents the story from the perspective of Eshkar, a shepherd who is a loner traveling among the exiled tribes. She portrays Moses as an antihero, hardly the stuff of myth, and the purveyor of miracles—not justice—to the wandering Hebrews. "This is not a story for the pious," Alan Lelchuk maintained in the *New York Times Book Review.*

For both its style and content, *The Miracle Hater* garnered high praise from reviewers. "The triumph of *The Miracle Hater . . .* is not so much to be found in its modern, realistic view, as it is in the rich and convincing imagining of the historical past," opined Lelchuk, who also had praise for the author's narrative skill and the translation skills of Hillel Halkin. Other commentators, however, did find Harevens treatment of the biblical tale to have relevancy to modern concerns. According to Jane Mendelsohn in the *Voice Literary Supplement,* "*The Miracle Hater* attests to the fact that a good story can benefit from a retelling, that the nature of a tale changes over time, and that new ages require new modes of mythmaking." Describing the work as "a powerfully imagined novella," Susan P. Willens of *Belles Lettres* added, "it makes the old Exodus story as current as this morning's headlines." "The message for contemporary existence is clear," asserted Karen Alkalay-Gut in *American Book Review.* "The call for justice that concentrates on the daily life of the individual, the absolute agreement with the wonder and beauty of life, the overall assertion of the limited value of leaders and ideals—all this is so close to the present situation of the same people so many years later that we ignore these aspects of Hareven's story at our peril."

Like *The Miracle Hater,* "*Prophet,* too, rejects the supernatural and the romantic," remarked Penny Kaganoff in the *Voice Literary Supplement.* In the novel, published in English in 1990, the prophet Hivai, who believes in many gods, undergoes a spiritual crisis when his city is attacked by nameless invaders. He joins the Hebrews, a nomadic desert tribe, and tries unsuccessfully to commune with their one God. Only years later, exiled by the Hebrews, does Hivai return to his home to find that he has been declared a traitor by his own people. He then takes up a near-solitary existence by the Jordan River, with a mute boy as his companion. Mary Banas, writing for *Booklist,* stated that Hareven's imaginative use of Biblical themes in *Prophet* "deftly gives poetic voice to the ineffable in humankind's ceaseless search for . . . meaning."

After Childhood is a work that first appeared in 1996 with the publication of *Thirst: The Desert Trilogy,* which also included reprintings of *The Miracle Hater* and *Prophet*. This last volume in the trilogy revolves around Moran, a shy young woman from the mountains who has dreamed of moving to the desert. She gets her wish when she marries Salu, an older Hebrew who has become an outcast because he blinks constantly, the result of an attempt by his father to offer him as a sacrifice. She later finds solace in the land when Salu deserts her. Discussing the trilogy as a whole, Ray Olson in *Booklist* found the combined works "much more thoughtful and poetic than the average novel." While finding the three novels "hindered by a lack of convincing character development," a *Publishers Weekly* critic concluded; "These are apocryphal tales that, at their best, possess a shimmering, timeless quality." In a *Library Journal* review of the trilogy, Molly Abramowitz praised Hareven's "great narrative skill in a spare style that complements the desert landscape described." Writing in the *New York Times Book Review*, Lore Dickstein also lauded the author's writing style, stating that "the success of *Thirst* rests entirely on the author's evocative and lush prose. . . . Her best writing is about the land itself."

With one exception, the stories in Hareven's 1992 collection, *Twilight*, are set in contemporary Jerusalem and deal with the fragmented lives of Jewish women who have come from other countries in order to start a new life there. The stories elicited widely varying reviews. Barbara Short, reviewing *Twilight* in the *Women's Review of Books*, felt that while the author demonstrated "finely honed powers of observation and narrative technique," the women and their world do not come alive to readers. A critic for *Kirkus Reviews* was disappointed with the "sharp, overly hurried tone" of the stories. But Emanuel Rubin in *World Literature Today* saw the author's use of simple declarative sentences as a useful stylistic device in which words are "applied meticulously, like tiles lovingly placed into a mosaic." Rubin continued, "Hareven excels in making the reader understand what people are feeling, rather than what they think. . . . It is in their psychological landscape that these superbly crafted stories really take place." Maxine Rodberg, a critic for *Belles Lettres*, also had praise for the collection, declaring that "Hareven crafts these seven stories with exquisite poetic detail and great range."

BIOGRAPHICAL/CRITICAL SOURCES:

PERIODICALS

American Book Review, September, 1989, pp. 13, 15.

Belles Lettres, winter, 1989, p. 18; spring, 1993, p. 49.
Booklist, March 1, 1990, p. 1264; April 1, 1996, p. 1342.
Kirkus Reviews, January 15, 1992, p. 66.
Library Journal, May 1, 1995, p. 96; April 1, 1996, pp. 120-21.
New York Times Book Review, March 27, 1977, p. 47; July 9, 1978, p. 43; June 12, 1988, p.16; December 15, 1996, p. 37.
Publishers Weekly, February 2, 1990, pp. 76-77; January 13, 1992, p. 51; April 10, 1995, p. 58; February 26, 1996, p. 98.
Voice Literary Supplement, April, 1988, p. 5; May, 1990, p. 11.
Washington Post Book World, June 12, 1977, p. E6.
Women's Review of Books, July, 1992, p. 27.
World Literature Today, winter, 1990, pp. 189-90; winter, 1994, p. 206.*

*   *   *

HARRELL, Beatrice Orcutt 1943-

PERSONAL: Born April 23, 1943, in Claremore, OK; daughter of A. D. and Juanita (Walker) Orcutt; married Orville Morris (deceased); married Robert Harrell (a welder), February 3, 1969; children: (first marriage) Richard, Lisa Morris Green, Theresa; (second marriage) Vicky. *Education:* Attended Tulsa Junior College, 1981. *Politics:* "Yellow Dog Democrat." *Religion:* "Deist/Native American Church." *Avocational interests:* Environmental ecology, literacy, social services for children, crocheting.

ADDRESSES: Home and office—13962 Hickory Pl., Glenpool, OK 74033.

CAREER: Indian Health Care, Tulsa, OK, social service counselor, 1975-77; Green Bay Packaging, Tulsa, personnel assistant, 1987-91; Sapulpa Indian Education, Sapulpa, OK, tutor, 1995—. Adult Literacy Program, volunteer tutor, 1990—; Habitat for Humanity, volunteer coordinator, 1991—.

MEMBER: Wordcraft Circle of Native American Writers & Storytellers.

WRITINGS:

(Reteller) *How Thunder and Lightning Came to Be: A Choctaw Legend*, illustrated by Susan L. Roth, Dial (New York City), 1995.

Choctaw Mother (story), Snowbird Publishing (Kimball, NE), 1995.

Contributor to magazines.

WORK IN PROGRESS: Long Walkers Journey, a "trail of tears" story, seen through the eyes of a nine-year-old Choctaw boy; research on the land run and its effects on the tribes in Indian Territory; two new novels.

SIDELIGHTS: Beatrice Orcutt Harrell commented: "I have always wanted to write. My parents, however, said that was well and good, but it wasn't possible to make a living writing, and I had better think of something I could do to support myself. I quit school, married, and had four children. When they were nearly all grown and gone, I went back to school for two years. I did well in most of my classes (except algebra), but I earned straight A's in composition. I had to go to work in a manufacturing plant, so that I could have such luxuries as a car and electricity, but the seed had been planted. I was sure I could write, but I didn't know if I could earn a living doing it. I still don't know that!

"I had always heard that you must write what you know, so that's what I did. I took my lifelong interest in my Choctaw culture and began to gather the stories and legends of my people. I heard about a Native American writers' conference being held in Norman, at the University of Oklahoma. I couldn't afford the conference fee, but I desperately wanted to go. I called to see if they might have a fee waiver. A very nice lady sent me a form to complete, and I was in! That conference changed my life. I heard other Indians talking about their work, and I was so motivated that I met with some publishing representatives, there at the conference. It just happened that Dial Books was looking for exactly the kind of work I was doing! I submitted some of my stories, and they bought one of them. I had been prepared to deal with years of rejections, but it never happened. I advise aspiring writers, no matter what their age, to submit their work. Stop rewriting and put it in the mail. Then you are doing something constructive, and you will get valuable input.

"My goal is to preserve all of the stories and legends I can find that tell about the Choctaw people. I was very lucky to get to go to the Newberry Library in Chicago, to get copies of sixteenth-century travel journals kept by the French as they explored Choctaw country. There were long-lost stories there, but now they will be preserved for future generations. *How Thunder and Lightning Came to Be* is one of the lost stories, found in a bulletin of the U.S. Bureau of American Ethnology. I am hard at work on a new fiction story about the ancient Choctaw burial custom of bonepicking.

"I try to write at least two hours a day, but when I'm on a roll, I may work for six or eight hours and never notice the passing time. Sometimes I won't write for a day or two, because I need to think about where I'm trying to go with a story. Then I write it in longhand on a legal pad and do all my first editing. Only when that's complete will I put it on the word processor, a new and very scary tool! One final edit, and I'm ready to submit it.

"Writing has opened up my world. If there is one single person responsible for my having the confidence to try my hand at this wonderful art form, that would be Chuck Sasser, a wonderful writer and teacher who I am proud to call my friend."

BIOGRAPHICAL/CRITICAL SOURCES:

PERIODICALS

Booklist, August, 1995, p. 1592.
Kirkus Reviews, May 15, 1995, p. 710.
Publishers Weekly, May 8, 1995, p. 295.
School Library Journal, August, 1995, p. 134.

*　　*　　*

HAUSDORFF, Felix 1868-1942
(Dr. Paul Mongre)

PERSONAL: Born November 8, 1868, in Breslau, Germany (now Wroclaw, Poland); committed suicide to avoid deportation to a concentration camp, January 26, 1942, in Germany; son of Louis (a dry goods merchant) and Johanna Tietz Hausdorff; married Charlotte Goldschmidt, 1899; children: Lenore. *Education:* Leipzig University, Ph.D., 1891. *Religion:* Jewish.

CAREER: Mathematician and writer. Hausdorff and Company (publishing firm), partner, beginning in 1896; Leipzig University, lecturer, 1896-1903, associate professor, 1903-10; University of Bonn, associate professor, 1910-13, professor, 1921-35; professor at a university in Greifswald, Germany, 1913-21.

Military service: Served in Infantry Regiment 106 in Leipzig, achieved rank of vice-sergeant, 1891-94.

WRITINGS:

(Under the pseudonym Dr. Paul Mongre) *Sant' Ilario: Thoughts from the Landscape of Zarathustra,* [Germany], 1897.

(As Mongre) *Chaos in Cosmic Choice,* [Germany], c. 1898.

(As Mongre) *Ecstasies* (poetry), [Germany], 1900.

(As Mongre) *The Doctor's Honor* (play), produced in Hamburg and Berlin, Germany, c. 1900.

Grundzuge der Mengenlehre (title means "Basic Features of Set Theory"), Chelsea, 1965.

Set Theory, 2nd edition, Chelsea Publishing, 1978.

Author (as Mongre) of the essays "Death and Return," 1899, and "God's Shadow," 1914.

SIDELIGHTS: Felix Hausdorff was a mathematician who contributed to the subject of topology, a field of geometry which studies the shapes of objects. His greatest contributions were the assertions that geometric spaces could be regarded as sets of points and sets of relationships among those points. These proposals have come to be called Hausdorff's Topological Spaces and Hausdorff's Neighborhood Axioms. His work had an impact on set theory, the study of relationships between sets of similar items.

Hausdorff was born on November 8, 1868, in the German city of Breslau, which is now Wroclaw, Poland. His father, Louis Hausdorff, was a successful dry goods merchant; his mother was Johanna Tietz Hausdorff. The family moved to Leipzig, Germany, in 1871. The young Hausdorff attended public school until the age of ten, when he enrolled at the Nicolai Gymnasium; he graduated in 1887. After studying astronomy and mathematics in Freiburg and Berlin, Hausdorff earned his Ph.D. in 1891 in Leipzig. His dissertation explored the theory of astronomic refraction, and his first four published papers dealt with topics in optics and astronomy.

In 1891, Hausdorff volunteered to serve in Infantry Regiment 106 in Leipzig. He achieved the rank of vice-sergeant before removing himself from consideration for further promotion in 1894. He was Jewish, and no acknowledged Jews had been commissioned as officers in the German military for nearly fifteen years. In 1896, following his father's death, Hausdorff succeeded him as a partner in the publishing firm Hausdorff and Company, which produced the leading trade magazine for spinning, weaving, and dyeing. That same year, he was accepted as a lecturer at Leipzig University.

Hausdorff had a lively interest in the fine arts and in philosophy. He was an accomplished pianist, and would have devoted his advanced studies to music except for the objections of his father. Throughout his life, his closest friends were musicians and artists, as well as several prominent mathematicians (including Pavel S. Aleksandrov). He developed a lifelong interest in the philosophy of Friedrich Nietzsche, carefully examining the philosopher's ideas, sometimes agreeing with them and sometimes not. He associated with other followers of Nietzsche, and even corresponded with the philosopher's sister.

In 1897, the first of Hausdorff's four full-length literary works was published. He wrote these books under the pseudonym Dr. Paul Mongre so that he could express himself freely without jeopardizing his university position. The first book, *Sant' Ilario: Thoughts from the Landscape of Zarathustra,* was primarily a collection of aphorisms relating to Nietzsche's *Thus Spoke Zarathustra.* It was published by the same company that had published Nietzsche's book, and was even produced with a similar cover.

The second book written under the name Mongre, *Chaos in Cosmic Choice,* dealt with metaphysical relationships between space and time. Hausdorff presented the same concepts in "The Space Problem," his inaugural lecture upon being appointed as an associate professor at Leipzig University in 1903. He had worked as a lecturer at Leipzig since 1896, but his promotion was opposed by a fourth of the faculty on the grounds that Hausdorff was of the "faith of Moses."

Mongre's third major literary work was *Ecstasies,* a volume of sonnets and poems published in 1900. He also wrote *The Doctor's Honor,* a satirical play that was successfully produced in Hamburg and Berlin; the work is an attack on the resurgence of the duel as a means of defending one's honor, a practice that accompanied the movement to establish an intellectual and political elitism in society.

In 1897, Hausdorff began publishing papers on topics in mathematics, including non-Euclidean geometry, complex numbers, and probability. He became interested in Georg Cantor's work on set theory—the study of the relationships between groups of similar items, such as numbers or letters—and during the summer semester of 1901 taught what may have been the first course on set theory to be presented in Germany. Also about this time, David Hilbert was publishing work applying set theory to geometry; his work may have been the inspiration for Hausdorff's greatest mathematical accomplishment.

In 1910, Hausdorff accepted a position as associate professor at the University of Bonn. Although he had written one or two technical articles per year for two decades, he published nothing from 1910 until 1914. He moved to Greifswald in 1913 to become a professor at the university there. The following year, he published his monumental *Grundzuge der Mengenlehre* (Basic Features of Set Theory). The *Grundzuge* was a comprehensive text dealing with set theory and point set topology (the idea that geometric shapes can be thought of as sets of points). Although the book was written for students at the advanced undergraduate level, Hausdorff noted in the preface that the volume also offered new ideas and methods to his professional colleagues. By organizing point set theory with just the right choice of axioms, he so thoroughly revised the related existing work that his book became the foundation on which modern topology has been developed.

In 1919, Hausdorff introduced another revolutionary concept. He generalized the notion of dimension (e.g., a two-dimensional triangle or a three-dimensional cube) to include the possibility of objects with fractal dimensions. (Fractals are geometric forms which, when examined from whatever distance, exhibit the same general shape.) The study of fractals has applications to such diverse areas as weather forecasting and the fracturing of glass or metal.

As Hausdorff noted in his preface to the *Grundzuge,* "in an area where simply nothing is obvious, conclusions frequently paradoxical, [and] the plausible wrong, there is hardly a remedy besides a consistent deduction to save oneself and the reader from deceptions." Indeed, one of his talents was that of clear exposition. A review of the *Grundzuge* appearing in the *Bulletin of the American Mathematical Society* praised its "happy choice and arrangement of subject matter, the careful diction, the smooth, vigorous and concise literary style, and the adaptable notation; above all . . . the highly pleasing unifications and generalizations and the harmonious weaving of numerous original results into the texture of the whole."

In 1921 Hausdorff returned to the University of Bonn, where he worked as a professor for the rest of his career. He was respected as the most capable mathematician in Bonn and as a professor whose lectures were well reasoned and clearly delivered. He taught until 1935, when he reached the mandatory retirement age of sixty-seven. He continued to publish mathematical papers until 1938.

In 1899, Hausdorff married Charlotte Goldschmidt, the daughter of a doctor. His only child, a daughter named Lenore (usually called Nora), was born the following year. Although Charlotte came from a Jewish family, she had been baptized a Protestant Christian in 1896 and Lenore was similarly baptized. The members of the Hausdorff family held an enduring devotion for one another. Though Hausdorff was high-strung, he loved to listen to beautiful music with friends who were so close to him that they could share the experience without need of words. He maintained a congenial but reserved demeanor with acquaintances and was prone to depression; yet, he enjoyed dining with friends, and in their company he could relax, have some wine, and be quite jovial. When the family moved to Bonn in 1921, they bought a lovely home on a quiet street (which would be renamed Hausdorffstrasse in 1949). Hausdorff's normal routine was to spend the evenings enjoying the company of family or guests; taking advantage of the quiet nighttime hours, he would then work quite late in his study, enjoying strong tea and stout cigars. He would sleep until late in the morning and then go to the university.

Although he had been a member of the German Democratic Party for three years following the end of World War I, Hausdorff did not participate actively in politics. He believed in freedom and individual rights. In his 1904 essay "God's Shadow," written under the Mongre pseudonym, Hausdorff had warned against the "blonde beast" and the mysticism of racial purity. In 1921, he inscribed a copy of his book *Sant' Ilario* as a birthday gift to his friend Theodor Posner with a newly-written poem bemoaning the failure of the intelligentsia in the Weimar Republic and the decreasing political wisdom of the populace.

The anti-Semitism that had blocked his promotion in the infantry and threatened to prevent his promotion at Leipzig University continued to plague Hausdorff throughout his lifetime. For instance, a young professor whose 1926 appointment Hausdorff had supported became openly anti-Semitic in 1933, repudiating any former contacts with Jews and refusing to join the rest of the faculty in attending seminars given by Jewish mathematicians. Some of Hausdorff's Jewish friends emigrated to escape the persecution; others whose emigration was thwarted committed suicide.

Suicide was a topic addressed by Nietzsche; consequently, it had been a subject for reflection by Hausdorff. Zarathustra advocated "voluntary death" as a consummation of life for the noble man. "Death and Return," an 1899 essay by Mongre, treated the subject in the form of a letter to a fictitious depressed friend. In it, the author advises that "this final remedy really helps, that it does not [merely] plunge one into a futile expense for morphine or revolver cartridges."

The infamous November pogrom of 1938, in which government-fostered attacks resulted in the arrest of twenty thousand Jews and twenty-five million marks' worth of damage to hundreds of Jewish homes, shops, and synagogues, occurred the day after Hausdorff's seventieth birthday. Charlotte Hausdorff and her sister, Edith Pappenheim (who had come to live with them a few months earlier), tried to bolster Hausdorff's spirits. After this pogrom, Hausdorff was required to adopt the additional first name Israel, and his wife the name Sara. He continued to work on his mathematics, but no longer published his results; instead, he put them into storage. Another ugly incident from this period happened in late 1941 when Hausdorff took his wife to the university dental clinic. As she was being treated, a senior staff doctor rushed toward her, ripped the napkin from her neck, and said, "Get out, get out. When Jews are sick, they should hang themselves."

In mid-January of 1942, the Hausdorffs received notification to report to an internment camp located at a former monastery; this would probably be followed by deportation to a concentration camp. After organizing their affairs and leaving property disposal and cremation instructions with trusted friends, Hausdorff, his wife, and her sister committed suicide on January 26, 1942. That evening, each of them took an overdose of the sedative barbital and sat down to read. Hausdorff died with his glasses on, holding a copy of the novel *Renate* by Theodor Storm.

On January 25, 1980, a memorial plaque honoring Hausdorff was placed at the entrance of the Mathematical Institute at the University of Bonn. From January 24 to February 28, 1992, an exhibition of photographs and personal, literary, and mathematical documents was held at the University of Bonn, commemorating the fiftieth anniversary of Hausdorff's death.

BIOGRAPHICAL/CRITICAL SOURCES:

BOOKS

Boyer, Carl B., *A History of Mathematics,* Wiley, 1991, pp. 620-622.
Gillispie, Charles Coulston, editor, *Dictionary of Scientific Biography,* Volume VI, Scribner, 1974, pp. 176-177.

PERIODICALS

Mathematical Intelligencer, winter, 1989, pp. 6-9; winter, 1990, pp. 4-5.

OTHER

Brieskorn, Dr. Egbert, letters to Loretta Hall, 1993-94.
Felix Hausdorff—Paul Mongre—1868-1942, (in German), catalog for the 1992 memorial colloquium and exhibition, University of Bonn, 1992.*

* * *

HAWKINS, W(alter) Lincoln 1911-1992

PERSONAL: Born March 21, 1911, in Washington, DC; died of heart failure, August 20, 1992, in CA; son of William Langston (a lawyer for the Census Bureau) and Maude Johnson (a science teacher) Hawkins; married Lilyan Varina Bobo, August 19, 1939; children: two sons. *Education:* Rensselaer Polytechnic Institute, graduated, 1932; Howard University, M.S. (chemistry), 1934; McGill University, Ph.D. (chemistry), 1938.

CAREER: Chemical engineer and writer. Taught at a trade school, c. 1934; Columbia University, instructor, 1938-42; Bell Laboratories, Murray Hills, NJ, began as researcher and inventor, became assistant director of the Chemical Research Laboratory, 1942-76, consultant on the education and employment of minorities, beginning in 1976; Plastics Institute of America, Hoboken, NJ, research director, 1976-83. American Chemical Society's Project SEED (a campaign to promote science careers to minority students around the country), chair, 1981; worked with the National Action Council for Minorities in Engineering (NACME), a committee set up by several major companies to get minorities into the field; member and chair of the board of trustees of Montclair State College, New Jersey.

AWARDS, HONORS: Fellowship in chemistry, 1938, from McGill University; National Research Council Fellowship in alkaloid chemistry, 1938; Honor Scroll, 1970, from the American Institute of Chemistry; Percy Julian Award, 1977, from the National Organization of Black Chemists and Chemical Engineers; International Medal, 1984, from the Society of Plastics Engineering; National Medal of Technology, 1992, for his work in chemical engineering and for his efforts to bring minorities into the sciences.

WRITINGS:

Polymer Degradation and Stabilization, Springer Verlag, 1984.

SIDELIGHTS: A longtime employee of Bell Laboratories, W. Lincoln Hawkins was a chemical engineer whose work helped make universal telephone service possible. Until the late 1940s telephone cables were insulated with a lead coating, which was very expensive; this coating was also too heavy for use in the multi-cable conduits which would be required if most homes were to have telephones. It was clear to many that plastics could be a cheaper and lighter insulating alternative, but every plastic then in existence broke down rapidly when exposed to the elements. Hawkins, working at Bell Laboratories, helped to solve the problem by co-inventing a plastic coating that withstood heat and cold and had a life span of many decades.

Hawkins was always a tinkerer. Born Walter Lincoln Hawkins on March 21, 1911, in Washington D.C., he was the son of William Langston Hawkins, a lawyer for the Census Bureau, and Maude Johnson Hawkins, a science teacher. As a child, he was fascinated with how things worked, and he made spring-driven model boats to sail on Washington's Reflecting Pool. He also constructed a simple radio to listen to baseball games. "I always loved building things," he told Kim E. Pearson in a 1983 interview for *Crisis.* "When I was about eleven years old, a friend and I tried to build a perpetual motion machine. We didn't know anything about thermodynamics—we had no idea that it couldn't be done." Hawkins's parents hoped their son would pursue a career in medicine, but it was engineering that captured his imagination. He attended Dunbar High School in Washington, a segregated public school renowned for its science and engineering programs—the faculty consisted primarily of African Americans with doctoral degrees who could not get a job elsewhere because of their race. One of his teachers had a new car every year, and when Hawkins learned it was partial compensation

for the man's patent on a component of the car's self-starter, he realized that tinkering could actually earn a person a living.

After graduation from Dunbar High School, Hawkins and one other African American student attended the well-known engineering school in Troy, New York, Rensselaer Polytechnic Institute. They were the only black students in the school. The next year they were followed by two more African American students from Dunbar. While nearly two out of three students dropped out of Rensselaer, Hawkins and the three other black students completed their studies in four years. But the Depression awaited Hawkins upon graduation in 1932, so he continued his studies, and by 1934 he had earned a master's degree in chemistry at Howard University in Washington. Following this, he taught for a time in a trade school and then was convinced by a counselor at Howard University to apply for a fellowship in chemistry at McGill University in Canada. He won the fellowship and completed his Ph.D. in chemistry at McGill in 1938. That same year he won a National Research Council Fellowship in alkaloid chemistry and he accepted a position at Columbia University, where he would remain until 1942. During his time at Columbia he met Lilyan Varina Bobo, whom he married on August 19, 1939. They would have two sons.

In 1942 Hawkins joined Bell Laboratories in Murray Hills, New Jersey, the first African American scientist to be hired there. Hawkins would stay at Bell for the next thirty-four years, researching and inventing new materials and products for the preservation and recycling of plastics; he completed his career as assistant director of the Chemical Research Laboratory. "I had a ball," Hawkins told Pearson, describing his years of service at the research lab. "There's a world of excitement there that's like nowhere else." Of the eighteen domestic and 129 foreign patents Hawkins himself held, by far the most important was that to replace the lead insulation of telephone cables with a new weather-resistant plastic coating. Working together with Vincent Lanza in the late 1940s, he developed additives to create a new polymer that could resist both thermal degradation and the effects of oxidation and last up to seventy years in the elements. "Hawkins's work is arguably one of the major achievements which made universal telephone service economical," a colleague at Bell Laboratories told John Burgess of the *Washington Post.*

But engineering was only part of Hawkins's long and distinguished career. Retiring at age sixty-five, he remained a consultant to Bell on the education and employment of minorities. He also became research director for the Plastics Institute of America in Hoboken, New Jersey, from 1976 to 1983, and he worked privately as a materials consultant. In addition, he often spoke to minority youth about the importance of education. In 1981, he became the first chairman of the American Chemical Society's Project SEED, a campaign to promote science careers to minority students around the country.

Hawkins worked for many years with the National Action Council for Minorities in Engineering (NACME), a committee set up by several major companies to propel minorities into the field. He was also a member and chair of the board of trustees of Montclair State College in New Jersey. This second career in counseling was as successful as his first in engineering, and the students listened to him as if he were a member of their own family. Robert Stephens of Montclair State College told Burgess of the *Washington Post* that the students said to themselves: "This guy is my uncle, this guy is my grandfather, but this guy is also somebody important."

Hawkins was widely honored for his pioneering work in polymers, winning the Honor Scroll of the American Institute of Chemistry in 1970, the Percy Julian Award from the National Organization of Black Chemists and Chemical Engineers in 1977, and the International Medal of the Society of Plastics Engineering in 1984. But by far his most important honor was the 1992 National Medal of Technology, awarded to him not only for his work in chemical engineering, but also for his labors in attempting to bring minorities into the sciences.

Hawkins remained vital and active through his eighth decade. He and his wife traveled around the world and then moved to San Marcos, California, to be near one of their sons. On August 20, 1992, Hawkins died of heart failure at the age of eighty-one. Shortly after his death, an undergraduate research fellowship was established in his name by the National Action Council for Minorities in Engineering.

BIOGRAPHICAL/CRITICAL SOURCES:

BOOKS

Sammons, Vivian Ovelton, *Blacks in Science and Medicine,* Hemisphere Publishing Corporation, 1990, pp. 114-115.

PERIODICALS

About . . . Time, March, 1993, p. 9.
American Chemical Society Chemunity News, September, 1992, p. 3.
Crisis, April, 1983, pp. 192-193.
New York Times, August 23, 1992, p. L46.
Washington Post, June 24, 1992, pp. F1-F2.*

* * *

HAWORTH, Walter (Norman) 1883-1950

PERSONAL: Born March 19, 1883, in Chorley, Lancashire, England; died of a heart attack, March 19, 1950, in Birmingham, England; son of Thomas and Hannah Haworth; married Violet Chilton Dobbie, 1922; children: two sons. *Education:* Manchester University, received degree (with first-class honors in chemistry), 1906, D.Sc. (organic chemistry), 1911; University of Goettingen, Ph.D., 1910.

CAREER: Chemist and writer. Imperial College of Science and Technology, senior demonstrator, 1911-12; University of St. Andrews, lecturer at United College, 1912-20; University of Durham, professor of organic chemistry at Armstrong (later King's) College, 1920-25; University of Birmingham, Mason Professor of Chemistry, 1925-48, dean of the faculty, 1943-46. British Chemical Panel for Atomic Energy, chair, during World War II.

MEMBER: British Chemical Society (president, 1944-46).

AWARDS, HONORS: Fellow of the Royal Society, 1928; Nobel Prize in chemistry (with Paul Karrer), 1937, in recognition of his work on carbohydrates and on vitamin C; Longstaff Medal, 1933, from the British Chemical Society; Davy Medal, 1934; Royal Medal, 1942, from the Royal Society; knighted, 1948.

WRITINGS:

The Constitution of Sugars, Longmans, Green, 1929.

Contributor to journals and periodicals, including *Chemische Berichte, Proceedings of the Royal Society,* and *Journal of the Chemical Society.*

SIDELIGHTS: Walter Haworth's earliest research was influenced by his contact with William Perkin at the University of Manchester and involved a study of terpenes, a class of hydrocarbons often found in plants. The work for which he is best known, however, involves his studies of various carbohydrates, including a number of important monosaccharides, disaccharides, and polysaccharides. Among his finest achievements was the determination of the molecular structure for glucose, perhaps the most important of all monosaccharides. The method he used for designating the formula of glucose and those of other carbohydrates is well known today to any student of organic chemistry as the Haworth formula. The 1937 Nobel Prize in chemistry was awarded to Haworth in recognition not only of his work on carbohydrates but also for his elucidation of the structure of vitamin C and the first artificial synthesis of this important compound.

Haworth was born in Chorley, Lancashire, England, on March 19, 1883. He was the fourth child and second son of Thomas and Hannah Haworth. Thomas Haworth, whose family enjoyed a distinguished reputation in business, was the manager of a linoleum factory and took it for granted that his son would follow him into that business. And, indeed, after completing school at the age of fourteen, young Haworth did take a job at the linoleum factory. He soon decided, however, that he had no interest in making his career in that kind of work. Instead, he had become fascinated with the chemical applications he saw all around him and had decided that he wanted a career in that field.

That road was made all the more difficult, however, when Haworth's parents withheld their approval and support for any additional education for their son. It was only through great personal effort and the aid of a private tutor that he was finally able in 1903 to pass the entrance examination at Manchester University. There he studied chemistry under the department chair, William Perkin, Jr., and became particularly interested in Perkin's own specialty, the chemistry of terpenes. Haworth received his degree in 1906, earning first-class honors in chemistry, and then stayed on at Manchester to work as Perkin's assistant.

In 1909 Haworth left Manchester to spend a year at the University of Gottingen studying with future (1910) Nobel Prize winner Otto Wallach, an expert on terpenes. In only one year, Haworth had earned his Ph.D. and was on his way back to Manchester. One year later, he had qualified for his second doctorate, a D.Sc. in organic chemistry. Over the next

fifteen years, Haworth held posts at three institutions. He was senior demonstrator at the Imperial College of Science and Technology in London from 1911 to 1912, lecturer at United College in the University of St. Andrews from 1912 to 1920, and professor of organic chemistry at Armstrong (later King's) College in the University of Durham from 1920 to 1925. In the latter year he was appointed Mason Professor of Chemistry at the University of Birmingham, a post he held until his retirement in 1948.

The most important period for Haworth in his pre-Birmingham days was his tenure at St. Andrews. It was there that he was introduced to the new field of carbohydrate chemistry by Thomas Purdie and James Colquhoun Irvine, two of England's foremost authorities in the field. In the early 1910s, scientists knew a fair amount about the chemical composition of the carbohydrates, but relatively little about their molecular structure. It was to the question of molecular structure that Haworth soon turned his attention at St. Andrews, and before long, he had abandoned his work on terpenes.

World War I interrupted Haworth's new line of research, however. For the duration of the war, the chemical laboratories at St. Andrews (like other such facilities) were completely given over to the manufacture of chemicals with military importance. At the war's conclusion, however, Haworth returned to his work on carbohydrates. The first stages of that research were devoted to the monosaccharides, the simplest of the carbohydrates. Haworth developed a method by which he could determine the sequence of linkages within a molecule and was able to elucidate the detailed formulas for many compounds. Among the most important of these was glucose, which Haworth showed in 1926 to exist as a six-membered ring consisting of five carbon atoms and one oxygen atom. The convention he used to represent the glucose structure, showing the three-dimensional orientation of its components, has since become known as a Haworth formula or Haworth projection.

In his later work at Birmingham, Haworth took on more and more complex structures, eventually finding formulas for lactose and sucrose, two important disaccharides. He also took on yet another challenge—the determination of the structure for hexuronic acid. Hexuronic acid had been discovered in 1932 by Albert Szent-Gyorgyi in extracts taken from the adrenal gland, in cabbages, and in oranges. Szent-Gyorgyi suspected that his hexuronic acid might be identical to vitamin C, the antiscurvy agent, that had also been discovered recently.

In his own research, Haworth was able to elucidate the structure of this compound and then to synthesize it in his laboratory. That accomplishment was historic since it was the first time that a vitamin had been produced synthetically. Because of the compound's antiscurvy properties, Haworth suggested that it be renamed ascorbic acid ("notscurvy" acid), a name by which it is now universally known. For his work both with carbohydrates and with vitamin C, Haworth was awarded a share of the 1937 Nobel Prize in chemistry along with Paul Karrer.

Haworth's health failed him in 1938, but three years later he had recovered sufficiently to return to his research and other commitments. Included among those other commitments were a number of political and professional responsibilities. He served as chairperson of the British Chemical Panel for Atomic Energy during World War II. He also became dean of the faculty at Birmingham from 1943 to 1946 and served as president of the British Chemical Society from 1944 to 1946. At the same time, he continued an active program of research, concentrating on the most complex of all carbohydrates, the polysaccharides.

Haworth was married to Violet Chilton Dobbie in 1922. The couple had two sons. Haworth died at his home in Birmingham of a heart attack on March 19, 1950, his birthday. In addition to the Nobel Prize, he had been awarded the Longstaff Medal of the British Chemical Society in 1933, the Davy Medal in 1934, and the Royal Medal of the Royal Society in 1942. He was made a fellow of the Royal Society in 1928 and was knighted in 1948.

BIOGRAPHICAL/CRITICAL SOURCES:

BOOKS

Dictionary of Scientific Biography, Volume 6, Scribner, 1975, pp. 184-186.
Legg, L. G. Wickham, and E. T. Williams, *Dictionary of National Biography: 1941-1950,* Oxford, 1959, pp. 368-369.

PERIODICALS

Journal of the Chemical Society, 1951, pp. 2790-2806.*

HEDGECOE, John 1937-

PERSONAL: Born March 24, 1937; son of William Hedgecoe and Kathleen Don; married Julia Mardon, 1960 (divorced, 1995); children: two sons, one daughter. *Education:* Guildford School of Art. *Avocational interests:* Sculpture, building, gardening.

ADDRESSES: Home—47 Riverside Ct., Nine Elms Lane, SW8 5BY England.

CAREER: Queen Magazine, London, staff photographer, 1957-72; freelance photographer for international magazines, 1958—; freelance photographer for the London *Sunday Times* and *Observer,* 1960-70; Royal College of Art, Kensington Gore, London, reader in photography and head of photography department, 1965-74, chair of photography department, 1975, professor of photography, 1975-94, professor emeritus, 1994—, fellow, 1973, managing trustee, 1983, senior fellow, 1992. John Hedgecoe Ltd., director, 1965-95; Perennial Pictures Ltd., director 1980, 1991; Lion & Unicorn Press Ltd., director 1986-94. Works have been exhibited in London, Sydney, Toronto, Edinburgh, Venice, and Prague; photographs are also featured in a number of permanent collections, including the Victoria & Albert Museum, Art Gallery of Ontario, National Portrait Gallery, and Citibank (all in London), Henry Moore Foundation, Museum of Modern Art (New York City), Leeds City Art Gallery, England, and Ministry of Culture (Morocco).

AWARDS, HONORS: Prize for best art book, 1969, for *Henry Moore;* Kodak Photobuchpreis Stuttgart, 1979, and Grand Prix Technique de la Photographie, Musee Francais de la Photographie, 1980, both for *The Art of Colour Photography;* laureate and medal for contribution to photography, the government of Czechoslovakia, 1989.

WRITINGS:

The Book of Photography, 1976, revised and updated edition published as *The Book of Photography: How to See and Take Better Pictures,* Knopf (New York), 1984.
John Hedgecoe's Pocket Guide to Practical Photography, 1979, revised and expanded as *The Photographer's Workbook,* Mitchell Beazley (London), 1983.
What a Picture!, 1983, published under the title *John Hedgecoe's Taking Great Photographs,* Simon and Schuster (New York), 1984.

(With Jack Tresidder and Richard Platt) *The Art of Colour Photography,* 1978, revised and updated edition published as *The Art of Color Photography,* Simon and Schuster (New York), 1989.

John Hedgecoe's Nude Photography, Simon and Schuster (New York), 1984.

John Hedgecoe's Darkroom Techniques, Simon and Schuster (New York), 1985, published as *The Workbook of Darkroom Techniques,* Mitchell Beazley (London), 1990.

John Hedgecoe's Photographer's Workbook, Simon and Schuster (New York), 1985.

John Hedgecoe's Photographic Techniques, Simon and Schuster (New York), 1985.

John Hedgecoe's Nude and Portrait Photography, Simon and Schuster (New York), 1985.

John Hedgecoe's New Manual of Photography, Weidenfeld and Nicolson (London), 1986.

John Hedgecoe's Pocket Guide to Vacation Photography, Simon and Schuster (New York), 1986.

(With Ron van der Meer) *The Working Camera: The World's First Three-Dimensional Guide to Photography Made Easy,* Harmony Books (New York), 1986.

John Hedgecoe's Practical Portrait Photography, Simon and Schuster (New York), 1987.

The Photographer's Sourcebook, Knopf (New York), 1987.

John Hedgecoe's Practical Landscape Photography, Simon and Schuster (New York), 1988, published as *John Hedgecoe's Landscape Photography,* Sterling (New York), 1994.

Hedgecoe on Video: A Complete Creative and Technical Guide to Making Videos, Pyramid Books (London), 1989.

John Hedgecoe's Complete Video Course: A Step-by-Step, Self-Instruction Guide to Making Great Videos, Simon and Schuster (New York), 1989.

The Workbook of Photographic Techniques, Mitchell Beazley (London), 1990.

John Hedgecoe's Practical Portrait Photography, Collins and Brown (London), 1991, published as *John Hedgecoe's Complete Guide to Photographing People,* Sterling (New York), 1992.

The Workbook of Nudes and Glamour, Mitchell Beazley (London), 1991.

The Photographer's Handbook, third revised edition, Knopf (New York), 1992.

John Hedgecoe's Complete Guide to Video, Sterling (New York), 1992.

(With Salma Samar Damluji) *Zillij: The Art of Moroccan Ceramics,* Garnet, 1992.

John Hedgecoe's Photography Basics, Sterling (New York), 1993.

John Hedgecoe's Compete Guide to Black and White Photography: And Darkroom Techniques, Sterling (New York), 1994.

John Hedgecoe's New Book of Photography, Dorling Kindersley (London), 1994.

John Hedgecoe's Camcorder Basics, Amphoto (New York), 1995.

Author of other books, including *Kevin Crossley-Holland Book of Norfolk Poems,* 1970; *Sculptures of Picasso,* 1970; (with others) *Photography, Material and Methods* (annual publication), 1971-74; *Henry Moore, Energy in Space,* 1973; *Handbook of Photographic Techniques,* 1977; *Possessions,* 1978; *Introductory Photography Course,* 1979; *Master Classes in Photography: Children and Child Portraiture,* 1980; *The Book of Advanced Photography,* 1982; *Aesthetics of Nude Photography,* 1984; *The Workbook of Photo Techniques,* 1984; *The Workbook of Darkroom Techniques,* 1984; *Pocket Book of Travel and Holiday Photography,* 1986; *Henry Moore: His Ideas, Inspirations and Life as an Artist,* 1986; *The Three Dimensional Pop-up Photography Book,* 1986; *Photographer's Manual of Creative Ideas,* 1986; *Hedgecoe on Photography,* 1988; *Complete Photography Guide,* 1990; *Video Photographer's Handbook,* 1992; *The Spirit of the Garden,* 1994; *Black and White Photography,* 1994; *John Hedgecoe—A Complete Introductory Guide—Video,* 1995; *Breakfast with Dolly* (novel), 1996; *Figure and Form,* 1996; and *John Hedgecoe's New Introductory Photography Course,* 1996.

Contributor of photographs to books, including *Poems of Thomas Hardy,* 1981; *Poems of Robert Burns,* 1981; *Henry Moore,* edited by Suzanne Webber, Chronicle (San Francisco), 1986; *Shakespeare's Land: A Journey through the Landscape of Elizabethan England* by A. L. Rowse, Chronicle, 1987; and *A. L. Rowse's Cornwall: A Journey through Cornwall's Past and Present* by A. L. Rowse, Weidenfeld and Nicolson, 1988.

SIDELIGHTS: John Hedgecoe is considered both a master photographer and an expert in the art of explaining photographic techniques via the written word. His book-length treatises have represented not only various types of photography, from landscapes to children's portraits, but also explanations of various photographic techniques, including film development, working in black-and-white, and the use of video. These instructional volumes have received high marks from reviewers for Hedgecoe's clear expository style as well as for his well-selected and generous use of photographs to illustrate details of his discussions.

Many of Hedgecoe's books are considered excellent tools for use in the classroom. *John Hedgecoe's Complete Guide to Photography,* for example, is divided into seventy-one projects of increasing difficulty. This type of organization "provides an excellent way of teaching . . . through hands-on exercises," noted a reviewer for *Library Journal.* Critics have also lauded the usefulness of Hedgecoe's books for photographers of various skill levels. *Library Journal* contributor Raymond Bial noted that a beginner may read *John Hedgecoe's New Book of Photography,* for example, from cover to cover, while more experienced picture-takers will more likely dip into the book at various places for help with specific problems. Similarly, R. Bruce Schauble, in a *Kliatt* review, dubbed the third edition of Hedgecoe's *Photographer's Handbook* "an ideal reference text or hobbyist's companion." In an assessment of *John Hedgecoe's Complete Course of Photographing Children,* a *Kliatt* contributor praised the author's clear instructional style, observing that "Hedgecoe offers a guiding hand to acquaint the reader with the feel of the camera and what it can do."

Hedgecoe has written several books that delve further into specialized areas of photography. One such work is *John Hedgecoe's Practical Portrait Photography,* a book that was considered "an excellent in-depth introduction to the subject" by a *Kliatt* reviewer. The subject of video photography is explored in *John Hedgecoe's Complete Video Course,* which Clarence Petersen of the *Chicago Tribune* called "so good . . . that I suspect it will sell a lot of video cameras to people who never knew they wanted one."

Hedgecoe is also the co-author of *Zillij: The Art of Moroccan Ceramics,* a 1992 book created with Salma Samar Damluji, also of the Royal College of Art in London. This scholarly book offers a historical perspective on a distinctive Islamic cut-tile decorative art which has contributed significantly to the Moroccan architectural landscape. According to G. A. Anderson in *Choice,* the book's high-quality photos and well-written text make the work "a magnificent volume."

BIOGRAPHICAL/CRITICAL SOURCES:

PERIODICALS

Booklist, April 15, 1985, p. 1149; June 15, 1992, p. 1798; September 1, 1993, p. 24.

Books, May, 1988, p. 9.
Chicago Tribune, August 20, 1989, sec. 14, p. 7.
Choice, December, 1993, p. 594.
Kliatt, spring, 1985, pp. 57-58; April, 1988, p. 52; January, 1990, p. 46; March, 1993, p. 46.
Library Journal, February 1, 1985, p. 91; May 1, 1985, p. 55; July, 1992, p. 45; July, 1994, p. 88; November 15, 1994, p. 65.
School Library Journal, September, 1989, p. 165; April, 1995, pp. 168-169.
Spectator, November 15, 1986, p. 37.
Voice of Youth Advocates, February, 1993, p. 369.*

* * *

HEIM, Michael Henry 1943-

PERSONAL: Born January 21, 1943, in New York, NY; son of Emery and Blanche (Lake) Heim; married Priscilla Smith Kerr, 1975. *Education:* University of Michigan, participated in a summer study tour of the Soviet Union, 1962; Sprachen-und Dolmetscher Institut, Munich, Germany, received an advanced certificate in German, 1963; Columbia College, A.B. (magna cum laude), 1964; Charles University, Prague, received an advanced certificate in Czech and Slovak, 1965-66; Harvard University, M.A., 1966, Ph.D., 1971.

ADDRESSES: Home—500 Levering Ave., Los Angeles, CA 90024-1912. *Office*—Department of Slavic Languages and Literatures, 115 Kinsey Hall, University of California, 405 Hilgard Ave., Los Angeles, CA 90095-1502; fax 310 825 7894. *E-mail*—heim@humnet.ucla.edu.

CAREER: Czech Commission for Cooperation with UNESCO, Prague, Czechoslovakia, translator, summers of 1965, 1966, and 1968; Czechoslovak Academy of Sciences, Prague, lexicographer, summers of 1966 and 1968; Harvard University, Cambridge, MA, teaching fellow, 1966-69, visiting associate professor, 1985-86; University of Wisconsin, Madison, assistant professor, 1970-72; University of California, Los Angeles, assistant professor, 1972-79, associate professor, 1979-86, professor, 1986—; University of California, Berkeley, visiting assistant professor, 1977-78.

MEMBER: National Endowment for the Arts (translation program), National Endowment for the Humanities (translation program), American Council of

Learned Societies (joint committee on Eastern Europe), American Association for the Advancement of Slavic Studies (language committee), American Association of Teachers of Slavic and East European Languages (book awards committee).

AWARDS, HONORS: Hungarian Government Prize for Translation; Translation Center Prize, Columbia University; American Literary Translators Association Prize; Prize for Service to the Field, American Association of Teachers of Slavic and East European Languages.

WRITINGS:

NONFICTION

Contemporary Czech, Slavica (Ann Arbor, MI), 1976.
The Russian Journey of Karel Havlicek Borovsky, O. Sagner (Munich, Germany), 1979.

TRANSLATOR

The Letters of Anton Chekhov, Harper, 1973, published as *Anton Chekhov's Life and Thought: Selected Letters and Commentary,* Northwestern University Press, 1996.
The Death of Mr. Baltisberger by Bohumil Hrabal, Doubleday (Garden City, NY), 1975.
Three Sisters (play) by Anton Chekhov, first produced at Mark Taper Forum, Los Angeles, CA, 1976.
Uncle Vanya (play) by Anton Chekhov, first produced at Pittsburgh Public Theatre, 1976.
The Seagull (play) by Anton Chekhov, first produced at Pittsburgh Public Theatre, 1979.
The Cherry Orchard (play) by Anton Chekhov, first produced at Cincinnati Playhouse, 1980.
The Book of Laughter and Forgetting by Milan Kundera, Knopf (New York City), 1980.
The Joke by Milan Kundera, Harper (New York City), 1982.
The Island of Crimea by Vassily Aksyonov, Random House (New York City), 1983.
Novel With Cocaine by M. Ageyev, E. P. Dutton (New York City), 1984.
The Unbearable Lightness of Being by Milan Kundera, Harper, 1984.
Jacques and His Master: An Homage to Diderot in Three Acts (play; first produced at American Repertory Theatre, Cambridge, MA, 1986) by Milan Kundera, Harper, 1985.
Crime and Punishment (play), adaptation of Fyoder

Dostoevsky's novel by Yuri Lyubimov, first produced at Arena Stage, Washington, DC, 1986.
Chekhov by Henri Troyat, Dutton, 1986.
Master and Margarita (play), adaptation of Mikhail Bulgakov's novel by Yuri Lyubimov, American Repertory Theatre, Cambridge, MA, 1987.
(With Antonina W. Bouis) *In Search of Melancholy Baby* by Vassily Aksyonov, Random House, 1987.
The White Plague (play; first produced at Northlight Theatre, Evanston, IL, 1988) by Karel Capek, Theatre Communications Group (New York City), 1988.
The Encyclopedia of the Dead (short stories) by Danilo Kis, Farrar, Straus (New York City), 1989.
Astrophobia by Sasha Sokolov, Grove Weidenfeld (New York City), 1990.
Too Loud a Solitude by Bohumil Hrabal, Harcourt (New York City), 1990.
Helping Verbs of the Heart by Peter Esterhazy, Grove Weidenfeld, 1991.
A Certain Finkelmeyer by Felix Roziner, Norton (New York City), 1991.
Fording the Stream of Consciousness (short stories) by Dubravka Ugresic, Virago Press (London), 1991, Northwestern University Press (Evanston, IL), 1993.
(With Celia Hawkesworth) *In the Jaws of Life* (short stories) by Dubravka Ugresic, Virago Press (London), 1992, Northwestern University Press, 1993.
Uncle Fedya, His Dog, and His Cat (children's book) by Eduard Uspensky, illustrated by Vladimir Shpitalnik, Knopf, 1993.
Prague Tales (short stories) by Jan Neruda, Chatto & Windus (London), 1993.
Migrations, Volume 1, by Milos Tsernianski, Harcourt (New York City), 1994.
(And selector and author of afterword) *The Melancholy of Rebirth: Essays from Post-Communist Central Europe, 1989-1994* (nonfiction) by George Konrad, Harcourt, 1995.
Dancing Lessons for the Advanced in Age by Bohumil Hrabal, Harcourt Brace, 1995.

EDITOR

(With Olga Matich) *The Third Wave: Russian Literature in Emigration,* Ardis (Ann Arbor, MI), 1984.
(With Zlata Meyerstein and Dean Worth) *Readings in Czech,* Slavica Publishers (Columbus, OH), 1985.

Maria and the Angels (play) by Pavel Kohout, first produced at Actors Theatre, St. Paul, MN, 1989.

Magic Prague, by Angelo Maria Ripellino, translated by David Newton Marinelli, University of California Press, 1993.

Talks With T. G. Masaryk (nonfiction), by Karel Capek, translated by Dora Round, Catbird/Garrigue (North Haven, CT), 1995.

Member of editorial board for *Cross Currents, East European Politics and Societies,* and *Slavic and East European Journal;* contributor of articles and reviews to journals; contributor of reviews of contemporary East European literature to periodicals, including *New York Times, Los Angeles Times,* and *Washington Post.*

WORK IN PROGRESS: Translations of *A Bohemian Youth* by Josef Hirsal (from the Czech), *The Number Devil* by Hans Magnus Enzensberger (from the German), *Mediterranean: A Cultural Landscape* by Predrag Matvejevic (from the Croatian), and *Early Sorrows* by Danilo Kis (from the Serbian).

SIDELIGHTS: A prolific translator of Russian, Czech, Hungarian, and Serbo-Croatian texts, Michael Henry Heim has made available in English the work of some of the most prominent names in contemporary Central and Eastern European literature, such as Milan Kundera and Danilo Kis. Heim, a university professor of Slavic languages and literatures, is a fluent speaker of Czech, French, German, Italian, Russian, and Serbo-Croatian and can also read Danish, Hungarian, Latin, Slovak, Romanian, and Spanish. He published a Czech grammar textbook in 1976 and produced a revised edition in 1982; according to Heim, *Contemporary Czech* has been the primary Czech textbook for Slavists in the United States and to a large extent in Europe and Asia consistently for the past twenty years. Aimed at beginners, the textbook strives to provide both a reading and a speaking knowledge of the Czech language. Peter Herrity, a contributor to *Modern Language Review,* called the book "thoughtfully and intelligently compiled" and added that "it is to be welcomed as a very useful aid to those learning Czech from scratch." In 1987 Heim co-compiled *Readings in Czech,* which was billed as the first Czech reader to be readily available in the United States. Laura A. Janda, in *Modern Language Journal,* predicted that the book would "challenge and delight students and spare teachers . . . the burden of gathering materials."

By the time *Readings in Czech* was published, Heim's career as translator was well under way since the 1973 release of *The Letters of Anton Chekhov.* He

translated *The Book of Laughter and Forgetting* by Milan Kundera in 1980, a novel which Heim believes is among the author's best work. Reviewing the work in the *New York Review of Books,* Janet Malcolm remarked that "Heim's translation . . . hasn't a trace of the awkwardnesses and weirdnesses of its predecessors; its distinction lies in the clean precision and elegant leanness of diction through which the novel's taut modernist tone is rendered."

In 1989 came a translation of Yugoslav writer Danilo Kis's short story collection *The Encyclopedia of the Dead,* which received a good deal of critical coverage. Calling the book "one of the finest fantastic collections since [Jorge Luis] Borges's *Ficciones,"* *Nation* reviewer Brendan Lemon stated that "praise is due Michael Henry Heim's fluid translation" for the transfer into English of Kis's "linguistic acuity." Heim translated Sasha Sokolov's parodistic, experimental novel of future history *Astrophobia* in 1990. *New Republic* reviewer Donald Fanger, in discussing the translation, praised "the discreet felicities of Michael Henry Heim's heroic Englishing." And in the *New York Times,* Angela Carter described Heim's contribution to *The Encyclopedia of the Dead* as "a seamlessly perfect translation."

Heim switched back to Czech for Bohumil Hrabal's *Too Loud a Solitude* in 1990. Hrabal, although not a dissident, was considered a brilliantly talented, darkly comic writer of Czech fiction. Writing in the *New York Times Book Review,* Sven Birkerts commented that Heim's translation "seems expert"; John Banville of the *New York Review of Books* termed Heim's version of *Too Loud a Solitude* "excellent."

Heim translated from the Hungarian when he worked on Peter Esterhazy's *Helping Verbs of the Heart.* Banville reviewed that novel enthusiastically in the same *New York Review of Books* article as Hrabal's *Too Loud a Solitude;* John Simon of the *New Republic,* on the other hand, found fault with both author and translator. *Helping Verbs of the Heart* was the first novel to appear in the United States by Esterhazy, a renowned Hungarian writer. Heim performed the same service in 1991 for Russian writer Felix Roziner, author of *A Certain Finkelmeyer,* a comic novel about a Russian-Jewish writer who is compelled to become a literary hoaxer. Karen Karbo of the *New York Times Book Review* found Heim's translation of Roziner's novel "jaunty."

In 1992, Heim's translation of Kundera's *The Joke* was revised by Kundera. Originally pleased with the translation, the author had developed second thoughts over the years and changed some words, phrases, and sentences to make them more idiomatic or clearer. Marie Bednar of *Library Journal* gave the revised version high praise, finding it more natural and comprehensible than its predecessor.

Heim took a turn into children's fiction when he translated *Uncle Fedya, His Dog, and His Cat* by the Russian writer Eduard Uspensky in 1993; this fantasy about a small boy who runs away from home with his talking dog and cat was warmly greeted by reviewers at both *Publishers Weekly* and *School Library Journal.* Heim continued to show his versatility by translating the first volume of the Serbo-Croatian historical novel *Migrations* by Milos Tsernianski in 1994. He translated another novel by Bohumil Hrabal, *Dancing Lessons for the Advanced in Age,* in 1995. This comic novel is narrated in the form of one immense sentence by an old man whose reminiscences blend Czech history and vivacious private hijinks.

Heim has also worked on nonfiction projects. He edited a book called *Magic Prague* by the Italian author Angelo Maria Ripellino for an English-speaking audience in 1993. The book, according to a *Library Journal* critic, combines fact and fiction in its dense evocation of the essence of the romantic city of Prague. Heim both edited and translated selected essays by the Hungarian author George Konrad in *The Melancholy of Rebirth: Essays from Post-Communist Europe, 1989-1994;* Heim's afterword help put the essays in context for the American reader. Heim also edited *Talks with T. G. Masaryk,* in which Czech author Karel Capek (inventor of the word "robot" in the 1920s) interviewed Masaryk, the former Czech leader and democratic activist.

BIOGRAPHICAL/CRITICAL SOURCES:

PERIODICALS

Library Journal, September 15, 1989, p. 137; April 1, 1991, p. 155; July, 1992, p. 126; September 1, 1993, p. 211; April 1, 1994, p. 135; April 15, 1995, p. 100.
Modern Language Journal, Autumn, 1984, pp. 283-284, Summer, 1987, pp. 204-205.
Modern Language Review, October, 1984, pp. 1007-1008.
Nation, March 6, 1989, pp. 313-314.
New Republic, April 10, 1989, p. 36; March 12, 1990, pp. 39-42; April 15, 1991, p. 35-38.

New York Review of Books, May 10, 1984, p. 5; February 14, 1991, pp. 14-17.
New York Times, April 23, 1989, p. 14.
New York Times Book Review, December 9, 1990; August 4, 1991.
Publishers Weekly, January 20, 1989, pp. 139-40; September 22, 1989, p. 39; July 27, 1990, p. 222; October 12, 1990, p. 46; March 1, 1991, pp. 60-61; November 8, 1993, p. 68, p. 77; April 4, 1994, p. 58; February 27, 1995, p. 100; June 26, 1995, p. 86; July 24, 1995, pp. 58-59.
School Library Journal, November, 1993, p. 95.
Time, August 31, 1997, p. 62; January 19, 1987, p. 76.

OTHER

http://www.humnet.ucla.edu/humnet/slavic/faculty/heim.

*   *   *

HEO, Yumi

PERSONAL: Born in Korea. *Education:* Graduated from the New York School of Visual Arts.

ADDRESSES: Home—New York, NY.

CAREER: Author and illustrator of children's books.

WRITINGS:

SELF-ILLUSTRATED

One Afternoon, Orchard (New York), 1994.
Father's Rubber Shoes, Orchard, 1995.
(Reteller) *The Green Frogs: A Korean Folktale,* Houghton Mifflin (Boston, MA), 1996.

ILLUSTRATOR

Suzanne Crowder Han, reteller, *The Rabbit's Judgment,* Holt, 1994.
Han, reteller, *The Rabbit's Escape,* Holt, 1995.
Verna Aardema, reteller, *The Lonely Lioness and the Ostrich Chicks: A Masai Tale,* Knopf, 1996.
Cynthia Chin-Lee, *A Is for Asia,* Orchard, 1997.

SIDELIGHTS: Yumi Heo's distinctive artwork, which appears in her own picture books as well as some written by others, has garnered enthusiastic responses from critics impressed with her eccentric use of perspective, her energetic use of color, and her unique blend of primitive and sophisticated styles. The illustrator described her excitement at getting the assignment for her first book, Suzanne Crowder Han's retelling of a Korean folktale entitled *The Rabbit's Judgment,* to Sally Lodge in a *Publishers Weekly* interview. "This was a tale I had known since I was a child in Korea, and I felt a real connection with it," Heo said. "I was very comfortable with it from the start," she remarked of the artistic process that culminated in the illustrations for Han's text. "I would say that this art came from inside of me."

The story of *The Rabbit's Judgment* tells of a man lured into rescuing a tiger from a pit; though the tiger promises not to attack the man, once he is freed from the pit he changes his mind. The man looks first to a pine tree, then to an ox, and finally to a rabbit for a judgment that will rescue him; the first two are unsympathetic, but the rabbit slyly tricks the tiger back into the pit, and the man goes on his way. "The text . . . highlights amusingly eloquent interchanges" between the characters, noted a *Publishers Weekly* contributor, "while arrestingly skewed illustrations in a rich, natural palette illuminate the story's childlike wisdom." Other reviewers similarly highlighted Heo's winning addition to Han's well-told story; a *Kirkus Reviews* critic characterized the artist's style as "a pleasing blend of sophisticated design, ethnic reference, and visual storytelling."

Heo paired up with Han for another adaptation of a Korean folktale in *The Rabbit's Escape,* in which a rabbit is tricked into visiting the Dragon King of the East Sea, who wants to eat the rabbit's liver in order to cure his own illness. The fast-talking rabbit assures the king that he keeps his liver in a safe place and manages to escape when given permission to return to land to retrieve it. "Yumi Heo's original, quirky illustrations, with their Klee-like seas of floating figures, contribute significantly to the book's appeal," averred Nancy Vasilakis in *Horn Book.* The judgment was echoed by other reviewers, who, as with the duo's earlier collaborative effort, commented on the happy synergy between author and artist. Lisa S. Murphy, a contributor to *School Library Journal,* concluded: "Whimsical details [in the illustrations] reveal themselves with each new look, and this folktale is engaging enough to warrant many such readings!"

Equally successful are Heo's collaborations with other writers, including Verna Aardema, who adapted *The Lonely Lioness and the Ostrich Chicks,* and Cynthia Chin-Lee, whose alphabet book, *A Is for Asia,* provides information about the languages, people, and customs of the countries of Asia. As in her collaborations with Suzanne Han, Heo's illustrations for *The Lonely Lioness and the Ostrich Chicks* combine several art forms, including pencil, paper collage, and oil paints, and a style that characteristically tosses details or smaller elements in an almost wallpaper-like manner across the background. "Unique compositions and perspectives, combined with a subdued palette . . . challenge existing geometric notions of African art," remarked a *Kirkus Reviews* critic. Heo's artwork for *A Is for Asia* experiments in both traditional and tradition-breaking styles, according to a *Publishers Weekly* reviewer who concluded, "Heo's illustrations make turning every page an adventure into contemporary and historical Asia."

Heo's own picture books combine her signature illustrations with a variety of stories. In her first effort, *One Afternoon,* "the kinetic energy of life in the big city motors this zippy picture book right along," according to a *Publishers Weekly* critic. The story of a little boy who spends his day running errands with his mother, *One Afternoon* emphasizes the loud noises the pair encounter everywhere they go, noises which appear as words within the illustrations. In addition, the illustrator presents each destination from the child's viewpoint; "perspective, comparative size, and realistic details are forgotten" in the process, explained Nancy Seiner in *School Library Journal,* who feared that Heo's "extraordinary arrangements of details" in her pictures might captivate some children, but would confound others. Nancy Vasilakis reveled in the author-artist's "freewheeling style," and concluded that the "vibrant look at bustling city life . . . offers ample opportunity for creative applications in group story sessions."

Father's Rubber Shoes, Heo's second self-illustrated picture book, tells the story of a young boy whose family has just moved to the United States from Korea. Yungsu is understandably lonely at his new school, but his father tells the story of the poverty he endured as a child in Korea—carrying his precious rubber shoes instead of wearing them—and explains that they came to America so that Yungsu would have an easier childhood. "Heo's innovative compositions—flat, kinetic paintings incorporating many patterns and details—reflect Yungsu's changing feelings," observed Martha V. Parravano in *Horn Book.* While some critics found "the understated story too elusive for young children," as did *Booklist* reviewer Hazel Rochman, Heo's illustrations, which John Philbrook described in his review for *School Library Journal* as "primitive and appealing in [their] simplicity," were almost universally admired.

Heo tried her hand at retelling a Korean folktale in her third self-illustrated picture book, *The Green Frogs: A Korean Folktale,* a pourquoi tale that explains why green frogs sing when it rains. The story of two naughty little frogs who love to disobey their mother comes to its "gleefully fatalistic" ending, according to a *Kirkus Reviews* critic, when their dying mother tries to trick them into burying her on a sunny hill by requesting that they bury her by the side of the stream. For once the frogs obey their mother's wish and thus, every time it rains, they sit by the side of the stream and cry, afraid that the rain will wash her grave away.

"This is a quirkier pourquoi tale than most," *Horn Book* critic Nancy Vasilakis observed, "but it's too mischievous to be morbid." Others concurred, some pointing to what a critic for *Kirkus Reviews* called Heo's "magnificently eccentric illustrations" as the most successful element in the book. A reviewer for *Publishers Weekly* enthusiastically enjoined, "This Korean folktale is so beguilingly retold and visualized with such individuality that it deserves a wide audience."

BIOGRAPHICAL/CRITICAL SOURCES:

PERIODICALS

Booklist, June 1, 1994, p. 1825; August, 1994, p. 2048; September, 15, 1995, p. 175; November 15, 1996, p. 589.
Bulletin of the Center for Children's Books, February, 1997, p. 198.
Horn Book, November, 1994, pp. 719-720; September, 1995, p. 613; November, 1995, p. 733; November, 1996, pp. 748-749.
Kirkus Reviews, March 1, 1994, p. 305; June 1, 1996, p. 823; September 1, 1996, p. 1318; March 15, 1997, p. 459.
Publishers Weekly, March 7, 1994, pp. 70-71; July 4, 1994, p. 39; July 11, 1994, p. 77; April 3, 1995, p. 62; August 26, 1996, pp. 96-97; October 7, 1996, p. 73; February 3, 1997, p. 106.
School Library Journal, June, 1994, p. 119; November, 1994, pp. 81-82; June, 1995, pp. 101-102; November, 1995, p. 74.*

HIGH, Linda Oatman 1958-

PERSONAL: Born April 28, 1958, in Ephrata, PA; daughter of Robert (a miner and bus driver) and Mary Myrna Millard (an office worker) Haas; married John High (a recycler); children: J.D. High (stepson), Justin Oatman, Kala High (stepdaughter), Zachary High. *Religion:* Christian.

ADDRESSES: Home and office—1209 Reading Rd., Narvon, PA 17555.

CAREER: News reporter and feature writer; contributor of a weekly column, "Jake's View," to local newspapers.

MEMBER: Society of Children's Book Writers and Illustrators, Pennwriters.

AWARDS, HONORS: John Crane Memorial Scholarship, Highlights Foundation, 1993; work in progress grant, Society of Children's Book Writers and Illustrators, 1994.

WRITINGS:

Maizie (young adult novel), Holiday House (New York), 1995.
Hound Heaven (young adult novel), Holiday House, 1995.
The Summer of the Great Divide (young adult novel), Holiday House, 1996.
A Stone's Throw from Paradise (novel), William B. Eerdmans (Grand Rapids, MI), 1997.
A Christmas Star (picture book), illustrated by Ronald Himler, Holiday House, 1997.

WORK IN PROGRESS: Picture books *The Barn Savers,* illustrated by Ted Lewin, *Winter Shoes for Shadow Horse,* illustrated by Lewin, and *The Beekeepers,* illustrated by Doug Chayka, all for Boyds Mills Press; picture books *The Horse Carvers,* illustrated by Floyd Cooper, and *Under New York,* both for Holiday House; *Last of the Diving Horses,* set on the Atlantic City Boardwalk in 1977; research on Atlantic City, New Jersey.

SIDELIGHTS: Linda Oatman High commented: "I was born and raised in Lancaster County, Pennsylvania, living in the boondocks on Swamp Road. Swamp Road was just a road like any other country road, with no swamp in sight. There were woods and trails and trees and creeks and relatives for neighbors. And there was me, wondering why in the world somebody named it Swamp Road when there was no swamp in sight. That wondering was probably one of the first signs that I'd be a writer. We writers spend lots of time thinking about titles and names and words and why people call things something they're not.

"So there I was, growing up on Swamp Road with two parents, one brother, and an assortment of pets. We had many pets: a nervous Chihuahua named Vester, who trembled whenever we looked his way; a yellow canary named Tweety-Bird, who threw bird-seed all over my bedroom; an aquarium full of fish; a strawberry roan pony, Pedro the Burro; a sheep named Lambchop, who thought she was a dog; and Whitey, a fluffy Samoyed dog I loved with all my heart. It was my memory of the love I felt for Whitey which formed the backbone of *Hound Heaven*. In the book, twelve-year-old Silver Nickles longs for a dog to love, to maybe make up for the hurt she's felt since her family died in a car wreck. Silver covers her ceiling with pictures of dogs from the *Sunday News* adoption column, an idea which came to me when my son Justin began clipping pictures of dogs and saving them as a sort of dream dog collection.

"I was a child who believed in everything: angels, fairies, ghosts, UFOs, Santa Claus, the Easter Bunny. Once, I swore I saw Rudolph the Red-Nosed Reindeer through my bedroom window, and it wasn't anywhere near Christmas. Mom said that I had a crazy imagination, and Dad said I ate too many bananas before bed. You need a crazy imagination to write, but you don't necessarily need bananas.

"For first grade, I was lucky enough to attend California School. California School was a one-room school with a hill for sledding and the best spring water ever and a creek out back where I threw my bologna sandwiches. The teacher said that was why I was so skinny, but he never could explain why California School was on California Road, smack-dab in the center of Pennsylvania.

"My year in first grade—1964—was the last year of California School. The next year, I went to a brand-new school in a nearby town called Churchtown, which of course had lots of churches. The new school had unscratched desks, fresh paint, a cafeteria, a gym, and a black macadam playground with hoops and nets and hopscotch squares. The brand-new school had lots of rooms, but no creek for bologna sandwiches. No hill for sledding. No spring water. No coal stoves in the corners or creaking wooden floors. I thought they should have built another church instead.

"Speaking of churches, they seem to pop up in most of the novels I write. My characters attend church, probably because I began going to church when I was twelve years old. I wrote a poem about that fact, titled 'Faith':

"'Never heard much of Heaven or faith, till I went to California Church on California Road with Aunt Julia and Uncle Dave one day.

"'Sunday.

"'Twelve years old, didn't know Matthew from Mark or Luke from John, but I went anyway, with Aunt Julia and Uncle Dave on Sunday.

"'Little white church with a bell and an organ and pews full of relatives, the ones who were still living.

"'And, after I went to California Church that day, I finally figured out where the ones who were dead went.'

"As a child, I had an obsessive fear of death, until I found faith in California Church that day. In *Hound Heaven,* Silver Nickles is dealing with the death of her mama and daddy and baby sister, and faith plays a large part in the novel.

"When I was in the tenth grade, I wrote an essay about the Fireman's Fair in a nearby town. I wrote about the greasy French fries and the hillbilly music and the spinning roulette wheels that steal your money away. I wrote the essay for a creative writing class taught by Mrs. Severs (who we secretly called by her first name, Susie). Mrs. Severs—*Susie*—loved my essay and hung it on the bulletin board for everybody to see. She raved and raved about my writing and said that I should be a writer. From that moment on, I was. That's all I needed: to hear the words out loud.

"I wasn't officially published until 1984, after my first child was born. I had quit my job as a secretary and wanted to stay home with my baby, while still bringing in some money. Writing fit in my plans perfectly, and I wrote feature articles for local newspapers until 1987, when I decided that I wanted to write from my heart and not my head, as I'd been doing with newspaper reporting.

"In 1987, Justin was four years old, and I was reading a lot of picture books to him, becoming very interested in children's literature in the process.

That's when I began writing for magazines, selling some stories to *Highlights for Children, Hopscotch,* and *Children's Digest.* I loved writing fiction for magazines, but I had a dream. My dream was to write *books*—picture books, novels, chapter books. So I wrote and I wrote and I wrote, creating and submitting and collecting rejection slips as I acquired three more children: my stepchildren J.D. and Kala, then Zachary.

"There were times when I almost gave up, because it was hard. The writing was hard, the waiting was hard, the competition was tough. I had lots of kids and little time for writing. I almost gave up, but not quite.

"In 1990, right after my son Zachary was born, I wrote a novel called *Maizie,* published by Holiday House in April of 1995. It was my first published book, and *Hound Heaven* was to follow on the fall list of Holiday House, then *The Summer of the Great Divide,* in the spring.

"My dream has come true, with a bit of faith, a dash of determination, and lots of hard work. In *Hound Heaven,* Silver Nickles never gives up. She has faith and determination, and she works hard toward her goal. I try to instill all my fictional characters with these very real attributes . . . they can make dreams come true! In giving advice to aspiring writers, I would quote Ben Franklin: 'Never, ever, ever, ever, ever give up.'"

Linda Oatman High's novels for young adults feature spunky heroines whose unwillingness to give up their dreams, even in the face of unpleasant realities, helps ease the passage from childhood to adolescence. In *Maizie,* High's twelve-year-old central character has taken care of her alcoholic father and her four-year-old sister since her mother ran off with a vacuum-cleaner salesman. Maizie and Grace, her little sister, keep their dreams alive by making "wish" books from pictures cut out of magazines. Maizie's most ardent wishes are for a horse and to see her mother again. In pursuit of her dreams, she takes a job at a nursing home to raise money to buy a horse, and writes to her mother.

"The characters [in *Maizie*] are fresh, and their dialogue is natural, with just a hint of mountain flavor," observed Elizabeth S. Watson in the *Horn Book.* Several reviewers noted Maizie's ability to keep her spirits up, even when faced with seemingly insurmountable troubles. This feature of High's nar-

rative "keeps the book from being dreary but makes [Maizie] unrealistically plucky," complained Susan Dove Lempke in the *Bulletin of the Center for Children's Books,* though she admitted, that "overall, readers will find Maizie both likable and admirable." "Maizie is a character readers will not soon forget," Carrie Eldridge asserted in *Voice of Youth Advocates,* adding that High's first effort deserves comparison to Vera Cleaver's classic tale about Mary Call, the strong female protagonist of *Where the Lilies Bloom.*

Like Maizie, Silver Nickles, the main character in *Hound Heaven,* lives in rural poverty on a mountain in the eastern United States. Silver has lived with her grandfather since the death of her parents and little sister in a car crash and only wishes she could have a dog to love, a thing she feels will soothe her aching sadness. "High creates a rich and at times humorous cast of characters around Silver," reviewer Jeanne M. McGlinn remarked in *Voice of Youth Advocates* concerning High's second novel for young adults.

Other reviewers found the plot of *Hound Heaven,* which includes a one-sided schoolboy crush with overtones of stalking and a beauty pageant, strains the story's credibility. But, according to a critic for *Kirkus Reviews,* "this quirky novel is satisfying despite its odd detachment from reality." *Bulletin of the Center for Children's Books* contributor Deborah Stevenson credited the ultimate success of *Hound Heaven* to Silver's first-person narration, which "is touching in its yearning and appealing in its gentle humor."

Also told in the first-person is *The Summer of the Great Divide,* High's third novel for young adults. Set in the turbulent 1960s, this novel finds High's heroine spending the summer on her aunt and uncle's farm while her parents decide whether they should divorce. There, thirteen-year-old Wheezie is confronted by strange and arduous tasks connected with life on a farm, as well as making peace with a retarded cousin, the onset of puberty, and the ongoing war in Vietnam. *Summer of the Great Divide* failed to maintain the standard of characterization found in High's earlier novels, some reviewers observed, particularly in the book's secondary characters, who were faulted as sketchy. But readers are likely to sympathize with Wheezie's problems, according to Leone McDermott in *Booklist,* and "the 1960s time frame gives an interesting twist to a familiar theme."

BIOGRAPHICAL/CRITICAL SOURCES:

PERIODICALS

Booklist, April 15, 1995, p. 1500; June 1 & 15, 1996, p. 1718.
Bulletin of the Center for Children's Books, April, 1995, p. 277; December, 1995, p. 129.
Horn Book, May, 1995, p. 332.
Kirkus Reviews, October 15, 1995, p. 1493.
School Library Journal, April, 1995, p. 132; April, 1996, p. 134.
Voice of Youth Advocates, October, 1995, p. 220; February, 1996, p. 372.

*   *   *

HIRSCHHORN, Joel 1937-

PERSONAL: Born December 18, 1937, in Bronx, NY; son of Irving (a postal supervisor) and Evelyn (a homemaker; maiden name, Slatoff) Hirschhorn; married Jill Williams, April 18, 1969 (divorced, June, 1984); married Jennifer Carter (a documentary producer), June 18, 1985; children: (stepchildren) Derek, Brent, Kevin. *Education:* Attended Hunter College. *Religion:* Jewish.

ADDRESSES: Home—2727 3rd St., Santa Monica, CA 90405. *Office*—9762 West Olympic Blvd., Beverly Hills, CA 90212.

CAREER: Nightclub singer and pianist, New York City, 1959-63; songwriter, 1959—; recording artist, 1960-62; court reporter, New York City, 1963-65.

MEMBER: Broadcast Music, Inc., National Association of Songwriters, Musicians' Union, Dramatists' Guild, Academy of Motion Picture Arts and Sciences, American Film Institute.

AWARDS, HONORS: Academy Award for Best Song, Academy of Motion Picture Arts and Sciences, 1973, for "The Morning After" (the theme song from *The Poseidon Adventure*), and 1975, for "We May Never Love Like This Again" (the theme song from *The Towering Inferno*); received Golden Globe nominations for Best Music, Original Song, 1973, for the song "The Morning After" from *The Poseidon Adventure,* 1975, for the song "We May Never Love Like This Again" from *The Towering Inferno,* and 1978, for *Pete's Dragon;* received Academy Award

nomination for Best Song, Academy of Motion Picture Arts and Sciences, 1978, for the song "Candle on the Water" (the theme song from *Pete's Dragon*); received Academy Award nomination for Best Music, Original Song Score and Its Adaptation or Best Adaptation Score, 1978, for *Pete's Dragon;* received Antoinette Perry "Tony" Award nominations for *Seven Brides for Seven Brothers* and *Copperfield.*

WRITINGS:

(With Al Kasha) *If They Ask You, You Can Write a Song,* Simon & Schuster (New York City), 1979, revised edition, 1990.
Rating the Movie Stars for Home Video, TV, Cable, Beekman House (New York City), 1985.
(With Kasha) *Notes on Broadway: Conversations with the Great Songwriters,* Contemporary Books (Chicago, IL), 1985, published as *Notes on Broadway: Intimate Conversations with Broadway's Greatest Songwriters,* Simon & Schuster, 1987.
(With Kasha) *Reaching the Morning After,* Nelson (Nashville, TN), 1986.

Also coauthor (with Kasha) of the libretto to *Copperfield,* produced at the ANTA Theater, New York City, 1980; columnist and contributing editor, *Songwriter;* film critic and contributing editor, *Video Times.*

SIDELIGHTS: Joel Hirschhorn's involvement with the Broadway stage dates back to the 1950s. The native New Yorker, who attended the city's High School of Performing Arts, was by his early twenties earning a living as a songwriter, nightclub singer, and pianist; he later even recorded a few songs himself. For a time in the 1960s, he worked as a court reporter, but returned to show business to write songs for movies and stage works. In 1981, Hirschhorn's collaboration with Al Kasha on a stage version of the Charles Dickens novel *David Copperfield* debuted at Broadway's ANTA Theater. *David Copperfield* was not Hirschhorn's first joint work with Kasha. The two had scored hits—and two Academy Awards—with theme songs to the early 1970s disaster films *The Poseidon Adventure* and *The Towering Inferno* (both directed by Irwin Allen). They also penned their first book, 1979's *If They Ask You, You Can Write a Song,* followed seven years later by *Reaching the Morning After,* which took part of its title from the *Poseidon Adventure* theme song.

In their 1987 work, *Notes on Broadway: Intimate Conversations with Broadway's Greatest Songwriters,*

Hirschhorn and Kasha interviewed 27 Broadway composers, including Marvin Hamlisch and Leonard Bernstein, to provide readers with a behind-the-scenes look at what constitutes a hit musical—or perhaps more interestingly, what yields a flop. The reader learns that Barbra Streisand was only a last-resort choice for the career-making lead in *Funny Girl,* and Bernstein recounts the agony behind his *1600 Pennsylvania Avenue,* of one of the Great White Way's most notorious turkeys. Donna Perlmutter, reviewing *Notes on Broadway* for the *Los Angeles Times Book Review,* asserted that the authors placed a slight overemphasis on their interviewees' hairstyles, but conceded they excelled in "eliciting candid comments." *People* critic Ralph Novak called *Notes on Broadway* "a real treat for anyone who's ever wondered" about the process of songwriting for the stage, and contended the book "was obviously a labor of love for Kasha and Hirschhorn."

BIOGRAPHICAL/CRITICAL SOURCES:

PERIODICALS

Los Angeles Times Book Review, December 22, 1985, p. 6.
New York Times, April 19, 1981.
People, February 17, 1986.

* * *

HITCHCOCK, Alfred (Joseph) 1899-1980

PERSONAL: Born August 13, 1899, in London, England; came to the United States in 1939; naturalized U.S. citizen, 1955; died of kidney failure in Los Angeles, CA, April 29, 1980; son of William (a poultry dealer, greengrocer, and fruit importer) and Emma (Whelan) Hitchcock; married Alma Reville (an assistant film director and screenwriter), December 2, 1926; children: Patricia (Mrs. Joseph O'Connell). *Education:* Attended Salesian College, Battersea, London, 1908; attended St. Ignatius College, Stamford Hill, London, 1908-13; attended School of Engineering and Navigation, 1914; attended drawing and design classes under E. J. Sullivan at London University, 1917.

CAREER: Film director, 1925-76. W. T. Henley Telegraph Co., London, England, technical estimator, advertising artist, 1914-19; Famous Players-Lasky Co. (now Paramount Pictures Corp.), Islington,

England, began as silent picture title card writer and artist, became scriptwriter, art director, and assistant director to Graham Cutts, 1920-22; Gainsborough Pictures, Islington, began as scenario writer, became art director, production manager, and assistant director, 1923-25, produced and directed first film, 1925; director of motion pictures for Michael Balcon in Germany, 1925-27; director of motion pictures for studios in England, including British International Pictures, 1927-33, Elstree Studio Centre, 1927-39, Lime Grove Studios, 1934-39, and Gaumont-British Studios, 1935-38; director of motion pictures for studios in the United States, including Selznick International, Hollywood, CA, 1940-48, Warner Bros., Burbank, CA, 1948-54, Paramount Pictures, Beverly Hills, CA, 1954-60, and Universal Pictures, Universal City, CA, 1960-80. Executive producer, host, and occasional director, *Alfred Hitchcock Presents,* Columbia Broadcasting System (CBS), 1955-60, retitled *The Alfred Hitchcock Hour,* National Broadcasting Co. (NBC), 1960-65; Shamley Productions, founder and production supervisor of television series *Suspicion,* 1957, and series of programs for *Ford Star Time,* 1960.

Director of films, including *Blackmail,* Sono-Art, 1929; *Juno and the Paycock* (also known as *The Shame of Mary Boyle*), Wardour, 1929; *The Skin Game,* British International, 1931; *Number Seventeen,* Wardour, 1932; *Rich and Strange* (also known as *East of Shanghai*), Power, 1932; *Waltzes from Vienna* (also known as *Strauss's Great Waltz* and *The Great Waltz*), Gaumont, 1933; *The Man Who Knew Too Much,* Gaumont, 1935; *The Thirty-Nine Steps,* General Films, 1935; *Secret Agent,* Gaumont, 1936; *Sabotage* (also known as *The Woman Alone*), Janus, 1936; *Young and Innocent* (also known as *The Girl Was Young*), Gaumont, 1937; *The Lady Vanishes,* Metro-Goldwyn-Mayer, 1938; *Jamaica Inn,* Paramount, 1939; *Rebecca,* United Artists, 1940; *Foreign Correspondent,* United Artists, 1940; *Mr. and Mrs. Smith,* RKO, 1941; *Suspicion,* RKO, 1941; *Saboteur,* Universal, 1942; *Shadow of a Doubt,* Universal, 1943; *Life Boat,* Fox, 1944; *Spellbound,* United Artists, 1945; (and producer) *Notorious,* RKO, 1946; *The Paradine Case,* United Artists, 1947; (and producer with Sidney Bernstein) *Rope,* Warner Bros., 1948; (and producer with Sidney Bernstein) *Under Capricorn,* Warner Bros., 1949; (and producer) *Stage Fright,* Warner Bros., 1949; (and producer) *Strangers on a Train,* Warner Bros., 1951; (and producer) *I Confess,* Warner Bros., 1953; (and producer) *Dial M for Murder,* Warner Bros., 1954; (and producer) *Rear Window,* Paramount, 1954; (and producer) *To Catch a Thief,* Paramount, 1954; (and producer) *The Trouble with Harry,* Paramount, 1954; (and producer) *The Man Who Knew Too Much* (remake of the 1935 film of the same title), Gaumont, 1955; (and producer) *The Wrong Man,* Warner Bros., 1956; (and producer) *Vertigo,* Paramount, 1957; (and producer) *North by Northwest,* Metro-Goldwyn-Mayer, 1959; (and producer) *Psycho,* Paramount, 1960; (and producer) *The Birds,* Universal, 1963; (and producer) *Marnie,* Universal, 1964; (and producer) *Torn Curtain,* Universal, 1966; (and producer) *Topaz,* Universal, 1969; (and producer) *Frenzy,* Universal, 1972; (and producer) *Family Plot,* Universal, 1976.

Also director of the uncompleted silent film *Number Thirteen* (also known as *Mrs. Peabody*), 1922; director, with Seymour Hicks, of the silent film *Always Tell Your Wife,* 1923. Director of the silent films *The Pleasure Garden* (also known as *Irrgarten der Leidenschaft*), 1926; *The Mountain Eagle* (also known as *Der Bergadler* and *Fear o' God*), 1926; *The Lodger,* 1926; *A Story of the London Fog* (also known as *The Case of Jonathan Drew*), 1926; *Easy Virtue,* 1926; *Downhill* (also known as *When the Boys Leave Home*), 1927; *The Ring,* 1927; *The Farmer's Wife,* 1928; *Champagne,* 1928; *The Manxman,* 1928; (co-director) *Elstree Calling,* 1930; *Murder!,* (released in Germany as *Mary* and *Sir John greift ein!,* 1931), 1930; and *An Elastic Affair* (short film), 1930. Director of short films *Bon Voyage,* 1944, and *Aventure Malgache* (also known as *The Malgache Adventure*), 1944. Producer of *Lord Camber's Ladies,* British International, 1932, and *The Directors,* 1963.

Also inter-title designer of *The Great Day,* 1920; *The Call of Youth,* 1920; *The Princess of New York,* 1921; *Appearances,* 1921; *Dangerous Lies,* 1921; *The Mystery Road,* 1921; *Beside the Bonnie Brier Bush* (also known as *The Bonnie Brier Bush*), 1921; *Three Live Ghosts,* 1922; *Perpetua* (also known as *Love's Boomerang*), 1922; *The Man from Home,* 1922; *Spanish Jade,* 1922; *Tell Your Children,* 1922. Assistant director, art director, and editor of *Woman to Woman,* 1923; art director and editor of *The White Shadow* (also known as *White Shadows*), 1923; assistant director and art director of *The Passionate Adventure,* 1924; assistant director and art director of *The Prude's Fall,* 1924; assistant director and art director of *The Blackguard* (also known as *Die Prinzessin under der Geiger*), 1925; director of additional scenes for *The House Across the Bay,* 1940; conducted re-editing and dubbing for U.S. version of *Men of the Lightship* (short film), 1940; supervisor of

re-editing for U.S. version for *Target for Tonight,* 1941.

Actor, with cameo appearances in his own films, including *A Story of the London Fog, Blackmail, Murder, The Thirty-Nine Steps, Young and Innocent, The Lady Vanishes, Rebecca, Foreign Correspondent, Mr. and Mrs. Smith, Saboteur, Shadow of a Doubt, Life Boat, Spellbound, Notorious, The Paradine Case, Rope, Stage Fright, Strangers on a Train, I Confess, Dial M for Murder, Rear Window, To Catch a Thief, The Trouble with Harry, The Man Who Knew Too Much, The Wrong Man, Vertigo, North by Northwest, Psycho, The Birds, Marnie, Torn Curtain, Topaz, Frenzy,* and *Family Plot.* Appeared in *The Directors,* 1963, the documentary *Makin' It,* 1970, and as an interviewee in *Once Upon a Time . . . Is Now,* 1977. Contributor of voice (on telephone) in *The Gazebo,* 1960.

AWARDS, HONORS: Best Director, New York Film Critics, 1938, for *The Lady Vanishes;* Academy Award for Best Picture, 1940, for *Rebecca;* Academy Award Best Director nominations, 1940, for *Rebecca,* 1944, for *Lifeboat,* 1945, for *Spellbound,* 1954, for *Rear Window,* and 1960, for *Psycho;* Milestone Award, Producers Guild of America, 1954; Golden Globe Award for best television show, Hollywood Foreign Press Association, 1958, for *Alfred Hitchcock Presents;* Chevalier, Legion of Honor, 1962; D. W. Griffith Award, Directors Guild of America, 1968; Irving G. Thalberg Memorial Award, Academy of Motion Picture Arts and Sciences, 1968; D.F.A., University of California, Santa Cruz, 1968; Officier des Arts et des Lettres, 1969; Cecil B. De Mille Award, Hollywood Foreign Press Association, 1972; D.H.L., Columbia University, 1972; Commander, National Order of Arts and Letters, 1976; Life Achievement Award, American Film Institute, 1979; Knight Commander of the Order of the British Empire, 1980.

WRITINGS:

SCREENPLAYS

(Adapter with others) *Blackmail* (based on the play by Charles Bennett), Sono-Art, 1929.
(With Alma Reville) *Juno and the Paycock* (based on the play by Sean O'Casey; also known as *The Shame of Mary Boyle*), Wardour, 1929.
(With Alma Reville) *The Skin Game* (based on the play by John Galsworthy), British International, 1931.

(With Alma Reville and Rodney Ackland) *Number Seventeen* (based on the play and novel by J. Jefferson Farjeon), Wardour, 1932.

(With Alma Reville and Val Valentine) *Rich and Strange* (based on a novel by Dale Collins; also known as *East of Shanghai*), Power, 1932.

(Author of story) *Saboteur*, Universal, 1942.

(Author of story) *Notorious*, RKO, 1946.

Also co-scriptwriter of *A Story of the London Fog* (also known as *The Case of Jonathan Drew*), 1926; *The Ring*, 1927; *The Farmer's Wife*, 1928; *Woman to Woman*, 1923; and *The Passionate Adventure*, 1924. Adapter of *Champagne*, 1928; and (with Alma Reville and Walter C. Mycroft) *Murder!* (based on the play *Enter Sir John* by Clemence Dane and Helen Simpson; released in Germany as *Mary* and *Sir John greift ein!*, 1931), 1930.

EDITOR

Suspense Stories, Dell, 1945.

Bar the Doors: Terror Stories, Dell, 1946.

Fireside Book of Suspense, Simon & Schuster, 1947.

Fear and Trembling: Shivery Stories, Dell, 1948.

Alfred Hitchcock Presents: Stories They Wouldn't Let Me Do on TV, Simon & Schuster, 1957.

Alfred Hitchcock Presents: My Favorites in Suspense, Random House, 1959, published as *Alfred Hitchcock Presents: Fourteen of My Favorites in Suspense*, Dell, 1959.

(And author of introduction) Henry Slesar, *Clean Crimes and Neat Murders*, Avon, 1960.

Alfred Hitchcock Presents: Stories for Late at Night, Random House, 1961.

Alfred Hitchcock Presents: Thirteen More Stories They Wouldn't Let Me Do on TV, Dell, 1961.

Haunted Houseful, illustrated by Fred Banbery, Random House, 1961, new edition illustrated by Anthony Colbert, Reinhardt, 1962.

Ghostly Gallery: Eleven Spooky Stories for Young People, illustrated by Fred Banbery, Random House, 1962.

Alfred Hitchcock Presents: Sixteen Skeletons from My Closet, Dell, 1963.

Alfred Hitchcock Presents: Stories My Mother Never Told Me, Random House, 1963.

Solve-Them-Yourself Mysteries, illustrated by Fred Banbery, Random House, 1963.

Alfred Hitchcock Presents: Stories Not for the Nervous, Random House, 1965.

Alfred Hitchcock's Monster Museum, illustrated by Earl E. Mayan, Random House, 1965.

Alfred Hitchcock's Sinister Spies, illustrated by Paul Spina, Random House, 1966.

Alfred Hitchcock Presents: Stories That Scared Even Me, Random House, 1967.

Alfred Hitchcock's Spellbinders in Suspense, illustrated by Harold Isen, Random House, 1967.

Alfred Hitchcock Presents: A Month of Mystery, Random House, 1969, published as *Alfred Hitchcock Presents: Dates with Death*, Dell, 1976.

Murders I Fell in Love With, Dell, 1969.

Death Can Be Beautiful, Dell, 1972.

A Hearse of a Different Color, Dell, 1972.

Alfred Hitchcock Presents: Stories to Be Read with the Lights On, Random House, 1973.

Alfred Hitchcock's Supernatural Tales of Terror and Suspense, illustrated by Robert Short, Random House, 1973.

Alfred Hitchcock Presents: Stories to Be Read with the Door Locked, Random House, 1975.

Alfred Hitchcock Presents: Stories That Go Bump in the Night, Random House, 1977.

Alfred Hitchcock's Witch's Brew, illustrated by Stephen Marchesi, Random House, 1977.

Alfred Hitchcock Presents: The Master's Choice, Random House, 1979.

SIDELIGHTS: "I am out to give the public good, healthy, mental shake-ups," the late film director Alfred Hitchcock said in 1936. The quote is taken from *Hitchcock on Hitchcock: Selected Writings and Interviews*, a collection of interviews, essays, and speeches edited by Sidney Gottlieb. The director continued, "Civilization has become so screening and sheltering that we cannot experience sufficient thrills at first hand. Therefore, to prevent our becoming sluggish and jellified, we have to experience them artificially, and the screen is the best medium for this." This was a vision he would maintain throughout his life. That Hitchcock, who was sometimes simply called "Hitch" for short, was an accomplished and highly influential director of thrillers is beyond question, even among his most stalwart critics. Years after his death in 1980, his name is still familiar to young and old as the creative hand behind such films as *Psycho*, *The Birds*, *North by Northwest*, *Rear Window*, *Vertigo*, *The Man Who Knew Too Much*, and many more. Hitchcock is known as a scriptwriter as well, particularly early in his career with writing credits on such films as *The Skin Game* and *Number Seventeen*. He is also author of the story to *Saboteur*.

During a career that spanned five decades, Hitchcock directed fifty-three feature films. He has been both hailed as a master technician and lambasted for caring too much about technique and not enough about the characters in his film. Despite the praise and many awards he has received, Hitchcock, for some critics, falls short of being "an artist." As William S. Pechter averred in his *Twenty-Four Times a Second,* "[Hitchcock's] films veer schizophrenically toward empty entertainment on the one hand, and something like art on the other." Other critics, however, have looked more deeply into the director's films to find a unifying and fascinating preoccupation. Robin Wood, writing in the *International Directory of Films and Filmmakers,* asserted that in Hitchcock there is "so much more than the skillful entertainer and master-craftsman he was once taken for. His films overall represent an incomparable exposure of the sexual tensions and anxieties (especially *male* anxieties) that characterize a culture built upon repression, sexual inequality, and the drive to domination." In addition to the sexual tones in many of his films, however, are the distinctive preoccupations with feelings of guilt and fear. Still other experts have simply acknowledged, as Andrew Sarris did in *The American Cinema: Directors and Directions, 1929-1968,* that "Hitchcock's art is full of paradoxes."

Hitchcock was born in London, England, in 1899. His family loved to go to the theater, and so young Alfred was exposed early to the entertainment world, even before movies. Raised in a Catholic family, he attended the Jesuit school of St. Ignatius College in London. "It was probably during this period with the Jesuits," Hitchcock said in Francois Truffaut's *Hitchcock,* "that a strong sense of fear developed—moral fear—the fear of being involved in anything evil. Why? Perhaps out of physical fear. I was terrified of physical punishment. In those days they used a cane made of very hard rubber. I believe the Jesuits still use it." This sense of fear was combined with a love of crime stories. "I was reading . . . all the real-life crime stories I could get hold of," he recalled in a *Sight and Sound* article by John Russell Taylor, "but it never occurred to me as a practical possibility that my professional life might take that turn."

Instead, Hitchcock at first planned to be an engineer, and so his parents obligingly sent him to the School of Engineering and Navigation, where he studied mechanics, electricity, acoustics, and navigation. After leaving school, Hitchcock was employed at Henley Telegraph Company, where he became a technical estimator at the young age of nineteen. At the same time, however, he was also studying art at the University of London. Both his studies in engineering and art would prove helpful in his later film career.

Though his parents' early influence on him led to a fondness for the theater, Hitchcock was even more drawn to movies. "I preferred the movies and was more attracted to American films than to the British," he said in Truffaut's book. "I was very keen on pictures and the stage and very often went to first nights by myself. From the age of sixteen on I read film journals. Not fan or fun magazines, but always professional and trade papers. And since I was studying art at the University of London, Henley's transferred me to the advertising department, where I was given a chance to draw."

The year was 1920 when Hitchcock read in a trade paper that Paramount was opening a branch studio of Famous Players-Lasky in Islington, London. Seeing an opportunity, he read one of the books that the studio was planning to turn into a movie. This was still the era of silent films, and dialogue and narration was displayed on the screen as titles shown between scenes to help the audience follow the story. These titles were often illustrated with pictures. Hitchcock employed his drawing skills and designed several pictures to serve as title illustrations. Submitting his work to the studio, he was hired as a title designer, and his first job was doing the titles for the 1920 film *The Great Day.*

"At this time," Hitchcock recalled in Truffaut's book, "I met several American writers and I learned how to write scripts. And sometimes when an extra scene was needed—but not an acting scene—they would let me shoot it. However, the pictures made by Famous Players in England were unsuccessful in America. So the studio became a rental studio for British producers." Practicing his scriptwriting abilities, Hitchcock wrote an adaptation for the screen based on a serial novel published in a magazine. Upon showing his work to a British company that had taken over the Islington studio, Hitchcock impressed the filmmakers enough to land a job as an assistant director. When another company came to the studio in 1922 to film an adaptation of the play *Woman to Woman,* Hitchcock offered to write the screenplay. Not only did he become co-screenwriter, he also worked on that film as assistant director, art director, and editor.

Michael Bacon, the man who formed the company Hitchcock was working for, offered the young assistant his first chance to direct an entire film with *The Pleasure Garden* in 1925. Hitchcock went on to direct ten silent features. *The Lodger,* the 1926 film about a man accused of being Jack the Ripper, was a thriller that was a sensation in England. Even more important of these early films was 1929's *Blackmail,* in which the unique Hitchcock style—and his interest in the theme of guilt—first becomes truly discernible. Though originally without sound, *Blackmail* later had a soundtrack added to it, allowing Hitchcock to display more of the inventiveness he had already begun to show in his imagery. Hitchcock called his technique "subjective sound." In *Blackmail,* the story of a woman who has stabbed her seducer to death, he uses subjective sound to slowly distort dialogue until only the word "knife" can be heard, thus focusing in on the woman's sense of guilt and anxiety.

The Pleasure Garden and Hitchcock's second film, *The Mountain Eagle,* were shot in German studios. In the 1920s, German film was highly influenced by Expressionism. Expressionism, as Robin Wood explains in the introduction to his book *Hitchcock's Films,* "evades simple definition, but a central impulse was clearly the attempt to 'express' emotional states through a distortion or deformation of objective reality, 'expression' taking precedence over representation." Hitchcock's interest in showing his audiences subjective views of reality as expressed through various cinematic techniques thus begins in Germany. A second early influence on the director came when he first saw films from the Soviet Union, which introduced him to the technique of montage, or piecing together various elements of a film to convey a certain impression. From the Soviet filmmakers, Hitchcock learned that skillful editing can be used "for deceiving the spectator, for playing tricks with time and space." As Wood noted, Hitchcock learned that showing images in certain sequences can lead the audience to impose emotions onto a scene. For example, if a picture of an actor's face is shown, followed by a picture of a bowl of soup, the audience might think that the actor is hungry, even if he isn't trying to convey that feeling.

By the time *Blackmail* was released, Hitchcock was already developing a reputation as a fine director of thrillers. Yet in the 1930s he was still honing his skills, and, consequently, some of his early works were not successful. Films such as *The Skin Game* and *Number Seventeen* were damaged by ridiculous villains or even boring plots (such as in the stultifying musical piece, *Waltzes from Vienna*). On the other hand, movies such as the spy thrillers *The Thirty-Nine Steps, Secret Agent,* and 1935's *The Man Who Knew Too Much,* which Hitchcock remade in 1955, rewarded audiences with strong acting and flashes of brilliant directing. Of Hitchcock's English

films, David Thomson wrote in *A Biographical Dictionary of Film,* "The English films are playful, and sometimes facetious or silly. But they have dark moments and there are stirrings of sexual menace. The comic adventure of *The Lady Vanishes,* for instance, turns into a parable on appeasement, in which stock English fools get hurt. The first *Man Who Knew Too Much* is startlingly grim and cruel, and *Sabotage* is not unworthy of Conrad's novel *The Secret Agent.*" Still, Hitchcock was not satisfied with the limitations of working in English studios. He had always admired American cinema more than British, and so it did not take much for producer David O. Selznick to lure Hitchcock to Hollywood in 1939.

Thomson credits Selznick with teaching Hitchcock something about the importance of character and plausible plots in films. The director being a good student, his first American film, *Rebecca,* proved an auspicious beginning to his new life. The film, based on the Daphne du Maurier novel, won an Academy Award for best picture and received wonderful reviews from critics. Selznick had expected Hitchcock to make another spy film, but the director surprised him with a psychological thriller instead. *Rebecca* is the story of a young woman who becomes the second wife of the rich widower Mr. de Winter. Upon arriving at her husband's mansion, she discovers that the staff hates her for replacing the beloved, deceased Rebecca. Especially nasty is the housekeeper, Ms. Anderson, who torments the new Mrs. de Winter to the brink of insanity. Later, it is revealed that the late Mrs. de Winter was actually a horrible person who cheated on and tormented her husband, and that she wanted to destroy him. Her death at Mr. de Winter's hand is shown to be accidental, and the horrible Ms. Anderson dies when the mansion catches fire.

Although *Rebecca* is not typical of Hitchcock's films, it does contain characteristic elements, especially when it comes to the question of whether Mr. de Winter is guilty of killing his wife. The question of guilt is a central strain in the director's oeuvre, a theme that is often laced with sexual implications. Interestingly, the male characters in his films are usually innocent of any crimes in which they are suspects (with very few exceptions, such as *Shadow of a Doubt*), while his female characters are often guilty of murder, conspiracy, or sexually immoral acts such as adultery.

Shadow of a Doubt, released in 1943, is often considered one of Hitchcock's best works, and it was also one of his personal favorites. Based on a real-life murderer, Earle Leonard Nelson, who strangled several women during the 1920s, Hitchcock created an urbane and witty villain who kills his victims in a small, middle-class town. Charming villains and violence in ordinary settings are two Hitchcock trademarks, for the director enjoyed doing anything to catch his audience off balance. Instead of keeping the murderers' identities a secret—Hitchcock was not interested in mysteries, wanting instead to create suspenseful thrillers—he made them unsettlingly appealing. Having a murder occur in an ordinary household instead of a back alley or gloomy mansion was equally disturbing to most audiences. But Hitchcock particularly liked *Shadow of a Doubt* because he was able to blend character so well with action.

More typical of his early films, however, are movies such as *Suspicion* (1941) and *Spellbound* (1945), in which the hero might be a killer but proves in the end not to be. (In the case of *Suspicion,* the studio did not want the film's star, Cary Grant, to be a villain). In *Suspicion,* Grant plays Johnnie Aysgarth, a man whose wife suspects him of murder, and who fears that he will kill her too. However, in the end he actually saves her life and proves his love. *Spellbound* is another psychological thriller. Here, Gregory Peck plays psychiatrist John Ballantine, whose odd behavior makes him the suspect of a murder. Dr. Peterson, played by Ingmar Bergman, becomes convinced that his peculiar actions are caused by some kind of trauma, which turns out to be the time when Ballantine accidentally caused his brother's death.

During the 1940s, Hitchcock was still evolving as a director. *Foreign Correspondent* (1940), *Saboteur* (1942), and *Notorious* (1946) are spy thrillers; *Under Capricorn* (1949) was considered a failure; and in 1941 Hitchcock even uncharacteristically tried his hand at comedy with *Mr. and Mrs. Smith* (he also later tried black comedy in *The Trouble with Harry,* a flop about a natural death mistaken for a murder, and *Family Plot,* one of his most successful works). Though still not viewed as his most brilliant period, Hitchcock was assuredly coming into his own. *Lifeboat* (1944) is an intense drama in which several passengers from an American ship are stuck on a lifeboat with a German submarine captain after both vessels have sunk. *Rope* (1948), a film in which two homosexual men strangle another friend to death just for the thrill of it, is unique in that Hitchcock filmed it so that the entire movie appeared to be one continuous shot with all the action occurring in real time. With such films, Hitchcock was always proving himself an inventive director, composing innovative shots

to add visual impact to his films. In *Suspicion,* for example, Hitchcock placed a lit lightbulb within a glass of milk to make it glow ominously because the wife suspects her husband has poisoned the drink.

It was with 1951's *Strangers on a Train* that some critics maintain Hitchcock reached the top of his form. In this movie, Hitchcock mixes a concoction of fear, anxiety, and dread into one of his most suspenseful potions. After meeting for the first time on a train, as the title implies, Bruno Antony, a young playboy with rich parents who has been expelled from three colleges, makes an unusual proposal to Guy Haines, a tennis pro who is trying to start a career in politics. Bruno hates his father, whom he feels is too demanding, and promises that if Guy will murder Mr. Antony, then he, in turn, will kill Guy's money-grubbing wife. When Guy calls the plan ridiculous, Bruno backs off. But then he begins to pursue Guy, repeatedly insisting that he murder Bruno's father. When Bruno actually kills Guy's wife, the suspense builds even more until the final climactic confrontation between Bruno and Guy.

Some movie critics, who had judged Hitchcock to be in somewhat of a slump since *Shadow of a Doubt,* asserted that the director had regained his stride with *Strangers on a Train.* As Richard Winnington remarked in *Sight and Sound,* "*Strangers on a Train* . . . recalls the old virtuoso of the art of suspense. Here again fear and paranoia are let loose in the open against normal backgrounds." Guilt, too, is central to the story. Guy wished to be rid of his wife, and when Bruno actually kills her Guy must question his own involvement. Is he guilty—through his association with Bruno—of the murder, too? "*Strangers on a Train,*" remarked Wood in *Hitchcock's Films,* "draws together many themes already adumbrated in earlier films, which will be taken further in later ones: the theme of what Conrad calls the 'sickening assumption of common guilt' (developed especially in *Psycho*); the theme of the search for identity (*Vertigo*); the theme of the struggle of a personality torn between order and chaos (perhaps the most constant Hitchcock theme); and, in close conjunction with this, the notion of experience-therapy—the hero purged of his weaknesses by indulging them and having to live out the consequences (*Rear Window*)."

Though Hitchcock's heroes often suffer through some sort of emotional or moral crisis, they are seldom guilty of a crime. However, this is not the case with the heroines in the director's movies. Women are guilty of murder in films such as *The Paradine Case,* or conspiracy to murder, as in *Vertigo,* or adultery, as in *Dial M for Murder,* or theft, as in *Psycho.* Wood argued in the *International Directory of Film and Filmmakers* that Hitchcock's tendency to make his female characters guilty of crimes has a distinct sexual connotation, especially when one considers how the male characters are often drawn toward and "contaminated" by the females' guilt. "On the whole," wrote Wood, "it is the guilty woman films that are the more disturbing . . . here, the potentially threatening and subversive female sexuality . . . erupts to demand recognition [and], is answered by an appalling violence." It is these films, concluded Wood, that are Hitchcock's most disturbing.

Whether or not these trends in his films were conscious decisions on Hitchcock's part is a matter for debate. What is much more certain, however, is the director's interest in applying technique to get the best reaction from his audience. "I don't want to film a 'slice of life,'" he told Truffaut, "because people can get that at home, in the street, or even in front of the movie theater. . . . Making a film means, first of all, to tell a story. . . . The next factor is the technique of film-making, and in this connection, I am against virtuosity for its own sake. Technique should enrich the action. One doesn't set the camera at a certain angle just because the cameraman happens to be enthusiastic about that spot. The only thing that matters is whether the installation of the camera at a given angle is going to give the scene its maximum impact. The beauty of image and movement, the rhythm and the effects—everything must be subordinated to the purpose."

Because he felt each shot was so important, Hitchcock was known for his obsessive planning before any scene was filmed. "The secret," he told Pete Martin in the *Saturday Evening Post,* "is the way in which the story is pieced together. With me, all the little bits of business and the situations must be planted and established before the camera rolls. Sometimes I plan as many as six hundred camera setups before I begin to shoot." Actress Janet Leigh, who played Marion in *Psycho,* recalled in an *American Film* article by Stephen Rebello: "His camera was absolute. . . . Every move was planned. . . . He said, 'You can do almost anything with Marion and I won't interfere, so long as it's within my concept.'" Leigh later added, "Hitchcock's films had so little cutting, he told me, because he had learned the hard way. . . . Before he had the clout to have his pictures the way he wanted, someone else would cut them their own way. . . . He learned to preplan so precisely to not give them

extra material, because it was either going to work or not. If it worked, he didn't want anybody to muck it up."

Hitchcock had a reputation for not only being meticulous with his camera, but also for his sense of wit he deployed in his shots. For example, in one scene in *Marnie* Hitchcock films a kind of split screen shot, with Marnie on one side stealing the contents of her boss's safe and, on the other, a maid cleaning up the boss's office. Some critics have seen the director's wit as being integral to his ability to create suspense. In *Films in Review,* for example, Steve Sondheim remarked "Hitchcock's brilliance is his wit, and his flawless technique for using that wit to support and counterpoint suspense. When his wit fails, his suspense fails."

Hitchcock was not only known for his cleverness on camera, but also off, when he would indulge in practical jokes, although he later told Martin: "I have pretty much outgrown that now. And I'm afraid that if I tried to describe them to you, they'd seem pretty flat and contrived." One trick Hitchcock was particularly noted for on camera, however, was his penchant for cameo appearances. Usually these are simple bits, such as Hitchcock playing a passerby in *The Thirty-nine Steps* or as a man standing in a railway station in *The Lady Vanishes.* At other times, he would add a little humor, such as when he played a man who misses a bus in *North by Northwest.*

Despite this sense of humor, Hitchcock was also notorious for his poor treatment of his actors and for other people with whom he worked. He saw actors not as fellow artists who could contribute something to his films but, rather, as props to be used. "Hitchcock's thing about actors was very strange," said Joseph Stefano in Rebello's article. Stefano was a screenwriter who worked on *Psycho* and who commented that Hitchcock viewed actors as "spoiled children. . . . It was as though he really didn't live in the same world with them—or they in his." The director sometimes treated his coworkers with similar contempt. He often did not give others credit for contributing to his films, a deliberate omission that gave the false impression that Hitchcock did more work on his films than he actually did. He could also hold heavy grudges. For example, when screenwriter John Michael Hayes, who had done the writing for famous Hitchcock films like *Rear Window* and *The Man Who Knew Too Much,* refused to write the script for *The Wrong Man* for free, the director threatened to end their partnership. Hayes recalled in *Premiere,*

"He said, 'If you don't do this, I'll never speak to you again,'" and he never did.

Many of Hitchcock's most well-known and talked-about films were made from the mid-1950s through the mid-1960s, including *Rear Window, Vertigo, North by Northwest, Psycho,* and *The Birds.* Each is a very distinct work that convey different ideas. *Rear Window,* which debuted in 1954 and starred Jimmy Stewart, who had been in other Hitchcock films such as *Rope,* is about a magazine photographer who takes to observing his neighbors through a pair of field glasses while he is convalescing from a broken leg. One night, unable to sleep, he sees his neighbor, Mr. Thorwald, doing something suspicious. Thorwald's wife has disappeared, and the photographer begins to suspect that Thorwald has killed her. The theme of voyeurism in the film is clear, and, since the audience is watching Stewart watching his neighbor, that sense of voyeurism is also implied on the audience's part. Francois Truffaut, writing in his *The Films in My Life,* felt that in *Rear Window* one can see by implication the director's opinion of humanity—his audience—because everything the photographer sees shows people at their worst. "*Rear Window,*" wrote Truffaut, "is a film about indiscretion, about intimacy violated and taken by surprise at its most wretched moments; a film about the impossibility of happiness, about dirty linen that gets washed in the courtyard." Truffaut compared the courtyard in the film to "the world, the reporter/photographer is the film maker, the binoculars stand for the camera and its lenses. And Hitchcock? He is the man we love to be hated by."

Stewart also starred in 1957's *Vertigo.* Stewart plays John "Scottie" Ferguson, a policeman who develops a severe case of acrophobia (a fear of heights) and a sense of dizziness and disorientation (vertigo) after almost falling to his death while pursuing a criminal on the roof of a building. Retiring from the force, Scottie agrees to help his old college friend Gavin keep track of his wife, Madeleine, who has been acting peculiarly. Madeleine is obsessed with the idea that she is possessed by the spirit of an ancestor who killed herself. Scottie follows Madeleine for some time and begins to fall in love with her. When Madeleine climbs to the top of a tower and leaps to her death, Scottie is torn by guilt because his vertigo prevented him from following her. Later, he meets Judy Barton, who bears an uncanny resemblance to Madeleine. Scottie becomes obsessed with Judy and insists she change her appearance to look like Madeleine. Actually, Judy is, in fact, Madeleine,

having played the role as a favor to Gavin to cover up the real murder Gavin committed. Realizing he has been duped, Scottie, enraged, drags Judy to the top of a church bell tower. He has overcome his vertigo, but he can't bring himself to murder Judy. Judy, however, is accidentally startled when a nun suddenly appears, and she falls to her death.

Vertigo falls into the category of one of Hitchcock's "guilty women" films. However, Judy is highly sympathetic because she falls in love with Scottie, who can't return that love because he is obsessed with Madeleine. Often acclaimed as one of the director's most fascinating films, the most common criticism of *Vertigo* is that Hitchcock reveals too soon the fact that Judy and Madeleine are the same person (something the French novel *D'entre les morts,* upon which the film is based, does not do until the end). Hitchcock explained in David Zinman's *50 from the 50's: Vintage Films from America's Mid-Century* that *Vertigo* is a prime example of his intention not to surprise viewers so much as to create a suspenseful plot. The suspense lies in the question of what Scottie will do once he finds out Judy is Madeleine. "I felt that the second part of the novel was written as if nothing came next," said Hitchcock.

Hitchcock followed *Vertigo* with 1959's *North by Northwest,* starring Cary Grant as Roger Thornhill. *North by Northwest* is a spy/chase film like 1955's *The Man Who Knew Too Much,* and a good example of Hitchcock's penchant for putting ordinary people in extraordinary situations. *The Man Who Knew Too Much,* the film Hitchcock liked so much he made it twice, places two tourists (played by Doris Day and Stewart) in Morocco, where they unwittingly stumble into a spy ring, kidnappers, and murderers. *North by Northwest* features an advertising executive who is mistaken for another man and kidnapped because he is suspected of being a spy. While *North by Northwest* is an exciting chase film tinged with Hitchcock's black sense of humor, his movie *The Wrong Man* (1956), which also has the theme of mistaken identity, is much bleaker. In this film, Manny, played by Henry Fonda, is accused of murder. Manny is imprisoned, and his wife, unable to cope, is committed to a sanatorium. Though the real criminal is eventually found and Manny is released, he loses his wife to her mental disorder. Audiences found *The Wrong Man* disturbingly bleak, and so it was not as popular as the more upbeat *North by Northwest* and *The Man Who Knew Too Much.*

Psychological disturbance was a theme Hitchcock had touched on in several of his films—most notably,

Shadow of a Doubt and *Strangers on a Train*—but it was later in his career that he made his most famous film on the subject, *Psycho. Psycho,* whose murderous psychopath character is based on the real-life Ed Gein, a cannibal and murderer who lived in Wisconsin, has everything one could expect of a Hitchcock film: the guilty woman stealing money from her boss, sexual overtones and voyeurism (a la *Rear Window*) with Norman Bates (Anthony Perkins) looking through the peephole at Marion Crane (Janet Leigh), and brilliant camera work (the famous shower scene in which Norman stabs Marion to death). *Psycho* also begins with a scene—very controversial for its time—in which Marion (appearing in her undergarments) is having a hotel tryst with her lover, Sam. Sam, who is in debt and has to pay his ex-wife alimony, says he can't afford to get remarried. Marion, desperate to make a new life for herself, steals money from her boss and leaves town. She stops at the Bates motel, where she meets Norman, a shy young man who seems like he is oppressed by his domineering mother, whom Marion is not allowed to meet. That night, while Marion (who has decided to return the money) is taking a shower, the curtain is drawn back and a figure wearing a dress stabs her.

Marion's sister, Lila, worried about her sister's disappearance, contacts Sam and a detective. The detective, checking motels in the area where Marion was last seen, enters the Bates motel and is killed by the same figure in a dress. Lila and Sam next go to the hotel, where Sam distracts Norman while Lila goes to talk to Norman's mother. To her horror, she finds that Norman's mother is a corpse. Just then, the figure in a dress comes in to attack Lila, but Sam enters, pulls away the wig and reveals that Norman is the murderer. Norman, who killed his mother and her lover years ago in a fit of jealousy, has become insane.

Psycho was a sensation when it was released in 1960. Critics called it ingeniously grisly, and audiences flocked to see it. Theaters created more interest with certain tricks, as Danny Peary remarked in *Cult Movies 3:* "In 1960, theaters wouldn't let you in if you missed the beginning of *Psycho* (a gimmick that attracted enormous crowds) and it's a good thing because the opening scene in the hotel is vital." There is much sexual tension in the film. Marion, as the opening scene shows, is uncomfortable with her sexuality; Norman is a sexually repressed voyeur; Norman's mother was puritanical and controlling. It is thus Norman's pent-up sexual anxieties that lead him to murder both his mother (and her lover) and

Marion. His killing of the detective, however, is more the result of his fear of being found out.

The violence, of course, is the most disturbing part of the film. Hitchcock keeps his audience off balance by having the murders occur when they are least expected: in a well-lit shower; in a comfortable, ordinary room; and on a staircase, well before the detective reaches the door to Mrs. Bates' room. Ernest Callenbach, writing in *Film Quarterly,* called *Psycho* "the sickest film ever made. It is also one of the most technically exciting films of recent years." Of course, there were also critics who did not like the film. Dwight Macdonald asserted in his *D. M. on Movies* that *Psycho* was "third-rate Hitchcock," calling it "a reflection of a most unpleasant mind, a mean, sly, sadistic little mind."

The next film Hitchcock made, 1963's *The Birds,* was also a horror film, but of a very different sort. The first color feature Hitchcock ever made, it is based on a story by Daphne du Maurier, who also wrote the novel *Rebecca* that the director adapted. In *The Birds* Hitchcock juxtaposes tense human relationships with the bizarre and completely unexplained attack of thousands of birds upon the citizens of Bodega Bay. When Melanie Daniels (played by Tippi Hedren), a spoiled young socialite, arrives in town in pursuit of her love interest, lawyer Mitch Brenner (played by Rod Taylor), tensions grow between her and Mitch's former girlfriend and his mother. The reason for the birds' sudden attack on the town has been a matter of debate. In *Hitchcock's Films,* author Robin Wood addresses three possibilities: "1) *The birds are taking revenge for man's persecution of them....* 2) *The birds are sent by God to punish evil humanity....* 3) *The birds express the tensions between the characters.*" Of the first two, Wood feels that the events in the film are not supportive, whereas the third choice "is more interesting, and seems to gain some support when one considers the original attack on Melanie by the seagull [when she is about to meet Mitch to give him a present of love birds]. But objections soon pile up: the birds attack innocent schoolchildren and kill Dan Fawcett, of whose possible tensions we know nothing."

Another theory expounded upon by John Thomas in *Film Society Review* is that the birds simply represent the irrationality of the world: "The birds . . . are but an analogue for those violent irrational forces that Hitchcock sees underlying our civilized world." Peter Bogdanovich, writing in *Film Culture,* favored the theory that *The Birds* "is a modern fable about the complacency of Man and the uncertainty of his position in the universe." The critic praised the film for its disturbing, Hitchcockian combination of horrible events within an ordinary setting. "There are sequences in *The Birds* that will literally leave you limp," Bogdonavich reported. Other critics, however, have been disappointed by *The Birds*. Comparing *The Birds* to *Psycho*, Callenbach said that *The Birds* does not build-up tension the way *Psycho* does: "*The Birds* uses up its excitement early, then tries to rise to what is only an anticlimax—the escape of the four individuals in the sports car." Wood, too, did not like the film—but only before gaining a better appreciation of it: "At first it seemed to me a great disappointment; now, after repeated viewings, it seems to me among Hitchcock's finest achievements."

Marnie, released in 1964, readdresses Hitchcock's interest in psychological disturbances. Marnie Edgar (played by Tippi Hedren) is a woman who takes jobs at rich firms under various aliases and steals from them. She then gives the money to her mother, who, for some reason, seems to hate Marnie, even though Marnie loves her. Marnie is also troubled by nightmares and becomes unreasonably frightened by thunderstorms and the sight of anything that is the color of blood. When Marnie is hired by Mark Rudland (played by Sean Connery), she does not know he has heard she is a thief. Mark is strangely attracted to Marnie, however, and when he catches her stealing from him, he offers to let her off the hook if she will marry him. Marnie agrees, but it is an uneasy union, for Marnie hates all men. Mark becomes aware that something horrible happened to Marnie in her past that makes her act the way she does. One day, he insists they go to the home of Marnie's mother, where Mark confronts Mrs. Edgar. When Marnie tells him to leave her mother alone, a memory comes to the surface of when she saw her mother, who was once a prostitute, being attacked by one of her clients. Marnie killed the man with a poker from the fireplace. Finally understanding her past, Marnie is able to accept Mark's love.

Marnie once again mixes murder and guilt with themes about sexual transgressions, including a scene in which Mark takes advantage of Marnie. It also harkens back to earlier Hitchcock films, such as *Blackmail* and *Notorious,* in which the heroine is "saved" by the male lead. Although *Marnie* was not one of the director's more successful films at the box office, it is a prime example of the Hitchcockian theme of the search for identity. Marnie slips in and out of aliases to hide her identity as a thief, which in

itself is an alter ego of the real Marnie—the one who committed murder as a child. "Hitchcock considered *Marnie* an unusual mystery," stated Peary in *Cult Movies 2,* "because the search is not for a criminal but for a criminal's motivations." George Kaplan, writing in *Film Comment,* called *Marnie* "the culmination of Hitchcock's concept of cinema as an artificially fabricated construct; it is also among the films in which one senses him most emotionally engaged. The paradox is only apparent: it is in the nature of Hitchcock's art that it is most intense when it leaves daily reality, the 'normal,' behind to explore unnatural relationships and extreme mental states, especially the obsessive compulsive, in a kind of abstraction only cursorily disguised as naturalism."

Hitchcock did not break any new ground with his last four films. Indeed, some critics, like Thomas, felt that his color films suffered from "sloppiness" not seen in his earlier black-and-white movies. *Torn Curtain* (1966) and *Topaz* (1969) are spy films, *Frenzy* (1972) is a thriller, and *Family Plot* (1976) is another dark comedy harkening back to *The Trouble with Harry. Torn Curtain* was one of the director's least successful films financially, part of which might be due to what has been called poor casting and acting by stars Julie Andrews and Paul Newman, who plays Professor Michael Armstrong, a nuclear scientist defecting to East Germany to give the enemy a secret formula. Although Wood, writing in *Hitchcock's Films,* called *Torn Curtain* "a remarkably rich film," he also felt it left one with "a certain sense of emptiness. This is partly due to what is in other ways so admirable—the undermining of the morality of what Michael is doing on a political level: we are left wondering what it has all been for, and not finding very much of an answer." *Topaz* again involves East-West international intrigue. Set in the year 1962, while the Soviet Union was sending missiles to Cuba, the plot involves a French spy who is trying to uncover an information leak to the enemy.

Of his final films, *Frenzy,* for which he returned to England for the first time in twenty years, is one of the more successful. Although a reiteration of earlier thrillers, Hitchcock delivers some of his best material in this 1972 feature. The film concerns an ordinary man, Jon Finch, who is falsely accused of murdering his ex-wife and his girlfriend, and a debonair man who is the actual psychopathic rapist and killer. Hitchcock garnishes his movie with a dollop of humor, most notably a chef who insists on serving elaborate cuisine when all Finch really longs for is meat and potatoes. Hitchcock displays a most playful mood with his audience in *Frenzy*. As Joseph Sgammato stated in *Sight and Sound*, "Much of the vitality of *Frenzy* results from this implied relationship between director and audience. Hitchcock plays with our anticipations." Sgammato later added that *"Frenzy* is not about a sex killer; it's about looking at a sex killer. Its manner is its matter."

Gabriel Miller, writing in *Film Heritage*, expressed his belief that *Frenzy*, despite its touches of humor, "is Hitchcock's most pessimistic film." It is a pessimism that Miller felt was evident in all of Hitchcock's later features (though it is also present in films like *Rear Window*). "It seems that over the years Hitchcock's belief in the possibilities of man to save himself and his world have diminished." As further evidence, Miller pointed to the conclusion of *The Birds*, in which the menace of the birds remains even at the end, and *Topaz*, in which war has been avoided but humanity is indifferent to its fate.

Hitchcock concluded his career with *Family Plot*, which was second only to *Psycho* in terms of box office sales, earning over seven million dollars. In this film, Hitchcock intertwines two stories: a spiritual medium and her boyfriend are hired by an heiress to locate her heir, and two thieves are planning a kidnapping in order to get a ransom of diamonds. The four characters meet accidentally in a graveyard, and Hitchcock ties them all together in a suspenseful, humorous ride. Although popular with his audiences, some critics did not regard it as one of the director's best. "Ultimately," concluded Roger Greenspan in *Film Comment*, "*Family Plot* may be more fun to think about than to see. . . . There are moments of quite stunning intensity. . . . But some of the principle action sequences seem relatively lax and unfocused."

In the latter decades of his life, Hitchcock was known not only for his film directing, but also as the host of the television program *The Alfred Hitchcock Hour* and as the editor of the *Alfred Hitchcock Presents* horror and thriller short story collections. His true fame, however, will always rest with his feature movies. Though his films have been both praised and condemned, there is little question that he gave the world such a unique and memorable theatrical contribution that he is well remembered years after his death in 1980. Hitchcock stands out among other directors for what Wood called in the *International Directory of Films and Filmmakers* the "extreme peculiarity of [his] art." Sometimes criticized for not making films about "real life" or "the human condition," Hitchcock never pretended to be anything other than what he was: a man who delighted in the art of film. As Eric Rhode declared in *Encounter*, "Hitchcock may well be the last commercial director to think of the cinema as a new medium and the camera as a fresh toy." "I'm not interested in content," Hitchcock reiterated in a *Rolling Stone* article by James Toback published after the director's death. "It's the same as a painter not worrying about the apples he's painting—whether they're sweet or sour. Who cares? It's his style, his manner of painting them—that's where the emotion comes from."

BIOGRAPHICAL/CRITICAL SOURCES:

BOOKS

Arginteanu, Judy, *The Movies of Alfred Hitchcock*, Lerner Publications, 1994.

Bouzereau, Laurent, *The Alfred Hitchcock Quote Book*, Carol Publishing Group, 1993.

Boyd, David, editor, *Perspectives on Alfred Hitchcock*, G. K. Hall, 1995.

Finler, Joel W., *Hitchcock in Hollywood*, Continuum, 1992.

Freeman, David, *The Last Days of Alfred Hitchcock: A Memoir Featuring the Screenplay of "Alfred Hitchcock's The Short Night,"* Overlook Press, 1984.

Gottlieb, Sidney, editor, *Hitchcock on Hitchcock: Selected Writings and Interviews*, University of California Press, 1995.

Humphries, Patrick, *The Films of Alfred Hitchcock*, Portland House, 1986.

Hurley, Neil P., *Soul in Suspense: Hitchcock's Fright and Delight*, Scarecrow Press, 1993.

Kapsis, Robert E., *Hitchcock: The Making of a Reputation*, University of Chicago Press, 1992.

LaValley, Albert J., editor, *Focus on Hitchcock*, Prentice-Hall, 1972.

Macdonald, Dwight, *D. M. on Movies*, Prentice-Hall, 1969, pp. 303-304.

Nevins, Francis M., Jr., and Martin Harry Greenberg, editors, *Hitchcock in Prime Time*, Avon, 1985.

Peary, Danny, *Cult Movies 2: 50 More of the Classics, the Sleepers, the Weird, and the Wonderful*, Delta, 1983, pp. 84-87.

Peary, Danny, *Cult Movies 3: 50 More of the Classics, the Sleepers, the Weird, and the Wonderful*, Simon & Schuster, 1988, pp. 187-93.

Pechter, William S., *Twenty-Four Times a Second*, Harper, 1971, pp. 177-78.

American Film, April, 1990, pp. 38-48.

Phillips, Gene D., *Alfred Hitchcock,* Twayne, 1984.

Rohmer, Eric, and Claude Chabrol, *Hitchcock, the First Forty-four Films,* Frederick Ungar, 1979.

Sarris, Andrew, *The American Cinema: Directors and Directions, 1929-1968,* Dutton, 1968, pp. 56-61.

Sloan, Jane, *Alfred Hitchcock: A Guide to References and Resources,* G. K. Hall, 1993.

Sloan, Jane, *Alfred Hitchcock: A Filmography and Bibliography,* University of California Press, 1995.

Spoto, Donald, *The Art of Alfred Hitchcock: Fifty Years of His Motion Pictures,* Doubleday, 1992.

Taylor, John Russell, *Cinema Eye, Cinema Ear: Some Key Film-Makers of the Sixties,* Hill & Wang, 1964.

Taylor, John Russell, *Hitch: The Life and Times of Alfred Hitchcock,* Da Capo Press, 1996.

Thomson, David, *A Biographical Dictionary of Film,* third edition, Knopf, 1994, pp. 341-343.

Truffaut, Francois, *Hitchcock,* Simon & Schuster, 1968.

Truffaut, Francois, *The Films in My Life,* Simon & Schuster, 1978.

Wood, Robin, *Hitchcock's Films,* A. S. Barnes, 1966.

Wood, Robin, "Alfred Hitchcock," *International Directory of Film and Filmmakers,* second edition, Volume 2: *Directors,* edited by Nicholas Thomas, St. James Press, 1991, pp. 388-92.

Zinman, David, *50 from the 50's: Vintage Films from America's Mid-Century,* Arlington House, 1979, pp. 381-87.

PERIODICALS

American Scholar, spring, 1970, pp. 295-304.

Encounter, October, 1963, p. 44.

Film Comment, November-December, 1972, pp. 46-53; May-June, 1976, pp. 20-22.

Film Culture, winter, 1955, p. 31; spring, 1963, pp. 69-70.

Film Heritage, winter, 1969-70, pp. 17-23; winter, 1972-73, pp. 19-24; February 4, 1974, pp. 17-23; spring, 1976, pp. 1-10.

Film Quarterly, fall, 1960, pp. 47-49; winter, 1962-63, pp. 3-16; summer, 1963, pp. 44-46; summer, 1968, pp. 21-27.

Films and Filming, October, 1974, pp. 51-54.

Films in Review, October, 1954, p. 427.

Film Society Review, September, 1965, pp. 13-14.

Nation, January 7, 1939, p. 45; November 10, 1945, p. 506.

New Republic, October 19, 1938, p. 307; February 8, 1943, p. 182; December 3, 1945, p. 477; September 13, 1948, pp. 29-30.

New Yorker, November 22, 1941, p. 98; January 15, 1944, pp. 56-57; November 3, 1945, pp. 69-70.

New York Magazine, April 19, 1976, pp. 84-86.

Premiere, February, 1994, p. 36.

Rolling Stone, December 25-January 8, 1981.

Saturday Evening Post, July, 1956.

Saturday Review, June 8, 1940, p. 21.

Sight and Sound, August-September, 1951, pp. 21-22; October-December, 1954, pp. 89-90; summer, 1956, pp. 30-31; spring, 1957, p. 211; summer, 1973, pp. 134-37.

Time, September 23, 1935, pp. 44-45.

Village Voice, April 2, 1979, pp. 45-46.

OBITUARIES:

PERIODICALS

London Times, April 30, 1980.

New York Times, April 30, 1980.

Washington Post, May 4, 1980.*

* * *

HOBBS, Valerie 1941-

PERSONAL: Born April 18, 1941, in Metuchen, NJ; daughter of Herbert Trevor Evans and Alise (a painter; maiden name, Hansen) Minney; married Gary Johnson, 1962 (divorced, 1973); married Jack Hobbs (a teacher), June 18, 1978; children: (first marriage) Juliet. *Education:* University of California, Santa Barbara, B.A., 1968, M.A., 1978. *Politics:* Democrat. *Avocational interests:* Golf, hiking, travel, poker.

ADDRESSES: Home—69 Skyline Cir., Santa Barbara, CA 93109. *Office*—Writing Program, University of California, Santa Barbara, CA 93106. *E-mail*—hobbs @humanitas.ucsb.edu. *Agent*—Barbara Markowitz, 117 North Mansfield Ave., Los Angeles, CA 90036.

CAREER: High school English teacher, Oahu, HI, 1971-74; University of California, Santa Barbara, lecturer in writing, 1981—.

MEMBER: PEN Center West, Society of Children's Book Writers and Illustrators, South Coast Writing Project.

AWARDS, HONORS: Best Young Adult Novels citation, American Library Association, 1995, for *How Far Would You Have Gotten If I Hadn't Called You Back?*

WRITINGS:

How Far Would You Have Gotten If I Hadn't Called You Back? (young adult fiction), Orchard Books (New York City), 1995.
Get It While It's Hot. Or Not (young adult fiction), Orchard Books, 1996.

Work represented in anthologies, including *California Childhoods,* edited by Gary Soto, 1987. Contributor of stories to magazines, including *Northeast Corridor, Chrysalis, American Fiction, New Renaissance,* and *Kansas Quarterly.*

WORK IN PROGRESS: Jeronimo: A Love Story.

SIDELIGHTS: Valerie Hobbs is the author of the young adult novel *How Far Would You Have Gotten If I Hadn't Called You Back?* The story of a young woman with a love of both racing cars and the men who drive them, Hobbs's 1995 coming-of-age novel has been praised by critics for its original and sensitive portrait of a teenager struggling to find herself amid a sea of contradictory influences. In addition to publishing numerous short stories in magazines, Hobbs has also written *Get It While It's Hot. Or Not,* another young adult novel with a focus on friendships and teen sexual relationships.

Although to Hobbs it seems as though she has been writing all her life, she did not begin to write seriously until her late teens, after one of her friends met with a tragic accident. "Actually, my first novel was born when I was eighteen and wrote a truly awful short story about the death of a young man I was involved with at the time," she revealed. "Then, in 1986, I picked up the thread of that story and wrote 'Ojala 1959' for *California Childhoods,* a collection of short stories by California writers. Then I got real bold and decided there was more to tell," Hobbs added, "so I wrote a novel that ended with the same tragedy that impelled me to write the story in the first place."

That first novel was published in 1995 as *How Far Would You Have Gotten If I Hadn't Called You Back?.* The title derives from an expression often used by the author's father; the is based upon incidents in her own childhood that likely prompted her father's question. In the novel, sixteen-year-old

Bronwyn Lewis isn't a typical high school student. Growing up in the late 1950s, in a generation in which young women her age chose such role models as Doris Day and Donna Reed and looked forward to marriage and a future spending hours in the kitchen, Bronwyn would rather be drag-racing. Like her creator, Hobbs, the fictional Bronwyn moved from urban New Jersey to rural California at age fifteen; her interests and hobbies are different than those of the teens in her new town and fitting in at her new high school has been almost impossible. The fact that her family is now poor and her out-of-work dad has already attempted suicide makes Bronwyn feel even more withdrawn. Finally, friendship with Lanie, a pretty but poor young woman from the "wild side" of town allows Bronwyn a way "in" to a peer group: she falls behind in school, dumps her interest in playing classical piano for rock 'n' roll, and starts dating, drinking, and hanging out with the drag-racing crowd. A sexual fling with the much older racer known as J. C. is interrupted by a budding love affair with the mature and far more suitable Will, but when Will leaves for his first year at West Point, Bronwyn returns to her old ways, with tragic consequences.

Calling Bronwyn "a believable and realistic voice," Joel Shoemaker praised *How Far Would You Have Gotten* in his review in *School Library Journal,* noting that the novel's "themes are subtly evoked and life's lessons are learned the hard way." *Booklist* reviewer Stephanie Zvirin called *How Far Would You Have Gotten* "an enticing coming-of-age story," asserting that Hobbs "manipulates the elements (including the sex) with energy, confidence, and surprise."

How Far Would You Have Gotten wasn't written with a young adult audience in mind, although the novel was later marketed for young adult readers. Instead, Hobbs wanted to write down her personal recollections of her teen years, complete with her bout with personal tragedy and her own growing awareness of her maturing attitudes. "I think it was probably best that I didn't write [the novel] for young adults," Hobbs told Nathalie Op de Beeck in *Publishers Weekly,* "because I didn't know enough to pull punches. I just wanted to say it the way it is, the way people forget that it is. I always see those years as fraught with danger."

"No matter what we think we're writing about, we're probably always writing about ourselves," Hobbs believes. "My second novel has four entirely made-up characters, but I think, at heart, they're all just different parts of who I am and have been in my life." In that second novel, entitled *Get It While It's Hot. Or Not,* Hobbs weaves different aspects of herself into the lives of four best friends. Constant companions since the eighth grade, Megan, Mia, Elaine, and Kit begin their junior year of high school in difficult circumstances. Weak-willed Kit, who lives with her mother in a poor part of town, finds herself pregnant and bedridden; dependable Megan risks cutting classes and lying to her parents to help Kit get through her difficult pregnancy. A boyfriend pressuring her for sex, a stint on the school newspaper during which she decides to educate her fellow students about sex issues, and serving as matchmaker for her friend Mia all keep Megan busy, but not too busy to gain an understanding of several matters of common interest to teens: birth control, HIV/AIDS, unwanted pregnancy, and dealing with parents. Hobbs's novel allows readers to "relate to Megan's struggle to define the boundaries of friendship and her responsibilities to her family and community," explained Marcia Mann in her review of *Get It While It's Hot. Or Not* in *Voice of Youth Advocates.* Janice M. Del Negro of the *Bulletin of the Center for Children's Books* added that teen readers would likely find the "friends' group dynamics and the contemporary themes appealing." *Horn Book* reviewer Lauren Adams called the novel "well paced and highly readable, taking on serious issues with humor and intelligence."

While Hobbs would like to have a regular writing schedule, she has found that it doesn't suit her lifestyle. "I try very hard to write every morning, but I'm just not that disciplined," she confided. "I write in spurts, long ones. Once I get going, I don't want to stop. Then I might go two or three days without writing at all. The writing process (how and when people write and for how long) is unique to everybody. There aren't any 'shoulds' that are universal."

From her home in California, Hobbs teaches academic writing at the University of California-Santa Barbara. "The shift between the two kinds of writing is probably a good one for me," Hobbs notes. "There are many similarities, of course, between writing for the academy and creative writing, the most obvious being that if you are invested in what you're writing, if you do it with heart and passion, it will turn out fine."

BIOGRAPHICAL/CRITICAL SOURCES:

PERIODICALS

Booklist, October 1, 1995, p. 304.

Bulletin of the Center for Children's Books, November, 1996, p. 99.
Children's Bookwatch, March, 1997.
Horn Book, December, 1996, p. 744.
Kirkus Reviews, September 15, 1995, p. 1351; August 15, 1996.
Publishers Weekly, October 16, 1995, p. 63; December 18, 1995, pp. 28-30.
School Library Journal, October, 1995, p. 155.
Voice of Youth Advocates, December, 1995, p. 302; December, 1996, p. 270.

* * *

HOESTLANDT, Jo(celyne) 1948-

PERSONAL: Born May 13, 1948, in Le Pecq, Yvelines, France; daughter of Daniel (a mushroom producer) and Evelyne (a mushroom producer; maiden name, Gooden) Ravary; married Dominique Hoestlandt (an executive vice president), 1970; children: Maud, Bertrand, Olivier. *Education:* B.A., University of Sorbonne. *Politics:* "I don't like parties. I want to avoid being biased. Every day I meet children and work for acknowledgment of each other." *Religion:* Catholic.

ADDRESSES: Home—5 rue Felix Faure, 92500 Rueil Malmaison, France.

CAREER: Teacher in Paris, France, 1969-72; writer. Organizer of reading and writing animations for children in art centers and schools.

AWARDS, HONORS: Sydney Taylor Book Award and Das Rote Tuch Award, 1996, both for *Star of Fear, Star of Hope.*

WRITINGS:

Le petit Pousse, Ecole des Loisirs, 1980.
Le Moulin a paroles: Abecedaire (title means "The Word Mill: An ABC"), illustrated by Frederic Stehr, Ecole des Loisirs, 1980.
La rentree de mamans, Bayard Presse, 1990, translation published as *Back to School with Mom: A Story,* illustrated by Claude and Denise Millet, Child's World (Mankato, MN), 1992.
La grande peur sous les etoiles, Syros, translation by Mark Polizzotti published as *Star of Fear, Star of Hope,* illustrated by Johanna Kang, Walker (New York), 1995.

Les passants de Noel, Syros, 1996.
Les amoureue de Leonie, Casterman, 1996.

Other books in French include *Emile bille de clown,* published by Bayard Presse, and *Peurs,* published by Syros.

WORK IN PROGRESS: Six books, including a book of poems for children and an Easter book.

SIDELIGHTS: While the works of children's author Jo Hoestlandt are primarily in French, a few of them have been translated into English. One such work, described by Maria W. Posner in *School Library Journal* as an "extraordinarily moving picture book . . . [with] spare prose and appropriately stark illustrations," is *Star of Fear, Star of Hope.*

The story begins with the narrator, an aging woman named Helen, taking the reader back to Nazi-occupied France in 1942 on the eve of her ninth birthday. Her best friend Lydia, who is Jewish, spends the night at Helen's apartment. During the night, however, Lydia wants to go home after being frightened by strangers outside Helen's home. As Lydia leaves, Helen tells her that she is no longer her friend. Helen soon realizes her mistake and she tries to find Lydia the next day. But she is too late—Lydia and her family have disappeared. By telling her story to the world, Helen hopes that she and Lydia will meet again one day. "Fluidly written and centered in events a child can comprehend, the book is an ideal starting point for serious discussions about the Holocaust," noted a reviewer in *Publishers Weekly.* Similarly, *Horn Book* commentator Mary M. Burns appreciated how "the book translates history into a form accessible to young audiences."

Hoestlandt commented: "I think words hide secrets, and stories tell secrets more or less hidden by the words.

"The most important book of my career is *Star of Fear, Star of Hope.* None of my family who lived during World War II suffered deportation, though my grandfather was a political prisoner. When I was very young, however, I understood that many children died just because they were Jewish, and I felt concerned just because I was alive.

"When I was a child, I decided I was a dancer-writer, because I liked to dance and to write. Later, I understood I have found exactly the same thing in writing and in dancing. I stood on tiptoe, or I was poised at the end of the pen, just as on a leg, light and grave, high and low together, touching earth and sky at the same moment.

"I always try to write unaffectedly, sincerely, with words so simple that they can touch hearts and minds just like sunlight or darkness or dancing snow. People say that all of my books tell love or friend stories. Maybe all that we need to learn during life is actually included in our love and friend stories."

BIOGRAPHICAL/CRITICAL SOURCES:

PERIODICALS

Booklist, February 15, 1985, p. 850; May 1, 1995, p. 1573; March 15, 1996, p. 1289.
Bulletin of the Center for Children's Books, June, 1995, p. 347.
Horn Book, September-October, 1995, pp. 588-89.
Kirkus Reviews, May 15, 1995, p. 711.
Publishers Weekly, June 5, 1995, pp. 63-64.
School Library Journal, August, 1995, p. 124.
Tribune Books, September 10, 1995, p. 396.

*   *   *

HOLLY, Ellen (Virginia)   1931-

PERSONAL: Born January 16, 1931, in New York, NY; daughter of William (a chemical engineer) and Grayce (a librarian; maiden name, Arnold) Holly. *Ethnicity:* "African American." *Education:* Hunter College (now Hunter College of the City University of New York), B.A., 1952; studied acting at Perry-Mansfield School of the Theater, and with Barney Brown, Uta Hagen, Charlotte Perry, Eli Rill, and Mira Rostova. *Avocational interests:* Writing.

ADDRESSES: Agent—Starkman Agency, 1501 Broadway, Suite 301A, New York, NY 10036.

CAREER: Actor and writer. Actor in theatrical productions, including "The Anniversary" and "A Switch in Time," *Two for Fun* (double-bill), Greenwich Mews Theatre, New York City, 1955; *A Florentine Tragedy* and *Salome,* Davenport Theatre, New York City, 1955; *Too Late the Phalarope* (Broadway debut), Belasco Theatre, New York City, 1956; *Tevya and His Daughters,* Carnegie Hall Playhouse, New York City, 1957; *Othello,* Belvedere

Lake Theatre, 1958; *Face of a Hero,* Eugene O'Neill Theatre, New York City, 1960; *Moon on a Rainbow Shawl,* East Eleventh Street Theatre, New York City, 1962; *Tiger, Tiger, Burning Bright,* Booth Theatre, New York City, 1962; *Antony and Cleopatra,* New York Shakespeare Festival, Delacorte Theatre, New York City, 1963; *Funny House of a Negro,* East End Theatre, New York City, 1964; *A Midsummer Night's Dream,* New York Shakespeare Festival, Delacorte Mobile Theatre, 1964; *King Henry V* and *The Taming of the Shrew,* New York Shakespeare Festival, Delacorte Mobile Theatre, 1965; *The Owl Answers,* White Barn Theatre, Westport, CT, then Theatre de Lys, New York City, 1965.

Also *An Evening of Negro Poetry and Folk Music,* Delacorte Theatre, 1966, produced as *A Hand Is on the Gate,* Longacre Theatre, New York City, 1966; *Macbeth,* New York Shakespeare Festival, Delacorte Mobile Theatre, 1966; *The Comedy of Errors,* National Repertory Theatre, U.S. cities, 1967; *Camino Real,* Playhouse in the Park, Cincinnati, OH, 1968; *The Comedy of Errors,* Ford's Theatre, Washington, DC, 1968; *Crime on Goat Island,* Playhouse in the Park, Cincinnati, OH, 1968; *The Cherry Orchard,* New York Shakespeare Festival, Public/Anspacher Theatre, New York City, 1973; *King Lear,* New York Shakespeare Festival, Delacorte Theatre, 1973; *'Tis Pity She's a Whore,* U.S. cities, 1974-75. Also appeared in stage productions of *Orchids in the Moonlight,* American Repertory Theatre, Cambridge, MA, and in *John Brown's Body.* Member of Playhouse in the Park, Cincinnati, OH, 1968.

Actor in films, including *Take a Giant Step,* United Artists, 1959; *Cops and Robbers,* United Artists, 1973; *School Daze,* Columbia, 1988. Actor in television series, including *One Life to Live,* ABC, 1968-81 and 1983-85; *Guiding Light* (also known as *The Guiding Light*), CBS, 1989—; and *Love of Life,* CBS. Actor in television episodes, including *Odyssey,* CBS, 1957; "King Lear," *Great Performances* (also known as *Theatre in America*), PBS, 1974; "High School Narc," *ABC Afterschool Special,* ABC, 1985; *The Big Story,* NBC; *Confidential File,* syndicated; *The Defenders,* CBS; *Dr. Kildare,* NBC; *Look Up and Live,* CBS; *The Nurses,* CBS; *Sam Benedict,* ABC. Actor in television movies, including *Sergeant Matlovich vs. the U.S. Air Force,* NBC, 1978.

MEMBER: Actors Equity Association, Screen Actors Guild, American Federation of Television and Radio Artists, Delta Sigma Theta.

WRITINGS:

One Life: The Autobiography of an African American Actress, Kodansha (New York City), 1996.

SIDELIGHTS: Ellen Holly turned to writing relatively late in life, after working over forty years as an actress. *One Life: The Autobiography of an African American Actress* depicts her struggles to succeed as an African American woman in the entertainment industry. Throughout much of Ellen Holly's career there were few acting jobs for women of color, and Holly did not win many of them because she was considered too fair-skinned for African American roles. Hence, the acclaim she received for her acting abilities, both on stage and film, never materialized into concrete opportunities to perform.

Holly made her acting debut on a New York Stage in 1955, but she did not climb into the national spotlight until 1968. That year she won the part of Carla Benari on the daytime television drama *One Life to Live.* This character would be a fixture on the show for the next seventeen seasons, until a dispute with the soap's director pushed her to move to a competitor's drama. Noting the many facets of Ellen Holly's career, a reviewer for *Publishers Weekly* noted how Holly "depicts the mercurial world of show biz" and "displays a vivid sense of justice in this outspoken memoir." Writing in *Booklist,* Ilene Cooper shared similar opinions, remarking on the "raw emotion behind Holly's often quite elegant prose."

BIOGRAPHICAL/CRITICAL SOURCES:

BOOKS

Contemporary Theatre, Film, and Television, Volume 10, Gale (Detroit, MI), 1993.

PERIODICALS

Booklist, November 15, 1996, p. 563.
Publishers Weekly, October 28, 1996, p. 69.*

* * *

HORNBOSTEL, Lloyd 1934-

PERSONAL: Born May 27, 1934, in Beloit, WI; son of Lloyd, Sr., and Dorothy Hornbostel; married Julia

Conkling, September 10, 1960; children: John, Julia Hornbostel Batholomew. *Ethnicity:* "White." *Education:* University of Wisconsin—Madison, B.S.; Oak Ridge Associated Universities, Nuclear Materials License. *Politics:* Independent. *Religion:* Anglican. *Avocational interests:* Archaeology, horological restoration.

ADDRESSES: Home—7062 Kinnikimmick Dr., Roscoe, IL 61073.

CAREER: Business Technology Services, partner. Worked in manufacturing operations and research and in corporate executive positions; holder of more than twenty U.S. patents. *Military service:* U.S. Army, 1954-56.

WRITINGS:

An Act of God (science fiction), Galde Press (Lakeville, MN), 1996.
War Kids, 1941-1945 (historical fiction), Galde Press, 1996.

WORK IN PROGRESS: Research on pre-Columbian cultures and trades.

SIDELIGHTS: Lloyd Hornbostel told *CA:* "*An Act of God* is science fiction written in the classic style. The book details an adventure resulting from global cooling and the interaction of government and special interests to deal with and profit from the situation. It is not a 'special effects' novel, but one which questions extra-terrestrial life and its possible effect on the United States.

"*War Kids, 1941-1945* is stories about children, written for children to create interest in the war years. Characters are fictitious, but incidents are drawn from real events. I felt that there was a real need to document the home-front war effort as it was seen by children. The length and style of the book are designed for young adult readers."

*   *   *

HOROWITZ, Renee B(arbara)   1932-

PERSONAL: Born March 4, 1932, in NY; daughter of Hyman (a pharmacist) and Anne (a homemaker) Braunstein; married Arthur Horowitz (a pharmacist), August 26, 1951; children: David Robert, Steven Jay. *Education:* Brooklyn College (now of the City University of New York), B.A., 1955; University of Colorado, M.A., 1971, Ph.D., 1974. *Religion:* Jewish.

ADDRESSES: Home—6257 East Calle Camelia, Scottsdale, AZ 85251. *Office*—Department of Information and Management Technology, College of Technology and Applied Sciences, Arizona State University, Tempe, AZ 85281. *E-mail*—rbhorow @asu.edu. *Agent*—Teresa Chris, Teresa Chris Literary Agency, 43 Musard Rd., London W6 8NR, England.

CAREER: U.S. Department of Commerce, Institute for Telecommunication Sciences, writer and editor, 1974-80; Sperry Flight Systems, editor in publications engineering, 1980-81; AlliedSignal Companies, Documentation and Data Management Group, senior documentation engineer, 1981-86; Arizona State University, Tempe, associate professor, 1986-91, professor of information and management technology, 1991—, course coordinator, 1989—. University of Colorado, Boulder, visiting lecturer and instructor, 1974-80; Metropolitan State College, Denver, CO, instructor, 1977-79. Volunteer computer Braille transcriber and teacher for Foundation for Blind Children, Desert Volunteer Braille Guild, and Library of Congress; public speaker.

MEMBER: Society for Technical Communication (senior member), Association of Teachers of Technical Writing, National Association for Industrial Technology (regional director, 1991-93), Council for Programs in Technical and Scientific Communication, Institute of Electrical and Electronics Engineers, IEEE Professional Communication Society, Delta Kappa Gamma.

AWARDS, HONORS: National Association of Industrial Technology, outstanding professor award, 1990, leadership award, 1992-93.

WRITINGS:

(Contributor) *Publications Management: Essays for Professional Communicators,* Baywood Press, 1994.
Rx for Murder (mystery novel), Avon (New York City), 1997.
Deadly Rx (mystery novel), Avon, 1997.

Contributor to professional journals, including *Issues in Writing, Technical Writing Teacher, IEEE Trans-*

actions on *Professional Communication,* and *Industrial Management.* Editor of *Frontiers: A Journal of Women's Studies,* 1974-80.

WORK IN PROGRESS: Two mysteries, *Rx Alibi* and *Killer's Rx.*

SIDELIGHTS: Renee B. Horowitz told *CA:* "I believe you're never too old to make your dreams come true. I realized my own long-time dream with the publication of my first two mystery novels. In them, readers get a behind-the-scenes look at pharmacy, as amateur detective Ruthie Kantor Morris, pharmacy manager in an Arizona supermarket, uses her pharmaceutical knowledge to solve murders. In *Deadly Rx,* Ruthie is accused of making a fatal prescription error, and she must find the real culprit to clear herself.

"Reviewers have found my work authentic. It should be. My husband Arthur is the pharmacy manager for an Arizona supermarket chain. It is just a coincidence, of course!

"I am a professor of technology at Arizona State University. For many years now, I've had to concentrate on scholarly writing to feed the publish-or-perish syndrome, but fiction is my first love. I decided to break into the highly competitive mystery field because I love reading mysteries. I enjoy the cozies or mysteries of manners, so that's the kind of novel I write—no gore or graphic violence."

*   *   *

HORWITT, Sanford D. 1943-

PERSONAL: Born September 19, 1943, in Milwaukee, WI; son of Morton and Mary (Strawitz) Horwitt; married Joan Engel (a food writer), December 26, 1970; children: Matthew, Jeffrey. *Citizenship:* United States. *Education:* Northwestern University, B.S., 1965, Ph.D., 1970.

ADDRESSES: Home—5935 North Fifth Rd., Arlington, VA 22203. *E-mail*—shorwitt@aol.com.

CAREER: University of Illinois, Chicago, assistant professor of communications studies, 1970-74; The Office of United States Representative Abner Mikva (D-Ill.), Washington, DC, senior legislative aide, 1974-79; writer and policy advisor for public interest organization, Washington, DC, 1980—.

WRITINGS:

Let Them Call Me Rebel: Saul Alinsky: His Life and Legacy, Knopf (New York City), 1989.

Contributor to *New York Times Book Review, San Francisco Chronicle Book Review* and *Washington Post Book World.*

SIDELIGHTS: Sanford D. Horwitt's biography of Saul Alinsky shed new insight into the decades-long work of one of Chicago's most radical personalities. Horwitt, himself familiar with Chicago politics and history from his student days at Northwestern University, a teaching stint at the University of Illinois's Chicago campus, and later as an aide to a Chicago congressman, retraces the path of Alinsky's career as a community organizer in the 1989 book *Let Them Call Me Rebel: Saul Alinsky: His Life and Legacy.*

Alinsky died in 1972, just two years after Horwitt earned his Ph.D. from Northwestern. By then, the activist had been somewhat forgotten by history, though certain radical groups had eagerly espoused his no-nonsense ideas to empower the poor. Alinsky, as *Let Them Call Me Rebel* details, was himself a product of the Chicago streets with origins in the city's lively immigrant Jewish quarter. He attended the University of Chicago, where he thrived in the intellectually challenging and liberal sociology department. There, as Horwitt explains, his professors encouraged a spirited, involved approach to tackling the problems of the growing class of urban poor. For his graduate work, he planned to write his dissertation on the underworld organization of Al Capone.

Alinsky later abandoned these studies, however, and took a job in the Joliet penitentiary; by the late 1930s he had affiliated himself with the Congress of Industrial Organizations (CIO), a powerful labor union during the era. The tactics used by the CIO Alinsky carried over into his work with the Chicago Area Project, an ambitious anti-delinquency program. As Horwitt demonstrates, Alinsky had a thorough disdain for the traditional urban "do-gooder" channels, which were primarily run by Protestant organizations, or were at least Protestant in flavor, and staffed by women.

Alinsky's next ambitious project was a community organizing plan for the Back of the Yards, the foul-smelling, crime-ridden neighborhoods just downwind of Chicago's meat-packing plants. As *Let Them Call Me Rebel* explains, Alinsky had a genius for shoring up allies from the most unlikely corners: the Catholic archdiocese, for instance, provided support as well as financial help for the Back of the Yards Neighborhood Council (BYNC), recognizing the practicality of Alinsky's message: that empowering the poor, proving to them that they could effect change on their own, was a surefire path to community stability and prosperity—and thus the viability of their churches. From this grew Alinsky's Industrial Arts Foundation, which survives in twenty-three American cities as a grass-roots, urban aid foundation run by the very people it was designed to assist.

Horwitt writes about Alinsky and his ideals, and the way in which they subtly lost support among certain liberal elements over the course of time. But later, radical tacticians fully espoused Alinsky and his community-organizing methods. Both the Student Nonviolent Coordinating Committee, a civil-rights group of 1960s, and the Black Panthers learned much through Alinsky's work.

Ed Marciniak, reviewing *Let Them Call Me Rebel* for *Tribune Books,* found Horwitt's "behind the scenes" tour of leftist politicking noteworthy. In the *New York Times Book Review,* Nelson Lichtenstein termed it "a highly readable, exhaustively researched biography that is full of both playful anecdote and thoughtful political analysis." Lichtenstein especially praised Horwitt's ability to navigate through the complex territory of social-work movements and ideological nuances. *New Republic* writer Sean Wilentz also praised the way in which the biographer "mastered the historical elements that swirled around his subject," and though Wilentz faulted Horwitt for including too many superfluous tidbits, he found *Let Them Call Me Rebel* "one of the most thorough and sensitive of all the modern biographies of American radicals. . . . It ought to be mandatory reading for anyone concerned with the enduring issues of American poverty."

BIOGRAPHICAL/CRITICAL SOURCES:

PERIODICALS

Los Angeles Times Book Review, December 3, 1989, p. 3.
New Republic, December 25, 1989, p. 30-38.
New York Times Book Review, November 12, 1989, p. 23.
Tribune Books (Chicago), October 8, 1989, p. 1.
Washington Post Book World, November 19, 1989, pp. 1-2.

HULL, H. Braxton
See JACOBS, Helen Hull

*   *   *

INGERSOLL, Earl G(eorge)   1938-

PERSONAL: Born May 6, 1938, in Spencerport, NY; son of Earl D. (a carpenter) and Rose (a homemaker; maiden name, Neth) Ingersoll; married Mary Cosgrove (a teacher), June 17, 1960; children: Jeffrey, Timothy. *Education:* University of Rochester, B.A., 1960; Syracuse University, M.A., 1963; University of Wisconsin—Madison, Ph.D., 1971. *Avocational interests:* Gardening.

ADDRESSES: Home—173 Dewey St., Churchville, NY 14428. *Office*—State University of New York College at Brockport, Brockport, NY 14420; fax 716-395-2391. *E-mail*—eingerso@po.brockport.edu.

CAREER: State University of New York College at Brockport, instructor, 1964-71, assistant professor, 1971-87, associate professor, 1987-91, professor, 1991-96, distinguished teaching professor of English, 1996—.

MEMBER: International Association for the Fantastic in the Arts, D. H. Lawrence Society of North America (member of executive council, 1994-96; president-elect, 1996), Modern Language Association of America, College English Association, Doris Lessing Society, Margaret Atwood Society, Lawrence Durrell Society, Canadian Association of Irish Studies, New York College English Association (president, 1994-96), Irish-American Cultural Institute.

WRITINGS:

(Editor with Judith Kitchen and Stan Sanvel Rubin) *The Post-Confessionals: Conversations with American Poets of the Eighties,* Fairleigh Dickinson University Press (Madison, NJ), 1989.
Margaret Atwood: Conversations, Ontario Review Press (Princeton, NJ), 1990, revised edition, Virago Press (London, England), 1992.
Conversations with May Sarton, University Press of Mississippi (Jackson, MS), 1991.
Representations of Science and Technology in British Literature since 1880, Peter Lang Publishing (New York City), 1992.
Doris Lessing: Conversations, Ontario Review Press,

1994 (published in England as *Putting the Question Differently,* HarperCollins, 1996).

Engendered Trope in Joyce's "Dubliners," Southern Illinois University Press (Carbondale, IL), 1996.

Lawrence Durrell: Conversations, Associated University Presses (Madison, NJ), 1998.

Contributor of articles to language and literature journals, including *Conradiana, College Language Association Journal, Journal of Men's Studies, Midwest Quarterly, Studies in the Novel, Journal of the Fantastic in the Arts,* and *Doris Lessing Newsletter.*

WORK IN PROGRESS: D. H. Lawrence and a New Psychoanalytic Criticism, an investigation of Lawrence's novels, using contemporary, rather than traditional, psychoanalytic approaches to literary texts.

SIDELIGHTS: Earl G. Ingersoll told *CA:* "As a reader of literary criticism, I have often been attracted to the connections writers make between contemporary theory and literary works that I may have read many times in preparation for the classroom. Often, if the theorizing is especially provocative, it stimulates me to see ways in which theory can open other texts. When I write, I would like to create a little of that excitement as I work at opening a text, so that readers can participate in the process and go on to do their own. What I write is an effort toward repaying the debt I owe to the dozens of critics and theorists who have opened familiar texts for me.

"I like to think that my book *Engendered Trope in Joyce's 'Dubliners'* is a case in point. I first read Joyce as a college student some forty years ago, and I have discussed at least some of these stories with students almost every year since. The *Dubliners* study grew out of a half-dozen essays that I wrote on individual stories after reading material by several readers of Jacques Lacan. Of these, Barbara Johnson, Jane Gallop, and Jerry Aline Flieger helped me to read Joyce's stories in the context of the gender associations implicit in Lacan's two key tropes of metonymy and metaphor. I hope to be carrying forward what I have called a New Psychoanalytic Criticism. Following in the footsteps of Peter Brooks, I want to redirect attention away from psychoanalyzing authors or fictional characters toward looking at the text as a structure of conflicting desires.

"I would like also to put in a word for the impact of technology. Virtually all of my professional writing and editing dates from my discovery of word processing. There is just no way to exaggerate how much I have benefited from being freed of the drudgery involved in transforming handwritten manuscripts into work that can be sent out for evaluation. Also, I was never one of those who could compose at a typewriter because I was inhibited by the continual appearance of typographical errors. Now I find myself writing very little by hand. I have been fascinated by this 'interface' with the computer monitor with its pulsating prompt signal, encouraging me to make words appear. I am struck by the tropes we use in word processing, such as 'memory.' In my less rational moments I can almost convince myself that, if the machine has memory, perhaps it has stored away somewhere all the brilliant and eloquent writing I *think* I have done—that is, until I go back later to revise it and discover it has vanished."

*   *   *

INGRAMS, Doreen   1906-1997

OBITUARY NOTICE—See index for *CA* sketch: Born January 24, 1906, in London, England; died July 25, 1997. Author. Ingrams was an authority on the Arab world. She began her studies of socio-economic conditions in Arabia in 1934 when her husband, Harold, was stationed in Aden. She spent a great deal of time researching the lives of Arab women and was responsible for founding a Bedouin Girls' School, the first of its kind. Her first book, *Survey of Social and Economic Conditions in the Aden Protectorate,* was published in 1949 after her return to England. She joined the staff of the British Broadcasting Corp. (BBC) in 1956 as a senior assistant in Arabic Service, a position she held until 1968. Ingrams also lectured extensively and served on the Council for the Advancement of Arab-British Understanding. Her other works include *Palestine Papers, 1917-1922: Seeds of Conflict, Mosques and Minarets, Tents to City Sidewalks,* and *The Awakened: Women of Iraq.* She also served as co-editor of a sixteen-volume work entitled *Records of Yemen 1798-1960.*

OBITUARIES AND OTHER SOURCES:

BOOKS

Writers Directory, St. James Press, 1996.

PERIODICALS

Times (London; electronic), August 11, 1997.

J

JACOBS, Helen Hull 1908-1997
(H. Braxton Hull)

OBITUARY NOTICE—See index for *CA* sketch: Born August 6, 1908, in Globe, AZ; died of heart failure, June 2, 1997, in Easthampton, NY. Athlete, farmer, designer, and author. Jacobs is best remembered for her early career as a tennis star and for the numerous instructional books she wrote about the sport. In the 1920s and 1930s she was a competitor for many women's tennis titles, earning nine major championship awards. Among these awards are the United States national title in 1932, 1933, 1934, and 1935. She was ranked in the top ten in women's tennis between 1928 and 1939, and she won the singles at Wimbledon in 1936. Jacobs retired from the sport in 1947.

During World War II Jones joined the U.S. Naval reserve on active duty at the WAVES Training School. Jacobs also worked as a public information officer at the Naval Gun Factory and served at the Naval Proving Ground. She retired in the rank of commander in 1968. During her career, she also worked as a senior editor with Grolier Council for Education Research in New York City. Her first book, *Modern Tennis,* was published in 1933. She wrote many other books based on the sport as well as on her experiences in the Navy. These works include *Beyond the Game: An Autobiography, "By Your Leave, Sir": The Story of a WAVE, Gallery of Champions, Proudly She Serves: The Realistic Story of a Tennis Champion Who Becomes a WAVE, Famous American Women Athletes, Beginner's Guide to Winning Tennis, The Savage Ally,* and *Courage to Conquer.* In 1962 she was admitted to the international Tennis Hall of Fame.

OBITUARIES AND OTHER SOURCES:

BOOKS

Who's Who in America, Marquis, 1997.

PERIODICALS

New York Times, June 4, 1997, p. D24.

* * *

JACOBS, Jonnie

PERSONAL: Born in northern CA. *Education:* University of California, Berkeley, B.A., Boalt Hall School of Law, law degree; California State University, M.A. (counseling); University of Michigan, M.A.

ADDRESSES: Home—Northern CA. *E-mail*—Jonnie @netcom.com. *Agent*—Deborah Schneider, Gelfman Schneider Literary Agency, 250 West 57th St., New York, NY 10017.

CAREER: Mystery writer. Has worked as a high school English teacher, a high school counselor, and an attorney for a San Francisco, CA, law firm.

WRITINGS:

MYSTERY NOVELS

Murder among Neighbors, Kensington (New York), 1994.
Murder among Friends, Kensington, 1995.

Shadow of Doubt, Kensington, 1996.
Evidence of Guilt, Kensington, 1997.
Murder among Us, Kensington, 1998.

WORK IN PROGRESS: A third "Kali O'Brien" novel.

SIDELIGHTS: Jonnie Jacobs has written several mystery novels featuring female sleuths. In the "Kate Austen" series of novels, the protagonist's domestic duties and family relationships often compete with the pursuit of clues, while in the "Kali O'Brien" series the lead character is an unmarried female attorney. Though some critics find these works unambitious and tame, others are quick to note Jacobs's apt social commentary aimed at the suburban lives of her Northern California protagonists and their friends.

In Jacobs's first novel, *Murder among Neighbors,* published in 1994, the author introduces Kate Austen, an unemployed suburban mother whose next-door neighbor is found dead under suspicious circumstances. While Kate's husband takes off for Europe to find himself, Kate and her best friend begin to gather clues about the suspected murder that call into question the police's theory. In the process, Kate begins to fall for Michael Stone, the officer in charge of the case. A *Kirkus Reviews* critic found the heroine's unflappably domestic nature to be a bit overdone, noting that despite her adventures, "Kate still chooses dresses and makeup as carefully as ever, and she manages to spot the murderer without seriously disrupting her day care arrangements." A reviewer for *Publishers Weekly,* however, dubbed *Murder among Neighbors* an "entertaining debut," concluding that "Jacobs tops off this slice of suburban life with a dollop of romance and a twist of suspense."

Murder among Friends, Jacobs's second book to feature Kate Austen, finds the protagonist again disputing her lover Stone's theory about the death of one of her friends. When Kate finds client Mona Sterling—for whom she works as an art consultant—dead from an apparent suicide, she immediately begins casting about for potential murder suspects. "Kate's always phoning people to ask if they might be the killer," a *Kirkus Reviews* contributor noted. Jacobs's heroine finds plenty of suspects, however, from Sterling's ex-husband to her most recent lover and the husband of one of her students. "Jacobs's domestic tale takes a few well-aimed jabs at suburban life," noted a *Publishers Weekly* critic. A contributor to *Library Journal* stated that *Murder among Friends* has qualities that make it "an appealing choice for many readers," singling out the book's "minimal violence" as one such trait.

With 1996's *Shadow of Doubt,* which reached the bestseller list of the *San Francisco Chronicle,* Jacobs introduces a new protagonist in the person of San Francisco lawyer Kali O'Brien. When Kali returns to her hometown for the funeral of her father, she finds her former best friend accused of murdering her husband. The attorney decides to stay on to help. Kali's inner turmoil, as her assumptions about herself and her life in San Francisco are thrown into doubt in the context of her hometown, provides a strong subplot to an otherwise light mystery, some critics noted. "Jacobs spins a merely adequate mystery plot here," observed a reviewer for *Publishers Weekly,* "but she portrays Kali's return to her home—and the self-revelations the trip engenders—with a sure sense of character."

Kali returns in *Evidence of Guilt,* a 1997 novel in which she has opened a solo law practice in her hometown. She finds herself reluctantly agreeing to defend a local man whom everyone believes guilty of murdering a waitress and her daughter. Again, the reviewer for *Publishers Weekly* found Jacobs's plot to be one of the weaker aspects of this mystery, though her protagonist "is likable enough."

Jacobs told *CA:* "As wonderful as it is to lose yourself in reading a good book, it's even better (when things are going well) to find yourself immersed in a fictional world of your own creation. I love having the opportunity to be so many different people and to have so many different experiences.

"I see all fiction, including mystery fiction, as a framework on which to hang human drama. It's the personal side of things—relationships, secrets, underlying tensions—that interest me most, and mysteries offer a wonderful opportunity to explore these. That's what crime is about—relationships that have broken down, human nature pushed to the limits. In writing mysteries, my focus is less on the violence of the crime itself, than the passions that led up to it."

BIOGRAPHICAL/CRITICAL SOURCES:

PERIODICALS

Kirkus Reviews, August 1, 1994, p. 1027; July 1, 1995, p. 903; January 15, 1996, p. 102.
Library Journal, June 1, 1995, p. 168; February 1, 1996, p. 103.
Publishers Weekly, August 29, 1994, p. 64; July 24, 1995, pp. 50-51; January 29, 1996, p. 87; December 30, 1996, p. 57.

JAFFE, (Andrew) Michael 1923-1997

OBITUARY NOTICE—See index for *CA* sketch: Born June 3, 1923, in London, England; died July 13, 1997. Educator, museum director, and author. Jaffe is remembered for his contributions to the field of art. After serving in the Royal Naval Volunteer Reserve during World War II as a lieutenant commander, he received his M.A. from King's College in 1949. He began a fellowship at King's College in 1952, then worked as a professor of Renaissance art at Washington University in St. Louis in 1960. In 1961 he returned to England's Cambridge University, first as a lecturer until 1968, then as a reader, followed by stints as professor in the history of Western art and head of the department. In 1973 he was named director of Fitzwilliam Museum, where he worked until his retirement in 1990. During his career, Jaffe was famous for acquiring precious works of art for various museums. Among his acquisitions were Van Dyck's "Madonna and Child" and Renoir's "Place Clichy." He also published *Van Dyck's Antwerp Sketchbook* in 1966. Among his other books are *Rubens and Italy* and *Jordaens.* Jaffe also edited *The Devonshire Collection of Italian Drawings.* He was named CBE in 1989.

OBITUARIES AND OTHER SOURCES:

BOOKS

Who's Who, St. Martin's, 1996.

PERIODICALS

Times (London; electronic), July 17, 1997.

* * *

JAFFREY, Zia

PERSONAL: Daughter of Madhur Jaffrey (a culinary writer).

ADDRESSES: Agent—c/o Pantheon Books, 201 East 50th St., New York, NY 10022.

CAREER: Writer.

WRITINGS:

The Invisibles: A Tale of the Eunuchs of India, Pantheon Books (New York City), 1996.

Contributor to periodicals, including *New York Times, Nation, Village Voice, Progressive, Elle,* and *Harper's Bazaar.*

SIDELIGHTS: While visiting India for a family wedding, Zia Jaffrey became aware of the presence of eunuchs in Indian society, a nearly invisible vestigial caste left over from a bygone era. "They still constitute a shadowy subculture," noted Richard Bernstein in the *New York Times,* who added that Jaffrey "does a fine job of exploring" the eunuchs' lives in her first book, *The Invisibles: A Tale of the Eunuchs of India.* Jaffrey, who spent part of her childhood in India, takes on this task as a way of exploring her own ambiguous identity as Indian by ethnicity yet American by upbringing.

Rather than report her findings in a systematic way, the author "takes us along on her journey of discovery, disclosing the confusingly contradictory pieces of information she receives, the obstacles she encounters, the questions that are raised and that remain unanswered," Bernstein remarked. The result of the book's subjectivity is, according to several critics, an element that adds to the mysteriousness of the subject and highlights Jaffrey's lyrically written, beautiful prose that a conclusive report could never yield.

The eunuchs are called "hijras" in India, where they are a perennial sight at wedding ceremonies and birth celebrations. They are considered both holy and disgusting, and thus are paid both for their presence at these gatherings and for leaving them. Neither men nor women in appearance, but a curious hybrid of both, they bless the ceremonies in vulgar language, singing and dancing without any pretence of musicality, presenting themselves as completely equivocal beings. "Yet they emerge . . . with a touching concreteness and dignity as they struggle against misfortune and intolerance," Bernstein contended in his review of *The Invisibles.* Extremely secretive about their ways, the hijras themselves were not the only source of information on the eunuch societies Jaffrey sought. Indeed, according to Lee Siegel in the *New York Times Book Review,* Jaffrey's book "is an eloquent compilation of, and compassionate contemplation on, historical and contemporary accounts of hijras by travelers of old, scholars, journalists, policemen, housewives, an auto mechanic, a chauffeur and—but not most reliably—the hijras themselves."

Jaffrey's book, *The Invisibles: A Tale of the Eunuchs of India,* introduces readers to a facet of Indian life Westerners may find anachronistic. Feared and despised for their reputed role in kidnapping and castrating young boys to incorporate into their caste, India's hijras are also considered holy men whose mutilation allows them to dedicate their lives to God. As both clowns and fakirs, the hijras occupy an ambivalent place in modern-day Indian society, a stance the author—of mixed heritage—could understand. Critics praised Jaffrey's compassionate and lyrical account of her quest to uncover the secrets of this mysterious sect. "Ms. Jaffrey is a sympathetic but hardheaded observer, not just of her subject but, sometimes more interestingly, of herself as well," wrote Bernstein in his laudatory review.

BIOGRAPHICAL/CRITICAL SOURCES:

PERIODICALS

New York Times, November 20, 1996, p. C22.
New York Times Book Review, November 24, 1996, p. 24.
Publishers Weekly, September 23, 1996, p. 65.

*   *   *

JANSSEN, Marian (L. M.) 1953-

PERSONAL: Born October 23, 1953, in Deventer, the Netherlands; daughter of Guillaume (a factory manager) and Margaretha (a homemaker; maiden name, Graefenhain) Janssen; *Education:* University of Nijmegen, M.A. (cum laude), 1980, Ph.D. (cum laude), 1987.

ADDRESSES: Home—Nonnenstraat 24, 6511 VN Nijmegen, Netherlands. *Office*—English department, University of Nijmegen, Erasmusplein 1, 6525 HT Nijmegen, Netherlands.

CAREER: University of Nijmegen, Nijmegen, Netherlands, research assistant, 1977-80, research fellow, 1980-84, instructor in American literature, 1985-86, coordinator of American studies program, 1986—, post-doctoral research fellow, 1988-92. International Student Exchange Program, consultant; also affiliated with the Catholic University of Nijmegen.

MEMBER: International Society for Contemporary Literature and Theatre, Society for the Study of Southern Literature.

AWARDS, HONORS: "Voluntary Visitor," United States Information Agency, 1987; research grant, Nether

lands Organization for Scientific Research, 1988; fellowship, American Council of Learned Societies, 1989-90.

WRITINGS:

The Kenyon Review: 1939-1970: A Critical History, Louisiana State University Press (Baton Rouge), 1990.

WORK IN PROGRESS: A biography of the poet Isabella Gardner.

SIDELIGHTS: Marian Janssen's love of the English language compelled her to make it her field of academic study as well as her career. Dutch by birth and a professor of American studies at the University of Nijmegen in the Netherlands, Janssen expanded her doctoral dissertation on a small but influential literary quarterly of the mid-twentieth century into her 1990 book *The Kenyon Review: 1939-1970: A Critical History.* In it, Janssen traces the founding of this journal of poetry, fiction, and literary criticism within the English department of a small, rather obscure Ohio college of the same name. Its guiding light, John Crowe Ransom, was an up-and-coming young scholar of his day; he founded the *Review* with the blessing of the Kenyon College president in 1939 partly to propagate what came to be known as the New Criticism, a fresh movement in literary examination that stressed the text of the work, rather than the life and personality of its writer or the time in which he or she wrote.

In her book, Janssen demonstrates the wide-ranging influence the *Kenyon Review* had upon American academia during its heyday. Along with Arthur Mizener and a host of other editors and advisors throughout the years, the journal published articles on Robert Lowell (a protege of Ransom's) and Wallace Stevens, and the criticism of Lionel Trilling and Richard Ellmann. Later, it offered its small group of devoted readers the work of Flannery O'Connor and Joyce Carol Oates. Within a decade or so after its founding, New Criticism was an integral part of collegiate English studies, the standard way of dissecting a work of literature. Janssen cites numerous details from the *Kenyon Review*'s archives in showing its stellar history and the way in which its philosophies secured a place in academia.

The *Review,* many have determined, was a victim of its own success—its ideas no longer fresh and iconoclastic once they became the norm, and a continual target of hostility from Kenyon college faculty and administration. It folded in 1970, though it was later revived. "Janssen's history is a model of thorough, thoughtful research," wrote Sam Pickering in the *Sewanee Review,* while *Washington Post Book World* critic Michael Dirda also lauded her "conscientious, accountant-like survey of the magazine's history." A *Times Literary Supplement* critique echoed that sentiment, with Philip Hobsbaum's remark that "Janssen has told the story conscientiously, though not captivatingly." William E. Cain termed it in *American Literature* as "rather thin in critical insights and ideas . . . yet comprehensive and enlightening in its details."

Janssen told *CA:* "As an *au pair* in the Seventies in Great Britain, I became interested in British literature, and decided to major in English after my return to the Netherlands. I received my B.A. in English, but then my youngest brother, a student of mathematics, taunted me with his knowledge of American literature. As I regarded any literature in English *my* field, I started reading American authors and was immediately hooked. Consequently, in my M.A. studies I specialized in American, rather than British literature. Through my doctoral research on the *Kenyon Review,* I came to know a number of wonderful, but now almost forgotten contributors to its pages: one of them was the poet Isabella Gardner, whose biography I am now writing. I do not know yet where she will lead me, but I look forward to continuing to write about the American literary landscape."

BIOGRAPHICAL/CRITICAL SOURCES:

PERIODICALS

American Literature, September, 1990, p. 521.
Kenyon Review, summer, 1990.
Kirkus Reviews, October 15, 1989.
Publishers Weekly, October 27, 1989.
Sewanee Review, spring, 1990.
Times Literary Supplement, January 25, 1991, p. 8.
Washington Post Book World, April 1, 1990, p. 11.

* * *

JAQUES, Faith   1923-1997

OBITUARY NOTICE—See index for *CA* sketch: Surname pronounced "Jakes"; born December 13, 1923, in Leicester, England; died July 12, 1997. Illustrator, educator, and author. Jaques was a well established illustrator of children's books, including works such as Roald Dahl's *Charlie and the Chocolate Factory* and Philippa Pearce's *What the Neighbours Did.* She worked to gain recognition for illustrators, particularly in regard to receiving royalties along with authors for the work. Jaques served with the Women's Royal Naval Service during World War II, becoming a petty officer. Beginning in 1950 she worked as a visiting lecturer at the Guildford School of Art in England, followed by a stint at the Hornsey College of Art beginning in 1958. She worked as an illustrator with various firms, including Folio Society Books, Reader's Digest Educational Books, BBC School Publications, and Cape, Heinemann, Methuen, and Penguin. In addition to illustrating the books of others, she created the artwork for books of her own, including *Tilly's House, Frank and Polly Muir's Big Dipper,* and *The Christmas Party.* Her illustrator credits include *The Twelve Days of Christmas,* Louisa May Alcott's *Little Women,* Eric Mathieson's *Jumbo the Elephant,* Robert Louis Stevenson's *Treasure Island,* Allan Ahlberg's *Mr. Buzz the Beeman,* and Charles Dickens' *The Magic Fish-Bone.* She also illustrated books in "The Apprentices" series by Leon Garfield such as *Labour in Vain* and *The Filthy Beast.*

OBITUARIES AND OTHER SOURCES:

PERIODICALS

Times (London; electronic), August 1, 1997.

* * *

JENKINS, Fred W(illiam)   1957-

PERSONAL: Born April 13, 1957, in Cincinnati, OH; son of Fred E. and Ethel M. Jenkins; married Nancy Courtney, October 31, 1992. *Education:* University of Cincinnati, B.A. (summa cum laude), 1979; University of Illinois at Urbana-Champaign, A.M., 1981, Ph.D., 1985, M.S., 1986.

ADDRESSES: Home—Dayton, OH. *Office*—105-F Roesch Library, University of Dayton, 300 College Park, Dayton, OH 45469. *E-mail*—jenkins@data.lib. udayton.edu.

CAREER: College of Physicians of Philadelphia, Philadelphia, PA, historical collections cataloger, 1986-87; University of Dayton, Dayton, OH, instructor, 1988-89, assistant professor, 1987-96, associate professor, 1996—, catalog specialist, 1987-96, rare book librarian, 1993-96, coordinator and head of collection management, 1996—.

MEMBER: American Library Association, Association of College and Research Libraries (chairperson of Classical, Medieval, and Renaissance Discussion Group, 1993-94, 1997-98), American Society of Papyrologists, Academic Library Association of Ohio, Phi Beta Kappa, Phi Kappa Phi, Phi Beta Mu.

AWARDS, HONORS: Grants from Academic Library Association of Ohio, 1993, 1997; *Classical Studies* was selected an outstanding academic book by *Choice,* 1996.

WRITINGS:

Classical Studies: A Guide to the Reference Literature, Libraries Unlimited (Englewood, CO), 1996.

Contributor of articles and reviews to library and papyrology journals.

WORK IN PROGRESS: French Language and Literature, publication by Libraries Unlimited expected in 1999; research on Greek papyrology, Latin literature, and the history of classical scholarship.

*   *   *

JINKS, Catherine   1963-

PERSONAL: Born November 17, 1963; daughter of Brian and Rhonda (Dickings) Jinks; married Peter Dockrill (November 22, 1992); children: one child. *Education:* University of Sydney, B.A. (with honors), 1986. *Politics:* "Left."

ADDRESSES: Agent—Margaret Connolly, 16 Winton St., Warrawee, Sydney, NSW 2074, Australia.

CAREER: Westpac Banking Corp., Sydney, Australia, journalist, 1986-93.

AWARDS, HONORS: Australian Children's Book of the Year Award shortlist, Children's Book Council of Australia, 1993, for *Pagan's Crusade,* and 1997, for *Pagan's Scribe;* Victorian Premier's Award shortlist, 1993, for *Pagan's Crusade;* Australian Children's Book of the Year Award (Older Readers category), Children's Book Council of Australia, and Adelaide Festival Award shortlist, both 1996, both for *Pagan's Vows.*

WRITINGS:

This Way Out, Omnibus (New York), 1991.
Pagan's Crusade, Hodder & Stoughton (Kent, England), 1992.
The Future Trap, Omnibus, 1993.
Pagan in Exile, Omnibus, 1994.
Witch Bank, Penguin (New York City), 1995.
Pagan's Vows, Omnibus, 1995.
Pagan's Scribe, Omnibus, 1996.
An Evening with the Messiah (adult novel), Penguin, 1996.
Eye to Eye, Penguin, 1997.
Little White Secrets (adult novel), Penguin, 1997.
The Secret of Hermitage Isle (cartoon book), ABC Books, 1997.

WORK IN PROGRESS: Piggy in the Middle.

SIDELIGHTS: Catherine Jinks commented: "In Australia I'm best known for my medieval historical series, the 'Pagan' books—*Pagan's Crusade, Pagan in Exile, Pagan's Vows,* and *Pagan's Scribe.* So far only *Pagan's Crusade* has made a low-key appearance outside this country—in the United Kingdom and Canada. They are humorous books, written in present tense/first person. My interest in medieval history was fuelled by my study of it in university; it's an abiding interest, and will probably result in more medieval books.

"I've always wanted to produce books, and sent my first 'novel' off to a publisher when I was twelve. I feel shocking if I'm not working on a book and have no problem applying myself to their creation—no writer's block for me. I love creating stories; if I didn't, I wouldn't be doing it. It's the best job in the world (I just wish it paid more!).

"P.S. I grew up in Papua New Guinea and spent eighteen months in Nova Scotia from 1993 to 1994 (being married to a Canadian). Canada will be the subject of my next published adult book."

When *Pagan's Vows* won the Australian Children's Book of the Year Award for the older readers category from the Children's Book Council of Australia, Jinks remarked in her acceptance speech: "In a funny sort of way I see the award as more of a tribute to Pagan than to me. . . . He's been through a lot, yet he's kept his humour and his courage and his loving heart. More than any other character I've created . . . he's the one who deserves, and has the strength, to live on a bit—instead of disappearing into the black hole of the remainders bin. So I'd like to express my gratitude on Pagan's behalf."

Jinks's first book for young adults, *This Way Out,* is unique in her body of published work. This novel is a contemporary story that focuses on a fifteen-year-old girl's dissatisfaction with her life and her search for a job that will pay for photographs that she hopes will begin her modeling career. "*This Way Out* reveals the author's awareness of some of the frustrations and longings of youth," stated Cathryn Crowe in *Magpies.*

The author is better known for creating a twelfth-century ragamuffin character named Pagan Kidrouk, squire to Lord Roland during the last days of the Crusades. *Pagan's Crusade,* Jinks's first installment in what has become a series of novels, is "a curious, and curiously fascinating, novel," commented Marcus Crouch in *Junior Bookshelf.* Critics have noted the author's unusual choice of modern vernacular speech for her medieval characters, a choice that yields "a style which is elliptical and abrupt and, at times, wildly funny," according to a reviewer for *Magpies.*

The focus of *Pagan's Crusade* is the relationship that develops between Pagan, a boy from the streets, and Lord Roland, who is the epitome of upper-class strength and valor. "The interplay between these two strong characters, each of which supplies a need in the other, underpins the whole fabric of the book," remarked Joan Zahnleiter in *Magpies.* "The aristocratic Templar [Roland] and his scruffy squire make an unlikely partnership and it is a measure of the success of Ms. Jinks' story that we accept the mutual respect that grows up between the partners under the stress of violent action," continued Marcus Crouch in *Junior Bookshelf.* In the first sequel, *Pagan in Exile,* Lord Roland takes Pagan back to his estate in France, where he becomes involved in the domestic wars among the twelfth-century landed aristocracy. Both books are noted for Pagan's humorous first-person narration. "Though the time and setting may not sound conducive to hilarity," Karen Jameyson admitted in her review of *Pagan's Crusade* in *Horn Book,* "the book certainly has elements of the hysterical historical." Indeed, echoed the reviewer in *Magpies,* Jinks's sense of humor enables her to "present the historical novel in an accessible style for today's readers."

BIOGRAPHICAL/CRITICAL SOURCES:

PERIODICALS

Horn Book, July, 1993, p. 498.

Junior Bookshelf, December, 1993, pp. 246-47.
Magpies, November, 1992, p. 14; March, 1993, p. 32; May, 1993, p. 24; July, 1995, p. 24.
Reading Time, November, 1996, pp. 7-8.

*   *   *

JOAS, Hans 1948-

PERSONAL: Born November 27, 1948, in Munich, Germany; son of Alois and Gertrud (Buckel) Joas; married Heidrun Boehme, May 26, 1976; children: Christian. *Education:* Free University of Berlin, diploma in sociology, 1972, Ph.D., 1979, Habilitation, 1981. *Religion:* Roman Catholic.

ADDRESSES: Office—Free University of Berlin, Lansstrasse 5-g, 14 195 Berlin, Germany.

CAREER: University of Chicago, Chicago, IL, visiting professor, 1985; University of Toronto, Toronto, Ontario, Canada, visiting professor, 1986; University of Erlangen, Erlangen, Germany, associate professor, 1987-90; Free University of Berlin, West Berlin, Germany, professor of sociology and North American studies, 1990—.

MEMBER: International Sociology Association (vice president of research committee on theory, 1988—).

AWARDS, HONORS: Heisenberg fellowship, Max Planck Institute, Berlin, Germany, 1984.

WRITINGS:

Die gegenwaertige Lage der soziologischen Rollentheorie, Akademische Verlagsgesellschaft (Frankfurt am Main, Germany), 1975.
Praktische Intersubjektivitaet, Suhrkamp (Frankfurt am Main, Germany), 1980, translation by Raymond Meyer published as *G. H. Mead: A Contemporary Re-examination of His Thought,* MIT Press, 1985.
(With Axel Honneth) *Soziales Handeln und menschliche Natur: Anthropologische Grundlagen der Sozialwissenschaften,* Campus-Verlag (Frankfurt am Main, Germany), 1980, translation by Raymond Meyer published as *Social Action and Human Nature,* Cambridge University Press (Cambridge, England), 1988.
(Editor) *Das Problem der Intersubjektivitaet: Neuere Beitraege zum Werk George Herbert Mead,* Suhrkamp, 1985.

(Editor) *Kommunikatives Handeln: Beitraege zu Juergen Habermas' "Theorie des kommunikativen Handelns,"* Suhrkamp, 1986, translation by Jeremy Gaines and Doris L. Jones published as *Communicative Action: Essays on Juergen Habermas's "The Theory of Communicative Action,"* MIT Press (Cambridge, MA), 1991.

(With Michael Bochow) *Wissenschaft und Karriere: Der berufliche Verbleib des akademischen Mittelbaus,* Campus (Frankfurt am Main, Germany), 1987.

(Editor with Helmut Steiner) *Machtpolitischer Realismus und pazifistische Utopie: Krieg und Frieden in der Geschichte der Sozialwissenschaften,* Suhrkamp, 1989.

Die Kreativiteat des Handelns, Suhrkamp, 1992, translation by Jeremy Gaines and Paul Keast published as *The Creativity of Action,* University of Chicago Press (Chicago, IL), 1996.

(Editor with Martin Kohli) *Der Zusammenbruch der DDR: Soziologische Analysen,* Suhrkamp, 1993.

Pragmatism and Social Theory, University of Chicago Press, 1993, originally published in German.

(Editor with Wolfgang Knoebl) *Gewalt in den USA,* Fischer Taschenbuch Verlag (Frankfurt am Main, Germany), 1994.

SIDELIGHTS: Hans Joas is a German sociologist who has taught at the Free University of Berlin since 1990. Among Joas's publications in English translation is *G. H. Mead: A Contemporary Re-examination of His Thought.* The volume focuses on the American pragmatist G. H. Mead, whose own ideas, though significantly influenced by Darwinism, nonetheless questioned the issues of behaviorism to which Charles Darwin's theories often led. Joas particularly concentrates on Mead's notion of practical intersubjectivity, which contends that action inevitably involves what Howard L. Sacks, writing in *Contemporary Sociology,* described as "fundamentally interpenetrative conduct carried out in an ongoing dialectical confrontation in the natural and social world." In reconsidering Mead's work, Joas compares him with other American pragmatists and such European thinkers as Juergen Habermas, Edmund Husserl, Maurice Merleau-Ponty, and Jean Piaget. In his *Contemporary Sociology* review, Sacks wrote that "in Joas's hands Mead's work defines a task for empirical science that is potentially practical, political, and ethical in extending the boundaries through which intelligent action is possible in the contemporary world."

Pragmatism and Social Theory, another of Joas's works in English translation, explores the increasingly important ties between pragmatism and sociology. Here Joas perceives pragmatism as it is evident in a range of social theories. In addition, he indicates the necessity of understanding pragmatism if one is to fathom contemporary notions of action and interaction. *Contemporary Sociology* contributor David R. Maines urged people to read *Pragmatism and Social Theory* since "it addresses issues that are at the core of an array of current sociological practices. If read with understanding, it will help the reader to comprehend better why sociology has no alternative but to adopt a pragmatist framework."

BIOGRAPHICAL/CRITICAL SOURCES:

PERIODICALS

Choice, February, 1986, p. 879.
Contemporary Sociology, May, 1986, pp. 488-489; January, 1995, pp. 134-135.

OTHER

http://diogenes.baylor.edu/WWWproviders/Larry _Ridener/DSS/Me
ad/MEAD2.HTM L, October 9, 1997.
http://diogenes.baylor.edu/WWWproviders/Larry_ Ridener/DSS/Mead/MEAD5.HTM L, October 9, 1997.*

*   *   *

JOHNSON, Clarence L(eonard)   1910-1990

PERSONAL: Born February 27, 1910, in northern MI; died of undisclosed causes following a long illness, December 21, 1990, in Burbank, CA; son of Peter (a mason) and Christine (a launderer and housecleaner; maiden name, Anderson) Johnson; married first wife, Althea (a paymaster at Lockheed), 1936 (died); married second wife, Maryellen Elberta Meade (died); married third wife, c. 1990. *Education:* Attended Flint Junior College, c. 1927-29; University of Michigan, B.S. (engineering), 1932, graduate study, 1933.

CAREER: Aeronautical engineer and writer. Lockheed Aircraft Corporation, Burbank, CA, engineer, 1933-41, director of the "Skunk Works" division for secret military projects, 1941-c.76.

AWARDS, HONORS: Medal of Freedom, 1964, presented by President Lyndon B. Johnson; National Security Medal, 1983, presented by President Ronald Reagan; received honorary doctorate degrees.

WRITINGS:

Kelly: More Than My Share of It All, Smithsonian Institution Press, 1985.

SIDELIGHTS: Clarence L. Johnson designed some of America's most advanced airplanes. As an engineer for Lockheed Aircraft Corporation, Johnson served as flight test engineer, stress analyst, weight engineer, and performed countless aerodynamic tests with wind tunnels. During his tenure as chief research engineer Johnson created the Skunk Works, a division within Lockheed that designed advanced, secret military projects. It became associated with some of Lockheed's most impressive achievements in aviation.

Johnson's father, Peter, left his native Sweden in 1882 to avoid military service and embarked for the United States. After settling in northern Michigan, he sent for his fiancee, Christine Anderson. They had nine children, of whom Clarence was the seventh; he was born February 27, 1910. Johnson's father eked out a living as a mason. His mother earned money by washing other people's laundry on her wash board and by scrubbing floors. Although they were poor, Johnson recalled happy memories of his childhood. Even in the dead of winter he liked to hike in the forests and explore nature.

Learning appealed to the young Johnson, and he received good grades. He would spend hours poring over Tom Swift adventure books admiring Swift's exploits as a builder, engineer, and designer. By watching his father, whom he described as a skilled craftsman, Johnson acquired an early appreciation of what human hands could accomplish. Johnson's interest in things mechanical seem to have been nurtured by these early influences. By the time he was twelve, Johnson had already developed a love for airplanes and had decided that he would one day build them. His parents and the local school principal supported this interest. The principal even invited Johnson to address the Lions Club on aviation.

Johnson acquired the nickname "Kelly" from an incident that transpired during his early years in school. As Johnson told the story in his autobiography, *Kelly: More Than My Share of It All,* a boy from the wealthy part of the village had tormented Johnson by calling him "Clara." To pay him back, Johnson jumped on the boy's leg from behind and broke it. Johnson's schoolmates were impressed and gave him "a good fighting

Irish name" from the popular song "Kelly from the Emerald Isle."

In 1923, when Johnson was thirteen, his family moved to Flint, Michigan, where prospects for employment were more encouraging. The family's economic position improved and Johnson saved enough money by working to attend Flint Junior College, where he studied mathematics and physics. He did well, and in 1929 the University of Michigan in Ann Arbor accepted him to study aeronautical engineering. Johnson graduated with a bachelor's degree in 1932. He returned the following year for graduate work after having spent the summer searching in vain for a position as an aeronautical engineer. Although Lockheed Aircraft Corporation in Burbank, California, did not hire him then, the chief engineer suggested that Johnson get a master's degree and then apply for a position. The company had recently been purchased and was in a state of uncertainty.

Events went as planned and Lockheed hired Johnson in 1933. Johnson lost no time in telling his new employers that he disagreed with their design of the reorganized company's first aircraft, the Lockheed Electra. He said the airplane would be unstable. Hall L. Hibbard, Lockheed's chief engineer and a graduate of the Massachusetts Institute of Technology, had helped design the aircraft. He was uncertain of Johnson's argument but was willing to let the new employee have a chance.

Hibbard sent Johnson back to the University of Michigan to test a model of the aircraft in the university's wind tunnel, where Johnson had recently worked as a student. After many trials Johnson solved the problem of instability by adding a double vertical stabilizer to the tail. Lockheed included the idea in its early metal aircraft. It appeared as a three-tail design in Lockheed's famous Constellation, which remained in production until the mid-1950s.

As tensions grew in Europe during the late 1930s, the Army Air Corps sought development of a new fighter. Lockheed's P-38 was a response to this need. The new airplane set speed records of over four hundred miles per hour and became one of the most versatile aircraft in the U.S. fighter fleet. Various models served as strafers, reconnaissance aircraft, rocket carriers, and ambulances. By 1945 some ten thousand of these airplanes had rolled off the assembly line.

Although the P-38 had impressive speed, its piston engine imposed limitations both on the airplane's speed and performance. Lockheed urged the Army Air Corps to consider letting it design a jet aircraft. The Air Corps rebuffed Lockheed's overtures and urged the company to correct existing bugs in the P-38. Developments with Frank Whittle's jet engine in the United Kingdom in 1941, however, alerted the Air Corps to possibilities for jet aircraft in the United States.

Johnson promised to deliver a prototype jet aircraft in 180 days. The aircraft would be powered by a jet engine Whittle had designed in the United Kingdom. To make good on his promise, Johnson corralled a number of Lockheed engineers and workers and made work space from wooden shipping crates. Johnson and his crew cobbled together a rudimentary administration, including a purchasing department, so that their design and production efforts would not interfere with Lockheed's already overburdened main plant. The new administration and production facilities acquired the name "Skunk Works." Under Johnson's direction the Skunk Works created some of the most radical and most successful designs in aircraft.

Having established the Skunk Works, Johnson and his crew set about to create the first American operational jet fighter. The experimental version, the XP-80, first flew at Muroc Dry Lake (later Edwards Air Force Base) on January 8, 1944, at speeds over five hundred miles per hour. Johnson had fulfilled his promise to deliver a jet airplane within 180 days. Production models did not come off the assembly line until 1948, however, when the plane was redesignated the F-80.

When the Korean conflict broke out in 1950, the F-80 Shooting Star performed well against the North Korean MiG-15. American pilots complained, however, that the MiGs could elude American fighters by ascending to higher altitudes. This demand for altitude and speed set Johnson again to designing new capabilities. The outcome was Lockheed's F-104 Starfighter, the "missile with a man in it." Designed as an interceptor-fighter, the F-104 was the first aircraft to hold speed and altitude records at the same time. In 1958, for example, an F-104 set a speed record of 1,404.19 miles per hour and (in a separate flight) an altitude record of 91,243 feet. In 1959 an F-104 set a new altitude record of 103,395.5 feet.

Johnson had also made his mark on non-fighter aircraft. Lockheed's Constellation, designed as a commercial airliner, saw service as a military transport during World War II. General Dwight D. Eisenhower flew in a Constellation named *Columbine I* when he was commander of the North American Treaty Organization (NATO). As president, he flew in another Constellation, named *Columbine II.*

The versatile military cargo airplane, the C-130 Hercules, also bore Johnson's imprint as did the high-flying reconnaissance airplane, the U-2. Francis Gary Powers was flying a U-2 when the Soviets shot him down on May 1, 1960, leading to a tense face-off between President Eisenhower and Soviet premier Nikita Khrushchev. As designer of the U-2 and other important military aircraft, and corporate vice president since 1956, Johnson was now an important figure in the Cold War calculations of parry and riposte. During this period Johnson slept with a pistol near his bed. After the Soviets released Powers from captivity in 1962, he worked for Johnson at the Skunk Works.

Johnson's last and most difficult project was in designing the SR-71, a high-altitude, long-range strategic reconnaissance airplane that repeatedly set speed and distance records. The Blackbird, as it was unofficially called, could reach speeds of over 2,200 miles per hour at an altitude of 80,000 feet. This airplane was the first to incorporate "stealth " technology to avoid (or lessen) radar detection.

Johnson retired with his wife, Althea, to their ranch near Santa Barbara, California. She had been the paymaster at Lockheed when Johnson first joined the company. After a four-year courtship they married in 1936. She later died, and Johnson married his secretary, Maryellen Elberta Meade. Together they enjoyed horseback riding and golf at their ranch, but she died only a year and a half after their marriage. Johnson married again shortly thereafter but died in Burbank of undisclosed causes on December 21, 1990, after a prolonged illness.

Johnson's many awards, most of them received after retirement, included honorary doctorates; the Medal of Freedom, presented in 1964 by President Lyndon B. Johnson; and the National Security Medal, presented by President Ronald Reagan in 1983.

BIOGRAPHICAL/CRITICAL SOURCES:

BOOKS

Johnson, Clarence L., *Kelly: More Than My Share of It All,* Smithsonian Institution Press, 1985,

PERIODICALS

Air Progress, September, 1986, pp. 60-61.
Aviation Week & Space Technology, January 7, 1991.
New York Times, December 22, 1990, p. 33.*

* * *

JOHNSON, Fenton 1953-

PERSONAL: Born October 25, 1953, in New Haven, KY; son of Patrick D. and Nancy Lee (Hubbard) Johnson. *Education:* Stanford University, B.A. (with honors); University of Iowa Writers' Workshop, M.F.A.

ADDRESSES: Agent—Malaga Baldi Literary Agency, 2112 Broadway, No. 403, New York, NY 10023, mbaldi@aol.com. *E-mail*—johnfenton@aol.com.

CAREER: Novelist, short fiction writer, essayist, critic, and journalist. U.S. Representative Ron Mazzoli, Washington D.C., legislative assistant/press secretary, 1975-77; San Francisco State University, San Francisco, CA, adjunct faculty, 1988—; Columbia University Program in Writing, New York City, adjunct assistant professor, 1996-97. Streetside Stories, volunteer at writing workshops with the elderly and with AIDS/HIV students, 1990-94; Department of English, Santa Clara University, visiting faculty, 1992; San Francisco State University Journalism Department, summer faculty, 1992; Napa Valley Writer's Conference, fiction faculty, 1995; Provincetown Fine Arts Work Center, summer session teacher, 1997. Served as freelance consultant, writer, and editor, on grantmaking/evaluation panels for the Rockefeller Foundation, 1987, National Endowment for the Arts, 1989, and the Knight Foundation, 1993; served as judge, Jackson/Phelan Literary Awards, 1996, and the San Francisco Bay *Guardian* fiction competition, 1988. Frameline/San Francisco International Lesbian and Gay Film Festival, board of directors, 1987-90; Mercury House (literary press), board of directors, 1994—.

MEMBER: PEN-America, National Writers Union, National Lesbian and Gay Journalists' Association.

AWARDS, HONORS: Michener Fellowship, Iowa Writers Workshop, 1982-83; Wallace Stegner Fellowship in Fiction, Stanford University Program in Creative Writing, 1985-86; Joseph Henry Jackson Award for outstanding fiction by a California writer, 1986; *Chicago Tribune*/Nelson Algren Fiction Award, 1986; *Transatlantic Review*/Henfield Foundation Award, 1986; fellowship, National Endowment for the Arts in literature, 1989, and creative nonfiction, 1995; fellow, MacDowell Colony, 1991; nominations for best fiction, San Francisco Bay Area Book Reviewers, *Boston Book Review* Fisk Award, American Library Association, *Lambda Review* Book Awards, Quality Paperback Bookclub, 1993, all for *Scissors, Paper, Rock;* residency, Headlands Center for the Arts, 1994-95.

WRITINGS:

Crossing the River: A Novel, Carol Publishing Group, 1989.
Scissors, Paper, Rock, Pocket Books, 1993.
Geography of the Heart: A Memoir, Scribner (New York City), 1996.

Short fiction published in periodicals, including *Los Angeles Times Magazine, Chicago Tribune, Turnstile Quarterly, Sewanee Review, Greensboro Review,* and *Fiction Network,* and anthologies, including *Best of the West,* Peregrine Smith Books, 1989. Articles and essays published in periodicals, including *Harper's, New York Times Magazine, Mother Jones, Out, American Voice,* and *Virgina Quarterly Review,* and in anthologies, including *How We Live Now,* St. Martin's/Bedford Books, 1992; *Writers for Life,* Persea Books, 1994; *Wrestling with the Angel: Gay Men Write on Religion,* edited by Brian Bouldrey, G. P. Putnam's, 1995; and *The Writer's Journal,* Bantam/Doubleday, 1996; *A Free Library in This City,* Peter Wiley, 1996. Book reviews published in periodicals, including *San Francisco Chronicle, San Jose Mercury, San Francisco Review of Books, Washington Post, Louisville Courier-Journal,* and *Chicago Tribune.*

Also author of scripts for interactive CD-ROM projects and for documentaries, including Academy Award nominee Lourdes Portillo's *La Ofrenda: Days of the Dead;* and *Stranger with a Camera,* produced by Appalshop. Member of editorial board, *San Francisco Review of Books,* 1983-88; editor, *Release Print,* 1983-85; free-lance editor for publishing companies, including North Point Press and HarperCollins.

WORK IN PROGRESS: Dialogue in Silence: The Contemplative Life in America.

SIDELIGHTS: Fenton Johnson is a writer whose novels have earned praise for their detailed evocation of the land and people of the Appalachian mountains. In addition, his memoir of life with a lover dying of acquired immunodeficiency syndrome (AIDS) is considered a moving tribute to love and loss. According to reviewers, Johnson—the youngest of nine children born to a Catholic family in Kentucky—exhibits in his writings an intimate knowledge of Appalachian culture, with its emphasis on family ties and stories of the past. Though occasionally faulted for relying on an overly episodic framework, especially in his second novel, *Scissors, Paper, Rock,* Johnson is also recognized as a gifted storyteller whose works display wisdom and compassion.

Crossing the River, Johnson's first novel, centers on Martha Bragg Pickett, who on a dare crosses the river that separates her fundamentalist Baptist community from the town of Catholics on the other side in order to buy beer. There she instantly falls in love with Bernie Miracle, the town's innkeeper. She finds herself twenty years later in a life as stifling in its own way as the one she had impetuously abandoned in her youth. At the graduation party for Martha and Bernie's son, Martha meets and falls in love with a Yankee contractor who is building a bridge that will span the two communities. "This is essentially the story of a woman's awakening, not so much sexually as in terms of her identity," noted Sybil Steinberg in *Publishers Weekly.* Steinberg added praise for Johnson's "sly humor" in relaying the foibles of his Kentucky characters. Leita Kaldi, a contributor to *Bloomsbury Review,* had some reservations about the work, stating that, with the exception of Martha, most of Johnson's characters are less vivid than his setting. "The delightful descriptions of the two rural towns linked by a fragile bridge and the river that separates them, are as important as the characters portrayed," Kaldi contended.

Johnson returned to Kentucky for the setting of his second novel, *Scissors, Paper, Rock.* The book is "less a novel than a series of linked short stories," according to Charles Solomon in the *Los Angeles Times Book Review.* When Raphael Hardin returns to his rural hometown of Strang Knob in the novel's first chapter to reconcile with his dying father, he is determined to hide the fact of his own impending death from AIDS. Subsequent chapters skip backward and forward in time, focusing on Raphael's siblings and parents, the author "less interested in how one incident leads to another than in how one memory leads to another," David Morgan observed in *Rapport.* Although some reviewers reacted to *Scissors, Paper, Rock* as an AIDS novel, *New York Times Book Review* contributor Lauren Picker noted that the novel's structure gives it an added theme—"the ways in which truth is reshaped and memory custom fitted to create

the myths that families live by." The book was widely admired, not least for its stylistic and tonal adroitness. "Almost as if he is whispering in your ear," according to Morgan, Johnson "subtly evoke[s] all the complexities of family and community both past and present."

In 1990, Johnson's lover of three years, Larry Rose, died of complications arising from AIDS. The author wrote *Geography of the Heart* as a tribute to Rose, who was a teacher, and as a document of what Johnson learned about love and living from him. Continuing his emphasis on roots and family, Johnson's memoir details the two men's diverse family histories—Rose was the late-born child of Holocaust survivors, Johnson the product of a large Catholic family brought up in rural Appalachia. The two met at the funeral for a mutual friend and began a love affair that in its earliest stages found Rose the pursuer, the one more certain of his feelings.

David L. Kirp, who reviewed the book for the *Nation,* pronounced John-son's account of his romance with Rose the most successful portion of the memoir, as the author successfully avoids the pitfalls of writing about love. "In fact," Kirp remarked, "the greatest strength of the book is its persistent rejection of the cliches of romance, its insistence on acknowledging ambiguities and imperfections of character." Ted Loos, contributor to the *New York Times Book Review,* noted the presence of Johnson's novelistic skills in this "lyrical memoir" which "marries his eye for detail with graceful writing to tell the story of a survivor." Indeed, "this is a remarkable memoir," echoed Genevieve Stuttaford in *Publishers Weekly,* "touching, searing, eloquent, beautifully alive."

BIOGRAPHICAL/CRITICAL SOURCES:

PERIODICALS

Bloomsbury Review, July 1990, p. 29.
Entertainment Weekly, August 13, 1993, p. 69.
Library Journal, July 1989, p. 109.
Los Angeles Times Book Review, July 10, 1994, p. 12.
Nation, July 15, 1996, pp. 36-37.
New York Times Book Review, August 15, 1993, p. 18; September 11, 1994, p. 44; September 22, 1996, p. 24.
Publishers Weekly, June 16, 1989, pp. 56-57; May 17, 1993, pp. 63, 66; April 15, 1996, p. 57.
Rapport, September 1993, p. 26.

JOHNSON, Nancy 1948-

PERSONAL: Born July 11, 1948, in Bethlehem, PA; daughter of Wallace R. and Ellen B. Johnson; married Arthur Y. Bryant (an attorney), August 17, 1991; children: Wallace Johnson. *Ethnicity:* "White." *Education:* Randolph-Macon Woman's College, B.A., 1970; Lehigh University, M.Ed., 1972; Johns Hopkins University, M.A., 1987; University of Arizona, M.F.A., 1989.

ADDRESSES: Home—3612 Newark St. N.W., Washington, DC 20016; fax 202-363-4175. *E-mail*—nkjohn son@mindspring.com.

WRITINGS:

Zoo and Cathedral (poems), White Pine Press (Fredonia, NY), 1996.

*   *   *

JOHNSON, Owen (McMahon) 1878-1952

PERSONAL: Born August 27, 1878, in New York, NY; died January 27, 1952, in Vineyard Haven, MA; son of Robert Underwood (a poet, writer, and editor) and Katherine McMahon Johnson; married Mary Galt Stockly, 1901 (died, 1910); married Esther (or Elaine) Cobb (later known as Cobina Wright), 1912 (divorced, 1917); married Cecile Denis de la Garde, 1917 (died, 1918); married Catherine Sayre Burton, January, 1921 (died March, 1923); married Gertrude Bovee Boyce, 1926. *Education:* Lawrenceville School, Lawrenceville, NJ, graduated 1895; Yale University, graduated, 1900. *Politics:* Republican, later Bull Moose, later Democrat. *Avocational interests:* Golf, tennis, fencing, music, painting.

CAREER: American novelist. *The Lit* (school magazine), Lawrenceville, NJ, founding editor, 1895. *Yale Literary Magazine,* editor, 1900. Worked as reporter in police court, first decade of twentieth century; was unsuccessful Democratic candidate for U.S. House of Representatives, First Congressional District of Massachusetts, 1936 and 1938; served on Republican National Committee before 1920.

MEMBER: Authors League (co-founder), Berkshire Symphonic Festival (co-founder), Alpha Delta Phi.

AWARDS, HONORS: Chevalier of the Legion of Honor (France), 1919.

WRITINGS:

NOVELS

Arrows of the Almighty, Macmillan (New York City), 1901.

In the Name of Liberty: A Story of the Terror, Century (New York City), 1905, published as *Nicole, or In the Name of Liberty: A Story of the Terror,* Macmillan (London), 1905.

Max Fargus, Baker & Taylor (New York City), 1906.

The Eternal Boy: Being the Story of the Prodigious Hickey, Dodd, Mead (New York City), 1909, published as *The Prodigious Hickey,* Baker & Taylor, 1910.

The Humming Bird, Baker & Taylor, 1910.

The Varmint, Baker & Taylor, 1910.

Lawrenceville Stories, Baker & Taylor, 1910.

The Tennessee Shad, Chronicling the Rise and Fall of the Firm of Doc Macnooder and the Tennessee Shad, Baker & Taylor, 1911.

Stover at Yale, Stokes (New York City), 1912, reprinted with an introduction by Kingman Brewster, Jr., Simon & Schuster (New York City), 1967.

The Sixty-first Second, Stokes, 1913.

Murder in Any Degree, Century, 1913.

The Salamander, Bobbs-Merrill (Indianapolis, IN), 1914.

Making Money, Stokes, 1915.

The Spirit of France, Little, Brown (Boston, MA), 1916.

The Woman Gives: A Story of Regeneration, Little, Brown, 1916.

Virtuous Wives, Little, Brown, 1918.

The Wasted Generation, Little, Brown, 1921.

Skippy Bedelle: His Sentimental Progress from Urchin to the Complete Man of the World, Little, Brown, 1922.

Blue Blood: A Dramatic Interlude, Little, Brown, 1924.

Children of Divorce, Little, Brown, 1927.

Sacrifice, Longmans, Green (New York City), 1929.

The Coming of the Amazons: A Satiristic Speculation on the Scientific Future of Civilization, Longmans, Green, 1931; microfiche, Greenwood Press (Westport, CT), 1985.

The Lawrenceville Stories (includes *The Prodigious Hickey, The Varmint,* and *The Tennessee Shad*), illustrated by F. R. Gruger, with an introduction by Cleveland Amory, Simon & Schuster, 1967, reprinted with a new introduction, Touchstone/ Simon & Schuster, 1987.

PLAYS

The Comet, produced in New York City, at the Bijou Theatre, December 30, 1907.

The Salamander (based on his novel), produced in New York City, at the Harris Theatre, October 23, 1914.

OTHER

Contributor to periodicals, including *Colliers* and *The Lit.*

ADAPTATIONS: The Salamander was directed by Arthur Donaldson and released by B. S. Moss Motion Picture Corporation, 1916; *The Happy Years,* based on some of the Lawrenceville stories, was produced by Metro-Goldwyn-Mayer, 1951; "Stover at Yale," *Omnibus VI, vol. 1,* was adapted by Douglas Wallop, directed by Richard Dunlap, and produced Robert Saudek Associates in association with NBC, broadcast October 20, 1957. "The Prodigious Hickey," *American Playhouse,* was adapted by Jan Jaffe Kahn, directed by Robert Iscove, and co-produced by Ronald J. Kahn Productions and Scholastic Productions, Inc., broadcast January 26, 1987.

SIDELIGHTS: It is not unusual for a writer to have works that are extremely popular during his or her lifetime fall out of favor after his or her death. Much rarer is the writer who has works that are extremely popular, then fall out of favor—but still retains legendary status. Such was fate of the school and college novels of Owen Johnson, particularly his 1912 *Stover at Yale,* which follows the fortunes of John Humperdink Stover, widely known as Dink Stover. That name, as Michael J. Halberstam observed in a 1967 article in *The American Scholar,* "still epitomizes the clear-eyed college man of the early 1900's," to such an extent that Dink Stover was still being used in an ad campaign for the Boston newspaper at the time Halberstam wrote.

Yet as Halberstam pointed out, the novel *Stover at Yale* drew anything but a rosy picture of American college life. It was according to Halberstam, not at all the "rah-rah classic" that a 1987 reviewer for the *Washington Post Book World* would later mistakenly assume it to be. It was, wrote Halberstam, "a very bitter, almost subversive book, an American classic that not only saturates us with the values and atmosphere of an earlier time but, like any good book, starts us thinking about our own condition."

The novel, Halberstam asserted, brings Stover to Yale full of grand illusions, "and then destroys them all."

In the words of Samuel Irving Bellman in *Dictionary of Literary Biography,* "*Stover at Yale* reads like a reform document of academic muckraking." The preppie sophomore, Hugh Le Baron, who tries to take Stover in hand when the latter arrives as a freshman, is revealed to be shallow and snobbish; the more attractive characters are those students who come from diverse backgrounds: among them an older, working-class freshman and a Jew. Dink, as a sophomore, leads a rebellion against the entrenched system of secret societies typified by Skull and Bones; he forms a discussion group, one of whose members, Brockhurst, serves as the apparent mouthpiece for author Johnson's own disillusionment with Ivy League values.

Given, in Halberstam's words, "all Johnson's best lines, and Johnson was a very good writer indeed," Brockhurst criticizes not only the preppie types, but the hard-working outsiders who, he claims, are not taking advantage of the precious opportunity to gain a liberal education. Brockhurst calls American universities "admirably organized instruments for the prevention of learning," set up for the handing out of degrees. "We are business colleges, and the business of our machines is to stamp out so many businessmen a year, running at full speed and in competition with the latest devices in Cambridge and Princeton."

The novel also depicts Stover's disenchantment with athletics, where, despite the zest of action and the relative democracy of the locker room, he is "appalled" by "the weight of the seriousness, the deadly seriousness of the American spirit which seizes on everything that is competition and transforms it, with the fanaticism of its race, for success." Bellman faulted Johnson for a compromise ending in which, because of his personal magnetism, Stover is allowed into a secret society anyway—the last man chosen. Perceived by some as an artistic flaw, a forgivable yielding to commercial realities, or the ambiguity of a complex work, is a matter of discussion among critics.

Stover at Yale was the capstone of a series of novels which, earlier, showed Dink and other boys at prep school. The school was Lawrenceville School both in fiction and in real life, and the characters, who were given colorful nicknames such as Doc Macnooder and the Tennessee Shad, were based on youthful friends of Johnson's (Dink Stover, it is said, was a composite character, one of the models for whom was a great Yale football end, James Shevlin). The three Lawrenceville School novels, republished in 1967 as *The Lawrenceville Stories,* consisted of *The Eternal Boy: Being the Story of the Prodigious Hickey* (1909), *The*

Varmint (1910), and *The Tennessee Shad* (1911). They established fame and fortune for Johnson after the relative obscurity of his earlier, apprentice novels; John R. Tunis, in the *New York Times Book Review,* quoted a contemporaneous history as saying, "every fourteen-year-old everywhere was on his stomach reading *Stover at Yale* and *The Varmint.*"

The Lawrenceville novels were noted for their depictions of schoolboy pranks, but of something more as well; declared Bellman, "Johnson was not by any means attempting to rival the hackwriting syndicates that were shamelessly grinding out titles like *The Rover Boys at School* and *The Motor Boys at Boxwood Hall.* Lawrenceville life was real, and earnest." The books gave, for their time and perhaps for later times, a realistic view of the painful process of adolescent boys' maturation. Of the three, *The Varmint,* which focuses on Stover's arrival in and difficult absorption into the Lawrenceville School, is usually considered the finest; it is, claimed Jared C. Lobdell in the *National Review* in 1969, "the best American story I know of a man's development 'out of the dirtied, hopeless cocoon of the boy.'" Lobdell went on to say that "I am astonished to find in these [three] republished novels a statement, a description, an understanding of adolescence which says more to me than, and is at least as good as . . . Salinger's [in *The Catcher in the Rye*]."

Lobdell felt that the Lawrenceville novels had not dated; Tunis, on the other hand, felt that they had dated to some extent, becoming period pieces despite real merits. Nevertheless, Tunis called Johnson "a supreme storyteller" and "a craftsman with a sure technique and a simple style," and commended his "original mind." Johnson, Tunis wrote, explored previously unused realms in writing, such as describing an athletic competition through the eyes of one of the players. Though Tunis did not enjoy all the Lawrenceville tales equally, he assured *Times* readers that "some of these stories are so good your immediate reaction is a low whistle of delight."

Those four novels were the peak of a career that declined steeply afterward. Most of Johnson's later novels dealt with the adult world of high society, a subject which, although he knew it well, he was unsuccessful with in print. Divorces, near-divorces, and broken homes predominated. In addition, there was a 1916 novel of bohemian life, *The Woman Gives: A Story of Regeneration;* a weak, 1921 melodrama of World War I, *The Wasted Generation;* a failed 1922 attempt to revive the schoolboy series, *Skippy Bedelle: His Sen-*

timental Progress from Urchin to the Complete Man of the World; and a 1931 science-fiction novel, *The Coming of the Amazons: A Satiric Speculation on the Scientific Future of Civilization,* in which the female gender dominates the world. Bellman singles out one novel, the 1914 *The Salamander,* as almost reaching the level of the Stover works; it concerns gold-digging young women in Manhattan. "The sociology . . . is explored by Johnson in his highly informative foreword and throughout the story," Bellman attested, but the melodramatic outcome of the plot makes it, he felt, "an interesting if literarily unsophisticated story."

The decline in quality in Johnson's writing was the subject of speculation at the time, as is demonstrated by a passage in a letter F. Scott Fitzgerald wrote to H. L. Mencken on May 4, 1925; as quoted by Bellman, Fitzgerald analyzed, "'There's nothing the matter with some of Johnson's later books, they're just rotten that's all. He was tired. . . .'" If Johnson was indeed tired, the fact may be evidenced by his exceptionally busy life. Married five times, he was an excellent amateur golfer as well as a tennis player, fencer, portrait painter, patron of the arts, and aficionado of politics. Tunis called him "a social lion of the early 1900's," someone who "knew everyone, went everywhere." He served on the Republican National Committee at a time when Republicanism meant Theodore Roosevelt; he followed that President into the Bull Moose Party, and later became a staunch supporter of Franklin D. Roosevelt. Johnson's second wife, Elaine (or Esther) Cobb, later known as Cobina Wright, wrote about him in a memoir entitled *I Never Grew Up.* As quoted by Tunis, she stated that Johnson was "a man of distinction. He stood out in any gathering, whether people knew him or not. The top athlete's controlled grace, the enormous vitality, the poise and carriage of that handsome head always seemed to fill any room and dominate it."

BIOGRAPHICAL/CRITICAL SOURCES:

BOOKS

Johnson, Owen, *Stover at Yale,* Stokes (New York City), 1912, reprinted with an introduction by Kingman Brewster, Jr., Simon & Schuster (New York City), 1967.
Dictionary of Literary Biography Yearbook 1987, Gale (Detroit, MI), 1987, pp. 316-325.

PERIODICALS

American Scholar, summer, 1969, pp. 470-480.

National Review, March 11, 1969, pp. 238-239.
New York Times Book Review, September 24, 1967, p. 8.
Washington Post Book World, March 1, 1987, p. 12.

* * *

JONES, George (Glenn) 1931-

PERSONAL: Born September 12, 1931, in Saratoga, TX; son of George Washington (a pipe fitter) and Clara (a church pianist) Jones; married first wife, Dorothy, c. 1949 (divorced); married second wife, Shirley, 1954 (divorced, 1968); married Tammy Wynette (a singer), September, 1968 (divorced, 1975); married Nancy Sepulvado (a telephone company worker), March 4, 1983; children: Susan (first marriage); Jeffrey, Brian (second marriage); Tamala Georgette (third marriage); stepchildren: Adina, Sherry (fourth marriage). *Religion:* Raised Penecostal.

ADDRESSES: Home—Brentwood, TN. *Office*—c/o Buddy Lee Attractions, 38 Music Alley, Nashville, TN 37212-2311. *Agent*—Talent Agency, 1005-A Lavergne Circle, Hendersonville, TN 37075. *E-mail*—mcanash @mca.com.

CAREER: Professional singer and guitar player, c. 1945—; performed on Texas radio stations and in honky-tonks, 1945; signed with Starday Records, 1953 (some sources say 1954), had first country hit "Why Baby Why," 1955; signed with Mercury Records, 1958, moved to United Artists label, 1961, moved to Musicor label, 1965, and moved to Epic Records, 1967. Operated (with Nancy Sepulvado) Jones Country theme park, Woodville, TX. Also worked as a house painter. *Military Service:* U.S. Marine Corps, 1950-53.

AWARDS, HONORS: Male Vocalist of the Year, Country Music Trade Association, 1962, 1963; *Rolling Stone* Magazine Music Awards Critics' Pick, Best Artist, country, 1976; Top Male Vocalist, Academy of Country Music, 1980; Country Music Association Male Vocalist of the Year, 1980, 1981; Grammy Award, Best Country Vocal Performance by a Male, 1980, for "He Stopped Loving Her Today"; TNN *Music City News* Country Awards, Single, 1981, for "He Stopped Loving Her Today"; Video Award, Country Music Association, 1986, for "Who's Gonna Fill Their Shoes"; TNN *Music City News* Country Awards Living Legend Award, 1987; American Music Awards

Country Video Award, Favorite Male Video Artist, 1987; inducted into the Country Music Hall of Fame, 1992; Grammy Award nomination, Best Country Male Vocal, for "I Don't Need Your Rockin' Chair."

WRITINGS:

(With Tom Carter) *I Lived to Tell It All* (memoir), Villard (New York City), 1996.

RECORDINGS:

The Great George Jones, Mercury-Wing, 1958.
George Jones Sings, Mercury, 1959.
George Jones Sings "White Lightning" and Other Favorites, Mercury, 1960.
George Jones Sings Country and Western Hits, Mercury, 1961.
Country Church Time, Mercury, 1961.
Greatest Hits of George Jones, Mercury, 1961.
The Crown Prince of Country Music, Starday, 1961.
The Best of George Jones, United Artists, 1962.
(With Margie Singleton) *Duets Country Style,* Mercury, 1962.
The Fabulous Country Music Sound of George Jones, Starday, 1962.
George Jones's Greatest Hits, Starday, 1962.
George Jones Sings Bob Wills, United Artists, 1962.
George Jones Sings from the Heart, Mercury, 1962.
George Jones Sings the Hits of His Country Cousins, United Artists, 1962.
I Wish Tonight Would Never End, United Artists, 1962.
My Favorites of Hank Williams, United Artists, 1962.
The New Favorites of George Jones, United Artists, 1962.
The Ballad Side of George Jones, Mercury, 1963.
Duets Country Style, Mercury, 1963.
George Jones Sings More New Favorites, United Artists, 1963.
Homecoming in Heaven, United Artists, 1963.
Novelty Styles, Mercury, 1963.
Blue and Lonesome, Mercury, 1964.
Bluegrass Hootenanny, United Artists, 1964.
Country and Western's Number One Male Singer, Mercury, 1964.
George Jones Salutes Hank Williams, Mercury, 1964.
George Jones Sings Like the Dickens, United Artists, 1964.
Grand Ole Opry, United Artists, 1964.
The Great George Jones, Mercury, 1964.
I Get Lonely, United Artists, 1964.
More Favorites by George Jones, United Artists, 1964.
What's In Our Hearts, United Artists, 1964.

Heartaches and Tears, Mercury, 1965.

New Country Hits, Musicor, 1965.

Singing the Blues, Mercury, 1965.

Close Together (As You and Me), Musicor, 1966.

Country Heart, Musicor, 1966.

We Found Heaven Right Here at 4033, Musicor Records, 1966.

George Jones Golden Hits, Volume Two, United Artists, 1967.

The George Jones Story, Musicor, 1968.

My Country, Musicor, 1968.

Golden Hits, Volume Three, United Artists, 1969.

George Jones Sings Hank Williams and Other Great Country Hits, World Wide Records, 1970.

If My Heart Had Windows, Musicor, 1970.

Mr. Country and Western George Jones, Musicor, 1970.

A Picture of Me (Without You), Epic, 1972.

Wrapped around Her Finger, RCA Victor, 1972.

The Best of George Jones, Volume Two, RCA Records, 1973.

I Can Still See Him in Your Eyes, RCA Victor, 1973.

(With Tammy Wynette) *Let's Build a World Together,* Epic, 1973.

Nothing Ever Hurt Me, Epic, 1973.

In a Gospel Way, Epic, 1974.

The Grand Tour, Epic, 1974.

I Can Love You Enough, RCA Victor, 1974.

You Gotta Be My Baby, RCA, 1974.

The Best of George Jones, Epic, 1975.

(With Tammy Wynette) *George and Tammy and Tina,* Epic, 1975.

Memories of Us, Epic, 1975.

Alone Again, Epic, 1976.

The Battle, Epic, 1976.

George Jones—The Greatest, Realm Records, 1976.

(With Tammy Wynette) *Golden Ring,* Epic, 1976.

All-Time Greatest Hits, Volume One, Epic, 1977.

The Best of George Jones, Musicor, 1977.

(With Tammy Wynette) *Greatest Hits,* Epic, 1977.

I Wanta Sing, Epic, 1977.

Bartender's Blues, Epic, 1978.

My Very Special Guests, Epic, 1979.

The Pick of George Jones, 51 West, 1979.

The Best of George Jones, CSP, 1980.

(With Johnny Paycheck) *Double Trouble,* Epic, 1980.

I Am What I Am, Epic, 1980.

Mr. Country, Piccadilly, 1980.

Encore, Epic, 1981.

(With Tammy Wynette) *Encore,* Epic, 1981.

George Jones, Time-Life Records, 1981.

George Jones's Greatest Hits, Phoenix, 1981.

Golden Hits, Gusto Records, 1981.

Still the Same Ole Me, Epic, 1981.

Anniversary: Ten Years of Hits, Epic, 1982.

Down Home Country, 51 West, 1982.

A Helping of Hits, 51 West, 1982.

Once You've Heard the Best, CSP, 1982.

(With Merle Haggard) *A Taste of Yesterday's Wine,* Epic, 1982.

That Jones Boy, 51 West, 1982.

George Jones, CSP, 1983.

Heartaches and Hangovers, Rounder Records, 1983.

Jones Country, Epic, 1983.

Shine On, Epic, 1983.

By Request, Epic, 1984.

Ladies' Choice, Epic, 1984.

The Living Legend, CBS Special Products, 1984.

A Tribute to Merle Haggard and George Jones, CBS Special Products, 1984.

You've Still Got a Place in My Heart, Epic, 1984.

First Time Live, Epic, 1985.

Rockin' the Country, Mercury, 1985.

Who's Gonna Fill Their Shoes, Epic, 1985.

Texas Tornado, Crown, 1986.

Wine Colored Roses, Epic, 1986.

Don't Stop the Music, Ace, 1987.

Super Hits, Epic, 1987.

Too Wild Too Long, Epic, 1987.

Twenty Greatest Hits, Highland Music, 1987.

(With Merle Haggard and Willie Nelson) *Walking the Line,* Epic, 1987.

One Woman Man, Epic, 1989.

Hallelujah Weekend, Epic, 1990.

You Oughta Be Here with Me, Epic, 1990.

And Along Came Jones, MCA, 1991.

Friends in High Places, Epic, 1991.

You Couldn't Get the Picture, MCA, 1991.

Live at Dancetown, U.S.A., Ace, 1992.

Walls Can Fall, MCA, 1992.

High Tech Redneck, MCA, 1993.

All Time Greatest Hits, Liberty, 1994.

Country Songs, Mercury, 1994.

Cup of Loneliness, Poly Tone, 1994.

(With Tammy Wynette) *Super Hits,* Epic, 1995.

Also recorded *George Jones' Greatest Hits,* Volume Two, Mercury; *George Jones with Love,* Musicor; *I Get Lonely in a Hurry,* United Artists; *I'll Share My World with You,* Musicor; *Walk through This World with Me,* Musicor; and *Where the Grass Won't Grow,* Musicor; recorded (with Melba Montgomery) *George Jones and Melba Montgomery,* Guest Star. Contributor to albums, including *Country Music Spectacular: The Golden Country Hits of the Fifties,* Starday, 1959; *The Country Music Hall of Fame,* Volume Two, Starday, 1962; *Hall of Fame,* Volume Nine, Starday, 1969; *Greatest Country Hits of the 80s,* Columbia,

1981; *Music for On and Off the Road,* Epic, 1983; *Rip Roarin' Country,* K-Tel, 1983; *Tammy Wynette,* Time-Life Records, 1983; *For the Record—The First Ten Years,* David Allan Coe, Columbia, 1984; *Seven Spanish Angels and Other Hits,* Ray Charles, CBS Records, 1989; *Duets,* Emmylou Harris, Reprise, 1990; *Heroes and Friends,* Randy Travis, Warner Bros., 1990; *Feelin' Good Train,* Sammy Kershaw, Mercury, 1994; *Guest Stars of the Hee-Haw Show,* Hilltop Records; and *Opry Time in Tennessee,* Starday.

SIDELIGHTS: According to David Gates in *Newsweek,* George Jones is "arguably the greatest living country singer." It is an assessment shared by many critics. In a career that has spanned more than three decades, Jones has played to adoring fans, "recorded so many albums and singles that even he has lost count" (according to a contributor to *Contemporary Musicians*), and overcome alcohol and cocaine addictions to restart his faltering career and earn himself a place in the Country Music Hall of Fame. It is Jones's remarkably emotive voice that has for years kept the record-buying public listening.

In 1996 Jones's autobiography, *I Lived to Tell It All,* was published. Jones wrote the book with ghostwriter Tom Carter, who had also written books with Reba McEntire and Ralph Emery. In *I Lived to Tell It All,* Jones describes his early years growing up in Texas, where, as the son of Pentecostal parents, he played the guitar from the age of nine and listened to Grand Ole Opry radio shows. He ran away from home at age fourteen, earning a living playing backup for radio shows. After serving in the United States Marine Corps, Jones painted houses and began playing country shows locally. In 1955 he recorded the singles "Why Baby Why" and "You Gotta Be My Baby," his first popular hits. More soon followed. During the 1960s Jones toured almost nonstop, recorded prolifically, and saw a different one of his songs reach the country music top ten each year.

However, Jones also became notorious in the country music business for his drinking, hard living, and frequently raucous behavior. Between approximately 1949 and 1975 Jones married and divorced three times, leaving his four children to be raised by others. His tempestous third marriage, to fellow country singer Tammy Wynette, was marked by frequent duets and public battles, both of which continued after their 1975 divorce. He earned the reputation of a brawler, and he often performed while intoxicated by drugs or alcohol—or stood up audiences altogether. "When you're just a kid out of the country," Jones told Jim Jerome in *People Weekly,* "and never had nothing, and all of a sudden you got everything at your feet, it can really ruin you in more ways than one. Mine was just self-destruction." After being sued by his former wives and by show promoters whose concerts he missed, Jones declared bankruptcy.

In the 1980s Jones began to take control of both his personal life and career. He married Nancy Sepulvado in 1983, and the following year he was told by doctors that he must quit drinking or die. "I did a lot of thinking," Jones told Jerome. "Got thousands of encouraging letters. Said a lot of prayers. And I made up my mind—enough of that." The recovery process was a challenging one, but Jones survived and learned to quell his pre-performance jitters without drugs or alcohol. And to his delight, the audiences still loved his music.

Gates remarked that *I Lived to Tell It All* depicts Jones's "humility before the primal forces of self-hatred and selfless love that tore him apart and put him back together." Likewise, a contributor to *People Weekly* remarked that two things make the memoir worthwhile: "the account of the rich music Jones has made" and "the tribute to his fourth wife, Nancy."

BIOGRAPHICAL/CRITICAL SOURCES:

BOOKS

Allen, Bob, *George Jones: The Life and Times of a Honky Tonk Legend,* Carol Publishing Group (Secaucus, NJ), 1994.
Allen, Bob, *George Jones: The Saga of an American Singer,* Doubleday (Garden City, NY), 1984.
Carlisle, Dolly, *Ragged But Right: The Life and Times of George Jones,* Contemporary Books (Chicago, IL), 1984.
Contemporary Musicians, Volume 4, Gale (Detroit, MI), 1991, pp. 139-144.

PERIODICALS

Newsweek, May 6, 1996, p. 82.
People, November 23, 1992, pp. 109-112; May 20, 1996, pp. 36, 40.
Publishers Weekly, March 11, 1996, p. 50.*

K

KANDEL, Michael 1941-

PERSONAL: Born December 24, 1941, in Baltimore, MD. *Education:* Indiana University, Ph.D. in Slavic Languages and Literature, 1971.

ADDRESSES: Office—Modern Language Association, 10 Astor Pl., New York, NY 10003. *Agent*—Matthew Bialer, William Morris Agency. *E-mail*—michael. kandel@mla.org.

CAREER: Editor at the Modern Language Association; Consultant science fiction editor for Harcourt Brace; Translator of Stanislaw Lem.

MEMBER: P.E.N. Club; Science Fiction Writers of America.

WRITINGS:

Strange Invasion, Bantam, 1989.
In Between Dragons, Bantam, 1991.
Captain Jack Zodiac, Bantam, 1993.
Panda Ray, St. Martin's, 1996.

WORK IN PROGRESS: Scholar, a fantasy novel.

SIDELIGHTS: Michael Kandel commented: "Although the protagonists of my novels are often children and although my style is humorous, the humor is dark, because it deals with the pain of the world, the cruelty of the world, and our imperfection. My genre is science fiction and fantasy but what I do with it tends to be unconventional."

The unconvention to which Kandel refers is often cited in reviews of his works. "Michael Kandel's *Strange Invasion* is a strange item indeed," asserted *Analog's* Tom Easton in a favorable assessment of the book. In *Strange Invasion,* protagonist Wally Griffith, who suffers from frequent hallucinations, has an alien spaceship land in his backyard with warnings of the imminent arrival of a horde of tourists whose presence generally spells doom for their host worlds. Easton dubbed Kandel's first work "a morality play" satirizing "the impact of the arrogant and self-satisfied who go abroad only to condescend." *Voice of Youth Advocates* contributor Margaret Mary Ptacek called *Strange Invasions* "an amusing tale filled with fun," praising Kandel's "truly clever" use of insects and animals in the work.

Panda Ray is the story of an adolescent alien faced with the prospect of losing his magic powers and being turned into a normal straight-A student by his mother. A *Kirkus Reviews* critic commented that Kandel's story is "tirelessly inventive but amorphous, with humorous intentions that never quite break through into real amusement: impressive yet difficult to approach. Rather like . . . yes, like Stanislaw Lem." References to Lem, the Polish science fiction writer, are often found in reviews of Kandel's work. Kandel was twice nominated for a National Book Award for his translations of Stanislaw Lem's writings. A *Publishers Weekly* reviewer thus similarly maintained that *Panda Ray,* "understated, surreal, and intensely ironic, is unlikely to appeal to readers who see space opera as the epitome of good SF but should find an audience among admirers of the work of Lem." In another favorable review of *Panda Ray,* Carl Hays of *Booklist* asserted that Kandel's "picaresque romp strikes just the right balance between whimsy and seriousness to keep things interesting, and Lem's fans will hear echoes of the

Polish master's mercurial wit in Kandel's abundant satirical quips."

BIOGRAPHICAL/CRITICAL SOURCES:

PERIODICALS

Analog, April, 1990, p. 184.
Booklist, July, 1996, p. 1811.
Kirkus Reviews, May 15, 1996, p. 718.
Library Journal, June 15, 1996, p. 96.
Publishers Weekly, June 10, 1996, p. 90.
Voice of Youth Advocates, February, 1990, p. 371; April, 1991, p. 44; December, 1992, p. 293.
Washington Post Book World, October 28, 1990, p. 10.

*　*　*

KANT, Hermann 1926-

PERSONAL: Born June 14, 1926, in Hamburg, Germany; son of Paul and Luise (Visser) Kant. *Education:* Attended Arbeiter-und Bauernfakul-taet (Workers' and Farmer's College), University of Greifswald, 1949-52; studied German, Humboldt University, Berlin, 1952-1956. *Politics:* SED/RDS.

ADDRESSES: Home—Dorfstr. 4, 17235 Praelank, Germany. *Agent*—c/o Aufbau-Verlag, Postfach 193, 10105 Berlin, Germany.

CAREER: Novelist and short story writer. Journalist and freelance writer; apprentice electrician during World War II; worked briefly as research assistant during the 1950s. *Wartime Service:* German army, 1944-45. Prisoner of war, Poland, 1945-49.

MEMBER: East German Writers' Union, board of directors, 1963-89; president, 1978-89. Academy of the Arts, German Democratic Republic, 1969-89.

AWARDS, HONORS: Heinrich Heine Prize, 1963; Erich Weinert Medal, 1966; Heinrich Mann Prize, 1967; National Prize of the German Democratic Republic, 1973, 1983.

WRITINGS:

NOVELS

Die Aula (title means "The Auditorium"), Ruetten & Loening (Berlin), 1965.

Das Impressum (title means "The Journal" or "The Masthead"), Ruetten & Loening, 1972.
Der Aufenthalt (title means "The Stay"), Ruetten & Loening, 1977.
Kormoran, Aufbau-Verlag (Berlin), 1994.
Escape: Ein Word-Spiel, Aufbau-Verlag, 1995

SHORT STORY COLLECTIONS

Ein Bisschen Suedsee (title means "A Bit of the South Seas"), Ruetten & Loening, 1962.
Eine Uebertretung (title means "An Infringement"), Ruetten & Loening, 1975; selections republished as *Andrede der Aertzin O. an den Staatsenwalt F. gelegentlich einer Untersuchung,* Neuwied & Darmstadt (Luchterhand), 1978.
Der Dritte Nagel (title means "The Third Nail"), Ruetten & Loening, 1981.
Schoene Elise (title means "Beautiful Elise"), Reclams Universal-Bibliothek (Leipzig), 1983.
Bronzezeit: Geschichten as de Leben des Buchhalters Farssmann (title means "The Bronze Age"), Ruetten & Loening, 1986.

NONFICTION

In Stockholm, Volk und Welt, 1971.
Zu de Unterlagen: Publizistik 1957-1980 (collected public writings), Aufblau (Berlin and Weimar), 1981.
My Alphabet of GDR Literature, Department of Foreign Languages, West Virginia University (Morgantown, WV), 1981.
Unterlagen zur Literatur und Politik, Neuwied & Darmstadt, 1982.
Die Summe: Eine Begebenheit, Luchterhand, 1988.
Abspann: Erinnerung an meine Gegenwart (memoir), Aufbau-Verlag (Berlin), 1991.

Frequent contributor to *Neues Deutschland.*

SIDELIGHTS: From 1978 to 1989, Hermann Kant was a novelist who also held political power. He was president of the East German Writers' Union during those years, and as such, influenced cultural policy, sometimes to the extent of affecting concretely the work of his fellow writers. His political position—what Manfred Bansleben in the *Dictionary of Literary Biography* referred to as "the writer who comes closest to representing an official East German view of literature"—made him controversial both in political and in literary terms. Since the downfall of the German Communist regime in 1989, critics have sometimes taken Kant to task for not grappling with the injustices of that government. Reviewing Kant's memoir *Abspann: Erinnerung an meine Gegenwart* for *World Literature Today,* Wes Blomster observed: "Kant takes his countrymen's inability to confront their past and to accept either personal or collective responsibility for it to nauseating extremes. . . . His autobiography . . . intensifies the ambiguity that haunts the intellectual world of this century." Similarly, when Blomster reviewed Kant's collection of journalistic writings *Zu den Unterlagen: Publizistik 1957-1980* for *World Literature Today,* he surmised that "the two phases of Kant's career are necessarily linked by a number of sleepless nights." On one hand, Blomster noted "party-line loyalty," and on the other—in Kant's fiction—an exquisite "sensitivity to injustice." Blomster called the collection "an important book" and "a cultural history of the [German] Democratic Republic."

Blomster and other Western critics have consistently preferred Kant's novels over his other work. These novels, wrote Blomster, "stand as superb accomplishments within the totality of postwar German literature." Perhaps the work that gained the most attention was *Die Aula* ("The Auditorium"), which brought Kant to public and critical attention when it was published in magazine serialization in 1963 and in book form in 1965. According to Bansleben in the *Dictionary of Literary Biography,* the novel was widely translated and frequently reprinted; it became a standard text in East German schools and a stage adaptation ran for nine years in East Berlin. The novel itself features those stylistic qualities which Bansleben listed as "virtuosity with language, an occasional tendency toward mannerism, and a general avoidance of metaphor." Its plot documents one small section of postwar East German life: the special colleges which, from 1949 to 1962, trained working-class youth to assume positions of importance in socialist society. Kant, a youth of working-class background, had himself benefitted from such an institution, and the novel traces the successful careers of several characters who are uplifted in that way. The novel was praised for its use of techniques such as flashback, jumbled time sequence, and interior monologue. It also criticized East German society to a certain extent: Bansleben argued, in fact, that critics on both sides of the Iron Curtain underestimated its critical intentions: "Although in *Die Aula* Kant does not violate any taboos, he does significantly enlarge the room for debate." A *Times Literary Supplement* critic, commenting on the German edition in the context of a review of Kant's second novel, called *Die Aula* "a fine example of the socialist novel rising above the potentially drab earnestness of its subject-

matter . . . with fluent irony and a remarkable lightness of touch."

According to Bansleben, Kant's next novel, *Das Impressum* ("The Journal" or "The Imprint") may have been written in response to an official policy decree at the second Bitterfield Conference in 1964, urging East German novelists to write about social problems from the viewpoint of management. In response, *Das Impressum* was about the editor-in-chief of an East German magazine. Taking place on a single day, the novel shows its lead character resisting a promotion to minister during the morning, but then later accepting the post that same night. Bansleben missed in *Das Impressum* the complexity of character and theme that he felt marked *Die Aula.* A reviewer in the *Times Literary Supplement* wrote: "The overriding impression is of a gifted short-story writer . . . stringing episodes together in the hope that their individual brilliance and social relevance will permit the emergence of a substantial general statement."

Kant's third novel, 1977's *Der Aufenthalt* ("The Stay"), was better-received than *Das Impressum.* Autobiographical in content, the novel portrays a young German prisoner of war in Poland beginning in 1945, who undergoes personal growth as a result of confronting his national and personal history. Blomster, again in *World Literature Today,* called the novel "a work of gentle beauty . . . among the major achievements of the 1970s," offering particular praise for two sections of the book: an "essay on 'the many ways of saying German' (a masterpiece of verbal facility) and the description of the walk through the ruins of the Warsaw ghetto." Bansleben characterized *Der Aufenthalt* as "perhaps Kant's most impressive and certainly his most honest novel," with its honesty arising, he noted, from the absence of any commentary on the East Germany of the 1970s.

A fourth novel, *Kormoran,* was published in 1994 during the post-Communist era, and takes place on a summer day in 1992 when a Kant-like character named Kormoran gathers with friends to celebrate his sixty-sixth birthday. According to the synopsis on the book's jacket, Kant wrote the novel "not following events but against them," and according to Sigrid Bauschinger in *World Literature Today,* it criticizes sharply the end of socialism. Calling the novel "the swan song of an unhappy segment of society," Bauschinger commented that "Kant's reckoning with the changed circumstances in East Germany is, as was to be expected, devastating."

Kant has also written several volumes of short stories. The title story of his 1981 collection, *Der Dritte Nagel* ("The Third Nail"), has as its protagonist a bookkeeper named Farssmann, who was also the narrator of all five stories in Kant's 1986 collection, *Bronzezeit* ("The Bronze Age"). "All the stories [in *Bronzezeit*] are superbly narrated and entertaining," asserted Bansleben, who singled out "Schoene Elise" ("Beautiful Elise") as the best. That story, in turn, became the title story of a later volume of stories, which Blomster reviewed for *World Literature Today* and characterized as pleasant "light reading."

BIOGRAPHICAL/CRITICAL SOURCES:

BOOKS

Elfe, Wolfgang D., and Hardin, James, editors, *Dictionary of Literary Biography,* Volume 75: *Contemporary German Fiction Writers, Second Series,* Gale (Detroit, MI), 1988, pp. 133-38.

PERIODICALS

World Literature Today, spring, 1978; spring, 1982; autumn, 1982; summer, 1984, pp. 413-14; winter, 1987, p. 92; autumn, 1992, pp. 717-18; summer, 1995.
Times Literary Supplement, September 22, 1972.

*   *   *

KARMA KAREN
  See KENT, Karen

*   *   *

KELLER, Debra   1958-

PERSONAL: Born September 25, 1958, in New York, NY; daughter of Herbert B. (a mathematician) and Loretta (an artist) Keller; married James Muldavin (an executive director), July 11, 1991; children: Noah, Elana. *Education:* Attended University of California, San Diego; California State University, Long Beach, B.A. *Avocational interests:* Hiking, biking, gardening.

ADDRESSES: Office—1220 H St., No. 102, Sacramento, CA 95814.

CAREER: Advertising copywriter in Los Angeles and San Francisco, CA, 1984-90; freelance copywriter, Sacramento, CA, 1990—.

MEMBER: Society of Children's Book Writers and Illustrators.

AWARDS, HONORS: The Trouble with Mister was an *American Booksellers Association* "Pick of the List," 1995, and a Junior Library Guild selection, 1996.

WRITINGS:

The Trouble with Mister, illustrated by Shannon McNeill, Chronicle Books (San Francisco, CA), 1995.

WORK IN PROGRESS: A mystery picture book.

SIDELIGHTS: Debra Keller commented: "I've always loved to write. I wrote my first (unpublished) children's book when I was nine years old. My teacher read it to the class, and no one laughed when he (or she) was supposed to. I wrote my second (unpublished) children's book in college. My professor, who was also a freelance editor, said she would help me revise the text and submit the manuscript, but I didn't believe her.

"I went on to become an advertising copywriter at a big Los Angeles agency. My first job was to write dog food coupons. My first (published) children's book was about a dog.

"Although I only have one book out, I write stories all the time. When I write, I begin with something I want to say. *The Trouble with Mister* began with my wanting to tell children, 'You're safe. You're okay. Use your imagination, and your world will be just right.'

"My favorite picture book authors are William Steig and Peggy Rathmann, which is funny because they were both illustrators first. Although their books are very different, they each speak to my heart in an honest, warm manner, which is what I think the best children's books do.

"My advice to aspiring authors is just to do it. If you have never written, but want to, just try it. No one has to read a word you write, and it's really very safe. If you have written a little, but want to write more, just do. As I once learned at a writer's conference, you can't fail unless you stop trying."

In her first children's book, *The Trouble with Mister,* Keller writes about a young boy who desperately wants a dog. When his parents refuse, Alex paints himself a picture of a dog, complete with long purple hair and bright yellow socks. One evening, his dream dog Mister comes alive, and the two play together all night. The next morning Mister runs away, and Alex is afraid his dog is gone forever until he receives a mysterious envelope with his original painting of Mister inside. Writing in *School Library Journal,* reviewer Jody McCoy praised Keller's well constructed text and claimed the book was "a treat for the eye, the ear, the imagination, and the heart." Ilene Cooper remarked in *Booklist* that children should enjoy the picture book, "especially the frisky Mister." A reviewer in *Kirkus Reviews* praised the "winning combination" of Keller's story with Shannon McNeill's illustrations, going on to describe *The Trouble with Mister* as "a colorful, bouncy romp."

BIOGRAPHICAL/CRITICAL SOURCES:

PERIODICALS

Booklist, January 1, 1996, p. 846.
Boston Book Review, November, 1995, p. 28.
Family Fun, November, 1995, p. 152.
Kirkus Reviews, October 1, 1995, p. 1431.
Publishers Weekly, October 16, 1995, p. 60.
School Library Journal, February, 1996, p. 86.
Working Mother, April, 1996, p. 68.

*　　*　　*

KELLY, Gene 1912-1996

PERSONAL: Born Eugene Curran Kelly, August 23, 1912, in Pittsburgh, PA; died February 2, 1996, in Beverly Hills, CA; son of James Patrick Joseph (a gramophone salesperson) and Harriet (a dance instructor and actress; maiden name, Curran) Kelly; married Betsy Blair (an actress), September 22, 1941 (divorced, 1957); married Jeanne Coyne (a dancer and assistant choreographer), August 6, 1960 (died, 1973); married Patricia Ward (a writer), July, 1990; children: (first marriage) Kerry; (second marriage) Timothy, Bridget. *Education:* Attended Pennsylvania State College; University of Pittsburgh, A.B. (economics), 1933; attended law school.

CAREER: Dancer, singer, actor, choreographer, director, producer, and author. Actor in stage produc-

tions, New York City, including *Leave It to Me,* 1938; *Hold Your Hats,* 1938; *The Time of Your Life,* 1939; *One for the Money,* 1939; and *Pal Joey,* 1941. Dance director and choreographer of stage productions, New York City, including *Hold Your Hats,* 1938; *The Emperor Jones,* 1938; *Green Grow the Lilacs,* 1939; *Billy Rose's Diamond Horseshoe Revue,* 1940; and *Best Foot Forward,* 1941. Stage director of productions, New York City, including *Flower Drum Song,* 1958. Actor in films, including *Me and My Girl,* 1942; *Pilot #5,* 1942; *DuBarry Was a Lady,* 1943; *Thousands Cheer,* 1943; *The Cross of Lorraine,* 1943; *Christmas Holiday,* 1944; *Ziegfeld Follies,* 1945; *The Three Musketeers,* 1948; *The Black Hand,* 1949; *Summer Stock,* 1950; *It's a Big Country,* 1952; *The Devil Makes Three,* 1952; *Crest of the Wave,* 1954; *Les Girls,* 1957; *Marjorie Morningstar,* 1958; *Inherit the Wind,* 1960; *Let's Make Love,* 1960; *What a Way to Go,* 1964; *The Young Girls of Rochefort,* 1968; *Forty Carats,* 1973; *Viva Knievel,* 1977; and *Xanadu* 1980. Actor and choreographer of films, including *Cover Girl,* 1944; *Anchors Aweigh,* 1945; *Living in a Big Way,* 1947; *The Pirate,* 1947; "Slaughter on Tenth Avenue" sequence, *Words and Music,* 1948; *Take Me Out to the Ball Game,* 1948; *An American in Paris,* 1951; *Brigadoon,* 1954; and *Deep in My Heart,* 1955. Actor, choreographer and director of films, including *On the Town,* 1949; *Singin' in the Rain,* 1952, *It's Always Fair Weather,* 1955; and *Invitation to the Dance,* 1956. Actor, producer, and director of films, including *The Happy Road,* 1957. Director of films, including *The Tunnel of Love,* 1958; *Gigot,* 1962; *A Guide for the Married Man,* 1967; and *Hello, Dolly!,* 1969. Director and producer of films, including *The Cheyenne Social Club,* 1970. Narrator of films, including *That's Entertainment!,* 1974; *That's Entertainment! Part II,* 1976; *That's Dancing!,* 1985; and *That's Entertainment! Part III,* 1994. Performer in shows, including *The Gillette Summer Sports Reel,* 1954; "The Life You Save," *Schlitz Playhouse of Stars,* 1957; "A Man's Story," *Wide Wide World,* 1957; "Dancing, A Man's Game," *Omnibus,* 1958; "The Gene Kelly Show," *Pontiac Star Parade,* 1959; *Going My Way,* 1962-63; *Jack and the Beanstalk,* 1967; *The Funny Side,* 1971; *The Academy Awards Presentation,* 1975; *North and South,* 1986; and *Sins,* 1986. Performer in video recordings, including *The Ultimate Swan Lake,* 1985; and *American Treasure, A Smithsonian Journey,* 1986.

Also worked for a dancing school owned by his mother in Pittsburgh, PA, 1933-35 (school renamed Gene Kelly School of the Dance, 1935, with branch added in Johnstown, PA); performed in a dance act with his brother Fred, various locations, including 1934 World's Fair, Chicago, IL; directed vaudeville acts, Pittsburgh, PA, c. mid-1930s. Worked variously in a gas station, in construction, and as a gymnastics teacher. Served as vice president of the Screen Actors Guild. *Wartime Service:* U.S. Navy, became lieutenant junior grade, 1944-46.

AWARDS, HONORS: Academy Award nomination, best actor, 1945, for *Anchors Aweigh;* Special Academy Award for "for versatility as an actor, singer, director, and dancer, and specifically for his achievements in the art of choreography of film," 1951; *Dance Magazine* Annual Award, 1958; Medal of the City of Paris, 1960; Emmy Award, 1967, for *Jack and the Beanstalk;* Cecil B. De Mille Award, Hollywood Foreign Press Association, 1981; Kennedy Center Honors, John F. Kennedy Center for the Performing Arts, 1982; Life Achievement Award, American Film Institute, 1985; National Medal of the Arts, 1994. Named chevalier of French Legion of Honor.

WRITINGS:

SCREENPLAYS

Invitation to the Dance, Metro-Goldwyn-Mayer, 1956.

TELEPLAYS

"Dancing, A Man's Game," *Omnibus,* NBC, 1958.

STORY IDEAS

(With Stanley Donen) *Take Me Out to the Ball Game,* Metro-Goldwyn-Mayer, 1948.

RECORDINGS:

Nursery Songs, Columbia, 1949.
The Pied Piper of Hamelin, Columbia, 1949.
The House That Wouldn't; The King Who Couldn't Dance; The Cuckoo Who Lived in a Clock, Columbia, 1950.
Gene Kelly, Song and Dance Man, Stet, 1978.
The Happiest Birthday in the World, 51 West, 1979.
Songs and Stories for Children, CBS Records, 1979.
Xanadu: From the Original Motion Picture Soundtrack, MCA, 1980.
The Best of Gene Kelly: From MGM Classic Films, MCA, 1987.

An American in Paris: Original MGM Soundtrack, CBS Special Products, 1990.
Brigadoon, 1990.
Singin' in the Rain, CBS Special Products, 1990.

Performer on the original soundtrack albums for films, including *Deep in My Heart,* Metro-Goldwyn-Mayer; *For Me and My Gal,* Soundtrack; *It's Always Fair Weather,* Metro-Goldwyn-Mayer; *Les Girls,* Metro-Goldwyn-Mayer; *The Pirate,* Metro-Goldwyn-Mayer; *Singin' in the Rain,* Metro-Goldwyn-Mayer; and *Summer Stock,* Metro-Goldwyn-Mayer. Performer on the sound recording *Peter Rabbit.*

SIDELIGHTS: Skilled in front of, and behind, the camera as well as onstage, Gene Kelly became a film icon in the 1940s and 1950s for his roles in such musical classics as *On the Town* (1949) and *Singin' in the Rain* (1952). An athletic dancer with a vigorous, yet graceful air, he represented the typical American male at a time when the typical American male was likely to disdain the art of dance. His style was often contrasted with that of another great American film dancer, Fred Astaire, whose image was that of a sleek, top-hatted society beau. Perhaps more importantly, Kelly was an innovator in the filming of dance, creating adventurous techniques for the relatively new big-screen medium and rendering dance sequences into character and plot devices. In the words of a *Contemporary Theatre, Film, and Television* obituary, "Whether he was 'singing in the rain,' spending time 'on the town,' or just being 'an American in Paris,' Kelly delighted audiences with his exceptional dancing, acting, wit, and charm."

Kelly was born in Pittsburgh, Pennsylvania, where his mother, who ran a dancing school, enlisted all five of her children in music and dance lessons. An athletic child, Kelly played football and hockey in high school and dreamed of playing baseball for the Pittsburgh Pirates. Compelled by the Depression to interrupt his education at Pennsylvania State College, he found a job teaching gymnastics at a summer camp. He later graduated from the University of Pittsburgh and went to work in his mother's successful dancing school, which was renamed for him two years later. During the hard years of the Depression, Kelly, often with his brother Fred, danced on local and regional stages and helped direct vaudeville acts. In 1938 he ventured to New York City and landed a job as chorus boy in the musical *Leave It To Me,* featuring Mary Martin. The following year, he was noticed in a considerably larger part, acting the role of a dancer in William Saroyan's play *The Time of*

Your Life, which led to Kelly's role in the 1940 hit musical, *Pal Joey. New York Times* critic John Martin (as quoted by Albin Krebs in the *New York Times* obituary for Kelly), lauded the dancer's performance in *Pal Joey,* noting how Kelly "is not only glib-footed, but he has a feeling for comment and content that give his dancing personal distinction and raise it several notches as a dancing art."

Kelly's success in *Pal Joey* prompted Hollywood film producer David O. Selznick to sign the up-and-coming star to a film contract. Selznick lent Kelly to Metro-Goldwyn-Mayer (MGM), and MGM soon bought out Kelly's contract. It was in Hollywood that Kelly made his permanent mark on the arts of dance and cinema, but it took him a few more years to achieve notable success. Although his first film role, opposite Judy Garland in *For Me and My Gal,* was a hit, his subsequent films offered only small roles. Then MGM lent Kelly to Columbia Pictures for the 1944 *Cover Girl.* For *Cover Girl,* Kelly and director (and future directing collaborator) Stanley Donen created a revolutionary sequence in which Kelly danced with a second image of himself, representing his conscience, producing an effect possible only on screen. Critical response was enthusiastic. A contributor to the *New York Times* (as quoted by Krebs) raved that "for once, a dance on the screen is not merely a specialty but actually develops character and advances plot." Kelly called his cinematic innovations "cine-dancing," and later admitted, "I tried to invent the dance to fit the camera and its movements." He took his innovations a step further in 1945 when, for the film *Anchors Aweigh,* after much lobbying of studio officials, he won permission to film a sequence in which he danced with the animated mouse Jerry, of the *Tom and Jerry* cartoon series. His film innovations were invariably resisted by studio powers, who relented in the face of Kelly's strong, self-confident persuasiveness.

Other filmed dance milestones for Kelly were a duet with Fred Astaire in *Ziegfeld Follies* (1945), a recreation of "Slaughter on Tenth Avenue" in *Words and Music* (1948), and two films with Frank Sinatra: *Take Me Out to the Ball Game* (1948), which Kelly also choreographed, and *On the Town* (1949), which Kelly co-directed with Donen. *On the Town,* filmed mainly in its New York setting, was the first musical to be shot on location. Recalling that film in a 1977 interview, Kelly said, "The picture has dated a bit, but it's the closest to my heart." The 1951 film *An American in Paris* was even more successful. Kelly acted in and choreographed *An American in Paris,*

and won a special Academy Award for his versatile talents as actor, singer, and director, and for his contributions to screen choreography. This film contains a groundbreaking seventeen-minute dance sequence in which Kelly appears against sets inspired by notable painters such as Raoul Dufy, Auguste Renoir, Henri Rousseau, Henri de Toulouse-Lautrec, Maurice Utrillo, and Vincent van Gogh.

Kelly's most famous work is probably the 1952 musical *Singin' in the Rain,* in which he acted as well as choreographed and co-directed with Donen. Dancing to the title song, Kelly larked his way through a downpour, umbrella in hand, in a scene that has been shown on innumerable film clips. One of Kelly's dance partners in that film, Debbie Reynolds, was a novice in her first starring role, and remembered that although director Kelly sometimes became angry with her, "it took a lot of patience for him to work with someone who had never danced before." *Singin' in the Rain* was among the first twenty-five films chosen for preservation in the National Film Registry of the Library of Congress, and has appeared on numerous critics' lists of the top films of all time. According to Scott Harris of the *Los Angeles Times, Singin' in the Rain* is "often called the best musical ever made."

Kelly appeared in several other successful film projects in the 1950s, but the great age of the movie musical was ending. He adapted well to the television era, appearing in specials and, for one season, playing a priest in the series *Going My Way,* a role originated on film by Bing Crosby. His dramatic roles for the big screen included the memorable part of E. K. Hornbeck, the worldly, pro-evolution journalist (modeled upon H. L. Mencken) in *Inherit the Wind* (1960). Kelly also directed movies, such as *Hello, Dolly!* (1969), and narrated three installments of the theatrically released film compilation, *That's Entertainment!* He was engaged in other dance projects as well. In 1956 he created, wrote, starred in, directed, and choreographed a plotless, dialogueless dance film, *Invitation to the Dance.* He created, wrote, narrated, and appeared in a 1958 television special on the dance, "Dancing, A Man's Game," on the series *Omnibus.* In 1958 he also directed the Broadway stage production of the hit musical *Flower Drum Song.* In 1960 he accepted an invitation from the Paris Opera ballet troupe to create a jazz ballet; Kelly's work, set to George Gershwin's *Concerto in F* and entitled *Pas de Dieux,* received more than twenty curtain calls. Kelly received many well-deserved honors for the remainder of his life, without stopping to rest on his laurels. As quoted in a *Los*

Angeles Times obituary, he told an interviewer in 1976, "My only problem is learning how to loaf. . . . I still find it almost impossible to relax for more than one day at a time." He danced onscreen for the last time in *Xanadu* in 1980.

At the time of his death in 1996, Kelly was working on a book in collaboration with his third wife, writer Patricia Ward. He had suffered a series of strokes in 1994 and 1995, and passed away peacefully in his sleep. Hearing of his death, former costar Reynolds told the *Los Angeles Times,* "He made me a star. He taught me how to dance and how to work hard, to be dedicated and yet still loving, as he was to his family and friends." She called Kelly "a cinematic genius [whose] work will influence films forever."

BIOGRAPHICAL/CRITICAL SOURCES:

BOOKS

Basinger, Jeanine, *Gene Kelly,* Pyramid Publications (New York City), 1976.
Burrows, Michael, *Gene Kelly—Versatility Personified,* Primestyle Ltd. (St. Austell, England), 1972.
Hirschorn, Clive, *Gene Kelly: A Biography,* Regnery (Chicago, IL), 1974.
Thomas, Tony, *The Films of Gene Kelly, Song and Dance Man,* Citadel Press (Secaucus, NJ), 1974.

PERIODICALS

American Film, March, 1985, pp. 20-27.
Dance Magazine, December, 1980, p. 108; April, 1996, p. 126.
Entertainment Weekly, February 16, 1996, pp. 15-16; fall, 1996, p. 58.
Good Housekeeping, August, 1983, p. 17.
Harper's Bazaar, January, 1985, pp. 166-169.
Interview, May, 1994, pp. 110-113.
Los Angeles Magazine, May, 1994, pp. 72-79.
New Yorker, March 21, 1994, pp. 166-169.
New York Times Magazine, April 17, 1994, p. 58.
People Weekly, June 15, 1992, p. 86.
Saturday Evening Post, July-August, 1980, pp. 54-57.
Washington Post, February 3, 1996, pp. C1, C6.

OBITUARIES:

BOOKS

Contemporary Theatre, Film, and Television, Volume 16, Gale (Detroit, MI), 1997.

PERIODICALS

Chicago Tribune, February 3, 1996, pp. 1, 11.
Dance Magazine, April, 1996, pp. 94-95.
Entertainment Weekly, February 16, 1996, pp. 14; December 27, 1996, pp. 110-114.
Life, January, 1997, pp. 82-101.
Los Angeles Times, February 3, 1996, p. A1.
Maclean's, February 12, 1996, p. 7.
Newsweek, February 12, 1996, p. 83.
New York Times, February 3, 1996, pp. 1, 13.
People Weekly, February 19, 1996, pp. 36-41.
Time, February 12, 1996, p. 82.
Time for Kids, February 16, 1996, p. 8.
Times (London), February 5, 1996, p. 19.
Variety, February 5, 1996, p. 46.
Washington Post, February 3, 1996, pp. A1, A12.*

*   *   *

KENT, Karen   1941-
(Karma Karen, a pseudonym)

PERSONAL: Born May 19, 1941, in IA; daughter of Norman (a farmer, in business) and Dorothy (Johnson) Blass; married Harold Dean Kent, March, 1956 (marriage ended, May, 1964); children: April Shultz, Alan. *Education:* University of Iowa, B.A., 1969, M.A., 1971, M.F.A., 1972. *Politics:* Liberal democrat. *Religion:* Nondenominational. *Avocational interests:* Art, music, film, theater, swimming, walking, vegetarianism, the occult.

ADDRESSES: Home—Red Hook, NY. *Office*—Read Head Press, P.O. Box 552, Red Hook, NY 12571; fax 518-398-7962. *E-mail*—readhead@taconic.net.

CAREER: Professional photographer, New York City, 1976—.

MEMBER: Professional Women Photographers.

AWARDS, HONORS: Grants from Agfa Corporation and Ilford Corporation.

WRITINGS:

Reflections of New York, Smithmark (New York City), 1991.
Plains and Prairies: Where the West Begins, Smithmark, 1995.
(Under pseudonym Karma Karen) *Love Me Tender: The True Story of Marilyn and the King as Told*

by Karma Karen (fiction), Read Head Press (Red Hook, NY), 1997.

WORK IN PROGRESS: At Home in America, a collection of family photographs.

SIDELIGHTS: Karen Kent told *CA:* "I was married at fifteen, divorced at twenty-two. I returned to finish high school with two young children, and graduated at the top of my class. I then moved to Iowa City, and entered the University of Iowa, earning a Master of Fine Arts degree from the Writer's Workshop there in 1972.

"I moved to New York City in 1976 to pursue a career in photography, which was for me 'visual poetry.' As a photographer, I worked with many clients in corporate, advertising, and editorial capacities. I show my photographs in exhibitions, galleries, and other spaces—public places—in the United States and abroad. The major influences on my work are the poet William Carlos Williams, the painter Edward Hopper, and the photographer Bernice Abbott. In 1991 I did my first book, *Reflections of New York.*

"In 1995 I did another book, *Where the West Begins: America's Plains and Prairies.* I explored the Missouri River states, photographing and writing about the people, the landscape, and the architecture. The book took five years to complete. It gave me a chance to do my home state of Iowa as well.

"In 1994 I started work on *Love Me Tender: The True Story of Marilyn and the King as told by Karma Karen.* This is a fictional work, in which I rewrite [popular culture] mythology in a send-up of kiss-and-tell biographies, with a pulp-fiction attitude. I wanted to give a new interpretation of the circumstances surrounding the deaths of Marilyn Monroe and Elvis Presley, and the death of President John Kennedy. Instead of focusing on their insecurities, I focused on what these people did as revolutionary pioneers in the 1950s and their stature as enduring cultural icons.

"Their secret passion is revealed by their friend and confidant, Karma Karen, a lesbian psychic astrologer, channeler, and tarot reader. They tell their story through her. In spite of the inherent tragedy in the lives of these people, I wanted the book to be a fun read, so I used the pulp-fiction writing style to achieve this.

"After delving into the writing for almost two years, I discovered that what I created also created me.

Even as I wrote, under the pseudonym Karma Karen, I became her in many ways and was compelled to tell this story to answer the question 'What happened?' regarding Elvis's, Marilyn's, and JFK's untimely deaths. This grew out of a desire to find a new way to look at the losses in my own life—by looking at their lives, and retelling their stories, even with the same outcome, the circumstances give a new mythology to them while skewering conventionally held images in history."

*   *   *

KERR, Philip 1956-

PERSONAL: Born in 1956, in Scotland; married Jane Thynne (a journalist); children: two. *Education:* Law school graduate.

ADDRESSES: Home—Wimbledon, England. *Office*—c/o Viking Penguin USA 375 Hudson St. New York, NY 10014.

CAREER: Writer. Previously worked in law, advertising, and journalism.

WRITINGS:

NOVELS

March Violets, Viking (London), 1989.
The Pale Criminal, Viking (London), 1990.
A German Requiem, Viking (London), 1991.
Berlin Noir (contains *March Violets, The Pale Criminal,* and *A German Requiem),* Penguin Books (London), 1993.
A Philosophical Investigation, Chatto & Windus (London), 1992.
Dead Meat, Mysterious Press (New York, NY), 1994.
Gridiron, Chatto & Windus (London), 1995, published as *The Grid,* Warner Books (New York, NY), 1996.

EDITOR

The Penguin Book of Lies (anthology), Penguin (New York, NY), 1990.
The Penguin Book of Fights, Feuds, and Heartfelt Hatreds: An Anthology of Antipathy, Penguin (London), 1993.

OTHER

Also author of screenplays.

WORK IN PROGRESS: A "techno-thriller" entitled *Esau;* a novel entitled *A Five-Year Plan.*

SIDELIGHTS: In 1989, Philip Kerr launched his career as a novelist with *March Violets,* the first of three well-received mysteries set in Nazi-era Berlin that feature a private investigator named Bernhard Gunther. A hard-boiled ex-cop who is always ready with a sarcastic observation or two about life in the Third Reich, Gunther has been described by more than one reviewer as a German Philip Marlowe. In fact, as reviewer Ed Strosser notes in *Armchair Detective,* Kerr's portrayal of his hero "is solidly in the [Raymond] Chandler tradition of the tough guy with a sensitive heart."

The plot of *March Violets* places elements of the standard detective novel against the backdrop of an entire country sliding in dictatorship. A specialist in tracking down missing persons—mostly Jews—Gunther takes on a very different assignment when a powerful German industrialist hires him to find out who murdered his daughter and son-in-law and stole a valuable diamond necklace from their safe before burning down their house. The investigation plunges the detective into a full-blown political scandal involving Hermann Goering and Heinrich Himmler, two of Adolf Hitler's closest aides, and assorted other scrapes with various Gestapo agents, criminals, and even a famous actress.

Writing in the London *Times,* Lisanne Radice praises *March Violets* as "highly original" and finds Gunther "wonderfully sharp and satirical." Fellow *Times* critic Tim Heald notes Kerr "is exceptionally accomplished at time, place, and pace" and has the ability to create "good characters too." A reviewer for *Publishers Weekly* says the author "re-creates the period accurately and with verve. . . . Gunther is a spirited guide through the chaos of 1930s Berlin." Strosser declares *March Violets* to be "a promising first novel."

Gunther surfaces again in Kerr's second novel, *The Pale Criminal.* Set in 1938, a couple of years after *March Violets,* it focuses on a conspiracy involving homosexuality, blackmail, serial murder, and the occult, all of which ultimately have connections with Hitler's brutal SS. Gunther's search for answers once more draws him into the seamy underworld of pre-war Berlin and gives him cause to reflect on the darkness and evil inherent in mankind.

While *Times Literary Supplement* reviewer Savkar Altinel finds Kerr's treatment of his themes "a touch perfunctory" and his slangy language suggestive of "an inept translation," Altinel notes that "the plot . . . is handled with some skill." On the other hand, Tom Nolan of the *Wall Street Journal* thinks Kerr's language is perfectly suited to his subject matter and his main character, a "tarnished knight" who is "by turns vulgar and starkly lyrical." Continues Nolan: "Gunther travels some truly awful boulevards. . . . Kerr renders this dire place and time in an effective and aptly stilted prose that often reads as if translated from the German."

Chris Petit of the London *Times* also hails the author's "notable recreation" of an especially sordid era and reserves special praise for the fact that he makes his historical figures "eerily believable" and "doesn't cheat with hindsight, but lets time and place control his story." In short, observes Strosser in *Armchair Detective,* Kerr uses "mordant humor" and "an abundance of period detail" to fashion "a vivid portrait of life in a city ruled by madmen and doomed to nearly total destruction."

Kerr's third installment in the Gunther series, *A German Requiem,* takes place for the most part not in pre-war Berlin but in postwar Vienna. It is there that Gunther becomes involved in Cold War intrigue with ex-Nazis, the Soviet KGB, and U.S. intelligence. "Rooted in historical details, driven by a powerful narrative, this atmospheric novel traces a frightening course amid a multiplicity of ironies," declares a reviewer for *Publishers Weekly.* Petit, once again commenting in the London *Times,* lists Kerr's strengths as "thorough research" and "evocation of place," noting that both Vienna and Berlin "are artfully recreated" in the pages of *A German Requiem.* Looking back over the entire Gunther series, Christopher Wordsworth concludes in the *Observer* that it is "brutally powerful stuff."

More recently, Kerr has turned his attention to the present and even the near-future as the author of a couple of "techno-thrillers" and a detective story set in modern Russia. *A Philosophical Investigation,* for instance, takes place in London in the year 2013. Technology is being used to help control crime by means of genetic "fingerprinting" and brain scanning that identify those who are prone to violence. But one of these potential killers succeeds in breaking into the computer containing information on his fellow misfits, all of whom have code names corresponding to famous philosophers and writers. He then erases his own name from the database and begins murdering the others one by one in a misguided attempt to purge society of its most dangerous elements. Assigned to solve the case is a tough, man-hating detective named Isadora "Jake" Jakowicz. She is soon drawn into the killer's bizarre game.

Nolan of the *Wall Street Journal* calls *A Philosophical Investigation* "one of the more imaginative thrillers in quite a while," adding that the "inventive procedural [moves] swiftly as [Kerr] combines teleological speculations with nitty-gritty futuristic police work." Scott Veale makes a similar observation in the *New York Times Book Review,* noting that "Kerr clearly has more on his mind than standard slasher fiction" as he lays out his "bleak, nasty vision of a future world." The vivid depiction of that vision is, in fact, what Lucasta Miller of the *New Statesman & Society* finds most impressive about *A Philosophical Investigation.* She admires "the plausibility with which Philip Kerr constructs his sinister vision of Britain in the 21st century. . . . With an observant eye for detail, [he] reveals a fine-tuned ability to make his fiction credible by combining the futuristic with the familiar."

Others take *A Philosophical Investigation* a bit less seriously than its subject matter might dictate. Commenting in the *Spectator,* for instance, Harriet Waugh says that the inclusion of so much moral philosophy in the novel proves to be "rather fun and gives Mr. Kerr leeway for some amusing high jinks. . . . The only real criticism of [his book] is that it is enjoyable rather than truly racy and hair raising." S.M. Tyson of the *Armchair Detective* also praised the book's "wicked humor and social satire," declaring it to be "true brain candy . . . that deserves a wide general audience beyond the mystery and science fiction lovers who are bound to delight in it."

Kerr followed *A Philosophical Investigation* with a more conventional thriller entitled *Dead Meat.* It follows two Russian detectives who join forces in St. Petersburg as they battle corruption, bureaucracy, and a lack of resources while trying to contend with the organized crime syndicate known as the Russian Mafia. As with his previous novels, reviewers praise Kerr's skillful evocation of the grim and desperate land in which the action takes place—perhaps the book's "most interesting" feature, in fact, according to Newgate Callendar in the *New York Times Book*

Review. Donald H. Buck, writing in *Armchair Detective,* also found that the author "successfully blends a fascinating picture of daily life and an equally engrossing police investigation."

With his next novel, *The Grid,* Kerr returned to the techno-thriller genre, cementing his reputation as one of Great Britain's most successful young writers. His setting this time is Los Angeles in the near future, where the central computer ("Abraham") that runs a brand-new, fully automated, high-rise office tower suddenly (and with deadly intent) turns on the people who designed, built, and work in it. Stopping Abraham becomes the responsibility of a police detective and an assistant to the tower's architect. Woven throughout the plot of what *People* magazine critic J.D. Reed describes as a "tale of ego and electronics run riot" are Kerr's thought-provoking observations on modern technology and architecture and big-city life, all of which he regards with pessimism.

Commenting in the *Times Literary Supplement,* Julian Ferraro remarks that "the fictional world of *[The Grid]* is in many respects familiar" and "reads like the 'book of the film' before the film has even been made." Continues Ferraro: "It does, however, add some entertaining postmodern twists to the computer paranoia movies of the 1970s. . . . [It] is well constructed and reasonably gripping."

A reviewer for *Publishers Weekly* is more enthusiastic, calling *The Grid* a "mindbending thriller, sure and savvy" adding that the book "will make readers think twice the next time they enter a high-rise—and thrice the next time they boot up a computer."

BIOGRAPHICAL/CRITICAL SOURCES:

PERIODICALS

Armchair Detective, fall, 1990, p. 473; summer, 1991, p. 345; winter, 1994, p. 104; fall, 1994, pp. 486-487.
Economist, November 10, 1990, p. 109.
Kirkus Reviews, May 15, 1989, pp. 720-721.
London Review of Books, October 11, 1990, pp. 10-12.
Maclean's, May 13, 1996, p. 49.
Nation, June 7, 1993, pp. 788-800.
New Statesman & Society, October 5, 1990, p. 44; September 25, 1992, pp. 53-54.
New York Times Book Review, June 13, 1993, p. 20; May 22, 1994, p. 39.
Observer, May 14, 1989, p. 50; December 6, 1992, p. 57; April 25, 1993.

People, June 3, 1996, p. 36.

Publishers Weekly, June 9, 1989, p. 56; August 16, 1991, pp. 49-50; April 25, 1994, p. 60; February 5, 1996, p. 75; April 8, 1996, pp. 43-44.

Spectator, August 28, 1993, pp. 32-33.

Times (London), June 3, 1989; May 17, 1990; May 19, 1990; April 18, 1991.

Times Literary Supplement, June 29, 1990, p. 704; December 4, 1992, p. 32; June 9, 1995, p. 29.

Wall Street Journal, September 20, 1990, p. A12; May 17, 1993, p. A14.*

*   *   *

KHALID, Farooq   1950-

PERSONAL: Born May 27, 1950, in Lahore, Pakistan; immigrated to the Netherlands; son of Mohammad Hussain (in bank service) and Nazar (a homemaker; maiden name, Begam) Khalid; married Nicolette Munting (a homemaker), December 30, 1984; children: Mubeen, Shasha Nazar.

ADDRESSES: Home—Amsterdam, The Netherlands.

CAREER: Freelance writer and translator, c. 1977—.

MEMBER: PEN International, Holland.

AWARDS, HONORS: Aadamji Award (Pakistan) for *Black Mirrors,* 1978.

WRITINGS:

NOVELS

Siah Ainey, Maktaba Meri Library (Lahore, Pakistan), 1977; translated by Eric Cyprian as *Black Mirrors,* J. Cape (London, England), 1987.

Apni Duaoon Kay Aseer (title means "Prisoners of Their Own Prayers"), Qausain (Lahore, Pakistan), 1986.

Also translator of several Dutch novels into the Urdu language, including *Max Havelaar* by Multatuli; and *Van Oude Mensen de dingen die voorbijgaan* and *Eline Vere* by Louis Couperus.

SIDELIGHTS: Pakistani novelist Farooq Khalid's first book, *Black Mirrors,* saw print in his native country in 1977, then was translated for readers of English by Eric Cyprian in 1987. He followed this with another novel published in Pakistan, 1986's *Apni Duaoon Kay Aseer.* In addition to creating his own fiction, Khalid is responsible for the translation of several Dutch novels into the Urdu language.

Black Mirrors is the story of several quirky characters who live in and around a dilapidated hotel in Pakistan, and who interact with each other after a dead newborn baby is found nearby. There is a narrating character, Munir, a friend of Aziz, one of the hotel's occupants, but many other sections of the novel are related in third person. Andrew Hislop, reviewing *Black Mirrors* in the *Times Literary Supplement* described it as "part metaphysical black mystery tale, part philosophical, comically seedy soap." He had high praise for Khalid's use of metaphor in the story, because the metaphor is rooted in the Urdu language (and faithfully translated), and therefore fresh to English-language readers. Hislop asserted, however, that "*Black Mirrors* seems born of an imagination whose associations would startle in any language, and whose metaphors would never age easily into 'naturalness.'" Alamgir Hashmi in *World Literature Today* also affirmed that "the English translation . . . retains strongly the flavor of the original idiom."

BIOGRAPHICAL/CRITICAL SOURCES:

PERIODICALS

Times Literary Supplement, April 3, 1987, p. 361.

World Literature Today, summer, 1989, p. 539.

*   *   *

KIDMAN, Fiona (Judith)   1940-

PERSONAL: Born March 26, 1940, in Hawera, New Zealand; daughter of Hugh and Flora Cameron (Small) Eakin; married Ernest Ian R. Kidman, August 20, 1960; children: one son, one daughter.

ADDRESSES: Home—28 Rakau Rd., Hataitai, Wellington 3, New Zealand. *Agent*—Ray Richards, Richards Literary Agency, P. O. Box 31-240, Milford, Auckland, New Zealand.

CAREER: Writer. Worked as high-school librarian, 1961-62; writer, 1962—.

MEMBER: International P.E.N., New Zealand Book Council (president, 1992-95), New Zealand Writers' Guild, Media Women.

AWARDS, HONORS: Scholarships in letters, 1981, 1985, and 1991; Mobil Short Story Award, 1987, for "Earthly Shadows"; Award for Achievement from Queen Elizabeth II Arts Council, 1988; Fiction Award, New Zealand Book Council 1988, for *The Book of Secrets;* named officer of Order of British Empire, 1988; writing fellowship, Victorian University, 1988; President of Honour, New Zealand Book Council, 1997.

WRITINGS:

NOVELS

A Breed of Women, Harper (Australia), 1979, Viking Penguin (New York City), 1988.
Mandarin Summer, Heinemann (Exeter, NH), 1981.
Paddy's Puzzle, Heinemann, 1983, published as *In the Clear Light,* Norton (New York City), 1985.
The Book of Secrets, Heinemann, 1987.
True Stars, Random Century, 1990.
Richochet Baby, Vintage, 1996.
The House Within, Vintage, 1997.

SHORT STORIES

Mrs. Dixon and Friends, Heinemann, 1982.
Unsuitable Friends, Heinemann, 1988.
The Foreign Woman, Vintage (Auckland, New Zealand), 1993.

POETRY

Honey and Bitters, Pegasus Press (Christchurch, New Zealand), 1975.
On the Tightrope, Pegasus Press, 1978.
Going to the Chathams, Poems: 1977-1984, Heinemann (Auckland, New Zealand), 1985.
Wakeful Nights: Poems Selected and New, Vintage, 1991.

OTHER

Search for Sister Blue (radio play), Reed (Wellington, New Zealand), 1975.
(With Jane Ussher) *Gone North* (travel), Heinemann, 1984.
(With Grant Sheehan) *Wellington,* Random, 1989.
Palm Prints (biographical sketches), Vintage, 1994.

Author of column in *Listener,* 1972-76. Contributor to periodicals.

WORK IN PROGRESS: A novel.

SIDELIGHTS: Fiona Kidman is a versatile New Zealand writer who has received particular attention for both her novels and her short story collections. Kidman's first novel, *A Breed of Women,* sparked controversy by grimly portraying the plight of women in 1970s New Zealand. The novel's central figure is Harriet, a young farm girl who becomes a successful poet and television host. Fleur Adcock, writing in the *Times Literary Supplement,* affirmed that Kidman "takes Harriet through all the bloody transition points of female life, from first menstruation to defloration to the birth of her first child, each of them traumatic and attended by ritually brutal male contempt."

Mandarin Summer, Kidman's next novel, is an unsettling tale of deceit and incest as related by an adolescent girl. In the tale, rich European settlers swindle and enslave a family of war-traumatized aboriginal New Zealanders. The domineering European patriarch, however, has difficulties maintaining both his drug-addicted wife and his mistress. Events culminate in an immense fire.

In 1983 Kidman issued *Paddy's Puzzle,* which was later published in the United States as *In the Clear Light.* This novel charts the hardships endured by a mother and daughter from the Depression to the aftermath of World War II. Among the mother's tribulations are poverty and the sudden departure of her husband. The daughter finds love and understanding briefly with an African American marine but eventually enters into prostitution before falling ill with tuberculosis. Barbara Fisher Williamson, writing in the *New York Times Book Review,* noted that "a mournful, elegiac quality runs through this novel."

The Book of Secrets, published in 1988, is among Kidman's more structurally complex novels. Unfolding through correspondence, recollection, and journal entries, *The Book of Secrets* recounts the experiences of three generations of women and the patriarch who dominated them. Aging, eccentric, and witch-like, Marie McClure lives isolated in a simple cottage at the outskirts of her village and is haunted by the memories of her mother and grandmother and the family that rejected her for having a love affair. *Times Literary Supplement* reviewer Tom Aitken observed that "the moral argument—feminist but never shrill—is sustained and illuminated by sharp visual images."

Kidman's next novel, *True Stars,* details romance and political intrigue during the decline of a Labor Party government in New Zealand. The novel features a range of characters from the spectrum of social classes, and it delineates the manner in which political enthusiasm degenerates into despair.

Aside from writing novels, Kidman has also published such short story-collections as *Mrs. Dixon and Friends, Unsuitable Friends,* and *The Foreign Woman. The Foreign Woman,* like many of Kidman's novels, concentrates on women's issues and predicaments. In the *Australian Book Review,* Heather Neilson wrote: "The women who inhabit Fiona Kidman's short stories are foreign in different ways, and with varying degrees of self-awareness. For some the struggle is to establish themselves in a new environment, or in a profession; others are estranged from their own histories, or within their own families." Notable among the tales in *The Foreign Woman* are "Nobody Else," in which a young girl, who is gradually realizing that she is a lesbian, listens as her parents' budding relationship is recalled by her mother; "Border Country," wherein a woman accompanies her husband to Vietnam, where he hopes to somehow fathom the recent suicide of a fellow veteran; and the title tale, in which a New Zealand woman comes to realize the value of her father's foreign ancestry.

Kidman has published several volumes of poetry, including *Wakeful Nights: Poems Selected and New,* which appeared in 1991. She has also written radio plays, including *Search for Sister Blue;* published, in collaboration with Jane Ussher, the travel volume *Gone North;* and completed *Palm Prints,* which features biographical sketches of various women.

BIOGRAPHICAL/CRITICAL SOURCES:

PERIODICALS

American Studies International, October, 1995, pp. 1-16.
Australian Book Review, July, 1994, pp. 44-45.
New York Times Book Review, July 28, 1985, p. 18; February 5, 1988, p. 133.
Times Literary Supplement, March 13, 1981, p. 279.
Washington Post Book World, September 14, 1986, p. 12.

*   *   *

KIHLMAN, Christer Alfred 1930-

PERSONAL: Born June 14, 1930, in Helsinki, Finland; son of Bertel Lorenzo (a translator, novelist, and editor) and Karin (Bolinder) Kihlman; married Selinda Enckell, June 1, 1956; children: Nina, Jerker. *Politics:* Social Democrat.

ADDRESSES: Home—Sveinsgatan 27 B, Esbo, Finland 02730. *Agent*—Peter Owen, London, England.

CAREER: Novelist. Reviewer, Helsinki *Nya Pressen,* and Stockholm *Dagens Nyheter.* Co-publisher (with Jorn Donner), *Arena* (literary magazine).

MEMBER: International PEN.

WRITINGS:

Den Bla Modern, 1963, translated by Joan Tate as *The Blue Mother,* afterword by George C. Schoolfield, University of Nebraska Press (Lincoln, NE), 1990.
Dyre Prins, 1975; translated by Joan Tate as *Sweet Prince,* Peter Owen (London), 1983.
Alla Mina Soner, Alba (Stockholm), 1980; translated as *All My Sons,* 1984.
Livsdrommen Rena: Bok om Maktloshet (title means "The Pure Dream of Life: Book about Powerlessness"), Soderstrom (Helsinki)/Alba (Stockholm), 1982.
De Nakna Och de Saliga (erotic poems), illustrations by Henrik Tikkannen, Soderstrom (Helsinki), 1983.
Pa Drift i Forlustens Landskap (title means "Adrift in the Landscape of Loss"), Alba (Stockholm), 1986.
Gert Bladhs Undergang, Soderstrom (Helsinki), 1987, translated by Joan Tate as *The Downfall of Gerdt Bladh,* Peter Owen (London), 1989.

Also the author of *Se Upp Salige!* (title means, "Pay Heed, O Blest!"), 1960, *Madeleine,* 1965, *Inblandningar, Utmaningar,* 1969, and *Manniskan Som Skalv* (title means "The Human Being Who Trembled"), 1971.

PLAYS

Tio Steg Pa Manens Yta, 1970.
Hundarna i Casablanca, 1976.
(With Frej Lindkvist) *SK 911 till Acapulco,* 1978.

OTHER

Author of the article "Svenskhetens Slgskugga," 1959, translation published as "The Shadow Cast by Swedishness" in 1986.

SIDELIGHTS: One of the most prominent contemporary Finnish novelists, Christer Alfred Kihlman was born into the Swedish-speaking upper class of his country in 1930. One of his great-grandfathers was a well-known politician, teacher, and industrialist, a grandfather was a renowned anti-Czarist judge, and Kihlman's father was a man of letters who edited an important Finnish journal, *Nys Argus*. Kihlman rebelled against his privileged background, criticizing the bourgeoisie of his country throughout his career and posing as an angry rebel in his youth; yet in another sense he followed in the literary tradition of his family. After gaining initial attention with an article critical of the influence of Swedish culture on the upper class of Finland, Kihlman became a full-fledged national celebrity with his first novel, the 1960 *Se Upp Salige!* ("Pay Heed, O Blest!"). Set in a provincial town, the novel portrays hypocrisies among the town's rulers and the tragedies that befall the family of the newspaper editor who uncovers those hypocrisies. The book's reception in Finland was divided, with some readers and reviewers hailing it as a masterpiece of contemporary literature and others reviling it for its criticisms of Finnish society.

Three years later, Kihlman followed his first novel with *Den Bla Modern* ("The Blue Mother"), a work set in the same provincial town and involving the same newspaper editor and his family, as well as another family, the Lindermanns. The book is narrated by the two Lindermann brothers: Benno, a sexually abused homosexual who fantasizes about being a World War II Nazi commandant at the Auschwitz concentration camp, and Raf, a bitterly satirical author. Both brothers yearn for an idealized maternal figure, the 'blue mother' of the title. On the book's American publication in 1990, a *Publishers Weekly* contributor described Kihlman's writing as "passionate and, ultimately, hopeful," though the reviewer found some of the book's extremes unsavory. *Booklist* critic Danny Rochman called the novel "brutally honest" and recommended it as "strong stuff." The third novel by Kihlman, the 1965 *Madeleine,* takes place on the day of the assassination of U.S. president John F. Kennedy and is narrated in diary form. In contrast to its predecessors, it is short and idyllic in tone.

In 1966, Kihlman vowed not to write any more novels; he turned to a confessional mode in 1971 with *Manniskan som Skalv* ("The Human Being Who Trembled"). Providing an autobiographical account that includes tales of alcoholism and bisexuality, the author insists that his motive for telling his own story

is a desire to help reform society through candor. The book was a best-seller in both the Swedish and the Finnish languages and persuaded its author to reconsider his self-imposed ban on fiction writing.

His novel *Dyre Prins* ("Sweet Prince") appeared in 1975. The book, which again follows the fortunes of the Lindermann family (through a member by marriage, the industrialist Donal Blaadh), has been compared to Thomas Mann's *Buddenbrooks,* a classic European bourgeois family chronicle. It was published in English in 1983 as *Sweet Prince.* The book received a largely negative review in the *Times Literary Supplement* from the British poet and critic D. J. Enright, who found fault with both the author and the translator on stylistic grounds and also criticized the author for thematic weaknesses. In the *Observer,* however, Hermione Lee called the novel "sprawling, verbose, patchy, but interesting."

Kihlman returned to confessionals with the 1980 *Alla Mina Soner* ("All My Sons") and the 1982 *Livsdrommen Rena: Bok om Maktloshet* ("The Pure Dream of Life: Book about Powerlessness"), both of which describe the author's involvements with young male prostitutes in South America. (Kihlman had gone to that continent in order to research further volumes of his family chronicle fiction). George C. Schoolfield, reviewing the books in separate volumes of *World Literature Today,* admitted discomfort with both, and referred to Kihlman as "a fine intelligence that can also be maudlin and bland." In 1983, Kihlman's book of erotic poems was published, with pictures by a deceased friend, Henrik Tikkanen. Schoolfield, in *World Literature Today,* did not find the sexual aspects of the book shocking, but called the volume "a sometimes mysterious and by no means nugatory addition to the bibliography/iconography" of its author and its illustrator.

The author's next volume of memoirs, the 1986 *Pa Drift i Forlustens Landskap* ("Adrift in the Landscape of Loss") is a bitter work about Kihlman's wife's infidelity and Kihlman's own struggle with writing. Schoolfield, reviewing the work in *World Literature Today,* expressed fundamental doubts about Kihlman's "compulsion" to continue in the confessional mode, which the critic felt had reached an impasse. Nevertheless, Schoolfield admitted, "no more graceful or memorable artist of prose is at work in the Swedish language today."

In 1987, Kihlman offered a sequel to *Sweet Prince: Gerdt Bladhs Undergang,* published in English as *The*

Downfall of Gerdt Bladh. The title character, the head of a department store, undergoes a personal and financial breakdown in what a *Publishers Weekly* contributor called "an unremittingly bleak but compelling" novel. The reviewer savored both the novel's "straightforward yet powerful" narrative sections and Gerdt's "apocalyptic" interior monologues. Schoolfield, in *World Literature Today,* was disturbed by the apparent layers of semi-autobiography in the novel and by the author's tendency to inject political commentary into fiction; he added, however, "Kihlman still has his acute powers of social observation, and he has kept his ability to re-create atmospheres." The reviewer concluded that the 1987 novel would be "of great interest to any faithful Kihlman observer . . . and the author's career remains worthy of close observation."

BIOGRAPHICAL/CRITICAL SOURCES:

PERIODICALS

Booklist, April 15, 1990, p. 1607.
Observer, July 10, 1983.
Publishers Weekly, November 10, 1989, p. 50; March 2, 1990, p. 79.
Times Literary Supplement, July 29, 1983, p. 804.
World Literature Today, autumn, 1981, p. 687; winter, 1984, p. 118; winter, 1985, pp. 113-14; summer, 1987, p. 460; autumn, 1988, pp. 673-74.*

*   *   *

KILLEBREW, Harmon (Clayton, Jr.) 1936-

PERSONAL: Born June 29, 1936, in Payette, ID; son of H. C. (a house painter and sheriff) and Katherine Pearl May (Culver) Killebrew; married Elaine Roberts, October 1, 1955; children: Cameron, Kenneth, Shawn, Kathryn, Erin. *Education:* Attended College of Idaho. *Religion:* Mormon. *Avocational interests:* Hunting.

ADDRESSES: Home—P. O. Box 1969, Kansas City, MO 64141.

CAREER: Washington Senators (professional baseball team), Washington, DC, player, 1954-60; Minnesota Twins (professional baseball team), Minneapolis, MN, player, 1961-74; Kansas City Royals (professional baseball team), Kansas City, MO, player,

1975; WTCN-TV, Minneapolis, broadcaster, 1976-78; KPIX-TV, San Francisco, CA, broadcaster of Oakland A's baseball games, 1979-82; KTLA-TV, Los Angeles, CA, broadcaster of California Angels baseball games, 1983; Spectrum Sports, Minneapolis, broadcaster of Minnesota Twins baseball games, 1984—. Partner and agent of Killebrew, Harding & Harper Insurance and Securities Sales, 1976—; owner and dealer of Killebrew Motors, 1984. Organizer and director of Danny Thompson Memorial Golf Tournament, 1977—.

MEMBER: Elks.

AWARDS, HONORS: Named to American League All-Star Team, 1959-71; named American League Player of the Year by *Sporting News,* American League Most Valuable Player, and recipient of Babe Ruth Sultan of Swat Award, all 1969; Lou Gehrig Award, 1971; named to Idaho Sports Hall of Fame, 1979; Idaho Distinguished Citizen Award, 1981; named to Baseball Hall of Fame, 1984; honorary captain of American League All-Star Team, 1985.

WRITINGS:

(With Dave Campbell, Brooks Robins, and Duke Snider) *The Scouting Report: 1986,* edited by Marybeth Sullivan, Harper (New York), 1986.

SIDELIGHTS: Harmon Killebrew is a former baseball player who ranks among the game's all-time greatest sluggers. Killebrew began his major-league career with the Washington Senators in 1954. Throughout Killebrew's first five years in the Senators organization, he played only occasionally at the major-league level, and he marked himself as both an undisciplined batter and a mediocre fielder. But in 1959 Senators' management finally decided to play Killebrew regularly at third base. Killebrew quickly repaid the favor by blasting several home runs, including eight in less than two weeks. He ended the 1959 season with forty-two home runs, enough to tie him with the Cleveland Indians' Rocky Colavito for leadership of the American League.

In 1960, after the Senators moved to Minnesota and renamed themselves the Twins, Killebrew began the season with a batting slump, but he revived himself and managed thirty-one homers. The following season ranks among his greatest: he hit forty-six home runs and realized a batting average of .288. In 1962 Killebrew continued his impressive production rate by smashing forty-eight home runs, enough for him to again lead the American League, and he drove in 126 runs, also leading the league. During the next two seasons he continued to lead the American League in home runs, with forty-five and forty-nine, respectively, and he began showing some prowess as a fielder.

Killebrew's 1965 season was abbreviated by injury, though he still managed twenty five home runs. That season, the Twins won the American League pennant but lost the World Series to the National League's Los Angeles Dodgers. The next season, Killebrew hit thirty-nine homers and finished with a batting average of .281. In 1967 he hit another forty-four home runs, best in the American League, but in 1968 he once again suffered an injury. He proved himself fully recovered by 1969, though, and blasted a league-leading forty-nine home runs. In addition, he led the league by driving in 140 runs. That year, the Twins finished first in the American League's West Division, but the team lost the league championship series to the Baltimore Orioles, leaders of the East Division. Killebrew, however, won significant personal honor, being accorded both the American League's Most Valuable Player Award and the Sporting News's Player-of-the-Year Award.

The year 1970 would prove Killebrew's last great season as a slugger. That year he hit forty-one home runs and managed a batting average of .271. The next year his home run production dropped to twenty eight and his batting average declined to .254, although he once again led the league in runs batted in with 119. Killebrew played only four more seasons, finishing in 1975 with the Kansas City Royals.

Killebrew retired with 573 home runs, which ranked him fifth as of 1995, and a home-run percentage of 7.0, good enough for third as of 1995. On six occasions he led the American League in home runs, and six seasons he also led the league in home-run percentage. His career batting average was .256, while his career fielding average was .981. In addition he scored 1283 runs and drove in 1584. Killebrew also finished with 1699 strikeouts, placing him tenth as of 1995. And he ended with 1559 walks, including a league-leading 145 in 1969, the year he was acknowledged as the league's most valuable player.

After ending his professional playing career, Killebrew turned to sports broadcasting. From 1976 to 1978 he worked as an announcer on television broadcasts of Twins games. He next spent four years announcing televised games of the Oakland A's In 1983 he switched to televised games of the California Angels.

But in 1984 he returned to Minneapolis to resume work broadcasting Twins games.

In addition to his broadcasting endeavors, Killebrew has participated in various business ventures, including an insurance company and an automobile dealership. He has also served as organizer and director of the Danny Thomas Memorial Golf Tournament, a charitable event held in Sun Valley, Idaho.

In 1986 Killebrew collaborated with Dave Campbell, Brooks Robinson, and Duke Snider on *The Scouting Report: 1986,* which profiles various baseball players. Killebrew was named to the Baseball Hall of Fame in 1984.

BIOGRAPHICAL/CRITICAL SOURCES:

PERIODICALS

Globe and Mail (Toronto), May 10, 1986.
Sports Illustrated, June 1, 1959; April 8, 1963.
Time, August 14, 1964, p. 44.*

* * *

KIMBALL, Robert (Eric) 1939-

PERSONAL: Born August 23, 1939, in New York, NY; son of Morris Harold and Eve (Schulman) Kimball; married Abigail Leon Kuflik, May 23, 1972; children: Philip Zachary, Miranda Erica. *Education:* Yale University, B.A., 1961, LL.B., 1967.

ADDRESSES: Home—180 W. 58th St., New York, NY 10019.

CAREER: Yale Collection of Literature and American Musical Theatre, New Haven, CT, curator, 1967-71; *New York Post,* New York City, music and dance reviewer, 1973-87, chief classical music critic, 1987-88; Roxbury Records, president, 1988—; writer. Lecturer at Yale University, 1970 and 1974; senior research fellow and visiting professor of music at Brooklyn College of the City University of New York's Institute for Studies in American Music, 1974-75; lecturer in Drama at New York University, 1979-80; lecturer in music at Yale University, 1980-81.

MEMBER: Theatre Library Association, Folio Society, Trollope Society, Dutch Treat Club, Elihu Club, Elizabethan Club of Tale, Freighter Travel Club.

AWARDS, HONORS: Carnegie fellowship, 1961-62; *Drama Desk* Award, 1987, for recovering lost manuscripts.

WRITINGS:

(With William Bolcom) *Reminiscing with Sissle and Blake,* Viking (New York), 1973.
(With Alfred Simon) *The Gershwins,* Atheneum, 1973.
(With Tommy Krasker) *Catalog of the American Musical: Musicals of Irving Berlin, George and Ira Gershwin, Cole Porter, Richard Rodgers and Lorenz Hart,* National Institute for Opera and Musical Theatre, 1988.

Contributor to *Grove's Dictionary of Music.* Contributor to periodicals. Contributor of notes—sometimes in collaboration with Alfred Simon—to recordings.

EDITOR

Cole, Holt (New York), 1971.
The Complete Lyrics of Cole Porter, foreword by John Updike, Knopf (New York), 1983.
(With Dorothy Hart) *The Complete Lyrics of Lorenz Hart,* Knopf, 1986.
The Complete Lyrics of Ira Gershwin, Knopf, 1993.

Also the editor of *The Unpublished Cole Porter,* 1975.

SIDELIGHTS: Robert Kimball is a musicologist with particular expertise in twentieth-century musical theatre. Among his early publications is *Cole,* a volume devoted to songwriter Cole Porter, who enjoyed widespread popularity in the 1930s. This comprehensive book, which Kimball edited, features numerous photographs and a generous number of Porter's lyrics. In addition, it includes a biographical essay supplied by Brendan Gill, a longtime theatre writer for the *New Yorker.* John Lahr, writing in the *New York Times Book Review,* praised *Cole* as "everything Porter would have wanted out of literature," and he noted that Kimball "has made a fine selection of his songs . . . and given us a definitive discography and chronology." Another reviewer described *Cole* in the *Times Literary Supplement* as "rather more than a casual book," and Robert Mazzocco, in his *New York Review of Books* appraisal, called Cole Porter "the purest of the pop composers," deeming the volume "a splashy affair." Mazzocco concluded that "the selections, on the whole, seem just." *Newsweek's* Walter Clemons, meanwhile, affirmed that *Cole* "lifts

one's spirits the way [Porter's] tunes do." Clemons also acknowledged the book's "remarkable personal photographs from the 1920s and '30s" and declared that *Cole* manages "to evoke the era of which Porter was as representative a figure as Erte, Lindbergh or Scott Fitzgerald."

In 1973 Kimball and Alfred Simon published *The Gershwins,* an account of composer George Gershwin and his lyricist brother, Ira. The Gershwin brothers collaborated on many of the twentieth century's most memorable songs before George's untimely death at age thirty nine. Like the earlier *Cole, The Gershwins* includes numerous photos and a broad range of documentation. Hans Keller, writing in the *Times Literary Supplement,* ranked Gershwin with Ludwig van Beethoven as "arguably the most successful composers ever." Keller noted Kimball and Simon's feat in having unearthed "fascinating documents" in *The Gershwins,* while Walter Clemons wrote in the *New York Times Book Review* that *The Gershwins* "is a collage biography distinguished by solid, unobtrusive scholarship and filled with evocative, unfamiliar photographs."

Kimball has also written and edited various volumes devoted to the works of various lyricists of distinction. In 1984 he finished the compiling of *The Complete Lyrics of Cole Porter,* which Stefan Kanfer described in *Time* as "a model of typography, design, and scholarship." Two years later, Kimball produced, in collaboration with Dorothy Hart, *The Complete Lyrics of Lorenz Hart,* which includes the lyrics that Lorenz Hart supplied to composer Richard Rodgers's music in creating such tunes as "Blue Moon," "My Funny Valentine," and "Isn't It Romantic," as well as such stage productions as *Pal Joey* and *On Your Toes. New York Times* reviewer Michiko Kakutani, who described the Rodgers-Hart ouvre as "a huge, sparkling body of work," deemed *The Complete Lyrics of Lorenz Hart* "sumptuous." And in 1993 Kimball completed his work as editor of *The Complete Lyrics of Ira Gershwin,* which features the lyrics to nearly three hundred songs, including such collaborations with George Gershwin as "The Man I Love," "S' Wonderful," and "I Got Rhythm." Sheldon Harnick, writing in the *New York Times Book Review,* called this volume "a book that should be in every library in the country, instantly available to all budding lyricists, and in the home of everyone who has an interest in the art of the musical theater."

Kimball has taught at Yale University and has been a music critic for the *New York Post.* Among his other publications are *Reminiscing with Sissle and Blake,* written with William Bolcom; *Catalog of the American Musical: Musicals of Irving Berlin, George and Ira Gershwin, Cole Porter, Richard Rodgers and Lorenz Hart,* written with Tomy Krasker; and *The Unpublished Cole Porter.*

BIOGRAPHICAL/CRITICAL SOURCES:

PERIODICALS

Chicago Tribune, May 24, 1987.
Newsweek, December 20, 1971.
New York Review of Books, January 27, 1972, pp. 3-4.
New York Times, November 22, 1986.
New York Times Book Review, December 19, 1971, p. 1; September 23, 1973, pp. 3, 49-50; December 5, 1993, p. 6.
Time, February 6, 1984, pp. 71-72.
Times Literary Supplement, September 13, 1974, p. 970.*

*   *   *

KNEELAND, Linda Clarke   1947-

PERSONAL: Born May 29, 1947, in Baltimore, MD; daughter of Julian Sangston (in sales) and Beatrice (a homemaker; maiden name, Cookling) Clarke; married Chase E. Kneeland (a psychotherapist), December 16, 1972; children: Stephanie, Katie. *Education:* Ursinus College, B.A., 1970; Chestnut Hill College, M.S., 1991. *Religion:* Protestant. *Avocational interests:* Botanical illustration, choir, gardening, developing friendships.

ADDRESSES: Home and office—2021 Berks Rd., Lancaster, PA 19446. *E-mail*—LindaCKnee@aol.com.

CAREER: Northwestern Corp., Philadelphia, PA, group therapist, 1991-93; writer, 1993—.

MEMBER: American Association of University Women, Pennsylvania Horticulture Society, Down Syndrome Interest Group.

WRITINGS:

Cookie, illustrated by Todd Fargo, Jason & Nordic (Hollidaysburg, PA), 1989.

SIDELIGHTS: Linda Clarke Kneeland commented: "I was brought into writing by the publishers at Jason & Nordic because I had written for a local newspaper and was the parent of a five-year-old daughter with Down Syndrome. There is a lack of reading material for children with disabilities, and the mission of the publisher was to provide such books in a story context relevant to these kids.

"The book I wrote was based on our actual experience of having difficulty communicating with my daughter and both her frustrations and our frustrations with that. With the help of a speech therapist who introduced a visual/sensory approach to communication (children's sign language) we were finally, delightedly, able to understand one another.

"I am so grateful to those people who were able to help us, and I was delighted to contribute our story in a way that might help others."

*   *   *

KNOX, Elizabeth (Fiona)   1959-

PERSONAL: Born February 15, 1959, in Wellington, New Zealand; daughter of Ray Knox (a journalist) and Heather Douglas (a librarian) Knox; married Fergus Barrowman (a publisher), 1989; children: one son. *Education:* Victoria University, B.A., 1986. *Religion:* "Atheist."

ADDRESSES: Home—74 Glen Rd., Kelburn, Wellington, New Zealand. *Agent*— Christina Arneson, Christina Arneson Agency.

CAREER: Writer. Worked as tutor in film studies at Victoria University, 1989-95; worked variously as a clerk, printer, insurance underwriter, computer operator, editor, web page editor, publicity officer, and shop assistant.

AWARDS, HONORS: Award from P.E.N., 1988, for *After Z-Hour;* P.E.N. fellowship, 1991; New Zealand Book Award, shortlisting, for *Treasure.*

WRITINGS:

NOVELS

After Z-Hour, Victoria University Press (Wellington, New Zealand), 1987.

Paremata, Victoria University Press, 1989.
Treasure, Victoria University Press, 1992.
Pomare, Victoria University Press, 1994.
Glamour and the Sea, Victoria University Press, 1996.

Contributor to *Cherries on a Plate: New Zealand Writers Talk About Their Sisters,* edited by Marilyn Duckworth, Random House New Zealand (Auckland), 1996.

OTHER

Short stories represented in anthologies, including *Now See Hear!,* edited by Ian Wedde and Gregory Burke, Victoria University Press, 1990; *Soho Square 4,* edited by Bill Manhire, Bloomsbury, 1991; *Pleasures and Dangers,* edited by Wystan Curnow and Trish Clark, Moet and Chandon/Longman Paul, 1992; *Into the Field of Play,* edited by Lloyd Jones, Tandem, 1992; and *The Picador Anthology of Contemporary New Zealand Fiction,* edited by Fergus Barrowman, Picador, 1996.

Author of screenplay, *The Dig (Un Certain Regard),* 1994.

Contributor to periodicals, including *Landfall, Metro, New Zealand Listener, Sport,* and *Stout Centre Review.* Assistant editor of *Sport,* 1988-93.

Contributor to *Privacy: The Art of Julia Morrison* (Jonathan Jensen Gallery), 1994.

WORK IN PROGRESS: Tawa, forthcoming from Victoria University Press, *The Vintner's Luck,* and *Black Oxen.*

SIDELIGHTS: Elizabeth Knox is a noted novelist from New Zealand. Her first novel, *After Z-Hour,* is a complex tale concerning three individuals who take shelter in an old house while a storm rages. The story is told variously by the three individuals, and its tone—and even its genre—seems to shift whenever another character assumes narration. During the initial storytelling, for example, the tale seems essentially concerned with the supernatural. A second narration, however, emphasizes the story's elements as a mystery. In addition to the various narrations, storytelling forms within the novel include both correspondence and journal entries.

Knox's next novel, *Paremata,* details the interactions of several children. Knox followed *Paremata* with *Treasure,* another tale involving both mystery and the

supernatural. Here a graduate student, who is romantically involved with her supervisor where she works at a museum, learns that a co-worker has received a box that may hold strange powers. Meanwhile, a North Carolina youth, who finds himself at odds with the family's religious bent, discovers that he possesses the power to heal ailing individuals. The two narratives eventually converge at a meeting devoted to miraculous healing, whereupon the North Carolina youth is given the mysterious box.

Knox is also the author of the novel *Pomare.* In addition, she has written a screenplay, *The Dig (Un Certain Regard),* and has published several short stories in various periodicals. Some of her essays have been collected in anthologies such as *Now See Hear!* and *Pleasures and Dangers.*

BIOGRAPHICAL/CRITICAL SOURCES:

BOOKS

Contemporary Novelists, St. James Press (Chicago), 1991.

PERIODICALS

Australian Book Review, August, 1993.
Canadian Literature, fall, 1994, p. 253.
Landfall, May, 1997.
New Zealand Books, November, 1996.

*   *   *

KOCHENDOERFER, Violet A. 1912-

PERSONAL: Born November 7, 1912, in Winona, MN; daughter of Hugo H. (a machinist) and Maumie (a homemaker; maiden name, Ziebell) Kochendoerfer. *Education:* Attended Reed College, Portland, OR; Starr King School for the Ministry, Berkeley, CA, Master of Divinity. *Politics:* Democrat. *Religion:* Unitarian.

ADDRESSES: Home—226 North 60 Ave. E., Duluth, MN 55804.

CAREER: Chamber of Commerce, Santa Fe, NM, officer manager, c. 1950s. Ordained as a Unitarian Minister, 1962. Worked in the Unitarian ministry at churches in Cape Cod, MA, Kent, OH, Tallahassee, FL, and Calgary, Alberta, Canada. *Military service:*

Member of the Women's Army Auxiliary Corps, 1943, American Red Cross volunteer, 1944-47.

WRITINGS:

One Woman's World War II (memoir), University Press of Kentucky (Lexington, KY), 1994.
A Modern Pioneer: One Woman's Ministry (memoir), Skinner House (Boston, MA), 1996.

WORK IN PROGRESS: "My third book, *Santa Fe in the Fifties,* is about the ten years I spent there as office manager for the Chamber of Commerce, and after that I have plans for another book about growing up in Minnesota during the Great Depression."

SIDELIGHTS: Violet A. Kochendoerfer recounts her wartime experiences in *One Woman's World War II,* which was praised by the *Register of the Kentucky Historical Society* as "a forthright and honest account" and "a welcome addition to the growing body of literature" from service men and women.

Kochendoerfer told *CA:* "Some years back, I wrote over a thousand pages of my autobiography for family and friends. At a writers' conference I was told, "Vi, you have at least two books there!" The University Press of Kentucky published *One Woman's World War II* in 1994, in time for the fiftieth anniversary of D-Day.

"Being one of more than two-hundred authors invited by the Tennessee Humanities Council to the Southern Festival of Books in late 1994 put me on a panel with Stephen Ambrose, a leading historian of World War II and director of the Eisenhower Museum at the University of New Orleans. He was fascinated that I'd once had dinner with Ike, and has written to me that he's now working on another history of World War II, and wishes to use some of my stories."

BIOGRAPHICAL/CRITICAL SOURCES:

PERIODICALS

Register of the Kentucky Historical Society.

* * *

KOHON, Gregorio 1943-

PERSONAL: Born October 7, 1943, in Buenos Aires, Argentina; immigrated to England, 1970; immigrated to Australia, 1988; son of Jose Israel (a piano technician) and Elizabeth (a homemaker; maiden name, Bartscherer) Kohon; married Valli Shaio (a child psychotherapist), August 3, 1974; children: Sebastian Jose, Silvana Iris Liliana, Mariela Vera. *Education:* Attended Universidad Nacional de la Plata, 1964-69. *Religion:* Jewish.

ADDRESSES: Home—P. O. Box 584, 4004 Spring Hill, Australia.

CAREER: Hospital Dr. Araoz Alfaro, Buenos Aires, Argentina, clinical psychologist for the adolescent department, 1969-70; Institute de Orientacion Familiar, Buenos Aires, psychotherapist for adult department, 1969-70; private practice as a psychotherapist in London, England, 1970-88; Arbours Crisic Centre/Arbours Association, London, team leader, 1971-74, director of training program, 1972-74; Tavistock Clinic, London, clinical associate of the marital unit of the adult department, 1975-76; Open Door-Young People's Counseling Service, London, psychotherapist, 1976-77; Personal Consultation Centre Camden Counseling and Social Services, London, psychotherapist, 1980-83; private practice in Australia, 1988—. Member of the Archway Therapeutic Community in London, 1970-71; member of the management committee for the Arbours Association, 1971-74; member of board of directors for the Brisbane Centre for Psychoanalytic Studies, 1988—.

MEMBER: International Psychoanalytical Association; British Psychoanalytical Society; British Psychological Society; British Association of Psychotherapists; Australian Psychoanalytical Association; Balint Society; Queensland Association of Psychotherapy.

WRITINGS:

POETRY

Puntos de partida, Ediciones Agua Viva (Argentina), 1963.
(Contributor) *Nueva Poesia Argentina* (anthology), Editorial Leitura (Rio de Janeiro, Brazil), 1963.
Ebrio sale el sol, Montanari Editores (Argentina), 1967.
(Contributor) *Mano de obra* (anthology), Ediciones Sunda (Buenos Aires, Argentina), 1968.
Odetta en Babilonia y el rapido a Canada, Ediciones del Mediodia (Argentina), 1969.
20 Nuevos Narradores Argentinos (anthology), Monte Avila Editores (Caracas, Venezuela), 1970.

Generacion poetica del 60 (anthology), Ediciones Culturales Argentinas (Buenos Aires, Argentina), 1975.

Antologia de la poesia Argentina (anthology), Ediciones Libreria Fausto (Buenos Aires, Argentina), 1979.

NONFICTION

(Editor) *The British School of Psychoanalysis: The Independent Tradition,* Yale University Press (New Haven, CT), c. 1986.

Also contributor of poetry to Latin American journals and literary magazines; contributor of articles to professional journals, including *Cuadernos Sigmund Freud, Contemporary Psychoanalysis, International Journal of Psychoanalysis,* and *Free Associations.*

SIDELIGHTS: Gregorio Kohon has had a long career as a psychotherapist. First, he worked briefly in that capacity in his native Argentina, then moved to London, where he had a private practice for eighteen years before relocating to Australia and going into practice in that country. He first gained fame as a writer, however—at least in Argentina and other Latin American countries—for his poetry. His first collection, *Puntos de partida,* saw print in 1963; his most recent volume of poems, *Odetta en Babilonia y el rapido a Canada,* was published in 1969. Kohon's poetry has gained a place in several Latin American anthologies as well, including 1975's *Generacion poetica del 60* and 1979's *Antologia de la poesia Argentina.*

Kohon has contributed scholarly writing to the mental health profession as well. In 1986 he edited *The British School of Psychoanalysis: The Independent Tradition.* In this volume, interested readers already somewhat knowledgeable about psychoanalysis are provided first with an introductory history of psychoanalysis in Great Britain, then with essays from the independent branch of a three-part field. According to *The British School,* there were very few psychoanalysts in England prior to the First World War, and those that existed formed a small group around the leadership of Ernest Jones in London. Then in 1926 Melanie Klein moved from Berlin, Germany, to London. She differed in her psychoanalytic theories from Anna Freud, a disciple of her famous father, Sigmund Freud. Klein's presence and influence produced a schism in the English group between her teachings and those of Freud, a schism which widened when Anna Freud herself immigrated to London in 1938,

fleeing Nazi Germany's persecution of Jews. Yet there was yet another branch of English psychoanalysts who wanted to follow neither Klein nor Freud. As Paul Roazen, reviewing *The British School* in the *New Statesman,* explained, "the largest group of analysts, called the Middle Group or the Independents, who wanted to be free from either of the two rival doctrines, sought to evolve a separate path of their own."

The group of psychoanalysts did evolve "a separate path," and Kohon includes essays from noted practitioners and theorists among the Independents on subject matter such as early childhood, regression, transference and counter-transference, and female sexuality—all areas in which the Independents are considered to have made great contributions. The book includes case histories to illustrate its points; many of the histories concern intensely disturbed patients.

The British School was generally well-received by critics. Roazen judged the first section—on early childhood—to be the least valuable, and the third section—on transference and counter-transference—to have the most value. Of the book as a whole, he observed that "all the papers in this volume share a genial kind of harmony." Harold J. Fine, critiquing *The British School* in *Contemporary Psychology* praised it highly, saying that reading it, "you feel the enthusiasm for a volume that springs into its own life the conflicts, resolutions, and clinical theory that are so British and so compelling that it makes psychoanalysis so alive, so bloody mysterious, so experiential that one is euphoric (perhaps unrealistically) about its future." Elizabeth Wright in *British Book News* concluded that the collection's essays "reflect both the pragmatic outlook of this group and its commitment to the practice of psychoanalysis."

BIOGRAPHICAL/CRITICAL SOURCES:

PERIODICALS

British Book News, June, 1986, p. 351.
Contemporary Psychology, October, 1987, pp. 862-864.
New Statesman, February 28, 1986, pp. 26-27.

*   *   *

KOPELEV, Lev (Zinovievich)   1912-1997
   (E. Lepko, L. Yakovenko)

OBITUARY NOTICE—See index for *CA* sketch: Some sources transliterate given name as Lew, middle name as Synovyevich or Zinovevich, and surname as Kopelew; born April 9, 1912, in Kiev, Ukraine, Russia; died of heart disease, June 18, 1997, in Cologne, Germany. Human rights activist, educator, and author. Kopelev was a Russian dissident who wrote the details of his life in books such as *To Be Preserved Forever.* The work recounts time he spent in Soviet prison camps because of his political views and activities. Early in his career, he worked for the Kharkov Trainbuilding Factory in the Ukraine as a metal worker, teacher, journalist, and editor of the factory's newsletter. In the late 1930s he joined the faculty of the Moscow Institute of Philosophy, History, and Literature as an assistant professor of German Literature.

During World War II Kopelev was in the Soviet Army and served in Germany as a propagandist because of his ability to speak the language fluently. He was accused of sympathizing with the enemy when he protested the harsh treatment civilian Germans were receiving at the hands of the Soviet soldiers, was sent to prison and wasn't released until the mid-1950s. His book *To Be Preserved Forever,* named after a stamp placed on Soviet political prisoner files, recounted his imprisonment with such cellmates and fellow dissidents as Alexander Solzhenitsyn. Released from prison, he began work as a freelance writer before venturing to the Poligrafical Institute to teach in 1957.

From 1960 to 1968 Kopelev was a scientific fellow at the Moscow Institute of History of Arts. Kopelev encountered trouble with authorities again and again during his lifetime when he stood up for various human rights causes. He was thrown out of the Communist Party, expelled from the Writers Union in 1977, and stripped of his Soviet citizenship during the early 1980s. His citizenship was revoked after Kopelev and his wife left the country for Germany on a trip to conduct scientific research. The Kopelevs were granted honorary German citizenship in 1981. In 1990, by a decree of Russian President Mikhail Gorbachev, Kopelev's citizenship was restored. While in Germany Kopelev continued to write and teach. Among his books were other autobiographical accounts, including *Ease My Sorrows* and *The Education of a True Believer,* as well as books such as *Common Memories: We Lived In Moscow, 1956-1980, Myths and Truths of the American South, The Heart Is Always on the Left,* and *Without Past and Without Future: Notes of Contemporary Young People* (with his wife, Raisa Orlova).

OBITUARIES AND OTHER SOURCES:

BOOKS

The Facts on File Encyclopedia of the Twentieth Century, Facts on File, 1991.

PERIODICALS

Chicago Tribune, June 20, 1997, sec. 1, p. 12.
New York Times, June 20, 1997, p. B8.
Washington Post, June 19, 1997, p. B6.

*　*　*

KORCHILOV, Igor 1941-

PERSONAL: Born March 3, 1941, in Murmansk, Russia; son of Dmitry (an architect) and Anna (a homemaker; maiden name, Besedina) Korchilov; married Inna Samokhina, 1975. *Ethnicity:* "Caucasian." *Education:* Attended First Moscow State Institute of Foreign Languages, 1961-67, United Nations special training courses for translators and interpreters, 1967-68, and Foreign Ministry Diplomatic Academy, 1985-86. *Religion:* Christian Orthodox. *Avocational interests:* Reading, writing, music, painting.

ADDRESSES: Home—310 East 46th St., No. 17-D, New York, NY 10017. *Agent*—Mary Yost, Mary Yost Associates, Inc., 59 East 54th St., Suite 73, New York, NY 10022.

CAREER: United Nations, New York City, conference interpreter, 1968-73; Soviet Foreign Ministry, Moscow, U.S.S.R., diplomatic interpreter, 1973-80; United Nations, senior conference interpreter, 1980-85; Soviet Foreign Ministry, senior diplomatic interpreter, 1986-90.

WRITINGS:

Translating History: Thirty Years on the Front Lines of Diplomacy with a Top Russian Interpreter (memoir), Scribner (New York City), 1997.

WORK IN PROGRESS: A novel about the world of diplomacy and politics.

SIDELIGHTS: Igor Korchilov told *CA:* "I was an interpreter for Mikhail Gorbachev, the first and last president of the Soviet Union, an extraordinary personality and a great reformer of our time. The idea of writing a memoir to describe my experiences with him began to germinate in my mind even before I actually began to work for him in the mid-1980s. When I did begin, I started keeping notes in the form of diaries or journals in which I recorded, 'hot on the heels' of events, my observations, impressions, and reflections. I realized that I was in a unique position to observe this fascinating man at close range, interacting with top world leaders such as Ronald Reagan, George Bush, Margaret Thatcher, and some other figures. I wanted to record what I saw and heard and recreate the atmosphere in which they interacted in the hope that one day it would be possible to share with the public at large my observations and impressions of the way high-stakes superpower diplomacy operated at the highest levels of government at one of the most critical periods of history. It proved, in fact, to be a major turning point in the twentieth century, when the Cold War came to an end, communism collapsed, the Soviet empire disintegrated, and the Soviet Union imploded, altering radically the world as we had known it. All this happened peacefully, without major bloodshed. The public has a right to know history as it happened, and not as some others wanted it to happen or as they tried to skew it to suit their own purposes.

"I was lucky enough to be involved in some of the most important history-making events of the day. Their impact on mankind would be felt for a long time to come. One can never know the whole truth right away, however, especially historical truth. The whole truth takes too long to emerge and it consists of too many strands, so I decided to try to make up at least a few essential strands of the whole truth that was Gorbachev by writing a book of my own memoirs. Few of us become involved in history-making, in whatever capacity, and when it happened to me, it understandably dominated a good chunk of my life. Rather than keep the story bottled up inside me for the rest of my life, I thought it was a good idea to get it out of my system.

"I did some research in the course of actual writing, but mostly I relied on the notes that I had kept during the numerous and unprecedented summit meetings between Gorbachev and his major Western counterparts that took place in Washington, Moscow, London, Ottawa, Bonn, Helsinki, Geneva, and elsewhere. During those summits I would make it a point to jot down my immediate impressions and observations at the earliest opportunity during the day. Then,

later at night, before going to bed, I would complete the notes with more details. I knew even then that memory is fallible and unreliable. If I wanted to present an accurate and truthful story later on, in sufficient detail, I had to do the rough work right away. Subsequently, of course, after I had left diplomatic service, I used those notes to write what I hoped would be an interesting and readable literary account of my impressions, and not just another pedestrian recital of the who, where, and when of events. I found the computer to be a marvelous tool, which made it possible to improve continuously and polish the text almost *ad infinitum*. Since English is not my mother tongue, I would sometimes turn to dictionaries for help. Last but not least, inspiration, ideas, and thoughts seemed to visit me at the worst possible time one could think of: at night, when I was fast asleep. Then I would wake up, force myself out of bed, turn on the table lamp, and write them down while they were still fresh in my mind. Alas, this happened almost every night, making me almost a nervous wreck. Normally, I would spend between six and ten hours writing every day of the year.

"What inspired me to write was my love of history. I happen to be keen on modern history. I believe that people, particularly those with lively, curious, and probing minds, do themselves a tremendous favor when they expand their knowledge of the great events that shaped our history and way of life by reading memoirs and biographies by and of great men in history. This allows us to know better and remember our past, to learn lessons from it, and perhaps even to act, if need be, to prevent bad things from happening again. It is true that history often repeats itself, precisely because people tend to forget its lessons."

*   *   *

KULA, Witold 1916-1988

PERSONAL: Born April 18, 1916, in Warsaw, Poland; died February 12, 1988. *Education:*University of Warsaw, Krakowskie Pzedmiescie, graduate (philosophical faculty), 1937; Free Polish University, studied economics, 1934-39; Besancon University, doctorate in Historical Science, 1939; Dr. habil., 1947.

CAREER: Lodz University, Lodz, Poland, staff member, 1945-49; University of Warsaw, Poland, staff member, 1949-88, associate professor, 1950-63, chair of Economic History of Political Sciences Faculty, 1950-74, dean of Political Economics Faculty, 1962-63, professor, 1963-88, professor at Institute of Economic Sciences, 1975. Co-organizer and secretary of Institute of History of Polish Academy of Sciences, 1954-56; head of Social Structures Research Center of Institute of History, c. 1954-69.

MEMBER: PAN Committee of Historical Sciences (vice president, 1965-68, president, 1968-70), Association Internationale d'Histoire Economique (honorary president, 1970), Comite International pour la Metrologie Historique (vice president, 1975), Polish Academy of Science.

AWARDS, HONORS: Officer's Cross of Polish Restituta, honorary doctorate, Besancon University, 1965.

WRITINGS:

Historia gospodarcza Polski w dobie popowstaniowej 1864-1918, [Warsaw], 1947.

Ksztaltowanie sie kapitalizmu w Polsce, Panstwowe Wydawn Naukowe (Warsaw), 1955.

Szkice o manufakturach w PolaceXVIII wieku (title means, "Studies on Manufactures in Poland in the Eighteenth Century"), Panstwowe Wydawn Naukowe, 1956.

Rozwazania o historii (title means "Reflections on History"), Panstwowe Wydawn Naukowe, 1958.

Teoria ekonomiczna ustroju feudalnego, Panstwowe Wydawn Naukowe, 1962, translated as *An Economic Theory of the Feudal System,* London, 1976.

(With N. Assorodobraj and M. Kula) *Problemy i metody historii gospodarczej* (title mean "Problems and Methods of Economic History"), Panstwowe Wydawn Naukowe, 1963.

Miary i pudzie, Panstwowe Wydawn. Naukowe, 1970, translated by R. Szreter as *Measures and Men,* Princeton University Press (Princeton, NJ), 1986.

Miedzy feudalizmem a kapitalizmem, Zaktad Narodowy im. Ossolinskich (Wroclaw, Poland), 1976.

Historia, zacofanie, rozwoj, Czytelnik (Warsaw), 1983.

(With Nina Assorodobraj-Kula and Marcin Kula) *Listy emigrantow z Brazylii i Stanow Zjednoczonych, 1890-1891,* translated by Josephine Wtulich as *Writing Home—Immigrants in Brazil and the United States, 1890-1891,* East European Monographs (Boulder, CO), 1986.

Wokol historii, Pastwowe Wydawn Naukowe, 1988.

Rozwoj gospodarczy Polski XVI-XVIII w (title means, "Economic History of Poland in the Sixteenth through Eighteenth Centuries"), Wydawn Naukowe PWN, 1993.

EDITOR OF SERIES

Badania nad Dziejami Przemyslu i Klasy Robotniczej w Polsce (title means, "Research on History of Industry and Working Class in Poland,"), nine volumes, 1956.

Spoleczenstwo Krolestwa Polskiego, six volumes, Society of the Congress Kingdom of Poland, 1965.

Also editor with J. Leskiewiczowa of *Spoleczenstwo Polskie XVIII i XIX wieku* (title means, "Polish Society of Eighteenth and Nineteenth Century").

SIDELIGHTS: Polish economic historian Witold Kula would have attained a place as one of the foremost historians of the twentieth century, according to a contributor to *Twentieth-Century Culture: A Biographical Companion*—if he had written in a "world language." His ideas were not deprived of originality despite the fact that Kula, a Marxist, worked under communist rule for decades, the contributor suggested. His first major work was *Szkice o manufakturach w Polace XVIII wieku,* a 1956 study of twenty-four eighteenth-century Polish manufacturing concerns, including textile factories, mines, and blast furnaces. In 1958, in *Rozvazania o historii,* he considered questions of historical method. His best-known book in English, *An Economic Theory of the Feudal System,* hypothesizes that the validity of an economic proposition is limited to certain times and places. *Miary I pudzie,* known in English as *Measures and Men,* examines the history of weights and measures as a problem in intellectual history; the author theorizes that early measures were based on human characteristics. Reviewing *Measures and Men* for *Choice,* J. C. Murdock described the book's subject as "extremely broad, deep, and complex." In the *American Historical Review,* August W. Giebelhaus found the volume "always informative, usually interesting, but sometimes confusing in its eclecticism and large number of topics covered.

Of the numerous books by Kula, perhaps the one that garnered most attention in the United States was the volume published in 1986 as *Writing Home: Immigrants in Brazil and the United States, 1890-1891,* written with two relatives. The volume originated in

1941 when Kula, searching the Polish Archives, found a set of 352 letters from Polish immigrants written in Yiddish, Lithuanian, German, and Russian, which the Kulas later translated into Polish. An English translator, Josephine Wtulich, came upon the book while doing her own research in Poland on the status of women, and provided a major contribution to all Polish researchers by verifying the translations. In *Contemporary Sociology,* Helena Znaniecka Lopata stated that *Writing Home* is "good reading for scholars interested in the early experiences of immigrants from Europe to the new world." The reviewer concluded, "We are grateful to both the Kulas and Josephine Wtulich for all the work involved." A reviewer for *Choice* wrote, "These letters offer insight into the journey to the new land, the difficulty of the work, and the squalor of living conditions."

BIOGRAPHICAL/CRITICAL SOURCES:

BOOKS

Stroynowski, Juliusz, editor, *Who's Who in the Socialist Countries of Europe,* K.G. Saur (Munich, Germany), 1989.
Twentieth-Century Culture: A Biographical Companion, edited by Alan Bullock and R. B. Woodings, Harper, 1983, pp. 413-414.

PERIODICALS

American Historical Review, December, 1987, pp. 1193-1194.
Choice, November, 1986, p. 504; November, 1994, p. 412.
Contemporary Sociology, March, 1988, pp. 164-165.*

* * *

KURALT, Charles (Bishop) 1934-1997

OBITUARY NOTICE—See index for *CA* sketch: Born September 10, 1934, in Wilmington, NC; died of complications from lupus, July 4, 1997, in New York, NY. Television news reporter, producer, writer. Kuralt is remembered as the television anchor who shun-piked his way across the backroads of the United States, searching for unique stories about ordinary people. His "On the Road" segments for the *CBS Evening News with Walter Cronkite,* aired from 1967 to 1980, and eventually led to a position as

anchor for *CBS News Sunday Morning.* Broadcasting and reporting were a way of life for Kuralt. At the age of fourteen he announced minor-league baseball games and edited the student newspaper while in college. In 1955 he joined the staff of the *Charlotte News* as a reporter. In 1957 he went to work for the Columbia Broadcasting System (CBS) in New York as a writer; by 1959 he was the host of *Eyewitness to History.* For the next eight years Kuralt covered hard news stories in Latin America and Vietnam. His career changed in 1967 when he began covering human interest stories. Traveling more than 50,000 miles each year in a motorhome from 1967 to 1980, Kuralt and his camera crew set off in search of the real America. According to Arthur Unger of the *Christian Science Monitor,* Kuralt convinced CBS into sponsoring his "On the Road" segment by explaining: "I got the idea . . . one night in an airplane as I looked down at the lights in the countryside and wondered . . . what was going on down there. There are a lot of Americans who don't live in cities and don't make headlines. I was interested in finding out about them."

His forty-year career afforded Kuralt three George Foster Peabody Awards, thirteen Emmy Awards, and a 1985 broadcaster of the year award from the International Radio and Television Society. His television credits are numerous and include *Dateline America, America Tonight, 60 Minutes . . . 25 Years* (also known as *60 Minutes Turns 25*), *On the Road with Charles Kuralt,* and *An American Moment.* His written works include *Charles Kuralt's America, To the Top of the World: The Adventures and Misadventures of the Plaisted Polar Expedition, March 28-May 4, 1967, Southerners: Portrait of a People,* and *A Life on the Road.* He also wrote two companion pieces for his television shows: *Dateline America* and *On the Road with Charles Kuralt.*

OBITUARIES AND OTHER SOURCES:

BOOKS

Who's Who in America, Marquis Who's Who, 1996.

PERIODICALS

Chicago Tribune, July 5, 1997, section 1, p. 4.
Christian Science Monitor, July 24, 1974.
CNN Interactive (electronic), July 4, 1997.
Los Angeles Times, July 5, 1997, p. A1.
MSNBC (electronic), July 5, 1997.
New York Times, July 5, 1997, p. 24.

USA Today (electronic), July 4, 1997.
Washington Post, July 5, 1997, p. B4.

* * *

KVASNOSKY, Laura McGee 1951-

PERSONAL: Born January 27, 1951, in Sacramento, CA; daughter of Harvey C. (a newspaper publisher) and Helen (a comptroller; maiden name, McDonald) McGee; married John Kvasnosky (a public relations executive) on December 16, 1972; children: Timothy John, Noelle Helen. *Education:* Occidental College, B.A., 1973; studied writing with Jane Yolen at Centrum, Port Townsend, WA, 1994; studied illustration with Keith Baker at Seattle's School of Visual Concepts. *Religion:* "Northwest pantheist." *Avocational interests:* Gardening, cross-country skiing, hiking.

ADDRESSES: Home and office—4425 51st Ave., Seattle, Washington, 98105. *E-mail*—Kvasjl@wolfenet. com.

CAREER: Writer and illustrator. Graphic Designer, proprietor of one-person design shop, Seattle, WA, 1980—. Board of Directors, NW Girlchoir, 1992-96; Washington Region board member, Society of Children's Book Writers and Illustrators, edited newsletter, 1992-94.

MEMBER: Society of Children's Book Writers and Illustrators; Authors Guild.

AWARDS, HONORS: Best Books selection, *Parents* Magazine, and Children's Book of the Month Club selection, both 1995, both for *See You Later, Alligator;* "Pick of the Lists," American Booksellers Association, 1996, for *A Red Wagon Year* (written by Kathi Appelt).

WRITINGS:

FOR CHILDREN; SELF-ILLUSTRATED, EXCEPT AS NOTED

Pink, Red, Blue, What are You?, Dutton, 1994.
One, Two, Three, Play with Me, Dutton, 1994.
See You Later, Alligator, Harcourt, 1995.
Mr. Chips!, Farrar, Straus, Giroux, 1996.
What Shall I Dream?, Dutton, 1996.

Also illustrator of *There Once Was a Puffin,* by Florence Page Jaques, Dutton, 1995; *A Red Wagon Year,*

by Kathi Appelt, Harcourt, 1996; and *If Somebody Lived Next Door,* by Libby Hough, Dutton, 1997.

WORK IN PROGRESS: Zelda and Ivy, a picture book about fox sisters, for Candlewick; *Speedy and Lulu,* an early chapter book for Dutton.

SIDELIGHTS: Laura McGee Kvasnosky commented: "Creating children's books is my dream job. The experiences I value most—nurturing a family, writing, graphic design, reading—all meet in this one enterprise.

"I come from a long line of California newspaper writers. Perhaps we feel a genetic urge to organize a story as a way to understand life. Being part of [a larger] family also affects what I choose to write about. I'm the middle of five kids. In many ways my childhood was like growing up in a summer camp. My mother even put name tags in our underwear.

"Three things happened in third grade that led me to become a writer and illustrator: 1) We moved, so I was a new kid at school. As an outsider looking in, I developed observation skills. 2) I made up tremendous stories in hopes of attracting friends, thus developing a keen understanding of the blend of fact and fiction that a good 'believable' story requires. 3) My reading improved to the point where I could really read. I became (and still am) a bookworm.

"I began my work career at the age of eight, sharpening pencils for my editor-father. Over the years I contributed in the advertising and editorial departments of his newspaper, too. When my children were small, I created over 10,000 Christmas ornaments in my kitchen. Then, in 1980, I started my own graphic design firm. I decided to go for a lifelong dream of publishing a children's book when I turned 40. Now, six years later, I am harvesting my eighth title."

Kvasnosky's first published works for children were the self-illustrated board books *One, Two, Three, Play with Me* and *Pink, Red, Blue, What are You?,* published in 1994. Using short, rhyming phrases and bright pictures to introduce colors and numbers, these works also employ various groupings of multiethnic children to illustrate learning concepts. In *Pink, Red, Blue, What are You?,* animals define themselves by their color, temperament and sometimes their olfactory qualities: "We're pink, we stink" proclaim a group of pigs; "We're green, we're mean" warn the alligators. A *Publishers Weekly* reviewer found these board books "simple, fun and effective," while

School Library Journal contributor Linda Wicher praised Kvasnosky's illustrations, asserting that "the sketched figures are full of movement and wit." Another of Kvasnosky's self-illustrated books for preschoolers, *See You Later, Alligator,* features a group of young reptiles whose parents begin the day by dropping them off at River Bottom School. A variety of reptilian variations of the title phrase, including "In a shake, garter snake," and "In a blizzard, little lizard," attempt to convey the book's emphasis on "upbeat separations," according to *School Library Journal* contributor Nancy Seiner.

Kvasnosky has also written picture books for independent readers, including the stories *What Shall I Dream?* and her self-illustrated *Mr. Chips!. What Shall I Dream?,* called "a lovely bedtime story" by *School Library Journal* contributor Judith Constantinides, takes us into the world of young Prince Alexander, who worries over what to dream. His royal family uses their power and influence to summon Dream Brewers, Dream Weavers and Dream Sweepers to assist him; but when the dreams these masters concoct prove unsatisfying, it is the shrewd observation of the humble nursemaid that saves the day. *Mr. Chips!* is a simple story of the affectionate bond between a dog and a child. In this instance, the dog, Mr. Chips, is away for days and does not return home before his little companion Ellie and her family move to a new town. "Stories about lost pets who manage to find their families despite vast distances are always touching, and this one is no exception," asserted a *Kirkus Reviews* critic. *School Library Journal* contributor Marianne Saccardi called *Mr. Chips!* "a heartwarming story," adding: "Kvasnosky's cartoon art is bright and appropriately childlike as well."

"The seeds that grow into future books are often planted in young children," Kvasnosky asserted. "I know that because it is my experience. It is one reason I enjoy working with young writers and artists."

BIOGRAPHICAL/CRITICAL SOURCES:

PERIODICALS

Booklist, July, 1996, p. 1830.
Bulletin of the Center for Children's Books, November, 1996, p. 105; January, 1997, pp. 177-78.
Kirkus Reviews, July 1, 1996, p. 970.
Publishers Weekly, May 2, 1994, p. 305; June 24, 1996, p. 58.
School Library Journal, August, 1994, p. 139; November, 1995, p. 74; August, 1996, p. 126; September, 1996, p. 182.

L

LACY, Allen 1935-

PERSONAL: Born January 7, 1935, in Dallas, TX; son of David Allen Lacy Jr. (a commodities broker) and Jetta (a homemaker; maiden name, Surles) Lacy; married Hella Goethert (a nurse, now retired), November 28, 1958; children: Paul David, Michael Loren Bernhard. *Education:* Duke University, A.B., 1956; Vanderbilt University Divinity School, 1958; Duke University, Ph.D., 1962. *Politics:* Independent. *Religion:* Episcopalian.

ADDRESSES: Home—1511 Shore Rd., Linwood, NJ 08221. *Office*—Richard Stockton College of New Jersey, Pomona, NJ 08290. *Agent*—Helen Pratt, Inc., 1165 Fifth Ave., New York, NY 10029.

CAREER: Professor of philosophy and gardening writer. Clemson College, Clemson, SC, instructor in English, 1961-62; James Madison University, Harrisonburg, VA, assistant professor, 1962-65, associate professor of philosophy and English, 1965-66; Michigan State University, East Lansing, MI, assistant professor of humanities, 1966-68; Kirkland College, Clinton, NY, assistant professor, 1968-69, associate professor of philosophy and humanities, 1969-71; Richard Stockton College of New Jersey, Pomona, NJ, associate professor, 1971-72, professor of philosophy, 1972—. Founding editor, *Allen Lacy's Homeground* (quarterly journal), 1993—. Member of advisory boards for Sarah P. Duke Gardens, Duke University, 1990-92, and North Carolina State University Arboretum, 1992-93.

MEMBER: Perennial Plant Association, Authors Guild.

AWARDS, HONORS: National Endowment for the Humanities fellowship, 1970; citation for excellence in horticultural writing, American Horticulture Society, 1985; Quill and Trowel Award, Garden Writers Association of America, 1991, for *The Garden in Autumn.*

WRITINGS:

Home Ground: A Gardener's Miscellany, Farrar, Straus & Giroux (New York City), 1984.
Farther Afield: A Gardener's Excursions, Farrar, Straus & Giroux, 1986.
The Garden in Autumn, Atlantic Monthly Press (New York City), 1990.
The Glory of Roses, photographs by Christopher Baker, Stewart, Tabori & Chang (New York City), 1990.
The Gardener's Eye and Other Essays, Atlantic Monthly Press (New York City), 1991.
Gardening with Groundcovers and Vines, photographs by Cynthia Woodyard, HarperCollins (New York City), 1993.

Gardening columnist for *Wall Street Journal,* 1979-85, and for *New York Times,* 1986—; author of gardening articles for periodicals, including *Horticulture, Connoisseur, American Photographer, American Horticulturalist, House and Garden, House Beautiful, Organic Gardening, Harrowsmith,* and *New York Times Magazine.*

EDITOR

(And translator, with Martin Nozick and Anthony Kerrigan) *Peace in War,* by Miguel de Unamuno, Princeton University Press (Princeton, NJ), 1983.
(And translator, with others) *The Private World,* by Unamuno, Princeton University Press, 1984.

Gardening for Love: The Market Bulletins, by Elizabeth Lawrence, Duke University Press (Durham, NC), 1987.

The American Gardener: A Sampler, Farrar, Straus & Giroux, 1988.

(With Nancy Goodwin) *A Rock Garden in the South,* by Lawrence, Duke University Press, 1990.

OTHER

Miguel de Unamuno: The Rhetoric of Existence (philosophy), Mouton (The Hague, Netherlands), 1967.

Contributor of book reviews to periodicals, including *Philadelphia Inquirer, New York Times Book Review, Washington Post, Washington Star, Newsday, Dallas Morning News, San Francisco Chronicle,* and *Los Angeles Times.* Author of scholarly articles for *Christian Scholar* and *Hispanic Review.*

WORK IN PROGRESS: The Inviting Garden: Gardening for the Sensory Mind and Body, to be published by Holt, in 1998.

SIDELIGHTS: If ever a philosopher took literally Voltaire's advice to Candide that he should tend his own garden, it was Allen Lacy. An expert on Spanish philosopher Miguel de Unamuno and a professor at Richard Stockton College of New Jersey—but a lifelong avocational gardener—Lacy became a gardening columnist for the *Wall Street Journal* by chance in 1979. He remained in that post for six years, moving to the *New York Times* at the beginning of 1986. Lacy described his career path for *CA:* "After paying my scholarly dues, I set out to become a novelist. As an undergraduate at Duke, I was admitted to the legendary writing class taught by the equally legendary William Blackburn, whose students included Mac Hyman, William Styron, Reynolds Price, Fred Chappell, and many other novelists of note. I did not become a novelist of note, nor even a published one. In 1979, serendipity struck, in the form of an unexpected invitation to initiate a garden column for the *Wall Street Journal.* It seems that I found my way as a writer in the gardens I had been tending for most of my life, since my childhood in Texas."

Lacy's first gardening book was the 1984 publication *Home Ground: A Gardener's Miscellany,* which brought together many of Lacy's short pieces written for periodicals between 1979 and 1983. Averring that the collection had the "enjoyable crispness" of celery, Allen Paterson of the *Times Literary Supplement* called Lacy's work "a jolly good write, provocative, robust and

knowledgeable." Charles Solomon, reviewing the book in the *Los Angeles Times Book Review,* praised the "informal, *entre nous* tone" of this "genial" book, and complimented Lacy for not being "resolutely upbeat."

A second collection of Lacy's short pieces was published two years later under the title *Farther Afield: A Gardener's Excursions.* Assessing the volume for the *Washington Post Book World,* Paul Hodge observed, "What sets Lacy above the common garden-variety journalist is not just his good humor and good sense . . . but his fascination with the origin of the plants we grow." Hodge singled out a long essay on "the Seed King of Costa Rica"—a renowned Texas-born hybridizer—as "a fascinating study of how modern plant hybrids are born." The critic also enjoyed a chapter on garden theft, stating that "Lacy's delightful, light-hearted rambles are almost always informative and fun to read." A *Publishers Weekly* reviewer called the book "a source of delight" for readers interested in the subject. In a critique of the book for the *New York Times Book Review,* Susan Brownmiller described Lacy as being "among that admirable elite who elevate the pleasant pastime of writing personally and with firm opinions about their private gardens into something that approaches literature." Brownmiller expressed a preference for the essays Lacy wrote about his own gardens, rather than those which, in obedience to the title, went farther afield.

In his 1990 work, *The Garden in Autumn,* Lacy provides a unique discussion of gardening in the later months of the year. About the book Lacy noted: "*The Garden in Autumn* was the first book ever written on this topic, because British gardening books have been influential in the way Americans see their own, very different, gardens. The realities of latitude and climate mean that there is no autumn worth mentioning for English gardens. Here [in the United States], the season is prolonged and given to some of our best weather, the kindest to many plants. There was an obvious hole in our gardening literature. I saw it and leaped in to fill it—but the realization about autumn came to me very suddenly. Seeing the obvious is sometimes very difficult." Gardening and cooking writer Bill Neal, reviewing the book for the *New York Times Book Review,* applauded Lacy for his choice of subject, and also noted, "The difference between a good gardener and a great one is the practice of an observant eye." *Bloomsbury Review* contributor Pat Wagner singled out the book's "beautiful photographs and a wealth of ideas," praising the amount of "sensible advice" Lacy had managed to include in a book of just over two hundred pages.

Another collection of Lacy's essays, *The Gardener's Eye,* appeared in 1992. The work contains pieces on various gardeners—including gardening writer Elizabeth Lawrence—as well as on more traditional gardening topics. A *Publishers Weekly* critic praised Lacy for including philosophical musings on such topics as etymology and architecture within his gardening essays; the reviewer particularly liked the essay "Listening to Miss Lawrence" for illuminating the posthumous author-editor relationship that Lacy had with the late North Carolina gardening writer. Said Lacy, "Duke Press gave me Lawrence's text shortly before she died. The voice I 'listened' to was the voice that often came through in that text—which guided me in editing it." Charles Solomon, in the *Los Angeles Times Book Review,* wrote, "horticulturists everywhere will enjoy Lacy's delight in his subject."

Lacy's next book, published in 1993, examined the specialized topic of *Gardening with Groundcovers and Vines.* Here, Lacy staked out new ground by arguing that instead of lawns or other traditional groundcovers, gardeners might use mixtures of plants that arc usually placed in borders of gardens. Saying that Lacy "could probably write about sawdust and make it sound delightful," Melanie Fleischmann in the *New York Times Book Review* found the chapters on vines "the most fun." *Library Journal* writer Dale Luchsinger called the book "remarkable" and added, "anyone with a year or two of gardening experience will be able to use this book to enhance his or her knowledge of garden plants." *Washington Post Book World* reviewer Constance Casey called the book an "elegant and beautifully illustrated long essay."

The Glory of Roses, published in 1990, features photographs by Christopher Baker and accompanying text by Lacy. Robert Smaus, garden editor of the *Los Angeles Times,* praised the "almost universal appeal" of the subject, calling Lacy's text "interesting and amusing" and Baker's photographs "gorgeous." Lacy also was editor of the 1988 collection of garden writing, *The American Gardener: A Sampler.* The book includes works by about fifty horticultural writers, including Louise Beebe Wilder, Henry Mitchell, Thalassa Cruso, Celestine Sibley, and Harlan J. Hand. A *Booklist* contributor called Lacy's volume a "delightful anthology" and *Library Journal* writer Luchsinger declared that in Lacy's collection "readers will discover joys of gardening beyond their initial appreciation of beauty."

Lacy told *CA:* "In 1992, I quit the *New York Times.* Shortly afterwards with my younger son, Michael, a graphic designer who is art director for a corporation that publishes a number of city and regional magazines, I began publishing *Homeground,* a quarterly newsletter or mini-magazine. The content is mostly essays on particular plants or the life of a gardener. *Homeground* has now finished its fifth year.

"For fours years now I have been working on a book, *The Inviting Garden,* with Cynthia Woodyard as photographer. This book, to be published in 1998 by Henry Holt, is the first that combines my philosophical training and experience with my horticultural interest and passion."

BIOGRAPHICAL/CRITICAL SOURCES:

PERIODICALS

Bloomsbury Review, April/May 1991.
Booklist, April 15, 1988, p. 1380.
Library Journal, May 15, 1988, p. 88; November 15, 1993, p. 92.
Los Angeles Times Book Review, August 14, 1988, p. 2; November 25, 1990; March 1, 1992; July 23, 1995.
New York Times Book Review, June 1, 1986, p. 30; December 2, 1990; December 15, 1993, p. 30.
Publishers Weekly, March 14, 1986, p. 99; December 20, 1991, p. 19.
Times Literary Supplement, May 3, 1985, p. 507.
Washington Post Book World, June 6, 1986, p. 15; March 8, 1992, p. 13; December 5, 1993, p. 8.

*   *   *

LANDIS, Geoffrey A(lan) 1955-

PERSONAL: Born May 28, 1955, in Detroit, MI; son of John Lloyd and Patricia L. Landis. *Education:* Massachusetts Institute of Technology, B.S., B.E.E., 1980; Brown University, M.S., M.E.E., Ph.D., 1988.

ADDRESSES: Office—NASA Lewis Research Center 302-1, 21000 Brookpark Rd., Cleveland, OH, 44135.

CAREER: Physicist and writer. Spire Corporation, Bedford, MA, staff scientist, 1977-82; Solar Energy Research Institute, Golden, CO, research associate, 1986-87; National Aeronautics and Space Administration (NASA) Lewis Research Center, Cleveland, OH, research associate, 1988-90; Ohio Aerospace Institute, Brook Park, OH, adjunct professor, 1990-92, senior research associate, 1995—; Sverdup Technology, Brook

Park, OH, physicist, 1994-95; NYMA, Inc., Brook Park, senior engineer, 1994—. National Association of Rocketry, PA, trustee, 1978-81; Spacemodeling World Championships, Jambol, Bulgaria, member of U.S. team, 1978; Vision-21 Conference, Cleveland, technology chair, 1990, 1993.

MEMBER: American Physical Society, Science Fiction Writers of America, Artemis Society.

AWARDS, HONORS: Nebula Award, Science Fiction Writers of America, 1990; Hugo award for best science fiction short story, 1992.

WRITINGS:

Myths, Legends, and True History, Pulphouse Publishing (Eugene, OR), 1991.
(Editor) *Vision-21, Space Travel for the Next Millennium,* National Aeronautics and Space Administration (NASA), Scientific and Technical Information Division (Washington, DC), 1991.
(Editor) *Vision-21, Interdisciplinary Science and Engineering,* NASA, Scientific and Technical Information Division, 1993.

Contributor to the anthology *Future Boston: The History of a City 1990-2100.* Author of over fifty published science-fiction short stories; contributor of over two hundred articles to professional journals.

SIDELIGHTS: Geoffrey A. Landis told *CA:* "In a climate where authors are increasingly being forced by commercial concerns toward trilogies, series, and media tie-in books, it is becoming very difficult to attract attention as a short-story writer."

*   *   *

LANGLEY, Lee 1932-

PERSONAL: Born in 1932, in Calcutta, India; married Theo Richmond (a writer); children: three.

ADDRESSES: Home—6 Chiselhurst Rd., Richmond, Surrey, United Kingdom. *Office*—c/o Milkweed Editions, 430 First Ave. N., Suite 400, Minneapolis, MN 55401.

CAREER: Writer.

MEMBER: Writers' Guild of Great Britain.

AWARDS, HONORS: Award for Best Fiction, Writers' Guild of Great Britain, and the Commonwealth Writers' Prize for Best Novel in the Eurasia region, both 1993, both for *Persistent Rumours; Changes of Address* and *A House in Pondicherry* were shortlisted for the Hawthornden Prize.

WRITINGS:

NOVELS

The Only Person, Heinemann (London), 1972.
Sunday Girl, Heinemann, 1973.
From the Broken Tree, Dutton (New York City), 1978.
The Dying Art, Heinemann, 1983.
Changes of Address, Collins (London), 1987.
Persistent Rumours, Heinemann, 1992, Milkweed Editions (Minneapolis, MN), 1994.
A House in Pondicherry, Heinemann, 1995.

PLAYS

Baggage: A Comedy, French (New York City), 1977.

SCREENPLAYS

A Woman of Substance (miniseries), based on the novel by Barbara Taylor Bradford, 1983.
(With Marjorie Deane and Geoffrey Kerr) *The Tenth Man,* based on the novel by Graham Greene, CBS Entertainment Productions/Metro-Goldwyn-Mayer, 1988.
(With Jim Henshaw and Lyle Slack) *Another Woman,* based on the novel by Margot Dalton, Alliance Communications, 1994.
September (also known as *Rosamunde Pilcher's September*), based on the novel by Rosamunde Pilcher, Hallmark Entertainment, 1996.

Also author of several dramatizations for the BBC and ITV. Contributor to *Guardian, Daily Telegraph,* and *London Evening Standard.*

SIDELIGHTS: British writer Lee Langley has written a number of novels that examine middle-class lives and the sometimes flawed personalities that lurk just beneath the surface. Midway through her career, Langley began allowing her characters to roam the subcontinent of India. It was a milieu she herself knew well having spent much of her childhood traveling the region with her dissipated mother. "Because I lived all my childhood on the sidelines, watching other people and observing rather than participating, I had very good training to be a writer," Langley told Liz Hodgkinson in the London *Times.*

The first of Langley's books to attract attention was her 1972 novel, *The Only Person,* which chronicles the tale of Lydia Carter, a bored suburban housewife who begins an affair with her children's schoolmaster. The two eventually flee to Spain, but, surprisingly, Lydia returns to her life of dullness. "Langley creates [Lydia] and her environment with wit and originality," praised Diane LeClercq in *Books and Bookmen,* but noted that the real strength of *The Only Person* seemed to be in its wryly written scenes of Lydia in the suburbs, not in her break for freedom and ultimate personal growth.

Langley's next novel chronicles the tale of a young woman writing a flip-diary-type column for a newspaper. In the column *Sunday Girl,* Suzi Walters lets readers in on what is new and exciting in the world of fashion, food, and fun, and lives the fast-lane lifestyle that her readers imagine, rife with dinner dates and parties. Eventually, tragedy occurs in Suzi's life and she is forced to re-examine her morals and lifestyle.

Pamela Marsh of the *Christian Science Monitor* gave *Sunday Girl* a mixed review, calling it "as refreshing as a crisp tart apple on a muggy day," yet noting "it can also be sour enough to set your teeth on edge," while a reviewer for *Publishers Weekly* called the book "a superficial look at a superficial life." Though Douglas Dunn, writing for *New Statesman and Society*, felt that "a nastier book would have been more convincing" and that a less sympathetic portrayal of the characters would have strengthened the novel, he noted Langley's "gift of comedy," stating that a more straightforward style of satire would display her talents to their advantage.

Langley takes her protagonist on an unusual journey in *The Dying Art.* Widowed Rosemary Nightingale is bored by her middle-class London existence, and swaps homes with a Southern Californian for a time, taking her young son with her. Rosemary encounters a cast of strange characters in the neighbors surrounding her new idyllic suburban setting, and her eleven-year-old adapts admirably, watching television and painting freckles on his face. Yet the glossy surface of suburban Los Angeles cracks when a family is murdered; one of Rosemary's neighbors begins warning of an imminent outbreak of bubonic plague, and the bottled-water delivery boy begins making unexpected visits. "Indulgent readers will enjoy much of the cheerful gab and most of the gormless people in this busy frolic," noted a *Kirkus Reviews* critic. A *Publishers Weekly* reviewer called Rosmary's character a study of "an interesting woman whose self-doubts and quirky humor make her engagingly real to the reader."

The 1987 publication of *Changes of Address* marked a change of sorts for Langley as well: it was the first of her works to return to India, where she had spent a difficult childhood. Her parents were transplanted Britons whose marriage dissolved early in Langley's life; Langley moved around with her mother to a series of seedy hotels as her mother drifted from boyfriend to boyfriend, with alcohol the only constant. Intensely autobiographical, *Changes of Address* lets its young protagonist, Maggie, reflect this part of Langley's life, even up to the point where she left home at age sixteen and never spoke to her mother again.

In *Changes of Address,* the mother, Moti, exists in her own dimension, unable to distinguish fact from fiction and unable to provide any sort of parental guidance for her fatherless child. Sex, alcohol, and financial worries are all a part of Maggie's young life. Langley herself told Hodgkinson in the *Times* that "with a little luck, and less reliance on alcohol, my mother could have shone. The trouble was, she had not been brought up to look after herself and she never managed to do this. She was a supreme non-coper." Maggie yearns for a boring English existence, away from the chaotic foreignness of the colonial outpost in its last days as part of the British Empire. "It is very vivid and poignant, the heat and smells of India, the atmosphere of English hotels, teeming bazaars and sordid lodgings," noted James Simmons in the *Spectator.*

Persistent Rumours, Langley's sixth novel, also deals with the legacy of colonialism and its effects on seemingly ordinary British families. The protagonist of the 1992 novel is an aging cartographer, James Oakley, who was born on an island off the coast of India where his father was an officer at a notorious penal colony. James's free-spirited mother chafed at the colonial lifestyle, and often consorted with Indians or others deemed unsuitable company by the local British community. When James reaches school-age, he is sent back to England, an act of betrayal that serves to haunt him the rest of his life. He is told as a teenager that his mother is dead, apparently a victim of a hurricane and subsequent shipwreck, but "rumors persist" to the contrary, with tales that she has been murdered, committed suicide, gone native, or run off with another man.

In his late seventies, James returns to the island to uncover the truth with his long-suffering wife Daisy in tow. Gradually, *Persistent Rumours* shifts and becomes a tale of Daisy's ultimate liberation from the brutal treatment she has endured at the hands of her emotionally damaged husband for so many years. Francis King, reviewing the work for the *Spectator,* remarked that the Indian-born Langley "is always at her best when writing of the country. She brings out both the lush, gaudy beauty of the place and its hidden dangers." Writing in *Washington Post Book World,* Dwight Garner asserted that "this strange, supple book catches you from its first pages and draws you steadily along. . . . The novel radiates a startling intelligence, not only about the elusive quality of history and memory but about the often unbridgeable gaps between cultures—and between men and women."

Langley's next novel, 1995's *A House in Pondicherry,* also returns to India as a setting, but this time in the little-known former French quarter of the country. "I was absolutely fascinated by [Pondicherry] . . . because it's unlike any other India town, very French," the author told *Books* magazine. The novel uses several colorful personalities from the region's history, such as the half-Indian Sri Aurobindo Ghosh, educated in England at the turn of the twentieth century only to return to Pondicherry to establish an ashram, or spiritual retreat. A trio of women make up the fictional segment of the novel's cast of characters, including the daughter of a French innkeeper who continues Aurobindo's legacy, and an English free spirit who stays at the ashram for a time only to become pregnant by its arrogant French architect; her daughter is the last of the created characters, who returns as an adult to India to seek out the mysteries of her origins.

Spectator critic Francis King lauded Langley's portrayal of the town and its climate in *A House in Pondicherry.* "She is particularly skillful at evoking the city's changes of light, as abrupt and dramatic as its changes of fortune," noted King, though the critic faulted "the blurred, decorative shapes" of many of her characters. In the *Books* interview, Langley herself described the novel as being "about the persistence of love really. It looks at the way even though a love story may not always have a happy ending it can actually survive many years and enrich people in many different ways."

BIOGRAPHICAL/CRITICAL SOURCES:

PERIODICALS

Best Sellers, November 1, 1968, p. 320.
Books, summer, 1995, p. 15.
Books & Bookmen, July, 1972, p. 62.
Christian Science Monitor, July 25, 1973, p. 9.
Drama, autumn, 1977, p. 78.
Globe & Mail, November 3, 1984.
Kirkus Reviews, August 1, 1968, p. 849; July 15, 1978, p. 766; September 1, 1983, p. 968.
Library Journal, December 1, 1983, p. 2262.
New Statesman & Society, May 25, 1973, pp. 773-775.
New York Times Book Review, October 30, 1994, p. 29.
Publishers Weekly, June 25, 1973, p. 69; July 24, 1978, p. 82; September 23, 1983, p. 60; August 29, 1994, p. 62.
Spectator, January 2, 1988, p. 24; June 13, 1992, p. 32; July 15, 1995, p. 31.
Times (London), March 10, 1983; September 4, 1987; October 1, 1987.
Times Literary Supplement, December 14, 1979, p. 142; October 23, 1987, p. 1175; June 26, 1992, p. 20.
Washington Post Book World, August 28, 1994, p. 6.

*   *   *

LANGLEY, Stephen G(ould)   1938-1997

OBITUARY NOTICE—See index for *CA* sketch: Born December 25, 1938, in Gardner (one source says Athol), MA; died of cardiac arrest, June 7, 1997, in Brooklyn, NY. Theater manager, educator, and author. Langley is remembered for his contributions to the performing arts, particularly in regard to theater management. Langley worked as publicity director for the Falmouth Playhouse in Massachusetts from 1959 to 1964 and then became its general manager until 1979. In 1963 he began a lengthy association with Brooklyn College of the City University of New York, first as an instructor, then as associate professor of theater administration and later as professor of performing arts management. He also served the school as general manager of the performing arts office and of its performing arts center. Beginning in 1976, he was director of the performing arts management division of Brooklyn College's department of theater.

He also wrote several books, including *Theater Management and Production in America, Jobs in Arts and Media Management,* and *Producers on Producing.*

OBITUARIES AND OTHER SOURCES:

BOOKS

Who's Who in Entertainment, Marquis Who's Who, 1992.

PERIODICALS

New York Times, June 15, 1997, p. 31.

* * *

LASSERRE, Philippe 1939-

PERSONAL: Born May 27, 1939, in Bordeaux, France; married Michelle Gauthier, July 26, 1960; children: Virginie, Benoit, Marion. *Ethnicity:* "Caucasian." *Education:* Bordeaux Junior College Michel Montaigne, baccalaureat (with honors), 1958; University of Paris, master's degree, 1961; University of Texas at Austin, Ph.D., 1975. *Religion:* Roman Catholic.

ADDRESSES: Home—Samois sur Seine, France. *Office*—INSEAD, Blvd. de Constance, 77309 Fontainebleau, France; fax 33-16-072-4049. *E-mail*—Philippe Lasserre1@compuserve.com.

CAREER: French Foundation for Management Education, Paris, France, vice-general secretary, 1962-72; INSEAD, Fontainebleau, France, professor, 1975—. SNECMA, Paris, controller, 1963-69. Community of Samois sur Seine, council member. *Military service:* Served in the French military, 1961-63; became a lieutenant.

MEMBER: Strategic Management Society, Long Range Planning Society (London).

WRITINGS:

Business Strategy and Management, Tinu Academic Press (Singapore), 1986.
Strategies for Asia Pacific, New York University Press (New York City), 1995.

WORK IN PROGRESS: Joint Ventures in Asia.

LEADER, Mary 1948-

PERSONAL: Born January 9, 1948, in Pawnee, OK; daughter of Joe (a men's clothing merchant) and Katharine H. (a poet) Privett; married Neal Leader (divorced); children: Sarah, Edward. *Education:* University of Oklahoma, B.A., 1975, J.D., 1980; Warren Wilson College, M.F.A., 1991; Brandeis University, A.B.D.

ADDRESSES: Home—916 Oakbrook Dr., Norman, OK 73072.

CAREER: Office of Oklahoma Attorney General, Oklahoma City, OK, assistant to attorney general, 1980-81; Oklahoma Supreme Court, Oklahoma City, referee, 1982-91; Emory University, Atlanta, GA, creative writing fellow in poetry and lecturer in literature and law.

AWARDS, HONORS: National Poetry Series, 1996, for *Red Signature.*

WRITINGS:

Red Signature (poetry), Graywolf Press (St. Paul, MN), 1997.

Contributor of poems to journals, including *Western Humanities Review, Membrane, Virginia Quarterly Review, Beloit Poetry Journal, Denver Quarterly,* and *Malahat Review.*

WORK IN PROGRESS: Books of poetry, including *House Afire, Inkstone, Harlequinade,* and *They Vibrate;* research on the use of documents in poems, especially by Muriel Rukeyser.

* * *

LENO, Jay 1950-

PERSONAL: Born James Douglas Muir Leno, April 28, 1950, in New Rochelle, NY; son of Angelo and Cathryn Leno; married Mavis Nicholson, November 30, 1980. *Education:* Emerson College, graduated, 1973. *Avocational interests:* Antique motorcycles and automobiles.

ADDRESSES: Office—P.O. Box 7885, Burbank, CA 91510-7885.

CAREER: Rolls Royce auto mechanic and deliveryman; stand-up comedian at venues, including Carnegie Hall and Caesar's Place; performed as opening act for Henry Mancini, Johnny Mathis, John Denver, James Brown, Tom Jones, and Perry Como; *Good Times,* CBS, writer, 1974; *Jay Leno and the American Dream,* Showtime, host and producer, 1986; *The Tonight Show,* NBC, exclusive guest host, 1987-92, host, 1992—. Appeared on television show episodes, including *Laverne and Shirley,* ABC, 1976; *Alice,* CBS, 1976; *The Marilyn McCoo and Billy Davis, Jr. Show,* CBS, 1977; *Saturday Night Live,* NBC, 1986; *Baywatch,* syndicated, 1989; *Seinfeld,* NBC, 1990; *Fresh Prince of Bel-Air,* NBC, 1990; *Home Improvement,* ABC, 1991; *Mad About You,* NBC, 1992; *The Larry Sanders Show,* 1992; *Homicide: Life on the Street,* NBC, 1993; *The Nanny,* CBS, 1993; *Ellen,* ABC, 1994; *Dennis Miller Live,* 1994; *Friends,* NBC, 1994; *Caroline in the City,* NBC, 1995; *Third Rock from the Sun,* 1996; *Just Shoot Me,* 1997; and *Late Night with David Letterman,* NBC. Other television appearances include *Jay Leno's Family Comedy Hour,* 1987; *The 42nd Annual Primetime Emmy Awards,* 1990; *Happily Ever After: Fairy Tales for Every Child,* 1995; and *Our Planet Tonight.* Appeared in films, including *The Silver Bears,* EMI Films, 1977; *Fun with Dick and Jane,* Columbia, 1977; *American Hot Wax,* Paramount, 1978; *Americathon,* Lorimar/Warner Bros., 1979; *Collision Course,* De Laurentiis Entertainment/ Interscope Communications, 1988; *Dave,* Warner Bros., 1993; *Wayne's World 2,* Paramount, 1993; *We're Back! A Dinosaur's Story,* Amblin, 1993; *The Flintstones,* Universal/Hanna-Barbera/Amblin, 1994; *Major League II,* Warner Bros., 1994; *The Birdcage* (also known as *Birds of a Feather*), Metro-Goldwyn-Mayer/United Artists, 1996; *Meet Wally Sparks,* Trimark, 1997; *Contact,* Warner Bros., 1997; *In & Out,* Paramount, 1997; and *Mad City,* Warner Bros., 1997.

AWARDS, HONORS: Writers Guild of America nomination, 1987; Emmy Award for Best Musical or Variety Series, 1995, for the *Tonight Show;* Emmy Award for Best Musical or Variety Series nomination, 1996 and 1997, for the *Tonight Show;* Best Political Humorist, *Washingtonian Magazine; Tonight Show* named Favorite Television Show in Europe.

WRITINGS:

(Editor) *Headlines: Real but Ridiculous Samplings from America's Newspapers,* Warner, 1989.
(Editor) *More Headlines: Real but Ridiculous Samplings from America's Newspapers,* Warner, 1991.
(Editor) *Headlines III: Not the Movie, Still the Book: Real but Ridiculous Samplings from America's Newspapers,* Warner, 1991.

(Editor) *Headlines IV: The Next Generation: More Out-of-This World Headlines from the Bestselling Series,* Warner, 1992.
(Editor) *Jay Leno's Headlines. Books I, II, III,* Wings (New York City), 1992.
(Editor) *Jay Leno's Police Blotter: Real-Life Crime Headlines from "The Tonight Show with Jay Leno,"* Andrews & McMeel (Kansas City, MO), 1994.
(With Bill Zehme) *Leading with My Chin,* Harper-Collins (New York City), 1996.

SIDELIGHTS: Born in New Rochelle, New York, and raised in Andover, Massachusetts, late-night television host Jay Leno began his show-business career as a standup comedian. Performing his comedy routines around the country, making as many as three hundred appearances a year, Leno eventually procured a spot as the guest host of the popular late-night program *The Tonight Show,* which starred Johnny Carson. With Carson's retirement from the show, Leno stepped in as his successor, beating out other contenders, including David Letterman. Now dubbed by the media as "The King of Late Night," Leno's *Tonight Show* began topping late-night television ratings in 1995.

Leno's autobiography, *Leading with My Chin,* details his rise to fame from small comedy clubs to his late-night television success. The son of an Italian American father and a Scottish mother who immigrated to the United States alone at the age of eleven, Leno has apparently always had a heart for comedy. His fifth grade report card read: "If Jay spent as much time studying as he does trying to be a comedian, he'd be a big star." Leno's autobiography does not break from his comedic tendencies. In the book, he lightheartedly shares anecdotes of his rise to fame, including early gigs in mental institutions and strip clubs. One memorable appearance Leno describes in his book is performing for a group of Orthodox Jews only to find that the audience was really expecting to be entertained by a Yiddish storyteller.

Leading with My Chin is not the first book that Leno has issued. He capitalized on his affiliation with *The Tonight Show* to compile and edit more than four hundred newspaper headlines, material from one of the show's featured routines, to create *Headlines: Real but Ridiculous Samplings from America's Newspapers.* Over the years, five more *Headlines* books have emerged. When *Headlines* was published in 1989, *Booklist* reviewer Steve Weingartner, citing the book's entertaining material and the popularity of

Leno, stated, "This material should attract an avid audience." Excerpts from the book include, "Researchers call murder a threat to public health" and "Condom week starts with a cautious bang." When *More Headlines* was published in 1991, a *Kliatt* reviewer commended, "Leno's . . . follow-up is equally humorous." Book five in the *Headlines* series concentrated on crime headlines, but is similar to the first four books.

Critics and fans have found Leno to be a nice guy. The royalties from his second book, *More Headlines,* were donated to a foundation that funds pediatric AIDS programs. The "nice-guy image," as perceived by some reviewers of *Leading with My Chin,* is at odds with their expectations from a Hollywood autobiography. Alex Tresniowski, in *People,* pointed out that "no one is criticized, no action regretted, no demon wrestled with." Tresniowski described the book as "a homey, joke-filled whitewash of any splotches on Leno's squeaky-clean facade." *Entertainment Weekly* reviewer Bret Watson questioned how Leno survived the battle to inherit Johnny Carson's throne as host of *The Tonight Show* as well as the inside story on Leno's "agonizing decision to fire Helen Kushnick, his manager of seventeen years." Watson was left wishing Leno had offered "insights into his private struggles or intriguing perspectives on the famous people he has known." *New York Times Books Review* contributor Bill Carter felt that such criticism was beside the point. "That's not what Mr. Leno is about; he is about performing," Carter declared.

BIOGRAPHICAL/CRITICAL SOURCES:

BOOKS

Celebrity Register, 1990, Gale Research (Detroit, MI), 1990.
Contemporary Newsmakers, Gale Research, 1989.
Contemporary Theatre, Film, and Television, Gale Research, 1989.
Leno, Jay, editor, *Headlines: Real but Ridiculous Samplings from America's Newspapers,* Warner (New York City), 1989.
Leno, Jay, *Leading With My Chin,* with Bill Zehme, HarperCollins (New York City), 1996.

PERIODICALS

Advertising Age, May 25, 1992, p. 24; November 30, 1993, pp. 1-3.
Booklist, January 1, 1990, p. 870.
Boston Magazine, May, 1992, pp. 16-21.

Chicago Tribune Books, January 14, 1990, p. 4.
Cosmopolitan, December, 1993, pp. 70-72; May, 1996, pp. 180-185.
Entertainment Weekly, August 14, 1992, pp. 20-27; February 11, 1994, p. 63; April 22, 1994, p. 12; November 3, 1995, p. 19; March 15, 1996, p. 52; October 11, 1996, pp. 84-85; November 8, 1996, p. 11.
Esquire, October, 1995, pp. 98-105.
Insight on the News, July 22, 1991, pp. 42-44.
Kliatt, January, 1991, p. 55.
Ladies Home Journal, February, 1997, p. 166.
Life, November, 1993, p. 100.
Newsweek, June 29, 1992, p. 56; January 25, 1993, pp. 60-63.
New Yorker, November 9, 1992, pp. 46-65.
New York Times Book Review, November 17, 1996, p. 24.
New York Times Magazine, January 30, 1994, p. 28.
People Weekly, December 24, 1990, pp. 56-59; August 23, 1993, pp. 46-49, October 14, 1996, p. 39.
Playboy, December 1990, pp. 57-69; October 1996, pp. 51-60.
Publishers Weekly, January 15, 1996, p. 320.
Redbook, July, 1992, pp. 48-51.
Runner's World, November, 1994, pp. 42-45.
Time, March 16, 1992, pp. 58-62.
TV Guide, April 11, 1992, pp. 16-21; August 15, 1992, p. 27; January 30, 1993, pp. 49-51; August 28, 1993, pp. 18-23; October 22, 1994, pp. 28-33; October 5, 1996, pp. 14-22.
Vanity Fair, July, 1991, pp. 48-50.
Washingtonian, November, 1993, pp. 76-80.
Woman's Day, March 10, 1992, pp. 36-40.

OTHER

Amazon, http://www.amazon.com/exec/obidos/ISBN=0060186941/7208-1512015-857663, August 20, 1997.
E! Online, http://www.eonline.com/Hot/Qa/Leno/index. html, August 25, 1997.
Mr. Showbiz, http://web3.starwave.com/showbiz/memory bank/starbios/jayleno/b.
html, August 25, 1997.
NBC website, http://www.nbc.com/entertainment/shows/tonight/bioleno.html, August 19, 1997.
New York Times Books, http://search.nytimes.com/books, August 20, 1997.
TV-Guide Online, http://www.iguide.com/tv/magazine/960930/ftr1a.sml, October 14, 1997.
"What other people have to say about Jay Leno" and *Esquire* article, http://users.cybercity.dk/~dko1225, October 14, 1997.

LEPKO, E.
See KOPELEV, Lev (Zinovievich)

* * *

LIPMANN, Fritz Albert 1899-1986

PERSONAL: Born June 12, 1899, in Koenigsburg, East Prussia (now Kaliningrad, Russia); became U.S. citizen; died following a stroke, July 17, 1986, in Poughkeepsie, NY; son of Leopold and Gertrud Lachmanski Lipmann; married Freda M. Hall (an artist), June 21, 1931; children: Stephen Hall. *Education:* University of Berlin, M.D., 1924, Ph.D., 1927. *Religion:* Jewish.

CAREER: Biochemist and writer. Kaiser Wilhelm Institute, Berlin and Heidelberg, Germany, researcher, 1927-30; Fischer's Laboratory, Berlin, Germany, researcher, 1930-31; Rockefeller Institute for Medical Research, New York, researcher, 1931-32; Carlsburg Foundation, Copenhagen, Denmark, researcher, 1932-39; Cornell University, Ithaca, NY, researcher, 1939-41; Massachusetts General Hospital, Boston, researcher and administrator, 1941-57; Harvard University, Cambridge, MA, professor, 1949-57; Rockefeller University, New York, professor, 1957-86.

AWARDS, HONORS: Carl Neuberg Medal, 1948; Mead Johnson and Company Award, 1948; Nobel Prize for medicine or physiology (with Hans Krebs), 1953, for his discovery of coenzyme A (CoA); National Medal of Science, 1966.

WRITINGS:

Wanderings of a Biochemist, Wiley-Interscience (New York), 1971.

Also author of numerous scientific papers. Contributor to journals and periodicals, including *Advances in Enzymology, Annual Review of Biochemistry, Nature,* and *Harvey Lectures.*

SIDELIGHTS: Fritz Albert Lipmann was a leading architect of the golden age of biochemistry. His landmark paper, "Metabolic Generation and Utilization of Phosphate Bond Energy," published in 1941, laid the foundation for biochemical research over the next three decades, clearly defining such concepts as group potential and the role of group transfer in biosynthesis. Most biochemists clearly recognized that

Lipmann had revealed the basis for the relationship between metabolic energy production and its use, providing the first coherent picture of how living organisms operate. His discovery of coenzyme A (CoA), which occurs in all living cells and is a key element in the metabolism of carbohydrates, fats, and some amino acids, earned him the 1953 Nobel Prize in physiology or medicine. He also conducted groundbreaking research in protein synthesis. Lipmann was an instinctual researcher with a knack for seeing the broader picture. Lacking the talent or inclination for self-promotion, he struggled early in his career before establishing himself in the world of biochemistry.

Lipmann was born on June 12, 1899, in Koenigsberg, the capital of East Prussia (now Kaliningrad, Russia). The son of Leopold, a lawyer, and Gertrud Lachmanski, Lipmann grew up in happy and cultured surroundings and fondly remembered the peaceful years at the turn of the century. He counted his only brother Heinz, who would pursue the arts as opposed to science, as one of the two people who most influenced him in his formative years. The other was Siegfried (Friedel) Sebba, a painter who would remain his friend for life. From these two, he first learned to appreciate the arts, an avenue of interest that he used to escape the confines and pressures of his laboratory investigations.

Early on, Lipmann demonstrated a diffidence in academic pursuit that would belie his future success. He admitted that he was never very good at school, even when he reached the university. After graduating from the gymnasium, Lipmann decided to pursue a career in medicine, largely due to the influence of an uncle who was a pediatrician and one of his boyhood heroes. In 1917 he enrolled in the University of Koenigsberg, but had his medical studies interrupted in 1918 as he was called to the medical service during World War I. Serving near the front during the last days of the war, he first learned to exert authority and never forgot the grim experience of severely wounded men receiving bad care.

In 1919 he was discharged from the army and went to study medicine in Munich and Berlin. Lipmann's brother was a literature student in Munich, and Lipmann became involved with his brother's circle of artistic friends while he lived in Schwabing, which Lipmann called the Greenwich Village of the city at that time. Throughout his life he maintained fond memories of Berlin. He eventually returned to Koenigsberg to complete his studies and obtained his medical degree from Berlin in 1922. Even though he cared about patients, Lipmann became more intrigued by what went on inside the human body. This interest was further cultivated when, during his practical year of medical studies, he worked in the pathology department in a Berlin hospital and took a three-month course in modern biochemistry taught by Peter Rona. At the same time, Lipmann was troubled by his concerns over the ethics of profiting from providing necessary medical services. The final turning point came when he went to the University of Amsterdam on a half-year stipend to study pharmacology. There, he first became versed in biochemical problems and the working of a biological laboratory. He left Amsterdam bent on a new career as a researcher.

Returning to Koenigsberg, Lipmann, who had no money, lived with his parents while he studied chemistry in the university for the next three years. Looking for a laboratory to do research in for his thesis, he chose to work with biochemist Otto Meyerhof, whose physiological investigations focused on the muscle. For the most part, Lipmann worked on inhibition of glycolysis (the breakdown of glucose by enzymes) by fluoride in muscle contraction and did his doctoral dissertation on metabolic fluoride effects. During this time in Berlin, Lipmann met many of the era's great biochemists, including Karl Lohmann, who discovered adenosine triphosphate (ATP—a compound that provides the chemical energy necessary for a host of chemical reactions in the cell) and who taught Lipmann about phosphate ester chemistry, which was to play an important role in Lipmann's later research. Lipmann also met his eventual lifelong companion while attending one of the masked balls popular at that time. Freda Hall, an American-born German and an artist, would become his wife in 1931.

Over the next ten years, Lipmann continued with a varied but not very lucrative research career. In *The Roots of Modern Biochemistry,* Freda remembered her husband as a very "unusual young man" who "seemed to be certain of a goal" but "had no position, no prospects, and it did not seem to trouble him." Although he was interested in his work, Freda recalled that "at no time was Fritz the obsessed scientist without other interests. He always had time for fun," which included tennis matches, bicycle races, and the theater.

Lipmann spent a short time in Heidelberg when Meyerhof moved his laboratory there, but then returned to Berlin and worked with Albert Fischer on tissue culturing and the study of metabolism as a method to measure cell growth. Soon, however, uniformed followers of Hitler began to appear in the streets of Berlin; both Lipmann and Freda had un-

pleasant encounters, and once Lipmann was beaten up. Realizing that they would soon have to leave Germany, Lipmann, through Fischer's intervention, received an offer to work at the Rockefeller Foundation (now Rockefeller University). Before leaving for the United States, Lipmann and Freda Hall were married on June 21, 1931. As it turned out, Freda's birth in Ohio made her an American citizen, thus greatly reducing obstacles to immigration.

At the Rockefeller Foundation, Lipmann worked in the laboratory of chemist Phoebus Aaron Theodor Levene, who had conducted research on egg yolk protein, which he called vitellinic acid, and found that it contained ten percent bound phosphate (phosphate strongly attached to other substances). Lipmann's interest in this protein, which served as food for growing animal tissues, led him to isolate serine phosphate from an egg protein.

At the end of the summer of 1932 Lipmann and his wife returned to Europe to work with Fischer, who was now in the Biological Institute of the Carlsberg Foundation in Copenhagen, Denmark. Free to pursue his own scientific interests, Lipmann delved into the mechanism of fermentation and glycolysis and eventually cell energy transformation. In the course of these studies, Lipmann found that pyruvate oxidation (a reaction that involves the loss of electrons) yielded ATP. Lohmann, who first discovered ATP, had also found that creatine phosphate provides the muscle with energy through ATP. Further work led Lipmann to the discovery of acetyl phosphate and the recognition that this phosphate was the intermediate of pyruvate oxidation. A discovery that Lipmann said was his most impressive work and had motivated all his subsequent research.

Despite his belief in his work, Lipmann had still to make his mark in research. In his book, *Wanderings of a Biochemist,* Lipmann would remember his efforts at the institute and throughout that decade as a time of personal scientific development that set the stage for his later discoveries. "In the Freudian sense," said Lipmann, "all that I did later was subconsciously mapped out there; it started to mature between 1930 and 1940 and was more elaborately realized from then on."

But before Lipmann could piece together his formula for the foundation of how organisms produce energy, once again the rise of the Nazis forced him and his wife to flee to the United States; they were nearly penniless. Fortunately, Lipmann acquired a research fellowship in the biochemistry department of Cornell University Medical College. His work with pyruvate oxidation and ATP had germinated and set him on a series of investigations that led to his theories of phosphate bond energy and energy-rich phosphate bond energy. During a vacation on Lake Iroquois in Vermont, Lipmann began his essay "Metabolic Generation and Utilization of Phosphate Bond Energy," in which he introduced the squiggle ($\sim$) to represent energy-rich phosphate, a symbol subsequently used by other researchers to denote energy-rich metabolic linkages. In this essay Lipmann also first proposed the notion of group potential and the role of group transfer in biosynthesis.

This essay was the turning point in Lipmann's career. Prior to its publication, Lipmann had contributed disparate pieces to the puzzle of biosynthesis, but through his natural scientific instinct and his ability to see the broader picture, he had now laid the foundation for the basis of how living organisms function. Although his essay covered a wide range of topics, including carbamyl phosphate and the synthesis of sulfate esters, his elucidation of the role of ATP in group activation (such as amino acids in the synthesis of proteins) foretold the use of ATP in the biosynthesis of macromolecules (large molecules). In more general terms, he identified a link between generation of metabolic energy and its utilization. A prime example of ATP's role in energy transmission was the transfer of phosphor potential from ATP to provide the energy needed for muscles to contract.

Despite the growing acknowledgement that Lipmann had written a groundbreaking paper in biochemistry, he soon found himself without a solid job prospect when Dean Burk, whose lab Lipmann worked in, left for the National Institutes of Health. Burk was reluctant to take Lipmann with him because of Lipmann's lack of interest in Burk's cancer research. While Lipmann's renown had grown, he had also antagonized other researchers, particularly as a result of his insistence that the term "bond energy" had been misused and his replacement of the term with "group potential" to refer to the capacity of a biochemical bond to carry potential energy for synthesis. It also took many years for the squiggle to be fully accepted as a way to denote energy-carrying bonds. Fortunately, Lipmann gained an unusual appointment in the Department of Surgery at Massachusetts General Hospital through the support of a CIBA Foundation fellowship. "This was really one of the lucky breaks in my life," Lipmann recalled in his autobiography. Soon he received growing support from the Commonwealth

Fund as more and more people began to recognize the importance of his work. Building upon his group transfer concept, Lipmann delved into the nature of the metabolically active acetate, which had been postulated as an "active" intermediary in group activation. In 1945, working with a potent enzyme from pigeon liver extract as an assay system for acetyl transfer in animal tissue, Lipmann and colleagues at Massachusetts General Hospital discovered Coenzyme A (CoA), the "A" standing for the activation of acetate. (Coenzymes are organic substances that can attach themselves to and supplement specified proteins to form active enzyme systems.) Eventually, CoA would be shown to occur in all living cells as an essential component in the metabolism of carbohydrates, fats, and certain amino acids. In 1953 Lipmann received the Nobel Prize in physiology or medicine for his discovery specifically of the acetyl-carrying CoA, which is formed as an intermediate in metabolism and active as a coenzyme in biological acetylations. (Lipmann shared the prize with his old colleague and friend, Hans Krebs, from Berlin.) Although proud of the Nobel Prize, Lipmann often stated that he believed his earlier work on the theory of group transfer was more deserving.

In 1957 Lipmann once again found himself at the Rockefeller Institute, twenty-five years after his first appointment there. Lipmann was to spend the next thirty years at the institute, primarily working on the analysis of protein biosynthesis. He and his colleagues contributed greatly to our understanding of the mechanisms of the elongation step of protein synthesis (stepwise addition of single amino acids to the primary protein structure).

Lipmann's productive career included 516 publications between 1924 and 1985. His 1944 paper on acetyl phosphate is a citation classic, having been cited in other works more than seven hundred times. His work on high-energy phosphate bonds and group transfer discoveries propelled biochemistry to the forefront of physiological research for nearly three decades. In addition to the Nobel Prize, Lipmann received the National Medal of Science in 1966 and was elected a foreign member of the Royal Society in London.

In 1959 the Lipmanns, who had a son Stephen Hall, bought a country home with Fritz's Nobel Prize money. Although his wife described him essentially as a city person, Lipmann enjoyed the country and often strolled the twenty acres of woods that surrounded his home with his Australian terrier, Pogo, named after the satiric comic strip character popular in the 1960s and 1970s. A private man who avoided political and social issues, Lipmann did, however, sign the Nobel laureate public appeal letters seeking prohibition of the hydrogen bomb and asking for freedom for the Polish Worker's Union. Lipmann's talent for writing was evident in the easy-to-follow and informative format of his scientific essays and in his autobiography. Still, he was given to preoccupation, and a colleague fondly recalled Lipmann once combing an auditorium after a lecture in search of his shoes, which he had left behind in going to the podium.

Lipmann's unique ability to see the entire scientific picture set him apart from many of his contemporaries. Interestingly, this ability also translated into his noted penchant for spotting four-leaf clovers almost anywhere. He kept them in books, manuscripts, and wallets, perhaps reflecting his own estimation that he had been fortunate in a life and career that allowed him to follow his instincts so successfully.

Despite failing strength, Lipmann continued to work until he suffered a stroke on July 17, 1986, and died seven days later. "One evening I heard him say: I can't function anymore," recalled Freda Hall in *The Roots of Modern Biochemistry,* "and that was that." Lipmann's ashes were scattered along his walking path in the woods that surrounded his home.

BIOGRAPHICAL/CRITICAL SOURCES:

BOOKS

Lipmann Symposium: Energy, Regulation, and Biosynthesis in Molecular Biology, de Gruyter, 1974.
McGraw-Hill Modern Men of Science, McGraw-Hill, 1966.
The Roots of Modern Biochemistry, de Gruyter, 1988.*

* * *

LISANDRELLI, Elaine Slivinski 1951-

PERSONAL: Born July 11, 1951, in Pittston, PA; daughter of Leo J. (a postal employee) and Gabriella A. (a registered nurse; maiden name, Sharek) Slivinski; married Carl A. Lisandrelli (a history teacher), June 20, 1980. *Education:* Marywood University, B.A., 1973, M.S., 1976; further graduate study at Marywood University, Indiana University—Bloomington, and Villanova University. *Avocational interests:* "Exer-

cise; research; visiting libraries; spending time with my husband, family, friends and animals (especially dogs); watching movies and documentaries; listening to music (especially Broadway tunes and love songs); lending a helping hand to others whenever I can."

ADDRESSES: Home—Moosic, PA. *Office*—North Pocono Middle School, Church St., Moscow, PA 18444.

CAREER: North Pocono Middle School, Moscow, PA, English teacher, 1973—; Marywood University, Scranton, PA, adjunct faculty member, 1986—. Member of Pennsylvania Writing Assessment Committee, Pennsylvania Department of Education, 1989. International Correspondence School, proofreader, summer, 1991; educational consultant.

MEMBER: Society of Children's Book Writers and Illustrators, National Council of Teachers of English, Kosciuszko Foundation, Polish Arts and Culture Foundation, Humane Society of the United States, La Plume (writer's group), Kappa Gamma Pi, Lambda Iota Tau.

WRITINGS:

(Co-author) *Easywriter,* Levels G and H, ERA/CCR, Inc., 1987.
(With Susan Campbell Bartoletti) *The Study Skills Workout,* Scott, Foresman, 1988.
Maya Angelou: More than a Poet (young adult nonfiction), Enslow (Hillside, NJ), 1996.
Bob Dole: Legendary Senator (young adult nonfiction), Enslow, 1997.

Contributor to magazines, including *Pockets* and *Cobblestone.*

WORK IN PROGRESS: A biography of Ignacy Jan Paderewski, publication by Morgan Reynolds expected in 1998; a biography of Ida B. Wells-Barnett and a biography of Jack London, both for Enslow Publishers.

SIDELIGHTS: Elaine Slivinski Lisandrelli commented: "I've always loved history. In grade school, I wanted to look up a different historical time, person, or place every night. Biographies are important to me because they bring people, events, and times past back to life.

"My parents, my older brother Dennis, and my teachers encouraged me to read on my own, and they also read to me. I found a fascinating world in books.

Books taught me so much and still do. I try to instill this love for reading in my students. I hope my writing will touch my readers in a special way and make them hungry to learn more. I believe in the words of Frederick Douglass: 'Education means emancipation; it means light and liberty.'

"I've been fortunate to belong to a writer's group whose members have helped me to grow as a writer. Their feedback is invaluable, and their support and encouragement gives me hope."

BIOGRAPHICAL/CRITICAL SOURCES:

PERIODICALS

Booklist, September 1, 1996, pp. 116, 118.
School Library Journal, June, 1996, p. 160.
Voice of Youth Advocates, October, 1996, p. 234.

* * *

LUKAS, J(ay) Anthony   1933-1997

OBITUARY NOTICE—See index for *CA* sketch: Born April 25, 1933, in New York, NY; died of asphyxiation resulting from suicide, June 5, 1997, in Manhattan, NY. Journalist, educator, and author. Lukas was a highly esteemed journalist who wrote about social and racial issues in twentieth-century America. His detailed writings earned him many awards, including two Pulitzer Prizes, the George Polk Memorial Prize, a Page One Award, and an American Book Award among others. After studies at Harvard University and the Free University of Berlin, he worked as a city hall correspondent with the *Baltimore Sun.* In 1962 he joined the staff of the *New York Times* working with the Washington, D.C. and United Nations bureaus. Later assignments took him to the Congo and India. He won his first Pulitzer in 1968 for local reporting. He also covered the trial of the "Chicago Seven," antiwar protestors accused of conspiring to incite riots at the 1968 Democratic National Convention in Chicago. He wrote a book about the experience titled *The Barnyard Epithet and Other Obscenities: Notes on the Chicago Conspiracy Trial.* In the 1970s he taught at Yale University's School of Public Communications and at the Kennedy School of Government at Harvard. He also issued *Don't Shoot—We Are Your Children!* and *Nightmare: The Underside of the Nixon Years.* In the 1980s he wrote *Common Ground: A Turbulent Decade in the Lives of Three American Families,* which detailed the controversy in Boston about school busing. The work earned him a second Pulitzer as well as a National Book Award. During his long career he became a freelance writer and was also co-founder of *More,* a magazine that examined the media. In 1997 he became president of the Author Guild. Shortly before his death he completed work on *Big Trouble,* a book about the murder of an Idaho governor and the labor leader brought to trial for the crime.

OBITUARIES AND OTHER SOURCES:

BOOKS

Who's Who in America, Marquis Who's Who, 1997.

PERIODICALS

Chicago Tribune, June 7, 1997, section 1, p. 23.
CNN Interactive (electronic), June 6, 1997.
Los Angeles Times (electronic), June 7, 1997.
New York Times, June 7, 1997, p. 11.

* * *

LYONS, Mary E(velyn)   1947-

PERSONAL: Born November 28, 1947, in Macon, GA; daughter of Joseph and Evelyn Lyons; married Paul Collinge (owner of a used and rare bookstore). *Education:* Appalachian State University, B.S., 1970, M.S., 1972; University of Virginia, doctoral study. *Avocational interests:* Playing Irish penny whistle and banjo, performing with the group Virgil and the Chicken Heads.

ADDRESSES: Home—Charlottesville, VA.

CAREER: Writer. Has worked as a reading teacher at elementary and middle schools in North Carolina and in Charlottesville, VA, and as a school librarian at elementary, middle, and high schools, Charlottesville.

AWARDS, HONORS: Best Books for Young Adults, American Library Association, and Carter G. Woodson Book Award, National Council for the Social Studies, both 1991, both for *Sorrow's Kitchen;* Teacher Scholar Award, National Endowment for the Humanities, 1991-92; Notable Children's Trade Book in the Field of Social Studies, National Council for the Social Studies and Children's Book Council (NCSS/CBC),

1992, for *Raw Head, Bloody Bones,* and 1996, for *Keeping Secrets;* Best Books for Young Adults, American Library Association, Golden Kite Award for fiction, Society of Children's Book Writers and Illustrators, both 1992, Honor Book, Jane Addams Children's Book Award, 1993, and Parents' Choice Award, 1996, all for *Letters from a Slave Girl;* Notable Book designation, American Library Association, 1993, and Carter G. Woodson Award, National Council for the Social Studies, 1994, both for *Starting Home;* Notable Children's Trade Book in the Field of Social Studies, NCSS/CBC, 1994, for *Stitching Stars;* Books for the Teen Age, New York Public Library, 1995, for *Deep Blues;* Carter G. Woodson Elementary Merit Book, National Council for the Social Studies, 1995, for *Master of Mahogany;* Jefferson Cup Series Award, Virginia Library Association, 1996, for the "African-American Artists and Artisans" series. Three fellowships from the Virginia Foundation for the Humanities.

WRITINGS:

FOR YOUNG PEOPLE

Sorrow's Kitchen: The Life and Folklore of Zora Neale Hurston, Scribner (New York City), 1990.
(Editor) *Raw Head, Bloody Bones: African-American Tales of the Supernatural,* Scribner, 1991.
Letters From a Slave Girl: The Story of Harriet Jacobs, Scribner, 1992.
The Butter Tree: Tales of Bruh Rabbit, illustrated by Mireille Vautier, Holt (New York City), 1995.
Keeping Secrets: The Girlhood Diaries of Seven Working Writers, Holt, 1995.

"AFRICAN-AMERICAN ARTISTS AND ARTISANS" SERIES

Starting Home: The Story of Horace Pippin, Painter, Scribner, 1993.
Stitching Stars: The Story Quilts of Harriet Powers, Scribner, 1993.
Master of Mahogany: Tom Day, Free Black Cabinetmaker, Scribner, 1994.
Deep Blues: Bill Traylor, Self-Taught Artist, Scribner, 1994.
Painting Dreams: Minnie Evans, Visionary Artist, Houghton (Boston, MA), 1996.

OTHER

A Story of Her Own: A Resource Guide to Teaching Literature by Women, National Women's History Project, 1985.

SIDELIGHTS: Born in Macon, Georgia, Mary Lyons displays a southern sensibility that is clearly evident in her many award-winning historical and biographical works for children. A former elementary and middle-school teacher of seventeen years and librarian for seven more in North Carolina and Virginia, Lyons claims that many of her books were inspired by her experiences in these professions. For instance, she undertook her first book, *Sorrow's Kitchen: The Life and Folklore of Zora Neale Hurston,* in response to the relative dearth of information on this important African-American figure who was admired by Lyons's students.

Sorrow's Kitchen vividly presents Hurston as an eccentric and often misinterpreted intellectual. Associated with the Harlem Renaissance in the 1920s and '30s, Hurston's reputation suffered through the middle of the century, but she has since become the subject of much critical attention. Lyons's succinct biography, directed to young readers, speaks with a laudatory but objective tone as it recounts Hurston's accomplishments and follows her life from her birth in Florida to her literary activities in Harlem. Praised by critics for its careful and precise documentation, the book records Hurston's anthropological work, especially in the preservation of African-American folktales and legends. Called "fascinating, enlightening, stimulating and satisfying" by Elizabeth S. Watson of *Horn Book, Sorrow's Kitchen* also features Lyons's brilliant use of eye-catching excerpts from Hurston's own writings.

Several of the stories that Zora Neale Hurston discovered and preserved appear in Lyons's second book, *Raw Head, Bloody Bones: African-American Tales of the Supernatural.* In this collection are fifteen tales of ghosts, demons, and other monsters, many of them retold by Lyons in their original Gullah dialect, a speech pattern used by some African-Americans living in the coastal regions of South Carolina. According to Lyons's introduction to these scary tales, most were originally unearthed by the Federal Writer's Project and were designed to teach moral lessons as well as to frighten and entertain listeners. Once again critics have noted that Lyons's excellent notes and bibliography makes this a valuable work for children interested in the history of African-American folklore.

After the publication of *Sorrow's Kitchen* and *Raw Head, Bloody Bones,* Lyons began to focus full-time attention on writing for children. Assisted by several honors and awards, including a National Endowment for the Humanities Teacher Scholar Award, Lyons has centered many of her efforts on important figures in

African-American culture, many of whom have been otherwise overlooked. *Letters from a Slave Girl* (1992) is an account of the life of Harriet Ann Jacobs. Depicting Jacobs's story through a series of fictionalized letters based upon her autobiography, Lyons recreates Jacobs's struggle with sexual harassment and the indifference of whites in the South to her plight. Lyons's book carries the reader through seven years that Jacobs spent in hiding, and to her eventual escape north in this tale that a *Kirkus Reviews* contributor called "a moving evocation of the tragedies inflicted by slavery."

Several of Lyons's next projects were undertaken as part of the "African-American Artists and Artisans" series. Focusing on the rich African cultural heritage in American art, Lyons has produced a superb collection of biographical sketches, stories, and images concerning some typically overlooked individuals in nineteenth and early twentieth-century American history. *Starting Home: The Story of Horace Pippin* renders the life of this self-taught painter. A soldier in World War I, Pippin produced several haunting works of folk-art, many of which depict his involvement in the Great War. Lyons's second volume for the series, *Stitching Stars: The Story Quilts of Harriet Powers,* recounts the life of this talented former slave whose quilts are considered valuable pieces of American social history. Reviewing the work for the *Bulletin of the Center for Children's Books,* Deborah Stevenson has observed that "Lyons's lively writing stitches concepts together with smoothness and clarity. . . . [This] is both an unusual take on history and a reminder of the democratic possibilities of art."

Master of Mahogany: Tom Day, Free Black Cabinetmaker, Deep Blues: Bill Traylor, Self-Taught Artist, and *Painting Dreams: Minnie Evans, Visionary Artist* are three more of Lyons's books for the "Artists and Artisans" series. Her story of Tom Day offers insights into the life of a free black man in the era of slavery. A successful businessman, Day used his carpentry skills to become an individual of considerable wealth, overcoming the suspicions of many whites in the prewar south. *Deep Blues* and *Painting Dreams* are both portraits of untutored artists who created their work under very unusual circumstances. Born into slavery in 1856, Bill Traylor did not begin painting until he was eighty years old. A talented folk-artist, he went on to earn a measure of fame when his works were "discovered" in 1939. Lyons's presentation of Minnie Evans's life investigates the work of this deeply religious woman haunted by dreams that provided the

inspiration for her art that was made from scrap materials. As with her other books, Lyons has been praised for her careful documentation and meticulous scholarship in these works.

Lyons's writings also include her versions of six African-American trickster tales in *The Butter Tree: Tales of Bruh Rabbit.* These retellings have been praised by critics for their simplicity and accessibility to young people. *Horn Book* reviewer Maeve Visser Knoth commented: "Lyon's skilled retellings are brief and uncluttered, recalling the oral tradition. She uses few adjectives, yet her language is colorful and evokes regional flavor."

Lyons has also written an important volume of literary scholarship titled *Keeping Secrets: The Girlhood Diaries of Seven Working Writers.* Focusing on the biographies of such individuals as Louisa May Alcott, Kate Chopin, Ida B. Wells, and Charlotte Perkins Gilman, *Keeping Secrets* combines enlightening excerpts from the writings of these famous women with an analysis of questions pertaining to women's identity and freedom in modern American society.

A socially active author, Lyons presents one constant theme in her writing: the importance and value of the various underrepresented sources of American culture, particularly the contributions of women and African-Americans. Considering this subject matter, Lyons is rarely surprised when people assume that she must be African-American; instead, she has commented, "I'm quite flattered when that happens because it means I'm an effective writer."

BIOGRAPHICAL/CRITICAL SOURCES:

BOOKS

Seventh Book of Junior Authors and Illustrators, H. W. Wilson, 1996, pp. 203-05.
Twentieth-Century Children's Writers, 4th edition, St. James Press, 1995, pp. 606-07.

PERIODICALS

Booklist, December 15, 1990, p. 816; January 1, 1992, p. 830; November, 1992, p. 79; November 15, 1993, p. 618; October 1, 1994, p. 322; November 15, 1994, p. 598; July, 1996, p. 1852.

Bulletin of the Center for Children's Books, January, 1991, p. 124; February, 1992, p. 162; December, 1993, p. 128; December, 1994, p. 136.

Horn Book, March-April, 1991, p. 216; January-February, 1992, pp. 81-82; November-December, 1992, pp. 729-730; March-April, 1995, p. 221; September-October, 1995, p. 614; October, 1995, pp. 620-621.

Kirkus Reviews, November 1, 1992, p. 1380; May 15, 1996, p. 747.

Publishers Weekly, October 25, 1991, p. 69; February 20, 1995, p. 206.

School Library Journal, January, 1991, p. 119; December, 1992, p. 113; May, 1994, p. 113; October, 1994, p. 136; January, 1995, p. 127; June, 1995, p. 103; July, 1995, p. 100; July, 1996, p. 93.

Voice of Youth Advocates, February, 1991, p. 378; December, 1992, p. 282; October, 1995, pp. 252, 254.

M

MAHARANI OF JAIPUR
See DEVI, Gayatri

* * *

MALCOLM, Noel

PERSONAL: Male.

ADDRESSES: Office—*Daily Spectator,* Spectator Ltd., 56 Doughty St., London WC1N 2LL, England; fax 242-0603. *Agent*—c/o Oxford University Press, Walton St., Oxford OX2 6DP, England.

CAREER: Historian and political columnist. *Daily Spectator,* London, England, political columnist covering the Balkan countries; *Daily Telegraph,* political columnist.

WRITINGS:

De Dominis, 1560-1624: Venetian, Anglican, Ecumenist, and Relapsed Heretic, Strickland & Scott (London), 1984.
George Enescu: His Life and Music, Toccata (London), 1990.
Bosnia: A Short History, New York University Press (New York City), 1994.
(Editor) *The Correspondence: Thomas Hobbes,* Oxford University Press (Oxford, England), 1994.
Kosovo: A Short History, New York University Press, 1998.

SIDELIGHTS: British journalist Noel Malcolm has covered the Balkan countries in his political column for the London *Daily Spectator* since the early 1980s. He has also used his experience at this post to write several books, either on historical figures, such as cleric Marcantonio de Dominis and composer George Enescu, or on a region of the Balkans, such as the republic of Bosnia. Malcolm's book-length efforts have met with praise from reviewers for their thoroughness and interest level.

De Dominis, 1560-1624: Venetian, Anglican, Ecumenist, and Relapsed Heretic was published in 1984, and has as its subject a priest born in sixteenth-century Dalmatia to Venetian parents. Marcantonio de Dominis was ordained in the Catholic Church, but for a time held heretical opinions that led him to seek refuge in England. He recanted his heresy and returned to Catholicism under Pope Gregory XV, but was imprisoned when Urban VIII was elected Pope. He died of natural causes five months later, before his trial began. Uberto Limentani in the *Modern Language Review* praised Malcolm's biographical efforts, noting that his "account of the vicissitudes and *volte-faces* of a bewildering personality goes a long way towards explaining the motives that lay behind his often contrasting attitudes."

The subject of Malcolm's next biography, 1990's *George Enescu: His Life and Music,* is a Romanian composer and musician who has been compared with Wolfgang Amadeus Mozart, according to David Matthews in the *Times Literary Supplement.* Known primarily for two pieces called the *Romanian Rhapsodies,* the rest of Enescu's body of work suffered from the governing regime's reluctance to support the composer, in part because of his marriage to a member of the former Romanian royal family and his opposition of the country's communist dictatorship, which lasted until the late 1980s. Furthermore, according to Matthews, "Enescu was not a modernist as Schoenberg, Stravinsky and Bartok were. He sought no overthrow of tonality, nor indulged in fashionable iconoclasm." The reviewer also judged that "Malcolm's study will surely do much to help the rehabilitation of Enescu as a composer. He is a passionately committed guide, interweaving well-researched biography with an account of all the music Enescu wrote."

Malcolm's 1994 volume, *Bosnia: A Short History,* details the history of Bosnia, the former Yugoslavian republic that has been divided by warfare. Many critics have found Malcolm's assertion, in the words of *Times Literary Supplement* reviewer Dimitri Obolensky, that "the root causes of Bosnia's collapse . . . were first, the political strategy of the Serbian leadership, and second, the total lack of understanding displayed by the leaders of the West" to be the most significant aspect of the work. *Bosnia: A Short History* also, however, examines the republic's religious and social history since medieval times, and attempts to refute the notion that Bosnia has always been divided from within by its diverse religious and ethnic groups. As John Fine stated in the *London Review of Books,* that "such ethnic hostility as did reveal itself in Bosnia between the |world| wars was usually exported there by its excitable neighbors. In fact, whenever violence has broken out in Bosnia over ideological causes . . . its source has lain beyond the borders."

Obolensky hailed *Bosnia: A Short History* as "a most impressive achievement. Combining wide and perceptive scholarship—evident in historical argument, illuminating notes and wide-ranging bibliography—it will do much for the professional historian while acting as a firm and skilful guide to the general reader." Michael Ignatieff in the *New York Review of Books* also applauded the volume, calling it "a thoughtful, lucid, and deeply informed study." Tom Gjelten, reviewing Malcolm's effort in the *Washington Post Book World* concluded that "it is a measure of the Bosnian conflict that a book on history . . . has the political significance that this one has."

BIOGRAPHICAL/CRITICAL SOURCES:

PERIODICALS

Kirkus Reviews, July 15, 1994, pp. 963-964.
London Review of Books, April 28, 1994, pp. 9-10.

Modern Language Review, January, 1986, pp. 225-226.
New York Review of Books, April 21, 1994, p. 3.
Publishers Weekly, July 25, 1994, p. 39.
Times Literary Supplement, January 11, 1991, p. 13; April 8, 1994, pp. 15-16.
Washington Post Book World, October 9, 1994, p. 6.*

* * *

MANHEIM, Ralph   1907-

PERSONAL: Born in 1907, in New York, NY.

ADDRESSES: Home—Paris, France. *Agent*—c/o Arcade Publishing, 141 Fifth Ave., New York, NY 10010.

CAREER: Translator of literature from German, French, Dutch, and Polish.

AWARDS, HONORS: Translation Prize, PEN Book-of-the-Month Club, 1964, for translation of *The Tin Drum,* by Gunter Grass; Schlegel-Tieck Translation Prize, Translators Association of the Society of Authors (UK), 1966, for translation of *Dog Years,* by Gunter Grass; National Book Award, 1970, for translation of *Castle to Castle,* by Louis-Ferdinand Celine; Goethe House-PEN Translation Prize, 1976, for translation of *A Sorrow Beyond Dreams,* by Peter Handke; John D. and Catherine T. MacArthur Foundation fellowship, 1983; Academy-Institute Award, American Academy and Institute of Arts and Letter, 1987; PEN Medal for Translation, 1988.

WRITINGS:

TRANSLATIONS

Konrad Heiden, *Der Fuehrer; Hitler's Rise to Power,* Houghton Mifflin (Boston, MA), 1944.
Karl Jaspers, *Way to Wisdom: An Introduction to Philosophy,* Yale University Press (New Haven, CT), 1951.
Ernst Cassirer, *The Philosophy of Symbolic Forms,* Yale University Press, 1953.
(With R. F. Hull) Joseph Campbell (from Eranos Yearbooks), *Spirit and Nature,* University Press (Princeton, NJ), 1954.
Erich Neumann, *Amor and the Psyche: The Psychic Development of the Feminine: A Commentary on the Tale by Apoleius,* Pantheon, 1956.

(With Hull) Joseph Campbell (from Eranos Yearbooks), *Man and Time,* Princeton University Press, 1957.

Karl Kerenyi, *Archetypal Images in Greek Religion: Asklepios: Archetypcal Image of the Physician's Existence,* Pantheon (New York, NY), 1959.

Erich Neumann, *Art and the Creative Unconscious,* Princeton University Press, 1959.

Jolande Jacobi, *Complex Archetype in the Psychology of C. G. Jung,* Princeton University Press, 1959.

Martin Heidegger, *An Introduction to Metaphysics,* Yale University Press, 1959.

(With Hull) Joseph Campbell (from Eranos Yearbooks), *Spiritual Disciplines,* Princeton University Press, 1960.

Gunter Grass, *The Tin Drum,* Pantheon, 1962.

Adolf Hitler, *Mein Kampf,* Houghton Mifflin, 1962.

Carl Kerenyi, *Archetypal Images in Greek Religion: Prometheus, Archetypal Image of Human Existence,* Princeton University Press, 1963.

Erich Neumann, *The Great Mother: An Analysis of the Archetype,* Pantheon, 1963.

(With Hull) Joseph Campbell (papers from Eranos Yearbooks), *Man and Transformation,* Princeton University Press, 1964.

Jakov Lind, *Soul of Wood,* J. Cape (London), 1964, Hill & Wang (New York City), 1986.

Erich Maria Remarque, *The Night in Lisbon,* Hutchinson (London), 1964.

Karl Jaspers, *Socrate, Buddha, Confucius & Jesus: The Paradigmatic Individuals* (taken from *Great Philosophers, Volume 1*), edited by Hannah Arendt, Harcourt (New York City), 1966.

Jakov Linde, *Landscape in Concrete,* Methuen, 1966.

Karl Jaspers, *Kant* (taken from *Great Philosophers, Volume 1*), Harcourt, 1966.

Louis-Ferdinand Celine, *Death on the Installment Plan,* New Directions (New York City), 1966.

Myth, Religion, & Mother Right: Selected Writings of Johann Jakob Bachofen, Princeton University Press, 1967.

Jakov Linde, *Ergo,* Random House (New York City), 1967.

Gunter Grass, *The Plebians Rehearse the Uprising,* Secker & Warburg (London), 1967.

Louis-Ferdinand Celine, *Castle to Castle,* Delacorte (New York City), 1968, with a new introduction by Kurt Vonnegut, Jr., Penguin, 1976.

Jakov Lind, *The Silver Foxes Are Dead and Other Plays,* Methuen (London), 1968, Hill & Wang, 1969.

Karl Jaspers, *Perennial Scope of Philosophy,* Archon (North Haven, CT), 1968.

(With Teresa Dziduszycka) Slawomir Mrozek, *Tango* (play), Grove Press (New York City), 1968.

Henry Corbin, *Creative Imagination in the Sufism of Ibn Arabi,* Princeton University Press, 1969.

Gunter Grass, *Speak Out: Speeches, Open Letters, Commentaries,* Harcourt, 1969.

Gunter Grass, *Local Anaesthetic,* Secker & Warburg (London), 1969, Harcourt (New York City), 1970.

Jurgen Neven-Du Mont, *After Hitler: Report from a West German City,* Pantheon, 1970.

Alfred Andersch, *Efraim's Book,* Doubleday, 1970.

Peter Hacks, *Amphitryon* (play), produced in New York City, 1970.

Hermann Hesse, *Rosshalde,* Farrar, Straus (New York City), 1970.

(Also editor, with John Willett) Bertolt Brecht, *Collected Plays,* nine volumes, Methuen (London), 1970-1973, Vintage (New York City), 1971-.

Yambo Ouologuem, *Bound to Violence,* Sphere (London), 1971.

Hermann Hesse, *If the War Goes On . . . . : Reflections on War and Politics,* Farrar, Straus, 1971.

Hermann Hesse, *Knulp: Three Tales from the Life of Knulp,* Farrar, Straus, 1971.

Hajo Holborn, *Republic to Reich: The Making of the Nazi Revolution* (ten essays), Pantheon (New York City), 1972.

Louis-Ferdinand Celine, *North,* Delacorte, 1972.

Michel Tournier, *Friday and Robinson: Life on Esperanza Island,* Knopf (New York City), 1972.

Erich Maria Remarque, *Shadows in Paradise,* Harcourt, 1972.

(With Denver Lindley) Hermann Hesse, *Stories of Five Decades,* edited and with an introduction by Theodore Ziolkowski, Farrar, Straus, 1972.

Slawomir Mrozek, *Vatzlav,* Cape (London), 1972, Applause Theatre Book Publishers, 1986.

Republic to Reich; the Making of the Nazi Revolution, Pantheon, 1972.

Victor Serge, *From Lenin to Stalin,* Anchor (New York City), 1973.

Jolande Jacobi, *Psychology of C. G. Jung,* Routledge and K. Paul (London), 1968, Yale University Press, 1973.

Erich Neumann, *The Child: Structure and Dynamics of the Nascent Personality,* C. G. Jung Foundation for Analytical Psychology (New York City), 1973.

Arnold Metzger, *Freedom and Death,* Human Context Books (London), 1973.

Andre Schwarz-Bart, *A Woman Named Solitude,* Atheneum (New York City), 1973.

Gunter Grass, *From the Diary of a Snail,* Harcourt, 1973.

Pascual Jordan, *Science and the Course of History,* Greenwood Press (Westport, CT), 1974.

Peter Handke, *Short Letter, Long Farewell,* Farrar, Straus, 1974.

Marie-Claire Blais, *St. Lawrence Blues,* Farrar, Straus, 1974.

Wilhelm Reich, *Listen, Little Man!,* illustrated by William Steig, Farrar, Straus (New York City), 1974.

Hans Erich Nossack, *To the Unknown Hero,* Farrar, Straus, 1974.

Karl Jaspers, *Spinoza, Taken from the Great Philosophers Series,* edited by Hannah Arendt, Harcourt, 1974.

Hermann Hesse, *Reflections,* selected by Volker Michels, Farrar, Straus, 1974.

(Translator with Denver Lindley) Hermann Hesse, *My Belief: Essays on Life and Art,* edited and with an introduction by Theodore Ziolkowski, Farrar, Straus, 1974.

(With Hull) Sigmund Freud and C. G. Jung, *The Freud-Jung Letters,* edited by William McGuire, Princeton University Press, 1974.

Louis-Ferdinand Celine, *Rigadoon,* Delacorte, 1974.

Hermann Broch, *The Guiltless,* Little, Brown (Boston), 1974.

The Hesse/Mann Letters, The Correspondence of Hermann Hesse and Thomas Mann, 1910-1955, edited by Anni Carlsson and Volker Michels, with a foreword by Theodore Ziolkowski and annotations by Wolfgang Sauerlander, Harper (New York City), 1975.

Peter Handke, *A Sorrow beyond Dreams,* Farrar, Straus, 1975.

Georges Simenon, *Letter to My Mother,* Harcourt, 1976.

Tales of Student Life, edited by Theodore Zialkowski, Farrar, Straus, 1976.

Marthe Robert, *From Oedipus to Moses: Freud's Jewish Identity,* Anchor (Garden City, NY), 1976.

Bertolt Brecht, *Poems, 1913-1956,* Methuen (New York City), 1976.

Abdallah Laroui, *The History of the Maghrib: An Interpretive Essay,* Princeton University Press, 1977.

Jacob Grimm, *Grimm's Tales for Young & Old: The Complete Stories,* Doubleday (Garden City, NY), 1977.

C. G. Jung Speaking: Interviews & Encounters, edited by R. F. Hull and William McGuire, Princeton University Press (Princeton, NJ), 1977.

Peter Handke, *The Left-Handed Woman,* Farrar, Straus, 1978.

Gunter Grass, *The Flounder,* Harcourt, 1978.

Emile Ajar, *Momo,* Doubleday, 1978.

Franz Babinger, *Mehmed the Conqueror and His Time,* Princeton University Press, 1978.

Alfred Andersch, *My Disappearance in Providence,* Doubleday, 1978.

(Also editor, with John Willett and Erich Fried) Carl Kerenyi, *Dionysos: Archetypal Image of Indestructible Life* (part of the "Archetypal Images in Greek Religion" series), Princeton University Press, 1979.

The Invisible Jew: The Story of One Man's Survival in Nazi Germany, Dutton (New York City), 1980.

Louis-Ferdinand Celine, *Journey to the End of the Night,* New Directions, 1980.

Hermann Hesse, *Hesse as Painter,* Suhrkamp Publishers (New York City), 1980.

Slawomir Mrozek, *Three Plays,* Grove Weidenfeld, 1981.

Gunter Grass, *The Meeting at Telgte,* Harcourt, 1981.

Rare Treasures from Grimm (selection from *Grimm's Tales for Young and Old, The Complete Stories*), paintings by Erik Blegvad, Doubleday, 1981.

Marthe Robert, *As Lonely as Franz Kafka,* Harcourt, 1982.

Gunter Grass, *Headbirths: Or the Germans Are Dying Out,* Harcourt, 1982.

Michel Tournier, *The Four Wise Men,* Doubleday, 1982.

Adolf Eichmann, *Eichmann Interrogated: Transcripts from the Archives of the Israeli Police,* edited by Jochen Von Lang, Farrar, Straus (New York City), 1983.

Gunter Grass, *Drawings & Words 1954-1977,* Harcourt, 1983.

Jona Oberski, *Childhood,* Doubleday, 1983.

(With Michael Mok) Anne Frank, *Anne Frank's Tales from the Secret Annex,* Doubleday, 1983.

Michael Ende, *The Neverending Story,* Doubleday, 1983.

Joachim Maass, *Kleist: A Biography,* Farrar, Straus, 1984.

Marie-Gisele Landes-Fuss, *A Red Brick Building, Ugly as Hell, in Venice, California,* Doubleday, 1984.

E. T. A. Hoffmann, *The Nutcracker,* illustrated by Maurice Sendak, Crown (New York City), 1984.

Peter Handke, *The Weight of the World,* Farrar, Straus, 1984.

Gunter Grass, *Etchings and Words 1972-1982,* Harcourt (San Diego), 1985.

Gunter Grass, *On Writing and Politics: 1967-1983,* with an introduction by Salman Rushdie, Harcourt, 1985.

Peter Handke, *Slow Homecoming,* Farrar, Straus, 1985.

Romain Gary, *The Life before Us: Madame Rosa,* New Directions (New York City), 1986.

Peter Handke, *Across,* Farrar, Straus, 1986.

Elias Canetti, *The Play of the Eyes,* Farrar, Straus, 1986.

The Plays of Elias Canetti, Farrar, Straus, 1986.

Hans C. Buch, *The Wedding at Port-au-Prince,* Harcourt, 1986.

Gunter Grass, *The Rat,* Harcourt, 1987.

Erich Auerbach, *Dante: Poet of the Secular World,* University of Chicago Press (Chicago), 1988.

Wilhelm Grimm, *Dear Mili,* illustrated by Maurice Sendak, Farrar, Straus, 1988.

Margarete Buber-Neumann, *Milena,* Seaver (New York City), 1988.

Peter Handke, *Repetition,* Farrar, Straus, 1988.

Marcel Proust, *Selected Letters, 1880-1903,* edited by Philip Kolb and J. M. Cocking, University of Chicago Press, 1988.

Horst Bienek, *Earth and Fire,* Atheneum (New York City), 1989.

Fritz Raddatz, *The Survivor,* Little, Brown (Boston), 1989.

(Also editor with John Willett) Bertolt Brecht, *Brecht Letters,* Routledge (New York City), 1989.

Peter Handke, *The Afternoon of a Writer,* Farrar, Straus, 1989.

Peter Handke, *Absence,* Farrar, Straus, 1990.

Danilo Kis, *Hourglass,* Farrar, Straus, 1990.

Helme Weine, *The Marvelous Journey through the Night,* Farrar, Straus, 1990.

Carl Kerenyi, *Eleusis: Archetypal Image of Mother & Daughter,* Princeton-Bollingen (Princeton, NJ), 1991.

Helme Heine, *Mollywoop,* Farrar, Straus, 1991.

Jean Rouaud, *Fields of Glory,* Arcade Publishing (New York City), 1992.

Gunter Grass, *The Call of the Toad,* Harcourt, 1992.

Erich Auerbach, *Literary Language and Its Public in Late Latin Antiquity and in the Middle Ages,* Princeton University Press, 1993.

Bertolt Brecht, *The Threepenny Opera, Baal, and The Mother,* Arcade Publishing, 1993.

EDITOR

(With John Willett) Bertolt Brecht, *Short Stories, 1921-1946,* translated by Yvonne Kapp, Hugh Rorrison, and Anthony Tatlow, Methuen, 1983.

(With Willett) Bertolt Brecht, *Fear and Misery in the Third Reich,* translated by Willett; bound with *Seora Carrar's Rifles,* translated by Wolfgang Sauerlander, Methuen (London),1983.

(With Willet) Bertolt Brecht, *The Good Person of Szechwan,* translated by John Willet, Arcade, 1994.

(With Willet) Bertolt Brecht, *Mother Courage and Her Children,* translated by John Willet, Arcade, 1994.

(With Willet) Bertolt Brecht, *The Caucasian Chalk Circle,* translated by James and Tania Stern with W. H. Auden, Arcade, 1994.

(With Willet) Bertolt Brecht, *Life of Galileo,* translated by John Willet, Arcade, 1994.

(With Willet) Bertolt Brecht, *The Rise and Fall of the City of Mahagonny* and *The Seven Deadly Sins of the Petty Bourgeoisie,* translated by W. H. Auden and Chester Kallman, Arcade, 1996.

(With Willet) Bertolt Brecht, *Mr. Puntila and His Man Matti,* translated by John Willet, Arcade, 1997.

Contributor to magazines, including *Time.*

SIDELIGHTS: When *Time* magazine correspondent Patricia Blake wrote a feature story on translators, calling them (in the words of Russian poet Alexander Pushkin) "couriers of the human spirit," Ralph Manheim was one of a handful of the professionals featured. According to *New York Times* contributor John Leonard (as quoted in a *Publishers Weekly* interview with Manheim), "When they get around to giving Gunter Grass his Nobel Prize, they should give one as well to Ralph Manheim." Manheim is the translator of more than one hundred books, primarily from German and French. Widely considered the dean of professional translators into the English language, he was awarded a MacArthur fellowship in 1983, in the amount of $60,000 tax-free dollars per year for the rest of his life. Questioned by *Publishers Weekly's* Herbert R. Lottman as to the effect of the money on his life and work, Manheim responded, "It allows me to spend more time on difficult books. If I had to think about making a living all the time, I'd go faster with [his then-current project by German novelist Peter] Handke and perhaps make more mistakes. And if I want to visit the scene of the story. . . . I can do that, to get a better picture of the terrain he describes."

Manheim began his career in the United States and, since 1950, has continued pursuing it in Paris, where he has made his home in a Montparnasse apartment.

Born in New York to American parents, he spent an adolescent year in Vienna and some time after college in Germany before the Hitler regime took power. He began translating in the field of philosophy, often working on books by major figures such as Karl Jaspers and Ernst Cassirer, and the field of Jungian psychology. His first major translation of a novel was Gunter Grass's *The Tin Drum,* a first novel that drew the worldwide attention to its author and earned Manheim the 1964 PEN Book-of-the-Month Translation Prize. The same year, Manheim translated Adolf Hitler's autobiographical *Mein Kampf.* That translation, too, was critically praised, as was Manheim's translation, a few years later, of the transcripts of the Adolf Eichmann trial.

Manheim has continued to translate nonfiction in such disciplines as history, philosophy, and psychology, often by writers he has worked with repeatedly, such as Erich Neumann. However, since the mid-1960s his reputation has been increasingly associated with the translation of fiction and other imaginative literature.

It has been said that a list of the authors Manheim has translated reads like a roll-call of twentieth-century European literature: Grass, Handke, Hermann Hesse, Erich Maria Remarque, Georges Simenon, Louis-Ferdinand Celine, Marcel Proust (the letters), Bertolt Brecht, and in nonfiction, C. G. Jung and Sigmund Freud, to name only the most noted. He has also translated Grimm's fairy tales, E. T. A. Hoffmann's *Nutcracker,* and more. Although book reviews often refrain from commenting on the quality of a translation, in the case of Manheim a tip of the hat from the reviewer of a work has become almost obligatory. A full citation of comments would require a volume; a sampling will give the flavor of the critical consensus. "Ralph Manheim, as usual, has done an excellent translation of [*The Afternoon of a Writer,* by Handke] from the German," said Herbert Mitgang writing for the *New York Times.* As for Handke's 1990 novel, *Absence,* said reviewer Rikki du Cornet in the Toronto *Globe and Mail,* "Ralph Manheim's translation is brilliant, limpid, graceful, perfectly fluid and beautiful." Gunter Grass's *The Rat* is, according to the *New York Times*'s Christopher Lehmann-Haupt, "as always superbly translated by Ralph Manheim." Said the London *Times Literary Supplement* of Manheim's work on Grass's *Local Anaesthetic,* "Like many translations, it reads well; like far fewer, it is also done well." Grass is a reputedly difficult writer to

translate from German, his work full of local allusions and colloquialisms.

Selected comments about Manheim's translations of other challenging books may also be illuminating. When Manheim translated Hoffmann's *Nutcracker,* reviewer Michael Steinberg of the *New York Times Book Review* wrote, "Mr. Manheim has put *Nutcracker* into delightful and lucid English; it moves fluently, it is full of ingenious solutions to tricky problems . . . and you would never guess that you are reading a translation." This, despite Steinberg's opinion that Manheim's "first-rate translation into prose" had inevitably lost some of Hoffmann's poetic effects. Jerry Griswold, contributor to the *Los Angeles Times Book Review,* meanwhile declared that Manheim had created "a finally readable translation" of Hoffmann's classic. When Manheim translated Grimm's fairy tales, he was competing with many previous versions, and did so successfully. *Library Journal*'s R. D. Roffman said, "[B]ecause Manheim has a wonderful ear, the tales are exciting to read aloud" as well as remaining close to the spirit of the German version.

In addition, Roffman asserted, "Manheim's translation doesn't screen out the violence, depravity, or the gratuitous moment; it is the least remote, yet the one truest to the magic of the original." The *New Yorker*'s reviewer announced that "Manheim's English reads as if it were dateless, and retains the stories' feeling of having been oral literature." And *School Library Journal*'s M. J. Laflan praised a "fluent and well paced" rendition, "in uncomplicated and unembellished language, free of . . . archaisms." Reviewing a later selection of fifteen of the lesser-known Grimm tales, *Rare Treasures* from Grimm, *Horn Book*'s E. L. Heins referred to the complete version as Manheim's "excellent prodigious 1977 work." The *New York Times Book Review*'s Joyce Milton commented of *Rare Treasures,* "Mr. Manheim narrates . . . with no-nonsense relish. . . . Manheim's translations make the most of the suspense." Perhaps one of Manheim's most difficult translation projects has been on the novels of Louis-Ferdinand Celine, the notoriously profane, anti-Semitic French novelist of the 1930s, who later wrote in the vernacular of Parisian criminals. Reviewing Celine's *Castle to Castle* for the *New York Times,* Anatole Broyard called the French author's style an "'emotive subway' . . . a non-stop stutter of short clauses separated by three dots." Wrote Broyard, "Ralph Manheim has captured intact this difficult, un-English poetry of *'moi, je.'* With the exception of the single word 'zounds' . . . the translation is a masterpiece." Reviewing the same Celine novel for *Newsweek,* Raymond A. Sokolov wrote that although translation inevitably made Celine's rough prose too smooth, "Sipping Celine through Manheim's straw is almost as good as the real thing and far simpler than joining the Parisian underworld for a few years to learn to read the original."

In old age, Manheim continues to work hard, walking each day from his apartment to his small office in a former maid's room near the Luxembourg Gardens. He turns out about a thousand pages, or three books, per year, working five hours a day, and breaking for a sandwich for lunch. He sometimes has critical words for other translators (such as Vladimir Nabokov, translator of Pushkin's *Eugene Onegin,* which Manheim termed "unreadable"), and sometimes expresses irritation with authors and publishers. "There's a moment in the middle of a job when a certain antagonism develops," he told *Publishers Weekly*'s Lottman, "because the author is making you work so hard. I think this resistance is good for me. If a translator finds the going too easy, it can be dangerous; perhaps he has failed to notice things." His devotion to the works he translates is unquestioned, and includes, at times, consulting specialists on difficult technical terms. For various works by Grass, he consulted dentists, stonecutters, and conchologists. As for his own talents, Manheim modestly summed up his efforts this way: "My main pride is that I know how to be simple. When inexperienced people run into an everyday expression in a foreign work that seems weird to them, they change it into something equally weird. But when you know a language well, you can translate the natural into the natural."

BIOGRAPHICAL/CRITICAL SOURCES:

PERIODICALS

Atlantic, January, 1969, pp. 102-104.
Bookworld, February 9, 1969; May 18, 1969.
Chicago Tribune Book World, February 2, 1972; February 12, 1984, p. 28.
Detroit Free Press, March 8, 1970.
Detroit News, January 30, 1972.
Globe and Mail (Toronto), July 21, 1990.
Horn Book, April, 1982.
Kenyon Review, number 4, 1968.
Library Journal, November 15, 1977.
Los Angeles Times Book Review, September 4, 1983, p. 5; November 11, 1984, pp. 1, 6; August 31,
1986, p. 2; July 16, 1989, pp. 3, 11; July 1, 1990.
Nation, March 17, 1969; December 13, 1971.
New Republic, June 20, 1970, pp. 23-25.
Newsday, June 26, 1971.
Newsweek, January 27, 1969; May 26, 1969.
New Yorker, December 12, 1977.
New York Times, January 6, 1968; May 22, 1969; March 3, 1970; May 17, 1970; March 5, 1970; May 29, 1970; November 6, 1970; March 5, 1971; July 4, 1978; April 29, 1981; January 19, 1983; June 28, 1983; July 16, 1983; July 12, 1984; June 25, 1986; June 29, 1987; November 8, 1988; August 28, 1989.
New York Times Book Review, January 5, 1969, pp. 3, 18; February 10, 1980, February 7, 1982, p. 26; March 14, 1982; October 24, 1982; May 29, 1983; July 10, 1983; November 6, 1983; November 20, 1983; November 11, 1984, pp. 1, 63; July 5, 1987; June 26, 1988; August 4, 1988; January 15, 1989.
Observer Review, July 19, 1970.
Publishers Weekly, February 22, 1985, p. 159.
School Library Journal, November, 1977.
Time, April 13, 1970; November 19, 1984, pp. 118-123; July 20, 1987.
Times Literary Supplement, November 23, 1967; December 28, 1967; September 19, 1968; July 23, 1970; February 17, 1984; August 28, 1987.
Voice Literary Supplement, March, 1982, pp. 11-12; October, 1982.
Washington Post Book World, March 10, 1971; August 9, 1981; November 21, 1982; June 5, 1983; July 31, 1983; August 7, 1983; October 16, 1983; May 16, 1984; August 26, 1984; July 12, 1987; November 6, 1988; August 26, 1990.*

*　　*　　*

MARTINEZ, Victor 1954-

PERSONAL: Born in 1954, in Fresno, CA; married; wife's name, Tina. *Education:* Attended California State University, Fresno; Stanford University, postgraduate fellowship (creative writing).

ADDRESSES: Agent—c/o HarperCollins, 10 East 53rd St., New York, NY 10022.

CAREER: Poet and novelist. Worked as a field laborer, welder, truck driver, firefighter, teacher, and office clerk.

AWARDS, HONORS: National Book Award, 1996, for *Parrot in the Oven: Mi Vida.*

WRITINGS:

Caring for a House, Chusma House Publications (San Jose, CA), 1992.
(With Juan Antonio Diaz) *A la Conquista del Corazon,* [Uruguay], 1993.
Parrot in the Oven: Mi Vida, HarperCollins (New York City), 1996.

Contributor to periodicals and journals, including *Iowa Review* and *Bloomsbury Review.*

SIDELIGHTS: Victor Martinez offers young adult readers an understanding of Chicano culture in the novel *Parrot in the Oven: Mi Vida.* The story relates the grave difficulties being experienced by Manny Hernandez's family, including his father's struggle with alcoholism and unemployment and Manny's attempts to cope with sometimes explosive family situations (the elder Hernandez is sent to prison after he threatens Manny's mother with a rifle). As *School Library Journal* contributor Sylvia V. Meisner pointed out, "Intense emotions and bursts of violence flare up in this story, tempered by true love and family ties."

Narrated in the first-person, *Parrot in the Oven* conveys Manny's feelings as he suffers through his sister's miscarriage, humiliation and taunts from white classmates, gang problems and run-ins with the law, and the deprivations of poverty. Throughout painful periods of his youth, Manny maintains a sense of dignity. A *Publishers Weekly* reviewer noted that "Martinez's honest voice, and descriptions sprinkled with elegant imagery, offer a rare and consummately believable portrait of barrio life."

BIOGRAPHICAL/CRITICAL SOURCES:

PERIODICALS

New York Times, November 7, 1996, p. C21.
Publishers Weekly, October 28, 1996, p. 83; November 11, 1996, p. 17.
School Library Journal, November 1996, p. 123.
Time for Kids, November 22, 1996, p. 8.

OTHER

bookwire.com (website), October 16, 1997.
latinolink.com (website), October 16, 1997.*

MASON, Marilyn (J.) 1933-

PERSONAL: Born May 17, 1933, in Chicago, IL; married Richard Donald Stelli, 1955 (divorced, 1974); children: Jerrod, Jeanine Alice. *Ethnicity:* "British-American." *Education:* Attended Culver-Stockton College and Northwestern University; University of Minnesota—Twin Cities, B.S., 1972, Ph.D., 1980. *Politics:* "Democrat." *Religion:* Unitarian. *Avocational interests:* Travel, bicycling, hiking, community work.

ADDRESSES: Home—510 Groveland, #522, Minneapolis, MN 55403. *Office*—Mason & Associates, 3033 Excelsior Blvd., #300, Minneapolis, MN 55416; fax 612-879-9177. *E-mail*—mjmason@ compuserve .com. *Agent*—Ellen Levine, Ellen Levine Agency, 15 East 26th St., Suite 1801, New York, NY 10010.

CAREER: Private practice, Minneapolis, MN, 1974-80; Family Therapy Institute, St. Paul, MN, co-owner, 1980-90; University of Minnesota—Twin Cities, clinical associate professor, 1985—, Mason and Associates, Minneapolis, MN, president, 1990—. Journeys Inward, president, 1980—; Rapid Change Technologies, training director. Voyageur Outward, member of board of directors, 1994-97; Tibetan-American Foundation of Minnesota, chairperson of board of directors, 1994-97; Hazelden Foundation, member of board of trustees, 1996-97.

MEMBER: Association for Marriage and Family Therapy (fellow), American Family Therapy Academy (member of board of directors, 1990-94).

AWARDS, HONORS: Distinguished Alumni Award, Culver-Stockton College, 1984; Minnesotans Who Make a Difference Award, 1994; Distinguished Service Award, Minnesota Association for Marriage and Family Therapy.

WRITINGS:

(With Merle Fosson) *Facing Shame: Families in Recovery,* Norton (New York City), 1986.
Making Our Lives Our Own: A Woman's Guide to Six Challenges of Personal Change, Harper (San Francisco, CA), 1991.
Seven Mountains: The Inner Climb to Commitment and Caring, Dutton (Bergenfield, NJ), 1997.

WORK IN PROGRESS: The Inner Life of Business.

SIDELIGHTS: Marilyn Mason told *CA:* "My primary motivation for writing has been a desire to take the relationship information held by professionals to the general public. Much of what the media presents is catering to quick-fix solutions and relationship hype. Many people are seeking common-sense guidance.

"I also write to know what I think; writing is powerfully therapeutic. My work is influenced by ongoing narratives about people's lives—their encounters with struggle and pain. I also write to learn, to discover. The research and reading hold the intrigue.

"My writing process requires stillness. I write with my first cup of coffee. I like to discover what comes forth. I write on my word processor. This was my first 'crush' on an inanimate object.

"My inspiration has come from my personal discoveries through life experiences—my own and those of others. People's experiences and stories fascinate me and often ignite my spirit. Stories awake the unconscious mind and help with raising all our conscious minds to move us toward a soul shift."

*   *   *

MAZZARINS, Laimdota 1945-

PERSONAL: Born September 28, 1945, in Flensburg, Germany; immigrated to the United States, 1950, naturalized citizen; daughter of Janis (a mechanical engineer) and Anita (a homemaker) Mazzarins; married Fritz Stavenhagen, February 1, 1980 (divorced February 13, 1989); children: Martin, Michael. *Ethnicity:* "Latvian-American." *Education:* Michigan State University, B.A., 1967; Harvard University, M.A., 1968, Ph.D., 1976. *Politics:* "Member of Green party in Germany." *Avocational interests:* Playing the flute, drawing, travel, hiking, reading.

ADDRESSES: Home—Duennwalder Strasse 12, 51063 Cologne, Germany. *Office*—International Association for Human Rights in Kurdistan, Postfach 200738, 53137 Bonn, Germany; fax +49-22-836-3297.

CAREER: Brooklyn College of the City University of New York, Brooklyn, NY, instructor, 1972-77,

assistant professor of literature, 1977-79; teacher of English language and literature at technical and vocational high schools in Aachen, Dueren, Stolberg, and Erkelenz, Germany, 1979-85; University of Cologne, Cologne, Germany, teacher of English language and literature, 1985; Volkshochschule der Stadt Koeln, Cologne, teacher of English language and literature, 1985-92; African National Congress, Bonn Mission, Bonn, Germany, performed administrative work, 1991-94; International Association for Human Rights in Kurdistan, Bonn, administrative assistant, 1994—. Second Programme of the European Communities to Combat Poverty, publications officer in Animation and Dissemination Service, 1987-89; worked as free-lance editor and translator for busines firms and other institutions, including Translation Service of the Bundestag, German Foreign Ministry, and Initiative for Human Rights in Kurdistan.

MEMBER: Alpha Lambda Delta, Pi Sigma Alpha.

AWARDS, HONORS: Woodrow Wilson fellowship and Fulbright fellowship, both 1967.

WRITINGS:

(Editor and translator) Helene Deutsch, *Confrontations with Myself,* Norton (New York City), 1973.
(Translator) Elisabeth Beck-Gernsheim, *The Social Implications of Bioengineering,* Humanities (Atlantic Highlands, NJ), 1995.
(Translator) Noerbert Bolz and Willem van Reijen, *Walter Benjamin,* Humanities, 1996.
(Translator into German) Bernhard Press, *The Murder of the Jews in Latvia, 1941-1945,* Metropol Verlag (Berlin, Germany), 1992.

Biweekly theater reviewer, *Arts Review Letter,* 1976. Contributor of articles, translations, and reviews to periodicals, including *College Literature* and *In These Times.* Editor of *Exchange,* 1987-89.

WORK IN PROGRESS: Translating *Redlight Districts, Respectability, Prostitution, and the Bourgeois World,* by Regina Schulte, for Humanities.

SIDELIGHTS: Laimdota Mazzarins told *CA:* "I am particularly interested in translating works in the humanities and social sciences from German into English. This includes history, biography, sociology, women's studies, and literary criticism."

McKNIGHT, Linton W. 1942-

PERSONAL: Born March 3, 1942, in Baldwin County, GA; son of C. Wright and Winifred F. McKnight; married, wife's name Carolyn S. (divorced, June, 1992). *Ethnicity:* "White." *Education:* University of Georgia, B.B.A., 1969. *Politics:* Republican. *Religion:* Baptist. *Avocational interests:* Gardening, canoeing, sailing, motorcycles.

ADDRESSES: Home—161 Swint Ave., Milledgeville, GA 31061. *Office*—P.O. Box 1885-503, Milledgeville, GA 31061; fax 912-452-0008. *E-mail*—cpnet@hom.net.

CAREER: Real estate broker, Atlanta, GA, 1972-90; landscape contractor, Milledgeville, GA, 1991—. Past owner of a jewelry store.

MEMBER: Rotary International (member of board of directors), horticultural societies devoted to daffodil, rhododendron, iris, rose, hydrangea, hemerocallis, and chrysanthemum.

WRITINGS:

Birthflowers of the Landscape, Commercial Publishing Network, in press.

WORK IN PROGRESS: "Birthflowers of the Landscape" series, twelve volumes; research on garden color throughout the year.

* * *

McMOREY, James L.
See MOYER, Terry J.

* * *

MEAD, Alice 1952-

PERSONAL: Born January 11, 1952, in Portchester, NY; daughter of Richard (a teacher) and Jeanne (a secretary) Weber; married Larry Mead (a recreation director), November, 1983; children: Jeffrey O'Hara, Michael O'Hara. *Education:* Bryn Mawr College, B.A., 1973; Southern Connecticut State University, M.Ed., 1975; University of Southern Maine, B.A. (art education), 1985. *Politics:* Democrat. *Religion:* Quaker. *Avocational interests:* Flute, gardening, painting-nature, photography, video.

CAREER: Writer. Has worked as an art teacher in Connecticut and Maine, 1974-92, and as a preschool teacher in Maine, 1980-83. Board member for Project Co-Step for developmentally delayed preschoolers; active in efforts to aid children in Kosovo, Serbia. Flutist.

MEMBER: Maine Writers and Publishers Alliance, Maine Art Education Association.

WRITINGS:

Crossing the Starlight Bridge, Bradbury, 1994.
Walking the Edge, Albert Whitman (Morton Grove, IL), 1995.
Junebug, Farrar, Straus (New York City), 1995.
Journey to Kosovo, Loose Cannon Press, 1995.
(Editor, with Arnold Neptune) *Giants of the Dawnland: Ancient Wabanaki Tales,* Loose Cannon Press, 1996.
Adem's Cross, Farrar, Straus, 1996.
Junebug 2, Farrar, Straus, 1997.

WORK IN PROGRESS: Research on Scotland in 1606, the end of the Scottish clan system, and MacBeth.

SIDELIGHTS: Alice Mead's novels for young adults and middle graders often feature young people coping with dire circumstances, who with ingenuity, determination, and the aid of helpful adults make positive, if small, changes in their own lives and the lives of those around them. In *Crossing the Starlight Bridge,* Mead's first work, nine-year-old Rayanne's artistic abilities help smooth the transition when she and her mother move in with her grandmother, forcing Rayanne to adjust all at once to living in the city, making friends at a new school, and dealing with the break-up of her parents' marriage. Scott, the main character in *Walking the Edge,* Mead's next story, is also suffering the effects of his parents' broken marriage. In *Junebug,* Mead depicts life in the housing projects, with its ever-present drug dealers and gang warfare, and the efforts of one African American family not to be defeated by these circumstances. *Adem's Cross* takes place in the Eastern European country formerly known as Yugoslavia, where twelve-year-old Adem witnesses the death of his sister at the hands of soldiers, and must flee for his life as a consequence. Mead commented: "I have always been interested in writing about children who—for some reason—live on the edge of the mainstream society. I feel that authors and artists should travel to these edges, to widen the circle of inclusion through empathy and art.

"For many years I was an art teacher working with low-income children," Mead explained. "In America, wealth abounds yet a large proportion of American children are poor. Everyone tells poor kids to have hopes, to dream—but how do you go about it? We have a society that sees children in very negative ways. I like to celebrate the intensity and steadfastness of kids, their creativity and fresh energy."

Rayanne, the central character in *Crossing the Starlight Bridge,* is a member of the Penobscot tribe of Native Americans. She and her parents have always lived on their island reservation but now her father, who is unable to find work there, decides to leave. "Mead deftly establishes a child's point of view with simple and unpretentious language," observed Deborah Stevenson in the *Bulletin of the Center for Children's Books,* noting that Rayanne's misery over her father's absence is deepened when she realizes that she and her mother must leave the island, and her pet rabbit, behind. References to traditional Penobscot lore arise in the character of the grandmother with whom Rayanne and her mother go to live, "a strong, contemporary, optimistic woman whose warmth and encouragement are restorative," Susan Scheps asserted in *School Library Journal.* Though Scheps found the novel's ending a little too abrupt, a *Kirkus Reviews* critic called *Crossing the Starlight Bridge* "a believable and compelling portrayal of a Native American family coexisting with white society while retaining its own traditions."

Like Rayanne and other Mead protagonists, Scott, the main character in *Walking the Edge,* looks to something positive outside of himself to give him strength to endure the poverty and unhappiness of his life. Set in Maine and based on real events, the novel describes Scott's involvement in a science project that aims to restock the local bay with clams. *School Library Journal* contributor Connie Tyrrell Burns, commenting favorably on Mead's realistic depiction of the turbulent emotions of her adolescent hero, maintained that "Scott's amazement at the delicate and relentless process of life will be shared by readers."

Reeve McClain, known as Junebug, reluctantly approaches his tenth birthday in Mead's novel *Junebug,* knowing that he will then be recruited to join one of the gangs that terrorizes his housing project. Junebug develops an idea he hopes will help him realize his dream of learning to sail and captaining his own boat. He collects and cleans fifty glass bottles and seals in each a piece of paper describing his dream, then sets the bottles free on a boat trip around the harbor in New Haven, Connecticut. "The novel is a hopeful one," Maeve Visser Knoth commented in *Horn Book,* "in spite of the vivid portrait of the housing project's grim realities." Elizabeth Bush, on the other hand, writing in *Bulletin of the Center for Children's Books,* called *Junebug*'s happy ending "soothing but decidedly too easy," though her conclusion echoed that of a critic in *Kirkus Reviews,* who wrote that "readers will be rooting for Junebug and his dreams all the way." Mead commented: "I grew up near the water and have always loved boats. I wanted to be either a sea captain or a lighthouse keeper and live on an island. Writing a book is a lot like putting a message in a bottle and tossing it overboard—you never know who will read it! Or where!"

In *Adem's Cross,* Mead sets her story in Kosovo, a province of the former Yugoslavia that has been taken over by Serbian soldiers bent on "cleansing" the population of Albanians, descendants of the land's ancient conquerors. Twelve-year-old Adem and his family have been waiting for the Serb troops to leave their hometown for four years when Adem's older sister takes the bold stance of participating in a peaceful demonstration against the invaders. She is subsequently killed by Serb soldiers. Adem, enraged at his family's passivity, rebels by going out alone one night. He is caught by three soldiers who break his hand and carve a Serbian symbol, a Cyrillic cross, into his chest with a knife. He decides to leave Kosovo and is aided in his flight by a Serb and a gypsy. "Mead preps readers with a quick, efficient sketch of Yugoslavia's recent history before jumping into this disturbing society," observed Marilyn Payne Phillips in her review in *School Library Journal.* Critics noted that Mead does not take sides in the real-life deadly conflict. Instead, she "writes powerfully and eloquently about Adem's attempt to understand why people mistreat each other," Susan Dove Lempke remarked in *Booklist.*

Mead continued: "For the past two years, I have been traveling to Eastern Europe. When I was little

I was told that these countries lay behind the Iron Curtain, a place Americans didn't go. Since the collapse of communism, I have traveled there twice a year to document the conditions of children's lives. My novel, *Adem's Cross,* is about the cleansing of Albanian children in southern Serbia. I have brought nine teenagers to the U.S. to study in high schools in Maine. In addition, a group of schools got together and sent a truckload of toys to Kosovo, Serbia."

BIOGRAPHICAL/CRITICAL SOURCES:

PERIODICALS

Booklist, June 1, 1994, p. 1811; November 15, 1996, pp. 579, 581.
Bulletin of the Center for Children's Books, June, 1994, p. 329; December, 1995, pp. 133-34.
Children's Book Review Service, July, 1994, p. 155.
Children's Book Watch, January, 1996, p. 5.
Five Owls, January, 1996, p. 65.
Horn Book, September, 1994, p. 589; March, 1996, p. 198.
Instructor, April, 1996, p. 58.
Kirkus Reviews, May 1, 1994, p. 634; September 1, 1995, p. 1284; October 15, 1996, p. 1535.
New York Times Book Review, January 14, 1996, pp. 23, 66.
Parents, December, 1995, p. 232.
Publishers Weekly, April 18, 1994, p. 64; October 21, 1996, p. 84.
School Library Journal, June, 1994, pp. 132-33; December, 1995, p. 106; November, 1996, p. 109.
Voice of Youth Advocates, February, 1996, p. 374.

*   *   *

MEMMOTT, David R. 1948-

PERSONAL: Born December 10, 1948, in Grand Rapids, MI; son of Arthur L. and Mary Martha (Chinn) Memmott; married, wife's name Susan A. (an office manager), September 14, 1974; children: Liesle A. Memmott-Larson. *Ethnicity:* "White." *Education:* Eastern Oregon State University, B.A. (English) and B.A. (general studies), both 1977. *Politics:* "Proponent of integral culture." *Religion:* "Relative Holism—Panantheism." *Avocational interests:* Noetic sciences, study of exceptional human abilities, quantum physics, mysticism, shamanism, computers, photography, computer art, publishing, gardening, alternative lifestyles and medicine, futurology.

ADDRESSES: Home and office—1003 Y Ave., P.O. Box 3235, La Grande, OR 97850. *E-mail*—wordcraft @oregontrail.net.

CAREER: State of Oregon, La Grande, office specialist with Services to Children and Families; Wordcraft of Oregon, La Grande, editor and publisher of Jazz Police Books. *Ice River: Magazine of Speculative Writing,* managing editor, 1986-90; also worked as typesetter and book designer. Blue Mountain Designers and Craftsmen, Inc., member of board of directors, 1978-83; Grande Ronde Resource Council, member of board of directors, 1982-83, and chairperson of Land Use Planning Committee; League of Women Voters, director of public education program This Land Is Your Land: Conflicting Values in Land Use Planning; organizer of local literary activities such as arts festivals, poetry readings, film series, and performing arts programs. *Military service:* U.S. Air Force, 1972.

MEMBER: Institute for Noetic Sciences, Council for a Literature of the Fantastic.

AWARDS, HONORS: Grants from Coordinating Council of Literary Magazines, 1988, and Oregon Arts Commission, 1988, 1989; Pushcart Prize nominations, 1989 and 1996; Fishtrap fellow, Fishtrap Writers Gathering, 1990; Rhysling Award, Science Fiction Poetry Association, 1990; Oregon Book Award nominations, poetry category, 1992 and 1996; Literary Arts, Inc. fellowship, 1995.

WRITINGS:

(Poetry editor) *Alpha Gallery: Selections from the Fantastic Small Press,* Small Press Writers and Artists Organization, 1991.
House on Fire: Poetry and Collage, Jazz Police Books (La Grande, OR), 1992.
The Larger Earth: Descending Notes of a Grounded Astronaut (poems), Permeable Press (San Francisco, CA), 1996.
Watermark/Singing the Blues (poems and images), Ice River Press (La Grande, OR), in press.

Contributing editor, *Magazine of Speculative Poetry,* 1990, 1997.

WORK IN PROGRESS: Fractures, a Vietnam anti-war novel set in the Northwest; *Ghost Hunters in Dreamtime,* a collection of short stories and a one-act play; *Within the Walls of Jericho,* twenty-six books of poetry; *Dreamers' Round,* a metaphysical science fiction novel.

SIDELIGHTS: David R. Memmott told *CA:* "I took a rather circuitous route to write, with one thing leading to another until I found myself scratching out those first voluntary, tortured sentences. It actually began with my being a headthumper, thumping my head before I went to sleep and rocking back and forth singing to myself in the back seat of the car. This learned reflex of internalization in the face of traumatic events was an important first step in an unconscious strategy of avoiding confrontation with reality in favor of exploring inner worlds.

"I took up playing a trumpet in the seventh grade, practicing in the garage. I quickly learned to play it technically incorrectly, yet I managed to produce a decent tone. Music was my life. I played in the marching band, the concert band, the pep band, the stage band, a Tijuana Brass group, blasting my way through pep rallies and junior proms until my lips sagged. Then I took up guitar, fantasizing about become the next Roy Orbison, and quickly learned how to play it technically incorrectly. Soon I was thrumming guitar and singing at parties and coffee shops, making up songs, brooding along nicely in my folkrock rags. Then I decided writing lyrics might be easier if I learned something about poetry, so I quickly learned how to write technically incorrect poetry, deeply flawed and self-conscious posturing, using language to avoid confrontation with reality in favor of exploring inner worlds. Somewhere along the way, I found the process of writing was a process of self-discovery and, once I had gone beyond the point of no return, doors began to open and paths began to diverge, choices had to made, consequences were unavoidable, and the only way out was to see it through. My motivation for writing is mapping of the maze.

"My influences have changed as my writing has changed over the years. Early influences in poetry were T. S. Eliot, Theodore Roethke, Walt Whitman, William Stafford, George Venn. Early work tends to be in the style of regional realism, place-oriented, rooted in nature, rural and environmental. Those influences have, from the very beginning, been deflected by an ongoing interest in fantastic art, ranging from Betty Boop to the Wizard of Oz, from Ray

Bradbury to J. G. Ballard, *Twilight Zone* to *X-Files.* My favorite science fiction writer is Philip K. Dick, because he wasn't afraid to question the nature of consciousness and reality. I love magic realism, surrealism, cyberpunk, avant-pop, art whose imaginal landscapes follow the physics of dreams, the astounding implications of quantum physics, warp in and out of fringe science and Jungian psychology, overcome the tendency to retreat into what is known and comfortable and dance with the bizarre, confronting the anomalous at the outer edges of our culture and rediscovering at every turn the limits of our knowledge, invoking wonder and reaffirming our humanity.

"I am primarily a process writer, which basically means the process differs with each project and evolves organically. I am reasonably disciplined in that I maintain a writing schedule of working mornings for four days a week. Then I eat lunch, change for work, and listen to audiobooks as I walk to my half-time job. The walk allows me time to transition back into the 'real world' and get some much needed exercise to help balance a lifestyle dominated by keyboarding and clicking on menus. Occasionally, I will set a novel aside for a day or two and work on a short story or poem. Most of my work as a publisher occurs in the evenings, weekends, and Friday afternoons. I play music with friends on Saturday nights, and this, I have learned, is a wonderful way of keeping the creative juices flowing and a way of letting go for awhile so as not to be totally consumed by a novel. There are times when I avoid encounters with other people because the world of the novel is foremost in my mind. I also work some with photography and computer art based on the photography, and I plan to learn how to design web pages in the near future so I can explore a new direction in storytelling through hypertext and multimedia.

"What inspires me to write? I was listening to an audiotape by Dr. Wayne Dyer recently, and he talked about the old Buddhist saying, 'When the student is ready the teacher will appear.' In thinking about this, I realized the world was my teacher, and the challenge was to learn to pay attention. Inspiration can be anything from an article in a magazine to a cloud formation, from dreams to something said in a conversation. Quite often, for me, inspiration emerges from the process. It is part of the magic and the mystery that unravels in synchronicity when you open a book to the exact page with the answer to a problem, or wake up with lines in your head, or the scene develops on its own and the character says something that surprises you. It's part of another way of knowing, an intuitive, right-brained way of getting there that doesn't follow the usual road signs or take the usual turns. That's what makes it such an adventure and a royal road to discovery."

*   *   *

MEYER, Leisa D.

PERSONAL: Female. *Education:* United States Air Force Academy, cadet; University of Wisconsin, Ph.D..

ADDRESSES: Office—Department of History, College of William and Mary, Williamsburg, VA 23187-8795.

CAREER: Writer. College of William and Mary, assistant professor of history.

WRITINGS:

Creating GI Jane: Sexuality and Power in the Women's Army Corps during World War II, Columbia University Press (New York City), 1996.

SIDELIGHTS: Leisa D. Meyer "provides a key piece of the story of women's formal entrance into military life in the United States" in her 1996 book, *Creating GI Jane: Sexuality and Power in the Women's Army Corps,* according to Lori Ginzburg in the *Women's Review of Books.* Meyer, a historian and former Air Force Academy cadet, used oral histories, official archives, and wartime journalistic records to develop her vision of how the Women's Army Corps (WAC) was founded and, in particular, how its public-relations image was shaped.

Creating GI Jane is neither a full-fledged history of the WACs nor a broad critique of American gender roles; it maintains its focus on its carefully delineated topic, the creation of the image and reality of a specific military organization at a specific historical moment. The WACs were founded in order to correct a dearth of clerical and communications workers in the wartime army; they filled that role most capably, but were often the object of public skepticism and derision. At times they were viewed comically as mere providers of sexual services to male soldiers. Anticipating such public reactions,

WAC leaders imposed strict codes of behavior upon their enlistees in order to forestall possible sexual scandals, either heterosexual or homosexual in nature. So-called "mannish" women were anathema to this mindset, as was any attempt by women to overstep the then-current gender boundaries by taking over traditionally male roles. "Meyer's finest chapters," according to Ginzburg, are devoted to the WAC leaders' attempts to regulate the sexual behavior of their corpswomen. Other sociological factors surface in the story of the early WACs as well: African American women, for example, viewed successful enlistment as a step forward in their struggle for racial equality. Meyer also recounts the history of lesbians in the early WACs, and finds that they were relatively rarely prosecuted, perhaps because the resulting scandal would have hurt the corps.

Published at a time when debate over women's and gay men's roles in the military was much in the headlines, Meyer's book served as a "platform," according to *Library Journal* reviewer Jenny Presnell, for exploring this sensitive issue through a historical lens. Ginzburg, however, asserted that the book's usefulness in that capacity was limited by Meyer's reluctance to broaden her scope to include the ways in which society at large constructed gender and other social roles. For example, Ginzburg faulted the work for its absence of references to women who worked in the civilian industrial sector during World War II—the famous "Rosie the Riveter." Ginzburg also commented on Meyer's criticism of 1940s American feminists for not supporting more strongly women's right to become soldiers; in the 1940s, Ginzburg suggested, feminists were hardly in a position of strength to do so. Presnell applauded Meyer's work, declaring that it offered a "solid historical context" for its World War II subject and its 1990s parallels.

BIOGRAPHICAL/CRITICAL SOURCES:

PERIODICALS

Library Journal, October 15, 1996, p. 72.
Women's Review of Books, March, 1997, pp. 20-21.*

*   *   *

MILES, John
   See BICKHAM, Jack M(iles)

MILGRAM, Morris 1916-1997

OBITUARY NOTICE—See index for *CA* sketch: Born May 29, 1916, in New York, NY; died of a stroke, June 22, 1997, in Langhorne, PA. Builder, housing developer, author. The son of poor Russian immigrants, Milgram pursued a career as a developer who specialized in affordable multiracial housing projects. Despite his family's poverty, he attended City College (now City University of New York) until 1934 when he was expelled for contesting a reception that was being held for young Fascists from Italy. He continued his studies at the University of Newark (now Rutgers University). In 1941 he began six years as national secretary for the Workers Defense League in New York City. In 1947 he founded Milgram Companies in Philadelphia and worked as a housing developer. In all, he worked to create multiracial housing projects that benefitted about twenty-thousand people in locations such as Boston, Chicago, Virginia, Texas, California, and Washington, among others. He also worked to establish the Fund for an Open Society in Philadelphia, which helps provide low mortgages to those who move into such housing developments. Milgram resided in one of his housing projects in Greenbelt Knoll before he entered the Attleboro Nursing and Rehabilitation Center in 1990. His efforts were recognized with the National Human Rights Award from the Department of Housing and Urban Development. He was the first recipient of that honor in 1968. He authored several books, including *Good Neighborhood: The Challenge of Open Housing, Racial Integration in Housing,* and *Developing Open Communities.*

OBITUARIES AND OTHER SOURCES:

BOOKS

Who's Who in the East, Marquis Who's Who, 1994.

PERIODICALS

New York Times, June 26, 1997, p. B8.

*   *   *

MILLER, Andrew M. 1960-

PERSONAL: Born April 29, 1960, in Bristol, England; son of K. W. T. (a doctor) and M. A. (a counselor; maiden name, Hilton) Miller.

ADDRESSES: Home—Apartment 26, Marlborough Court, Marlborough St., Dublin 1, Ireland. *Agent*—Simon Trewin Sheil Land Associates, 43 Doughty St., London WC1N 2LF, England.

WRITINGS:

Ingenious Pain (novel), Harcourt (Orlando, FL), 1997.

WORK IN PROGRESS: A novel, *Casanova in England,* publication by Hodder & Stoughton expected in 1998.

*   *   *

MINTZ, Elizabeth E(mmons) 1913-1997

OBITUARY NOTICE—See index for *CA* sketch: Born December 31, 1913, in Minneapolis, MN; died June 23, 1997, in Bronxville, NY. Psychotherapist and author. Mintz gained prominence for her ideas on group therapy. As a psychotherapist, she was in private practice for nearly forty years, from 1953 to 1992. In addition she was the supervisor for the Community Guidance Service in Pleasantville, New York, as well as the group therapy director for the New York Clinic for Mental Health. She also taught at Cornell and Adelphi University. She was a contributor to numerous journals; she also contributed to books such as *Group Therapy 1974,* edited by Wolberg and Aronson, and *The Psychoanalytic Situation,* edited by L. Blank, G. Gottsegen, and M. Gottsegen. She also penned *Marathon Groups: Reality and Symbol,* which was published in 1971.

OBITUARIES AND OTHER SOURCES:

PERIODICALS

New York Times, July 7, 1997, p. B9.

*   *   *

MITCHELL, Ellinor R. 1930-

PERSONAL: Born August 26, 1930, in Lausanne, Switzerland; daughter of Francis Robinson (a writer) and Suzanne (Combes) Taylor; divorced; children: five. *Education:* Attended Radcliffe College, University of Lausanne, Barnard College, and University of California, Berkeley. *Politics:* Democrat. *Religion:* "No affiliation." *Avocational interests:* Amateur classical guitar, practicing Tai Ch'i.

ADDRESSES: Home—277 West End Ave., No. 15-A, New York, NY 10023; (summers) P.O. Box 266, Chilmark, MA 02535.

CAREER: Writer. Cell Block Theatre, instructor, 1974-80. Parents League of New York, member.

MEMBER: International Veterinary Acupuncture Society, American Association of Oriental Medicine, National Acupuncture and Oriental Medicine Alliance, Acupuncture Society of New York.

WRITINGS:

Plain Talk about Acupuncture, Whalehall (New York City), 1987.
Fighting Drug Abuse with Acupuncture: The Treatment That Works, Pacific View Press (Berkeley, CA), 1995.

Author of two unpublished novels, *The Old Boy* and *Have You Come to See Me Hanging?*

WORK IN PROGRESS: The Ch'i Factor (tentative title), a nonfiction work; *Morgan Island,* a novel about drugs set on an island in New England.

SIDELIGHTS: Ellinor R. Mitchell told *CA:* "Writing is one of my characteristics, like being nearsighted and right-handed. From the age of eight I have kept diaries and written stories and verse. As a child I was an omnivorous reader. When I was twelve I wanted to be Ernest Hemingway. Adventure stories sparked my imagination, but alas, the protagonists inevitably were boys. My stepfather wrote radio situation comedies and later became a Broadway playwright, well known in the fifties and sixties. Fame looked very attractive. At nineteen I wished I had written Francoise Sagan's *Bonjour Tristesse.* I am very inquisitive. Curiosity influences me most of all.

"It's like the Yin-Yang symbol—developing a piece of work from a notion means scribbling something about it on any handy bit of paper, then thinking about it, and maybe looking up some thing or some word that provokes more thought. The application of words to paper or screen provokes thought and research. I get feedback from seeing the words before me. With fiction, I write capsule biographies of characters, mainly to be sure that dates hang together coherently and to avoid anachronism. Whether I am writing fiction or nonfiction, I need a certain amount of product before I make an outline. In both forms, research is entirely too seductive. Whether nonfiction, short story, or novel, my writing improves toward the end. Lacking the daily journalist's skill of getting it right immediately, I rewrite relentlessly.

"In nonfiction and fiction, personal experience prompted me to write about the subject. Do we choose subjects, or do they choose us?"

*   *   *

MOK, Esther 1953-

PERSONAL: Born April 15, 1953, in Ipoh, Malaysia; daughter of Weng Pew (a supermarket manager) and Kon Yin (a homemaker; maiden name, Liew) Mok; divorced; children: Emmanuel Atsin, Aaron Atsin. *Education:* University of Malaya, B.S., 1977, Diploma in Education, 1978; University of Iowa, M.A., 1984. *Politics:* "Believer in democracy." *Religion:* Christian. *Avocational interests:* Film and television production, photography, swimming, outdoor activities, reading, cooking.

ADDRESSES: Home—1068 Wildwood Ave., Daly City, CA 94015. *Office*—Rosa Parks Elementary School, 3501 O'Farrel St., San Francisco, CA.

CAREER: San Francisco Unified School District, science teacher at middle school and math and biology instructor at high school, 1984—; kindergarten teacher, 1995—.

MEMBER: Society of Children's Book Writers and Illustrators, United Educators of San Francisco.

WRITINGS:

Sumo, the Wrestling Elephant, translated by Loraine Woodard, May Davenport Publishers (Los Altos Hills, CA), 1994.

Also author of poetry.

WORK IN PROGRESS: Wawa, the Wee-Wee Rabbit; Nunu; Amazing ABCs in Action; and *The Gingerbread Yeo-Yeos.*

SIDELIGHTS: Esther Mok commented: "When my children were little, they would say, 'Tell us a story, Mom!' On the spot, I would spin out an original story, be it on the way to school, waiting in line at the bank, at bedtime—anywhere, any time. I used stories to address some problems my kids were facing or to instill some moral values in them. My children are very creative and sometimes they would give me ideas; they are also the sounding boards for my new stories.

"I wrote *Sumo, the Wrestling Elephant* during a very hectic period of my life, a time when I was bracing a lot of dark storms. I wrote two lines, cooked, wrote another few lines, nursed my little son, wrote another few lines, played with my children (two boys, then three years old and one year old), then wrote again. I finished my first draft in two weeks. I would not have written had I not met a stranger in the park—a freelance writer—whose parting words to me were 'Don't just talk about it, do it!'"

*   *   *

MOLONEY, James   1954-

PERSONAL: Born September 20, 1954, in Sydney, Australia; son of Frank (a manager of truck manufacturing) and Betty (a teacher; maiden name, Wilkinson) Moloney; married Kate Hickey (a teacher and librarian), April 4, 1983; children: Siobhan, Julia, Bede. *Education:* Griffith University, Diploma in Primary Teaching, 1975; Queensland University of Technology, Graduate Diplomas in Computer Education, 1988, and Teacher Librarianship, 1979; University of Queensland, B.E.S., 1981. *Religion:* Roman Catholic. *Avocational interests:* Reading, family activities, travel.

ADDRESSES: Home and office—142 Buena Vista Ave., Coorparoo, Queensland 4151, Australia. *E-mail*—mcap@ozemail.com.au.

CAREER: Marist College Ashgrove, Brisbane, Australia, teacher and librarian at primary school, 1983-93, 1995-96; writer, 1994—.

AWARDS, HONORS: Family Award, Relationships Australia, 1992, for *Crossfire,* and 1993, for *Dougy;* Children's Book of the Year Honour Book, Children's Book Council of Australia (CBCA), 1994, for *Dougy,* and 1995, for *Gracey;* Multicultural

Award, Australian Department of Multicultural Affairs, 1995, for *Gracey;* Children's Book of the Year, CBCA, 1996, for *Swashbuckler;* Shortlist, Children's Book of the Year, CBCA, 1996, for *The House on River Terrace,* and 1997, for *A Bridge to Wiseman's Cove.*

WRITINGS:

Crossfire, University of Queensland Press (St. Lucia, Australia), 1992.
Dougy, University of Queensland Press, 1993.
Gracey, University of Queensland Press, 1994.
Swashbuckler, University of Queensland Press, 1995.
The House on River Terrace, University of Queensland Press, 1995.
A Bridge to Wiseman's Cove, University of Queensland Press, 1996.
The Pipe, Lothian, 1996.

WORK IN PROGRESS: Buzzard Breath and Brains, a sequel to *Swashbuckler.*

SIDELIGHTS: James Moloney commented: "The question I am most often asked in letters from my readers is 'Are you an Aborigine?' This is because my second and third books, *Dougy* and *Gracey,* tell the story of an Aboriginal family in outback Australia. Both are written in the first person, and I suppose my readers are wondering how much of the story is autobiographical.

"In fact, I am not an Australian Aborigine, though I feel a deep empathy for the traditional owners of this land. As a young man, I was posted to the small town of Cunnamulla to teach in the school there. Cunnamulla has a large Aboriginal population, and it was here that I became troubled by the latent racism hidden under the surface of otherwise cordial relations between white and black. I felt that the slightest spark could burn away the superficial tolerance, revealing the ugliness beneath. This is precisely the scenario I created in *Dougy.* I was also disturbed by the ease with which newcomers to the town would slide into the mind-set of prejudice. I highlighted this through the character of Trent Foster in *Gracey.*

"I have heard many authors say that their stories begin with a character, while others point to a particular setting. For me, stories usually begin with a big idea, some philosophical or political conundrum which niggles at me for weeks or months, or even years, until I feel compelled to express my feelings in a story. Gradually the issues at hand become less important as my interest turns to the characters I have invented. In fact, I use this transition to judge my literary progress, for only when the characters mean more to me than their predicaments do I know I am on the right track.

"There was much from my time in Cunnamulla to occupy my mind in this way. The first time this compulsion led to publication, the story was not concerned with racial relations, but with violence and the 'gun culture' so beloved of Australian, and I suspect American, men. The novel was *Crossfire*. *Dougy* followed quickly but, by the time I was plotting *Gracey,* I found that my growing family was taking more of my time in the evenings. I began rising at four o'clock in the morning and working until it was time to get ready for work. This has been a feature of my writing routine ever since, and it is likely to remain so until I become a full-time writer.

"*Swashbuckler* was my first attempt at a younger audience. Its success has encouraged me to focus more on this eight- to twelve-year-old age group. The wider critical acclaim for my work also prompted people to point out that all of my stories tend to explore the child's alienation from family, particularly son from father. This reaches its extreme in my novel *A Bridge to Wiseman's Cove*. The strange thing is that, having discovered this theme in my work, I now feel the urge to turn away from it."

BIOGRAPHICAL/CRITICAL SOURCES:

PERIODICALS

Australian Book Review, February, 1992, p. 58; July, 1994, p. 65; June, 1995, p. 61; August, 1995, p. 60; February, 1996, p. 57.
Bookbird, summer, 1994, p. 54.
Horn Book, March-April, 1995, pp. 237-39.
Magpies, November, 1992, p. 33.
Reading Time, February, 1997, p. 30.

*   *   *

MONGRE, Dr. Paul
  See HAUSDORFF, Felix

*   *   *

MOONDOG, Junkyard
  See DWYER, Jim

MOORE, Brenda L(ee)   1950-

PERSONAL: Born July 14, 1950, in Huntington, NY; daughter of Albert (a waiter) and Hester W. (a psychiatric social worker) Moore. *Ethnicity:* "African American." *Education:* State University of New York at Stony Brook, B.A. (with high honors), 1980; University of Chicago, M.A., 1984, Ph.D., 1987.

ADDRESSES: Home—90 Meyer Rd., Apt. 503, Amherst, NY 14226. *Office*—454 Park Hall, Department of Sociology, State University of New York at Buffalo, Buffalo, NY 14260; fax 716-645-3934. *E-mail*—socbrend@acsu.buffalo.edu.

CAREER: National Study of Internal Medicine Manpower, project assistant, 1983, field supervisor, 1984; Ameritech Corp., researcher-consultant, 1985; NORC Social Science Research Center, assistant survey director, 1985-86; Chicago Urban League, Chicago, IL, research assistant, 1986-87; field evaluator and consultant for public schools in Chicago, 1987-88; State University of New York at Buffalo, assistant professor, 1988-96, associate professor of sociology, 1996—, director of undergraduate studies, 1996-97. Indiana University Northwest, visiting assistant professor, 1987-88; guest speaker at Towson State University and University of Maryland at College Park; guest on radio and television programs; public speaker. Veterans Braintrust, Inc., member of board of directors, 1991—; American Battle Monuments Commission, member, 1994—; Defense Advisory Committee on Women in the Services, member, 1997—. *Military service:* U.S. Army, equal opportunity specialist, 1973-79.

MEMBER: American Sociological Association (member of board of directors, Peace and War Section, 1995—), Association of Black Sociologists, Joint Center for Political Studies Associates Program, Inter-University Seminar on Armed Forces and Society (member of board of directors, 1991-93), Women's Army Corps Veterans Association.

AWARDS, HONORS: Lilly Endowment grant, 1989-90; American Society for Engineering Education, visiting scholar awards for Navy Personnel Research and Development Center, 1991, and Defense Equal Opportunity and Management Institute, 1994; Outstanding Veteran Achievement Award, Veterans Benefits Clearinghouse, 1991; postdoctoral fellow, University of Maryland at College Park, 1991-92; Battelle-U.S. Army grants for Army Research Institute, 1992, 1993; visiting scholar award for Peace Studies Program at Cornell University, Ford Foundation, 1995.

WRITINGS:

(Contributor) Henry Louis Taylor, editor, *African Americans and the Rise of the Post Industrial City: The Case of Buffalo, 1940-Present,* Volume II, Urban League (Buffalo, NY), 1990.
To Serve My Country, to Serve My Race: The Story of the Only African American WACs Stationed Overseas during World War II, New York University Press (New York City), 1996.
(Contributor) Judith Stiehm, editor, *Men and Women in the Military,* Temple University Press (Philadelphia, PA), 1996.

Contributor of articles and reviews to journals, including *Armed Forces and Society, Minerva: Quarterly Report on Women in the Military,* and *National Journal of Sociology.*

WORK IN PROGRESS: Serving with Honor: Nisei Women in the Army Corps during World War II, completion expected in 1999.

*   *   *

MOORE, Judith   1940-

PERSONAL: Born in 1940.

ADDRESSES: Office—c/o Farrar, Straus, & Giroux, 19 Union Square, New York, NY 10003. *Home*—Berkeley, CA.

CAREER: Writer and editor. *San Diego Reader,* San Diego, CA, editor.

WRITINGS:

The Left Coast of Paradise: California and the American Heart, Soho Press (New York City), 1987.
Never Eat Your Heart Out, Farrar, Straus (New York City), 1997.

SIDELIGHTS: Judith Moore stepped onto the turf long held by Joan Didion when in 1987, she published *The Left Coast of Paradise,* her collection of sketches, interviews, observations and profiles pri-

marily concerned with the West Coast. Included are a tribute to the Frankfurt School Marxist philosopher Herbert Marcuse, who taught for many years at the University of California at San Diego and had a major influence on the New Left of the 1960s; an interview with the novelist Leonard Michaels, mourning the Hollywood treatment to his *The Men's Club;* a profile of an African American mortician; and, in the collection's departure from the Western shores, a remembrance of her grandmother in Arkansas in the 1940s. Doug Bolling, writing in the *American Book Review,* said of Moore: "She writes with a probing eye, with a view both humane and committed and yet distanced just enough to keep things honest." A reviewer for the *New York Times Book Review* commented, "Moore writes like an old pro."

In her second novel, *Never Eat Your Heart Out,* Moore reflects on food and its relation to life, especially her own. When she has an affair, the foods she makes become rich and sensual. However, after she leaves her husband, she does not eat for months. Nancy McKeon in *Washington Post* called the work "an idiosyncratic combination of memoir, mea culpa and food reporting." Simply stated by Susan Cheever in *New York Times Book Review,* "the food we eat is a way to tell about the life we live" and "the meals [Moore] has made for herself, for family and friends have been deeply complicated." Cheever found the book to be "tart, satisfying."

BIOGRAPHICAL/CRITICAL SOURCES:

PERIODICALS

American Book Review, March-April, 1989, pp. 7, 9.
Ms., November, 1987, p. 66.
New York Times Book Review, March 13, 1988, p. 21.
Times Literary Supplement, February 17-23, 1989, p. 157.
Washington Post, April 13, 1997, p. X10.*

OTHER

New York Times Books, http://search.nytimes.com/books, June 17, 1997.
Salon Magazine, http://www.salonmagazine.com/march97/food/moore970319.html, June 13, 1997.

MOULTON, Forest Ray 1872-1952

PERSONAL: Born April 29, 1872, in MI; died December 7, 1952, in Wilmette, IL; son of Belah G. (a farmer) and Mary G. (a schoolteacher; maiden name, Smith) Moulton; married Estella Laura Gillette, March 25, 1897 (marriage ended, 1938); married Alicia Pratt, July 28, 1939 (divorced, 1951); children: (with Gillette) Gail Francis, Vieva Gillette, Mary Elizabeth, and Merle Gordon. *Education:* Albion College, B.A., 1894, Sc.D. (astronomy and mathematics), 1923; University of Chicago, Ph.D. (summa cum laude), 1899; Drake University, LL.D., 1939. *Avocational interests:* Tennis, handball, billiards, opera, farming, poetry, classical literature, and painting.

CAREER: Astronomer and writer. Teacher in a rural school in Michigan, 1888-89; Albion College, teacher of astronomy, 1892-c.96; University of Chicago, assistant instructor of astronomy, 1896-98, associate instructor of astronomy, 1898-1900, instructor of astronomy, 1900-03, assistant professor of astronomy, 1903-08, associate professor of astronomy, 1908-12, became professor and eventually department chair, 1912-26; Utilities Power and Light Corporation, director, 1926-38. Carnegie Institution, research associate, 1908-23; trustee and president of the board of Albion College, 1919-23; trustee and director to Concessions of the Chicago World's Fair (also known as the Century of Progress Exposition), 1933-34. *Military service:* U.S. Army, worked at Fort Sill as a major in the Ordinance Department during World War I, 1918-19; became a lieutenant colonel in the U.S. Army Reserve.

MEMBER: Society for Visual Education (founder), National Academy of Sciences, American Association for the Advancement of Science (elected permanent secretary, 1937-46, administrative secretary, 1946-48), American Mathematical Society, American Astronomical Society.

AWARDS, HONORS: Honorary Sc.D., Case School of Applied Science, 1940.

WRITINGS:

(With T. C. Chamberlin) *The Tidal and Other Problems,* Carnegie Institution of Washington, 1909.
New Methods in Exterior Ballistics, University of Chicago Press, 1926.
The World and Man as Science Sees Them, University of Chicago Press, 1937.

(Editor, with J. J. Schifferes) *The Autobiography of Science,* second edition, J. Murray, 1963.

Associate editor of the *Transactions of the American Mathematical Society,* 1907-12; editor of twenty-five science symposium volumes for the American Association for the Advancement of Science. Contributor to journals and periodicals, including *Science.*

SIDELIGHTS: Forest Ray Moulton is best remembered for his hypothesis, conceived with Thomas Chrowder Chamberlin, that the planets formed when gas emitted by our sun was compressed under gravitational influence from a passing star. In this so-called Chamberlin-Moulton hypothesis, the gas solidified and condensed into "planetesimals," which later accumulated into the existing planets. While this model was superseded by later ideas, it brought to light certain theories about spiral motion in gas clouds that preceded important measurements of spiral galaxies. Moulton also served as chair of the University of Chicago's astronomy department; and, as secretary of the American Association for the Advancement of Science in Washington, D.C., saw the organization double its membership and find permanent housing. Moulton's interests also led to pioneering work in radio broadcasting and motion picture technology as well as contributions to the field of ballistics.

Moulton was born on April 29, 1872, to Belah G. Moulton, a farmer, and Mary G. (Smith) Moulton, a schoolteacher in a small school. Moulton was raised on a farm in southern Michigan's forest-rich Osceola County, near the town of Reed City (which later became Le Roy, Michigan). As noted in *Dictionary of American Biography Supplement 5 (1951-1955),* his mother named him Forest Ray because he was, in her words, "a perfect ray of light and happiness in that dense forest." The oldest child in his family, Moulton had five brothers and a sister: Mary, Charles, Vern, E. L., Elton J. (later a professor of astronomy at Northwestern University), and Harold G. (later a president of the Brookings Institution in Washington, D.C.). Moulton was sixteen when he began his teaching career, in a rural school near home, from 1888 to 1889. Moulton didn't begin secondary school until he was seventeen. He attended Albion College in 1892, where he played on the football team and taught astronomy, receiving his B.A. in 1894. He earned a Ph.D. in astronomy, summa cum laude, from the University of Chicago in 1899. Three years earlier he had begun working as an assistant instructor in the University of

Chicago's astronomy department. In 1898 he was promoted to associate instructor and to instructor in 1900. In 1903 he became assistant professor, then served as associate professor from 1908 to 1912. From then on he was a professor and department chair, until his resignation in 1926.

In 1898 Moulton first met with Thomas Chrowder Chamberlin, chair of the geology department at the University of Chicago. A few years later, under the sponsorship of the University of Chicago and the Carnegie Institution of Washington, the two scientists studied photographs of the total eclipse of the sun occurring on May 28, 1900. They were impressed by the flares of gas flying off the sun's surface. In 1904 they published the first complete statement of their theory of planetesimals to account for the solar system's formation. Chamberlin had been critical of Pierre-Simon Laplace's nebular hypothesis, which said a gas cloud contracted to form the sun, with rings of matter being left out at their present-day distances and later condensing into the planets. This scenario presupposed a warmer past for the Earth, but Chamberlin's study of ice ages on Earth contradicted this. Moulton and Chamberlin thought a star had passed close to the sun, which had caused the sun to throw off material. Over time, the smaller pebbles that solidified became rocks, then boulders, etc., with gravity speeding up the process. (Today, it is believed that gas thrown off of the sun will *not* condense into solid matter.) Moulton prepared tables showing that if the Earth had really been much hotter in the past, as Laplace had implied, all its water vapor would have escaped into space. Chamberlin and Moulton theorized that our own solar system, in its primitive gaseous state, might have exhibited spiral structure. This part of the Chamberlin-Moulton hypothesis may have influenced later observations of the rotation in spiral galaxies, as well as specific observations of the Andromeda Galaxy's rotation.

During World War I, Moulton worked at Fort Sill as a Major in the Ordnance Department of the U.S. Army. He was in charge of ballistics in the American Artillery from 1918 to 1919, and carried out mathematical and test research on high-velocity guns (and on improving the accuracy of firing data). He helped increase the range of guns by streamlining shells, and after the war, became a lieutenant colonel in the U.S. Army Reserve.

Moulton took on a variety of academic responsibilities, serving as associate editor of the *Transactions*

of the American Mathematical Society from 1907 until 1912, and more significantly, as a research associate at the Carnegie Institution from 1908 to 1923. After leaving the University of Chicago in 1926, Moulton became director of the Utilities Power and Light Corporation until 1938. In perhaps his most influential administrative role, Moulton was elected permanent secretary of the American Association for the Advancement of Science (AAAS) in 1937, a duty he carried out until 1946 (staying on as administrative secretary for two more years). During Moulton's tenure as secretary, the AAAS took over the publication of *Science* magazine, found permanent housing for the association in Washington, D.C., and saw its membership rise from less than twenty-thousand in 1937 to 43,000 in 1946. Moulton also edited twenty-five science symposium volumes for the AAAS.

For several years Moulton gave weekly broadcasts on astronomy, mathematics, and physics over the Columbia Broadcasting Company's radio network. From 1919 until 1923 Moulton was a trustee and president of the board of Albion College, and he received a Sc.D. in astronomy and mathematics there in 1923. From 1933 to 1934 Moulton served as trustee and director to Concessions of the Chicago World's Fair, also known as the Century of Progress Exposition. Trying to make ends meet during the Depression proved stressful, and Moulton suffered (but recovered from) heart problems during this time. In 1939 Moulton received an LL.D. from Drake University, and an honorary Sc.D. from the Case School of Applied Science the following year.

Moulton founded the Society for Visual Education, gave the first radio address broadcast from the University of Chicago, and invented a way to prevent the flickering of motion pictures. He gave hundreds of public lectures across the United States, and enjoyed membership in the AAAS, the National Academy of Sciences, the American Mathematical Society, and the American Astronomical Society. Moulton played tennis and handball, occasionally played billiards, and enjoyed opera. He was also fond of farming, poetry, classical literature, and painting. Moulton died at age eighty on December 7, 1952, at the home of a friend in Wilmette, Illinois.

Moulton married twice and divorced twice. He married Estella Laura Gillette in Owosso, Michigan, on March 25, 1897, and with her had four children: Gail Francis, Vieva Gillette, Mary Elizabeth, and Merle Gordon. This first marriage ended in 1938, and Moulton remarried on July 28, 1939, to Alicia Pratt, in Norristown, Pennsylvania. This marriage ended in a 1951 divorce.

BIOGRAPHICAL/CRITICAL SOURCES:

BOOKS

Encyclopedia of Cosmology, Garland, 1993, p. 56.
Garraty, John A., *Dictionary of American Biography Supplement 5 (1951-1955),* Scribner, 1977, pp. 508-509.
National Cyclopedia of American Biography, Volume 43, James T. White, 1961, p. 314.

PERIODICALS

New York Times, December 9, 1952, p. 33.*

* * *

MOYER, Terry J. 1937-
   (James L. McMorey)

PERSONAL: Born January 27, 1937, in Idaho Falls, ID; son of Hushul B. and Verna Mary (Metcalf) Moyer; married Donna Mae Schipper (a teacher); children: Cynthia Anne Moyer Manning, Vikki Vreni Moyer Bolich, Adrian C. *Education:* Brigham Young University, B.A., 1960; University of Southern California, M.S.Ed., 1964; attended California State University, Northridge, 1965-68. *Politics:* Conservative Republican. *Religion:* Church of Jesus Christ of Latter-Day Saints (Mormon). *Avocational interests:* Mountain climbing, genealogical research, the Civil War, gardening, hiking.

ADDRESSES: Home—3202 Sagebrush Cir., Salt Lake City, UT 84121. *Office*—50 East North Temple St., 21st Fl., Salt Lake City, UT 84150.

CAREER: High school teacher in Simi Valley, CA, 1961-75; Latter-Day Saints Social Services, Salt Lake City, UT, administrator of program development, 1975-90; Latter-Day Saints Translation, Salt Lake City, translation supervisor and linguist, 1991—. State coordinator for Civil War database project, U.S. National Parks. Has held various leadership positions within Church of Jesus Christ of

Latter-Day Saints. *Military service:* Army National Guard, 1960-66; became staff sergeant.

MEMBER: National Right to Life Organization.

WRITINGS:

Crescendo (young adult novel), Horizon (Bountiful, UT), 1995.
Have I Got a Story for You! (inspirational stories), Horizon, 1996.

Author of writings under the pseudonym James L. McMorey.

WORK IN PROGRESS: Ritter, a young adult novel; *Remembering Brigham Young University; The Defector,* a Latter-Day Saints novel.

ADAPTATIONS: Movie rights to *Crescendo* have been sold.

* * *

MURCHIE, Guy 1907-1997

OBITUARY NOTICE—See index for *CA* sketch: Born January 25, 1907, in Boston, MA; died July 8, 1997, in Anaheim (one source says Fullerton), CA. Journalist, photographer, artist, aviator, educator, author. Murchie had a varied career, first as a reporter with the *Chicago Tribune.* He began work with the paper as a feature writer in 1934 and later became one of its war correspondents during World War II. Murchie was said to be the first correspondent who was wounded during the conflict; he was injured in the leg during a bombing raid in Dover, England. During the war, he used his talents as a photographer and artist as well to capture scenes of the war from his posts in England and Iceland. In 1942 he began work as a navigation instructor with American Airlines' Air Transport Command. He worked from 1943 to 1944 as a navigator. In 1945 he founded the Apple Hill Camp for children in Pepperell, Massachusetts, and Nelson, New Hampshire, and served as its director from 1945 to 1955. He also found time to teach at the Landhaven School in Maine and to serve as a navigator for Seaboard and Western Airlines. He wrote and edited books, including *Men on the Horizon, Mutiny of the Bounty and Other Sea Stories, Song of the Sky: An Exploration of the Ocean of Air* (self-illustrated), *Music of the Spheres:*

The Material Universe from Atom to Quasar, Simply Explained (self-illustrated), *The Seven Mysteries of Life: An Exploration in Science and Philosophy* (self-illustrated), and *The Soul School.* His *Song of the Sky* was awarded the John Burroughs Medal for best nature book in 1955. He was also nominated for the American Book Award in 1982 for *The Seven Mysteries of Life.*

OBITUARIES AND OTHER SOURCES:

BOOKS

Writers Directory, St. James Press, 1996.

PERIODICALS

Chicago Tribune, July 11, 1997, section 3, p. 12.
New York Times, July 13, 1997, section 1, p. 26.

* * *

MUSSEN, Paul Henry 1922-

PERSONAL: Born March 21, 1922, in Paterson, NJ; son of Harry and Taube Mussen; married Ethel Foladore, October 30, 1953; children: Michele, James. *Education:* Stanford University, A.B., 1942, M.A., 1943; Yale University, Ph.D., 1949. *Politics:* Democrat.

ADDRESSES: Office—Department of Education, University of California, Los Angeles, CA. 90024.

CAREER: University of Wisconsin, Madison, assistant professor of psychology, 1949-51; Ohio State University, Columbus, assistant professor, became associate professor of psychology, 1951-56; University of California, Berkeley, member of faculty, 1956—, professor of psychology, 1961—, director of Institute of Human Development, 1969-80; University of California, Los Angeles, faculty member; writer. Social Sciences Research Council, member of board of directors. *Military service:* U.S. Naval Reserve, 1944-46; became lieutenant.

MEMBER: American Psychological Association, Society of Research of Child Development, Phi Beta Kappa, Sigma Xi.

AWARDS, HONORS: Fulbright fellowship, 1960-61; National Institute of Humanities grant.

WRITINGS:

NONFICTION

(With John Janeway Conger and Jerome Kagan) *Child Development and Personality,* Harper (New York City), 1956.
The Psychological Development of the Child, Prentice-Hall (Englewood Cliffs, NJ), 1963.
(With Mark R. Rosenzweig and Elliot Aronson) *Psychology: An Introduction,* Heath (Lexington, MA), 1973.
(With Nancy Eisenberg) *Roots of Caring, Sharing, and Helping: The Development of Prosocial Behavior in Children,* W.H. Freeman (San Francisco, CA), 1977.
(With others) *Psychological Development: A Life-Span Approach,* Harper, 1979.
(With Conger, Kagan, and Diana Steen) *Essentials of Child Development and Personality,* Harper, 1980.
(With Nancy Eisenberg) *The Roots of Prosocial Behavior in Children,* Cambridge University Press (London), 1989.

EDITOR

(With Alfred L. Baldwin and others) *Handbook of Research Methods in Child Development,* Wiley (New York City), 1960.
(With Conger and Kagan) *Readings in Child Development and Personality,* Harper, 1965.
(With Martin Covington and Jonas Langer) *Trends and Issues in Developmental Psychology,* Holt (New York City), 1969.
Carmichael's Manual of Child Psychology, Wiley, 1970, fourth edition published in four volumes as *Handbook of Child Psychology,* Volume 1: (with William Kessen) *History, Theories, and Methods,* Volume 2: (with Marshall M. Haith and Joseph J. Campos) *Infancy and Developmental Psychobiology,* Volume 3: (with John H. Flavell and Ellen M. Markman) *Cognitive Development,* Volume 4: (with E. Mavis Hetherington) *Socialization, Personality, and Social Development,* 1983.
(With Rosenzweig) *Concepts in Psychology: Introductory Readings,* Heath, 1974.
(With Conger and Kagan) *Basic and Contemporary Issues in Developmental Psychology,* Harper, 1975.
(With Conger and Kagan) *Readings in Child and Adolescent Psychology: Contemporary Perspectives,* Harper, 1980.

Also editor of *Annual Review of Psychology,* 1968-73.

SIDELIGHTS: Paul Henry Mussen is an authority on child psychology. He has taught at such institutions as Ohio State University and the University of California, Los Angeles, and he has written—and collaborated in writing—numerous volumes, including *Child Development and Personality, The Psychological Development of the Child, Roots of Caring, Sharing, and Helping: The Development of Prosocial Behavior in Children, Psychology: An Introduction, Psychological Development: A Life-Span Approach,* and *Essentials of Child Development and Personality.* In addition, he has served as editor, and co-editor, of such works as *Readings in Child Development and Personality* and *Carmichael's Manual of Child Psychology,* which was later published in four volumes as *Handbook of Child Psychology.*

*   *   *

MYERS, W. David 1956-

PERSONAL: Born April 17, 1956, in AZ; son of Catherine Myers. *Education:* Yale University, Ph.D., 1991. *Politics:* Liberal/Democrat.

ADDRESSES: Office—Department of History, Fordham University, Bronx, NY 10458.   *E-mail*—dmyers@ murray.fordham.edu.

CAREER: Georgetown University, Washington, DC, instructor in history, 1987-88; University of Maryland at College Park, visiting instructor in history, 1988-89; Catholic University of America, Washington, DC, instructor in history, 1990; Fordham University, Bronx, NY, associate professor of history, 1990—.

AWARDS, HONORS: Charlotte W. Newcombe fellow, Woodrow Wilson Foundation, 1985.

WRITINGS:

"Poor, Sinning Folk": Confession and Conscience in Counter-Reformation Germany, Cornell University Press (Ithaca, NY), 1996.

WORK IN PROGRESS: Sin and Crime in Early Modern Europe; research on the history of the conscience in Europe, 1500-1800.

N-O

NELSON, James L. 1962-

PERSONAL: Born April 5, 1962, in Lewiston, ME; son of David (an English professor) and Selma (an English teacher) Nelson; married Lisa Page, April 11, 1993; children: Elizabeth (Betsy) Clare Nelson. *Education:* Attended University of Massachusetts—Amherst, 1981-83; University of California at Los Angeles, B.A., 1986; graduate studies at Sonoma State University, 1993-94. *Avocational interests:* Sailing, travel, model building and woodworking, "though they are much intertwined with my vocation."

ADDRESSES: Agent—Nat Sobel, Sobel Weber Associates, Inc., 146 East 19th St., New York, NY 10003-2404.

CAREER: Writer, sailor, and television producer. The Landsburg Company (television production), Los Angeles, CA, assistant editor, 1986-88; *Golden Hinde* (ship), boatswain, 1988-89; *Lady Washington* (ship), rigger/sailor, 1990-91; "H.M.S." *Rose* (sail training ship), third mate/director of education, 1991-92; writer, 1992—.

MEMBER: American Sail Training Association, National Maritime Historical Society.

AWARDS, HONORS: Ray Stark Award, Hollywood Radio and Television Society Award, both earned while a student at UCLA, both for excellence in the field of television production.

WRITINGS:

By Force of Arms (historical fiction), Pocket Books (New York City), 1996.

The Maddest Idea (historical fiction), Pocket Books, 1997.

WORK IN PROGRESS: The Common Defense, the third in the Isaac Biddlecomb series, due from Pocket Books in 1998. Research for *The Guardship,* a novel set in Virginia in 1712.

SIDELIGHTS: James L. Nelson's first novel, *By Force of Arms,* draws on the author's experience as a sailor and his lifelong love of the sea to provide the setting for a historical novel set during the American Revolution. The book centers on Isaac Biddlecomb, who has worked his way up through the ranks to command of a merchant ship, and follows him as his fortunes, and those of his country, take a different turn. "Nelson's seagoing experience is evident in his clear, convincing description of the sailing," remarked a reviewer for *Publishers Weekly.* While the author's dialogue and straightforward plot were at times faulted, his rich characterizations, realistic action, and the rare naval view he presents of revolutionary times earned praise. *By Force of Arms* is "an engaging start to what promises to be a fine adventure series," the *Publishers Weekly* critic concluded.

Nelson told *CA:* "I was born and raised in Lewiston, Maine. My passion for ships and the sea goes back as far as I can recall. While other boys' interests moved from cars to dinosaurs to airplanes, I remained steadfastly interested in sailing ships. I built ship models, and later, in my early teens, a seventeen-foot sailboat.

"Most of the books I read were on maritime subjects, both fiction and nonfiction. Like so many others I fell in love with C. S. Forester's Hornblower books. I have read them all, including *The Hornblower Companion,* many times. In reading the histories of other authors of historical fiction I find many who were inspired to become writers by these wonderful books. I am not at all surprised.

"Mr. Forester's reputation has taken something of a beating in past years, largely in light of Patrick O'Brian's admittedly superior handling of the subject. Indeed, there is no author that I know of who understands and recreates the eighteenth century as perfectly as Mr. O'Brian. Still, the Hornblower books are as marvelous now as they ever were, and C. S. Forester must be given due credit for having invented the genre of the historic naval series and for inspiring so many young writers with his books.

"After graduating from Lewiston High School, I spent a year hitchhiking and motorcycling around the country, hoping to sate a wanderlust that I then erroneously believed could be sated. I went to the University of Massachusetts, Amherst, for two years, and then to UCLA, graduating in 1986 with a degree in motion picture and television production.

"I worked as an assistant editor at a television production company for two years, the longest I ever worked a real job and the longest I ever intend to. By 1988 I was living on a sailboat and directing all my energy toward the sea, that passion having been reawakened several years earlier.

"In 1988 I gave in to my growing wanderlust (it can never be sated, I had come to realize) and began to sail professionally. I joined the crew of the sailing ship *Golden Hinde*. My intention had been to sail with the *Hinde* for six months and then return to Los Angeles and my television career. A year later I left the *Hinde,* sold my boat and never thought again about working in television.

"For five years I worked with sailing ships, 'tall ships' as they are often called. I worked in the state of Washington aboard the brig *Lady Washington,* and on the east coast aboard the replica frigate *Rose*.

"While sailing aboard the *Golden Hinde* I met Lisa Page, a fellow sailor. She and I became involved in 1989 in a relationship that was often long-distance when one or the other of us was off to sea. In 1992 I was moved by two forces to give up sailing professionally; a desire to be with Lisa permanently, and a desire to write.

"The idea of becoming a novelist was one that I had entertained since childhood. From time to time I had even taken a stab at writing, always very badly. Like many neophyte writers I was more enamored with the romance of the whole thing—the Jack London/Ernest Hemingway image, sitting before the old manual Remington late at night, cigarette in my lips, bottle of bourbon on the desk, pounding out a novel—than I was in actually writing a book.

"It's laughable, but I actually tried to write that way. It was only some years later that I realized that neither Jack London, nor Ernest Hemingway, nor any other real writer works like that. The fact that one rarely finds a successful novelist under the age of thirty does not surprise me. The discipline and maturity needed to see a book through is something that tends to come about only after you have gotten the other stuff out of the way.

"In 1992, at age thirty, I realized I was ready to write. No cigarettes, no bottle of bourbon, just early mornings in front of the typewriter (being, at the time, too poor to afford a computer). I completed my first book, *By Force of Arms,* in December of 1994. The book introduces the character Isaac Biddlecomb, an American sea captain and smuggler, in the year 1775. Biddlecomb is caught by the British navy in his illegal activities, escapes to sea and is impressed onto another British man-of-war, where he leads a mutiny in order to escape. *Arms* is the first in an intended series that will tell the story of the naval aspects of the American revolution.

"The old adage goes 'write about what you know,' and I think most writers would agree with me that this is nonsense. It is true, however, that you must know about what you write. It was inevitable for me that I should write about ships and the sea, and indeed I never seriously considered writing about any other subject. My personal experiences at sea have greatly aided me in my writing, though they have not relieved me of the need for copious research into all aspects of eighteenth-century life.

"In 1993 Lisa and I were married. In February of 1994 we found out that Lisa was pregnant. Then in April my (now) agent, Nat Sobel, managed to sell *Arms* as well as two more books in the Isaac Biddlecomb series. Our daughter, Elizabeth Clare, was born on November 12, 1994.

"As of this writing I have completed the second and third books in the series and am waiting to find out if the series will be continued beyond that. If it is not I hope to continue my fictional documentation of America's maritime past with books covering other periods in that history. With so long and rich a heritage it is unlikely that I will run out of material."

BIOGRAPHICAL/CRITICAL SOURCES:

PERIODICALS

Publishers Weekly, January 8, 1996, p. 64.

*   *   *

NESAULE, Agate 1938-

PERSONAL: Born January 23, 1938, in Riga, Latvia; immigrated to United States, 1950; naturalized U.S. citizen, 1956; daughter of Peteris (a Lutheran minister) and Valda (a teacher, dishwasher, and professor; maiden name, Kness-Knezinskis) Nesaule. *Education:* Indiana University, B.A., 1961, M.A., 1963; University of Wisconsin-Madison, Ph.D., 1972.

ADDRESSES: Home—Madison, Wisconsin. *Office*—Women's Studies Department, University of Wisconsin—Whitewater, Whitewater, WI, 53190. *Agent*—c/o Soho Press, 853 Broadway, New York, NY, 10003.

CAREER: Writer. University of Wisconsin, Whitewater, professor of English and women's studies, 1963-96.

MEMBER: Latvian Writers' Association, Association for the Advancement of Baltic Studies, Writers' Place, Phi Beta Kappa, Phi Kappa Phi.

AWARDS, HONORS: Saunders Award for Excellence in Teaching in the Humanities, 1988; Outstanding Teaching Award in Letters and Sciences, University of Wisconsin—Whitewater, 1994; Before Columbus Foundation American Book Award, 1996, for *A Woman in Amber: Healing the Trauma of War and Exile;* Outstanding Achievement Award, Wisconsin Library Association, 1996, for *A Woman in Amber;* Outstanding Research Award, University of Wisconsin—Whitewater, 1996.

WRITINGS:

A Woman in Amber: Healing the Trauma of War and Exile (memoir), Soho Press (New York City), 1995.

WORK IN PROGRESS: Shopping for Relatives (working title), a novel; another memoir focusing on the author's father.

SIDELIGHTS: Agate Nesaule won critical and popular acclaim for her 1995 memoir *A Woman in Amber: Healing the Trauma of War and Exile.* The woman in the title was Nesaule herself, who as a young Latvian girl who suffered some of the worst hardships of World War II and who preserved those sufferings in the amber-like protective casing of her memory. Later, as an adolescent and adult in the United States, teaching herself English by reading *Gone with the Wind,* then earning a doctorate and becoming a professor at a well-recognized public university, Nesaule tried to keep her memories safely trapped in amber. They were revealed, however, through the questions of her therapist and her lover, and it is with those questions, asked of her while she was in bed with her lover, that the book begins.

In a flashback, Nesaule reveals her harrowing early life to the reader as she tells stories from the past to her gray-haired male partner; the book's chronology follows that of recollection rather than of history. Its path winds through the Nesaule family's peaceful life in Latvia, where her father was a Lutheran minister and her mother was a woman of much intelligence and culture, who keenly regretted that history had deprived her of a university degree.

The memoir traces Nesaule's internment by the Nazis and a stay in a Lutheran home for the mentally defective near Berlin; the home turned out to be a relatively safe location because of the compassion of its commandant, a German pastor. *A Woman in Amber* then delineates the horrendous suffering Nesaule endured at the hands of the Russian invaders who replaced the Nazis: the German pastor is executed, there are gang-rapes, witnessed killings, and starvation. The Nesaule family eventually escaped to a British-run displaced persons' camp and spent the years 1945-1950 there. Nesaule immigrated to the United States in 1950, and spent her adolescence struggling in the Latvian community and the slums of Indianapolis. Although she achieved the higher education her mother had hoped for, she spent years in an unhappy marriage and she was estranged from her mother. Eventually, however, Nesaule discovers a way to tell her story, to reconcile with and love her deceased mother, and to find meaning in her experiences.

Nesaule's memoir, in the opinion of many reviewers, is a searing work of literature. According to Patricia

Hampl in the *New York Times Book Review:* "It is a story both heroic and achingly humble. It draws the reader forward with the suspense of a novel, a tale told in the unmistakable voice of one searching urgently for integrity as if it were a cure. And in this memoir the cure is found."

Gabriele Annan, writing for the *London Review of Books,* called Nesaule's recounting of her life in Europe "deadpan factual," asserting that this portion of the memoir contained "no fine writing, no interpretive nudging, no drawing of lessons and no moralizing." Moreover, Annan asserted that "the tension, the climaxes of apprehension, horror, relief are brilliantly managed." Similarly, *Library Journal*'s Rena Fowler assessed the book as "well-written and insightful," and *Women's Review of Books* critic Mary L. Felstiner called Nesaule "a master storyteller," while asserting that "sometimes the detail is too abundant, like those nineteenth-century paintings that competed with photography." Hampl praised Nesaule's book's suspense and its accuracy of vision: "The evils Ms. Nesaule observes are rendered with the clear-eyed regard of a child who misses nothing," and concluded: "Ms. Nesaule's ability to escape at last from the evil enchantment of the war is not so much a triumph (which would be a crude resolution of such a story) as it is a benediction upon all that she bears as her family and national history."

Nesaule told *CA:* "I hope that, in however small a way, *A Woman in Amber* shows what happens to civilians during war and contributes to work for peace. The after-effects of war are long lasting and I fervently hope for greater understanding of all its victims. I want tenderness for them long after atrocities end.

"*A Woman in Amber,* while containing some grim passages, is also a love story, an immigrant story; it has a happy ending. I hope my book, begun after a writer's block lasting more than forty years, helps others to tell their stories and experience the integration and joy that it can bring."

BIOGRAPHICAL/CRITICAL SOURCES:

PERIODICALS

Library Journal, November 1, 1995, p. 74.
London Review of Books, March 21, 1996, p. 18.
New York Times Book Review, January 14, 1996, pp. 14-15.
Women's Review of Books, February, 1996, p. 4.

NETHERY, Mary

PERSONAL: Born in Eureka, CA; daughter of Louis Dante and Helen Jane (Gierek) Scuri; married Harry Arthur Nethery III (an environmental health administrator), August 8, 1970; children: Harry Arthur IV. *Education:* Humboldt State University, B.A. (magna cum laude), and Teaching Credential; University of San Francisco, M.A. *Politics:* Democrat. *Religion:* Roman Catholic. *Avocational interests:* Ballet, travel, animals, interior design, going to the movies, theater.

ADDRESSES: Home—6301 Eggert Rd., Eureka, CA 95503. *Office*—Humboldt County Office of Education, 901 Myrtle Ave., Eureka, CA 95501. *E-mail*—nethery@tidepool.com.

CAREER: Humboldt County Office of Education, Eureka, CA, staff development coordinator and editor, 1977—.

MEMBER: Society of Children's Book Writers and Illustrators, Association of Supervision and Curriculum Development, National Staff Development Council, Humane Society of America.

WRITINGS:

Hannah and Jack, illustrated by Mary Morgan, Simon & Schuster (New York City), 1996.
Orange Cat Goes to Market, Candlewick, 1997.

Contributor to children's magazines, including *Ladybug* and *Spider.* Editor, *Humboldt Highlights* (education journal), 1992—.

WORK IN PROGRESS: The Incredible Remy Hicks, a contemporary middle-grade novel of mystery, set in Paris and involving a young photographer.

SIDELIGHTS: Mary Nethery commented: "Sister Mildred, my first-grade teacher at St. Bernard's Elementary School, would always read my stories to the class. Then she'd add, 'This is a perfect example of fine writing.' I don't think her comments added to my popularity, but shortly thereafter, in second grade, I began my first novel. Of course it was fully illustrated.

"I've always loved to write. In junior high school, my friend Katy and I wrote adventure and romance stories during math class, then compared them, chapter by chapter. It was much more fun than fumbling around with numbers. But it wasn't until my son was born that I became intrigued with children's literature. Reading him stories by such writers as James Marshall, Tomi Ungerer, Graham Oakley, Daniel Pinkwater, Jane Yolen, James Howe, Steven Kellogg, and Dr. Seuss gave us so many moments of joy and laughter, as well as insights. I came to admire the extraordinary skill and brilliance of these writers.

"I write today because of their influence and inspiration, and because my voice tends to be either that of a five-, six-, or twelve-year-old. There's something magical about those times in life that continues to capture my attention. My first book *Hannah and Jack* is about a girl, five or six years old, who loves her cat Jack. When her family takes a trip to Grandma's, Hannah has to leave Jack behind. This is a story of how one small child empowers herself to deal with separation, as well as to luxuriate in a reunion that has them 'lolling like fat rabbits in the sweet grass, just being together again.'

"I can also remember the enormous energy and sense of anticipation that comes with being eleven or twelve years old, that time of transition from child to young adult. I read Margaret Mitchell's *Gone with the Wind* when I was eleven and was extremely annoyed to discover that she hadn't written a sequel. I could relate to Scarlet's spunk and ambition. I was a tomboy who loved animals and wanted a horse more than anything in the world. I used to draw reams of horse pictures and sneak bareback rides on other people's horses. When I was ten years old, I took care of my grandfather's farm—milking the cows and feeding the chickens and goats—while he was in Europe, so that I could earn money to buy my very own horse. I can also remember wanting desperately to travel, especially to Paris. Currently I am writing a novel set in Paris, about a twelve-year-old photographer who finds herself wrapped in mystery and danger. I love the characters in the book so much that there will definitely be a sequel!

"I write every morning before I go to work. When I can't write because of other obligations, I tend to become quite grumpy. Needless to say, my husband Han, my son H. A., and my Bengal cat Asta make sure that it's easy for me to write every morning. In fact, Asta lays on a big pillow by my desk in my studio while I write, giving me advice and ideas for getting his favorite characters out of the many pickles into which I get them.

"I have had the good fortune to work with and learn from other authors, such as Nancy Farmer, Tricia Gardella, Barbara Kerley, Helen Ketteman, Kirby Larson, Ann Paul, Dian Curtis Regan, Vivian Sathre, Aaron Shephard, Jane Yolen, Tasha Wing, and magazine editor Kim Griswell. They've inspired me with their talent and skill and have generously shared their knowledge with me.

"My goal is to write books that children will read with a flashlight under the bed covers, long after their parents have kissed them goodnight. If they wake up the next morning with my characters still in their heads, then I am in heaven."

BIOGRAPHICAL/CRITICAL SOURCES:

PERIODICALS

Booklist, May 1, 1996, p. 1512.
Horn Book, July-August, 1996, p. 543.
School Library Journal, March, 1996, p. 179.

                              *   *   *

NGOR, Haing S.   1947(?)-1996

PERSONAL: Born in 1947 (some sources say 1941, 1950, or 1951), in Samrong Yong, Cambodia; died February 25, 1996, in Los Angeles, CA; immigrated to Thailand, 1979; immigrated to United States, 1980; son of an Chinese father and a Khmer mother; engaged to Chang My Houy (died, June 2, 1978). *Education:* Graduated from medical school in Cambodia; attended Khmer Rouge school of acting. *Religion:* Buddhist. *Avocational interests:* Fluent in nine languages.

CAREER: Cambodian physician and actor. Ran an obstetrics-gynecology clinic in Phnom Pen, ending 1975; imprisoned by Khmer Rouge regime, Cambodia, 1975-79; worked in refugee assistance in Thailand at Cambodian border; worked in United States as actor, author, physician, security guard, and as job counselor at Chinatown Service Center, Los Angeles; co-founder, Aid to Displaced Persons, Brussels, Belgium, and Enfants d'Angkor, Paris, France. Appeared in films, including *The Killing Fields,* Goldcrest, 1984; *Dong fang tu ying* (also known as *Eastern Condors*), 1987; *Nadie Escuchaba,* 1988; *The Iron Triangle,* Eurobrothers/International Video Entertainment/Scotti Brothers, 1989; *Vietnam, Texas,* Eric Productions/Epic Productions, 1990; *Ambition,* Spirit, 1991; *Heaven and Earth,* 1993; *My Life,*

Columbia, 1993; *The Dragon Gate,* 1994; *Fortunes of War,* New Moon, 1994; and *Hit Me,* Slough Pond, 1996. Appeared on television, including *In Love and War* (television movie), 1987; "The Doctors Wilde" (also known as "Zoovets"), *CBS Summer Playhouse,* 1987; "The Last Outpost," *Vietnam War Story,* HBO, 1989; "Last Flight Out," *AT & T Presents,* 1990; *Earth and the American Dream* (documentary), 1993; *Vanishing Son,* 1994; appeared on television episodes, including *China Beach,* ABC,1988; *Highway to Heaven,* NBC, 1984; *Miami Vice,* NBC, 1984; *Hotel,* ABC; and as 1990 Miss Universe Pageant judge. *Military Service:* Cambodian army, served as a physician before 1975.

AWARDS, HONORS: Academy Award for best supporting actor, British Academy of Film and Television Arts Awards for best actor and best newcomer to film, and Golden Globe Award for best supporting actor, all 1984, all for *The Killing Fields.*

WRITINGS:

AUTOBIOGRAPHY

(With Roger Warner) *Haing Ngor: A Cambodian Odyssey* (also known as *A Cambodian Odyssey*), Macmillan (New York City), 1987, audio book distributed as *Surviving the Killing Fields,* read by Crawford Logan, Dual Dolphin, 1990.

ADAPTATIONS: Haing Ngor's life has been the subject of two film documentaries, *A Man Without A Country* and *Beyond the Killing Fields.*

WORK IN PROGRESS: The Healing Fields, a book unfinished at author's death.

SIDELIGHTS: Haing Ngor survived the killings fields of Cambodia's brutal Pol Pot dictatorship, but he did not survive the streets of Los Angeles. Born in 1947 (some sources give different years) in a farming village south of Phnom Penh, his earliest impressions of Cambodia were of a beautiful, peaceful land. He was still a boy, however, when civil war came.

As Ngor relates in his autobiography, *Haing Ngor: A Cambodian Odyssey,* a childhood experience of being harassed by soldiers while trying to take his mother to the doctor gave young Ngor the ambition of helping his people by becoming a physician. Although coming from a poor agricultural family, he went to live in a temple with Buddhist monks, and later pursued his medical education. Having obtained his de-

gree, he set up an obstetrics-gynecology clinic in Phnom Penh, and served as a Cambodian army doctor.

In 1975 the Khmer Rouge, a group of Maoist guerrillas led by Pol Pot, took control of the country and began a campaign of genocide aimed at ridding Cambodia of all Western cultural influences. This included killing anyone who displayed even the slightest signs of education, such as wearing eyeglasses. Ngor was operating on a wounded soldier in a hospital when Khmer Rouge soldiers burst in and asked him, "Are you the doctor?" Knowing his life was at stake, Ngor replied that the doctor had just fled. He himself then left the operating room, compelled to abandon the patient "with his body cavity still open," according to a *Washington Post* obituary of Ngor.

Captured by the Khmer Rouge, Ngor, like all other urban dwellers in Phnom Penh, was force-marched into the countryside, where he worked as a slave laborer, breaking rocks. He pretended to be an illiterate taxi driver, for "If you know only ABC, Khmer Rouge say, 'You CIA!'" he later told *People* magazine's Lois Armstrong and Deirdre Donahue. In a situation in which some three million Cambodians died from such causes as beating or starvation, Ngor managed to survive, foraging for small bits of food, and acting the part of an illiterate despite being frequently suspected. More than once, he had to look on silently while viewing the illnesses of fellow captors who, as a physician, he ought to have been able to heal. Twice he was tortured almost to the point of death after having been accused of being a doctor by a former medical school acquaintance. Once, the tip of a finger was cut off after he was caught stealing food (one source says the cause of the amputation was that he called his fiancee "sweet"). His weight dropped from 140 pounds to seventy pounds during his incarceration.

In the forced labor camp, Ngor fell in love with a woman, Chang My Houy, who conceived a child with him. They were unable to marry, and she died of labor complications resulting from malnutrition on June 2, 1978. Though Ngor was a trained obstetrician, he was unable to assist her without also losing his own life.

In May, 1979, the Pol Pot regime collapsed, and Ngor, whose parents, two sisters, and two of three brothers had been killed, rescued a young niece and escaped with her and a friend over the border into Thailand. For eighteen months he worked as a doctor in refugee camps there. He was at first denied entry into Australia and the United States because he did not have relatives in those countries. However, he was eventually allowed into the United States in leaving Thailand on October 1, 1980, and arriving in his new country with four dollars in his pocket.

Without a license to practice medicine in the U.S., Ngor took a job as a night security guard. One month after his arrival, he became a caseworker for the Chinatown Service Center in Los Angeles, helping Cambodian refugees find work. He found life in the United States good. Urged to take acting roles by fellow Cambodian refugees, he was uninterested at first, but met a casting director for *The Killing Fields* while at a party. Some seven thousand Cambodian refugees were trying to obtain parts in the film. Ngor approached the tryouts ambivalently, and as something of a lark. Director Roland Joff made him read a particularly emotional scene five times; each time, he found Ngor's performance affecting. "At that point, I knew this was an actor, not a gifted amateur," Joff told *People*. By that point, Ngor was changing his own mind about acting: he was deciding that through the film, he could, as he had promised Houy on her deathbed, tell the world about Cambodia's sufferings.

It was not until Ngor arrived with the film company in Thailand that he learned he had been given the co-starring role of Dith Pran, a real-life Cambodian news photographer who had helped *New York Times* reporter Sydney Schanberg escape that country, had then been caught by the Khmer Rouge, and had, much like Ngor, escaped after years of terrible hardship. His performance as Dith Pran was widely acclaimed, and when Ngor won the Best Supporting Actor award at the Oscars, it was the first time since 1946's *The Best Years of Our Lives* that a nonprofessional had won such a tribute.

Although the role of Dith Pran was Ngor's first paid performance as an actor, he told *People*, "I spent four years in the Khmer Rouge school of acting." His theory of acting, expressed in a profile in *Notable Asian Americans*, relied on the eyes to reveal a character's heart and to convince the audience of the character's reality. Discussing his award-winning performance, Ngor said modestly, "My best performances were over before I left Cambodia. And the prize there was much greater." Yet he clearly enjoyed such perks of fame as riding in limousines and being asked for his autograph. "I am very comfortable here," he told *People*. "It's a happy life."

Ngor acted periodically in other films, notably Oliver Stone's *Heaven and Earth* (1993), the story of a Vietnamese woman who is victimized by all sides in the Vietnam War. Yet Ngor continued his work as a job counselor, and spent a good deal of his time working on behalf of Cambodian refugees in Thailand, France, and Belgium. His ambition was to establish a medical center for refugees in Thailand. However, on a Sunday evening in February, 1996, he was shot in the chest after pulling into the driveway of his two-bedroom apartment near Los Angeles' Chinatown. Many people believed that he was killed because of his involvement in helping bring the perpetrators of Cambodian genocide to justice. However, the police eventually reported that Ngor was the victim of a street gang called the Oriental Lazyboys who robbed Ngor in order to purchase drugs. The Los Angeles County Coroner's Office estimated Ngor's physical age as fifty-five, although records showed him to be up to a decade younger than that.

In 1987 Ngor co-authored an autobiography, *A Cambodian Odyssey,* with journalist Roger Warner. It unsparingly told of Ngor's experiences. Reviewing the audio book version, *KLIATT* contributor Pat Dole commented on the "incredible horrors" its author had gone through. *Library Journal* reviewer Peter Josyph stated, "This highly compelling account . . . of cruel, sadistic oppression masquerading as ideology and should be heard in full by anyone who cares about freedom," and added that its importance is so great, any collection should contain it in order to be complete. Ngor, in a 1985 interview with *People,* had summed up his post-Khmer Rouge experience with this comment about his *Killing Fields* performance: "I wanted to show the world how deep starvation is in Cambodia, how many people die under Communist regime. My heart is satisfied. I have done something perfect."

BIOGRAPHICAL/CRITICAL SOURCES:

BOOKS

Contemporary Film, Theater, and Television, Volume 16, Gale (Detroit, MI), 1997.
Notable Asian Americans, Gale (Detroit, MI), 1995, pp. 284-287.

PERIODICALS

KLIATT, March, 1996, pp. 55-56.
Library Journal, November 1, 1995, p. 124.
People, February 4, 1985, pp. 43-44, 47.

OBITUARIES:

PERIODICALS

New York Times, February 27, 1996, p. A6.
Washington Post, February 27, 1996, p. B6.*

* * *

NIEMEYER, Gerhart   1907-1997

OBITUARY NOTICE—See index for *CA* sketch: Born February 15, 1907, in Essen, Germany; came to the United States, 1937; naturalized U.S. citizen, 1943; died of cancer, June 22, 1997, in Greenwich, CT. Philosopher, educator, and author. Niemeyer devoted more than forty years to teaching and public service, first at Madrid University as a lecturer in law in 1933. Positions at the University of Princeton and Oglethorpe University followed. In 1950 he became a foreign affairs officer with the U.S. Department of State.

Niemeyer joined the Council of Foreign Relations as a research analyst in 1953. He finished out his career at the University of Notre Dame as a professor of political science beginning in 1955; he reached pro-fessor emeritus status in 1976. He also lectured briefly at colleges and universities such as Yale, Munich, and Hillsdale. He wrote various books, in-cluding *Law without Force, An Inquiry into Soviet Mentality, Handbook on Communism, Between Noth-ingness and Paradise, Deceitful Peace, Within and Above Ourselves,* and *Aftersight and Foresight: Se-lected Essays.*

OBITUARIES AND OTHER SOURCES:

BOOKS

Who's Who in America, Marquis, 1996.

PERIODICALS

New York Times, June 29, 1997, p. 29.

* * *

NOVIS, Emile
  See WEIL, Simone (Adolphine)

NUNN, Kem

PERSONAL: Born in Pomona, CA. *Education:* Uni-versity of California, Irvine, degree in studio art.

CAREER: Novelist.

AWARDS, HONORS: American Book Award Best First Novel nomination, 1984, for *Tapping the Source.*

WRITINGS:

NOVELS

Tapping the Source, Delacorte (New York), 1984.
Unassigned Territory, Delacorte, 1987.
Pomona Queen, Pocket Books (New York), 1992.
The Dogs of Winter, Scribner (New York), 1996.

SIDELIGHTS: Kem Nunn earned critical acclaim in 1984 with his debut novel, *Tapping the Source,* a coming-of-age tale set in 1980's Huntington Beach, California. Nunn's protagonist, Ike Tucker, a young man from the backwoods, heads for the coast after he is warned that his sister is in danger. Driven by fear for his sister's life, Ike relentlessly searches for the runaway girl and simultaneously encounters unfamil-iar characters—surfers, addicts, gang members, and others unlike himself. His quest also becomes a per-sonal journey, as Ike loses his virginity and opens his eyes to the immense world beyond his own.

Tapping the Source was a huge success for Nunn, with reviewers comparing him to other well-known authors. Carolyn See, for example, writing for the *Los Angeles Times Book Review,* felt Nunn's novel was a step beyond the legacy of writers such as Horace McCoy, James Cain, Paul Cain, Raoul Whit-field, Ross Macdonald, and Hammett and Chandler. She added, "We live in a narrow paradise between sky, sand, ocean. We love it, maybe, but we foul it up, pig it up. Worse, we forget to even look at it. Kem Nunn brings it all back with the force of one of those brutal socks poor Ike is always taking on the chin."

A writer for *Publishers Weekly* also applauded *Tap-ping the Source,* deeming it "highly accomplished" and praised the novel's "strong atmosphere, an un-usual setting, great narrative drive and a highly vi-sual style." *Saturday Review* writer Frank Gannon wrote: "The book . . . builds its grip slowly and carefully so you're totally hooked." And Wendy Lesser, in her *New York Times Book Review* piece on Nunn's debut, felt that Nunn's talents as a writer were evident "in the portrayal of the young hero, Ike Tucker, whose rich internal reflections partially ameliorate the destitution of the external scene."

Nunn's second novel, *Unassigned Territory,* centers on religious cults and supernatural activities in the Mojave desert. The main figure in the book is preacher Obadiah Wheeler, who flees his Christian sect with the beautiful Delandra Hummer, the daughter of a desert museum creator who was murdered. As the story progresses, Obadiah and Delandra steal an artifact, referred to as "the Thing," that her father had created for the museum. The couple intends to sell it to repay Delandra's bail bondsman. The interested buyers of the piece are followers of a new age scientist, Ceton Verity, who, at the time of his death by murder, was searching for the crystals he believed would fuel a machine he was constructing to slow time and aging. Pursued across the desert by Delandra's brother, who wants to preserve the museum's artifacts, the couple works to unlock the mystery surrounding the deaths of Delandra's father and Verity.

Unassigned Territory, was not received as warmly as Nunn's first effort. Elizabeth Tallent, for example, wrote in her *New York Times Book Review* assessment of the book: "Sometimes self-consciously, sometimes playfully, 'Unassigned Territory' flirts with the conventions of grade B movies. In a horror flick, where violence is promised, it must be delivered; the more brutal and arbitrary the delivery, the better. But 'Unassigned Territory,' with its swift stream of events, its incidental gore and stray moments of self-mockery, hands out violence at the expense of coherence." Reviewer Josph Olshan, writing in the *Chicago Tribune Books,* was also among critics who were unenthusiastic about the plot of Nunn's second novel. Olshan commented: "The author has an inveterate preoccupation with cults. Unfortunately, . . .the energy spent on resolving the crystal connection ends up distancing the reader from the characters. . . . Nunn . . . is clearly talented and no doubt has many more books in him."

Nunn, according to Gary Dretzka writing in the *Chicago Tribune Books,* rebounded in 1992 "from a sophomore slump with his third novel, *Pomona Queen.*" Again set in southern California and peopled with rather seedy characters, *Pomona Queen* is the story of Earl Dean, who has returned to his childhood home, where his family once owned a thriving citrus grove. Now a door-to-door salesman, he knocks one day on the door of Dan Brown, a biker, convicted killer, and former schoolmate of Earl. The two recognize each other, Earl recalling Dan as a dangerous rowdy, and Dan remembering Earl as a local rock singer. Unfortunately for Earl, Dan is in the process of mourning his brother, Buddy, who has been stabbed to death and is lying on ice in Dan's living room. Earl, Dan decides, will sing at his brother's funeral. Before he knows it, Earl has also been coerced into looking for Dan's brother's killer. The book's title, *Pomona Queen,* has a dual reference to Earl's great-grandfather's citrus crops and to a band, of which Buddy's killer is a member.

While sharing the adventures of Earl and Dan, Nunn also highlights the history of Pomona, a once-burgeoning center of fruit production now in decline. His descriptions of the town particularly impressed critic Cassandra Smith, who wrote in the *Los Angeles Times Book Review:* "He depicts the squalid underbelly of a soiled landscape, a legacy of decay inhabited by foul-mouthed lowlifes and racist scumbags. . . . [and] displays an impressive knowledge of the ecological factors that have warped a once pristine prairie. His flair for language and explicit vision put him among the disaffected who warn of an environmental apocalypse."

Nunn's fourth novel, *The Dogs of Winter,* also explores the California landscape, this time focusing on a peninsula that protagonist Drew Harmon believes hosts the most treacherous waves a surfer could challenge. Enlisting a fledgling photographer and several young surfers to accompany him, Drew sets out to explore the area, only to find himself facing a conflict potentially more life-threatening than the monster waves. Critic John Motyka, writing in the *New York Times Book Review,* wrote that Nunn's "dark vision yields an effective lesson about the limits of two men's quest for redemption."

In a *New York Times Book Review* interview with Lori B. Miller, Nunn commented that he enjoys creating characters who "do crazy things," and said that his literary style may be influenced by his study of art. "Some people tell me the stuff I write has a visual quality to it," Nunn told Miller. "If it does, it might owe something to the fact that I'm interested in the use of color and the visual."

BIOGRAPHICAL/CRITICAL SOURCES:

BOOKS

Contemporary Literary Criticism, Volume 34, Gale (Detroit, MI), 1984.

PERIODICALS

Chicago Tribune, July 12, 1987, p. 5; April 5, 1992, p. 5.
Christian Science Monitor, April 5, 1985, p. B8.
Library Journal, November 15, 1996, pp. 89-90.
Los Angeles Times Book Review, April 8, 1984, pp. 1, 10; June 28, 1987, p. 9; April 12, 1992, pp. 2, 7.
New Yorker, August 31, 1987, p. 97.
New York Times Book Review, March 4, 1984, pp. 22-23; March 3, 1985, p. 34; July 5, 1987, pp. 7-8; March 23, 1997.
Publishers Weekly, January 20, 1984, pp. 74-75.
Saturday Review, March/April, 1985, p. 68.
Washington Post Book World, August 2, 1987, p. 7; April 5, 1992, p. 9.*

*　　*　　*

OESTERLE, Virginia Rorby
See RORBY, Ginny

*　　*　　*

O'KELLEY, Mattie Lou   1908-1997

OBITUARY NOTICE—See index for *CA* sketch: Born March 30, 1908, in Bank County, GA; died July 26, 1997, in Decatur, GA. Artist and author. Although she only began painting at the age of sixty, O'Kelley quickly established a reputation as a folk artist who vividly depicted nostalgic scenes of rural life in the South. She began painting to help ease the pain of an illness. O'Kelley grew up on the family farm and only attended school up to the ninth grade. She worked in a series of jobs, including cook, seamstress, and waitress, retiring in 1968. Upon her retirement she took up painting and so impressed art dealer Robert Bishop with her art that he helped introduce her work to museum professionals and art buyers.

O'Kelley's paintings included scenes of the Georgian countryside and featured gardens, animals, barns, and other folksy themes. She also lived briefly in New York City and turned her talents to urban settings. However, she longed to return to Georgia and settled in Decatur. She wrote several books, including *Circus* and *From the Hills of Georgia: An Autobiography*

in Paintings. She also illustrated Ruth Yaffe Radin's *A Winter Place.* In addition, O'Kelley's work was also featured in calendars and on a cover of *Life* magazine.

OBITUARIES AND OTHER SOURCES:

PERIODICALS

New York Times, July 31, 1997, p. B6.

*　　*　　*

OKUDZHAVA, Bulat Shalvovich   1924-1997

OBITUARY NOTICE—See index for *CA* sketch: Surname also transliterated as Okudjava; given name also transliterated as Boulat; born May 9, 1924, in Moscow, U.S.S.R. (now Russia); died of pneumonia and kidney failure, June 12, 1997, in Clamart, France, while visiting the country. Educator, journalist, poet, singer, author. Okudzhava is remembered for his songs and verse, which some considered dissident despite lyrics that spoke of love, life, and emotions.

Okudzhava was no stranger to political strife—his father was executed under Stalin's regime in 1937 and his mother was detained in forced labor camps for ten years. Okudzhava himself was expelled from the Communist Party in 1972. He was sometimes prohibited from performing but not jailed. He taught Russian language and literature in the Soviet Union in the 1940s and worked as a journalist in the mid-1950s. He worked at the Young Guard Publishing House on the editorial staff in the late 1950s and went on to serve as poetry editor for *Literaturniya gazeta* ("Literary Gazette") in the early 1960s.

Okudzhava's volumes of verse include *Lirica, Po doroge k Tinatin* ("On the Way to Tinatin"), *Veselyi barabanshchik* ("The Merry Drummer"), *Mart velikodushnyi* ("March the Generous"), and *Arbat, Moi Arbat* ("Arbat, My Arbat"; also includes songs). He also wrote *The Extraordinary Adventures of Secret Agent Shipov in Pursuit of Count Leo Tolstoy in the Year 1862, Appointment with Buonaparte,* and *Abolished Theatre* (also called *The Closed-Down Theatre*). For the latter work, he was awarded the Russian equivalent of the Booker Prize in 1994.

OBITUARIES AND OTHER SOURCES:

BOOKS

International Who's Who, Europa, 1996.

PERIODICALS

Chicago Tribune, June 14, 1997, sec. 1, p. 21.
Los Angeles Times, June 14, 1997, p. A18.
New York Times, June 14, 1997, p. 11.
Times (London; electronic), June 16, 1997.
Washington Post, June 14, 1997, p. B4.

* * *

OLIVER, Lawrence J. 1949-

PERSONAL: Born March 14, 1949, in Wilkes-Barre, PA; son of Lawrence and Constance (Saba) Oliver; married Mary Jane Charles, August 26, 1973; children: Cory and Craig (twins). *Ethnicity:* "White." *Education:* King's College (Wilkes-Barre, PA), B.A., 1971; Pennsylvania State University, M.A., 1973, Ph.D., 1981.

ADDRESSES: Home—1308 Todd Trail, College Station, TX 77845. *Office*—Department of English, 227 Blocker Bldg., Texas A&M University, College Station, TX 77843. *E-mail*—l-oliver@tamu.edu.

CAREER: Texas A&M University, College Station, assistant professor, 1984-90, associate professor of English, 1991—.

MEMBER: Modern Language Association of America, American Studies Association, Society for the Study of Multi-Ethnic Literature of the United States, South Central Modern Language Association.

WRITINGS:

Brander Matthews, Theodore Roosevelt, and the Politics of American Literature, 1880-1920, University of Tennessee Press (Knoxville, TN), 1992.
(Editor) *The Letters of Theodore Roosevelt and Brander Matthews,* University of Tennessee Press, 1995.
(Co-editor) *Critical Essays on James Weldon Johnson,* G. K. Hall/Macmillan, 1997.

WORK IN PROGRESS: Research on African American literature and culture of the 1930s.

* * *

O'NEILL, Thomas Philip, Jr. 1912-1994
(Tip O'Neill)

PERSONAL: Born December 9, 1912, in North Cambridge, MA; died of a heart attack, January 5, 1994, in Boston, MA; son of Thomas P. I. (a bricklayer, city councilor, and superintendent of sewers) and Rose Anne (Tolan) O'Neill; married Mildred Anne Miller (a homemaker), June 17, 1941; children: Rosemary, Thomas III, Susan, Christopher, Michael Tolan. *Ethnicity:* Irish-American. *Education:* Boston College, A.B., 1936. *Politics:* Democrat. *Religion:* Catholic. *Avocational interests:* Golf.

CAREER: Politician, beginning in 1936. Massachusetts state legislature, minority leader, 1947-48, speaker, 1948-52; U.S. representative for the 11th district of Massachusetts, 1953-63; U.S. representative for the 8th district of Massachusetts, 1963-87. Also served as House Majority Whip 1971-73, House Majority Leader, 1973-77, and Speaker of the House, 1977-87. Member of Cambridge School Committee, 1946.

AWARDS, HONORS: Laetare medal, Notre Dame University, 1980; Grand Cross, Order Orange-Nassau, from the government of the Netherlands, 1983; Legion of Honor, from the government of France, 1984; Presidential Medal of Freedom, 1991. Recipient of thirty-four honorary degrees from various universities and colleges, including Harvard University, 1987.

WRITINGS:

(With William Novak) *Man of the House: The Life and Political Memoirs of Speaker Tip O'Neill,* Random House (New York City), 1987.
(With Gary Hymel) *All Politics Is Local and Other Rules of the Game,* Times Books (New York City), 1994.

SIDELIGHTS: A former Speaker of the House, Democrat Thomas Philip O'Neill, Jr.—best-known as "Tip" O'Neill—served in the state legislature of Massachusetts for sixteen years before serving his country in the U.S. House of Representatives for more than two decades. During his tenure in national politics, he remained a loyal believer in former president Franklin D. Roosevelt's New Deal policies, even when the Democratic Party's liberal stance was changing. Remembered as a larger-than-life character, O'Neill came from a middle-class, Irish-Catholic family, getting his start in politics as a young man when he became a campaigner for presidential candidate Al Smith, who was defeated by Herbert Hoover in 1928. He was described in *Time* magazine as "a living caricature, like a Thomas Nast drawing come to life—the hulking 6-foot 3-inch frame, the sly smile, the W. C. Fields nose, the thicket of white hair."

O'Neill felt that Republican policies greatly contributed to the Great Depression of the 1930s and that, until Roosevelt's New Deal, middle-class Americans had no chance to prosper. These ideals spurred his continuing activities in Democratic politics, leading him at the age of thirty-seven to become the youngest speaker of the Massachusetts state house since the Civil War. Later, he served as speaker of the U.S. House of Representatives for a decade, the longest consecutive period of time spent in that role in congressional history. O'Neill was known for his ability to generate unity and party loyalty. In 1987 he teamed up with William Novak to write of his political exploits in *Man of the House: The Life and Political Memoirs of Speaker Tip O'Neill.* Hugh Brogan, for the *Times Literary Supplement,* praised the work, stating, "The most abiding impression left by this book will probably be that of the warmth and decency of the author." An example of this concern for others is a sign quoting Hubert Humphrey that O'Neill kept on his office wall: "The moral test of government is how it treats those who are in the dawn of life, the children; those who are in the twilight of life, the aged; and those who are in the shadows of life—the sick, the needy and the handicapped."

O'Neill's reminiscences include his roles in the difficult times of the Vietnam War and the Watergate scandal. He also has a great deal to say about former Republican president Ronald Reagan. O'Neill judged Ronald Reagan to be the worst of the eight presidents he had known, even worse than Richard Nixon. About Reagan, O'Neill once quipped, "He would have made a hell of a king." Reviewers of *Man of the House* lauded O'Neill's use of his Irish charm and storytelling abilities to enhance his many stories in what a *Time* critic referred to as "amiable siftings."

Besides his stories, O'Neill was famous for his distinctive quotes, one of which—O'Neill's favorite—became part of the title of his best-selling book, *All Politics Is Local and Other Rules of the Game,* writ-

ten with his former press secretary Gary Hymel. "All politics is local," was an axiom he credited to his father. Another memorable O'Neill statement found in the book is "For me, politics always was about values combined with instincts. Put those together and you get a rule." A *Publishers Weekly* reviewer summarized some of O'Neill's "rules": "No contribution is too small; never get introduced to the crowd at a sporting event, only boos will ensue; to be a successful public speaker, memorize poetry; avoid bunk; remember names; tip well."

Robert Dallek, writing in the *Los Angeles Times Book Review,* summarized O'Neill's life in 1987: "He is a blunt, practical man whose personal integrity (he left office with only 2,900 dollars in the bank), and compassion for the disadvantaged make him something of an anomaly in an age of manipulated images, ideological passions, and private greed. Tip O'Neill is a consensus politician who makes American government work." O'Neill retired from politics in 1987 and died seven years later, in 1994.

BIOGRAPHICAL/CRITICAL SOURCES:

BOOKS

Clancy, Paul R., *Tip, a Biography of Thomas P. O'Neill, Speaker of the House,* Macmillan (New York City), 1980.
Newsmakers: The People behind Today's Headlines, Gale (Detroit, MI), 1994.
O'Neill, Thomas, Jr., and William Novak, *Man of the House: The Life and Political Memoirs of Speaker Tip O'Neill,* Random House (New York City), 1987.
O'Neill, Thomas, Jr., and Gary Hymel, *All Politics Is Local and Other Rules of the Game,* Times Books (New York City), 1994.

PERIODICALS

American Spectator, March, 1988, p. 36.
Booklist, August, 1987, p. 1700.
Boston Review, December, 1987, p. 9.
Business Week, October 12, 1987, p. 20.
Christian Science Monitor, October 7, 1987, p. 20.
Commentary, December, 1987, p. 76.
Common Cause Magazine, January/February, 1990, pp. 9-10.
Commonweal, December, 1987, p. 707.
Contemporary Review, June, 1988, p. 329.
Economist, October 3, 1987, p. 102.
Guardian Weekly, April 3, 1988, p. 29.

Human Events, September 26, 1987, p. 5; March 5, 1988, p. 15.

Kirkus Reviews, August 1, 1987, p. 1140; November 15, 1993, p. 1449.

Library Journal, October 15, 1987, p. 84; January 1988, p. 43; January 1994, p. 142.

Los Angeles Times Book Review, September 13, 1987, p. 1.

Nation, October 10, 1987, p. 382; January 31, 1994, pp. 112-14.

National Review, October 5, 1987, p. 65.

New Leader, November 30, 1987, p. 20.

New Republic, October 5, 1987, p. 36.

New Yorker, April 18, 1988, p. 139.

New York Times, September 3, 1987, p. 17.

New York Times Book Review, September 6, 1987, p. 17; September 4, 1988, p. 24.

Observer, March 20, 1988, p. 43.

Publishers Weekly, July 31, 1987, p. 61; June 24, 1988, p. 109; November 22, 1993, pp. 51-52.

Rapport, January 1994, p. 32.

Spectator, March 19, 1988, p. 42.

Time, September 14, 1987, p. 78.

Times Educational Supplement, May 27, 1988, p. B3.

Times Literary Supplement, April 1, 1988, p. 352.

Tribune Books, August 28, 1988, p. 8.

USA Today, September 11, 1987, p. 4D.

U.S. News and World Report, January 17, 1994, pp. 6-7.

Wall Street Journal, September 3, 1987, p. 17.

Washington Monthly, October 1987, p. 58.

Washington Post Book World, January 23, 1994, pp. 2-3.

Wilson Library Bulletin, January 1988, p. 90.

Yankee, June 1994, pp. 82-91.

OBITUARIES:

PERIODICALS

Newsweek, January 17, 1994, p. 22.

Time, January 17, 1994, p. 19.*

*   *   *

O'NEILL, Tip
  See O'NEILL, Thomas Philip, Jr.

OVED, Iaacov
  See OVED, Yaacov

*   *   *

OVED, Yaacov 1929-

PERSONAL: Given name is sometimes transliterated "Iaacov;" born February 14, 1929, in Haskovo, Bulgaria; son of Ovadia (a merchant) and Bella Varsano; married, wife's name Tehila, June 7, 1951; children: Adva Oved Lloyd, Inbal, Renana Oved Barak, Raz. *Education:* Attended Hakibutz Hameucha Seminar of Social Studies, Tel Aviv University, and St. Antony's College, Oxford. *Politics:* Labour. *Religion:* Jewish. *Avocational interests:* Music, painting.

ADDRESSES: Home—Kibbutz Palmahim, D.N. Emek Sorek 76890, Israel. *Office*—Yad Tabenkin, Ramat Efal 52960, Israel. *E-mail*—ovedyac@ccsg.tau.ac.il.

CAREER: Representative of the kibbutz movement in Buenos Aires, Argentina; kibbutz member, officer, and teacher. Tel Aviv University, professor emeritus and executive director of international communal studies. *Military service:* Israel Defense Forces Reserve.

MEMBER: International Communal Studies Association.

WRITINGS:

Two Hundred Years of American Communes, Transaction Books (New Brunswick, NJ), 1988.

The Witness of the Brothers, Transaction Books, 1996.

Also author of *Anarchism and Workers Movement in Argentina* (in Spanish), 1978.

WORK IN PROGRESS: Research for a comparative history of communes and kibbutz.

P

PARK, Roberta J. 1931-

PERSONAL: Born July 15, 1931, in Oakland, CA; daughter of Robert D. (a mechanic) and Grace E. (a homemaker; maiden name, Faulkes) Park. *Education:* University of California, Berkeley, A.B., 1953; Ohio State University, M.A., 1954; University of California, Berkeley, Ph.D., 1971. *Avocational interests:* Opera, backpacking, cooking, swimming, travel, carpentry, cabinet making.

ADDRESSES: Office—Department of Human Biodynamics, University of California, Berkeley, CA 94720.

CAREER: Teacher in Oakland, CA, 1956-59; University of California, Berkeley, assistant supervisor of physical education, 1959-63, associate supervisor of physical education, 1963-69, supervisor of physical education, 1969-76, associate professor, 1976-80, professor of physical education (now human biodynamics), 1980—, chairman of department, 1982-92, associate of Center for Studies in Higher Education, 1984—; writer. Peter V. Karpovich Lecturer at Springfield College, 1991; Michael Osten, M.D., Lecturer at Catholic University, Leuven, 1992.

MEMBER: International Association for the History of Sport and Physical Education (vice president, 1989—), American Academy of Physical Education (fellow), American Academy of Kinesiology and Physical Education, British Society for Sports History (fellow),

AWARDS, HONORS: Fellowships from Danforth Foundation, and Research Consortium of American Alliance for Health, Physical Education, and Welfare; scholarship from American Alliance for Health, Physical Education, Recreation and Dance, 1992; writing award from Research Consortium of American Alliance for Health, Physical Education, Recreation, and Dance, 1993.

WRITINGS:

(With William W. Harper, Donna Mae Miller, and Elwood C. Davis) *The Philosophic Process in Physical Education,* third edition, Lea & Febiger (Philadelphia, PA), 1977.
The Body as Icon and Object: Sport, Exercise, and Gender, 1660-1980, University of Illinois Press, in press.

Contributor to anthologies, including *Dimensions of Physical Education,* edited by Charles Bucher, C. V. Mosby, 1974; *The History, Evolution, and Diffusion of Sports and Games in Different Cultures,* edited by Roland Renson, Peter P. DeNayer, and M. Ostyn, Bestuur voor de Lichamelijke Opvoeding (Brussels), 1976; (with Joan Hutt) *Sports in Modern America,* edited by William J. Baker and John M. Carroll, River City, 1981; *Sport History Research Methodology,* edited by Robert Day and Peter Lindsey, University of Alberta Press, 1981; *Perspectives on the Academic Discipline of Physical Education,* edited by George A. Brooks, Human Kinetics Publishers, 1981; *The Paradoxes of Play,* edited by John Loy, Leisure Press, 1982; *The Hero in Transition,* edited by Ray B. Browne and Marshall W. Fistwick, Bowling Green University Press, 1983; *The Masks of Play,* edited by Brian Sutton-Smith and Diana Kelly-Byrne, Leisure Press, 1984; *The Many Faces of Play,* edited by Kendall Blanchard, Leisure Press,

1985; *1984 Olympic Scientific Congress Report,* edited by Norbert Muller and Joachim K. Ruhl, Schors Verlag, 1985; *Manliness and Morality: Images of the Male in the Old World and the New,* edited by James A. Mangan and James Walvin, University of Manchester Press, 1987; *The Cutting Edge in Physical Education and Exercise Science Research,* edited by Margaret J. Safrit and Helen M. Eckert, Human Kinetics Publishers, 1988; *Physical Activity in Early and Modern Populations,* edited by Robert M. Malina and Helen M. Eckert, Human Kinetics Publishers, 1988; *Fitness in America: Images of Health, Sport, and the Body, 1830-1940,* edited by Kathryn Grover, University of Massachusetts Press, 1989; *The Olympic Games through the Ages: Greek Antiquity and Its Impact on Modern Sport,* edited by Roland Renson, Manfred Lammer, James Riordan, and Dimitrios Cassiotis, Hellenic Research Institute, 1991; *Sport: Le Troisieme millenaire,* edited by Fernand Landry, Marc Landry, and Magdeleine Yerles, Sainte Foy (Quebec), 1991; and *Women and Sport,* edited by D. Margaret Toohey and Sharon R. Guthrie, Human Kinetics Publishers, 1993.

Contributor to periodicals, including *British Journal of History of Sports, Journal of Sport History, Journal of the West, Quest,* and *Research Quarterly for Exercise and Sport.*

EDITOR

(With Janet C. Harris) *Play, Games, and Sports in Cultural Contexts: Readings in the Anthropology of Sport,* Human Kinetics Publishers (Champaign, IL), 1983.

(With James A. Mangan) *From Fair Sex to Feminism: Sport and the Socialization of Women in the Industrial and Post-Industrial Eras,* Cass (London), 1987.

(With Helen M. Eckert) *New Possibilities?/New Paradigms!,* Human Kinetics Publishers (Champaign, IL), 1991.

(With Jack W. Berryman) *Sport and Exercise Science: Essays in the History of Sports Medicine,* University of Illinois Press, 1992.

Editor of National Association for Sport and Physical Education's *Philosophy Newsletter,* 1980-81; editor of *Quest,* 1987-90; American editor of *International Journal of the History of Sport,* 1987—. History and philosophy editor for *Research Quarterly for Exercise and Sport,* 1977—. Member of editorial board of *Journal of Sport History,* 1980—, and *British Journal of the History of Sport,* 1984-87.

WORK IN PROGRESS: "Investigations of the scientific congresses held in connection with the 1928 Amsterdam Olympics; 'the Blacksmith's arm' as a metaphor that condensed important physiological, biological, psychological, and sociological issues in the nineteenth century; the reporting of athletic injuries in the Anglo-American medical press from 1870 to 1920; the body as *icon* and object with regard to health, exercise, and gender from 1850 to 1930."

SIDELIGHTS: Roberta J. Park told *CA:* "In 1959 I was invited to join the faculty of the Department of Physical Education (now Human Biodynamics) at the University of California, Berkeley. There I have taught applied biomechanics and curriculum. In obtaining a doctorate in 1971 in the history of education, I had begun researching pedagogical issues in Europe—especially France—during the eighteenth century. I produced a series of articles that brought together health, hygiene, and exercise from 1660 to 1800 in France, England, and Spain. I spent considerable time over the years in various European libraries, archives, and depositories while pursuing these and similar topics.

"Since the late 1970s my interests have been especially, but not exclusively, directed to bringing together various aspects of the emerging biological sciences, medicine, health, hygiene, exercise, athletics, and pedagogy as these emerged and expanded in the nineteenth and early twentieth centuries. Some of these themes are extremely important as antecedents to what has come to be known in the twentieth century as 'sports medicine.'"

*   *   *

PARKER, Frank R.   1940-1997

OBITUARY NOTICE—See index for *CA* sketch: Born May 11, 1940, in Mount Pleasant, PA; died of a heart attack, July 10, 1997, in Lexington, VA. Lawyer, human rights activist, educator, author. Parker is remembered for his work in the area of civil rights, particularly his involvement with the Lawyer's Committee for Civil Rights under Law in Mississippi. Early in his career, he worked as a staff attorney for the office of general counsel for the U.S. Commission on Civil Rights. In 1968 he joined the Lawyers' Committee as a staff attorney working out of Jackson, Mississippi. In 1972 he was named assistant chief counsel, taking on duties as chief counsel in 1976. In 1981 he began serving as director of the committee's voting rights project in Washington, D.C. In 1985 and 1986 he became a MacArthur Foundation Distinguished Scholar with Washington's Joint Center for Political Studies. During this time he conducted research for his award-winning book, *Black Votes Count: Political Empowerment in Mississippi after 1965.* He later conducted research at the Center for use in a book on affirmative action. In 1992 he joined the faculty of the District of Columbia School of Law and remained on staff until 1995. After a year teaching at American University, he became a visiting professor at Washington and Lee University, teaching constitutional law. He was still affiliated with the University at the time of his death. Among his many accomplishments was his work toward the passage of the Voter Registration Act of 1993. He also contributed to various anthologies, including *Minority Vote Dilution, One Nation Indivisible: The Civil Rights Challenge for the 1990s, Lost Opportunities: The Civil Rights Record of the Bush Administration Mid-Term,* and *From Exclusion to Inclusion: The Long Struggle for African American Political Power.*

OBITUARIES AND OTHER SOURCES:

BOOKS

Writers Directory, St. James Press, 1996.

PERIODICALS

New York Times, July 14, 1997, p. B9.
Washington Post, July 12, 1997, p. B6.

*   *   *

PARLOFF, Roger (Harris) 1955-

PERSONAL: Born September 21, 1955, in Washington, DC; son of Morris B. (a psychologist) and Gloria H. (an editor) Parloff. *Education:* Harvard University, B.A., 1977; Yale University, J.D., 1982.

ADDRESSES: Home—New York, NY. *Office*—*American Lawyer,* 600 Third Ave., New York, NY 10016. *E-mail*—rparloff@counsel.com. *Agent*—Jane Gelfman, Gelfman Schneider, 250 West 57th St., New York, NY 10107.

CAREER: Law clerk to U.S. District Judge William Wayne Justice, Tyler, TX, 1982-83; Office of the District Attorney, New York City, assistant district attorney, 1983-84; Goldman & Hafetz, New York City, criminal defense attorney, 1984-87; American Lawyer Media, New York City, senior writer, 1988—.

AWARDS, HONORS: National Magazine Award, essays and criticism, 1993.

WRITINGS:

Triple Jeopardy: A Story of Law at Its Best—and Worst, Little, Brown (Boston, MA), 1996.

*   *   *

PERENYI, Constance (Marie) 1954-

PERSONAL: Born November 30, 1954, in Denver, CO. *Education:* Colorado Women's College, B.A., 1977.

CAREER: Artist, children's book author and illustrator. Has worked at animal shelters, veterinary clinics, zoos, and for animal rescue programs.

WRITINGS:

(And illustrator) *Growing Wild: Inviting Wildlife into Your Yard,* Beyond Words, 1991.
(And illustrator) *Wild Wild West: Wildlife Habitats of Western North America,* Sasquatch, 1993.
(Contributor) *The Soul Unearthed,* edited by Cass Adams, Putnam, 1996.

WORK IN PROGRESS: Thirteen in a Million Cats—"about cats I knew while working in an animal shelter."

SIDELIGHTS: Constance Perenyi commented: "My life as an artist and illustrator has never followed a predictable path, but has always been guided by my deep love of animals and a concern about the environment. I have written and drawn as long as I can remember, but nothing has been as fulfilling for me as bringing those passions together with hands-on work with animals.

"Over time, my art has grown to reflect that inspiration. My first work after college was with fabric and for years, I showed wearables and wall-hangings in galleries and juried shows across the nation. It was not until moving to Seattle in 1980 that I realized how isolated I felt in the studio and how much I wanted to work with animals. What began as a once-a-week volunteer commitment at Woodland Park Zoological Gardens led to a job in the education department and countless hours spent in the feline and birds units, an unlikely pairing, I realize, but one that still sustains my imagination. My wearable art changed, taking on abstract animal forms and very clear allusions to fur and feathers.

"At that stage, I decided to start making my work more representative and accessible. I experimented cutting, tearing, and layering paper; and by the time my focus had shifted from captive animals at the zoo to wild animals in my own environment, I was ready to write and illustrate my first book. *Growing Wild: Inviting Wildlife into Your Yard* is intended to inspire young and experienced gardeners alike to create habitats for the animals with whom they share the outdoors.

"My second book, *Wild Wild West,* looks at eleven remaining wilderness areas in the west and the plants and animals they sustain. It also reflects an evolution in my collage process, with each habitat carefully detailed in several layers of paper. By the time I wrote and illustrated the book, I had much more experience with wild animals as well. I worked at a wildlife rehabilitation center, and had helped birds injured in oil spills at several clinics in Washington.

"In recent years, I have also expanded my understanding of issues affecting companion animals, especially my much-admired cats. The two years I worked in an animal shelter were the most painful, and the most fulfilling, of my life. I have written about those experiences for adults, and am beginning to write and illustrate my next children's book about some of the very special cats I encountered. For inspiration, I continue to do author/artist programs in the schools, sharing my interests with children, and being refueled and refreshed by their enthusiasm for everything I value."

BIOGRAPHICAL/CRITICAL SOURCES:

PERIODICALS

Booklist, December 15, 1993, p. 758.
Horticulture, February, 1992, p. 65.

Kirkus Reviews, August 15, 1993, p. 1077.
School Library Journal, December, 1993, p. 107.

* * *

PETRUCCI, Armando 1932-

PERSONAL: Born May 1, 1932, in Rome, Italy; son of Alfredo (an art historian) and Petronilla (Ruggiero) Petrucci; married Franca Nardelli (a historian), June 14, 1958. *Education:* Attended University of Rome.

ADDRESSES: Home—Via Latinta, 6/A, Pisa, Italy, 56125. *Office*—Scuola Normale Superiore, Piazza dei Cavalieri, 7, Pisa, 56126.

CAREER: Accademia dei Lincei, Rome, Italy, librarian, 1958-72; University of Salerno, Italy, professor, 1972-74; University of Rome, professor, 1974-91; Scuola Normale Superiore, Pisa, Italy, 1991—.

MEMBER: Academie Royale de Belgique, Bruxelles (Royal Academy of Belgium, Brussels).

WRITINGS:

Le Tavolette Cerate Fiorentine di Casa Majorfi, Edizione di storia e letteratura (Rome), 1965.
La Scrittura di F. Petrarca (title means "The Writings of Petrarch"), Biblliteca Vaticana (Rome), 1967.
Coluccio Salutati, Instituto della Enciclopedia italiana (Rome), 1972.
(With Giulia Barone) *Primo, Non Leggere: Biblioteche e Pubblica Lettura in Italia dal 1861 ai Nostri Giorni* (title means "First, Not to Read: Libraries and Public Reading in Italy from 1861 to the Present"), G. Mazzotta (Milan), 1976.
(Editor) *Libri, Editore e Pubblico nell'Europa Moderna: Guida Storica e Critica* (title means "Books, Publishing and the Public in Modern Europe: Historical and Critical Guide"), Laterza (Rome), 1977.
(Editor) *Catologo Sommavio dei Manoscritti del Fondo Rossi, Sezione Corsiniana,* Accademia Nazionale dei Lincei (Rome), 1977.
Libri, Scrittura, e Pubblico nel Rinascimento: Guida Storica e Critica (title means "Books, Writing and the Public in the Rennaissance: A Historical and Critical Guide"), Laterza (Rome), 1979.

Scrittura e Popolo nella Roma Barocca (title means "Writing and the People in Baroque Rome"), Quasar (Rome), 1982.

La Descrizione del Manoscritto: Storia, Problemi, Modelli (title means "The Description of the Manuscript: History, Problems, Models"), Nuova Italia Scientifica (Rome), 1984.

La Scrittura: Ideologia e Rappresentazione (title means "The Writings: Ideology and Representation"), Einaudi (Turin), 1986.

(Contributor) Luca Orfei. *Alfabeto delle Maiuscole Antiche Romane* (title means "Capital Letters of the Ancient Roman Alphabet"), Il Polifilo (Milan), 1986.

La Scrittura (title means "Writing"), Einaudi, 1986.

Scrivere e No (title means "Literacy and Illiteracy"), Riuniti (Rome), 1987.

(Editor, with Alessandro Pratesi) *Un Secolo di Paleografia e Diplomatica (1887-1986): Per il Centenario dell'Instituto di Paleografia dell'Universita di Roma* (title means "A Century of Paleography and Diplomatics (1887-1986): For the Centenary of the Institute of Paleography of the University of Rome"), Gela (Rome), 1988.

Scriptores in Urbibus: Alfabetismo e Cultura Scritta nell'Italia Altomedievale (title means "Writers in the Cities: Literacy and Written Culture in Early Middle Ages"), Il Mulino (Bologne), 1992.

Medioevo da Leggere: Guida allo Studio delle Testimonianze Scritte del Medioevo Italiano (title means "Reading the Middle Ages: For the Study of the Written Records of the Italian Middle Ages"), Einaudi, 1992.

I Piau Antichi Documenti Originali del Commune di Lucera (1232-1496) (title means "The Earlier Records of Lucera, 1232-1496"), Societa di Storia Patria per la Puglia (Bari), 1994.

Le Scritture Ultime: Ideologia della Morte e Strategie dello Scrivere nella Tradizione Occidentale (title means "The Last Writings: The Death's Ideology and the Strategy of the Script in Western Tradition"), Einaudi, 1995.

WORK IN PROGRESS: A history of the epistolography in the Middle Ages and research on medieval letters.

SIDELIGHTS: Armando Petrucci told *CA:* "I am a paleographer and a historian of writing. My interest for these subjects of study and research was born in my youth and was reinforced with the experience of work and teaching that I completed in the library in the University in which I worked. I have always considered the history of writing a subject suitable to help understand all of the aspects of the society and culture of an area, of a nation, or of a period; and like a global experience, either for a chronological extension or for typology and technique.

"The major influence on my work with history was in part from the figure of my father Alfredo, an art historian, and from another strong interest in politics, that I have never abandoned. My studies and work have resulted in spending more time in foreign countries, especially London, Paris, and the United States. I owe very much, for stimulus and critcism, to my students and in particular to my wife Franca Nardelli."

*　　*　　*

PITTENGER, W(illiam) Norman   1905-1997

OBITUARY NOTICE—See index for *CA* sketch: Born July 23, 1905, in Bogota, NJ; died in England, June 19, 1997. Theologian and author. Pittenger was an Anglican priest whose book *Time for Consent* discussed openly accepting gays into the church. He was ordained an Episcopal deacon in 1936 and was made a priest in 1937. From 1935 until 1966 he served at the General Theological Seminary in New York City, first as a tutor and later as a professor. Upon his retirement in 1966, Pittenger relocated to England and accepted a post as a lecturer in the theology department at Cambridge University. He also was a senior resident at King's College at Cambridge.

During his career Pittenger also taught at Columbia University for seven years, served as chaplain with the Episcopal Guild of Scholars for two decades, and was chair of the World Council of Churches' North American Theological Commission on Faith and Order. Pittenger, who later was open about his homosexuality, also wrote *Gay Life-Styles.* Among his other books, totalling about ninety, are *The Word Incarnate, The Approach to Christianity, Sacraments, Signs and Symbols, Theology and Reality, Rethinking the Christian Message, Love Is the Clue, Martin Luther, Henry VIII of England, Freed to Love, Becoming and Belonging,* and *Making Sexuality Human.*

OBITUARIES AND OTHER SOURCES:

BOOKS

Writers Directory, St. James Press (Detroit), 1996.

PERIODICALS

Chicago Tribune, June 30, 1997, sec. 1, p. 8.
Times (London; electronic), July 2, 1997.

* * *

POLKINHORN, Harry   1945-

PERSONAL: Born March 3, 1945, in Calexico, CA;
son of William (a customhouse broker) and Virginia
(a homemaker; maiden name, Griswold) Polkinhorn;
married Christa Umiker (a translator), 1972 (divorced); married Armida Romero (a teacher), March
1, 1986 (divorced, 1991); children: Cecilia. *Education:* University of California, Berkeley, B.A., 1967;
San Diego University, M.A. (English), 1970, M.A.
(art), 1982; New York University, Ph.D., 1975.

ADDRESSES: Home—Box 927428, San Diego, CA
92192.   Office—c/o San Diego State University,
San Diego, CA 92182. *E-mail*—hpolkinh@ mail.
sdsu.edu.

CAREER: Poet, artist, teacher, editor, translator,
and critic.

WRITINGS:

POETRY

Excisions, privately published (Zurich), 1976.
Radix Zero, Atticus Press (San Diego, CA), 1981.
Volvox, Atticus Press (San Diego, CA), 1981.
Anaesthesia, Textile Bridge Press (New York),
1985.
Bridges of Skin Money (visual poetry), Xeroxial
Editions (Madison, WI), 1986.
Summary Dissolution (visual poetry), Runaway Spoon
Press (Port Charlotte, FL), 1988.
Begging for Remission, Score Publications (Oakland,
CA), 1989.
Teraphim (visual poetry), Runaway Spoon, 1995.
Mount Soledad, Left Hand Books (New York), 1996.
Throat Shadow, 3300 Press (San Francisco), 1997.

EXPERIMENTAL FICTION

Travelling with Women, Atticus Press, 1983.
Lorenia La Rosa: A Travelogue, Institute of Culture
(Mexicali, Baja CA), 1989.

OTHER

(With Alfredo Velasco and Malcolm Lambert) *El
Libro de Calo: Pachuco Slang Dictionary,*
Atticus Press, 1983, revised as *El Libro de Calo:
Chicano Slang Dictionary,* Floricanto Press
(Oakland, CA), 1986.
(Editor) *Border Literature/Literatura Fronteriza: A
Binational Conference,* Border Studies Series,
Institute for Regional Studies of the Californias
(San Diego, CA), 1987.
(Co-editor)   *Literatura Frontera Mexico-Estados
Unidos/Mexican-American Border Writing: Pro-
ceedings of the First Conference of Writers from
the Californias,* Direccion de Asuntos Culturales
(Mexicali, Baja California), 1987.
(Co-editor) *Mexican/American Border Literature:
Short Stories,* Binational Press (Mexicali, Baja
California/Calexico, CA), 1987.
Jerome Rothenberg: A Descriptive Bibliography,
McFarland (Jefferson, NC), 1988.
(Co-editor) *The Line: Essays on Mexican/American
Border Literature,* Binational Press, 1988.
(Editor and author of introduction) *Post-Art: Interna-
tional Exhibition of Visual/Experimental Poetry,*
San Diego State University, 1988.
(Co-editor) *Border Literature: Proceedings of the
Border Literature Conference (Tijuana, June-
July, 1988),* Institute for Regional Studies of the
Californias/ Culture Institute of Baja California
(Mexicali, Baja California/San Diego, CA), 1989.
*The Illusion of Reality: An Interview with Dick
Higgins,* Score Publications (Oakland, CA), 1990.
(Co-editor) *Border Literature: Towards an Inte-
grated Perspective,* XIII Ayuntamiento de
Mexicali/Institute for Regional Studies of the
Californias (Mexicali, Baja California/San Di-
ego, CA), 1990.
(Translator) *Corrosive Signs* (essays on experimental
poetry), edited by Cesar Espinosa, Maisonneuve
Press (Washington, DC), 1990.
(Co-editor) *Visual Arts on the U.S./Mexican Border,*
Binational Press, 1991.
(Co-editor) *The Flight of the Eagle: Poetry on the
U.S.-Mexico Border,* Binational Press, 1993.
(Co-editor and translator) *Bodies beyond Borders:
Dance on the U.S.-Mexico Border,* Binational
Press/San Diego State University Press, 1993.

(Translator) Jose Manuel Di Bella, *Nailed to the Wound* (short fiction), San Diego State University Press, 1993.

(Co-editor) *Open Signs: Language and Society on the U.S.-Mexico Border,* Binational Press, 1993.

(Translator) Sergio Gomez Montero, *The Border: The Future of Postmodernity* (critical essays), San Diego State University Press, 1994.

(Co-editor and translator) *Visual Poetry: An International Anthology,* Visible Language (Providence, RI), 1994.

(Translator) Philadelpho Menezes, *Poetics and Visuality: A Trajectory of Contemporary Brazilian Poetry* (theoretical text), San Diego State University Press, 1995.

(Editor) Raymond Starr, *San Diego State University: A History in Word and Image,* San Diego State University Press, 1995.

(Translator) Clevente Padin, *Art for Life: Latin American Art in Our Time,* www.grist.light&dust (website), 1997.

Blueshift (poetry), 3300 Press, 1998.

Contributor of poetry, graphics, and articles to periodicals, including *American Book Review, Afterimage, Poetics Journal, Photostatic, Moody Street Irregulars, Smile, Uno Mas Uno, Score, Tempus Fugit, La Poire d'Angoisse, Sink,* and *Kaldron.*

WORK IN PROGRESS: Seeing Power (essays), forthcoming to the website www.grist.light&dust.

SIDELIGHTS: Harry Polkinhorn attributes growing up less than one hundred yards from Mexico, in Calexico, California, as having great influence on his work as a poet, artist, and educator. He has produced numerous works embracing the culture of this area. In an autobiographical essay for *Contemporary Authors Autobiographical Series,* Polkinhorn said that his first fifteen years of adulthood, beginning in the 1960s, were "lock, stock, and barrel under the influence of the likes of Kerouac, Ginsberg, Burroughs, and company, it became incumbent upon me to reject social convention, 'experiment' with drugs, sleep on the floor, dress like a bum, and ride the rails." Somehow he managed to complete his education during these riotous years, while also attempting to obtain a deferment from military service in Vietnam by training for the Peace Corps. Polkinhorn never made it into the Peace Corps, he explained; he was stopped as he was boarding the plane heading to India to begin his tour, even though he had completed his training and mastered Tamil, the language spoken by millions of the Indian people. Polkinhorn found out later that a member of his hometown draft board was indignant that Mexican-Americans were being drafted more than "gringos," and was trying to make amends.

When Polkinhorn was found unfit (psychologically, he professes) for the military, he started teaching English in Vermont to foreign students, including Christa Umiker, with whom he fell in love. In 1972, they married and moved to Manhattan where Polkinhorn taught language to students from Harlem. Moving once again, Polkinhorn taught English in Zurich, in his wife's home country of Switzerland for five years before returning to the United States. During these years, he mastered a number of languages, continued to write, and developed his art.

In 1982, while obtaining a second master's degree, in printmaking, Polkinhorn bought a letterpress and began to teach himself printing. He credits his Aunt Dorothy, "a major influence in my life," with helping to publish his first book, a long poem titled *Volvox.* She helped him hand-set and distribute the type to print the work. Polkinhorn's interest was intense in researching the history of printing in the Western culture, bookbinding, graphic design, typography and the culmination, publishing. "It had a liberating effect on me as an artist. I quickly came to realize that I could do whatever I wanted, I was not beholden to anonymous publishers or editors to validate my work," he said in his autobiographical essay. From 1982 to 1992, in San Diego, California, Polkinhorn and business partner Ralph Cook published *Atticus Review,* a literary magazine, and eventually books and broadsides with silk-screen or block-print illustrations. They were in the research process of writing the book, *Jerome Rothenberg: A Descriptive Bibliography* together when Cook ended the partnership and left the work for Polkinhorn to complete. Shortly there after he and his wife separated and they eventually divorced.

Polkinhorn had been fascinated with the people and culture of United States-Mexican border—known as "the line"—since he was a boy. This fascination continued to lead him back to Calexico where he made contact with other writers and artists in Mexico, co-sponsoring a series of conferences, workshops, and cultural activities connected to exploring what it meant to live on the border and to produce culture there. In addition to writing, Polkinhorn began a series of translations from Spanish, Portuguese, and Italian. His own work began to be translated abroad as well.

In 1986, though skittish about a second marriage, he and Armida Romero wed. Her attention wandered, however, and shortly after the birth of their daughter she asked for a divorce. After one failed marriage and for the sake of their daughter Polkinhorn was driven towards reconciling, and endured years of the calamitous relationship, he stated, before finally divorcing.

Eventually, he returned to San Diego, taking over San Diego State University Press and editing numerous books relating to the United States/Mexican border. In 1983 he co-wrote *El Libro de Calo: Pachuco Slang Dictionary*. A *Choice* reviewer averred that the dictionary is not only valuable for its English translations of the slang of young Mexican-Americans in Southern California, but also for "the broader function of documenting the culture of this same group of people." In 1986 Polkinhorn co-wrote a revised edition, *El Libro de Calo: Chicano Slang Dictionary*.

While much of Polkinhorn's work focuses on narrow regions and topics that are primarily of interest to border area residents, he has occasionally broadened his scope. One example of this is *The Flight of the Eagle: Poetry on the U.S.-Mexico Border,* which he co-edited. This bilingual anthology examines the border experience through the work of eight Mexican writers. In a review of the volume, Lawrence Olszewski for *Library Journal* stated, "The poems express the quest for identity and acceptance in two conflicting, equally unattractive worlds and successfully persuade readers of the dilemma."

Besides editing, translating, and writing poetry, Polkinhorn also produces visual poetry and photography. In the 1970s he began to turn his camera lens on the problems he saw around him. One of his series portrayed the living conditions of undocumented farm workers in San Diego's North County.

After the photographs were viewed by members of the Select Commission on Immigration Reform in Washington, D.C., Polkinhorn was invited to exhibit the work in the city museum in Quito, Ecuador. This international exposure led to his being invited to serve residencies at the Pontifical Catholic University of Sao Paulo, Brazil in 1992 and 1996, working with Ph.D. candidates in semiotics and communications as well as doing sound-poetry performances and introducing the *Contemporary Brazilian Theory* series.

BIOGRAPHICAL/CRITICAL SOURCES:

BOOKS

Contemporary Authors Autobiography Series, Volume 25, Gale (Detroit, MI), 1996.

PERIODICALS

Choice, May 1984, p. 1280; February 1988, p. 882; October 1989, p. 307.
Library Journal, May 15, 1994, p. 76.

*   *   *

POLLACK, Robert (Elliot)   1940-

PERSONAL: Born September 2, 1940, in Brooklyn, NY; married Amy Steinberg, 1961; children: Marya. *Education:* Columbia University, B.A. (physics), 1961; Woods Hole Marine Biological Laboratory (Falmouth, MA), summer, 1963; Brandeis University, Ph.D. (biology), 1966; New York University Medical Center, National Institutes of Health postdoctoral fellowship, 1966-68; Weizmann Institute (Rehovot, Israel), National Institutes of Health special fellowship, 1969-70.

ADDRESSES: Home—445 FDR Dr., New York, NY 10002-5901; P.O. Box 307, North Main St., Chelsea, VT 05038. *Office*—Department of Biological Sciences, 749 Fairchild Bldg., M.C. 2419, 1212 Amsterdam Ave., Columbia University, New York, NY 10027.

CAREER: New York University Medical Center, New York City, instructor, 1968-69, assistant professor, 1969-70; State University of New York at Stony Brook School of Medicine, Stony Brook, NY, adjunct assistant professor, 1971-75, associate professor, 1975-77, professor, 1977-78; Columbia University, New York City, professor, 1978—, dean of Columbia College, 1982-89. Laboratory researcher funded by agencies including the National Institutes of Health, the National Cancer Institute, and the National Science Foundation, 1966-93; Cold Spring Harbor Laboratory, senior scientist, 1971-75, director of summer program, 1972-74; Albert Einstein College of Medicine, visiting associate professor, 1977-93; Dartmouth College, visiting scholar, summer, 1988, 1989-90, 1993.

Trustee for New York Foundation, 1989—, Brandeis University, 1989-94, Community Impact, 1989—, Alliance for Raising Educational Achievement, 1989—, Solomon Schechter High School, 1996—; advisory board member for scientific, educational, and civic organizations including U.S.-Israel Binational Science Foundation, American Association for the Advancement of Science, National Alzheimer's Disease Foundation, National Science Foundation, New York Academy of Sciences, New York City Board of Education, Campus Jewish Life Fund; editorial board member for publications including *Journal of Virology, Journal of Cell Biology, Molecular and Cellular Biology, BBA Reviews on Cancer, The Scientific Prospect, Environmental Management and Health,* and the *Concise Encyclopedia* (Columbia University Press).

MEMBER: American Association for the Advancement of Science, American Society for Microbiology, New York Academy of Sciences, National Grange (Chelsea, VT, chapter).

AWARDS, HONORS: National Institutes of Health Research Career Development Award, 1974; Commendation for Teaching, American Association for Higher Education, 1986; Who's Who in America, American Men and Women of Science, 1986—; Alexander Hamilton Medal, Columbia University, 1989; American Association for the Advancement of Science, fellow, 1992; John Simon Guggenheim Foundation, fellow, 1993; Lionel Trilling Award, 1995, for *Signs of Life: The Language and Meanings of DNA;* grants from Abe Wouk Foundation, 1985—, Hughes Foundation, 1989-94, National Science Foundation, 1990-93, Sloan Foundation, 1993, 1995-97, and Ford Foundation, 1996-97.

WRITINGS:

(With S. Pfeiffer) *Animal Cell Culture Cell Manual,* Cold Spring Harbor Press (Cold Spring Harbor, NY), 1970.
(Editor with S. Hellman and M. Oxman) *Biohazards in Biological Research,* Cold Spring Harbor Laboratory Press, 1973.
(Editor) *Readings in Mammalian Cell Culture,* Cold Spring Harbor Laboratory Press, 1973, revised, 1975 and 1981.
Signs of Life: The Language and Meanings of DNA, Houghton (Boston), 1994.
(With H. Goldstein, J. Gross, and R. Blumberg) *The Scientific Experience,* Columbia University Press (New York City), 1995.

Contributor of more than one hundred articles to periodicals, including *Cancer Research, Journal of Virology, Molecular and Cellular Biology, New York Times,* and *Science.*

* * *

PORTE, Barbara Ann   1943-

PERSONAL: Born May 18, 1943, in New York, NY; daughter of a pharmacist and a lawyer. *Education:* Attended Iowa State University; Michigan State University, B.S., 1965; Palmer Graduate Library School, Long Island University, M.S., 1969.

ADDRESSES: Home—P.O. Box 16627, Arlington, VA 22215.

CAREER: Writer. Nassau Library System, Uniondale, NY, chief, Children's Services Division, 1974-86.

AWARDS, HONORS: Notable Book designation, American Library Association (ALA), for *Harry's Visit, Harry's Dog,* and *Harry in Trouble;* "Pick of the List," American Booksellers Association, 1985, for *The Kidnapping of Aunt Elizabeth;* Children's Books of the Year, Child Study Association of America, 1986, for *Harry's Mom,* and 1992, for *Harry Gets an Uncle;* Best Books, *Parents Magazine* and *Learning,* for *Ruthann and Her Pig;* Best Books for Young Adults, ALA, for *Something Terrible Happened;* "Pick of the List," American Booksellers Association, and Parents' Choice Picture Book Honor, Parents' Choice Foundation, both 1995, both for *Chickens! Chickens!*

WRITINGS:

Harry's Visit, illustrated by Yossi Abolafia, Greenwillow (New York City), 1983.
Jesse's Ghost and Other Stories, Greenwillow, 1983.
Harry's Dog, illustrated by Abolafia, Greenwillow, 1984.
Harry's Mom, illustrated by Abolafia, Greenwillow, 1985.
The Kidnapping of Aunt Elizabeth, Greenwillow, 1985.
I Only Made Up the Roses, Greenwillow, 1987.
Harry in Trouble, illustrated by Abolafia, Greenwillow, 1989.
The Take-along Dog, illustrated by Emily Arnold McCully, Greenwillow, 1989.

Ruthann and Her Pig, illustrated by Sucie Stevenson, Orchard Books (New York City), 1989.

Fat Fanny, Beanpole Bertha, and the Boys, illustrated by Maxie Chambliss, Orchard Books, 1991.

Harry Gets an Uncle, illustrated by Abolafia, Greenwillow, 1991.

Taxicab Tales, illustrated by Abolafia, Greenwillow, 1992.

A Turkey Drive and Other Tales, illustrated by Abolafia, Greenwillow, 1993.

"Leave That Cricket Be, Alan Lee," illustrated by Donna Ruff, Greenwillow, 1993.

When Grandma Almost Fell Off the Mountain and Other Stories, illustrated by Maxie Chambliss, Orchard Books, 1993.

Something Terrible Happened (for young adults), Orchard Books, 1994.

When Aunt Lucy Rode a Mule and Other Stories, illustrated by Chambliss, Orchard Books, 1994.

Harry's Birthday, illustrated by Abolafia, Greenwillow, 1994.

Chickens! Chickens!, illustrated by Greg Henry, Orchard Books, 1995.

Black Elephant with a Brown Ear (in Alabama), with illustrations by Bill Traylor, Greenwillow, 1996.

Surprise! Surprise! It's Grandfather's Birthday (picture book), illustrated by Bo Jia, Greenwillow, 1997.

Harry's Pony, illustrated by Abolafia, Greenwillow, 1997.

Tale of a Tadpole (picture book), illustrated by Annie Cannon, Orchard Books, 1997.

Work represented in anthologies, including *Funny You Should Ask,* edited by David Gale, Delacorte (New York City), 1992; *Don't Give Up the Ghost,* edited by Gale, Delacorte, 1993; *Birthday Surprises,* edited by Johanna Hurwitz, Morrow Junior Books (New York City), 1995; and *New Handbook for Storytellers,* edited by Caroline Feller Bauer, ALA, 1993.

Contributor of stories, poems, essays, and reviews to literary magazines, including *Advocate, Book Links, Confrontation, Earth's Daughters, Green's Magazine, Hanging Loose, Karamu, Newsday, New York Times, Phoebe, 13th Moon, San Jose Studies,* and *School Library Journal.*

ADAPTATIONS: Jesse's Ghost and Other Stories is available as a talking book from the Library of Congress. *Harry's Dog* is available as a cassette tape, from Random House.

WORK IN PROGRESS: Hearsay: Strange Tales from the Middle Kingdom, for Greenwillow; *Living Arrangements* (short stories), for Hanging Loose Press (Brooklyn, NY).

SIDELIGHTS: Best known for her popular "Harry" books for beginning readers, versatile author Barbara Ann Porte has also written a wide variety of books for the middle grader, including a collection of macabre stories and several funny family tales, as well as thought-provoking novels for young adults dealing with biracial families and painful subjects like AIDS, divorce, and death. Critics have praised her for her skillful storytelling, lively dialogue, convincing characterization, and humor.

Born in New York City, the daughter of a lawyer mother and a storytelling pharmacist father, Porte and her two sisters grew up telling stories to one another. Every night their mother read aloud to them, even after they could read on their own. Every day their father told them: "Read something everyday and write something every day, no matter what else you do with your lives." And, as Porte stated in the *Sixth Book of Junior Authors and Illustrators,* "We did, and we do."

Despite her love of books, however, Porte majored in the more practical subject of agriculture in college, in both Iowa and Michigan. After she married and had children, however, she returned to school to become a librarian. Porte began her writing career with three stories for the "Read-alone Books" series about the small boy narrator, Harry, who lives with his single-parent dentist dad. *Harry's Visit* describes his reluctance when invited to spend a day with old friends of his father and their children. That is, until one of the children invites him to shoot a few baskets. "Shoot some baskets? He must be joking. I am just a little taller than one of Snow White's dwarfs," is Harry's first reaction.

As Zena Sutherland of the *Bulletin of the Center for Children's Books* observed, "The treatment is light but the emotions are deep and universal." In *Harry's Dog,* Harry makes up some wild tales when his allergic father discovers a dog in the house. However, a home is found for the dog, and Harry finds his father a suitable pet: a goldfish. "As logical and winsome as ever," commented Karen Jameyson of *Horn Book Magazine.* Although the theme of *Harry's Mom* is serious, beginning with the opening "I, Harry, am an orphan," Zena Sutherland of the *Bulletin of the Center for Children's Books* stated, "The author has proved herself adept at investing simply presented situations with emotional substance—here, both humor and sadness." The wise father helps Harry recognize all the loving people in his life, including an aunt and four grandparents, and from them Harry learns about his daredevil, sports-reporter mother. A "quietly satisfying story," commented Denise M. Wilms of *Booklist*. Interspersed with books about other families and books for older readers, several other stories, including *Harry in Trouble, Harry Gets an Uncle,* and *Harry's Birthday,* continue the series with the slightly over-anxious lad inevitably discovering his worries were in vain and that lost library cards, wedding responsibilities, and birthday surprises can have happy conclusions.

In another series of books aimed for the preschooler or beginning independent reader, *The Take-along Dog* introduces Sam Rabinowitz, his sister Abigail, and their parents, a taxi driver father and artist mother. Because of their mother's fear of dogs, the children must take their little dog Benton with them wherever they go, even to places where dogs are not permitted, until the day Benton protects Mother from a larger dog and wins her appreciation and friendship. *School Library Journal* contributor Pamela Miller noted that *The Take-along Dog,* which among other summer activities depicts Sam taking ballet lessons, "subtly emphasizes important human values [such as] acknowledgment of a parent's fear . . . and the negation of gender stereotypes."

In the second of the series, *Taxicab Tales,* Father entertains his family with tales of his day and the unusual passengers he has met. "Porte is an expert at creating unity from bits and pieces, half-truths, absolutes, and maybes—the stuff that real life and great stories are made of," asserted Heide Piehler in a *School Library Journal* review.

A Turkey Drive and Other Tales, the third chapter book of the series, is narrated by Abigail and uses Mother's artwork as a springboard. A *Kirkus Reviews* commentator maintained that Porte "keeps the book moving with unexpected plot-twists, comical detail, impeccable timing, and a rare ear for natural, funny dialogue." Quraysh Ali of *Booklist* enthused that in *A Turkey Drive* Porte "ties together little pieces of sense, nonsense, and stream-of-consciousness to arrive at the wittiest conclusions." A *Publishers Weekly* reviewer described the book as a collection of "quirky, loosely connected tales," adding: "Porte's energetic imagery and plotting keep the pages turning."

Diverging from her normal population of urban children, Porte turns to a Chinese-American boy in *"Leave That Cricket Be, Alan Lee."* Determined to catch a cricket he hears chirping, Alan learns that crickets sing by rubbing their wings, that his great-uncle Clem used to make cricket cages as a boy in China, and that Chinese legend has it that crickets bring good luck. Once caught, however, the cricket no longer sings, so Alan lets it go and is rewarded by its song. A *Kirkus Reviews* critic contended that the narrative is rather long, but added that it is "propelled by plenty of lively realistic dialogue [and] artfully reveals a lot" about the family interrelationships. Jody McCoy in *School Library Journal* concurred that the text is a bit long for reading at one sitting, but praised the "deliciously poetic passages [that] beg to be read aloud."

Middle-graders can enjoy Porte's *Jesse's Ghost and Other Stories,* a collection of twelve eerie short stories that *Publishers Weekly* advised "be read in daylight, with people around." *Booklist* reviewer Denise M. Wilms described them as "sometimes elegant stories [that] have a haunting quality to them." Zena Sutherland of the *Bulletin of the Center for Children's Books* noted that the writing style "often [captures] the cadence of the oral tradition." This same oral tradition is particularly evident in tales featuring two sisters, Stella and Zelda, who prevail upon their grandmother to tell them a story in *When Grandma Almost Fell Off the Mountain and Other Stories,* and hear her account of traveling to Florida by car with the girls' parents in the 1930s. The grandmother's "colorful words, brisk descriptions, and unerring choice of subjects" entertain the sisters (and readers) and add a "rich multigenerational flavor," according to a *Kirkus Reviews* commentator.

In a companion book, *When Aunt Lucy Rode a Mule and Other Stories,* the girls prod their aunt to recount her childhood memories, which include visiting her grandmother in the mountains and getting stung by bees. A *Publishers Weekly* reviewer stated that Porte "liberally sprinkles the text with the kind of rich natural phrasing associated with oral storytelling." *School Library Journal* contributor Nancy Menaldi-Scanlan points out that for today's children who equate vacation with "a trip to Disneyworld or to some other prepackaged funhouse," Porte offers "a sense of old-fashioned good times and down-home humor."

"A fresh and innovative present-tense narrative," as Betsy Hearne described it in the *Bulletin of the Cen-*

ter for Children's Books, Porte's *Ruthann and Her Pig* tells of Ruthann and her pet pig, Henry Brown. Visitor Cousin Frank, however, also becomes attached to Henry. The ensuing correspondence between cousins, the discovery of a long-lost grandfather, and Henry's fate all add up to reading-aloud fun that Hearne pronounced "distinctively done."

Hearne offered a similar estimation of *Fat Fanny, Beanpole Bertha, and the Boys,* noting that "with the same present-tense immediacy that distinguished her narrative in *Ruthann and Her Pig,*" Porte relates the story of two fifth-grade girls, friends since kindergarten, who share a difficult time. Bertha's father has vanished in the Bermuda Triangle, and Fanny's parents are secretly divorced. Sally T. Margolis stated in *School Library Journal* that "Porte approaches the problem novel from left field with zesty humor, unique characters, and unlikely plot developments." Harried Bertha has to look after her eight-year-old younger brothers (triplets) while her mother works two jobs, and overweight Fanny eats excessively while brooding about her folks. "It's the characterizations of this odd lot that make the story a standout," commented Ilene Cooper in *Booklist.* "Fresh and funny, yet it packs a punch."

For older readers, *The Kidnapping of Aunt Elizabeth* features fifteen-year-old Ashley Rush who, for a school project on family history, collects stories from assorted relatives. *School Library Journal* contributor Heide Piehler noted that "Porte establishes herself as a masterful storyteller, [who can create] memorable characters and a seemingly endless supply of engaging tales." A mixture of invention and authenticated folk and fairy tales, the combination makes for "fast moving and captivating reading," according to *Voice of Youth Advocates* contributor Margaret J. Porter.

Another of Porte's well-received books for teens, *I Only Made Up the Roses,* focuses on a seventeen-year-old narrator, Cydra, who lives with her white mother, black stepfather, and younger half-brother Perley. "A wonderful, intelligent book," Myrna Feldman wrote in *Voice of Youth Advocates,* with all the feelings and experiences of a bi-racial family "explored and handled by contemporary, educated, liberal individuals." Beginning with southern step-grandfather's funeral and concluding with Thanksgiving, the string of short stories revolve around incidents in a family spanning three continents. "Thematic reflections on racial prejudice,

family adjustment, and life cycles are delivered by a personable protagonist," wrote Betsy Hearne in the *Bulletin of the Center for Children's Books.*

Selected as one of ALA's Best Books for Young Adults, and a departure from Porte's usual light-hearted tales, *Something Terrible Happened* tells the story of Gillian, whose father died of addictions brought home from Vietnam, and whose mother is stricken with AIDS. Although raised in New York, Gillian identifies with her mother and grandmother, "Island" women of Caribbean heritage. As her mother's condition worsens, Gillian is sent to Tennessee to stay with her white uncle and his family. Her mother's death forces Gillian to grow up, gaining strength from the wealth of folktales she had been brought up on, and learning acceptance and self-reliance.

Horn Book reviewer Ellen Fader praised this "compelling" story and predicts readers will be captivated by "this gritty, engaging, fast-moving tale of one young girl's fight for emotional survival." A *Kirkus Reviews* critic commented that the author "enlivens a refreshingly cliche-free narrative with the folktales this multiracial family of strong women tell each other." Deborah Stevenson of *Bulletin of the Center for Children's Books* concluded, "the final effect is dreamy and somewhat adult, but there's a verisimilitude in the wandering and an intimacy in the portrayals that keep the book an absorbing read." A reviewer for *Publishers Weekly* observed, "Once in concert with its unique rhythm, the reader will burrow into this story and relish its nuggets of insight."

Porte first met illustrator Greg Henry at a faculty art exhibition at Hampton University, her husband's alma mater. When she discovered that the young painter had grown up on a chicken farm in Guyana, she was ecstatic. "I majored in agriculture in college and received a two-year foundation grant, partially based on my own interest in chickens," she explained. The serendipitous result was the book *Chickens! Chickens!,* of which Betsy Hearne of the *Bulletin of the Center for Children's Books* commented: "This buoyant story will snag listeners with its infectious silliness." Hearne identified the theme as "follow your dream" and summarized the book as "a lot of fun."

In another book inspired by pictures, *Black Elephant with a Brown Ear (in Alabama),* ten stories describe what a survivor of slavery and farmer, almost ninety years old, drew and painted. Deborah Stevenson quotes Porte in *Bulletin of the Center for Children's Books* as saying, "When I look at many of Bill Traylor's pictures, I think of them as stories that he told himself. Seeing them, I tell myself different stories."

The stories range from hilarity to heroism, pieces about pigs and dogs, run-away goat carts and circus performers. *School Library Journal* contributor Pam Gosner explained how Porte chose ten out of over twelve hundred paintings the African American artist had made and how she created imaginative tales about each. "Porte's writings, which are light and folksy in tone, explore a world of possibilities," she declared. Susan Dove Lempke in *Booklist* observed that "while the stories tend to wander and be somewhat insubstantial, they have a certain charm," and Lempke suggested that creative writing and art teachers might find this book useful in encouraging their own students to try out the method.

In an article for *School Library Journal,* Porte examined the philosophy underlying author visits to schools and libraries. She was encouraged by author Betty Miles, who sought to give children a better understanding of writing as a worthwhile skill to be developed. At the same time, however, Porte was disturbed by the response of several other authors who admitted they spent hours, weeks, maybe more, to prepare for an adult audience, but hardly any time preparing for an audience of children.

Porte was delighted with fellow writer Esther Hautzig, who said she prepared more carefully for children because it means more to them. Porte herself has asserted: "I believe that children are the audience to whom we owe the greatest responsibility and effort. . . . Children are most likely to believe and remember what we tell them. We owe it to them to take them seriously."

BIOGRAPHICAL/CRITICAL SOURCES:

BOOKS

Sixth Book of Junior Authors and Illustrators, edited by Sally Holmes Holtze, H. W. Wilson, 1989, pp. 231-32.

PERIODICALS

Book Links, March, 1997, p. 21.
Booklist, October 15, 1983, p. 366; October 15, 1985, p. 343; October 1, 1989, p. 354; March 1, 1991, p. 1388; April 15, 1993, p. 156; May 15, 1996, p. 1584.
Bulletin of the Center for Children's Books, July-August, 1983, p. 217; March, 1984, p. 134; July-August, 1984, p. 211; December, 1985, pp. 75-76; June, 1987, p. 194; February, 1989, p. 155; January, 1990, p. 119; April, 1991, p. 202; May, 1994, p. 298; December, 1994, p. 143; April, 1995, p. 284; June, 1996, p. 350.
Horn Book, June, 1983, p. 299; August, 1984, pp. 463-464; May-June, 1985, p. 313; January-February, 1992, pp. 66-67; May-June, 1993, p. 330; November-December, 1994, p. 737; March-April, 1995, p. 187.
Kirkus Reviews, February 1, 1993; April 1, 1993, p. 463; July 15, 1993, p. 939; May 15, 1994, p. 704; October 15, 1994, p. 1414.
New York Times Book Review, May 21, 1995, p. 22.
Publishers Weekly, September 16, 1983, p. 126; April 19, 1993, p. 62; August 1, 1994, p. 79; October 10, 1994, p. 70.
School Library Journal, May, 1983, p. 88; April, 1985, p. 91; March, 1989, pp. 124-125; June, 1989, p. 91; February, 1991, p. 82; April, 1992, pp. 98-99; October, 1993, p. 108; November, 1994, p. 88; May, 1996, p. 96.
Voice of Youth Advocates, June, 1985, p. 134; June, 1987, p. 82.
Wilson Library Bulletin, June, 1995, p. 117.

R

RANDALL, Richard H(arding), Jr. 1926-1997

OBITUARY NOTICE—See index for *CA* sketch: Born January 31, 1926, in Baltimore, MD; died of heart failure, July 3, 1997, in Baltimore, MD. Curator, educator, author. An expert on medieval art, Randall devoted much of his career to overseeing collections at the Metropolitan Museum of Art, the Museum of Fine Arts, and the Walters Art Gallery. After receiving degrees from Princeton and Harvard, he started work as an assistant curator at New York City's Metropolitan Museum of Art in 1953. He eventually became an associate curator of medieval art. In 1959 he joined the staff at Boston's Museum of Fine Arts as assistant curator of decorative arts. He moved on to Baltimore's Walters Art Gallery in 1964 as its assistant director, later serving as director from 1965 to 1981. He served as the Gallery's curator of medieval art from 1981 until 1985. During his career he also served as an assistant professor at Columbia University and he worked as a member of the furnishing committee to the White House. A member of the Maryland Historical Society, he served on its board of trustees in the mid-1990s. He wrote several books, including *The Golden Age of Ivory: Gothic Carvings in North American Collections, A Bestiary of the Cloisters, American Furniture, Jewelry: Ancient to Modern* (with others), and *Masterpieces of Ivory* (with others).

OBITUARIES AND OTHER SOURCES:

BOOKS

Who's Who in America, Marquis, 1995.

PERIODICALS

New York Times, July 7, 1997, p. B9.

RATHMANN, Peggy (Margaret Crosby) 1953-

PERSONAL: Born March 4, 1953, in St. Paul, MN; married John Wick. *Education:* University of Minnesota, B.A. in psychology; attended American Academy, Chicago, IL, Atelier Lack, Minneapolis, MN, and Otis Parson's School of Design, Los Angeles, CA.

ADDRESSES: Office—c/o Putnam/Berkeley Publicity Department, 200 Madison Ave., New York, NY 10016.

CAREER: Children's book writer and illustrator, 1991—.

AWARDS, HONORS: "Most promising new author" mention, Cuffies Awards, *Publishers Weekly,* 1991, for *Ruby the Copycat;* Notable Children's Book, American Library Association, 1994, for *Good Night, Gorilla;* Chicago Public Library, Best Books of the Year list, 1995, *School Library Journal*'s Best Books of 1995 list, and Caldecott Medal, 1996, all for *Officer Buckle and Gloria.*

WRITINGS:

AND ILLUSTRATOR

Ruby the Copycat, Scholastic Inc. (New York City), 1991.

(Illustrator) Barbara Bottner, *Bootsie Barker Bites,* Putnam (New York), 1992.

Good Night, Gorilla, Putnam, 1994.

Officer Buckle and Gloria, Putnam, 1995.

SIDELIGHTS: With her first children's book, *Ruby the Copycat,* Peggy Rathmann turned an embarrassing personal incident into a well-received story and earned the "most promising new author" distinction in the 1991 Cuffies Awards. Her second self-illustrated book, *Good Night, Gorilla,* was an American Library Assocation Notable Children's Book. And for her third title, *Officer Buckle and Gloria,* Rathmann was awarded the Caldecott Medal in 1996.

In her Caldecott acceptance speech, as reported in *Horn Book,* Rathmann explained the genesis of her writing/illustrating career. "Ten summers ago," Rathmann recalled, "I was vacationing with my two nieces. The girls were three and five years old, and as far as I could tell, they didn't like me nearly enough." One day on a car trip the nieces both wanted to sit in front next to another aunt. "Now, this aunt cannot help that she is extremely attractive, intelligent, and pleasant to be around. *I* wanted to sit next to her, too." But there was only room for one, so the younger niece was sent howling to the back seat with Rathmann. "She glowered at me; I was the booby prize." In desperation, Rathmann pulled out her sketch pad and began drawing a story "that starred my niece and me as extremely attractive people with good personalities and high IQs. It worked." It was also the start of an award-winning career. According to Diane Roback and Shannon Maughan in *Publishers Weekly,* Rathmann creates "characters with built-in kid appeal: a copycat, a girl who bites, a young gorilla who slips the keys away from the zookeeper." Roback and Maughan also noted that while Rathmann's books may be "spare in text," they are "long on action, much of it related through her cleverly expressive pictures."

Rathmann was born in St. Paul, Minnesota, in 1953, one of five children. She grew up in the suburbs of St. Paul and started her illustrating career in the seventh grade, with campaign posters for her older brother's successful bid for student council. After graduation from Mounds View High School in New Brighton, Minnesota, Rathmann attended several colleges before settling down at the University of Minnesota where she took a degree in psychology. Rathmann once said that she "wanted to teach sign language to gorillas, but after taking a class in signing, I realized what I'd rather do was draw pictures of gorillas." There followed various career plans from commercial artist to fine artist, but meanwhile she continued to work on the picture book she had begun with her nieces, a book that became "endless," as she described it in her Caldecott acceptance speech. "A whopping 150 pink-and-purple pages. . . . The book had everything—except conflict and a plot."

A publisher's rejection and a subsequent tip from a published writer sent Rathmann back to school, this time to a children's book-writing and illustration class. It was there that Rathmann began an assignment on an embarrassing incident in her life that led to her first published book. The teacher of this class suggested the students develop a story idea from the worst or most embarrassing thing they knew about themselves. At first Rathmann was unsuccessful, but as her classmates began presenting *their* stories, she developed the "overwhelming compulsion to swipe" the embarrassing incidents of other students, as she confessed in her Caldecott acceptance speech. Eventually she decided that this very tendency toward copying was the shameful thing she could use for the assignment which eventually turned into the book, *Ruby the Copycat.* "Since then, all of my books have been based on embarrassing secrets," Rathmann said in her Caldecott speech.

Ruby the Copycat, a book that *Kirkus Reviews* dubbed "a solid debut," tells the story of a new girl in class named Ruby who tries to act just like the popular girl, Angela. Ruby's poem is almost exactly like Angela's; Ruby was a flower girl in a wedding, just like Angela. Initially, the popular girl finds such adulation flattering, but ultimately it is flat out irritating. Ruby even copies the painted nails of the teacher, Miss Hart, who finally takes Ruby in hand and lets her know it is okay to be herself. In fact, the kindly teacher advises her that is the only way she will really fit in and win friends. So Ruby shows off her hopping ability, and the other kids soon are copying her. This feat even wins Angela's friendship.

Martha Topol, reviewing *Ruby the Copycat* in *School Library Journal,* noted that this was a "book with a strong story and complementary illustrations that addresses the philosophical question of individuality vs. conformity." Topol concluded the book "a small gem." Other critics noted the originality of Rathmann's artwork and how integrally it fitted in and helped develop the story. Ilene Cooper in *Booklist* commented that Rathmann's "colorful artwork adds new bits of humor to the text," and a *Publishers Weekly* reviewer asserted that her "expressively illustrated, quirky and individualistic first book" inspired confidence in children and taught them "not to take skills . . . for granted."

Rathmann followed up this success with the illustrations for Barbara Bottner's *Bootsie Barker Bites,* and then with her own story, *Good Night, Gorilla,* inspired by another classroom assignment and aided by a childhood memory. The writing and illustrating, however, were not the matter of a quick study session. The initial draft of the manuscript had value, but everyone concurred that the ending was problematic. It took two years and ten more endings to put together the final manuscript for *Good Night, Gorilla,* which went on to win an ALA Notable Book citation in 1994. This book relies heavily on pictures to convey story; words are limited to a bubbled "Good night," as the keeper of a zoo makes his rounds, tucking in the various animals he cares for. There is a gorilla, a lion, a giraffe, an armadillo, a hyena, and even a non-zoo mouse. But little does the zookeeper know that the gorilla in the first cage has lifted his keys and is setting free the animals in back of him, and that they are all following him home to the cozy security of a surrogate "parent." The zookeeper's wife finally takes the menagerie back to their proper places—all except the gorilla and the mouse who in the end snuggle down next to the zookeeper and his wife.

Deborah Stevenson of the *Bulletin of the Center for Children's Books* noted both the story and pictorial value of the book in her review. Indicating that it was a "livelier bedtime story" than *Good Night, Moon,* Stevenson went on to comment on Rathmann's lines, "rounder here than in her previous work," on the animals, which "have a cheerful simplicity of mien," and the palette, which "relies on a twilit glow of pink and green that lends a gentle circus flavor to the proceedings." *Booklist*'s Ilene Cooper noted that Rathmann's "Jaunty four-color artwork carries the story and offers more with every look," while *Kirkus Reviews* dubbed the book "delightful" and *Horn Book*'s Ann A. Flowers called it "an outstanding picture book." Considering the effect of both picture and story, Jan Shepherd Ross in *School Library Journal* concluded that *Good Night, Gorilla* is "a clever, comforting bedtime story."

"There's a funny thing that happens between words and pictures," Rathmann said in her interview with Roback and Maughan for *Publishers Weekly.* Rathmann learned the symbiotic nature of the two in her classes at Otis Parsons. She also learned that neither could exist without the other. In fact, it was yet another class assignment that led to her Caldecott Medal with *Officer Buckle and Gloria.* "The assignment was to write and illustrate a story which could not be understood by reading the text alone," she related in her Caldecott acceptance speech. "I did it because the teacher told us to, but in the process I discovered that this challenge was the very definition of a picture book. Officer Buckle was the words, Gloria was the pictures, and neither could entertain or enlighten without the other." Employing the acrobatic and clowning talents of her own family dog, Rathmann wrote and illustrated a story about a school safety officer and the dog who makes him fabulously popular for a time. Officer Buckle knows more about safety than just about anybody in the town of Napville, but he is a tremendous bore when he gives assemblies to impart his safety tips. One day, though, the Napville Police Department buys a police dog with the improbable name of Gloria. Buckle begins taking Gloria with him to his demonstrations and, behind his back, the jolly dog performs a series of skillful acrobatic tricks, much to the amazement and amusement of the audience. Suddenly, Officer Buckle is much in demand, and things go along wonderfully until the policeman sees a video of his performance on the television news and understands that the cheers have been for Gloria, and not for him. Outraged, Officer Buckle refuses to visit any more schools, and when Gloria goes on her own, she is a bomb. In fact, the two need each other, and when they return to the stage, they present a final safety tip: "Always stick with your buddy."

Deborah Stevenson in *Bulletin of the Center for Children's Books* noted that "This is at heart the old story of the importance of friendship, but the safety tips . . . and the rest of the plot devices give it a fresh twist." Indeed, Rathmann spent much time and money on the 101 safety tips that are posted throughout the book and on the endpapers. With deadlines approaching and more tips needed, Rathmann offered her nieces and nephews twenty-five dollars apiece for any safety tips that made it past her editor. "The response was very expensive," Rathmann recalled in her Caldecott acceptance speech. Though many such tips are quite humorous, Stevenson went on to note in her review that the illustrations are "the lifeblood" of the book: "scratchy-edged watercolors in a luminous palette." Carolyn Phelan, writing in *Booklist,* commented that "the deadpan humor of the text and slapstick wit of the illustrations make a terrific combination." Kathie Krieger Cerra in *Five Owls* noted especially how Rathmann's illustrations "move beyond the story and enrich it," and concluded that *Officer Buckle and Gloria* "is a book that children return to repeatedly, for there is much to be discovered in the illustrations and the language." A

Publishers Weekly reviewer asserted that Rathmann "brings a lighter-than-air comic touch to this outstanding, solid-as-a-brick picture book," and *Horn Book*'s Ann A. Flowers called it "a glorious picture book." Lisa S. Murphy in *School Library Journal* summed up critical opinion in the conclusion of her review: "A five-star performance."

BIOGRAPHICAL/CRITICAL SOURCES:

BOOKS

Rathmann, Peggy, *Officer Buckle and Gloria,* Putnam, 1995.

PERIODICALS

Booklist, November 15, 1991, p. 631; July, 1994, p. 1956; November 1, 1995, p. 471.
Bulletin of the Center for Children's Books, May, 1994, p. 299; October, 1995, p. 66.
Five Owls, March-April, 1996, pp. 85-86.
Horn Book, July-August, 1994, pp. 443-44; November-December, 1995, pp. 736-37; July-August, 1996, pp. 424-27.
Kirkus Reviews, November 15, 1991, p. 1474; April 15, 1994, p. 562; August 15, 1995, p. 1193.
Los Angeles Times Book Review, February 25, 1996, p. 11.
Publishers Weekly, November 8, 1991, p. 64; March 14, 1994, p. 71; February 20, 1995, p. 125; July 17, 1995, p. 229.
School Library Journal, January, 1992, p. 96; July, 1994, p. 87; September, 1995, p. 185.
Wilson Library Bulletin, February, 1995, p. 94.

*　　*　　*

RAU, Dana Meachen 1971-

PERSONAL: Born October 15, 1971, in CT; married Christopher Rau (a teacher), July 2, 1994. *Education:* Trinity College, Hartford, CT, B.A., 1993. *Avocational interests:* Reading, watching movies, eating pizza.

ADDRESSES: Home—621 Courtland Ave., Bridgeport, CT 06605.

CAREER: Children's book writer and editor.

MEMBER: Society of Children's Book Writers and Illustrators, Phi Beta Kappa.

AWARDS, HONORS: Trumbull Arts Festival Literary Competition, first place award, 1993, for the story "The Date," honorable mentions, 1996, for the stories "The Traveler" and "Delusions of Grandeur."

WRITINGS:

FOR CHILDREN

Robin at Hickory Street, illustrated by Joel Snyder, Soundprints (Norwalk, CT), 1995.
One Giant Leap: The First Moon Landing, illustrated by Thomas Buchs, Soundprints, 1996.
A Box Can Be Many Things, illustrated by Paige Billin-Frye, Children's Press (Chicago, IL), 1997.
Undersea City: A Story of a Caribbean Coral Reef, illustrated by Katie Lee, Soundprints, 1997.
Arctic Adventure: Inuit Life in the 1800s, illustrated by Peg Magovern, Soundprints, 1997.
The Secret Code, illustrated by Bari Weissman, Children's Press, 1998.

OTHER

Wall (play), produced by Company One Theater in Hartford, CT, 1993.

Also author of short stories for adults.

WORK IN PROGRESS: Thomas Edison (tentative title), for Soundprints.

SIDELIGHTS: Dana Meachen Rau commented: "Currently, my career can be defined as writer and editor. I have been a children's book editor for the past four years, working on both fiction and nonfiction. I coordinate the entire book process and collaborate with a diverse group of authors and illustrators. In my free time, I have been writing fiction for all ages.

"I have always thought that one of the most important things an author can have is an active imagination. When I was little, my brother and I always used our imaginations. We pretended our beds were pirate ships, and the hallway was a bowling alley. The best creation of all was setting up the boxes in the basement to look like a palace!

"Now that I am an adult, I find that I am still always using my imagination. I pretend that driving my car is a roller coaster ride. I pretend that a walk in the woods is a safari adventure. When I look around my small apartment, I still pretend that I live in a palace!"

BIOGRAPHICAL/CRITICAL SOURCES:

PERIODICALS

Booklist, October 15, 1996, p. 419.

*   *   *

REED, Philip (Chandler) 1952-

PERSONAL: Born March 17, 1952, in Minneapolis, MN; son of Thomas B. (an inventor) and Vivian (a teacher; maiden name Odh) Reed; married Vivian Blackwell Swigle, August 11, 1979; children: Andrew Wesley, Anthony Wilson. *Education:* Attended Dean Junior College, Franklin, MA, 1970-73; University of North Carolina, Chapel Hill, B.A. (English), 1975. *Politics:* Democrat. *Religion:* Presbyterian. *Avocational interests:* Beer making, carpentry, tennis, golf, free throw shooting, mountain climbing.

ADDRESSES: Home—Long Beach, CA. *Agent*—John Hawkins, John Hawkins & Associates, 71 West 23rd St., No, 1600, New York, NY 10010. *E-mail*—philreed@aol.com.

CAREER: City News Bureau of Chicago, Chicago, IL, reporter, 1976-78; Sentinel Newspapers, Denver, CO, reporter, 1978; *Rocky Mountain News,* Denver, reporter, 1978-82; *Hollywood Drama-Logue,* Hollywood, CA, critic and columnist, 1982-90.

MEMBER: Writers' Guild of America, Mystery Writers of America.

WRITINGS:

True Blues (play), produced in Hollywood, CA, 1984.
Nightside (play), produced in Los Angeles, CA, 1987, produced in Chicago, IL, Victory Gardens Theater.
Candidly, Allen Funt: A Million Smiles Later (biography), Barricade Books (New York City), 1994.

Free Throw, HarperCollins (New York City), 1996.
Bird Dog (thriller), Pocket Books (New York City), 1997.

Author of the plays *Boondoggle* and *Vacancy in Paradise;* has written for television shows, including *Miami Vice, Beauty and the Beast,* and *Probe;* contributor of reviews to periodicals, including *USA Today, Hollywood Drama-Logue,* and *Long Beach Press Telegram;* ghost writer of the books *Used Cars—How to Buy One* and *Lease Cars—How to Get One;* author of unproduced screenplays; author of scripts for production company training videos and videos used to educate juries.

WORK IN PROGRESS: Low Rider, a sequel to *Bird Dog,* for Pocket Books, expected in 1998; research on sports-related topics as well as additional story ideas for mystery-thrillers, particularly in regards to the subject of cars.

SIDELIGHTS: Philip Reed told *CA:* "When I was growing up we moved from Buffalo, New York, to Danville, Indiana, and finally to Concord, Massachusetts, a town steeped in literary history and the home of Henry David Thoreau, Nathanial Hawthorne, and Louisa May Alcott. These writers influenced me somewhat. A greater influence was the fact that my grandfather had written short stories for pulp magazines in the 1920s. He later became a news reporter and ad man in Chicago.

"At an early age I became interested in writing short stories and novels. Some of the first authors I remember reading were Mark Twain and Jack London. When I was thirteen or fourteen, we spent a year in Oxford, England, and while I was there, I read many of the great American writers: Steinbeck, Salinger, and Hemingway. While in England I built a raft and sailed it down the Thames hoping to reach London (the current turned out to be extremely sluggish and we barely made twenty-five miles in a week). I wrote a memoir of this trip. And in the same year I wrote a short story in the style of O. Henry with a 'surprise' ending.

"Through high school I continued to write short stories that were not very good and novels that I never finished. I continued this into junior college, took a year off and traveled in Europe, then returned attend the University of North Carolina at Chapel Hill. I went to U.N.C. because the soccer coach helped me bypass admissions, and because it was the alma mater of my favorite writer at that time—Thomas Wolf.

"In 1975, when I was ready to graduate, I found I was still three credits short. I enrolled in a correspondence course for playwriting. To complete the class I wrote two one-act plays (one of those plays was produced in Hollywood eight years later).

"After college I spent a year working in a hotel in Boston and writing in my spare time. I had several newspaper articles published, but I had no luck with fiction. Finally, I concluded I didn't have anything to write about and began looking for a job as a reporter. A friend was moving to San Francisco and gave me a ride as far as Chicago, which I had heard was 'a good newspaper town.' Ten days later I began working for the City News Bureau of Chicago, a wire service for the three city dailies and radio and TV stations.

"For two years I was a police reporter. I covered murders, robberies, assaults, explosions, accidents, and many, many fires. This gave me a first-hand look at crime and the aftermath of crime and a working knowledge of police investigations. While riding the train to work and back I began writing a mystery, which was never finished.

"In 1978 I moved to Denver, Colorado, and began working for the Sentinel Newspapers, a string of suburban weeklies. Nine months later I landed a job as night reporter for the *Rocky Mountain News*. I drove a car equipped with a police scanner and a two-way radio to communicate with the city desk. In this position, I continued my education of crime and police work, but in a more in-depth fashion than in Chicago. A year later I was given a new assignment and covered many murder trials in Denver area courts. This gave me a look at how crimes are handled once they get into the judicial system.

"While working the night police beat, I wrote a mystery, *Dead Beat*. I also wrote several plays which I began mailing to contests and production companies.

"I was married in 1979 to Vivian Swingle who, although trained as a librarian, was interested in screenwriting. She wrote several screenplays which she mailed to Hollywood agents. Several agents wrote back, interested in her material. In 1982 we decided to move to California so Vivian could pursue screenwriting while I tried to get my plays produced. Once in Los Angeles, however, we were overwhelmed by the competition in the writing game and began to reassess our decision. Vivian got a job

as a librarian in Long Beach, and I began writing theater reviews for *USA Today, Hollywood Drama-Logue,* and the *Long Beach Press Telegram.*

"In 1984 the owner of a small Hollywood theater offered to let me use his space to produce my play *True Blues* which was based on an incident I witnessed as a police reporter in Chicago. However, he required me to direct the show myself, and double-cast the play. *True Blues* was given a lukewarm review by the *Los Angeles Times.* But later, a police reporter from the *Times* saw the play and praised it as a realistic assessment of the relationship between blacks and the L.A.P.D. Some producers from *Hill Street Blues* saw my play and recommended me to the staff of the then-unseen *Miami Vice.* I was hired to write an episode of that series.

"For the next few years I wrote and produced my plays in Los Angeles. I also wrote several other episodes for TV shows: *Beauty and the Beast* and *Probe.* In 1987 my full length play *Nightside* was produced in West L.A. It was based on the colorful old-school police reporters I had met working the midnight shift in the central police headquarters pressroom. A two-character play, it was later produced in Long Beach, California, and then at the Victory Gardens Theater in Chicago.

"In most of my playwriting I seemed to be exploring the importance of work in our lives. Also, two plays looked at racial relations: *True Blues* is about police brutality while *Nightside* is more understated, showing the changing of the guard as more blacks entered the workplace and were given promotions over many whites.

"In 1985 my son Andrew was born and this increased the need to make money and gain some measure of security. I began working for a production company in Beverly Hills writing scripts for training videos. I also wrote scripts for videos that would be used to educate juries in trial.

"In 1990 I optioned the rights to a screenplay *Flying Blind* to a young producer named Barin Kumar. After several failed attempts to rewrite my movie, we began rewriting the script together. Tragically, Barin died of a heart attack at the age of thirty-six and the movie was never made. However, he caused a breakthrough in my writing. With his help, I learned to write a story from multiple points of view.

"In 1990 my second son, Anthony, was born and the need for money increased. This also came at a time when Los Angeles was entering a deep recession. I was hired to ghost-write a how-to book about car buying, *Used Cars—How to Buy One,* which was self-published and nationally distributed. The following year I wrote another such book, *Lease Cars— How to Get One.* Both of these experiences showed me I was capable of writing a full-length manuscript.

"In 1992 I tried screenwriting again, co-writing a script called *Green Light* with a friend who worked for the *Los Angeles Times.* However, in May, the Los Angeles riots broke out. I knew my friend would be tied up covering the riots so I began work on a novel I had been thinking about for some time. For a long time I had been intrigued with the idea of writing a novel that borrowed heavily from the screenplay and stage play format. My idea was to write in such a way as to view the story from the outside, like a camera, with only occasional eavesdropping on the character's thoughts. I also wanted to write scenes that would be told entirely in dialogue. The novel that I began that morning became *Bird Dog.* However, after writing forty-two pages I could not decide what would happen next. I put it down and didn't pick it up again for two years.

"In 1993 I was offered the chance to write Allen Funt's autobiography. That was another chance to prove to myself I could create book-length work. Funt had attempted to write his memoirs several times, with other writers, but the efforts failed. I wrote four chapters of *Candidly, Allen Funt* and secured a contract from Barricade Books. The book was published in 1994.

"During this time, I began to develop a process for writing that I still use today. I get up early, about five a.m., and write quickly by hand, for about an hour. Then, after breakfast, I type this material into the computer, revising it as I go. This gives me two passes at a first draft. Sometimes I reject this handwritten material completely. Sometimes it goes in with little editing. But it helps me break the ice, and gets me past the blank page.

"After the publication of the Funt autobiography, I became more determined to finish my novel. One morning, while in the shower, another large section of the story unfolded to me. I began writing again and made it up to page 170. Finally, I decided to finish the book, whether I liked the ending or not. Once I did this I saw my way to the right ending and finished the book a few months later.

"After finishing *Bird Dog,* I learned that the world's champion free throw shooter, Dr. Tom Amberry, who made 2,750 free throws in a row, lived in Long Beach. I met him and asked him to teach me how he shot free throws. After a year of writing and shooting baskets, I sold *Free Throw* to HarperCollins Publishers. In almost the same month, my agent sold *Bird Dog* to Pocket Books and got me a two-book contract for the sequel. That book, with the working title *Low Rider,* is scheduled for publication in spring 1998."

*   *   *

REESE, Roger R(oi) 1959-

PERSONAL: Born May 18, 1959, in Fort Knox, KY; son of Ronald R. and Carleen H. (Smith) Reese; married Alison Winslow, July 9, 1988; children: Emily, Alexander, Helen. *Ethnicity:* "Caucasian." *Education:* Texas A&M University, B.A., 1981; University of Texas at Austin, M.A., 1986, Ph.D., 1990.

ADDRESSES: Home—1205 Pershing, College Station, TX 77840. *Office*—Department of History, Texas A&M University, College Station, TX 77843-4236; fax 409-862-4314. *E-mail*—rreese@tamvml. tamu.edu.

CAREER: Texas A&M University, College Station, assistant professor, 1990-96, associate professor of history, 1996—. *Military service:* U.S. Army, Infantry, 1981-84; became second lieutenant; received Commendation Medal. U.S. Army Reserve, 1984-94; became captain.

MEMBER: American Association for the Advancement of Slavic Studies.

AWARDS, HONORS: Fellow at University of Illinois at Urbana-Champaign, 1987, 1989; grants from Kennan Institute for Advanced Russian Studies, Woodrow Wilson Center for International Scholars, 1990, 1997, and National Endowment for the Humanities, 1993.

WRITINGS:

Stalin's Reluctant Soldiers: A Social History of the Red Army, 1925-1941, University Press of Kansas (Lawrence), 1996.

Contributor of articles and reviews to periodicals, including *Soviet Studies, Soviet and Post-Soviet Review,* and *Slavic Review.* Contributor to *Stalinist Terror: New Perspectives,* edited by J. Arch Getty and Roberta Manning, Cambridge University Press (Cambridge, England), 1993.

WORK IN PROGRESS: A History of the First Five-Year Plan: A Survey and Synthesis; editing a book on the Soviet Red Army and society.

* * *

RIGG, Sharon
   See CREECH, Sharon

* * *

RISSINGER, Matt 1956-

PERSONAL: Born November 2, 1956, in Sacramento, PA; son of Robert B. (a farmer) and Mary C. (a registered nurse; maiden name, Downey) Rissinger; married Margaret L. Loeb (a teacher), November 20, 1982; children: Rebecca, Emily. *Education:* Pottsville Hospital School of Nursing, R.N., 1977; Kutztown University, B.A., 1981; Temple University, M.A, 1990. *Politics:* Democrat. *Religion:* Roman Catholic. *Avocational interests:* "Listening to little kids tell their jokes."

CAREER: Health care professional, journalist, actor, storyteller. American Red Cross Penn-Jersey Blood Service, Philadelphia, PA, assistant director of donor services, 1983-90; Phoenixville Hospital, Phoenixville, PA, director of patient relations, 1990—. Eagleville Drug and Alcohol Hospital, Eagleville, PA, part-time nurse-counselor, 1983-96; humorist/industrial film actor/storyteller, 1983—; freelance journalist for health care publications, 1985—.

Methacton Community Theater, board of directors, 1984-86; United Way Charity, work-site chairperson, 1993-96; Lower Providence New Library Fund Raising Committee, 1995; Art Goes to School, educational volunteer, 1995, 1996; Phoenixville Area Committee of Social Concerns, member, 1995-96.

MEMBER: Authors' Guild, National Association for Storytelling, American Association for Therapeutic Humor, Southeastern Pennsylvania Patient Represen-

tatives (vice president, 1996), Pennsylvania Society for Patient Representatives (member of board of directors, 1992-96).

AWARDS, HONORS: Kutztown Faculty Awarded Scholarship, Kutztown University, 1980; winner, writing contest (humor category), Methacton School District, 1986; winner, writing contest, Hospital Association of Pennsylvania/Patient Representation Society, 1993.

WRITINGS:

(With Philip Yates) *The Great Book of Zany Jokes,* illustrated by Lucy Corvino, Sterling, 1994.
(With Yates) *The Biggest Joke Book in the World,* illustrated by Jeff Sinclair, Sterling, 1995.
(With Yates) *The World's Silliest Joke Book,* Sterling, 1997.

WORK IN PROGRESS: The Official Class Clown's Joke Book.

SIDELIGHTS: Matt Rissinger commented: "I've always been able to smile as effortlessly as I've been able to breathe. Humor is a fascination and a comfort to me. Growing up on a farm, I delighted in watching the antics of the pigs, cows, horses, and ducks. I never, however, found anything funny about vegetables.

"Life on a farm can be somewhat solitary, so reading was a wonderful way to go beyond the fields. As a kid, I read just about everything, except horror. I think having to feed and water the animals after dark in our windswept, creaking old barn had something to do with that.

"I still prefer humor over horror. However, there are some similarities between humor and horror. The surprise ending of a joke is the 'punch-line.' 'Bombing' is the horrible term when the audience isn't laughing and you're just 'dying' in front of them. Even the term for doing well is brutal—when your jokes are working well a comic says 'I'm killing 'em.' However, good or bad, performing is a tough business.

"A fellow performer, Philip Yates, and I used to write and do stand-up comedy. After a while we found out we enjoyed writing more than performing. When you see a comedy club on TV like *Seinfeld* the audience is bright, intelligent, attentive, and sober. Unfortunately, in real life almost none of those descriptions apply. We decided to perform less for adults and write more for children. To date, Phil and I have co-authored three books and performed for thousands of kids. We hope our books and stories help children and adults to laugh.

"An important part of growing up is developing the ability to laugh at yourself. Each person has their own unique type of humor. It is almost like a fingerprint. Some people ask me why I choose to write humor for children. The answer is easy: when I was a baby my mother accidentally spilled ink on my funny bone. I've been making a humorous impression ever since."

*   *   *

RIVARD, David 1953-

PERSONAL: Born December 2, 1953, in Fall River, MA; son of Norman and Barbara Rivard; married Michaela Sullivan, December 17, 1982; children: Simone. *Education:* Southeastern Massachusetts University, B.A., 1975; University of Arizona, M.F.A., 1982.

ADDRESSES: Home—72 Inman St., Apt. A., Cambridge, MA 02139. *Office*—English Department, Tufts University, Medford, MA 02155.

CAREER: Writer. Tufts University, Medford, MA, member of English department; poetry editor for the *Harvard Review.*

AWARDS, HONORS: Agnes Lynch Starrett Poetry Prize, University of Pittsburgh, 1987, for *Torque;* fellowships from National Endowment for the Arts 1986, 1991, and from Fine Art Work Center in Provincetown, MA, 1984-85, 1986-87; Pushcart Prize, 1994; Massachusetts Cultural Council fellow, 1994; James Laughlin Award, Academy of America Poets, 1996, and finalist for poetry prize, *Los Angeles Times,* 1997, both for *Wise Poison.*

WRITINGS:

Torque (poetry), University of Pittsburgh Press (Pittsburgh, PA), 1988.
Wise Poison (poetry), Graywolf Press (St. Paul, MN), 1996.

Contributor to periodicals, including *Ploughshares* and *Poetry.*

SIDELIGHTS: With his first verse collection, *Torque,* David Rivard distinguished himself as a writer of volatile poems with striking imagery. In this work Rivard concentrates on the working-class tenor. Fast automobiles, assembly lines, basketball games, and drug users are all developed to tell the stories of childhood, relationships, and life that are prominent in Rivard's work, along with a sense of despair and an awareness of life's hardships. His work, however, is not entirely downbeat. Concerned parents and committed lovers are also recognized, though they are not, perhaps, as widespread as are more disturbing elements of human nature and life. And though the author concedes in his discourse that good does exist along with evil, his characters in *Torque* display a "psychological paralysis," according to a *Booklist* reviewer, and are resolutely affixed in their barely tolerable lives. He creates, said a *Publishers Weekly* critic, "dramatic tension" in depicting our human weaknesses.

Rivard followed *Torque* with *Wise Poison,* another award-winning volume of visceral, unsettling verses that prompted some critics to hail him as a distinctive and compelling poet. Although Rivard has published only two books, he has won impressive recognition for his work. Among his awards are both the Agnes Lynch Starrett Poetry Prize and the Academy of American Poets's James Laughlin Award.

BIOGRAPHICAL/CRITICAL SOURCES:

PERIODICALS

Booklist, October 1, 1988, p. 214.
Boston Review, February/March, 1997.
Publishers Weekly, August 26, 1988.

OTHER

Amazon.com (website), April 7, 1997.

*   *   *

ROBERTS, (Ray) Clayton (Jr.) 1923-

PERSONAL: Born November 10, 1923, in Changsha, China; son of Ray Clayton (a nonprofit organization secretary) and Eva (a merchant; maiden name, Rewalt) Roberts; married Margaret Anne Vail (an occupational therapist), 1952; children: Cecily Holloway Roberts Selling, Robert Geoffrey Roberts

Donjacour, Cathy Denshaw, David Dylan. *Ethnicity:* "White." *Education:* Attended Whitman College, 1941-43, 1946; University of Washington, Seattle, B.A., 1947, M.A., 1948; attended University of Glasgow, 1949-50, and Institute of Historical Research, London, 1950-51; Cornell University, Ph.D., 1952. *Politics:* Democrat. *Avocational interests:* Tennis, ice dancing, hiking, wind surfing.

ADDRESSES: Home—R.R.1, Miller Lake, Ontario, Canada N0H 1Z0; (winters) 26 Ridgmount St., London WC1E 7AA, England.

CAREER: Ohio State University, Columbus, instructor, 1952-56, assistant professor, 1956-61, associate professor, 1961-66, professor of history, 1966-91. Columbus Figure Skating Club, president, 1970-72.

MEMBER: North American Conference on British Studies (president of Midwestern Conference, 1984), American Historical Association, Samuel Johnson Society, Royal Historical Society (fellow), Ohio Academy of History.

AWARDS, HONORS: Award for best historical work, Ohio Academy of History, 1966, for *The Growth of Responsible Government in Stuart England;* senior fellow, National Endowment for the Humanities, 1987.

WRITINGS:

The Growth of Responsible Government in Stuart England (first volume of a trilogy), Cambridge University Press (Cambridge, England), 1966.
A History of England, Volume I, Prentice-Hall (Englewood Cliffs, NJ), 1980, 3rd edition, 1991.
(Contributor) Stephen Baxter, editor, *England's Rise to Greatness,* University of California Press (Berkeley), 1983.
Schemes and Undertakings: A Study of English Politics in the Seventeenth Century (second volume of a trilogy), Ohio State University Press (Columbus), 1985.
The Logic of Historical Explanation, Pennsylvania State University Press (University Park), 1996.

Contributor to scholarly journals, including *Albion, Historical Journal, Journal of British Studies, Journal of Modern History, English Historical Review,* and *American Historical Review.*

WORK IN PROGRESS: The Struggle for the Sceptre: A Study of Politics in Eighteenth Century Britain, the third volume of a trilogy.

SIDELIGHTS: Clayton Roberts told *CA:* "I had the good fortune to be an antediluvian scholar, by which I mean that I received my first university appointment before the publish-or-perish flood washed over the campuses of America. I did not need to write a book in order to gain tenure; I already had it. Why then did I write one? Probably for three reasons: I had something to say, I enjoy writing, and I wanted to be famous. I wrote my second book because the history editor of Prentice-Hall asked me to. I agreed less for the money (the royalties are modest) than to force myself to bring up to date my lectures on the history of England for my students at Ohio State University. I wrote my third book to develop a theme—the importance of parliamentary undertaking in achieving responsible government—that had emerged out of my first book.

"The genesis of my fourth book occurred in the following manner. In 1962 I gave an informal seminar in the philosophy of history to a group of interested graduate students. In the course of that seminar I suddenly saw that the positivists, who advocated the covering-law model of explanation, failed to see that no historian ever used it at the macro-level (the level of wars, revolutions, depressions, enlightenments) but that the humanists, who rejected the covering-law model, failed to see that all historians use covering laws at the micro-level (to connect discrete events in a historical narrative). The seminar having come to an end, I said to myself, 'Surely, some philosopher will see this.' Twenty years later none had, so I wrote a book setting forth that key insight into the nature of historical explanation.

"The most important influence on my work has been the Whig historians whom I read in college and graduate school, historians such as C. H. Firth, G. M. Trevelyan, and S. R. Gardiner, as well as more recent historians such as Wallace Notestein, Conyers Read, and David Harris Wilson. Bred in such a school, I have remained skeptical of revisionists such as Sir Lewis Namier and Conrad Russell. Cleansed of its exaggerations, romanticism, and naivete, the Whig interpretation of history offers a truer account of the past than the rampant revisionism of the Namierites and Russellites. The corpus of my work seeks to show this.

"In 1949 and 1950 I spent a year at Glasgow University on an exchange scholarship. I spent much of the year searching for a subject for my doctoral dissertation. After several false starts, I finally seized on a suggestion that some scholar should correlate all the impeachments voted by the English Parliament in the seventeenth century. Halfway through my researches on these impeachments, I realized that my interest was not in the law of impeachment, but in the use of impeachment to enforce responsible government; that is, government by ministers responsible to Parliament. This was in 1951. Ever since, for nearly fifty years, I have written articles and books on the growth of responsible government in England. I am still doing so."

* * *

RODEN, Claudia

PERSONAL: Born in Cairo, Egypt.

ADDRESSES: Home—London, England.

CAREER: Cookbook writer. British Broadcasting Corporation, London, host of television cooking series.

WRITINGS:

A Book of Middle Eastern Food, illustrated by Edward Bawden, Nelson (London), 1968, illustrated by Alta Anne Parkins, Knopf (New York City), 1972.

Coffee, Faber (London), 1977, published as *Coffee: A Connoisseur's Companion,* Random House (New York City), 1994.

Everything Tastes Better Outdoors, illustrated by Parkins, Knopf, 1984, revised edition, Wings Books (Avenael, NJ), 1995.

A New Book of Middle Eastern Food, Viking (New York City), 1985.

Mediterranean Cookery, Knopf, 1987.

The Good Food of Italy, Region by Region, Knopf, 1990.

The Book of Jewish Food: An Odyssey from Samarkand to New York, Knopf, 1996.

Invitation to Mediterranean Cooking, Rizzoli (New York City), 1997.

SIDELIGHTS: Claudia Roden, a resident of London, was born and raised in Egypt. She started her cook-

book writings in 1968 with *A Book of Middle Eastern Food,* which not only presented hundreds of recipes, but also included extensive notes on their origins and interpretations. The book has been recommended by numerous reviewers over the years. An enlarged, 1985 edition is described by Derek Cooper in the *Listener* as "beautifully written and as aromatically tempting as a walk through the spice stalls of an Arab souk." Reviewing the volume for *Books,* broadcaster Denis Curtis lauded the paperback version as "more stylish." He also related his first encounter with Roden in the sixties, after she immigrated to London. Roden's tales of her life in the Middle East and tales of her childhood food eventually served as the basis of a British Broadcasting Corporation series.

In 1977 Roden again drew from old memories with her book, *Coffee.* Victoria Glendinning, writing for the *Times Literary Supplement,* praised the fifty pages of historical details, from the "gamier and muskier" coffee of the first coffee-house in Oxford, England, in 1650, to Roden's remarks about modern instant coffee, where "the poorer blends find oblivion." A *Publishers Weekly* reviewer found *Coffee* to "be a treat for the real coffee lover" with a wealth of coffee lore and recipes for food to accompany the beverage.

The English edition of *Everything Tastes Better Outdoors* was written in 1984 and revised in 1995 after Roden came to the United States to study outdoor cooking in America. Phyllis Hanes, in the *Christian Science Monitor,* summarized the new book: "Iranian omelets, Japanese lunch boxes, and English tea on the lawn are described along with beanhole baked beans, hush puppies, New England clambakes, and barbecue recipes from Texas and India." This is similar to the original book, which had been commended by Charles Monaghan in the *Washington Post Book World* for its "daffy and garrulous air" and sentimentality, which he felt was a far cry from American cookbooks which are simply crammed with recipes.

Mediterranean Cookery, published in 1987, is a guide to the many recipes gathered by Roden for her television series in London. A *Christian Science Monitor* reviewer noted that the cookbook delves beyond the typical recipes associated with the Mediterranean region also including classics such as calzones and meat and fruit stews.

In 1990, *Book World* food editor and reviewer Monaghan reproved Roden in another of her books,

The Good Food of Italy, Region by Region, for recommending a raw shellfish dish popular with Ligurians, "without a peep about their subsequent hurried visits to the gastroenterologist." Despite feeling that Roden's recipes romanticize the cooking of generations gone by in which women had the time and inclination to prepare pasta from scratch, Monaghan commended the wealth of information about the dishes and the easy-to-prepare recipes. Angela Carter, writing for *New Statesman and Society,* called the volume "visually voluptuous" and appreciated the Italian atmosphere infused in the book.

The Book of Jewish Food: An Odyssey from Samarkand to New York, published in 1996, "chronicles the lives of Jews all over the world in short segments on unusual Jewish communities past and present," explained a *Publishers Weekly* reviewer, citing groups in Salonika, Greece, and China as examples. *Booklist* critic Mark Knoblauch felt that the was a definitive book of Jewish cooking throughout history and remarked that the book is a "masterful historical, sociological, religious, and culinary compendium of Jewish eating habits." Judith C. Sutton of *Library Journal* concurred that Roden's "exhaustively researched and impressive new book is obviously a labor of love." Besides writing intriguing cookbooks, Roden gives cooking lessons in her London home as well as in cities around the world.

BIOGRAPHICAL/CRITICAL SOURCES:

BOOKS

Roden, Claudia, *Coffee,* Nelson, 1977.
Roden, Claudia, *The Good Food of Italy, Region by Region,* Knopf, 1990.

PERIODICALS

Booklist, February 15, 1973, p. 544; May 15, 1984, p. 1284; October 15, 1987, p. 354; November 15, 1990, p. 589; December 15, 1996, p. 702.
Books, July, 1987, p. 12; Jun,e 1989, pp. 8-9.
Books and Bookmen, January, 1969, p. 52.
Books of the Times, August, 1980, p. 383.
Changing Times, November, 1982, p. 65.
Christian Science Monitor, October 31, 1984, p. 24; December 11, 1987, p. 24.
Kirkus Review, July 1, 1972, p. 784; April 15, 1984, p. 416; September 15, 1987, p. 1385; September 15, 1990, p. 1319; January 15, 1992, p. 108.

Library Journal, August 1972, p. 2600; May 15, 1984, p. 982; October 15, 1990, p. 100; December 1996, p. 135.
Listener, December 12, 1985, p. 16; December 11, 1986, p. 16; December 6, 1990, p. 36.
Ms., February, 1980, pp. 54-55.
New Statesman and Society, November 24, 1989, pp. 32-33.
New York Times Book Review, December 3, 1972, p. 96; December 6, 1987, p. 38.
Observer (London), November 29, 1981, p. 27; November 30, 1986, p. 21.
Publishers Weekly, December 26, 1977, p. 63; April 20, 1984, p. 76; September 18, 1987, p. 173; September 21, 1990, p. 71; January 4, 1991, p. 37; October 25, 1991, p. 60; November 4, 1996, p. 73.
Punch, July, 1987, p. 69.
Saturday Review, December 2, 1972, p. 82.
Spectator, December 20/27, 1986, pp. 56-57; December 1, 1990, p. 48.
Times Literary Supplement, December 2, 1977, p. 1404.
Washington Post Book World, July 8, 1973, p. 8; July 29, 1984, p. 3; December 2, 1990, p. 14.*

* * *

ROHLFS, Anna Katharine Green
See GREEN, Anna Katharine

* * *

ROJANY, Lisa
(Adriana Gabriel)

PERSONAL: Born February 14, in Los Angeles, CA; daughter of Avi Rojany and Mary Marks. *Education:* University of California, Los Angeles, B.A. (magna cum laude), 1986; Sorbonne, Universite de Paris, and Alliance Francaise, Translation Certificate and Diplome des Hautes Etudes en Francais, 1987; Brown University, M.A., 1989.

ADDRESSES: Office—Gateway Learning Corp., c/o Rosewood Capital, 1 Maritime Plaza, San Francisco, CA 94111. *E-mail*—lrojany@aol.com.

CAREER: Triangle Publications, Los Angeles, CA, writer and editor for *TV Guide,* 1987-88; Brown

Daily Herald Newspaper Services, Providence, RI, staff editor, 1989; Ligature, Inc., Boston, MA, textbook editor, 1989-90; Intervisual Books, Inc., Santa Monica, CA, senior editor, 1991-93; Price Stern Sloan, Inc., Los Angeles, editorial director, 1993-97; Gateway Learning Corp., San Francisco, CA, editorial director, 1997—. Also works as a freelance writer and editor, including ghostwriter for other authors; public speaker.

MEMBER: International Women's Writing Guild, PEN Center USA West, Society of Children's Book Writers and Illustrators, Women's National Book Association (Los Angeles chapter), National Writers Club (Los Angeles chapter), Book Publicists Club of Southern California, Phi Beta Kappa.

AWARDS, HONORS: King Arthur's Camelot was a Book-of-the-Month Club selection; *Exploring the Human Body* was named among "Ten Best New Parenting Books," *Child,* 1993; *Giant Animal Fold-Outs* books were included in *American Bookseller* "Pick of the List," 1995.

WRITINGS:

The Hands-on Book of Big Machines, illustrated by Joel Snyder, Little, Brown (Boston, MA), 1992.

(With Stacie Strong) *Exploring the Human Body,* illustrated by Linda Hill Griffith, Barron's, 1992.

(Adapter) *King Arthur's Camelot* (pop-up), four volumes, illustrated by Laszlo Batki, Dutton, 1993.

The Story of Hanukkah, illustrated by Holly Jones, Hyperion, 1993.

Where's That Pig?, illustrated by John Wallner, Price Stern Sloan, 1993.

Santa's New Suit, illustrated by Mike Lester, Price Stern Sloan, 1993.

Jake and Jenny on the Town, illustrated by Barney Saltzberg, Price Stern Sloan, 1993.

Mr. Bump, illustrated by Adam Hargreaves, Price Stern Sloan, 1993.

Mr. Funny, illustrated by Hargreaves, Price Stern Sloan, 1993.

Mr. Silly, illustrated by Hargreaves, Price Stern Sloan, 1993.

Walt Disney's Alice in Wonderland: Down the Rabbit Hole, illustrated by Robbin Cuddy, Disney Press, 1994.

Token of Love, illustrated with antique changing pictures by Ernest Nister, Philomel, 1994.

Spring Gardens, illustrated with antique changing pictures by Nister, Philomel, 1994.

Mickey Mouse: Where's the Picnic?, Mouse Works, 1994.

Winnie the Pooh: The Surprise Party, Mouse Works, 1994.

(With Craig Walker) *Make Your Own Valentines,* illustrated by Wendy All, Price Stern Sloan, 1994.

(Compiler) *Birthday Celebrations,* illustrated by Kathy Hendrickson, Andrews & McMeel, 1994.

(Compiler) *Cats: Those Wonderful Creatures,* illustrated by Kathy Mitchell, Andrews & McMeel, 1994.

(Compiler) *Flowers for My Friend,* illustrated by Karen Lidbeck, Andrews & McMeel, 1994.

(Compiler) *Friendship: What You Mean to Me,* illustrated by Mitchell, Andrews & McMeel, 1994.

(Compiler) *Thoughts for a Sunny Day,* illustrated by Mitchell, Andrews & McMeel, 1994.

(Compiler) *Wedding Sentiments,* illustrated by Gwen Connelly, Andrews & McMeel, 1994.

Melvin Martian, illustrated by David Crossley, Price Stern Sloan, 1995.

Dena Dinosaur, illustrated by Crossley, Price Stern Sloan, 1995.

Morty Monster, illustrated by Crossley, Price Stern Sloan, 1995.

Wanda Witch, illustrated by Crossley, Price Stern Sloan, 1995.

Casper: The Junior Novelization (based on the screenplay by Sherri Stoner and Deanna Oliver), Price Stern Sloan, 1995.

Dumbo's Circus Train: A Rolling Wheels Book, Mouse Works, 1995.

Cinderella's Coach: A Rolling Wheels Book, Mouse Works, 1995.

Kangaroo and Company (fold-out book), illustrated by Cristina Mesturini and Tranquillini, Price Stern Sloan, 1995.

Hippo and Pals (Giant Animal Fold-Outs), illustrated by Michele Tranquillini, Gianni Ronco, and Elena Rozzo, Price Stern Sloan, 1995.

(Reteller) *The Magic Feather: A Jamaican Legend,* illustrated by Philip Kuznicki, Troll Associates, 1995.

Tell Me about When I Was a Baby, illustrated by K. A. Bickle, Price Stern Sloan, 1996.

Gold Diggers: The Secret of Bear Mountain (based on the screenplay by Barry Glasser), Price Stern Sloan, 1996.

(Under pseudonym Adriana Gabriel) *Dragonheart: The Junior Novelization,* Price Stern Sloan, 1996.

Big Trucks and Bigger Diggers (fold-out book), Price Stern Sloan, 1996.

Giant Giants and Magic Mermaids (fold-out book), Price Stern Sloan, 1996.
Leave It to Beaver: The Novelization (based on the screenplay by Brian Levant and Lon Diamond), Price Stern Sloan, 1997.

Author of two books in the series "Code Blue: In the Emergency Room," HarperCollins, 1996; author of *Making the Grade,* 1997. Author of *Pandora's Box* and *Over in the Meadow* (CD-ROM books for children), Rose Studios, 1995. *Center: Publication of PEN Center USA West,* editor in chief, 1992-95, then member of editorial board; member of editorial staff, *Clerestory: Brown/RISD Journal of the Arts* and *Hwaet! Graduate Journal of Medieval Studies,* 1989; founding editor, *Together,* 1985-86.

WORK IN PROGRESS: She-Pirate, the first title for a proposed adventure series for girls.

SIDELIGHTS: Lisa Rojany commented: "I was born and grew up in Los Angeles. After college, where I wrote for newspapers and a women's news magazine, I spent three years in New England going to graduate school at Brown. There I free-lanced at various publishing houses in Boston and embarked upon my children's book writing and editorial career.

"I have had over thirty children's books published, both fiction and nonfiction. My favorite projects are the ones for which I have conceived paper engineering/interactive elements as well as text, such as *The Hands-On Book of Big Machines, The Story of Hanukkah,* and *Tell Me about When I Was a Baby.* I have also written quote books, pop-up books, books about animals and machines, board books, original YA novels, movie tie-in novelizations—you name it, I'm willing to try it.

"The most impressive-*looking* book that I wrote was an Intervisual Books package called *King Arthur's Camelot.* The artist for this project—an oversized book with a huge pop-up castle and four storybooks based on the King Arthur legend—was Hungarian and, although we had trouble understanding one another, we communicated so well that, with the help of the designer, the end result was something very exciting.

"I also wrote two interactive CD-ROM titles for children, *Over in the Meadow* and *Pandora's Box.* Because the story lines are nonlinear, I had to relearn what it means to tell a story, while helping the animators and 'techies' learn how a story must be a larger total than the sum of its parts. Writing animation sequences is the zaniest experience, because the writer gets to translate visual humor and drama into words and then watch them transmogrify back into moving visual images. For someone who has a facility with words but absolutely no hands-on artistic talent, that's quite an experience.

"What I like most about writing for children is that there are very few *real* boundaries. Kids don't see limitations like we do, and I love being in the imaginative place where children live, a place where anything is possible. The world becomes a place with an infinite amount of adventure just waiting to happen."

BIOGRAPHICAL/CRITICAL SOURCES:

PERIODICALS

Horn Book Guide, spring, 1995, p. 53.
Learning, March, 1995, p. 43.
Publishers Weekly, September 20, 1993, p. 32.

*   *   *

RORBY, Ginny   1944-
   (Virginia Rorby Oesterle)

PERSONAL: Born August 9, 1944, in Washington, DC; adopted daughter of Noel (in sales) and Kathryn (a homemaker; maiden name, Loonan) Rorby; married Stan Clarke, August 29, 1964 (marriage ended, December 29, 1965); married Douglas Oesterle (an accountant), May 22, 1971 (separated, 1980); stepchildren: Robert A., Mark W. *Education:* University of Miami, FL, A.B. (biology and English), 1985; Florida International University, M.F.A. (creative writing), 1991. *Politics:* Democrat. *Avocational interests:* Wildlife photography, kayaking, canoeing, travel.

ADDRESSES: Home and office—Fort Bragg, CA. *Agent*—Barbara Kouts, P.O. Box 558, Bellport, NY 11713.

CAREER: National Airlines (later Pan American Airways), Miami, FL, flight attendant, 1966-89; writer. Chair, Glass Beach Access Committee; member, Leadership Mendocino.

MEMBER: National Audubon Society (president, Mendocino Coast chapter), Phi Kappa Phi.

AWARDS, HONORS: Keystone to Reading Book Award nomination, Keystone State Reading Association, 1997, for *Dolphin Sky.*

WRITINGS:

Dolphin Sky (juvenile novel), Putnam (New York City), 1996.

WORK IN PROGRESS: At Home in the Dark, a fictionalized memoir; *Without Voices,* a young adult novel; a natural history of the Mendocino coast.

SIDELIGHTS: Ginny Rorby commented: "I was born in the Florence Crittenton Home for unwed mothers in Washington, D.C. My birth mother was forced to care for me for about three months, throughout the adoption process. I was adopted by Kathryn and Noel Rorby, who lived in Detroit at the time. When I was two, we moved to Maitland, Florida. I have always loved animals. Before we left Detroit, I got my head stuck between the bars of the lions' cage at the Detroit Zoo.

"I lived the next twenty years in central Florida, first in Maitland in the house that is now the headquarters of the Florida Audubon Society, then in Winter Park. By the time I was four, it was discovered that I had a weak muscle in my right eye, which caused it to turn inward when I was tired. The doctors tried a patch, then glasses. All through school, my greatest fear was being called on to read aloud in class. I barely got out of high school.

"I excelled at nothing as a youngster. I was a moderately good swimmer, singer, and painter, but I started smoking when I was fifteen, ruining my chances at two out of three, and I lost interest in painting. I attended a junior college in Orlando, where I was admitted on academic probation. I took remedial English three times before I finally received a 'D.' I still can't diagram a sentence.

"In 1964 I married to get away from home. The marriage lasted eleven months, and only that long because I felt guilty about the wedding gifts. In 1966 I was hired by National Airlines as a 'stewardess.' Pan American Airways bought the company in 1980. I flew for twenty-three years. It was a wonderful life for about the first fifteen, then I began to feel trapped. In 1977, when I went back to school, it was

with the intention of someday becoming a veterinarian. As it worked out, it took me eight years to get my undergraduate degree. By the time I graduated, I had begun to write.

"That I am now a writer was an accident. Until August, 1982, I had only written a couple of searing letters, one to a store owner in Orlando who had fired a former co-worker with breast cancer, and one to an eye doctor who went to a patient's deathbed to collect his fee. Some time in 1981, a friend of mine (who did become a vet) found a starving dog. Maggots were already consuming its flesh. When I came home from a trip, she had gained its trust. We collected every sleeping pill and valium that we had between us, drugged the dog, took it to a vet, and had it put to sleep. The first thing I ever wrote, aside from those letters, was about that dog.

"A year later, I found the 'story' stuffed in the side pocket of my uniform purse. It made my heart hurt all over again, so I typed it and took it to the smaller of our two Miami newspapers. They published 'We Found Your Dog' in 1982. An editor called me at home and said, 'If you can write like that, we will publish anything you write.' Of course, I couldn't. It would be years before I found my way back to writing about what knots my guts. In the interim, I started taking writing courses and ended up with an M.F.A. in creative writing. In 1991 I moved to the north coast of California. *Dolphin Sky* was sold five days before my fiftieth birthday."

Dolphin Sky tells the story of twelve-year-old Buddy, who empathizes with the mistreated dolphins she sees in a cut-rate tourist show near her Florida home. Buddy herself feels neglected by her single father and confused and "dumb" in school. She has the love and respect of her elderly grandfather, however, and with his help and that of a new biologist friend, she grows in self-esteem. She learns that she is not stupid but has a learning disability, and she comes up with a plan to free her mistreated dolphin friends. Buddy's boating trips with her grandfather "bring suspense, and the theme of our inhumane treatment of other mammals adds substance and tenderness," Susan DeRonne noted in *Booklist.* While *School Library Journal* contributor Susan Oliver found some of the events implausible, she praised Rorby's "sensitively drawn" characters and her "provocatively and emotionally discussed" treatment of animal rights. As a *Publishers Weekly* reviewer concluded, "convincingly portrayed relationships, a deeply moving plot," and interesting detail on the Florida Everglades "combine to make this debut a real winner."

BIOGRAPHICAL/CRITICAL SOURCES:

PERIODICALS

Booklist, March 1, 1996, p. 1184.
Publishers Weekly, March 25, 1996, p. 85.
School Library Journal, April, 1996, p. 140.

*   *   *

ROSEN, Leora N(adine) 1950-

PERSONAL: Born January 16, 1950, in South Africa; naturalized U.S. citizen, 1984; daughter of Abraham and Miriam (a teacher; maiden name, Kahnevsky) Rosen; married Norman Rosenthal, 1974 (divorced, 1983), remarried, July 21, 1986; children: Joshua. *Ethnicity:* "White, Jewish." *Education:* University of the Witwatersrand, Ph.D., 1976; Columbia University, M.P.H., 1980. *Religion:* Jewish.

ADDRESSES: Home—11110 Stephalee Lane, Rockville, MD 20852.

CAREER: University of the Witwatersrand, Johannesburg, South Africa, lecturer in social anthropology, 1974-75; New York State Psychiatric Institute, research assistant in lithium clinic, 1977-78, research assistant in child psychiatry, 1978; Psychiatric Institutes of Washington, DC, research assistant, 1981-85; Walter Reed Army Institute of Research, research social scientist in Department of Military Psychiatry, 1985—.

AWARDS, HONORS: Department of the Army, Certificate of Customer Service Excellence, 1993, Certificate of Achievement, 1995.

WRITINGS:

(With Michelle Etlin) *The Hostage Child: Sex Abuse Allegations in Custody Disputes,* Indiana University Press (Bloomington), 1996.

Contributor of more than fifty articles to professional journals, including *African Studies, Journal of Affective Disorders, The Anthropology of the Body,* *Archives of General Psychiatry, Biological Psychiatry, Journal of Nervous and Mental Disease, American Journal of Psychiatry, Southern Medical Journal, The Psychoanalytic Study of Society, Acta-Psychiatica Scandinavica, Behavioral Medicine, Military Medicine, Psychiatry Research, Psychology of Women Quarterly, Journal of Applied Psychology, Journal of Applied Social Psychology, Child Abuse and Neglect, Journal of Occupational Health Psychology, Journal of Traumatic Stress, Sex Roles, Armed Forces and Society, Military Psychology, Women's Health Journal,* and *Violence against Women.*

SIDELIGHTS: Leora N. Rosen told *CA:* "I became interested in child sexual abuse as a result of the Elizabeth Morgan case. Dr. Morgan spent two years in jail without having been tried and convicted of any crime. In apartheid South Africa, where I grew up, imprisonment without trial was commonly practiced as a method of coercing political dissidents to stop criticizing the government and to stop trying to effect change in a corrupt and evil system. Outside South Africa, imprisonment without trial was regarded as a human rights violation. It was no less a human rights violation in Dr. Morgan's case, but in the land of the free and the brave, it was not recognized as such. That this could happen in a country that prides itself on its human rights record appalled me, but also compelled me to conduct the research that eventually led me to write *The Hostage Child.*"

*   *   *

ROSENKRANZ, E. Joshua 1961-

PERSONAL: Born December 3, 1961, in New York, NY; son of Herbert S. (a scientist) and Deanna (an artist; maiden name, Green) Rosenkranz; married Sydney Martin, June 6, 1997. *Education:* Attended Columbia University, 1979-81; Case Western Reserve University, B.A. (summa cum laude), 1983; Georgetown University, J.D. (magna cum laude), 1986.

ADDRESSES: Home—55 Liberty St., No. 11-A, New York, NY 10005. *Office*—Brennan Center for Justice, New York University, 161 Avenue of the Americas, New York, NY 10013; fax 212-995-4550. *E-mail*—joshua.rosenkranz@nyu.edu. *Agent*—F. Joseph Spieler, 154 West 57th St., 13th Floor, Room 135, New York, NY 10019.

CAREER: U.S. Court of Appeals for the District of Columbia Circuit, law clerk, 1986-87; Supreme Court of the United States, Washington, DC, law clerk to Justice William J. Brennan Jr., 1987-88; Office of the Appellate Defender, founding attorney in charge, 1988-96, vice president, 1988-92, president and chief executive officer, 1992-96; New York University, New York City, founding president and executive director of Brennan Center for Justice, 1994—. Training and Resources for Assigned Counsel, Inc., member of board of directors, 1990-91. Speaker at colleges and universities, including University of Connecticut, Yale University, and School for the Visual Arts.

MEMBER: New York State Association of Criminal Defense Lawyers (chairperson of Strategic Litigation Committee, 1992-93; co-chairperson of Committee on Ethics, 1992-93), New York State Defenders Association, Association of the Bar of the City of New York, Phi Beta Kappa.

AWARDS, HONORS: First Annual Scribes Brief-Writing Award, 1993; New York State Bar Association Award, outstanding contribution to the delivery of defense services, 1995; named among forty-five top public sector lawyers under forty-five, *American Lawyer,* 1997.

WRITINGS:

A Practitioner's Guide to Harmless Error, New York State Defenders Association, 1991.
(Editor, with B. Schwartz) *Reason and Passion: Justice Brennan's Enduring Influence,* Norton (New York City), 1997.

Author of the books (with M. Gimpel) *A Guide to Criminal Appeals,* 1995; *Voter Choice '96: A Fifty-State Report Card on the Presidential Elections,* 1996; and (with R. Winger) *What Choice Do We Have?,* 1997. Contributor to periodicals, including *Hastings Law Journal, Cancer Research, Mutation Research, Nation, Boston Review, Nova Law Journal,* and *Capital Defender Manual.*

* * *

ROSIS, Brendan
 See TILLY, Chris

ROSS, Donald H. 1928-

PERSONAL: Born August 30, 1928, in Jerome, ID; married, 1955; children: five. *Education:* University of Oregon, B.A., 1952, M.A., 1955; University of Colorado, Ph.D., 1963.

ADDRESSES: Office—Department of English, Washington State University, Pullman, WA 99163.

CAREER: Washington State University, Pullman, WA, assistant professor, 1961-73, associate professor of English, 1973—. *Military service:* U.S. Army, Signal Corps, 1952-54.

AWARDS, HONORS: Summer grant for humanities studies, 1968.

WRITINGS:

The Black Bull, Sage Publications (Thousand Oaks, CA), 1967.
Writer vs. Reader, Writer's Digest Books (Cincinnati, OH), 1972.
The Writing Performance, Lippincott (Philadelphia, PA), 1973.*

* * *

ROTH, Gerhard (Jurgen) 1942-

PERSONAL: Born June 24, 1942, in Graz, Austria; son of Emile (a doctor) and Erna (Druschnitz) Roth; married Erika Wolfgruber, September 16, 1963 (divorced, 1986); married Senta Thonhauser, 1995; children: Eva, Petra, Thomas. *Education:* Attended University of Graz Medical School, 1961-67.

ADDRESSES: Home—Am Heumarkt 714137, N030 Wien, Austria.

CAREER: Writer and photographer. Graz Center for Statistics, Styria, Austria, computer operator, then manager, 1966-77; freelance writer, 1978—.

AWARDS, HONORS: State of Styria Literaturpreis, Austria, 1972, 1973, 1976; Kritikerpreis, Southwestern Broadcasting System (Baden/Baden, Germany), 1978; fellowship from City of Hamburg, Germany, 1979-80; Alfrid Doeblin Prize, 1983; Silver Bear award, Berlin Film Festival, 1982, for film production of *Der stille Ozean;* wuerdigungspreis, Bundes

Ministeriums fuer Unterricht und Kunst, 1990; Marie Luise Kaschnitz Prize, Literary Prize of Vienna, and Manuscripte Prize, all 1992.

WRITINGS:

FICTION; "DIE ARCHIVE DES SCHWEIGENS" SERIES

Der stille Ozean, Fischer (Frankfurt), 1980, translated by Helga Schreckenberger and Jacqueline Vansant as *The Calm Ocean,* Ariadne Press (Riverside, CA), 1993.

Landlaufiger Tod, Fischer, 1984, portions translated as *Between Heaven and Earth* in *Black Letters,* Atlas Press (London), 1989.

Am Abgrund, Fischer, 1986.

Der Untersuchungsrichter: Die Geschichte eines Entwurfs, Fischer, 1988.

Im tiefen Oesterreich (photographs), Fischer, 1990.

Die Geschichte der Dunkelheit: Ein Barracked, Fischer, 1991.

Eine Reise in das Innere von Wien, Fischer, 1991.

FICTION; OTHER

Die Autobiographie des Albert Einstein (novel), Suhrkamp (Frankfurt am Main), 1972, translated as *The Autobiography of Albert Einstein,* Atlas Press, 1993.

Der Ausbruch des Ersten Weltkriegs und andere Romane (stories), Suhrkamp, 1972.

Der Wille zur Krankheit (novel), Suhrkamp, 1973.

Herr Mantel und Herr Hemd (for children), Insel (Frankfurt am Main), 1974.

Der grosse Horizont (novel), Suhrkamp, 1974.

Ein neuer Morgen (novel), Suhrkamp, 1976.

Winterreise (novel), Fischer, 1978, translated by Joachim Neugroschl, Farrar Strauss (New York City), 1980.

Menschen, Bilder, Marionetten (collected works), Fischer, 1979.

Circus Saluti (novel), Fischer, 1981.

Die schoenen Bilder beim Trabrennen, Fischer, 1982.

Das Toeten des Bussards, Droschl (Graz), 1982.

Dorfchronik zum "Landlaufiger Tod," Fischer, 1984.

Die Vergessenen (novel), Fischer, 1986.

Das doppelkoepfige Oesterreich, S. Fischer, 1995.

PLAYS

Lichtenberg (Graz, 1973), Autoren (Frankfurt am Main), 1973.

Sehnsucht (Graz, 1977), Fischer, 1977.

Daemmerung (Graz, 1978), Suhrkamp-Theaterverlag, 1977.

Erinnerungen an die Menschheit (Graz, 1985), Droschl, 1985.

Also author of television plays, including *Beobachtungen in Amerika—Ankuft,* 1976; *Der grosse Horizont* (adapted by Roth from his novel), 1976; *Der stille Ozean* (adapted by Roth from his novel), 1982; *Der Bien,* 1990; and *Das Geheimnis,* 1992. Author of radio plays, including *In Groenland,* 1977; *Die Unmoeglichkeit der Naturwissenshaften,* 1985; and *Ein Schneetag,* 1987.

OTHER

(With Konrad R. Mueller and Peter Turrini) *Bruno Kreisky,* Nicolai (Berlin), 1981.

Grenzland, Hannibal (Wien), 1981.

Ueber Bienen, Jugend & Volk (Vienna), 1989.

Ueber Bilder: Oesterreichische Malerei seit 1945: Aus der Sammlung der Zentralsparkasse (nonfiction), Jugend & Volk, 1990.

(With Edith Hoerander and others) *Von Bienen und Imkern. von Wachs und vom Honig* (nonfiction), Brandstaetter (Wien), 1993.

SIDELIGHTS: Known for works of experimental fiction that focus on the isolation of individuals within an increasingly complex and dehumanizing society, Gerhard Roth has been hailed as one of Austria's most significant contemporary authors. The recipient of numerous awards throughout his career as a writer, Roth is noted both for novels and dramatic works, all of which break with stylistic and grammatical conventions. He has strived to, in the words of *Dictionary of Literary Biography* essayist Peter Ensberg, "escape traditional and systematic orders in language and thought and to open up new surrealistic ways of perceiving reality."

After his first novel, known in English as *The Autobiography of Albert Einstein,* was published in Austria in 1972, Roth was praised by critics as a writer of prodigious talent and as one of the foremost members of the avant-garde literary groups of Graz, "City Park Forum" and "Gathering of Graz Authors." In succeeding novels, the promising young writer's prose underwent a transformation: "Between 1967 and 1973 Roth's language became more economical, realistic, and impressive," noted Sigrid Bauschinger in the *Dictionary of Literary Biography.* In 1980 Roth published *Der stille Ozean* (translated in 1993 as *The Calm Ocean*), the first of a multi-part series of fiction that chronicles the history of modern Austria by straying into a surrealistic world full of metaphors pointing to the inscrutability of modern life. Death, insanity, paranoia, exploitation, and the powerlessness of the individual: these themes serve as common threads throughout the four novels in Roth's "Archive des Schweigens" (the story and history of his Austria), which includes along with *Der stille Ozean,* 1984's *Landlaufiger Tod* ("Common Death"), *Am Abgrund* ("On the Abyss") and *Der Untersuchungsrichter* ("The Investigating Judge"). The series also includes a volume of photographs *Im tiefen Osterreich,* and essay collections *Eine Reise in das Innere von Wien* and *Ein Bericht.*

Roth's dramatic works, which include *Daemmerung* ("Dawn") and *Sehnsucht,* drew mixed reactions from critics when they were first produced in the mid-1970s. In 1977's *Sehnsucht* ("Desire"), no consistent story line is apparent, a condition that is characteristic of Roth's other works for the stage. After his first three plays drew criticism from reviewers, Roth decided to concentrate on his prose fiction for several years. Then, in 1985, he returned to the stage with *Erinnerungen an die Menschheit* ("Recollections of Mankind"), which presents a dreamscape that "dispenses . . . with any semblance of a plot," according to Ensberg. "The often highly associative remarks of the characters cannot be explained by applying normal methods of interpretation," Ensberg explained. "Roth emphasizes the illogical and concentrates on fantastic, surrealistic phenomena." Although *Erinnerungen an die Menschheit* drew high praise for its depiction of the inadequacy of human reason and the scientific method, since its stage debut Roth has again returned his attention to his prose fiction, with occasional forays into writing for Austrian radio and television.

BIOGRAPHICAL/CRITICAL SOURCES:

BOOKS

Bauschinger, Sigrid, "Gerhard Roth," in *Dictionary of Literary Biography,* Volume 85: *Austrian Fiction Writers after 1914,* Gale (Detroit), 1989, pp. 263-269.
Ensberg, Peter, "Gerhard Roth," in *Dictionary of Literary Biography,* Volume 124: *Twentieth-Century German Dramatists, 1919-1992,* Gale, 1992, pp. 364-369.

PERIODICALS

German Quarterly, Vol. 54, 1981, pp. 427-446.
Voice Literary Supplement, May 1993, p. 27.
World Literature Today, summer 1992, pp. 505-506.

S

SAENZ, Benjamin Alire

PERSONAL: Male.

ADDRESSES: Office—Department of English, University of Texas, El Paso, 500 West University Ave., El Paso, TX 79968-8900.

CAREER: Writer. University of Texas, El Paso, teacher of creative writing.

AWARDS, HONORS: American Book Award from Before Columbus Foundation, 1992, for *Calendar of Dust.*

WRITINGS:

Calendar of Dust (poetry), Broken Moon Press, 1991.
Flowers for the Broken (short stories), Broken Moon Press, 1992.
Carry Me like Water (novel), Hyperion, 1995.
Dark and Perfect Angels (poetry), Cinco Puntos, 1995.
The House of Forgetting (novel), HarperCollins (New York City), 1997.

Contributor to periodicals.

SIDELIGHTS: Benjamin Alire Saenz is a poet and fiction writer who has won particular praise for his expressions of Mexican American life in the United States.

Saenz's first publication was *Calendar of Dust,* a collection of poems that articulate, as Roberto Bedoya stated in the *Hungry Mind Review,* the "ex-periences of injustice, both personal and social, specific to Native American and Mexican-Americans." Among the subjects of Saenz's poems are childhood, the mistreatment of Native Americans by the U.S. government, and the human capacity to overcome adversity. This debut volume includes the poems "Ring of Life," which concerns the author's vision of the birth-death-rebirth cycle, and "Walking," a complex work integrating a hymn to the earth with a chronicle of one individual's self-illuminating journey.

Calendar of Dust signified Saenz as an ambitious new poet. Bert Almon, writing in *Western American Literature,* cited what he saw as shortcomings in the author's style, but also declared that Saenz "appears to be an author with important, interesting stories to tell." Bedoya, in *Hungry Mind Review,* observed that "the momentum of Saenz's poems never escapes the predictable sadness that resounds throughout [*Calendar of Dust*]," but he also described Saenz as a poet whose work "is honest, economic and keen in the shaping of a poetry of lament."

In 1992 Saenz produced his second volume, the short-story collection *Flowers for the Broken.* These tales, set largely in the contemporary American southwest, concern Mexican Americans, but the themes of the stories are essentially universal. "Obliterate the Night," for example, is the story of a wealthy woman who regrets having rejected an impoverished but loving student in favor of a wealthier, but emotionally shallow man embodying the Anglo-Saxon cultural ties that she desired. And in the title tale, a young woman spends a day delivering flowers and comes to realize that she must break free from the influence of her man-hating mother and make her own decisions.

Paul J. Ferlazzo told *Western American Literature* readers that the title story in *Flowers for the Broken* is "a good example of Saenz's ability as an effective and moving storyteller," adding that "the same awareness and honesty about the complications and contradictions of life are present in every story."

Saenz followed *Flowers for the Broken* with his first novel, *Carry Me like Water,* which depicts a host of characters inhabiting the border town of El Paso, Texas. Included among the characters are Maria Elena, who has rejected her Mexican American culture and moved to California but who later returns home to find Diego, her deaf-mute brother; Diego himself, a poor laborer endlessly rewriting a suicide note; Elena's husband, Eddie, who is searching for his own long-lost brother, Jake, who has, in turn, been driven from the home of their wealthy but abusive parents; and Maria Elena's friend, Lizzie, who has been misled by her shamed adoptive parents into thinking she is Anglo-Saxon instead of Mexican American. Lizzie is able to periodically leave her body through astral projection. These and other characters, as Melita Marie Garza wrote in *Tribune Books,* "run around trying to figure out who they really are at the risk of losing something more dear than their country of residence: their souls."

Garza further described *Carry Me like Water* as "at once epic and fantastic in tone." She added that the novel is "strange and hot, but it is never dull, desolate or poor." Another reviewer, Norma E. Cantu, was likewise impressed, writing in the *Washington Post Book World* of Saenz's "evocative prose" and his "ability to tell a story using not one voice, but many." Cantu hailed *Carry Me like Water* as "a significant addition to the growing body of Chicano literature and to American literature in general."

In 1995 Saenz published a second verse collection, *Dark and Perfect Angels.* In this volume, the author once again writes of clashing Anglo-Saxon and Mexican American cultures in the American southwest.

BIOGRAPHICAL/CRITICAL SOURCES:

PERIODICALS

Booklist, September 1, 1991, p. 24; April 1, 1995, pp. 1378-1379.

Tribune Books (Chicago), August 20, 1995, p. 5.
Hungry Mind Review, fall, 1992, pp. 56, 59.
Los Angeles Times Book Review, August 23, 1992, p. 11.
Nation, June 7, 1993, pp. 772-774.
Publishers Weekly, January 23, 1995, p. 43; April 24, 1995, p. 57; July 31, 1995, p. 74.
Washington Post Book World, September 17, 1995, p. 10.
Western American Literature, November, 1992, pp. 275-276; February, 1994, pp. 366-367.*

* * *

SALVADORI, Mario (George) 1907-1997

OBITUARY NOTICE—See index for *CA* sketch: Born March 19, 1907, in Rome, Italy; came to the United States, 1939; naturalized U.S. citizen, 1944; died June 25, 1997, in Manhattan, NY. Engineer, educator, author. Salvadori was a successful structural engineer who made the study of architecture accessible to inner-city youths. Working with the New York Academy of Sciences, he taught the principles of building construction to Harlem and South Bronx junior high school students.

Born in Italy, Salvadori first taught at the University of Rome from 1933 to 1938, eventually escaping fascism in Italy in 1939 to come to the United States. He first worked for the Lionel Corporation as a time and motion engineer. In 1940 he began a lengthy association with Columbia University in New York City, first as a lecturer and ultimately as a professor of civil engineering and architecture. In 1975 he became a professor emeritus of architecture and the James Renwick Professor Emeritus of Civil Engineering. In addition to his duties as an educator, he served as vice president of the Industrial Products Trading Corporation from 1939 to 1942, as a consultant to the Manhattan Project from 1942 to 1944, and as consulting engineer to the firm of Paul Weidlinger. In 1962 he began three years as vice president of Advanced Computer Techniques Corporation and in 1963 he became a partner with Weidlinger Associates. He became honorary chairperson with Weidlinger Associates in 1991. His work with junior high school students began in 1975. That year also saw the establishment of the Salvadori Educational Center on Built Environment, which he chaired until 1991, becoming honorary chairperson in 1993. During his career he also found time to write. Among his books are *The Mathematical Solution of Engineering Problems, Numerical Methods in Engineering* (with Melvin L. Baron), *Differential Equations in Engineering Problems* (with Ralph J. Schwarz), *Structure in Architecture* (with Robert Heller), *Structural Design in Architecture* (with Matthys Levy), *Statics and Strength of Structures* (with Jeremiah Eck and Giuseppe de Campoli), *Building: The Fight against Gravity* (for children), and *Why Buildings Stand Up: The Strength of Architecture.* In addition, he translated verse by Emily Dickinson into the Italian language.

OBITUARIES AND OTHER SOURCES:

BOOKS

Who's Who in America, Marquis, 1996.

PERIODICALS

New York Times, June 28, 1997, p. 28.

*　　*　　*

SALYER, Lucy E.   1956-

PERSONAL: Born October 30, 1956, in IL; daughter of Oswald (a minister and teacher) and Frances Helen (a teacher; maiden name, Pyeatt) Salyer; married Lee Rubin (a mechanical designer), June 17, 1989; children: Nathanael, Naomi. *Education:* University of California, San Diego, B.A. (cum laude), 1979; University of California, Berkeley, M.A., 1983, Ph.D., 1989. *Politics:* Democrat. *Religion:* Methodist.

ADDRESSES: Office—Department of History, Horton Social Science Center, 20 College Rd., University of New Hampshire, Durham, NH 03824; fax 603-862-0178. *E-mail*—les@christa.unh.edu.

CAREER: California Judicial Council, San Francisco, research intern, 1982; University of California, Berkeley, research assistant, 1981-85, teaching assistant, 1983-86; Federal Litigation Assessment Project, U.S. District Court for the Northern District of California, San Francisco, research coordinator, 1985; University of New Hampshire, Durham, associate professor of history, 1989—, Gustafsen fellow at Center for the Humanities, 1996-97. New Hamp-

shire Bar Foundation, member of legal history committee, 1992.

MEMBER: Organization of American Historians (membership committee, 1992-96).

AWARDS, HONORS: Regents fellow, 1981-82, 1982-83; Distinguished Teaching Assistant Award, University of California, Berkeley, 1984; National Graduate Student fellowship, 1986-87; fellow of Bancroft Library and American Bar Foundation, both 1986-87; Jacob Javits fellow, 1987-88, 1988-89; Louis Pelzer Memorial Award, Organization of American Historians, 1988, for an essay; Northern District of California Prize, U.S. District Court, 1989, for an essay; grants from American Bar Association, 1990, and Judicial Conference of the United States, 1991; fellow, National Endowment for the Humanities, 1991-92; Theodore Saloutos Memorial Book Award in American Immigration History, 1996, for *Laws Harsh as Tigers.*

WRITINGS:

(Contributor) *Entry Denied: Exclusion and the Chinese Community in America, 1882-1943,* edited by Sucheng Chan, Temple University Press (Philadelphia, PA), 1991.
(Contributor) *Asian Immigrants and American Law: Historical and Contemporary Perspectives,* edited by Charles McClain, Garland Publishing (New York City), 1994.
Laws Harsh as Tigers: Chinese Immigrants and the Shaping of Modern Immigration Law, University of North Carolina Press (Chapel Hill), 1995.

Contributor of articles and reviews to academic journals, including *Law and History Review, Journal of the West, Journal of American History, Focus on Law Studies,* and *Legal Studies Forum.* Member of editorial board, *Law and History Review.*

WORK IN PROGRESS: "The History of the California Supreme Court: 1910-1949," for *The History of the California Supreme Court,* edited by Harry N. Scheiber.

*　　*　　*

SANDEEN, Ernest (Emanuel) 1908-1997

OBITUARY NOTICE—See index for *CA* sketch: Born December 15, 1908, in Warren County, IL; died

July 12, 1997, in South Bend, IN. Educator, poet, author. Sandeen devoted his career to teaching, first at Knox College in Galesburg, Illinois, as an English instructor beginning in 1935. After working at the University of Iowa from 1937 to 1943, he began a lengthy association with the University of Notre Dame in Indiana. After serving as an assistant professor, then as an associate professor, he became a full professor of English in 1960 and began heading the department in 1965. In all, his work at Notre Dame lasted fifty years; he became professor emeritus of American literature in 1976. That year he received the Sheedy Award from the College of Arts and Letters. In addition to his teaching, Sandeen wrote poetry. His verse was compiled in books such as *Antennas of Silence, Children and Older Strangers, Like Any Road Anywhere,* and *Collected Poems, 1953-1977.* He also contributed to volumes, including *Fifty Years of the American Novel* and *American Classics Reconsidered.*

OBITUARIES AND OTHER SOURCES:

BOOKS

Directory of American Scholars, Volume 2: *English, Speech, and Drama,* eighth edition, R. R. Bowker, 1982.

PERIODICALS

Chicago Tribune, July 16, 1997, sec. 2, p. 11.

*   *   *

SANDIN, Joan 1942-

PERSONAL: Born April 30, 1942, in Watertown, WI; daughter of Robert L. (a teacher) and Frances K. (an interviewer; maiden name, Somers) Sandin; married Sigfrid Leijonhufvud (a journalist), April 30, 1971 (divorced, 1986); children: Jonas, Jenny. *Education:* University of Arizona, B.F.A., 1964.

ADDRESSES: Home—Tucson, AZ.

CAREER: Illustrator, author, and translator of children's books. Illustrations for *The Long Way to a New Land* have been exhibited in solo shows in Sweden and the United States. Artwork is represented in the Kerlan Collection.

MEMBER: FST, Swedish Society of Illustrators.

AWARDS, HONORS: Best Children's Books, American Institute of Graphic Artists, 1970, for *Crocodile and Hen;* travel and work grants from Forfattarfonden (Swedish Writers' Fund); exhibition grant from Bildkonstnarsfonden (Swedish Artists' Fund); Notable Children's Trade Books in the Field of Social Studies, National Council for the Social Studies and Children's Book Council, for *Hill of Fire,* 1971, *The Lemming Condition,* 1976, *The Long Way to a New Land,* 1981, and *Time for Uncle Joe,* 1981; Georgia Children's Award, 1973, for *"Hey, What's Wrong with This One?";* Outstanding Science Trade Book for Children, National Science Teachers Association and Children's Book Council, 1974, for *Woodchuck;* nominee, Edgar Allan Poe Award, Mystery Writers of America, 1975, for *The Mysterious Red Tape Gang;* Notable Book, American Library Association, 1981, for *The Long Way to a New Land,* and 1988, for translation of Christina Bjork's *Linnea's Windowsill Garden.*

WRITINGS:

SELF-ILLUSTRATED

The Long Way to a New Land, Harper (New York City), 1981.
The Long Way Westward, Harper, 1989.
Pioneer Bear: Based on a True Story, Random House (New York City), 1995.

ILLUSTRATOR

Carol Beach York, *The Blue Umbrella,* F. Watts, 1968.
Randolph Stow, *Midnite: The Story of a Wild Colonial Boy,* Prentice-Hall, 1968.
Harold Felton, *True Tall Tales of Stormalong: Sailor of the Seven Seas,* Prentice-Hall, 1968.
Edith Brecht, *The Little Fox,* Lippincott (Boston), 1968.
Eleanor Hull, *A Trainful of Strangers,* Atheneum (New York City), 1968.
Ellen Pugh, *Tales from the Welsh Hills,* Dodd, 1968.
Maia Wojciechowska, *"Hey, What's Wrong with This One?,"* Harper, 1969.
Joan Lexau, *Crocodile and Hen,* Harper, 1969.
Jan M. Robinson, *The December Dog,* Lippincott, 1969.
Constantine Georgiou, *Rani, Queen of the Jungle,* Prentice-Hall, 1970.
Joan Lexau, *It All Began with a Drip, Drip, Drip,* McCall/Dutton, 1970.

Jean Little, *Look through My Window,* Harper, 1970.

Joanna Cole, *The Secret Box,* Morrow, 1971.

Thomas P. Lewis, *Hill of Fire,* Harper, 1971.

Barbara Brenner, *A Year in the Life of Rosie Bernard,* Harper, 1971.

Ellen Pugh, *More Tales from the Welsh Hills,* Dodd, 1971.

Jean Little, *From Anna,* Harper, 1972.

Nathaniel Benchley, *Small Wolf,* Harper, 1972.

Edna Mitchell Preston, *Ickle Bickle Robin,* F. Watts, 1973.

Alison Morgan, *A Boy Called Fish,* Harper, 1973.

Joan L. Nixon, *The Mysterious Red Tape Gang,* Putnam, 1974.

Hans Eric Hellberg, translated by Patricia Crampton, *Grandpa's Maria,* Morrow, 1974.

Faith McNulty, *Woodchuck,* Harper, 1974.

Kathryn Ewing, *A Private Matter,* Harcourt, 1975.

Liesel Skorpen, *Michael,* Harper, 1975.

Liesel Skorpen, *Bird,* Harper, 1976.

Sandra Love, *But What about Me?,* Harcourt, 1976.

Alan Arkin, *The Lemming Condition,* Harper, 1976.

Thomas P. Lewis, *Clipper Ship,* Harper, 1978.

Clyde Robert Bulla, *Daniel's Duck,* Harper, 1979.

Nancy Jewell, *Time for Uncle Joe,* Harper, 1981.

Eleanor Coerr, *The Bell Ringer and the Pirates,* Harper, 1983.

Doreen Rappaport, *Trouble at the Mines,* Crowell, 1987.

Aileen Fisher, *The House of a Mouse: Poems,* Harper, 1988.

Aileen Fisher, *Always Wondering: Some Favorite Poems of Aileen Fisher,* HarperCollins, 1991.

Nancy Smiler Levinson, *Snowshoe Thompson,* Harper Collins, 1992.

Elaine Marie Alphin, *A Bear for Miguel,* HarperCollins, 1996.

TRANSLATOR

Gunilla Bergstrom, *Who's Scaring Alfie Atkins?,* Farrar, Straus, 1987.

Christina Bjork, *Elliot's Extraordinary Cookbook,* Farrar, Straus, 1991.

Christina Bjork, *The Other Alice: The Story of Alice Liddell and Alice in Wonderland,* R & S Books/Farrar, 1993.

Christina Bjork, *Big Bear's Book: By Himself,* Farrar, Straus, 1994.

Olof Landstrom, *Boo and Baa in a Party Mood,* Farrar, Straus, 1996.

Olof Landstrom, *Boo and Baa in Windy Weather,* Farrar, Straus, 1996.

SIDELIGHTS: Joan Sandin once commented: "I most enjoy working with folk tales and books demanding research and/or travel." Sandin lived in Sweden for more than a decade before returning to the United States in the mid-1980s. Her extensive travels in Europe and Mexico as well as the United States have inspired her work. A prolific illustrator, Sandin is also a skilled translator and a storyteller in her own right.

Among the many books Sandin has illustrated is *A Bear for Miguel,* by Elaine Maria Alphin, an unusual story for early readers, according to reviewers, but one that is effectively done and sensitively rendered in pictures and words. When Maria brings her stuffed toy bear, Paco, along to the market with her father, she has no intention of trading him. However, her realization of what the ongoing war in their country of El Salvador has meant for her father's ability to find work, and her understanding that a little boy injured in the war would love to have Paco, impels Maria to trade the toy for food for her family. "Sandin's watercolors add to the emotional impact . . . and do an effective job of setting the scene," remarked Gale W. Sherman in *School Library Journal.*

Sandin has translated several books from Swedish into English. Among those for children is *Boo and Baa in a Party Mood* and *Boo and Baa in Windy Weather,* two picture books written by Olof and Lea Landstrom featuring a couple of hapless lambs. In *Boo and Baa in a Party Mood,* the two prepare for a birthday party by practicing their dance steps, but things get sticky when they try to wrap the present. In *Boo and Baa in Windy Weather,* the two go to the grocery store, but dragging home a sled laden with their purchases through a snow storm presents a problem. *Big Bear's Book,* according to *School Library Journal* contributor Marilyn Taniguchi, is not a picture book but "a whimsical reminiscence of childhood" best suited to sentimental adults. Written by Christina Bjork, *Big Bear's Book* tells the story of a toy bear's relationship to his owner, from childhood, through a sojourn in the attic, to a place in the child's adult life and a career in the movies. Sandin is also the translator of Bjork's tribute to the children's classic, *Alice in Wonderland.* In *The Other Alice,* Bjork describes the model for Lewis Carroll's main character, Alice Liddell, and explains some of the games and other trivia associated with the book. The result is "a unique pleasure," Ann A. Flowers maintained in *Horn Book.*

Sandin's own background—her ancestors immigrated to the United States from Sweden in the nineteenth century—inspired the research that went into *The Long Way to a New Land* and *The Long Way Westward,* two self-illustrated early readers that tell the story of an immigrant family's journey from Sweden to the United States in the 1860s. Told from the perspective of Carl Erik, the family's older son, *The Long Way to a New Land* describes a drought that forces Erik's family to sell their farm and try to make a fresh start in America, and the trip by boat to the United States, where bad weather, bad smells, and crowding mean long days of discomfort before they reach their destination. Critics noted that Sandin utilizes her illustrations effectively to augment a necessarily spare text intended for beginning readers. "It isn't always easy to make history comprehensible to younger children," remarked Zena Sutherland of the *Bulletin of the Center for Children's Books,* "[but] Sandin does a nice job of it." Similarly praised as "an interesting, well-researched slice of history" by a critic for *Kirkus Reviews, The Long Way Westward* completes the story of the Erik family's journey as they travel from New York by railroad to Minnesota to live among their relatives.

Also set in the nineteenth century, *Pioneer Bear* tells the story of John Lacy, a photographer who has heard that young Andrew Irwin has taught a bear to dance. Lacy travels thirty miles to the Irwin farm to photograph the bear; but when he arrives Bearly the Bear is nowhere to be found, and Sandin provides a visual survey of pioneer life on a farm as the family goes from room to room, from barn to outhouse, in search of the cub. "Pioneer activities such as washing laundry in tubs . . . and smoking meats are realistically presented in warm watercolor illustrations," Mary Ann Bursk observed in *School Library Journal.* Reviewers also noted Sandin's sly infusion of humor into the story through her illustrations. "Primary schoolers will enjoy sighting Bearly . . . as he peeks from behind outbuildings and foliage," remarked Elizabeth Bush in *Bulletin of the Center for Children's Books.*

BIOGRAPHICAL/CRITICAL SOURCES:

PERIODICALS

Booklist, November 1, 1996, pp. 507-508.
Bulletin of the Center for Children's Books, March, 1982, p. 138; July, 1995, p. 397.

Horn Book, February, 1982, p. 39; March, 1994, p. 215; May, 1996, pp. 331-332.
Kirkus Reviews, November 15, 1981, pp. 1406-1407; August 15, 1989, p. 1250.
Publishers Weekly, August 25, 1989, p. 63; August 5, 1996, p. 440.
School Library Journal, April, 1995, p. 130; October, 1995, p. 117; June, 1996, p. 92.

*   *   *

SCARNE, John   1903-1985

PERSONAL: Surname is pronounced *scar*-nee; born March 4, 1903, in Steubenville (one source says Niles), OH; died July 7, 1985, in Englewood, NJ; son of Fiorangelo and Maria (Tamburro) Scarne; married Steffi Norma Kearney, 1956; children: John Teeko. *Education:* Attended public schools in Guttenberg, NJ, and Fairview, NJ; left school after eighth grade.

CAREER: Authority and author on games and gambling. John Scarne Games, Inc., North Bergen, NJ, president, 1950-85. Served as gambling consultant to Hilton Hotels International, to the FBI, and to the governments of Great Britain, Lesotho, and The Netherlands Antilles. Magician on stage and screen, and teacher of magicians. *Wartime Service:* Served as consultant to U.S. Armed Forces, 1941-45.

AWARDS, HONORS: Man of the Year, Police Chiefs of the United States, 1960.

WRITINGS:

NONFICTION

(With Clayton Rawson) *Scarne on Dice,* photographs by George Karger, Telegraph Press (Harrisburg, PA), 1944, revised edition, 1962, revised and updated edition, Stackpole Books (Harrisburg, PA), 1974, eighth revised edition, 1980.
Scarne on Cards, illustrations by George Karger, including a photographic section on cheating at cards, Crown (New York City), 1949, updated and enlarged edition, 1974.
Scarne on Card Tricks, Crown, 1950.
Scarne's Magic Tricks: 200 Best Tricks That Anyone Can Do, Crown, 1951, portions reprinted as *One Hundred of Scarne's Magic Tricks,* Cornerstone Library (New York City), 1961, and *One Hun-*

dred More of Scarne's Magic Tricks (also known as *Scarne's Magic Tricks*), Cornerstone Library, 1963.

Scarne on Teeko, Crown, 1955.

The Amazing World of John Scarne, A Personal History (autobiography), Crown, 1956.

Complete Guide to Gambling, Simon & Schuster (New York City), 1961; revised, expanded, and updated edition published as *Scarne's New Complete Guide to Gambling,* 1974.

Scarne, the Greatest in Board Games: Complete Official Rules for Forty New and Different Games of Skill (also known as *Rules for Playing Scarne: Forty New and Different Games of Skill Created by John Scarne*), John Scarne Games (Fairview, NJ), 1962.

The Odds against Me (autobiography), Simon & Schuster, 1966.

Scarne: A New Era in Card Playing, John Scarne Games, 1967.

The Woman's Guide to Gambling, Crown, 1967.

Scarne's Encyclopedia of Games, Harper (New York City), 1973.

The Mafia Conspiracy, Scarne Enterprises (North Bergen, NJ), 1976.

Scarne's Guide to Casino Gambling, Simon & Schuster, 1978.

Scarne's Guide to Modern Poker, Simon & Schuster, 1979.

Scarne's Encyclopedia of Card Games, Harper, 1983.

OTHER

Collaborator on *John Scarne Explains Why You Can't Win: A Treatise on Three Card Monte and Its Sucker Effects* by Audley V. Walsh, originally produced c. mid-1930s; and Gambler's Book Club (Las Vegas), 1972. Contributor to *World Book Encyclopedia,* 1970, and *Encyclopedia Britannica,* 1975.

SIDELIGHTS: The name John Scarne has been synonymous with cards, gambling, and magic tricks for decades, just as the name Hoyle has been synonymous with the rules for games. Writer John Lardner, quoted in a *New York Times* obituary, stated, "Scarne is to games what Einstein is to physics."

Born in Ohio, in 1903, Scarne grew up in New Jersey, where his skill with cards and other magician's devices became evident from a very early age. Leaving school after the eighth grade, he assiduously studied the magic tricks and card manipulation that

were to bring him fame and some degree of fortune in his adult life. He honed his skills through constant practice; the *New York Times* obituary related that "his skill derived, in part at least, from the fact that he himself had been dealing from the bottom of the deck since he was old enough to tell a deuce from a trey." His dexterity at sleight of hand was remarkable; it has been said that Scarne could "cut to an ace at will," in the words of the *New York Times* contributor.

Scarne first achieved fame during World War II when, working for the Armed Forces, he strove to rid the Army and Navy of crooked gambling. At the end of the war he published his first book, *Scarne on Dice,* coauthored with Clayton Rawson, and it has remained a perennial seller through several editions and updatings. His second book, the 1949 *Scarne on Cards,* has also remained popular. As Scarne's fame grew, so did the scope of his writings. He produced encyclopedic tomes on games and gambling, such as the 1973 *Scarne's Encyclopedia of Games* and the 1978 *Scarne's Guide to Casino Gambling.* In the early 1960s he invented a new form of card game, Scarne (pronounced like his last name), which had many variations but which, despite its inventor's efforts, did not become as widely successful as he had hoped. Over the years he also wrote two autobiographical volumes, the 1956 *The Amazing World of John Scarne, A Personal History* and the 1966 *The Odds against Me.*

A book less directly related to gambling was the 1976 *The Mafia Conspiracy,* in which Scarne, an Italian-American, expressed his views on the image of Italian-Americans in the United States as a civil liberties matter. The versatile Scarne was also a teacher of celebrity magicians such as Orson Welles and the Duke of Windsor, and a consultant to corporations and governments that had casino interests, as well as to the FBI. Scarne contributed articles on his area of expertise to two major encyclopedias, the *World Book Encyclopedia* and the *Encyclopedia Britannica.*

Scarne, whom the *Times* described as wearing a double-breasted pinstripe suit and talking from the side of his mouth, was an energetic reformer in his field, one who tried to educate the general public on how not to get cheated by hustlers. The 1972 treatise by Audley V. Walsh, *John Scarne Explains Why You Can't Win: A Treatise on Three Card Monte and Its Sucker Effects,* was but one of Scarne's efforts along those lines, and despite its publication date, its creation stemmed from the Thirties. In recognition of such efforts Scarne was named Man of the Year by the Police Chiefs of the United States in 1960.

BIOGRAPHICAL/CRITICAL SOURCES:

BOOKS

Who's Who in America, Marquis (New Providence, NJ), 1994.

OBITUARIES:

PERIODICALS

Los Angeles Times, July 9, 1985.
New York Times, July 9, 1985.
Washington Post, July 11, 1985.*

* * *

SCHACHTER, Stanley   1922-1997

OBITUARY NOTICE—See index for *CA* sketch: Born April 15, 1922, in New York, NY; died of colon cancer, June 7, 1997, in East Hampton, NY. Psychologist, educator, author. Schachter is remembered for his work in the field of psychology, studying the social habits of ordinary people. After serving in the Army Air Forces during World War II, he joined the faculty of the University of Minnesota, a post he held until 1961. At that time he became professor of psychology at Columbia University in New York until his retirement in 1992. His studies focused on addictions, emotions, obesity, and the stock market. He also acted as a consultant for the National Institute of Mental Health, as well as other organizations. His writings include *Obese Humans and Rats* (with Judith Rodin), *Emotion, Obesity and Crime, The Psychology of Affiliation: Experimental Studies of the Sources of Gregariousness, When Prophecy Fails* (with Festinger and Rieckin), and *Social Pressures in Informal Groups* (with Festinger and Bock). He was also the editor (with others) of *Extending Psychological Frontiers.*

OBITUARIES AND OTHER SOURCES:

BOOKS

Who's Who in America, Marquis (New Providence, NJ), 1996.

PERIODICALS

New York Times, June 11, 1997, p. B13.

* * *

SCHMIECHEN, Peter   1938-

PERSONAL: Born April 15, 1938; married Janet Hoffman (a teacher and librarian); children: Timothy, Nathan. *Education:* Elmhurst College, B.A., 1959; Eden Theological Seminary, B.D., 1962; Harvard University, Ph.D., 1969.

ADDRESSES: Home—1502 Hillcrest Rd., Lancaster, PA 17603. *Office*—Lancaster Theological Seminary, 555 West James St., Lancaster, PA 17603.

CAREER: Ordained minister of United Church of Christ, 1962; pastor of United Church of Christ in Everett, MA, 1962-65; United Church of Christ, staff member, Biennial Emphasis Committee on Urbanization and the Church, 1965-66; Elmhurst College, Elmhurst, IL, began as instructor, became professor of theology and religion, 1966-85, dean of the college, 1975-85; Lancaster Theological Seminary, Lancaster, PA, professor of theology and president of seminary, 1985—. United Church of Christ, member of Council for Higher Education, 1975—; Council of Presidents of the Closely Related Seminaries of the United Church of Christ, chairperson, 1989-93.

MEMBER: American Academy of Religion, Association of Theological Schools, American Association for Higher Education, American Association of Colleges for Teacher Education, American Association of University Professors, American Conference of Academic Deans, American Theological Society, North Central Association of Academic Deans (president, 1981-82).

AWARDS, HONORS: D.D., Franklin and Marshall College, 1987; D.Hum., Tohoku Gakuin University, Sendai, Japan, 1989.

WRITINGS:

The Gift and the Promise: Becoming What We Are in Christ, United Church Press (New York City), 1989.
Christ the Reconciler, Eerdmans (Grand Rapids, MI), 1996.

Contributor to theology journals and religious magazines, including *Christian Ministry, Prism: A Theological Forum for the United Church of Christ, New Conversations, Scottish Journal of Theology,* and *Christian Century.*

* * *

SCHWARTZ, Joyce R. 1950-

PERSONAL: Born April 24, 1950, in New Orleans, LA; daughter of Wallace (a physician) and Elsie (Gelpi) Rubin; married Richard E. Schwartz (a lawyer), June 13, 1970; children: Eric Thomas, Sara Leslie. *Education:* Vassar College, B.A., 1971. *Politics:* Democrat. *Religion:* Jewish. *Avocational interests:* Cooking, gardening, bicycling.

ADDRESSES: Home—106 Hesketh St., Chevy Chase, MD 20815.

CAREER: University of Michigan, Ann Arbor, laboratory assistant in physiology, 1972-73; Murch Elementary School, Washington, DC, science lab instructor, 1982-84; Somerset Elementary School, Chevy Chase, MD, Science Lab Aide, 1986-87; Sidwell Friends Middle School, Washington, DC, substitute science teacher, 1989—. I Have a Dream Foundation, science teacher, 1989; Business Enterprise, mathematics instructor, 1992. National Museum of Natural History, docent, 1976—; Calvert Marine Museum, intern, 1983.

MEMBER: Vassar Club of Washington.

WRITINGS:

(With Ellen R. Butts) *May Chinn: The Best Medicine,* illustrated by Janet Hamlin, Scientific American Books for Young Readers (New York City), 1995.

Contributor to magazines, including *Kitchen Bazaar Times* and *Science Weekly.*

WORK IN PROGRESS: A biography of a woman scientist.

SIDELIGHTS: Joyce R. Schwartz commented: "The two subjects which most fascinate me are cooking and science. My love of good food is a part of my New Orleans heritage. I grew up in a city where people live to eat, and I learned to cook by helping out in my mother's and grandmother's kitchens. Now I frequently do without recipes and create dishes based on ones I've enjoyed elsewhere or on what I have around at the moment. I've also had fun teaching cooking classes for young children, who seem willing to taste even the most exotic dish if they've helped create it.

"My interest in science developed later than my love of good food. Having previously been more comfortable with subjects like history and languages, I was surprised to discover during my senior year of high school that not only was I good at chemistry, but I liked it. I went on to college thinking that I would pursue chemistry as a side interest, but eventually decided to major in it. For the past twenty years, I've taught grade school and middle school science and given tours of the paleontology exhibits at the Natural Museum of Natural History here in Washington. As a teacher and tour guide, I love breaking down difficult concepts into easily digestible bits of information and watching the understanding dawn on a child's face.

"I've often thought there must be a connection between my interests in cooking and science. Perhaps the common ground lies in my desire to understand why things work the way they do: it doesn't matter whether I'm studying atomic structure or trying to make a perfect loaf of bread—in both cases, I enjoy learning about the invisible processes that explain the world around us. And I love sharing that knowledge with others."

BIOGRAPHICAL/CRITICAL SOURCES:

PERIODICALS

Appraisal, autumn, 1995, pp. 89-90.
School Library Journal, September, 1995, p. 206.
Science Books and Films, January-February, 1996, p. 20.

* * *

SCOTT, William L.
See FINLEY, Joseph E(dwin)

SEBALD, W(infried) G(eorg)   1944-

PERSONAL: Born in 1944, in Wertach im Allgaeu, Germany; immigrated to England, 1966. *Education:* Educated in Germany.

ADDRESSES: Office—University of East Anglia, Norwich, Norfolk NR4 7TJ, United Kingdom. *Agent*—c/o New Directions Publications, 80 Eighth Avenue, New York, NY 10011.

CAREER: Writer. University of East Anglia, Norwich, England, professor of European literature, 1970—. Director, British Center for Literary Translation, University of East Anglia, 1989-94.

AWARDS, HONORS: Berlin Literature Prize, Johannes Bobrowski Medal, and Literature Nord Prize, and *Jewish Quarterly* Literary Prize for fiction, 1997, all for *The Emigrants;* Henrich Boell Preis, Cologne, Germany;

WRITINGS:

FICTION

Nach der Natur: Ein Elementardgedicht, photographs by Thomas Becker, Greno (Noerdlingen, Germany), 1988.
Schwindel, Gefuehle (also known as *Schwindelgefuehle*), Eichborn (Frankfurt am Main, Germany), 1990.
Die Ausgewanderten, Eichborn, 1992, translated by Michael Hulse as *The Emigrants,* Harvill (London), 1996, New Directions (New York City), 1997.
Die Ringe des Saturn: Eine Englische Wallfahrt (title means "The Rings of Saturn: An English Pilgrimage"), Eichborn, 1995.

Also the author of works of poetry.

NONFICTION

(As Winfried Georg Sebald) *Carl Sternheim: Kritiker und Opfer der Wilhelminschen Aera,* Kohlhammer (Stuttgart, Germany), 1969.
(As Winfried Georg Sebald) *Der Mythus der Zerstoerung im Werk Doeblins,* Klett (Stuttgart), 1980.
Die Beschreibung des Ungluecks: Zur Oesterreichischen Literatur von Stifter bis Handke, Residenz-Verlag (Salzburg, Austria), 1985.

(Editor and contributor) *A Radical Stage: Theatre in Germany in the 1970s and 1980s,* Berg (Oxford, England), 1988.
Unheimliche Heimat: Essays zur Oesterreichischen Literatur, Residenz-Verlag, 1991.

SIDELIGHTS: Literary and theatrical scholar W. G. Sebald, who immigrated to England in 1966 at age twenty-six, has become widely known in the German-speaking world for his genre-crossing works of creative prose as well as for his literary criticism. In 1996 his work *Die Ausgewanderten* was translated into English as *The Emigrants.* This volume is the second in a series of books of fiction written by Sebald. Its 1990 predecessor, *Schwindel, Gefuehle,* is an autobiographical tale in which the narrator traverses four loosely related stories that occur at various times in European history. The third volume, *Ringe des Saturn: Eine Englische Wallfahrt,* is more linear in its narration than the previous books in the series; it uses a journey through Suffolk, England, as the central element in a work that features dreams, observations, and memories on a variety of topics.

The Emigrants is, in the words of Lisa Cohen in the *Boston Review,* "a complex attempt to track and dislodge the tenacious insanities of the Holocaust." Its four parts portray four different characters from Sebald's own past, all of whom who are destroyed, one way or another, during World War II. The book contains numerous old photographs that, according to reviewer Carole Angier of the *Spectator,* "are part of the artistry and originality of the text." Cohen also noted the unique format of Sebald's work, stating that the proper classification for *The Emigrants* is as "a novel-essay in the form of a scrapbook, a joint biography, an oral history, and a memoir." Sebald himself, Cohen reports, has disclaimed the status of novelist with the observation that "his 'medium is prose, not the novel.'" He has called *The Emigrants* "a metaphor or allegory" of historical experiences. Angier noted that the narratives "move like memory itself—not logically or openly, but mysteriously, through images, echoes and accidents."

Sebald's prose has been highly praised for its simplicity and lyrical qualities, as has its English rendering by Michael Hulse. Angier found the book "exquisitely written and exquisitely translated" and declared, "I think it may be a masterpiece." Dennis Drabelle for *Washington Post Book World* called the translation a "gem." "The brilliance of this book lies in the fact that Sebald never loses sight of either the power of metaphor or the viciousness of history," wrote Cohen, who appreciated the "uncanny vividness and specificity" of the stories Sebald tells. Martin Chalmers in the *New Statesman* stated that *The Emigrants* is "marvelous" and suggested that "we need stories like those of *The Emigrants*" to ensure that the lessons of history are not lost. A reviewer for the *New York Times Book Review,* Larry Wolff, wrote "the impact of the Holocaust on the novel's emigrant survivors lies at the silent heart of the book, the suppressed tragedy they find so difficult to address directly." Andre Aciman in *Commentary* described "Sebald's world" as "haunting, hypnotic, and, at times, even hallucinatory."

In his career as a scholar of German theater and literature, Sebald has also produced a number of nonfiction books. Some of his volumes have dealt with the works of individual playwrights, including Carl Sternheim and Alfred Doeblin. In 1985, he published a collection of ten previously published essays on Austrian literature under the title *Die Beschreibung des Ungluecks: Zur Oesterreichischen Literatur von Stifter bis Handke.* Martin Swales, a reviewing the volume for *Modern Literature Review,* stated that "Sebald writes well and there is a splendid urgency to every analysis that he offers." A second collection on the same subject, *Unheimliche Heimat: Essays zur Oesterreichischen Literatur,* appeared in 1991. Sebald "writes deftly and with clear inner involvement all the while maintaining a salutary critical attitude towards the writers under view" commented Sidney Rosenfeld on *Unheimliche Heimat* for *World Literature Today.* Readers were able to sample Sebald's critical writing in English in his contribution to the 1988 volume *A Radical Stage: Theatre in Germany in the 1970s and 1980s,* which he edited, and which John Brosnahan, a reviewer for *Booklist,* called "illuminating."

BIOGRAPHICAL/CRITICAL SOURCES:

PERIODICALS

Booklist, February 15, 1989, p. 972.
Boston Review, February/March 1997, pp. 44-45.
Commentary, June, 1997.
German Quarterly, March 1983, pp. 341-343; winter, 1987, pp. 135-137.
Modern Language Review, April 1972, pp. 471-472; January 1987, pp. 248-250; July 1993, pp. 803-805.
New Statesman, July 12, 1996, pp. 44-45.
New York Times Book Review (electronic), March 30, 1997.
Spectator, August 17, 1996, pp. 28-30.
Times Literary Supplement, July 12, 1996, p. 22.
Washington Post Book World, December 15, 1996, p. X6.
World Literature Today, winter, 1992, pp. 127-128.*

* * *

SHAH, Jami J. 1950-

PERSONAL: Born July 11, 1950; U.S. citizen; son of Maqsood (a lawyer) and Nasim (a college professor) Shah. *Education:* N.E.D. Engineering College, B.S., 1973; University of Pittsburgh, M.S., 1976; Ohio State University, Ph.D., 1984. *Politics:* Democrat. *Religion:* Muslim. *Avocational interests:* Hiking, mountain climbing.

ADDRESSES: Office—Department of Mechanical and Aerospace Engineering, Arizona State University, Mail Code 6106, Tempe, AZ 85287-6106. *E-mail*—jami.shah@asu.edu.

CAREER: PASMIC Steel Mills, project engineer, including a visiting position at Cherepovets Steels Mills, U.S.S.R., 1973-75; P.O.L., product engineer, 1976-78, product manager for welding products, 1978-80; Ohio State University, Columbus, lecturer in mechanical engineering, 1981-84; Arizona State University, Tempe, assistant professor, 1984-88, associate professor, 198-93, professor of mechanical and aerospace engineering, 1994—, coordinator of Mechanical Engineering Design Group, 1990-91. Held summer positions with General Electric, 1986, Garrett Engines, 1990, General Motors, 1991, and Philips Co. (Netherlands), 1991; consultant to Crown-Zellerbach, Universal Propulsion, and Allied Signal.

MEMBER: North American Manufacturing Research Institute, American Society of Mechanical Engineers, Sigma Xi (president, 1994-95).

AWARDS, HONORS: Grants from National Science Foundation and various manufacturers.

WRITINGS:

(Editor, with M. Mantyla and D. Nau, and contributor) *Advances in Feature-based Manufacturing,* Elsevier-North Holland, 1994.

(With Mantyla) *Parametric and Feature-Based CAD/ CAM: Concepts, Techniques, and Applications,* Wiley (New York City), 1995.

Contributor to periodicals, including *Journal of Intelligent Manufacturing, Computer Aided Design, Journal of Integrated Computer Aided Engineering, Research in Engineering Design, Computing and Control Journal,* and *Manufacturing Review.*

SIDELIGHTS: Jami J. Shah told *CA:* "I am motivated by a desire to make the latest developments in computer-aided design (CAD) technology more easily available to graduate students, researchers, and engineers in industry.

"My co-authors and I prepared outlines and gradually filled in topics, starting with more stable and better established areas and moving on to newer and more controversial subjects. Each co-author had primary responsibility for certain chapters. We then reviewed each other's work and edited one another's contributions."

*   *   *

SHAW, George
  See BICKHAM, Jack M(iles)

*   *   *

SHEPPARD, Harold L(loyd)   1922-1997

OBITUARY NOTICE—See index for *CA* sketch: Born April 1, 1922, in Baltimore, MD; died of heart failure, July 10, 1997, in Tampa, FL. Educator, civil servant, author. Sheppard devoted much of his career to the issue of aging in the United States. In conjunction with his studies, he served on various governmental committees, wrote books on the subject, and worked as a consultant. In his early career, Sheppard was an instructor at Wayne State University from 1947 to 1953, then he became an associate professor of sociology from 1953 to 1959. A post as research director with the U.S. Senate Committee on Aging followed; he later served as the Committee's staff director. He then joined the U.S. Department of Commerce's Area Redevelopment Administration. From 1963 to 1975 he was staff social scientist for the W. E. Upjohn Institute for Employment Re-

search. He then became senior research fellow at the American Institute for Research in Washington, D.C., a post which ended in 1980 when he became counselor on aging to the Carter Administration. In 1981 Sheppard began work as associate director of the National Council of Aging, before joining the faculty of the University of South Florida in 1983 as director of its International Exchange Center. He also was a professor in the gerontology department at the University. Sheppard's other career posts included chairing the task force on poverty and the older American for the Office of Economic Opportunity, serving on the President's task force on economic security and welfare for the White House Conference on Civil Rights, chairing the advisory council of the U.S. Senate Committee on Aging, and working as consultant to the U.S. Senate Subcommittee on Manpower, Employment, and Poverty. He wrote, edited, and translated various books. They include *When Labor Votes: A Study of Auto Workers, Too Old to Work, Too Young to Retire, The Job Hunt: Job-seeking Behavior of Unemployed Workers in a Local Economy* (with A. Harvey Belitsky), *Civil Rights, Employment, and the Social Status of American Negroes* (with Herbert Striner), *Employment Aspects of the Economics of Aging, The Graying of Working America,* and *Future of Older Workers.*

OBITUARIES AND OTHER SOURCES:

BOOKS

Who's Who in America, Marquis, 1995.

PERIODICALS

New York Times, August 4, 1997, p. B6.

*   *   *

SHERMAN, Vincent   1906-

PERSONAL: Original name, Abram Orovitz; born July 16, 1906, in Vienna, GA; son of Harry and Vinnie (Scherman) Orovitz. *Education:* Oglethorpe University, B.A. *Politics:* Democrat.

ADDRESSES: Home—6355 Sycamore Meadoes Dr., Malibu, CA 90265. *Agent*—c/o University Press of Kentucky, 663 South Limestone St., Lexington, KY 40508-4008.

CAREER: Actor, writer, dialogue director, producer, and director. Actor in stageplays, and, beginning in 1933, in motion pictures, including *Counsellor-at-Law, Midnight Alibi, Speed Wings, The Crime of Helen Stanley, One Is Guilty, Girl in Danger,* and *Hell Bent for Love;* director of motion pictures, including *Doctor X, Saturday's Children, Man Who Talked Too Much, Underground, Flight from Destiny, The Hard Way, All Through the Night, Old Acquaintances, In Our Time, Mr. Skeffington, Pillow to Post, Janie Gets Married, Nora Prentiss, The Unfaithful, Adventures of Don Juan, Somewhere in the City, Hasty Heart, Damned Don't Cry, Goodbye, My Fancy; Lone Star,* and *Assignment—Paris;* producer and director of motion pictures, including *Affair in Trinidad, The Young Philadelphians, The Naked Earth, Second Time Around, Ice Palace, Fever in the Blood,* and *Garment Jungle;* director of numerous television series, including episodes of *Medical Center, Westside Medical, Baretta, The Waltons, Doctors Hospital,* and *Trapper John;* director of made-for-television movies, including *The Last Hurrah, Women at West Point, The Yeagers, Bogey, The Dream Merchants, Trouble in High Timber Country,* and *High Hopes—The Capra Years.*

CAREER: Directors Guild of America, Academy of Motion Picture Arts and Sciences.

AWARDS, HONORS: National Film Award (London), 1950; honorary doctorate (fine arts), Oglethorpe University (Atlanta, GA), 1997.

WRITINGS:

Crime School (screenplay), produced by Brian Foy, 1938.
Studio Affairs: My Life as a Film Director (autobiography), University Press of Kentucky (Lexington), 1996.

WORK IN PROGRESS: Screenplays: *Redneck, The Man Behind the Moon,* and *Life of George Washington.*

SIDELIGHTS: Vincent Sherman, whose original name was Abram Orovitz, was a leading man on the stage and in motion pictures before writing the screenplay for the 1938 film *Crime School.* A year later, Sherman embarked on a career as a producer and director, garnering a lengthy list of film and television credits before his retirement. His 1996 autobiography, *Studio Affairs: My Life as a Film*

Director, chronicles Sherman's colorful career in Hollywood.

BIOGRAPHICAL/CRITICAL SOURCES:

BOOKS

Sherman, Vincent, *Studio Affairs: My Life as a Film Director,* University Press of Kentucky (Lexington), 1996.

*   *   *

SHPAKOW, Tanya   1959(?)-

PERSONAL: Born c. 1959. *Education:* Graduated from the Rhode Island School of Design.

ADDRESSES: Home—Albuquerque, NM.

CAREER: Author and illustrator of children's books.

WRITINGS:

SELF-ILLUSTRATED

Baba, Knopf (New York), 1989.
On the Way to Christmas, Knopf, 1991.

WORK IN PROGRESS: *The Island of the Six-Toed Cats,* about fifty-six felines adrift at sea after a hurricane, and *Bear Thanksgiving,* about a missing eight-year-old boy and a bear cub.

SIDELIGHTS: Tanya Shpakow described the best and worst aspects of illustrating her own children's books to Fran Rogers Krajewski of *Writer's Digest:* "When I write a book, I don't have to wait six months to a year to find out what it's going to look like. At the same time, if I'm disappointed, I can only blame myself for not drawing the characters correctly or not creating just the right atmosphere." One disadvantage, however, is that "when you're blocked, you're *really* blocked," Shpakow continued in the same interview. "If you can't think of how your story should go, you're probably not going to be able to dig yourself out by doodling around and drawing a picture of it.

"The story can become your enemy. What happens is, you sour yourself on all sorts of things in terms of pictures if you're really having a struggle. . . . But the text must *always* come first.

"If you don't have the text in your mind—not only seeing the characters, but knowing that character's habits, where and how he lives, what he thinks about, who he meets—then you can't draw the pictures."

Shpakow's advice for beginning illustrators is to stay away from "putting a character or an object in the middle of a page, drawing it beautifully—like it's a museum specimen—and letting it go at that. It's beautiful, but it's boring. If you're not showing a lot of movement and activity in a picture, it can be quite dull.

"I try to do a certain number of pictures where there is some kind of space that the child can jump into, so that there's some perspective used in the actual drawing. That way, children can project themselves into the picture plane and feel like they're really there *in* the story."

As regards the written portion of her picture books, Shpakow told Krajewski, "Even though my characters have to experience and get through a trauma or dilemma, I don't ever write stories that are straightforward morality tales. The plot will be related to everyday life, but it can still be fantastical or improbable.

"The fear of being left behind—at a rest stop, in a grocery store, never to be found again—is every kid's worst nightmare, and possibly every adult's. But when I address the abandonment issue, as I did in *On the Way to Christmas,* I don't want it to be an actual child being left behind. I want the story to be less threatening, so I'll write about a teddy bear being blown off a car or, as happens in *The Island of the Six-Toed Cats,* about fifty-six cats set adrift at sea following a hurricane.

"It's easier for children if they can emote along with characters who are safer. . . . They can scream and cry and yell and laugh all the way through the stories (which all have happy endings). It makes it an emotionally safe experience for them."

Tanya Shpakow's self-illustrated picture books feature unusual stories accompanied by illustrations that have brought comparisons to Chris Van Allsburg and Susan Jeschke. While her stories are sometimes considered less accomplished than her illustrations,

Shpakow's first two works, *Baba* and *On the Way to Christmas,* were generally well received. In *Baba,* a young girl listens to her grandmother's tales of being born in Russia and sold for a penny to the gypsies, from whom she learned to fly. Due to the combination of fantasy and reality, it is not clear if "Baba is flying through the air or attending a Bingo game, and this may confuse or put off some children," remarked Betsy Hearne in the *Bulletin of the Center for Children's Books.* Nonetheless, Marilyn Iarusso, a *School Library Journal* contributor, praised Shpakow's visual depiction of the "mischievous and appealing" Baba in drawings "with dramatic shading and lighting effect." Likewise, a *Kirkus Reviews* critic singled out Shpakow's "eerie" illustrations which, while "clearly influenced by Van Allsburg . . . have their own unique, fey humor."

In *On the Way to Christmas,* Walter the teddy bear gets lost when the movers fail to pack him inside the car, a mishap that leads to many adventures before he finds his way back to the little boy with whom he lives. The story is "beautiful," averred Ellen J. Brooks in the *Children's Book Review Service,* full of "suspense, warmth and the magic of Christmas."

BIOGRAPHICAL/CRITICAL SOURCES:

PERIODICALS

Bulletin of the Center for Children's Books, January, 1990, pp. 120-21.
Children's Book Review Service, October, 1991, p. 17.
Children's Bookwatch, September, 1991, p. 5.
Kirkus Reviews, September 1, 1989, p. 1332.
Language Arts, April, 1990, p. 430.
School Library Journal, January, 1990, p. 90; October, 1991, p. 33.
Writer's Digest, April, 1996, pp. 25-27.*

* * *

SIDAHMED, Abdel Salam 1956-

PERSONAL: Born June 28, 1956, in Hassaheisa, Sudan; son of Mohamed Sidahmed. *Education:* University of Khartoum, B.Sc. (with honors), M.Sc., 1983; Charles University, Ph.D., 1991. *Avocational interests:* Reading, classical music.

ADDRESSES: Home—27 Quernmore Rd., London N4 4QT, England. *Office*—Middle East Program, International Secretariat, Amnesty International, 1 Easton St., London WC1X 8DJ, England; fax 44-171-413-5719. *E-mail*—asidahme@amnesty.org.

CAREER: Sudanow, Khartoum, Sudan, senior reporter and sub-editor for current affairs, beginning in 1985; Cambridge University, Cambridge, England, researcher and lecturer in modern Middle Eastern history, 1991-95; Amnesty International, London, England, human rights researcher specializing in the Middle East, 1995—. Consultant to Sudan Studies Centre.

MEMBER: British Society of Middle Eastern Studies (fellow), Association of Clerical, Technical, and Supervisory Staff.

WRITINGS:

(Co-editor) *Islamic Fundamentalism,* Westview (Boulder, CO), 1996.
Politics and Islam in Contemporary Sudan, Curzon (England), 1997.

WORK IN PROGRESS: Sudan: Contemporary Affairs and Society, publication by Harwood Academic Publishers expected c. 1998-99; *Islam and Human Rights: Thoughts on Universality and Cultural Relativism,* completion expected in 1998; *The Desert and the Nile: A Personal Account; Discourse on Contemporary Islamism;* continuing research on human rights in the Middle East.

SIDELIGHTS: Abdel Salam Sidahmed told *CA:* "Since my early school years I have developed an interest in writing. This ranged from keeping bits and pieces of observations and personal experiences in my diary to experimenting in short story writing and school journalism. Subsequently, and throughout my educational and career years, writing became first a necessity and then a profession. I now see writing as an essential part of my life. Through writing I hope to contribute some input to those who may share my concerns and interests, and/or those who are in one way or another being influenced by the issues addressed in my works.

"My preliminary inspiration has been the issues confronting my country of origin. Sadly, Sudan, the largest country in Africa and a country of ancient history and civilization, has gone from one disaster to another. Therefore, Sudan's history and its current affairs, as well as its problems and complications, have been both a field of interest and a motivation for my writing. On another level, the trend that contemporary Sudanese politics has taken and its increased association with Islam and Islamist ideology has enlarged the scope of my writing and research interests to include Islamic history, contemporary Islamism, and Middle Eastern affairs in general.

"Notwithstanding my preliminary, or even primary, interest in Sudanese issues, Middle Eastern politics and contemporary Islamism have also assumed greater margins in my schemes of research for professional and other reasons. For me the question is not just a matter of academic curiosity. Rather, it is an attempt to contribute to an ongoing debate directly concerned with the essential issues confronting Muslims and their societies and the way they perceive their religion in view of today's realities. These issues include the question of Islam and modernity, modernism or postmodernism; the secular or Islamist challenge; and Islam and politics.

"Although currently my main field is academic writing, I love feature writing and do occasionally run pieces in journals and newspapers whenever my time and other commitments allow."

*   *   *

SIMON, Ulrich E(rnst)   1913-1997

OBITUARY NOTICE—See index for *CA* sketch: Born September 21, 1913, in Berlin, Germany; relocated to England, 1933; died July 31, 1997. Theologian, educator, author. Although he was born in the Jewish faith in Germany, Simon converted to Christianity and became a priest in the Church of England. He escaped Germany along with his mother during the Nazi's rise to power in 1933; his father and brother were victims of the Holocaust. In 1942 Simon began to serve the Church of England as a priest in Upton, Buckinghamshire, England. He later served as a priest in Millbrook, Bedfordshire, from 1950 to 1954. Then he joined the faculty of King's College at the University of London, first as an assistant professor and later as a professor in the department of theology. In 1958 he became chair in Christian literature. He also served as dean of King's College from 1978 to 1980. During his career he also worked as a visiting professor at St. Mary's

University in Baltimore. He wrote a number of books, including *A Theology of Crisis, A Theology of Salvation, Heaven in the Christian Tradition, The Ascent to Heaven, Theology Observed, A Theology of Auschwitz, The Trial of Man, Story and Faith, Atonement,* and *Pity and Terror.* He also penned the semi-autobiographical *Sitting in Judgment.*

OBITUARIES AND OTHER SOURCES:

BOOKS

Who's Who, St. Martin's Press, 1994.

PERIODICALS

Times (London; electronic), August 5, 1997.

* * *

SINYAVSKY, Andrei (Donatevich)   1925-1997
(Abram Tertz)

OBITUARY NOTICE—See index for *CA* sketch: Born October 8, 1925, in Moscow, U.S.S.R. (now Russia); immigrated to France, 1973; Russian citizenship restored, 1990; died of cancer, February 25, 1997, in Fontenay-aux-Roses, France. Educator and author. A novelist, essayist, and short story writer, Sinyavsky received international attention when he and fellow writer Yuli M. Daniel were arrested and brought to trial for allegedly creating works that the U.S.S.R. government considered "anti-Soviet." Some of the novelist's works had been secretly taken out the country for publication abroad under the pseudonym Abram Tertz—a move that angered Soviet authorities when they discovered the true identity of Tertz. Ultimately Sinyavsky was sentenced to six years in a labor camp, but was released after about five. In his early career, he worked as a senior research fellow at the Gorki Institute of World Literature in Moscow. He also was a lecturer on Russian literature at Moscow University. Both of these posts ended with his imprisonment in 1966. Released in 1971 Sinyavsky had difficulty finding work and ultimately was allowed to leave the Soviet Union for France in 1973 for a job at the Sorbonne. Sinyavsky was a prolific author. Among his books written as Abram Tertz are *The Trial Begins* and *The Make-peace Experiment.* He also issued short stories as Tertz, including *Fantastic Stories,* which was also

published as *The Icicle, and Other Stories.* He also wrote nonfiction titles such as *Pikasso* ("Picasso"), *For Freedom of Imagination* (essays), *A Voice from the Chorus, Strolling with Pushkin, In the Shadow of Gogol, Goodnight, Ivan the Simple: Paganism, Magic and Religion of the Russian People, Soviet Civilization,* and *On Socialist Realism* and *Unguarded Thoughts* (both as Tertz). Along with his wife, M. Rozanova-Sinyavskaya, he founded the publication *Sintaksis* and served as one of its main contributors.

OBITUARIES AND OTHER SOURCES:

BOOKS

International Who's Who, Europa, 1996.

PERIODICALS

Chicago Tribune, March 27, 1997, sec. 3, p. 10.
New York Times, February 26, 1997, p. D22.
Times (London), February 26, 1997, p. 21.
Washington Post, February 27, 1997, p. D5.

* * *

SLAYTON, Donald K(ent)   1924-1993

PERSONAL: Born March 1, 1924, in Sparta, WI; died June 13, 1993, in League City, TX; married Marjory Lunney, 1955 (divorced); married Bobbie Osborn, 1983; children: one son. *Education:* University of Minnestoa, B.S., 1949; Michigan Technological University, honorary Ph.D., 1965. *Avocational interests:* Formula One airplane racing.

CAREER: American astronaut, 1959-74. Boeing Company, aeronautical engineer, 1949-51; fighter test pilot, 1955-59; National Aeronautics and Space Administration (NASA), director, flight crew operations, 1963-74, manager, space shuttle approach and landing tests, 1975-77, manager, space shuttle orbital flight tests, 1978-82; Space Services, Inc., president, 1982; Mercury Seven Foundation, vice-president. *Military Service:* U.S. Army Air Corps, 1942-46; U.S. Air National Guard, 1951-63, became major.

MEMBER: Society of Experimental Test Pilots (fellow), American Astronautical Society, Order of Daedalians, American Fighter Aces.

WRITINGS:

(With M. Scott Carpenter, L. Gordon Cooper Jr., John H. Glenn Jr., Virgil I. Grissom, Walter M. Schirra, and Alan B. Shepard Jr.) *We Seven,* Simon and Schuster (New York City), 1962.

(With Alan B. Shepard Jr., Jay Barbree, and Howard Benedict) *Moon Shot: The Inside Story of America's Race to the Moon,* introduction by Neil Armstrong, Turner Publishing (Atlanta, GA), 1994.

(With Michael Cassutt) *Deke!: An Autobiography,* St. Martin's Press (New York City), 1995.

SIDELIGHTS: Known to his friends and to the world as "Deke," Donald K. Slayton was one of the seven original Mercury astronauts—and the only one who did not make it into space in the Mercury program. A minor heart problem, discovered after John Glenn's 1962 orbital flight, prevented Slayton from following Glenn as the fourth American into space. Fortunately, both space technology and Slayton's health improved to the point where, thirteen years later, in 1975, he became crew leader of Apollo 18.

His journey began in Wisconsin, where Slayton fully expected, as a boy, to spend his life following in his father's earthbound footsteps as a farmer. While a teenager, however, he took a five-minute recreational ride on a flying boat over Lake Michigan. The experience changed his life: it made him want to be a pilot. Joining the Army Air Corps (the predecessor of the U.S. Air Force) in 1942, he was trained as a bomber pilot, and flew fifty-six combat missions over Europe. Then he himself became a trainer of bomber pilots, before flying seven more missions, this time over Japan.

After the war, Slayton earned a degree in aeronautical engineering and went to work for Boeing. But the Korean War was on the horizon, and during that conflict, Slayton, as an activated member of the Air National Guard, flew fighter missions as a squadron commander. (It was during this period that a senior officer gave Slayton the name "Deke," to distinguish him from the many other Donalds on the base.) After Korea, Slayton became a test pilot at Edwards Air Force base in California—a center of what journalist Tom Wolfe, in *The Right Stuff,* would call "pushing the envelope." Chosen by the National Aeronautics and Space Administration (NASA) to be one of the first seven U.S. astronauts in 1959, Slayton, with his cohorts, underwent the grueling psychological and physical training regimen that prepared them for the unforeseen conditions of space flight. After the disappointment of being deleted from the list of active astronauts, Slayton was made director of NASA flight operations in 1963 and remained in that position till 1974. He had a major behind-the-scenes role in establishing a rotating crew roster for flights. His work as flight director has been immortalized in the film *Apollo 13,* where Slayton (played by Ed Harris, who had played John Glenn in *The Right Stuff*) is shown to be heroic in his calm long-distance handling of the astronauts on the nearly fatal moon flight.

Even at that time, however, Slayton was privately training his body to return to flight. He had abstained from cigarettes and coffee for years, as well as reducing his alcohol consumption; daily exercise, added to these changes, enabled him to qualify in 1972. The Apollo 18 flight came three years later, and was noted for its rendezvous with the Soviet spaceship Soyuz 19. (In a typical display of diligence, Slayton had studied Russian before the flight, and had traveled to Russia to train with the cosmonauts.) The flight, which began July 15, 1975, lasted nine days, during two of which the two spacecraft were linked. Slayton, 51, was at that time the oldest man ever to fly in space. Although the mission was on the whole successful, a fuel leak during splashdown severely burned Slayton's lungs. Ironically, however, a medical examination related to the burning uncovered an unsuspected lung tumor, which was successfully removed. Slayton retired from NASA in 1981, then became president of Space Services, Inc., a company that developed rockets for small commercial space flights. The company was billed as the first privately financed space enterprise in the United States; it hoped to attract a variety of customers who wished to put satellites into orbit. In 1985 the company contracted with a group of Florida funeral homes to conduct burials in space; however, Space Services, Inc. was abandoned by its major corporate investor in 1990. Slayton also served as vice president of the Mercury Foundation, an organization founded by six of the original astronauts and the widow of the seventh, Virgil I. Grissom, with the aim of raising money for science scholarships. Despite the earlier removal of a malignancy, Slayton became ill with a brain tumor, and died at his home in Texas. He was sixty-nine.

As an author, Slayton participated with his six Mercury colleagues in the creation of the 1962 book *We Seven,* produced at the height of public enthusiasm for the space program. More than thirty years later, he and one of the original seven, Alan B. Shepard, Jr., co-authored *Moon Shot: The Inside Story of America's Race to the Moon,* along with two experienced space journalists, Jay Barbree and Howard Benedict. The book received pre-publication publicity because of its six-figure advance from Turner Publishing and its tie-in to a four-part Turner television documentary. The authors promised fuller characterizations than had been shown in previous astronaut books, and also declared that they would set right misconceptions, such as the mistaken rumor that Virgil I. Grissom, the second American in space, panicked and blew the hatch off his capsule on landing. The book, published shortly after Slayton's death, received a front-page review in the *New York Times Book Review;* Alex Roland, the reviewer, called it "lively and readable." Roland expressed surprise at the presence of some factual mistakes and of invented dialogue; however, he applied the adjectives Roland "visionary and reverential" and "swashbuckling" to the book. Another posthumous book, also co-written, followed a year later; it was *Deke: An Autobiography.*

BIOGRAPHICAL/CRITICAL SOURCES:

BOOKS

Annual Obituary 1993, St. James Press (Detroit, MI), 1994, pp. 504-507.

PERIODICALS

New York Times Book Review, July 17, 1994, pp. 1, 25.
Publishers Weekly, March 15, 1993, pp. 16-17; April 25, 1994, p. 21.

OTHER

Nemesis Formula 1 Airplane Racing (home page), June 17, 1997.*

*   *   *

SMART, Mary (Spencer Simpson) 1915-

PERSONAL: Born December 26, 1915, in Lyons, NY; daughter of R. Spencer (a surgeon) and Tusanelda (a homemaker and civic leader; maiden name, Nusbickel) Simpson; married William J. Smart (retired), November 4, 1949; children: Stuart Spencer Smart, Sarah Robinson Smart. *Education:* Wellesley College, A.B., 1937. *Religion:* Christian. *Avocational interests:* Gardening, reading, cooking, and local history.

ADDRESSES: Home—8841 Lock Berlin Rd., Lyons, NY 14489.

CAREER: Writer.

WRITINGS:

A Flight with Fame, the Life and Art of Frederick MacMonnies, Sound View Press (Madison, CT), 1996.

Contributor of short stories and historical pieces to periodicals, including *Woman's Day, Wayne County Supervisors and Historical Society,* and *Woman's Art Journal.*

WORK IN PROGRESS: Contribution of biographical entry on Mary MacMonnies to *Dictionary of Women Artists,* Fitzroy Dearborn (London), 1997.

SIDELIGHTS: Writer Mary Smart spent two decades researching the sculptor and painter Frederick MacMonnies, an artist who has often been overlooked in American art history. Smart's book, *A Flight with Fame, the Life and Art of Frederick MacMonnies,* corrects this oversight. Smart's interest in MacMonnies developed after a new neighbor in her small town in northern New York, one of the artist's eleven grandchildren, showed her a box of family papers. Smart gathered documents and reminiscences about MacMonnies across the United States and in France where MacMonnies lived for about thirty years, compiling her findings in her 1996 book.

A reviewer for *Art Times* applauded Smart's volume on the artist as an "eminently readable monograph" that discusses the man behind some of America's familiar landmarks. These landmarks include the central set of bronze doors that adorn the Library of Congress and the statue of Nathan Hale in New York's City Hall Park.

Because of Smart's extensive research on MacMonnies, she has served as a consultant on the artist for museums and art historians. She has also written a number of articles on regional history, short fiction, and a biographical sketch on MacMonnies' first wife.

Smart told *CA:* "By interviewing friends and family members of the artist before their deaths, I was able to reconstruct the almost-forgotten details of his life and preserve them in my biography. This voluminous research is on file at the Smithsonian's Archives of American Art."

BIOGRAPHICAL/CRITICAL SOURCES:

BOOKS

Smart, Mary, *A Flight with Fame, the Life and Art of Frederick MacMonnies,* Sound View Press (Madison, CT), 1996.

PERIODICALS

Art Times, September, 1996.
Woman's Art Journal, fall/winter, 1983-84.

*　*　*

SMITH-REX, Susan J. 1950-

PERSONAL: Born August 27, 1950, in Philadelphia, PA; daughter of William (in the U.S. Navy) and Joyce (in the U.S. Navy; maiden name, Moyer) Kodad; married Jeffrey Smith (a manufacturer), 1972 (divorced, 1992); married James H. Rex (a university vice president), November 5, 1994; children: Jeffrey, Siri, Adam, Nathan. *Education:* Lock Haven State College, B.S., 1972; Bloomsburg State College, M.Ed., 1973; Shippensburg State College, Supervisor's Certificate in Special Education, 1978; University of South Carolina, Ed.D., 1983. *Politics:* Democrat. *Religion:* Roman Catholic.

ADDRESSES: Home—340 Woodside Dr., Winnsboro, SC 29180. *Office*—College of Education, Winthrop University, Rock Hill, SC 29733. *E-mail*—SmithSJ@Winthrop.edu.

CAREER: Winthrop University, Rock Hill, SC, professor of education, 1979—, director of Winthrop's Project for At Risk Initiatives, 1985—, director of Winthrop's Involvement in Nurturing and Graduating Students (WINGS) Program, 1990—. Director, PhoneFriend (talk line for York County children), 1984—; member of board of directors, Charlotte (NC) Drug Education Center, 1989-90; director, York County Parent Educators in the Work Force Program, 1990—. Host of the South Carolina public

television programs *Winthrop Challenge,* 1988-91, and *Perceptions,* 1990-91.

AWARDS, HONORS: Jefferson Award, WBTV program *Jefferson Pilot,* 1988; South Carolina Human Rights Award, South Carolina School Counselor Association, 1990; Point of Light Award, President George Bush, 1992, for the WINGS Program; grants from federal and state offices for education, health, and human services.

WRITINGS:

Art, Fine Motor, and Cognitive Ideas for Special Education, Communication Skill Builders, 1985.
(With Kim "Tip" Frank) *Getting a Grip on A.D.D.: A Kid's Guide to Understanding and Coping with Attention Disorders,* illustrated by Jan Hanna Elliott, Educational Media, 1994.
(With Frank) *Getting a Life of Your Own: A Kid's Guide to Understanding and Coping with Family Alcoholism,* Educational Media, 1995.
(With Frank) *Getting over the Blues: A Kid's Guide to Understanding and Coping with Unpleasant Feelings and Depression,* Educational Media, 1996.
(With Frank) *Getting with It,* Educational Media, 1997.
(With Frank) *ADHD: 102 Practical Strategies for Reducing the Deficit,* Youthlight, 1997.

Contributor to journals and newspapers, including *Principals' Journal.*

SIDELIGHTS: Susan J. Smith-Rex commented: "After twenty-five years in the field of special education, I have become very interested in helping children better understand different disabilities and 'at risk' issues, so that they can learn to take increased responsibility for reaching their own potential. Four of the six books I've written are for children. The other two offer ideas for parents and teachers to help students learn strategies for success in the mainstream.

"Five of my books were written with Mr. Kim 'Tip' Frank, a guidance counselor in Rock Hill, South Carolina. Our books have been illustrated by either teachers or high school students, who know our audience well. Educational disabilities is a growing field of study, and I am excited to be a part of it through teaching, writing, and parenting."

SOSNOWSKI, David (J.) 1959-

PERSONAL: Born March 9, 1959, in Dearborn, MI; son of Eugene Joseph (a high school maintenance person) and Florence Dorothy (a homemaker; maiden name, Nalezyty) Sosnowski. *Ethnicity:* "Polish." *Education:* University of Michigan—Dearborn, B.A. (with high distinction), 1982; University of Alaska—Fairbanks, M.F.A., 1985. *Politics:* Liberal Democrat. *Religion:* "Catholic (somewhat lapsed)." *Avocational interests:* Computer and general science, humor writing, contemporary fiction, philosophy, current events.

ADDRESSES: Home—6410 Mayfair, Taylor, MI 48180. *Office*—U.S. Environmental Protection Agency, 2565 Plymouth Rd., Ann Arbor, MI 48105. *Agent*—Linn Prentis, Virginia Kidd Agency, 538 East Harford, Milford, PA 18337. *E-mail*—sosnowskid @aol.com.

CAREER: University of Michigan—Dearborn, tutor in English, 1980-85; University of Detroit, Detroit, MI, instructor in composition, 1985-86; University of Michigan—Dearborn, instructor in composition, 1986-88; U.S. Environmental Protection Agency, Washington, DC, budget and program analyst for Office of Mobile Sources, Office of Air and Radiation, 1988-90, environmental protection specialist at National Vehicle and Fuels and Emission Laboratory, Ann Arbor, MI, 1990—. University of Alaska—Fairbanks, instructor, 1983-85; Madonna College, instructor, 1985; Wayne State University, instructor, 1985-88; University of Michigan—Dearborn, instructor, 1986-88. *Philosophy and Literature,* editorial assistant intern, 1981; *Monthly Detroit,* proofreader, 1983; National Staff Development Council, proofreader and copy editor, 1988-91.

MEMBER: Phi Kappa Phi.

AWARDS, HONORS: First place, Fejes Fiction Prize, 1985; resident at Ragdale Foundation, 1993, 1994, 1995; first place, Thomas Wolfe Fiction Prize, 1994; grant from Arts Foundation of Michigan, 1995.

WRITINGS:

Rapture (fiction), Villard Books (New York City), 1996.

Contributor of stories, poems, and articles to periodicals, including *Heartland, Passages North,* *MacGuffin, Lip Service, Alaska Today, River City,* and *Metro Times* (Detroit, MI).

Contributor to *Tales of the Marvelous Machine: Thirty-Five Stories of Computing,* edited by Robert Taylor and Burchenal Green, Creative Computing (New York City), 1980.

WORK IN PROGRESS: Dot, Dot, Dot (tentative title), a "black comedy novel about spirit possession;" research on spirit possession, serial killers, Catholic nuns, auras, channeling, and paralysis victims.

SIDELIGHTS: It took a decade between David Sosnowski's initial inspiration for his first novel, *Rapture,* and its 1996 publication, according to an interview conducted by Scott Martelle for Detroit's *Metro Times.* Sosnowski, a student at the University of Alaska in the 1980s, remembers being all alone in an eight-story building, reading about heroin addicts and wondering what would happen if addicts sprouted wings. This was the seed of the idea for a short story, and subsequently for the novel, in which a virus randomly attacks human beings, leaving them winged. The first publicized victim is a drug dealer who goes on the talk-show circuit; later, a diverse selection of humans succumb, forming a new "race" that is sometimes the object of prejudice. Sosnowski's "angels" are thoroughly human rather than supernatural, and he uses their special condition as a lens through which to satirize "normal" humanity. *Library Journal* contributor Patricia Almer had praise for the work, stating that it is "written with much wit and humor." Sybil S. Steinberg of *Publishers Weekly* called the novel "original and sometimes clever," though she felt that Sosnowski had perhaps attempted to load too many ideas into his story. *Metro Times* reviewer Susan Whitall wrote that Sosnowski was particularly successful at entering the consciousness of his female characters and added, "*Rapture* ultimately lives up to its name, and Sosnowski reveals himself to be a romantic, even if his is a darkly imagined romanticism."

Sosnowski told *CA:* "I write primarily to alleviate the overwhelming guilt I feel when I'm not writing. That said, I also write to have fun, to feel complete and vital. These two motivators aren't as contradictory as they might seem. It's the guilt that gets me to turn on the computer and start tapping half-heartedly at the keys, but, after a half-hour or so of swimming through molasses, something clicks, the words flow, time stops, and I become ecstatic. Once I get past the wall of resistance, it is this sense of ecstasy that keeps me going.

"I also write because it is really fun to make stuff up—lie—and be praised for it instead of punished. Writing is also a way of making the meaningless junk of your life relevant by transforming it into source material that can be bent, a little bit this way and a little bit that way, to make the latest lie all the more believable. Getting all the pieces to fit together into something new that makes people laugh and cry and turn pages past the point when they really should be going to bed . . . well, I like being able to do that. It is the sort of thing that makes my dark, mischievous heart smirk.

"I have been influenced by a wide range of writers, for better or worse. For example, I like the serio-comic quirkiness and convoluted plotting of Kurt Vonnegut, Thomas Pynchon, Tom Robbins, John Irving, and Jeremy Leven. At the same time I strive for the clean subtlety and depth of writers like Charles Baxter, Ethan Canin, J. D. Salinger, James Joyce, Carol Shields, Barbara Kingsolver, and Michael Cunningham. I like the magic realism of Kafka, Calvino, Ionesco, and Marquez, and the science fiction of Ray Bradbury, Orson Scott Card, and Arthur C. Clarke. When I need inspiration and a laugh, Anne Lamott's *Bird by Bird* always does the trick.

"I usually start writing with a 'What if . . .?' premise, try to figure out what the obvious or conventional conclusion or treatment of that premise would be, and then react against it. Then I start taking notes, and that process can take up to a year or more. Coming up with the right opening scene is critical when it comes to moving me out of the simple notetaking phase into the actual drafting phase.

"My novel *Rapture* grew out of a short story I wrote in the early 1980s called 'Fix,' about a heroin addict who inexplicably sprouts wings and becomes as fatally addicted to flight as she had been to heroin. The novel is about a lot of addicts with a lot of wings."

BIOGRAPHICAL/CRITICAL SOURCES:

PERIODICALS

Library Journal, July, 1996, p. 164.

Metro Times (Detroit), January 15-21, 1997, p. 16.
Publishers Weekly, July 22, 1996, p. 227.

* * *

SPENCER, Jon Michael

PERSONAL: Male.

ADDRESSES: Agent—c/o Africa World Press, 11 Princess Rd., Lawrenceville, NJ 08648.

CAREER: Authority on African American hymnal music and music history. Duke University Divinity School, Durham, NC, faculty member; Bowling Green State University, Department of Popular Culture, Bowling Green, OH, faculty member; University of North Carolina, Chapel Hill, NC, faculty member; University of Richmond, Richmond, VA, faculty member.

WRITINGS:

As the Black School Sings: Black Music Collections at Black Universities and Colleges with a Union List of Book Holdings, Greenwood Press (New York City), 1987.
Sacred Symphony: The Chanted Sermon of the Black Preacher, Greenwood Press, 1987.
Protest and Praise: Sacred Music of Black Religion, Fortress Press (Minneapolis, MN), 1990.
Theological Music: Introduction to Theomusicology, Greenwood Press, 1991.
Black Hymnody: A Hymnological History of the African-American Church, University of Tennessee Press (Knoxville, TN), 1992.
Blues and Evil, University of Tennessee Press, 1993.
The Rhythms of Black Folk: Race, Religion, and Pan-Africanism, Africa World Press (Trenton, NJ), 1995.
Sing a New Song: Liberating Black Hymnody, Fortress Press, 1995.
Researching Black Music, University of Tennessee Press, 1996.
Self-Made and Blues-Rich, Africa World Press, 1996.
The New Negroes and Their Music: The Success of the Harlem Renaissance, University of Tennessee Press, 1997.
The New Colored People: The Mixed-Race Movement in America, New York University Press (New York City), 1997.

Contributor of chapters to books, including "Les Eglises Noires entre l'Excentrique et le Sublime" in *Harlem 1900-1935: De la Metropole Noire au Ghetto, de la Renaissance Culturelle al'Exclusion,* and "The Performed Word: Music and the Black Church" in *The Black Church in the African-American Experience;* contributor of articles to periodicals, including *Black Sacred Music: A Journal of Theomusicology, Black Scholar, American Music, Hymn, Theology Today,* and *Journal of Black Sacred Music.*

SIDELIGHTS: Jon Michael Spencer is a leading authority in the field of African American history and music. In 1987 Spencer started his career by writing an extensive compilation of musical resources for scholars and researchers in black music titled *As the Black School Sings: Black Music Collections at Black Universities and Colleges with a Union List of Book Holdings.* G. T. Johnson, a *Choice* reviewer, described "this unique bibliography" as "a detailed inventory of published and unpublished compositions."

Again in 1987 Spencer tackled music, this time that of the chanted sermon with *Sacred Symphony: The Chanted Sermon of the Black Preacher.* Commentator R. G. O'Meally, writing for *Choice,* explained that "'spirituals' often sprang from exalted, antiphonal preaching: from musical inventions by preachers and the spontaneously orchestrated responses by their congregations," but wished more explanation was given to the sermon-fragments.

With his intense focus on music, Spencer's search for hymn texts and other material has been relentless. In 1993 Stephen A. Marini, for the *Journal of American History,* commented, "a historical monograph devoted entirely to black church hymnals, *Black Hymnody: A Hymnological History of the African-American Church* has a narrower focus than Spencer's wide-ranging *Protest and Praise: Sacred Music of Black Religion* (1990)" and further that the author "used black hymnals as a textual lens through which to assess the theological and social development of the black church." Not only did Spencer examine hymns from the civil rights period, but he offered a hymnal history of ten denominations. Starting with the African Methodist Episcopal church hymnal compiled in 1801 by Richard Allen, Spencer's examination included Episcopalian, Catholic, Holiness and Pentecostal, Methodist, and Baptist traditions. The author's word for this study is "theomusicology."

According to Bishop W. J. Walls, there was a historical period when black Americans viewed the singing of spirituals as evidence of a lack of education. But after the civil rights movement, according to Spencer, spirituals were viewed as a "precious gift squeezed out of the toils and tears of our ancestral afflictions." Stephen W. Angell told *American Historical Review* readers that "Spencer hopes for replacing extant hymnody with a radically aggressive song dedicated to removing remaining racial barriers and enhancing a corporate sense of black personhood, although he admits that this may be impractical at present."

In 1993 *Blues and Evil,* Spencer's sixth work, debunked the concept of the blues being the "devil's music." In it Spencer examines the mythologies, theologies, and theodicies of the blues. Reviewer Carolyn M. Jones, in the *Journal of the American Academy of Religion,* described Spencer's blues theology as being "like the spirituals." She added that "the blues is a form of prayer, concerned both with life in the world and with the after life, and the blues can also be eulogy, mourning loss in times of tragedy. The performance, the preaching, of the blues lays bare the theological meaning of African-American life." While advancing his argument, Spencer tied in Biblical aspects of his conjectures with scholarship.

Peter R. Aschoff, in the *Journal of Southern History,* remarked that Spencer discusses issues in *Blues and Evil* relating to "the nature of sin and evil, the relationship between the sacred and the profane within the duality of the human spirit, the concept of the devil and its ties to West African spirits and/or trickster characters, the workings of an essentially animistic cosmology, and the place of men and women within such a universe."

Blues and Evil was written shortly after Spencer left Duke University Divinity School for an appointment at Bowling Green State University's Department of Popular Culture. Spencer has written four other books, each focusing on black theological music or black history and their connection to race, rhythm, freedom, and Africanism.

BIOGRAPHICAL/CRITICAL SOURCES:

BOOKS

Spencer, Jon Michael, *Black Hymnody: A Hymnological History of the African-American Church,*

University of Tennessee Press (Knoxville, TN), 1992.

PERIODICALS

American Historical Review, October, 1993, pp. 1332-1333.
American Reference Books Annual, 1988, p. 509.
Black Scholar, fall, 1992, p. 71; spring, 1995, p. 73; winter, 1995, p. 66.
Choice, November, 1987, p. 458; April, 1988, p. 1264; December, 1990, p. 641; December, 1991, p. 605; April, 1993, p. 1324; November, 1993, p. 468.
Come-All-Ye, summer, 1993, p. 9; fall, 1993, p. 7.
Entertainment Weekly, October 18, 1996, p. 82.
Journal of American History, December, 1993, pp. 1077-1078.
Journal of the American Academy of Religion, spring, 1996, pp. 181-185.
Journal of Southern History, November, 1994, pp. 834-835.
Library Journal, March 15, 1991, p. 122; April 1, 1993, p. 101.
Music Educators Journal, December, 1987, p. 14.
Newsweek, October 17, 1994, p. 84.
New York Times, December 17, 1996, pp. B3, C18.
Notes, September, 1988, p. 66.
Reference and Research Book News, fall, 1987, p. 25.
Religious Studies Review, July, 1992, p. 224.
Theology Today, October, 1991, p. 360; July, 1992, p. 286.*

*　　*　　*

SPRINGER, Claudia 1956-

PERSONAL: Born May 13, 1956, in Lawrence, KS; daughter of George (a professor of mathematics and computer studies) and Annemarie (an art historian) Springer; married Geoff Adams, August 16, 1992; children: Jack. *Education:* Northwestern University, B.A., 1978, M.A., 1981, Ph.D., 1986.

ADDRESSES: Home—Providence, RI. *Office*—Department of English, Rhode Island College, Providence, RI 02908. *E-mail*—CLSpringer@earthlink.net.

CAREER: Rhode Island College, Providence, professor of English and film studies, 1986—.

WRITINGS:

Electronic Eros, University of Texas Press (Austin, TX), 1996.

*　　*　　*

STEELE, Mary 1930-

PERSONAL: Born November 11, 1930, in Newcastle, New South Wales, Australia; daughter of William H. (a minister) and Frances D. (a homemaker; maiden name, De Chair) Johnson; married Bruce Steele (an academic), 1963; children: one son, one daughter. *Education:* University of Melbourne, B.A. (with honors), 1951, M.A., 1952; University of London, post-graduate certificate in education, 1960. *Religion:* Anglican. *Avocational interests:* Gardening, choral singing, music, crafts, reading, travel, attending the theater.

ADDRESSES: Home—Balwyn, Australia. *Office*—c/o Hyland House Publishing, 387-9 Clarendon St., South Melbourne, Victoria 3205, Australia.

CAREER: Office of the Federal Attorney General, Melbourne, Australia, research officer, 1953-54; Melbourne University, Melbourne, tutor, 1955-57; Australian Scientific Liaison Office, London, England, research officer, 1958-59; Monash University, Melbourne, lecturer in English, 1961-62; part-time work as school librarian, university tutor, research assistant, and book reviewer, 1965-80; writer.

AWARDS, HONORS: Arkwright was named Australian Junior Book of the Year, Children's Book Council of Australia, 1986.

WRITINGS:

Arkwright (self-illustrated), Hyland House (South Melbourne, Australia), 1985.
Mallyroots' Pub at Misery Ponds, Hyland House, 1988.
Citizen Arkwright (self-illustrated), Hyland House, 1990.
Featherbys (self-illustrated), Hyland House, 1993, Peachtree Publishers (Atlanta, GA), 1996.
A Bit of a Hitch and Other Stories, Hyland House, 1995.

Work represented in anthologies published in the United States.

WORK IN PROGRESS: Tenderhooks, a novel for young teenagers and preteens; a book about the author's own childhood.

SIDELIGHTS: Mary Steele commented: "Words and writing have always been important to me, as I studied language and literature at university and then went on to teach in the same discipline. I didn't attempt to write fiction until I was involved part-time in a school library. My first book was published in 1985, by which time I was nearly fifty-five years old. Since then I have produced a book every two or three years. My busy family life prevents me from writing full-time, so I am not very prolific. This doesn't worry me; there are more than enough books in the world! Encouraged by my publishers, and rather to my surprise (as I am not a trained artist), I illustrated three of my books. Young readers seem to like my pictures, I think because they recognize the work of a fellow amateur.

"I grew up before the advent of television, videos, and computers. Our main entertainment came from simple games, the radio, and reading. I had my own small collection of books, which I read over and over again, and in them I could lose myself in another world. I write for young readers now, hoping that they will find the same entry into that imaginary world and the same companionship. One need never be bored or lonely in the company of a good book— by the fire, in bed, up a tree, on the beach, in the bath, or on a train. Can the same be said of a television or a computer screen?

"My father had a great sense of humor, and our family life has always been pretty hilarious, so writing in a comic vein comes naturally to me. I believe that most children are born with a natural tendency toward fun and laughter but, unless this is nourished, it won't necessarily develop. Serious and pessimistic issues are so often emphasized in children's books these days, and I feel there is a need to lighten up and take an optimistic view. In any case, one can deal most effectively with human follies through humor and satire.

"As a child I had a great menagerie of animals, and most of my stories include animal characters, especially the first one, *Arkwright.* Arkwright is a giant anteater from South America who wants to see the world. He becomes attached to an old sea captain who is sailing to Australia, where he plans to retire. Arkwright behaves like any immigrant as he adjusts to the customs and creatures of his new home. His adventures carried over into a second book, *Citizen Arkwright.*"

BIOGRAPHICAL/CRITICAL SOURCES:

PERIODICALS

Magpies, March, 1991, p. 2; March, 1994, p. 31.
Publishers Weekly, September 23, 1996, p. 77.

*   *   *

STEIN, Kevin 1954-

PERSONAL: Born January 1, 1954, in Anderson, IN; son of Joseph and Mary Rita (Kelly) Stein; married Debra Lang (a registered nurse), May 26, 1979; children: Kirsten Anne, Joseph Kevin. *Education:* Ball State University, B.S. (summa cum laude), 1976, M.A., 1978; Indiana University, M.A. (creative writing), 1982, Ph.D. (American literature), 1984.

ADDRESSES: Home—6127 West Legion Hall Rd., Dunlap, IL 61525. *Office*—Department of English, Bradley University, 418 Bradley Hall, Peoria, IL 61625.

CAREER: Ball State University, Muncie, IN, instructor, 1978-79; Indiana University, Bloomington, IN, associate instructor, 1980-84; Bradley University, Peoria, IL, assistant professor, 1984-88, associate professor, 1988-94, professor of English, 1994—; writer.

MEMBER: Modern Language Association, Illinois Writers.

AWARDS, HONORS: Fellowship, Illinois Arts Council, 1986; chapbook award, Illinois Writers, 1986, for *A Field of Wings;* Stanley Hanks Chapbook Award, 1988, for *The Figure Our Bodies Make;* Frederick Bock Prize, *Poetry,* 1987; Faculty Member of the Year, Bradley University, 1989; fellowship, National Endowment for the Arts, 1991; Devins Award for Poetry, University of Missouri Press, 1992, for *A Circus of Want.*

WRITINGS:

POETRY

A Field of Wings, Illinois Writers Inc. (Normal, IL), 1986.

The Figure Our Bodies Make, St. Louis Poetry Center (St. Louis, MO), 1988.

A Circus of Want, University of Missouri Press (Columbia), 1992.

Bruised Paradise, University of Illinois Press (Urbana), 1996.

Contributor to periodicals, including *Black Warrior Review, Crazyhorse, Denver Quarterly, Kansas Quarterly, Kenyon Review, Mid-American Review, North American Review, Plainsong, Ploughshares, Poetry Northwest, Quarterly West, Seattle Review, Southern Poetry Review, Spoon River Quarterly,* and *Zone 3.*

OTHER

James Wright: The Poetry of a Grown Man (literary criticism), Ohio University Press (Athens), 1988.

Private Poets, Worldly Acts: Public and Private History in Contemporary American Poetry (essays), Ohio University Press, 1996.

Contributor of essays to periodicals, including *American Poetry Review, Concerning Poetry, Indiana Review, Iowa English Journal,* and *Ohio Review.* Editor of *Illinois Writers Review,* 1988-92; associate poetry editor of *Crazyhorse,* 1992—.

WORK IN PROGRESS: Black and Blue in Poetry, poems; essays on "'history' as subject matter in contemporary poetry and on the intersection of 'public' and 'private' history"; essays on James Wright, Philip Levine, Frank O'Hara, and Yusef Komunyakaa.

SIDELIGHTS: Kevin Stein is a poet who is primarily concerned with the nature of significance and appreciation. Sally Thomas, writing in *Quarterly West,* declared that "Stein's poems represent the part of the story that can be told: what we can see, know, and say, all we can mean when we say we love our lives." Thomas noted that in the volume *A Circus of Want* Stein explores "what it means to live in a universe in which life is not easily lovable, and beauty and despair are often the same thing."

Stein told *CA:* "What most interests me is the way our lives continually surprise us, how the common may suddenly glint with uncommon light or darken with horror. How these quotidian events change our lives, or fail to. How what matters comes to matter, or matter not at all. It is precisely this mysterious process, through which we sort our lives and apply to their vagaries intellectual or emotional significance, that fascinates me. My poems, and to some extent my critical essays, reflect that, for what else is an essay if not a sorting out of what attracts or repels us as readers?

"I've always been interested in muting the line between lyric and narrative poetry, a fictional boundary created and maintained by writerly convention. A number of poems in *A Circus of Want* experiment with ways to invoke elements of story with an essentially lyric form and, conversely, ways to make lyrical the telling of a story. This enables the speaker to follow meditative tangents along the way, to delay and transgress. Recently, I've worked with the dramatic monologue in poetry. Doing so offers me— because dramatic monologue is seemingly out of fashion—the enviable opportunity to be radical using traditional forms. I worked from a small packet of my great-great-grandfather's personal papers: a few letters, his immigration documents, a note absolving him of chicken thievery, some bills and receipts. I researched county historical records where he settled in Richmond, Indiana, in the 1850s, and found mention of him and his family in microfilmed copies of old newspapers. The result, a series of twelve or so dramatic monologues spoken in his voice, are part fact and part fiction, some measure real and much more imagined, an invented flesh of history stitched over skeletal facts.

"Those writers whom I find most compelling are characterized by what James Wright called a 'furious and unceasing growth.' I admire those writers who, while not abandoning all they've learned to do, journey into the unknown spreading before them like Arctic tundra and see in its vast emptiness only possibility. Not nothingness but something they've yet to discover. That fierce embracing of aesthetic change first attracted me to Wright and led to my critical study, *James Wright: The Poetry of the Grown Man.* In the process of my research, however, I was startled by the continuity of themes beneath the surface of Wright's stylistic alterations. The need for change and the will for order provided a useful, generative tension throughout his career. For the last two years, I've focused on poets whose work demands an intersection of public and private 'history,' poets such as Wright, Philip Levine, and Yusef Komunyakaa. I'm thinking, for example, of the importance of work and workers in Wright's poetry, or the significance of the Spanish Civil War in Levine's. Given the day's vertiginous theory and ideology, it's more necessary than ever for writers to enter the dialogue by examining and responding to the work of others. Silence, while protective, amounts to the worst sort of abnegation."

BIOGRAPHICAL/CRITICAL SOURCES:

PERIODICALS

Quarterly West, winter, 1992, pp. 232-236.

* * *

STEINBERG, Norman 1939-

PERSONAL: Born June 6, 1939, in Brooklyn, NY; son of Morris Alex and Lillian May Steinberg; married Bonnie Strock (an interior designer), October 8, 1977. *Education:*University of Maryland, A.B., 1961; University of Pittsburgh, L.L.B., 1964.

ADDRESSES: Office—c/o Paramount Studios, 5555 Melrose Ave., Los Angeles, CA 90038.

CAREER: Screenwriter, director, and actor. Television writer for programs, including *The Flip Wilson Show,* NBC, 1970-74; writer and executive producer of the CBS-TV programs *Doctor, Doctor,* 1989-91, and *Teech,* 1991.

Also appeared in roles in films, including Dr. Barmen, *Yes, Giorgio,* Metro-Goldwyn-Mayer/United Artists (MGM/UA), 1982; Sandy, *My Favorite Year,* MGM/UA, 1982; Reporter Duffy, *Johnny Dangerously,* Twentieth Century-Fox, 1984; and Charlie, *Miami Rhapsody,* Buena Vista, 1995.

MEMBER: Writers Guild of America, Directors Guild of America, Screen Actors Guild.

AWARDS, HONORS: Emmy Award, outstanding writing achievement in a variety or music series, 1971, for *The Flip Wilson Show;* Writers Guild of America West Award, 1973, for *Blazing Saddles.*

WRITINGS:

SCREENPLAYS

(With Mel Brooks and others) *Blazing Saddles,* Warner Bros., 1974.
(With Dennis Palumbo) *My Favorite Year,* MGM/ UA, 1982.
Yes, Giorgio, MGM/UA, 1982.
(With others) *Johnny Dangerously,* Twentieth Century-Fox, 1984.
(With David Frankel) *Funny about Love* (also known as *New York Times*), Paramount, 1990.

SIDELIGHTS: Norman Steinberg was in his early thirties when his writing first attracted notice through his work on *The Flip Wilson Show,* a weekly sketch-comedy variety hour for which he won an Emmy Award. The Brooklyn-born Steinberg, who had earned a law degree prior to pursuing a career in the entertainment field, next teamed up with a host of writers for the 1974 comedy *Blazing Saddles.* Director Mel Brooks and several others also received writing credit for this spoof of the traditional Western that starred Cleavon Little, Gene Wilder, and Madeline Kahn. "Loaded to bursting with one-liners, four-letterers, skits and sketches, slapsticks and pratfalls, the movie goes beyond spoofery of Westerns into just about every gag that comes to mind—and a lot of minds were involved," noted *New York* film critic Judith Crist. "It is a pity that Brooks has brought in so many cooks to stretch out his own witty brew and somehow dilute and divert it in the process," Crist concluded.

Steinberg's next major project was the acclaimed 1982 film *My Favorite Year.* The comedy was a homage to the golden era of television, when young writers such as Mel Brooks, Neil Simon, and Woody Allen were launching careers in the entertainment industry by writing jokes for Hollywood actors appearing on television variety programs. Steinberg wrote a script with Dennis Palumbo that revolves around the appearance of Peter O'Toole's Errol Flynn-like character on a variety show during the early 1950s. His comic foil is a young comedy writer from Brooklyn, "a small chipmunk called Benjy, whose actions are probably based partly on the exploits of the young Mel Brooks," according to *New Yorker* film critic Pauline Kael. The critic also noted that Brooks' production company helped bring *My Favorite Year* to the screen. "The plot appears to be casual—even a bit scatty," Kael contended, "yet when you think the movie over, the layers of reference in the script come together. They chime the way they do in the best-constructed farces."

Steinberg's screenwriting talents had less success that same year with the movie *Yes, Giorgio.* The film was a romantic comedy starring Italian tenor Luciano Pavarotti in his first screen role. David Denby, reviewing it for *New York,* called it a "fiasco." The *New York Times*'s Janet Maslin termed "Steinberg's script . . . too hokey to have any energy or any surprises." Steinberg later co-authored the 1984 Michael Keaton film *Johnny Dangerously* with several others before returning to the television medium. He is credited as a writer for the 1989-91 CBS medical spoof *Doctor, Doctor,* starring Matt Frewer, which he also directed and produced. Howard Rosenberg of the *Los Angeles Times* lambasted the pilot, but conceded that Steinberg's writing sometimes landed on "an appealingly off-center edge." Steinberg again served as writer and producer for the 1991 CBS sitcom *Teech,* in which an African American music teacher takes a job at a tony private school.

Steinberg returned to the silver screen with *Funny about Love,* released in 1990. The movie was directed by Leonard Nimoy and starred Gene Wilder and Christine Lahti. Roger Ebert in the *Chicago Sun-Times* wrote a disparaging review that began "*Funny about Love* provides an opportunity to spend 101 minutes in the presence of the most cloying, inane and annoying dialogue I've heard in many a moon, punctuated only by occasional lapses into startling bad manners." Chris Hicks in *Deseret News* agreed, remarking that "most of the audience will likely [give] up on this film."

BIOGRAPHICAL/CRITICAL SOURCES:

BOOKS

Contemporary Theatre, Film and Television, Volume 1, Gale (Detroit), 1984.
Magill's Cinema Annual, Magill, 1980 edition, pp. 184-187; 1983 edition, pp. 241-245.

PERIODICALS

Chicago Sun-Times, September 21, 1990.
Deseret News (Salt Lake City, UT), September 21, 1990.
Los Angeles Times, June 12, 1989.
New Statesman, February 25, 1983, p. 28.

Newsweek, February 18, 1974, p. 101; October 4, 1982, p. 77.
New York, February 25, 1974, p. 52; October 11, 1982, p. 86; October 18, 1982, p. 72.
New Yorker, February 18, 1974, p. 100; October 4, 1982, p. 132.
New York Times, June 30, 1974, sec. 2, p. 1; September 24, 1982, p. C8; October 1, 1982, p. C10; November 7, 1982, sec. 2, pp. 15, 16; December 21, 1984, p. C25.
Rolling Stone, March 28, 1974, p. 54.
Time, March 4, 1974, p. 62; October 11, 1982, p. 93; September 27, 1982, p. 71.
Times (London), February 25, 1983.
Variety, June 21, 1989, p. 57; September 16, 1991, p. 92.
Washington Post, October 8, 1982.*

*   *   *

STEVENS, Diane   1939-

PERSONAL: Born April 27, 1939, in Berkeley, CA; daughter of Mike (in sales) and Shyrle (a writer; maiden name, Pedlar) Hacker; married Joe Stevens (a psychiatrist), August 27, 1961; children: Scott, Dana, Tracy. *Education:* University of California, Berkeley, B.A., 1960; Our Lady of the Lake University, M.A., 1982. *Avocational interests:* Cooking, skiing, travel, reading, poetry.

ADDRESSES: Home—P.O. Box 422, Cambria, CA 93428. *E-mail*—fruitheart@aol.com.

CAREER: Special education teacher, San Antonio, TX, 1970-80; family therapist, San Antonio, 1980-87; writer.

MEMBER: Society of Children's Book Writers and Illustrators.

AWARDS, HONORS: Liza's Blue Moon was chosen Best Children's Book for 1995, Book Publishers of Texas.

WRITINGS:

Liza's Blue Moon, Greenwillow Books, 1995.
Liza's Star Wish, Greenwillow Books, 1997.

WORK IN PROGRESS: True Blue, an adult novel.

SIDELIGHTS: Diane Stevens commented: "I grew up to the sound of my mother's typewriter. She wrote novels behind that closed door that my brother and I knew not to go near during her working hours. I watched her over the years as she dealt with rejection, always sending her manuscripts out again immediately, before she let herself get too discouraged. Now she is over eighty years old and still writing every day, on a computer instead of the Underwood typewriter. Her book *The Goldminer's Child* was published in 1996, and she now edits my work before I send it out. She has been an inspiration, but more important, she is an example of the kind of commitment it takes to achieve success."

BIOGRAPHICAL/CRITICAL SOURCES:

PERIODICALS

Booklist, April 1, 1995, p. 1388.
Bulletin of the Center for Children's Books, March, 1995, p. 251.
Kirkus Reviews, March 15, 1995, p. 396.
Publishers Weekly, January 30, 1995, p. 101.
School Library Journal, April, 1995, p. 136.
Voice of Youth Advocates, August, 1995, p. 166.

* * *

STILLE, Alexander

PERSONAL: Male.

ADDRESSES: Office—c/o Pantheon Books, 201 East 50th St., New York, NY 10022.

CAREER: Journalist for *Boston Globe* and *U.S. News & World Report* in Italy, 1990-93.

AWARDS, HONORS: Los Angeles Times Book Award, 1992, for *Benevolence and Betrayal: Five Italian Jewish Families under Fascism.*

WRITINGS:

Benevolence and Betrayal: Five Italian Jewish Families under Fascism, Summit Books (New York City), 1991.
Excellent Cadavers: The Mafia and the Death of the First Italian Republic, Pantheon (New York City), 1995.

SIDELIGHTS: Alexander Stille writes about the problems of the modern Italian state in his books *Benevolence and Betrayal: Five Italian Jewish Families under Fascism* and *Excellent Cadavers: The Mafia and the Death of the First Italian Republic.* The first, which won the *Los Angeles Times* Book Award in 1992, is a study of the Italian Jewish community under Mussolini. The second looks at the uneasy relationship between the crime families of Italy and Sicily and the Italian government, and especially at the recent attempts of the judicial system to bring criminals to trial. He writes from his own and his family's experience: his "paternal grandparents," explained Istvan Deak in the *New York Review of Books,* "were Jews who emigrated to Italy from Russia after World War I." His father was a writer who published under the joint pseudonym Ugo Stille (German for "silence") after Mussolini passed racial laws in 1938 restricting the freedom of Jews to write and work. Stille's father immigrated to the United States in 1941. From 1990 to 1993, Alexander Stille worked as a journalist in Italy, during the period when the crime families made "excellent cadavers" out of some of the leading governmental reformers. "Mr. Stille," wrote *New York Times* contributor Richard Bernstein, "is a writer to watch."

"The story of Italian Jews under Fascism brings home not only the outrage and disastrous consequences of the racial laws, but the illusions and willful blindness of the Jewish communities," declared Victor Brombert in his review of *Benevolence and Betrayal* for the *Times Literary Supplement.* Brombert continued, "It also tells of the humanity, courage and plain decency of the many who stood up to oppose the spreading evil." "In 1984," stated Edith Kurzweil in the *Partisan Review,* "Alexander Stille decided to find out what had happened to Italian Jews under fascism which, after all, had been in power for sixteen years before the racial laws were put into effect in 1938." "Italy has always been the least anti-semitic of European nations," wrote Carole Angier in the *New Statesman and Society,* "and Italian Jews, accordingly have been the most secure and assimilated." This was as true in ancient times as it was in the late 1930s. "The Jewish community of Rome," declared *Commonweal* contributor Philip P. Hallie, "was the oldest in the Western world . . . two hundred years before the birth of Jesus Christ there were tens of thousands of Jews in Rome," he explained, "and . . . at Julius Caesar's death Jews kept watch and wept over Caesar's tomb out of gratitude for his tolerance."

Many Italian Jews celebrated the coming to power of the fascists as a good thing for Italy and supported Mussolini "by praising him to the skies," Hallie continued, "and by melting down some of their most precious gold and silver religious objects 'for the Fatherland.'" "Out of a Jewish population of 47,000 in 1938," wrote Edward Alexander in *Commentary,* "more than 10,000—that is, one third of the adults—belonged to the Fascist party." So assimilated were Italian Jews into Italian culture in 1938 that they minimized the impact that Nazi racism could have on them. "Nearly all Jewish Italians had relatives who had intermarried with Catholics, had many children and friends, and were as attached to their fatherland as they were to their families," Kurzweil said in the *Partisan Review.* "Thus they all started out by assuming that the Germans' racial laws could not possibly damage them, or even touch them."

This was not the case. Stille covers the lives of five representative Jewish families in *Benevolence and Betrayal,* trying to determine how these people dealt with the sudden onset of oppression. Ettore Ovazza of Turin responded by increased dedication to the Fascist party, even going so far as to attack his fellow Jews. In 1943 he was denounced to the S.S. and summarily executed. The family of anti-fascist Vittorio Foa, also of Turin, "supplied the resistance with one of its most vigorous fighters," stated Stefan Kanfer in the *Los Angeles Times Book Review.* The Di Verolis of Rome were devastated in 1943. Many family members died in the aftermath of the city's purge in that year. Two members of the Schoenheit family of Ferrara spent the last years of World War II in the concentration camp at Buchenwald; both father and son survived the war.

Stille's "stunning achievement," *New York Times Book Review* critic Barbara Grizzuti Harrison declared, "—the result of meticulous research and comprehensive understanding—is to give faces and personalities to people who might otherwise have remained consigned to anonymity, to generalized categories rather than to be seen with their own peculiar natures, motives and characters." Angier concluded: "He is clearly a most sympathetic interviewer, and a most judicious user of the results; and he makes superb use of contemporary letters, diaries, and—startlingly—of police and secret police files. I have never read a more immediate and moving retelling of personal stories of the Holocaust, or indeed of anything else."

Stille's *Excellent Cadavers* is "a fascinating and horrifying book," stated Denis Mack Smith in the *New York Times Book Review,* which "explain[s] in great detail how in the last twenty-five years the Mafia has terrorized Sicilian society and helped to bring the first Italian Republic close to collapse." Stille draws connections between organized crime and political corruption, showing how each draws on the other for support. During the 1980s, government reformers—including prosecutors Paolo Borsellino and Giovanni Falcone—began moving against the Sicilian Mafia, or Cosa Nostra. Each of them was targeted by the crime families. "The magistrates lived for years in virtual isolation," wrote Martin Clark in the *Times Literary Supplement,* "could have no social life, exposed their families to reprisals, and often had little support from their superiors. They did manage to break up many Mafia families, and they paid for this success with their lives."

Despite the ambiguity of criminal prosecution in Italy in the mid-1990s, Stille views the struggle led by Falcone and his compatriots as a victory for the forces of law and order. "Mr. Stille demonstrates how this victory of law was, necessarily, coincidental with the end of the first Italian republic, which occurred in 1993 with the radical reform of the electoral system," declared *Wall Street Journal* contributor Roger Kaplan. "Whether the second republic—with its reforms, its new men and its invigorated civil society—can sustain the work begun by the Sicilian judges is far from certain." "*Excellent Cadavers* is an act of faith that humans will work and sacrifice to live decently," asserted Art Elsenson in the *Los Angeles Times Book Review,* "It is a fine monument to those who died and those who live to act on that hope."

BIOGRAPHICAL/CRITICAL SOURCES:

PERIODICALS

Booklist, March 15, 1995, p. 1292.
Business Week, May 22, 1995, p. 22.
Christian Science Monitor, May 31, 1995, p. 13.
Commentary, May, 1992, pp. 56-59.
Commonweal, April 24, 1992, pp. 15-18.
Los Angeles Times Book Review, November 8, 1992, p. 11; April 30, 1995, p. 2.
New Statesman and Society, March 13, 1992, pp. 48-49.
New York Review of Books, November 5, 1992, pp. 22-26.

New York Times, June 21, 1995, p. C16.
New York Times Book Review, January 12, 1992, pp. 3, 15; April 23, 1995, p. 7.
Partisan Review, Volume 59, number 2, 1992, pp. 325-28.
Publishers Weekly, February 6, 1995, p. 68.
Time, May 8, 1995, pp. 91-92.
Times Literary Supplement, June 5, 1992, p. 12; September 1, 1995, p. 7.
Wall Street Journal, April 25, 1995, p. A18.
Washington Post Book World, June 4, 1995, pp. 1, 14.*

*   *   *

SUFRIN, Sidney Charles 1910-1997

OBITUARY NOTICE—See index for *CA* sketch: Born March 4, 1910, in New York, NY; died after a long illness with renal failure, June 6, 1997, in Amherst, MA. Economist, educator, author. Sufrin was known for his work in the field of public policy and economics. He held a series of positions with the U.S. Government beginning in the 1930s, including working with the National Recovery Administration, the Department of Labor, and the War Production Board. During World War II, he served in the U.S. Army's Service Forces. After the war he took up teaching at Syracuse University in New York, while serving as a consultant to the American Embassy in London.

Sufrin was appointed to the Economic Cooperation Administration and led an economic mission to Spain in 1950 and 1951, resulting in Spain's inclusion in the North Atlantic Treaty Organization (NATO). Beginning in 1952 Sufrin devoted his time to teaching. He left Syracuse in 1969 to take a post at the University of Massachusetts. He wrote numerous articles and books on labor policy, economics, and politics. They include *Annotated Bibliography of Labor in Emerging Society* (with F. E. Wagner), *What Price Progress* (with M. Buck), *Management of Business Ethics, Bhopal, The Decentralization of America: The Breakup of Washington,* and *Ethics, Markets, and Policy.*

OBITUARIES AND OTHER SOURCES:

BOOKS

Who's Who in the East, Marquis, 1990.

PERIODICALS

New York Times, June 11, 1997, p. B13.

*   *   *

SUMARSAM 1944-

PERSONAL: Born July 27, 1944, in Dander, Bojonegoro, East Java, Indonesia. *Education:* Indonesian National Conservatory of Music, Teaching Diploma, 1964; Indonesian National Academy of Music, B.A., 1968; Wesleyan University, M.A., 1976; Cornell University, Ph.D., 1992.

ADDRESSES: Home—576 Millbrook Rd., Middletown, CT 06457.

CAREER: Indonesian National Conservatory of Music, Surakarta, teacher, 1966-71; Indonesian Embassy, Canberra, Australia, instructor in Gamelan, 1971-72; Wesleyan University, Middletown, CT, visiting artist and instructor, 1972-76, artist in residence and lecturer, 1976-90, director of Wesleyan Gamelan Ensemble, 1972-90, member of various committees, 1974—; adjunct associate professor, 1990-92, adjunct professor of music, 1992—.

Kasatriyan Junior High School, Surakarta, Indonesia, Gamelan instructor, 1965-69; Indonesian National Academy of Music, Surakarta, Indonesia, assistant lecturer, 1967-71; University of Wisconsin—Madison, director of Gamelan Ensemble, summers, 1977, 1979; Brown University, Providence, RI, visiting instructor of Javanese music, 1980; Cornell University, Ithaca, NY, consultant on exhibition of Javanese puppet at the Herbert F. Johnson Museum, 1980-88, co-director of Gamelan Ensemble, 1983-84, director, 1984; member of National Screening Committee for Fulbright research award, 1985, 1988; member of advisory committee for program of performing arts of the Festival of Indonesia, 1987-91; consultant for documentary film *Art of Indonesia: Tales from the Shadow World,* produced by the National Gallery of Art and the Metropolitan Museum of Art, 1990; Williams College, Williamstown, MA, visiting instructor of Javanese music, 1991; Smith College, Northampton, MA, visiting instructor of Javanese music, 1995-97; speaker at colleges and universities, including University of California,

Berkeley, University of Chicago, Australian National University, Vassar College, and London School of Oriental and African Studies, London; performer as gamelan director and musician and Javanese puppeteer; musical composer.

MEMBER: International Council for Traditional Music, Society for Ethnomusicology (member of council, 1991-96), Society for Asian Music (member of board of directors, 1991—), Association for Asian Studies, Koninklijk Instituut voot Taal-, Land-, and Volkenkunde, Masyarakat Seni Pertunjukan Indonesia.

AWARDS, HONORS: Grant from American Council of Learned Societies, 1994.

WRITINGS:

Kendhangan Gaya Sala: Kendag Kalih & Setunggal Dengan Selintas Pengetahuan Gamelan, Indonesian National Academy of Music (Surakarta, Indonesia), 1976.

(Translator) *Menakjingga Lena* (title means "The Death of Menakjingga"), Department of Music, Wesleyan University (Middletown, CT), 1981.

(Contributor) *Aesthetic Tradition and Cultural Transition in Java and Bali,* edited by Stephanie Morgan and Laurie Jo Sears, Center for Southeast Asian Studies, University of Wisconsin (Madison, WI), 1984.

Introduction to Javanese Gamelan (monograph), Department of Music, Wesleyan University, 1988.

(Contributor) *Music-Cultures in Contact: Convergences and Collisions,* edited by Margaret Kartomi and Stephen Blum, Currency Press (Sydney, Australia), 1994.

Gamelan: Cultural Interaction and Musical Development in Central Java, University of Chicago Press (Chicago, IL), 1995.

Contributor of articles and reviews to periodicals, including *Indonesia, Kompas Minggu, Seni Pertunjukan Indonesia: Jurnal Masyarakat Musikologi Indonesia, Ethnomusicology, Asian Music,* and *Puppetry Journal.* Member of advisory board of *Balungan Journal,* a publication of the American Gamelan Institute, Oakland, CA, 1987—; consultant on the translation from Indonesian to English of *Source Reading in Javanese Gamelan and Vocal Music,* a theory text of Javanese music, University

of Michigan Center for South and Southeast Asian Studies (Ann Arbor, MI), 1980-88.

*   *   *

SUSSEX, Lucy (Jane)   1957-

PERSONAL: Born in 1957, in New Zealand; immigrated to Australia, c. 1971.

ADDRESSES: Agent—c/o Omnibus Books, 52 Fullarton Rd., Norwood, SA 5067, Australia.

CAREER: Editor and author, c. 1985—; co-editor of *Australian Science Fiction Review,* 1986-87.

WRITINGS:

(Editor with Jenny Blackford, Russell Blackford, and Norman Talbot) *Contrary Modes: Proceedings of the World Science Fiction Conference, Melbourne, Australia, 1985* (literary criticism anthology), Ebony Books (Melbourne), 1985.

The Peace Garden (juvenile novel), [Australia], 1989.

My Lady Tongue, and Other Tales (short stories), W. Heinemann Australia (Melbourne), 1990.

Deersnake (juvenile novel), Starlight (Australia), 1994.

(Editor) *The Patternmaker* (short story anthology), Omnibus (Australia), 1994.

(Editor) *Shadow Alley* (short story anthology), Omnibus, 1995.

(Editor with Judith Raphael Buckrich) *She's Fantastical* (short story anthology), with foreword by Ursula K. LeGuin, Sybylla (Australia), 1995.

The Scarlet Rider (novel), Forge (New York City), 1996.

SIDELIGHTS: New Zealand-born author and editor Lucy Sussex is well known in the genres of science fiction and mystery in her adopted country of Australia. With three others, she edited a nonfiction anthology of science fiction criticism, *Contrary Modes: Proceeding of the World Science Fiction Conference,* in 1985. In the following year, Sussex began co-editing the *Australian Science Fiction Review,* a task she stayed with until 1987. She has edited the fiction anthologies *The Patternmaker* and *Shadow Alley,* which feature science fiction and mystery, respectively, and in 1995 she co-edited a collection of speculative fiction by Australian women, *She's Fantastical*. Sussex has also written fiction of her own; her short works fill the 1990 collection *My Lady Tongue, and Other Stories,* and she is author of two novels for young adult readers, *The Peace Garden* and *Deersnake.* Her 1996 mystery novel, *The Scarlet Rider,* reached readers in the United States through the Forge publishing firm of New York City.

Sussex's work as both editor and author has received favorable notices from critics. *The Patternmaker* was praised by Stephen Matthews in the *Australian Book Review* for providing readers with stories that "are thought-provoking in the way that good science fiction tends to be." He especially praised Sussex's "juxtapositions" of the individual tales, judging that they "work well in emphasising the diversity of the collection."

In 1994, the same year that *The Patternmaker* saw print, Sussex also published her juvenile novel *Deersnake.* Its narrator, Kate, is drawn into a group whose teacher leads them to an alternate world through the use of a hallucinogenic drug. While in this different world, one of the group disappears, and Kate is the only member who notices. She resolves to take another drug-induced journey in order to find him, despite warnings from her guardian, the writer Aunt Gray. Kate eventually learns that the group's teacher has what Matthews described in the *Australian Book Review* as "unworthy sexual intentions." Matthews enjoyed *Deersnake,* applauding the way in which "Sussex raises plenty of fascinating ideas," although he mentioned what he felt to be the "untidiness" of the novel's ending.

Sussex combined her interest in juvenile fiction with her interest in the mystery genre when she edited 1995's *Shadow Alley.* This collection features stories from well-known Australian writers in which most of their beloved sleuths are seen solving mysteries during their adolescence or childhood. J. R. Carroll, discussing the anthology in *Australian Book Review,* cited many individual tales as meritorious, and declared: "*Shadow Alley* succeeds in assembling a disparate array of authors who all manage to unlock a secret or two in the dark—or not so dark—side of the human heart." Also reaching readers in 1995 was Sussex's editorial collaboration with Judith Raphael Buckrich, *She's Fantastical.* The volume includes, as Jenny Digby reported in the *Australian Book Review,* "short stories, poems, extracts from novels and experimental writings" by Australian women writers of speculative fiction. Stories include Leanne Frahm's tale of a housewife obsessed with cleanliness and Carmel Bird's piece about a mother whose baby disappears when she takes its picture. Digby asserted that "the many women involved in creating *She's Fantastical* are to be congratulated for this marvelous anthology."

The Scarlet Rider is, according to a *Publishers Weekly* reviewer, "a mystery within a mystery." Young heroine Mel Kirksley takes a temporary job with a feminist press, and her first task is to discover the name of an anonymous author whose 1865 novel the press wishes to reissue. During the course of her investigations, she comes to believe that she is a descendant of the author and learns that the novel in question was semiautobiographical. She also meets a direct descendant of the basis for the novel's romantic hero. While the *Publishers Weekly* reviewer cautioned against "too many coincidences," the commentator noted that "Sussex shows a flair for lively narrative."

BIOGRAPHICAL/CRITICAL SOURCES:

PERIODICALS

Australian Book Review, August, 1994, pp. 65-66; September, 1994, pp. 67-68; July 1995, p. 70; November, 1995, p. 47.
Publishers Weekly, August 5, 1996, p. 432.*

* * *

SUTTON, Roger 1956-

PERSONAL: Born October 26, 1956, in Manchester, CT; son of Franklin T. (in sales) and Mary Sheila (a secretary; maiden name, McNally) Sutton; married Richard L. Asch (a realtor), April 17, 1989. *Education:* Pitzer College, B.A., 1978; University of Chicago, M.L.S., 1982.

ADDRESSES: Office—Horn Book, Inc., 11 Beacon St., Boston, MA 02108. *E-mail*—rsutton@hbook. com.

CAREER: Chicago Public Library, librarian, 1982-88; *Bulletin of the Center for Children's Books,* editor, 1988-96; Horn Book, Inc., editor-in-chief, 1996—.

MEMBER: American Library Association.

AWARDS, HONORS: Best Books for Young Adults, American Library Association, Children's Book of Distinction, *Hungry Mind Review,* and Society of Midland Authors Best Juvenile Nonfiction, all 1994, all for *Hearing Us Out: Voices from the Gay and Lesbian Community.*

WRITINGS:

Hearing Us Out: Voices from the Gay and Lesbian Community, Little, Brown (Boston, MA), 1994.

SIDELIGHTS: Roger Sutton's *Hearing Us Out: Voices from the Gay and Lesbian Community* is a collection of interviews he conducted with fifteen gay and lesbian people in Chicago. Although some of the subjects are teenagers, many are adults because, as Sutton stated in the introduction, "I thought it was important to show teenage gays and lesbians . . . life goes on past junior-high humiliation and high-school ostracism."

Sutton's book has garnered a number of favorable assessments from reviewers who note that it fills an important need for many young readers. In a foreword to the book, novelist M. E. Kerr ponders "what this book might have meant to me, growing up gay, but also to a parent like my mother." *Booklist* reviewer Carolyn Phelan cited the "wide diversity of experiences, backgrounds, and points of view" brought together in Sutton's work, concluding that "readers wondering about what it means to be gay or lesbian will find this an intriguing and informative book of personal reflections." In a review in *School Library Journal,* Claudia Morrow stated that *Hearing Us Out* "succeeds largely because the narrators' words bespeak qualities such as humor, honesty, generosity, and commitment." *Voice of Youth Advocates* contributor Keith McCoy similarly asserts: "In all, the angst from discovering one's differentness comes across, but not at the expense of hearing how normal these people are."

BIOGRAPHICAL/CRITICAL SOURCES:

PERIODICALS

Booklist, September, 1994, p. 124.
Horn Book, January-February, 1995, p. 71; March-April, 1996, p. 133.
Publishers Weekly, November 21, 1994, p. 79.

School Library Journal, December, 1994, p. 140.
Voice of Youth Advocates, February, 1995, p. 365.

* * *

SWANSON, Helen M(cKendry)   1919-

PERSONAL: Born October 3, 1919, in Waukesha, WI; daughter of James Banford (a minister) and Helen Amy McKendry; married Neil H. Swanson Jr. (a minister and writer), August 30, 1941; children: David, Shirley, Kenneth, Howard. *Education:* Cornell College, B.A., 1941; Marquette University, teaching certificate, 1963. *Politics:* Registered Republican. *Religion:* Protestant. *Avocational interests:* Reading, hiking, birds.

ADDRESSES: Home and office—824 West Pitcher, Nevada, MO 64772.

CAREER: Elementary schoolteacher in Milwaukee, WI, 1964-65, Toledo, OH, 1966-67, and Maui, HI, 1968-82. Chair and member of board of directors, Maui Special Learning Center; community volunteer.

MEMBER: Phi Beta Kappa.

WRITINGS:

Angel of Rainbow Gulch, Bess Press (Honolulu, HI), 1992.
The Secret of Petroglyph Cave, Bess Press, 1995.
Angel and Tutu, Bess Press, 1997.

Contributor of about a dozen stories to children's magazines.

WORK IN PROGRESS: Ilima Miller, Hapa Haole (tentative title).

SIDELIGHTS: Helen M. Swanson commented: "After reading hundreds of children's books to the youngsters in my primary classes, I convinced myself that I could do it, too. My setting was Maui, where I taught local children in an 'up-country' plantation setting; hence, my choice of Angel. He is a young Hawaiian boy being raised in a *hanai* (adopted) family. His grandmother took him in, simply because she was lonely when her husband died.

"Because I hiked all the Hawaiian islands extensively and was constantly involved with the local culture, it was inevitable that I should choose to write what I knew. Angel has now become a three-book series for young readers aged eight to twelve.

"My editor at Bess Press encouraged me to try a 'girl' series, and now I am doing just that.

"In 1990 my husband and I returned to life on the mainland, in Nevada, Missouri, but my head and heart remain in Hawaii."

* * *

SZASZ, Suzanne (Shorr) 1915-1997

OBITUARY NOTICE—See index for *CA* sketch: Born October 20, 1915, in Budapest, Hungary; came to the United States; died in 1997 in Budapest, Hungary, while visiting relatives. Photographer and author. Szasz was a popular photographer of children, often capturing their images in unsentimental ways. Born in Budapest, she relocated to the United States following World War II. Her career as a photographer began in New York when she borrowed a camera and began taking pictures. Szasz, who worked as a camp counselor, submitted a photograph in a *Ladies' Home Journal* competition and won, prompting her to pursue a career behind the camera. Later, she became a founding member of the Pinewoods Folk Music Club (now the Folk Music Society of New York) and the American Society of Magazine Photographers. Her work was featured in magazines, including *Look, Good Housekeeping, Life,* and many others. Szasz also had her work exhibited in solo shows with the New York City Camera Club, Donnell Library, Nassau Community College, and the Hungarian National Gallery, among others. Her work was also featured in *Family of Man* by Edward Steichen, *Helping Your Child's Emotional Growth* by Anna W. Wolf, *The Silent Miaow* by Paul Gallico, and *Now I Have a Daddy Haircut* by Morey and Clara Appell. She also studied women in Puerto Rico who used birth control pills and presented a photographic report of the results in 1962. She was responsible for a number of photographic books, including *Young Folks' New York* (with Susan E. Lyman), *Child Photography Simplified, Modern Wedding Photography, The Body Language of Children, Sisters, Brothers and Others* (with Elizabeth Taleporos), and *We Are Six: The Story of a Family*

(with Morey and Clara Appell). In 1959 she was named one of the ten best women photographers in the United States.

OBITUARIES AND OTHER SOURCES:

BOOKS

Authors of Books for Young People, third edition, Scarecrow Press, 1990.

PERIODICALS

New York Times, July 10, 1997, p. B12.

* * *

SZYMCZAK, Leonard K. 1947-

PERSONAL: Born November 9, 1947, in Chicago, IL; son of Stanley and Estelle (Petrola) Szymczak; divorced; children: Melissa, Nathaniel. *Ethnicity:* "Polish." *Education:* Loyola University of Chicago, B.A., 1969; University of Illinois at Chicago Circle, M.S.W., 1971; further study at Family Institute of Chicago, 1974-76.

ADDRESSES: Home—5970 West Lakebluff Dr., Unit 501, Tinley Park, IL 60477. *E-mail*—szymczak @aol.com.

CAREER: Psychotherapist and educator in the United States and Australia. Northwestern University, Evanston, IL, senior affiliate therapist, Family Institute; Marriage Guidance Council of New South Wales, Australia, director of family therapy program; Royal North Shore Hospital, Sydney, Australia, senior social worker, Child and Family Psychiatry Department; Wollongong Marriage and Family Centre, Australia, director; currently therapist and consultant, Chicago, IL.

MEMBER: National Association of Social Workers, Academy of Certified Social Workers.

WRITINGS:

Cuckoo Forevermore (novel), Evanston Publishing (Louisville, KY), 1996.

Contributor to social work journals.

WORK IN PROGRESS: Kookaburra Hereafter, a novel, completion expected in 1998; continuing research on men's issues, particularly masculine psychology.

SIDELIGHTS: Leonard K. Szymczak told *CA:* "My first article was published in a professional book on social work in 1976. My first novel, *Cuckoo Forevermore,* was published in 1996. During that twenty-year span, my burning desire for creative expression became realized when I forged my love of writing with my career in psychotherapy. A satirical novel was born.

"I addressed many of the paradoxes and problems of my profession in *Cuckoo Forevermore,* which plucks the feathers off psychotherapy. Set in Australia, where I had lived and worked for fourteen years, the novel draws upon my therapeutic background and Polish heritage. The story describes a man's journey toward manhood as the twenty-nine-year-old psychologist, Peter Pinowski, who still lives with his parents, lands his first job in a child and adolescent psychiatric department in a Sydney hospital. He soon finds the sex offenders, suicidals, paranoids, and delusionals are driving him to extreme anxiety—and that's just his co-workers! The scenes are meant to shock, titillate, and even infuriate, but one thing can be guaranteed—your preconceived ideas about therapy or therapists will never be the same.

"I believe that all writers should attempt to fulfill their heartfelt ambitions. With this in mind, I dedicated my novel to all those inspired to dream who have mustered the courage to turn a dream into reality. I am currently working on another dream, the sequel."

T

TAINTER, Frank H(ugh) 1941-

PERSONAL: Born April 13, 1941, in Winona, MN; son of Hugh F. (a fish culturist) and Rose M. (a homemaker; maiden name, Brommerich) Tainter; married M. Magdalena Hemard, February 12, 1966; children: Rebecca Marie, Jennifer Adella. *Ethnicity:* "English-French-German." *Education:* Attended Winona State College (now University), 1959-60; University of Montana, B.S.F., 1964; University of Minnesota—Twin Cities, M.S., 1968, Ph.D., 1970. *Politics:* Independent. *Religion:* Roman Catholic.

ADDRESSES: Home—436 Patterson Rd., Central, SC 29630. *Office*—Department of Forest Resources, Clemson University, Clemson, SC 29634-1003; fax 864-656-3304. *E-mail*—ftntr@clemson.edu.

CAREER: U.S. Forest Service, lookout fireman, summer, 1961, smokejumper, summer, 1962; U.S. Peace Corps, Washington, DC, volunteer forestry technician at Instituto Forestral, Santiago, Chile, 1964-66; University of Minnesota—Twin Cities, St. Paul, instructor in forest pathology, 1966-70; University of Arkansas, Fayetteville, assistant professor, 1970-74, associate professor, 1974-79, professor of forestry, 1979; Clemson University, Clemson, SC, professor of forest resources, 1979—.

MEMBER: American Phytopathological Society, Sigma Xi, Phi Kappa Phi, Xi Sigma Pi, South Appalachian Botanical Club.

AWARDS, HONORS: Grants from Partners of the Americas, European Economic Community, National Lumber Exporters Association, U.S. Forest Service, National Science Foundation, U.S. Department of Agriculture, Horticultural Research Institute, International Society of Arboriculture, and several U.S. corporations.

WRITINGS:

How the Biltmore Forest School Came to Be (coloring book), Cradle of Forestry in America Interpretive Association, 1992.
Deforestation in Southwestern Colombia (bilingual coloring book), Partners of the Americas, 1995.
(With F. A. Baker) *Principles of Forest Pathology,* Wiley-Liss (New York City), 1996.

Contributor of more than a hundred articles to scientific journals. Associate editor, *Plant Disease,* 1979-82.

WORK IN PROGRESS: The Plant Doctor, a coloring book; research on tree pathology, specifically oak decline and root diseases, bacterial wetwood of oaks, and international forest pathology in general.

SIDELIGHTS: Frank H. Tainter told *CA:* "My primary motivation for writing is a sense of obligation to put my knowledge into a form that can be used by others. Writing is like pulling teeth, but once I start, it seems to flow, if I can avoid interruptions. I write mainly about my professional work (pathology), but also about some life experiences."

*   *   *

TAYLOR, Joe 1949-

PERSONAL: Born January 27, 1949, in Cincinnati, OH; son of Mary Louise Cox (a registered nurse);

married Linda Bramse (divorced, 1973); married Patricia Willey (a registered nurse), December 18, 1982. *Education:* University of Kentucky, B.A., 1976; Florida State University, Ph.D., 1985. *Religion:* Roman Catholic.

ADDRESSES: Home—R.R. No. 2, Box 90-D, Coatopa, AL 35470. *Office*—University of West Alabama, Station 22, Livingston, AL 35470. *Agent*—Richard DeRus, Claudia Menza Literary Agency, 1770 Broadway, New York, NY 10001.

CAREER: University of West Alabama, Livingston, professor, 1990—. Livingston Press, director, 1990—.

MEMBER: Associated Writing Programs, Modern Language Association of America.

WRITINGS:

Oldcat and Ms. Puss: A Book of Days (comic novel), Black Belt Publishers (Montgomery, AL), 1997.
The Once and Future Bunion (comic novel), Black Belt Publishers, in press.

WORK IN PROGRESS: "The First Spinning Moment," a literary trilogy, completion expected in 1999; two comic novels, *Feather Truth* and *The Baron, the Bear, and the Bees.*

SIDELIGHTS: Joe Taylor told *CA:* "My work has been influenced by my upbringing as a Roman Catholic and my undergraduate degree in philosophy. The fact that I was raised by a single, working parent in the fifties surely has also influenced my writing—prompted it, even. Other writers I consciously admire include Graham Greene, Laurence Stern, Robertson Davies, and Angela Carter."

*   *   *

TERTZ, Abram
   See SINYAVSKY, Andrei (Donatevich)

*   *   *

THIEMANN, Ronald F. 1946-

PERSONAL: Born October 4, 1946, in St. Louis, MO; son of Frank J. and Marie M. (Gruser) Thiemann;

married Beth Arlene Barkow, June 15, 1968; children: Sarah, Laura. *Education:* Attended Concordia College, River Forest, IL, 1964-66; Concordia Senior College, Fort Wayne, IN, B.A. (magna cum laude), 1968; Concordia Seminary, St. Louis, MO, M.Div., 1972; Yale University, M.A., 1973, M.Phil., 1974, Ph.D., 1976; attended University of Tuebingen, 1974-75. *Religion:* Lutheran.

ADDRESSES: Home—Jewett House, 44 Francis Ave., Cambridge, MA 02138. *Office*—Office of the Dean, Divinity School, Harvard University, 45 Francis Ave., Cambridge, MA 02138. *E-mail*—rthiemann@harvard.edu.

CAREER: Yale University, New Haven, CT, acting instructor in religious studies, 1975-76; Lutheran Theological Seminary, Philadelphia, PA, visiting assistant professor, 1977; Haverford College, Haverford, PA, faculty member, 1978-82, associate professor, 1982-85, professor of religion, 1985-86, department head, 1978-84, acting provost, 1985, acting president, 1986; Harvard University, Cambridge, MA, John Lord O'Brian Professor of Divinity and dean of Divinity School, 1986—. Villanova University, visiting professor, 1981; Trinity Lutheran Seminary, Fendt Lecturer, 1984; University of Virginia, distinguished visiting theologian, 1988; Valparaiso University, O. P. Kretzmann Lecturer, 1988; University of California, Davis, St. Augustine Lecturer, 1993; Lutheran Southern Seminary, Yost Lecturer, 1995. Lecturer at colleges and universities in the United States and abroad, including Union Theological Seminary (Richmond, VA), University of Marburg, Brown University, Providence, RI, Marquette University, Houghton, MI, Oklahoma City University, Hamline University, St. Paul, MN, and Middlebury College, VT; guest on television programs; public speaker. Evangelical Lutheran Church in America, member of task force on Lutheran-Reformed Theological Conversations, 1988—, and task force on Theological Education, 1989-91; Trinity Press International, member of board of directors, 1989-92, and board of governors, 1992—. Center of Theological Inquiry, Princeton, NJ, member, 1982-83; member editorial board, *dialog,* 1987—.

MEMBER: American Academy of Religion (chairperson of Narrative Interpretation and Christian Theology Research Group, 1982-86), Handel and Haydn Society.

AWARDS, HONORS: Fellow of Deutscher Akademischer Austauschdient, 1974-75; distinguished teaching award, Christian and Mary Lindback Foundation, 1981-82; Mellon humanities fellow, 1982-83.

WRITINGS:

(Contributor) *Christianity and the Many Faces of Marxism,* Augsburg (Minneapolis, MN), 1984.

Revelation and Theology: The Gospel as Narrated Promise, University of Notre Dame Press (Notre Dame, IN), 1985.

(Contributor) *Scriptural Authority and Narrative Interpretation,* Fortress (Philadelphia, PA), 1987.

(Contributor) *Friedrich Schleiermacher and Karl Barth: Beyond the Impasse?,* Fortress, 1988.

Toward an American Public Theology: The Church in a Pluralistic Culture, Westminster-John Knox Press (Louisville, KY), 1991.

(Editor) *The Legacy of H. Richard Niebuhr,* Fortress (Minneapolis), 1991.

Religion in Public Life: A Dilemma for Democracy, Georgetown University Press (Washington, DC), 1996.

Contributor of articles and reviews to theology journals and newspapers, including *Theology Today, Harvard Theological Review, Theological Education, Interpretation, Thomist,* and *Journal of Ecumenical Studies.*

WORK IN PROGRESS: Religion and Secularity in the Modern World.

*   *   *

THONDUP, Tulku   1939-

PERSONAL: Born in 1939, in Golok, Tibet; son of Malha Cha and Dolma Wangrol. *Ethnicity:* "Tibetan." *Education:* Dodrupchen Monastery, Vajracharya, 1957; research scholar at Visva-Bharati University, India, 1963-66. *Religion:* Buddhist.

ADDRESSES: Office—Buddhayana Foundation, 3 Barnaba Rd., Marion, MA 02738; fax 508-748-0806.

CAREER: Lucknow University, Lucknow, India, lecturer, 1967-76; Visva-Bharati University, West Bengal, India, reader, 1976-80; Harvard University, Cambridge, MA, visiting scholar, 1980-83; Buddhayana Foundation, Marion, MA, presiding officer, 1983—.

WRITINGS:

The Tantric Tradition of the Nyingmapa: The Origin of Buddhism in Tibet, Buddhayana, 1984.

Buddhist Civilization in Tibet, Routledge (England), 1987.

The Dzogchen Innermost Essence Library of Tibetan Preliminary Practice, second edition, Works and Archives, 1989.

(Translator) *The Assemblage of Vidhyadharas,* second edition, Dodrupchen, 1992.

(Translator) *The Queen of Great Bliss,* second edition, Dodrupchen, 1992.

Enlightened Journey: Buddhist Practice as Daily Life, Shambhala (Boulder, CO), 1995.

(Translator and author of introduction and annotations) *The Practice of Dzogchen,* Snow Lion, 1995.

The Healing Power of Mind: Simple Meditation Exercises for Health, Well-Being, and Enlightenment, Shambhala, 1996.

Masters of Meditation and Miracles: The Longchen Nyingthig Lineage of Tibetan Buddhism, Shambhala, 1996.

(Translator) *Enlightened Living: Teachings of Tibetan Buddhist Masters,* second edition, Rangchung Yeshe, 1997.

(Translator) *Hidden Teachings of Tibet: An Explanation of the Terma Tradition of Tibetan Buddhism,* second edition, Wisdom Publishing, 1997.

Thondup's books have been published in German, Italian, Spanish, Portuguese, French, Chinese, Danish, Swedish, and Hebrew.

SIDELIGHTS: Tulku Thondup told *CA:* "I was born in a tent and grew up as a nomad child in Eastern Tibet. At the age of four, I was recognized as an incarnation of a high Lama of the famed Dodrupchen Monastery. There I went through intensive studies for thirteen years and became a *Vajracharya.*

"At the age of eighteen, barely escaping with my life, I sought refuge in India. After getting accustomed to my new-found life, I taught for thirteen years at Lucknow University and Visva Bharati University. I came to the United States as a visiting scholar at Harvard University in 1983, and I have since been living in Cambridge.

"I have engaged my whole life in writing and translating the history, meditation, and philosophy of Tibetan Buddhism, in order to preserve and propagate the endangered, rich Tibetan Buddhist tradition. Under the auspices of the Buddhayana Foundation I have published more than ten original Tibetan Buddhist works and translations. *The Healing Power of Mind* is the result of my lifelong Buddhist training, my Tibetan cultural background in which healing through spiritual means is greatly emphasized, my experience of consulting Westerners for nearly twenty years, and especially my own life, which has been filled with afflictions and healing, pain and pleasure.

"The healing principle of *The Healing Power of Mind* is the universal nature and omnipresent power envisioned in Mahayana Buddhism. We can heal simply by being what we truly are, and by allowing our own natural healing qualities—peaceful and open mind, the right and positive attitude, warm and joyful energy in the state of balanced and harmonious life—to manifest themselves."

* * *

THWAITES, Reuben Gold 1853-1913

PERSONAL: Born May 15, 1853, in Dorchester, MA; died October 22, 1913, in Madison, WI; son of William George (a farmer) and Sarah (a farmer; maiden name, Bibbs) Thwaites; married Jessie Inwood Turville, 1882; children: one son. *Education:* Attended Dorchester, MA, public schools; self-educated at college level in Oshkosh, WI; pursued graduate studies as special student, Yale University, 1874-75.

CAREER: Librarian, historian, editor, educator, and administrator in Wisconsin. Newspaper correspondent, *Oshkosh Times,* Oshkosh, WI, 1872-74, and *Oshkosh Northwestern,* Oshkosh, 1875-76; *Wisconsin State Journal,* city editor, then managing editor, 1876-85. State Historical Society of Wisconsin, assistant to secretary, 1885-86, secretary, 1886-1913. Lecturer on American history, University of Wisconsin.

MEMBER: American Library Association (president, 1900, later member of executive council), American Historical Association (chair of Historical Manuscripts Commission, 1900-06, member of program committee, 1904), Conference of Historical Societies (later American Association for State and Local History; co-founder), Mississippi Valley Historical Association (president, 1912), Wisconsin Free Library Commission (vice chair), Wisconsin History Commission (secretary and editor).

AWARDS, HONORS: Honorary LL.D., University of Wisconsin, 1904.

WRITINGS:

Historical Sketch of the Public Schools of Madison, Wisconsin, 1838-1885, M. J. Cantwell (Madison, WI), 1886.

Historic Waterways: Six Hundred Miles of Canoeing down the Rock, Fox, and Wisconsin Rivers, McClurg (Chicago, IL), 1888; revised as *Down Historic Waterways: Six Hundred Miles of Canoeing upon Illinois and Wisconsin Rivers,* McClurg, 1902, reprinted in *The Trail of the Serpent: The Fox River Valley: Lore and Legend,* compiled by Robert E. Gard and Elaine Reetz, with photographs by Edgar G. Mueller, Wisconsin House (Madison, WI), 1973.

The Story of Wisconsin, Lothrop (Boston), 1890, revised and enlarged, 1899.

The Colonies, 1492-1750, Longmans, Green (New York City and London), 1891, revised, 1892.

The Story of the Black Hawk War, State Historical Society of Wisconsin (Madison, WI), 1892.

Our Cycling Tour in England, from Canterbury to Dartmoor Forest, and Back by Way of Bath, Oxford and the Thames Valley, McClurg, 1892.

Afloat on the Ohio: An Historical Pilgrimage of a Thousand Miles in a Skiff, from Redstone to Cairo, Way & Williams (Chicago, IL), 1897, revised as *On the Storied Ohio: An Historical Pilgrimage of a Thousand Miles in a Skiff, from Redstone to Cairo,* McClurg, 1903, Arno Press (New York City), 1975.

Stories of the Badger State, American Book Co. (New York City and Cincinnati, OH), 1900.

Daniel Boone, Appleton (New York City), 1902, Books for Libraries Press (Freeport, NY), 1971.

Father Marquette, Appleton, 1902.

How George Rogers Clark Won the Northwest, and Other Essays in American History, McClurg, 1903, Books for Libraries Press, 1968.

A Brief History of Rocky Mountain Exploration, with Especial Reference to the Expedition of Lewis and Clark, Appleton, 1904.

France in America, 1497-1763, Harper (New York City and London), 1905, Greenwood Press (Westport, CT), 1970.

Wisconsin: The Americanization of a French Settlement, Houghton (Boston, MA, and New York City), 1908, AMS Press (New York City), 1973.

(With Calvin Noyes Kendall) *A History of the United States for Grammar Schools,* Houghton Mifflin, 1912.

The History of Winnebago County & the Fox River Valley, 1541-1877 (originally published in serial form in *Oshkosh Times*, 1877), The County (Winnebago Co., WI), 1984.

EDITOR

Proceedings of the State Historical Society of Wisconsin, Volumes 35-60, 1888-1912.

Wisconsin Historical Collections, Volumes 11-20, 1888-1912.

(And compiler, with Daniel Steele Durrie) *Triennial Catalogue of the Portrait Gallery of the State Historical Society of Wisconsin,* two volumes, Democrat Printing Co. (Madison, WI), 1889, 1892.

(And compiler) *Arguments for a Joint Building for the State Historical Society and the State University,* Democrat Printing Co., 1895.

Alexander Scott Withers, *Chronicles of Border Warfare; or, A History of the Settlement by Whites, of North-Western Virginia, and of the Indian Wars and Massacres in that Section of the State, with Reflections, Anecdotes, &c.,* Clark (Cincinnati), 1895.

The Jesuit Relations and Allied Documents: Travels and Explorations of the Jesuit Missionaries in New France, 1610-1791; The Original French, Latin and Italian Texts, with English Translations and Notes, seventy-three volumes, Burrows (Cleveland, OH), 1896-1901.

(And contributor) *The University of Wisconsin, Its History and Its Alumni, with Historical and Descriptive Sketches of Madison,* Purcell (Madison, WI), 1900.

The State Historical Society of Wisconsin: Exercises at the Dedication of Its New Building, October 19, 1900; Together with a Description of the New Building, Accounts of the Several Libraries Contained Therein, and a Brief History of the Society, Democrat Printing Co., 1901.

Mrs. John H. Kinzie (Juliette Augusta Magill), *Wau-Bun, the "Early Day" of the Northwest,* Caxton Club (Chicago), 1901.

Father Louis Hennepin, *A New Discovery of a Vast Country in America,* two volumes, McClurg, 1903, Coles Pub. Co. (Toronto, Ontario, Canada), 1974.

Original Journals of the Lewis and Clark Expedition, 1804-1806; Printed from the Original Manuscripts in the Library of the American Philosophical Society and by the Direction of Its Committee on Historical Documents, together with Manuscript Material of Lewis and Clark from other Sources, Including Notebooks, Letters, Maps, etc., and the Journals of Charles Floyd and Joseph Whitehouse, Now for the First Time Published in Full and Exactly as Written, eight volumes, Dodd, Mead (New York City), 1904-05.

Early Western Travels, 1748-1846: A Series of Annotated Reprints of Some of the Best and Rarest Contemporary Volumes of Travel, Descriptive of the Aborigines and Social and Economic Conditions in the Middle and Far West, During the Period of Early American Settlement, thirty-two volumes, Clark, 1904-07.

(With Louise Phelps Kellogg) *Documentary History of Dunmore's War, 1774,* State Historical Society of Wisconsin, 1905, bicentennial edition, C.J. Carrier Co. (Harrisonburg, VA), 1974.

Louis Armand de Lom d'Arce, Baron de Lahontan, *New Voyages to North-America,* two volumes, McClurg, 1905.

Descriptive List of Manuscript Collections of the State Historical Society of Wisconsin; together with Reports on Other Collections of Manuscript Material for American History in Adjacent States, State Historical Society of Wisconsin, 1906.

State Historical Society of Wisconsin Handbooks, numbers 1-7, State Historical Society of Wisconsin, 1906-13.

Joel Palmer, *Journal of Travel over the Oregon Trail in 1845,* Clark, 1906, in *Early Western Travels, 1748-1846,* portion republished as commemorative edition by Oregon Historical Society Press (Portland, OR), 1993.

(With Kellogg) *The Revolution on the Upper Ohio, 1775-1777,* State Historical Society of Wisconsin, 1908, Kennikat Press (Port Washington, NY), 1970; portion republished as *Report of a Treaty with the Western Indians: Conducted at Pittsburgh September 12-October 21, 1775 and Now for the First Time Published* by Lewis Morris and others, Commissioners, from the Colonial Congress, Wisconsin Historical Society, 1908.

Wisconsin Historical Commission, *Original Papers,* seven volumes, State Historical Society (Madison, WI), 1908-12.

Wisconsin Historical Commission, *Reprints,* two volumes, State Historical Society (Madison), 1908-1912.

(With Kellogg) *Frontier Defense on the Upper Ohio, 1777-1778,* State Historical Society of Wisconsin, 1912, Kraus Reprint Co. (Millwood, NY), 1973.

(And compiler, with Annie Amelia Nunns) *Checklist of Publications of the Society, 1850-1913,* State Historical Society of Wisconsin, 1913.

Editor, *State Historical Society of Wisconsin Bulletins of Information,* numbers 1-70.

OTHER

Author of "Early Lead-Mining in Illinois and Wisconsin" in *Annual Report of the American Historical Association for the Year 1893,* Government Printing Office (Washington, DC), 1894; "State-Supported Historical Societies and Their Functions" in *Annual Report of the American Historical Association for the Year 1897,* Government Printing Office, 1898; "Historical Outline of the Admission of Wisconsin to the Union" in *Constitution of the State of Wisconsin,* edited by Henry Casson, Democrat Printing Co. (Madison, WI), 1898; "The Story of Lewis and Clark's Journals" in *Annual Report of the American Historical Association for the Year 1903,* two volumes, Government Printing Office, 1904, Volume One; "Report of the Committee on Methods of Organization on the Part of State and Local Historical Societies" in *Annual Report of the American Historical Association for the Year 1905,* two volumes, Government Printing Office, Volume One; "The Romance of Mississippi Valley History" in *Proceedings of the Fiftieth Anniversary of the Constitution of Iowa,* edited by B. F. Shambaugh, State Historical Society of Iowa (Iowa City), 1907; "The Ohio Valley Press before the War of 1812-1815" in *Proceedings of the American Antiquarian Society,* Volume Nineteen, 1909; and "At the Meeting of the Trails: The Romance of a Parish Register" in *Proceedings of the Mississippi Valley Historical Association,* Volume Six, 1912-1913.

Contributor of articles to *Oshkosh Times, Magazine of Western History, Wisconsin Journal of Education, Evening Wisconsin, Madison Times, Library Journal, Christendom, American Historical Review, Scribner's Magazine, Sunset Magazine, Independent,* and *Wisconsin Library Bulletin.*

Thwaites's papers are housed at the State Historical Society of Wisconsin.

SIDELIGHTS: A prolific historian and editor of historical materials, Reuben Gold Thwaites worked for a generation as secretary of the State Historical Society of Wisconsin, taking over that post in 1886 from the esteemed Lyman C. Draper. During his tenure at the Historical Society, Thwaites changed it from a relatively small collection of antiquarian papers intended for the reading pleasure of an intellectual elite, to, in the words of Steven P. Gietschier in

Dictionary of Literary Biography, "an instrument for public education" whose "varied resources" were to be used by the public at large. In the process, Gietschier asserted, Thwaites "created the modern idea of the historical society."

Active in civic educational affairs during a progressive period of American, and especially Wisconsin, history, Thwaites helped oversee a historically important, and still enduring, union between the State Historical Society of Wisconsin and another great state-supported institution, the University of Wisconsin. These two mutually assisting institutions still share space on the University of Wisconsin campus in Madison. As secretary of the Historical Society, Thwaites hired a staff which by the end of his lifetime, in 1913, numbered forty-one professionals plus three students and a staff of caretakers. His aggressive acquisitions policy—the Historical Society acquired some 6,900 volumes per year under his leadership—enlarged the Society's collection to more than 350,000 volumes, tripling its 1887 holdings.

Through his work for the American Historical Association, Thwaites was largely responsible for the establishment of a number of historical organizations, including the Conference of American Archivists, later known as the Society of American Archivists, and the Conference of Historical Societies, later known as the American Association for State and Local History. His educational work for the state of Wisconsin was equally admirable. Thwaites, a strong believer in what Gietschier termed "the perfectibility of man through broad-based public education," was a founder of the Wisconsin Library Association and of various local library associations, and of Wisconsin's Free Library Commission, which encouraged the growth of public libraries in that state. He was actively involved in erecting markers at Wisconsin historical sites and in restoring the state capitol building, which is still considered one of the finest state capitols in the United States. He lectured in American history at the University of Wisconsin, and spoke before audiences at local schools. He was, Gietschier asserted, "the best-known man in Wisconsin outside politics" when he suddenly died of a heart attack at age sixty, after entering a hospital for what was first diagnosed as a kidney problem.

As historian and editor of historical materials, Thwaites produced some work that it still available and of historiographic interest, including Father Louis Hennepin's *A New Discovery of a Vast Country in America* (originally written 1698), Joel Palmer's

Journals of Travel over the Oregon Trail in 1845 (1906), *The Revolution on the Upper Ohio, 1775-1777* (with Louise Kellogg, 1908), *Frontier Defense on the Upper Ohio, 1777-1778* (also with Kellogg, 1912), and his own *Daniel Boone* (1902, the "Appleton Life Histories Series"), *How George Rogers Clark Won the Northwest and Other Essays in Western History* (1903), *On the Storied Ohio* (1903), *France in America, 1497-1763* (1905), and *Wisconsin: The Americanization of a French Settlement* (1908).

His early writings, such as the 1888 *Historic Waterways,* were in many cases the fruit of Thwaites's summer canoe trips, as well as of his reading of the great American historian Francis Parkman. According to Gietschier, Thwaites was a man of enormous energy who "demanded much of his staff," but also one of great personal charm. Standing five feet seven inches, slightly round of figure and wearing rimless eyeglasses and a cheerful expression, he made friends easily and treated his workers like members of a family. Although his writing "has been faulted for lack of critical insight," according to Gietschier, he was "a gifted lecturer and storyteller, both in person . . . and in his writing." Thwaites's editing of various series of historical documents remain "a cherished resource," but his greatest legacy was his democratization of an important information resource, the historical society. As Gietschier put it, "The goals to which Thwaites aspired have become accepted standards in his profession."

BIOGRAPHICAL/CRITICAL SOURCES:

PERIODICALS

American Historical Review, April, 1906; October, 1906; January, 1907; October, 1908; April, 1909.
Critic, April, 1906.
Dial, July 1, 1906.
Nation, January 18, 1906; June 14, 1906; November 22, 1906; April 1, 1909.
New York Times, January 13, 1906; January 9, 1909.
Outlook, March 3, 1906; February 20, 1909.

BOOKS

Wilson, Clyde N., *Dictionary of Literary Biography,* Volume 47: *American Historians, 1866-1912,* Gale (Detroit), 1986, pp. 302-312.
Who Was Who in America, Volume 1: *1897-1942,* Marquis (Chicago), 1943, p. 1238.*

TILDON, J(ames) Tyson 1931-

PERSONAL: Born August 7, 1931, in Baltimore, MD; married Sania Amr, 1988; children: Levia, Jay, Sharon, Sania. *Education:* Morgan State College, B.S., 1954; Johns Hopkins University, Ph.D. (biochemistry), 1965; Brandeis University, post-doctoral study, 1965-67.

ADDRESSES: Office—Department of Pediatrics, University of Maryland School of Medicine, 655 West Baltimore St., Rm. 10-033 BRB, Baltimore, MD 21201.

CAREER: Biochemist and writer. Sinai Hospital, Baltimore, MD, research assistant, 1954-59; Institut de Biologie Physico-Chimique, Paris, France, Fulbright Scholar, 1959-60; Brandeis University, Helen Hay Whitney fellow in biochemistry, 1965-67; Goucher College, Baltimore, MD, assistant professor of chemistry, 1967-68; University of Maryland School of Medicine, Baltimore, MD, research assistant professor of pediatrics, 1968-69, assistant professor in biological chemistry, 1969-74, professor of pediatrics, 1974—, professor of biological chemistry, 1982—, Carter Clinical Laboratories director for six years, director of pediatric research in the Department of Pediatrics for nine years, helped establish the Sudden Infant Death Syndrome (SIDS) Institute; Antioch College, Baltimore campus, lecturer, 1972—.

Visiting scientist in the Laboratory of Developmental Biochemistry and Josiah Macy Junior Faculty Scholar at the University of Groningen in the Netherlands, 1975-76. Has served on the boards of directors of the Mental Health Association of Metropolitan Baltimore, the Maryland Academy of Sciences, and the Associated Black Charities.

MEMBER: American Chemical Society, Association for the Advancement of Science, American Society for Biochemistry and Molecular Biology, Society for Experimental Biology and Medicine, Sigma Xi.

AWARDS, HONORS: Maryland State Senate Citation, 1983, for work with SIDS; City of Baltimore Citizen Citation, 1986; Joseph S. Tyler, Jr., Award for Achievement in Science, Baltimore Chapter of the National Technical Association, 1986; National Association of Negro Business and Professional Women's Club's Community Service Award, 1987; Humanitarian Award, Associated Black Charities, 1991.

WRITINGS:

The Anglo-Saxon Agony, Whitmore Publishing, 1972.
Sudden Infant Death Syndrome, Academic Press, 1983.

Contributor to journals and periodicals, including *Archives of Biochemistry and Biophysics* and *Journal of Clinical Investigation.*

SIDELIGHTS: J. Tyson Tildon, the discoverer of Coenzyme A Tranferase Deficiency, a cause of disease in infants, has made major contributions to the establishment of the Sudden Infant Death Syndrome (SIDS) Institute at the University of Maryland School of Medicine. His research interests include developmental neurochemistry and the processes that control metabolism.

Tildon was born April 7, 1931, in Baltimore, Maryland. He received his B.S. degree in chemistry from Morgan State College in 1954 and then worked for five years as a research assistant at Sinai Hospital, where he developed and used biochemical techniques to study vitamin deficiencies in humans and animal models. Subsequently, he spent a year as a Fulbright Scholar at the Institut de Biologie Physico-Chimique in Paris and, upon his return, matriculated to the doctoral program in biochemistry at Johns Hopkins University. After receiving his Ph.D. in 1965, Tildon accepted a two-year postdoctoral fellowship at Brandeis University, where his studies included an examination of how cells assume specialized functions during development. Tildon returned to Baltimore in 1967 to assume the post of assistant professor in the department of chemistry at Goucher College. The following year he became research assistant professor in the department of pediatrics at the University of Maryland School of Medicine, and, in 1969, assistant professor in the department of biological chemistry. He has been a full professor of pediatrics since 1974 and a professor of biological chemistry since 1982. Tildon has also served as director of the Carter Clinical Laboratories for six years and director of pediatric research in the medical school's Department of Pediatrics for nine. In addition, he was a visiting scientist in the Laboratory of Developmental Biochemistry at the University of Groningen in the Netherlands, where he did research in the developmental neurobiology.

Among Tildon's contributions is the discovery of Coenzyme A (or CoA) Transferase Deficiency in infants. In his research, he demonstrated that the brains of infants use organic molecules called ketone bodies as an energy source during their first several weeks of life, disproving the previously held theory that glucose was the major energy source of the human brain at all ages of life. Tildon was also instrumental in establishing the SIDS Institute at the University of Maryland, one of the largest research programs dedicated to the study of SIDS, a disorder that causes an infant to abruptly stop breathing. Included in the discoveries made at the Institute are those of researcher Robert G. Meny, who found that babies suffered bradycardia, or abnormally slow heartbeat, before they stopped breathing. This finding has stimulated new research into the role of the heart in SIDS.

Tildon's interests extend beyond medicine and biochemistry and into other realms of research. In his book *The Anglo-Saxon Agony,* he points out that Western societies rely predominately on sight and hearing to gather information while ignoring the more personal senses of taste, smell, and touch. Rather than integrating all of the brain's responses to stimuli, Tildon suggests, the Anglo-Saxon approach is to separate thinking and feeling in an effort to be dispassionate. Yet, by excluding the emotional component, he writes, westerners fail to understand fully the human condition.

Among the many societies Tildon belongs to are Sigma Xi, the American Chemical Society, the Association for the Advancement of Science, the American Society for Biochemistry and Molecular Biology, and the Society for Experimental Biology and Medicine. He received the Maryland State Senate Citation for his work with SIDS in 1983, the City of Baltimore Citizen Citation in 1986, the Baltimore Chapter of the National Technical Association's Joseph S. Tyler, Jr. Award for Achievement in Science in 1986, the National Association of Negro Business and Professional Women's Club's Community Service Award in 1987, and the Humanitarian Award from the Associated Black Charities in 1991. In addition, he has served on several boards of directors, including those of the Mental Health Association of Metropolitan Baltimore, the Maryland Academy of Sciences, and the Associated Black Charities.*

*　　*　　*

TILGHMAN, Christopher 1948(?)-

PERSONAL: Born c. 1948.

ADDRESSES: Home—Harvard, MA.

CAREER: Has worked as a carpenter, in a sawmill, renovating buildings, and writing copy for corporate reports; freelance writer, 1971—. *Military service*—served in U.S. Navy until 1971.

WRITINGS:

In a Father's Place (short stories; contains "On the Rivershore," "Loose Reins," "Norfolk, 1969," "Hole in the Day," "A Gracious Rain," "In a Father's Place," and "Mary in the Mountains"), Farrar Straus (New York City), 1990.
Mason's Retreat (novel), Random House (New York City), 1996.

Also contributor of short stories to periodicals, including the *New Yorker*.

SIDELIGHTS: Fiction writer Christopher Tilghman began writing when he left the U.S. Navy in 1971. He had to support himself with odd jobs, however, including carpentry and writing copy for corporations, because he didn't sell his first story until 1986. Tilghman's first book-length publication is the acclaimed 1990 short story collection *In a Father's Place.* He followed this critical success with another in 1996—his first novel, *Mason's Retreat.* Though he writes about other locations as well, the Chesapeake Bay area of Maryland features strongly in his books.

Nicholas Clee, writing in the *Times Literary Supplement,* asserted that "Tilghman writes prose that is lyrical, alert and warm; he is engagingly unafraid to let it swell, risking sentimentality." Many critics have agreed about the merit of *In a Father's Place,* though there was dissent about the relative quality of some of the individual stories.

"On the Rivershore," is about the tension between Maryland watermen and farmers, and how these are played out and resolved when a handyman kills a fisherman who had molested his daughter. Richard Eder, critiquing *In a Father's Place* in the *Los Angeles Times Book Review,* called "On the Rivershore" a "beautifully drawn" story. Ann Hulbert in the *New Republic* cited the tale as memorable as well, calling its use of description "metaphorically as well as physically telling." Robert Towers in the *New York Review of Books* marveled over how, in the "only twenty-two pages" of "On the Rivershore," "a small society, with its occupations, its class structure, and its codes . . . has been revealed."

"Loose Reins," concerns a grown son revisiting the ranch he grew up on after his widowed mother has married a once-drunken ranch hand. Eder found the story to be too "stiffly arranged around its point, although it boasts one shining scene." John Casey in the *New York Times Book Review* noted that "Loose Reins" "has some of the abrupt complexity of comedy," and summed up the tale as being "about what all of these people have worked out with one another, the way the place works them loose from the predestinations of family and class." Towers applauded the fact that "the Montana landscape [is] evoked carefully and knowledgeably" and "so are the language and attitudes of the old ranch hand."

"Norfolk, 1969" describes a marriage that comes apart after the husband is drafted into the Navy and the wife joins the peace movement. In Eder's opinion the story "arranges its characters woodenly," but he conceded "there is some lovely writing in it." Casey, by contrast, found it "plausible and intelligent." Hulbert praised the subtle ways in which "the political contours" of the couple's "trouble emerge" in "Norfolk, 1969," as well as how "just as subtly they are complicated by a deeper, unideological perspective."

"Hole in the Day" portrays a woman's attempt to run away from her marriage when she learns she is pregnant with a fifth child, and details her husband's quest to find her. Eder praised "Hole in the Day" as "touching and comic," explaining that in it, "Tilghman has accomplished what only a true storyteller can do: make the impossible inevitable." Casey labeled "Hole in the Day" "elegantly balanced," while the same tale prompted Thomas D'Evelyn in the *Christian Science Monitor* to declare that "Tilghman is wonderful with children." Similarly, Towers assessed that in "Hole in the Day" the author "dramatizes the situation of the desperate young couple without condescension and the children are remarkably real."

"A Gracious Rain," gives readers the thoughts of a young, married man who suddenly dies. This story came in for criticism from Eder, who found the focus on a character who had passed to the afterlife "contrived." Michiko Kakutani of the *New York Times* did not care for that tale either, labeling it "an awkward ghost story." Casey liked "A Gracious Rain," however, and added that "it leads to a vision that is more than worth the jolt." Hulbert enjoyed it as well, and observed that "this unusual story . . . nonchalantly steps into the afterlife as though barely a doorsill stood in the way." D'Evelyn affirmed that "Tilghman manages the transition from this character's life to his afterlife without skipping a beat."

The title story for the collection, which illustrates a man's reactions to his son's obnoxious girlfriend, brought mixed reviews. Malcolm Jones in *Newsweek* praised "In a Father's Place" for its "almost Dickensian sense of drama and possibility," while Eder lamented that the obnoxious girlfriend of the piece, Patty, "is not simply a mean effigy; she is a regular Guy Fawkes stuffed to the sneer with gunpowder." Similarly, Casey described the same character as an "onstage villain," but judged that the tale is "still riveting in its progress." Hulbert, interestingly, praised Patty as "quite comically drawn." Towers, however, singled out "In a Father's Place" as the only tale in the collection in which "Tilghman's touch seems less than sure." "Mary in the Mountains" is the tale of a woman conveyed predominantly in letters to her ex-husband. D'Evelyn praised the letter-writer heroine of this final piece of *In a Father's Place*: "She writes with the vehemence of [twentieth-century American poet] Sylvia Plath and the aching wisdom of [nineteenth-century American poet] Emily Dickinson."

"*In a Father's Place* is a moving and pictorially vivid collection—a collection that signals the appearance of a gifted new writer, blessed with an instinctual feel for the emotional transactions that make up family life," wrote Kakutani. Casey summed up the collection as "a wonderful surprise," while D'Evelyn, citing the author's wide range of experience as well as his maturity, concluded that Tilghman's "eloquent stories are works of intelligence, craft, and time."

Mason's Retreat seems to have fulfilled critical expectations for Tilghman's first novel. It uses a contemporary frame and a narrator looking back upon his own family history to tell a story that takes place during the late 1930s. Edward Mason has inherited a two-hundred-year-old Maryland estate from a maiden aunt, and decides to leave his floundering manufacturing business in England to take up life as a rich farmer. With him, he brings Edith, the wife he has promised never again to be unfaithful to, and their two sons, thirteen-year-old Sebastien and six-year-old Simon. Though he is resistant to the move at first, Sebastien soon comes to see the estate as his long-lost spiritual home. Edith finds happiness there as well; in fact, the only one who cannot adjust, let alone prosper, is Edward. His plans to return to England and

his family's subsequent resistance bring about a tragedy that changes the family forever.

Thomas Mallon, discussing *Mason's Retreat* in the *New York Times Book Review,* wrote that "Tilghman writes with the same authoritative elegance that he displayed in his earlier stories," and went on to praise the novel as a "finely imagined book." Similarly, Gene Lyons in *Entertainment Weekly* appraised it as "beautifully written" and "fully imagined." *Mason's Retreat* prompted Paula Chin in *People* to call Tilghman "a master of mood and atmosphere," while Jonathan Yardley in the *Washington Post Book World* concluded: "In all respects, *Mason's Retreat* is exemplary."

BIOGRAPHICAL/CRITICAL SOURCES:

PERIODICALS

Christian Science Monitor, June 15, 1990, p. 13.
Entertainment Weekly, June 7, 1996, pp. 52, 55.
Los Angeles Times Book Review, April 29, 1990, pp. 3, 7.
New Republic, June 4, 1990, pp. 40-41.
Newsweek, April 2, 1990, pp. 59-60.
New York Review of Books, August 16, 1990, p. 46.
New York Times, April 3, 1990, p. C17.
New York Times Book Review, May 6, 1990, p. 12; April 28, 1996, p. 13.
People, August 19, 1996, p. 33.
Times Literary Supplement, July 5, 1996, p. 22.
Washington Post Book World, April 7, 1996, p. 3.*

—*Sketch by Elizabeth Wenning*

* * *

TILLY, Chris 1955-
(Brendan Rosis)

PERSONAL: Born November 9, 1955, in France; U.S. citizen; son of Charles (a professor) and Louise (a professor) Tilly; married Marie Kennedy (a professor), 1984; children: Kaaren, Amanda. *Ethnicity:* "USA." *Education:* Harvard University, A.B., 1976; Massachusetts Institute of Technology, Ph.D., 1989. *Politics:* "Progressive." *Avocational interests:* Popular music.

ADDRESSES: Home—185 Davis Ave., No. 8, Brookline, MA 02146. *Office*—University of Massachusetts, Lowell, MA 01854. *E-mail*—tillyc@woods.uml.edu.

CAREER: University of Massachusetts, Lowell, associate professor of regional economic and social development, 1988—. Grassroots International, member of program committee.

MEMBER: American Economic Association, Union for Radical Political Economics.

WRITINGS:

(With Yohel Camayd-Freixas) *Fifteen Years of Community-Based Development: An Annotated Bibliography, 1968-1983,* CPL Bibliographies (Chicago, IL), c. 1985.

Short Hours, Short Shrift: Causes and Consequences of Part-Time Work, Economic Policy Institute (Washington, DC), c. 1990.

(With Randy Albelda) *It'll Take More Than a Miracle: Income in Single-Mother Families in Massachusetts, 1979-1987,* University of Massachusetts Press (Boston), 1992.

(With Barry Bluestone and Mary Huff Stevenson) *Public Policy Alternatives for Dealing with the Labor Market Problems of Central City Young Adults: Implications from Current Labor Market Research,* University of Massachusetts Press, 1994.

Half a Job: Bad and Good Part-Time Jobs in a Changing Labor Market, Temple University Press (Philadelphia, PA), 1996.

(With Randy Albelda) *Glass Ceilings and Bottomless Pits: Women's Work, Women's Poverty,* South End Press (Boston, MA), 1997.

(With Charles Tilly) *Work under Capitalism,* Westview Press (Boulder, CO), 1997.

Also uses the pseudonym Brendan Rosis. Member of editorial collective, *Dollars and Sense.*

WORK IN PROGRESS: A book on discrimination, Russell Sage (New York City), 1999.

* * *

TORRES, John A(lbert) 1965-

PERSONAL: Born August 18, 1965, in New York, NY; son of Americo, Jr. (a retail manager) and Carmen (Calderon) Torres; married Julie Perry (a secretary), June 9, 1990; children: Daniel, Jacqueline. *Education:* Fordham University, B.A., 1987. *Politics:* Independent. *Religion:* Roman Catholic.

ADDRESSES: Home—2-D Millholland Dr., Fishkill, NY 12524. *E-mail*—JohnnyPitt@aol.com.

CAREER: Writer. Little League coach.

WRITINGS:

FOR YOUNG PEOPLE

(With Michael J. Sullivan) *Sports Great Darryl Strawberry,* Enslow Publishers (Hillside, NJ), 1990.

(Self-illustrated) *Home-Run Hitters: Heroes of the Four Home-Run Game,* Simon & Schuster (New York City), 1995.

Sports Reports: Hakeem Olajuwon, Enslow Publishers, 1997.

Sports Great Jason Kidd, Enslow Publishers, 1997.

Greg Maddux, Lerner Publications (Minneapolis, MN), 1997.

WORK IN PROGRESS: Sports Great Oscar De La Hoya and *Top Ten Three-Point Shooters* for Enslow Publishers; a novel about a sportswriter.

SIDELIGHTS: John A. Torres commented: "Ever since I can remember, I have wanted to be a writer. My idol as a child was Ernest Hemingway. Since I also love sports, I tried to combine my two loves: writing and sports. My ultimate dream is to have my novel published and to be able to become a full-time writer. The most important development in my evolution as a writer was when I read [Ernest] Hemingway's *The Old Man and the Sea* during the summer I spent interning at United Press International. That was truly a baptism by fire."

BIOGRAPHICAL/CRITICAL SOURCES:

PERIODICALS

Horn Book Guide, July, 1990, p. 145; fall, 1995, p. 373.

School Library Journal, November, 1990, p. 124; May, 1995, p. 116.*

* * *

TRAIN, Arthur (Cheney) 1875-1945

PERSONAL: Born September 6, 1875, in Boston, MA; died of cancer, December 22, 1945, in New

York, NY; son of Charles Russell (attorney general of the Commonwealth of Massachusetts) and Sarah Maria (Cheney) Train; married Ethel Kissam, April 20, 1897 (died May 15, 1923); married Helen C. Gerard, January 6, 1926; children: (first marriage) Mrs. Boris Samsonoff, Mrs. Lucy Worcester, Arthur K.; (second marriage) John. *Education:* Harvard University, A.B. (cum laude), 1896, LL.B., 1899.

CAREER: American lawyer and author. Admitted to Massachusetts bar, 1899; Robinson Biddle and Ward (law firm), lawyer, 1900; New York County, NY, assistant district attorney, 1901-08, and 1913 (some sources say 1914)-45; Train and Olney (law firm), member, 1908-13; State of New York, Special Deputy Attorney General, 1910, to investigate and prosecute political offenders in Queens County; Perkins and Train (law firm), member, 1916-23.

MEMBER: Author's League of America (co-founder, 1912), National Institute of Arts and Letters (twice elected president), Century Club, University Club, Harvard Club.

WRITINGS:

CRIME NOVELS

The Confessions of Artemas Quibble, Scribner (New York City), 1911.
"C.Q."; or, In the Wireless House, Century (New York City), 1912.
The Hermit of Turkey Hollow, Scribner, 1921.
The Blind Goddess, Scribner, 1926.
The Adventures of Ephraim Tutt, Scribner, 1930.
Manhattan Murder, Scribner, 1936, published as *Murderers' Medicine,* Constable (London), 1937.
Yankee Lawyer—The Autobiography of Ephraim Tutt, Scribner, 1943.

OTHER NOVELS

The Butler's Story, Scribner, 1909.
(With Robert Williams Wood) *The Man Who Rocked the Earth* (science fiction), Doubleday (New York City), 1915, Arno Press (New York City), 1975.
The World and Thomas Kelly, Scribner, 1917.
The Earthquake, Scribner, 1918.
As It Was in the Beginning, Macmillan (New York City), 1921.
His Children's Children, Scribner, 1923.
The Needle's Eye, Scribner, 1924.
The Lost Gospel (novella, with postscript by Train), Scribner, 1925.

High Winds, Scribner, 1927.
Ambition, Scribner, 1928.
The Horns of Ramadan, Scribner, 1928.
Illusion, Scribner, 1929.
Paper Profits, Liveright (New York City), 1930.
Princess Pro Tem, Scribner, 1932.
No Matter Where, Scribner, 1933.
Jacob's Ladder, Scribner, 1935.
Tassels on Her Boots, Scribner, 1940.
(With Robert Williams Wood) *The Moon Maker* (science fiction), Krueger (New York City), 1958.

SHORT STORY COLLECTIONS

McAllister and His Double, Scribner, 1905, Books for Libraries Press (Freeport, NY), 1970.
Mortmain, Appleton (New York City), 1907.
Tutt and Mr. Tutt, Scribner, 1920.
By Advice of Counsel, Scribner, 1921.
Tut, Tut! Mr. Tutt, Scribner, 1923.
Page Mr. Tutt, Scribner, 1926.
When Tutt Meets Tutt, Scribner, 1927.
Tutt for Tutt, Scribner, 1934.
Mr. Tutt Takes the Stand, Scribner, 1936.
Mr. Tutt's Case Book (omnibus), Scribner, 1936.
Old Man Tutt, Scribner, 1938.

NONFICTION

The Prisoner at the Bar, Scribner, 1906, Arno Press, 1974, revised edition, 1908, revised edition published as *From the District Attorney's Office,* 1939.
True Stories of Crime from the District Attorney's Office, Scribner, 1908, Arno Press, 1974.
Courts, Criminals, and the Camorra, Scribner, 1912.
Courts and Criminals (selections from *The Prisoner at the Bar* and *Courts, Criminals and the Camorra),* Scribner, 1921, Arno Press, 1974.
On the Trail of the Bad Men, Scribner, 1925.
Puritan's Progress, Scribner, 1931.
The Strange Attacks on Herbert Hoover, Day (New York City), 1932.
My Day in Court (autobiography), Scribner, 1939.

EDITOR

The Goldfish, Being the Confessions of a Successful Man, Century, 1914.

OTHER

Author of more than one hundred short stories. Manuscripts and correspondence collected at the

American Academy of Arts and Letters, New York, Princeton University, and the Beinecke Rare Book and Manuscript Library, Yale University.

SIDELIGHTS: Into his allotted seventy years, Arthur Train packed two remarkably full careers: that of lawyer and that of man of letters. His two callings were neatly intertwined, although Train more than once expressed regret at the influence of legal training on his writing. In *Yankee Lawyer: The Autobiography of Ephraim Tutt,* published in 1943, there is a conversation between Train's fictional creation, Tutt, and Train himself, in which Train says, "No lawyer can spend ten years drawing papers and retain his freedom of expression. . . . It's not only the saids, aforesaids, whereases, hereinafters and befores, it's because the factual attitude becomes part of his makeup. His style ceases to be free. He becomes literal, pedantic, over-precise." On the other hand, there is no doubt that the law gave Train a wealth of material for many of his most popular books and stories.

Train was bred to the legal profession, growing up as the son of the attorney general of Massachusetts. Although he had literary aspirations from an early age, the profession of writing was looked at with askance in the upper-class circles to which the Train family belonged. Train took literature courses at Harvard, then entered the University's law school and practiced briefly in Boston. He soon moved to New York City, where he persistently pursued a job with the reformer William Travers Jerome and was ultimately hired as an assistant district attorney. Among other cases, he successfully prosecuted a famous investment banker named Henry Siegel.

During this period, the human interest of criminal cases and the atmosphere of the "Tombs" prison fascinated Train, and he began writing fictionalized cases. By 1905 he was regularly contributing to the *Saturday Evening Post* and *Scribner's* magazines. Although aware of modernist experiments such as those of Henry James, Train's own narrative gift was a straightforward one, and his legal subject-matter offered, as quoted by Philip Stevick in the *Dictionary of Literary Biography,* "a ready-made plot of its own."

At the same time, Train was writing and publishing nonfiction accounts of the legal system, for which he was becoming well known. His volumes in the true-crime genre included *The Prisoner at the Bar* (1906), *True Stories of Crime from the District Attorney's Office* (1908), *Courts, Criminals and the Comorra* (1912), and the selection *Courts and Criminals* (1921), some of which were republished in the 1970s.

In 1919 Train had the inspiration for a fictional character who was to bring him his greatest popular success: Ephraim Tutt, a tall, elderly Yankee lawyer who wore a stovepipe hat, frock coat, and smoked a cigar. This figure's physical appearance came from a painted portrait in a clamshell ashtray in Train's childhood home. Spiritually, Train accounted for Tutt's genesis, quoted in the *Dictionary of Literary Biography,* as follows: "I suppose that Mr. Tutt is a combination of most of the qualities which I would like to have, coupled with a few that are common to all of us. One critic has disposed of him by saying that his popularity is due to the fact that he is a hodgepodge of Puck, Robin Hood, Abraham Lincoln, and Uncle Sam. I am willing to let it go at that." Stevick found this assessment accurate in that it positions Tutt as a mythic character: "Tutt is less a character . . . than he is a myth. . . . Like many mythic figures, Tutt is aristocratic in his bearing, populist in his compassion."

J. Randolph Cox, in *Twentieth-Century Crime and Mystery Writers,* observed that the Tutt tales follow a formula that includes the "triumph of justice over the technicalities of the law" against all odds. Cox added, "Mr. Tutt is a figure from American folklore, the shrewd Yankee on the side of the underdog." To this consensus, Stevick added as a further reason for the Tutt stories' appeal that they "always rest upon a basis of fact which is both interesting in itself and integral to the story."

A keen researcher, Train filled his tales with convincing descriptions of specific New York buildings, streets, businesses, and people, in addition to the workings of technical trades ranging from oil prospecting to railroad signalling to legerdemain. The legal touches in the stories are so credibly presented that, in the 1936 omnibus volume *Mr. Tutt's Case Book,* they are annotated by a lawyer and preceded by a foreword by a former dean of Northwestern University Law School. "Finally," declared Stevick, "the stories are executed in a style at once elegant, knowing, often arch, ingratiating, charming—in a word, comfortable."

All told, more than a hundred Tutt stories were published in magazines and subsequently collected in books. But the most memorable Tutt volume was a

novel in the form of Tutt's autobiography, the 1943 *Yankee Lawyer,* which Stevick termed "a remarkable tour de force." Train presents Tutt's life from boyhood—including photographs—through his Harvard education, law practice, personal life, and most famous cases. Included are Tutt's fictional friendships with real celebrities such as Edith Wharton and Calvin Coolidge. The book ends with a chapter in which Tutt philosophizes on law, justice, ethics, and the condition of the United States. Train's name did not appear on the book cover or title page, and the copyright notice read, "Copyright, 1943, by Ephraim Tutt." According to Stevick, "The illusion is never broken: the book seems, from start to finish, a book by Tutt, not Train."

The illusion was so successful that readers widely refused to believe that Tutt was an invented character or that Train himself had written the autobiography. Letters addressed to Tutt came from would-be clients and from self-proclaimed long-lost relatives; *Who's Who* invited Tutt to submit his resume. Train, in turn, published disclaimers in the *Saturday Evening Post,* as well as a later, more serious essay in the *Saturday Review,* which Stevick recommended as "an urbane and thoughtful defense of the long tradition of the fictional 'autobiography.'"

Train's own autobiography appeared in 1939 under the title *My Day in Court.* According to Stevick, the book displays not only narrative skill and an eye for interesting anecdotes, but "a mind immensely engaged by experience" and "a capacity to reflect . . . on the nature of authorship." Reviewing *My Day in Court* for the *Saturday Review of Literature,* Stephen Vincent Bent wrote, "These are the memories and comments of a shrewd and civilized observer who has seen a great deal more of the human comedy than most of us and played his part in it with gusto—and sometimes with his tongue in his cheek." For the benefit of aspiring writers, Bent averred, "The last hundred pages of *My Day in Court* . . . contain a great deal of sound, skillful, and honest comment on the business of writing. . . . A good many writers' autobiographies waver between professional mock modesty and a beautifully naive Jack Hornerism. There isn't a trace of either here. This is the advice of a skilled craftsman . . . and he talks about his own career objectively and without bunkum." According to Robert Van Gelder, who reviewed the autobiography for the *New York Times Book Review,* Train's examination of the business side of writing went deeper than Anthony Trollope's in that Victorian novelist's autobiography.

It was Train's dual awareness of the law and of the difficulties of a literary career that impelled him to co-found the Author's League of America in 1912, after he discovered an inequity in publishers' payments for serial rights to short stories. The founding of this institution, which has helped writers with contractual and other legal problems ever since, would in itself be enough to earn the gratitude of Train's colleagues in the literary profession, and doubtless contributed to Train's twice being elected president of the National Institute of Arts and Letters.

Even setting aside Train's legal career and his fiction and nonfiction writings about the law, he would have amassed a reasonably prolific life's work as a writer. His work included two co-written science fiction novels, one of which, *The Man Who Rocked the Earth,* published in 1915, included an early account of the possible uses of atomic energy. The *New York Times Book Review* called this effort "an ingenious yarn with an excellent basic idea." Train's 1924 short story, "The Lost Gospel," first published in the *Saturday Evening Post,* concerned the discovery of a biblical manuscript in some Libyan desert ruins. It was republished as a book with a postscript by Train in response to the many letters he had received about the story.

A noteworthy novel of Train's from 1918 was *The Earthquake,* a study of the effects of World War I on the American upper class, which the *New York Times Book Review* hailed in that year as "by far the best piece of work he has ever done." Five years later, a *Times* reviewer applied similar praise to another of Train's non-crime novels, *His Children's Children,* the saga of a rich American family: "an excellently sustained novel with a high degree of able characterization, by far the most ambitious and successful piece of work [Train] has ever turned out." The reviewer concluded that *My Children's Children* was "a more than ordinarily excellent piece of genre painting," and "a book that should add immeasurably to his reputation." According to Cox in *Twentieth-Century Crime and Mystery Writers, His Children's Children* can be compared with John Galsworthy's *The Forsyte Saga.*

Another work of Train's that deserves specific mention is the 1931 *Puritan's Progress,* a well-researched nonfictional recreation of the Train family history and of American manners in the 1800s. The historian Allan Nevins, reviewing this book for the *Saturday Review of Literature* labeled it "enjoyable" and "irreverent" and, although not finding profound insights in it, said, "It would be difficult to find a more entertaining work on national manners."

Train was a crime writer in several veins, a mainstream novelist, a historian of manners, an innovator in the use of the radio in fiction plots, the creator of a mythic crime-fighting character, an early parodist, according to Van Gelder, of Gertrude Stein, the co-founder of an important institution in the modern publishing world, and a successful lawyer. Noting that few people still read Train's work, Stevick concluded that, "a reader who happens upon his fiction now will be struck with its ease and grace and the wisdom with which he takes the measure of his fellow man and woman. . . . the historian of our culture's myths will be obliged to acknowledge the extraordinary power . . . of the image of Ephraim Tutt."

BIOGRAPHICAL/CRITICAL SOURCES:

BOOKS

Dictionary of Literary Biography, Volume 86: *American Short-Story Writers, 1910-1945,* edited by Bobby Ellen Kimbel, Gale (Detroit, MI), 1989, pp. 298-305.

Train, Arthur, *Yankee Casebook—The Autobiography of Ephraim Tutt,* Scribner (New York City), 1943.

Twentieth-Century Crime and Mystery Writers, third edition, St. James Press (Chicago, IL), 1991, pp. 1016-1017.

PERIODICALS

Nation, February 7, 1907, p. 133; November 21, 1907, p. 474; April 27, 1909, p. 419; November 14, 1912, p. 462; January 10, 1918, p. 43; August 24, 1918, pp. 206-207; May 2, 1923, pp. 522-523.

New Republic, March 24, 1926, p. 152; November 22, 1943, p. 726.

New York Times Book Review, November 23, 1907, p. 743; September 19, 1908, p. 514; April 17, 1909; September 15, 1912, p. 511; May 30, 1915, p. 206; November 18, 1917, p. 475; March 24, 1918, p. 122; April 18, 1920, p. 199; April 17, 1921, p. 22; May 15, 1921, p. 24; February 18, 1923, p. 22; September 30, 1923, p. 5; September 28, 1924, p. 8; October 11, 1925, p. 21; March 7, 1926; December 12, 1926, p. 37; April 17, 1927, p. 19; November 6, 1927, p. 23; February 26, 1928, p. 6; De-

cember 2, 1928, p. 52; April 13, 1929, p. 9; May 12, 1929, p. 16; February 22, 1931, pp. 1, 17; July 17, 1932, p. 6; August 13, 1933, p. 7; March 18, 1934, p. 12; March 3, 1935, p. 7; March 22, 1936, p. 21; June 5, 1938, p. 7; February 19, 1939, p. 5; August 27, 1939, p. 3, 21; August 11, 1940, p. 6; April 27, 1941, p. 7; August 29, 1943, p. 1; March 18, 1945, p. 25.

Saturday Review of Literature, October 25, 1924, p. 224; May 15, 1926; July 23, 1927; November 26, 1927, p. 353; April 28, 1928, p. 830; April 5, 1930, p. 904; July 11, 1931, p. 955; September 2, 1933, p. 84; March 24, 1934, p. 581; August 31, 1935; August 29, 1936, p. 21; June 4, 1938, p. 20; February 18, 1939, p. 5; September 16, 1939, p. 12; August 17, 1940, p. 11.

Spectator, July 27, 1907, p. 128.

Times Literary Supplement, October 11, 1923, p. 672; September 27, 1928, p. 689; October 24, 1929, p. 848; October 19, 1940.*

*   *   *

TRELL, Bluma L(ee)   1903-1997

OBITUARY NOTICE—See index for *CA* sketch: Born March 10, 1903, in New York, NY; died June 10, 1997, in Englewood, NJ. Educator, historian, numismaticist, author. Trell studied ancient coins and their depictions of the architecture of ancient Greek civilization. Her studies of the coins led her to write her dissertation, *Architectura Numismatica: The Temples of Asia Minor,* and draft blueprints and a reconstruction of the Temple of Artemis in Ephesus, Turkey—one of the seven ancient wonders of the world. The reconstructed temple is on display in London at the British Museum.

Trell received a degree in law and was in private practice from 1926 to 1932. She returned to her studies and in 1935 received a bachelor's degree in the arts. She taught briefly at the University of California, Los Angeles, and at Hunter College (now City University of New York) before joining the faculty at New York University in 1959. She contributed many articles to journals and wrote for the *Dictionary of Arts.* Her other works are *Coins and Their Cities: Architecture on the Ancient Coins of Greece, Rome, and Palestine* (with Martin Jessop Price), and *The Temple of Artemis at Ephesos.*

OBITUARIES AND OTHER SOURCES:

PERIODICALS

New York Times, June 12, 1997, p. B17.
Washington Post, June 16, 1997, p. B4.

*   *   *

TUTUOLA, Amos   1920-1997

OBITUARY NOTICE—See index for *CA* sketch: Born in 1920, in Abeokuta, Nigeria; died from hypertension and diabetes, June 8, 1997, in Ibadan, Nigeria. Author. Tutuola is credited as the first internationally recognized Nigerian writer for his novels and short stories retelling folktales. After attending the Salvation Army School in Lagos, Tutuola trained as a metalsmith. He served with Britain's Royal Air Force during World War II and later worked for the Nigerian Broadcasting Corporation (now the Federal Radio Corporation of Nigeria). Tutuola's first book, *The Palm-Wine Drinkard and His Dead Palm-* *Wine Tapster in the Dead's Town,* published in 1952, received critical acclaim and was later adapted for the stage. His use of the Yoruba language combined with English brought a truly African flavor to his writings, which are considered by many as African classics. Many of his stories appear in anthologies such as *An African Treasury: Articles, Essays, Stories, Poems by Black Africans,* edited by Langston Hughes, and *African Writing Today,* edited by Ezekiel Mphahlele. His works include the volumes *Pauper, Brawler, and Slanderer, The Witch-Herbalist of the Remote Town, The Feather Woman of the Jungle, The Brave African Huntress,* and *My Life in the Bush of Ghosts.*

OBITUARIES AND OTHER SOURCES:

BOOKS

International Who's Who, Europa Publications, 1996.

PERIODICALS

New York Times, June 15, 1997, p. 31.
Washington Post, June 22, 1997, p. B8.

V

VAIL, Rachel 1966-

PERSONAL: Born July 25, 1966, in New York, NY; married; husband's name, Mitchell; children: Zachary. *Education:* Georgetown University, B.A., 1988.

ADDRESSES: Home—New York, NY. *Office*—c/o Writers House, 21 West 26th St., New York, NY 10010.

CAREER: Writer.

MEMBER: Authors Guild.

AWARDS, HONORS: Editor's Choice, *Booklist,* 1991, for *Wonder,* and 1992, for *Do-Over;* "Pick of the List," American Booksellers Association, 1991, for *Wonder;* Blue Ribbon designation, *Bulletin of the Center for Children's Books,* 1992, for *Do-Over;* Books for the Teen Age citation, New York Public Library, 1992, for *Do-Over,* and 1994, for *Ever After;* Best Books designation, *School Library Journal,* 1996, for *Daring to Be Abigail.*

WRITINGS:

Wonder, Orchard Books (New York City), 1991.
Do-Over, Orchard Books, 1992.
Ever After, Orchard Books, 1994.
Daring to Be Abigail, Orchard Books, 1996.

SIDELIGHTS: Born in Manhattan, Rachel Vail grew up in New Rochelle, New York. In her youth she never intended to be a writer, but she received the encouragement of various teachers, both in high school and later at Georgetown University, who helped her to develop her talent. In an autobiographi-cal sketch for *Horn Book,* Vail recalls one instructor in particular named Doc Murphy. A theater professor, Murphy encouraged her to focus on the essentials of character. Vail observed: "I think writing would be so much more exciting and less daunting to children if the emphasis were put on the details, the questions that propel the writer to create astonishing, unique characters who, by their juxtaposition with other astonishing, unique characters, make stories happen."

Vail's emphasis on character is apparent in her first novel for children, a coming-of-age story titled *Wonder.* As twelve-year-old Jessica enters seventh grade she finds that she has suddenly become unpopular. Sheila, her former best friend, and five other girls succeed in ostracizing Jessica, giving her the humili-ating nickname "Wonder" after one of the girls describes her new polka-dot dress as "a Wonder Bread explosion." With determination, and with the welcome attentions of Conor O'Malley, the object of her first crush, Jessica perseveres. Lauded by critics for its skillful rendering of character, *Wonder* proved to be a highly successful debut novel for its author. "Vail has the measure of this vulnerable age and its painful concern about identity within the group," noted a *Kirkus Reviews* commentator, who added: "Gauche, likable Jess . . . is a character to remember." *School Library Journal* contributor Debra S. Gold also spoke favorably of Vail's characterization of her central protagonist in *Wonder,* commenting: "Jessica's first-person account reveals a three-dimensional character with whom readers will laugh and empathize." Deborah Abbott of *Booklist* asserted: "Piercing and funny, Vail's breezy story describes the hazards of junior high, sketched with the emotional chasms universal to the age."

One of Jessica's schoolmates, Whitman Levy, becomes the hero of Vail's next story, *Do-Over*. Eighth-grader Whitman is faced with some severe family problems, including his parents' imminent break-up, while struggling with his first real boy-girl relationships and a part in the school play. Vail balances the comical tale of his various escapades with other thorny issues, including Whitman's discovery that his best friend Doug is a bigot. Eventually the self-conscious and somewhat bewildered Whitman comes to understand how to deal with all that confronts him, in a moment of self-realization while on stage: "I could screw up or I could be amazing, and there's no turning back, no do-overs."

Reviewers of Vail's work in *Do-Over* again highlighted her strengths with character and dialog in a number of positive assessments. *School Library Journal* contributor Jacqueline Rose asserted: "Vail is a master at portraying adolescent self-absorption, awkwardness, and fickleness, all with freshness and humor." In the *Bulletin of the Center for Children's Books,* Roger Sutton compared Vail favorably with popular children's writer Judy Blume, writing: "Vail is funnier than Blume, and more moving, partly because of her natural ear for teenaged talk, and partly because she never, ever preaches. This is the real thing." Stephanie Zvirin of *Booklist* likewise spoke of the "sharp and genuine" dialogue in *Do-Over,* commending Vail's "remarkable talent for capturing so perfectly the pleasure and pain of being thirteen—in a real kids' world."

In her third novel, *Ever After,* Vail employs a new narrative technique, presenting much of her story in the form of diary entries written by fourteen-year-old Molly. Best friends Molly and Vicky live year-round on a small Massachusetts island. The presence of a new friend, summer visitor Grace, causes Vicky to feel insecure and puts a strain on her relationship with Molly. Vicky's possessiveness begins to disturb Molly, and eventually destroys their friendship when Molly learns that Vicky has been reading her personal journal without permission. "That Vicky and Molly's rift is likely to be permanent . . . is just one hallmark of the authenticity of this carefully conceived story," noted a *Publishers Weekly* reviewer. A *Kirkus Reviews* commentator praised *Ever After* as "an unusually immediate portrayal of a thoughtful teen finding her balance among her peers while making peace with her own capabilities." *School Library Journal* contributor Ellen Fader characterized the book as "a breezy, smart-talking novel that explores the ever-fascinating arena of young teen friendship,"

while Hazel Rochman of *Booklist* expressed a common critical refrain when noting that "the contemporary teenage voice is exactly right."

Daring to Be Abigail features a narrative format similar to the one that Vail employs in *Ever After.* The story unfolds in the letters of Abby Silverman, an eleven-year-old girl who has decided to "reinvent herself" while away at Camp Nashaquitsa for the summer. Her newly adopted boldness wins the acceptance of her fellow campers, but also seems to require that Abby, now Abigail, forsake Dana, an unpopular girl in her cabin. Although she likes Dana, Abigail succumbs to peer pressure by accepting a dare to urinate in Dana's mouthwash. Unable to stop Dana before she uses the rinse, Abigail is thrown out of the camp, and addresses a final, poignant letter to her dead father, whose apparent disappointment with Abby inflamed her crisis of identity and prompted her efforts at "reinvention." Deborah Stevenson of the *Bulletin of the Center for Children's Books* noted that Abigail's "vulnerability and her poignantly, desperately upbeat letters home will engender reader sympathy and understanding." *Booklist* reviewer Stephanie Zvirin praised Vail for once again being "right on target when it comes to the reality of preadolescent girls, catching how they act and what they say, their nastiness and envy and sweetness, and how confusing it is to long for independence, yet be afraid of the freedom and responsibility that come with it." Lauren Adams, reviewing *Daring to Be Abigail* for *Horn Book,* commented: "As in her other books, Vail displays her talent for capturing the humor and angst of early adolescence; this latest novel . . . is her most sophisticated yet."

BIOGRAPHICAL/CRITICAL SOURCES:

BOOKS

Seventh Book of Junior Authors and Illustrators, H. W. Wilson, 1996.

PERIODICALS

Booklist, September 1, 1991, p. 54; August, 1992, p. 2013; March 1, 1994, p. 1254; March 1, 1996, p. 1184.
Bulletin of the Center for Children's Books, September, 1991, p. 24; December, 1992, pp. 125-126; February, 1996, p. 207.
Horn Book, November-December, 1992, p. 731; May-June, 1994, pp. 301-304; May-June, 1996, pp. 337-339.

Kirkus Reviews, August 8, 1991, p. 1095; July 15, 1992, p. 927; April 1, 1994, pp. 486.

Publishers Weekly, August 9, 1991, p. 58; December 20, 1991, p. 24; February 21, 1994, pp. 255-256.

School Library Journal, August, 1991, p. 196; September, 1992, p. 282; May, 1994, p. 136; March, 1996, p. 198.

*   *   *

VALKO, Peter 1950-

PERSONAL: Born July 4, 1950, in Budapest, Hungary; son of Ivan Peter and Anna (Selymes) Valko; married Vilma Horvath, December 2, 1974; children: Benedek, Luca, Lili. *Ethnicity:* "Hungarian." *Education:* Veszprem University, B.Sc. and M.S.; Novosibirsk Institute for Catalysis, Ph.D.

ADDRESSES: Office—Department of Petroleum Engineering, Texas A&M University, 1403 Langford, College Station, TX 77840. *E-mail*—valko@spindle top.tamu.edu.

CAREER: Eotvos L. University, Budapest, Hungary, assistant professor, 1975-77, associate professor, 1981-89; Hungarian Oil Co., Budapest, research scientist, 1989-91; Lfoben Mining University, Austria, associate professor, 1991-93; Texas A&M University, College Station, associate professor of petroleum engineering, 1993—.

MEMBER: Society of Petroleum Engineers.

WRITINGS:

Sonnenbestrahlung von Gebeauden feur verschiedene Bauformen und Fassadenrichtungen: Isolation bes baatiments en fonction de leur forme et de leur orientation, Hallwag (Stuttgart, Germany), 1975.

(With Vajda Saandor) *Miuszaki-tudomaanyos feladatok megoldaasa szemaelyi szaamaitaogaeppel,* Miuszaki Keonyvkiadao (Budapest, Hungary), 1986, Elsevier Science (New York City), 1989.

(With Michael J. Economides) *Hydraulic Fracture Mechanics,* Wiley (New York City), 1995.

Author of the volume *Advanced Scientific Computing in Basic,* 1989. Member of editorial board, *SPE Journal.*

WORK IN PROGRESS: A chapter to be included in a book on petroleum well construction.

*   *   *

VIRAMONTES, Helena Maria 1954-

PERSONAL: Born February 26, 1954, in East Los Angeles, CA; daughter of a construction worker and a homemaker; children: two. *Education:* Immaculate Heart College, B.A., 1975; attended University of California at Irvine.

ADDRESSES: Agent—c/o Dutton/Signet, 375 Hudson St., New York, NY 10014.

CAREER: Fiction writer. Co-founder of Southern California Latino Writers and Film Makers group; teaches at Cornell University.

AWARDS, HONORS: Statement Magazine first prize for fiction, California State University, for the short stories "Requiem for the Poor, 1977, and "The Broken Web," 1978; first prize for fiction, University of California at Irvine Chicano Literary Contest, for the short story "Birthday," 1979; National Endowment for the Arts fellowship, 1989.

WRITINGS:

The Moths and Other Stories, Arte Publico Press (Houston, TX), 1985.

Under the Feet of Jesus, Dutton (New York City), 1995.

NONFICTION

(Co-editor, with Maria Herrera-Sobek) *Chicana Creativity and Criticism: Charting New Frontiers in American Literature,* Arte Publico Press (Houston, TX), 1988.

(Co-editor, with Maria Herrera-Sobek) *Chicana (w)rites: On Word and Film,* Third Woman Press (Berkeley, CA), 1995.

OTHER

Works represented in anthologies, including *Cuentos: Short Stories by Latinas,* Kitchen Table/Women of Color Press, 1983; *Woman of Her Word,* edited by Evangelina Vigil, Arte Publico Press (Houston, TX), 1984; *Breaking Boundaries: Latina Writings and*

Critical Readings, edited by Asuncion Horno-Delgado, Eliana Ortego, Nina M. Scott, and Nancy Saporta Sternbach, University of Massachusetts Press (Amherst, MA), 1989; and *New Chicana/Chicano Writing,* edited by Charles M. Tatum, University of Arizona Press (Tuscon, AZ), 1992. Contributor of short stories to periodicals, including *XhismeArte, Hispanic Link, America's 2001, Pearl,* and *Blue Mesa Review*; adapted one of her stories for film, 1991.

WORK IN PROGRESS: Their Dogs Came with Them, a novella about interracial violence in Los Angeles.

SIDELIGHTS: A Chicana writer whose work addresses social issues, Helena Maria Viramontes "believes that writing can bring about social change," related Kayann Short in her interview with the author in the *Bloomsbury Review.* The stories in her debut collection, *The Moth and Other Stories,* many of which were published previously in small magazines and are set mostly in Los Angeles, present everyday incidents of oppression—economic, racial, and sexist—in the lives of ordinary, often Chicana, women of all ages. "Viramontes' relentlessly serious stories," a *Kirkus Reviews* critic remarked, "are really a series of poignant vignettes, slices of Latina life. Were she to lighten up a bit and sacrifice ideology for artistry, she might become [an] important new voice." *Village Voice* book reviewer Laurie Stone found most of the stories in *Moth* "tense, direct, and powerfully imagined," but also noted that in some stories "her characters sink under rhetorical points about the condition of women."

Viramontes's novel, *Under the Feet of Jesus,* is narrated by a young female migrant worker, Estrella, who rebels against her rural community's racial and sexual restrictions, and offers a Chicana perspective on corporate agricultural practices. "If they read the book, and if they think about the piscadores when they eat their salad, that would bring me great satisfaction as a writer," Viramontes told Short. *Booklist* reviewer Gilbert Taylor praised *Under the Feet of Jesus:* "in Viramontes' hands the canvas . . . teems with color." A *Kirkus Reviews* contributor wrote that her novel is "a compelling debut with prose that sometimes stumbles but more often soars in describing human suffering and faith." Sonia Saldivar-Hull, writing in the *Dictionary of Literary Biography,* assessed Viramontes's literary contributions thusly: "Her groundbreaking narrative strategies, combined with her sociopolitical focus, situate her at the forefront of an emerging Chicana literary tradition that redefines Chicano literature and feminist theory."

BIOGRAPHICAL/CRITICAL SOURCES:

BOOKS

Dictionary of Literary Biography, Volume 122: *Chicano Writers,* Gale (Detroit, MI), 1992.
Notable Hispanic American Women, Gale (Detroit, MI), 1993.

PERIODICALS

Bloomsbury Review, January/February, 1996.
Booklist, April 15, 1995, pp. 1481-1482.
Kirkus Reviews, October 1, 1985, p. 1046; February 15, 1995, pp. 180-181.
Publishers Weekly, March 20, 1995, pp. 42-43.
Village Voice, April 15, 1986, p. 55.
Washington Post Book World, May 14, 1995, p. 4.*

*   *   *

VITOLA, Denise 1957-

PERSONAL: Born October 13, 1957, in Olney, MD; daughter of Anthony (in U.S. Navy) and Mary (Sorrell) DeMartino; married Gregory Vitola, February 1, 1980. *Ethnicity:* "Caucasian." *Education:* Northern Virginia Community College, A.A. (cum laude). *Avocational interests:* Reading, public speaking.

ADDRESSES: Home—HCO2, Box 6760, Sandia, TX 78383. *E-mail*—gvitola@aol.com. *Agent*—Irene Kraas, 220 Copper Trail, Santa Fe, NM 87505.

CAREER: Writer.

WRITINGS:

Half Light (science fiction novel), TSR, Inc., 1992.
The Winter Man (horror novel), Berkley (New York City), 1995.
Quantum Moon (supernatural mystery novel), Ace Books (New York City), 1996.
Opalite Moon (supernatural mystery novel), Ace Books, 1997.
Manjinn Moon (supernatural mystery novel), Ace Books, in press.

Author of a young adult horror novel published by Scholastic, Inc. (New York City). Work represented in anthologies, including *Realms of Infamy.* Contributor to magazines, including *Amazing Stories.*

WORK IN PROGRESS: Delora Moon, publication expected in 1999.

SIDELIGHTS: Denise Vitola told *CA:* "My primary motivation for writing is to explore the ordinary human condition by revealing how extraordinary it really is. My characters are called upon to discover who they are while being soundly smacked in the face by the hard realities of life and society. It is a question as old as man himself—how do we mark our days with wonder and joy instead of hardship and pain?

"I want to know what drives a person to create or to kill. Are we shaped by our environment or our heredity? Perhaps, it is nothing so mundane as all that. Perhaps, we are indeed the pawns of an all-powerful God, and if that is true, then how would we even know the difference? What are the signs in the road of life that tell us we have entered the ramp toward enlightenment?

"My work is influenced by the timeless myths of humanity. I look back into the past and pick and choose from the folklore I find. My writing process is simple. I start a story with a germ of an idea and then brainstorm until the idea grows a little. I then decide what theme I will be exploring and what characters would be best to carry off the whole deal. Once that begins, I rely on synchronicity to help me along. By that I mean: I am open to concepts that will fit in my stories and enhance the theme. I may find these by watching television, reading, or eavesdropping on a conversation. I can't explain it, but the process works. Things pop up because I am aware of them.

"Myths and legends have always been the inspiration for my subjects. The fact that I love science fiction was a gift of those writers who have dreamed the possible realities before me. They forged my interest in the future and took me beyond the limits of this planet. For that, I am eternally grateful."

*   *   *

VON AHNEN, Katherine 1922-

PERSONAL: Born April 22, 1922, in Cape May, NJ; daughter of Edward Y. (on school maintenance staff) and Mary Elizabeth (Bennett) Rott; married Rudolph Von Ahnen (divorced, 1991); children: Regina Davis, Patricia Peckham, Susan Qualls. *Education:* Attended Augustana College (Moline, IL) and St.

Ambrose College (Davenport, IA), 1982-84; attended Institute for Children's Literature, 1984-88. *Religion:* Baptist.

ADDRESSES: Home and office—304 St. James Place, Cape May, NJ 08204.

CAREER: Writer, speaker, and poet. Women's editor, WCMC Radio, Wildwood, NJ, 1945-55; editor of *Fireglow* (a three-state newsletter for the Camp Fire Girls), Davenport, IA, 1965-70. Special events coordinator and admissions person for Cape May Lighthouse; editor of *Homespun* (newsletter of the Cape May, NJ, Historical Society); founder of two writing groups, Write-On, Cape May, and Write-On-Two, Ocean City, NJ. Frequent speaker on local culture and heritage in school programs and for community and civic organizations.

MEMBER: Cape May Historical Society (vice president), Wisconsin Regional Writer's Association, New Jersey Lighthouse Association, U.S. Lighthouse Association, Mid-Atlantic Center for the Arts, National Association for Children's Authors and Illustrators.

AWARDS, HONORS: First place, Garden State Writer's Challenge, 1995, for the poem "Me an' the Squirrels"; first place, State Poetry Award, first place, State Juvenile Story, first place, humorous article, all from the University of Wisconsin, all 1996; New Jersey State Poet of the Year, 1997.

WRITINGS:

Charlie Young Bear, illustrated by Paulette Livers Lambert, Roberts Rinehart, 1994.
Heart of Naosaqua, illustrated by Lambert, Roberts Rinehart, 1996.
Mary Elizabeth and the Cape May Lighthouse, Northwest, 1997.

Also author of *The Cape May Collection* (poetry), self-published, 1991, and *Lighthouse and Three Little Pigs,* self-published, 1994.

WORK IN PROGRESS: The Mystery of Emily's House, a young adult romance-mystery, set in Cape May; a sequel to *Heart of Naosaqua;* and poetry for *Highlights* magazine. Research into customs of Mesquakie Indians of the Tama, Iowa, area.

SIDELIGHTS: Katherine Von Ahnen commented: "I've been writing since I was in the sixth grade. During my high-school days, I was editor of the school paper and the senior yearbook for my graduating class. Now I am a seventy-four-year-old grandmother going on forty-five. . . . My two target areas for writing books are lighthouses and Native American children. I also write much poetry and have made more money on the 'Olde Cape May Lighthouse' poem than any of my books. I attended the Chautauqua Children's Writer's Conference in New York in 1995, and flew to Wisconsin in the fall of 1995 to present book programs in six schools and to be the featured speaker at the Wisconsin Regional Writer's Conference on the subject, 'How to Self-Publish and Make Money.' I live in a little seashore inland town, Cape May Court House, with my ninety-four-year-old mother, who is the Mary Elizabeth in my first book. Sometimes she goes on autograph signings with me.

"Currently, I have a finished manuscript, *The Mystery of Emily's House,* a young-adult mystery romance set in the Victorian National Landmark city of Cape May, that is out in the mail looking for a publisher. I am also a speaker for a three-county librarians' organization, Wildwood Golf and Country Club, Linwood Historical Society, and several school programs. It's a good life!"

BIOGRAPHICAL/CRITICAL SOURCES:

PERIODICALS

Booklist, July, 1996, p. 1827.
School Library Journal, April, 1995, p. 119.

VON ZELEWSKY, Alexander 1936-
(AvZ, a pseudonym)

PERSONAL: Born July 17, 1936, in Zurich, Switzerland; married Hedwig Ebner; children: Katja Von Zelewsky Flueler, Thomas. *Education:* Swiss Federal Institute of Technology, diploma (chemistry), 1960, Ph.D. (chemistry), 1964.

ADDRESSES: Home—La Vertschire, 1637 Charmey (FR), Switzerland. *Office*—Institute of Inorganic Chemistry, University of Fribourg, Perolles 1700, Fribourg, Switzerland; fax 41-026-300-9738. *E-mail*—Alexander.vonzelewsky@unifr.ch.

CAREER: University of Fribourg, Fribourg, Switzerland, professor of inorganic chemistry, 1969—. Swiss National Science Foundation, vice president.

MEMBER: Swiss Chemical Society (president), American Chemical Society, Royal Society of Chemistry, New York Academy of Sciences.

WRITINGS:

Science et Responsibilitae: Wissenschaft und Verantwortung, Editions Universitaires (Fribourg, Switzerland), 1982.
Stereochemistry of Coordination Compounds, Wiley (New York City), 1996.

Some writings appear under the pseudonym AvZ.

W-Z

WAGNER, Linda W.
  See WAGNER-MARTIN, Linda (C.)

*   *   *

WAGNER, Linda Welshimer
  See WAGNER-MARTIN, Linda (C.)

*   *   *

WAGNER-MARTIN, Linda (C.) 1936-
  (Linda Welshimer Wagner; Linda W. Wagner)

PERSONAL: Born in 1936.

ADDRESSES: Home—907 Whittier Dr., East Lansing, MI 48823. *Office*—Department of English, University of North Carolina, Chapel Hill, NC 27514.

CAREER: Writer. Michigan State University, professor of English, beginning 1968; University of North Carolina, Hanes Professor of English and Comparative Literature, beginning 1988; affiliated with Wayne State University, Detroit, MI, and Bowling Green State University, Bowling Green, OH. Editor, *Centennial Review.*

WRITINGS:

Denise Levertov, Twayne (New York City), 1967.
The Prose of William Carlos Williams, Wesleyan University Press (Middletown, CT), 1970.

Phyllis McGinley, Twayne, 1971.
(As Linda Welshimer Wagner) *Hemingway and Faulkner: Inventors/Masters,* Scarecrow Press (Metuchen, NJ), 1975.
(As Linda Welshimer Wagner) *Ernest Hemingway: A Reference Guide,* G. K. Hall (Boston, MA), 1977.
(As Linda Welshimer Wagner) *William Carlos Williams: A Reference Guide,* G. K. Hall, 1978.
(As Linda W. Wagner) *Dos Passos: Artist as American,* University of Texas Press (Austin, TX), 1979.
(As Linda W. Wagner) *American Modern: Essays in Fiction and Poetry* (essays), Kennikat Press (Port Washington, NY), 1980.
(As Linda W. Wagner) *Ellen Glasgow: Beyond Convention,* University of Texas Press, 1982.
Sylvia Plath: A Biography, Simon & Schuster (New York City), 1987, published as *Our Missing Companion: Sylvia Plath: A Biography,* Vermilion Books (New York City), 1987.
The Modern American Novel, 1914-1945: A Critical History, Twayne (Boston, MA), 1990.
Wharton's "The House of Mirth": A Novel of Admonition, Twayne, 1990.
Plath's "The Bell Jar": A Novel of the Fifties, Twayne, 1992.
Telling Women's Lives: The New Biography, Rutgers University Press (New Brunswick, NJ), 1994.
Favored Strangers: Gertrude Stein and Her Family, Rutgers University Press, 1995.
"The Age of Innocence": A Novel of Ironic Nostalgia, Twayne, 1996.

Also author of *The Poems of William Carlos Williams,* 1964, *Intaglios,* 1967, and *Songs for Isadora,* 1981.

EDITOR

William Faulkner: Four Decades of Criticism, Michigan State University Press (East Lansing, MI), 1973.

T. S. Eliot: A Collection of Criticism, McGraw-Hill (New York City), 1974.

Ernest Hemingway: Five Decades of Criticism, Michigan State University Press, 1974.

(As Linda W. Wagner; and compiler with C. David Mead) *Introducing Poems,* Harper (New York City), 1976.

(As Linda Welshimer Wagner; and author of introduction) *Speaking Straight Ahead: Interviews with William Carlos Williams,* New Directions (New York City), 1976.

(As Linda W. Wagner; and author of introduction) *Robert Frost: The Critical Reception,* B. Franklin (New York City), 1977.

(As Linda Welshimer Wagner; and author of introduction) *Denise Levertov, In Her Own Province* (interviews), New Directions (New York City), 1979.

(As Linda W. Wagner) *Critical Essays on Joyce Carol Oates,* G. K. Hall, 1979.

(As Linda W. Wagner) *Critical Essays on Sylvia Plath,* G. K. Hall, 1984.

New Essays on "The Sun Also Rises", Cambridge University Press (Cambridgeshire, England), 1987.

Ernest Hemingway: Six Decades of Criticism, Michigan State University Press, 1987.

Sylvia Plath: The Critical Heritage, Routledge (London), 1988.

Critical Essays on Anne Sexton, G. K. Hall, 1989.

Virginia by Ellen Glasgow, 1989.

Critical Essays on Denise Levertov, G. K. Hall, 1991.

(Editor of contemporary section) *The D. C. Heath Anthology of American Literature,* Heath (Boston), 1990.

(With Cathy N. Davidson) *The Oxford Book of Women's Writings in the United States,* Oxford University Press (New York City), 1995.

(Editor-in-chief with Cathy N. Davidson others) *The Oxford Companion to Women's Writing in the United States,* Oxford University Press (New York City), 1995.

New Essays on "Go Down, Moses", Cambridge University Press, 1996.

SIDELIGHTS: A literary critic of modern American fiction and poetry, Linda Wagner-Martin is perhaps best known as a biographer of twentieth-century American poet Sylvia Plath. The major elements of Plath's life are well known to American readers, for in the decades since her suicide in 1963 at the age of thirty, her work has become greatly esteemed. Plath's novel *The Bell Jar,* and her poetry, published in the volume *Ariel,* have achieved perennial popularity, and the autobiographical nature of her work has created an interest in her life as well. The events of that life, including Plath's stormy six-year marriage to the British poet Ted Hughes, her increasingly desperate attempts to balance homemaking with a poet's life, and her tragic death by oven gas and sleeping pills during the coldest London winter in a century—have become part of the mythology of contemporary literature. The fact that Hughes and Plath destroyed some of their own—and each other's—letters, journals, and drafts at crucial times in their lives—a tendency described in Plath's poem "Burning the Letters"—has created historical gaps, not so much in the literal record of events as in the record of the writers' motivations and emotions. Plath's last journals are not due to be made public until 2013, and therefore have not been available to any of her biographers thus far. In the meantime, Wagner-Martin, like others, has tried to fill in the blanks.

Although the Hughes estate tried to convince Wagner-Martin to cut some fifteen thousand words from her biography, she resisted doing so, and was thus denied permission to make extensive quotes from Plath's writing. Nevertheless, her 1987 work, *Syvlia Plath: A Biography,* was well received by the reading public and by many reviewers. Betty Abel, in *Contemporary Review,* was among the most enthusiastic, asserting that Wagner-Martin's book "should be read by all who wish to understand how close to her life Plath's poetry was." Calling the volume "a clear, straightforward account of the events of Plath's life," Abel praised the biographer for crafting "an interpretation unclouded by psychological theorising and, at the same time, full of useful pointers to a permanently troubled state of mind." Anne Stevenson in the London *Sunday Times,* whose authorized biography of Plath was in progress at the time of her review, praised "the impressive picture of 1950s American culture which emerges, despite clumsy writing, from the first six or seven chapters" of Wagner-Martin's book. Stevenson also found "the final chapter, describing Sylvia's desperate last weeks in London," to be "moving." Yet Sevenson was dissatisfied with Wagner-Martin's analysis of Plath's poetry, stating, "The critical limitations of this book are too many to enumerate." Several critics applauded the energy of Wagner-Martin's research. Stevenson called her "an indefatigable . . . researcher and interviewer," and Elaine Kendall, in the *Los Angeles Times Book Review,* commended Wagner-Martin for "diligent interviews and conscientious perusal of letters and papers."

Stevenson, Kendall, and others found *Syvlia Plath* to be somewhat thin in the area of critical analysis. Kendall called the biographer's approach "matter-of-fact" and asserted that "there are no value judgments here, either personal or professional." Claiming that "Wagner-Martin avoids all but the most rudimentary speculation," she called the book "an inconclusive account of a tragically abbreviated life." Stevenson took the author to task for attributing too much of Plath's psychopathology to her marriage rather than to earlier experiences, yet she also wrote that Wagner-Martin's biography "is of interest as a revealing document—perhaps even now of a past phase—in the history of literary feminism." Claire Tomalin in the *Observer* remarked that the biography "is respectful but fails to get inside the skin of its subject." Jeffrey Meyers, in the *National Review,* and Mark Ford, in the *Times Literary Supplement,* both expressed the view that the world still awaited a definitive biography of Plath. Victoria Glendinning in the *Spectator,* alluding to Plath's desire for recognition and honors as well as a perfect family life, wrote that "what this interestingly imperfect book suggests most strongly is the destructiveness of the success ethic."

Some reviewers maintained that Wagner-Martin's view of Plath's life cast Hughes and patriarchy as villains, and was therefore limited in its critical power; Stevenson called Wagner-Martin "a sincere but naive feminist." Bruce Bawer, in the *Washington Post Book World,* wrote that the author "seems a bit too eager to believe the worst about Hughes." Glendinning, however, asserted that Wagner-Martin was "not a flame-thrower" and that "her interpretation of Plath's life has a justifiably feminist slant." Diane Middlebrook, a biographer of Plath's friend and colleague Anne Sexton, praised Wagner-Martin's book in the *Nation* for its "sociological consistency," but argued that for an understanding of Plath's growth of an artist, the poet's own journals, letters, and poems were the best source.

Wagner-Martin was troubled by some of the critical reaction to her book, especially on the part of British critics. "Telling a woman's life . . . had become a dangerous cultural and literary project," she wrote in her 1994 book, *Telling Women's Lives: The New Biography,* which began in part as Wagner-Martin's

written response to some of the controversy surrounding the Plath book. *Telling Women's Lives* surveys the history of female biographies in English. The study comments critically on such issues as the difference between male-written and female-written biographies of women. Elaine Showalter, a contributor to the *London Review of Books,* wrote that despite Wagner-Martin's intriguing subject, her approach was lacking in originality: "a disappointingly sedate historical overview." Allyson F. McGill, reviewing the book for the journal *Belles Lettres,* declared that Wagner-Martin "raises important questions about the ethics of biography, points to the dangers of sentimentalizing one's subject, and cautions against stereotype. . . . Wagner-Martin attempts to get it all in, and on the level of pointing her readers in the right direction in their pursuit of biography, she succeeds." Carol Muske, in the *New York Times Book Review,* called the book "a shaky platform from which to leap headlong into the swirling waters of controversy"; but *Library Journal*'s Sharon Firestone was more enthusiastic, calling the book "insightful" and "cogent." A *Publishers Weekly* critic termed *Telling Women's Lives* "a lively and perceptive historical overview."

Wagner-Martin followed *Telling Women's Lives* with 1995's *The Oxford Book of Women's Writing in the United States,* which she edited with Cathy N. Davidson. The editors included works from many genres into their anthology, rather than limiting it to the familiar genres of fiction and poetry. The result, said Donna Seaman in *Booklist,* was "a wonderful spectrum" of writing that added up to a "meandering and happily idiosyncratic anthology." A *Publishers Weekly* commentator labeled the anthology "as remarkable for its quality as it is for its breadth. . . . an outstanding editorial achievement"; *Library Journal*'s Amy Boaz called the anthology "masterly and comprehensive."

In addition to these major works, Wagner-Martin has, since the 1960s, been continually involved in scholarly writing, and has written or edited numerous studies of individual authors, including William Carlos Williams, Ernest Hemingway, William Faulkner, Anne Sexton, Joyce Carol Oates, Phyllis McGinley, Denise Levertov, John Dos Passos, and Edith Wharton.

BIOGRAPHICAL/CRITICAL SOURCES:

PERIODICALS

Belles Lettres, fall, 1994, pp. 18-19.

Booklist, June 1 and 15, 1995, pp. 1718, 1720.
Contemporary Review, March, 1988, pp. 166-167.
Library Journal, June 15, 1994, p. 70; August, 1995, p. 92.
London Review of Books, September 22, 1994, p. 19.
Los Angeles Times Book Review, January 31, 1988, p. 12.
Nation, November 28, 1987, pp. 656, 658-659.
National Review, March 18, 1988, pp. 52-54.
New Statesman, March 11, 1988, pp. 32-33.
New York Times Book Review, October 25, 1987, pp. 12-13; December 13, 1987, p. 46; November 6, 1994, p. 18.
Observer (London), March 6, 1988, p. 43.
Publishers Weekly, June 13, 1994, p. 56; May 8, 1995, p. 288.
Spectator, March 5, 1988, p. 34.
Sunday Times (London), February 28, 1988, p. G3.
Times Literary Supplement, April 29-May 5, 1988, p. 468.
Washington Post Book World, October 25, 1987, p. 4.*

*　　*　　*

WALD, George 1906-

PERSONAL: Born November 18, 1906, in New York, NY; son of Isaac (a tailor and foreman in a clothing factory) and Ernestine (Rosenmann) Wald; married Frances Kingsley, May 15, 1931 (divorced); married Ruth Hubbard, 1958; children: (first marriage) Michael, David; (second marriage) Elijah, Deborah. *Education:* New York University, B.S., 1927; Columbia University, M.A., 1928, Ph.D., 1932.

ADDRESSES: Home—21 Lakeview Ave., Cambridge, MA 02138-3325. *Office*—Department of Biology, Harvard University, Cambridge, MA 02138.

CAREER: Biochemist, writer, and educator. National Research Council fellow at Kaiser Wilhelm Institute, Berlin and Heidelburg, Germany, the University of Zurich, and the University of Chicago, 1932-34; Harvard University, tutor in biochemical sciences, 1934-35, instructor in biology, 1935-39, faculty instructor, 1939-44, associate professor of biology, 1944-48, professor, 1948-77, Higgins Professor of Biology, 1968-77, professor emeritus, 1977—. University of California— Berkeley, visiting professor of biochemistry, 1956. National Sigma Xi lecturer, 1952; participant in the United States-Japan eminent scholar exchange, 1973; Permanent Peoples' Tribunal, Rome, Italy, vice president, 1980—.

MEMBER: Optical Society of America.

AWARDS, HONORS: Eli Lily Prize, American Chemical Society, 1939; elected to the National Academy of Science, 1950; Albert Lasker Award, American Public Health Association, 1953; Proctor Award, Association for Research in Ophthalmology, 1955; elected to the American Philosophical Society, 1958; Rumford Premium, American Academy of Arts and Sciences, 1959; Guggenheim fellow, mid-1960s, and Overseas fellow of Churchill College, 1963-64, Cambridge University; Ives Medal, Optical Society of America, 1966; Nobel Prize in Physiology or Medicine (with Haldan K. Hartline and Ragnar Granit), 1967, for his work with vision; Paul Karrer Medal in Chemistry, University of Zurich, 1967; T. Duckett Jones Award, Helen Hay Whitney Foundation, 1967; Bradford Washburn Medal, Boston Museum of Science, 1968; Max Berg Award, 1969; Joseph Priestley Award, Dickinson College, 1970; Award for Distinguished Achievement, Columbia University, 1990. Awarded numerous honorary degrees, including M.D.s from the University of Berne, 1957, and the University of Leon—Nicaragua, 1984; D.Sc.s from Yale University, 1958, Wesleyan University, 1962, New York University, 1965, McGill University, 1966, Amherst College, 1968, University of Rennes, 1970, University of Utah, 1971, Gustavas Adolphus University, 1972, Hamline University, 1977, and Columbia University, 1990; and a D.H.L. from Kalamazoo College, 1984.

WRITINGS.

(Co-author) *General Education in a Free Society,* Harvard University Press (Cambridge, MA), 1945.
Visual Pigments and Photoreceptors: Review and Outlook, Academic Press, 1974.

Also coauthor of *Twenty-Six Afternoons of Biology,* 1962. Contributor to journals and periodicals, including *American Scientist.*

SIDELIGHTS: George Wald first won a place in the spotlight as the recipient of a Nobel Prize in Physiology or Medicine for his discovery of the way in which hidden biochemical processes in the retinal pigments of the eye turn light energy into sight. Among Wald's important experiments were the effects of vitamin A on sight and the roles played by rod and cone cells in black and white and color vision. Outside the laboratory, his splendid lectures at Harvard to packed audiences of students generated great intellectual excitement. It was as a political activist during the turbulent 1960s, however, that Wald garnered further public recognition. Wald's personal belief in the unity of nature and the kinship among all living things is evidenced by the substantial roles he played in the scientific world as well as in the political and cultural arena of the 1960s.

Wald's father, Isaac Wald, a tailor and later a foreman in a clothing factory, emigrated from Austrian Poland, while his mother, Ernestine Rosenmann Wald, emigrated from Bavaria. Most of Wald's youth was spent in Brooklyn, New York, where his parents moved after his birth on the Lower East Side of Manhattan on November 18, 1906. He attended high school at Brooklyn Tech, where he intended to study to become an electrical engineer. College changed his mind, however, as he explained to the *New York Times Magazine* in 1969, "I learned I could talk, and I thought I'd become a lawyer. But the law was man-made; I soon discovered I wanted something more real."

Wald's bachelor of science degree in zoology, which he received from New York University in 1927, was his ticket into the reality of biological research. He began his career at Columbia University, where he was awarded a master's degree in 1928, working under Selig Hecht, one of the founders of the field of biophysics and an authority on the physiology of vision. Hecht exerted an enormous influence on Wald, both as an educator and a humanist. The elder scientist's belief in the social obligation of science, coupled with the conviction that science should be explained so the general public could understand it, made a great impression on the young Wald. Following Hecht's sudden death in 1947 at the age of fifty-five, Wald wrote a memorial as a tribute to his colleague.

In 1932 Wald earned his doctorate at Columbia, after which he was awarded a National Research Council Fellowship in Biology. The two-year fellowship helped to support his research career, which first took him to the laboratory of Otto Warburg in Berlin. It was there, in 1932, that he discovered vitamin A as one of the major constituents of retinal pigments, the light sensitive chemicals that set off the cascade of biological events that turns light into sight.

Warburg sent the young Wald to Switzerland, where he studied vitamins with chemist Paul Karrer at the University of Zurich. From there Wald went to Otto Meyerhof's laboratory of cell metabolism at the Kaiser Wilhelm Institute in Heidelberg, Germany, finishing his fellowship in the department of physiology at the University of Chicago in 1934. His fellowship completed, Wald went to Harvard University, first as a tutor in biochemistry and subsequently as an instructor, faculty instructor, and associate professor, finally becoming a full professor in 1948. In 1968 he became Higgins Professor of Biology, a post he retained until he became an emeritus professor in 1977.

Wald did most of his work in eye physiology at Harvard, where he discovered in the late 1930s that the light-sensitive chemical in the rods—those cells in the retina responsible for night vision—is a single pigment called rhodopsin (visual purple), a substance derived from opsin, a protein, and retinene, a chemically modified form of vitamin A. In the ensuing years, Wald discovered that the vitamin A in rhodopsin is "bent" relative to its natural state, and light causes it to "straighten out," dislodging it from opsin. This simple reaction initiates all the subsequent activity that eventually generates the sense of vision.

Wald's research moved from rods to cones, the retinal cells responsible for color vision, discovering with his co-worker Paul K. Brown, that the pigments sensitive to red and yellow-green are two different forms of vitamin A that co-exist in the same cone, while the blue-sensitive pigments are located in separate cones. They also showed that color blindness is caused by the absence of one of these pigments.

For much of his early professional life, Wald concentrated his energy on work, both research and teaching. His assistant, Brown, stayed with him for over twenty years and became a full-fledged collaborator. A former student, Ruth Hubbard, became his second wife in 1958, and they had two children, Elijah and Deborah. (His previous marriage to Frances Kingsley in 1931 ended in divorce; he has two sons by that marriage, Michael and David.) Wald, his wife, and Brown together became an extremely productive research team.

By the late 1950s Wald began to be showered with honors, and during his career he received numerous honorary degrees and awards. After Wald was awarded (with Haldan K. Hartline of the United States and Ragnar Granit of Sweden) the Nobel Prize in Physiology or Medicine in 1967 for his work with vision, John E. Dowling wrote in *Science* that Wald and his team formed "the nucleus of a laboratory that has been extraordinarily fruitful as the world's foremost center of visual-pigment biochemistry."

As Wald's reputation flourished, his fame as an inspiring professor grew as well. He lectured to packed classrooms, inspiring an intense curiosity in his students. The energetic professor was portrayed in a 1966 *Time* article that summarized the enthusiasm he brought to teaching his natural science course: "With crystal clarity and obvious joy at a neat explanation, Wald carries his students from protons in the fall to living organisms in the spring, [and] ends most lectures with some philosophical peroration on the wonder of it all." That same year, the *New York Post* said of his lectures, "His beginnings are slow, sometimes witty. . . . The talk gathers momentum and suddenly an idea *pings* into the atmosphere—fresh, crisp, thought-provoking."

Six days after he received the Nobel Prize, Wald wielded the status of his new prestige in support of a widely popular resolution before the city council of Cambridge, Massachusetts—placing a referendum on the Vietnam War on the city's ballot of November 7, 1967. Echoing the sentiments of his mentor Hecht, he asserted that scientists should be involved in public issues.

The Cambridge appearance introduced him to the sometimes stormy arena of public politics, a forum from which he has never retired. The escalating war in Vietnam prompted Wald to speak out against the U.S. government's military policy. In 1965, during the escalation of that war, Wald's impromptu denunciation of the Vietnam War stunned an audience at New York University, where he was receiving an honorary degree. Shortly afterward, he threw his support and prestige behind the presidential campaign of Eugene McCarthy. His offer to speak publicly on behalf of McCarthy was ignored, however, and he became a disillusioned supporter, remaining on the fringe of political activism.

Then on March 4, 1969, he gave an address at the Massachusetts Institute of Technology (M.I.T.) that, "upended his life and pitched him abruptly into the political world," according to the *New York Times Magazine*. Wald gave "The Speech," as the talk came to be known in his family, before an audience of radical students at M.I.T. The students had helped to organize a scientists' day-long "strike" to protest the influence of the military on their work, a topic of much heated debate at the time.

Although much of the M.I.T. audience was already bored and restless by the time Wald began, even many of those students who were about to leave the room stopped to listen as the Nobel laureate began to deliver his oration, titled "A Generation in Search of a Future." "I think this whole generation of students is beset with a profound sense of uneasiness, and I don't think they have quite defined its source," Wald asserted as quoted in the *New York Times Magazine*. "I think I understand the reasons for their uneasiness even better than they do. What is more, I *share* their uneasiness."

Wald's discourse evoked applause from the audience as he offered his opinion that student unease arose from a variety of troublesome matters. He pointed to the Vietnam War, the military establishment, and finally, the threat of nuclear warfare. "We must get rid of those atomic weapons," he declared. "We cannot live with them." Speaking to the students as fellow scientists, he sympathized with the their unease at the influence of the military establishment on the work of scientists, intoning, "Our business is with life, not death."

The speech was reprinted and distributed around the country by the media. Through these reprints, Wald told readers that some of their elected leaders were "insane," and he referred to the U.S. "war crimes" enacted in Vietnam. In the furor that followed, Wald was castigated by critics, many of whom were fellow academics, and celebrated by sympathizers. A letter writer from Piney Flats, Tennessee, was quoted in the *New York Times Magazine* as saying, "So good to know there are still some intellects around who can talk downright horsesense." Wald summed up his role as scientist-political activist in that same article by saying, "I'm a scientist, and my concerns are eternal. But even eternal things are acted out in the present." He described his role as gadfly as putting certain controversial positions into words in order to make it, "easier for others to inch toward it."

Wald's role as a Vietnam War gadfly expanded into activism in other arenas of foreign affairs. He served for a time as president of international tribunals on El Salvador, the Philippines, Afghanistan, Zaire, and Guatemala. In 1984 he joined four other Nobel Prize laureates who went with the "peace ship" sent by the Norwegian government to Nicaragua during that country's turmoil.

In addition to his interests in science and politics, Wald's passion includes collecting Rembrandt etchings and primitive art, especially pre-Columbian pottery. This complex mixture of science, art, and political philosophy was reflected in his musings about religion and nature in the *New York Times Magazine:* "There's nothing supernatural in my mind. Nature is my religion, and it's enough for me. I stack it up against any man's. For its awesomeness, and for the sense of the sanctity of man that it provides."

In addition to the Nobel Prize, Wald has received numerous awards and honors, including the Albert Lasker Award of the American Public Health Association in 1953, the Proctor Award in 1955 from the Association for Research in Ophthalmology, the Rumford Premium of the American Academy of Arts and Sciences in 1959, the 1969 Max Berg Award, and the Joseph Priestley Award the following year. In addition, he was elected to the National Academy of Science in 1950 and the American Philosophical Society in 1958. He is also a member of the Optical Society of America, which awarded him the Ives Medal in 1966. In the mid-1960s Wald spent a year as a Guggenheim fellow at England's Cambridge University, where he was elected an Overseas Fellow of Churchill College for 1963-64. Wald also holds many honorary degrees.

BIOGRAPHICAL/CRITICAL SOURCES:

PERIODICALS

New York Post, May 1, 1966, p. 32.
New York Times Magazine, August 17, 1969, pp. 28-29.
Science, October 27, 1967.
Time, May 6, 1966.*

*   *   *

WARREN, Cathy 1951-

PERSONAL: Born January 24, 1951, in Larned, KS; daughter of Robert (an optometrist) and Margaret (an artist and teacher; maiden name, Bellinger) Bair; married Russell Warren (an artist), January 2, 1970; children: Tasha, Tanya Marie. *Education:* University of St. Thomas, B.A. (cum laude), 1975; graduate work at the University of North Carolina, 1979-80. *Religion:* Roman Catholic.

ADDRESSES: Home—Davidson, NC.   *Office*—P.O. Box 991, Davidson, NC 28036.

CAREER: Methodist Hospital, Houston, TX, assistant psychiatric counselor, 1973-75; Mother Earth Early Child Development Center, San Antonio, TX, director, 1976-77; Beacon Hill Elementary School, Lakeland, FL, teacher, 1977-78; Children's Schoolhouse (a cooperative preschool), Davidson, NC, creative arts teacher and director, 1980-85; freelance writer, 1983—; Queen College, Charlotte, NC, instructor in continuing education, 1988—.

MEMBER: Authors Guild, Society of Children's Book Writers, North Carolina Writers Network.

AWARDS, HONORS: Parents' Choice Remarkable Book Award, Parents' Choice Foundation, 1983, for *The Ten-Alarm Camp-Out; Roxanne Bookman: Live at Five* was selected for inclusion in Children's Books of the Year at Bank Street College, 1988.

WRITINGS:

The Ten-Alarm Camp-Out, illustrated by Steven Kellogg, Lothrop, (New York City), 1983.
Victoria's ABC Adventure, illustrated by Patience Brewster, Lothrop, 1984.
Fred's First Day, illustrated by Pat Cummings, Lothrop, 1984.
Springtime Bears, illustrated by Cummings, Lothrop, 1986.
Saturday Belongs to Sara, illustrated by DyAnne DiSalvio-Ryan, Bradbury (New York City), 1988.
Roxanne Bookman: Live at Five, Bradbury, 1988.

Author of a weekly column "Art and Artists" for the *Charlotte Observer,* 1981-82.

SIDELIGHTS: Cathy Warren's books for young readers are inspired by the child in herself, the author has claimed. Born in Kansas in 1951, Warren earned a degree from Houston's University of St. Thomas—where she often read children's literature in the school library for pleasure—and became a mental health professional after graduation. For the latter part of the 1970s she worked in the child care field, eventually becoming director of a preschool in North Carolina. Married with two young daughters, it was during a summer-camp stint with her school that Warren came up with the idea for her first book, *The Ten-Alarm Camp-Out.* Published in 1983 and aimed at four- to six-year-old readers, the book recounts the story of a family of armadillos who embark on a camping trip in the city park. "I thought it would be funny for animals to create some kind of havoc, just because their sense of order might not always jibe with our sense of order," Warren explained. "Armadillos seemed the perfect animals for this situation because they are such awkward yet benevolent little creatures."

Warren's second book, aimed at the same age group, appeared in 1984. The title character in *Victoria's ABC Adventure* is a young snake, the only brown one out of a brood of twenty-six, and her green sisters shun her because of it; all are named after a different letter of the alphabet. Saddened, Victoria takes off on her own; at a cookout she finds some hot dogs on a grill, and assumes that these are her true relatives. The humans panic and organize a snake hunt, but Victoria saves them from capturing her family. A *Publishers Weekly* reviewer called *Victoria's ABC Adventure* "a dazzler, brimful of fun." In her next book, also published in 1984, Warren utilized her experiences in the day-care field to craft a story depicting one young boy's first-day-at-school jitters. *Fred's First Day* provides young readers with a tale in which nervousness is overcome and new friends are made.

Warren also wrote *Springtime Bears,* about a family of young cubs who try to evade spring cleaning and in doing so, evoke the wrath of their mother. *Saturday Belongs to Sara,* published in 1988, is aimed at a slightly older readership than Warren's previous works. It tells the story of a young girl and her mother who have planned a day-long outing. As a favor, they stop to visit an elderly woman who is housebound. Mrs. Ivey winds up coming along on Sara's picnic, and the girl's special day with her mother is further interrupted when her mother does errands for Mrs. Ivey. Yet Sara learns that the day she coveted for having her mother all to herself had other unexpected rewards; "children will appreciate the dignity given to her feelings," noted a *Booklist* reviewer.

BIOGRAPHICAL/CRITICAL SOURCES:

BOOKS

Something about the Author, Volume 62, Gale, 1990, pp. 184-185.

PERIODICALS

Booklist, November 15, 1983, p. 503; November 1, 1984, p. 376; July, 1986, p.1628; May 15, 1988, p. 1613.
Publishers Weekly, April 27, 1984, p. 86.

School Library Journal, December, 1983, p. 61; October, 1984, pp. 152-53; January, 1985, pp. 69-70; September, 1987, p. 172; June-July, 1988, p. 95.

*   *   *

WEAVER, Robert C(lifton)   1907-1997

OBITUARY NOTICE—See index for *CA* sketch: Born December 29, 1907, in Washington, DC; died July 17, 1997, in Manhattan, NY. Politician, civil rights activist, consultant, and author. Remembered for his work in human rights causes, Weaver was the first African American to be named to a presidential cabinet post when Lyndon B. Johnson appointed him as secretary of Housing and Urban Development. In his early career, he served as an aide to Interior Secretary Harold Ickes. Under President Franklin D. Roosevelt, Weaver was a member of the "Black Cabinet," an informal group of African Americans that the president consulted on urban issues. During World War II he served as an administrative assistant for the War Planning Board. In 1949 he joined the J. H. Whitney Foundation in New York City as director of opportunity fellowships. He left the post to become the deputy commissioner of housing and rent-control administrator for the State of New York in 1955. His post as rent commissioner was the first New York State cabinet position given to an African American.

From 1959 to 1960 Weaver was a consultant to the Ford Foundation, then became vice chairperson of the Housing and Redevelopment Board until 1961. From 1961 to 1966 he served the U.S. Government as administrator of the Housing and Home Finance Agency. President John F. Kennedy had sought to make the position part of his cabinet, but he ran into staunch opposition from the South. By the time Lyndon Johnson assumed the presidency, the civil rights movement had made great strides for equality and the president was able to appoint Weaver to secretary of Housing and Urban Development. In 1969 Weaver became president of the Bernard M. Baruch College of Business and Public Administration, where he stayed until 1970 when he accepted a post as distinguished professor of Urban Affairs at Hunter College. He remained at Hunter until his retirement. During his career, Weaver also served as national chairperson of the National Association for the Advancement of Colored People

(NAACP) and as a member of the School of Urban and Public Affairs' visiting committee at Carnegie-Mellon University. He also found time to write books, including *The Negro Ghetto, Hemmed In: ABC's of Race Restrictive Housing Covenants, The Future of the American City, The Urban Complex: Human Values in Urban Life, Housing for Senior Citizens: A Progress Report, The Urban Environment: How It Can Be Improved* (with William E. Zisch and Paul H. Douglas), and *Negro Labor: A National Problem.*

OBITUARIES AND OTHER SOURCES:

BOOKS

Who's Who among African Americans, Gale (Detroit, MI), 1996.

PERIODICALS

Chicago Tribune, July 19, 1997, sec. 1, p. 21.
Los Angeles Times, July 22, 1997, p. A20.
New York Times, July 19, 1997, p. 50.

*   *   *

WEBER, Thomas 1950-

PERSONAL: Born September 26, 1950, in Melbourne, Australia; son of Alec and Elizabeth Weber; married Marja Koskela; children: Hanna. *Ethnicity:* "Hungarian." *Education:* University of Melbourne, Australia, LL.B., 1973, post-graduate diploma in criminology, 1974; La Trobe University, College of Northern Victoria, Bundoora, Victoria, Australia, M.A., 1982, Ph.D., 1991. *Avocational interests:* Birdwatching, bush-walking.

ADDRESSES: Home—737 Chum Creek Rd., Healesville, Victoria 3777, Australia. *Office*—Department of Politics, La Trobe University, Bundoora, Victoria 3083, Australia; fax 039-479-1997. *E-mail*—t.weber @latrobe.edu.au.

CAREER: La Trobe University, Bundoora, Australia, teacher of politics and peace studies and coordinator of Interdisciplinary Studies, Peace Studies Area, both 1996—, Institute for Peace Research, inaugural peace research scholar, 1987, member of governing committee, 1987—. Community Aid Abroad, member of India Projects Committee, 1989-94.

WRITINGS:

(With K. L. Milte) *Police in Australia: Development, Functions, and Procedures,* Butterworth (Sydney, Australia), 1977.
(With Milte and S. I. Miller) *Principles of Police Planning: Armed Robbery,* Government Printer (Melbourne, Australia), 1978.
(With Roger Douglas) *Guilty, Your Worship: A Study of Victoria's Magistrates' Courts* (monograph), Legal Studies Department, La Trobe University (Bundoora, Australia), 1980.
Hugging the Trees: The Story of the Chipko Movement, Viking (New Delhi, India), 1988, Penguin, 1989.
Conflict Resolution and Gandhian Ethics, Gandhi Peace Foundation (New Delhi), 1991.
Gandhi's Peace Army: The Shanti Sena and Unarmed Peacekeeping, Syracuse University Press (Syracuse, NY), 1996.
On the Salt March: The Historiography of Gandhi's March to Dandi, HarperCollins (New Delhi), 1997.
(Contributor) A. Copley and G. Paxton, editors, *Gandhi and the Contemporary World,* Indo-British Historical Society, 1997.

Contributor to periodicals, including *Nonviolence Today. Interdisciplinary Peace Research/Pacifica Review,* founding member of editorial committee, 1988—, editor, 1990-96.

WORK IN PROGRESS: The Recurring Vision: Nonviolent Intervention and Unarmed Peacekeeping, with Yeshua Moser-Puangsuwan, on grassroots peace team initiatives; *Gandhi, Gandhism, and the Gandhians,* a collection of previously published articles.

*   *   *

WEIL, Simone (Adolphine) 1909-1943
(Emile Novis, a pseudonym)

PERSONAL: Born February 3, 1909, in Paris, France; died of starvation and pulmonary tuberculosis, August 24, 1943, in Ashford, England; daughter of Bernard (a physician) and Salomea (also known as Selma) Weil. *Education:* Studied under Alain at Henri IV Lycee, Paris, 1925-28; graduated from Ecole Normale Superieure, agregation (diploma), 1931. *Religion:* Jewish, converted to Christianity, c. late 1930s.

CAREER: French religious philosopher, essayist, dramatist, and poet. Taught philosophy at five girls' lycees, 1931-38; worked as a machine operator in three Paris factories for one year, c. 1930s; briefly worked in fall grape harvest near Marseilles, 1941. *Military service:* Volunteer for Republican forces during Spanish Civil War and for Free French forces in London during World War II.

WRITINGS:

(As Emile Novis) "L'Iliade, ou, Le Poeme de La Force" (essay), *Cahiers du Sud* (journal), 1940, published in the U.S. as "The Iliad, or The Poem of Force," translated by Mary McCarthy, in *Politics* (journal), November, 1945, reprinted as a pamphlet by Pendle Hill Publications (Wallingford, PA), 1956; 150 copies republished with preface by George P. Elliott, Stone Wall Press (Iowa City, IA), 1973.

La Pesanteur et La Grace (essays), introduction by Gustave Thibon, Librairie Plon (Paris), 1947, published as *Gravity and Grace,* translated by Arthur Wills, Putnam (New York City), 1952, Ark Paperbacks (London), 1987.

L'Enracinement: Prelude a une Declaration des Devoirs Envers L'Etre Humain (essay), Gallimard (Paris), 1949, published in U.S. as *The Need for Roots: Prelude to a Declaration of Duties toward Mankind,* translated by Arthur Wills, preface by T. S. Eliot, Putnam, 1952, Octagon Books, 1979, Ark Paperbacks, 1987.

L'Attente de Dieu (letters and essays), preface and notes by Joseph-Marie Perrin, La Colombe (Paris), 1950, published as *Waiting on God,* foreword by Malcolm Muggeridge, Routledge (London), 1951, published as *Waiting for God,* translated by Emma Craufurd, introduction by Leslie A. Fiedler, Putnam, 1951, Harper (New York), 1985.

La Connaissance Surnaturelle (title means "Supernatural Knowledge," also known as *Cahiers d'Amerique;* notebooks), Gallimard, 1950, published as *First and Last Notebooks* (containing *New York Notebook* and *London Notebook*), translated by Richard Rees, Oxford University Press (London), 1970.

La Condition Ouvriere (title means "The Workers' Condition," essays), Gallimard, 1951.

Les Intuitions Pre-chretiennes, La Colombe, 1951.

Lettres a un Religieux (letters), Gallimard, 1951, also published as *Letters to a Priest,* translated by Arthur Wills, Routledge, 1953, Putnam, 1954.

Cahiers (notebooks), three volumes, Librairie Plon, 1951-56, portions published as *The Notebooks of Simone Weil,* two volumes, translated by Arthur Wills, Routledge, 1956, Putnam, 1956.

La Source Grecque (essays), Gallimard, 1953.

Oppression et Liberte (essays), Gallimard, 1955, published as *Oppression and Liberty,* translated by Arthur Wills and John Petrie, introduction by F. C. Ellert, University of Massachusetts Press (Amherst, MA), 1958, reprinted 1978.

Venise Sauvee: Tragedie en Trois Actes (play), Gallimard, 1955, revised with an introduction and notes by Jean-Marie Lhote, Theater Universitaire (Marseilles, France), 1965.

Ecrits de Londres et Dernieres Lettres (essays and letters), Gallimard, 1957.

Intimations of Christianity among the Ancient Greeks (contains translated selections from *La Source Grecque* and *Les Intuitions Pre-chretiennes*), edited and translated by Elisabeth Chase Geissbuhler, Routledge, 1957, reprinted 1976, also published in U.S. by Beacon Press (Boston), 1958.

Lecons de Philosophie de Simone Weil (Roanne 1933-1934) (lectures), edited by Anne Reynaud, Librairie Plon, 1959, published as *Lectures on Philosophy,* translated by Hugh Price, introduction by Peter Winch, Cambridge University Press (Cambridge), 1978.

Ecrits Historiques et Politiques (title means "Historical and Political Writings"; essays), Gallimard, 1960.

Selected Essays: 1934-1943, translated and arranged by Richard Rees, Oxford University Press (London), 1962.

Pensees sans Ordre Concernant L'Amour de Dieu (aphorisms), Gallimard, 1962.

Sur La Science (essays), Gallimard, 1965.

Seventy Letters, translated and arranged by Richard Rees, Oxford University Press, 1965.

Poemes, Suivis de "Venise Sauvee" (poetry and drama), 1968.

On Science, Necessity, and the Love of God, collected, translated, and edited by Richard Rees, Oxford University Press, 1968.

Gateway to God, edited by David Raper with collaborations by Malcolm Muggeridge and Vernon Sproxton, Fontana (London), 1974, Crossroad (New York City), 1982.

The Simone Weil Reader, edited by George A. Panichas, McKay (New York City), 1977.

Reflexions sur Les Causes de La Liberte et de L'Oppression Social (title means "Reflections on the Causes of Liberty and Social Oppression"), Gallimard, 1980.

Two Moral Essays: Draft for a Statement of Human Obligations and Human Personality, edited by

Ronald Hathaway, Pendle Hill, 1981.

Simone Weil, an Anthology, edited and introduced by Sian Miles, Virago (London), 1986, Weidenfeld & Nicholson (New York City), 1986.

Formative Writings, 1929-1941, edited and translated by Dorothy Tuck McFarland and Wilhelmina Van Ness, University of Massachusetts Press, 1987.

COLLECTED WORKS

Oeuvres Completes, Edition Publiee sous La Direction d'Andre A. Devaux et de Florence de Lussy (title means "Complete Works, Edition Published under the Direction of Andre A. Devaux and Florence de Lussy"), six volumes, Gallimard, 1989-94.

SIDELIGHTS: During her lifetime, Simone Weil published only a few poems and articles in obscure left-wing journals. Since her death by starvation and pulmonary tuberculosis in a British sanitorium in 1943, however, Weil's essays, notebooks, and letters have been widely published, with the result that she has become one of the influential—and also one of the more controversial—religious thinkers of the twentieth century. Born in 1909 in Paris, the daughter of an Alsatian physician and his Austrian-Galician wife, Weil was doubly an outsider in French culture by virtue of her immigrant background and of being Jewish. Intelligent and sensitive, she refused to eat sugar at age five because no sugar was rationed to French soldiers who currently were fighting World War I. She graduated at age fifteen from a prestigious lycee, or high school, where she studied under the philosopher Alain (Emile Chartier). Her adolescence was marked by near-breakdowns and thoughts of suicide. She suffered from a lifelong feeling of inferiority to her older brother Andre, who had been considered a math prodigy from his earliest years. Anne Fremantle in *Saturday Review* physically described Simone Weil as "clumsy and unattractive" and that "she purposely wore dowdy clothes." After graduating from the Ecole Normale Superieure in 1931 (another excellent French school), Weil taught philosophy at girls' schools, but was unpopular with students and employers, and went through five jobs in seven years. According to a 1979 article by Jean Amery, Weil's students were bored by her, so much so that most failed the final exam.

For one year during the 1930s, Weil took a self-assigned furlough by working in factories. Amery described her as a "hopelessly inept worker." Weil, in the 1930s, was a leftist activist who participated in picket lines, published articles on the workers, and gave most of her salary to the poor, leaving herself only with the amount given to the unemployed as relief. Nevertheless, she expressed contempt for the revolutionary rhetoric of Lenin and others, which she considered unauthentic. She served briefly with an anarchist group during the Spanish Civil War, but left the experience feeling disenchanted by the brutality on both sides. The years 1936 through 1938 marked the crucial spiritual change in Weil's life. She began to study Christianity, which she considered the "religion of slaves"—a compliment in her view, since she identified with the oppressed. Afflicted with severe migraine headaches (which she suffered from all her life) and possibly malnourished, Weil experienced several mystical episodes. At the chapel of St. Francis of Assisi, in Assisi, Italy, in 1937, she felt pulled to her knees by an overpowering force. Other pivotal experiences occurred in 1938 while listening to Gregorian chants at an Easter mass, and while reciting British metaphysical poet George Herbert's "Love." During the latter experience, as she later wrote, "Christ Himself came down and took possession of me." In 1940, with the fall of France to the Nazis, her life changed of necessity. She moved to Marseilles and came under the influence of a Catholic priest, Jean-Marie Perrin, who in turn introduced her to Gustave Thibon, a farmer who was also a Catholic philosopher, and who hired Weil to work in the grape harvest. Weil left Thibon her notebooks for use in his own writing.

Weil then went to London to work with the Free French. She pleaded to be allowed to parachute into France, an action that would probably have been suicidal if permitted, since she was both Jewish and in frail physical health. In England she contracted tuberculosis and refused treatment, insisting that her food be limited to the rations given to French civilians. She died in a sanitorium at Ashford, Kent. The coroner's diagnosis, according to Amery, was "heart failure due to myocardial insufficiency caused by hunger and pulmonary tuberculosis," but Amery rephrased this as "suicide resulting from a religious compulsion neurosis." According to a *Twentieth-Century Literary Criticism* contributor, the cause of death was "voluntary starvation," although "it is still a matter for debate whether her death was a result of anorexia, actual suicide, mental illness, or a self-imposed martyrdom due to her unbending asceticism." In any event, the manner of Weil's death contributed greatly to her posthumous mystique, which in turn contributed to a welcome reception to the first publications of her works in the late 1940s and 1950s.

Responses to Weil have tended toward extremes. According to Amery, Charles de Gaulle, who, as the leader of the Free French knew Weil slightly, considered her *folle*, or mad. On the other hand, Albert Camus, after winning the Nobel Prize for literature, spent an hour meditating in the deceased Weil's room before boarding the plane for Stockholm. Eminent thinkers such as T. S. Eliot and Gabriel Marcel admired her greatly. Eliot, in 1952, wrote of her as "a woman of genius, of a kind of genius akin to that of the saints." Said Amery, "she was, and has remained until today [1979], a rare jewel that it would be blasphemous to touch. The prestige of her death has shielded her from criticism." Since that essay, however, criticism has mounted. Especially vocal has been criticism of Weil for being a Jewish anti-Semite. She denied the presence of any divine revelation in the Jewish religion, but found it in many other faiths besides Christianity. Discussing this phenomenon in 1957, Hans Meyerhoff wrote, "what makes her case so dramatic is that she launched her Gnostic revolt against the Jewish religion at a time when the Jewish people were suffering the worst agonies and tortures. . . . She was driven to indict the religion of her own people in the language of their worst enemies and persecutors." Weil also has been criticized on the grounds that her specific worldly and political suggestions were misguided. She advocated sacrificing Czechoslovakia to Hitler in the 1930s, and wrote in her 1943 notebook that the French ought to have used Gandhi-like passive resistance against the Nazis.

Weil's theology was highly personal and unorthodox, and has received both praise and criticism from all sides of the philosophical spectrum. She felt drawn to the Roman Catholic Church, but criticized it sharply for its rejection of other religions (although she criticized it equally for its absorption of Jewish influences), and refused to be baptized. The true Christian, she felt, did not consider herself worthy of baptism. Commentators have at times sought among the Christian heresies of the past for labels to apply to Weil. Eliot claimed that Weil fell into "something very like the Marcionite heresy" while Nobel Prize-winning poet Czeslaw Milosz called Weil, "at least by temperament, an Albigensian, a Cathar." Others have found Manichean dualistic elements in her writings. Weil's thought also was inspired by elements of Platonic philosophy, Greek tragedy, Hindu Upanishads, and ancient Egyptian and Chaldean worldviews. The *Twentieth-Century Literary Criticism* contributor

summed up Weil's beliefs by saying that she considered God to have abandoned the world after creating it, and to have brought Christ into the world so that humanity could approach God. However, Weil did not see the crucifixion of Jesus as a sacrifice that relieved mankind of its burden of sin, but rather as an inspirational model which the believer ought to strive to follow. "Weil's philosophy centers on the abandonment of God by God, signified by Christ's cry, 'My God, My God, why hast Thou forsaken Me?'" stated the *Twentieth-Century Literary Criticism* contributor. The experiences of abandonment and self-sacrifice—of the ache of the absence of God—were, for Weil, necessary preludes to redemption by God's love.

In the first two decades after her death, Weil's work was variously edited and brought out in individual volumes. Her first title available in English was *Waiting for God* (1951), which was a collection of letters and essays from the early 1940s, all but one to the Dominican Father Jean-Marie Perrin. Anne Fremantle in *Saturday Review* commented that Weil's intelligence displayed in *Waiting for God* was "high." "So sharp are her analyses of ordinary human situations that these situations seem clearly visible for the first time," noted Fremantle. A reviewer for the *Times Literary Supplement* described Weil's attraction to Roman Catholicism and her refusal of complete attachment to it: "like the beggar at the gate of heaven, she lived on the threshold of the Roman Church, refusing to come in but ever gazing through the open door at the distant altar." The reviewer for *Times Literary Supplement* felt that the reader was "likely to feel well rewarded with the many things, unexpected, profound, and true which he will find her uttering."

The second volume available in English was *The Need for Roots: Prelude to a Declaration of Duties toward Mankind* (1952). Arthur Wills (a prominent translator of Weil's writings) translated the work and T. S. Eliot wrote the introduction. The subject of *The Need for Roots*, according to a reviewer for *Times Literary Supplement*, was "politics in the widest Aristotelian understanding of the term, and the treatment is of exceptional originality and breadth of human sympathy." Weil wrote the volume at the request of the French in London, who were curious about her thoughts on the potential of France's reconstruction after World War II, but as the *Times Literary Supplement* critic reported, "the [book] is of equal interest and appeal . . . no matter what country." Jenny Turner in *New Statesmen* stated that Weil specifically wrote the piece for General de Gaulle for "it was intended to provide a philosophical foundation for the Fifth Republic." The reviewer for *Times Literary Supplement* also related that the reaction of feeling "provocation to agree with her, and more often to disagree, is . . . strong." S. M. Fitzgerald in *New Republic* observed: "[Weil's] thinking is sometimes idiosyncratic in the extreme, displaying a lack of objectivity that seems almost willful, and some of her outbursts are so emotional as to be almost altogether untrustworthy."

In *Letters to a Priest,* 1953, Weil related thirty-five of her essential beliefs to Father Perrin to see if they violated any of the doctrines of the Roman Catholic faith. A reviewer in *New Yorker* called Weil's writing "an interesting work, but chiefly" it was a "picture of a brilliant mind caught in the web of comparative religions." The *Times Literary Supplement* noted that "so far as is known the letter went unanswered." The reviewer further describes the thirty-five beliefs as "a series of philosophic queries which go to the very roots of religion." The essays contained in another work, *Oppression and Liberty,* 1958, related, according to a reviewer for *New York Times Book Review,* "discerning appraisals of Marxism." This work is the only one to outline Weil's responses to Marxism and her personal reactions to the political ideology. A young student of Weil's at the girls' lycee in Roanne, Anne Reynaud, kept thorough notes in class and the notes were eventually translated and gathered into a book, *Lectures on Philosophy,* which was first published in French in 1951. The lectures, according to a reviewer for *Choice,* "systematically explore" many of Weil's prevalent issues, including ethics, moral psychology, and theories of knowledge. The *Lectures* shed light on the events leading up to Weil's final embrace of Christianity.

Two volumes of *The Notebooks of Simon Weil* were released in 1956. A reviewer for the *Times Literary Supplement* observed that "it is a great pity that the *Notebooks* have not been more imaginatively edited. There is no introduction . . . the footnotes . . . are totally inadequate. At best the *Notebooks* will send the reader back to other works." Anne Fremantle in the *New York Times Book Review* stated: "It is unfortunate that these volumes lack an editor. The reader longs for some signposts." A reviewer for the *Times Literary Supplement,* impressed by Weil's mind, made this observation: "The kind of all-around scholar who could grasp Simone Weil's every thought in its 'incandescent stage' hardly exists today: [the scholar] would have to be familiar with theology,

ancient and modern literature, comparative religion, folklore, geometry, algebra, physics, mechanics, astrology, the history of science, sociology, economics, and of course, philosophy."

A translation by Richard Rees, *Selected Essays, 1934-1943* (1962), contained a variety of essays on several subjects, aiding in the illumination of Weil's thought. "By nature Weil seems to have thought in aphorisms rather than in sequences of ideas," noted a reviewer for *Times Literary Supplement.* John Ratte, in *Commonweal,* attempted to define Weil's thoughts: "In its ranging, her mind draws parallels, suggests analogies and makes connections (both safe and wild) in a tireless effort to increase man's understanding of his own nature and of his society in order to create new possibilities for action." The reviewer for the *Times Literary Supplement* set forth the attraction of Weil: "The fact remains that we value her not because she supplies us with a coherent philosophy but because she sets our minds working."

In 1965 Richard Rees translated and arranged another compilation of Weil's writings, titled *Seventy Letters.* A *Times Literary Supplement* reviewer decided that "these letters, though they cannot be compared for depth with other works by Simone Weil . . . will serve as an introduction to her thoughts and life and tempt readers to ask more." Rees also translated *On Science, Necessity, and the Love of God* (1968). This book, according to a reviewer for the *Times Literary Supplement,* relates that "what obsessed Simone Weil here, as always, was the problem of God: God as conceived by Plato, God as revealed by Jesus Christ." The reviewer added, "we might reach the conclusion that Simone Weil is a far more profound philosopher of the absurd that Camus." Rees translated *First and Last Notebooks* (1970), which received favorable reviews. Weil's writings here were described by a reviewer for *Times Literary Supplement:* "Simone Weil not only makes hard reading, which is doubtless why she has been passed by in superficial sociology or journalistic theology, but she also took a poor view of our technological civilization and of our ecclesiastical Establishments."

In 1977 George A. Panichas edited a volume simply called *The Simone Weil Reader.* Edmund White in the *Washington Post Book World,* describing Weil as "an uncompromising, bristly thinker" who at times was driven to "outrageous remarks" by her "severity," enjoyed *The Simone Weil Reader:* "her thought is beautifully and copiously introduced in this volume." Unlike previous titles, this volume was arranged according to themes, not chronology, and Doris Grumback in the *New York Times Book Review* found Weil's "central thought . . . intact and available." Joyce Carol Oates in the *New Republic* offered praise for the book: "this massive collection of Simone Weil's writings is an extraordinary book. An extraordinary experience." Oates continued to relate her thoughts on Weil: "What would be a trivial sin in another person is a mortal sin in Weil. Her curious inflation of her own self-worth is never questioned, not by Weil at least, and if others attempted to point it out to her, there is no indication from her side. *She is the object of God's attention; God is most vulnerable to her.*" Oates continued: "Yet it is doubtful that she was at heart a very compassionate person, or even a Christian in the usual sense of the word. She seems to have been charged with a self-righteous zeal that is, at times, rather chilling." Weil, Oates expressed, also had "contempt" for "the Hebrews" and the *Old Testament,* which defied logic since she was born Jewish: "One reads Weil, then with a variety of emotions. Fascination at first. Exasperation. Disappointment. Even anger at her willfulness, her refusal to recognize her own narcissism though she is quick to see it in others."

Yet another compendium, *Formative Writings, 1929-1941* (1987), was translated by Dorothy Tuck McFarland and Wilhelmina Van Ness. Kate Soper in *New Statesmen* felt this volume was to "direct attention to the 'other Weils'—to Weil the political activist and Weil the philosopher-teacher." Soper also commented on Weil's "intellect almost stumbling over itself" attempting "to gain a grip on historical momentum rapidly about to escape from all rational control." "[The writings] reveal an intelligent and sensitive woman deeply engaged in the travails of the world, one whose commitment is to the underdog, the exploited and destitute," wrote George L. Farre in *America.* Farre found the book "well worth reading and pondering," but was taken by Weil's inconsistency, which he felt "was rooted in a naive conception of a brotherhood of men." Elizabeth Kamarck Minnich in *Women's Review of Books* found *Formative Writings* rewarding: "I was left once again stunned by Weil's brilliance, troubled—almost repelled—by her passion for suffering, awed by her extreme independence, and then troubled again by some of her views." Minnich noted that "as the agonies of Weil's world increased, so did her need to participate in them."

Simone Weil: An Anthology, edited by Sian Miles, was another volume of arranged writings, but a re-

viewer for *Observer* decided that the *Notebooks* contained "the best of Weil's work." French publishing company Gallimard began publishing a uniform edition of her complete works in 1988. With voluminous writings by Weil in print, in so many arrangements, compiled from such diverse sources, and with an industry of commentary arising, perhaps the most conclusive statement that could be made about her came from Elisabeth Young-Bruehl, reviewing *Formative Writings, 1929-1941* in the *New York Times Book Review:* "Simone Weil can no longer be reduced to a noun's worth, or even two, of doctrinal type or ideology. She has become again the puzzle she was while she lived."

BIOGRAPHICAL/CRITICAL SOURCES:

BOOKS

Amery, Jean, "Simone Weil: 'Beyond the Legend,'" in *Radical Humanism: Selected Essays,* edited and translated by Sidney Rosenfeld and Stella P. Rosenfeld, Indiana University Press, 1984.

Dictionary of Twentieth-Century Culture, Volume 2, Gale (Detroit), 1995.

Meyerhoff, Hans, "Contra Simone Weil: 'The Voices of Demons for the Silence of God,'" in *Arguments and Doctrines: A Reader of Jewish Thinking in the Aftermath of the Holocaust,* edited by Arthur A. Cohen, Harper, 1970.

Milosz, Czeslaw, "The Importance of Simone Weil," in *Emperor of the Earth: Modes of Eccentric Vision,* University of California Press, 1977.

Twentieth-Century Literary Criticism, Volume 23, Gale, 1987.

Weil, Simone, *The Need for Roots: Prelude to a Declaration of Duties toward Mankind,* translated by Arthur Wills, introduction by T. S. Eliot, Putnam, 1952.

PERIODICALS

America, September 19, 1987, p. 139.

Choice, April, 1974, p. 274; May, 1979, p. 405.

Commonweal, March 22, 1963, pp. 669-670; November 6, 1987, pp. 638-639.

Library Journal, January 15, 1979, pp. 195-196.

Ms., December, 1985.

New Republic, August 18, 1952, p. 18; July 2, 1977, p. 33-37.

New Statesman, August 28, 1987, p. 24; September 4, 1987.

New Yorker, April 3, 1954, p. 133.

New York Times Book Review, March 14, 1954, p. 7;

December 16, 1956, p. 6; September 11, 1977, pp. 16, 20; June 25, 1978; August 2, 1987, p. 19.

Observer (London), February 16, 1986.

Saturday Review, March 8, 1952, p. 26; May 10, 1952, pp. 20-21.

Times Literary Supplement, October 26, 1951, p. 681; May 30, 1952, p. 365; March 20, 1953, p. 192; November 16, 1956, p. 685; December 28, 1962, p. 1003; October 17, 1968, p. 1174; August 14, 1970, p. 904; January 4, 1980, p. 19; July 28, 1989, p. 821; July 13, 1990, p. 747; August 23, 1991, p. 7.

Washington Post Book World, October 2, 1977, p. E5; January 24, 1993, p. 15.

Women's Review of Books, October, 1987, pp. 13-14.*

* * *

WELCH, Robert 1947-

PERSONAL: Born November 25, 1947, in Cork, Ireland; son of Patrick (a factory worker) and Kathleen (a homemaker; maiden name, Kearney) Welch; married, wife's name Angela, June 30, 1970; children: Rachel, Killian, Egan, Tiernan. *Ethnicity:* "Irish." *Education:* National University of Ireland, University College, Cork, B.A., 1968, M.A. (first class honors), 1971; University of Leeds, Ph.D., 1974. *Politics:* "Nationalist." *Religion:* Roman Catholic. *Avocational interests:* Gardening, walking, wine, fishing.

ADDRESSES: Home—34 Station Rd., Portstewart, County Derry BT55 7DA, Northern Ireland. *Office*—Centre for Irish Literature and Bibliography, University of Ulster, Coleraine, County Londonderry BT52 1SA, Northern Ireland.

CAREER: University of Leeds, Leeds, England, temporary lecturer, 1971-73; University of Ife, Ile-Ife, Nigeria, lecturer, 1973-74; University of Leeds, lecturer, 1974-84; University of Ulster, Coleraine, Northern Ireland, professor of English, 1984—, head of Department of English, Media, and Theatre Studies, 1984-94, director of Centre for Irish Literature and Bibliography, 1994—. National University of Ireland, University College, Cork, visiting lecturer, 1982; speaker at colleges and universities, including York University, Chuo University, University of Caen, St. Michael's College, Winooski, VT, Tokyo University, Trinity College, Dublin, University of Graz, Ulster Polytechnic, University of Wuppertal, and University of Newcastle-upon-Tyne. Arts Council of Northern Ireland, member of board of directors, 1988-96, vice chairperson, 1994-95, chairperson of Literature Committee, 1990-96; O'Casey Theatre School, director, 1994-96; member of board of directors of a theater company, 1997—.

MEMBER: International Association for the Study of Anglo-Irish Literature (chairperson, 1988-91).

AWARDS, HONORS: Visiting fellow, St. John's College, Oxford, 1986; grants from Leverhulme Trust, 1989, Community Relations Council, 1990, and British Academy, 1996; Critics Award, O'Reachtas, 1996.

WRITINGS:

Irish Poetry from Moore to Yeats, Barnes & Noble (New York City), 1980.

(Editor and contributor) *The Way Back: George Moore's "The Untilled Field" and "The Lake,"* Barnes & Noble, 1982.

A History of Verse Translation from the Irish, 1789-1897, Barnes & Noble, 1988.

(Editor with Suheil Badi Bushrui) *Literature and the Art of Creation: Essays in Honour of A. N. Jeffares,* Barnes & Noble, 1988.

Muskerry (poems), Dedalus Press (Dublin, Ireland), 1991.

(Editor and author of introduction) *Irish Writers and Religion,* Barnes & Noble, 1991.

Changing States: Transformations in Modern Irish Writing, Routledge (London), 1993.

(Editor and author of introduction and notes) *W. B. Yeats: Irish Folklore, Legend, and Myth,* Penguin, 1993.

The Kilcolman Notebook (novel), Brandon Press, 1994.

(Editor) *The Oxford Companion to Irish Literature,* Clarendon Press (Oxford, England), 1996.

Irish Myths, Appletree Press (Belfast, Northern Ireland), 1996.

(Editor with Greg Delanty, and co-author of introduction and notes) *Patrick Falvin: New and Selected Poems,* Cork University Press, 1996.

Groundwork (novel), Blackstaff Press, 1997.

Secret Societies (poems), Dufour (New York City), 1997.

Tearmann (novel; in Gaelic), Coisceim (Dublin), 1997.

The Blue Formica Table (poems), Dedalus Press, in press.

A History of the Abbey Theatre, Oxford University Press, in press.

General editor and founder of "Ulster Editions and Monographs," a series, Colin Smythe, 1988—; member of editorial board of the series "Irish Writers," Colin Smythe. Contributor of articles and reviews to periodicals, including *Religion and Literature, Writing Ulster, Threshold, Gaeliana, Irish University Review,* and *Literary Review.* Editor, *IASAIL Newsletter,* 1982-85.

Contributor to books, including *Lady Gregory Fifty Years After,* edited by Anne Saddlemeyer and Colin Smythe, Barnes & Noble, 1986; *Tradition and Influence in Anglo-Irish Poetry,* edited by Terence Brown and Nicholas Grene, Macmillan (London, England), 1989; *The Achievement of Brian Friel,* edited by Alan Peacock, Barnes & Noble, 1993; *Seamus Heaney,* edited by Elmer Andrews, Macmillan, 1993.

WORK IN PROGRESS: The Plays and Poems of J. M. Synge, publication by Penguin expected in 1999; *The Concise Companion to Irish Literature,* Oxford University Press, 2000.

SIDELIGHTS: Robert Welch told *CA:* "I have tried in my work to bring to light the variousness of Irish literary tradition and to link the Gaelic tradition with writings in English. I have attempted to deal with as extensive a period of Irish literary culture as possible, from the earliest beginnings in saga to contemporary writings. I have been concerned to understand, as far as I could, the pain and shame of colonialism, the subject to one degree or another of my two published novels in English and my novel in Irish. My poetry seeks to speak of what is hidden, shameful, oppressed and sad, but to do it with buoyancy and as much fearlessness as I can muster."

*   *   *

WELCH, Willy 1952-

PERSONAL: Born April 8, 1952, in Madison, WI; son of Wayne (a professor and scientist) and Dorothy (Dunlap) Welch; married Wendy Jackson (a singer), September 8, 1984; children: Grady, Molly Bess. *Education:* Boston University, B.F.A., 1976. *Politics:* "Progressive." *Religion:* "Charismatic Episcopalian." *Avocational interests:* Bicycling, canoeing, fishing, baseball, reading.

ADDRESSES: Home and office—817 Berkinshire Dr., Dallas, TX 75218.

CAREER: Actor in Boston, MA, and New York City, 1975-83; singer and songwriter, New York City and Dallas, TX, 1983—.

MEMBER: American Society of Composers, Authors, and Publishers, Actors' Equity Association, Society of Children's Book Writers and Illustrators, Dallas Songwriters Association.

WRITINGS:

Playing Right Field, illustrated by Marc Simont, Scholastic, Inc., 1995.
Home Made Cookie, Scholastic, Inc., 1997.

SIDELIGHTS: Willy Welch commented: "I am in love with the *sounds* of words. I've loved them from my earliest days, and I've made up rhymes and stories for as long as I can remember. I woke up to Shakespeare's and Yeats's musical/poetical use of language when I was about fourteen, and these authors are still my primary inspirations when the muse seems to abandon me. I decided at fourteen that all I wanted to do was use the English language as art, and I've used it as an actor, a singer, a writer, and a lyricist. (I've also used it as a word processor, waiter, and taxi driver!)

"I rather fell into writing children's books in the course of being a songwriter. As more and more of my songs came to be for and about young people, I decided to take a course on the children's book business. Shortly after I completed the course, I was contacted by Scholastic Inc., who expressed an interest in publishing my song 'Playing Right Field' as a children's book. They had heard the song performed by Peter, Paul, and Mary on PBS-TV. They got the wonderful illustrator Marc Simont to do the pictures. The song has been used as a television commercial for Pizza Hut, and the book will soon be published in Japan.

"My next book, *Home Made Cookie,* is also a children's picture book. I put it to music as well and sing it in my concerts, which I perform alone or with my wife Wendy. Sometimes my daughter Molly sings with us. My son Grady sells the books and tapes and T-shirts!

"What is important for me is to try to hear what God is telling me. This isn't easy for me, but I keep trying, either by prayerful solitude or through what my friends and family say.

"My writing, which usually emerges as a song, comes from everyday experiences, thoughts, and memories. It is like exploring a strange land, because writing brings out parts of me that I'm not always aware of. It is an adventure like reading is!

"Writing *Playing Right Field* helped me think about my own self-esteem, my fears of being rejected by others, and my desire to be a hero even though I felt I wasn't big and strong enough."

BIOGRAPHICAL/CRITICAL SOURCES:

PERIODICALS

Booklist, January 15, 1995, p. 925.
Bulletin of the Center for Children's Books, July-August, 1995, p. 400.
Horn Book, September-October, 1995, pp. 593-94.
Kirkus Reviews, February 15, 1995, p. 234.
Publishers Weekly, April 17, 1995, p. 56.
School Library Journal, March, 1995, p. 188.

*   *   *

WHEAT, Joe Ben   1916-1997

OBITUARY NOTICE—See index for *CA* sketch: Born April 21, 1916, in Van Horn, TX; died June 12, 1997, in Denver, CO. Curator, archaeologist, author. Wheat gained recognition for his work with Navajo textiles and weaving. As the curator of the archaeology museum of the University of Colorado for more than thirty years, Wheat studied Navajo blankets of the nineteenth century. *Navajo Blankets from the Collection of Anthony Berlant* was a result of his research. Wheat began his career in the field of archaeology at Texas Technological College (now Texas Tech University) as a field director for the Works Progress Administration in 1939. He also conducted field research for the Smithsonian Institution and the National Park Service, and taught for many years. He contributed numerous articles to journals and, in addition, contributed to the *Encyclopaedia Britannica;* he served as the Southwest editor of *Abstracts of New World Archaeology.* His other works include *An Archaeological Survey of Addicks Dam Basin, Mogollon Culture Prior to A.D. 1000, Crooked Ridge Village, The*

Olsen-Chubbuck Site: A Paleo-Indian Bison Kill, and *The Gift of Spiderwoman: Southwestern Textiles, the Navajo Tradition.*

OBITUARIES AND OTHER SOURCES:

BOOKS

Who's Who in America, Marquis, 1996.

PERIODICALS

New York Times, June 16, 1997, p. B11.
Washington Post, June 16, 1997, p. B4.

*   *   *

WHYTE, Mary   1953-

PERSONAL: Born December 10, 1953, in Cleveland, OH; daughter of Donald Robert (an executive) and Elizabeth Reid (Patton) Whyte; married Smith B. Coleman (a gallery owner), April 23, 1977. *Education:* Temple University, Tyler School of Art, B.F.A., 1976. *Religion:* Christian.

ADDRESSES: Home—1007 Embassy Row Way, Johns Island, SC 29455. *Office*—Coleman Fine Art, 45 Hasell St., Charleston, SC 29401.

CAREER: Writer; professional artist, 1976—. Artwork represented in collections at Bell Atlantic, Easter Seals Society, University of Pennsylvania, and West Chester University; work exhibited in solo and group shows, including those of the American Watercolor Society, Allied Artists of America, Pennsylvania Watercolor Society, South Carolina Watercolor Society, Pennsylvania State Capitol, and Adirondacks National Exhibition of American Watercolors.

MEMBER: Pennsylvania Watercolor Society, South Carolina Watercolor Society, Philadelphia Watercolor Club, Charleston Artists Guild.

AWARDS, HONORS: I Love You the Purplest was chosen as one of the Best Books for 1996 by both *Parents Magazine* and *Child.*

WRITINGS:

(Self-illustrated) *Watercolor for the Serious Beginner,* Watson-Guptill (New York City), 1997.

Contributor to art magazines.

ILLUSTRATOR

Constance W. McGeorge, *Boomer's Big Day,* Chronicle Books (San Francisco, CA), 1994.

McGeorge, *The Snow Riders,* Chronicle Books (San Francisco, CA), 1995.

McGeorge, *Boomer Goes to School,* Chronicle Books (San Francisco, CA), 1996.

Barbara Joosse, *I Love You the Purplest,* Chronicle Books (San Francisco, CA), 1996.

WORK IN PROGRESS: Illustrating children's books for Chronicle Books and Dial; numerous portrait commissions.

SIDELIGHTS: Mary Whyte commented: "Art has always been a major focus of my life. I sold my first drawing when I was fourteen years old and had my first solo art exhibition when I was sixteen. My husband and I have an art gallery, Coleman Fine Art, located in the historic district of Charleston, South Carolina.

"I illustrated my first children's book *Boomer's Big Day* in 1994. The book, a collaborative effort with author Constance McGeorge, was inspired by my golden retriever, Boomer. The book prompted the sequel *Boomer Goes to School,* and since then Boomer and I have made many delightful visits to schools and bookstores.

"I live on a barrier island, and from my studio I can hear owls and the faint sound of the ocean. I generally spend forty hours per week in my studio, illustrating books, painting portraits, and writing for artists' magazines. Boomer is always by my side, either under the drawing table asleep, or jangling his leash to tell me it's time for a walk on the beach."

BIOGRAPHICAL/CRITICAL SOURCES:

PERIODICALS

Booklist, July, 1994, pp. 1955-56; January 1, 1996, pp. 847-48; April 15, 1996, p. 1446; October 15, 1996, p. 436.

Book World, May 8, 1994, p. 18.

Kirkus Reviews, March 15, 1996, p. 450.

Publishers Weekly, April 29, 1996, p. 74; September 16, 1996, p. 82.

School Library Journal, July, 1996, p. 68.

WICK, Steve 1951-

PERSONAL: Born June 15, 1951, in Haddonfield, NJ; son of David, Jr. (an engineer) and Margaret (a nurse; maiden name, Elberson) Wick; married, wife's name Deborah, April 16, 1979; children: Larisa, Kathryne, Andrew. *Ethnicity:* "White." *Education:* Attended Colorado State University, 1973. *Politics:* Independent. *Religion:* Roman Catholic. *Avocational interests:* Skiing, fly fishing, sailing.

ADDRESSES: Home—P.O. Box 985, Cutchogue, NY 11935. *Office*—Newsday, Long Island, NY 11747. *E-mail*—wick@newsday.com. *Agent*—Stuart Krichevsky, 381 Park Ave. S., Suite 899, New York, NY 10016.

CAREER: Newsday, Long Island, NY, staff writer, 1978—.

MEMBER: Writers Guild of America East.

AWARDS, HONORS: Numerous journalism awards, including two Pulitzer Prizes.

WRITINGS:

Bad Company: Drugs, Hollywood, and the Cotton Club Murder (nonfiction), Harcourt (New York City), 1989.

Heaven and Earth: The Last Farmers of the North Fork (nonfiction), St. Martin's Press (New York City), 1996.

SIDELIGHTS: Steve Wick told *CA:* "I became a newspaper reporter after I read Frederick Forsythe's *The Odessa File,* about a young German journalist who tracks down the Nazi who murdered his father. I owe Forsythe a lot—he turned me into a reporter, which turned me into a writer. As a newspaper reporter, I searched and searched for a story that could be expanded into a book. I found the story I was looking for in the 1983 murder of theatrical producer Roy Radin. The circumstances of his death are the heart of a book I called *Bad Company: Drugs, Hollywood, and the Cotton Club Murder.*

"I wrote my second book, *Heaven and Earth: The Last Farmers of the North Fork,* because I wanted to get back to American history, and to combine journalism with historical research. I also live on the North Fork of Long Island, and I knew many of the farmers in the book. It took four years to finish it. I taped most of my interviews with the farmers. I wrote at night after work and on weekends. I am so darn proud of this book, even though it is of purely local interest. In the summer of 1997, it became a play at Bay Street Theater, in Sag Harbor.

"Two books inspired me to write *Heaven and Earth*. One was Peter Matthiessen's *Men's Lives,* about the baymen on the South Fork of Long Island. The other was Melissa Fay Greene's *Praying for Sheetrock,* about blacks living on an island off the coast of Georgia. Beautiful books, both of these.

"I don't know exactly where I'm going next. I have some ideas, which is nice."

* * *

WIGGINS, Melanie 1934-

PERSONAL: Born October 15, 1934, in Fort Smith, AR; daughter of Ralph J. (in business) and Melanie (Holt) Speer; children: William Fiveash, Edward Fiveash. *Ethnicity:* "White." *Education:* Hollins College, B.A., 1956; attended Newcomb College. *Politics:* Republican. *Religion:* Episcopalian. *Avocational interests:* Photography, piano, choir.

ADDRESSES: Home and office—League City, TX.

CAREER: Manages twelve thousand acres of family land on Texas's Bolivar Peninsula, beginning c. 1978.

MEMBER: Texas Gulf Historical Association, Galveston Historical Foundation (member of board of advisors), Galveston County Historical Commission.

WRITINGS:

NONFICTION

They Made Their Own Law: Stories of Bolivar Peninsula, Rice University Press (Houston, TX), 1990.
Torpedoes in the Gulf: Galveston and the U-Boats, 1942-43, Texas A & M University Press (College Station, TX), 1995.

WORK IN PROGRESS: A collection of factual U-boat stories from World War II; research on factual stories of Vietnamese people in the United States.

SIDELIGHTS: Melanie Wiggins is descended from Charles Taylor Cade, who owned large quantities of land in Texas's Bolivar Peninsula at the turn of the twentieth century. At present, Wiggins manages these lands for her family, and the peninsula, as well as other Texas locales on the Gulf of Mexico, have helped provide her with inspiration for her books, 1990's *They Made Their Own Law: Stories of Bolivar Peninsula* and 1995's *Torpedoes in the Gulf: Galveston and the U-Boats, 1942-43.*

In *They Made Their Own Law,* Wiggins tells the history of the Bolivar Peninsula, from the prehistoric Native Americans who were the dwellers there to events of the 1980s. She focuses on the turn of the twentieth century, however, and includes interviews with elderly denizens who remember those times. The work's title comes at least in part from the fact that most of the peninsula lies in Chambers County, but that county's seat was extremely far away in pre-automotive days, and therefore so was official government.

As the title of *Torpedoes in the Gulf* implies, the book concerns a little-known but interesting facet of World War II history—that twenty-four German submarines entered the Gulf of Mexico between May, 1942, and December, 1943, sinking fifty-six ships and damaging fourteen more. U-boat successes in the Gulf Sea frontier raised German naval victories to a new high, according to Wiggins. The author interviewed German U-boat personnel, including several commanders, and procured rare photographs for her second full-length work.

British film director Nigel Turner has filmed part of a three-hour U-boat documentary in the Galveston-Texas City area, which includes interviews with Wiggins and other local people used as sources for *Torpedoes in the Gulf.* The documentary was scheduled to run on the Discovery Channel.

Wiggins told *CA:* "I never intended to be a writer, but my job as family business manager necessitated letters and reports about various wild happenings on our Bolivar Peninsula land. At the urging of my sister, I attempted to produce a book dealing with peninsula history, but the manuscript was rejected many times. One editor advised me to take some writing courses, and I followed his advice, rewrote the book, and *They Made Their Own Law: Stories of Bolivar Peninsula* was published. However, in reworking the manuscript I kept the individual oral histories intact, because I felt they were too charming and original to integrate into the text.

"About a year passed while I searched for ideas for a second book. One presented itself when a friend pointed out the old blimp base at Hitchcock, close to Galveston. When he said that blimps in World War II had patrolled the Gulf of Mexico looking for U-boats, I really didn't believe it. At the library I found that he was correct and that no one had written a complete book on the subject. Therefore, my second effort, *Torpedoes in the Gulf: Galveston and the U-Boats, 1942-1943.* Because oral histories were such an important ingredient in my first book, I sought out as many German submarine veterans as possible, and especially any who had patrolled the Gulf. The few that I did find added immeasurably to the overall picture, giving the reader a chance to travel with commanders and crew members inside submarines and to understand their thinking.

"Project number three is a result of *Torpedoes,* in that my searches in Germany turned up many U-boat veterans of all ranks, who remembered their adventures in other seas and countries during and just after the war. Their old diaries, photographs, letters, and reports are the basis for my present work, and I am hoping again to provide an intimate insight into a world seldom glimpsed.

"More than anything, I want to make reading history *fun.*"

*   *   *

WILBUR, C(larence) Martin 1908-1997

OBITUARY NOTICE—See index for *CA* sketch: Born May 13, 1908, in Dayton, OH; died of leukemia, June 18, 1997, in Haverford, PA. Educator, curator, author. Wilbur devoted his attention to Asian studies and became a well-known authority on the political history of China. He grew up in Japan and China where his parents were missionaries. In 1936 he became the curator of Chinese archaeology for the Field Museum of Natural History in Chicago, a post he held until 1942. During World War II, he served as a research analyst for the U.S. Office of Strategic Services and later for the U.S. Department of State. In 1947 he joined the faculty of Columbia University where he taught Chinese history until his retirement in 1976. He also served as the director of Columbia's East Asian Institute from 1957 to 1963. He contributed many articles to scholarly journals and books, including the *Cambridge History of China,* edited by

John K. Fairbank. His major works include *Slavery in China during the Former Han Dynasty, Documents on Communism, Nationalism, and Soviet Advisers in China, 1918-1927* (with Julie Lien-ying How), and *Sun Yat-sen, Frustrated Patriot.*

OBITUARIES AND OTHER SOURCES:

PERIODICALS

New York Times, June 20, 1997, p. B7.

*   *   *

WILES, Peter John de la Fosse 1919-1997

OBITUARY NOTICE—See index for *CA* sketch: Born November 25, 1919, in Rugby, England; died July 11, 1997. Educator, Sovietologist, author. Wiles devoted his career to teaching, first at All Souls College at Oxford University as a fellow in 1947. This position followed five years with the Royal Artillery during World War II. He then served as fellow at Oxford's New College from 1949 to 1960. Next he ventured to the United States for a stint at Brandeis University as professor of economics before heading to Sweden's Institutet for International Ekonomi in Stockholm as a research officer in 1963. After a brief visiting professorship at City College of New York, Wiles joined the faculty at London University as professor of Russian social and economic studies from 1965 to 1985. The British Academy elected him as a fellow in 1990. During his career, he earned a name for himself as an authority on communist economies. He also held visiting professorships at College de France and the University of Windsor, among others. He wrote several books, including *Price, Cost and Output, The Political Economy of Communism, Distribution of Income East and West, Economic Institutions Compared,* and *Communist International Economics.* He also edited *The New Communist Third World* and *Economics in Disarray.*

OBITUARIES AND OTHER SOURCES:

BOOKS

Who's Who, St. Martin's Press, 1994.

PERIODICALS

Times (London; electronic), July 31, 1997.

WILLIAMS, Vernon J(ohnson, Jr.) 1948-

PERSONAL: Born April 25, 1948, in Marshall, TX; children: Vella L., Alexander M. *Ethnicity:* "African American." *Education:* University of Texas at Austin, B.A., 1969; Brown University, A.M., 1973, Ph.D., 1977.

ADDRESSES: Office—Department of History, Purdue University, West Lafayette, IN 47907.

CAREER: University of Rhode Island, Kingston, instructor in history, 1978; Clark University, Worcester, MA, lecturer in history, 1978-79; Northwestern University, Evanston, IL, research associate in history, 1979-84; University of Iowa, Iowa City, visiting adjunct assistant professor of history, 1985; Rhode Island College, assistant professor of history, 1985-90; Purdue University, West Lafayette, IN, associate professor, 1990-97, professor of history, 1997—. Elmhurst College, lecturer, 1981; University of Massachusetts—Boston, research associate at William Monroe Trotter Institute, 1987-88; Boston University, lecturer and research associate at Afro-American Studies Center, 1989-90; guest lecturer at educational institutions, including University of Houston, University of California, Irvine, and Boston College. Edit, Inc., researcher and writer, 1979-80; consultant to Henry Rasof Literary Agency and Boston Athenaeum.

MEMBER: Afro-American Historical Association, American Studies Association, Association of Black Sociologists, Association of Social and Behavioral Scientists, Immigration History Society, National Association for Ethnic Studies, National Council for Black Studies, Organization of American Historians, Southern Historical Association, Southern Conference on Afro-American Studies, Indiana Historical Society.

AWARDS, HONORS: Grants from National Endowment for the Humanities, 1989, and American Council of Learned Societies, 1990-91; Clio grant, Indiana Historical Society, 1994-95.

WRITINGS:

(Contributor) *Contemporary Black America,* Southwestern Publishing (Nashville, TN), 1980.
(Contributor) Earl S. Davis, editor, *The Bicentennial of the U.S. Constitution: Reflections on the Black Experience,* Institute of Afro-American Affairs, New York University (New York City), 1988.
From a Caste to a Minority: Changing Attitudes of

American Sociologists toward Afro-Americans, 1896-1945, Greenwood Press (Westport, CT), 1989.
Rethinking Race: Franz Boas and His Contemporaries, University Press of Kentucky (Lexington, KY), 1996.
(Contributor) Thomas D. Boston, editor, *A Different Vision: African American Economic Thought,* Volume I, Routledge (London, England), 1997.
(Contributor) Nancy L. Grant, V. P. Franklin, and Genna Rae McNeil, editors, *Blacks and Jews: An American Historical Perspective,* University of Missouri Press (Columbia, MO), 1997.

Contributor of articles and reviews to professional journals, including *Griot: Journal of Black Heritage, Western Journal of Black Studies, Explorations in Ethnic Studies: Journal of the National Association for Ethnic Studies, Afro-Americans in New York Life and History,* and *Afrocentric Scholar: Journal of the National Council for Black Studies. New England Journal of Black Studies,* member of editorial board, 1989, editor, 1990-93.

WORK IN PROGRESS: Editing *George W. Ellis and Liberia.*

*   *   *

WILLIAMS-GARCIA, Rita

PERSONAL: Born April 13, in Jamaica, Queens, NY; father was in the U.S. Army; mother was a domestic servant; married Peter Garcia; children: Michelle, Stephanie. *Education:* Graduated from Hofstra University; pursuing a master's degree in creative writing at Queens College; studied dance under Alvin Ailey and Phil Black. *Avocational interests:* Chess, playing Tetris, jogging, sewing.

ADDRESSES: Home—Jamaica, NY.

CAREER: Writer. Interactive Market Systems, New York City, manager of software distribution and production. Has also worked as a dancer and reading teacher.

MEMBER: Authors Guild, Society of Children's Book Writers and Illustrators.

AWARDS, HONORS: Notable Books for Children and Young Adults citation, American Library Association

(ALA), 1991, for *Fast Talk on a Slow Track; Booklist* Editors' Choice selection, 1995, Best Books for Young Adults citation, ALA, and Coretta Scott King Honor Book selection, ALA, both 1996, all for *Like Sisters on the Homefront;* PEN/Norma Klein Award for Children's Fiction, 1997.

WRITINGS:

Blue Tights, Lodestar, 1988.
Fast Talk on a Slow Track, Lodestar, 1991.
Like Sisters on the Homefront, Lodestar, 1995.

WORK IN PROGRESS: Every Time a Rainbow Dies, a novel about a young boy who falls in love with a rape victim.

SIDELIGHTS: "Focusing her attention on contemporary African American youth," wrote Susan P. Bloom in *Twentieth-Century Young Adult Writers,* "Rita Williams-Garcia informs her fictional teenagers with her own experiences as student, as teacher, as dancer." Her three young adult novels to date show young black men and women living and coping with difficulties in an honest, uncontrived manner. "Williams-Garcia's portrayal of these urban black adolescents and their worlds feels genuine, neither sensationalized nor romanticized," stated *Horn Book* contributor Rudine Sims Bishop. "Her work is marked by an authentic rendering of the styles and cadences of urban black language, some touches of humor, and strong, dynamic characterization." Together with such African American writers as Jacqueline Woodson, Dolores Johnson, and Angela Johnson, said Bishop, Williams-Garcia "show[s] great promise, and with continuing support and nurturing . . . may well turn out to be among the most prominent African-American literary artists of the next generation."

"I was born in Queens, New York, at the tail end of the fifties," Williams-Garcia told Susan Pais, Phyllis Brown, Ann Gartner, and Kay E. Vandergrift in a specially conducted interview posted on the web page "Learning about Rita Williams-Garcia." "My father was in the army so we traveled by car across the country. Our first stop was to Arizona when I was three—a sweeping contrast to our Far Rockaway projects." The family then settled in the California town of Seaside, where Rita and her siblings spent their childhood. "We played a lot outdoors; we were very athletic children," she explained to *Booklist* interviewer Hazel Rochman. "We were always doing things. My sister was an artist. My brother was into

math. I loved words; I just thought that was normal. To characterize me as a kid, you could say that I was definitely a geek."

Perhaps the most important influence on Williams-Garcia's life was her mother, whom she calls "Miss Essie": "My sister, brother and I grew up thinking our mother, 'Miss Essie,' discovered Pop Art," the author states in a publisher's biography released by Penguin Books. "When she wasn't cleaning, working or in school, Miss Essie painted every little thing that needed color."

Williams-Garcia developed her reading skills early in life. She recalls in her "Learning about Rita Williams-Garcia" interview that she taught herself to read at age two by learning to associate letters with their sounds, partly through looking at billboards and partly through the efforts of her older sister, who would often share her books with young Rita. By the time she entered school, Williams-Garcia was already an accomplished reader and a writer of poetry and stories, "mostly adventures that involved the heroic exploits of my sister Rosalind, brother Russell and I."

Williams-Garcia was exposed to racial issues while growing up during the 1960s. She remembers discussing race relations and racism in the classroom in the aftermath of the 1968 riots, the assassination of Dr. Martin Luther King, Jr., and the militant political views of the Black Panthers. At the age of twelve, she left California for Georgia for six months, then settled in Jamaica, New York. In the sixth grade, she reported in her interview, she went looking for literature for young adults that featured black protagonists. She discovered biographies of historical figures, such as Harriet Tubman and Sojourner Truth, and a single novel (*Mary Ellen, Student Nurse*), but little else. "When I brought this up to the school librarian . . . she gave me three books about a West African girl who would rather hunt with her father, the chief, than do traditional girl things," the author recalled. "I'll pay a king's ransom to know the title and author of the aforementioned books!" Her teachers encouraged her to write for herself, and at the age of fourteen she published her first story in *Highlights* magazine.

"None of my characters are truly me," Williams-Garcia stated in her interview, "although there is always some aspect of me in each and every one. Joyce in *Blue Tights* is a voluptuous teen with dance inside of her. Denzel in *Fast Talk* is a bright young man who must face himself. Gayle in *Like Sisters on the Homefront* has lived through a lot of pain but refuses to acknowledge it. That's where similarities between myself and my characters pretty much end. Outside of watching football and baseball with my sister, my adolescence was uneventful."

When Williams-Garcia enrolled in Hofstra University, she temporarily dropped writing for other activities. "In college, real life seemed to displace my need to 'make' stories," she explained in the Penguin publishers biography, "so I didn't write for nearly three years. (Real life was running my dance company and being political.)" She declared a major in economics, auditioned for dancing roles in musicals, and performed community outreach work through her sorority, Alpha Kappa Alpha. In her senior year in college, Williams-Garcia enrolled in a creative writing class. She combined her outreach work—teaching high school girls remedial reading—with her writing workshop training and penned an early version of the story that became *Blue Tights*.

Blue Tights is partly based on Williams-Garcia's own experiences, but it is mostly a conglomeration of the stories of many young women. The book tells the tale of Joyce Collins, an ambitious African American girl who loves to dance and exhibits great talent. However, Joyce finds that she is shut out of her school's European-oriented dance program because the dance instructor believes her body shape is not suited to ballet. Besides dealing with this great disappointment, Joyce has to come to terms with her home life—she has been raised by an often absent mother and a religiously fanatic aunt—and her identity. "A volatile combination of worldliness and innocence," Bishop stated, "Joyce seeks love and popularity in all the wrong places and with all the wrong people." "Williams-Garcia does not shy away from the harsh circumstances that define Joyce and her family," explained Bloom. "Aunt Em's severe treatment of Joyce stems from a horrific self-induced coat hanger abortion she suffered in her adolescence. Williams-Garcia provides less sensational, daily evidence of the grinding poverty that eats at this family." "Through her work with an African-American dance troupe," Bishop concluded, Joyce "discovers her own special talents as a dancer and achieves a new appreciation of her own self-worth."

It took Williams-Garcia almost ten years to get *Blue Tights* published. While she worked on the book, revising and collating the stories she had assembled from her own life and the lives of her reading students, she went to work for a marketing company in Manhattan, churning out manuscripts on an old typewriter in the company mailroom. The manuscript of *Blue Tights* (originally titled *Blue Tights, Big Butt*), however, kept returning to the author with depressing regularity. Editors complained that the protagonist had a poor self-image and was too focused on her appearance. "The letters I got back from editors and agents were more or less on the same lines," the author explains to Rochman. "Can you make the girl older, about seventeen, if there's going to be any kind of sexual content in the book? Or, this is not a good role model; she's not positive; she doesn't have anything uplifting to offer to young African American women growing up; can you do something about her attitude? Can you do something about all these references to black culture? Readers aren't going to understand them. Can you make it more universal?" Williams-Garcia put the manuscript away after three years of marketing it unsuccessfully.

Williams-Garcia continued to write and submit stories during the 1980s until her job was cut in a company restructuring. In the meantime she had married and given birth to two daughters. She brought the *Blue Tights* manuscript to Lodestar Books, a publishing house known for its history of publishing challenging books. The novel was released in 1988 and won recognition from many reviewers. "By writing about urban black teenagers and a young girl who aspires to be a dancer," Nancy Vasilakis stated in *Horn Book,* "Rita Williams-Garcia incorporates a setting and a subject that she obviously knows well." "The novel vividly evokes [Joyce's] neighborhood and the rigor and joy of her dancing," commented a *Booklist* critic, adding, "Joyce's sexual conflicts are treated with candor." "Joyce's understanding is believably paced and powerfully realized," declared a *Publishers Weekly* reviewer, "and her story is uplifting."

While Joyce Collins's story becomes uplifting through her realization of her own potential and self-respect, Denzel Watson's story becomes uplifting in the way he deals with failure while moving from high school to college. Denzel, the smooth-talking valedictorian of his high school, attends a summer program for minority students at Princeton University. Denzel had relied on his winning personality throughout high school, but he quickly discovers that he cannot use the same tricks in college. "While he is involved with the summer program, he struggles with the feeling of inadequacy and decides not to return to Princeton in the fall," wrote Jo Holtz in *Voice of Youth Advocates.* "For the first time in his life, he feels like a failure." Denzel turns to a part-time job as a door-to-door salesman to regain his self-esteem, and experiments briefly with the world of black street culture. Finally, however, he bows to family pressure and resolves to enter Princeton in the fall, "to find that, with a little humility and some serious study, he *can* hack it," explained a *Kirkus Reviews* contributor. "The author puts it to her college-bound readers: When the time comes, will *they* have what it takes to step up to a new, very challenging world?"

Fast Talk on a Slow Track won as much attention from reviewers as *Blue Tights* had. It was also cited on the American Library Association's Notable Books for Children and Young Adults list. "Williams-Garcia writes just as authoritatively about teenage boys as she did about girls in her first novel," stated Nancy Vasilakis in *Horn Book.* "She understands the forces and fears driving a young man in search of his true self." "Teens everywhere," wrote Hazel Rochman in *School Library Journal,* "will be able to identify and commiserate with Denzel as he goes through his options, gains confidence, and matures."

The heroine of *Like Sisters on the Homefront,* fourteen-year-old Gayle, also has her own set of problems and needs to gain maturity in order to cope with them. After she becomes pregnant for a second time (her first pregnancy resulted in a son, Jose, now seven months old), her mother takes her to an abortion clinic and then ships her off to the family home in Georgia. At first Gayle feels uncomfortable in the rural environment; she is away from her boyfriend and homegirls and has to cope with her uncle's disapproval, her aunt's insistence on proper child care for her young son, and her cousin Cookie's religious standards. She begins to change when her aunt gives her the responsibility for caring for her great-grandmother, Great, who is sick and near death. The relationship between Great and Gayle deepens as the old woman's condition worsens. Great "exhibits a strength of spirit and a stubbornness that Gayle recognizes in herself," remarked reviewer Nancy Vasilakis in *Horn Book.* "Great understands Gayle, too. 'When you lay down your deviling,' she tells her great-granddaughter, 'you'll be stronger than those who lived by the rule all their lives.'"

Great finally chooses Gayle to receive the Telling, the source of family history that keeps the family together. "Strong-willed, self-absorbed, and impulsive," stated Vasilakis, Gayle "is not unlike the hero-

ine of Williams-Garcia's earlier novel, *Blue Tights,* imbued with a lively mix of naivete and worldliness, particularly in sexual matters, that gives her characterization depth and vibrancy." "Painting Gayle as a hard-edged, high-spirited young woman clearly headed for either trouble or triumph," commented Deborah Stevenson in the *Bulletin of the Center for Children's Books,* "Williams-Garcia breathes life into what could have been a stereotypical portrait of a trash-talking, streetwise city teen, and while its scales are tipped in favor of a responsible life, the book is honest enough to acknowledge the pleasures of the other kind."

Williams-Garcia plans to continue her pattern of writing strong, hard-hitting books about African-American teens living in the modern world—not in times of great crisis, but in the small crises of everyday life. "I really don't think we deal with the complex issues of our young people's lives," she told Rochman. "We tell them about racism and those kinds of things . . . but then there's that real person who has to deal with the fact that he is not a symbol, he is not a model, he is a real, flesh-and-blood person who makes mistakes and has to keep moving and learning and accepting all these things as part of life. . . . It's what you come to know about yourself that is more important than any big thing that might happen to you."

BIOGRAPHICAL/CRITICAL SOURCES:

BOOKS

Bloom, Susan P., "Rita Williams-Garcia," *Twentieth-Century Young Adult Writers,* St. James Press (Detroit, MI), 1994, pp. 709-710.
Children's Literature Review, Volume 36, Gale (Detroit, MI), 1995.

PERIODICALS

ALAN Review, winter, 1996.
Booklist, December 15, 1987, pp. 696-697; April 1, 1991, p. 1561; February 15, 1996, pp. 1002-1003.
Bulletin of the Center for Children's Books, January, 1988, p. 106; June, 1991, pp. 253-254; September, 1995, p. 34.
Dance, November, 1993, p. 81.
Horn Book, March-April, 1988, pp. 215-216; July-August, 1991, p. 466; September-October, 1992, pp. 616-620; November-December, 1995, pp. 748-749.

Kirkus Reviews, December 1, 1987, p. 1680; February 1, 1991, pp. 179-180.
Publishers Weekly, November 13, 1987, p. 73; February 8, 1991, pp. 58-59.
School Library Journal, June-July, 1988, p. 120; April, 1991, p. 143.
Voice of Youth Advocates, August, 1988, p. 136; June, 1991, pp. 104-105.

OTHER

Pais, Susan, Phyllis Brown, Ann Gartner, and Kay E. Vandergrift, compilers and interviewers, "Learning about Rita Williams-Garcia," http://www.scils.rutgers.edu/special/kay/williamsgarcia.html.
"Rita Williams-Garcia" (publishers' release), http://www.penguin.com/usa/childrens/bios/garcia.htm.*

* * *

WILSON, Edmund Beecher 1856-1939

PERSONAL: Born October 19, 1856, in Geneva, IL; died of bronchial pneumonia, March 3, 1939, in New York, NY; son of Isaac Grant (a lawyer and judge) and Caroline Louisa (Clark) Wilson; married Anne Maynard Kidder, September 27, 1904; children: Nancy. *Education:* Attended Antioch College, 1873-74, and University of Chicago, 1974-75; Sheffield Scientific School, Yale University, B.S., 1878; Johns Hopkins University, Ph.D., 1881; postdoctoral studies at Johns Hopkins University, Cambridge University, University of Leipzig, and the Zoological Station at Naples. *Avocational interests:* Music, especially playing the flute and the cello.

CAREER: Zoologist and embryologist. Schoolteacher, 1872-73; Williams College, Williamstown, MA, instructor, 1883-84; Massachusetts Institute of Technology, Cambridge, instructor, 1884-85; Bryn Mawr College, Bryn Mawr, PA, professor of biology, 1885-91; Zoology Department, Columbia University, New York City, professor of zoology, 1891-1928, became department chair, became DaCosta Professor. Worked at Marine Biological Laboratory, Woods Hole, MA.

WRITINGS:

(With William T. Sedgwick) *General Biology,* [New York], 1886.

The Cell in Development and Inheritance, [New York], 1896, second edition, 1900, third edition, revised and enlarged as *The Cell in Development and Heredity,* 1925, Garland (New York City), 1987.
(With Edward Leaming) *An Atlas of Fertilization and Kayokinesis of the Ovum,* Macmillan (New York City), 1895.
The Physical Basis of Life, Yale University Press (New Haven, CT), 1923.

Contributor to journals and periodicals, including *Science.*

SIDELIGHTS: Edmund Beecher Wilson emphasized careful experimentation and analysis in biology at a time when the field was rife with theories based on little more than speculation. Indeed, Wilson's work was instrumental in transforming biology into a rigorous, scientific discipline. Although known for his meticulous approach to the study of the structure and function of the cell, he never lost sight of biology as a unified field that included embryology, evolution, and genetics. His influence in biology was felt through his position as a professor first at Bryn Mawr College and then at Columbia University, and through his highly influential textbook, *The Cell in Development and Inheritance.* His study of chromosomes, and especially his discovery of the sex chromosomes, helped lay the foundation for the study of genetics and evolution in the early twentieth century. Many of the problems that Wilson tackled, including the details of cell development, remain unsolved today.

Wilson was born on October 19, 1856, in Geneva, Illinois. He was the second of four surviving children of Isaac Grant Wilson, a lawyer and eventually judge, and Caroline Louisa Clark, both of whom were originally from New England. When Edmund was two years old, his father was appointed a circuit court judge in Chicago. Rather than separate him from her childless sister and brother-in-law in Geneva, Edmund's mother left him to live with them while the rest of the family moved to Chicago. In this manner, he was "adopted" by Mr. and Mrs. Charles Patten and grew up counting himself very lucky to have two homes and four parents.

Shortly before he turned sixteen, Wilson taught school for one year from 1872 to 1873. As his older brother, Charles, had done the previous year, Wilson taught everything, including reading and arithmetic, to twenty-five pupils aged six to eighteen in a one-room schoolhouse. The following year he attended Antioch College in Yellow Springs, Ohio, following in the footsteps of an older cousin, Samuel Clarke. At Antioch, Wilson decided to devote himself to the study of biology, which, at that time, largely meant natural history.

In the fall of 1874 Wilson did not return to Antioch because he wished to prepare for studying at the Sheffield Scientific School of Yale University, which had been highly recommended to him by his cousin. To ready himself for Yale, Wilson moved to Chicago, where he lived with his parents and took courses at the old University of Chicago from 1874 to 1875. He entered Yale in 1875 and received his bachelor's degree in 1878.

Although Wilson's particular focus of research changed many times in his long career, his work was always concerned with gaining a better understanding of how the single fertilized egg gave rise to a complete individual, whether that individual be an earthworm, jellyfish, or human. This interest in the development of the organism led Wilson to study cell structure and function, heredity, and evolution.

During his years of graduate and postgraduate work, Wilson studied the embryology and morphology of earthworms, sea spiders, the colonial jellyfish (renilla), and other invertebrates. After Yale, he again followed Sam Clarke's educational path, this time to Johns Hopkins University. A close friend, William T. Sedgwick, entered Johns Hopkins along with him. From 1878 to 1881, Wilson worked closely with William Keith Brooks, obtained his Ph.D. in 1881, and remained at Johns Hopkins for an additional year of postdoctoral work. In 1882 Wilson studied in Europe with the help of a loan from his older brother, Charles. He studied in Cambridge, and, with Thomas H. Huxley's recommendation, gave a paper on renilla before the Royal Society in London. From England, he went to Leipzig, Germany, and then to the Zoological Station at Naples. Wilson worked for almost a year there and formed strong friendships with director Anton Dohrn and zoologist Theodor Boveri. (For Wilson, the embryos of marine invertebrates were more easily studied than those of terrestrial animals, and for almost fifty years, Wilson spent his summers working at the Marine Biological Laboratory in Woods Hole, Massachusetts.)

To visit Naples, Wilson had worked out an arrangement with Clarke, who was then teaching at Williams College in Massachusetts. The college would pay for a laboratory bench at Naples for two years as part of a professorship at Williams. Wilson would work at Naples the first year while Clarke taught at Williams, then the two would switch places. Wilson's stint at Williams College lasted between 1883 and 1884.

From Williams, Wilson moved to the Massachusetts Institute of Technology as an instructor from 1884 to 1885. There, he collaborated with his friend, William T. Sedgwick, in the creation of a textbook titled *General Biology* (1886). Wilson's next teaching appointment, unlike his previous two, offered him the time and opportunity to continue his research. M. Carey Thomas, the first dean of Bryn Mawr College, invited Wilson to become the first professor of biology at the new women's college. He taught there between 1885 and 1891. While at Bryn Mawr, the scientist tackled the problem of cell differentiation— the way in which the fertilized egg gives rise to many kinds of specialized cells. To do this, he studied the cell-by-cell development of the earthworm and Nereis, a marine worm. This work, known as "cell lineage," established Wilson's reputation as a biologist of considerable skill. His 1890 and 1892 papers on Nereis demonstrated the value of cell lineage and inspired other scientists to pursue this fruitful avenue of research.

In 1891 Wilson accepted an appointment to become an adjunct professor of zoology in the new zoology department at Columbia University being organized by Henry Fairfield Osborn. He spent the rest of his career at Columbia, eventually becoming chair of the department, and retiring as DaCosta Professor in 1928. Before settling on campus, however, Wilson spent another fruitful year in Munich and Naples from 1891 to 1892. A series of lectures on the study of the cell that he gave during his first teaching year at Columbia formed the basis of his textbook *The Cell in Development and Inheritance,* published in 1896. Written before the fundamentals of heredity were understood, the book added a balanced, careful voice to the fierce debates over modes of inheritance and cell development that were occurring in biology at that time. The book, which illuminated Wilson's penchant for observation and experimentation, was hugely influential and further cemented his already substantial reputation. The book was dedicated to Boveri, the Italian zoologist.

On September 27, 1904, Wilson married Anne Maynard Kidder. Kidder and her family lived in Washington, D.C., but spent their summers at their cottage in Woods Hole, and it was there that the two met. Their only child, Nancy, became a professional cellist. Wilson himself was an avid amateur musician, and his trips to Europe were warmly remembered as much for the music he heard as for the science he learned. A flutist as a young man, he began taking cello lessons while he was living in Baltimore. For the rest of his life, in Bryn Mawr and then New York, he always found himself a quartet of amateur musicians with which to play.

In 1900 the modern era of genetics was born. Three scientists, working independently from each other, stated that inherited characteristics were determined by the combination of two hereditary units, one from each parent. (Today, those two hereditary units are known as genes.) This theory had actually been published thirty-six years earlier by Gregor Johann Mendel, but had lain dormant until it was "revived" at the turn of the nineteenth century by Hugo De Vries, Karl Erich Correns, and Erich Tschermak von Seysenegg.

Wilson quickly saw the connection between the rediscovery of the laws of heredity and his own work with cells and cell structures. The laws of heredity stated that the fertilized egg received half of the blueprint for its own expression from each parent. Chromosomes, he theorized, were the cell structures responsible for transmitting the units of inheritance. By following instructions from the chromosomes, the fertilized egg gave rise to a complete individual.

In 1905 Wilson and Nettie Maria Stevens of Bryn Mawr College independently showed that the X and Y chromosomes carried by the sperm were responsible for determining gender: in many species, including humans, females had an XX pair of chromosomes while males had an XY pair. In eight papers published from 1905 to 1912 titled "Studies on Chromosomes," Wilson brilliantly extended his study of the chromosomal theory of sex determination, and it is for this work with chromosomes that he is best remembered. He is also recognized for setting the stage for the zoology department's future excellence in genetics, as personified by Thomas Hunt Morgan and Hermann Joseph Muller.

In the last years of his career, Wilson continued his study of cell structures. Despite failing health, he also wrote the third edition of *The Cell in Development and Inheritance,* over twelve hundred pages, which was published in 1925. In most respects, this was actually a completely new book that included the new discoveries in biology of the twentieth century.

Wilson retired from Columbia University in 1928. He died in New York, on March 3, 1939, of bronchial pneumonia, and his ashes were buried in the churchyard of the Church of the Messiah in Woods Hole, Massachusetts.

BIOGRAPHICAL/CRITICAL SOURCES:

BOOKS

Biographical Memoirs, Volume 21, National Academy of Sciences, 1941, pp. 315-342.
Obituary Notices of the Fellows of the Royal Society, Volume 3, Royal Society (London), 1939-41, pp. 123-138.

PERIODICALS

American Naturalist, January/February, 1943, pp. 5-37; March/April, 1943, pp. 142-172.*

*   *   *

WILSON, Robert Charles 1953-

PERSONAL: Born in 1953; Canadian citizen.

ADDRESSES: Home—Nanaimo, British Columbia; Toronto, Ontario. *Office*—c/o Doubleday, 666 Fifth Avenue, New York, NY 10103.

CAREER: Writer.

WRITINGS:

NOVELS

A Hidden Place, Bantam (New York City), 1986, Orbit (London), 1990.
Memory Wire, Bantam, 1988, Orbit, 1990.
Gypsies, Doubleday (Garden City, NY), 1989, Orbit, 1990.
The Divide, Doubleday, 1990, Orbit, 1990.
A Bridge of Years, Doubleday, 1991, New English Library (London), 1994.
The Harvest, Bantam, 1992, New English Library, 1993.
Mysterium, Bantam, 1994, Hodder & Stoughton (London), 1995.

SIDELIGHTS: Through a series of novels beginning in the mid-1980s, science fiction novelist Robert

Charles Wilson has earned high praise from both readers and critics. Henry Leperlier, writing in *Twentieth-Century Science-Fiction Writers,* stated, "It is quite possible that Wilson will be one of the few writers of the 1980s that will survive his own era. His treatment of contemporary themes such as alienation and the loss of identity puts him in the same league with many science fiction and mainstream writers who have managed to resist the passage of time."

Wilson gained critical recognition with his first novel, the 1986 love story *A Hidden Place,* which is set in a small prairie town. Wilson's consideration of human emotion in the novel brought him comparisons, according to Leperlier, with novelist Theodore Sturgeon. The two human protagonists, Travis Fisher and his girlfriend Nancy Wilcox, come under the influence of a woman from the realm of Faery, Anna Blaise, whose quest is to reunite with her male half, a hobo named Bone who does not remember his true origin. Tom Easton, in *Analog,* noted that the novel was about misfits, as did Leperlier, who called the characters "estranged persons." According to Easton, the novel contains "salutary vicarious lessons for its readers." In a review of Wilson's second novel, *Memory Wire,* Easton reflected on *A Hidden Place* as "fine and moving and instructive." He liked *Memory Wire* even more, finding it "more plausible" than its predecessor and containing "marvelous science fictional devisings"; indeed, Easton predicted possible Hugo and Nebula nominations for the book, which is a study of a man cybernetically altered to be a perfectly objective "Recording Angel." In *Quill & Quire,* reviewer Kim G. Kofmel found *Memory Wire* "compelling" as an adventure tale, a love story, a "welldrawn" vision of the future, and "an examination of the function of memory, of the freedoms and constraints contained in both remembering and forgetting."

Wilson's third novel, *Gypsies,* comprises "[a] blend of science fiction, mystery, and thriller," according to a reviewer in *Publishers Weekly*—a combination which that commentator found "spellbinding." The "gypsies" of the title are actually adult siblings, abused in childhood, who possess the power to move among invented worlds. The protagonist, Karen, has settled for a normal married life in Toronto, but divorce and the return of a mysterious "Grey Man" from her past prompt her, and her similarly gifted teenage son, to seek refuge with her sister Laura, who lives in a West Coast utopia of her own invention. More than one critic commented that the novel straddles genres; Sharon Oard Warner, in the *New York Times Book Review,* found the book's turn to-

ward fantasy and away from realism somewhat awkward; Leperlier, while praising the realistic psychology of the work, regretted that its fantastic aspects relied on magic rather than adhering to the conventions of science fiction.

One year later, in *The Divide* (1989), Wilson produced what Gerald Jonas, in the *New York Times Book Review,* called "a literate thriller, a superbly crafted novel of character and a thoughtful exploration of what it might feel like to be a superman." The superman in question is John Shaw, who has been created by a government experiment that closes down, leaving Shaw estranged—as so many of Wilson's characters are—from everyday society. Shaw develops a second personality in order to deal with the world around him; a love triangle arises, as each of his personalities is involved with a different woman. Reviewer and science fiction writer Jonas expressed wonder at Wilson's ability to "satisfy the demands of plausibility while contriving a 'happy ending'" for *The Divide.* Pippa Wysong, in *Quill & Quire,* however, found the book's ending "predictable."

Jonas, though continuing to voice admiration for Wilson's gifts, was nevertheless somewhat disappointed by the author's next work, *Bridge of Years,* in which a young man in the Pacific Northwest, recovering from alcoholism and divorce, discovers a time-travel mechanism that takes him to Greenwich Village in 1962. Jonas regretted, in particular, a plot turn in which the custodian of the device, a time-traveling cyborg soldier from the future, tries to get it back; the reviewer maintained that the two major plot strands, while seperately interesting, interfered with one another. A critic writing in the *Los Angeles Times Book Review* found the novel too intricately plotted but wrote that the protagonist, Tom Winter, was "particularly well drawn" and that Wilson's prose was "lovingly crafted." A *Chicago Tribune Books* commentator found the novel "an entertaining mix of human foible and heroic action, held together by vivid imagination."

Wilson's 1992 novel, *The Harvest,* combined an up-to-date science fiction premise with a "cozy" Northwest setting, according to R. John Hayes in *Quill & Quire.* In the novel, an extraterrestrial starship, whose inhabitants are masters of nanotechnology and virtual reality, appears above the Earth, offering a high-tech immortality on another world for all humans who choose it. The Earth is soon depopulated, except for one-hundredth of one percent of the human species, who have refused the offer for various individual reasons. The novel follows a selected sample of those people and in the process presents a view of human motivation and its emotional complexity. As with *The Divide,* critics were themselves divided over the book, especially over its ending. In the *New York Times Book Review,* Jonas called *The Harvest* "an intelligently conceived, fully realized novel," and singled out the ambiguities of the ending for special praise: "Because he eschews pat answers, Mr. Wilson manages to derive great suspense from the questions that the survivors pose to themselves and to one another." Meanwhile, Easton, in *Analog,* said he "enjoyed *The Harvest* a great deal," yet found it less satisfying than *A Bridge of Years* and other works by Wilson, precisely because of the ending's ambiguity.

In 1994 Wilson produced a seventh novel, *Mysterium.* It is set in the small town of Two Rivers in the Upper Peninsula of Michigan—a town that, in this fictional treatment, has been transported into an alternate reality, a North America governed by a French-English confederacy whose religion is Gnostic Christian. Searching for the how and why of their startling situation, the townspeople discover that they are to be the subjects of this society's first experiment in exploding an atomic bomb. Their task, from that point on, is to find a way out of their predicament, and they do so with the help of a Nobel-winning physicist, Alan Stern, who never appears in the book but guides its spirit throughout. A *Publishers Weekly* reviewer said of *Mysterium,* "Wilson . . . blends science, religion, philosophy and alternate history into an intelligent, compelling work of fiction." Other critics were united in praise of Wilson's literary skill, especially his characterizations. Jonas wrote in the *New York Times Book Review* that "Mr. Wilson is adept at drawing fully rounded characters in a few paragraphs. Everyone in the large cast is seen from the inside." In *Quill & Quire,* fantasy novelist Michelle Sagara sounded a similar note: "There are no cardboard people in Wilson's hands; even glimpsed for only a page, his people become real. He is that rarest of writers—one who writes both truthfully and with great affection for his characters." Jonas added that the book's ending was "as poignant as it is unexpected."

BIOGRAPHICAL/CRITICAL SOURCES:

BOOKS

Twentieth-Century Science-Fiction Writers, edited by Noelle Watson and Paul E. Schellinger, third edition, St. James Press, 1991.

PERIODICALS

Analog, September, 1987, pp. 181-182; July, 1988, pp. 178-179; May, 1993, pp. 131-133.
Los Angeles Times Book Review, July 29, 1990, p. 6; January 5, 1992, p. 4.
New York Times Book Review, May 28, 1989, p. 18; February 11, 1990, p. 29; October 27, 1991, p. 30; December 27, 1992, p. 22; July 10, 1994, p. 30.
Publishers Weekly, November 18, 1988, p. 71; March 7, 1994, p. 67.
Quill & Quire, April, 1988, p. 23; April, 1990, p. 25; March, 1993, p. 49; March, 1994, p. 70.
Tribune Books (Chicago), October 27, 1991, p.6. *

*   *   *

WINCH, Julie 1953-

PERSONAL: Born in 1953. *Education:* Attended Bryn Mawr College.

CAREER: Affiliated with the University of Massachusetts, Boston, MA.

WRITINGS:

Philadelphia's Black Elite: Activism, Accommodation, and the Struggle for Autonomy, 1787-1848, Temple University Press (Philadelphia), 1988.

Contributor of book reviews to periodicals.

SIDELIGHTS: Julie Winch, an instructor at the University of Massachusetts in Boston, drew upon research that she conducted for her doctoral dissertation at Bryn Mawr College to produce the 1988 work, *Philadelphia's Black Elite: Activism, Accommodation, and the Struggle for Autonomy, 1787-1848.* The book examines the lives and accomplishments of privileged black citizens in Philadelphia in the decades preceding the U.S. Civil War. Throughout those years, Philadelphia had the largest concentration of free blacks in the United States; by 1848, free African Americans made up five percent of the city's population. "Throughout the antebellum era," Winch observes in *Philadelphia's Black Elite,* "leadership was rooted in a complex network of autonomous Black organizations, which offered able and articulate men and women within the community a basis for asserting their authority and developing the skills they would require to oversee citywide and, in some cases, national organizations." One such organization was the American Moral Reform Society. Another influential force in Philadelphia's black community was the new African Methodist Episcopal church.

According to Sheldon Harris in an *American Historical Review* assessment, "Winch, in her perceptive study, offers the thesis that the leaders produced by Philadelphia's black community belonged to a higher socioeconomic class than ordinary blacks and were among the leadership element for all free blacks in the antebellum era. Leadership, she contends, emerged from the business class and from the clergy." Winch mentions various leaders and the role they played, especially in the difficult times after 1838 when the state legislature, with the approval of white voters, disfranchised the black population. Larry A. Greene, in a review of the study for the *Journal of American History,* pointed out that *Philadelphia's Black Elite* provides valuable insight as it "determines the basis of [the black elite's] influence, explores the course they steered between the sometimes conflicting demands of white and black communities, and analyzes the strategies they developed for the racial betterment of slaves and free blacks." Greene maintained that the volume goes beyond just examining issues in Philadelphia to present "a thorough, national analysis of black leadership."

BIOGRAPHICAL/CRITICAL SOURCES:

BOOKS

Winch, Julie, *Philadelphia's Black Elite: Activism, Accommodation, and the Struggle for Autonomy, 1787-1848,* Temple University Press (Philadelphia), 1988.

PERIODICALS

American Historical Review, February 1990, p. 259; April 1994, pp. 658-659; June 1996, pp. 910-911.
Journal of American History, March 1989, p. 1311; September 1994, pp. 691-692.
Journal of American Studies, December 1990, p. 449.
Journal of Southern History, November 1989, p. 704.
Journal of Urban History, May 1990, p. 319.
Library Journal, May 1, 1988, p. 79.*

WINDLEY, Carol 1947-

PERSONAL: Born June 18, 1947, in Tofino, British Columbia, Canada; daughter of Anthony (an artist) and Mavis (retired) Guppy; married Robert Windley (a teacher), October 8, 1970; children: Tara. *Avocational interests:* Drawing, piano.

ADDRESSES: Home—5989 Tweedsmuir Crescent, Nanaimo, British Columbia, Canada. *E-mail*—oolichan@mail.island.net. *Agent*—c/o Oolichan Books, P.O. Box 10, Lantzville, British Columbia, VOR 2HO Canada.

CAREER: Short-story writer. Malaspina University-College, instructor of fiction-writing workshops, 1995-97.

MEMBER: Writers' Union of Canada.

AWARDS, HONORS: Bumbershoot/Weyerhaeuser Publication Award, 1993, for *Visible Light;* Canadian Broadcasting Corporation Radio Literary Competition winner; shortlisted for the Journey Prize and the Ethel Wilson Fiction Award; Governor General's Fiction Prize nomination; Canada Council "B" grants, 1995 and 1997.

WRITINGS:

Visible Light, Oolichan Books (Lantzville, British Columbia, Canada), 1993.

Work included in *The Journey Prize Anthology: The Best Short Fiction from Canada's Literary Journals,* McClelland & Stewart (Toronto, Ontario, Canada), 1993; *Best Canadian Stories,* Oberon (Ottawa, Ontario, Canada), 1996; *Paper Guitar: 27 Writers Celebrate 25 Years of Descant Magazine,* edited by Karen Mulhallen, HarperCollins (Toronto, Ontario, Canada), 1996.

WORK IN PROGRESS: City of Ladies, a novel, Oolichan, expected in spring, 1998; *Homeschooling: Stories,* in progress.

SIDELIGHTS: Carol Windley's first collection of stories, *Visible Light,* won the 1993 Bumbershoot/Weyerhaeuser Publication award and was a candidate for Canada's Governor General's Fiction Prize. Windley has also been a winner in the Canadian Broadcasting Corporation Radio Literary Competition. Praising the descriptive qualities of Windley's stories in evoking the landscape of British Columbia's west coast, *Canadian Literature* reviewer Timothy

Paleczny noted that several pieces depicted "people longing to retreat into a private Eden, remote and protected from the threatening world of twentieth century 'progress.'"

In one such story, "Dreamland," Lillian discovers there is no road out of the village she and her husband will settle in. Lillian notes that this is a "land which makes what it wants of you," rather than being "a place waiting to be discovered" as her husband says. Reviewer John Oughton, in *Books in Canada,* commented that Windley's work as "quiet, poetic, full of civilized characters busily trying to recreate the past or imagine themselves in the future." Her stories capture insights and inner terrors in regards to relationships, places, and even moths. *Canadian Materials for School & Libraries* reviewer, Barbara J. Graham, remarked, "Locality acts as an important catalyst in human experience," when detailing a number of Windley's stories.

BIOGRAPHICAL/CRITICAL SOURCES:

BOOKS

Journey Prize Anthology, McClelland & Stuart, 1993.
Windley, Carol, *Visible Light,* Oolichan Books (Lantzville, British Columbia, Canada), 1993.

PERIODICALS

Books in Canada, October 1993, pp. 28-29.
Canadian Literature, Autumn 1995, pp. 143-144.
Canadian Materials for School & Libraries, January 1994, p. 18.

*   *   *

WISEMAN, Frederick   1930-

PERSONAL: Born January 1, 1930, in Boston, MA; son of Jacob Leo and Gertrude Leah (Kotzen) Wiseman; married Zipporah Batshaw, May 29, 1955; children: David B., Eric T. *Education:* Williams College, B.A., 1951; Yale University, L.L.B., 1954; also attended Harvard University.

ADDRESSES: Office—1 Richdale Ave., Number 4, Cambridge, MA 02140-2627.

CAREER: Admitted to the bar of the state of Massachusetts, 1955; lawyer and filmmaker, Paris, France,

1956-58; Boston University Law School, Boston, MA, lecturer, 1958-61; Brandeis University, Waltham, MA, research associate, 1962-66; Organization for Social and Technical Innovation, treasurer, 1966-70; WNET Channel 13, New York City, filmmaker, 1968-81; Zipporah Films, Cambridge, MA, filmmaker, 1970—; theatre director, c. late 1980s; visiting lecturer at numerous schools. Director and/or producer of nonfiction documentary films broadcast on the Public Broadcasting System (PBS), including *Titicut Follies,* 1967; *High School,* 1968; *Law and Order,* 1969; *Hospital,* 1970; *Basic Training,* 1971; *Essene,* 1972; *Juvenile Court,* 1973; *Primate,* 1974; *Welfare,* 1975; *Meat,* 1975; *Canal Zone,* 1977; *Sinai Field Mission,* 1978; *Manoeuvre,* 1979; *Model,* 1981; *The Store,* 1983; *Racetrack,* 1985; *Deaf,* 1986; *Blind,* 1986; *Multi-Handicapped,* 1986; *Adjustment and Work,* 1986; *Missile,* 1987; *Near Death,* 1989; *Central Park,* 1989; *Aspen,* 1991; *Zoo,* 1993; *High School II,* 1994; *Ballet,* 1995; and *La Comedie Francaise,* 1996; also producer of *The Cool World,* c. early 1960s. Director and producer of feature film, *Seraphita's Diary,* 1982. Director of stage productions, including *Tonight We Improvise,* 1986-87; *Life and Fate,* 1988; *Hate,* 1991; and *Welfare: The Opera,* American Music Theater Festival, 1992. *Military service:* U.S. Army, 1955-56.

MEMBER: American Academy of Arts and Sciences.

AWARDS, HONORS: Fellow, Russell Sage Foundation, 1961-62; Emmy Award for best documentary direction, 1970, for *Hospital;* grant, Guggenheim Foundation, 1980-81; MacArthur Prize, 1982-87; Peabody Award, 1991; fellow, National Academy of Television Arts and Sciences, 1991.

WRITINGS:

SCREENPLAYS

The Thomas Crown Affair, Mirisch-Simkoe-Solar/United Artists, 1968.
Seraphita's Diary, Zipporah Films, 1982.

DOCUMENTARIES BROADCAST ON PBS; CREATOR AND EDITOR

Titicut Follies, 1967.
High School, 1968.
Law and Order, 1969.
Hospital, 1970.
Basic Training, 1971.
Essene, 1972.

Juvenile Court, 1973.
Primate, 1974.
Welfare, 1975.
Meat, 1975.
Canal Zone, 1977.
Sinai Field Mission, 1978.
Manoeuvre, 1979.
Model, 1981.
The Store, 1983.
Racetrack, 1985.
Deaf, 1986.
Blind, 1986.
Multi-Handicapped, 1986.
Adjustment and Work, 1986.
Missile, 1987.
Near Death, 1989.
Central Park, 1989.
Aspen, 1991.
Zoo, 1993.
High School II, 1994.
Ballet, 1995.
La Comedie Francaise, 1996.

Also contributor of articles and interviews to periodicals, including *Ecran, Film Library Quarterly, Filmmaker's Newsletter, New Yorker,* and *Sight and Sound.*

SIDELIGHTS: American filmmaker Frederick Wiseman has written screenplays for his 1982 film *Seraphita's Diary* and for Norman Jewison's 1968 film *The Thomas Crown Affair.* As the creator of numerous documentary films, he is active in many aspects of filmmaking. A practitioner of the philosophy of *cinema verite* (which tries to keep as little outside commentary from intruding on the film as possible), Wiseman shoots hours of film on a particular subject, then edits it and puts it together without narration or even music. In this manner, he has created several documentaries televised on the Public Broadcasting System (PBS), such as *Titicut Follies, High School, Hospital, Basic Training, Model,* and *High School II.* His work on *Hospital* garnered him an Emmy Award for best documentary direction in 1970.

Wiseman began his career as an attorney, and was admitted to the bar in his native Massachusetts in 1955. Around that time, he began filmmaking, first producing director Shirley Clarke's version of *The Cool World* in the early 1960s, then working on his own first documentary creation, *Titicut Follies,* in 1967. *Titicut Follies* has had a history of controversy. The film portrays typical events at the Bridgewater State Hospital for the Criminally Insane in Massachu-

setts, and for many years it was banned by that state from screening to anyone but mental health specialists. Some of the source of controversy was that Wiseman had allowed the inmates' faces to be shown in his film; some of it was the degrading ways that the inmates were treated. With *Titicut Follies,* Wiseman launched his practice of showing the ways in which various institutions and bureaucracies lose the purpose for which they came into existence and become more concerned with perpetuating themselves than with any legitimate, useful mission. Yet, with *Titicut Follies,* Wiseman also displayed his trademark objectivity—an objectivity that has brought him both praise and blame from critics. Robert Coles observed in the *New Republic:* "Ironically [*Titicut Follies*] is so effective because it is not another *Snake Pit,* another brutal and unrelenting expose of life behind the closed doors of a mental hospital."

Other reviewers of *Titicut Follies* have lauded the film, including Robert Hatch, who noted in the *Nation* that "as far as content is concerned, Mr. Wiseman is relentlessly explicit." Nancy Ellen Dowd in *Film Quarterly* explained the effect of *Titicut Follies:* "the film is not sensationalist . . . ; nor does it try to make a succinct statement about mental hospitals. The film reveals. To its credit, *Titicut Follies* defies interpretation."

Wiseman turned his camera to a high school for his 1968 work, *High School.* As Joseph Featherstone reported in the *New Republic,* the filmmaker "sets out to portray a reputable high school, not a blackboard jungle." Featherstone added that *High School's* "message can be reduced to a string of cliches: the schools are authoritarian, repressive, and so on. On film—on this film, anyway—the cliches take on density and complexity, carrying us beyond slogans into artistic truth." Pauline Kael, writing in the *New Yorker,* gave high praise to *High School* as well, labeling it "extraordinarily evocative," and asserting that "it's a good sign when a movie sends us out wanting to know more and feeling that there is more to know." Stephen Mamber, contributing to *Film Quarterly,* hailed *High School* as "a marvel of visual expressiveness, a display of a fully engaged sensibility adding a quiet commentary all its own."

After documenting the experience of American adolescent students, Wiseman turned his camera upon law enforcement, resulting in the 1969 film *Law and Order.* Wiseman later recalled for *American Film's* Frank Spotnitz his motivation and then education while making the film: "I, like everybody else after the Democratic Convention in Chicago in 1968, assumed, based on my middle-class experience with parking tickets, that the police were all pigs." Yet he added that "after you ride around in the police cars for about twenty seconds, you realize that the piggeries are in no way restricted to the police, because you see that what people do to each other makes it necessary to have police in the first place. This is not to excuse or condone police brutality, but rather to put it into the context of human brutality." Similarly, Donald E. McWilliams, discussing *Law and Order* in *Film Quarterly,* declared that the film "at the deepest level is not about police at all, but about individuals, what they do and say to each other and the ambiguity of behavior."

In 1970 Wiseman made *Hospital,* the documentary that brought him an Emmy Award. Though it was filmed at Metropolitan Hospital in New York City and depicts a staff dealing with the many crises of urban health care, many critics declared that the documentary's participants are treated more sympathetically than the subjects of most of Wiseman's other works. For instance, Kael noted in another *New Yorker* review that the film "is not an expose of man's inhumanity to man. The revelation of *Hospital* is the many surprising forms of man's humanity to man." Though *Hospital* sometimes depicts patients in embarrassing situations such as vomiting after a drug overdose, Richard Schickel in *Life* magazine asserted that "one never feels the voyeur, no matter how intimate or revealing the scene [Wiseman] asks us to observe."

For his next subject, Wiseman chose the U.S. Army, or at least the first part of a soldier's experience within it. The result was the 1971 documentary *Basic Training.* The film prompted Mamber in *Film Comment* to compare it with *High School:* "In *High School* Wiseman repeatedly points up militaristic aspects of the high school experience; in *Basic Training* he emphasizes the highschoollike aspects of the training process. . . . [They] come to be seen as two steps in much broader processes of molding and regulation of citizens in nonvoluntary situations." Jane Larkin Crain, discussing *Basic Training* along with other Wiseman films in *Commentary,* remarked that "*Basic Training* is in many ways the most satisfying of the movies simply because it tells a story that has a beginning, a middle, and an end."

One of Wiseman's more unusual documentary subjects was that of an Anglican monastery, which he filmed for the 1972 effort, *Essene.* Most reviewers agreed that an important aspect of *Essene* was its portrayal of the ways in which a cloistered community was still deeply affected by the political and philosophical arguments of the world around it. As Patrick Sullivan explained in *Film Quarterly,* the documentary "portrays a small society at work redefining itself both in the light of its particular members but also in light of larger cultural forces it both moves toward and with." Sullivan went on to assess *Essene* as "a film with a special resonance which may make it Wiseman's most important to date."

After *Essene* Wiseman filmed *Juvenile Court* in 1973. Crain remarked that the most striking aspect of *Juvenile Court* is "the sense, strongly held by the participants themselves . . . that many problems, the majority in fact, can be resolved satisfactorily." Margaret Tarratt, reviewing *Juvenile Court* in *Films and Filming,* objected to Wiseman's usual *cinema verite* technique, noting that "no-one ever speaks directly to the camera and the film functions as an outsider's exploration of an institution."

Wiseman's 1974 film, *Primate,* examines the daily occurrences within the Yerkes Primate Research Center in Atlanta, Georgia. Though the film includes many explicit scenes of animal experimentation, it does not necessarily take a stand on questions of animal rights, according to Chuck Kraemer in the *New York Times.* "*Primate* is never sentimental. Although the animals appear pitiful, the point of the film is not just to protest cruelty." Kraemer and other critics, however, including Richard Schickel of *Time,* did argue that Wiseman's choices as a director and filmmaker led to the conclusion that he was definitely questioning the necessity of extensive primate research. Schickel labeled *Primate* an "assault on scientism and social scientism, the unquestioning belief that 'pure' research must—perhaps because people insist on calling it pure—be valuable for its own sake."

Karl E. Meyer, critiquing Wiseman's 1975 documentary *Welfare* in the *Saturday Review,* noted that the film often "is very good indeed, if one can use the word *good* about a film whose subject is appalling and depressing." Shot at a welfare center in New York City, *Welfare* contains interviews with welfare applicants and shows the bureaucracy connected with the welfare system. Meyer also asserted that *Welfare* "argues powerfully for a fresh approach to the problem of poverty." James Wolcott in the *Village Voice* differed somewhat in his opinion of *Welfare,* commenting: "When discreet the movie is superb but at the end, when Wiseman tries for dramatic thunder, he allows people to stridently perform for the lens."

Joining *Welfare* in 1975 was another Wiseman documentary, *Meat.* The latter documentary takes viewers through the production of meat, from cattle grazing in the fields, to the slaughterhouse, to the cutting and packing of the final product. The tight control of the process impressed Mamber, this time writing in the *New Republic.* He reported: "Life and death, food and work, are governed according to projected weekly kill figures. Labor reorganizations seek maximum efficiency. We feel ourselves grasping for trivial indications of humanity."

Wiseman captures another unique documentary subject in 1981's *Model.* Focusing on the fashion world, he uses his *cinema verite* method to present viewers with scenes ranging from interviews at a modeling agency to backstage activities at a fashion show. This technique prompted a variety of interpretations from critics. Mary Frazer, in the *Times Literary Supplement,* stated that "everybody involved [in *Model*] comes out quite well." Meanwhile, David Denby in *New York* saw *Model* as a film depicting "a world in which physical strength, character, intelligence, and even, amazingly, beauty itself are put aside in favor of a ruthlessly arbitrary definition of style." Similarly, David R. Slavitt in the *New Republic* declared: "The film raises the question: whom to blame for this madness? Where does the buck stop?" The critic also predicted that *Model* "will be welcomed by all those who have learned to see with Wiseman's eyes the absurdities of institutions and corporate structures in his films."

One of Wiseman's most important projects of the 1980s was his four-part examination of student life at the Alabama Institute for the Deaf and Blind (AIDB). All four films, *Deaf, Blind, Multi-Handicapped,* and *Adjustment and Work,* were presented to audiences in 1986. Robert Coles in the *New Republic* quoted Wiseman about his motivation for the series: "Before I made these films my experience and knowledge of deaf and/or blind people was limited, practically nonexistent. When I began to think about it I realized that I had never gone to school with anyone who was deaf or blind, nor did I have any contact in my work or social life with anyone who was without one or both of these basic senses." Coles concluded that Wiseman "and his camera attend the contours of our daily life, and in the end, as with fiction, help us better see and hear ourselves—what such films as *Blind* and *Deaf* do so very well, indeed."

Wiseman ushered in the 1990s with *Aspen,* a 1991 film documenting the popular resort city of Aspen, Colorado. This film captures both nature and people, both the rich and the middle-class denizens of the area. *Aspen* also contains scenes of a young girl consulting with a plastic surgeon about altering the shape of her nose, as well as scenes of New Age religious seminars. Reviewers of *Aspen* tended to fault Wiseman for either approaching the subject too lightly or for not being critical enough of the town's wealthy citizens. Frank Rich in the *New Republic,* for instance, lamented that "the decent Aspen cancels out the decadent Aspen; and the snow, that great visual leveler, gently and finally cloaks everything, until the viewer cannot see the forest *or* the trees." Harry F. Waters in *Newsweek* observed that "in Wiseman's viewfinder, at least, Aspen throbs with spiritual yearning: maybe it's the altitude." Speaking of a sequence in which a family celebrates a fortieth wedding anniversary, he affirmed that "the best of the human spirit glows like a full Aspen moon."

In 1994 Wiseman returned to the subject matter of one of his best-known efforts with *High School II.* The sequel, according to Stuart Klawans in the *Nation,* is a much more optimistic depiction than the original. Shot at New York City's Central Park East Secondary School, the film depicts typical interactions between a largely ethnic student body and a largely Caucasian group of teachers and counselors. Klawans reported that "as you watch *High School II,* you come to understand that Central Park East is run by people who might almost be creatures of legend. Level-headed, nondogmatic and down-to-earth, these are activists who really improve people's lives." Klawans also noted how "Wiseman once more comes as close as a filmmaker can to relying on pure observation."

BIOGRAPHICAL/CRITICAL SOURCES:

BOOKS

Contemporary Literary Criticism, Volume 20, Gale (Detroit, MI), 1982.

Thomas, Nicholas, editor, *International Directory of Films and Filmmakers,* second edition, Volume 2: *Directors,* St. James Press (Chicago, IL), 1991.

PERIODICALS

America, March 15, 1980, p. 218.
American Film, May, 1991, pp. 16-21.

Christianity and Crisis, November 28, 1977, pp. 286-287.
Commentary, December, 1973, pp. 70-75.
Film Comment, fall, 1969, pp. 60-61; November/ December, 1973, pp. 9-15.
Film Library Quarterly, spring, 1971, pp. 29-33.
Film Quarterly, spring, 1969, pp. 26-31; spring, 1970, pp. 48-51; fall, 1970, pp. 17-26; fall, 1973, pp. 55-57; winter, 1983, pp. 2-10.
Films and Filming, August, 1974, pp. 43-44.
Life, February 6, 1970, p. 9.
Nation, October 30, 1967, p. 446; July 25, 1994, pp. 136-137.
New Republic, January 20, 1968, pp. 18, 28-30; June 21, 1969, pp. 28-30; December 4, 1976, pp. 21-22; September 23, 1981, p. 40; August 29, 1988, pp. 58-60; February 24, 1992, pp. 34-38.
Newsweek, December 30, 1991, p. 55.
New York, September 14, 1981, pp. 61-62.
New Yorker, October 18, 1969; January 31, 1970; April 2, 1980, pp. 91-101; October 24, 1988, pp. 31-32; January 20, 1992, pp. 26-27; March 21, 1994, pp. 162-163.
New York Review of Books, October 21, 1971, pp. 19-22; November 8, 1990, pp. 24-28.
New York Times, December 1, 1974, sec. 2, pp. 1, 31.
Saturday Review, September 20, 1975, p. 52.
Sight and Sound, winter, 1977-78, pp. 59-60.
Time, December 9, 1974, p. 95; March 24, 1980, pp. 76-77.
Times Literary Supplement, March 27, 1981, p. 349.
Village Voice, September 29, 1975, p. 126.
Vogue, June, 1993, pp. 84-85.*

—Sketch by Elizabeth Wenning

*   *   *

WITCHEL, Alex

PERSONAL: Married Frank Rich (a columnist for *New York Times*).

ADDRESSES: Agent—c/o Random House, 201 East 50th St., New York, NY 10022.

CAREER: New York Times, New York City, style reporter.

WRITINGS:

Girls Only (autobiography), Random House (New York City), 1996.

SIDELIGHTS: Alex Witchel is a style writer for the *New York Times.* She is also the author of *Girls Only,* an autobiographical account that provides a perspective on sibling relationships, mother-daughter relationships, and male-female relationships. In addition, *Girls Only* touches on such subjects as vanity, love, and mortality. *New York Times* reviewer Patricia Volk, who described the tone of *Girls Only* as "pajama-party intimate," observed that Witchel manages to be "sardonic, mournful and hilarious, sometimes all at once."

Several critics took note of a chapter in *Girls Only* that discusses sex as particularly humorous. Here, the author recounts introducing her mother to William Shatner, who played Captain Kirk on the original *Star Trek* television series, "weaving this priceless encounter around a discussion of diaphragm insertion, underwear fetishism and a severe case of static cling," according to Volk. A *Publishers Weekly* reviewer commented that Witchel "shows a flair for genuine comedy," citing the chapter about sex and the Shatner encounter as an example. A reviewer for *Booklist* described Witchel as "sharp and wry." Volk wrote in her *New York Times* review that Witchel is "the kind of person you want on your volleyball team. Her wickedly observant eye drew me to her and made me laugh."

BIOGRAPHICAL/CRITICAL SOURCES:

PERIODICALS

Booklist, November 15, 1996, p. 551.
Library Journal, November 1, 1996, p. 74.
New York Times, January 29, 1997, p. B9.
Publishers Weekly, October 28, 1996, p. 64.*

*   *   *

WOLKOFF, Judie (Edwards)

PERSONAL: Born in MT. *Education:* Attended University of Utah.

CAREER: Writer. Has taught primary school in California and New York City.

WRITINGS:

Wally, Bradbury (New York City), 1977.
Where the Elf King Sings, Bradbury, 1980.

(With Barbara B. Murphy) *Ace Hits the Big Time,* Delacorte (New York City), 1981.
Happily Ever After . . . Almost, Bradbury, 1982.
(With Murphy) *Ace Hits Rock Bottom,* Delacorte, 1985.
In a Pig's Eye, Bradbury, 1986.

SIDELIGHTS: Judie Wolkoff has written several books for young readers, often presenting realistic problems faced by young people in narratives leavened with humor. Her work ranges widely from zany tales that some commentators have described as farce, to more serious depictions of topics such as alcoholism and the Vietnam War. Wolkoff has earned her highest marks from critics, however, for her more humorous books, including two co-written with Barbara B. Murphy, which many have suggested as good candidates to capture the attention of reluctant readers.

In *Wally,* Wolkoff's first book, a little boy named Michael agrees to care for a chuckwalla despite his mother's refusal to allow pets in the family home. With the help of younger brother Roger, Michael rigs a secret cage for the lizard, which looks like a miniature dinosaur, in a closet. *School Library Journal* contributor Christine McDonnell described the series of mishaps that result from this arrangement as "fast, fresh, and funny." Although a *Kirkus Reviews* critic dismissed the novel as "a kid's sitcom about a lizard in the house," McDonnell praised the "quick sure strokes" with which Wolkoff painted her comical situations, and asserted that *Wally* "will be popular with middle grade and older reluctant readers."

Wolkoff did an about-face with her second novel, addressing serious and emotionally-laden contemporary themes in *Where the Elf King Sings.* Centering on twelve-year-old Marcie and her younger brother David, the plot hinges on the disturbing outbursts of the children's alcoholic father, a veteran of the war in Vietnam who suffers from flashbacks of the horrifying death of his friend, a death for which he feels responsible. The children's primary means of escape from their troubles at home lies in their secret visits to elderly Mrs. King, who reads poetry to them, encourages their artistic expression, teaches them yoga, and offers them a relatively sane refuge from their unhappy homelife. Critics generally felt that these scenes were handled credibly, though some found the subject matter too depressing for young adult audiences. "Wolkoff draws a vivid picture of the misery alcoholism brings to an entire family, and a convincing picture of the adjustment problems of veterans, but these are heavily stressed and seem at times to overburden the narrative," remarked Zena

Sutherland of the *Bulletin of the Center for Children's Books.* A *Kirkus Reviews* commentator similarly complained that the novel is "both depressing and uninvolving because the children are merely victims, incapable of effective action on their own behalf." However, Judith Goldberger, who reviewed *Where the Elf King Sings* for *Booklist,* praised the realism with which Wolkoff depicts the painful and gradual recovery of Marcie and David's father. The novel "lingers in the mind and will surely speak to children who have war-worn fathers or parents deeply troubled in other ways," Goldberger concluded.

Wolkoff's third book was the first of two comic tales written with Barbara B. Murphy. *Ace Hits the Big Time* relates the story of Horace Hobart, an awkward sixteen-year-old who prepares to attend a new school after moving with his parents during the summer. Horace leaves for his first day wearing an eye patch to cover an ugly sty in his eye and borrowing a red jacket his uncle had sent from Japan when he can't find his own. Horace's desperate attire appeals to members of a gang at school (especially the dragon on the back of his Japanese jacket), and another mishap—his ballpoint pen waiting until the fourth letter of his name to begin dispensing ink—sets "Ace" on track for a series of happy coincidences that combine to give him instant popularity. "Fast-paced, written with humor and flair, the first-person narrative is a side-splitting comedy of errors in the Damon Runyon tradition," enthused *Horn Book* reviewer Mary M. Burns. A *Kirkus Reviews* critic also commended *Ace Hits the Big Time* as "alertly, entertainingly plotted."

Wolkoff and Murphy followed this successful collaboration with another "Ace" tale, *Ace Hits Rock Bottom.* In this story, Ace and his gang-member friends are desperate for summer jobs, eventually accepting work as gardeners and busboys at a home for retired actors in the Bronx—which also happens to be the home turf of a rival gang, the Piranhas. "Behind the zany humor is an appealing picture of youth interacting with the aged—played for a few heart tugs as well as laughs," noted *Booklist* reviewer Sally Estes. *School Library Journal* contributor Sharon Morrison agreed, commenting: "The book alternates between being funny—the boys dress like bag ladies as a disguise to keep the Piranhas from recognizing them—and touching."

The critical response to Wolkoff's *Happily Ever After . . . Almost,* a lighthearted novel about the creation of a hybrid family when a divorced woman with children marries a divorced man with a son, was also generally favorable. At the center of Wolkoff's story is Kitty, an eleven-year-old girl whose mother remarries, bringing into the family not only a stepfather for Kitty and her younger sister, but also a stepbrother, R. J. Together they all move from a house in the suburbs to a loft in the Soho district of New York City, occasioning a period of adjustment during which Kitty's father's new wife has a baby, and R. J.'s father attempts to fight his ex-wife in court for custody of the brother Kitty has come to love. "There is a 'Key to Family Trees' to keep everyone straight, and most episodes are funny, with an authentic ring," noted Betsy Hearne in *Booklist,* who praised Wolkoff's "entertaining and genuinely optimistic look at the extended families sometimes created by a divorce." Zena Sutherland of the *Bulletin of the Center for Children's Books* maintained: "There's a great deal of warmth and humor in the story, a brisk pace to its development, and a satisfying, believable happy ending."

Wolkoff received further high marks for humor in reviews of her 1986 story for middle graders, *In a Pig's Eye.* This tale features the escapades of fourth-grade pals Maisie Blumm and Glenda Jax, who participate in a dog show, create a neighborhood newspaper, and exhibit Maisie's extraordinarily messy teenage brother's room to younger children as an official "pig's eye." *Booklist* reviewer Ilene Cooper called the work "uneven," but added that "the funny parts are very funny indeed." A *Kirkus Reviews* critic dubbed *In a Pig's Eye* "an entertaining romp, full of action and funny conversations."

BIOGRAPHICAL/CRITICAL SOURCES:

PERIODICALS

Booklist, January 15, 1981, p. 704; November 1, 1982, p. 375; September 1, 1985, p. 53; August, 1986, p. 1695.
Bulletin of the Center for Children's Books, November, 1980, p. 104; November, 1982, p. 59.
Catholic Library World, December, 1983, p. 232.
Children's Book Review Service, October, 1980, p. 20; winter, 1983, p. 62.
Horn Book, February, 1982, p. 55.
Kirkus Reviews, December 15, 1977, p. 1321; January 15, 1981, p. 80; February 15, 1982, p. 209; July 1, 1986, p. 1019.
Reading Teacher, March, 1982, p. 752.
School Library Journal, January, 1978, p. 92; November, 1980, p. 81; November, 1982, p. 93; November, 1985, p. 100; October, 1986, p. 184.

Voice of Youth Advocates, June, 1981, p. 34; April, 1983, p. 43.*

* * *

WOODSON, Jacqueline 1964-

PERSONAL: Born February 12, 1964, in Columbus, OH. *Education:* Received a B.A. (English).

ADDRESSES: Home—Brooklyn, NY. *Agent*—c/o Bantam Doubleday Dell, 1540 Broadway, 20th Fl., New York, NY 10036.

CAREER: Writer. Former faculty member of the Goddard College M.F.A. Writing Program; former fellow at the MacDowell Colony and at the Fine Arts Work Center, Provincetown, MA. Has also worked as a drama therapist for runaway children in New York City.

AWARDS, HONORS: Kenyon Review Award for Literary Excellence in Fiction, 1992; Best Books for Young Adults, American Library Association (ALA), 1993, for *Maizon at Blue Hill;* Coretta Scott King Honor Book, ALA, 1995, for *I Hadn't Meant to Tell You This,* and 1996, for *From the Notebooks of Melanin Sun.*

WRITINGS:

FOR CHILDREN

Martin Luther King, Jr., and His Birthday (nonfiction), illustrated by Floyd Cooper, Silver Burdett, 1990.
We Had a Picnic This Sunday Past, illustrated by Diane Greenseid, Hyperion (New York City), 1997.

FICTION; FOR YOUNG ADULTS

Last Summer with Maizon (first book in trilogy), Delacorte, 1990.
The Dear One, Delacorte, 1991.
Maizon at Blue Hill (second book in trilogy), Delacorte, 1992.
Between Madison and Palmetto (third book in trilogy), Delacorte, 1993.
Book Chase ("Ghostwriter" series), illustrated by Steve Cieslawski, Bantam (New York City), 1994.

I Hadn't Meant to Tell You This, Delacorte, 1994.
From the Notebooks of Melanin Sun, Scholastic, Inc. (New York City), 1995.
The House You Pass on the Way, Delacorte, 1997.

OTHER

(With Catherine Saalfield) *Among Good Christian Peoples* (video), A Cold Hard Dis', 1991.
Autobiography of a Family Photo (novel), New American Library/Dutton (New York City), 1994.
(Editor) *A Way Out of No Way: Writing about Growing Up Black in America* (short stories), Holt (New York City), 1996.

Contributor to short story collection *Am I Blue?,* edited by Marion Dane Bauer, HarperTrophy, 1994; contributor to *Just a Writer's Thing: A Collection of Prose & Poetry from the National Book Foundation's 1995 Summer Writing Camp,* edited by Norma F. Mazer, National Book Foundation, 1996.

SIDELIGHTS: Jacqueline Woodson writes about "invisible" people: young girls, minorities, homosexuals, the poor, all the individuals who are ignored or forgotten in mainstream America. They are the people, as the author wrote in a *Horn Book* article, "who exist on the margins." An African American and lesbian herself, Woodson knows first-hand what it is like to be labelled, classified, stereotyped, and pushed aside. Nevertheless, her stories are not intended to champion the rights of minorities and the oppressed. Rather, they celebrate people's differences. Her characters are not so much striving to have their rights acknowledged as they are struggling to find their own individuality, their own value as people. "I feel compelled to write against stereotypes," says Woodson, "hoping people will see that some issues know no color, class, sexuality. No—I don't feel as though I have a commitment to one community—I don't want to be shackled this way. I write from the very depths of who I am, and in this place there are all of my identities."

Woodson's sense of not really belonging to one community might be grounded in her childhood. During her adolescent years, she moved back and forth between South Carolina and New York City, and "never quite felt a part of either place," according to a *Ms.* article by Diane R. Paylor. But Woodson began to feel "outside of the world," as she explained in *Horn Book,* even before her teen years. The turning point for her came when Richard Nixon resigned the presidency in 1974 and Gerald Ford took his place instead of George McGovern. "McGovern was my first 'American Dream.' Everyone in my neighborhood had been pulling for him." When Ford stepped into the Oval Office, Woodson felt that she and all of black America had been abandoned. "The word *democracy* no longer existed for me. I began to challenge teachers, and when they couldn't give me the answers I wanted, I became sullen, a loner. I would spend hours sitting underneath the porch, writing poetry and anti-American songs."

Writing soon became Woodson's passion. In the fifth grade, she was the literary editor of her school's magazine. "I used to write on everything," she commented for a Bantam Doubleday Dell web site. "It was the thing I liked to do the most. I never thought I could have a career as a writer—I always thought it was something I would have to do on the side." Her seventh-grade English teacher encouraged Woodson to write and convinced her that she should pursue whatever career she felt would make her happiest. Deciding that writing was, indeed, what she wanted to do, Woodson endeavored "to write about communities that were familiar to me and people that were familiar to me. I wanted to write about communities of color. I wanted to write about girls. I wanted to write about friendship and all of these things that I felt like were missing in a lot of the books that I read as a child."

Woodson has always had a deep empathy for young girls, who often suffer from low self-esteem in their preteen and adolescent years. "I write about black girls because this world would like to keep us invisible," she wrote in *Horn Book.* "I write about *all* girls because I know what happens to self-esteem when we turn twelve, and I hope to show readers the number of ways in which we are strong." Woodson's first published book, *Last Summer with Maizon,* begins a trilogy about friends Margaret and Maizon. Set in the author's hometown of Brooklyn, the story tells of two eleven-year-olds who are the closest of friends. Their friendship is strained, however, when Margaret's father dies of a heart attack and Maizon goes to boarding school on a scholarship. While her friend is away, Margaret, who is the quieter of the two, discovers that she has a talent for writing. She also finds comfort in her family, who support her in her attempt to deal with her father's death. Maizon, meanwhile, finds that she does not like the almost all-white Connecticut boarding school and returns home after only three months. Glad to be with her loved ones again, Maizon, along with Margaret, goes to a gifted school in her own neighborhood.

Critics praised *Last Summer with Maizon* for its touching portrayal of two close friends and for its convincing sense of place. Julie Blaisdale, writing in *School Librarian,* also lauded the work for its "positive female characters . . . who provide the enduring sense of place and spiritual belonging" in the tale. Roger Sutton of the *Bulletin of the Center for Children's Books,* while generally commending the book, found fault with the way Margaret eases her sadness by writing poetry. "Although underdeveloped," Sutton concluded, "this story will appeal to readers who want a 'book about friends.'" Similarly, *Horn Book* writer Rudine Sims Bishop commented on the story's "blurred focus," but asserted that "the novel is appealing in its vivid portrayal of the characters and the small community they create."

Woodson continues Margaret and Maizon's stories with *Maizon at Blue Hill* and *Between Madison and Palmetto.* The former is not really a sequel but, rather, an "equal" to the first book in the trilogy. *Maizon at Blue Hill* focuses on what happens to Maizon while she is at the Connecticut boarding school. Maizon, who is a very bright girl, likes the academic side of Blue Hill, but she is worried about fitting in socially. Most of the other girls are white and are either snobbish or, at least, not eager to be her friend. Although she is welcomed by a small clique of other black students, Maizon sees this group as rather elitist, too. She decides to return to Brooklyn, where she can comfortably just be herself. An American Library Association Best Book for Young Adults, *Maizon at Blue Hill* has been acclaimed for its strong and appealing characters. "More sharply written than its predecessor, this novel contains some acute characterization," remarked Roger Sutton in *Bulletin of the Center for Children's Books.* Noting that the issues about self-esteem and identity that are addressed in the story spring appropriately from the characters rather than vice versa, *Voice of Youth Advocates* contributor Alice F. Stern asserted: "We are in the hands of a skilled writer here. . . . Woodson is a real find."

The last book in the trilogy, *Between Madison and Palmetto,* picks up where the first book left off, with Maizon and Margaret entering eighth grade at the academy. Again, Woodson covers a lot of ground in just over one hundred pages, including Margaret's bout with bulimia, issues of integration as the two girls' neighborhood begins to change and white families move in, and the testing of Margaret and Maizon's friendship as Maizon spends more time with another girl named Carolyn. A *Publishers*

Weekly reviewer applauded Woodson's gift with characterization, but noted that the effect is "somewhat diluted by the movie-of-the-week problems." In another *Voice of Youth Advocates* review, Alice F. Stern acknowledged that Woodson has "a lot of ground to cover," but noted that "she manages admirably." A *Kirkus Reviews* critic described *Between Madison and Palmetto* as a fine portrayal of a "close-knit community . . . [that] comes nicely to life."

In her *Horn Book* article, Woodson grouped her books into two categories: her "good" books, which deal with relationships between family members and friends, and her more controversial books, which address issues of alcoholism, teenage pregnancy, homosexuality, and other issues that skirt the delicate problem of what is "appropriate" for children to read. She reflected on how, after writing her second book, *The Dear One,* the speaking invitations she had formerly received suddenly stopped coming. "Even after *Maizon at Blue Hill,* another relatively 'nice book,' school visits were few and far between. Yet I often wonder, If every book had been like *Last Summer with Maizon,* and I was a young woman with a wedding band on my hand, would I get to visit schools more often?"

The central character of *The Dear One* is twelve-year-old Feni, a name meaning "The Dear One" in Swahili. Feni lives in an upper-class African American home and basks in her family's attention. This all changes, however, when fifteen-year-old Rebecca is invited by Feni's mother to stay with them. Rebecca, the daughter of an old college friend, is a troubled, pregnant teenager from Harlem. Feni becomes jealous because she is no longer the center of attention. "But gradually and believably, with the patient support of Feni's mother and a lesbian couple who are longstanding family friends, the two girls begin to develop mutual trust and, finally, a redemptive friendship," related *Twentieth-Century Children's Writers* contributor Michael Cart.

The Dear One is a unique book in that it deals with tensions not between blacks and whites but between poor and wealthy blacks. Woodson gives a sympathetic portrayal of Rebecca, who is uncomfortable living in what she considers to be a mansion, and who is also reluctant to change her lifestyle. She misses her boyfriend and her family back in Harlem; she envies Feni and resents the privileges Feni has been given. The novel also offers a fresh perspective on adult relationships. As Hazel S. Moore noted in *Voice of Youth Advocates,* "The lesbian couple seems to be intact, while the straight couples have divorced and suffered." Marion and Bernadette, the lesbian couple, provide Feni with wise advice to add to the support she receives from her mother.

Taking things a step further than *The Dear One, I Hadn't Meant to Tell You This* explores a relationship that spans both race and class when Marie, a girl from a well-to-do black family, befriends Lena, whom Marie's father considers to be "white trash." Both girls have problems: Marie's mother has abandoned her family, and Lena is the victim of her father's sexual molestations. Told from Marie's point of view, the book details the twelve-year-old's internal conflicts as she tries to think of how she can help Lena. In the end, Lena, who has been able to find no other viable solutions to her problem, runs away from home, and Marie must accept the fact that there is nothing she can do about her friend's tragedy. Woodson has been praised by critics for not resolving her story with a pat conclusion. Cart commented: "Woodson's refusal to impose a facile resolution on this heartbreaking dilemma is one of her singular strengths as a writer." "Woodson's novel is wrenchingly honest and, despite its sad themes, full of hope and inspiration," concluded a *Publishers Weekly* reviewer.

The issue of homosexuality, which had been peripheral in Woodson's earlier books, comes to the forefront in *From the Notebooks of Melanin Sun* and *The House You Pass on the Way.* Thirteen-year-old Melanin Sun, the central character in the former novel, has a close relationship with his mother, whom he admires as a single working mother who is also putting herself through law school. Their bond is strained, however, when Melanin's mother tells him that she is a lesbian and that she is in love with a white woman. This development makes Melanin question his relationship with his mother, as well as making him wonder about his own sexuality. Torn between his emotional need for his mother and his fear about what her lesbianism implies, Melanin goes through a tough time as his friends also begin to abandon him. Gossip in the neighborhood that Melanin's mother is "unfit" also spreads, making matters even worse. Again, Woodson offers no clearcut resolution to the story, but by the novel's end Melanin has begun to grow and understand his mother. Critics have praised Woodson's portrayal of Melanin's inner conflicts as being right on the money. As Lois Metzger wrote in the *New York Times Book Review,* "Ms. Woodson, in this moving, lovely book, shows you Melanin's strength and the

sun shining through." "Woodson has addressed with care and skill the sensitive issue of homosexuality within the family . . . [without] becoming an advocate of any particular attitude," asserted *Voice of Youth Advocates* critic Hazel S. Moore. In *The House You Pass on the Way,* fourteen-year-old Evangeline, the middle child in a mixed-race family, struggles with feelings of guilt and dismay over her awakening sexual preference. "A provocative topic," noted a *Kirkus Reviews* critic, "treated with wisdom and sensitivity, with a strong secondary thread exploring some of the inner and outer effects of biracialism."

Although most of her works have been aimed at preteen and teenage audiences, Woodson has also written a novel for adults, *Autobiography of a Family Photo,* and a children's picture book, *We Had a Picnic This Sunday Past.* The latter, as with all of the author's work, is about the importance of family, while the former addresses issues of sexuality and sexual behavior for a more mature audience. However, its short length and central coming-of-age theme put *Autobiography of a Family Photo* within the reach of young adult audiences. Told in a series of vignettes spanning the 1960s and 1970s, the novel is a reminiscence related by an unnamed narrator. Her family has many problems, including her parents' troubled marriage, her brother Carlos's inclination to be sexually abusive, her brother Troy's struggles with homosexuality that compel him to go to Vietnam, and other difficulties. Despite all of this, the narrator survives adolescence, undergoing a "compelling transformation," according to Margot Mifflin in an *Entertainment Weekly* review. However, some critics have contended that the vignettes fail to form a unified whole. A *Kirkus Reviews* contributor, for example, commented: "Chapters build on each other, but the information provided is too scanty to really create any depth." Catherine Bush, writing in the *New York Times Book Review,* complained that the novel focuses too much on the narrator's growing sexual awareness. "I found myself wishing that the narrator's self-awareness and longing could be defined less exclusively in sexual terms," Bush says. Bush concluded, however, that "even in these restrictive terms, the novel is the best kind of survival guide: clear-eyed, gut true."

Woodson has never backed away from portraying truths about life in modern American society. She has written her "good" books about friendship and family that deal with safe, acceptable topics, but she clearly does not shy away from controversial subjects like homosexuality and sexual abuse. Woodson has asserted that she is not trying to force any kind of ideology on her readers, but rather is interested in all kinds of people, especially the socially rejected. "One of the most important ideas I want to get across to my readers," Woodson emphasizes, "is the idea of feeling like you're okay with who you are."

BIOGRAPHICAL/CRITICAL SOURCES:

BOOKS

Twentieth-Century Children's Writers, fourth edition, edited by Laura Standley Berger, St. James Press, 1995.

PERIODICALS

Booklist, November 15, 1991, p. 619; July, 1992, p. 1931; March 15, 1993, p. 1344; September 15, 1993, p. 152; February 15, 1994, p. 1072; December 15, 1994, p. 736; January 15, 1995, p. 860; April 1, 1995, pp. 1404, 1412; March 15, 1996, p. 1284.

Bulletin of the Center for Children's Books, October, 1990, pp. 49-50; September, 1991, p. 26; December, 1992, p. 128; December, 1993, p. 136; March, 1994, p. 239; July, 1995, p. 401.

Entertainment Weekly, April 21, 1995, pp. 50-51.

Essence, February, 1995, p. 52; April, 1995, p. 56.

Horn Book, November, 1991, p. 746; September, 1992, pp. 616-20; January, 1994, p. 72; September, 1994, p. 601; July, 1995, p. 468; November-December, 1995, pp. 711-15.

Kirkus Reviews, August 1, 1991, p. 1018; October 15, 1992, p. 1318; December 1, 1993, p. 1532; June 1, 1994, p. 782; October 1, 1994, pp. 1307-08; May 15, 1995, p. 717; July 1, 1997, p. 1038.

Ms., November-December, 1994, p. 77; July, 1995, p. 75.

New York Times Book Review, July 29, 1990, p. 33; May 10, 1992, p. 21; November 6, 1994, p. 32; February 26, 1995, p. 14; July 16, 1995, p. 27; April 28, 1996, p. 36.

Publishers Weekly, June 28, 1991, p. 103; January 20, 1992, p. 66; January 4, 1993, p. 74; November 8, 1993, p. 78; April 18, 1994, p. 64; November 7, 1994, p. 44; May 15, 1995, p. 74; December 11, 1995, p. 71.

School Librarian, November, 1991, p. 154.

School Library Journal, November, 1990, p. 121; June, 1991, p 129; November, 1992, p. 99; November, 1993, p. 111; May, 1994, p. 136; August, 1995, p. 158.

Voice of Youth Advocates, February, 1991, p. 360; October, 1991, p. 236; October, 1992, p. 235; April, 1994, p. 32; June, 1994, p. 95; October, 1995, p. 227; June, 1997, p. 114.

OTHER

Bantam/Doubleday Dell website, "Jacqueline Woodson," http://www.bdd.com./forum/bddforum.cgi/trc/index/wood (April 8, 1997).*

*   *   *

WU, Chien-Shiung 1912(?)-

PERSONAL: Born May 29, 1912 (some sources say 1913 or 1915), in Liu Ho, China; naturalized U.S. citizen; daughter of Wu Zhongyi (an engineer, revolutionary, and teacher) and Fan Fuhua (a teacher); married Chia Liu Yuan, 1942; children: Vincent Wei-Chen Yuan. *Education:* National Central University, Nanking, China, B.S., 1934; University of California—Berkeley, Ph.D., 1940.

ADDRESSES: Home—15 Clairmont Ave., Apt. 73, New York, NY 10027.

CAREER: Physicist. University of California, Berkeley, research fellow and lecturer, 1940-42; Smith College, Northampton, MA, assistant professor, 1942-43; Princeton University, Princeton, NJ, instructor, 1943-44; Columbia University, New York City, Manhattan Project, beginning 1944, research associate, 1945, associate professor, 1952-58, professor, 1958-81, Pupin Professor of Physics, 1972-81. Participated in war effort during World War II.

MEMBER: National Academy of Science, Royal Society of Edinburgh (honorary fellow), American Physical Society (president, 1975), Chinese Academy of Science, American Association for the Advancement of Science, American Academy of Arts and Sciences.

AWARDS, HONORS: Research Award, Research Corporation, 1959; award, American Asian University Women, 1960; Comstock Award, National Academy of Science, 1964; Achievement Award, Chi-Tsin Cultural Foundation, 1965; Scientist of the Year, *Industrial Research Magazine,* 1974; Tom Bonner Prize, American Physical Society, 1975; National Science Medal, 1975; Wolf Prize in Physics, 1978;

Nishina Memorial Lecturer, Universities of Tokyo, Osaka, and Kyoto, 1983; asteroid named in honor, 1990; honorary degrees from various universities and colleges, including Princeton University, Smith College, Goucher College, Rutgers University, Yale University, Russell Sage College, Harvard University, Bard College, and Adelphi University.

WRITINGS:

(With others) *An Experimental Test of Parity Conservation in Beta Decay,* [New York], 1957.

(Editor, with Luke C. L. Yuan) *Nuclear Physics,* Academic Press (New York City), 1961.

(Editor, with Vernon W. Hughes) *Muon Physics,* Academic Press, 1975-77.

SIDELIGHTS: For more than thirty years, Chien-Shiung Wu was a member of the physics department at Columbia University, where she earned a reputation as one of the world's foremost nuclear physicists. Wu is best known for a classic experiment on beta decay, completed in 1957, which confirmed a prediction made a year earlier by Tsung-Dao Lee and Chen Ning Yang regarding the conservation of parity (the basic symmetry of nature) in reactions involving the weak force. A number of observers have commented on the apparent inequity of the Nobel Prize committee's not having included Wu in the 1957 physics prize, which was awarded to Lee and Yang for this work.

Wu was born in May of 1912 (some sources say 1915; one source says 1913), in Liu Ho near Shanghai, China. Her father, Wu Zhongyi, was a former engineer who had abandoned his profession in 1911 to take part in the revolution that overthrew the Manchu dynasty. After the war, Wu returned to Liu Ho to open a school for girls. Still filled with revolutionary zeal, he saw it as his mission to make sure that girls as well as boys were able to have an education in the "new China." Chien-Shiung's mother, Fan Fuhua, helped her husband in this effort, providing education to their students' families in their own homes.

Wu attended her father's school until she was nine and then continued her education at the Soochow Girls School, about fifty miles from her home. During her high school years, Wu was active in a number of political causes; her fellow classmates chose her to represent them in some of the causes because, with her stellar scholastic record, she could not readily be dismissed from school on the basis of her involvement in political issues. In 1930 Wu graduated from Soochow as valedictorian of her class and then entered the National Central University in Nanking. By that time she had decided to pursue physics as a career, and in 1934 was awarded a bachelor's degree in that field. After teaching and doing research for two years, Wu left China in 1936, intending to obtain the graduate training in physics that was not then available in her native land. Her original plans to enroll in the University of Michigan changed abruptly when she reached San Francisco and was offered an opportunity to attend the University of California at Berkeley.

Among the factors influencing Wu's decision to remain in California was the presence of Ernest Orlando Lawrence, inventor of the atom-smashing cyclotron (a device that accelerates the speed of nuclear particles), on the Berkeley campus. The chance to study with Lawrence was, Wu decided, too important to pass up. Another factor in her decision was the presence of "Luke" Chia Liu Yuan—a young man she met soon after arriving in San Francisco. Wu and Yuan were married in 1942 and eventually had one son, Vincent Wei-Chen Yuan.

Wu received her Ph.D. in 1940, a time of great turmoil in her homeland and in the world at large. The Japanese army had already invaded China, and U.S. involvement in World War II was only a year away. Wu stayed on as a research assistant at Berkeley for two years after receiving her degree, but spent much of that time on war-related work. In 1942 she was offered her first teaching position, at Smith College in Northampton, Massachusetts. She remained at Smith for only one year before accepting an appointment at Princeton University, where she was assigned to teach introductory physics to naval officers. She held this position for only a few months before she was offered a post at Columbia University, where she would join the Manhattan Project—through which the world's first atomic bombs were designed and built. That job, which began in March 1944, was the beginning of a long relationship with Columbia; she eventually became a research associate in 1945, associate professor in 1952, and finally full professor in 1958. She retired from Columbia in 1981.

The work for which Wu gained fame took place in 1957. It was based on a revolutionary theory proposed by two colleagues, Tsung-Dao Lee, also of Columbia, and Chen Ning Yang, of the Institute for Advanced Study in Princeton, New Jersey. In 1956 Lee and Yang had raised the possibility that a property known as parity may not be conserved in certain types of nuclear reactions. Conservation laws had long been at the heart of physical theories. These laws said that a number of important physical characteristics—mass, energy, momentum, and electrical charge, for instance—were always conserved during physical or chemical changes. As an example, the law of conservation of electrical charge says that the total electrical charge on all particles involved in a physical change would be the same both before and after the event.

Lee and Yang found theoretical reasons to question the conservation of parity in some instances. Parity refers to the theory that the laws of nature are not biased in any particular direction, a concept long held by physicists. When beta particles are emitted by nuclei during radioactive decay, for example, classical theory predicts that they will be emitted without preference to any particular spin orientation. Lee and Yang developed a mathematical argument showing that this might not be the case and outlined experiments through which their theory could be tested.

Lee and Yang presented their ideas to Wu, already recognized as an authority on beta decay (a radioactive nuclear transformation) and the weak force that causes it. Even before her colleagues had published a paper on their theory, Wu had begun to design experiments to test their ideas. Working with colleagues at the National Bureau of Standards's Low Temperature Physics Group, Wu labored almost without rest for six months. In January of 1957, she announced her results: clear evidence for the violation of parity conservation had been observed. Later that same year, Lee and Yang were awarded the Nobel Prize in Physics—an award that many observers in the field believe might easily have been shared with Wu.

Although she did not receive a Nobel Prize, Wu has won a host of other awards, including the first Wolf Prize awarded by the state of Israel (1978), the first Research Corporation Award (1959) given to a woman, the Comstock Award of the National Academy of Sciences (1964), and the National Science Medal (1975). She was elected to the National Academy of Sciences in 1958.

BIOGRAPHICAL/CRITICAL SOURCES:

BOOKS

Kass-Simon, G., and Patricia Farnes, editors, *Women of Science: Righting the Record,* Indiana University Press, 1990, pp. 205-208.

McGraw-Hill Modern Men of Science, Volume 2, McGraw-Hill, 1984, pp. 541-542.

McGrayne, Sharon Bertsch, *Nobel Prize Women in Science,* Birchlane Press, 1993, pp. 255-279.

Yost, Edna, *Women of Modern Science,* Dodd, 1959, pp. 80-93.*

* * *

YAKOVENKO, L.
 See KOPELEV, Lev (Zinovievich)

* * *

YOUNG, J(ohn) Z(achary) 1907-1997

OBITUARY NOTICE—See index for *CA* sketch: Born March 18, 1907, in Bristol, England; died July 4, 1997. Zoologist, educator, author. Young was one of the foremost experts in zoology in his day. Among his topics of study was the anatomical function of the brain. In his early career, he was a demonstrator in zoology and comparative anatomy and a fellow of Magdalen College at Oxford University, beginning in 1931. In 1945 he left Oxford for the University of London as professor of anatomy; he became professor emeritus and fellow in 1975. During his career he also served as Fullerton Professor at the Royal Institution from 1958 to 1961 and was affiliated with the Wellcome Institute for the History of Medicine. He also delivered the BBC Reigh Lectures in 1950, the Croonian Lecture for the Royal Society in 1965, and the Gifford Lectures in 1973. From 1976 until 1986 he served as president of the Marine Biological Association of Great Britain. Among his many awards were honorary degrees from schools such as University of Bristol, University of Bath, Duke University, and University of Aberdeen, among others. He was awarded the Royal Society's Royal Medal in 1967 and the Zoological Medal from the London Zoological Society in 1974. The British Academy gave him an honorary fellowship. He was also an author and editor of books, including *Doubt and Certainly in Science: A Biologist's Reflections on the Brain, The Life of Mammals: Their Anatomy and Physiology, The Life of Vertebrates, A Model of the Brain, The Memory System of the Brain,* and *Philosophy and the Brain.* His book, tentatively titled *The Brains and Lives of Cephalopods,* was in progress at the time of his death.

OBITUARIES AND OTHER SOURCES:

BOOKS

Writers Directory, St. James Press, 1996.

PERIODICALS

Times (London; electronic), July 9, 1997.

*   *   *

YOUNG, James E. 1951-

PERSONAL: Born August 26, 1951, in CA; son of J. A. (an engineer) and Elizabeth J. (a nurse) Young; married Lori J. Friedman (a gallery director), June 21, 1987. *Education:* University of California, Santa Cruz, B.A., 1973; University of California, Berkeley, M.A., 1976; University of California, Santa Cruz, Ph.D, 1983. *Religion:* Jewish. *Politics:* Democrat. *Avocational interests:* Photography, art, film, baseball.

ADDRESSES: Office—Department of English, University of Massachusetts, Amherst, MA 01003. *Agent*—Deborah Karl Wylie, 250 West 57th St., New York, NY 10017.

CAREER: Bryn Mawr College, Bryn Mawr, PA, visiting assistant professor, 1983-84; New York University, New York City, assistant professor and Dorot Fellow in English and Hebrew/Judaic Studies, 1984-88; University of Massachusetts, Amherst, professor of English and Judaic Studies, 1988—. Ronald S. Lauder Foundation, on academic advisory board; New England Holocaust Memorial Committee, on design management committee; State Museum at Terezin, Czechoslovakia, on board of directors; Polish Ministry of Culture, on International Auschwitz Council; Hillel of Massachusetts, on board of directors; guest curator of "The Art of Memory," Jewish Museum, New York City, 1994.

AWARDS, HONORS: Visiting fellow, YIVO Institute for Jewish Research, New York City, 1981; Fulbright/Israel government grant, Hebrew University, Jerusalem, 1981-82; Alexander Silberman International Fellowship, Institute of Contemporary Jewry, Hebrew University, Jerusalem, 1982-83; National Endowment for the Humanities summer stipend, 1986; Memorial Foundation for Jewish Culture Fellowship Grant, 1987-88; Yad Hanadiv/Barecha Foundation Fellowship, Hebrew University, Jerusalem, 1988-89; *Choice* Outstanding Academic Book Award, for *Writing and Rewriting the Holocaust;* Lucius N. Littauer Foundation Grant, 1989-90; John Simon Guggenheim Memorial Foundation Fellowship, 1988; National Endowment for the Humanities exhibition planning grant, 1990; Egit Grant for Holocaust and Jewish Resistance Literature, 1992; National Endowment for the Humanities exhibition implementation grant, 1993.

MEMBER: Association for Jewish Studies, Modern Language Association, College Art Association.

WRITINGS:

Writing and Rewriting the Holocaust: Narrative and the Consequences of Interpretation, Indiana University Press (Bloomington, IN), 1988.
The Texture of Memory: Holocaust Memorials and Meaning, Yale University Press (New Haven, CT), 1993.

Contributor of articles to books and academic journals on aesthetics, Jewish culture, the Holocaust, propaganda, literary criticism, English, and Hebrew. Contributor of reviews to periodicals, including *Chicago Tribune, New York Times Book Review,* and the *Independent.* Served on the editorial advisory board of *Dimensions: A Journal of Holocaust Studies, Patterns of Prejudice* (London), and *Tikkun;* American associate editor of *Jewish Quarterly of London.*

WORK IN PROGRESS: "Two received histories of the Holocaust and after."

SIDELIGHTS: James E. Young told *CA:* "Because I was born after the Holocaust, I don't remember it outside the ways it has been passed down to me by the victims in their diaries or the survivors in their memoirs. I remember not the actual events but what I have read in history books and novels, what I have seen in photographs and film, what I have heard in the hours spent with survivors and their harrowing stories. With this in mind, I have devoted much of my writing to the ways I have received the Holocaust from literature, film and its memorials. All of which has shaped the ways I respond to contemporary suffering in light of the Holocaust.

"At the same time, I resist strongly the reduction of a thousand years of Jewish life in Europe to its terrible end. It has become very important to teach and write about the long continuum of Jewish history, its richness before World War II and its continuation after in Israel and America. My new work, therefore, concentrates explicitly on the relationships I have had with two survivors of the Holocaust, the manner in which I have received and responded to their life stories. As part of the next generation, I want to understand how their memory lives in me and in my actions, how the past makes itself palpable in my everyday present."

In the late 1790s, in the wake of the French Revolution, Friedreich Schiller wrote that "Humanity has lost its dignity, but art has rescued it and preserved it in significant stones." In a twentieth century context, the inhumanity of the Holocaust is preserved in the "significant stones" of memorials, according to Young, who has written two books that examine the public and private memory of the Holocaust. The first was *Writing and Rewriting the Holocaust: Narrative and the Consequences of Interpretation,* published in 1988. The second, *The Texture of Memory: Holocaust Memorials and Meaning,* focuses expressly on official, government-sponsored Holocaust memorials. These pieces of art, according to Young, enhance public memory. But what is remembered, the author points out, depends on the motivations behind the construction and design of the memorial—whether it pays homage to the victims, appeals to shared responsibility, expurgates collective shame and anger, builds an ideal of peacemaking, or perpetuates a political ideology.

According to Young, the responsibility to remember any historical event always includes the possibility of revising the memory to fit political exigencies. Reviewing *The Texture of Memory* in the *Nation,* Joanne Jacobson observed: "James Young's excellent and important book testifies eloquently to the inadequacy of a notion of 'memory' as the neutral recollection of experienced past: 'The motives of memory,' he insists, 'are never pure.'"

In Israel and the United States, Young notes, the Holocaust has become part of a broader mythology. Writes Jacobson: "The Shoah anchors a narrative that is essential to Israeli legitimacy and unity, around which Jewish history can be written out of powerlessness, marginality and victimization and into redemption." The memorials, museums and monuments in the U.S., writes Young, "reinforce America's self-idealization as a haven for the world's oppressed—the U.S. as liberator, sanctuary, international guarantor of freedom." Jacobson pointed to Young's discussions of the "politically motivated 'administration of

memory,'" especially by Eastern European Soviet bloc countries, who used the memory of the Holocaust to demonstrate the veracity of their Marxist interpretations, pointing to Germany's industrial excess and fascism as the enemy. For instance, Young notes that the design of the 1948 Warsaw Ghetto Monument was steeped in controversy as a conflict arose as to whether to depict the Jews as ghetto resistance fighters or proletarian heroes. And, until the disintegration of the Soviet Union and its potentate in Poland, the monument was a source of bitter contention between the state and Solidarity trade union leaders.

In Israel, Europe, and the United States, there are numerous Holocaust memorials that offer a range of aesthetic representations. Young focuses on the relationship between these memorials, public memory and national self-definition. Writing in the *New York Times Book Review,* Mark Lilla observed: "In four separate sections of the book [Young] systematically examines memorials built where the Final Solution was planned (Germany), where it was mainly carried out (Poland) and where the bulk of its survivors fled (Israel and the United States)."

Young's argument, according to Mark A. Pollock, writing in the *Chicago Tribune,* is that the "memorial representations" of the horrific memories of the Holocaust cannot be adequately explained merely by assessing their artistic merit or historical accuracy. By heightening critical awareness of all memorials and the potential uses and abuses of officially cast memory, Pollock asserts, Young "sheds light on how fictional and non-fictional representations shape our understanding of the Holocaust." Pollock concluded that Young's book "makes clear that much of who we are is shaped not only by what we remember but also by how we remember."

BIOGRAPHICAL/CRITICAL SOURCES:

BOOKS

Young, James E., *The Texture of Memory: Holocaust Memorials and Meaning,* Yale University Press (New Haven, CT), 1993.

Young, James E., *Writing and Rewriting the Holocaust: Narrative and the Consequences of Interpretation,* Indiana University Press (Bloomington, IN), 1988.

PERIODICALS

Chicago Tribune, July 18, 1993, sec. 14, p. 5.

Nation, October 18, 1993, pp. 431-432.
New York Times Book Review, September 19, 1993, pp. 31-32.

* * *

ZINSSER, Hans 1878-1940
(R. S., a pseudonym)

PERSONAL: Born November 17, 1878, in New York, NY; died of leukemia, September 4, 1940, in New York, NY; son of August (a manufacturing chemist) and Marie Theresa (Schmidt) Zinsser; married Ruby Handforth Kunz, 1905; children: Gretel, Hans Handforth. *Education:* Columbia University College of Physicians, M.A. and M.D., 1903; interned at Roosevelt Hospital. *Avocational interests:* Horse-back riding, foxhunting, shooting.

CAREER: Bacteriologist. Practiced medicine; Columbia University, New York City, instructor in bacteriology, until 1910, professor, 1913-15; Stanford University, Palo Alto, CA, associate professor of bacteriology and immunology, 1910-13, 1918-23; Harvard University Medical School, instructor, beginning 1923, became Charles Wilder Professor of Bacteriology, c. 1925; Made scientific expeditions around the world, including the Soviet Union, 1923; Mexico, 1931; and China, 1938. *Military service:* Member of Red Cross Typhus Commission; officer, U.S. Army Medical Corps., became lieutenant colonel.

MEMBER: American Association of Immunologists (president, 1919), Society of American Bacteriologists (president, 1926), Harvey Society, Sigma Xi.

AWARDS, HONORS: U.S. Distinguished Service Medal, French Legion of Honor, Order of Sava, all for contributions during World War I; honorary doctorates from universities, including Columbia University, 1929, Western Reserve University, 1931, Lehigh University, 1933, Yale University, 1939, and Harvard University, 1939.

WRITINGS:

(With Philip Hanson Hiss, Jr.) *A Textbook of Bacteriology,* D. Appleton, 1910.
Infection and Resistance, Macmillan (New York City), 1914.
(With J. G. Hopkins and Reuben Ottenburg) *Laboratory Course in Serum Study,* [New York], 1916.

(With R. P. Strong, G. C. Shattuck, A. W. Sellards, and J. G. Hopkins) *Typhus Fever with Particular Reference to the Serbian Epidemic,* Harvard University Press (Cambridge, MA), 1920.
Rats, Lice and History, Little, Brown (Boston, MA), 1935.
As I Remember Him: The Biography of R. S., Little, Brown, 1940.
Spring, Summer and Autumn, (poems), Knopf (New York City), 1942.
Microbiology, Appleton-Century-Crofts (New York City), 1968.

Contributor to journals and periodicals, including *Archives of Internal Medicine* and *American Journal of Hygiene.* Author of essays and poetry, sometimes under pseudonym R.S.

SIDELIGHTS: Hans Zinsser was one of the leading bacteriologists and immunologists in the United States during the first half of the twentieth century. His work in advancing the understanding of typhus fever as well as a number of fundamental features of immunology remains central to this day.

Zinsser was born on November 17, 1878, in New York City, and grew up in a household where German was the primary language that was spoken. Both of his parents had emigrated from Germany: His father, August Zinsser, was a wealthy manufacturing chemist originally from the Rhineland, and his mother, Marie Theresa (Schmidt), was from the Black Forest region, an area long dominated by French tradition. For this reason, the young Zinsser soon became fluent in a second language: French.

The youngest of August and Marie's four sons, Zinsser did not start formal schooling until age ten. At that time he was sent to a private school in New York City operated by Julius Sachs, and only then did Zinsser begin using English as his first language. The school emphasized the liberal arts, an area of learning especially valued by Zinsser, who had the fortune of spending some portion of every one of his first twenty years of life visiting the art galleries and concert halls of Europe. In 1895, at age seventeen, Zinsser entered nearby Columbia University where he was intent on studying literature and pursuing a writing career. Studying under comparative literature specialist George Edward Woodberry, the already broadly educated Zinsser showed great promise in the writing of poetry. In an article in *Memoirs of the National Academy of Sciences,* Zinsser's principal biographer, Simeon Burt Wolbach, noted that the "world of things and thoughts" had occupied Zinsser until that time. Although his intellectual life was about to change, Zinsser remained an accomplished poet and essayist as well as lucid writer of scientific prose for the remainder of his more than sixty years. On his deathbed, after battling leukemia for the final two years of his life, he wrote his last sonnet. The poem, which was published posthumously in his collection *Spring, Summer and Autumn,* ends with the lines: "Then, ageless, in your heart I'll come to rest / Serene and proud as when you loved me best."

It was only after his tutelage under biologists Edmund Beecher Wilson and Bashford Dean during his junior year at Columbia that Zinsser realized that the life sciences would be his career. He went on to Columbia's College of Physicians and Surgeons in 1899, deciding to devote his career to the application of his interest in biology to real human problems. Earning both an M.A. and an M.D. in 1903, he interned at Roosevelt Hospital, then began to practice medicine. He left that vocation after a short while, however, when Columbia offered him a post as instructor in bacteriology. In the meantime he had married Ruby Handforth Kunz in 1905.

Zinsser taught bacteriology for a short time at Columbia and teamed with Philip Hanson Hiss, Jr., with whom in 1910 he coauthored *A Textbook of Bacteriology,* which has become a standard microbiology text. Simultaneously, he served as assistant pathologist at New York's St. Luke's Hospital. The same year that *A Textbook of Bacteriology* was released, Zinsser moved his wife and first child, Gretel, to Palo Alto, California, to accept a position as associate professor of bacteriology and immunology at Stanford University. There he set up a bacteriology laboratory with the most minimal of equipment in some space borrowed from the anatomy department. In 1913 Zinsser returned to Columbia University, where he concentrated his research in the field of immunology.

As a professor of bacteriology and immunology at Columbia, Zinsser experienced a decade that was both exciting and dismaying. In 1915, in the midst of World War I, Zinsser served first as a member of the Red Cross Typhus Commission and later as an officer in the U.S. Army Medical Corps. Arriving in Serbia in 1915, Zinsser had his first field contact with an epidemic of typhus—a disease that is caused by the family of bacteria known as rickettsia, and is characterized by stupors, delirium, high fevers, severe headaches, and dark rashes. Approximately one hundred and fifty thousand cases of typhus existed at the Belgrade front, with a fatality rate of about sixty to seventy percent. During their experiences in the Eastern Front, the scientists in the commission began to gain a rudimentary understanding of the bacteriology and pathology of the disease. For his contributions during the war, Zinsser was awarded the U.S. Distinguished Service Medal, the French Legion of Honor, and the Order of Sava, a major Serbian citation.

In 1918 Zinsser left the U.S. Army Medical Corps as a lieutenant colonel and continued his professorial duties at Columbia, where he specialized in immunology. In particular, Zinsser focused on discovering a way to immunize patients against the chronic and contagious disease syphilis. Though he did not succeed in his quest to discover a successful method of immunization, he did contribute to the existing knowledge of spirochete, a type of bacteria that causes syphilis and relapsing fevers. In addition, Zinsser continued to study typhus, since he had became an expert on military sanitation, especially with regards to typhus, during his service in the war. He wrote articles and books on the subject in the course of his career, and during his lifetime took a number of trips to distant lands to study epidemic typhus or cholera—a diarrheal disease caused by bacteria. Among his expeditions were excursions to the Soviet Union in 1923, to Mexico in 1931, and to China in 1938, where he lectured at the Peiping, Beijing, Medical College. His Columbia years came to an end in 1923 when, at the age of forty-five, he was offered a teaching position at Harvard University Medical School. Within two years he was named the Charles Wilder Professor of Bacteriology. Zinsser remained in Boston for the remainder of his life. The Zinsser family, along with their second and last child, Hans Handforth Zinsser (who later graduated from Columbia's College of Physicians and Surgeons), lived in a house in the city and traveled often to their country farm in Dover, Massachusetts. The farm became a retreat and entertainment site for Zinsser's colleagues and his medical students.

By 1930 Zinsser had decided to concentrate his studies on typhus fever research, and began a lengthy friendship with Charles J. H. Nicolle, the Nobel Prize-winning French physician and bacteriologist who discovered that typhus is transmitted by body lice. During the 1930s Zinsser was able, either alone or with a variety of co-workers, to aid in the understanding of the cause of the several forms of typhus, including Brill's disease, named for American physician Nathan Edwin Brill, who investigated the malady.

Zinsser was able to prove that the disease is caused by the microorganism Rickettsia prowazekii as opposed to Rickettsia mooseri, as was commonly believed, and hypothesized that Brill's disease is a form of recrudescent (or renewing) typhus. His theory was confirmed by later studies, and the disease has since been renamed Brill-Zinsser's disease. In addition, Zinsser worked on a vaccine against typhus and assisted in conceiving of a way to prepare the vaccine commercially, thus making the treatment available to large numbers of people. These endeavors have guaranteed him a place in the history of bacteriology and medicine.

In addition to his significant contributions to bacteriology, Zinsser also made advancements in the field of immunology. He discovered that it is not possible to create a grand conceptual unification for an understanding of the phenomenon of allergic reaction. Near the beginning of the twentieth century, Austrian pediatrician Clemens von Pirquet and Hungarian pediatrician Bela Schick, then leading figures in immunology, sought to explain allergic reactions as if all were antibody-mediated. They also believed that an allergic reaction was a typical step in the recovery process. Zinsser showed that certain forms of bodily responses to infection, including those involving the body's reaction to tuberculin (a substance that was later, and to this day, used in the test for tuberculosis infection), are fundamentally different from other types of allergic responses.

In several books and papers Zinsser detailed his scientific studies in the fields of bacteriology and immunology; among the most well known of these volumes is his 1935 work *Rats, Lice and History*. An examination of the history of typhus, the book intermixes philosophy and wit along with scientific information. The book became a best-seller and was praised by several literary critics. Zinsser delved into his private life with his 1940 autobiography, *As I Remember Him: The Biography of R. S.* Made up of some of the author's thoughts regarding living with leukemia—the disease that eventually caused his death—*As I Remember Him* was a popular book whose somewhat odd subtitle was derived from Zinsser's use of a pseudonym for his literary writings. In these writings he often referred to himself as R. S. There is disagreement as to what R. S. stood for: Some say it meant "Romantic Self"; others believe that it was derived from a German author, Rudolf Schmidt, who in 1908 had written on pain and its significance in medicine.

During his lifetime Zinsser won numerous awards and was actively involved in many scientific societies, such as serving as president of the American Association of Immunologists in 1919 and of the Society of American Bacteriologists in 1926. His major honors include the receipt of honorary doctorates from Columbia University in 1929, Western Reserve University in 1931, Lehigh University in 1933, Yale University in 1939, and Harvard University in 1939. Among his other accolades are his elections to the Harvey Society and Sigma Xi. His published articles number more than 270.

Zinsser possessed a lifelong devotion to personal fitness—enjoying activities ranging from horseback riding to hounds (at which he was expert) to shooting. "Throughout his life," Wolbach reported in *Memoirs of the National Academy of Sciences,* "he carried the aura of youth." Zinsser died of leukemia in his native New York City on September 4, 1940.

BIOGRAPHICAL/CRITICAL SOURCES:

PERIODICALS

Memoirs of the National Academy of Sciences, Volume 24, 1947, pp. 323-360.*